Series on Bioengineering and Biomedical Engineering – Vol. 8

NEUROPROSTHETICS
Theory and Practice

Second Edition

SERIES ON BIOENGINEERING AND BIOMEDICAL ENGINEERING

Series Editor: John K-J Li *(Department of Biomedical Engineering, Rutgers University, USA)*

Series on Bioengineering and Biomedical Engineering – Vol. 8

NEUROPROSTHETICS
Theory and Practice

Second Edition

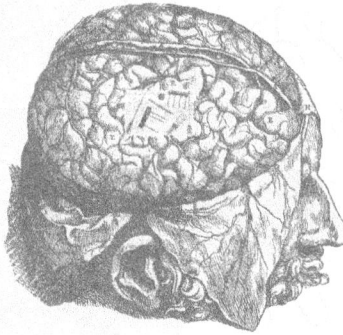

Editors

Kenneth Horch
Daryl Kipke

University of Utah, USA

World Scientific

NEW JERSEY · LONDON · SINGAPORE · BEIJING · SHANGHAI · HONG KONG · TAIPEI · CHENNAI · TOKYO

Published by

World Scientific Publishing Co. Pte. Ltd.

5 Toh Tuck Link, Singapore 596224

USA office: 27 Warren Street, Suite 401-402, Hackensack, NJ 07601

UK office: 57 Shelton Street, Covent Garden, London WC2H 9HE

Library of Congress Cataloging-in-Publication Data
Names: Horch, Kenneth W., editor. | Kipke, Daryl, editor.
Title: Neuroprosthetics : theory and practice / edited by Kenneth Horch, Daryl Kipke.
Other titles: Neuroprosthetics (Horch) | Series on bioengineering and biomedical engineering.
Description: 2nd edition. | Hackensack, NJ : World Scientific, 2017. | Series: Series on bioengineering and
    biomedical engineering | Includes bibliographical references and index.
Identifiers: LCCN 2016059280 | ISBN 9789813207141 (hardcover : alk. paper)
Subjects: | MESH: Neural Prostheses | Brain-Computer Interfaces |
    Nervous System Physiological Phenomena | Electric Stimulation--methods
Classification: LCC RC350.N48 | NLM WL 26 | DDC 616.8/046--dc23
LC record available at https://lccn.loc.gov/2016059280

British Library Cataloguing-in-Publication Data
A catalogue record for this book is available from the British Library.

Neuroprosthetics: Theory and Practice

Table of Contents

Section 1

Neuroanatomy and Physiology

Chapter 1.1

Peripheral Nervous System

Ken Horch

KWH Consulting, LLC
PO Box 20498, Fountain Hills, AZ 85269
KWHCarizona@gmail.com

This chapter provides an overview of the basic structure and physiology of peripheral sensory and motor nerves.

1. Introduction

All you know about the external world, and all you can do about it, depends on your peripheral nervous system and cranial nerves, the latter a rostral extension of the former. In this chapter we provide an overview focused on the structure of peripheral nerves responsible for cutaneous and proprioceptive sensation and for voluntary muscle control.

2. Structural Organization

The peripheral nervous system (PNS) consists of two major divisions, autonomic and somatic. The autonomic system consists of a preganglionic component (with nerve cells originating in the spinal column or skull) and a postganglionic component (with nerve cells lying wholly outside the axial skeleton). The somatic system consists of nerve cells with cell bodies located within or near the spinal column or skull. The autonomic system is largely concerned with functions not normally under voluntary control, while the somatic system is concerned with sensory inputs that can be perceived and with voluntary control of skeletal muscles.

The voluntary nervous system is divided on anatomical and functional grounds into sensory and motor components. Except for the cranial nerves, the sensory system consists structurally of nerve cells with somata located outside the spinal cord in aggregates called dorsal root ganglia. These cells have no dendrites, but instead possess a single process that bifurcates upon leaving the ganglion, one process travelling centrally through dorsal roots to enter the dorsal part of the spinal cord and the other process travelling distally through peripheral nerves to innervate or form distal sense organs. These nerve processes are called afferent nerve fibers because they conduct action potentials and, hence, information from the periphery to the central nervous system.

The sensory elements can be divided, following the example of Gray [7], into the "special" senses of audition and vestibulation, smell, taste, and vision, and the "general" senses which include just about everything else that gives rise to conscious sensation. The "general" senses fall into two major domains: somatosensory and proprioceptive. One can think of the somatosensory or exteroceptive system as providing information about the state of the external environment as it interacts with the body, and of the proprioceptive system as providing information about the orientation of the body in space. This reduces to a consideration principally of cutaneous receptors and muscle/joint receptors.

The motor system consists structurally of nerve cells with somata located in the ventral quadrant (horn) of the spinal cord. These cells have dendrites ramifying through the ventral portions of the spinal cord, and single axons that leave the spinal cord through the ventral roots and join with the sensory fibers to form the peripheral nerves and eventually innervate skeletal muscle fibers. These nerve process are called efferent nerve fibers because they conduct action potentials and, hence, information from the central nervous system to the periphery.

Active movement of joints is produced by contraction of extrafusal muscle fibers. A single motor neuron will typically innervate several muscle fibers in a given muscle. Since there is normally a one-to-one relationship between an action potential on a motor neuron and an action potential in the post synaptic muscle fiber, the axon and all its innervated muscle fibers is called a motor unit. Under normal conditions, only a single nerve fiber innervates a given muscle fiber, although multiple innervation can occur transiently in response to partial denervation of muscle. The electrical properties of muscle fiber membrane makes it difficult to active these fibers by externally applied currents. Thus, except in the case of totally denervated muscle, electrical stimulation of muscle by externally applied current normally consists of activation of the terminals of motor neurons that in turn activate the muscle.

Within the spinal cord, afferent process make local synapses and may terminate within a few segments of their entry point or they may travel directly, via the dorsal columns, to the medulla of the brainstem. On the efferent side, the dendrites of motor neurons receive input from local circuits, including feedback from sensors in the skin and muscle, and input from descending pathways originating in the brain.

3. Peripheral Nerves

Peripheral nerves consist of the axons of autonomic, dorsal root ganglion and ventral horn neurons, their associated ensheathing Schwann cells and basement membrane embedded in a collagen matrix called the endoneurium (Fig. 1). Collections of nerve fibers are segregated by a cellular perineurium, which, along with the capillary endothelium, also acts as a blood-PNS barrier [20]. The perineurial encapsulated structure is called a fascicle. Fascicles are bound together by a collagenous epineurium, which defines the nerve as a distinct anatomical entity and is its primary provider of strength. Within their fascicles, nerve fibers follow an undulating course. This is manifest in the appearance of the Bands of Fontana, seen as alternating light and dark bands under proper illumination of the nerve. Within a given fascicle, the fibers undulate in phase. Shifts in the phase of the appearance of the light and dark bands can be used intraoperatively as an indicator of different fascicles. The undulations allow a certain amount of stretch to occur in the nerve without damage to the delicate axons. Once the nerve fibers straighten out and the Bands of Fontana disappear, further stretch of the nerve will result in damage to the axons [22].

The best sources of information about the general anatomy and mechanical properties of peripheral nerves are found in the clinical nerve repair literature, such as the classic tomes by Sunderland [22] and Mackinnon and Dellon [12] as well as more specialized review articles such as the one on mechanical properties by Topp and Boyd [23].

3.1. *Nerve fibers*

Nerve fibers are grouped together into fascicles not on the basis of their function, but on the basis of their destination. That is, fascicles provide a topographic organization to peripheral nerves. As one moves proximally, fascicles tend to fuse, but the topographic segregation of fibers may continue quite some distance proximally within the fused fascicle [9, 21, 27]. There is also evidence that within the somatotopic organization peripheral nerve fibers may be segregated by functional modality [4, 10]. Proximal to the cervical or lumbar plexi, the distal topographic organization is replaced by a spinal segment organization. Therefore, in order to obtain receptor specific information, one cannot rely on whole nerve or whole dorsal rootlet recording methods [2, 6, 25].

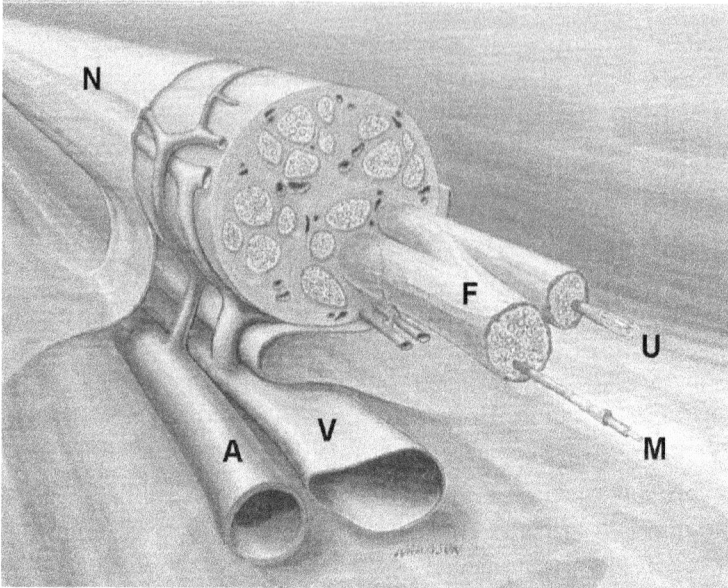

Fig. 1. Drawing of a peripheral nerve (N) with associated arterial (A) and venous (V) blood vessels. Shown as extending from the nerve epineurium are two fascicles (F) ensheathed in perineurium. Shown as extending from the endoneurium of the fascicles are a myelinated axon (M) and a bundle of unmyelinated axons encased in a single Schwann cell (U). (Adapted from Mackinnon and Dellon [12]).

In addition to the classification of nerve fibers based on their origin and overall function (autonomic, sensory or motor), nerve fibers are also classified on the basis of the type of structure they innervate, the presence or absence of myelin, and their size. Although the conduction velocity of action potentials increases with axon size, vertebrates (unlike their invertebrate cousins such as cephalopods and annelids) utilize a second mechanism to further increase conduction velocity in large axons: myelination [28]. In these axons, the Schwann cells, rather than simply enveloping a collection of nerve fiber axons as is the case with unmyelinated fibers, form a one-to-one association with a particular axon, with a different Schwann cell every 0.5 mm or so. These Schwann cells form elaborations of their cell membranes which wrap around the axon, leaving only a small gap between Schwann cells where the nerve membrane is directly exposed to the extracellular milieu (Fig. 2). This results in saltatory conduction: action potentials jump from one node of Ranvier to the next, rather that progress continuously along the membrane as is the case in unmyelinated fibers. This results in a significant increase in conduction velocity without a concomitantly large increase in axon diameter, saving space in the nerve and metabolic requirements in the parent soma. In addition, myelinated axons tend to have briefer action potentials than unmyelinated nerve fibers, allowing them to support higher firing rates than the latter.

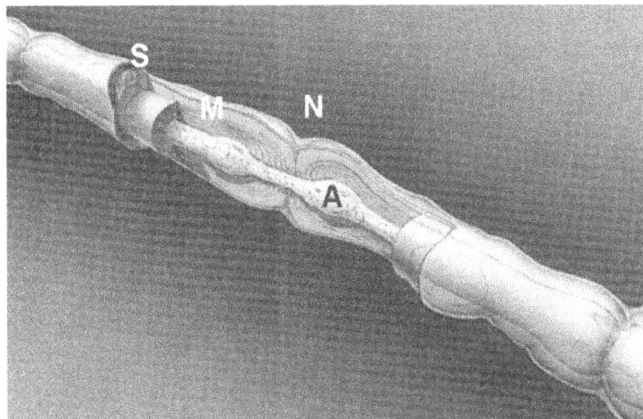

Fig. 2. Drawing of a myelinated nerve fiber axon (A) at the level of a node of Ranvier (N), where the myelin sheath (M) produced by the enveloping Schwann cell (S) terminates leaving a small gap before the next sheath begins. (Adapted from [Mackinnon and Dellon [12]).

In general, myelinated axons are used for tasks where speed (such as control of skeletal muscle contraction or signaling of temporally rapid and brief events) is required or where fine tactile or proprioceptive discriminations are to be made. The latter stems from the fact that the higher the signaling rate, the higher the information transfer rate. Unmyelinated fibers tend to be associated with control of smooth muscle or signaling diffuse, temporally sluggish events such as pain and temperature. The biophysics of nerve fibers and the electrical insulating properties of the perineurium are such that electrical currents applied outside the perineurium tend to excite large, myelinated fibers first [15, 26]. As the current is increased, successively smaller fibers are recruited. Activation of unmeylinated nerve fibers may require currents strong enough to block the large myelinated fibers. Intrafascicular nerve stimulation tends to recruit fibers based on size and distance from the electrode [8, 16].

A summary of the terminology used to anatomically classify nerve fibers appears below (see [13]).

- **Cutaneous nerves**
  - Large myelinated sensory neurons   Aαβ
  - Small myelinated sensory neurons   Aδ
  - Autonomic neurons   B
  - Unmyelinated sensory neurons   C

- **Muscle nerves**
  - Large myelinated sensory neurons
      (in order of decreasing size)   Ia, Ib and II
  - Small myelinated sensory neurons   III
  - Unmyelinated sensory neurons   IV

  - Large myelinated motor neurons α
  - Intermediate myelinated motor neurons β
  - Small myelinated motor neurons γ

3.2. *Electrical properties*

The electrical properties of peripheral nerve fibers and their surrounding milieu are well known [14, 17 - 19] and have served as the basis for increasingly sophisticated models of stimulation and recording methods as described elsewhere in this volume. For neuroprosthetic purposes it is critical that the methodology can selectively record from and/or stimulate peripheral nerve fibers on a chronic basis. This is where the perineurium plays a critical role.

In addition to its other functions, the perineurium acts as a high resistance barrier between the endoneurial contents of a nerve and its external environment [24, 29]. This has two major implications. From a recording perspective, that means the extracellular current flow associated with action potential production and conduction is largely confined to the interior of the fascicle. Thus, for moderate and large size fascicles, it is not possible to chronically record individual unit action potentials with extra-fascicular electrodes. On the other hand this confinement of current flow and the anisotropic properties of the endoneurium make it possible to do so with intra-fascicular electrodes [5, 6].

For stimulation, the perineurial barrier, in addition to keeping much of the current flow from externally placed electrodes outside the fascicle, tends to flatten the field curvature, thereby limiting the size-distance recruiting effects seen with punctate stimulation [8]. As a result in fibers are activated on the basis of size (large fibers first) and not location within the fascicle. Various techniques have been developed to provide size [1, 11] and location [8, 30 - 33] selectivity with extrafascicular stimulation, but these methods don't come close to the kind of selectivity seen with intrafascicular stimulation [3, 16, 34].

4. Summary

The peripheral nervous system consists of centrally located neuronal cell bodies and distally located sensors and effectors, linked by transmission lines called axons bundled together in fascicles, collections of which make up the peripheral nerves. Mechanoreceptors provide information about skin deformation, hair displacement, joint movement, tendon tension, and muscle length. Thermoreceptors provide information about skin or muscle temperature. Threatening or damaging chemical, mechanical and thermal events evoke activity in nociceptors, which gives rise to the sensation of pain. Skeletal muscle produces force by contraction of extrafusal muscle fibers.

Peripheral nerves consist of collections of afferent and efferent nerve fibers. Large nerve fibers are myelinated, have low thresholds for electrical excitation, conduct action potentials rapidly, constitute the dominant component contributing to normal tactile sensations, and control contraction of both intrafusal and extrafusal muscle fibers. Unmyelinated sensory fibers are small, have high thresholds for electrical activation, conduct action potentials slowly, and mainly subserve temperature and pain sensations.

Peripheral nerves tend to be organized somatotopically, both in terms of where the nerves go and in terms of how the nerve fibers within a nerve are segregated. Because of their accessibility, peripheral nerves are common targets for functional neuromuscular stimulation intervention. However, they are elastic, mobile structures that tend to react adversely to constraint or constriction, providing numerous technological challenges to neuroprostheticists.

References

1. Accornero, N., Bini, G., Lenzi, G. L. and Manfredi, M. (1977) Selective activation of peripheral nerve fibre groups of different diameter by triangular shaped stimulus pulses, *J Physiol.* **273**, 539-560.
2. Bradley, R. M., Cao, X., Akin, T. and Najafi, K.(1997) Long term chronic recordings from peripheral sensory fibers using a sieve electrode array, *J. Neurosci. Meth.* **73**, 177-186.
3. Branner, A., Stein, R. B. and Normann, R A. (2001) Selective stimulation of cat sciatic nerve using an array of varying-length microelectrodes, *J. Neurophysiol.* **85**, 1585–1594.
4. Ekedahl, R., Frank, O. and Hallin, R. G. (1997) Peripheral afferents with common function cluster in the median nerve and somatotopically innervate the human palm, *Brain Res. Bull.* **42**, 367–376.
5. Goodall, E. V., Horch, K. W., McNaughton, T. G. and Lybbert, C. M. (1993) Analysis of single-unit firing patterns in multi-unit intrafascicular recordings, *Med. Biol. Eng. Comput.* **31**, 257-267.

6. Goodall, E. V., Lefurge, T. M. and Horch, K. W.(1991) Information contained in sensory nerve recordings made with intrafascicular electrodes, *IEEE Trans. Biomed. Eng.* **38**, 846-850.
7. Gray, H. (1977) *Anatomy, Descriptive and Surgical*, (Bounty Books, New York).
8. Grill, W. M. (1999) Modeling the effects of electric fields on nerve fibers: Influence of tissue electrical properties, *IEEE Trans. Biomed. Eng.* **46**, 918–928.
9. Hallin, R. G (1990) Microneurography in relation to intraneural topography: somatotopic organisation of median nerve fascicles in humans, *J. Neurol. Neurosurg. Psychiatry* **53**, 736-744.
10. Hallin, R. G. and Wu, G. (2001) Fitting pieces in the peripheral nerve puzzle, *Exp. Neurol.* **172**, 482–492.
11. Lertmanorat, Z., Gustafson, K. J. And Durand, D. M. (2006) Electrode array for reversing the recruitment order of peripheral nerve stimulation: Experimental studies, *Ann. Biomed. Eng.* **34**, 152–160.
12. Mackinnon, S. E. and Dellon, A. L. (1988) *Surgery of the Peripheral Nerve*, (Thieme Medical Publishers, New York).
13. Mann, M. D. (1981) *The nervous system and behavior*, (Harper & Row Publishers, Philadelphia).
14. Mcintyre, C. C., Richardson, A. G. and Grill, W. M. (2002) Modeling the excitability of mammalian nerve fibers: Influence of afterpotentials on the recovery cycle, *J. Neurophysiol.* **87**, 995–1006.
15. Mortimer, J. T. (1990) Electrical excitation of nerve, In: *Neural Prostheses. Fundamental Studies*, eds. Agnew, W. F. and McCreery, D. B. (Prentice Hall, Englewood Cliffs, NJ) pp. 67-83.
16. Nannini, N., and Horch, K. (1991) Muscle recruitment with intrafascicular electrodes, *IEEE Trans. Biomed. Eng.* **38**, 769-776.
17. Richardson, A. G., Mcintyre, C. C. and Grill, W. M. (2000) Modelling the effects of electric fields on nerve fibres: influence of the myelin sheath, *Med. Biol. Eng. Comput.* **38**, 438-446.
18. Rubinstein, J. T. (1991) Analytical theory for extracellular electrical stimulation of nerve with focal electrodes II. Passive myelinated axon, *Biophys. J.* **60**, 538-555.
19. Rubinstein, J. T. and Spelman, F. A. (1988) Analytical theory for extracellular electrical stimulation of nerve with focal electrodes I. Passive unmyelinated axon, *Biophys. J.* **54**, 975-981.
20. Rydevik, B. L., Danielsen, N., Dahlin, L. B. and Lundborg, G.(1990) Pathophysiology of peripheral nerve injury with special reference to electrode implantation, In: *Neural Prostheses. Fundamental Studies*, eds. Agnew, W. F. and McCreery, D. B. (Prentice Hall, Englewood Cliffs) pp. 85-105.
21. Stewart, J. D. (2003) Peripheral nerve fascicles: Anatomy and clinical relevance, *Muscle Nerve* **28**, 525–541.
22. Sunderland, S. (1978) *Nerves and Nerve Injuries*, (Churchill Livingstone, New York).
23. Topp, K. S and Boyd, B. S. (2006) Structure and biomechanics of peripheral nerves: Nerve responses to physical stresses and implications for physical therapist practice, *Phys Ther.* **86**, 92-109.
24. Ubogu, E. E. (2013) The molecular and biophysical characterization of the human blood-nerve barrier: current concepts, *J. Vasc. Res.* **50**, 289-303.
25. Vallbo, A. B. Hagbarth, K. E., Torebjörk, H. E. and Wallin, B. G. (1979) Somatosensory, proprioceptive, and sympathetic activity in human peripheral nerves, *Physiol. Rev.* **59**, 919-957.

26. van Bolhuis, A. I., Holsheimer, J. and Savelberg, H. H. C. M. (2001) A nerve stimulation method to selectively recruit smaller motor-units in rat skeletal muscle, *J. Neurosci. Meth.* **107**, 87-92.

27. Velde, K., Ross, M. W., Orsini, J. A., Parente, E. J., Foley, B., Richardson, D. W. and Miselis, R. R. (2004) Tracing axons of peripheral nerves in rats: A potential technique to study the equine recurrent laryngeal nerve, *J. Invest. Surg.* **17**, 151–162.

28. Waxman, S. G. (1978) *Physiology and Pathobiology of Axons*, (Raven Press, New York).

29. Weerasuriya, A., Spangler, R. A., Rapoport, S. I. and Taylor R. E. (1984) AC impedance of the perineurium of the frog sciatic nerve, *Biophys. J.* **46**, 167-174.

30. Leventhal, D. K. and D. M. Durand (2003) Subfascicle stimulation selectivity with the flat interface nerve electrode, *Annals of Biomedical Engineering*, **31**(6), 643-652.

31. Leventhal, D. K. and D. M. Durand (2004) Chronic measurement of the stimulation selectivity of the flat interface nerve electrode, *IEEE Transactions on Biomedical Engineering*, **51**(9), 1649-1658.

32. Tyler, D. J. and D. M. Durand (2002) Functionally selective peripheral nerve stimulation with a flat interface nerve electrode, *IEEE Transactions on Neural Systems and Rehabilitation Engineering*, **10**(4), 294-303.

33. Veraart, C., W. M. Grill, et al. (1993) Selective control of muscle activation with a multipolar nerve cuff electrode, *IEEE Transactions on Biomedical Engineering*, **40**(7), 640-653.

34. Yoshida, K. and K. Horch (1993) Selective stimulation of peripheral nerve fibers using dual intrafascicular electrodes, *IEEE Transactions on Biomedical Engineering*, **40**, 492-494.

Chapter 1.2

The Autonomic Nervous System

Kip Ludwig[1], Erika Ross[1], Nicholas Langhals[2], Doug Weber[3], J. Luis Lujan[1,4] and
Dmitrios Georgakopoulos[5]

[1] Department of Neurologic Surgery, Mayo Clinic, Rochester, Minnesota
[2] National Institute of Neurological Disorders and Stroke, N. Bethesda, Maryland
[3] University of Pittsburgh, Pittsburgh, Pennsylvania
[4] Department of Physiology and Biomedical Engineering,
Mayo Clinic, Rochester, Minnesota
[5] Sunshine Heart, Eden Prairie, Minnesota
ludwig.kip@mayo.edu

This chapter provides an overview of the anatomy and function of the sympathetic and parasympathetic nervous system, with an emphasis on development of next-generation neuromodulation devices.

1. Introduction

The autonomic nervous system (ANS) is also known as the vegetative or involuntary nervous system because it functions largely without conscious, voluntary control. The ANS innervates cardiac muscle, smooth muscle and various endocrine and exocrine glands, and therefore influences the activities of most tissues and organ systems in the body. The ANS regulates myriad bodily processes including blood pressure, body temperature, digestion, inflammatory response, visual focus and contraction of the urinary bladder. Seminal studies by Claude Bernard and Walter Canon have elucidated the pivotal role of the ANS in keeping the amounts of fluid/ionic concentrations and energy stores in the body remarkably stable despite highly irregular rates of intake [3-7]. The ANS must work in concert with and modulate endocrine systems such as the renin-angiotensin-aldosterone system to regulate blood pressure and maintain normal homeostatic equilibrium in response to external perturbations.

Any discussion of the ANS as it pertains to the development of neuromodulation devices must begin with one caveat, namely, we have limited understanding of the functional anatomy of the human ANS. Our historical understanding of the human ANS is predicated upon extensive animal studies that have been supplemented with much more limited human work and post-mortem anatomical assessment. Animal studies are advantageous because they enable invasive procedures and measurement techniques to probe mechanisms of action that are technically and ethically problematic to conduct in a human study of any size. For example, techniques to evaluate functional anatomy in animal studies include chronic implantation of high-density electrodes to stimulate and record from multiple points on the neural axis, dialysis techniques to measure changes in neurochemical and other biomolecules, pharmacological and optogenetic techniques to manipulate specific neural pathways with high precision, post-mortem neuronal tracing to visualize the full extent of neural pathways to and from targets, and cell-type specific histological stains. These techniques present additional risks to the patient and/or require specialized and complex perfusion/fixation procedures performed immediately after death that would not be possible to perform outside of the highly controlled environment of an animal research laboratory.

Although much of our current knowledge of human neuroanatomy was derived from animal studies, these studies do not capture a number of key factors that are relevant to human therapies. First and perhaps foremost, modern animals are the result of a different evolutionary path; even non-human primates have numerous anatomical and functional differences with respect to humans. Second, animal models are often obtained from the same genetic line, and therefore do not represent the genetic diversity of the human population. Third, animal studies typically utilize disease models that are induced instead of naturally occurring, and represent only a fraction of the myriad possible root causes underlying complex disorders such as human hypertension. Moreover, these animal models may recapitulate the features of a disease or disorder relevant to the intended therapeutic effect of the neuromodulation device, but often do not incorporate side effects that limit the therapeutic intervention.

The reliance on animal research to elucidate the functional anatomy of the human ANS is particularly problematic for the study of implantable and non-invasive neuromodulation devices designed to electrically activate nerves of the ANS for therapeutic effect. As discussed elsewhere, activation thresholds for target nerves of interest are profoundly impacted by several factors that do not scale linearly or predictably from animals to humans. Some factors are a function of the nerves themselves, including fiber and fascicle size, degree of myelination, and the distance and orientation of those nerves with respect to the stimulating electrode. Still, other factors are related to the stimulating electrode design, including electrode size, distance between cathode and anode, electrode configuration, and geometry of insulation used to direct current from the stimulating electrode to the target nerve. For example, the activation thresholds of ß fibers from cuff electrodes placed on the epineurium of the vagus nerve in rodents have been estimated to be 1/25th of the activation thresholds of ß fibers from an epineural cuff on the vagus nerve in humans [11]. These factors of scale are not just relevant to nerves targeted for therapeutic effect, but are a key for determining therapy-limiting side effects caused by unintended activation of nearby neural circuitry.

A final and critical factor limiting the translatability of animal functional studies of neuromodulation therapies to human patients is that neuromodulation devices are often indicated as adjunct therapies to existing pharmacological treatments. As an example, animal studies of hypertension therapies such as carotid sinus nerve stimulation, baroreceptor stimulation, or renal denervation have typically been conducted in normotensive or obese-hypertension models without additional pharmacological therapies. By comparison, the average patient in the CVRx Rheos™ study, a large clinical trial evaluating the safety and efficacy of a neuromodulation device that activate the carotid baroreceptors to treat hypertension, received an average of 5.2 hypertension medications [1]. Most of these drugs were orally administered and worked directly or indirectly activating or blocking channels/receptors that modulate portions of the ANS that regulate points on the cardio/renal axis [1]. The impact of utilizing an electrical stimulation device to modulate the function of a neural circuit in conjunction with multiple drug therapies acting on the same circuitry is largely unknown.

In contrast to animal studies, the tools to study human neuroanatomy in clinical research are largely restricted to non-invasive imaging and sensing techniques with lower spatial and temporal resolution, as well as measurements of surrogate biomarkers of effect. Consequently, the physiological effects of a neuromodulation device in humans are often assessed by lower resolution, noisy, and often subjective observational measurements of effect. Even human studies that take advantage of short-term access provided during ongoing surgical procedures often rely on older generation research tools in comparison to animal research. Unfortunately, these tools have a costly bar for regulatory approval yet a small potential market, hampering investment into translating latest-generation research tools from animal studies to human research. Although some higher-resolution moderately invasive tools for human research do exist, they are typically used in single or small case studies to confirm animal findings, but are problematic to use in larger clinical studies requiring appropriate statistical power. Post-mortem analysis techniques are limited to methods that do not require active transport; many more advanced histological staining and immunohistochemistry techniques have not been developed for or routinely implemented in human studies. As a result, the majority of what is known about the innervation of end-organs in humans was obtained by simple anatomical hand-tracing from cadaveric studies during the early and mid-1900s [13-17].

Despite our limited functional knowledge of the human ANS, implantable neuromodulation devices designed to electrically activate neural targets have demonstrated compelling clinical efficacy to treat a variety of conditions such as epilepsy, depression, incontinence, hypertension, and obesity, which were refractory to or untreatable by conventional drug therapies. However, incomplete understanding of the mechanisms of action in human patients has also contributed to several recent high-profile failures in large scale clinical trials of ANS device therapies. As discussed later in this chapter, the underlying technology even for successful therapies has remained mostly stagnant for decades, as it is difficult to improve a therapy in a regulated environment that was predicated on phenomenology instead of a detailed scientific understanding of the biology.

Given the enormous scope of functions governed by the autonomic nervous system a full review of what is known and not known about the functional anatomy of the ANS could take several books. For a more detailed introduction to the ANS, the authors of this chapter refer the reader to the excellent 'Primer on the Autonomic Nervous System, 3rd Edition' [18]. The remainder of this chapter will provide an overview of the functional anatomy of the ANS, in order to provide the foundation for a discussion of recent developments in the clinical and commercial landscape for ANS neuromodulation devices.

2. Functional Anatomy of the Human Autonomic Nervous System (adapted from [16, 19])

Dysfunction of the ANS has been implicated in many disease conditions such as heart failure, hypertension, chronic kidney disease, and chronic fatigue syndrome [20]. There are many possible root causes of ANS dysfunction including diabetes, Parkinson's disease, or simple aging [21]. As ANS dysfunction manifests through abnormal neural activity, which in turn drives deleterious abnormal function in specific organs or tissues, neuromodulation therapies are predicated on using electrical stimulation to drive such aberrant neural activity towards a normal healthy state. Consequently a detailed understanding of the functional anatomy of the ANS as it pertains to control of end-organs and effector tissues is critical for the design of ANS neuromodulation devices.

2.1. *ANS regulation of function*

ANS efferent nervous activity is primarily regulated by autonomic reflexes. Sensory inputs are transmitted via afferent nerves to control centers in the brain, including the brainstem and hypothalamus, where this information is processed and integrated with information from other afferents and higher neural centers. Responses from these neural centers are then carried out through efferent nerve signals that modify the activity of preganglionic autonomic neurons. The majority of sensory information transmitted to the brainstem from the abdominal or thoracic viscera travels through afferent fibers of the vagus nerve, also known as cranial nerve X. In addition to the vagus nerve, numerous other cranial nerves send sensory input to the brainstem and hypothalamus. An example of an autonomic reflex is the baroreceptor reflex, which responds to changes in vessel stretch and rate of stretch caused by fluctuations in blood pressure to maintain homeostatic equilibrium. Baroreceptors are stretch receptors in diverse locations such as the adventitial-medial border of the aorta and the internal carotid artery that sense distortion of vessel walls resulting from changes in pressure. Signals from the carotid baroreceptors are sent through the glossopharyngeal nerve (cranial nerve IX) to the control center in the brain via the nucleus of the solitary tract, whereas signals from the aortic baroreceptors travel to the brain through the vagus nerve. (Carotid afferents synapse in the petrosal ganglion whereas aortic/vagal baroreceptor afferents synapse in the nodose ganglion.) Increases in blood pressure cause the walls of these vessels to stretch, increasing baroreceptor activity. If blood pressure decreases, the signal to the brain from the baroreceptors diminishes, and the brain in turn sends an efferent signal to the heart and blood vessels to increase heart rate and vascular resistance to restore blood pressure to normal.

Neural control centers in the brainstem and hypothalamus can also be modulated by activity associated with emotional responses in higher brain areas such as the cerebral cortex and limbic system. For example, when embarrassed, increases in heart rate, blood flow to the face (blushing), and nervous sweating are mediated by the ANS through hypothalamic-brainstem pathways. Some autonomic reflexes, such as the micturition and defecation reflex, can occur entirely at the level of the spinal cord without input from the brain. However, these reflexes can also sometimes be influenced by input from higher brain areas.

2.2. *ANS efferent pathways*

Impulses from the central nervous system (CNS) are transmitted to effector tissue through an ANS efferent pathway consisting of two neurons. These two neurons connect to each other via synapses at a cluster of nerve cells outside of the CNS called ganglia, and are therefore called 'preganglionic' and 'postganglionic' neurons. Ganglia are not merely passive relay stations, but can also integrate and process activity from multiple neural inputs. The preglanglionic neuron originates in the CNS, with its cell body located in the brainstem, or in the lateral horn of the gray matter in the spinal cord. (In contrast to ANS efferents, ANS afferents have their cell bodies outside of the CNS.) The axon of the preganglionic neuron travels to an autonomic ganglion located outside the central nervous system where it synapses with a post-ganglionic neuron. The post ganglionic neuron then innervates the effector tissue. At visceral organs such as the heart, ANS efferents and afferents form a branching network of intersecting nerves called a plexus.

Autonomic postganglionic neurons do not form synapses with effector tissue in the same manner as neuron-to-neuron synapses. When axons of postganglionic neurons enter a tissue they contain multiple swellings known as varicosities. Varicosities release neurotransmitters over a large portion of the length of the axon, which diffuse over a large area of effector tissue. Consequently neurotransmitter release driven by post-ganglionic discharges can alter the activity of a large portion of the entire tissue. This latter point is the fundamental basis of the emerging field of 'electroceuticals' or 'bioelectronic medicines' [22, 23]. Electroceuticals utilize electrical stimulation at a single point in a connected neural circuit to drive the downstream activity of post-ganglionic neurons at a specific effector tissue, and therefore control delivery of endogenous neurotransmitters to the target tissue. The goal for electroceuticals is to use the body's intrinsic wiring to instruct the delivery of endogenous biomolecules only to the target effector of interest in order maximize effect and minimize unwanted side effects in contrast to systemic delivery of an exogenous or manufactured drug that elicits a similar effect but with less precision

2.3. *ANS – major divisions*

The ANS has two anatomically and functionally distinct divisions: the sympathetic nervous system (SNS) and the parasympathetic nervous system (PSNS). The SNS controls 'fight or flight' responses to prepare the body for strenuous physical activity, whereas the PSNS controls "rest and digest" basic bodily functions. Both the SNS and the PSNS are tonically active, meaning they provide some degree of neural signal to a tissue at all times. This is important for regulating a tissue's function with high precision as the signal can be either increased or decreased, and therefore effector tissue activity may be enhanced or inhibited.

Most organs receive innervation from both the SNS and the PSNS, with one system typically being excitatory and the other inhibitory. The PSNS in general regulates visceral organs of the head and body cavities. The SNS regulates the same visceral organs as the PSNS, and in addition regulates visceral structures in the body wall and extremities including blood vessels and sweat glands. With the exception of sexual activity, when both SNS and PSNS are active simultaneously, increased activity in one system in general coincides with reduced activity of the other system.

2.3.1. *Sympathetic nervous system*

SNS preganglionic neurons branch from the thoracic and lumbar regions of the spinal cord (segments T1 through L2, Figure 1). SNS preganglionic axons are typically short, as they synapse within sympathetic ganglion chains that run immediately parallel to either side of the spinal cord. Ganglion chains consist of 22 ganglia. Preganglionic neurons leave the spinal cord and synapse with a post-ganglionic neuron at the same spinal cord level, or they may travel rostrally or caudally in the ganglion chain to synapse in ganglia at other levels. A single preganglionic neuron may synapse with several postganglionic neurons in many different ganglia, an example of divergence. Long postganglionic neurons extend from this synapse in the ganglion chain to terminate on effector tissues at a distance. The ratio of preganglionic to post-ganglionic fibers is about 1:20. As a result, excitation by a single preganglionic neuron can coordinate sympathetic activation of multiple tissues.

Some SNS preganglionic neurons do not synapse at the ganglion chains immediately to either side of the spinal cord, but instead pass through these chains and travel more peripherally to synapses with post-ganglionic neurons located in one of the sympathetic collateral ganglia. These ganglia are typically found halfway between the CNS and the effector tissue. Still other preganglionic neurons synapse directly with the adrenal medulla at the superior poles of the kidney instead of in sympathetic ganglion chains near the cord or at the collateral ganglia. More recently, descending inputs from motor cortex to the kidney have also been discovered [24]. Cells of the adrenal medulla behave similarly to post-ganglionic neurons, but instead of releasing neurotransmitters, they release other secretory products into the blood stream, which transports these products to sympathetic effector tissues throughout the body.

SYMPATHETIC DIVISION
(thoracolumbar)

Key:
- Preganglionic neurons
- Postganglionic neurons

Distributed primarily to smooth muscle of blood vessels of these organs:

Brain

Eye

Pineal gland

Lacrimal gland

Mucous membrane of nose and palate

Sublingual and submandibular glands

Parotid gland

Spinal cord

C1
C2
C3
C4
C5
C6
C7
C8

Superior cervical ganglion

Middle cervical ganglion

Inferior cervical ganglion

Heart

Atrial muscle fibers

SA/AV nodes

Ventricular muscle fibers

Cardiac plexus

Trachea

Bronchi

Lungs

Skin

T1
T2
T3
T4
T5
T6
T7
T8
T9
T10
T11
T12

Pulmonary plexus

Greater splanchnic nerve

Celiac ganglion

Transverse colon

Aorticorenal ganglion

Lesser splanchnic nerve

Least splanchnic nerve

Superior mesenteric ganglion

Renal ganglion

Liver, gallbladder, and bile ducts

Stomach

Spleen

Pancreas

Small intestine

Descending colon

Ascending colon

Sigmoid colon

Rectum

Adrenal gland

Kidney

Ureter

Sweat gland

Hair follicle smooth muscle

Blood vessels (each sympathetic trunk innervates the skin and viscera)

L1
L2
L3
L4
L5

S1
S2
S3
S4
S5

Sympathetic trunk ganglia (on both sides)

Lumbar splanchnic nerve

Inferior mesenteric ganglion

Prevertebral ganglia

Coccygeal (fused together)

Urinary bladder

External genitals

Uterus

Hypogastric plexus

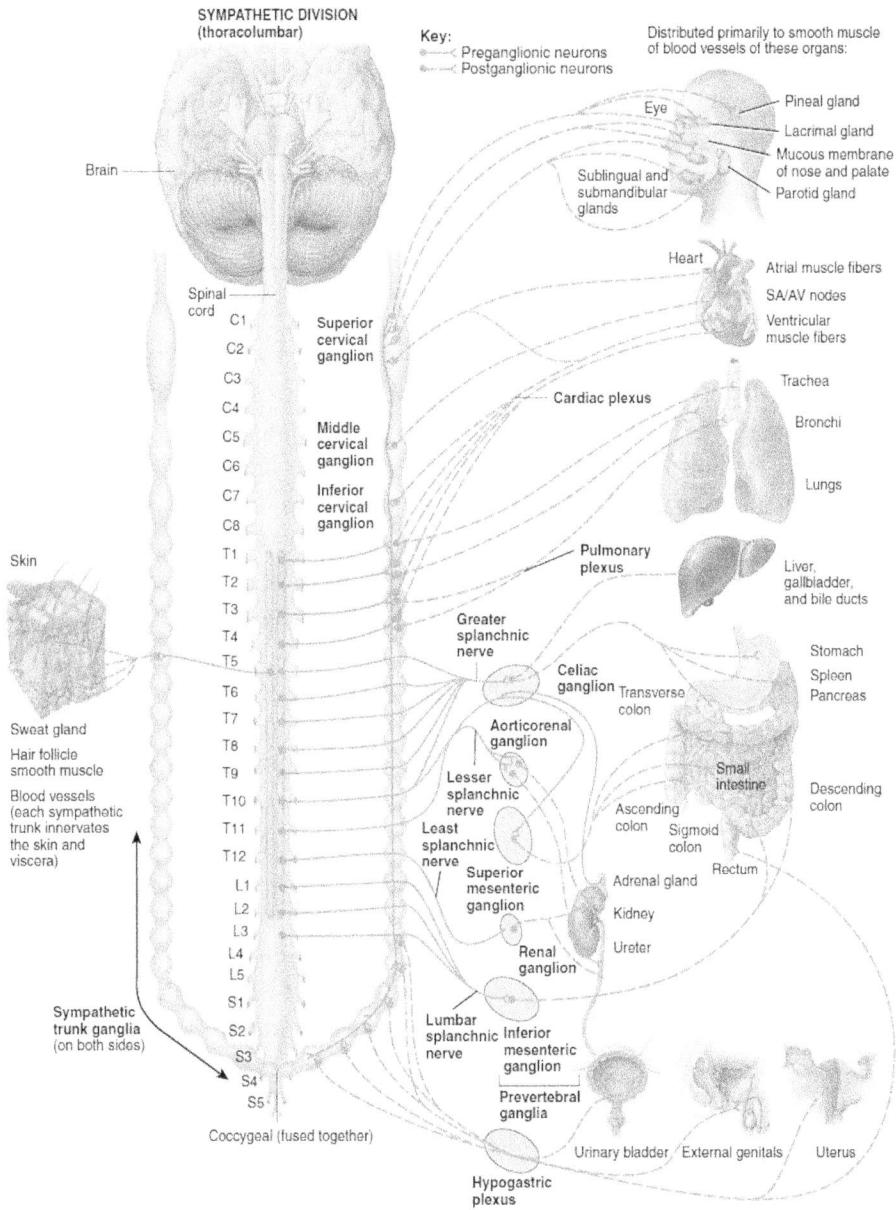

Fig. 1. Anatomy of the Sympathetic Nervous System. Adapted from [2]. (Note that although [10] states SNS preganglionic neurons branch from T1-L2, this figure shows T1-L3, underscoring that sources may conflict.)

In contrast to the parasympathetic system, post-ganglionic neurons of the sympathetic system travel within each of the 31 pairs of spinal nerves. Eight percent of the fibers comprising a spinal nerve are sympathetic, allowing for distribution of these fibers to peripheral blood vessels and sweat glands. Consequently, the majority of blood vessels in the body only receive input from sympathetic nerve fibers, and are therefore regulated by the SNS alone. The SNS also innervates structures of the head, the thoracic viscera, and the viscera of the abdominal and pelvic cavities (Figure 1).

2.3.2. Parasympathetic nervous system

Preganglionic neurons from the parasympathetic system originate from several nuclei of the brainstem and from segments S2 to S4 of the sacral region of the spinal cord (Figure 2). In comparison to SNS preganglionic axons, preganglionic PSNS axons are quite long, synapsing within terminal ganglia that are close to or embedded within the effector tissues. Consequently the axons of post-ganglionic PSNS neurons that provide input into effector tissue are quite short.

PSNS preganglionic neurons that originate in the brainstem leave the CNS as part of the cranial nerves. The oculomotor nerve innervates the eyes (cranial verve III); the facial nerve innervates the lacrimal gland, the salivary glands, and the mucus membranes of the nasal cavity (cranial verve VII); the glossopharyngeal nerve innervates the salivary gland (cranial nerve IX); and the vagus nerve (cranial nerve X) innervates the viscera of the thorax and abdomen (i.e., the spleen, stomach, pancreas, intestines, heart, and lungs). Approximately 75 percent of all parasympathetic fibers are in the vagus nerve, which terminate at widespread locations throughout the body. PSNS preganglionic nerves that originate at the sacral region of the spinal cord innervate the viscera of the pelvic cavity, leaving the CNS to form the pelvic nerves. The pelvic nerves innervate the lower half of the large intestine and organs of the renal and reproductive system.

In comparison to the SNS, there is little divergence in the PSNS, and in many organs, the ratio of preganglionic to post-ganglionic fibers is 1:1. Consequently, responses governed by the PSNS are more localized in comparison to widely distributed autonomic reflex responses governed by the SNS such as the 'fight or flight' response.

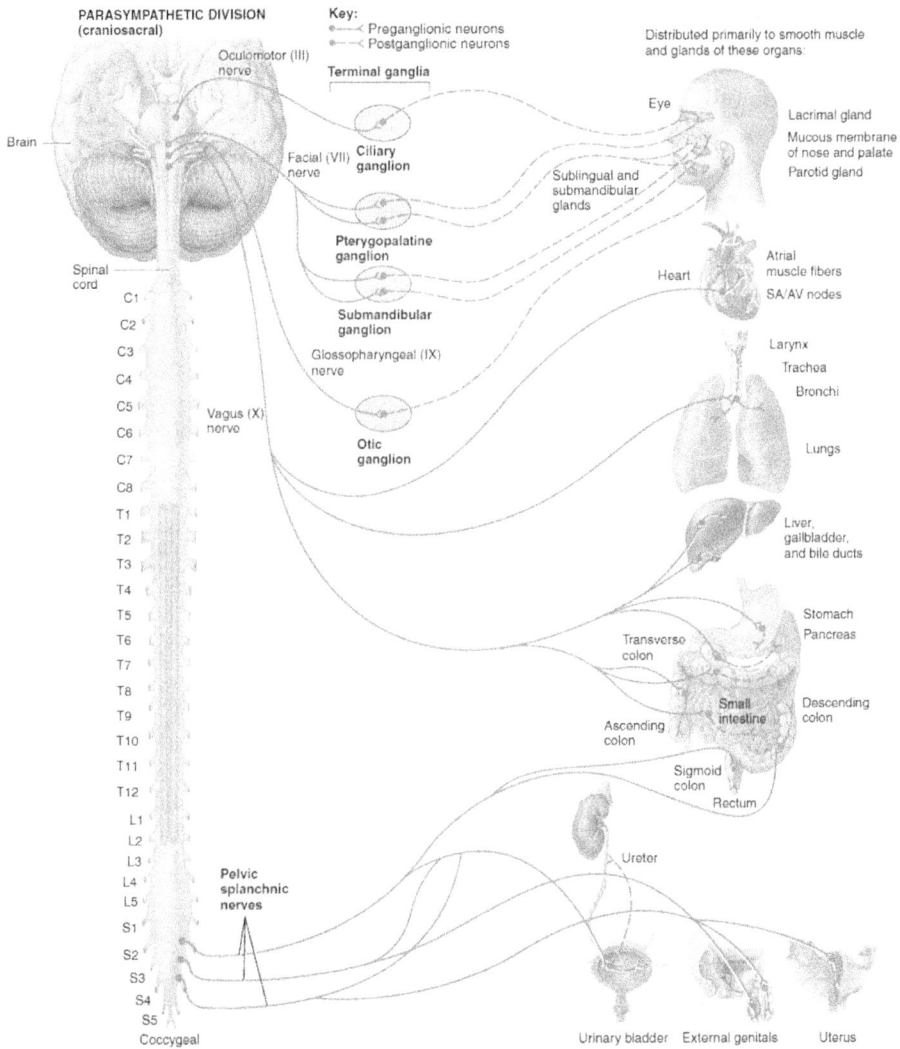

Fig. 2. Anatomy of the Parasympathetic Nervous System. Adapted from [2]

2.4. *ANS neurotransmitters and receptors*

The effects of ANS activity on effector tissue is determined by the neurotransmitter released by the post-ganglionic neuron and the type of receptor embedded in the post-synaptic cell membrane of the targeted effector tissue (Table 1). Consequently many ANS drugs create their therapeutic effect by directly binding to receptors to enhance or block the actions of these neurotransmitters, or by increasing the conversion of endogenous biomolecules and hormonal factors into forms that act on these receptors. For example administration of a "beta blocker" - a common treatment for hypertension and heart failure - would limit the excitatory effects of noradrenaline on β receptors located in the heart, thereby decreasing the force of the contraction of the heart and heart rate.

Table 1. Actions of the Sympathetic and Parasympathetic Nervous System.

Effector tissue	Parasympathetic effect	Sympathetic effect
Heart: Rate	Reduction	Increases
Heart: Force of Contraction	Reduction (especially in atria)	Increases
Arterioles and Veins	None	Constricts Dilates
Lungs	Constricts bronchioles	Dilates bronchioles
Glands: Nasal, Lacrimal, Submandibular, Parotid (salivary) and Gastric (stomach)	Stimulates copious secretion	Stimulates slight secretion & vasoconstriction
Digestive Tract	Increases motility & tone, relaxes sphinchter	Decreases motility & tone, contracts sphincter
Pancreas	Stimulates insulin & enzyme secretion	Inhibits insulin & enzyme secretion
Liver	Slight glycogen synthesis ("glucose store polymer")	Glucose release
Spleen	Decreases proinflammatory cytokines	Decreases proinflammatory cytokines
Bladder	Stimulates urination: Detrusor – contraction Trigone – relaxation	Inhibits urination: Detrusor – relaxation (slight) Trigone – contraction
Adipose tissue (fat)	None	Stimulates fat breakdown
Skeletal Muscle	None	Increases glycogenolysis
Male Sex Organ	Erection	Ejaculation
Eyes: Pupils	Constriction	Dilation
Ciliary Muscle	Slight relaxation (far vision)	Contraction (near vision)
Piloarrector Muscles	None	Contraction

The effects of ANS activity on effector tissue can be quite complex. Multiple neurotransmitters may be released at the same time, each with a different biological effect. For example some neurotransmitters might inhibit further release of additional neurotransmitters, whereas other neurotransmitters might promote the cellular reuptake of different neurotransmitters. Consequently the relative ratios of neurotransmitter release may ultimately determine the change in effector tissue function, commonly known as a 'ratiometric' effect.

The majority of SNS post-ganglionic neurons release noradrenaline and are therefore called adrenergic neurons, whereas the majority of PSNS neurons release acetycholine and are therefore called cholinergic neurons. Noradrenaline acts on α and β receptors in the effector tissue whereas acetycholine acts on muscarinic receptors in the effector tissue. Acetycholine may also act on nicotinic receptors that are primarily limited to synapses in the ANS ganglia, CNS, and at the skeletal muscle neuromuscular junction.

3. Neuromodulation Devices to Control the Autonomic Nervous System

The ANS is tasked with controlling multiple organ systems and is responsible for physiologic homeostasis. Therefore, it is not surprising that there is much effort to develop treatments aimed at controlling ANS function. Neuromodulation devices to control ANS function have seen a large increase in industry activity over the last decade. ANS devices are more amenable to minimally invasive surgical techniques than deep brain stimulators and can be effectively used to address a wide variety of large-market diseases and disorders. Cyberonics first received Premarket Approval (PMA) from the Food and Drug Administration (FDA) in 1997 for an implantable vagal nerve stimulator (VNS), relying on a epineural tripolar-cuff electrode design to reduce seizures associated with partial onset epilepsy that were unresponsive to drug treatment [25]. This same device received FDA market approval to treat depression in 2005 [26]. The manufacturing bar in a regulated environment for developing implantable devices that can safely and reliably stimulate nerves in human patients for a decade or more is exceptionally high. It is not unusual for a Pivotal Trial necessary for FDA Premarket Approval of a chronically implantable device to take up to a decade to complete and cost the manufacturer over $150 million. Moreover, benchtop and short (six months or less) animal tests are not fully predictive of safety or reliability for long term human implants at scale. As a result, the neuromodulation industry aggressively copycats successful clinical designs, drawing heavily from manufacturing processes with proven clinical and commercial success in a regulated market for new device concepts. Consequently the market approvals for the Cyberonics VNS device in 1997 and 2005 have led to a flurry of clinical studies utilizing variants of epineural cuff electrodes to interface with the ANS in new therapeutic indications.

Since 2010, the FDA has granted market approvals for Medtronic's InterStim System (sacral nerve stimulation for urinary and fecal incontinence [27]), Inspire's Upper Airway Stimulation System (hypoglossal nerve stimulation for obstructive sleep apnea [28]), Enteromedic's Maestro System (abdominal vagus blocking therapy for weight loss [29]), Medtronic's Enterra II System (stimulation of stomach for nausea/vomiting resulting from gastroparesis [30]), and CVRx's *neo*™ Legacy System (stimulation of baroreceptors in the carotid sinus for hypertension [31]). Even more prevalent are Conformité Européenne Markings (CE Mark), indicating that an ANS device may be legally marketed in Europe. Prominent CE Marks include several systems to treat heart failure (CVRx's neo™ baroreceptor stimulation system, BioControl's CardioFit vagal nerve stimulation system, and Cyberonics' VITARIA™ vagal nerve stimulation system), hypertension (CVRx's neo™ baroreceptor stimulation system, Boston Scientific's Vessix renal denervation system, Medtronic's Symplicity renal denervation system, and St. Jude's EnligHTN renal denervation system), type 2 Diabetes (Metacure's Diamond system for stimulation of the stomach), as well as bronchoconstriction and gastric motility disorders (electroCore's non-invasive vagal nerve stimulation system).

The difference in number of market approvals between the U.S. and Europe is largely attributable to different standards of clinical evidence necessary to obtain market approval. The FDA is mandated to provide a reasonable assurance of the safety and effectiveness of a medical device [32]. Accordingly, the FDA's Center for Devices and Radiological Health has a three phase system depending on clinical study stage: Early Feasibility, Feasibility, and Pivotal. The 'Pivotal' trial directly precedes market approval, and typically requires a randomized, double-blinded and sham-controlled trial design (RCT) for market approval demonstrating a statistically and clinically significant additional benefit in comparison to aggressive medical management to offset the risks of an invasive surgical procedure [32]. In double blinded designs both the patient and the investigator are deliberately kept unaware of which patient is in the therapy arm versus the control arm. True blinding of both the patient and the clinician may not be possible in some cases, as side-effects indicating the therapy is turned 'on' may be perceptible to both patients and clinicians. For invasive devices, sham controls are typically performed by implanting the neuromodulation device in all subjects and simply not turning it on in a randomized subset of subjects until later in the study.

A 510(k) market approval is a substantially less cumbersome regulatory path than a PMA, as the basis for the FDA submission is an already approved predicated device.

In contrast, the manufacturer need only provide proof that the devices 'works as intended' to receive a CE mark in Europe, even for high-risk medical devices [32]. The difference in regulatory systems creates a stark difference in burden on the manufacturer to obtain market approval; for example, a distal protection system for a coronary artery intervention received a CE mark after a single-arm study involving 22 patients [33, 34], whereas the same device was only approved for sale in the U.S. several years later on the basis of a randomized study involving 800 subjects [35].

Although the relative strengths and weaknesses of the U.S. and European regulatory systems can and have been debated, the U.S. requires a higher scientific standard of clinical evidence for market approval. This has recently led to a number of ANS systems receiving approval for sale in Europe based on single-arm or "open-label" studies, yet failing to meet their primary efficacy end-point in more rigorous, sham-controlled U.S. 'Pivotal' clinical studies to support PMA. Some recent examples include Enteromedic's Maestro system, CVRx's Rheos system and Medtronic's Symplicity System (Table 2). A common theme across these RCT studies is that a significant improvement in end-point metrics was observed in the untreated sham arm. Similarly large effects have been noted in the sham arm in clinical studies of central nervous system neuromodulation devices (NeuroPace, SANTE). It should be noted that some of these devices were able to achieve full FDA PMA (Enteromedics, NeuroPace) or more limited Humanitarian Device Exemptions (HDE, CVRx Rheos™) on the strength of their clinical studies, whereas many of the remaining neuromodulation devices still demonstrated significant improvements in pre-specified secondary efficacy end-points. It is also important to remember that the patients in these studies have severe life-threatening and/or life altering disease/disorders that have been demonstrated to be unresponsive to conventional pharmacologic/biologic treatments.

The inability to predict the outcomes of RCT studies for ANS neuromodulation is in part a function of our limited understanding of the functional neuroanatomy of in humans, and even more limited understanding of how the human autonomic nervous system responds to electrical stimulation delivered by a device at a single point in the system. It should be noted that our lack of understanding of how the functional anatomy relates to therapy limiting side-effects may be just as problematic as our understanding of intended effect.

Table 2. Recent Sham-Controlled Studies of Neuromodulation Devices

System	Description	Primary Clinical Efficacy End-Point	Result Treatment Arm	Result Sham Arm
CVRx Rheos™ [1]	Stimulation of the Carotid Baroreceptors for Hypertension	Percentage of patients with greater than 10mmHg in Systolic Blood Pressure versus sham at 6 months	54% response rate with at least 10-mm Hg reduction in systolic blood pressure from baseline	46% response rate with at least 10-mm Hg reduction in systolic blood pressure from baseline
Medtronic Symplicity [8]	Renal Denervation for Hypertension	Average reduction in systolic blood pressure versus sham at 6 months	14.1 mmHg average reduction in systolic blood pressure from baseline	11.7 mmHg average reduction in systolic blood pressure from baseline
Enteromedic's Maestro [9]	Stimulation of the Abdominal Vagus for Obesity	10 percent or greater average excess weight loss versus sham at 6 months	24.4 percent excess weight loss from baseline*	15.9 percent excess weight loss from baseline
Boston Scientific's NECTAR-HF study [10]	Stimulation of the Vagus for Heart Failure	Decrease in average left ventricular end-systolic diameter versus sham at 6 months	0.04 cm average decrease in left ventricular end-systolic diameter from baseline	0.08 cm average decrease in left ventricular end-systolic diameter from baseline
Medtronic SANTE Study [12]	Bilateral stimulation of the anterior thalamic nucleus for Epilepsy	Decrease in seizure rate per month versus sham	-40.4% median percentage in seizure frequency from baseline*	-14.5% median percentage in seizure frequency from baseline
NeuroPace [12]	Responsive Neural Stimulation for Epilepsy	Decrease in seizure rate per month versus sham	-37.9% median percentage in seizure frequency from baseline*	-17.3% median percentage in seizure frequency from baseline

* Statistically Significant versus Sham ($p < 0.05$)

4. Functional Anatomy - Key Principles for the Development of Neuromodulation Devices for the Autonomic Nervous System

The gold standard for implantable stimulation devices is the cardiac pacemaker. First developed in the early 1930s, over 300,000 patients receive a pacemaker implant each year in the United States alone and over 900,000 per year world wide [36]. The large commercial success of the cardiac pacemaker is a result of decades of development and smart engineering practices that have taken advantage of several features of human functional anatomy, including:

1) target anatomy that enables a simple, minimally invasive, surgical procedure,
2) activation of target effector tissue is easily separable from tissue the produces non-targeted side-effects,
3) low variability in functional anatomy from patient to patient, and
4) a clear and immediate biomarker of intended effect.

The modern pacemaker can be implanted under local anesthesia utilizing a small incision in the chest to provide access through the subclavian, cephalic, or femoral vein to the heart, as visualized using fluoroscopy. A lead is placed in both the atrium and the ventricle, where it is affixed to the endocardium either passively with tines or actively via a helical screw electrode design. These same lead locations can also be used for passive recording of ECG signals for closed-loop control of pacing, yielding an immediate biomarker of pacemaker effect without the need for additional invasive implants. As the cardiac muscle cells form a syncytium, meaning that they are interconnected to generate synchronized muscle activity, the target area for the stimulating electrode is comparatively large. This target area is also well isolated from nerves that could induce unwanted side effects; thus, unwanted side effects such as induced pain or diaphragmatic pacing are usually a result of lead migration or failure of insulation along the implanted lead.

Despite the decades of refinement and numerous favorable features of the human functional anatomy for cardiac pacemakers, surgeries are not without complications. The comprehensive FOLLOWPACE study, which followed over 1500 pacemaker patients over an average of 5.8 years, found that 12.4 percent of patients developed pacemaker complications within the first 2 months after surgery, while 9.2 percent of patients experienced complications thereafter [37]. Given the high complication rate of even the highly refined and established pacemaker technology, commercial development of neuromodulation devices targeting the autonomic nervous system relies heavily on the established manufacturing process used to develop the cardiac pacemaker. As FDA market approval requires the benefits of the product to outweigh the risks - and that the risks are clearly defined and quantified so that a fair evaluation can be made - there is great advantage for companies to develop devices based on previously successful examples where the risks are already well defined, or where the surgical strategy is anticipated to have less risk than standard procedures.

Market penetration and patient adoption also depends heavily on the perceived risk of the surgery. For example, the percentage of patients with Parkinson's disease indicated for deep brain stimulators that elect to receive a deep brain stimulator (DBS) implant vary from 5 to 20 percent depending on the country. Although many factors contribute to this low market penetration, risk perception on the part of patients is undoubtedly a large contributor. Thus, concerns about market viability can make companies reluctant to develop devices where the surgical risks are anticipated to exceed those of the refined pacemaker vascular implantation procedure. Not surprisingly, industry efforts into development of new therapeutic indications have been largely driven by identification of targets that offer similar advantages in local functional anatomy to those of pacemakers, with a primary emphasis on risk profile. Difficulties in meeting primary efficacy endpoints in Pivotal clinical studies can often be attributed to missing one of these enabling features. The following sections describe favorable features of the ANS functional anatomy as they pertain to neuromodulation devices currently undergoing or recently having completed clinical studies.

4.1. *Anatomy enables simple, minimally invasive surgical procedure*

The vagus nerve has become a popular target for autonomic neuromodulation therapies. At the mid-cervical level the vagus nerve lies superficially within the carotid sheath. As such, it can easily be accessed surgically via an incision in the neck. The vagus contains pathways to and from all the major organs in the viscera, and regulates critical systems implicated in numerous diseases and disorders such as the inflammatory reflex, digestion, and bronchoconstriction. A major advantage of targeting the vagus nerve at the mid-cervical level is that this location is typically directly visible via ultrasound, and its location is consistent relative to the carotid arteries, which are also visible. Since 1997 over 100,000 VNS devices have been implanted in 75,000 patients worldwide, providing considerable experience for the refinement of the surgical procedure, thus reducing complications and enhancing the mechanical reliability of the device [38].

Given the cost and difficulty to develop a stimulator that can be manufactured at scale and works reliably after ten years of implantation, existing VNS device designs and manufacturing processes are still largely drawn from practices established during the 1980s and 1990s in the cardiac pacemaker industry. Vagal nerve stimulation (VNS) devices are currently market approved in the United States to treat epilepsy, depression, and obesity. Additionally, VNS devices are market approved in Europe to treat cluster headache, heart failure, bronchoconstriction and type II Diabetes. Emerging indications for VNS devices at various stages of clinical testing include chronic inflammation, rheumatoid arthritis, anxiety, stroke rehabilitation, and tinnitus. Similar to the interest in leveraging the VNS platform for a myriad of ANS therapies, there has been a notable increase in clinical studies leveraging epidural spinal cord stimulators (SCS), which are already market approved for pain treatment, to provide ANS neuromodulation. Early clinical studies have demonstrated that existing SCS devices can be used to improve bladder function, sexual function, and cardiovascular responses in patients with spinal cord injury, in addition to some return of voluntary motor function [39, 40].

More recent ANS devices have focused on anatomical targets that can be accessed through a small surgical window. The CVRx first generation system to stimulate the baroreceptors for hypertension, Rheos™, consisted of vagal nerve tripolar cuff electrodes with a modified "glove" design that was wrapped around both carotid sinus bulbs [41]. The surgery for the Rheos™ system was a complex one, requiring the vascular surgeon to dissect 360° around the sinus bulb, internal and external carotid arteries, and associated substructures on each side of the neck [41]. This surgical complexity may have led to an increased number of adverse events such as nerve damage-related paresthesias. As a result, CVRx failed to meet their primary efficacy endpoint for the Pivotal trial of their first generation device. The CVRx second generation device, *neo™*, consists of a single, very small, monopolar electrode embedded within an insulating suture pad that can be attached to the carotid sinus bulb through a 2 cm unilateral incision [41]. Implantation of the *neo™* system required the development of a specialized surgical tool to enable mapping of the sinus bulb in order to identify the most efficacious implant location [42]. Additionally, implantation required suture of the electrode to the sinus bulb to prevent electrode migration post implantation [42]. Initial results utilizing the minimally invasive *neo™* have closely matched the results of the Rheos™ system, already leading to a CE mark in Europe and a new Pivotal trial in the U.S.

Laparoscopic or "needle-injection" implant surgeries are becoming increasingly commonplace for ANS neuromodulation therapies. The electrodes for the Medtronic Enterra (HDE) System to treat intractable nausea resulting from gastroparesis and the Metacure Diamond system (CE mark) to treat type II diabetes can both be implanted using minimally invasive laparoscopic procedures. The StimGuard tibial nerve stimulator for overactive bladder syndrome - which received an investigational device exemption for a clinical study from the FDA in 2015 - consists of an electrode that can be implanted non-surgically using only a needle, with power and telemetry provided by a small externally worn transmitter. One major advantage of the tibial nerve is that it is large enough to visualize via ultrasound, a critically enabling facet of a needle-stick procedure. Similarly, StimWave received an FDA 510(k) approval for their wireless spinal cord stimulation system, which is also amenable to surgical implantation via percutaneous needle stick. Typically an implantable device requires a PMA even if there are predicated devices, so the StimWave 510(k) approval based on not needing active implanted components has large positive implications for the wider industry. It should be noted that a minimally invasive surgical procedure such as a percutaneous needle stick does not guarantee fewer adverse events. A recent study of SCS implants suggests that adverse events such as dura puncture and cerebral spinal fluid leakage or lead migration are far more common in percutaneous implants than traditional open procedures, presumably due to the decreased visibility and more restricted access.

Although the electrode and lead designs for the StimWave and StimGuard system enable wireless power and telemetry, the size and configuration of the implanted electrode arrays are similar to existing systems powered through a wired connection to an implantable pulse generator. SetPoint Medical (inflammation) and Microtransponder (tinnitus, stroke rehabilitation), amongst others, are developing technology to reduce the size of the implantable electrode and transceiver to stimulate points along the vagus nerve. The end-goal is to reduce the size of the full implant- including electrodes and transceiver for power and telemetry - to fit within an injectable hermetic enclosure the size of a grain of rice. Although there has been considerable interest in developing vascularly implanted miniaturized wireless systems for indications other than cardiac pacing, developing a simple-to-implant device for other indications with the necessary focality of stimulation from within or across a vessel wall has remained elusive.

4.2. *Activation of target nerves is separable from off-target nerves*

There is a trade-off between a minimally invasive electrode design and an electrode design that can minimize the activation of off-target nerves and muscles that lead to side-effects that can limit the therapeutic efficacy. The simplest design for an injectable electrode is a simple small diameter insulated wire with an exposed tip that is bent or barbed, such as the Permaloc intramuscular electrodes for direct stimulation of the bladder wall [43]. These designs allow the wire to be implanted percutaneously through a needle or introducer, and the barb provides anchoring to maintain the position of the electrode once the introducer is retracted. Unfortunately, this simple design is not viable for many nerve stimulation applications as the applied current can create unwanted activation of nearby untargeted nerves or muscles at subthreshold levels for intended therapeutic stimulation of target nerves. In fact programming for many neuromodulation therapies - such as DBS electrodes or carotid baroreceptor stimulators – primarily entails slowly increasing energy delivered until side effects are first noted, and then applying the highest dosage that does not create observable side effects in order to maximize intended effect [44]. Programming procedures that are driven first and foremost by limiting side effects do not guarantee the device is engaging the intended neural target, especially when biomarkers of target engagement are often limited or unreliable.

The standard vagal nerve stimulator, for example, utilizes an insulating cuff that is wrapped around the cervical vagus in conjunction with a tripolar electrode design to limit the spread of current outside of the insulating cuff. Uninsulated electrodes similar to the Permaloc design that can be implanted via a needle injection have been attempted for vagal nerve stimulation in animals, but have been critically limited by unintended activation of the neck muscles at levels still too low for therapeutic activation of the vagus. The tripolar cuff design for existing VNS therapies provides adequate current steering to send current through the epineurium, but requires open surgical access to implant and to anchor the cuff to ensure conformance of the electrode and insulation during the healing-in process to create consistent current steering and prevent lead migration.

A number of commonly used techniques to maximize intended effect while minimizing unintended effects are critically dependent on the functional anatomy of the neural target and surrounding tissue. The first and most common technique is optimizing electrode location. The electric field created by a stimulating electrode falls off very rapidly (as a function of $1/r$ for monopolar configurations, $1/r^2$ for bipolar configurations, and $1/r^3$ for tripolar configurations, where 'r' is the distance from the stimulating electrode) [45, 46]. Consequently, targets with functional anatomy where the stimulating electrode can be consistently placed and maintained closer to target nerves are preferred. It is not unusual to implant an electrode array with electrodes in multiple locations to optimize stimulation based on location after implant; however, this requires a physically larger implant to span these locations and, consequently, can increase the invasiveness of the surgical procedure required.

There is also considerable interest in utilizing multiple cathode and anode electrode configurations to steer current to preferentially activate tissue between electrode contacts instead of at the location of the electrode. Although many market approved devices are capable of current steering, the ability of these techniques to create virtual electrodes for consistent preferential activation between electrode locations in long-term implants remains unproven. Many studies using optical recording techniques in isolated heart preps in animals have demonstrated that generation of virtual cathodes and anodes are dependent on both predictable and unpredictable anisotropies in the target tissue [47], which may vary as a function of edema and scarring from a chronic implant or from patient-to-patient difference in physiology. Therefore, the ability to predict and maintain a virtual cathode or anode for preferential activation of tissue to enhance desired effects and prevent unwanted side effects may be a valuable but limited tool.

A second common technique is manual calibration of the energy applied (pulse width and pulse amplitude) to find a setting that directly initiates action potentials in the fibers of interest while remaining sub-threshold for activating off-target fibers. Although distance from a given fiber to the stimulating electrode is by far the largest determinant of activation threshold, activation thresholds also depend on diameter, myelination, and orientation of the fiber with respect to the stimulating electrode [48]. Consequently, implant locations where there are clear morphological differences between target fibers and off-target fibers that can be differentiated through programming are preferred. Although there has been considerable research into preconditioning pulses and other asymmetrical waveforms to inactivate specific channel types of off-target fibers prior to applying a more general activation pulse, these techniques have yet to be proven or consistently practiced in market approved neuromodulation devices [49-51].

A third technique gaining in prevalence is temporal patterning to optimize on-target effects and minimize off-target effects by mimicking the temporal patterns of naturally occurring neural signals [52-54]. Historical ANS neuromodulation devices have stimulated at a continuous frequency, amplitude, and pulsewidth. Some systems have experimented with intermittent stimulation, such as stimulating one minute out of every five, but primarily to save battery life. Modern systems, however, are increasingly attempting to decipher and imitate the natural patterning of signals sent by nerve fibers to drive desired outcomes. For example, the BioControls system monitors the cardiac cycle to deliver stimulation in rhythm with the intrinsic beating of the heart, in order to mimic the rhythm of natural signals sent by sensory afferents from the heart during normal function. Whether more natural temporal patterning can enhance target effect while minimizing off-target effects compared to stimulation at a single fixed frequency in human patients remains unclear.

Lowering the percentage of the time in which the system is 'actively stimulating', known as duty cycle, is also being increasingly explored to reduce unwanted side effects. Intriguingly, rodent studies conducted by Tracey and colleagues suggest it may be possible to sustainably and beneficially modulate the inflammatory response at the spleen through epineural stimulation at the cervical vagus for as little as ten minutes a day to treat inflammatory conditions such as rheumatoid arthritis or system shock [55]. SetPoint Medical is currently exploring this idea using existing vagal nerve stimulators in exploratory clinical trials in Europe. Similarly closed-loop systems such as the NeuroPace Responsive Neural

Stimulation system use sensors to stimulate only when an active seizure is about to occur to minimize side effects and maximize battery life. Therapies in which stimulation only needs to be administered for a few minutes a day could potentially enable a host of less specific non-invasive neuromodulation techniques, as off-target effects that would be intolerable for a continuous therapy may be easily manageable for short periods.

4.3. *Low variability in functional anatomy from patient to patient*

Given a lack of high resolution tools for clinical research, variability in functional anatomy is difficult to assess from patient to patient, but has increasingly been implicated as a contributor to highly variable functional outcomes from patient to patient evident with many neuromodulation therapies. For example, African American patients in the Medtronic Symplicity-3 RCT study of renal denervation for hypertension showed a higher response to the sham procedure than non-African American patients. Earlier open-label studies did not enroll a large number of African Americans [56]. Although medical adherence and type of therapy administered as a function of race and cultural norms may have strongly contributed to this disparate result, genetic variability is also postulated as a root cause. African Americans have previously been demonstrated to respond differently to common high blood pressure drugs than other groups of people and may also be more sensitive to salt intake on average [57-59].

Similarly, very little is known about the variability in the organization of fibers from patient to patient in popular implant locations like the cervical vagus. The cervical vagus consists of approximately 100,000 fibers, of which 65-80 percent are unmyelinated visceral afferent sensory fibers from a multitude of visceral organs. The distance between afferents and efferents to and from a specific organ and the epineural cuff electrode at the level of the cervical vagus is largely unknown, and may vary greatly across a population. As distance is the largest determinant of activation thresholds, such variability could be partially, or even largely, responsible for the wide variability in patient outcomes to VNS therapy. Consequently, there is increasing interest in therapeutic targets with consistent functional organization of both intended and unintended neural targets from patient to patient, in order to develop a single therapy that maximizes the number of responsive patients.

4.4. *Need for clear and immediate biomarker of intended effect*

The time spent programming devices implanted in patients is both expensive and very burdensome on both the patient and the clinician, and therefore dramatically impacts the market viability of a neuromodulation therapy. Given the increasing number of variables that can be manipulated to impact therapy such as number of electrodes, stimulating electrode location, configuration, waveform amplitude, pulsewidth, pulse shape, frequency, and temporal patterning, the complexity of programming neuromodulation devices is constantly increasing. Consequently, therapeutic targets with clear and immediate direct or surrogate biomarkers of intended effect are critical in order to practically iterate through all potential combinations of therapy parameters. Clear, measurable biomarkers of effect and side effect not only make it easier for caretakers to iterate through the myriad programming options, but also may enable closed-loop systems that can continuously titrate the therapy based on changes in patient status over the course of the day.

An illustrative anecdotal example is from the personal experience of one of us (Ludwig) in programming both hypertension and heart failure patients in clinical studies of the CVRx Rheos™ and *neo*™ Systems. The CVRx device activates the carotid baroreceptors, sending an afferent signal through the carotid sinus nerve to the medulla, which in turn leads to sympathetic inhibition of the heart and blood vessels. In responsive hypertensive patients, therapy parameters resulting in baroreflex activation cause a quickly evident and clear acute drop in blood pressure presumably due to the intended sympathetic inhibition. However, as heart failure patients have a weakened heart, and therefore generate less force during contraction, blood pressure for heart failure patients is often comparatively low without therapy. Consequently, the surrogate biomarker of blood pressure to gauge the intended therapeutic sympathetic inhibition as a function of stimulating the carotid baroreceptors is notably less dramatic. This made it much more difficult to select programming parameters that maximized therapeutic sympathetic inhibition while minimizing side effects such as stimulation-induced pain or parasthesias, as the surrogate biomarker for inhibition of decreased blood pressure was much smaller and often obscured by normal fluctuations in pressure. Although the CVRx system is intended to achieve its therapeutic effect for both hypertension and heart failure by creating a change in vascular resistance via sympathetic inhibition, direct measurement of vascular resistance or sympathetic activity can be difficult to implement clinically for routine programming.

5. Conclusion

Recognizing the unique opportunity of phenomenology-based therapies that have demonstrated therapeutic effect in large clinical studies - but with limited understanding of mechanism of action - the National Institutes of Health (NIH), the Defense Advanced Research Projects Agency (DARPA), and pharmaceutical giant GlaxoSmithKline (GSK) recently convened a symposium of world experts to develop a research roadmap for the emerging field of ANS device therapies called "bioelectronic medicines" [23]. The ultimate vision for bioelectronic medicines is miniaturized, injectable wireless devices that can record, analyze and modulate neural signal patterns automatically, in a 'closed-loop' fashion to achieve therapeutic effects targeting organ functions. This technology would represent the ultimate in both precision and personalized medicine. Here, precise targeting of the nervous system would be used to direct location-specific delivery of endogenous biomolecules relevant to control end-organ function and avoid unwanted side effects, while biosensors would titrate the therapy in real-time based on patient-specific changes in measured physiological function. The research roadmap proposed three pillars necessary to realize this vision:

1) the open development of a detailed anatomical and functional nerve atlas in both humans and animal models establishing both intra and interspecies variation in organ innervation;

2) investment in next generation research platforms that can wirelessly stimulate, record and block nerve activity reliably in chronic animal preparations to better understand changes at the neural interface and systemic adaptation to therapy; and

3) investment in research tools and studies to support 'parallel translation'. Parallel translation means conducting high resolution, high-throughput animal studies *while simultaneously* conducting lower throughput human studies taking advantage of pre-existing surgical procedures, to hasten discovery compared to traditional serial translation efforts. Parallel translation is critically necessary to establish human relevance of the animal data, as well as to iteratively refine computational models to predict human results.

In support of this roadmap the NIH, DARPA, and GSK have all launched their own large-scale funding programs - known as the Stimulating Peripheral Activity to Relieve Conditions (SPARC, NIH), Electrical Prescriptions (ElectRx, DARPA), and Bioelectronic Medicines Programs (GSK). As neuromodulation devices are already a three billion dollar a year industry - yet predicated primarily on compelling clinical phenomenology - investment into elucidating the anatomy and physiology of the ANS will catalyze the development of completely new ANS device therapies while helping to optimize existing ones. ANS neuromodulation devices have the potential to become a minimally invasive frontline therapy, instead of a treatment of last resort, through capitalizing on advances on advanced in miniaturization, computing, and surgical tooling. Leveraging a keen understanding of the biology to optimize the number of responsive patients, ANS device therapies could both revolutionize clinical practice as well as create exponential economic growth.

References

1. J. D. Bisognano, G. Bakris, M. K. Nadim, L. Sanchez, A. A. Kroon, J. Schafer, P. W. de Leeuw, and D. A. Sica, Baroreflex activation therapy lowers blood pressure in patients with resistant hypertension: results from the double-blind, randomized, placebo-controlled rheos pivotal trial, *Journal of the American College of Cardiology*, **58**, pp. 765-773, 2011.
2. G. J. Tortora, and B. Derrickson, *Principles of Anatomy & Physiology*. 14th ed, (Wiley, Hoboken, NJ) 2014
3. C. Bernard, *Introduction à l'étude de la médecine expérimentale*, (J. B. Baillière et fils, Paris) 1865.
4. C. Bernard, *Leçons sur les phénomènes de la vie communs aux animaux et aux végétaux.* (J. B. Baillière et fils, Paris), 1878.
5. C. Bernard and P. Bert, *La science expérimentale.* (J. B. Baillière et fils, Paris), 1878.
6. W. B. Cannon, The mechanical factors of digestion, *International Medical Monographs*, (Longmans, Green & Co., New York) 1911.
7. W. B. Cannon, *Bodily Changes iIn Pain, Hunger, Fear and Rage; An Account of Recent Researches Into The Function of Emotional Excitement*, 2nd ed, (D. Appleton and Company, New York) 1929
8. H. C. Patel, C. Hayward and C. Di Mario, SYMPLICITY HTN 3: The death knell for renal denervation in hypertension?, *Global Cardiology Science & Practice*, **2014**(1), pp. 94-98, 2014.
9. G. Sinha, Weight loss 'electroceutical' device wins FDA okay, *Nature Biotechnology*, **33**(3): p. 226, 2015.
10. F. Zannad, G. M. De Ferrari, A. E. Tuinenburg, D. Wright, J. Brugada, C. Butter, H. Klein, C. Stolen, S. Meyer, K. M. Stein, A. Ramuzat, B. Schubert, D. Daum, P. Neuzil, C. Botman, M. Angeles Castel, A. D'Onofrio, S. D. Solomon, N. Wold, and S. B. Ruble, Chronic vagal stimulation for the treatment of low ejection fraction heart failure: results of the NEural Cardiac TherApy foR Heart Failure (NECTAR-HF) randomized controlled trial, *European Heart Journal*, **36**(7), pp. 425-433, 2015.
11. R. S. Terry, Vagus nerve stimulation therapy for epilepsy, in *Epilepsy Topics*, ed. M. D. Holmes, (InTech) 2014, pp. 139-160.
12. V. Krishna and A. M. Lozano, Brain stimulation for intractable epilepsy: Anterior thalamus and responsive stimulation, *Annals of Indian Academy of Neurology*, **17**(Suppl 1) pp. S95-S98, 2014.
13. G. A. G. Mitchell, ed., *Anatomy of the Autonomic Nervous System*, (Livingstone, London) 1953.
14. G. A. G.Mitchell, ed., *Cardiovascular Innervation*, (Livingstone, London) 1956.

15. J. Pick, ed., *The Autonomic Nervous System*, (Lippincott, Philadelphia) 1970.
16. L. K. McCorry, Physiology of the autonomic nervous system, *American Journal of Pharmaceutical Education*, **71**(4), p. 78, 2007.
17. W. Jänig, *Integrative Action of the Autonomic Nervous System: Neurobiology of Homeostasis*, (Cambridge University Press, Cambridge) 2008.
18. D. Robertson and I. Biaggioni, *Primer on the autonomic nervous system*, (Academic Press, Ne York), 2012.
19. G. S. Dhillon and K. W. Horch, Autonomic nervous system, in *Neuroprosthetics: Theory and Practice*, eds. K. Horch, and G. S. Dhillon, (World Scientific, New Jersey) 2004, pp. 137-157.
20. D. S. Goldstein, D. Robertson, M. Esler, S. E. Straus, and G. Eisenhofer, Dysautonomias: clinical disorders of the autonomic nervous system, *Annals of Internal Medicine*, **137**(9): pp. 753-763, 2002.
21. M. D. Esler, J. M. Thompson, D. M. Kaye, A. G. Turner, G. L. Jennings, H. S. Cox, G. W. Lambert, and D. R. Seals, Effects of aging on the responsiveness of the human cardiac sympathetic nerves to stressors, *Circulation*, **91**(2), pp. 351-358, 1995.
22. K. Famm, B. Litt, K. J. Tracey, E. S. Boyden, and M. Slaoui, Drug discovery: a jump-start for electroceuticals, *Nature*, **496**(7444). pp. 159-161, 2013.
23. K. Birmingham, V. Gradinaru, P. Anikeeva, W. M. Grill, V. Pikov, B. McLaughlin, P. Pasricha, D. Weber, K. Ludwig and K. Famm, Bioelectronic medicines: a research roadmap, *Nature Reviews. Drug Discovery*, **13**(6), pp. 399-400, 2014.
24. D. J. Levinthal and P. L. Strick, The motor cortex communicates with the kidney, *The Journal of Neuroscience*, **32**(19) pp. 6726-6731, 2012.
25. FDA *Cyberonics NeuroCybernetic Prosthesis System PMA p970003*. 1997.
26. FDA, *Cyberonics VNS Therapy System PMA P970003/S50*, 2005.
27. FDA, *Medtronic Interstim Threapy System PreMarket Approval P080025*, 2011.
28. FDA *Inspire Upper Airway Stimulation System PMA P130008*. 2014.
29. FDA, *Maestro Rechargeable System Premarket Approval P130019*, 2015.
30. FDA *Enterra II System Humanitarian Device Exemption H990014*. 2015.
31. FDA *CVRx Barostim neo Legacy System HDE H130007*. 2014.
32. D. B. Kramer, S. Xu, and A.S. Kesselheim, Regulation of medical devices in the United States and European Union, *The New England Journal of Medicine*, **366**(9), pp. 848-855, 2012.
33. A. V. Kaplan, D. S. Baim, J. J. Smith, D. A. Feigal, M. Simons, D. Jefferys, T. J. Fogarty, R. E. Kuntz, and M. B. Leon, Medical device development: from prototype to regulatory approval, *Circulation*, **109**(25), pp. 3068-3072, 2004.
34. J. G. Webb, R. G. Carere, R. Virmani, D. Baim, P. S. Teirstein, P. Whitlow, C. McQueen, F. D. Kolodgie, E. Buller, A. Dodek, G. B. J. Mancini, and S. Oesterle, Retrieval and analysis of particulate debris after saphenous vein graft intervention, *Journal of the American College of Cardiology*, **34**(2), pp. 468-475. 1999.
35. D. S. Baim, D. Wahr, B. George, M. B. Leon, J. Greenberg, D. E. Cutlip, U. Kaya, J. J. Popma, K. K. L. Ho, R. E. Kuntz, et al., Randomized trial of a distal embolic protection device during percutaneous intervention of saphenous vein aorto-coronary bypass grafts, *Circulation*, **105**(11), pp. 1285-1290, 2002.
36. G. Gregoratos, Indications and recommendations for pacemaker therapy, *American Family Physician*, **71**(8), pp. 1563-1570, 2005.

37. E. O. Udo, N. P. A. Zuithoff, N. M. van Hemel, C. C. de Cock, T. Hendriks, P. A. Doevendans, and K. G. M. Moons, Incidence and predictors of short- and long-term complications in pacemaker therapy: the FOLLOWPACE study, *Heart Rhythm*, **9**(5), pp. 728-735, 2012.

38. K. Chakravarthy, H. Chaudhry, K. Williams, P. J. Christo, Review of the uses of vagal nerve stimulation in chronic pain management, *Current Pain and Headache Reports*, **19**(12) p. 54, 2015.

39. M. R. Carhart, J. He, R. Herman, S. D'Luzansky, and W. T. Willis, Epidural spinal-cord stimulation facilitates recovery of functional walking following incomplete spinal-cord injury, *IEEE Transactions on Neural Systems and Rehabilitation Engineering*, **12**(1), pp. 32-42, 2004.

40. S. Harkema, Y. Gerasimenko, J. Hodes, J. Burdick, C. Angeli, Y. Chen, C. Ferreira, A. Willhite, E. Rejc, R. G. Grossman, and V. R. Edgerton, Effect of epidural stimulation of the lumbosacral spinal cord on voluntary movement, standing, and assisted stepping after motor complete paraplegia: a case study, *Lancet*, **377**(9781), pp. 1938-1947, 2011.

41. J. P. Gassler and J. D. Bisognano, Baroreflex activation therapy in hypertension, *Journal of Human Hypertension*, **28**(8), pp. 469-74, 2014.

42. A. Cates, E. Lovett, L. Murney, K. Ludwig, P. Pignato, and B. Soltis, Implant tool and improved electrode design for minimally invasive procedure, *U.S.Patent 8,788,066*, 2014.

43. J. S. Walter, J. Wheeler, L. Bresler, S. Sayers, and S. Singh, Neuroprosthetics for SCI bladder management: The argument for direct bladder stimulation, *International Journal of Physical Medicine & Rehabilitation*, **2**(5), p. 230, 2014.

44. J. Volkmann, E. Moro, and R. Pahwa, Basic algorithms for the programming of deep brain stimulation in Parkinson's disease, *Movement Disorders*, **21 Suppl 14,** pp. S284-S289, 2006.

45. R. Plonsey, Quantitative formulations of electrophysiological sources of potential fields in volume conductors, *IEEE Transactions on Bio-medical Engineering*, **31**(12), pp. 868-872, 1984.

46. R. Plonsey and D. B. Heppner, Considerations of quasi-stationarity in electrophysiological systems, The Bulletin of Mathematical Biophysics, **29**(4), pp. 657-664, 1967.

47. J. P. Wikswo, Jr., S. F. Lin, and R. A. Abbas, Virtual electrodes in cardiac tissue: a common mechanism for anodal and cathodal stimulation, *Biophysical Journal*, **69**(6), pp. 2195-2210, 1995.

48. M. A. Moffitt, C. C. McIntyre, and W. M. Grill, Prediction of myelinated nerve fiber stimulation thresholds: limitations of linear models, *IEEE Transactions on Bio-medical Engineering*, **51**(2) pp. 229-236, 2004.

49. C. C. McIntyre and W. M. Grill, Extracellular stimulation of central neurons: influence of stimulus waveform and frequency on neuronal output, *Journal of Neurophysiology*, **88**(4) pp. 1592-1604, 2002.

50. A. Wongsarnpigoon, J. P. Woock, and W. M. Grill, Efficiency analysis of waveform shape for electrical excitation of nerve fibers, *IEEE Transactions on Neural Systems and Rehabilitation Engineering*, **18**(3) pp. 319-328, 2010.

51. A. Wongsarnpigoon and W. M. Grill, Energy-efficient waveform shapes for neural stimulation revealed with a genetic algorithm, *Journal of Neural Engineering*, **7**(4), p. 046009, 2010.

52. M. J. McGee and W.M. Grill, Temporal pattern of stimulation modulates reflex bladder activation by pudendal nerve stimulation, *Neurourology and Urodynamics*, 10.1002/nau.22822, 2015.

53. M. J. Birdno, A. M. Kuncel, A. D. Dorval, D. A. Turner, and W. M. Grill, Tremor varies as a function of the temporal regularity of deep brain stimulation, *Neuroreport*, **19**(5) pp. 599-602, 2008.

54. W. M. Grill, A. M. Simmons, S. E. Cooper, S. Miocinovic, E. B. Montgomery, K. B. Baker, and A. R. Rezai, Temporal excitation properties of paresthesias evoked by thalamic microstimulation, *Clinical Neurophysiology*, **116**(5) pp. 1227-1234, 2005.

55. L. V. Borovikova, S. Ivanova, M. Zhang, H. Yang, G. I. Botchkina, L. R. Watkins, H. Wang, N. Abumrad, J. W. Eaton and K. J. Tracey, Vagus nerve stimulation attenuates the systemic inflammatory response to endotoxin, *Nature*, **405**(6785), pp. 458-462, 2000.

56. D. E. Kandzari, D. L. Bhatt, S. Brar, C. M. Devireddy, M. Esler, M. Fahy, J. M. Flack, B. T. Katzen, J. Lea, D. P. Lee, M. B. Leon, A. Ma, J. Massaro, L. Mauri, S. Oparil, W. W. O'Neill, M. R. Patel, K. Rocha-Singh, P. A. Sobotka, L. Svetkey, R. R. Townsend, and G. L. Bakris, Predictors of blood pressure response in the SYMPLICITY HTN-3 trial, *European Heart Journal*, **36**(4), pp. 219-227, 2015.

57. N. Kaperonis and G. Bakris, Blood pressure, antihypertensive therapy and risk for renal injury in African-Americans, *Current Opinion in Nephrology and Hypertension*, **12**(1), pp. 79-84, 2003.

58. J. G. Douglas, K. C. Ferdinand, G. L. Bakris and J. R. Sowers, Barriers to blood pressure control in African Americans. Overcoming obstacles is challenging, but target goals can be attained, *Postgraduate Medicine*, **112**(4), pp. 51-70, 2002.

59. G. L. Bakris, K. C. Ferdinand, J. G. Douglas and J, R. Sowers, Optimal treatment of hypertension in African Americans. Reaching and maintaining target blood pressure goals, *Postgraduate Medicine*, **112**(4), pp. 73-84, 2002.

Chapter 1.3

Anatomy and Physiology of the Central Nervous System

Doug Weber[1,2], James Harris[3], Tim Bruns[4], and Vivian Mushahwar[5]

[1]*Defense Advanced Research Projects Agency, Biological Technologies Office, Arlington, Virginia, USA*

[2]*Department of Bioengineering, University of Pittsburgh, Pittsburgh, PA, USA*

[3]*Information Systems Worldwide Corporation, Arlington, Virginia, USA*

[4]*Department of Biomedical Engineering, University of Michigan, Ann Arbor, Michigan, USA*

[5]*Division of Physical Medicine and Rehabilitation, Department of Medicine, University of Alberta, Edmonton, Alberta, Canada*

weber.doug@gmail.com

James.Harris@iswcorp.com

Bruns@umich.edu

Vivian.Mushahwar@ualberta.ca

Familiarity with the anatomy and physiology of the central nervous system (CNS) is essential for any student or researcher in the field of neural prostheses. Knowledge of CNS structure, organization, and function is crucial for understanding the effects of injury and disease on neurological function, and to design rational strategies for restoring or augmenting those functions with neural prostheses. Unlike mechatronic prostheses, which work by providing physical replacements for damaged or missing limbs, neural prostheses operate by leveraging intrinsic functions of the nervous system. Thus, to understand the capabilities and limitations of any neural prosthesis, one must consider the anatomy and physiology of the neural structures engaged by the technology. The goal of this chapter is to provide a general introduction to the CNS and serve as a reference when considering subsequent chapters that deal with particular components of this system. For brevity, we have focused more attention on structures that have been notable targets of previous efforts in neuroprosthetics. A brief description of the anatomy and physiology of each structure is provided. We have left the details of neuroprosthetic applications to subsequent chapters focusing on particular neural systems and functions.

1. Introduction

The central nervous system (CNS) comprises the brain and spinal cord, which contain vast networks of highly interconnected neurons that support myriad sensory, motor, cognitive, and autonomic functions. The CNS achieves most of these functions through interactions with the peripheral nervous system (PNS), described in more detail in chapter 1.1. This chapter will provide an overview of the CNS, divided in two sections covering the brain and spinal cord.

The CNS is composed of two main cell types, neurons and glia. Neurons conduct electrical impulses and form the basis for neuronal networks within the brain and spinal cord. In general, the main components of the neuron include dendrites, cell body (soma), axon hillock, axon, and axon terminals, which transmit chemical signals (i.e. neurotransmitters) to other neurons across connections called synapses. The dendrites form tree-like arborizations that integrate synaptic inputs from other neurons, resulting in graded changes in the transmembrane voltage that are called post-synaptic potentials (PSPs). At "rest", the transmembrane potential is approximately -70 mV, as measured between the inside of the cell relative to the extracelluar space. PSPs generated by synaptic inputs can be inhibitory or excitatory, depending on the type(s) of neurotransmitter released at the synapse and the type(s) of chemical receptors present on the postsynaptic neuron. Inhibitory PSPs (iPSPs) drive negative changes in the membrane potential (i.e. further polarization), while excitatory PSPs (ePSPs) serve to depolarize the membrane. When the neuron is depolarized to a critical "threshold", an action potential (AP) will be generated at the axon hillock of the neuron. The AP propagates along the length of the thin, elongated structure of the neurons called the axon. The size and length of axons varies depending on the neuron's function.

The vast majority of neurons are interneurons, neurons with axons that do not exit the central nervous system. Other neurons, known as motor neurons and sensory neurons, with cell bodies located in the brain and in or near the spinal cord (within the spinal column), extend their axons outside the central nervous system and form the efferent and afferent component of peripheral nerves, respectively. The ensuing sections will introduce different kinds of neuronal cells located throughout the central nervous system. Glial cells form the support matrix for neurons. Among their tasks is the provision of insulation or myelin for some axons which acts to increase the conduction velocity of electrical impulses, and the recycling of excess neurotransmitters released between cells.

The following planes of reference will be used when referring to the anatomical location of neuronal structures in the central nervous system (Fig. 1). The **sagittal** plane passes lengthwise through the body and divides it into left and right portions.

The term *lateral* refers to locations away from the midline in the sagittal plane while *medial* refers to locations close to the midline. The term *ipsilateral* means the same side in the sagittal plane while *contralateral* means the opposite side. The **frontal** or **coronal** plane passes lengthwise through the body and divides it into front and back portions. The terms *dorsal* and *posterior* refer to locations in the back part of the body in the frontal plane while *ventral* and *anterior* refer to locations in the front part. The **horizontal, transverse** or **cross-sectional** plane divides the body into upper (*rostral or superior*) and lower (*caudal or inferior*) portions.

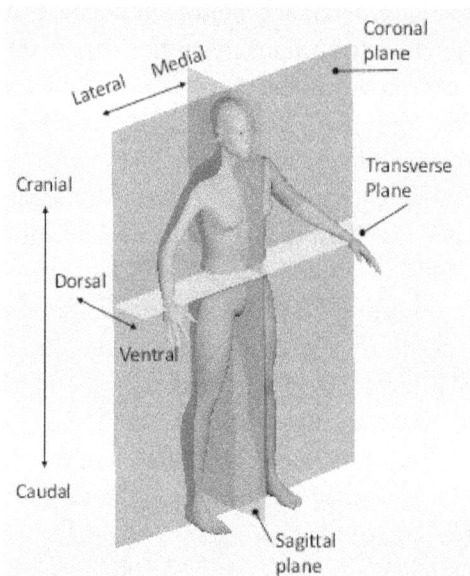

Fig. 1. Visualization of anatomical planes of reference and descriptive terms.

Starting caudally and moving rostrally, the central nervous system consists of the spinal cord, located within the spinal column (spine), a cranial swelling (medulla) connected through a bridge (pons) to the midbrain (mesencephalon) (Fig. 2). The roof (tectum) of the midbrain is the site of the superior and inferior colliculi, two important nuclei for vision and audition (see Chapters 1.7 and 1.8, respectively). As one travels "up" the system, progressing from the mesencephalon to the diencephalon (from which various forebrain structures extend), this simple linear progression breaks down, and various lateral branches, such as the cerebellum, make the anatomical system much more interesting and complicated. The thalamus and hypothalamus reside above the midbrain. The hypothalamus plays a critical role in the regulation of many autonomic nervous system functions (see Chap. 1.2), in the generation of emotional states and the motor patterns associated with them, and in the production of certain hormones (e.g., oxytocin and antidiuretic hormone) and regulation of others through the pituitary gland. The basal ganglia or cerebral nuclei consist of a collection of structures, some of which are related to the limbic system, but the majority of which are major players in the control of muscle tone and voluntary movement. Disorders of the basal ganglia function can be quite debilitating (e.g., Parkinson's disease) and are the subject of considerable current interest as candidates for neurostimulation based therapies. The limbic system is a collection of cortical and subcortical structures responsible for functions such as learning and memory, emotional states, and behavior associated with drives. Located most rostrally in the central nervous system is the cerebral cortex which is comprised of four lobes in each hemisphere, frontal, parietal, temporal and occipital.

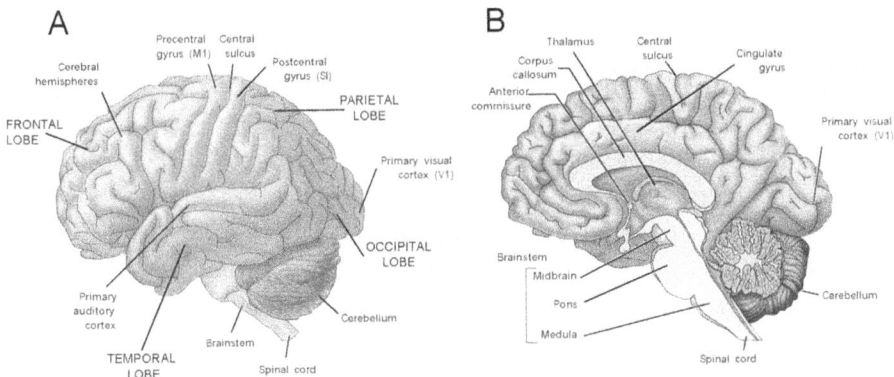

Fig. 2. Gross anatomy of the human brain, (A) lateral and (B) medial view. The spinal cord, brainstem, cerebellum, thalamus and cerebral cortex are shown. The wrinkled outer surface (composed of fissures or sulci and folds or gyri) that covers the majority of the brain is the cerebral cortex. In panel (A) labels illustrate some of the areas of localized function in the cerebral cortex including primary motor cortex on the precentral gyrus (M1) and primary somatosensory cortex on the postcentral gyrus (S1). Other primary sensory cortex areas for vision and audition are also shown. The cerebrum is divided in two hemispheres which are connected through the corpus callosum and anterior commissure. (Adapted from [1]).

The following sections provide a concise description of many components that are likely to be encountered in discussions of neuroprosthetic and neuromodulatory devices intended for application to the CNS. Though the chosen structures are segregated into individual sections, the reader is reminded that these structures are extensively interconnected. The reader is encouraged to examine the more specific descriptions on sensory, motor, and other systems that are covered in detail in subsequent chapters.

2. The Brain

While the complexity of the brain, its anatomy, and its function deserve a whole textbook, the following sections will serve as a primer to understand relevant structures (neural cell bodies, dendrites, and axons/fiber tracts) that enable or could enable applications in neuroprosthetics to treat clinical populations. We start with an examination of anatomy from a top-down perspective (cerebral cortex downward), with a focus on different functions that these structures play a role in mediating.

The majority of these discussions will describe neural cells and how to interface with those cells, but the reader is reminded that the non-neural cells, glia or neuroglia, are a large majority of the cells in the brain. The numbers of neural and non-neuronal cells are roughly equal, while in the cortex, neural cells make up only about 20% of the cells and in the cerebellum they make up about 80% of the cells [2]. Notably, the majority of non-neuronal cells is in the cortical white matter.

Regarding specific non-neuronal cells, microglia are the resident "first-responders" of the brain that respond to inflammation or other "invaders". Astrocytes are key in maintaining the immune privilege of the brain, working with pericytes and epithelial cells to govern the blood brain barrier. Astrocytes are also an important contributor to chemical and neurotransmitter buffering to maintain the well-controlled environment of the brain for the high energetic demands of the brain (15% of body energy consumption vs. 2% of body weight) [3]. Part of their function is to control blood flow [4]. Additionally, newer evidence is emerging about the differences in astrocytes among species where astrocytes in humans have distinct features versus rodents, including size and calcium wave conduction speed [5]. Similarly, the human neocortex has an additional type of astrocyte in comparison to the nonhuman primate [5]. A similar but different cell type is radial glia. These cells are vital in the development of the cortex; they are a main player in the inside out construction of the cortex where layer 6 (most inferior) is the first layer to develop and layer 1 (most superior) is the last layer created. In other words, a cell from layer 1 has to progress through layers 6-2 to get to its final location. Radial glia act as a guide rope to accomplish this. Another cell type is the oligodendrocyte that provides myelination of axons, much like Schwann cells in the peripheral nervous system. One notable difference between Schwann cells and oligodendrocytes is that Schwann cells interact with only one axon or cell where oligodendrocytes can interact with several axons or cells. One additional cell of note in the CNS is ependymal cells that create cerebrospinal fluid (CSF) for the brain and spinal cord. The constant generation and maintenance of this fluid helps maintain a stable environment for the brain. It also provides mechanical benefits by suspending the brain in the skull to minimize mechanical loading while at rest or during movement. While recent research has shown the interplay of neuronal and non-neuronal cells are vital in key brain functions and function of neurons themselves, further research is needed to tease apart the importance of all the relationships.

3. Forebrain

3.1. *Forebrain anatomy - overview*

The forebrain, or prosencephalon, contains some of the most evolutionary advanced structures in neuroanatomy. Most notably, the cerebral cortex, often referred to as the cerebrum, neocortex, or just the cortex, is often associated with many of our higher reasoning capabilities. The forebrain can be split into two different groups of structures: the telencephalon that contains the cerebral cortex, hippocampus, basal ganglia, among others and the diencephalon that contains the thalamus (as well as hypothalamus, subthalamus, epithalamus).

3.2. *Telencephalon – cerebral cortex anatomy*

The cerebral cortex or neocortex is often what we see when we picture the brain. The cortex has many functions and accounts for over 80% of the mass of the brain [2]. It is thought to be the foundation of consciousness, central processing of sensory information, integration of that information, memory, decision making, and generation of motor output commands, among other tasks. The undulating surface of the brain is composed of gyri (outfolds) and sulci (infolds). The folding increases the surface area of the cortex while not increasing skull volume, resulting in additional cortical areas not present in smaller brains. Therefore, in mammals with the smallest neocortices there are 10–20 different functional areas whereas this number can exceed 100 areas in humans [6, 7]. Notably, only higher-level mammals have this folding, or gyrencephalic brains. Lower level mammals, such as rodents, do not have the folding, which is dubbed lissencephalic brains [8]. This difference may impact which animal model is most relevant for preclinical work. Another difference to bear in mind is the ratio of white matter to gray matter volume. The volume ratio is 14:86 in rats and 10:90 in mice, white to gray matter, where in humans and swine it is 60:40 [9-11]. This difference can also dictate which animal model would be most relevant.

Packed into this large volume are 6 layers of neural cells that predominantly have different functions. While not all areas of the cortex have 6 layers, 90% of the cortex has 6 defined layers. The composition and complexity has evolved over time, and in humans, additional sublayers have been defined [8].

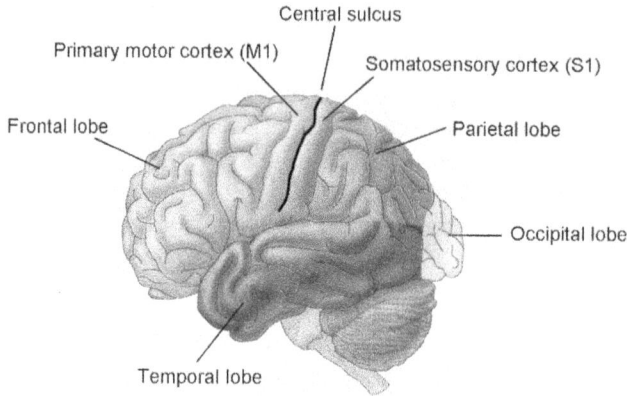

Fig. 3. The cerebral cortex has four lobes: frontal, parietal, occipital and temporal. Motor areas are located in the frontal lobe, in front of the central sulcus, while the somatosensory cortex lies in the parietal cortex immediately behind the central sulcus.

The cortex is divided into 4 lobes frontal, parietal, occipital, and temporal (Fig. 3). Each of these lobes can be further subdivided into areas that are specific to certain functions (e.g., primary motor cortex for motor function, primary visual cortex for vision, etc.). Several different maps of the cortex and its lobes are available, some which will be covered here. One of the most famous examples would a map of Brodmann areas (Fig. 4). In humans, he specified 43 areas, labeled 1-52 with areas 12-16 and 48-51 not present in his original human maps, but present in his maps of Old World monkeys. In the early 20th century, Campbell (1905 [12]), Smith (1907 [13]), and Brodmann (1909 [14]) painstakingly subdivided the neocortex into different regions based on the differences in the histological appearance. At the same time Sherrington [15] championed localization by meticulously "mapping" the cortex using electrical stimuli and noting the peripheral motor responses. The work by these researchers and others suggested that different areas of the cerebral cortex were specialized to perform discrete functions. Others built on these maps to further refine delineations (including Sarkisov [16], Fig. 4). Alternatively, others have built on these maps to address needs regarding stereotactic brain surgery, including Talairach space/coordinates and MNI (Montreal Neurological Institute and Hospital) space/coordinates [17-19]. Recent research has also used transmitter receptor mapping to further probe the composition of a particular area based on particular neurotransmitters [20].

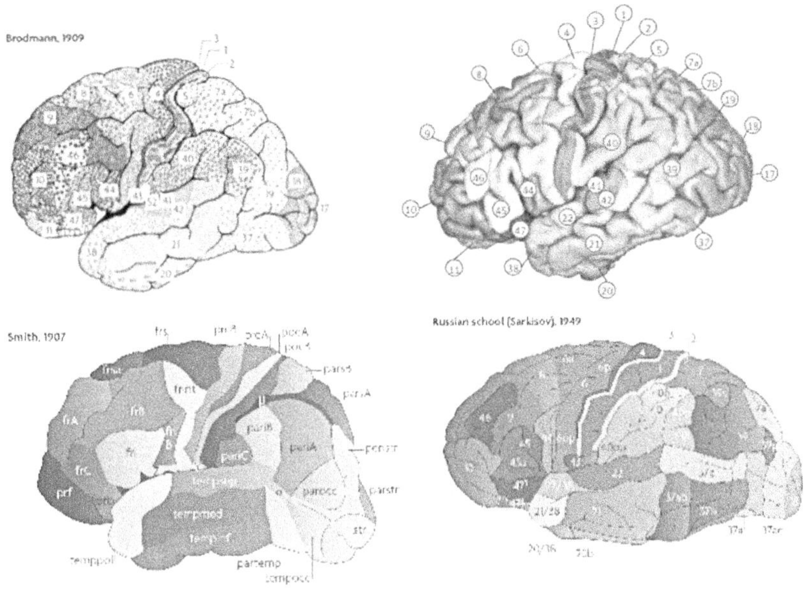

Fig. 4. Lateral views of the cortical maps of Brodmann (top row), Smith, and Sarkisov. (Adapted from [25]).

With the development of imaging techniques, such as magnetic resonance imaging (MRI), neuroscientists can non-invasively map the functions of the living human brain (Fig. 5). The newer techniques utilize features of MRI images to mark unique structures that enable transformations and delineation. An individual brain can be morphed to a universal brain (or coordinate system). Then, the brain can be parceled into different regions with several standards available, including the Desikan-Killiany atlas [21], the Destrieux et al. atlas [22], and the Desikan-Killiany-Tourville (DKT) atlas [23].

Other techniques can build upon these atlases and segmentation to map out task-specific activation of brain areas and how different areas of the brain are connected to each other, also known as the connectome. These methods use advanced tools such as functional magnetic resonance imaging (fMRI) or diffusion tensor imaging (DTI) (Fig. 6). When examined in parallel, a network analysis can be performed to understand the connectivity and function of the brain during different tasks, as illustrated in Fig. 6.

In addition to these anatomical and functional driven maps, there are many other maps associated with the brain. One such map, examines the blood supply (and outflow) to the cortex and the brain. A related map is the glymphatic system (waste clearance system of the brain). The influx and outflux of chemicals to

D. Weber et al.

neurons and the brain are vital to supporting its high metabolic load, so these maps and related work are important to bear in mind [24].

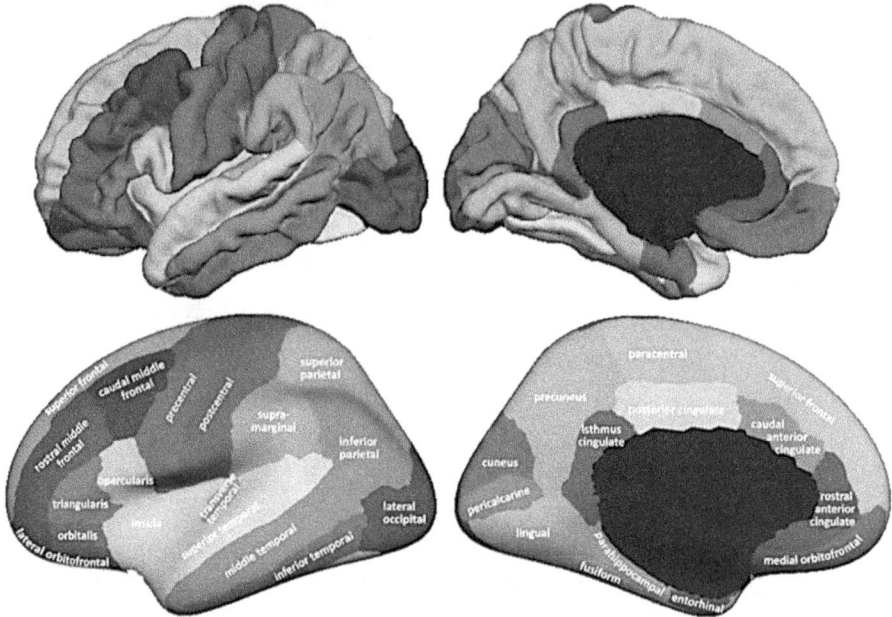

Fig. 5. Advanced MRI based cortical maps of lateral (left) and medial (right) views. Top row, pial surface projections of brain where areas are labeled according to "Desikan–Killiany–Tourville" (DKT) protocol with automatically generated labels. Bottom row, inflated surface projections of those viewed in top row, with shading and text of each region. Adapted from [23].

While the brain can be split up in many ways, distinct regions of the brain have a mapping on their own within their subsection. For example, the motor and somatosensory systems have maps in their respective cortices where different body parts are represented in different segments of the motor or somatosensory cortex (Fig. 7A, B). The maps were originally created by Penfield [27], but the homunculus is an important feature to bear in mind when designing neuroprostheses using the motor or sensory cortex to restore function associated with a particular body part. While cortical maps are the focus of this section, it should be noted that different maps of the body exist in other neural structures outside of the cortex. These include the motor and sensory maps in the cerebellum and thalamus, among others.

Vision (Fig. 7C-F), hearing (Fig. 7G-I), olfaction (not pictured, [28, 29]), and gustation (not pictured, [30]) have all shown organization and some type of mapping. For vision, there are many translations from the visual field to the visual cortex, but one of the main features is the enlarged projection of images to cortex for items in the center of the field of view (near the fovea). In terms of hearing, the most notable mapping is based on frequency where both the cochlea and auditory cortex are primarily responsive to particular frequencies (Fig. 7H, I). Similar to the non-cortical maps for somatosensory and motor function, the field of view has a defined mapping in the thalamus (lateral geniculate nucleus), hearing (cochlear nucleus, superior olivary complex, medial nucleus of the trapezoid body (MNTB), and inferior colliculus), and olfaction (olfactory bulb).

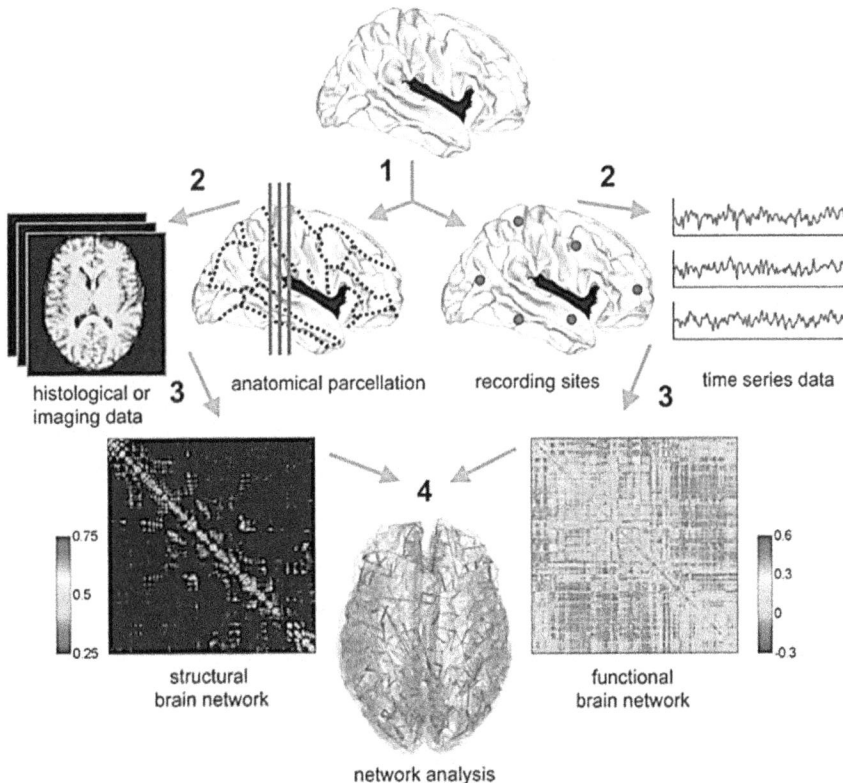

Fig. 6. Process to map brain networks relies on segmentation of the brain into regions or nodes, first. Then, in parallel, structural and functional networks are studied, resulting in matrices mapping connections. The final result is the merging of both networks to develop a structure showing regions of connectivity during certain tasks. Adapted From [26].

Regardless of the map or location, the reader should be warned that while the mapping and assignment of these areas tend to depict clear boundaries, these boundaries are never as sharp as drawn. While certain functions are fairly reliable to delineate (motor and sensory functions), some higher-level functions (like consciousness) may span several structures. Some of the imprecision may be due to lack of true understanding of the function of these higher-level functions.

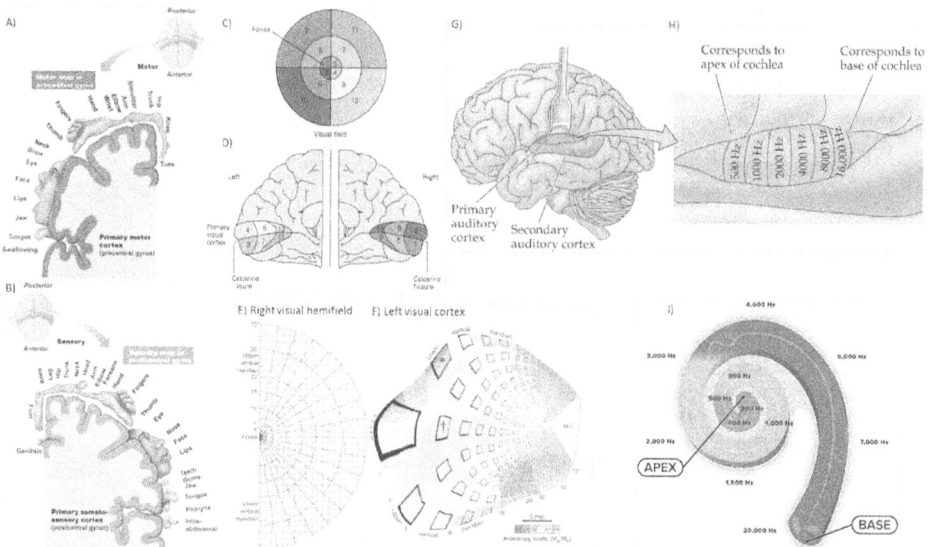

Fig. 7. Sensory maps in the nervous system. (A) The homunculi in M1 and (B) S1 as mapped by Penfield and colleagues is useful for illustrating the gross somatotopic organization of the cortex in these areas (Adapted from [31]). (C) Visual field split into different regions, 1-12, and (D) the projection of that visual field onto the visual cortex, V1 (Adapted from [32]). (E) The right visual hemifield featured with a uniform squares that is in turn (F) projected onto the visual cortex. Cortical areal magnification (Ma), linear magnification-isopolar rays (Mp), and linear magnification-isoeccentricity rings (Me) (Adapted from [33]). (G) Visualization of auditory corticies in the sulci and (H) the projection of frequency on the primary auditory cortex (Adapted from [34]). (I) Visualization of the cochlea and its tonotopic distribution across frequencies. The base of the cochlea is most responsive to high-frequency sounds while the apex of the cochlea is most responsive to low-frequency sounds (Adapted from [35]).

As mentioned previously, the cortex comprises 6 distinct cellular layers (Fig. 8). The density and number of cells varies from region to region, and this is well illustrated by the difference between the primary somatosensory area (Fig. 8, area type 4) and primary motor areas (Fig. 8, area type 1). The somatosensory area is primarily input whereas the motor area that is primarily output. In the somatosensory area, there are more layer 4 cells that receive primary input from the thalamus. In the motor area, there are more layer 5 cells (pyramidal) that project to subcortical/spinal targets (Fig. 8). While connections vary from area to area of the brain, layer 2 cells often project to other ipsilateral cortical areas, layer 3 cells project to the contralateral cortex, and layer 6 cells project to the thalamus [36] (Fig. 9). Additionally, the number of synapses per individual are markedly more in humans than rodents across cortical layers [8].

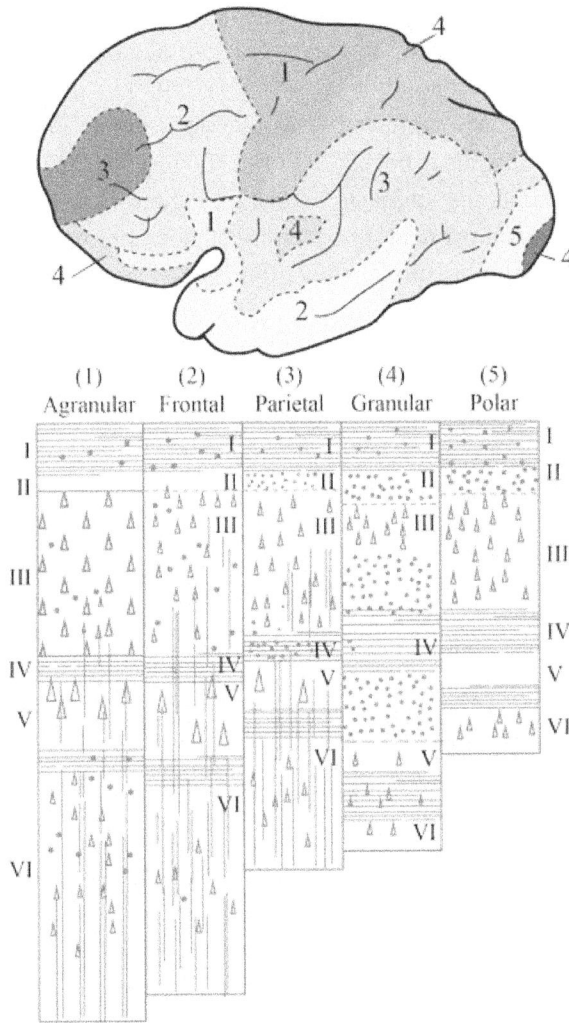

Fig. 8. Examples of types of layers of cerebral cortex and their distribution across cortex. The panel illustrates the layered nature of the cortex, showing the distribution of cell bodies and axons of cells in the cortex. The thickness in the primary motor cortex (agranular type) is slightly greater than that in primary somatosensory cortex (granular type). Adapted from [38].

Given all of these characteristics, layer 5 in the motor cortex would be a good layer to record activity when recording motor intent while layer 4 in the somatosensory cortex would be a good layer to record neural signals to understand touch and proprioception from the limbs, among other possible features and body parts. The sizes of cells in different layers change as well. A large layer 5 cell can often be the easiest to record and may mask recordings in other layers. Other neural types, such as smaller interneurons, may be important to record, but current recording methods are limited in their ability to accurately record signals from smaller cells. Therefore, the diversity of these cells has probably not been fully appreciated. The reader is referred to a thorough review and breakdown of the different interneuron cells types [37]. Further, many interneurons are inhibitory. With current methods the ability to record an inhibitory event on a postsynaptic neuron is difficult as most neuroprosthetic methods are extracellular and are only able to record excitatory neuronal activation.

In addition to the layering for vertical organization, there is a horizontal organization of cells into columns. One of the places that this is most evident is in the "barrel" field of the somatosensory region of rodents that maps to its whiskers. The columnar organization forms horizontal short-range connections within the column that is 300 – 500 μm in diameter with approximately 10,000 neuronal cell bodies [7]. In layer 4, where the sensory signals enter the cortex, the columns function almost totally independently of each other.

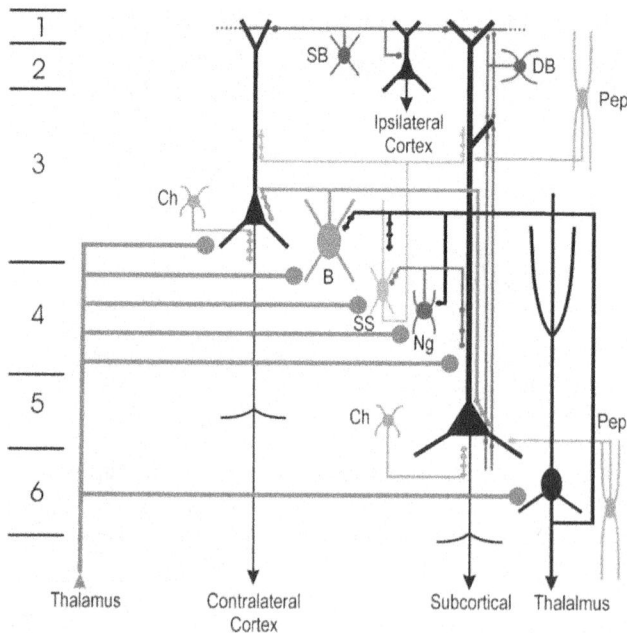

Fig. 9. The boundaries between the 6 layers of cortex are shown on the left side of the figure. Excitatory neurons that use glutamate are illustrated and include the afferent input from the thalamus, pyramidal neurons and spiny stellate (SS) neurons. Perisomatic inhibitory neurons are shown and include the chandelier (Ch) and large basket (B) neurons. The other inhibitory interneurons contacting the dendrites are shown and include the small basket (SB), double bouquet (DB), neurogliaform (Ng) and peptide (Pep) cells. The output targets of pyramidal neurons in different layers is also shown. (Adapted from [36]).

While many tend to focus on the primary areas associated with a function (e.g. primary motor area, primary sensory areas), other supporting areas of the brain for those particular functions are important as well. A primary output of the layer 5 cells are the corticospinal tracts that control muscle movement in the body (Fig. 10). The corticospinal tract fibers synapse to neurons in the spinal cord at the level where the muscle is to be controlled. The supplementary motor area, SMA, and premotor cortex also contribute axons to this tract along with a few other minor contributors in the cortex. In the case of the motor cortex, the premotor area and SMA contribute to complex and bilateral motor functions, among other functions [39, 40]. Much of the fundamental understanding comes from numerous experimental examples of correlation between the electrophysiological activity of neurons recorded in M1 (primary motor area and various parameters of movement including muscle force [41, 42], direction [43], speed [44] and the modulation of activity with different postures [45-47].

In addition to subcortical structures that will be discussed later, the parietal cortex and cingulate cortex also have different roles in motor function that may be associated with learning, intention, and action planning that could be useful targets for neuroprosthetics [48]. Specifically, the posterior parietal cortex features the spatial coordinates and the relationship between the body and its surroundings [49]. A complete model of how all these cortical (and subcortical) structures allows motor function has not been developed or validated. Future work will be needed to develop a complete understanding and model. Regardless, these structures allow for grossly and finely tuned control via neurons coding both low-level muscle activity and high-level spatial parameters. To enable this well-controlled system, the motor and sensory (specifically somatosensory) cortices have a large number of bidirectional interconnections. The close coupling of sensory and motor systems is a vital component in active sensing that results in improved sensation abilities. A good example of active sensing is the whisker system of rats that use controlled motion of whiskers to improve texture discrimination [50].

In terms of sensory input, many of the sensory modalities are similar to each other in that they use primary and secondary cortical areas to process sensory input where secondary areas often process the sensory information for more complex aspects, e.g. for vision, the secondary area would process visual detail and color, form, motion, 3-D position, etc. Therefore, the secondary sensory areas are often called association areas of that particular sensory modality. For example, if a person does not have a somatosensory association area on one side, the result is difficulty in recognizing the feeling of complex objects or forms on the opposite side of the body. The opposite side is due to the decussation of fibers as will be discussed in the section of the medulla.

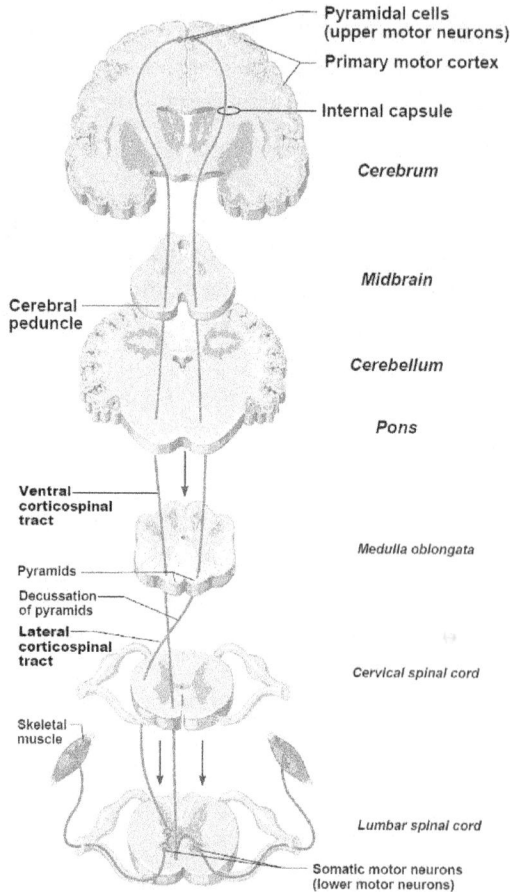

Fig. 10. Descending pathways. The corticospinal tract travels through the medullary pyramids and most axons cross in the caudal medulla (lateral pathway) while some axons remain uncrossed (ventral/anterior pathway). Adapted from [31].

The primary somatosensory cortex is divided into four strips parallel to the central sulcus that receive distinct sensory input modalities: skin, muscle, and joints. Input to the different sensory cortices mainly comes from the thalamus, ipsilaterial cortex, or contralateral cortex, but the majority of input will be from the contralateral side of the body. Except the sense of smell, almost all sensory input has a waypoint in the thalamus before ascending to cortex. None of the afferents projecting to S1 (primary somatosensory cortex) are first order sensory neurons; the information has been relayed across at least 2 synapses with the final projection coming from the thalamus [7]. Each sensory modality has a corresponding area in the cortex (vision = visual cortex, hearing = auditory cortex, somatosensation = somatosensory cortex, taste = gustatory cortex, smell = olfactory cortex). Some sensations are projected to multiple areas within the cortex, e.g. the sense of smell has many targets in the cortex (entorhinal, prepyriform, and pyriform cortices).

Another key feature of sensory systems is the wide dynamic range of these systems. For example, the automatic gain control of sensory systems is a distinguishing feature that allows humans to hear a wide range of sounds from faint voices to an explosion. While not all of the processing is done in the cortex, the cortex's role in this is to send descending signals to the thalamus, medulla, or spinal cord to control the sensitivity of input. A related feature of our sensory systems is surround or lateral inhibition. The ability of certain neurons to affect neighboring neurons allows for sharper delineations between sensations allowing finer resolution.

3.3. *Telencephalon – hippocampal anatomy*

Many assign the hippocampus with a central role in memory formation. Much of this association comes from studies of patients with epilepsy that had portions of their hippocampus removed: they are able to recall previous memories, but they are unable to form any new memories (anterograde amnesia). While the hippocampus could be seen as an elongated portion of the cerebral cortex that folds inward to form the ventral surface of the lateral ventricle, the hippocampus only has 3 cell layers in some of its areas, rather than the usual 6 of the cortex. From an evolutionary perspective the hippocampus was probably important in early decision-making mechanisms, and its role grew from there to include memory formation of many types, including spatial memory and navigation. Much of the role of the hippocampus in memory formation is termed consolidation, which denotes the translation of memories from short-term to long-term memory storage in the cortex.

Almost any type of sensory input causes activation of at least some part of the hippocampus. The hippocampus then distributes these outgoing signals to the anterior thalamus, hypothalamus, and other parts of the limbic system, mainly via the fornix. Note, the limbic system is a collection of structures across the forebrain that is largely assigned a role with emotions and memory formation. The main hippocampal pathway is largely unidirectional. The structure has resulted in many researchers using the hippocampus (or slices thereof) as a useful model to examine neuronal function (Fig. 11). Specifically, signals come in along the perforant pathway from layers II and III of the entorhinal cortex and synapse on the granule

cells in the dentate gyrus (DG). These cells form the Mossy fibers that synapse to
CA3 cells. The outputs of these cells form the Schaffer collaterals that synapse to
CA1 cells that generate output to the deep layers of the entorhinal cortex (among
other destinations). While only CA1 and CA3 are discussed here, the hippocampus
can be broken into domains CA1-4, where CA4 is often dubbed the hilus or hilar
region within the blade of the DG layer. The CA2 cells are located between CA1
and CA3, and comprise the cells that get input from the perforant path, but not
input from Mossy fibers from the DG.

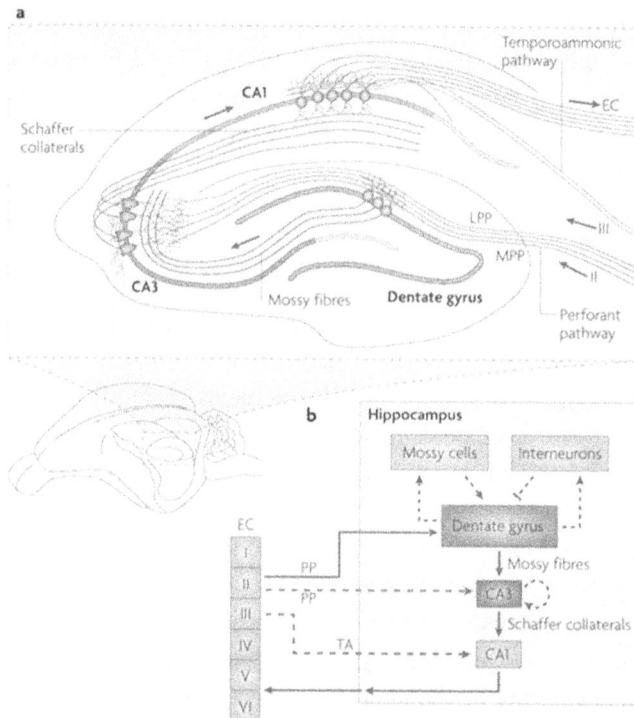

Fig. 11. The primary circuit of the hippocampus. (A) Depiction of hippocampus pathways and
neurons and its place in the rodent brain. (B) Block diagram of hippocampal circuit. Entorhinal
Cortex (EC), Dentate Gyrus (DG), Perforant Path (lateral and medial PP), Mossy Fibres (MF),
Schaffer Collateral Pathway (SC). Associational Commisural (AC) Pathway and and Subiculum (Sb)
neurons not illustrated. From [51].

3.4. Anatomy of the basal ganglia

The basal ganglia are a collection of subcortical nuclei, a cluster of neural cell
bodies that form accessory systems to both motor and limbic functions. In the case
of motor function, the basal ganglia work in conjunction with the cerebral cortex
and corticospinal motor control systems. Most of the input to basal ganglia comes

from the cortex, and most of the output returns to the cortex (Figure 12). Often the basal ganglia are split into dorsal and ventral components, with the dorsal section regulating motor function while the ventral division is involved in limbic functions. The dorsal section consists of the dorsal striatum (caudate nucleus and putamen), globus pallidus (GP), substantia nigra (SN), and subthalamic nucleus (STN). The ventral section consists of the ventral striatum (nucleus accumbens and olfactory tubercle), the ventral pallidum, and ventral tegmental area. While the basal ganglia are often placed in the telencephalon with the cerebral cortex, some of the basal ganglia structures are derived from other sections. Specifically, the GP (part of pallidum) and STN (part of subthalamus) are derived from the diencephalon and the substantia nigra is derived from the mesencephalon. The STN is thought to be involved in regulating somatic movements [52] and is the only nucleus of the basal ganglia that contains glutamatergic neurons. Additionally, in some cases texts lump the amygdala in with the basal ganglia, and we will discuss its functions in this section as well. Many of the components of the basal ganglia can be further split. The GP is composed of two portions, internal (GPi) and external (GPe) [53]. The SN has a portion called pars compacta (SNpc or SNc) and pars reticulate (SNpr or SNr).

For motor control, there are predominantly two pathways: "direct" and "indirect" that act in complementary fashion in the basal ganglia. When the "direct" pathway is activated, the result is the disinhibition (reduction of inhibition) of targets to facilitate movement. In the opposite fashion, the active "indirect" pathway will cause inhibition of targets to hinder movement. The primary targets of the basal ganglia are the thalamus and cortex. Several disease states can disrupt this balance to cause hypo- or hyper-kinetic movements. As can be seen in Figure 12 and Table 1, basal ganglia system utilizes many neurotrans-mitters in different forms to either excite or inhibit certain neural pathways and downstream targets. In addition to the direct and indirect pathways, a recent hyperdirect pathway has been shown. The activation of this pathway is thought to facilitate voluntary limb movement. Through these three pathways, the basal ganglia works in tandem with the thalamus and cortex to initiate, conduct, and end movements. A deeper discussion of the extensive signaling pathways inside and outside of the basal ganglia is saved for other textbooks.

In certain diseases the balance of these pathways can be disrupted, such as in Parkinson's disease (PD) or Huntington's disease (HD). Both diseases are represented by the accumulation of misfolded protein, alpha-synuclein for PD and huntingtin for HD. In PD, the exact mechanisms are unknown, but the accumulation of protein culminates in the degeneration of dopamine neurons in the

SNpc, resulting in a deficiency in dopamine in the striatum from projections from the SNpc (nigrostriatal pathway). By the time that PD symptoms first present, over 60% of dopamine neurons are already lost [56] (Figure 13A). The finding indicates that any future treatments will need early diagnostic tools as well.

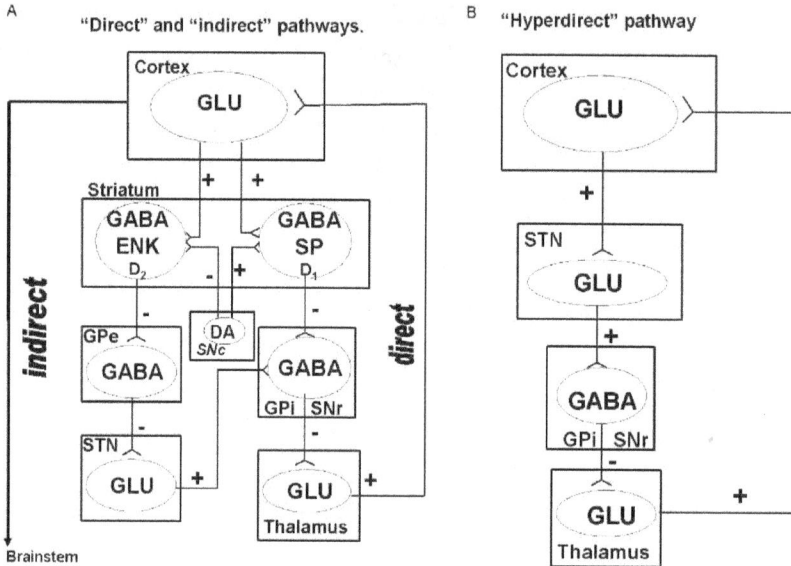

Fig. 12. (A) Schematic representation of the basal ganglia under normal conditions [54, 55]. The striatum receives excitatory (+) inputs from the cortex and excitatory or inhibitory (-) inputs from the SNc. The direct pathway projects to the GPi/SNr-thalamus-cortex, whereas the indirect pathway projects to the GPe-STN- GPi/SNr-thalamus-cortex. Output from all nuclei of the basal ganglia except the STN are inhibitory and are mediated by GABA. The STN is the only nucleus in the basal ganglia that contains glutamatergic neurons. Activation of the direct pathway leads to cortical excitation and movement facilitation, while activation of the indirect pathway leads to cortical inhibition and movement cessation. DA: dopamine, D1: DA D1 receptors, D2: DA D2 receptors, GLU: glutamate, GPe: external segment of the globus pallidus, GPi: internal segment of the globus pallidus, SNc: substantia nigra pars compacta, SNr; substantia nigra pars reticulate, and STN: subthalamic nucleus. (B) Schematic representation of the "hyperdirect" pathway. The STN receives direct excitatory inputs from the cortex and in turn projects to the GPi/SNr – thalamus and cortex. (+): excitatory. (-): inhibitory, GLU: glutamate, GPi: internal segment of the globus pallidus, SNr: substantia nigra pars reticulate and STN: subthalamic nucleus.

The degeneration of dopaminergic neurons culminates in the loss of ability to coordinate movement where tremor, rigidity, and hypokinesia or akinesia may be present. It is unknown why dopaminergic neurons are acutely vulnerable, but some postulate that the high-energy demands of these neurons make them more prone to degeneration. The degeneration is thought to impact both the direct and indirect pathway (Fig. 13), thereby affecting the starting and stopping of movements, resulting in the typical symptoms. Current medical treatments, both pharmacological and electrical, aim to restore dopamine levels in the striatum. L-dopa, a dopamine precursor that is permeable to the blood-brain barrier, is often used to treat PD symptoms by restoring a source of dopamine. Dopamine itself cannot cross blood brain barrier. Electrical stimulation via DBS is also used to restore the balance of the direct and indirect pathways. Note, that these treatments are to treat the symptoms of PD, and do nothing to reverse or stem the continued degeneration of dopamine neurons.

Table 1. The basal ganglia nuclei: Functional anatomy and pharmacology

Nucleus	Output	Function	Receptors
Striatum	GABA	Inhibitory (-)	NMDA, AMPA, Metabotropic glutamate receptors, D_1, D_2, Adenosine, GABA and serotonin
Globus Pallidum			
GPi	GABA	Inhibitory (-)	NMDA, AMPA, GABA and D_1
GPe	GABA	Inhibitory (-)	NMDA, Metabotropic glutamate receptors, D_1, D_2 and GABA
Subthtalamic Nucleus	Glutamtate	Excitatory (+)	NMDA, AMPA, Metabotropic glutamate receptors, D_1, D_2 and GABA
Substantia Nigra			
SNc	Dopamine	Excitatory (+) or Inhibitory (-)	NMDA and AMPA
SNr	GABA	Inhibitory (-)	GABA

In the case of Huntington's disease, many of the neurons affected are GABAergic neurons in the dorsal striatum. In the early stages of HD, the loss of neurons projecting to the GPe affects the indirect pathway that results in an increase of excitatory output to the thalamus and cortex (Fig. 13B). The increase results in hyperkinetic movements. As the disease progress GABAergic projections to the GPi are affected as well, and the direct pathway is affected resulting in symptoms similar to PD.

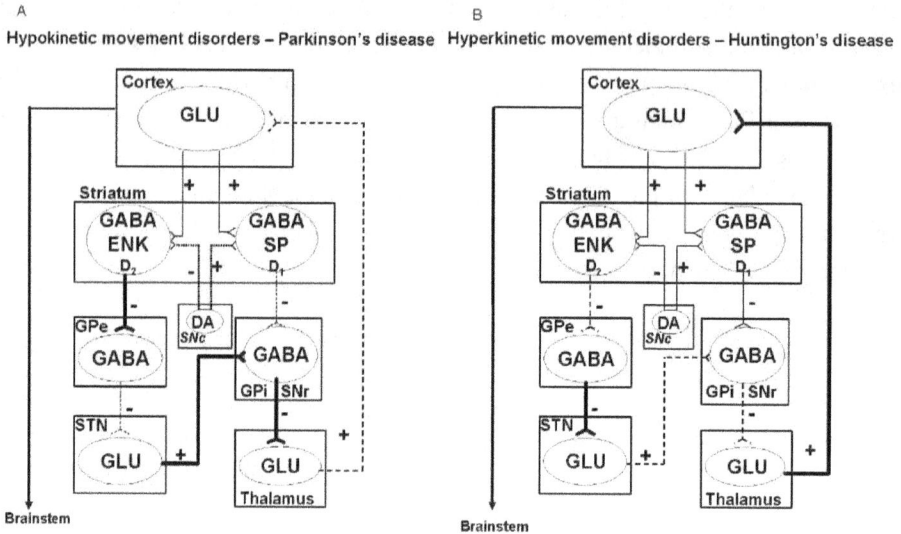

Fig. 13. (A) Schematic representation of the basal ganglia under Parkinsonian conditions [54, 57]. Degeneration of nigrostriatal DA neurons decreases striatal output through the "direct" pathway and increases output through the "indirect" pathway. The end result is increased GABA output to the thalamus and decreased thalamic glutamatergic output leading to cortical inhibition. Broken arrows represent decreased neurotransmission, thick arrows represent increased neurotransmission, (+): excitatory. (-): inhibitory, DA: dopamine, D_1: DA D_1 receptors, D_2: DA D_2 receptors, GLU: glutamate, GPe: external segment of the globus pallidus, GPi: internal segment of the globus pallidus, SNc: substantia nigra pars compacta, SNr; substantia nigra pars reticulata and STN: subthalamic nucleus. (B) Schematic representation of the basal ganglia under conditions of early Huntington's disease conditions [54, 57]. Degeneration of striatal GABA/ENK projection neurons increases GPe output to the STN leading to inhibition of the STN neurons and disinhibition of GPi/SNr and thalamus, thereby resulting in cortical excitation. Broken arrows represent decreased neurotransmission, thick arrows represent increased neurotransmission, (+): excitatory. (-): inhibitory, DA: dopamine, D_1: DA D_1 receptors, D_2: DA D_2 receptors, GLU: glutamate, GPe: external segment of the globus pallidus, GPi: internal segment of the globus pallidus, SNc: substantia nigra pars compacta, SNr; substantia nigra pars reticulata and STN: subthalamic nucleus.

In addition to the role that the basal ganglia play in motor control, they have an important role in limbic (cognitive) functions. Many of the reward pathways of the brain flow through the ventral tegmental area (VTA) and nucleus accumbens (NA), utilizing dopamine projections from the VTA to NA. This pathway involves many other non-basal ganglia structures including the prefrontal cortex, the thalamus, and amygdala. As mentioned previously, the amygdala is not always classified as part of the basal ganglia, but the complex of multiple small nuclei that compose the amygdala will be considered here. The amygdala has many other roles, with most of its primary outputs being mainly directed towards the hypothalamus as well as cortical targets, hippocampus, and thalamus. These effects include changes in visceral organ function (e.g. increase in gastrointestinal motility), movements (e.g. raising head, chewing, swallowing,), emotions (e.g. rage, pain, fear), or sexual function.

3.5. *Telencephalon – other noteworthy structures*

In addition to the neocortex, there is a region that is termed to be older evolutionary within the telencephalon, called the paleopallium or paleocortex. This region is also called the rhinencephalon, meaning smell-brain. The olfactory bulb and cranial nerve I (the olfactory tract) that route neural signals from olfactory cells to the brain are outgrowths of the forebrain. The brain also sends out inhibitory signals to cells in the olfactory bulb to finely tune the sense of smell. Sensation of smell proceeds primarily via two different pathways with a minor third pathway. The first is a pathway that routes signals to the medial olfactory area, most notably the septal nuclei. The second is to the lateral olfactory area that is primarily the prepyriform and pyriform cortices, along with the cortical portion of the amygdaloid nuclei. Disabling the medial olfactory area affects primitive responses to smell, such as licking, salivation, and other smelling of food responses. On the contrary, disabling the lateral area affects the more complex olfactory conditioned responses. These sensory inputs proceed straight to the paleocortex without passing through the thalamus first (as almost all other sensory input does). Another pathway is a minor pathway, but it does have a small set of fibers that pass through the medialdorsal thalamus on the way to the orbitofrontal cortex. Newer studies have shown that the majority of this pathway proceeds directly to the orbitofrontal cortex. Much more work needs to be completed to understand smell, but the third pathway probably aids in conscious analysis of odor.

Another collection of structures is the basal forebrain. The basal forebrain is composed of the nucleus basalis, medial septal nuclei, substantia innominate, and diagonal band of Broca. The nucleus accumbens is also in the basal forebrain, but as indicated above, it is considered to be part of the basal ganglia. While there are many subfunctions of the basal forebrain, its production and distribution of acetylcholine throughout the brain is the most notable function. Dissemination of the acetylcholine is thought to have a large role in neuroplasticity as a neuromodulator that may affect spike timing dependent plasticity. Another structure that has overlap with the basal ganglia is the claustrum, which some texts include in the basal ganglia. Much of its function is still not known, but it may act as a synchronizer of cerebral cortical activity, and therefore it may be a central player in consciousness and cognition.

3.6. Telencephalon – fiber tracts

While the sensing side of neuroprosthetics tends to focus on recording signals from cell bodies, deep brain stimulation (DBS) may impact both cell bodies and fibers of passage (fiber tracts). These tracts, or white matter, constitute important pathways in the brain. Additionally, dysfunction in one of the fiber tracts may be the underlying cause indicating the need for a potential neuroprosthesis. Therefore, we will briefly discuss a few major fiber tracts. We have already mentioned the pyramidal (corticospinal) tract to control movement and the nigrostriatal pathway in the basal ganglia from the SNpc to the striatum. One of the best known pathways is the corpus callosum that connects the two halves of the neocortex together to coordinate actions and/or processing. This is an example of a commissural fiber tract (connections between the two hemispheres). Additionally, the anterior and posterior commissures facilitate interhemispheric coordination.

Fibers that connect areas within the same hemisphere are called association fibers, and fibers that lie directly beneath layer VI cells connecting adjacent gyri are called short association fibers. Therefore, in the rostral – caudal axis, the arcuate fasciculus, an association fiber tract, forms a part of the superior longitudinal fasciculus that connects the frontal, occipital, parietal, and temporal lobes. Other long association fiber tracts of note are the cingulum (connecting parts of the limbic system and receiving input from the thalamus), external capsule (cortical-cortical connections), the extreme capsule (bidirectional communication between Wernicke's and Broca's areas), the uncinate fasciculus (connection between frontal and temporal lobes), and the fornix (main output of the hippocampus) among others. The last type, projection fibers, are efferent and afferent connections to lower parts of the brain and the spinal cord. The internal capsule that provides input and output of the cortex is predominantly composed of corticospinal tracts and represents a projection fiber tract.

3.7. Diencephalon – anatomy of the thalamus

One of the main areas that the cortex communicates with is the dorsal thalamus, often referred to as just the thalamus (Fig. 14). With the exception of the thalamic reticular nucleus, all thalamic nuclei project primarily to the cerebral cortex (layer IV) with a reciprocal connection from the same portion of the cortex to the thalamus. In many ways, the thalamus serves as a checkpoint for ascending and descending information for the cortex [58].

The thalamus is a large collection of different nuclei that are often classified based on location within thalamus. The thalamus is split into three regions via the internal medullary lamina: anterior, medial, and lateral (Fig. 14). Within each of these regions, there are distinct subnuclei, and each is often associated with a particular task or signal processing associated with an incoming or outgoing neural signal. Most nuclei can be paired into one of three categories: relay nuclei, association nuclei, or nonspecific nuclei [60]. Also, nuclei are classified as first order if the primary input is from subcortical brain structures and higher order if the primary input is from the cerebral cortex. Additionally, there is the thalamic reticular nucleus (TRN, not pictured) that is separated from the dorsal thalamus via the external medullary lamina. Fibers leaving the dorsal thalamus travel through and interact with neurons in the TRN before projecting to the cerebral cortex via the internal capsule[61].

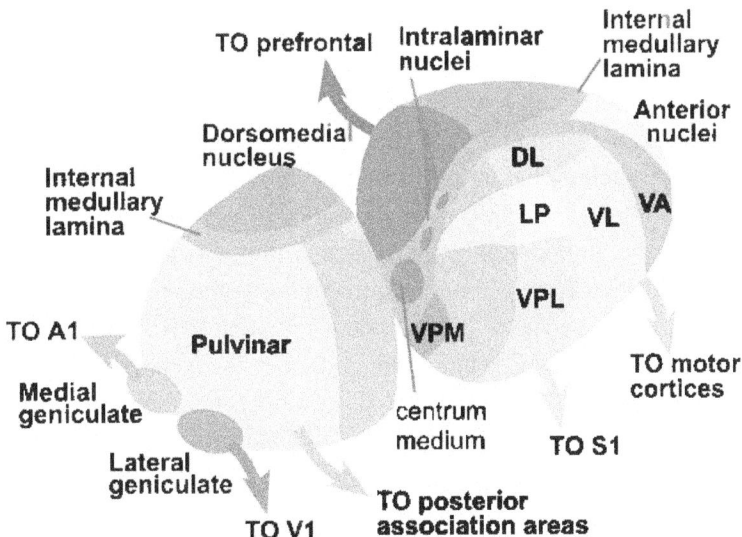

Fig. 14. Schematic diagram of the primate right thalamus. The major nuclei and some of the relevant inputs are shown. Inputs into VL from cerebellum and VA from basal ganglia are not shown. A1, primary auditory cortex; V1, primary visual cortex; S1, primary somatosensory cortex; DL, dorsolateral; LP, lateral posterior; VA, ventral anterior; VL, ventrolateral; VPL, ventral posteriolateral; VPM, ventral posteriomedial. Adapted from [59].

A significant portion of the incoming information to the thalamus is sensory information. Many nuclei are associated with one particular sensory modality (lateral genicular nucleus (LGN) for vision [62], medial geniculate nucleus (MGN) for hearing [63], ventral posteromedial (VPM) and ventral posterolateral (VPL) nuclei for somatosensation [64]) (Fig. 15). In the case of the VPM, it also processes taste signals [65], and therefore the VPM is mainly associated with input from the head (both taste and somatosensation) while the VPL is associated with somatosensation from the rest of the body, relaying leminical and spinothalamic signals. As discussed previously, most sensations of smell go straight to the cortex, but a small fraction of fibers do go to the mediodorsal thalamic nucleus before proceeding to the prefrontal and olfactory (medial and lateral orbitofrontal) cortices [66].

Likewise, the thalamus plays a central role in motor coordination, with basal ganglia and cerebellum acting as a relay for neocortex, basal ganglia, and cerebellum pathways, between and among those areas (Fig. 16). As previously noted, different thalamic nuclei can be split into 3 types, depending on their function. The relay nuclei have well defined inputs from noncortical structures, tune the signal, and relay it to distinct areas of the cerebral cortex. The association nuclei predominantly receive input from cortical structures, projecting information back to cortical structures. Lastly, the nonspecific nuclei, mostly intralaminar and midline nuclei, project broadly across the cerebral cortex and may be involved in general functions such as arousal and alertness.

The ventral anterior (VA) and ventral lateral (VL) nuclei are relay nuclei associated with motor function [67]. Input to these nuclei comes from the basal ganglia and cerebellum before projecting to the motor areas of the cerebral cortex. The VL mainly receives input from the cerebellum, but also receives input from the basal ganglia; its function is associated with motor feedback. The VA's main input is from the basal ganglia and its projections to the premotor cortex, including the SMA, are involved with planning and initiation of movement. Additionally, several association nuclei including the pulvinar (the largest association nucleus), lateral posterior (LP), and mediodorsal nuclei receive their primary inputs from layer V of particular cortical areas [60] and send projections back the cortex. In parallel with motor functions, limbic pathways also connect to the thalamus, playing a key role in consciousness and arousal as suggested by the broad innervation by nonspecific nuclei. Modulatory inputs also include feedback connections from the cortical area to which the nucleus projects. These feedback or reciprocal connections, as they are also called, seem to be especially important and there can be as many as ten times the number of feedback connections as feedforward connections[68]. Overall, the processing that the thalamus performs is key to enabling the cortex to pay attention to particular items through filtering extraneous information.

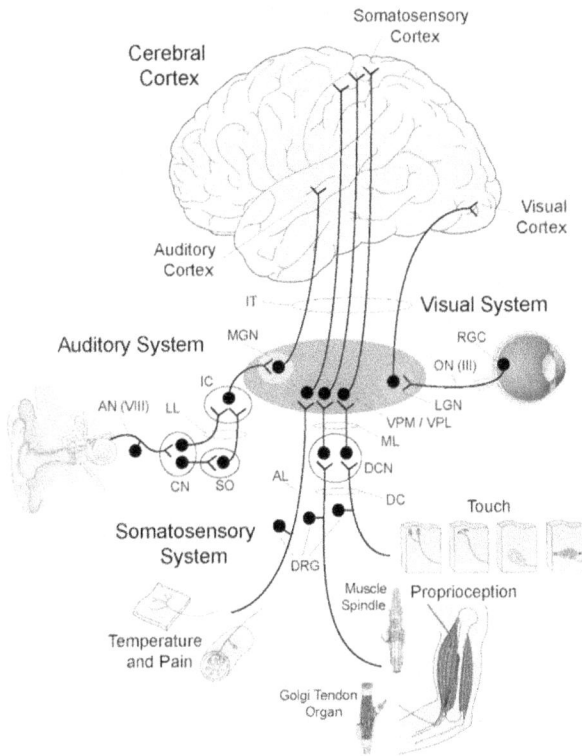

Fig. 15. The sensory systems showing major pathways, brainstem nuclei, thalamic nuclei, and primary processing areas of the cerebral cortex. Visual information from retinal ganglion cells (RGC) in the eye is transmitted to the lateral geniculate nucleus (LGN) of the thalamus via the optic nerve (ON). From there, LGN relay cells project via the internal capsule (IT) to primary visual cortex in the occipital lobe. Auditory information from the cochlea of the ear is transmitted along the auditory nerve (AN) to the cochlea nucleus (CN) in the brainstem. From there, CN cells form a direct and indirect auditory pathway to the inferior colliculus (IC). The indirect pathway is via the superior olivary nucleus (SO). Both pathways converge on the IC via the lateral lemniscus (LL). The IC then projects to the medial geniculate nucleus of the thalamus. From there, MGN relay cells project via the IT to primary auditory cortex in the temporal lobe. Somatosensory information from the three major submodalities is predominantly relayed through the ventral posteriolateral nucleus (VPL) and the ventral posteriomedial nucleus (VPM) of the thalamus. Dorsal root ganglion (DRG) fibres carrying information from the body for both touch and proprioception enter the spinal cord and ascend in the dorsal columns (DC) to reach the dorsal column nuclei (DCN) in the brainstem. From there, cells in the DCN project to the VPL via the medial lemniscus (ML). DRG fibres carrying information from the body about temperature and pain ascend in the anterolateral tract (AL) of the spinal cord and project directly to the VPL nucleus. Somatosensory information from the head enters the brainstem via the trigeminal nerve and similarly projects to VPM via the trigeminal nuclear complex (not shown). From there VPL / VPM relay cells project via the IT to primary somatosensory cortex in the parietal lobe.

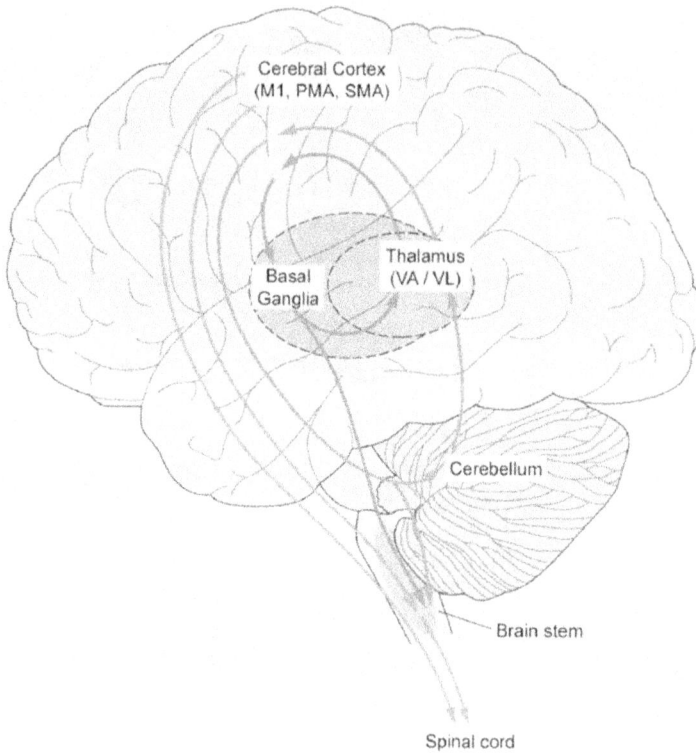

Fig. 16. The relationships between the motor nuclei of the thalamus and the basal ganglia and cerebellum. The motor nuclei of the thalamus provide access to the cerebral cortex. M1, primary motor cortex; PMA, premotor area; SMA, supplementary motor area; VA / VL, ventral anterior / ventral posterior nuclear complex. Adapted from [69].

While most focus on neural firing is concerned with trains of action potentials or spikes, the thalamic projection neurons have two physiological states: tonic and burst mode. In burst mode, also called oscillatory mode, cells have an intrinsic rhythm where the cells respond non-linearly and may by implementing a threshold function. In burst mode a special class of calcium channels governs rhythmic depolarization and hyperpolarization (Fig. 17). In tonic mode, neurons respond much like other neurons to depolarization and hyperpolarization events to represent the activity of their inputs. During sleep, most of the thalamic neurons are in burst mode, but it can be seen how the burst mode would be a key feature of the thalamic ability to filter information.

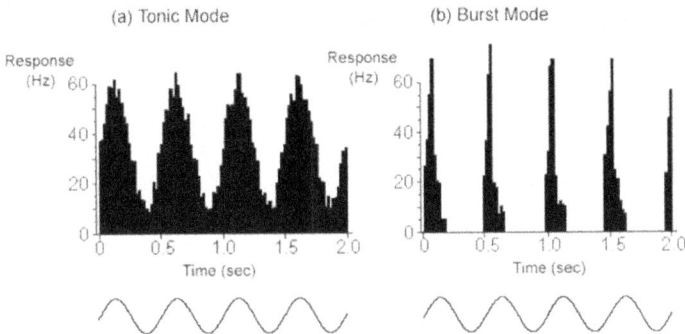

Fig. 17. Tonic and burst mode responses of relay cells in the lateral geniculate nucleus of a cat. The visual stimulus was a drifting grating. The upper histogram plot shows the responses of cells in each mode. The lower sine wave plot shows the time-varying contrast of the visual stimulus. Responses in tonic mode (a) faithfully represent the sine wave stimulus whereas in burst mode (b) only the contrast maxima are represented. Adapted from [70].

3.8. *Diencephalon – anatomy of the other thalami*

While an in depth review of other structures of the diencephalon will not be covered, some of the structures are important to cover at a high level. The subthalamus was already discussed in terms of the subthalamic nucleus (STN) in the basal ganglia section. The epithalamus has several structures contained under its umbrella, which is at the posterior part of the diencephalon. The main function of the epithalamus is to connect the limbic system to other parts of the brain, but the most notable structure in the epithalamus is the pineal gland. From comparative anatomy, it is the vestigial remnant of what was a third eye in the back of the head in some animals. Therefore, it is not surprising that this structure is key in light/dark rhythms (via suprachiasmatic nucleus and hypothalamus) and the secretion of melatonin among other chemicals. It also can play a role in modulating body temperature. In some animals, the inhibitory function of the pineal gland is a vital part of seasonal reproductive cycle.

The hypothalamus is a significant structure that is the main link between the brain and the body's endocrine system. The drive and processing to direct the endocrine system is through the main bidirectional connections the hypothalamus has with the limbic system. It is through these varied connections down to the brain stem and midbrain structures (e.g., pons, medulla), up to other structures of the diencephalon and cerebrum, or to control the adjoining pituitary gland that the hypothalamus can play a role in a myriad of body regulation functions including arterial pressure, water conservation, temperature, and hormones, to name a few

(Fig. 18). From previous experiments, it should be noted that it is unknown whether stimulation of particular areas in the hypothalamus is from stimulation of particular cell bodies or fiber tracts passing nearby. In addition to discrete regulation of body parameters, stimulation of different parts of the hypothalamus can affect the limbic system leading to rage, calm, fear, etc.

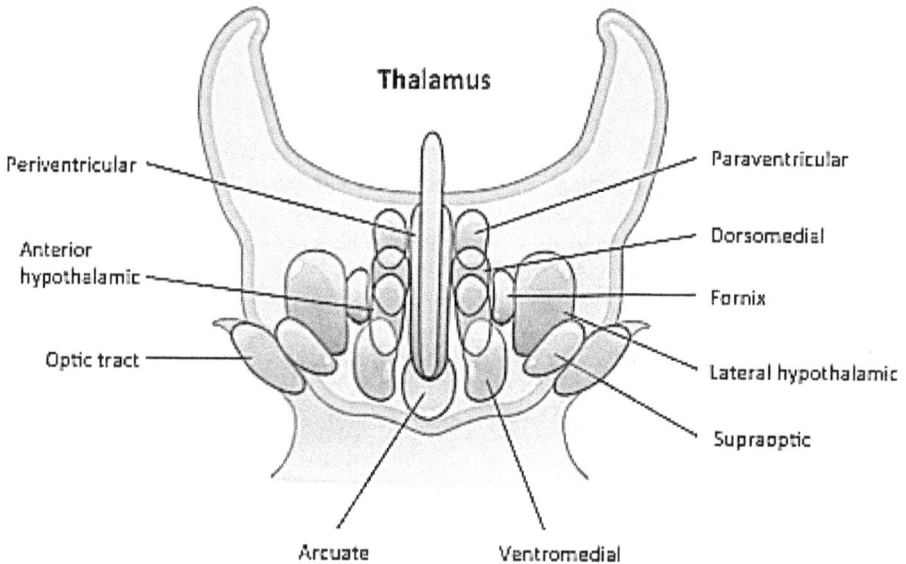

Fig. 18. Coronal view of control centers of the hypothalamus. Adapted from [3].

4. Midbrain

4.1. *Midbrain anatomy - overview*

The midbrain, or mesencephalon, is probably the least discussed of the forebrain, midbrain, and hindbrain areas. While important to functions of the body, its physical location between the better known forebrain and hindbrain means that on occasion some structures of the midbrain get lumped into the forebrain or hindbrain (e.g., substantia nigra into forebrain). Additionally, the term brainstem refers to the midbrain and portions of the hindbrain (pons and medulla oblongata) and is often used instead. The midbrain is often depicted by a horizontal section to visualize different regions (Fig. 19), but the main components of the midbrain are the tectum and cerebral peduncles (anything not in the tectum is usually binned in the peduncles and includes the tegmentum). The tegmentum forms the floor and the tectum forms the ceiling of the mesencephalon. In this section, we will cover some of the midbrain structures to familiarize the reader with some of its important structures.

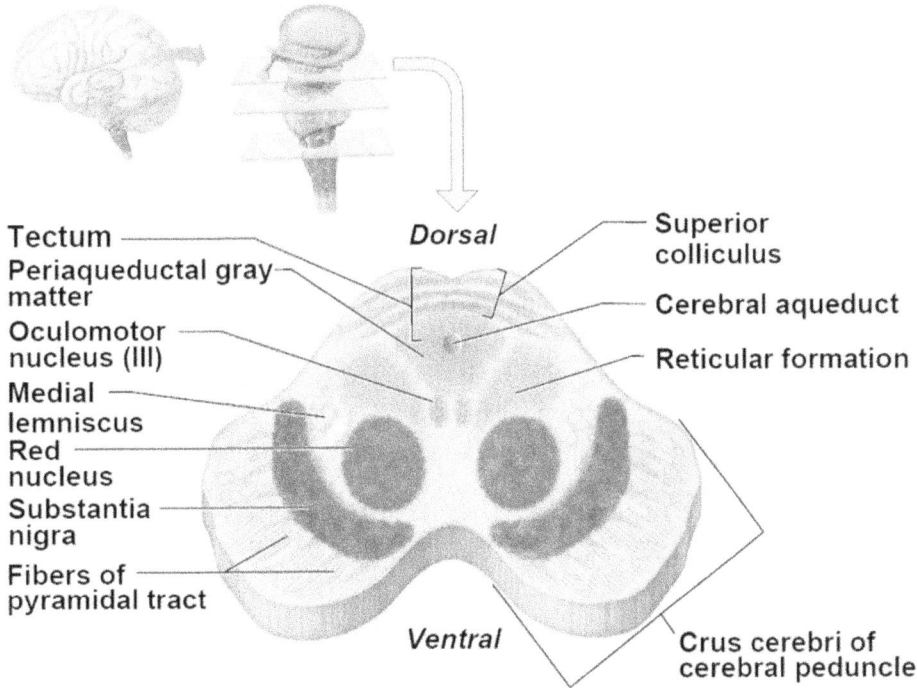

Fig. 19. Diagram of midbrain. The figure depicts a cross-section of the midbrain and its main structures at the level of the superior colliculus. Adapted from [31].

4.2. *Mesencephalon – anatomy of the tectum*

The tectum is comprised of the inferior and superior colliculi. A main function of the superior colliculus is associated with coordinated functions of the eyes. While higher levels of the superior colliculus take in sensory visual information, the lower levels deal with motor related activity of the eyes. With this construction, the superior colliculus is a key player in eye tracking and locking as the head or object moves. Note that the superior colliculus is referred to as the optic tectum in non-mammals. In comparison to the superior colliculus, the inferior colliculus primarily deals with auditory/vestibular input in addition to somatosensory input. The inferior colliculus receives auditory information from a wide range of auditory structures including the cochlear nucleus and auditory cortex while projecting to the MGN. In addition, the input from the lateral lemniscus suggests that the inferior colliculus (IC) is a significant control center for multimodal sensory information relating to sound and sensation. In this position, it would be a fitting center of how to best filter information and react to it. Therefore, it is a principal player in the startle response and vestibulo-ocular reflex.

4.3. *Mesencephalon – anatomy of the cerebral peduncles and fiber tracts*

The cerebral peduncles include the midbrain tegmentum, crus cerebri, substantia nigra, and pretectum. The nuclei for cranial nerves III and IV are in the midbrain tegmentum (see Table 2), but the majority of the peduncles are fiber tracts through the midbrain connecting other regions to each other, with the crus cerebri being a large bundle of efferent motor fibers. The several fiber tracts that run through the peduncles include the corticospinal, corticopontine, and corticobulbar tracts. In addition, the cerebral peduncles have 3 cerebellar peduncles as well. These are the communication links between the brainstem and cerebellum that are termed superior, middle, and inferior cerebellar peduncles. Through its connections, the cerebral peduncles play a role in motor tasks, including balance and posture.

Table 2. Functions of the Cranial Nerves (adapted from [71])

Cranial Nerve	Functions
olfactory (I)	Sensory: smell
optic (II)	Sensory: sight
oculomotor (III)	Motor: innervates all extraocular muscles except superior oblique and lateral rectus, innervates the striated muscle of the eyelid
	Parasympathetic: pupillary constriction, accommodation of lens for near vision
trochlear (IV)	Motor: innervates superior oblique muscle
trigeminal (V)	Sensory: mediates cutaneous and proprioceptive sensations from skin, muscles, and joints in face and mouth, sensory innervation of the teeth
	Motor: innervates muscles of mastication
abducens (VI)	Motor: innervates lateral rectus muscle
facial and intermediate (VII)	Sensory: taste from anterior two-thirds of tongue, sensation from skin of external ear
	Motor: innervates muscles of facial expression
	Parasympathetic: innervates lacrimal, mucous, and salivary glands
vestibulocochlear (VIII)	Sensory: hearing, balance, postural reflexes, orientation of head in space
glossopharyngeal (IX)	Sensory: visceral sensations from palate and posterior one-third of tongue, taste from posterior third of tongue, baroreceptors of carotid arch, chemoreceptors of carotid body
	Motor: swallowing
	Parasympathetic: parotid gland innervation
vagus (X)	Sensory: visceral sensation from pharynx, larynx, thorax, and abdomen, taste buds in epiglottis, baroreceptors of aortic arch, chemoreceptors of aortic bodies
	Motor: innervates striated muscle in larynx and pharynx and controls speech
	Parasympathetic: smooth muscle in heart, trachea, bronchi, esophagus, stomach, and intestine
spinal accessory (XI)	Motor: innervates trapezius and sternocleidomastoid muscles
hypoglossal (XII)	Motor: innervates intrinsic muscles of the tongue

The midbrain tegmentum, not to be confused with the pontine tegmentum, contains the red nucleus as well as other structures (e.g. the reticular formation). Likewise, some texts include the substantia nigra in the tegmentum as well, but the substantia nigra will not be covered in this section as it was already discussed under basal ganglia. Notably, the reticular formation and raphe nuclei are a collection of nuclei that span multiple levels of the brain, and these structures will be discussed here as well as in the hindbrain section. The reticular formation is composed of three columns: raphe nuclei (median), magnocellular (medial), and parvocellular (lateral) (Fig. 20). The reticular formation is involved with vestibular and neck reflexes while also regulating spinal reflexes. Specific actions of reticulospinal tracts on reflex activity may be modulated and even reversed during voluntary movements [72].

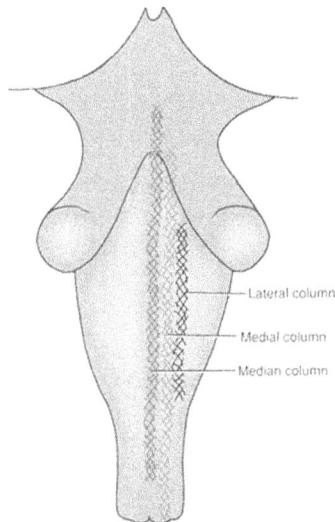

Fig. 20. Diagram of approximate locations of reticular formation (columns) in the brainstem. From [73].

The red nucleus consists of a magnocellular and parvocellular component. The corticorubral tract as well as branches from the corticospinal tract synapses to cells in the red nucleus. The red nucleus also receives input from the cerebellum. The output of the red nucleus is the rubrospinal tract (Fig. 21). The red nucleus serves as an alternative pathway for routing signals to the spinal cord, but the pathway seems to be more important in cats and monkeys than humans. The pathways through the red nucleus as well as descending signals through the basal ganglia, the reticular formation, and the vestibular nuclei are often termed the extrapyramidal system which includes the rubrospinal, pontine reticulospinal, medullary reticulospinal, lateral vestibulospinal, and tectospinal pathways). Similar to other motor structures, the red nucleus also contains a motor map (similar to cortical homunculus) of the muscles of the body, but in lesser detail than the motor cortex. Since the reticular formation is a loose amalgamation of cells from many sources, the roles of the reticular formation are varied from motor control, pain modulation, sleep, consciousness, and cardiovascular function.

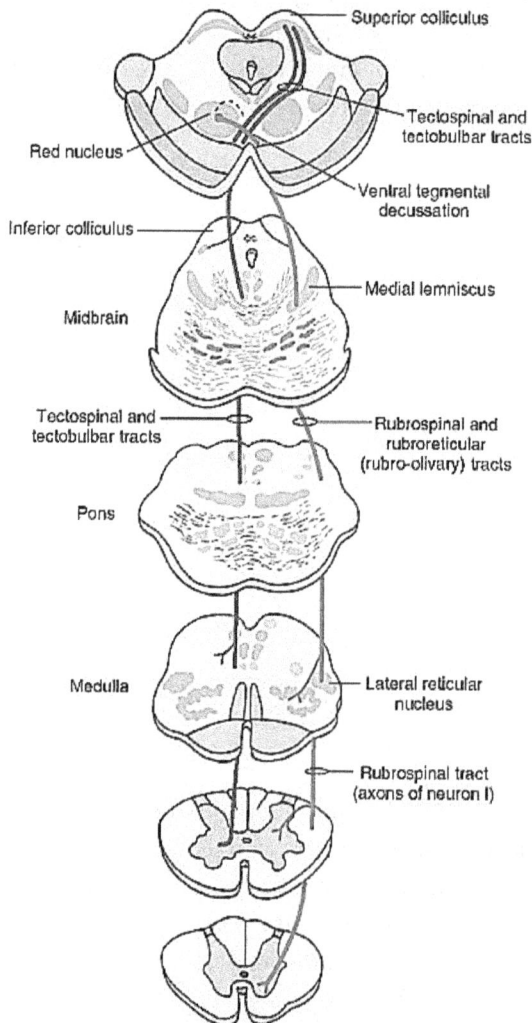

Fig. 21. Fibers of the rubrospinal tract decussate near their origin, the red nucleus. These neurons synapse on motor cells in the spinal cord. Fibers of the tectospinal (also called colliculospinal) tract decussate near the dorsal tegmental decussation and originate in the superior colliculus. The pathway is responsible for coordinating head, neck, and eye movements. The tectobulbar tracts refer to the pathways that terminate in the pons or medulla from the superior colliclus.

5. Hindbrain

5.1. *Hindbrain anatomy – overview*

The hindbrain (or rhombencephalon) is mainly composed of the myelencephalon that contains the medulla oblongata and the metencephalon which contains that pons and the cerebellum. As previously noted, the term brainstem refers to the midbrain, pons, and medulla with the cerebellum making its own category (Fig. 22). This section will consist of a discussion of those main structures (excluding the midbrain).

5.2. *Metencephalon – anatomy of cerebellum*

Much like the basal ganglia, the cerebellum works in concert with other brain structures to control movement (Fig. 23). The cerebellum sits caudal to the brainstem, directly below the occipital lobes of the cerebral hemispheres. The cerebellum's main function in motor control is to aid planning and timing of motor activities and to allow smooth transition from one muscle movement to the next while adjusting for changes in muscle loading conditions, mostly through the neocerebellum. To accomplish these feats, the cerebellum has many connections to/from the motor and sensory systems of the body. Therefore, it is not surprising that the cerebellum comprises 10% of the total volume of the brain, but it contains almost 80% of the neurons in the brain [2, 74]. The cerebellum can be split into three lobes: anterior, posterior, and flocculonodular (Fig. 24). The cerebellum has two hemispheres, and in the lateral to medial direction, the anterior and posterior lobes can be split into cerebrocerebellum (lateral zone or neocerebellum), medial spinocerebellum (intermediate zone or paleocerebellum), and a middle strip called the cerebellar vermis subdivisions (Fig. 24C,D) [74, 75]. The paleoecerebellum is mainly concerned with fine-tuning movements, using a rich source of proprioceptive and sensory input. The neocerebellum receives its input from the cortex via pontine nuclei and projects a wide set of outputs to different non-cortical regions that are associated with movement. Additionally, in the human, this region has been shown to have cognitive functions including word associations, solving puzzles, and sensory discrimination of complex spatiotemporal components [76]. The flocculonodular lobe mostly receives vestibular and other sensations, its output modulates muscles to coordinate balance and control eye activity to adjust for the head motion. The oldest part of the cerebellum is primarily concerned with balance. The intermediate zone and vermis also have a somatosensory homunculus similar to other brain structures. While the majority of work has tied the cerebellum to motor function, studies have indicated that the cerebellum plays a key role in cognition, language, memory, etc. The specific role of the cerebellum has been difficult to study since it often provides a parallel processing pathway to refine tasks.

Regarding the cellular construction of the cerebellum, it consists of two main neural structures (Fig. 25) [75]. There is an outer sheet of neurons, the cerebellar cortex (3 layers with the bottommost layer being granule cells and the middle layer being Purkinje cells), and a set of deep cerebellar nuclei. The neural types are Purkinje cells (15 million) and granule cells [77]. Additionally, there are predominantly three types of axons. Mossy fibers and climbing fibers terminate in the deep cerebellar nuclei as they enter from outside the cerebellum, and parallel fibers are the axons of the granule cells. Mossy fibers can project to deep nuclei (excitatory connection), but they also synapse to granule cells whereas climbing fibers project to Purkinje cells and send branches to deep cerebellar nuclei (excitatory connection). The main deep cerebellar nuclei is the dentate nucleus [75], but is joined by the globose, emboliform, and fastigial nuclei as the predominant source of cerebellar output. Purkinje cell input (inhibitory connection) from the cerebellar cortex comes into the deep nuclei synapsing to many large and small nuclear cells.

5.3. *Metencephalon – anatomy of pons*

Classically considered the middle of the brainstem, the pons serves many important functions, but the word pons, coming from bridge, denotes a primary function of white matter tracts to/from the brain. While a portion of the brainstem was covered in the midbrain section, we will continue our discussion of the key features of the pons (Fig. 24A). Similar to the midbrain, several cranial nerve nuclei are in the pons, including V (trigeminal), VI (abducens) , VII (facial) , and VIII (vestibulocochlear) (see Table 2). Therefore, the pons has a significant role in coordinating movements regarding the head. Most notably, the cranial nerve nuclei serve to control the oculomotor system that controls eye movements during rest or head movement when vestibulocochlear signal would provide input. Also similar to the midbrain, the pons has the pontine tegmentum, a portion of the reticular formation (including raphe nuclei), and the cerebellar peduncles pass through the pons.

One of the main functions of the brainstem (and pons) is to serve as a conduit of tracts with the peduncles comprising a large portion of the routing to/from the cerebellum. Additionally, ascending pain signals have synapses in the pons as does hearing pathways (in the superior olivary complex). Several spinoreticulo and reticulospinal loops associated with the reticular formation help in the modification of nociception. Since the reticular formation is spread out over the brainstem and the trigeminal nerve nuclei delivers sensations from the face, the boundaries of where different sensory modalities input into the brainstem are spread out.

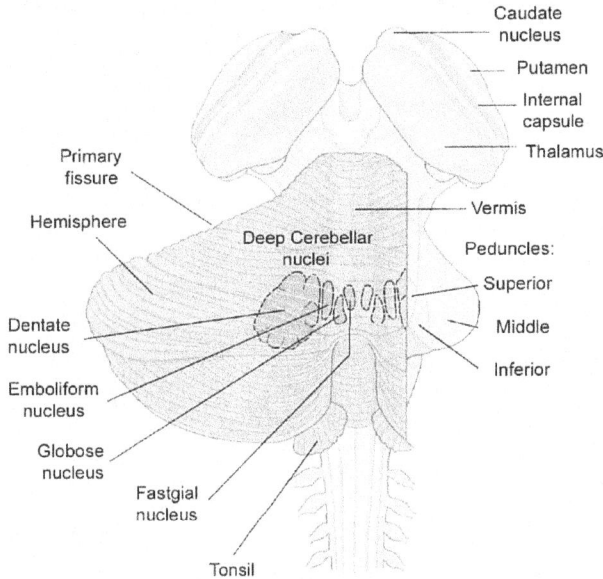

Fig. 22. Dorsal view of cerebellum and brainstem showing gross anatomical features including deep cerebellar nuclei. The right hemisphere has been removed to show cerebellar peduncles. Adapted from [74].

The medial (or pontine) reticulospinal tract and the lateral vestibulospinal tract are the descending pathways that have some cell bodies in the pons (Figure 26 + Figure 27). The majority of nuclei for the lateral vestibulospinal tract are in the medulla. The lateral vestibulospinal tract and the medial (or pontine) reticuluospinal tract coordinates muscles for postural stability and locomotion. The lateral (or medullary) reticulospinal tract affects actions that oppose the medial (or pontine) reticulospinal tract (Figure 27).

A significant component of the pons is the locus coeruleus (LC), a nucleus that some classify in the reticular formation. The LC is the main site for production of norepinephrine (NE) within the brain. Much like other biologic effects of norepinephrine, the LC has a role in the flight/fight response and stress. To this end, the LC has a wide range of outputs across all levels of the brain. NE is a neurotransmitter that can also be a neuromodulator to alter neuroplasticity via changes in spike timing dependent plasticity (see previous discussion regarding acetylcholine production in the basal forebrain).

There are other nuclei that regulate other body functions as well. Respiration, specifically inhalation versus exhalation is regulated by the pneumotaxic center while inspiration is regulated via the apneutstic center. In addition to the previous functions, other pontine nuclei may play a role in bladder control, swallowing, and sleep, among other functions.

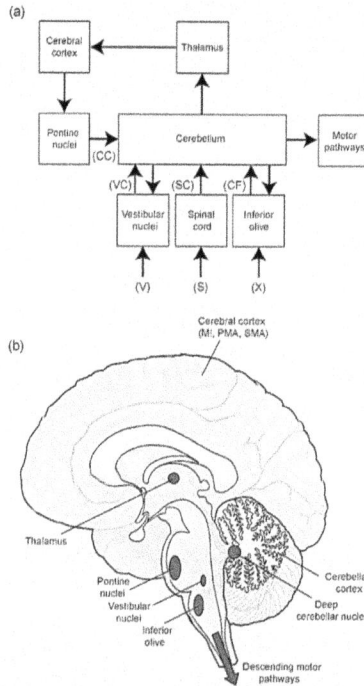

Fig. 23. Main inputs and outputs of the cerebellum. The schematic (a) shows the flow of information between the relevant structures. Mossy fibre inputs originate from three main regions and define the subdivisions of the cerebellum (VC, vestibulocerebellum; SC, spinocerebellum; CC, cerebrocerebellum). Climbing fibre (CF) inputs originate from the inferior olive and derive from multiple sources (X) including the spinal cord. Information from the vestibular system (V) is relayed via the vestibular nuclei. Sensory information concerning position and movement of the body (S) derives from the ascending spinal cord and trigeminal sensory systems. The anatomical diagram (b) shows the location of major structures.

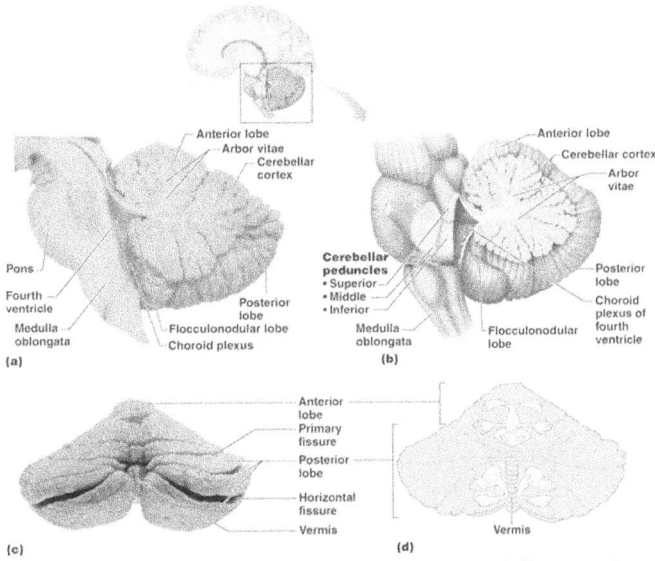

Fig. 24. Overview of cerebellum from two angles. (A,B) Image and diagram of a sagittal section of the cerebellum along its midline. (C,D) View from caudal viewpoint of the cerebellum. (D) Homunculus of the cerebellum. Spinocerebellum and cerebrocerebellum are not pictured. Adapted from [31].

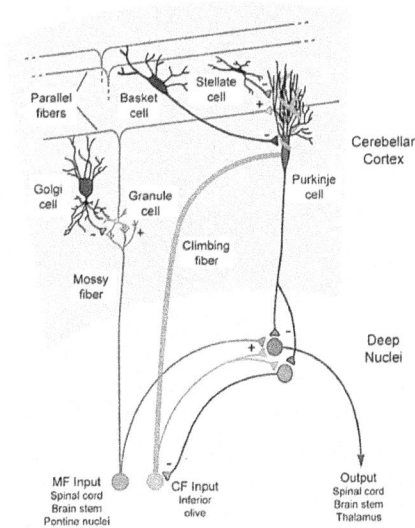

Fig. 25. Basic circuit module of cerebellum. Both cerebellar cortex and deep nuclei receive the same excitatory inputs from mossy fibre (MF) and climbing fibre (CF) systems. All local circuit neurons in the cerebellar cortex (Golgi cells, granule cells, basket cells, and stellate cells) are inhibitory. Purkinje cells are also inhibitory and provide the output system of the cerebellar cortex. Cells in the deep nuclei provide the output system for the cerebellum. Adapted from [74].

D. Weber et al.

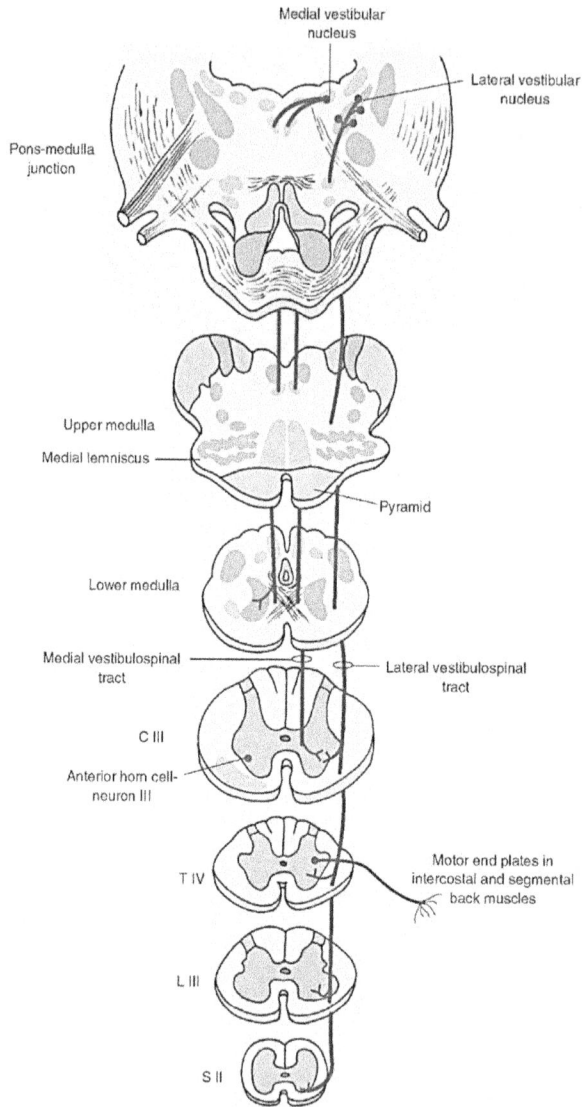

Fig. 26. The lateral vestibulospinal tract descends ipsilaterally. The medial vestibulospinal tract descends mainly ipsilaterally and only as far as the upper thoracic spinal cord.

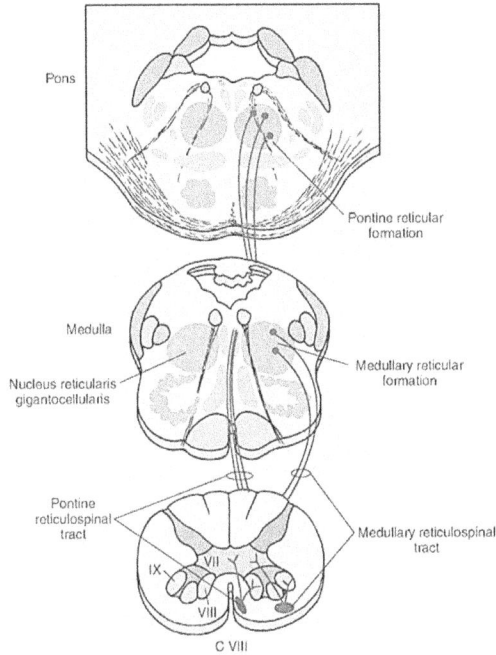

Fig. 27. The pontine/medial reticulospinal tract projects ipsilaterally to all levels of the cord and runs medially to the medullary/lateral reticulospinal tract. The medullary reticulospinal tract is largely from the gigantocellular nucleus and is ipsilateral, but the tract makes some contralateral connections (not shown).

5.4. *Myelencephalon – anatomy of medulla oblongata*

The last notable stop in the brainstem before the spinal cord, the medulla oblongata (or just medulla), is a significant waypoint in information into or out of the brain (Fig. 24A, B). Similar to the pons, several cranial nerves have their nuclei in the medulla, namely, IX (glossopharyngeal), X (vagus), XI (spinal accessory), and XII (hypoglossal) (see Table 2). The fibers from the facial (VII), glossopharyngeal, and vagus come together to innervate the solitary nucleus that is located in the medulla. While the solitary nucleus has a role in taste, it also has a large role in cardio-respiratory functions (mainly via nerves IX, X). Further, these cranial nerve nuclei and their associated connections with other nuclei in the medulla (some in pons or midbrain) play a role in digestion, inflammation, chemical balance, blood pressure (baroreceptors via IX), and many more.

D. Weber et al.

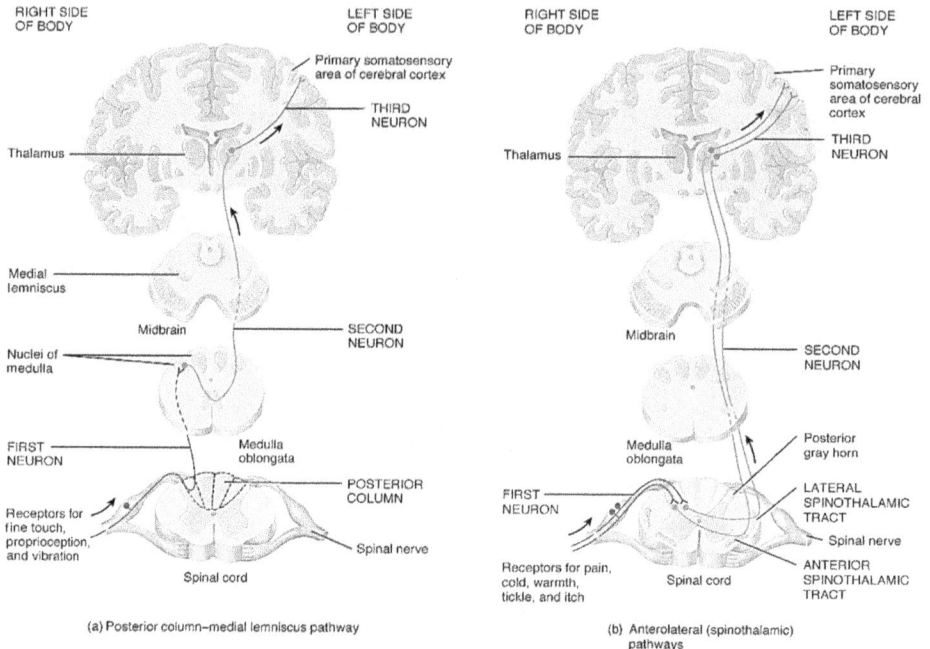

(a) Posterior column–medial lemniscus pathway

(b) Anterolateral (spinothalamic) pathways

Fig. 28. Ascending pathways. (a) The dorsal (or posterior) column-medial lemniscus pathway transmits touch, vibration, and proprioception information to the thalamus. The axons of the first order neurons run via the fasciculus cuneatus and fasciculus gracilis. Decussation occurs and axons synapse onto the cunneate and gracile nuclei, occurring in the medulla. (b) The anterolateral system carries pain and temperature modalities, and projects to the thalamus, pontine and medullary reticular formation, and superior colliculus (not shown). These axons decussate in the spinal cord. Adapted from [78].

As has been previously discussed in the pons and midbrain, several nuclei, or chains thereof, span the medulla. Specifically the reticular formation (Fig. 20), which includes the raphe nuclei, plays a significant role in somatosensory input, spinal reflexes, visceral reflexes (coughing/vomiting/sneezing), pain, and control of autonomic functions. For instance, the cochlear nuclei sit between the medulla and pons as an important pathway for higher-level hearing structures. Notably, the dorsal cochlear nucleus is layered while the ventral cochlear nucleus is not. Another notable nucleus is the inferior olivary nucleus that governs motor control and is a major source of input to the cerebellum via climbing fibers. The inferior olivary nucleus then receives inhibitory signals back from the cerebellum. Additionally, a significant portion of portion of the ascending somatosensory information synapses to the dorsal column nucleus (gracile and cuneate nuclei) in the medulla (actually between medulla and spinal cord) and decussates to form the dorsal column medial lemniscus pathway (Fig. 28). The alternative pathway of somatosensory feedback includes sensation for pain, heat, cold, crude tactile, and itch. This pathway is called the anterolateral pathway and is split into lateral and anterior components. The input decussates at the level of entry in the spinal cord and then ascends to the higher structures. Most of the tactile sensations continue onto the thalamus (spinothalamic) whereas pain sensations synapse to different nuclei in the reticular formation (spinoreticular). Still other fibers synapse in the midbrain (spinomesencephalic). While many of the descending pathways were discussed in the pons section, one additional aspect of the medullary reticulospinal tract is conveying descending signals for sleep paralysis during REM sleep.

6. Spinal Cord

The spinal cord forms the main communication link between the brain and the peripheral nerves. It transfers sensory information to various centers of the brain, conveying the status of body organs (e.g., muscle stretch) as well as exposure to changes in external environmental factors (e.g., temperature, pressure). It also carries descending commands from the brain resulting in muscle contractions that initiate movements or modulate ongoing ones. The spinal cord contains vast interneuronal networks which process the sensory information prior to its reception by supraspinal centers and modulate descending commands prior to their transfer to peripheral nerves. An injury to the spinal cord results in the loss of communication between the brain and the periphery but the neuronal networks below the lesion often remain largely intact.

6.1. *Spinal cord structure*

The spinal cord is a thin long tube that lies within the spinal column (Fig. 29). In contrast to the cerebrum and cerebellum, the center of the spinal cord forms the gray matter which is composed of densely located neural cells. Surrounding the gray matter is white matter, formed of axonal tracts that transfer ascending and descending information. The spinal cord is the caudal continuation of the brainstem medulla oblongata and is about 46 cm-long in adult humans. It extends from the base of the skull and comes to a tapering end (the conus medullaris) midway between lumbar vertebrae 1 and 2 (L1 and L2). The remaining space from vertebra L2 to the coccyx is filled with spinal roots, forming what is known as the cauda equina (horse's tail). With the exception of the cervical region, the spinal cord is divided into segments that correspond in number to the spinal vertebrae: 8 cervical (C1-C8), 12 thoracic (T1-T12), 5 lumbar (L1-L5), 5 sacral (S1-S5), and one coccyx (Co1) segment. The cord has two enlarged regions, the cervical and the lumbar enlargements, which correspond to the segments giving rise to the nerves that supply the upper and lower extremities, respectively.

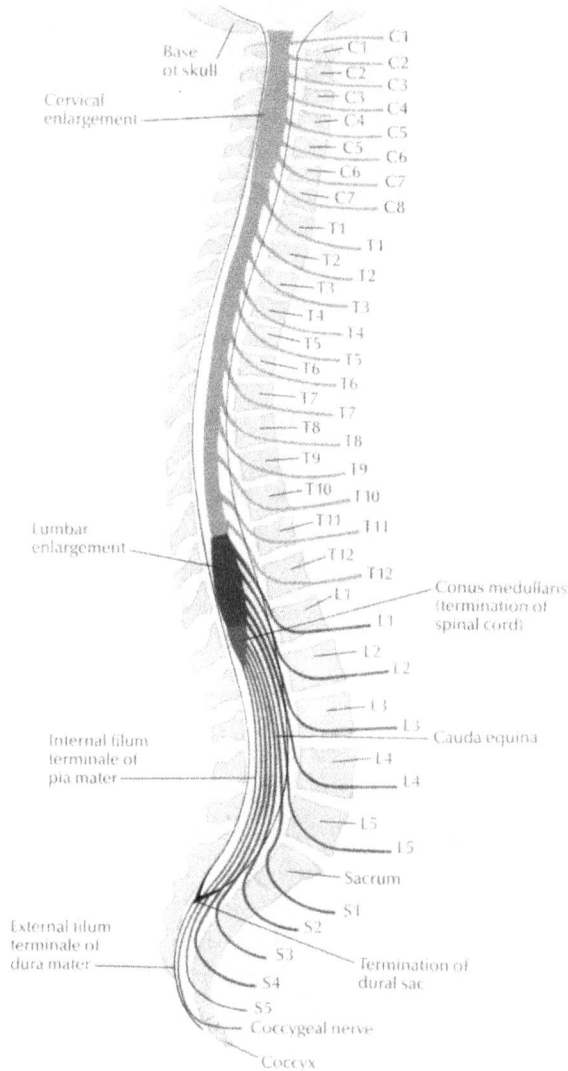

Fig. 29. Overview of spinal cord structure (adapted from [79]).

Similar to the brain, the spinal cord is ensheathed by three meningeal layers. The dura mater is the tough external fibrous sac encapsulating the cord and extends to the level of the second sacral vertebra. It also ensheaths the spinal roots, which penetrate through it to form spinal nerves, and fuses with the epineurium of peripheral nerves. Beneath the dura mater lies the arachnoid layer, the middle of the three meninges. The cerebrospinal fluid (CSF) circulates within the subarachnoid space as well as inside the central canal. The pia mater is the third meningeal layer and closest to the cord, tightly embracing it and the spinal roots. Lateral extensions of the pia mater, known as the denticulate ligaments, connect the cord to the dura mater at several locations. At the caudal end of the conus medullaris, the pia mater forms the thin filum terminale which descends within the cauda equina and terminates around the rostral end of the coccyx.

Fig. 30 shows a cross-section of the spinal cord illustrating the various components seen at each segmental level. Sensory fibers with endings in the periphery transmit their information to the dorsal root ganglia (located outside the spinal cord), where their cell bodies lie. The information continues to the spinal cord through the central axonal projections of the axons, which form the dorsal roots.

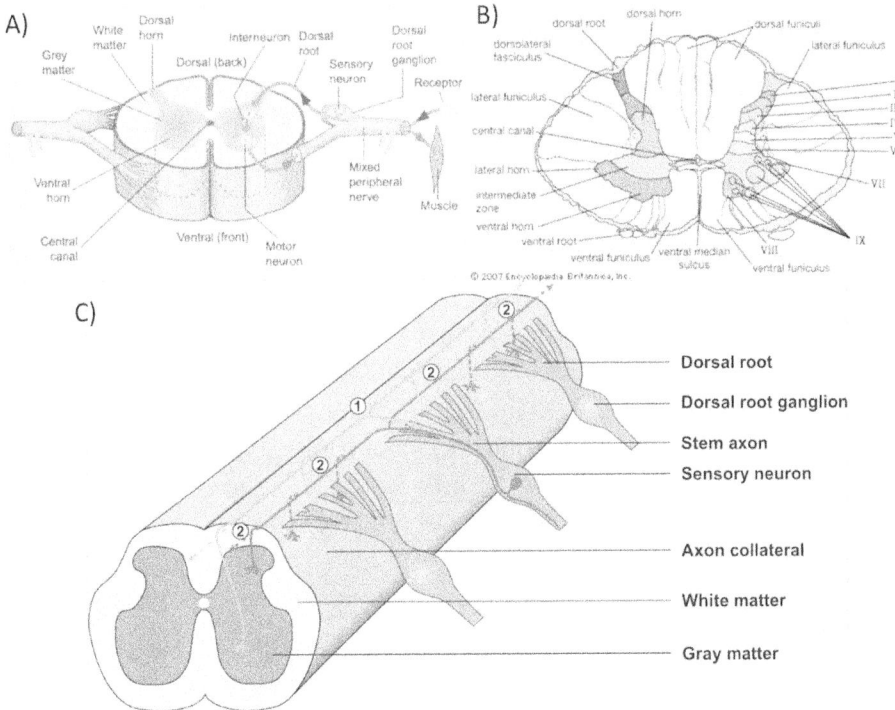

Fig. 30. (A) Cross-section of the spinal cord with spinal roots. (B) Laminar organization of the spinal cord gray matter. (C) Branching of Ia sensory neurons upon entry into the spinal cord.

The spinal cord receives sensory (or afferent) inputs from many peripheral elements which include skin, muscles and joints. This information is heavily integrated within the neuronal circuits of the spinal cord and the brain and strongly affects the motor commands transmitted to peripheral nerves (efferent output). The major classes of sensory afferents are cutaneous, nociceptive and proprioceptive. Cutaneous afferents are skin receptors transmitting several sensory modalities including touch, pressure and temperature. Nociceptive afferents are pain receptors and are located in soft tissue throughout the body. Proprioceptive afferents are often referred to as muscle sensors and transmit information regarding muscle length, stretch velocity and force.

Fig. 30B shows the organizational layers, or Rexed Laminae[80], of the gray matter within the spinal cord, divided based on the distinct cytological features of their resident neurons (interneurons and/or motoneurons). Interneurons are densely located in all laminae and are involved in processing and modulating sensory input at the local segmental level as well as integrating intersegmental input and descending input from supraspinal centers. Alpha motoneurons, whose axons exit through the ventral surface of the cord, forming the spinal ventral roots and subsequently giving rise to motor nerves in the periphery, are located in laminae IX of the ventral horn. Alpha motoneurons are known as the "final common pathway," as they integrate interneuronal and descending inputs which encode the motor commands to the periphery. Motor actions of the periphery are directly related to the action potentials generated in alpha motoneurons. Lamina IX also contains the cell bodies of gamma motoneurons which innervate the intrafusal fibers of the muscle spindle and act to modulate the sensitivity of the spindle depending on the skill level of the motor task [81, 82]. Cell bodies of motoneurons innervating a given muscle are arranged in the ventral horn in thin, spindle-shaped columns that span two or three segments and are called motor nuclei, motor columns, or motor pools[83-85] (Fig. 31A). There is little to no intermingling between the motoneuronal cells within the motor pools of various muscles. If any intermingling does occur, it is usually between the cells innervating synergistic muscles[85, 86]. However, motoneurons have extensive dendritic trees (Fig. 31B). The dendritic tree of a single motoneuron can span the full extent of the ventral horn, extend into the white matter, and even project to the contralateral ventral horn.

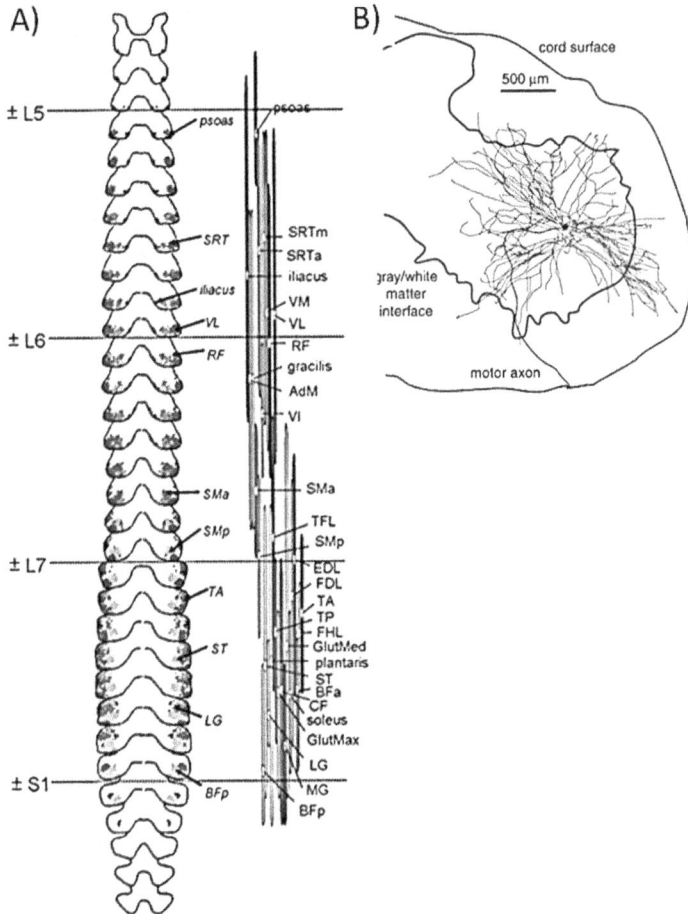

Fig. 31. (A) Organization of 28 motoneuronal pools in the lumbosacral enlargement of the spinal cord in the cat, the region controlling the muscles of the hind limb. Each cross-section represents a slice of spinal cord approximately 1 mm thick and the groups of dots refer to the locations of motoneuron pools in the enlargement; each dot representing a single motoneuron. The dotted lines approximately mark the rostral margins of the L5, L6, L7 and S1 spinal cord segments. Note that the cord of the cat has 2 additional lumbar segments and 2 less sacral segments relative to that of the human. The figure on the right displays the rostro-caudal extent of the motoneuron pools in the lumbosacral enlargement. The left to right position of each vertical bar reflects the approximate medial-lateral location of the corresponding motoneuron pool in the ventral horn (not to scale). The dorsal-ventral arrangement of the pools was ignored since some ventrally-located pools would be masked by dorsally-located ones. SRT: sartorius; SRTm and SRTa: medial and anterior heads of sartorius; VM, VL and VI: vastus medialis, lateralis and intermedius; RF: rectus femoris; AdM: adductor magnus; SMa and SMp: semimembranosus anterior and posterior; TFL: tensor fasciae latae; EDL and FDL: extensor and flexor digitorum longus; TA and TP: tibialis anterior and posterior; FHL: flexor hallucis longus; GlutMed and GlutMax: gluteus medius and maximus; ST: semitendinosus; BFa and BFp: biceps femoris anterior and posterior; CF: caudofemoralis; LG and MG: lateral and medial gastrocnemius. (Adapted from [87] and [88]). (B) Dendritic tree of a single motoneuron can extend throughout the ventral horn and into the white matter. Adapted from [89].

Sensory fibers entering the spinal cord bifurcate and send branches rostral and caudal to their respective dorsal entry point and synapse on interneuronal cells in various laminae (Fig. 30 A, C). Some sensory inputs have direct connections with motoneuronal cells in lamina IX. Branches of one sensory fiber span around three cord segments. Sensory input is transmitted to supraspinal centers in one of two patterns. Some fibers, particularly those associated with diffuse sensations like pain or temperature, branch locally in the dorsal parts of the gray matter and synapse with second-order (i.e., post-synaptic to the primary afferent fibers) cells that cross the midline and ascend to the brain in the lateral parts of the white matter (e.g., the spino-thalamic tract, Fig. 32). Other sensory fibers enter the cord and branch locally, but instead of synapsing with neurons forming the lateral tracts, they send a process up the dorsal part of the white matter (the dorsal columns) to synapse with second-order cells in the medulla. These sensory neurons tend to innervate structures associated with fine tactile discrimination.

The spinal cord white matter contains ascending and descending tracts transferring sensory information to supraspinal structures and modulatory commands affecting motor output. Ascending tracts often have names indicating the originating and termination points of the fibers, aiding one in identifying their function (e.g., "spino-thalamic" tracts carrying information from cutaneous receptors to the thalamic relay centers or nuclei of the brain, and "spino-cerebellar" tracts carrying sensory information from muscles to the cerebellum). Fibers descending from the brain to control motor activity in the spinal cord do so in the ventral and lateral tracts of the white matter. As with their ascending counterparts, these tracts can be named after their central source (e.g., "cortico-spinal" tract, Fig. 32) but sometimes are named based on morphological features (e.g., "pyramidal" tract). Descending fibers can synapse directly on motor neurons, but more commonly synapse on local neurons (interneurons) which interact indirectly through interneurons with motor neurons. See Table 3 for a summary of the spinal tracts. Fig. 32 provides a schematic representation of the location of ascending and descending tracts in the spinal cord and Table 3 summarizes the main features of select tracts. The location of cells of origin in the spinal cord of some ascending tracts is shown in Fig. 32A and B. The axons of most ascending and descending tracts cross to the opposite side along the course of their travel from origin to termination.

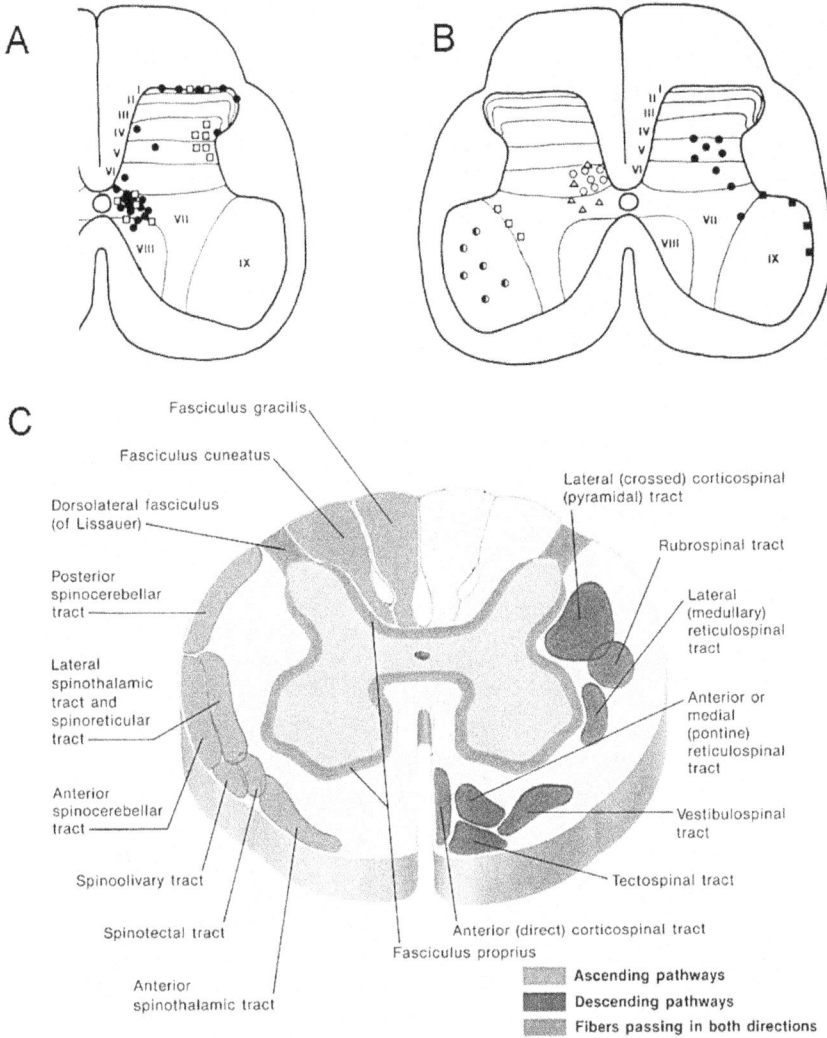

Fig. 32. Summary of location of some identified neuronal systems forming the ascending tracts of the spinal cord. (A) filled circle - spinothalamic tract in the cat; open square - spinothalamic tract in the monkey (adapted from [90]). (B) open circle - posterior spinocerebellar tract; open triangle - neurons projecting to cerebellum in the cat; filled circle and filled square - anterior spinocerebellar tract; open square - Ia inhibitory interneurons; half-filled circle - motoneurons (adapted from [90]). (C) Summary cartoon of ascending and descending spinal tracts in human. Adapted from [91].

Table 3. **Summary of select ascending and descending spinal tracts.**

Tract	Location of cells of origin	Primary site of termination	Information transferred/ function
Ascending tracts			
Anterior spinothalamic	Dorsal and intermediate laminae; tract crosses over to opposite side	Thalamus, then projects to cerebral cortex	Crude pressure and touch
Lateral spinothalamic	Dorsal and intermediate laminae; tract crosses over to opposite side	Thalamus, then projects to cerebral cortex	Pain and temperature
Fasciculus gracilis and fasciculus cuneatus (dorsal columns)	Peripheral afferent neurons from skin, muscles, tendons, and joints from lower extremities (gracilis) and upper extremities (cuneatus); tract does not cross over to opposite side	Gracilis and cuneatus nuclei in medulla, then projects to thalamus and subsequently to cerebral cortex	Fine touch, precise pressure, movements
Anterior spinocerebellar	Intermediate and ventral laminae; some fibers cross over to opposite side, others do not	Cerebellum	Proprioceptive input, necessary for coordinated muscle contractions
Posterior spinocerebellar	Intermediate laminae; tract does not cross over to opposite side	Cerebellum	Proprioceptive input, necessary for coordinated muscle contractions
Descending tracts			
Anterior corticospinal	Cerebral cortex; tract crosses to opposite side at the spinal cord level	Ventral horn	Coordination of precise voluntary movements
Lateral corticospinal	Cerebral cortex; tract crosses to opposite side at the level of the medulla	Ventral horn	Coordination of precise voluntary movements
Tectospinal	Brainstem; tract crosses to opposite side	Ventral horn	Coordination of head movements in response to visual, auditory and cutaneous inputs
Rubrospinal	Red nucleus of brainstem; tract crosses to opposite side	Ventral horn	Modulation of muscle tone and posture
Vestibulospinal	brainstem; tract crosses to opposite side	Ventral horn	Modulation of muscle tone and posture in response to movements of the head
Anterior and medial reticulospinal	Reticular formation of brainstem; tract does not cross over to opposite side	Ventral horn	Modulation of muscle tone and sweating
Lateral reticulospinal	Reticular formation of the brainstem; tract does not cross to opposite side	Ventral horn	Modulation of muscle tone and sweating

Cutaneous sensory innervation of the trunk consists of a series of bands, corresponding to the location at which each spinal root leaves the spinal column (Fig. 33). Sensory innervation of the skin of the limbs is similarly organized, not in bands but in patches corresponding to different spinal roots. For the arm, innervation progresses down the anterior (radial) side of the arm starting with segment C5, turns around at the middle of the hand with C7, and progresses back up the posterior (ulnar) side of the arm to T2, which also innervates the trunk at the level of the arm pit. A similar pattern occurs in the legs, which are innervated by segments L2 thorough S2. Each patch of innervation from a single root is called a dermatome. The innervation pattern of muscles is similarly organized except that, since muscles typically span more than one dermatome, innervation of a given muscle normally comes from more than one spinal root. Even so, the nerve supply for a single muscle always comes from adjacent roots, and there is a regular progression down the spinal cord of the roots involved as one moves down and back up the limb. Assessment of sensory and motor maps is used to determine the locus of injury after spinal cord damage. The extent of functional loss after spinal cord injury depends predominantly on the level of injury. Continued periodical assessments of these maps can help evaluate the recovery or further decline of sensation/motor activity as a function of time after injury, in response to rehabilitation interventions or due to complications associated with the injury.

6.2. *Spinal cord physiology*

The spinal cord is often thought of as a passive element of the central nervous system whose function is limited to transmission of ascending and descending information. However, the capacity of the spinal cord's inherent networks to process and modulate sensory and descending inputs, and to generate their own motor commands in the absence of both sensory and descending inputs, provide the primary building blocks of sensorimotor integration. Three types of basic spinal cord circuitry will be presented below: processing and modulation of pain, reflexive responses to proprioceptive and cutaneous inputs, and generation of locomotor rhythm. Other circuitry, such as the networks for bladder control, are discussed elsewhere.

6.2.1. *Pain*

Pain is the most distinctive of all sensory modalities. Sharp, acute pain serves as a protective mechanism against impending injury such as placing the hand on a hot stove. Pain can also be persistent or chronic. Persistent pain results from direct activation of nociceptors in soft tissue due to injury resulting in inflammation. Examples of persistent pain are sprains and strains, arthritis, and tumor invasion of soft tissue. Persistent pain also results from direct injury to the nervous system. While sharp pain serves as a warning mechanism, and the origin of persistent pain can usually be deduced and symptoms treated, chronic pain appears to occur for no clear reason and its treatment is far less successful. According to Basbaum and Jessell [92], chronic pain "appears to serve no useful purpose; it only makes patients miserable(!)."

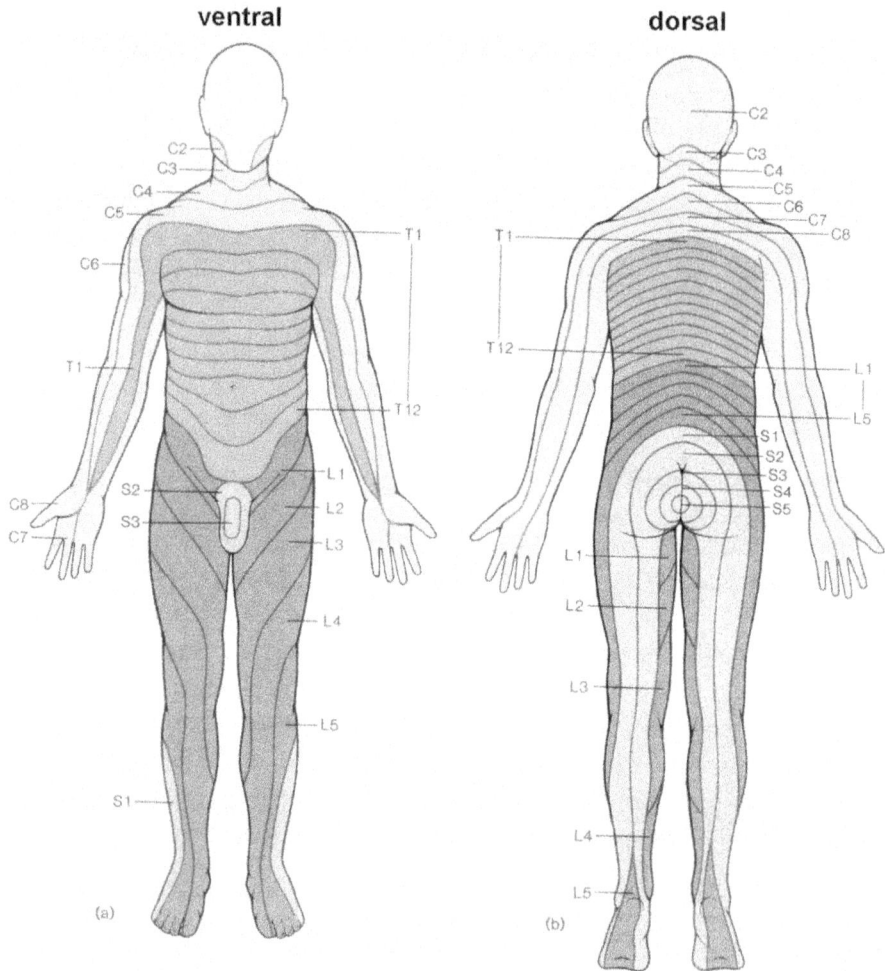

Fig. 33. The pattern of dermatomes or map of the projection of spinal nerves (usually based on dorsal root innervation) in the body. Adapted from [93].

The underlying mechanisms of pain perception have been extensively investigated. We consider here the spinal processing of nociceptive input. Fig. 34 shows the termination of nociceptive afferents, Aδ (myelinated) and C (unmyelinated), in the dorsal horn. Aδ fibers transmit sharp pain while C fibers transmit dull pain. Aδ fibers terminate with excitatory synapses on projection neurons (neurons whose axons travel towards the brain) in laminae I and V, thus increasing their level of activity. In contrast, C fibers form inhibitory connections with the inhibitory neurons in lamina II which in turn decreases their level of activity. Large diameter, myelinated Aα and Aβ mechanoreceptors also terminate on projection neurons of lamina V and inhibitory neurons of lamina II.

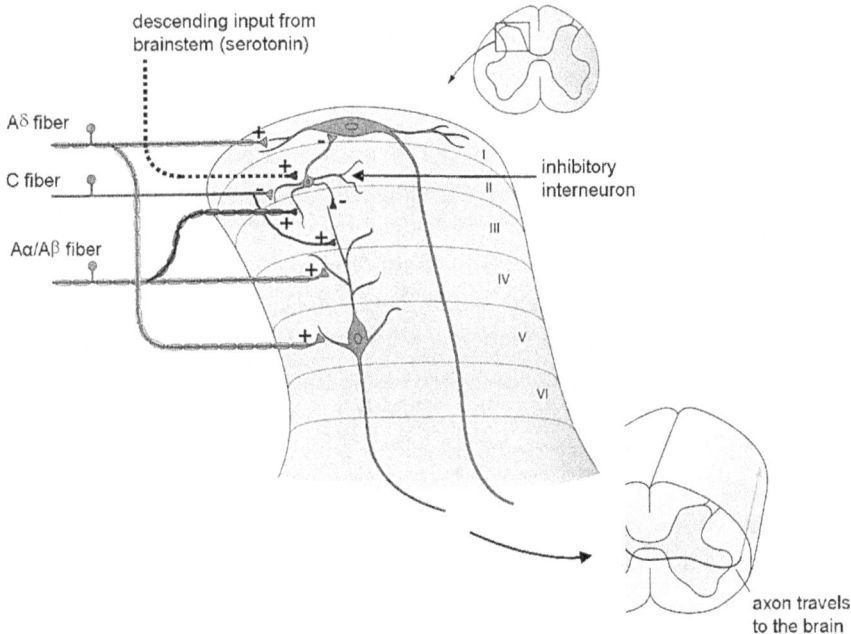

Fig. 34. Schematic of the spinal pain processing circuitry initially proposed by the "gate theory" of pain perception (adapted from [92]).

This connectivity was initially suggested in the 1960s [94] and formed the basis for the "gate theory" of pain perception. The circuitry allows for the balancing of nociceptive and nonnociceptive inputs prior to their projection to supraspinal centers. If noxious stimuli are the dominating input to a given spinal segment, the projection neurons are directly activated by excitatory connections from the Aδ fibers and indirectly activated by the disinhibition of the inhibitory neurons in lamina II from C fiber connections. The net result is an increased transmission of nociceptive input to the brain. However, if the large mechanoreceptors Aα and Aβ are activated simultaneously, they will strongly activate the inhibitory neurons of lamina II which would in turn reduce the activity in the projection neurons of laminae I and V. Therefore, activity in the large mechanoreceptors "gate" the transmission of nociceptive input to the brain. This is why rubbing the skin around an injured region in the body reduces the intensity of pain perception. Note that strong descending input from the brainstem can also gate the transmission of nociceptive input to supraspinal centers by directly activating the inhibitory neurons of lamina II.

6.2.2. *Spinal reflexes*

Spinal reflexes are automatic movements produced by motor commands generated in the spinal cord in response to sensory input from muscle or skin. It was postulated in the past that coordinated movements are but chains of spinal reflexes, initiated by sensory stimuli [15]. However, it soon became apparent that patterned and coordinated movements can be initiated and maintained in the absence of sensory input [95, 96] (e.g., rhythmic locomotion), giving rise to the current understanding that movements result from the adaptive integration of spinal reflexes and centrally generated motor commands. Indeed, it is through the ongoing modulation of motor commands by sensory information from muscle, joint, or skin that accurate movements are implemented successfully. Similarly, the level of synaptic transmission through reflex pathways can be modulated by descending input and spinally-generated motor commands.

Fig. 35 and Fig. 36 demonstrate three types of identified networks of spinal reflexes. The classical monosynaptic stretch reflex is shown in Fig. 35C. Ia afferents from muscle spindles (signalling rate of change in muscle length) in a given muscle have direct excitatory synapses on motoneurons innervating the homonymous (same) muscle as well as those innervating synergistic muscles (muscles with similar mechanical action). Each Ia afferent fiber branches extensively once entering the spinal cord (Fig. 35A) and makes synaptic connections with every motoneuron innervating the homonymous muscle. A reconstruction of the synaptic projections of a Ia afferent fiber on a motoneuron is shown in Fig. 35B. In addition to activating homonymous muscles, thereby causing them to contract and shorten (or resist lengthening), Ia afferents synapse indirectly on motoneurons innervating antagonistic muscles (muscles with opposite mechanical action) through an inhibitory interneuron (not shown in Fig. 35C). This disynaptic pathway forms the basis of reciprocal inhibition and acts to inhibit the activity in antagonistic muscles, thereby decreasing the amount and rate of stretch imposed in the homonymous muscle. Reciprocal inhibition is not only seen in reflex-evoked movements but is also evident during voluntary movements as the antagonistic muscles relax during the activation of prime movers. This enhances the efficiency of action of the prime movers as they are not required to work against the opposing contractions of antagonistic muscles.

A

dorsal

B

Ⅴ

Ⅵ

α

ventral

motoneuron

Ia afferent

500 μm

500 μm

C

Spinal cord

Axon of
sensory neuron

Cell body of
sensory neuron

monosynaptic
reflex

Direction of impulse

Dendrite of
sensory neuron

Receptor ends of
sensory neuron

Dendrite of
motor neuron

Axon of
motor neuron

Effector—
quadriceps
femoris
muscle

Patella

Cell body of
motor neuron

Femur

Tibia

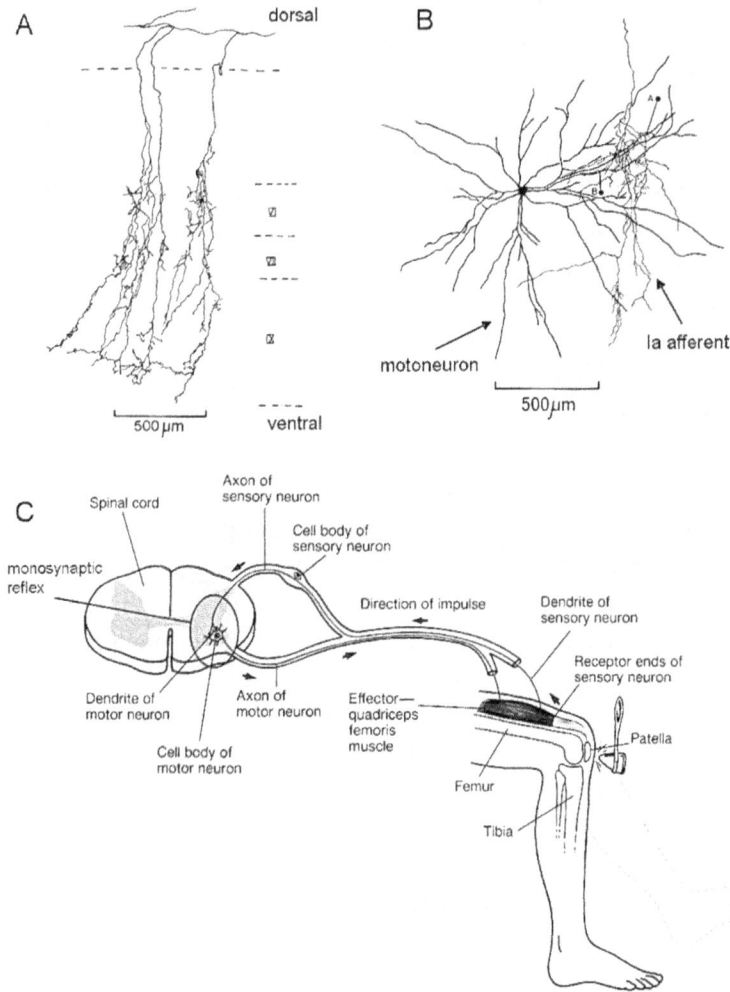

Fig. 35. Spinal reflexes. (A) Pattern of Ia afferent branching in the spinal cord (adapted from [90]).
(B) Reconstruction of Ia synapses on an alpha motoneuron (adapted from [90]). (C) Schematic
depicting the monosynaptic spinal stretch reflex Adapted from [93].

Another spinal reflex that has been extensively studied is the Ib afferent (or
Golgi tendon organ) reflex (Fig. 36B). Ib afferents have their endings in the
tendonous portions of skeletal muscles and convey information regarding the level
of force generated in a given muscle. This information provides the nervous system
with a precise measure of the state of muscle contraction at all times. At rest, the
Ib pathway acts as a negative feedback loop: activation of the Ib sensory endings
inhibits the homonymous muscle through a disynaptic inhibition pathway (Fig.

36B). However, Ib input to the spinal cord during weight bearing stepping, excites the motoneurons of homonymous muscles through polysynaptic connections (not shown) and acts to reinforce the level of tension in antigravity muscles (Fig. 36B). During locomotion, the disynaptic inhibition pathway is suppressed by descending input converging upon the inhibitory interneuron. This provides an example of the commonly seen state-dependent reflex reversal and highlights the malleability of spinal reflexes and their modulation by descending signals associated with the motor commands for walking.

Fig. 36A presents the flexion crossed-extension spinal reflex which involves the coordinated activation of muscles in both limbs. A noxious stimulus to one limb results in the activation of cutaneous nociceptive afferents which, through a network of inhibitory and excitatory interneurons, activate flexor motoneurons in the ipsilateral limb and extensor motoneurons in the contralateral limb. This causes the ipsilateral limb to flex and move away from the harmful stimulus and the contralateral limb to extend to support the shift in the center of mass and maintain postural stability. This spinal reflex further emphasizes the spinal cord's ability to process sensory information and generate appropriate motor responses in a large number of muscles. However, similar to the Ib disynaptic inhibition reflex, the flexion crossed-extension response is state-dependent. For example, an individual standing in place receiving a noxious stimulus to the foot reacts automatically by lifting the perturbed limb and supporting body weight with the contralateral limb. If, on the other hand, the noxious stimulus is presented to the stance limb during walking (i.e., limb fully supporting body weight), the flexor excitation in the ipsilateral limb will be suppressed. This is because flexion in the stance limb, while the contralateral limb is itself flexed as it undergoes the swing phase of stepping, will compromise upright posture and balance.

6.2.3. Locomotion

It was thought in the early 1900s that rhythmic movements, especially locomotion, are composed of chains of proprioceptive reflexes resulting in alternating flexion and extension movements of the limb [97]. However, this view was disproved by Graham Brown in 1911 [95] who showed that rhythmic locomotor patterns can still be generated in completely spinalized and deafferented animals (i.e., animals which complete spinal transaction and in which all dorsal roots were cut). Graham suggested that the spinal cord itself is capable of producing rhythmic locomotion and referred to this capacity as the "intrinsic factor of the spinal cord" [95]. Brown's theory has since been proven by several investigators. Experiments conducted throughout the course of the last century demonstrated that the neuronal networks necessary for basic rhythm generation reside within the spinal cord [96, 98-102]. However, even though descending and afferent inputs are not necessary for the production of rhythmic locomotion, in the intact nervous system, tonic descending input strongly activates the spinal locomotor networks and stepping is continuously modulated by sensory input.

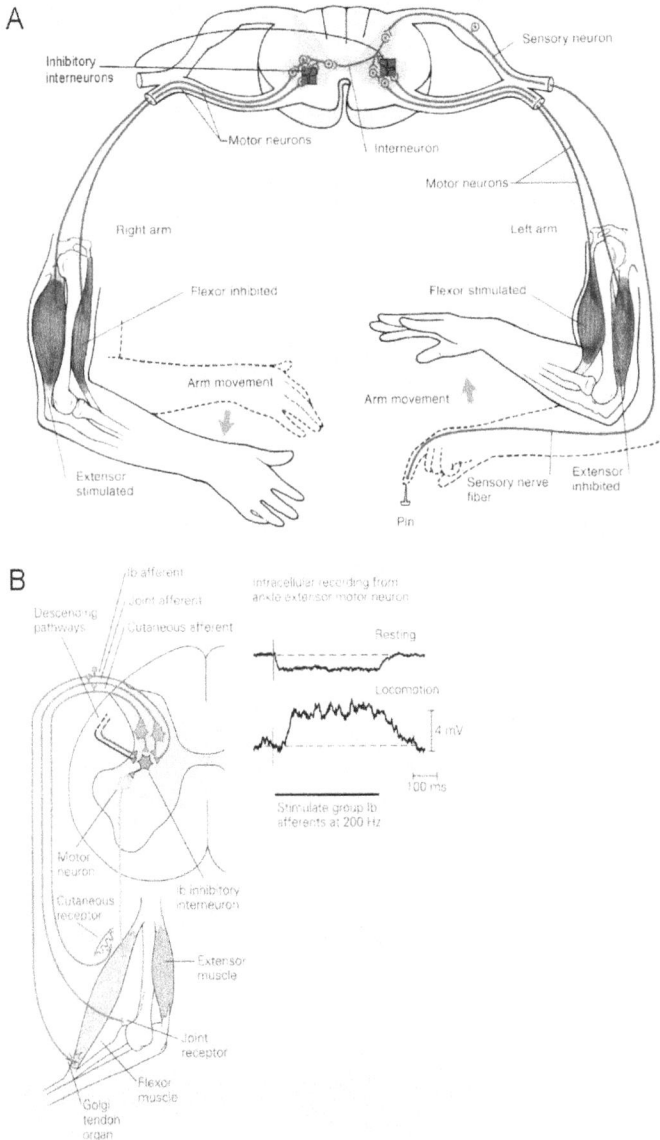

Fig. 36. Spinal reflexes. (A) Flexion crossed-extension reflex. Adapted from [93]. (B) Ib afferent reflex pathways. Adapted from [82].

A

B

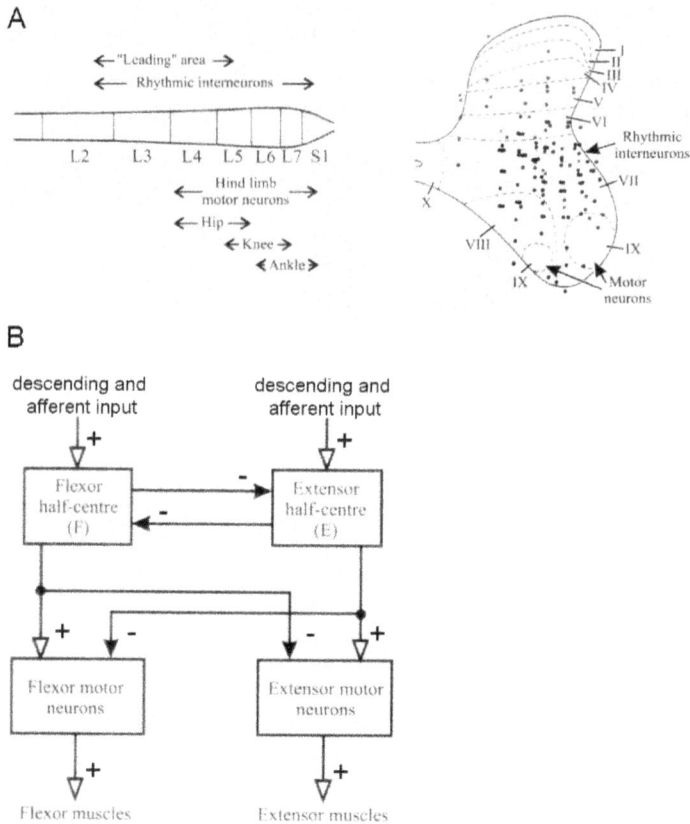

Fig. 37. Spinal cord rhythmic locomotor activity in the cat. (A) Rostral-caudal distribution of rhythmically active interneurons in the lumbosacral region of the cord and segments thought to exhibit strongest rhythm, or the "leading area" (left). Laminar distribution of rhythmically active interneurons (right). (B) Basic model of rhythm generation network in the spinal cord. Adapted from [103].

The location and nature of the spinal locomotor networks have been the topic of intense investigation [101, 103-109]. The motoneuron pools in the lumbar enlargement innervating the muscles of the hindlimbs extend from L4 to S1 in the cat (Fig. 37A, left). During rhythmic behaviours such as scratching and stepping, rhythmic activity is exhibited in all these pools [87]. Large numbers of interneurons situated throughout the enlargement also exhibit rhythmic activity similar to that of the motoneuron pools [109, 110] (Fig. 37A). Rhythmically active interneurons during fictive stepping were found in the same locations [110]. However, in vivo and in vitro studies in isolated spinal cords involving the use of pharmacological agents for the induction of rhythmic locomotor patterns combined with serial cutting of the spinal cord, suggested that the more rostral segments of the lumbar enlargement (segments L3 to L5 in the cat) are capable of generating stronger rhythms than the more caudal segments and are often referred to as the "leading segments" for locomotor pattern generation [103]. The leading and caudal segments of the lumbar enlargement are thought to be interconnected through propriospinal interneurons (intersegmental neurons with myelinated axons travelling within the white matter) [111]. These interneurons are also thought to play an active role in coupling forelimb and hindlimb activity in quadrupeds and upper and lower extremity activity in bipeds during stepping.

The connectivity of spinal neuronal networks and the mechanisms by which rhythmogenesis occurs have not been identified despite extensive efforts. The most common model proposed to explain the generation of rhythmic behaviours was initially proposed by Brown [95]. Brown [95] hypothesized that the main composition of a spinal locomotor network comprises two systems of interneurons in each side of the spinal cord, a flexor half-center and an extensor half-center, which mutually inhibit each other through reciprocal inhibitory connections (Fig. 37B). He suggested that the switching of activity between the half-centers depended on fatigue of these reciprocal inhibitory connections. Studies conducted in the 1960s provided support for Brown's half-center hypothesis [98, 99].

References

1. Purves, D. et al., *Neuroscience*, (Sunauer Associates, Sunderland, MA, 1997)
2. Azevedo, F. A., L. R. Carvalho, L. T. Grinberg, J. M. Farfel, R. E. Ferretti, R. E. Leite, W. Jacob Filho, R. Lent, and S. Herculano-Houzel, Equal numbers of neuronal and nonneuronal cells make the human brain an isometrically scaled-up primate brain, *Journal of Comparative Neurology*, **513**, pp. 532-541, 2009.
3. Hall, J. E., *Guyton and Hall textbook of medical physiology*, (Elsevier Health Sciences, Philadelphia, 2010).
4. Takano, T., G. F. Tian, W. Peng, N. Lou, W. Libionka, X. Han, and M. Nedergaard, Astrocyte-mediated control of cerebral blood flow, *Nature Neuroscience*, **9**, pp. 260-267, 2006.
5. Oberheim, N. A., T. Takano, X. Han, W. He, J. H. Lin, F. Wang, Q. Xu, J. D. Wyatt, W. Pilcher, J. G. Ojemann, B.R. Ransom, S. A. Goldman, and M. Nedergaard, Uniquely hominid features of adult human astrocytes, *J Neurosci*, **29**, pp. 3276-3287, 2009.
6. Porter, R. and R. N. Lemon, *Corticospinal function and Voluntary Movement*, (Oxford University Press, Oxford, 1993).
7. Mountcastle, V. B., *Perceptual neuroscience: The cerebral cortex*, (Harvard University Press, Cambridge, MA, 1998).
8. DeFelipe, J., The evolution of the brain, the human nature of cortical circuits and intellectual creativity, *Frontiers in Neuroanatomy*, **5**, p. 29, 2011.
9. Bailey, E.L., J. McCulloch, C. Sudlow, and J. M. Wardlaw, Potential animal models of lacunar stroke a systematic review, *Stroke*, **40**, pp. e451-e458, 2009.

10. Howells, D.W., M. J. Porritt, S. S. Rewell, V. O'Collins, E. S. Sena, H. B. van der Worp, R. J. Traystman, and M. R. Macleod, Different strokes for different folks: the rich diversity of animal models of focal cerebral ischemia, *Journal of Cerebral Blood Flow & Metabolism*, **30**, pp. 1412-1431, 2010.

11. Zhang, K. and T. J. Sejnowski, A universal scaling law between gray matter and white matter of cerebral cortex, *Proceedings of the National Academy of Sciences*, **97**, pp. 5621-5626, 2000.

12. Campbell, A. W. E. B. Schlesinger; H. A. Riley, *Histological studies on the localisation of cerebral function*, (Cambridge University Press, Cambridge, 1905).

13. Smith, G. E., A new topographical survey of the human cerebral cortex, being an account of the distribution of the anatomically distinct cortical areas and their relationship to the cerebral sulci, *Journal of Anatomy and Physiology*, **41**, p. 237, 1907.

14. Brodmann, K., *Vergleichende Lokalisationslehre der Grosshirnrinde in ihren Prinzipien dargestellt auf Grund des Zellenbaues*, (Barth, 1909). English translation available in Garey, L. J. *Brodmann's Localization in the Cerebral Cortex* (Smith Gordon, London, 1994).

15. Sherrington, C. S., *The Integrative Action of the Nervous System*, (Yale University Press, New Haven, CT, 1906).

16. Sarkisov, S., I. Filimonoff, and N. Preobrashenskaya, *Cytoarchitecture of the Human Cortex Cerebri*, (Medgiz, Moscow, 1949).

17. Talairach, J. and P. Tournoux, *Co-Planar Stereotaxic Atlas of the Human Brain. 3-Dimensional Proportional System: An Approach to Cerebral Imaging,*. (Georg Thieme Verlag, New York, 1988).

18. Talairach, J. and P. Tournoux, *Referentially Oriented Cerebral MRI Anatomy: An Atlas of Stereotaxic Anatomical Correlations for Gray and White Matter*, (Georg Thieme Verlag, New York, 1993).

19. Evans, A. C., et al. 3D statistical neuroanatomical models from 305 MRI volumes, *IEEE Nuclear Science Symposium and Medical Imaging Conference, 1993.*

20. Amunts, K., M. Lenzen, A. D. Friederici, A. Schleicher, P. Morosan, N. Palomero-Gallagher, and K. Zilles, Broca's region: novel organizational principles and multiple receptor mapping, *PLoS Biol*, **8**, p. e1000489, 2010.

21. Desikan, R.S., F. Ségonne, B. Fischl, B. T. Quinn, B. C. Dickerson, D. Blacker, R. L. Buckner, A. M. Dale, R. P. Maguire, B. T. Hyman, M. S. Albert, and R. J. Killiany, An automated labeling system for subdividing the human cerebral cortex on MRI scans into gyral based regions of interest, *Neuroimage*, **31**, pp. 968-980, 2006.

22. Destrieux, C., B. Fischl, A. Dale, and E. Halgren, Automatic parcellation of human cortical gyri and sulci using standard anatomical nomenclature, *Neuroimage*, **53**, pp. 1-15, 2010.

23. Klein, A. and J. Tourville, 101 labeled brain images and a consistent human cortical labeling protocol, *Frontiers in Neuroscience*, **6**, p. 171, 2012.

24. Iliff, J. J., M. Wang, Y. Liao, B. A. Plogg, W. Peng, G. A. Gundersen, H. Benveniste, G. E. Vates, R. Deane, S. A. Goldman, E. A. Nagelhus, and M. Nedergaard, A paravascular pathway facilitates CSF flow through the brain parenchyma and the clearance of interstitial solutes, including amyloid β, *Science Translational Medicine*, **4**, p. 147ra111, 2012.

25. Zilles, K. and K. Amunts, Centenary of Brodmann's map—conception and fate, *Nature Reviews Neuroscience*, **11**, pp. 139-145, 2010.

26. Sporns, O., The human connectome: a complex network, *Annals of the New York Academy of Sciences*, **1224**, pp. 109-125, 2011.

27. Penfield, W. and T. Rasmussen, *The Cerebral Cortex of Man,* (MacMillan, New York, 1952).

28. Arzi, A. and N. Sobel, Olfactory perception as a compass for olfactory neural maps, *Trends in Cognitive Sciences*, **15**, pp. 537-545, 2011.

29. Mori, K., Y. K. Takahashi, K. M. Igarashi, and M. Yamaguchi, Maps of odorant molecular features in the mammalian olfactory bulb, *Physiological Reviews*, **86**, pp. 409-433, 2006.

30. Carleton, A., R. Accolla, and S. A. Simon, Coding in the mammalian gustatory system, *Trends in Neurosciences*, **33**, pp. 326-334, 2010.

31. Marieb, E.N. and K. Hoehn, *Human Anatomy & Physiology*, (Pearson, Boston, 2013).

32. Jaygandhi786, https://commons.wikimedia.org/wiki/File:Retinotopic_organization.png, *Wikimedia Commons*, 2015.

33. Adams, D. L. and J. C. Horton, A precise retinotopic map of primate striate cortex generated from the representation of angioscotomas, *The Journal of Neuroscience*, **23**, pp. 3771-3789, 2003.

34. Purves, D., et al., The auditory system, in eds. D. Purves, G. J. Augustine, D. Fitzpatrick, L. C Katz, A.-S. LaMantia, J. O. McNamara, and S. M. Williams, *Neuroscience. 2nd edition*, (Sinauer Associates., Sunderland, MA, 2001).

35. Lahav, A. and E. Skoe, An acoustic gap between the NICU and womb: a potential risk for compromised neuroplasticity of the auditory system in preterm infants, *Frontiers in Neuroscience*, **8**, pp. 381-381, 2013.

36. Peters, A. and E. G. Jones, Cellular components of the cerebral cortex, in eds. A. Peters and E. G. Jones, *Cerebral Cortex, vol. 1*, (Plenum, New York, 1984).

37. Markram, H., M. Toledo-Rodriguez, Y. Wang, A. Gupta, G. Silberberg, and C. Wu, Interneurons of the neocortical inhibitory system, *Nature Reviews Neuroscience*, **5**, pp. 793-807, 2004.

38. Pansky, B., *Review of Medical Embryology*, (Macmillan, New York, 1982).

39. Hikosaka, O., K. Nakamura, K. Sakai, H. Nakahara, Central mechanisms of motor skill learning, *Current Opinion in Neurobiology*, **12**, pp. 217-222, 2002.

40. Sanes, J. N. and J. P. Donoghue, Plasticity and primary motor cortex, *Annual Review of Neuroscience*, **23**, pp. 393-415, 2000.

41. Evarts, E. V., Relation of pyramidal tract activity to force exerted during voluntary movement, *Journal of Neurophysiology*, **31**, pp. 14-27, 1968.

42. Sergio, L. E. and J. F. Kalaska, Changes in the temporal pattern of primary motor cortex activity in a directional isometric force versus limb movement task, *Journal of Neurophysiology*, **80**, pp. 1577-1583, 1998.

43. Georgopoulos, A.P., J. F. Kalaska, R. Caminiti, and J. T. Massey, On the relations between the direction of two-dimensional arm movements and cell discharge in primate motor cortex, *Journal of Neuroscience*, **2**(11): pp. 1527-1537, 1982.

44. Moran, D. W. and A. B. Schwartz, Motor cortical representation of speed and direction during reaching, *Journal of Neurophysiology*, **82**, pp. 2676-2692, 1999.

45. Caminiti, R., P. B. Johnson, and A. Urbano, Making arm movements within different parts of space: dynamic aspects in the primate motor cortex, *Journal of Neuroscience*, **10**, pp. 2039-2058, 1990.

46. Scott, S. H. and J. F. Kalaska, Reaching movements with similar hand paths but different arm orientations. I. Activity of individual cells in motor cortex, *Journal of Neurophysiology*, **77**, pp. 826-852, 1997.

47. Sergio, L. E. and J. F. Kalaska, Systemic changes in motor cortex cell activity with arm posture during directional isometric force generation, *Journal of Neurophysiology*, **89**, pp. 212-228, 2003.

48. Paus, T. and S. Breve, Primate anterior cingulate cortex: where motor control, drive and cognition interface, *Nature Reviews Neuroscience*, **2**, pp. 417-424, 2001.

49. Aflalo, T., S. Kellis, C. Klaes, B. Lee, Y. Shi, K. Pejsa, K. Shanfield, S. Hayes-Jackson, M. Aisen, C. Heck, C. Liu, and R. A. Andersen, Decoding motor imagery from the posterior parietal cortex of a tetraplegic human, *Science*, **348**, p. 906-910, 2015.

50. Diamond, M. E., M. von Heimendahl, and E. Arabzadeh, Whisker-mediated texture discrimination, *PLoS Biology*, **6**, p. e220, 2008.

51. Deng, W., J. B. Aimone, and F. H. Gage, New neurons and new memories: how does adult hippocampal neurogenesis affect learning and memory? *Nature Reviews Neuroscience*, **11**, pp. 339-350, 2010.

52. Parent, A. and L.N. Hazrati, Functional anatomy of the basal ganglia. II. The place of subthalamic nucleus and external pallidum in basal ganglia circuitry, *Brain Research Reviews*, **20**, pp. 128-154, 1995.

53. Parent, A., Extrinsic connections of the basal ganglia, *Trends in Neurosciences*, **13**, pp. 254-258, 1990.

54. Albin, R. L., A. B. Young, and J. B. Penney, The functional anatomy of basal ganglia disorders, *Trends in Neurosciences*, **12**, pp. 366-375, 1989.

55. Alexander, G. E. and M. D. Crutcher, Functional architecture of basal ganglia circuits: neural substrates of parallel processing, *Trends in Neurosciences*, **13**, pp. 266-271, 1990.

56. Dauer, W. and S. Przedborski, Parkinson's disease: mechanisms and models, Neuron, **39**, pp. 889-909, 2003.

57. Crossman, A., I. Mitchell, and M. Sambrook, Regional brain uptake of 2-deoxyglucose in N-methyl-4-phenyl-1, 2, 3, 6-tetrahydropyridine (MPTP)—induced parkinsonism in the macaque monkey, *Neuropharmacology*, **24**, pp. 587-591, 1985.

58. Hill, S. and G. Tononi, Thalamus, in ed. Arbib, M.A. *The Handbook of Brain Theory and Neural Networks (2nd edition)*, (The MIT Press, Cambridge, MA, 2003) pp. 1176-1180.

59. Hearn, R. A. Tc-models-thalamus.jpg, *http://www.scholarpedia.org/article/File:Tc-models-thalamus.jpg*, 2007.

60. Sherman, S. M. and C. Koch, Thalamus, in ed. Shepherd, G. M., *The Synaptic Organization of the Brain (4th edition)*, (Oxford University Press, New York, 1998) pp. 289-328.

61. Guillery, R. W., S. L. Feig, and D. A. Lozsadi, Paying attention to the thalamic reticular nucleus, *Trends in Neurosciences*, **21**, pp. 28-32, 1998.

62. Wurtz, R. H. and E. R. Kandel, Central visual pathways, in eds. E. R. Kandel, J. H. Schartz, and T. M. Jessell, *Principles of Neural Science*, (McGraw-Hill, New York, 2000) pp. 523-547.

63. Hudspeth, A. J., Hearing, in eds. E. R. Kandel, J. H. Schartz, and T. M. Jessell, *Principles of Neural Science*, (McGraw-Hill, New York, 2000) pp. 590-613.

64. Gardner, E.P., J.H. Martin, and T.M. Jessell, The bodily senses, in eds. E. R. Kandel, J. H. Schartz, and T. M. Jessell, *Principles of Neural Science*, (McGraw-Hill, New York, 2000) pp. 430-450.

65. Verhagen, J. V., B. K. Giza, and T. R. Scott, Responses to taste stimulation in the ventroposteromedial nucleus of the thalamus in rats, *J Neurophysiol*, **89**, pp. 265-275, 2003.

66. Shepherd, G. M., Perception without a thalamus: How does olfaction do it? *Neuron*, **46**, pp. 166-168, 2005.

67. Ilinsky, I. A. and K. Kultas-Ilinsky, Motor thalamic circuits in primates with emphasis on the area targeted in treatment of movement disorders, *Movement Disorders*, **17 Suppl 3**, pp. S9-14, 2002.

68. Rauschecker, J. P., Cortical control of the thalamus: top-down processing and plasticity, *Nature Neuroscience*, **1**, pp. 179-180, 1998.

69. DeLong, M. R., The basal ganglia, in eds. E. R. Kandel, J. H. Schartz, and T. M. Jessell, *Principles of Neural Science*, (McGraw-Hill, New York, 2000) pp. 853-867.

70. Sherman, S. M., Tonic and burst firing: dual modes of thalamocortical relay, *Trends in Neurosciences*, **24**, pp. 122-126, 2001.

71. Role, L. W. and J. P. Kelly, The brain stem: cranial nerve nuclei and the monoaminergic systems, in eds. E. R. Kandel, J. H. Schwartz, and T. M. Jessell, *Principles of Neural Science*, (Appleton & Lange, Norwalk, Connecticut, 1991) pp. 683-699.

72. Drew, T. and S. Rossignol, Phase-dependent responses evoked in limb muscles by stimulation of medullary reticular formation during locomotion in thalamic cats, *Journal of Neurophysiology*, **52**, pp. 653-675, 1984.

73. Snell, R. S., *Clinical Neuroanatomy*. (Lippincott Williams & Wilkins, Philadelphia, 2010).

74. Ghez, C. and W. T. Thach, The cerebellum, in eds. E. R. Kandel, J. H. Schartz, and T. M. Jessell, *Principles of Neural Science*, (McGraw-Hill, New York, 2000) pp. 832-852.

75. Barlow, J. S., *The Cerebellum and Adaptive Control*, (Cambridge University Press, Cambridge, 2002).

76. Desmond, J. E. and J. A. Fiez, Neuroimaging studies of the cerebellum: language, learning and memory, *Trends in Cognitive Sciences*, **2**, p. 355-362, 1998.

77. Llinas, R. R. and K. D. Walton, Cerebellum, in ed. Shepherd, G. M., *The Synaptic Organization of the Brain (4th edition)*, (Oxford University Press, New York, 1998) pp. 225-288.

78. Tortora, G. J., *Introduction to the Human Body: Essentials of Anatomy and Physiology - 8th edition*, (Wiley, New York, 2009).

79. Netter, F. H., *Atlas of Human Anatomy*, (CIBA-GEIGY Corporation, West Caldwell, New Jersey, 1989).

80. Rexed, B., A cytoarchitectonic atlas of the spinal cord in the cat, *Journal of Comparative Neurology*, **100**, pp. 297-379, 1954.

81. Hulliger, M., N. Dürmüller, A. Prochazka, and P. Trend, Flexible fusimotor control of muscle spindle feedback during a variety of natural movements, *Progress in Brain Research*, **80**, pp. 87-101, 1989.

82. Pearson, K. and J. Gordon, Spinal reflexes, in eds. E. R. Kandel, J. H. Schartz, and T. M. Jessell, *Principles of Neural Science*, (McGraw-Hill, New York, 2000).

83. Romanes, G. J., The motor cell columns of the lumbo-sacral spinal cord of the cat, *Journal of Comparative Neurology*, **94**, pp. 313-358, 1951.

84. Sharrard, W. J. W., The distribution of the permanent paralysis in the lower limb in poliomyelitis, *Journal of Bone and Joint Surgery*, **37B**, pp. 540-558, 1955.

85. Vanderhorst, V. G. J. M. and G. Holstege, Organization of lumbosacral motoneuronal cell groups innervating hindlimb, pelvic floor, and axial muscles in the cat, *Journal of Comparative Neurology*, **382**, pp. 46-76, 1997.

86. Mushahwar, V. K. and K. W. Horch, Selective activation of muscles in the feline hindlimb through electrical microstimulation of the ventral lumbo-sacral spinal cord, *IEEE Transactions on Rehabilitation Engineering*, **8**, pp. 11-21, 2000.

87. Yakovenko, S., V. Mushahwar, V. VanderHorst, G. Holstege, and A. Prochazka, Spatiotemporal activation of lumbosacral motoneurons in the locomotor step cycle, *Journal of Neurophysiology*, **87**, pp. 1542-1553, 2002.

88. Mushahwar, V. K., D. M. Gillard, M. J. Gauthier, and A. Prochazka, Spinal cord microstimulation generates locomotor-like and feedback-controlled movements, *IEEE Transactions on Neural Systems and Rehabilitation Engineering*, **10**, pp. 68-81. 2002.

89. Burke, R., Spinal motoneurons, in ed. D.W. Pfaff, *Neuroscience in the 21st Century: From Basic to Clinical*, (Springer, New York, 2013), pp. 1027-1062.

90. Brown, A. G., *Organization in the Spinal Cord: The Anatomy and Physiology of Identified Neurones*, (Springer-Verlag, Edinburgh, Great Britain, 1981).

91. Netter, F. H., *The CIBA Collection of Medical Illustrations, Volume I, Nervous System*, (CIBA, Summit, NJ, 1991).

92. Basbaum, A. I. and T. M. Jessell, The perception of pain, in eds. E. R. Kandel, J. H. Schartz, and T. M. Jessell, *Principles of Neural Science*, (McGraw-Hill, New York, 2000).

93. Van De Graaff, K. M., *Human Anatomy, 2nd ed.*, (Wm. C. Brown, Dubuque, Iowa, 1988).

94. Melzack, R. and P. D. Wall, Pain mechanisms: a new theory, *Science*, **150**, pp. 971-979, 1965.

95. Brown, T. G., The intrinsic factors in the act of progression in the mammal, *Proceedings of the Royal Society London B*, **84**, pp. 308-319, 1911.

96. Grillner, S. and P. Zangger, On the central generation of locomotion in the low spinal cat, *Exp. Brain Res.*, **34**, pp. 241-261, 1979.

97. Sherrington, C. S., Flexion-reflex of the limb, crossed extension-reflex, and reflex stepping and standing, *Journal of Physiology*, **40**, pp. 28-121, 1910.

98. Jankowska, E., M. G. M. Jukes, S. Lund and A. Lundberg, The effect of DOPA on the spinal cord. 5. Reciprocal organization of pathways transmitting excitatory action to alpha motoneurones of flexors and extensors, *Acta Physiologica Scandinavica*, **70**, pp. 369-388, 1967.

99. Jankowska, E., M. G. M. Jukes, S. Lund and A. Lundberg, The effect of DOPA on the spinal cord. 6. Half-centre organization of interneurones transmitting effects from the flexor reflex afferents, *Acta Physiologica Scandinavica*, **70**, pp 389-402, 1967.

100. Edgerton, V. R., et al., Central generation of locomotion in vertebrates, in ed. R. M Herman, *Neural Control of Locomotion, Advances in Behavioral Biology, v. 18*, (Plenum Press, New York, 1976) pp. 439-464.

101. Kremer, E. and A. Lev-Tov, Localization of the spinal network associated with generation of hindlimb locomotion in the neonatal rat and organization of its transverse coupling system, *Journal of Neurophysiology*, **77**, pp. 1155-1170, 1997.

102. Rossignol, S., C. Chau, E. Brustein, M. Bélanger, H. Barbeau, and T. Drew, Locomotor capacities after complete and partial lesions of the spinal cord, *Acta Neurobiologiae Experimentalis*, **56**, pp. 449-463, 1996.

103. Orlovsky, G. N., T. G. Deliagina, and S. Grillner, *Neuronal Control of Locomotion*, (Oxford University Press, New York, 1999).

104. Cazalets, J. R., M. Borde, and F. Clarac, Localization and organization of the central pattern generator for hindlimb locomotion in newborn rat, *Journal of Neuroscience*, **15**, pp. 4943-4951, 1995.

105. Kjaerulff, O. and O. Kiehn, Distribution of networks generating and coordinating locomotor activity in the neonatal rat spinal cord in vitro: a lesion study, *Journal of Neuroscience*, **16**, pp. 5777-5794, 1996.

106. Cowley, K. C. and B. J. Schmidt, Regional distribution of the locomotor pattern-generating network in the neonatal rat spinal cord, *Journal of Neurophysiology*, **77**, pp. 247-259, 1997.

107. Deliagina, T. G., G. N. Orlovsky, and G. A. Pavlova, The capacity for generation of rhythmic oscillations is distributed in the lumbosacral spinal cord of the cat, *Experimental Brain Research*, **53**, pp. 81-90, 1983.

108. Marcoux, J. and S. Rossignol, Initiating or blocking locomotion in spinal cats by applying noradrenergic drugs to restricted lumbar spinal segments, *Journal of Neuroscience*, **20**(22): pp. 8577-8585, 2000.

109. Berkinblit, M. B., T. G. Deliagina, A. G. Feldman, I. M. Gelfand, and G. N. Orlovsky, Generation of scratching. I. Activity of spinal interneurons during scratching, *Journal of Neurophysiology*, 1978, **41**, pp. 1040-1057.

110. Baev, K. V., A. M. Degtiarenko, T. V. Zavadskaia, and P. G. Kostiuk, [Activity of interneurons of the lumbar region of the spinal cord during fictive locomotion of thalamic cats], *Neirofiziologiia*, **11**, pp. 329-338, 1979.

111. Jordan, L. M. and B. J. Schmidt, Propriospinal neurons involved in the control of locomotion: potential targets for repair strategies? *Progress in Brain Research*, **137**, pp. 125-139, 2002.

Chapter 1.4

Muscle

Bethany R. Kondiles[1], Amirali Toossi[2], Vivian K. Mushahwar[2,3] and Stanley Salmons[4]

[1]Department of Physiology and Biophysics, University of Washington
[2]Neuroscience and Mental Health Institute, University of Alberta
[3]Department of Medicine, University of Alberta
5-005 Katz Group Centre, 116 St. and 85 Avenue, Edmonton, Alberta, Canada, T6G 2E1
vivian.mushahwar@ualberta.ca
[4] Department of Musculoskeletal Biology, Institute of Ageing & Chronic Diseases
University of Liverpool, William Henry Duncan Building
6 West Derby Street, Liverpool L7 8TX
s.salmons@liverpool.ac.uk

This chapter provides an overview of the basic anatomical, biochemical, physiological, and biomechanical properties of skeletal and smooth muscle.

1. Introduction

If cells were mere bags of cytoplasm they would, like soap bubbles, assume a spherical shape. In most cases cells are not spherical, even when they are separated from adjacent structures, and this is because they possess an internal skeleton. This structure is not permanent, however: some elements of the cytoskeleton are capable of lengthening or shortening, enabling the cell to undergo active changes of shape. How are such changes accomplished? Some filamentous proteins—actin and tubulin, for example—can vary their length by adding and subtracting subunits through a finely regulated process of polymerization and depolymerization. Other combinations of proteins—now referred to as molecular motors—can bring about changes of length much more rapidly by using energy from the hydrolysis of ATP to drive them past one another. Of these systems, one of the most widespread is based on the combination of actin with myosin.

In muscle cells the filaments of actin and myosin and their associated proteins are so abundant that they almost fill the interior of the cell. Furthermore they align predominantly in one direction, so that interactions at the molecular level are translated into linear contraction of the whole cell. The ability of these specialized

104

cells to change shape has thus become their most important property. Assemblages of muscle cells—the muscles—are, in effect, machines for converting chemical energy into mechanical work. The forces so generated move limbs, inflate the lungs, pump blood, close and open tubes, and so on. In man, muscle tissue constitutes 40-50% of the body mass.

The three major types of muscle are skeletal, cardiac and smooth muscle [67]. Both skeletal and cardiac muscle may be referred to as striated muscle, because in these types of muscle the myosin and actin filaments are organized into repeating elements called sarcomeres, which align in register across the cells and give them a finely cross-striated appearance when they are viewed in a light microscope.

2. The Structure of Skeletal Muscle

Skeletal muscle consists of parallel bundles of fibres. These long, cylindrical, multinucleate cells tend to be consistent in size within a given muscle, but in different muscles may range from 10-100 μm in diameter and from millimetres to many centimetres in length. Much of the cytoplasm of these cells is occupied by the contractile proteins. These are organized in an extremely regular and tightly packed fashion and, as a result, this type of muscle is capable of powerful contractions, around 100 watts per kilogram for human skeletal muscle. (For a more detailed account of subcellular structure and the molecular basis of force generation, see [67].)

The price paid for this organization is a limited range of contraction, but wherever a larger range of movement is required it is achieved through the amplification provided by the lever systems of the skeleton. These characteristic attachments give skeletal muscle its name. It is sometimes referred to as voluntary muscle, because the movements it brings about are often initiated under conscious control. This is, however, an unsatisfactory term, since many such movements—breathing, blinking, swallowing, and the actions of muscles of the perineum and the middle ear are examples—are usually or exclusively driven at an unconscious level. Skeletal muscle forms the bulk of the muscular tissue of the body.

Each muscle fibre is surrounded by a delicate network of connective tissue, collectively as known as the endomysium. This forms the immediate external environment of the muscle fibres. It is the site of metabolic exchange between muscle and blood, and capillaries together with small nerve branches run in this layer. Ion fluxes associated with the electrical excitation of muscle fibres take place through its matrix. The endomysium is continuous with more substantial septa of connective tissue which constitute the perimysium; this ensheathes groups of muscle fibres to form parallel bundles or fasciculi. The perimysium carries larger blood vessels and nerves and also accommodates sensory structures, the neuromuscular spindles. The perimysial septa are themselves the inward extensions of a collagenous sheath, the epimysium. This develops some thickness and forms part of the fascia that invests whole muscle groups. The epimysial, perimysial, and endomysial sheaths coalesce where the muscles connect to adjacent connective tissue structures, such as tendons. The result is to give such attachments great strength, since the tensile forces are distributed in the form of shear stresses, which are more easily resisted.

3. Innervation of Skeletal Muscle

Every skeletal muscle is supplied by one or more nerves which form part of the somatic (as opposed to autonomic) nervous system. In most cases the nerve travels with the principal blood vessels as a neurovascular bundle, approaches the muscle near to its least mobile attachment, and enters the deep surface, at a position that is more or less constant for each muscle.

Muscle nerves are frequently referred to as 'motor nerves', but they contain both motor and sensory components. The major motor component consists of the large, myelinated axons that supply the muscle fibres; these α-efferents, or α-motor axons, are among the fastest-conducting nerve fibres in the body. In addition, the nerve carries small, myelinated γ-efferents, or fusimotor fibres, which form part of the innervation of neuromuscular spindles, and fine, non-myelinated autonomic efferents (C fibres), which innervate smooth muscle in the walls of blood vessels. The sensory component consists of the large, myelinated Ia afferents from the neuromuscular spindles, the slightly smaller myelinated Ib afferents from the other major sensory structures, the Golgi tendon organs, and fine myelinated and non-myelinated fibres conveying pain and other sensations from free terminals in the connective tissue sheaths of the muscle.

Within muscles, nerves follow the connective tissue sheaths, coursing in the epimysial and perimysial septa before entering the fine endomysial tissue around the muscle fibres. Alpha-motor axons branch repeatedly before they lose their myelinated sheaths and terminate near the middle of muscle fibres. These terminals tend to cluster in a narrow zone towards the centre of the muscle belly known as the motor point. Clinically, this is the place on the muscle from which it is easiest to elicit a contraction with stimulating electrodes.

A specialized synapse, the neuromuscular junction, is formed where the terminal branch of an α-motor axon contacts the muscle fibre. The axon terminal gives off several short, curling branches over an elliptical area, the motor end plate. Under the end plate the membrane of the muscle cell, or sarcolemma, is thrown into deep synaptic folds. The arrival of an action potential at the motor end plate causes the transmitter substance acetylcholine to be released from storage vesicles into the 30-50 nm synaptic cleft that separates the nerve ending from the sarcolemma. The acetylcholine is rapidly bound by receptor molecules located in the junctional folds, triggering an almost instantaneous increase in the permeability, and hence conductance, of the postsynaptic membrane. This generates a local depolarization (the end-plate potential). The activity of the neurotransmitter is rapidly terminated by the enzyme acetylcholinesterase, which is located in the junctional folds. Because of the extended geometry of the neuromuscular junction, the end-plate potential is normally several times larger than is needed to initiate an action potential in the surrounding sarcolemma. This ensures that excitation is passed with high security to the muscle so that, except under conditions of extreme fatigue, a muscle action potential is generated for each nervous impulse. The action potential propagates along the length of the muscle fibre at about 5 m/s and initiates contraction.

This discrete type of neuromuscular junction is found on all muscle fibres that are capable of propagating action potentials. Other, less common, types of motor nerve ending are found on the slow tonic fibres present in the extrinsic ocular muscles and the stapedius muscle of the middle ear, and in the so-called intrafusal muscle fibres found inside the neuromuscular spindle.

4. Motor Units and Motor Control

4.1. *Motor units and their recruitment*

The terminal branches of α-motor axons are normally in a 'one-to-one' relationship with their muscle fibres: a muscle fibre receives only one branch, and any one branch innervates only one muscle fibre. When a motor neurone is excited, an action potential is propagated along the axon and its branches to all of the muscle fibres that it supplies. The motor neurone and the muscle fibres that it innervates can therefore be regarded as a functional unit, the motor unit, which accounts for the more or less simultaneous contraction of a number of fibres within the muscle. The actual size of the motor units varies considerably: in muscles that are employed for precision tasks, such as the external muscles of the eye, muscles between the fingers, and muscles of the larynx, each motor neurone innervates only about 10 muscle fibres, whereas in a large limb muscle the ratio may exceed 1000. Within a muscle, the fibres belonging to one motor unit are distributed over a wide territory, without regard to fascicular boundaries, and intermingle with the fibres of other motor units. The motor units become larger when the muscle nerve is damaged, because denervated fibres induce sprouting of the surviving axons, and each new branch can innervate a denervated muscle fibre.

The passage of a single action potential through a motor unit elicits a twitch contraction that lasts 25–75 ms. However, the motor neurone can deliver a second nervous impulse in less time than it takes for the muscle fibres to relax. When this happens, the muscle fibres contract again, building the tension to a higher level. Because of this mechanical summation, a sequence of impulses can evoke a larger force than a single impulse, and—within certain limits—the higher the impulse frequency, the more force is produced. This larger force, evoked by a sequence of nervous impulses, is called a tetanus. When the firing rate of the neurone is low, the tetanic force is quite oscillatory. As the frequency rises the contraction becomes smoother, until it is completely fused. Oscillatory forces are not normally observed in a voluntary contraction because the force developed at the whole muscle level is the net result of hundreds of individual motor unit contractions occurring asynchronously.

A given motor neurone does not usually fire at less than about 8 Hz. On the other hand, it is unusual to encounter rates of more than 100 or 200 Hz. It is common, however, to find one or two inter-pulse intervals as short as a few milliseconds at the beginning of a train of impulses (see §4.3).

The force-frequency relationship is one of the strategies used by the nervous system to gradate the contraction it elicits from the muscle. The other strategy is to recruit more motor units. In practice, the two mechanisms appear to operate in parallel, but their relative importance may depend on the size of the muscle: in large muscles with many motor units, recruitment is probably the more important mechanism.

Recruitment is not a random process. Low-level contractions are associated with low levels of excitation within the spinal cord, and—with only very minor exceptions—these conditions always produce regular firing of small motor neurones. As the force increases, motor neurones of larger size become involved, and the largest motor neurones are activated only when the highest forces have to be generated. Since large motor neurones have axons of large diameter, which divide into more numerous branches, the order of recruitment of motor units is in every sense one of increasing size. This 'size principle' was formulated by E. Henneman et al. [32 - 34] in a series of papers notable for their experimental elegance and rigour. The important concept is that motor units contribute to movement and posture in an orderly and predictable way.

4.2. *The fibre types of adult skeletal muscle*

With the exception of the rare tonic fibres mentioned earlier, mammalian skeletal muscles are composed entirely of fibres of the twitch type. These fibres can all conduct action potentials but they are not the same in other respects. Some fibres obtain their energy very efficiently by aerobic oxidation of substrates, particularly of fats and fatty acids. They have a high content of mitochondria and contain myoglobin, an oxygen-transport pigment related to haemoglobin. They are supported by a well-developed network of capillaries, which maintains a steady nutrient supply of oxygen and substrates. Such fibres are well suited to functions such as postural maintenance, in which moderate forces need to be sustained for prolonged periods. At the other extreme are fibres that have few mitochondria, little myoglobin, and a sparse capillary network. Their immediate energy requirements are met largely through anaerobic glycolysis, a route that provides prompt access to energy stores but is less efficient and less sustainable than oxidative metabolism. Such fibres are capable of brief bursts of intense activity, but these must be separated by extended quiescent periods during which glycogen and other reserves are replenished.

In many mammals these types of fibre tend to be segregated into different muscles: some muscles therefore have a conspicuously red appearance, derived from the rich blood supply and high myoglobin content associated with a predominantly aerobic metabolism, whereas others have a much paler appearance, reflecting a more anaerobic character. These variations in colour have been known for centuries, and 'red' and 'white' muscles were described clearly more than a hundred years ago by Ranvier [61].

In man, all muscles are of the mixed variety, in which fibres that are specialized for aerobic working conditions intermingle with fibres of a more anaerobic or intermediate metabolic character. These different types of fibre are not readily distinguished in sections stained by conventional histological techniques, but they emerge quite clearly when more specialized histochemical techniques are used. An example is seen in Fig. 1A. This section has been treated for the demonstration of an enzyme associated mainly with mitochondria, so that the colour develops most strongly in fibres that are rich in mitochondria.

On the basis of the metabolic differences that such a technique reveals, it is possible to classify the individual fibres as red (or oxidative), white (or glycolytic), and intermediate (or oxidative-glycolytic).

Ranvier also noted that 'red' muscles contracted and relaxed more slowly than 'white' muscles. The reason for this difference in contractile speed is now well understood. These types of muscle contain different forms (isoforms) of myosin, and that part of the myosin molecule known as the myosin heavy chain has a profound influence on contractile speed. The different myosin isoforms may be distinguished histochemically in microscopic sections by means of techniques that link the enzymatic, ATP-splitting, properties of the myosin heavy chain to a visualization reaction [10, 29].

Figure 1B shows an example of a muscle section that has been stained for ATPase activity after being exposed to formaldehyde and alkaline pH [87]. The dark fibres, which are termed Type 2B, contain a myosin heavy chain isoform that confers a fast contractile speed. Fibres of intermediate density are classified as Type 2A, and contain a slightly different 'fast' heavy chain. The lightly stained fibres are classified as Type 1; they contain a myosin heavy chain isoform that confers a slow contractile speed. There are sufficient structural differences between the isoforms of myosin that antibodies can be made which distinguish between them: these antibodies can then be used to label the fibres in a muscle section by attaching fluorescent or enzymatic markers to them (Fig. 1C, D).

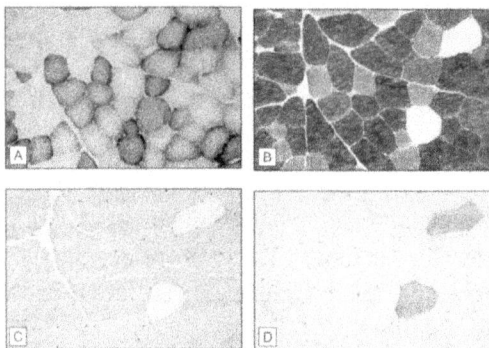

Fig. 1.   Light micrographs of serial transverse sections of a rabbit limb muscle, stained histochemically and by the immunoperoxidase technique to demonstrate differences between skeletal muscle fibre types. A. NADH tetrazolium reductase, an enzyme associated with oxidative metabolism. B. Myofibrillar ATPase after alkali and formaldehyde pre-incubation. Fibres that stain darkly are Type 2B, fibres with intermediate staining density are Type 2A, and fibres that are barely stained at all are Type 1. C. Monoclonal antibody to fast muscle myosin heavy chains. This antibody reacts with all Type 2 fibres, irrespective of subtype. D. Monoclonal antibody to slow muscle myosin heavy chain. This antibody reacts only with Type 1 myosin. Notice that the fibres staining strongly in D are the ones that stain very lightly in B. Note also in A that there is a considerable spectrum of metabolic activity, even within fibres of the same type.

In broad terms, Type 1 and Type 2A fibres tend to be predominantly oxidative in character, whereas Type 2B fibres rely more heavily on anaerobic glycolysis:

*   Type 2B fibres are fast-contracting but can sustain only brief bursts of activity;

- Type 2A fibres are fast-contracting and capable of sustained activity;
- Type 1 fibres are slow-contracting and capable of sustained activity.

Table 1 summarizes some of the major properties of these basic fibre types.

Table 1. Some physiological characteristics of the major histochemical fibre types.

Characteristics	Type 1	Type 2A	Type 2B
Function	sustained force, as in posture	—powerful, phasic movements—	
Motoneurone firing threshold	low	intermediate	high
Motor unit size	small	large	large
Firing pattern	tonic, low-frequency	—phasic, high-frequency—	
Maximum shortening velocity	slow	fast	fast
Rate of relaxation	slow	fast	fast
Fatigue sensitivity	resistant	resistant	susceptible
Power output	low	intermediate	high

All classification schemes tend to be oversimplified, for they disregard the considerable gradation of properties shown by the fibres of a given muscle. They are, however, convenient for directing attention to particular fibre populations in a muscle and as a means of describing—and to some extent quantitating—compositional differences between muscles. Such studies reveal, for example, that a named muscle may vary in terms of fibre type proportions between individuals of different age or athletic ability. It will also vary in composition from one species to another, especially where the normal posture of the limb requires it to perform a different functional role. Even the properties of the same fibre type vary between species: broadly speaking, all fibre types tend to be faster-contracting but more oxidative in small animals and slower-contracting but more glycolytic in large animals [19].

Although it is often feasible and convenient to classify fibres according to their content of Type 1, 2A or 2B myosin heavy chains, it is also necessary to recognize the limitations of such a simple scheme. The nomenclature can be modified to accommodate fibres that express a mixture of these isoforms, but it must be elaborated still further if it is to cope with the other isoforms of myosin whose existence has emerged in recent years [25, 75, 77].

Fibres that belong to one motor unit resemble one another much more closely than fibres derived from different motor units [15, 22, 56]. This is an important generality, but in sections of normal muscle, such as that of Figure 1A, it tends to be obscured by the overlap between different motor unit territories. It emerges much more clearly in muscles that have been partially denervated: the surviving axons reinnervate adjacent fibres, producing local aggregations of fibres with very similar histochemical staining characteristics. This phenomenon is referred to by muscle pathologists as fibre type grouping. The increased fibre type grouping that occurs with advancing age is probably due to a neurogenic process that results in a progressive reduction in the number of functioning motor units [45].

4.3. *Fatigue and the functional significance of motor unit organization*

Diversity of muscle fibre properties is an important element in the organization of the motor system, for it minimizes the possibility of muscle fatigue. Fatigue is the reduction in force observed when a muscle sustains a contraction or a regular sequence of contractions. It is usually expressed as a fatigue index, defined as the fraction (or percentage) of the original force that remains after the test contraction or series has been conducted for a specified interval.

Motor units that are active for much of the time are composed of slow, Type 1 fibres — the type of fibre that is best suited for sustaining tension without fatigue for long periods. Motor units that are active only infrequently are composed of fast, Type 2B fibres — the type of fibre that is best suited to generating powerful contractions on an intermittent basis. Between these extremes, the Type 2A motor units cope with routine activity against a background of more continuous postural tension provided by the Type 1 motor units. Thus the units that are recruited most frequently have the metabolic capability for sustained use. The units that are recruited only infrequently have time to replenish their anaerobic reserves between bouts of activity.

Fatigue can also be deferred if the muscle is activated in an economical way. Depolarization of the muscle membrane triggers contraction by releasing calcium ions within the muscle fibre; these calcium ions must then be reaccumulated, a process that consumes energy. Energy would therefore be conserved if the required force could be developed and maintained with fewer impulses. In practice this is achieved in three ways. First, motor units discharge at a rate that correlates closely with the contractile speed of the muscle fibres: thus, motoneurones innervating slow muscle fibres fire at lower frequencies than those innervating fast fibres [41]. Second, motor units discharge asynchronously, and as a consequence tension at the whole muscle level can develop smoothly at lower average impulse frequencies [60]. Third, individual motor units do not fire at a constant frequency. Fast motor units, in particular, tend to commence firing at a high frequency, usually in the form of a double pulse, which produces a rapid rise of tension. The impulse frequency then declines, but tension is sustained, a phenomenon sometimes referred to as the 'catch' property of skeletal muscle [43].

4.4. *Fibre type transformation and the adaptive capacity of skeletal muscle*

Mammalian skeletal muscle is a highly differentiated tissue, and it becomes still more specialized through the acquisition of distinct fibre type characteristics (Table 1), yet it has a remarkable capacity for changing these characteristics, even in adult life. This 'plasticity' was discovered by Buller, Eccles & Eccles in the course of cross-innervation experiments in which they cut and reconnected the nerves to a fast, white and a slow, red muscle so that each muscle would be reinnervated by the other's nerve [14]. Under these conditions a remarkable change in contractile speed took place, the fast muscle becoming slower-contracting and the slow muscle faster-contracting.

In order to explain these effects, the authors suggested that the muscles had responded to the influence of 'quickening' and 'slowing' chemical trophic factors transported to them along the motor nerves. There was, however, an alternative possibility. The nerves to fast muscles carry brief, high-frequency bursts of impulses, whereas those supplying slow muscles conduct prolonged, low-frequency trains [21]. The neural influence could therefore have something to do with these different patterns of impulse traffic in the nerves. Salmons developed an implantable miniature electronic stimulator, and for the first time it became possible to impose an artificial pattern of activity on the nerve supplying a fast muscle and to maintain it for long periods [63]. This led to the discovery that fast muscles that were stimulated continuously for several weeks at 10 Hz—a pattern similar to the one normally experienced by slow muscles—developed slow contractile characteristics [69]. Later it was shown that changes in the pattern of impulse activity could account fully for the cross-reinnervation experiments of Buller and his colleagues: on the one hand, chronic stimulation of a fast muscle via its own nerve made the muscle even slower than reinnervating it with a slow muscle nerve; on the other hand, chronic stimulation of a slow muscle could reverse completely the increase in contractile speed that normally took place when it was cross-reinnervated with a fast muscle nerve [69]. Chronically stimulated fast muscles resembled slow muscles in more than their speed of contraction; they acquired a red appearance and a resistance to fatigue that was even greater than that of slow muscles [69].

The transformation of fibre type induced by increased contractile activity led to the formulation of the idea of a natural adaptive capacity of skeletal muscle [64, 72]. According to this hypothesis, fibres adapt to sustained high levels of use by developing properties at the slow, fatigue-resistant end of the spectrum. These properties are suited to postural activity that involves maintenance of tension but little change of muscle length: the slow type of myosin is more energy-efficient under these conditions [3], and a well-developed aerobic metabolism provides the capacity for generating ATP on a continuous basis. Fibres that are less active retain, or revert to, a native fast state. Their properties are suited to dynamic activity, for which instantaneous power is more important than endurance. The concept emerges of a machine that can optimize its properties to suit the type of work most often demanded of it [64]. Thus muscle properties remain finely tuned throughout adult life through the ability to adapt continuously to changing conditions of use.

4.5. *The difference between voluntary activation and electrical stimulation*

From the viewpoint of a muscle fibre, the action potential received at its neuromuscular junction looks the same whether it is generated physiologically by the motor neurone or artificially by electrical depolarization of a segment of the motor nerve. The same is true whether the electrodes are placed on the nerve or on the muscle itself; in the latter case it is the intramuscular nerve branches that are excited preferentially, and these then activate the muscle fibres.

The physics of current flow in nerves dictates that large axons will be depolarized more readily by an electrical stimulus than small ones. If the force exerted by the muscle is gradually increased by raising the stimulus intensity from a subthreshold level, there is a tendency for the largest axons, corresponding to the largest motor units, to be excited first. This represents an inversion of the natural order of recruitment, and it has important functional consequences.

Inversion of recruitment order means that, even at submaximal intensities, the largest motor units — those least resistant to fatigue — are always in use. Moreover, electrical stimulation excites all motor units at the same frequency and synchronously, resulting in a contraction that is grossly oscillatory unless the frequency of stimulation is raised, further increasing the energy expenditure of the muscle. Thus the strategies used by the motor system to minimize fatigue are lost when a muscle is activated by electrically stimulating its motor nerve. In view of the increasing interest in clinical applications of electrical stimulation, it is important to overcome these drawbacks, and progress has been made in a number of directions, as described elsewhere in this volume.

These measures alone will not overcome all the problems of fatigue resulting from electrical stimulation, for two reasons. Firstly, in practice the so-called inversion of recruitment order is far from precise, and it may be more accurate to speak of disorderly recruitment. Secondly, a special situation arises when electrical stimulation is used to activate the muscles of individuals who have been paralysed by spinal cord injury. Where such an injury is of several years' standing, the muscles would have undergone a progressive adaptation to disuse, and 80-100% of the fibres would be of the fatigue-susceptible type [28].

It is the natural adaptive capacity of skeletal muscle that offers the main solution to these problems. Over an extended period, the changes induced by chronic stimulation enable the muscle to support sustained work without fatigue because they decrease the energy needed for contraction while they increase the capacity for generating that energy through aerobic routes. Thanks to this remarkable property, even the most energetically demanding of the clinical applications of electrical stimulation currently envisaged have now become feasible [68, 71, 85].

4.6 Denervation and disuse atrophy

Denervation occurs when the motor nerve is damaged by trauma or disease. It leads to atrophy of muscle fibres. Because motor unit territories overlap, and the corresponding muscle fibres intermingle, the atrophic fibres may occur singly or in small groups, and are compressed into angular shapes by the adjacent normal fibres. Note that the term atrophy simply refers to a reduction in size, although it is often used mistakenly to describe degenerative processes involving necrosis, or cell death. In man, disuse of muscles for 1 - 4 months leads to the atrophy of fast and slow muscle fibres [37, 74]. Longer term disuse caused by disease or injury results in the preferential atrophy of fast fibres [12].

5. Form and Function in Skeletal Muscles

5.1. Naming of muscles

The names given to individual muscles reflect the great variety they show in shape, size, number of heads or bellies, position, and action. It is helpful to know the meaning of some of the terms used.

Shape: deltoid (=triangular), quadratus (=square), rhomboid (=diamond-shaped), teres (=round), gracilis (=slender), rectus (=straight)

Size: major, minor, longus (=long), brevis (=short), latissimus (=broadest), longissimus (=longest)

Number of heads or bellies: biceps (=2 heads), triceps (=3 heads), quadriceps (=4 heads), digastric (=2 bellies), biventer (=2 bellies)

Position: anterior, posterior, interosseus (=between bones), supraspinatus (=above spine of scapula), infraspinatus (=below spine of scapula), dorsi (=of the back), abdominis (=of the abdomen), pectoralis (=of the chest), brachii (=of the arm), femoris (=of the thigh), oris (=of the mouth)

Depth: superficialis (=superficial), profundus (=deep), externus (or externi), internus (or interni)

Attachment: sternocleidomastoid (from sternum and clavicle to mastoid process), coracobrachialis (from the coracoid process to the arm)

Action: extensor, flexor; abductor, adductor; levator (=lifter), depressor; supinator, pronator; constrictor, dilator

These terms are often used in combination: thus, *flexor digitorum longus* (=long flexor of the digits), *latissimus dorsi* (=broadest muscle of the back).

The names should not be taken too literally. A given muscle may play different roles in different movements, and these roles may change if the movements are assisted or opposed by gravity.

5.2. *Fibre architecture*

In addition to their variation in shape, muscles differ in the predominant orientation of their fibres relative to the direction of pull. In some muscles the fibres are arranged largely parallel to the line of pull. The overall shape of the muscle may be flat and short (e.g. thyrohyoid) or long and straplike (e.g. sternohyoid, sartorius) but in either case individual fibres may run for its entire length. In a fusiform or spindle-shaped muscle, the fibres may run parallel in the 'belly', but converge to a tendon at one or both ends. Much more common are those muscles in which the fibres are oblique to the line of pull. The important term here is pennate (from the Latin *penna* = 'wing') or the alternative pinnate (from the Latin *pinna* = 'feather'). In a unipennate muscle, such as flexor pollicis longus, the fibres would typically pass at an oblique angle from fascia continuous with the tendon to the bone. The angle between the fibres and the axis of the tendon is known as the angle of pennation. In a bipennate muscle (e.g. rectus femoris, dorsal interossei) the tendinous fascia is in the centre of the muscle, and the fibres diverge from it in a symmetrical fashion. Various spiral arrangements may also be encountered.

5.3. *Functional implications*

Muscles that are organized symmetrically, such as strap, fusiform, bipennate and multipennate forms, exert tension along the line of the tendon. Unipennate forms generate a lateral component of force which is balanced by intramuscular pressure [88]. Muscles that incorporate a twist in their geometry unwind it as they contract, so that their action brings the attachments not just closer but also into the same plane. Similarly, muscles that spiral around a bone tend to reduce the spiral on contraction, imparting rotational force.

The force developed by an active muscle depends on the amount of contractile machinery that is assembled in parallel, and therefore on the cross-sectional area of the muscle. Fibre size itself is unimportant: if the fibres are small, the force will be influenced only to the extent that more of the cross-sectional area will be occupied by non-contractile elements, such as endomysial connective tissue; similarly, if there are many small fascicles this will increase the amount of perimysial connective tissue in the cross-section.

In vertebrate muscle, the internal construction of the sarcomeres limits the amount of shortening that can take place to about 30%. Since the sarcomeres are arranged in series, the muscle fibres shorten by the same percentage, and the actual range of contraction will depend on the number of sarcomeres in series—i.e., it will be proportional to fibre length.

Muscles in which the fibres are predominantly parallel to the line of pull are often long and thin. Such muscles develop rather low forces, but are capable of a long range of contraction. Where greater force is required, the cross-sectional area must be increased, and the pennate type of construction is a way of achieving this in a compact way. The range of contraction produced by such a muscle will be less than that of a straplike muscle of the same mass, because the fibres are short and because a smaller fraction of the shortening takes place in the direction of the tendon. The obliquely directed force can be resolved vectorially into two components, one acting along the axis of the tendon, and one at 90° to this. The functionally significant component is the one that acts along the tendon axis which provides less force than is developed by the fibres themselves. Thus angulation of a set of fibres is not, of itself, advantageous: it reduces both the force and the range of contraction along the axis of the tendon. These negative consequences are, however, outweighed by the design advantage conferred by pennation, which is the opportunity it affords to extend the area available for attachment of muscle fibres. A given mass of muscle can then be deployed as a large number of short fibres, increasing the total cross-sectional area, and hence the force, available. In a multipennate muscle, the effective cross-sectional area is larger still, and the fibres tend to be even shorter. The 'gearing' effect of pennation on a muscle thus results from the internal exchange of fibre length for total fibre area, which allows much greater forces to be developed, at the expense of a reduced range of contraction.

Although the terms power and strength are often used interchangeably with force, they are not synonymous. Power is the rate at which a muscle can perform external work and is equal to force times velocity. Since force depends on the total cross-sectional area of fibres, and velocity — the rate of shortening — depends on their length, power is related to the total mass of a muscle. Strength is usually measured on intact subjects in tasks that require the participation of several muscles; it is then as much an expression of the skilful activation and coordination of these muscles as it is a measure of the forces that they contribute individually. Thus it is possible for strength to increase without a concomitant increase in the true force-generating capacities of the muscles involved, especially during the early stages of training [40].

5.4. *Muscles and movement*

5.4.1. *Actions of muscles*

Contraction can be considered as an attempt on the part of the muscle to approximate its attachments. Whether it actually does so depends on the degree to which it is activated and the forces against which it has to act. These opposing forces are: gravitational and inertial forces; forces generated actively by opposing muscles; and forces generated passively by the elastic and viscous resistance of all the structures that undergo extension and deformation — some within the muscle itself, others in joints, inactive muscles and soft tissues. Depending on the conditions, therefore, an active muscle may maintain its original length, shorten, or lengthen, and during this time its tension may increase, decrease, or stay the same. Movements that involve shortening of the active muscle are termed concentric; movements in which the active muscle undergoes lengthening are termed eccentric.

Natural movements are accomplished by groups of muscles. Each muscle may be classified, according to its role in the movement, as a prime mover, antagonist, fixator, or synergist. It is usually possible to identify one or more muscles that are consistently active in initiating and maintaining a movement: they are its prime movers. Muscles that wholly oppose the movement, or initiate and maintain the opposite movement, are antagonists. As an example, brachialis has the role of prime mover in elbow flexion; triceps is the antagonist. To initiate a movement, a prime mover must overcome passive and active resistance and impart an angular acceleration to a limb segment until the required angular velocity is reached; it must then maintain a level of activity sufficient to complete the movement. Antagonists may be transiently active at the beginning of the movement; thereafter they remain electrically quiescent until the deceleration phase, when units are activated to arrest motion. During the movement, the active prime movers are not completely unrestrained, being balanced against the passive, inertial and gravitational forces already mentioned.

When prime movers and antagonists contract together they behave as fixators, stabilizing the corresponding joint, and creating an immobile base on which other prime movers may act. As an example, flexors and extensors of the wrist co-contract to stabilize the wrist when an object is grasped tightly in the fingers.

A prime mover, acting across a uniaxial joint, produces a simple movement. Prime movers that act at multiaxial joints or cross more than one joint may produce more complex movements, containing elements that have to be eliminated by contraction of other muscles. These muscles, which assist in accomplishing the movement, are considered to be synergists, although they may act as fixators, or even as partial antagonists of the prime mover.

In the context of different movements, a given muscle may act as a prime mover, antagonist, fixator or synergist. Even the same movement may involve a muscle in different ways if it is assisted or opposed by gravity. For example, under normal conditions when thrusting out the hand, triceps is the prime mover responsible for extending the forearm at the elbow, and the flexor antagonists are largely inactive. However, when the hand lowers a heavy object the extensor action of the triceps is replaced by gravity, and the movement is controlled by active lengthening of the flexors. This example should remind us that all movements take place against the background of gravity, and its influence must not be overlooked.

5.4.2. *Attachments and levers*

Skeletal muscles have a limited range of contraction, for two reasons. Firstly, the fibres themselves must work within inherent limits imposed by their sarcomeric construction. Secondly, the internal design of many muscles can reduce the excursion at the tendon still further if short, oblique fibres have been used to deliver force at the expense of range of contraction. Where it is necessary to produce a greater range of movement, this is achieved through the action of the muscles on the bony levers of the skeleton.

To produce a large range of movement, force has to be applied close to the axis of the joint. The closeness of the muscle attachment to the joint produces a large arc of motion; however, the motion can then be resisted by a force very much less than that developed by the muscle. In fact, the *force* available at any point is *reduced* by the same factor as the *range of motion* there is *increased*. In most cases the muscular force is applied close to the joint, either on the opposite side of the joint axis to the load (first class lever) or on the same side (third class lever). A less usual configuration is for the load to be closer to the joint axis than the force (second class lever). In this case the range of motion of the load is actually *less* than that produced by the muscle, and the force is *multiplied* by the same factor. The nutcracker action of molar teeth is obtained in this way.

Many muscles work from a more stable attachment to a more mobile one. The stable attachment, which would normally be part of a heavier and more proximal structure, is commonly referred to as the origin; the more mobile attachment, which would typically be lighter and more distal, is referred to as the insertion. Thus, in a muscle such as latissimus dorsi, the attachments to spine, pelvis and ribs constitute the origin, and the tendinous attachment to the highly mobile humerus constitutes the insertion. For other muscles, such as rectus abdominis, it is less easy to identify the more mobile attachment. It would not, therefore, be functionally meaningful to try to define an 'origin' and 'insertion' for every muscle.

6. Anatomy and Physiology of Smooth Muscle

Efforts to understand the physiology of the smooth muscles can be traced back to Engelmann's work in 1869 [24], when he reported on his electrophysiological experiments on the smooth muscles of the rabbit's ureter [7]. Since then, numerous research studies have focused on further understanding the anatomy and physiology of the smooth muscles as well as their relevant pathologies. In recent years, rapid technological developments have ushered in neuroprosthetic approaches as novel treatments of pathological conditions and disorders associated with smooth muscles.

Smooth muscles are found in many organs and structures throughout the body. Table 2 gives a brief overview of the structure and role of some examples of smooth muscles. For the most part, contraction of smooth muscles controls the diameter of an organ and moves contents inside the organ [80].

In smooth muscle cells the contractile elements are oriented in non-regular patterns, and are linked across multiple cells via connective tissue, allowing contraction to be conveyed across multiple cells [4] (Figure 2). In general, smooth muscle cells are mononuclear and are arranged such that the tapered end of one cell lies adjacent to the wide middle of the next cell, allowing for tight packing [80] (Figure 3). Inward folds in the cell membrane, known as caveoli, increase the surface area of the cell membrane, allowing for greater regions of ionic exchange [4]. The basic filaments of contraction in smooth muscles are the thin filaments, made up of actin and tropomyosin, and the thick filament, myosin. Thin filaments are present in higher concentration than thick filaments [4]. Many different cytoskeletal proteins form intermediate filaments [76], which are connected to the thick and thin filaments and the cell membrane at the dense bodies and dense areas [4] (Figure 2). Dense bodies and areas are attachment sites, against which filaments produce contraction force [1, 6].

Table 2. Examples of body systems and structures with smooth muscle components

Organ or Structure	Arrangement and Function
Iris	Surrounds pupil; responsible for dilation and constriction; receive sympathetic and parasympathetic innervation
Airway	Single unit cells in bronchi and trachea are arranged helically to constrict airway; receives neural and hormonal input
Arrector Pili	Attaches hair follicle to connective tissue; contraction causes hair erection; receives sympathetic input
Lymphatic Vessels	Maintain tone and contract rhythmically to propel lymphatic fluid; receives neural, hormonal and mechanical (e.g., lymph flow and pressure) inputs
Gastrointestinal Tract	See section 7.1
Cardiovascular Vessels	See section 7.2
Urinary Tract	See section 7.3
Penis	Involved in movement and ejaculation of semen, erectile function, and urination; receives parasympathetic and sympathetic innervation. Smooth muscle is in structures including the testes, epididymis, seminal vesicles, and prostate
Uterus	Allows for expansion and contractions; mainly hormonal control with no innervation

Refs: [4, 9, 17, 57, 80, 86, 89]

Innervation (neurogenic control), hormones, and adjacent cells (myogenic control) can control contraction in smooth muscles (Figure 2) [4]. Neurogenic control is mainly through the autonomic nervous system, which includes the sympathetic and parasympathetic branches. In addition, the gastrointestinal tract is innervated by the enteric system [4]. Neurotransmitters can either induce contraction or cause relaxation [4]. Hormones that circulate in the blood can diffuse to act on receptors on the surface of smooth muscle cells [4]. Finally, some smooth muscle cells exhibit intrinsic oscillatory activity, which can affect contraction. Special classes of smooth muscle cells, called atypical smooth muscle cells or pacemaker cells, generate rhythmic electrical activity that is conveyed to adjacent cells via gap junctions between their membranes [5].

B. R. Kondiles et al.

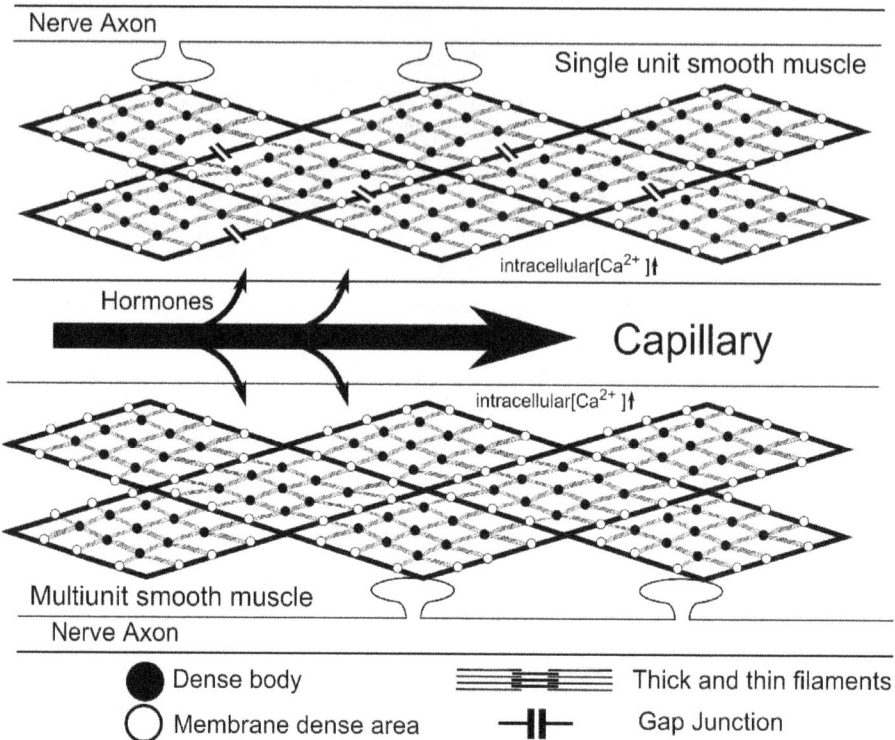

Fig. 2. Architecture of smooth muscle. Gap junctions transmit action potentials to adjacent cells forming a single unit. Multiunit smooth muscle cells are not electrically coupled. Thick and thin filaments attach at the dense body and dense areas to transmit contractive forces across the network of cells. Both innervation and hormones can increase intracellular calcium in smooth muscle.

Single unit smooth muscles are many smooth muscle cells that are connected via gap junctions. Changes in resting membrane potential and action potentials travel directly across multiple cells via the gap junctions, allowing for coordinated contraction (Figure 2). Multiunit smooth muscles do not possess many gap junctions; thus they are not as electrically coupled as single unit smooth muscles, and action potentials in one cell do not necessarily trigger action potentials in adjacent cells [4].

a) Single unit smooth muscle - relaxed

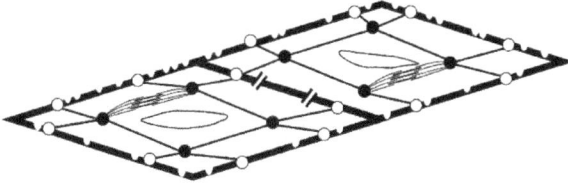

b) Single unit smooth muscle - contracted

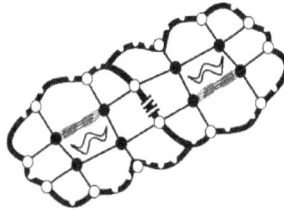

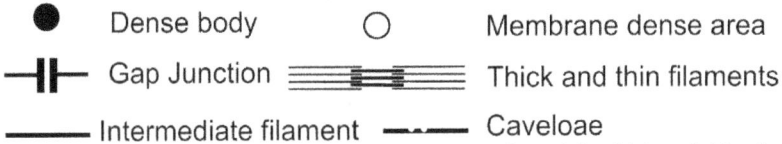

● Dense body	○ Membrane dense area
—‖— Gap Junction	≡≡≡ Thick and thin filaments
—— Intermediate filament	—·— Caveloae

Fig. 3. Smooth muscle cells are tightly packed, and contraction of the thick and thin elements is conveyed across the cytoskeleton.

In smooth muscles contraction can occur with or without an action potential, and is driven by increased concentrations in intracellular calcium. Calcium ions induce morphological shifts in the myosin fibers that are necessary for their interaction with actin fibers. The energy for cross-link formation between thin and thick filaments is derived from the hydrolysis of ATP [53]. Nonetheless, because smooth muscles must maintain long periods of contraction, once force is generated by cross-linking, it may not be ATP dependent, but instead may rely on calcium concentrations, phosphorylation state, and a unique contraction cycle [53]. The "latch-bridge" hypothesis presents the idea that once a cross-bridge is formed, dephosphorylation of myosin actually decreases the likelihood of its detachment [54]. Tropomyosin may bind together multiple actin fibers for multiple myosin binding sites [54]. Furthermore, the structural network of the contractile elements, cytoskeletal elements and attachments to the extracellular matrices in smooth muscle allows for force to be generated and distributed across the cell [79] (Figure 3). Thus, the cycling pattern and structure of smooth muscle allows cells to generate sustained contraction without significantly increasing energetic demands.

7. Examples of Smooth Muscle Systems

The following sections focus on smooth muscle systems that may benefit from electrical stimulation interventions, as described elsewhere in this volume. These are the smooth muscles in the gastrointestinal (GI) tract, the smooth muscles controlling cardiovascular vessel constriction and dilation, and the smooth muscles in the urinary tract.

7.1 *Smooth muscles of the gastrointestinal tract*

In general, two layers of smooth muscle, the inner circumferential and outer longitudinal, make up the smooth muscle of the hollow structures of the GI tract [4] (Figure 4). In the esophagus these muscle layers thicken at the junction with the stomach [80]. The lower esophageal sphincter is formed by bands of muscle from the esophagus and the longitudinal bands of the stomach. The stomach also has an additional inner oblique layer of muscles [80]. The pyloric sphincter is formed by the circumferential layer of the stomach at its most aboral (in the direction away from the mouth) point, and it expels the contents of the stomach into the small intestine [80]. The small intestine is split into three components: the duodenum, jejunum and ileum [80]. A thin longitudinal layer and thick circumferential layer make up the outer muscular layer of the small intestines, while an inner circular and longitudinal layer (the muscularis mucosae) extend muscle fiber projections into the villi, the projections into the lumen [80]. The large intestine is divided into the caecum, ascending, transverse, descending and sigmoid colons. For most of the large intestine, the longitudinal smooth muscle layers are divided into three bands, the taenia coli [80]. Finally, the rectum and anal canal lead to the internal and external anal sphincters. The smooth muscles of the inner sphincter are helical in shape, and the external sphincter muscle is striated and under voluntary control [80].

In general, the role of smooth muscle in the GI tract is to propel and mix its contents [4]. For example, in the esophagus, primary and secondary peristalsis are triggered by reflexes and the mechanosensation of distension caused by a bolus of food. The waves of muscle constriction above the bolus and relaxation below propel the bolus towards the stomach where gastric motility serves to mix and break down the contents with digestive enzymes [4]. In addition to the directional muscular movement, the valves and sphincters throughout the GI tract serve to prevent back flow of contents.

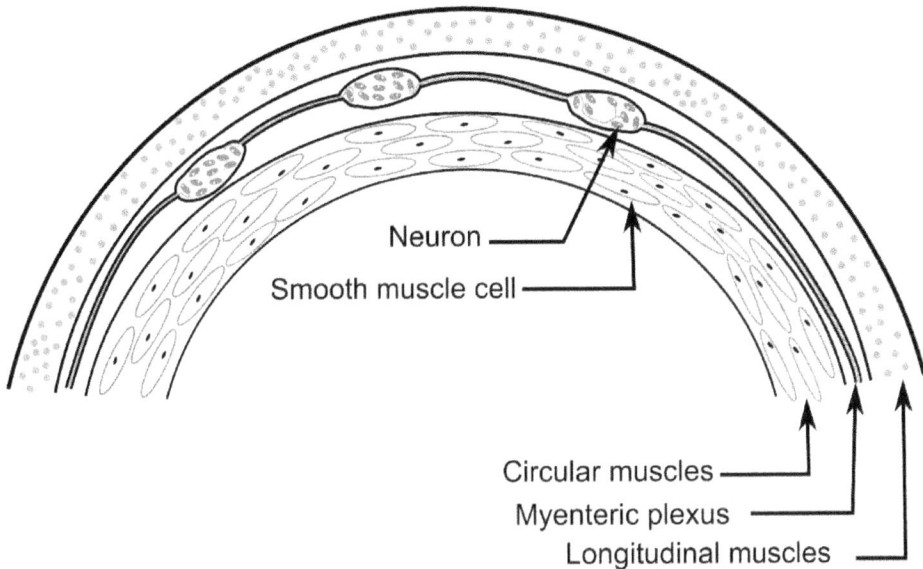

Fig. 4. General structure of smooth muscle in the GI tract. The myenteric plexus lies between the inner circumferential layer and outer longitudinal layer.

The semi-autonomous enteric nervous system regulates much of the activity of the GI tract [4]. In general, parasympathetic and sympathetic innervation, and intrinsic and extrinsic hormones can alter the speed of oscillatory activity [5]. Innervation from the enteric nervous system is responsible for low-level constant contraction, as well as peristalsis [80]. As a division of the enteric system, neurons of the myenteric plexus lie between the longitudinal and circumferential smooth muscle layers of the entire GI tract (Figure 4). Multiple additional circuits, including the submucosal plexus, also process signals including extrinsic input and internal sensory input and alter propulsion and mixing accordingly [4, 30].

The smooth muscles of the GI tract are mainly single units, meaning they are electrically coupled. In general, the cells of the inner circumferential layer are more closely coupled than the outer longitudinal layer [80]. This coupling serves to coordinate contraction to propel contents effectively through peristalsis. The circuits of the GI tract activate muscle cells in a directional pattern, causing coordinated excitation and contraction with a broad inhibition and relaxation [30]. Interstitial cells of Cajal (ICC) are also found within the two muscle layers and serve to control slow oscillations in the resting potential of smooth muscle cells, which cause weak contractions [4]. Even at the troughs of these oscillations, smooth muscles maintain some slight contraction. Action potentials can occur at the peak of these slow oscillations and induce a stronger contraction [4].

7.2. Smooth muscles of cardiovascular vessels

The musculature of the vascular system serves a different function than that of the GI tract. This difference is reflected in the structural and physiological differences between the two systems.

In the vasculature, the smooth muscles are one component of a layer, called the media, which surrounds the innermost layer of the vessel, the endothelium. The outermost layer of cardiovascular vessels, the adventita, includes the nerves. In general, arteries exhibit robust and thick smooth muscle layers. There are two main types of arteries, the elastic and muscular. In elastic arteries, the smooth muscle cells are layered with collagen and elastin, to accommodate large volumes of blood. In the muscular arteries, the muscle layers are circumferential and helical and make up the majority of the media layer [80]. In contrast to the highly muscular arteries, smooth muscle is thinner in veins [80]. Veins under 50 μm typically do not have musculature, and musculature is also absent in capillaries [80].

Changes in the contractile elements of smooth muscle result in the control of blood pressure via the maintenance of resistance against the blood. The smooth muscle cells have also been implicated in the production of extracellular matrix and repair of the arteries following injury or disease [44].

In general, changes in intracellular calcium are more dependent on ligands than changes in voltage in the smooth muscles of vessels [4]. For example, the endothelium can signal changes in contraction and relaxation via substances such as prostacyclin [4]. Nonetheless, smooth muscle of the vascular system is also under sympathetic control, with some minor innervation from the parasympathetic system [4].

Contraction in vascular smooth muscle is induced by increased intracellular calcium concentrations. Nonetheless, the intracellular calcium concentrations, and subsequent contraction of vascular smooth muscle, are not dependent on action potentials. Instead, changes in contraction reflect small changes in the membrane potential of muscle cells [4]. This tonic smooth muscle activity translates to a constant minor contractive force. This constant level of activity is typical of multiunit smooth muscle, where adjacent cells are not electrically coupled, as opposed to the single unit rhythmic smooth muscle of the GI tract [4].

7.3. Smooth muscles of the urinary tract

Urine is formed in the kidneys and moves through the ureter to the bladder and then is ultimately expelled from the body through the urethra. Layers of smooth muscle surround the ureter in longitudinal, circumferential and helical patterns

[38]. In particular, a stretch of longitudinal muscle at the entrance to the bladder prevents high pressure backflow of urine into the kidney when the bladder constricts during expulsion [38]. The bladder's smooth muscle layer, the detrusor, is particularly thick and controls the pressure inside the bladder, allowing for filling and expulsion [38]. The smooth muscle layers of the urethra lie both longitudinally and circumferentially, terminating at the inner involuntary sphincter and the voluntary external sphincter [38].

In general, the urinary tract smooth muscle serves a purpose similar to that in the GI tract: contents are moved towards expulsion with valves and sphincters to prevent backflow [38]. Many of the smooth muscle cells in the urinary tract are parts of a single unit system; therefore, increases in intracellular calcium are conveyed to adjacent cells via the gap junctions, maintaining coordinated activity.

In the ureter, two classes of cells display intrinsic oscillatory activity: the interstitial cells (referred to as ICC-like) and the atypical smooth muscle cells. These cells coordinate contraction and directional peristalsis [38]. There is also sympathetic and parasympathetic control, though this innervation is not necessary for peristalsis but instead modulates oscillatory activity. Three nerves, the pelvic nerve, the hypogastric nerve and the pudendal nerve coordinate the sensing of bladder distension, expulsion of the contents, and relaxation of the internal sphincter. The pudendal nerves also control the voluntary skeletal muscle components of the external sphincter, including the periurethral and intramural striated muscles. Thus, the control of voluntary and smooth muscles is coordinated to produce constriction of the detrusor, contraction of the longitudinal and circumferential smooth muscles of the urethra, and relaxation of the sphincters for voiding to occur [38].

8. Conclusion

This chapter has reviewed two classes of muscles: skeletal and smooth. In both, calcium signaling and contractile elements allow quick changes of a muscle cell's shape to exert forces and achieve movement. The forces generated can act on bones, organs, or other muscle cells. Muscle cells vary in structure, size, and interactions with neighboring cells. This variability allows muscles fill a wide variety of functional roles, ranging from voluntary skeletal muscle contractions used to play a piano concerto to involuntary peristaltic waves generated by smooth muscles to move food through the intestinal tract.

Acknowledgements

AT was supported by an Alberta Innovates – Health Solutions Graduate Studentship and a Vanier Canada Graduate Scholarship, BRK was supported by the Guy Tribble and Susan Barnes Graduate Discovery Fellowship from the University of Washington School of Medicine and VKM was an Alberta Heritage Foundation for Medical Research Senior Scholar. The authors thank Dr. Karen Martins for her input.

References

1. Aguilar, H. N. and B. F. Mitchell (2010) Physiological pathways and molecular mechanisms regulating uterine contractility, *Hum. Reprod. Update*, **16**(6), 725–744.
2. Baldwin, K. M. and F. Haddad (2001), Effects of different activity and inactivity paradigms on myosin heavy chain gene expression in striated muscle, *Journal of Applied Physiology*, **90**, 345-357.
3. Barclay, C. J., J. K. Constable and C. L. Gibbs (1993) Energetics of fast- and slow-twitch muscles of the mouse, *Journal of Physiology*, **472**, 61-80.
4. Berne, R. M. (2004) *Physiology*, 5th ed. (Mosby, t. Louis).
5. Berridge, M. J. (2008) Smooth muscle cell calcium activation mechanisms: Smooth muscle cell calcium activation mechanisms, *J. Physiol.*, **586**(21), 5047–5061.
6. Bond, M. and A. V. Somlyo (1982) Dense bodies and actin polarity in vertebrate smooth muscle, *J. Cell Biol.*, **95**(2), 403–413.
7. Bozler, E. (1973) Smooth muscle physiology, past and future, *Philos. Trans. R. Soc. Lond. B. Biol. Sci.*, **265**(867), 3–6.
8. Bredman, J. J., A. Wessels, W. A. Weijs, J. A. M. Korfage, C. A. S. Soffers and A. F. M. Moorman (1991) Demonstration of 'cardiac-specific' myosin heavy chain in masticatory muscles of human and rabbit, *Histochemical Journal*, **23**, 160-170.
9. Breslin, J. W. (2014) Mechanical forces and lymphatic transport, *Microvasc. Res.*, 96, 46–54.
10. Brooke, M. H. and K. K. Kaiser (1970) Muscle fiber types: how many and what kind? *Archives of Neurology, Chicago*, **23**, 369-379.
11. Brown, J. M. C., J. Henriksson and S. Salmons (1989) Restoration of fast muscle characteristics following cessation of chronic stimulation: physiological, histochemical and metabolic changes during slow-to-fast transformation, *Proceedings of the Royal Society of London Series B*, **235**, 321-346.
12. Budschu, H. D., R. Suchenwirth and W. Davis (1973) Histochemical changes in disuse atrophy of human skeletal muscle, in: ed. B. Kakulas, *Basic Research in Myology* (Excerpta Medica, Amsterdam), pp. 108-112.
13. Bugbee, M., N. N. Donaldson, A. Lickel, N. J. M. Rijkhoff and J. Taylor (2001) An implant for chronic selective stimulation of nerves, *Medical Engineering and Physics*, **23**, 29-36.
14. Buller, A. J., J. C. Eccles and R. M. Eccles (1960) Interactions between motoneurons and muscles in respect of the characteristic speeds of their responses, *Journal of Physiology*, **150**, 417-439.

15. Burke, R. E., D. N. Levine, P. Tsairis and F. E. Zajac (1973) Physiological types and histochemical profiles of motor units in the cat gastrocnemius, *Journal of Physiology*, **234**, 723-748.

16. Butler-Browne, G. S., P. O. Eriksson, C. Laurent and L. E. Thornell (1988) Adult human masseter muscle fibers express myosin isozymes characteristic of development, *Muscle and Nerve*, **11**, 610-620.

17. Clement, P. and F. Giuliano (2015) Anatomy and physiology of genital organs – men, *Handbook of Clinical Neurology*, **130**, 19–37.

18. Cummins, B. and S. Salmons (1999) Changes in the synthesis of total proteins induced by chronic electrical stimulation of skeletal muscle, *Basic and Applied Myology*, **9**, 19-28.

19. Davies, A. S. and H. M. Gunn (1972) Histochemical fibre types in the mammalian diaphragm, *Journal of Anatomy*, **112**, 41-60.

20. Duchenne, G. B. A. d. B. (1867) *Physiologie des Mouvements* (Librairie J.B. Baillières, Paris).

21. Eccles, J. C., R. M. Eccles and A. Lundberg (1958) The action potentials of the alpha motoneurones supplying fast and slow muscles, *Journal of Physiology*, **142**, 275-291.

22. Edström, L. and E. Kugelberg (1968) Histochemical composition, distribution of fibres and fatigability of single motor units. Anterior tibial muscle of the rat, *Journal of Neurology, Neurosurgery and Psychiatry*, **31**, 424-433.

23. Eisenberg, B. R. and S. Salmons (1981) The reorganisation of subcellular structure in muscle undergoing fast-to-slow type transformation: a stereological study, *Cell and Tissue Research* **220**, 449-471.

24. Engelmann, T. W. (1869) Zur Physiologie des Ureter, *Arch. Für Gesamte Physiol. Menschen Tiere*, **2**(1), 243–293.

25. Ennion, S., J. A. A. Sant'Ana Pereira, A. J. Sargeant, A. Young and G. Goldspink (1995) Characterization of human skeletal muscle fibres according to the myosin heavy chains they express, *Journal of Muscle Research and Cell Motility*, **16**, 35-43.

26. Geenen, I. L. A., M. J. Post, D. G. M. Molin, G. W. H. Schurink, J. G. Maessen, R. v. Oerle, H. ten Cate and H. M. H. Spronk (2012) Coagulation on endothelial cells: The underexposed part of Virchow's Triad:, *Thromb. Haemost.*, **108**(5), 863–871.

27. Gonyea, W. J. (1980) Role of exercise in inducing increases in skeletal muscle fiber number, *Journal of Applied Physiology*, **48**, 421-426.

28. Grimby, G., C. Broberg, I. Krotkiewska and M. Krotkiewski (1976) Muscle fiber composition in patients with traumatic cord lesion, *Scandinavian Journal of Rehabilitation Medicine*, **8**, 37-42.

29. Guth, L. and F. J. Samaha (1970) Procedure for the histochemical demonstration of actomyosin ATPase, *Experimental Neurology*, **28**, 365-367.

30. Hao, M. M., J. P. P. Foong, J. C. Bornstein, Z. L. Li, P. Vanden Berghe and W. Boesmans (2016) Enteric nervous system assembly: Functional integration within the developing gut, *Dev. Biol.*, in press.

31. Heilig, A. and D. Pette (1980) Changes induced in the enzyme activity pattern by electrical stimulation of fast-twitch muscle, in: ed. D. Pette, *Plasticity of Muscle* (Walter de Gruyter, Berlin) pp. 409-420.

32. Henneman, E., G. Somjen and D. O. Carpenter (1965) Excitability and inhibitability of motoneurones of different sizes, *Journal of Neurophysiology*, **28**, 599–620.

33. Henneman, E., G. Somjen and D. O. Carpenter (1965) Functional significance of cell size in spinal motoneurones, *Journal of Neurophysiology*, **28**, 560-580.

34. Henneman, E., H. P. Clamann, J. D. Gillies and R. D. Skinner (1974) Rank order of motoneurons within a pool: law of combination, *Journal of Neurophysiology*, **37**, 1338–1349.
35. Henriksson, J., M. M.-Y. Chi, C. S. Hintz, D. A. Young, K. K. Kaiser, S. Salmons and O. H. Lowry (1986) Chronic stimulation of mammalian muscle: changes in enzymes of six metabolic pathways, *American Journal of Physiology*, **251**, C614-C632.
36. Herring, S. W., A. F. Grimm and B. R. Grimm (1984) Regulation of sarcomere number in skeletal muscle: a comparison of hypotheses, *Muscle and Nerve*, **7**, 161-173.
37. Hikida, R. S., P. D. Gollnick, G. A. Dudley, V. A. Convertino and P. Buchanan (1989) Structural and metabolic characteristics of human skeletal muscle following 30 days of simulated microgravity, *Aviation Space and Environmental Medicine*, **60**, 664-670.
38. Hill, W. G. (2015) Control of urinary drainage and voiding, *Clin. J. Am. Soc. Nephrol.*, **10**(3), 480–492.
39. Holloszy, J. O. and F. W. Booth (1976) Biochemical adaptations to endurance exercise in muscle, *Annual Review of Physiology*, **38**, 273-291.
40. Jones, D. A. and J. M. Round (1990) *Skeletal Muscle in Health and Disease*, (Manchester University Press, Manchester).
41. Kernell, D. (1986) Organization and properties of spinal motoneurones and motor units, in: eds. H. J. Freund, U. Buttner, B. Cohen and J. Noth, *Progress in Brain Research*, (Elsevier Science Publishers, Amsterdam) pp. 21-30.
42. Kraus, W. E., C. E. Torgan and D. A. Taylor (1994) Skeletal muscle adaptation to chronic low-frequency motor nerve stimulation, **22**, 313-360.
43. Kwende, M. M. N., J. C. Jarvis and S. Salmons (1995) The input-output relationships of skeletal muscle, *Proceedings of the Royal Society of London Series B*, **261**, 193–201.
44. Lacolley, P., V. Regnault, A. Nicoletti, Z. Li and J.-B. Michel (2012) The vascular smooth muscle cell in arterial pathology: a cell that can take on multiple roles, *Cardiovasc. Res.*, **95**(2), 194–204.
45. Lexell, J. (1993) Ageing and human muscle: observations from Sweden, *Canadian Journal of Applied Physiology*, **18**, 2-18.
46. Lexell, J., C. Taylor and M. Sjöström (1988) What is the cause of ageing atrophy? Total number, size and proportion of different fiber types studied in whole vastus lateralis muscle from 15-83-year-old men, *Journal of Neurological Sciences*, **84**, 275-294.
47. Lexell, J., J. C. Jarvis, D. Y. Downham and S. Salmons (1992) Quantitative morphology of stimulation–induced damage in rabbit fast–twitch muscles, *Cell and Tissue Research*, **269**, 195–204.
48. Lexell, J., J. C. Jarvis, J. Currie, D. Y. Downham and S. Salmons (1994) Fibre type composition of rabbit tibialis anterior and extensor digitorum longus muscles, *Journal of Anatomy*, **185**, 95-101.
49. Lopez-Guajardo, A., H. Sutherland, J. C. Jarvis and S. Salmons (2000) Dynamics of stimulation-induced muscle adaptation: insights from varying the duty cycle, *Journal of Muscle Research and Cell Motility*, **21**, 725-735.
50. Mauro, A. (1961) Satellite cells of skeletal muscle fibers, *Journal of Biophysical and Biochemical Cytology*, **9**, 493-495.
51. Mayr, W., M. Bijak, D. Rafolt, S. Sauermann, E. Unger and H. Lanmüller (2001) Basic design and construction of the Vienna FES implants: existing solutions and prospects for new generations of implants, *Medical Engineering and Physics*, **23**, 53-60.

52. McCallum, R. W., I. Sarosiek, H. P. Parkman, W. Snape, F. Brody, J. Wo and T. Nowak (2013) Gastric electrical stimulation with Enterra therapy improves symptoms of idiopathic gastroparesis, *Neurogastroenterol. Motil.*, **25**(10), 815–e636.

53. Murphy, (1994) What is special about smooth muscle? The significance of covalent crossbridge regulation, *FASEB J.*, **8**(3), 311–318.

54. Murphy, R. A. and C. M. Rembold (2005) The latch-bridge hypothesis of smooth muscle contraction, *Can. J. Physiol. Pharmacol.*, **83**(10), 857–864.

55. Narusawa, M., R. B. Fitzsimons, S. Izumo, B. Nadal-Ginard, N. A. Rubinstein and A. M. Kelly (1987) Slow myosin in developing rat skeletal muscle, *Journal of Cell Biology*, **104**, 447-459.

56. Nemeth, P. M., L. Solanki, D. A. Gordon, T. M. Hamm, R. M. Reinking and D. G. Stuart (1986) Uniformity of metabolic enzymes within individual motor units, *Journal of Neuroscience*, **6**, 892-898.

57. O'Rahilly, R. and F. Muller (1982) *Basic Human Anatomy: A Regional Study of Human Structure* (W B Saunders Co, Philadelphia).

58. Pette, D. and G. Vrbova (1999) What does chronic electrical stimulation teach us about muscle plasticity? *Muscle and Nerve*, **22**, 666-677.

59. Pette, D. and R. S. Staron (1990) Cellular and molecular diversities of mammalian skeletal muscle fibers, *Reviews of Physiology, Biochemistry and Pharmacology*, **116**, 1-76.

60. Rack, P. M. H. and D. R. Westbury (1969) The effects of length and stimulus rate on tension in the isometric cat soleus muscle, *Journal of Physiology*, **204**, 443-460.

61. Ranvier, L. (1874) De quelques faits relatifs à l'histologie et à la physiologie des muscles striés, *Archives de Physiologie Normale et Pathologique*, **Deuxième Série**, 5-15.

62. Rowlerson, A., F. Mascarello, A. Veggetti and E. Carpène (1983) The fibre-type composition of the first branchial arch muscles in carnivora and primates, *Journal of Muscle Research and Cell Motility*, **4**, 443-472.

63. Salmons, S. (1967) An implantable muscle stimulator, *Journal of Physiology*, **188**, 13-14P.

64. Salmons, S. (1980) Functional adaptation in skeletal muscle, *Trends in Neurosciences*, **3**, 134-137.

65. Salmons, S. (1990) On the reversibility of stimulation-induced muscle transformation. in: ed. D. Pette, *The Dynamic State of Muscle Fibres*, (Walter de Gruyter, Berlin), pp. 401-414.

66. Salmons, S. (1994) Exercise, stimulation and type transformation of skeletal muscle, *International Journal of Sports Medicine*, **15**, 136-141.

67. Salmons, S. (1995) Section 7: Muscle, in: eds. P. L. Williams, L. H. Bannister, M. M. Berry, P. Collins, M. Dyson, J. E. Dussek and M. W. J. Ferguson, *Gray's Anatomy* (38th ed.), (Churchill Livingstone, London), pp. 737-900.

68. Salmons, S. (2009) Adaptive change in electrically stimulated muscle: a framework for the design of clinical protocols, Muscle and Nerve, **40**, 918-935.

69. Salmons, S. and F. A. Sréter (1976) Significance of impulse activity in the transformation of skeletal muscle type, *Nature*, **263**, 30–34.

70. Salmons, S. and G. Vrbová (1969) The influence of activity on some contractile characteristics of mammalian fast and slow muscles, *Journal of Physiology*, **201**, 535-549.

71. Salmons, S. and J. C. Jarvis (1992) Cardiac assistance from skeletal muscle: a critical appraisal of the various approaches, *British Heart Journal*, **68**, 333-338.

72. Salmons, S. and J. Henriksson (1981) The adaptive response of skeletal muscle to increased use, *Muscle and Nerve,* **4**, 94-105.
73. Salmons, S., G. T. Gunning, I. Taylor, S. R. W. Grainger, D. J. Hitchings, J. Blackhurst and J. C. Jarvis (2001). ASIC OR PIC? Implantable stimulators based on semi-custom CMOS technology or low–power microcontroller architecture, *Medical Engineering and Physics,* **23**, 37-43.
74. Sargeant, A. J., C. T. M. Davies, R. H. T. Edwards, C. Maunder and A. Young (1977) Functional and structural changes after disuse in humans, *Clinical Science & Molecular Medicine,* **52**, 337-342.
75. Schiaffino, S., L. Gorza, S. Sartore, L. Saggin, S. Ausoni, M. Vianello, K. Gundersen and T. Lømo (1989) Three myosin heavy chain isoforms in type 2 skeletal muscle fibres, *Journal of Muscle Research and Cell Motility,* **10**, 197-205.
76. Schwarz, N. and R. Leube (2016) Intermediate filaments as organizers of cellular space: How they affect mitochondrial structure and function, *Cells,* **5**(3), 30.
77. Smerdu, V., I. Karsch Mizrachi, M. Campione, L. Leinwand and S. Schiaffino (1994) Type IIX myosin heavy chain transcripts are expressed in type IIB fibers of human skeletal muscle, *American Journal of Physiology,* **267**, C1723-1728.
78. Solomonow, M., E. Eldred, J. Lyman and J. Foster (1983) Control of muscle contractile force through indirect high-frequency stimulation, *Am J Phys Med,* **62**, 71-82.
79. Stamenović, D. (2008) Cytoskeletal mechanics in airway smooth muscle cells, *Respir. Physiol. Neurobiol.,* **163**(1–3), 25–32.
80. Standring, S. (2008) *Gray's Anatomy: The Anatomical Basis of Clinical Practice,* 40th ed. (Churchill Livingstone Elsevier, London).
81. Stern, J. T., Jr. (1974) Computer modelling of gross muscle dynamics, *Journal of Biomechanics,* **7**, 411-428.
82. Sutherland, H., J. C. Jarvis, M. M. N. Kwende, S. J. Gilroy and S. Salmons (1998) The dose-related response of rabbit fast muscle to long-term low-frequency stimulation, *Muscle & Nerve,* **21**, 1632-1646.
83. Tabary, J. C., C. Tabary, C. Tardieu, G. Tardieu and G. Goldspink (1972) Physiological and structural changes in the cat's soleus muscle due to immobilization at different lengths by plaster casts, *Journal of Physiology,* **224**, 231-244.
84. Talonen, P. P., G. A. Baer, V. Häkkinen and J. K. Ojala (1990) Neurophysiological and technical considerations for the design of an implantable phrenic nerve stimulator, *Medical and Biological Engineering and Computing,* **28**, 31-37.
85. Thomas, G. A., R. L. Hammond, K. Greer, H. Lu, J. C. Jarvis, A. P. Shortland, D. M. Pullan, S. Salmons and L. W. Stephenson (2000) Functional assessment of skeletal muscle ventricles after pumping for up to four years in circulation, *Annals of Thoracic Surgery,* **70**, 1281-1289; discussion 1290.
86. Torkamani, N., L. Jones, N. Rufaut and R. Sinclair (2014) Beyond goosebumps: Does the arrector pili muscle have a role in hair loss? *Int. J. Trichology,* **6**(3), 88.
87. Tunell, G. L. and M. N. Hart (1977) Simultaneous determination of skeletal muscle fiber types I, IIA and IIB by histochemistry, *Archives of Neurology,* **34**, 171-173.

88. van Leeuwen, J. L. and C. W. Spoor (1993) Modelling the pressure and force equilibrium in unipennate muscles with in-line tendons, *Philosophical Transactions of the Royal Society of London Series B*, **342**, 321-333.

89. von der Weid, P.-Y. and D. C. Zawieja (2004) Lymphatic smooth muscle: the motor unit of lymph drainage, *Int. J. Biochem. Cell Biol.*, **36**(7), 1147–1153.

90. Williams, P. E. and G. L. Goldspink (1971) Longitudinal growth of striated muscle fibres, *Journal of Cell Science*, **9**, 751-767.

Chapter 1.5

Somatic Sensation

Sliman J. Bensmaia[1] and Kenneth W. Horch[2]

[1]Department of Organismal Biology and Anatomy, University of Chicago
Chicago, IL 60637
sliman@uchicago.edu
[2]Dept. Bioengineering, University of Utah
Salt Lake City, UT 84112
k.horch@utah.edu

This chapter provides an overview of the basic structure and physiology of cutaneous, muscle and joint sensory structures.

1. Introduction

Second perhaps to chemoreception, the sense of touch is the most universal source of information about the environment in the animal kingdom. Combined with proprioception, the awareness of the positions of our body parts relative to each other, it is provides us with our internal body image. Loss of these two modes of sensation produces distortions of this body image, leading to such pathologies as phantom limb sensations or neglect. It is the combination of input from tactile and proprioceptive sensors that gives rise to the sensations that identify us as real objects in the physical environment. That is, it provides us with a sense of embodiment. One of the principal functions of somatosensation is to guide our interactions with objects. Indeed, individuals who have lost this sense struggle to perform even the most basic activities of daily living, like turning a door knob [59]. One can think of the tactile or exteroceptive system as providing information about the state of the external environment as it interacts with the body, and of the proprioceptive system as providing information about the orientation of the body in that environment. This reduces to a consideration principally of cutaneous receptors and muscle/joint receptors.

2. Exteroceptive Receptors

2.1 *Basic response properties*

Cutaneous receptors fall into one of three groups, corresponding to the three psychophysically separable, distinct types of sensation: touch, temperature and pain [7, 36, 74]. The sense of touch is mediated by cutaneous mechanoreceptors. Cutaneous mechanoreceptors can be classified on the basis of their appearance (anatomy) or on the basis of what sorts of information they provide about mechanical stimuli (physiology) [11]. It turns out that there is generally a strict correspondence between the two.

Anatomically, distinctions between mechanoreceptor types are based on the size and myelination state of the axons that innervate them, the location of the nerve endings in the skin (e.g., dermis, dermal-epidermal junction, within the epidermis itself), and the presence or absence of specialized structures at the nerve terminal. Physiologically, distinctions are made on the basis of the structure to which the mechanical stimulus needs to be applied (e.g., hair deflection versus skin deformation), the nature of the deformation (e.g., skin indentation versus skin stretch), and the temporal properties of the most effective stimuli (e.g., steady deformation versus vibration). The correspondence between the anatomical and physiological classifications stems from the fact that function follows form: the location of the receptor ending determines what needs to be deformed to activate it, and the structure of the nerve ending determines what types of mechanical stimuli will be effective in activating it.

People who classify cutaneous mechanoreceptors fall into two classes: lumpers and splitters. Splitters assign significance to small, but reliable, differences in the way subsets of the members of the sets assigned by the lumpers respond to mechanical stimuli, such as the range of frequencies effective in activating vibration sensitive receptors. Table 1 shows a splitter's view of the cutaneous mechanoreceptor universe. A lumper would be inclined to merge, for example, the field receptor subgroups into one, and might use different terminology to identify the groups.

Mechanoreceptors of all sorts, cutaneous or otherwise, tend to exhibit the phenomenon of adaptation: a decline in response to a maintained stimulus [3, 41]. Slowly adapting receptors that respond to maintained indentation of the skin or displacement of a hair are called tonic; rapidly adapting receptors that respond only during movement of the innervated structure are called phasic. Tonic mechanoreceptors respond to both the displacement of the innervated structure from its rest position and the rate of change of displacement (velocity), and are better activated by movements away from the rest position than by movements back toward the rest position. That is, they are directionally sensitive. Phasic mechanoreceptors are not always directionally sensitive: many respond nearly equally well to movements toward the rest position as to movements away from the rest position. Considering the mechanoreceptor classes listed in Table 1 in terms of their general response properties, PC receptors are very phasic, responding principally to the acceleration components of a stimulus [39]. Their location deep in the dermis and in subcutaneous tissues together with their exquisite sensitivity allows them to respond to stimuli applied some distance from their actual physical locations, producing large receptive fields (the area of the skin from which a response can be elicited readily) [38]. The T1 and T2 receptors are tonic, continuing to respond to maintained skin indentation or stretch, respectively.

Most cutaneous receptors have a well developed phasic component with only a few having a pronounced tonic component to their response. This serves to make the system maximally sensitive to small changes in the status quo; without this property responses to such changes would be swamped by the ongoing background activity produced by the steady state deformation of the skin or hairs. In fact, even tonic receptors stop responding to an unchanging stimulus, as indicated by their designation as slowly adapting [3, 34, 41].

In general, phasic receptors respond better to high frequency vibration than do more tonic receptors. If one measures the vibratory sensitivity of receptors by looking at the minimum amplitude displacement required to elicit some criterion threshold response as a function of sinusoidal frequency, one finds that thresholds tend to decrease for phasic mechanoreceptors, whereas they are relatively flat for tonic ones [68].

The response properties of cutaneous mechanoreceptors are sufficiently rich and complex to provide for the variety of sensations elicited by cutaneous stimulation, which range from faint, evanescent tickles to strong and persistent feelings of skin indentation and pressure. Microneurographic recordings from humans, in which response properties of individual receptors have been related to unitary sensations evoked by stimulation of the axons innervating the receptors, have generally shown that activity in a given type of receptor is associated with a distinct type of sensation, supporting the idea that different submodalities lead to qualitatively different sensations [27, 71, 78]. Figure 1 summarizes the relationships between physiologically defined receptor type, receptive field size, innervation density, and anatomically recognized nerve terminal structure for the four major types of cutaneous mechanoreceptors innervated by large, myelinated nerve fibers in the glabrous skin of the hand. In hairy skin the picture would be similar, except that Pacinian corpuscles would be absent, replaced by richly innervated hair follicles.

Table 1. Characteristics of cutaneous receptors.

Class	Type	Axon size	Adequate stimulus	Receptor structure
Nociceptor	Mechano	Aδ, C	Threatening or damaging deformation of skin	Free nerve endings
	Thermo-mechano	Aδ, C	Above and noxious heat or cold	Free nerve endings
	Polymodal	C	Mechanical or thermal damage and irritant chemicals	Free nerve endings
Thermo-receptor	Warm	C	Skin temperature above 30° C*	Free nerve endings
	Cold	Aδ, C	Skin temperature below 35° C*	Intraepithelial free nerve endings
Mechano-receptor	PC	Aα	Accelerating displacements of skin and deeper tissue in any direction	Pacinian corpuscle receptor
	GI hair	Aα	Rapid movement of hair shaft in any direction	Endings around hair follicles
	G2 hair	Aα	Movement of hair shaft from rest position	Endings around hair follicles
	Fl field	Aα	Rapid indentation or retraction of skin from an indented position	Krause end bulb, Meissner's corpuscles, etc.
	F2 field	Aα	Movement of skin to an indented position	As above
	TI	Aα	Indentation of skin	Merkel cells
	T2	Aα	Skin stretch	Ruffini ending
	D mechano	Aδ	Movement of hair or skin in any direction	?
	C mechano	C	Lingering deformation of skin	?

*Response depends on acclimation temperature and rate of warming or cooling. (Adapted from [33])

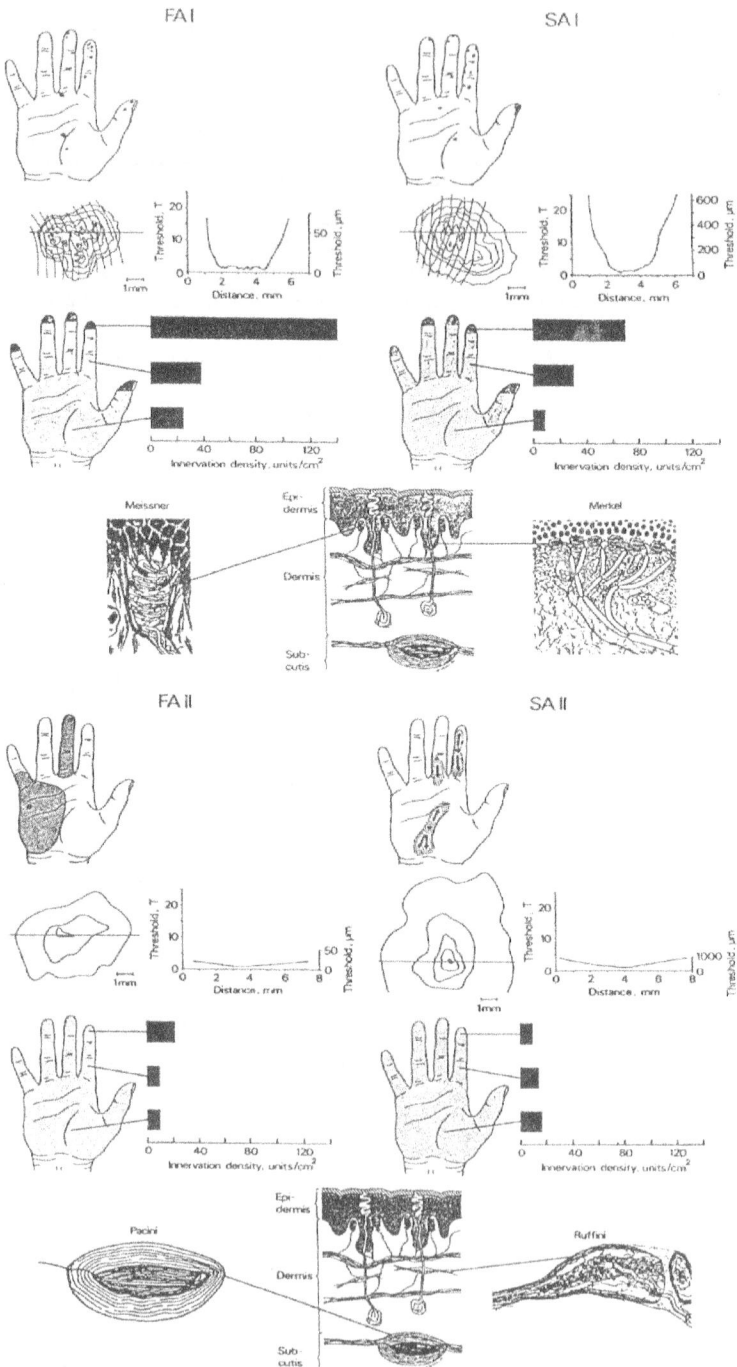

Fig. 1. Major cutaneous mechanoreceptor types in human glabrous skin and their properties. Shown are typical receptive field sizes, receptor densities, and locations in the skin. (Adapted from [70]).

Cutaneous temperature sensations arise from two classes of thermoreceptors in the skin: cold receptors and warm receptors. These are innervated by small myelinated or unmyelinated nerve fibers, show a mixed phasic and tonic response profile to changes in skin temperature, and acclimate over time to chronically maintained skin temperatures within the normal physiological range. This latter phenomenon shifts the sensitivity of the receptors to make them more responsive to changes in skin temperature than to absolute temperature. Interestingly, hot is a synthetic sensation caused by the simultaneous activation of warm and cold receptors, a result of the so-called paradoxical response of cold receptors to temperatures above about 45 °C.

True cutaneous pain (as distinct from central pain with a peripheral reference) arises from the activation of one or more of the several classes of peripheral nociceptors [47]. Like the thermoreceptors, these are innervated by small myelinated or unmyelinated nerve fibers. The former give rise to fast, sharp pain that typically has a distinct focus and tends to go away once the painful stimulus is removed. Activation of nociceptors innervated by unmyelinated fibers tends to produce slow, burning pain of ill defined focus that may persist even after the stimulus is removed. The nociceptors themselves may be specific to a given modality of stimulation (e.g., Aδ mechano-nociceptors), or to a variety of mechanical, thermal and chemical stimuli (e.g., C polymodal nociceptors). There is evidence that a subset of chemically sensitive receptors innervated by unmyelinated fibers are responsible for the sensation of itch [69, 75].

2.2 Tactile coding in the nerve

When we grasp an object, signals from cutaneous mechanoreceptors innervating the glabrous skin of the hand convey information about the shape, size, and texture of the object. These nerve fibers also signal movements of the object relative to the skin. Neural signals from the hand play a key role in our ability to dexterously manipulate objects [38]. Information about these multiple object features is multiplexed in the responses of populations of mechanoreceptive afferents [58]. That is, the same neural signals can be decoded in different ways to obtain different types of information.

Stimulus intensity: The strength of a stimulus contacting the skin is encoded in the strength of the response it evokes across all populations of afferents [79]. As mentioned above, all afferents respond better to dynamic stimuli than to static ones, so a tactile stimulus tends to feel more intense to the extent that it is dynamic (that is, when the degree to which it indents the skin changes over time). Of course, different fiber types are differentially sensitive to mechanical stimulation of the skin, and responses from the less sensitive receptors are weighted more than are those from the more sensitive ones [2]. Importantly, under normal circumstances, even a basic sensory dimension such as intensity involves the integration of signals from a large number of afferents spanning all classes.

Shape: When we interact with an object, different parts of our hand touch different parts of the object. At each contact point, the pattern of skin deformation reflects the contours of that object at that location. The spatial pattern of activation of afferents under the contact area also reflects the spatial configuration of the stimulus over that area. The representation of the stimulus is somewhat distorted by the fact that the forces applied to the skin's surface must propagate down to the location of the receptor [49, 65]. As a result, certain stimulus features are enhanced (edges, corners) and others obscured (small internal stimulus features). Nonetheless, the neural image carried by mechanoreceptive afferents – particularly by SA1 and RA fibers – is approximately isomorphic with the stimulus, drawing analogies with the neural image about a visual scene carried by the optic nerve. In downstream structures, the extraction of information about object shape is remarkably analogous to its visual counterpart. Indeed, neurons in somatosensory cortex, like neurons in visual cortex, respond best to edges at a specific orientation [2]. In fact, this orientation tuning may begin to emerge in the nerve, as information about local orientation is also conveyed in the responses of nerve fibers [54].

Texture: When we run our fingers across a surface, we acquire information about its surface microgeometry and material properties. Indeed, we can distinguish surfaces whose elements differ in size by tens of nanometers, and in inter-elements by hundreds of nanometers [61]. Again, a variety of receptors contribute to our remarkable sensitivity to texture. Coarse textural features, on the order of millimeters, are encoded in the spatial pattern of activation in SA1 (and maybe RA) fibers, by the same mechanism that mediates the tactile perception of shape (at those sizes, shape and texture overlap) [80]. Given the density of innervation of the skin, this spatial mechanism cannot account for our ability to discern fine textural features, which are orders of magnitude more tightly packed than are receptors. To feel fine texture, then, we run our fingers across a surface and, in so doing, set off small vibrations in our skin [42], the properties of which depend on the surface geometry. These skin vibrations are transduced by specialized receptors – Pacinian and Meissner's corpuscles – which then drive afferent responses that are highly patterned and texture-specific [72]. This temporal signal – a kind of Morse code – carried by PC and RA fibers allows us to perceive fine surface texture. Skin receptors, including Ruffini and Meissner's corpuscles, and Merkel receptors respond to tangential forces and can thus convey information about the frictional properties of a surface [81]. Finally, thermoreceptors convey information about the thermal conductivity of a surface: metals feel cold because they are highly conductive whereas plastics feel warm because they are insulating [83 - 86].

Motion: Pacinian and Meissner's corpuscles respond very strongly when something moves across the skin and are thought to drive reflexive grip adjustments when an object slips from our grasp [73]. The peripheral signal for tactile motion is thought to be carried in the sequential activation of nerve fibers with adjacent receptive fields [28], and the mechanisms by which motion information is extracted from this peripheral signal are highly analogous to their visual counterparts [46]. Stretch-sensitive receptors, whose response is modulated by the direction of tangential forces applied to the skin, may also contribute to the tactile perception of motion [87 - 88].

3. Proprioceptive Receptors

Like cutaneous mechanoreceptors, proprioceptive mechanoreceptors provide position or displacement signals and movement or transient signals. The former relay information about joint angle or muscle length continuously during a maintained position of a limb or digit, while the latter are available only during movement of a limb or digit. Movement-related signals can include information about the rate (velocity) at which a limb or digit changes its position and about acceleration or higher order derivatives. According to this scheme, static position signals (meaning signals continuously available while a limb or digit is stationary) can come only from slowly adapting receptors and are thought to give rise to static position sense. Dynamic position sense (awareness of limb or joint position during movement) is more perceptually salient than static position sense. These two senses appear to be distinct and mediated either by different sensory inputs or by different CNS pathways [18].

Similar to their cutaneous counterparts, kinesthetic receptors probably use both dedicated channels and pattern codes to provide information about the positions and movements of the limbs and digits. Ideas about the signaling of limb position have a complex, contradictory, and confusing history [16]. The current view is that proprioceptive information can be derived from several sources: neural signals from the skin, joints, and muscle are all potential sources of information about limb posture and movements. Humans can detect the occurrence of a movement without necessarily sensing its direction or speed, and they can independently judge the direction and the speed of a movement and the position of a limb. It seems reasonable, therefore, to expect that these features are either encoded independently by the receptor population utilizing different neural circuits [10] or that input from a common sets of receptors is decoded differently.

Since virtually any movement we make will stretch and bend some regions of skin and relax others, it has been suggested that cutaneous mechanoreceptors could play a significant role in kinesthesia [24]. Among cutaneous mechanoreceptors, the T2 receptor responds best to skin stretch and alters its discharge most in response to changes in joint position [22, 23], although T2 receptors do not appear to elicit any sensation at all when activated in isolation [71] and eventually adapt to a common resting discharge under static conditions [34]. On the other hand, anesthesia of the skin covering the tongue or the lips makes speech difficult, and anesthesia of the skin on the hands can produce a striking inability to use the fingers even with visual guidance, whereas anesthesia of a wide band of skin around the knee joint goes barely noticed [15].

Awareness of finger position is enhanced by somatosensory inputs from the finger that do not, in themselves, provide positional cues [18]. This suggests that the role of cutaneous mechanoreceptors in proprioception is supportive but not informative. Put simply, cutaneous input may be needed to support a body image of having, for example, a hand, but is not sufficient to provide reliable information about the configuration of the hand in space.

The ligaments and capsules of joints contain numerous slowly adapting mechanoreceptors that respond to stretching the ligament and stretching or bending the capsule [26, 60, 63, 76]. In the ligaments, slowly adapting responses arise mainly from Golgi type endings formed by a profuse branching of the nerve terminals. When tested in the isolated ligament, the Golgi receptors show a vigorous and almost non-adapting response to stretch, though tension appears a more relevant variable than stretch given the very low compliance of ligaments [1]. When one tests the responses of these receptors to movements of the intact knee, they respond only when high torques are applied or at the very extreme positions of the joint [30, 31, 35]. Thus, ligament receptors seem incapable of encoding position or movement of passively rotated or positioned joints, except perhaps to signal the extremes of flexion and extension.

In the joint capsule, slowly adapting responses arise mainly from Ruffini type endings [62, 82]. Ruffini endings appear very similar to the Golgi receptors, though a bit smaller, and they respond to stretch of the capsule. However, in their examination of knee joint mechanoreceptors, Burgess and Clark [9] concluded that joint receptors could not encode joint position during passive rotation, except perhaps at extreme positions of the joint. This conclusion is consistent with the finding of little or no impairment in proprioception associated with joint replacement in humans [32]. Rather, joint receptors likely play a protective role, such as providing a fast mechanism to prevent hyperextension of the joint during a vigorous movement.

Muscles contain two types of slowly adapting mechanoreceptors: the Golgi tendon organs and the muscle spindles. Golgi tendon organs lie in series with the main muscle fibers, well situated to measure tension in the muscle. Muscle spindles lie in parallel with the main muscle fibers, well situated to measure muscle length and rate of change of length.

The Golgi tendon organ consists of a thinly encapsulated bundle of small tendon fascicles with a fusiform (spindle-like) shape, innervated by a single large-diameter group Ib nerve fiber. This receptor ending responds to stretch of the tendon fascicles, but due to the very low compliance of tendon, tension seems the more appropriate variable. The tendon organ monitors the tension produced in its muscle and feeds the information back to the CNS. The role information from Golgi tendon organs plays during walking varies with the phase of the step cycle [67].

A muscle spindle measures muscle stretch and rate of change of stretch. A sophisticated sensory organelle, the spindle consists of a long, slender bundle of 2–12 modified muscle fibers (intrafusal fibers) encased in a fluid-filled capsule (Fig. 2). Each spindle receives innervation from one large, Group Ia primary sensory fiber and from 0 to 5 intermediate sized, Group II secondary sensory fibers. In addition, the spindle receives 6 to 12 small diameter motor fibers in the gamma range, the gamma efferents. Activity in the gamma efferent fibers can substantially alter the activity in the sensory fibers. Thus, the CNS is able to regulate the operating range and sensitivity of the muscle spindle receptors, presumably to optimize their response over a wide variety of muscle lengths and loading conditions.

There are two main types of muscle spindle sensory endings, the primary found at the middle of the intrafusal fibers and the secondary found just offset from the middle. The primary ending is formed by Group Ia nerve fibers and the secondary endings by Group II fibers. Many workers use the terms Group Iá afferents and Group II afferents in reference to the primary and secondary endings, respectively. Signals from muscle spindles provide the CNS with information about the length of a muscle and its rate of shortening. Both the length-related and the rate-related responses stand out clearly in the discharge of the sensory fibers, with the secondary endings showing mainly a length response and the primary endings showing a pronounced rate response as well as a more modest length response. Muscle spindles can signal increases in length much better than decreases because, during rapid shortening of a muscle, a pronounced velocity response can cause the spindles to go silent with a loss of information. During muscle shortening, activation of the gamma system can help to maintain the spindle discharge [51, 52]. In some cases gamma activation may actually cause spindle discharge to increase during muscle shortening [19].

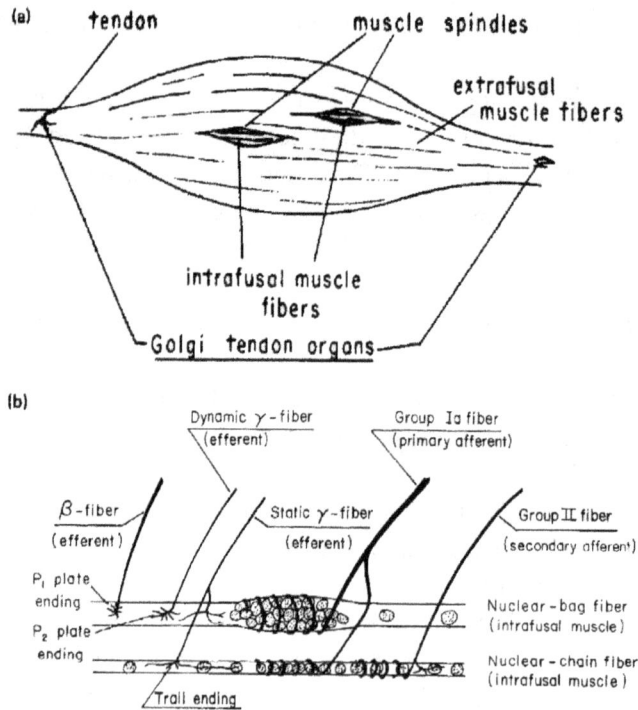

Fig. 2. Schematic drawings of Golgi tendon organ and muscle spindle receptors. (From [66]).

The primary endings respond especially strongly to the velocity of stretching, even with extremely small displacements. A sharp tap of a tendon produces a small but rapid stretch of the muscle that synchronously activates primary endings in many spindles. This volley of activity in the Ia fibers has a potent excitatory effect on the alpha motor neurons that innervate the extrafusal fibers of the muscle that contains the spindles, causing the muscle to contract (e.g., the knee jerk reflex). This stretch reflex can help compensate for unexpected changes in muscle length [37, 44]. Vibration applied to a muscle tendon also can powerfully excite primary spindle endings by virtue of their velocity sensitivity [56].

Gamma motor activity appears capable of independently altering both the length and the rate responses of primary and secondary spindle afferents [29]. Electrical stimulation of one type of gamma fiber (gamma static) in isolation can enhance the length response, whereas involvement of another type (gamma dynamic) can enhance the rate response. Gamma activity can thus serve to "bias" the spindle, adjusting its operating point so the spindle can respond optimally over the full range of possible muscle lengths. For instance, an ending that discharges at a long muscle length may go silent (because it goes slack) if the muscle shortens. However, an increase in gamma activity at the shorter length could return the sensory region to a portion of its operating range where it can once again signal small changes in length. Moreover, the static (length) and dynamic (rate) responses can be independently controlled.

One could argue that gamma control of the spindle discharge precludes the spindles from providing information about absolute muscle length and therefore limb position because the spindle responds not only to changes in length but also to changes in gamma activity [45, 57]. However, it is likely that downstream neurons take gamma drive into consideration when interpreting spindle output. Of all the candidates for position detectors, muscle spindle receptors, especially the secondary or Group II afferents, seem the best suited [12, 53]. Other muscle mechanoreceptors are most likely concerned with signaling painful events [43].

In summary, cutaneous Ruffini endings respond to skin stretch with a slowly adapting discharge and a population of these receptors may contribute information about static joint position. The skin also contains an abundance of rapidly adapting mechanoreceptors that could signal joint movement, but probably neither angular velocity nor absolute position, per se. Mechanoreceptors in joints seem poorly suited to signal joint position, except perhaps at the extremes of flexion and extension. Joint receptors might provide information about the rate and direction of movement of the joint, but they appear best suited to signal tension in the capsule and ligaments as the joint approaches one or the other limit of its range. This would suggest some sort of protective role for the receptors, probably to elicit fast acting spinal reflexes to prevent damage to the joint.

Mechanoreceptors in muscle are thought to convey the most information about limb position and movement (the muscle spindles) and muscle force (the Golgi tendon organs). Muscle spindles lie in parallel with the contractile elements of the muscle, well situated to encode muscle length, and produce a slowly adapting discharge that increases with stretch of the muscle. Thus, muscle spindles can encode both the static length of a muscle and the rate of length increase, and their sensitivity to these two components can be independently controlled by the gamma efferents. Moreover, in almost all situations muscles work in opposing groups, so for every muscle that shortens, another lengthens. Thus, spindles in antagonistic muscle pairs can keep the CNS informed of movement under any condition. Many, if not most, skeletal muscles, particularly in the appendages, cross more than one joint, so information about position of an individual joint is not directly available from receptors in an individual muscle or pair of muscles. Awareness of the position of the hand or fingers in space is more salient than awareness of the angles of the joints in the limb, suggesting that proprioception may be keyed to the former rather than to the latter [6, 18, 64]. The Golgi tendon organs lie in series with the tension producing elements of the muscles and display an exquisite sensitivity to the tension produced by contraction of the motor units within the muscles. As a group, the tendon organs provide a good sample of the overall tension developed in the muscle.

3.1. *Lumbrical muscles*

Intrafascicular micro-stimulation of ulnar and median nerve stumps in amputees can give rise to illusions of finger flexion but not extension, even though these nerves innervate only finger flexors and activation of stretch receptor afferents from these muscles should produce sensations of finger extension [20, 21].

The seeming discrepancy might be resolved by examining the nature of the sensations amputees report and in models of the intrinsic muscles of the hand by Leijnse and Kalker [40] and Biggs and Horch [4, 5]. Intrafascicular stimulation of tactile afferents in the median and ulnar nerve stumps of amputees restores or creates the illusion of a "normal" hand in the subjects with some location on the volar aspect of the hand or finger being touched [20]. The hand itself is perceived as being in a rest position with the fingers fully or nearly fully extended. Activation of proprioceptive afferents induces a sensation of one or more fingers curling (flexing) inward as if making a fist. The extent to which the fingers are flexed is a function of the rate of stimulation through the electrode [20, 21]. Since the fascicles in question innervate only the volar aspect of the hand and fingers, these sensations could not have arisen from stimulation of afferents from cutaneous stretch receptors on the back of the hand.

As Biggs and Horch [5] have pointed out, the lumbrical muscles of the hand are unique in that both their origins and insertions are on tendons: they extend between the extensor hood and the extrinsic flexor tendons of the fingers at the level of the metacarpal-phalangeal (MCP) joint. As such, they are stretched by flexion of any of the three finger joints by the extrinsic muscles, alone or in combination. Leijnse and Kalker [40] argued that the lumbrical muscles serve to make fine, rapid flexions of the MCP joint, but admit that their case is weakened by the relatively large displacements required for these muscles to do so. Rather, the large excursions experienced by these muscles during finger flexion, also noted by Biggs in his model, and their rich muscle spindle population make them prime candidates as sensors of finger position [55]. Since the spindles in these muscles cannot identify which of the three finger joints is being stretched, in the absence of any other information, the central nervous system would interpret increasing activity from these receptors alone as reflecting unloaded flexion of the fingers, which naturally assumes a fist-like pose.

On the basis of these considerations, it is possible that stretch receptors in the lumbrical muscles may constitute a major source of information about finger position and that proprioceptive sensations evoked by focal electrical stimulation of ulnar and median nerve stumps in amputees result from the activation of lumbrical muscle spindle afferents.

4. Summary

Mechanoreceptors provide information about skin deformation, hair displacement, joint movement, tendon tension, and muscle length. Thermoreceptors provide information about skin or muscle temperature. Threatening or damaging chemical, mechanical and thermal events evoke activity in nociceptors, which gives rise to the sensation of pain.

From a neuroprosthetics point of view, there is little reason to intentionally activate nociceptors and selective activation of thermoreceptors by electrical stimulation of peripheral nerves is a formidable challenge due to the small size of their nerve fibers which overlap nociceptive fiber sizes. For practical purposes, such as restoring distally referred sensations of touch and joint position, it is probably sufficient to focus on activation of large, myelinated (A) fibers. In that regard, the complex array of extero- and proprioceptive receptors and what they encode can be functionally simplified as follows.

Proprioception

    2° spindle > muscle strain

    1° spindle > muscle strain rate

Touch

    Merkel cell > skin strain

    F2 field   > skin strain rate

Vibrotaction

    F1 field   > flutter

    Pacinian corpuscle > vibration

References

1. Andrew, B. L. (1954) The sensory innervation of the medial ligament of the knee joint, *J. Physiol.* **123**, 241-250.
2. Bensmaia, S. J. (2008) Tactile intensity and population codes, *Behav Brain Res.* **190**, 165-173.
3. Bensmaia, S. J., Leung, Y. Y., Hsiao, S. S., and Johnson, K. O. (2005) Vibratory adaptation of cutaneous mechanoreceptive afferents, *J Neurophysiol.* **94**, 3023-3036.
4. Biggs, J. and Horch, K. (1999a) Biomechanical model predicts directional tuning of spindles in finger muscles facilitates precision pinch and power grasp, *Somatosensory & Motor Res.* **16**, 251-262.
5. Biggs, J. and Horch, K. (1999b) A three-dimensional kinematic model of the human long finger and the muscles that actuate it, *Med. Eng. Phys.* **21**, 625-639.
6. Biggs, J., Horch, K. and Clark, F. J. (1999) Extrinsic muscles of the hand signal finger tip location more precisely than they signal the angles of individual finger joints, *Exp. Brain Res.* **125**, 221-230.
7. Birder, L. A. and Perl, E. R. (1994) Cutaneous sensory receptors, *J. Clin. Neurophysiol.* **11**, 534-552.
8. Birder, I. A. (1954) The histological structure of the receptors in the knee joint of the cat correlated with their physiological response, *J. Physiol.* **124**, 476-488.
9. Burgess, P. R. and Clark, F. J. (1969) Characteristics of knee joint receptors in the cat, *J. Physiol.* **203**, 317-335.
10. Burgess, P. R, Horch, K. W. and Tuckett, R. P. (1983) Boring's formulation: a scheme for identifying functional neuron groups in a sensory system, *Fed. Proc.* **42**, 2521-2527.
11. Burgess, P. R., Horch, K. W. and Tuckett, R. P. (1999) Mechanoreceptors, In: *Encyclopedia of Neuroscience*, eds. Adelman, G. and Smith, B. H. (Elsevier Science, New York).
12. Burke, D. (1997) Unit identification, sampling bias and technical issues in microneurographic recordings from muscle spindle afferents, *J. Neurosci. Methods* **74**, 137-144.
13. Clark, F. J., Burgess, R. C., Chapin, J. W. and Lipscomb, W. T. (1985) Role of intramuscular receptors in the awareness of limb position, *J. Neurophysiol.* **54**, 1529-1540.
14. Clark, F. J., Grigg, P. and Chapin, J. W. (1989) The contribution of articular receptors to proprioception with the fingers in humans, *J. Neurophysiol.* **61**, 186-193.
15. Clark, F. J., Horch, K. W., Bach, S. M. and Larson, G. F. (1979) Contributions of cutaneous and joint receptors to static knee-position sense in man, *J. Neurophysiol.* **42**, 877-888.
16. Clark, F. J. and Horch, K. W. (1986) Kinesthesia, In: *Handbook of Perception and Human Performance*, eds. Boff, K. R., Kaufman, L. and Thomas J. P. (John Wiley and Sons, New York) pp. 13-1 - 13-62.
17. Collins, D. F., Refshauge, K. M., Todd, G. and Gandevia, S. C. (2005) Cutaneous receptors contribute to kinesthesia at the index finger, elbow, and knee, *J. Neurophysiol.* **94**, 1699-1706.
18. Cordo, P. J., Gurfinkel, V. S. and Levik, Y. (2000) Position sense during imperceptibly slow movements, *Exp Brain Res.* **132**, 1–9.
19. Critchlow, V. and von Euler, C. (1963) Intercostal muscle spindle activity and its γ motor control, *J. Physiol.* **168**, 820-847.
20. Dhillon, G. S., Krüger, T. B., Sandhu, J. S. and Horch, K. W. (2005) Effects of short-term training on sensory and motor function in severed nerves of long-term human amputees, *J. Neurophysiol.* **93**, 2625-2633.

21. Dhillon, G. S., Lawrence, S. M., Hutchinson, D. T. and Horch, K. W. (2004) Residual function in peripheral nerve stumps of amputees: Implications for neural control of artificial limbs, *J. Hand Surg.* **29A**, 605-615.

22. Edin, B. B. (1992) Quantitative analysis of static strain sensitivity in human mechanoreceptors from hairy skin, *J Neurophysiol.* **67**, 1105-1113.

23. Edin, B. B. and Abbs, J. H. (1991) Finger movement responses of cutaneous mechanoreceptors in the dorsal skin of the human hand, *J Neurophysiol.* **65**, 657-670.

24. Edin, B. B. and Johansson, N. (1995) Skin strain patterns provide kinaesthetic information to the human central nervous system. *J Physiol.* **487**, 243-251.

25. Ferrell, W. R. and Craske, B. (1992) Contribution of joint and muscle afferents to position sense at the human proximal interphalangeal joint, *Exp. Physiol.* **77**, 331-342.

26. Freeman, M. A. R. and Wyke, B. (1967) The innervation of the knee joint: An anatomical and histological study in the cat, *J. Anat.* **101**, 505-532.

27. Gandevia, S. C. and Hales, J. P. (1997) The methodology and scope of human microneurography, *J. Neurosci. Methods* **74**, 123-136.

28. Gardner, E. P. and Costanzo, R. M. (1980) Neuronal mechanisms underlying direction sensitivity of somatosensory cortical neurons in awake monkeys, *J Neurophysiol.* **43**, 1342-1354.

29. Goodwin, G. M., McCloskey, D. I. and Matthews, P. B. C. (1972) The contribution of muscle afferents to kinaesthesia shown by vibration induced illusions of movement and by the effects of paralysing joint afferents, *Brain* **95**, 705-748.

30. Grigg, P. (1975) Mechanical factors influencing response of joint afferent neurons from cat knee, *J. Neurophysiol.* **38**, 1473-1484.

31. Grigg, P. (1976) Response of joint afferent neurons in cat medial articular nerve to active and passive movements of the knee, *Brain Res.* **118**, 482-485.

32. Grigg, P., Fingerman, G. A. and Riley, L. H. (1973) Joint position sense after total hip replacement, *J. Bone Joint Surg. Am.* **55A**, 1016-1025.

33. Horch, K. W. and Burgess, P. R. (1980) Functional specificity and somatotopic organization during peripheral nerve regeneration, In: *Nerve Repair and Regeneration: Its Clinical and Experimental Basis*, eds. Jewett, D. and McCarrol, H. R. J. (Mosby, St. Louis) pp. 105-109.

34. Horch, KW and PR Burgess (1985) Long term adaptation of cutaneous type I and type II mechanoreceptors in the cat, Chinese J. Physiol. Sci. **1**, 54- 62.

35. Horch, K. W., Clark, F. J. and Burgess, P. R. (1975) Awareness of knee joint angle under static conditions, *J. Neurophysiol.* **38**, 1436-1447.

36. Horch, K. W., Tuckett, R. P. and Burgess, P. R. (1977) A key to the classification of cutaneous mechanoreceptors, *J. Invest. Dermatol.* **69**, 75-82.

37. Houk, J. C (1980) Homeostasis and control principles, In: *Medical Physiology* (14 ed.), ed. Mountcastle, V. B (Mosby, St. Louis).

38. Johansson, R. S. and Vallbo, A. B. (1980) Spatial properties of the population of mechanoreceptive units in the glabrous skin of the human hand, *Brain Res.* **184**, 353-366.

39. Kim, S. S., Sripati, A. P. and Bensmaia, S. J. (2010) Predicting the timing of spikes evoked by tactile stimulation of the hand, *J Neurophysiol.* **104**, 1484-1496.

40. Leijnse, J. N. A. L. and Kalker, J. J. (1995) A two-dimensional kinematic model of the lumbrical in the human finger, *J. Biomech.* **28**, 237-249.

41. Leung, Y. Y., Bensmaia, S. J., Hsiao, S. S. and Johnson, K. O. (2005) Time-course of vibratory adaptation and recovery in cutaneous mechanoreceptive afferents. *J Neurophysiol.* **94**, 3037-3045.
42. Manfredi, L. R., Saal, H. P., Brown, K. J., Zielinski, M. C., Dammann, J. F., 3rd, Polashock, V. S. and Bensmaia, S. J. (2014) Natural scenes in tactile texture, *J Neurophysiol.* **111**, 1792-1802.
43. Mense, S. (1996) Group III and IV receptors in skeletal muscle: are they specific or polymodal?, *Prog. Brain Res.* **113**, 83-100.
44. Merton, P. A. (1953) Speculations on the servo-control of movement. In: *The Spinal Cord*, ed. Wolstenholme, G. E. W. (Churchill London).
45. Merton, P. A. (1964) Human position sense and sense of effort, *Symp. Soc. Exp. Biol.* **18**, 387-400.
46. Pack, C. C. and Bensmaia, S. J. (2015) Seeing and feeling motion: Canonical computations in motion processing, *PLoS Biol.*, 100271.
47. Perl, E. R. (1996) Cutaneous polymodal receptors: characteristics and plasticity, *Prog. Brain Res.* **113**, 21-37.
48. Phillips, J. R., Johansson, R. S. and Johnson, K. O. (1992) Responses of human mechanoreceptive afferents to embossed dot arrays scanned across fingerpad skin, *J. Neurosci.* **12**, 827-839.
49. Phillips, J. R. and Johnson, K. O. (1981) Tactile spatial resolution. III. A continuum mechanics model of skin predicting mechanoreceptor responses to bars, edges, and gratings, *J Neurophysiol,* **46**, 1204-1225.
50. Pons, T. P. (1988) Representation of form in the somatosensory system, *Trends in Neuroscience* **11**, 373-375.
51. Prochazka, A.(1980) Muscle spindle activity during walking and during free fall, *Progress in Clinical Neurophysiology* **8**, 282–293.
52. Prochazka, A., Westerman, R. A. and Ziccone, P. (1976) Discharges of single hindlimb afferents in the freely moving cat, *J. Neurophysiol.* **39**, 1090-1104.
53. Proske, U., Wise, A. K. and Gregory, J. E. (2000) The role of muscle receptors in the detection of movements, *Prog. Neurobiol.* **60**, 85-96.
54. Pruszynski, J. A. and Johansson, R. S. (2014) Edge-orientation processing in first-order tactile neurons, *Nature Neurosci.* **17**, 1404-1409.
55. Ranney, D. and Wells, R. (1988) Lumbrical muscle function as revealed by a new and physiological approach, *Anat .Rec.* **222**, 110-114.
56. Ribot-Ciscar, E., Rossi-Durand, C. and Roll, J.-P. (1998) Muscle spindle activity following muscle tendon vibration in man, *Neurosci. Lett.* **258**, 147-150.
57. Rose, J. E. and Mountcastle, V. B. (1959) Touch and kinesthesis, In: *Handbook of physiology. Section 1: Neuro- physiology*, eds. Field, J. and Magoun, H. W. (American Physiological Society, Washington, D.C.).
58. Saal, H. P. and Bensmaia, S. J. (2014) Touch is a team effort: interplay of submodalities in cutaneous sensibility, *Trends Neurosci.* **37**, 689–697.
59. Sainburg, R. L., Ghilardi, M. F., Poizner, H. and Ghez, C. (1995) Control of limb dynamics in normal subjects and patients without proprioception, *J Neurophysiol.* **73**, 820-835.
60. Schmidt, R. F (1996) The articular polymodal nociceptor in health and disease, *Prog. Brain Res.* **113**, 53-81.
61. Skedung, L., Arvidsson, M., Chung, J. Y., Stafford, C. M., Berglund, B. and Rutland, M. W. (2013) Feeling small: exploring the tactile perception limits, *Sci. Rep.* **3**, 2617.

62. Skoglund, S. (1956) Anatomical and physiological studies of knee joint innervation in the cat, *Acta Physiol. Scand.* **36** (Suppl. 124), 1-101.

63. Skoglund, S (1973) Joint receptors and kinaesthesis, In: *Handbook of sensory physiology (Vol. 11); Somatosensory system*, ed. Iggo, A. (Springer-Verlag, New York).

64. Soechting, J. F. (1982) Does position sense at the elbow reflect a sense of elbow joint angle or one of limb orientation?, *Brain Res.* 248, 392-395.

65. Sripati, A. P., Bensmaia, S. J. and Johnson, K. O. (2006) A continuum mechanical model of mechanoreceptive afferent responses to indented spatial patterns, *J Neurophysiol.* **95**, 3852-3864.

66. Stein, R. B. (1974) Peripheral control of movement, *Physiol. Rev.* **54**, 215-243.

67. Stein, R. B. and Capaday, C. (1988) The modulation of human reflexes during functional motor task, *Trends in Neuroscience* **11**, 328-332.

68. Tuckett, R. P., Horch, K. W. and Burgess P. R. (1978) Response of cutaneous hair and field mechanoreceptors in the cat to threshold stimuli, J. Neurophysiol. **41**, 138-149.

69. Tuckett, R. P. and Wei, J. Y. (1987) Response to an itch-producing substance in cat. II. Cutaneous receptor populations with unmyelinated axons, *Brain Res.* **413**, 95-103.

70. Vallbo, A. B. and Johansson, R. S. (1984) Properties of cutaneous mechanoreceptors in the human hand related to touch sensation, *Hum. Neurobiol.* **3**, 3-14.

71. Vallbo, A. B., Olsson, K. A., Westberg, K.-G. and Clark, F. J. (1984) Microstimulation of single tactile afferents from the human hand, *Brain* **107**, 727-749.

72. Weber, A. I., Saal, H. P., Lieber, J. D., Cheng, J. W., Manfredi, L. R., Dammann, J. F. 3rd. and Bensmaia, S. J. (2013) Spatial and temporal codes mediate the tactile perception of natural textures, *Proc Natl Acad Sci U S A* **110**, 17107-17112.

73. Westling, G. and Johansson, R. S. (1987) Responses in glabrous skin mechanoreceptors during precision grip in humans, *Exp. Brain Res.* **66**, 128-140.

74. Winkelmann, R. K. (1988) Cutaneous sensory nerves, *Semin. Dermatol.* **7**, 236-268.

75. Wooten, M., Weng, H.-J., Hartke, T. V., Borzan, J., Klein, A. H., Turnquist, B., Dong, X., Meyer, R. A. and Ringkamp, M. (2014) Three functionally distinct classes of C-fiber nociceptors in primate, *Nature Commun.* **5**, 4122.

76. Wyke, B (1967) The neurology of joints, *Annals of the Royal College of Surgery* **41**, 25-50.

77. Yoshida, K. and Horch, K. (1996) Closed-loop control of ankle position using muscle afferent feedback with functional neuromuscular stimulation, *IEEE Trans. Biomed Eng.* **43**, 167-176.

78. Ochoa, J. and Torebjork, E. (1983) Sensations evoked by intraneural microstimulation of single mechanoreceptor units innervating the human hand, *Journal of Physiology,* **342**, 663-654.

79. Muniak, M. A., Ray, S., Hsiao, S. S., Dammann, J. F. and Bensmaia, S. J. (2007) The neural coding of stimulus intensity: linking the population response of mechanoreceptive afferents with psychophysical behavior, *J. Neurosci.,* **27**(43), 11687-11699.

80. Connor, C. E., Hsiao, S. S., Phillips, J. R. and Johnson, K. O. (1990) Tactile roughness: neural codes that account for psychophysical magnitude estimates, *J. Neurosci.,* **10**(12), 3823-3836.

81. Birznieks, I., Jenmalm, P., Goodwin, A. W. and Johansson RS. (2001) Encoding of direction of fingertip forces by human tactile afferents, *J. Neurosci.,* **21**(20), 8222-8237.

82. Boyd, I. A. (1954). The histological structure of the receptors in the knee joint of the cat correlated with their physiological response, *Journal of Physiology,* **124**, 476-488.

83. Ho, H. N. and Jones, L. A. (2006) Contribution of thermal cues to material discrimination and localization, *Percept. Psychophys.,* **68**(1), 118-128.

84. Ho, H. N. and Jones, L. A. (2008) Modeling the thermal responses of the skin surface during hand-object interactions, *J. Biomech. Eng.*, **130**(2), 021005.

85. Johnson, K. O, Darian-Smith. I. and LaMotte, C. (1973) Peripheral neural determinants of temperature discrimination in man: a correlative study of responses to cooling skin, *J. Neurophysiol.*, **36**(2), 347-370.

86. Johnson, K. O., Darian-Smit,h I., LaMotte C., Johnson, B. and Oldfield S. (1979) Coding of incremental changes in skin temperature by a population of warm fibers in the monkey: correlation with intensity discrimination in man, *J. Neurophysiol.*, **42**(5), 1332-1353.

87. Birznieks, I., Wheat, H. E., Redmond, S. J., Salo, L. M., Lovell, N. H. and Goodwin, A. W. (2010) Encoding of tangential torque in responses of tactile afferent fibres innervating the fingerpad of the monkey, *J. Physiol.*, **588**(Pt 7), 1057-1072.

88. Wheat, H. E., Salo, L. M. and Goodwin, A. W. (2010) Cutaneous afferents from the monkeys fingers: responses to tangential and normal forces, *J. Neurophysiol.*, **103**(2), 950-961.

Chapter 1.6

Visual System

Boshuo Wang[1] and James. D. Weiland[1,2]
¹Duke University, Durham, NC, USA
²University of Southern California, Los Angeles, CA, USA.
jweiland@med.usc.edu

The visual system is our part of the central neural system that gives us sight, one of the most important sensory functions. Disease of the visual system, especially of the retina, often leads to devastating blindness. The understanding of the anatomy, physiology, and pathology enables the development of neural prosthesis that restores partial sight to the blind.

1. Overview of the Visual System

Vision is arguably the most important and most complex of human sensory systems. It provides the predominant amount of information input, and it is estimated that 50% of the neural processing power of the brain is dedicated to vision and vision related computation [1].

The eye is the sensory component of the visual system receiving the light input from the outside world. Fig. 1 shows the cross section of human eyes, which is an approximately spherical structure consisting of several tissue layers surrounding the iris, lens, and vitreous humor in the inside. The external layers of the eye include the cornea in the very front and sclera covering the rest of the eyeball. The transparent cornea allows light to pass through and enter the eyeball through the pupil, which is an aperture formed by the center opening in the iris. The light is focused by the cornea and the lens, projected through the vitreous humor, and forms an image on the retina. The retina lines the back and inner surface of the eye. The eyeballs are rotated by extraocular muscles to allow the region of interest be aligned on the fovea centralis. The fovea is the central part of the retina with the highest visual acuity, while the peripheral retina attends to edges of the visual field, albeit with lower acuity. The retina converts the incoming light into electrical signals through a process called phototransduction (see section 3). The neural signal is carried by the optic nerve through the back of the eye to the visual cortex.

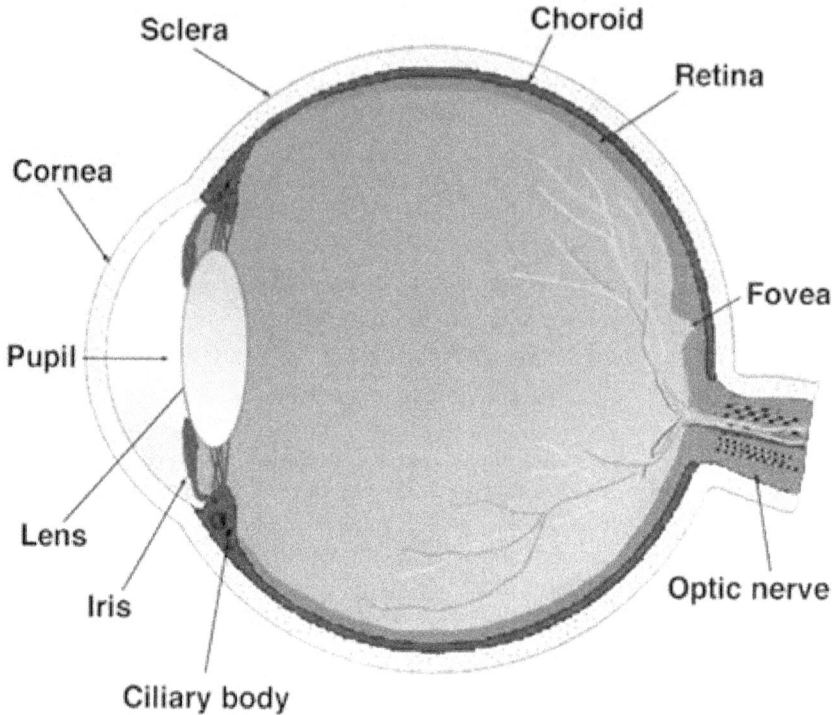

Fig. 1. Cross section of the eye. The cornea and lens focus the light passing through the pupil, and create an image on the retina, which lines the inner back of the eyeball. The visual information created by the retina is then transmitted to the cortex by the optic nerve. (Image from Webvision, http://webvision.med.utah.edu/.)

2. Anatomy of the Retina

The retina is a complex laminated structure about 300-μm thick [2], interfacing with the retinal pigment epithelium which provides functional and metabolic support to the retina. There are five major layers in the retina concerning neural circuitry—three contain cell bodies of retinal neurons and two contain synaptic connections (Fig. 2).

Specialized sensory cells, the photoreceptors, are located in the outermost layer. The photoreceptors include two types of cells, the rods and the cones. Rods are very sensitive, capable of detecting single photons. They operate in dimmer light, and therefore are almost entirely responsible for night (scotopic) vision. There are about 100 million rod cells in the human retina on average [3]. The cones operate under ambient daylight levels (photopic). The existence of three types of cone (red, green and blue), which are sensitive to photons of different wavelengths, provides color vision. On average, the human retina has about 4.6 million cones [3].The distribution of rods and cones in the retina is highly dependent on location relative to the fovea. The fovea is exclusively cones and the density of cones drops dramatically with distance from the fovea. Rods are absent from the fovea, have their highest density in the parafoveal region, then decrease in density in the peripheral retina. This distribution implies the function of these areas of the retina. The fovea is responsible for high acuity, color vision, while night vision and low-acuity tasks are mediated by peripheral retina (Fig. 3). The foveal region has a very specific neural circuitry that typically connects cone to the inner retina through one-to-one pathways, while in the peripheral retina the output layer receives converging input from many photoreceptors.

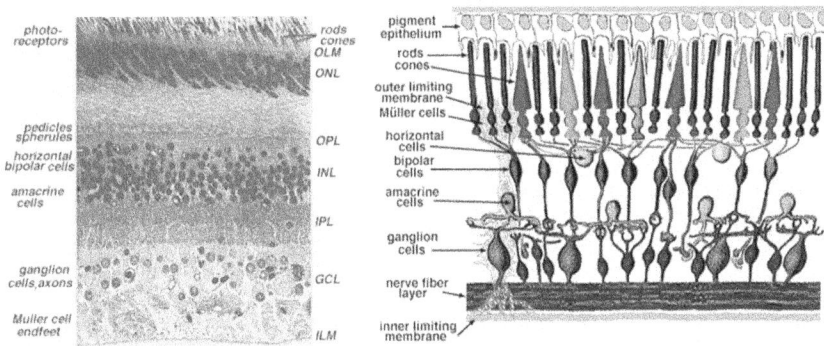

Fig. 2. Left: Light microscope of cross section of the central human retina. The three layers of neuronal soma are the outer nuclear layer (ONL), the inner nuclear layer (INL), and the ganglion cell layer (GCL). The two layers containing synaptic connections are the outer plexiform layer (OPL) and the inner plexiform layer (IPL). The inner limiting membrane (ILM) is formed by Muller cells and defines the inner border between the retina and the vitreous humor. Right: Simple diagram of retinal organization. Light enters the retina from the ganglion cell side, and travels through the retina before it is absorbed and converted into electrical signals by the photoreceptors. (Image from Webvision, http://webvision.med.utah.edu/.)

The photoreceptors form synaptic connections in the outer plexiform layer with the bipolar cells. The bipolar cells span the inner nuclear layer to interface with retinal ganglion cells (RGC) at the inner plexiform layer. The inner plexiform layer has sub-layers where the dendrites of different subtypes of bipolar cells and ganglion cell stratify and form synapses, thus separating different visual pathways. The horizontal cells and amacrine cells, which are also located in the inner nuclear layer, form local feed-forward and feedback neural networks at the outer and inner plexiform layers, respectively. The RGCs, which are the last layer in the retinal circuitry, projects axons into the nerve fiber layer in the inner most part of the retina. These axons coalesce at the optic disk and leave the eye forming the optic nerve.

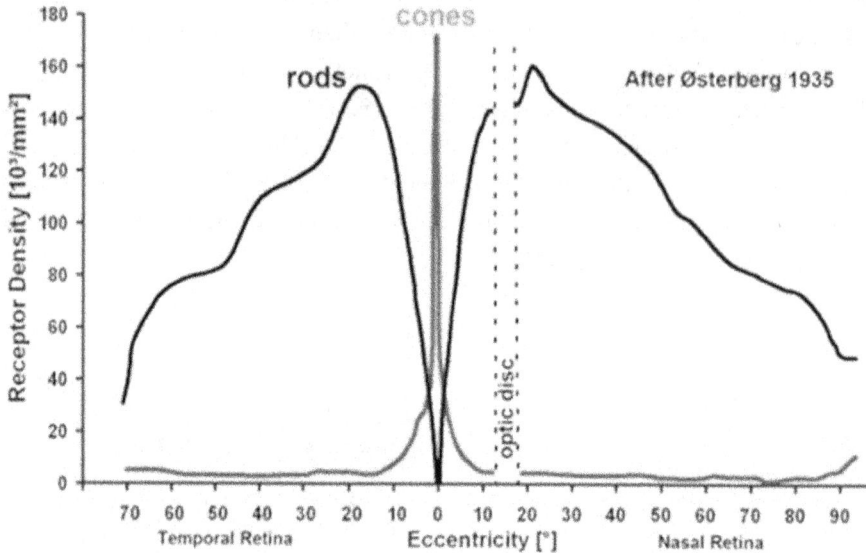

Fig. 3. Distribution of rod and cone photoreceptors in human retina. Cones are concentrated in the foveal region, responsible for high acuity vision and color. Rods are absent in the fovea, and have their peak density in the parafoveal region about 20 degrees from the fovea. (Image from Webvision, http://webvision.med.utah.edu/.)

Each retinal cell class has a great diversity in morphology and function (Fig. 4) [4]. These distinct neuron subtypes create specific pathways and circuits that allows for parallel visual processing in the retina. For example, subtypes of ganglion cells process specific visual information, forming different visual information channels for contrast, color, etc. [4]. By the time action potentials leave the retina through the optic nerve, the early processing has already compressed the information in the image focused on the retina into complex spatio-temporal patterns of activity.

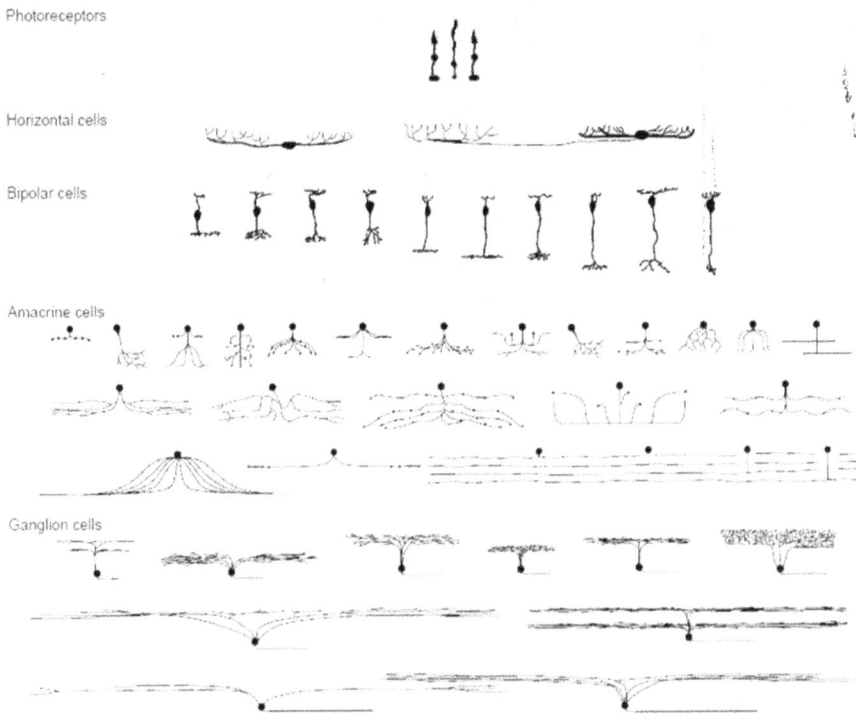

Fig. 4. Example of the diversity of morphology is shown for each retinal cell type. The structural classification is correlated with functional specifications. [4] (Reprinted from Current Opinion in Neurobiology, 11/4, R. H. Masland, Neuronal diversity in the retina, Pages 432, Copyright (2001), with permission from Elsevier.)

3. Electrophysiology of the Retina

When light hits the retina, the photons pass through the inner retinal layers, and initiate a process known as phototransduction when they are absorbed in the photoreceptors (Fig. 5). Opsins, a specific type of G-protein coupled receptors, signal a second-messenger cascade in response to the photon absorption. This amplifies the incoming light signal through several stages of biochemical reactions, and in the final step converts the information into electrical signals by closing ion channels on the cell membrane of the photoreceptors. Photoreceptors hyperpolarize as the dark current, which is maintained when no light stimulus is present, is reduced. This is quite unique, as most other cell types depolarize in response to external stimuli. The retina is the most metabolically active tissue in the body, due to the high turnover of the phototransduction machinery.

B. Wang & D Weiland

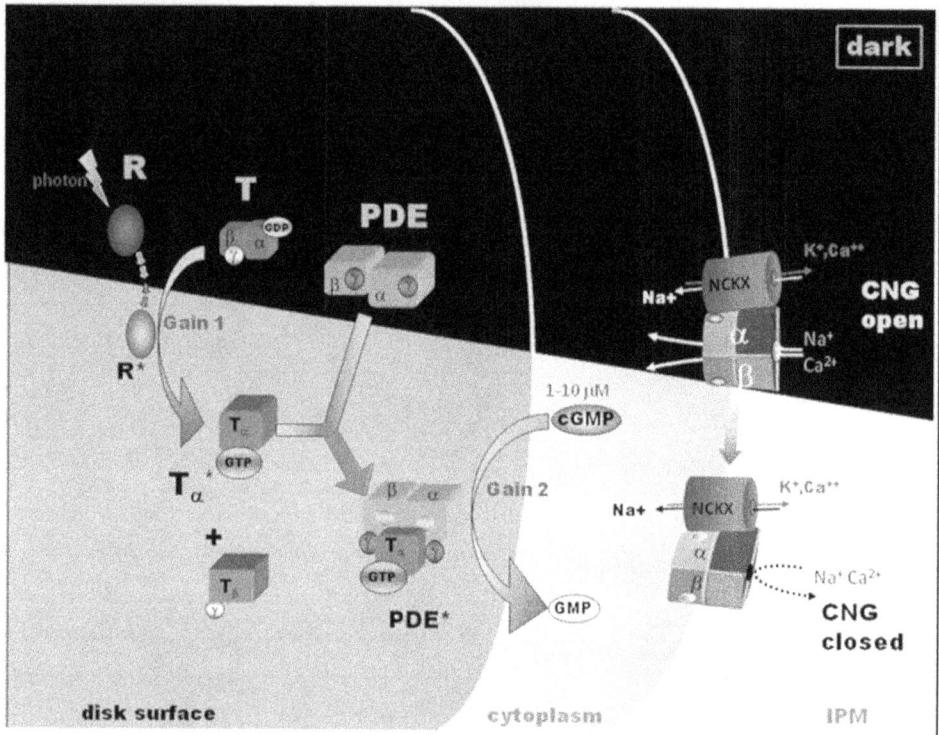

Fig. 5. Illustration of the phototransduction cascade in rods: 1. An incident photon is absorbed by the 11-*cis* retinal bound to the rhodopsin (R) on the rod's disk membrane, and the retinal undergoes isomerization from 11-*cis* to all-*trans* configuration. 2. The rhodopsin in response then activates transducin proteins, whose alpha subunit splits off. 3. The alpha subunit actives phosphodiesterase (PDE). 4. PDE breaks down cGMP to 5'-GMP, lowering the concentration of cytoplasmic cGMP. 5. The cGMP-gated sodium channels closes in response of the lower concentration, completing the transduction from light signal to electrical signal. The intracellular potential hyperpolarizes due to the reduced transmembrane sodium ion current. 6. Hyperpolarization closes the voltage-gated calcium channels, and reduces intracellular calcium. 7. The release of neurotransmitter in rods, which is regulated by calcium concentration, changes and neural signals are created in the retinal network. (Image from Webvision, http://webvision.med.utah.edu/.)

The hyperpolarization of the photoreceptors reduces the glutamate release at their synaptic terminals. Fluctuations of neurotransmitter release are detected by the bipolar cells, and with contributions of the local neural networks of horizontal cells and amacrine cells, are transmitted as a graded electrical signal down converging neural pathways towards the RGCs. Excitatory input from bipolar cells leads to RGCs firing action potentials, which are transmitted by their axons to the early visual processing nuclei, e.g. the lateral geniculate nucleus in the thalamus. The visual signal is then further transmitted to the primary visual cortex, and then higher visual centers in the cerebral cortex. The processing and sensory association of these cortical centers creates the sense of vision.

4. Visual Field and Pathways

Visual field is the spatial extent of visual perception without head movement [5]. The visual field consists of a binocular region perceived by both eyes, and monocular region only perceived by one eye. For each eye, the visual field extends to approximately 60 degrees nasally to 100 degrees temporally from the vertical meridian, and approximately 60 degrees above and 75 below the horizontal meridian. The visual field can be divided into left and right hemifields with respect to the fixation point, while the retina can also be divided into nasal and temporal hemiretina with respect to the fovea. Each hemifields projects on the nasal hemiretina of the ipsilateral eye, and temporal hemiretina of the contralateral eye.

The optic nerve carries information of the entire visual field of the corresponding eye when leaving the eyeball. The two optic nerves convene at the optic chiasm, from where two optic tracts lead to higher visual systems in the two cerebral hemispheres. At the chiasm, the nerve fibers of each optic nerve split in directions, so that each optic tracts combines nerve fibers of the temporal hemiretina of the ipsilateral eye and of the nasal hemiretina of the contralateral eye. This arrangement results in the projection of a visual hemifield exclusively into the contralateral subcortical regions and visual cortex.

The optic tracts project into three major subcortical region: the pretectum, the superior colliculus (SC), and the lateral geniculate nucleus (LGN). The projection into the pretectal areas of the midbrain and SC mediate functions such as pupillary reflexes and saccadic eye movement, whereas in the primate visual system, about 90% of the retinal ganglion cell axons terminate in the (LGN) of the thalamus. Three distinct pathways are present in the LGN: magnocellular pathways, parvocellular pathways and koniocellular pathways. Midget ganglion cells are considered to be the origin of the parvocellular pathway and constitute approximately 70% of the total cell population that project to the LGN. Parasol ganglion cells are the origin of the magnocellular pathway and bistratified ganglion cell make up most of the koniocellular pathway [6]. The retinal areas are not equally represented along the visual pathways and in the nucleus. The fovea, with the highest density of RGCs, has a larger representation than does the peripheral retina. Visual pathways leaving the LGN project to separate layers of the primary visual cortex, the first point in the visual pathway where the receptive fields of cells are significantly different from the retinal neurons. Like the LGN and SC, the primary visual cortex in each cerebral hemisphere receives information exclusively from the contralateral half of the visual field.

5. Retinal Degeneration

Visual impairment can take form in a wide range of symptoms, including blurry vision, reduced visual acuity and/or visual field, with complete blindness being most severe. Due to the importance of vision, visual impairment is a very debilitating condition, and, in fact, blindness has been considered worse than death in some cultures [7]. Visual impairment can arise from injury, degeneration and malfunction of different parts in the visual system, including the optical pathway (cornea, lens, and vitreous humor), retina, optic nerve, and central visual pathways and cortex. A significant part of the visual impairment is related to degenerative diseases of the retina such as age-related macular degeneration [8], which could be remedied by electrical prostheses.

Retinal degeneration (RD) is the deterioration of the retina caused by progressive photoreceptor death in the retina. RD impairs vision of the patient in the form of night blindness, reduced visual acuity, tunnel vision etc. They most commonly arise from inherited genetic mutations, but could also occur secondary due to vascular diseases such as artery or vein occlusion and diabetic retinopathy. The most prevalent types of retinal degeneration are age-related macular degeneration (AMD) and retinitis pigmentosa (RP). Together, they account for millions cases of blindness worldwide.

5.1. *Age-related macular degeneration*

AMD is a progressive degenerative ocular disease which usually affects older adults (mostly over the age of 55). Vision loss due to secondary dysfunction or loss of photoreceptors in the central retina (macular region) is caused by senescence and dysfunction of the retinal pigment epithelium (RPE), accumulation of subretinal drusen deposits, and in some patients, patchy loss of RPE or subretinal choroidal neovascularization [9]. The patients lose their visual field of highest acuity, but the peripheral vision is usually spared (Fig. 6, center). This makes it difficult and often impossible for patients to perform visual activities requiring fine resolution, such as reading, driving, and face recognition; and they also suffer from poor fixation stability, orientation discrimination, and shape discrimination [10]–[12].

Approximately 40 million people are affected by AMD worldwide. The World Health Organization estimates that 14 million people are legally blind or severely impaired, accounting for 8.7% of worldwide blindness [8]. AMD is mostly seen in Europe and in countries with European-based populations like the USA, Canada, and Australia. In the USA, for example, it is estimated that about 2 million Americans above the age of 55 have AMD [13]. Approximately 700,000 new cases occur each year in the United States alone, with 10% of the patients becoming legally blind [14], [15].

The exact cause of AMD is unknown, but risk factors include age, family history, genetic mutations, hypertension, obesity, smoking etc. [16]. AMD occurs in two forms: neovascular (wet, exudative) and non-neovascular (dry, nonexudative). The wet form is more severe, and involves abnormal blood vessel growth from the choroid behind retina, causing subretinal scarring and retinal detachment. In the dry form of AMD, the RPE atrophies and remodels, and extracellular deposits of debris known as drusen accumulated between the retina and the choroid. Treatment for either form of AMD is limited. For wet AMD, antiangiogenic drugs are administered through repeated injections into the eye to prevent the abnormal proliferation of blood vessels [17]. Nutritional supplements with antioxidant, anti-inflammatory, and cell protective effects have been used in dry AMD; however they show limited effectiveness only [18]. Stem cell therapies are experimental options under investigation.

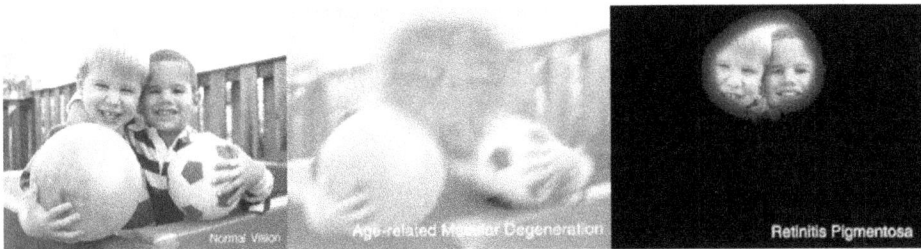

Fig. 6. Simulated vision of AMD (middle) and RP (right) compared to normal (left). (Image from National Eye Institute, http://www.nei.nih.gov/)

5.2. *Retinitis pigmentosa*

RP is the second most prevalent retinal degeneration that affects about 1.5 million people worldwide [19], [20]. The incident rate is 1:400 live births overall, however could vary depending on ethnicity [15], [19], [20]. RP is a group of inherited eye diseases that mostly affects rod photoreceptors, causing night blindness and tunnel vision (Fig. 6, right). The RP phenotype manifests through mutations in rhodopsin genes, with more than 100 genetic mutations identified [21], [22], [20]. More than half of all RP cases are autosomal recessive traits, a third are autosomal dominant, and the remainder are X-linked [20], [23]. Nutritional supplement of vitamin A has shown mitigation and postpone the disease progression [19]. Electronic retinal prostheses offer some improved vision for patients with severe RP. Two electronic retinal prostheses have received regulatory approval: Argus II (FDA and CE Mark) and Alpha-IMS (CE Mark). Ongoing research efforts involve retinal transplantation [24], gene therapy [25], and stem cells therapy [26].

5.3. *Inner retinal survival and remodeling in retinal degeneration*

In both AMD and RP, photoreceptors are lost as the disease progresses. However, much of the inner retina survives. In two studies, the inner retina of AMD patients is well preserved, with 70%-93% of the RGCs surviving and no significant difference in the inner nuclear layer cells [27], [28]. However, when comparing the two types of AMD, the exudative form has shown 50% ganglion cell loss, while the nonexudative form has no significant changes [9]. In RP, there is a varying degree of cell preservation, with about 78-88% of bipolar cells and 30-75 % of ganglion cells surviving [29], [30].

Due to the degeneration of the photoreceptors in RD, the retina tissue undergoes significant remodeling. Abnormalities such as glial hypertrophy, neurite sprouting, neuron migration, and rewiring of the remaining neural network occur in response to the loss of sensory input [31]–[35]. The remodeling will depend on the disease progression and occurs in phases [34]; and variability between individuals is always a possibility.

5.4. *Animal models of retinal degeneration*

The retinal remodeling due to RD poses a challenge to study the retinal prosthesis in the laboratory environment. Animal models that mimic the degeneration in human retina are required for electrophysiology studies, because the use of healthy animal/tissue could not reflect the realistic situation that the prostheses face in patient users. Models of retinal disease exist in dog, cat, chicken, mouse, and rat [36]. For example, the Abyssinian cat is an animal model of retinal degeneration that closely mimics recessive human RP [37], and the Irish Setter exhibits a genetic defect also found in *rd* mouse and recessive RP in human [38].

Many animal models have been developed in rodents to study the pathology, etiology, and electrophysiology of RD. For example, the Royal College of Surgeons (RCS) rat is the first known animal with inherited retinal degeneration and is widely used for research in hereditary retinal dystrophies [39], [40]. The

S334ter rat and P23H rat are transgenic models to express autosomal dominant mutations of the rhodopsin protein similar to that found in human RP patients [41].

A few dozens of mouse models are available for RP and AMD research, which have different genetic mutations, severity and progression of degeneration [42]. The *rd1* and *rd10* are widely studied models which reflect autosomal recessive traits of RP. The *rd1* mice have a much faster onset of retinal degeneration and normal development never occurs; while in *rd10* mice, the degeneration starts slower, and early retinal development is normal (Fig. 7) [42], [43].

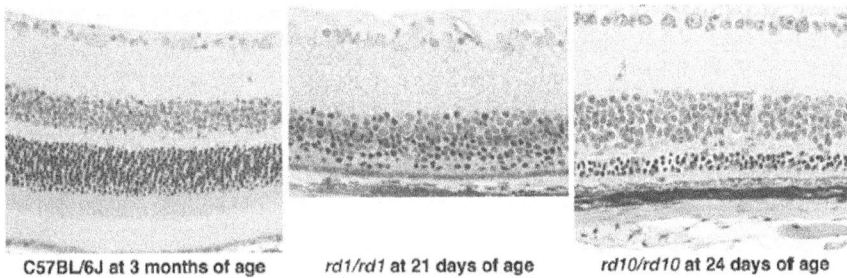

C57BL/6J at 3 months of age   *rd1/rd1* at 21 days of age   *rd10/rd10* at 24 days of age

Fig. 7. Histology sections of WT (left), *rd1* (middle), and *rd10* (right) mouse retina are shown side by side. The *rd1* retina has significant loss of the photoreceptor including outer nuclear layer. The *rd10* retina suffers from slower degeneration. While the outer and inner segments of the photoreceptors are completely degenerated, the loss of the outer nuclear layer is not so severe in *rd10* as compared to *rd1*. [42] (Reprinted from Current Opinion in Neurobiology, 11/4, R. H. Masland, Neuronal diversity in the retina, Pages 432, Copyright (2001), with permission from Elsevier.)

6. Summary

The visual system allows us to receive vivid and rich information of our surrounding, and is of great importance to the normal functioning in everyday life. The loss of visual function due to RD is devastating, and severely impairs the individuals. The understanding of the anatomy, physiology, and pathology of the retina is key to develop neuroprosthetic devices that interface with the diseased retina to restore partial vision. Continuous research in these area will further aid the improvement of retinal prostheses that will eventually provide viable treatment to RD.

References

1. J. S. Walker, Neuropsychological Assessment, in *Wiley Encyclopedia of Forensic Science*, (John Wiley & Sons, Ltd, New York) 2009.
2. M. T. B. C. Bonanomi, A. G. B. Nicoletti, P. C. Carricondo, F. Buzalaf, N. Kara-José Jr, A. M. V. Gomes, and Y. Nakashima, Retinal thickness assessed by optical coherence tomography (OCT) in pseudophakic macular edema, *Arq. Bras. Oftalmol.*, vol. **69**, no. 4, pp. 539–544, 2006.
3. C. A. Curcio, K. R. Sloan, R. E. Kalina, and A. E. Hendrickson, Human photoreceptor topography, *J. Comp. Neurol.*, vol. **292**, no. 4, pp. 497–523, 1990.
4. R. H. Masland, Neuronal diversity in the retina, *Curr. Opin. Neurobiol.*, vol. **11**, no. 4, pp. 431–436, 2001.
5. J. Smythies, A note on the concept of the visual field in neurology, psychology, and visual neuroscience, *Perception*, vol. **25**, no. 3, pp. 369–371, 1996.
6. J. J. Nassi and E. M. Callaway, Parallel processing strategies of the primate visual system, *Nat. Rev. Neurosci.*, vol. **10**, no. 5, pp. 360–372, 2009.
7. M. L. Rose, History of disability: ancient west, in *Encyclopedia of Disability*, vol. 2, ed. G. L. Albrecht (Sage Publication, Thousand Oaks, CA) 2006, pp. 852–854.
8. K. M. Gehrs, D. H. Anderson, L. V. Johnson, and G. S. Hageman, Age-related macular degeneration—emerging pathogenetic and therapeutic concepts, *Ann. Med.*, vol. **38**, no. 7, pp. 450–471, 2006.
9. N. E. Medeiros and C. A. Curcio, Preservation of ganglion cell layer neurons in age-related macular degeneration, *Invest. Ophthalmol. Vis. Sci.*, vol. **42**, no. 3, pp. 795–803, 2001.
10. H. E. Bedell, J. Tong, S. Y. Woo, J. R. House, and T. Nguyen, Orientation discrimination with macular changes associated with early AMD, *Optom. Vis. Sci.*, vol. **86**, no. 5, pp. 485–491, 2009.
11. K. Neelam, J. Nolan, U. Chakravarthy, and S. Beatty, Psychophysical function in age-related maculopathy, *Surv. Ophthalmol.*, vol. **54**, no. 2, pp. 167–210, 2009.
12. Y.-Z. Wang, E. Wilson, K. G. Locke, and A. O. Edwards, shape discrimination in age-related macular degeneration, *Invest. Ophthalmol. Vis. Sci.*, vol. **43**, no. 6, pp. 2055–2062, 2002.
13. G. J. Chader, J. D. Weiland, M. S. Humayun, J. Verhaagen, E. M. Hol, I. Huitenga, J. Wijnholds, A. B. Bergen, Gerald J. Boer, and D. F. Swaab, Artificial vision: needs, functioning, and testing of a retinal electronic prosthesis, *Progress in Brain Research*, vol. **175**, pp. 317–332, 2009.
14. C. A. Curcio, N. E. Medeiros, and C. L. Millican, Photoreceptor loss in age-related macular degeneration., *Invest. Ophthalmol. Vis. Sci.*, vol. **37**, no. 7, pp. 1236–1249, 1996.
15. E. Margalit and S. R. Sadda, Retinal and optic nerve diseases, *Artif. Organs*, vol. **27**, no. 11, pp. 963–974, 2003.
16. J. J. Wang, P. Mitchell, and R. Klein, Epidemiology of age-related macular degeneration early in the 21st century, in *Retinal Degenerations*, eds. J. Tombran-Tink and C. J. B. DPhil, (Humana Press, Ne York) 2007, pp. 23–59.
17. G. Menon and G. Walters, New paradigms in the treatment of wet AMD: the impact of anti-VEGF therapy, *Eye*, vol. **23**, pp. S1–S7, 2009.
18. J. S. L. Tan, J. J. Wang, V. Flood, E. Rochtchina, W. Smith, and P. Mitchell, Dietary antioxidants and the long-term incidence of age-related macular degeneration: The Blue Mountains eye study, *Ophthalmology*, vol. **115**, no. 2, pp. 334–341, 2008.
19. E. L. Berson, Retinitis pigmentosa. The Friedenwald Lecture, *Invest. Ophthalmol. Vis. Sci.*, vol. **34**, no. 5, pp. 1659–1676, 1993.

20. D. T. Hartong, E. L. Berson, and T. P. Dryja, Retinitis pigmentosa, *The Lancet*, vol. **368**, no. 9549, pp. 1795–1809, 2006.
21. J. K. Phelan and D. Bok, A brief review of retinitis pigmentosa and the identified retinitis pigmentosa genes, *Mol. Vis.*, vol. **6**, pp. 116–124, 2000.
22. J. R. Heckenlively, *Retinitis pigmentosa*. (J. B. Lippincott Company, Philadelphia) 1988.
23. J. R. Heckenlively, J. A. Boughman, and L. H. Friedman, Pedigree Analysis, in *Retinitis pigmentosa*, ed. J. R. Heckenlively (J. B. Lippincott Company, Philadelphia) 1988, pp. 14–24.
24. B. T. Sagdullaev, R. B. Aramant, M. J. Seiler, G. Woch, and M. A. McCall, Retinal transplantation–induced recovery of retinotectal visual function in a rodent model of retinitis pigmentosa, *Invest. Ophthalmol. Vis. Sci.*, vol. **44**, no. 4, pp. 1686–1695, 2003.
25. L. Stein, K. Roy, L. Lei, and S. Kaushal, Clinical gene therapy for the treatment of RPE65-associated Leber congenital amaurosis, *Expert Opin. Biol. Ther.*, vol. **11**, no. 3, pp. 429–439, 2011.
26. R. E. MacLaren, R. A. Pearson, A. MacNeil, R. H. Douglas, T. E. Salt, M. Akimoto, A. Swaroop, J. C. Sowden, and R. R. Ali, Retinal repair by transplantation of photoreceptor precursors, *Nature*, vol. **444**, no. 7116, pp. 203–207, 2006.
27. S. Y. Kim, S. Sadda, M. S. Humayun, E. de Juan, B. M. Melia, and W. R. Green, Morphometric analysis of the macula in eyes with geographic atrophy due to age-related macular degeneration, *Retina Phila. Pa*, vol. **22**, no. 4, pp. 464–470, 2002.
28. S. Y. Kim, S. Sadda, J. Pearlman, M. S. Humayun, E. de Juan, Jr., B. M. Melia, and W. R. Green, Morphometric analysis of the macula in eyes with disciform age-related macular degeneration, *Retina August 2002*, vol. **22**, no. 4, pp. 471–477, 2002.
29. A. Santos, M. S. Humayun, E. de Juan, Jr., R. J. Greenberg, M. J. Marsh, I. B. Klock, and A. H. Milam, Preservation of the inner retina in retinitis pigmentosa: A morphometric analysis, *Arch. Ophthalmol.*, vol. **115**, no. 4, pp. 511–515, 1997.
30. M. S. Humayun, M. Prince, E. de Juan, Jr., Y. Barron, M. Moskowitz, I. B. Klock, and A. H. Milam, Morphometric analysis of the extramacular retina from postmortem eyes with retinitis pigmentosa., *Invest. Ophthalmol. Vis. Sci.*, vol. **40**, no. 1, pp. 143–148, 1999.
31. R. N. Fariss, Z.-Y. Li, and A. H. Milam, Abnormalities in rod photoreceptors, amacrine cells, and horizontal cells in human retinas with retinitis pigmentosa, *Am. J. Ophthalmol.*, vol. **129**, no. 2, pp. 215–223, 2000.
32. R. E. Marc and B. W. Jones, Retinal remodeling in inherited photoreceptor degenerations, *Mol. Neurobiol.*, vol. **28**, no. 2, pp. 139–147, 2003.
33. R. E. Marc, B. W. Jones, C. B. Watt, and E. Strettoi, Neural remodeling in retinal degeneration, *Prog. Retin. Eye Res.*, vol. **22**, no. 5, pp. 607–655, 2003.
34. B. W. Jones, M. Kondo, H. Terasaki, Y. Lin, M. McCall, and R. E. Marc, Retinal remodeling, *Jpn. J. Ophthalmol.*, vol. **56**, no. 4, pp. 289–306, 2012.
35. K. E. Jones and R. A. Normann, An advanced demultiplexing system for physiological stimulation, *IEEE Trans. Biomed. Eng.*, vol. **44**, no. 12, pp. 1210–1220, 1997.
36. G. J. Chader, Animal models in research on retinal degenerations: past progress and future hope, *Vision Res.*, vol. **42**, no. 4, pp. 393–399, 2002.
37. K. Narfström, Hereditary and congenital ocular disease in the cat, *J. Feline Med. Surg.*, vol. **1**, no. 3, pp. 135–141, 1999.
38. M. L. Suber, S. J. Pittler, N. Qin, G. C. Wright, V. Holcombe, R. H. Lee, C. M. Craft, R. N. Lolley, W. Baehr, and R. L. Hurwitz, Irish setter dogs affected with rod/cone dysplasia contain

a nonsense mutation in the rod cGMP phosphodiesterase beta-subunit gene., *Proc. Natl. Acad. Sci.*, vol. **90**, no. 9, pp. 3968–3972, 1993.

39. M. C. Bourne, D. A. Campbell, and K. Tansley, Hereditary degeneration of the rat retina, *Br. J. Ophthalmol.*, vol. **22**, no. 10, pp. 613–623, 1938.

40. M. Pu, L. Xu, and H. Zhang, Visual response properties of retinal ganglion cells in the royal college of surgeons dystrophic rat, *Invest. Ophthalmol. Vis. Sci.*, vol. **47**, no. 8, pp. 3579–3585, 2006.

41. D. Lee, S. Geller, N. Walsh, K. Valter, D. Yasumura, M. Matthes, M. LaVail, and J. Stone, Photoreceptor degeneration in Pro23His and S334ter transgenic rats, in *Retinal Degenerations*, eds. M. M. LaVail, J. G. Hollyfield, and R. E. Anderson (Springer US, New York) 2003, pp. 297–302.

42. B. Chang, N. L. Hawes, R. E. Hurd, M. T. Davisson, S. Nusinowitz, and J. R. Heckenlively, Retinal degeneration mutants in the mouse, *Vision Res.*, vol. **42**, no. 4, pp. 517–525, 2002.

43. B. Chang, N. L. Hawes, M. T. Pardue, A. M. German, R. E. Hurd, M. T. Davisson, S. Nusinowitz, K. Rengarajan, A. P. Boyd, S. S. Sidney, M. J. Phillips, R. E. Stewart, R. Chaudhury, J. M. Nickerson, J. R. Heckenlively, and J. H. Boatright, Two mouse retinal degenerations caused by missense mutations in the β-subunit of rod cGMP phosphodiesterase gene, *Vision Res.*, vol. **47**, no. 5, pp. 624–633, 2007.

The Auditory System

Bryony A. Nayagam[1,2,3], Andrew K.Wise[1,2], and Robert K. Shepherd[1,2]

[1]*Bionics Institute, Melbourne, Victoria, Australia.*
[2]*Medical Bionics Department, University of Melbourne, Melbourne, Victoria, Australia.*
[3]*Department of Audiology and Speech Pathology, University of Melbourne, Melbourne, Victoria, Australia.*
RShepherd@bionicsinstitute.org

The development and clinical success of auditory prostheses rests, in part, on our knowledge of the structure and function of the auditory system. This chapter reviews the mammalian auditory pathway, placing considerable emphasis on the anatomy and physiology of the cochlea. This background is necessary to understand the pathological implications of a sensorineural hearing loss and its amelioration via an auditory prosthesis.

1. Introduction

Hearing loss afflicts approximately 360 million people world-wide (World Health Organisation). While many of these patients receive considerable benefit from amplification via a conventional hearing aid, those with a severe-profound loss of sensory hair cells (sensorineural hearing loss) receive no clinical benefit from these devices. It is only over the last three decades that these patients have been able to receive clinical benefit in the form of an auditory-based neural prosthesis known as a cochlear implant. These devices, together with central auditory prostheses (designed for use in patients without a functioning auditory nerve), will be described in some detail in Chapter 3.6.

2. External and Middle Ears

The external and middle ear consists of the pinna, the external auditory meatus (ear canal) and the middle ear (Fig. 1). The pinna and external auditory meatus provide efficient transmission of the acoustic stimulus to the tympanic membrane and protects the delicate structures of the middle ear. These key structures of the outer ear also assist in the selective amplification (approximately 1.5-5 kHz) and localization of environmental sounds. The middle ear cavity is bound by the tympanic membrane laterally and the inner ear (or cochlea) medially (Fig. 1). Its prime function is to efficiently couple sound energy from the air-filled external auditory canal to the fluid-filled cochlea. This is possible due to the action of the three smallest bones in the human body, the malleus, incus and stapes, collectively known as the auditory ossicles. The middle ear ossicles overcome the impedance mismatch between air and the fluid filled cochlea [1], thereby facilitating the efficient transfer of airborne sound waves into fluid pressure waves within the cochlea.

3. The Cochlea

The cochlea is responsible for the transduction of the mechanical pressure waves of the incoming acoustic signal into nerve impulses generated within the auditory nerve. The cochlea provides the initial intensity, timing and frequency analysis of the incident acoustic signal and outputs this information to the central auditory pathway for further analysis. This review of the cochlea is, by necessity, brief; more detailed accounts are available [3].

3.1. *Cochlear anatomy*

The mammalian cochlea is a spiral shaped labyrinth embedded within the temporal bone (Fig. 2a). In transverse section, three fluid-filled compartments, or scalae, are evident (Fig. 2b). The basilar membrane (BM) separates the scala tympani from the scala media while Reissner's membrane separates the scala media from the scala vestibuli. The human cochlea consists of two and a half turns and has a BM length of approximately 33 mm from base to apex. Both the scala tympani and scala vestibuli contain perilymph, an extracellular fluid with a similar electrolyte profile as cerebro-spinal fluid and plasma [4]. In contrast, the scala media contains a unique extracellular fluid called endolymph, which has a high concentration of potassium and a low concentration of sodium [5].

3.1.1. *Sensory hair cells*

The sensory cells of the cochlea are located within the organ of Corti, a complex structure attached to the BM (Fig. 2c), and extending along its entire length. There are two types of sensory hair cells, located on either side of the pillar cells. On the lateral side, three to four rows of outer hair cells (OHCs) are supported at their apex by a rigid plate known as the reticular lamina, and at their base by Deiters' cells. OHCs have a diameter of approximately 7 μm and a length that varies from 25 μm in the cochlear base to 45 μm in the apex. Inner hair cells (IHCs) lie on the medial or modiolar side of the pillar cells. Unlike the OHCs, the IHCs are completely surrounded by supporting cells. IHCs are approximately 10 μm in diameter and 35 μm long throughout the cochlea.

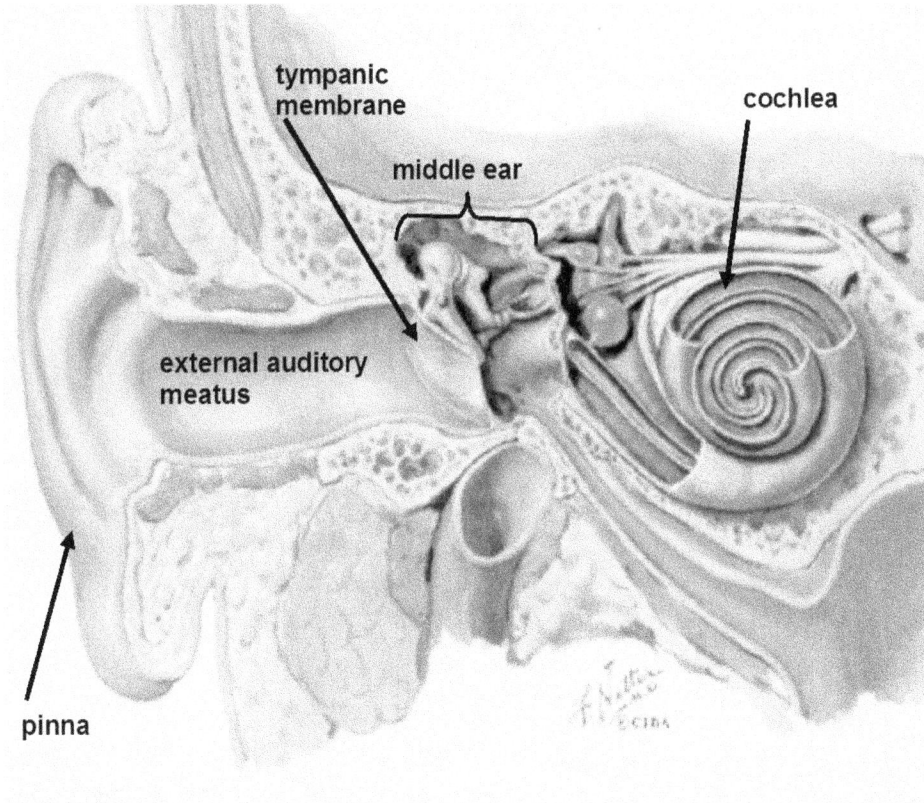

Fig. 1. Schematic diagram of the peripheral auditory system illustrating the pinna, external auditory meatus, the tympanic membrane, the middle ear cavity containing the ossicular chain (the malleus, incus and stapes), and the cochlea or inner ear. (adapted from[2]. Reprinted with permission Icon Learning Systems).

Both inner and outer hair cells contain a rigid cuticular plate at their apex, from which protrudes 50 to 150 stereocilia (Fig. 3) arranged in rows based upon their height. The short stereocilia are positioned towards the modiolus while the longer stereocilia are located towards the lateral wall of the cochlea. Stereocilia are mechanically coupled to one another via 'tip-links' [6] (Fig. 3) which are known to play an important role in the mechanoelectrical transduction process (see §3.5). Incredibly, the mammalian ear appears sensitive to deflections of the stereocilia of less than 1 nm [7, 8].

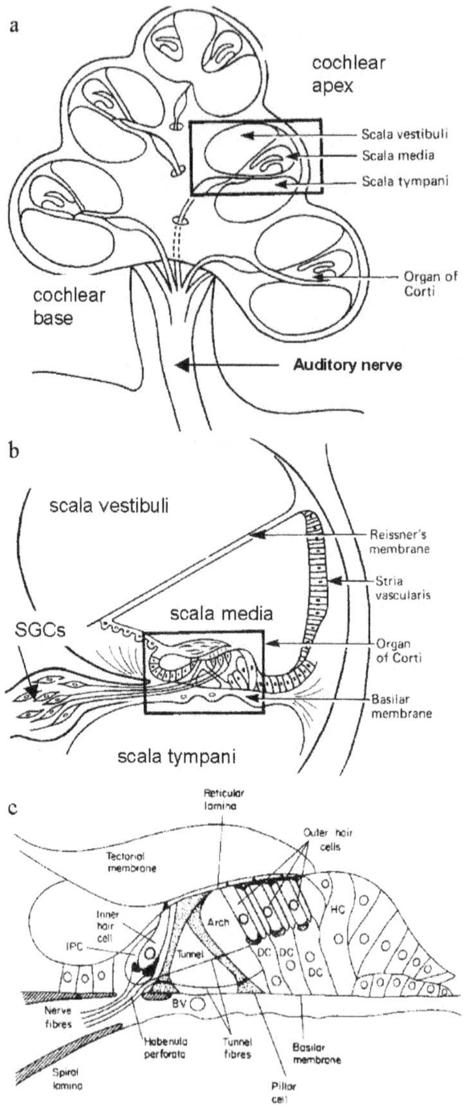

Fig. 2. (a) Transverse section of the mammalian cochlea illustrating the cochlear ducts spiraling around the modiolus, which contains the auditory nerve. (from [5]. Reprinted with permission Elsevier Science). (b) A magnified view of the cochlear duct in cross section illustrating the fluid filled scala tympani, scala media and scala vestibuli. (from [9]. Reprinted with permission Elsevier Science). (c) A diagram of the organ of Corti containing the sensory hair cells — a single row of inner hair cells and three rows of outer hair cells. Note that the organ of Corti is located on the basilar membrane, which separates the scala tympani from the scala media. DC, Deiters' cells; HC, Hensen's cells; IPC, Inner phalangeal cell; BV, blood vessel. (from [10]. Reprinted with permission Academic Press).

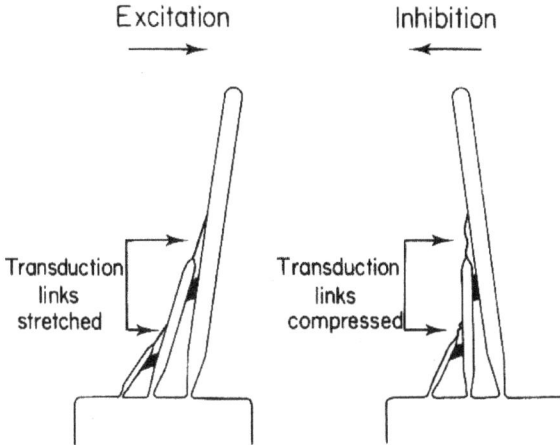

Fig. 3. Diagram illustrating the stereocilia located on the apical surface of both inner and outer hair cells. Stereocilia are coupled to one another via tip-links. Hair cell excitation occurs when the stereocilia are deflected towards the tallest stereocilium resulting in the stretching of tip-links, which then open to allow an influx of ions. In contrast, inhibition occurs when the stereocilia are deflected in the opposite direction, compressing the tip-links and thus preventing ion influx. (from [6]. Reprinted with permission Elsevier Science).

3.1.2. *Cochlear neuroanatomy*

There are three major components of cochlear innervation;
(i) afferent innervation;
(ii) efferent innervation; and
(iii) autonomic innervation.

We will discuss the afferent innervation of the cochlea in some detail, as this knowledge is central to our understanding of the principles of the cochlear implant (Chapter 3.6). This section will conclude with a brief description of efferent innervation of the cochlea.

3.1.2.1. *Afferent innervation of the organ of Corti*

There are approximately 30,000 afferent nerve fibres in the human cochlea [11]. As afferent neurons they convey information from the cochlea to the central auditory system. Their cell bodies, the spiral ganglion cells or auditory neurons, are located within Rosenthal's canal. This canal forms part of the modiolus. Rosenthal's canal follows the spiral course of the BM and borders the scala tympani via a thin shelf of bone known as the osseous spiral lamina (Fig. 4). Two types of auditory neurons are found within Rosenthal's canal; the most common (Type I) represents 90–95% of the total auditory neural population, and are characterized by a large myelinated cell body with a round nucleus and prominent nucleolus. In contrast, the Type II auditory neurons are half the size of the Type I cell body, possess a lobulated nucleus and an insignificant nucleolus. In most mammals Type II auditory neurons are unmyelinated and represent 5–10% of the auditory neural population [12] (Fig. 4).

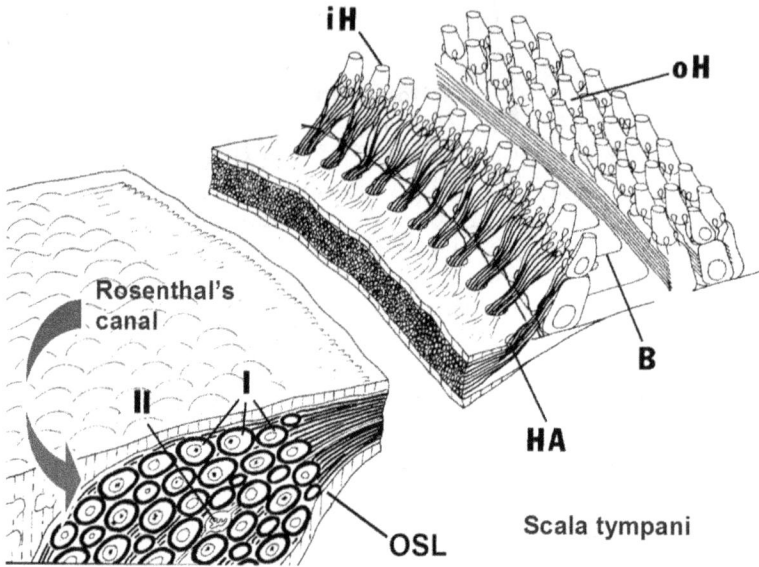

Fig. 4. Afferent innervation in the mammalian cochlea. Many Type I auditory neurons make direct synaptic contact with a single inner hair cell (iH); convergent innervation. In contrast, Type II auditory neurons project their processes across the floor of the basilar membrane (B) and make synaptic contact with numerous first, second and third row outer hair cells (oH); divergent innervation. HA — Habenula perforata, OSL — osseous spiral lamina. (adapted from [12]. Reprinted with permission Elsevier Science).

Auditory neurons are bipolar sensory cells which have a peripheral process that projects from the cell body to innervate the organ of Corti and a central axon that projects to the first relay center within the auditory brainstem, the cochlear nucleus [13]. Both the peripheral and central processes of Type I auditory neurons are myelinated while those of the Type II auditory neurons are typically unmyelinated.

The peripheral processes of auditory neurons project radially from their cell bodies to the organ of Corti. Processes from Type I auditory neurons lose their myelin as they pass through the habenula perforata (Fig. 4) and innervate the nearest IHC in a highly convergent manner; 20–30 Type I auditory neural processes make synaptic contact with a single IHC. In contrast, Type II auditory neural peripheral processes project in a basal direction along the floor of the organ of Corti and then innervate approximately 10 OHCs in a highly divergent manner (Fig. 4). The difference in afferent innervation of inner and outer hair cells reflects the different roles these two hair cell types play in the transduction process (see below).

3.1.2.2. Efferent innervation of the organ of Corti

The efferent pathways that innervate the organ of Corti originate in the superior olivary complex, located within the brainstem [14]. Being efferent neurons they exert some level of feedback and control over the cochlea from the central auditory system. Indeed there is evidence that they play a protective role for the organ of Corti in loud noise [15, 16].

There are two efferent pathways that project to the organ of Corti. The medial pathway consists of large myelinated fibres that synapse directly onto the OHCs, while the lateral system consists of small unmyelinated fibres that synapse onto the peripheral processes of the Type I auditory neurons just below the IHC (Fig. 5). The differences in the anatomy of efferent innervation onto the hair cells in the organ of Corti, suggests a more direct role of the medial efferents in modulating cochlea gain (by dampening the outer hair cell amplifier response; see §3.3.2). Conversely, the lateral efferents may have less direct modulatory effect on the response of the IHC, since this efferent synapse is axodendritic in nature and does not synapse directly onto the IHC, but rather the IHC afferent synapse (Fig. 5).

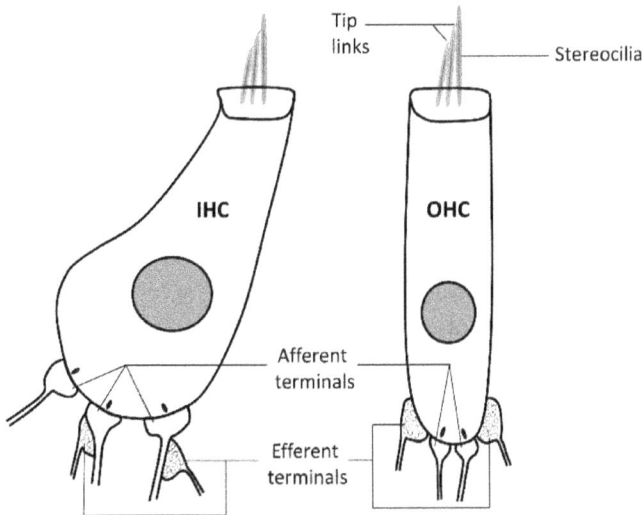

Fig. 5. Schematic representation of hair cell afferent and efferent innervation. The inner hair cells (IHCs) receive direct afferent innervation onto the basolateral surface of the cell, adjacent to the hair cell ribbon synapse (black filled discs). In addition, the IHCs receive indirect efferent innervation, with efferent terminals synapsing onto the Type I afferent terminal, prior to the afferent projection reaching the hair cell. Conversely, outer hair cells (OHCs) receive both afferent and efferent innervation directly onto the basolateral surface of the cell. Image adapted from [17].

3.2. Cochlear mechanics

3.2.1. The travelling wave and passive basilar membrane mechanics

The basilar membrane plays a key role in the analysis of sound by the auditory system. In cross section, the basilar membrane is narrow in length and relatively stiff in the base of the cochlear, while becoming wider and less stiff more apically. These mechanical characteristics provide the BM with a continuum of resonance frequencies along its length [18].

When sound pressure waves cause the tympanic membrane to vibrate, these oscillations are transmitted to the oval window via the middle ear ossicles. The stapes, which is fused to the cochlea oval window, faithfully reproduces these vibrations and causes a wave of displacement of the BM via movement of the cochlear fluids. This BM travelling wave propagates in an apical direction from the oval window. Different frequency components of the acoustic stimulus produce maximum displacement at specific sites along the BM; high frequencies cause maximal displacement in the base of the cochlea while lower frequencies cause maximal displacement at sites progressively more apical in the cochlea (Fig. 6). The BM travelling wave is an important stage in the analysis of sound, because the pattern of BM displacement is directly related to the frequency of the stimulus. Thus the cochlea is able to perform a spectral analysis of the incident acoustic stimulus by transposing acoustic frequency into position along the BM; a frequency-to-place or tonotopic transformation. The brain's decision as to the pitch of a sound is therefore determined, in part, on the basis of the site of maximum stimulation along the BM.

3.2.2. Active basilar membrane mechanics

The demonstration by von Békésy, of a tonotopic organization along the BM was performed in post mortem cochleae [18]. Research over the past 40 years has clearly demonstrated that there is also an active component to BM tuning that is only observed in living, healthy cochleae (Fig. 7). This active component of the tuning curve is known as the "active tip" and can add an additional 30–40 dB of sensitivity, thus providing the exquisite tuning associated with normal hearing. When the cochlea is in a poor physiological state, due for example to loud noise or ototoxic drug exposure, this sharply tuned component is lost and the tuning resembles that of the BM in the post mortem condition [8, 20, 21]. Clinically, this results in a loss of sensitivity in those individuals who may have damaged or non-functional outer hair cells. This indicates that the healthy cochlea contains both a sensitive, metabolically active and sharply tuned mechanism in addition to the relatively broadly tuned passive BM mechanics (Fig. 7).

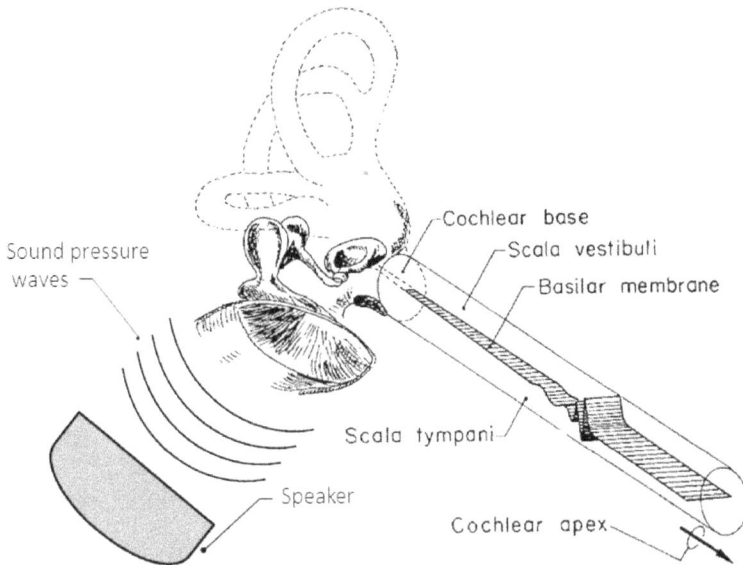

Fig. 6. Schematic diagram of the BM travelling wave in response to sound pressure waves on the tympanic membrane at one point in time. The high frequency components of the travelling wave (towards the middle ear) have already been removed in this example. As the wave propagates in an apical direction it becomes dominated by low frequency components and its velocity is reduced. The normally coiled mammalian cochlea has been straightened here for clarity. (Adapted from [*19*]. Reprinted with permission Journal of Neuroscience).

The exquisite tuning of the BM observed in physiologically normal cochleae, can also be detected at both the level of the hair cell (via receptor potentials [*22, 23*]) and single auditory nerve fibers (via neural spike activity [*24*]).

What is the source of this active component of BM mechanics? Studies of isolated OHC have revealed that these cells are capable of changing length in response to acoustic stimulation; OHCs shorten when depolarized and lengthen when hyperpolarized [*25-27*] (see §3.5). It is thought that this OHC motility feeds mechanical energy back into the BM, significantly enhancing its tuning properties [*19, 28*] (Fig. 8). Evidence suggests that large numbers of voltage-sensitive displacement motors are located along the lateral wall of the OHC, giving rise to this active process [*7, 29*]. This motor molecule has been identified as a membrane protein called prestin [*30, 31*]. Unlike most cellular motors (e.g., in muscle contraction), OHC motility does not require adenosine triphosphate (ATP) or calcium, but is driven by changes in the cells' membrane potential [*29, 32*]. Thus the OHC, which has little afferent input to the central auditory pathway, feeds additional mechanical energy into the BM thereby enhancing the BM's tuning characteristics in healthy cochleae. The rich efferent innervation of the OHC appears to exercise some control over this active process by reducing the efficiency of the OHC motor in the presence of loud noise [15, 16], thus reducing the potential damage caused by exposure to loud noise.

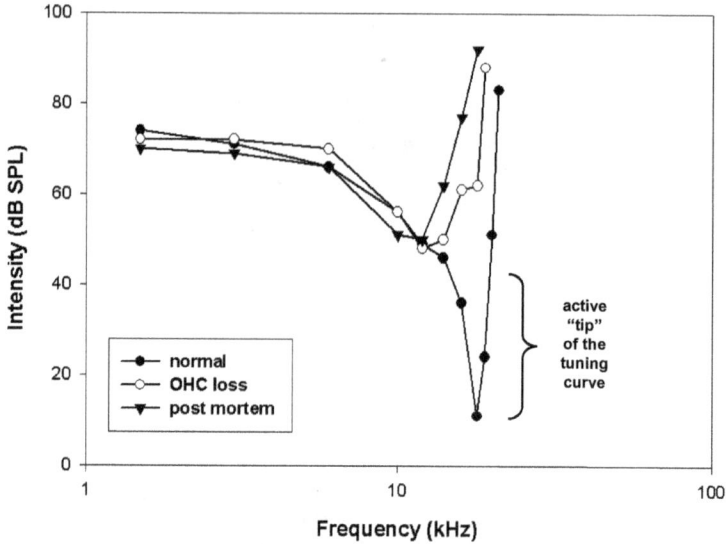

Fig. 7. Basilar membrane frequency threshold curve. Solid circles indicate data recorded from a normal cochlea; open circles show reduced tuning characteristics when the condition of the cochlea has deteriorated; triangles illustrate the post-mortem response of the BM. (adapted from [8]. Reprinted with permission Acoustical Society of America).

3.3. The endocochlear potential

In healthy cochleae, endolymph within the scala media is maintained at a resting DC potential of +80 mV relative to perilymph [34]. This so-called endocochlear potential (EP) is related to the high K^+ concentration of endolymph (Fig. 8). The EP is generated by an energy consuming process involving the active transport of multiple ions into the stria vascularis through the fibrocytes located on the lateral wall of the scala media [35] (Fig. 2b). In order to maintain the unique ionic composition of endolymph, the scala media is bounded by occluding tight junctions that minimize the movement of ions across membrane boundaries. The EP is integral to the hair cell transduction process and, therefore, for normal auditory function (Fig. 8). In contrast to endolymph, the DC potential of perilymph is similar to that of surrounding plasma and bone (i.e., 0 mV).

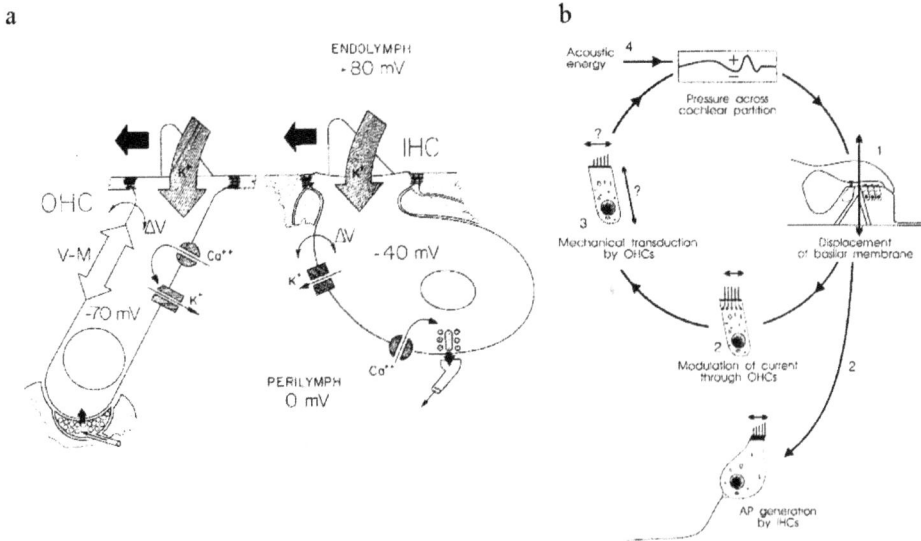

Fig. 8. (a) Diagram of inner and outer hair cells (IHC and OHC, respectively) illustrating the depolarization process. Deflection of the stereocilia towards the tallest stereocilium (black arrows) opens mechanical ion channels. Potassium ions (K^+) flow into the cell as a result of the electrical gradient created by the EP (+80 mV) and the cells polarization voltage (-40 mV IHC; -70 mV OHC). In the IHC, depolarization opens voltage sensitive Calcium (Ca^{2+}) channels that initiate the release of the excitatory neurotransmitter thereby giving rise to the generation of an action potential in the Type I auditory neurons. Finally, voltage sensitive K^+ channels are activated to remove K^+ and re-establish the polarization voltage. In the OHC, depolarization activates the voltage sensitive motile motor (V-M), feeding energy back into the BM. Voltage sensitive Ca^{2+} channels are then activated which in turn activates K^+ channels to re-establish the cells polarization potential. (from [19]. Reprinted with permission Journal of Neuroscience). (b) Schematic diagram illustrating the role of both inner and outer hair cells in the transduction process. 1. Displacement of the BM results in deflection of the stereocilia of both types of hair cells. 2. The inner hair cells initiate action potentials in Type I auditory neurons by release of the excitatory neurotransmitter. 3. Outer hair cells shorten and lengthen in response to depolarization and hyperpolarization, respectively. 4. Because the OHC is tightly coupled to the organ of Corti (via stereocilia attachment to the tectorial membrane) their motile activity is fed back into the BM as the active component, thereby improving the sensitivity of the cochlea by up to 40 dB. (from [33]. Reprinted with permission Elsevier Science).

3.4. *Hair cell transduction*

Sensory receptor cells and neurons maintain a negative DC potential at rest of typically 40–70 mV relative to their extracellular environment, i.e., they are polarized. In order to initiate the release of excitatory neurotransmitter (sensory receptor cells) or propagate an action potential (neurons), the cell must be depolarized — the negative DC potential must be lowered. This is achieved by the transport of positively charged ions into the cell via selective ion channels located in the cell membrane. As noted above, the apical surface of hair cells are bathed in

K$^+$-rich endolymph, which is maintained at +80 mV relative to perilymph (the base of the hair cells are bathed in a filtrate of perilymph and therefore rest at 0 mV). The EP, together with the resting polarizing voltage of hair cells (-40 mV for IHCs; -70 mV for OHCs), results in a voltage drop of 120 mV and 150 mV across the apical surface of the IHCs and OHCs, respectively (Fig. 8a). This large potential difference is central to the hair cell transduction process. Drugs that significantly reduce the EP are therefore capable of causing a profound hearing loss [36, 37].

Deflection of the hair cell stereocilia towards the tallest stereocilium in response to BM displacement, stretches tip-link coupling and opens mechanical ion channels containing transmembrane proteins [38] located in the sterocillia [7] (Fig. 3). Potassium ions then enter the cell down their electrical gradient leading to hair cell excitation [39, 40] (depolarization; Fig. 8a). Equally, deflection of stereocilia towards the smallest stereocilium compresses tip-links and reduces the probability of these mechanical ion channels opening. This in turn results in an increase in the hair cell polarizing voltage (hyperpolarization).

Depolarization of the IHC results in the release of the excitatory neurotransmitter glutamate, that in turn initiates the generation of an action potential (AP) in Type I auditory nerve fibres (ANFs). The response of IHCs following depolarization therefore contrasts with the motile response of the OHCs.

It is important to note that the transduction process is a graded one. Even at rest (i.e., in the absence of acoustic stimulation) some K$^+$ channels open and neurotransmitter is released spontaneously from the IHC. With increasing excitatory deflection of the stereocilia greater numbers of K$^+$ channels are opened, producing a graded depolarization of the hair cell and a graded increase in AP generation in the auditory nerve. Conversely, with increasing deflection of the stereocilia in the direction of the smallest stereocilium (i.e., inhibitory), a graded hyperpolarization of the cell membrane is observed due to greater numbers of K$^+$ channels closing. This in turn results in a graded reduction in neural spike activity below spontaneous activity (see below).

3.5. *Hair cell synapse with the auditory neuron*

During development, Type I auditory neurons extend their branched peripheral fibers towards the IHCs. The exuberant growth of the fibers is refined via neural repulsion mechanisms and the redundant branches eliminated [41-43]. The resultant innervation pattern is a single unbranched peripheral fiber of the Type I auditory neuron forming a synapse with one IHC. This arrangement is particularly suited for the rapid and temporally precise transmission of auditory information required for auditory processing [43]. Each IHC is innervated by multiple Type I ANFs with the number ranging from 10-30 [44, 45].

The cochlear hair cells contain specialised synapses, called ribbon synapses, which are particularly suited to high rate stimulation. The synaptic ribbons are found in both IHCs and OHCs [46] and are important for the release and replenishment of synaptic vesicles containing neurotransmitters. In recent years, these synapses can be labelled using sophisticated immunohistochemical techniques, and the number, size and distribution of puncta quantified (Fig. 9). Synaptic density is not uniform along the tonotopic gradient of the cochlea. For example, IHCs in the region of the cochlea most sensitive to sound (e.g. the most sensitive region in the audiogram) have the greatest density of synapses [43]. Furthermore, there is morphological and functional variability in the ribbon synapses within a hair cell, with ribbons located on the central side of the hair cell, closest to the ANFs, tending to be larger in size having greater synaptic strength than ribbon synapses on the lateral side of the hair cell [47]. The high threshold, low spontaneous rate ANFs (see §3.7.4) typically form synaptic connections on the central side of the hair cell [48] suggesting that ribbon synapse properties contribute to the heterogeneity in the functional properties of the ANFs. Interestingly it is these synaptic connections that are most susceptible to damage following exposure to sounds at moderate to high intensities [49, 50].

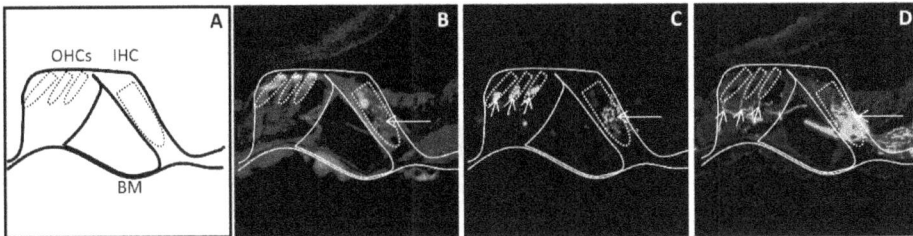

Fig. 9. Immunohistochemical studies can label various components of the hair cell to auditory neuron synapse. **(A)** Illustration of the organ of Corti in transverse section, showing one row of inner hair cells (IHCs) and three adjacent rows of outer hair cells (OHCs), located on the basilar membrane (BM). **(B)** Ribbon synapses located on the basolateral surface of the IHC (arrow) below the IHC nucleus. **(C)** Synapsin 1 immunochemistry as observed in the basolateral poles of both the IHC and OHCs (arrows), but with greater density on the IHC (longer arrow; reflecting synapses from up to 30 Type 1 auditory neurons which converge onto the base of each IHC). **(D)** The processes of the auditory neurons (both afferent and efferent) labelled with the pan neuronal marker, neurofilament. Note the concentration of fibres around the base of the IHC and the projecting neural fibres across the tunnel of Corti to the OHCs (smaller arrows). Scale bar = 10 µm. Perforated lines show approximate circumference of the inner and outer hair cell bodies. Images generously provided by Ms Tomoko Hyakumura.

3.6. *The response of the auditory nerve*

We have already noted that 90–95% of ANFs innervate the IHC. This means that almost all afferent input to the central auditory system comes via APs generated at the level of the IHC.

3.6.1. *Spontaneous activity*

Spontaneous activity in ANFs varies from levels as low as 0.5 spikes/s up to 120 spikes/s in the absence of acoustic stimulation. Spike rates increase above this spontaneous level during acoustic stimulation.

3.6.2. *Activity during acoustic stimulation*

Following the onset of an acoustic tone ANFs show an initial burst of neural activity which declines rapidly over the first 10–20 ms, and then more slowly over periods of minutes (Fig. 10). These periods of rapid and more long-term adaptation are thought to reflect changes in the neurotransmitter release process from the IHC [51]. The timing of the first action potential evoked by the acoustic stimulus is important for signalling the sound onset and also to signal fast amplitude transients required for the interpretation of temporal fine structure in complex sounds [52].

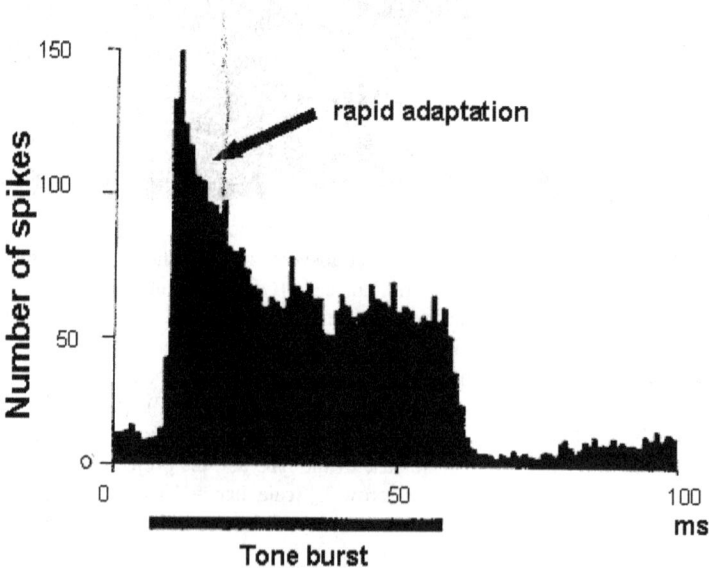

Fig. 10. A post-stimulus time histogram plotting the number of AP's following the onset of a tone burst (black bar). The tone-burst is repeated many times in order to obtain an accurate profile of the timing of APs. The small delay between the onset of the tone pip and the onset of AP activity reflects acoustic travel time, the propagation of the BM travelling wave and the IHC/ANF synaptic delay. (adapted from [24]. Reprinted with permission MIT Press).

3.6.3. *Frequency selectivity*

All ANFs exhibit highly tuned frequency response characteristics similar to the frequency-threshold curve measured at the level of the BM (Fig. 6). At the ANF level, these curves are obtained by measuring the intensity at frequencies where the rate of AP generation is increased above spontaneous level by some defined amount (Fig. 11a). The best or characteristic frequency (CF) of each ANF is determined by the location along the tonotopically organized BM at which that fiber innervates the organ of Corti [53]. High frequency CF fibers project to sites within the cochlear base, while lower frequency CF fibers project to more apical sites. Thus the orderly tonotopic organization of the BM is maintained within the auditory nerve. Our ability to discriminate high frequencies (>4–5 kHz) is thought to be solely based on the site of BM stimulation and is known as the place theory of frequency coding.

At lower frequencies, IHC receptor potentials preserve the phase information contained within the incident acoustic stimulus, i.e., they become phase-locked to the stimulus. This fine temporal information is also observed in ANF responses (Fig. 11b), and forms the basis of the volley theory of frequency coding [54].

Although an individual ANF can respond with a limited number of synchronized APs, within a population of these fibers an AP can be generated for each cycle of the acoustic stimulus, thus providing the central auditory system with temporally encoded frequency information. Therefore, for frequencies below 4–5 kHz, including almost all of the human speech-frequency range, phase-locked activity of ANFs provides important pitch or frequency cues.

3.6.4. *Intensity coding in ANFs*

Increasing the intensity of a tone at CF will produce an increase in the discharge rate of an ANF (Fig. 12). The majority of ANFs exhibit a relatively narrow dynamic range (~30–40 dB) over which their discharge rate increases. At intensities above the fiber's dynamic range the discharge rate fails to increase, i.e., the fiber saturates. Once saturated, the fiber can no longer provide an intensity cue. These ANFs are characterized by their high spontaneous rates and low thresholds [57]. Other ANF populations possess low rates of spontaneous activity, higher thresholds and wider dynamic ranges [57], and are believed to play an important role in intensity coding at high stimulus intensities. For example, at intensities above which the most sensitive ANFs saturate, these high threshold fibers are recruited and their discharge rate is sensitive to stimulus intensity over a wide dynamic range (50–70 dB; Fig. 12).

a

b

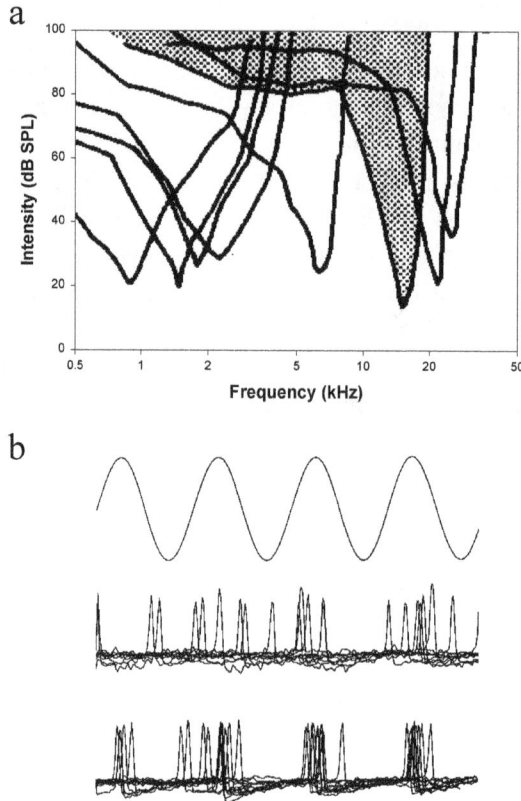

Fig. 11. (a) Typical ANF frequency-threshold curves from a normal mammalian cochlea. The eight examples shown here illustrate the highly tuned tip, the rapid high-frequency cut off (100–600 dB/octave) and a more gradual low frequency cut off. The stippled area illustrates the response area for a fiber with a CF of ~15 kHz, i.e., the neuron will respond to any combination of intensity and frequency within that area (from [55], reprinted with permission). (b) Phase-locking of ANFs to a 200 Hz tone. The neural responses at near-threshold (middle panel) and supra-threshold (bottom panel) represent several overlaid traces of an ANF response to the tone (top panel) (from [56]. Reprinted with permission Elsevier Science).

3.7. Conclusion

The role of the cochlea is central to our understanding of the function of the auditory system. It receives mechanohydraulic input from the middle ear and outputs spatio-temporal firing patterns over an array of 30,000 ANFs. In the following section we will briefly review the role of the central auditory pathway in interpreting information received from the cochlea, in order to provide the sense of hearing.

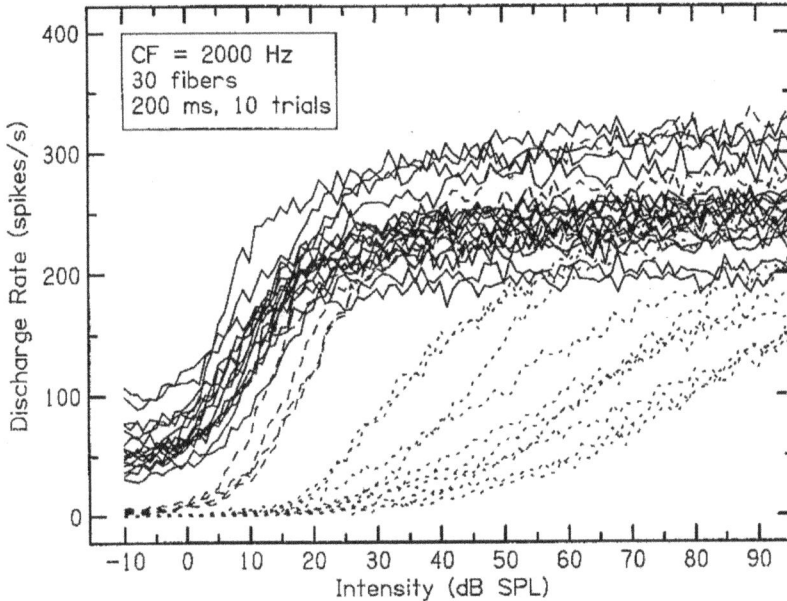

Fig. 12. Response of ANFs to stimulus intensity. Modeled data, illustrating the discharge rate of 30 ANFs connected to a single IHC (CF: 2 kHz) as a function of stimulus intensity. The majority of fibers are very sensitive (threshold <10dB SPL), have high levels of spontaneous activity (40–100 spikes/s), and narrow dynamic ranges (most saturate by 30dB SPL). Lower spontaneously active fibres (illustrated here as dashed and dotted lines) are less sensitive but exhibit wide dynamic ranges. While these curves are derived from a model they are physiologically realistic. (Reproduced with permission from Dr. E. Javel).

4. The Central Auditory System

The central auditory pathway is a highly complex structure containing over a dozen centers from brainstem nuclei to the cortex. This pathway is responsible for processing neural input from the cochlea, resulting in the perception of auditory stimuli as complex as human speech. An overview of the major centers within the central auditory pathway is illustrated in Fig. 13. An extensive review of this pathway is beyond the scope of this chapter. The interested reader is referred to several excellent books on this topic [*58-63*].

4.1. *Cochlear nucleus*

All ANFs terminate in the ipsilateral cochlear nucleus (CN; [*13*]). Based on cellular architecture, the CN has been divided into three distinct regions; the anteroventral (AVCN), posteroventral (PVCN) and dorsal (DCN) cochlear nuclei

[*64, 65*]. On entering the CN, ANFs bifurcate into an ascending branch projecting to the AVCN and a descending branch that projects to the PVCN and the DCN [*13*]. This projection is achieved in a highly organized manner, producing a precise tonotopic organization within all three subdivisions [*66, 67*]. The fact that the CN is tonotopically organized has important implication for the development of central auditory prostheses based on CN stimulation (see Chapter 3.6), although this organization is preserved throughout most central auditory centers [*68*].

The various cell types that help define the three distinct subdivisions of the CN correlate with the wide variety of response types observed electrophysiologically [*66, 68*]. These various cell types preserve specific spatio-temporal features of the ANF response, and marks the first stage of parallel processing of auditory information within the central auditory pathway.

4.2. *Superior olivary complex*

The superior olivary complex (SOC) consists of three major auditory nuclei, the medial (MSO) and lateral (LSO) superior olivary complex (Fig. 13) and the medial nucleus of the trapezoid body (MNTB; not illustrated in Fig. 13). The SOC receives input from both cochlear nuclei, and is therefore the first stage of the auditory pathway to process information from both ears. In particular, neurons from the MSO appear sensitive to interaural time delays while LSO neurons appear sensitive to interaural intensity or loudness differences. It is thought that the cells within these nuclei provide important cues for sound localization [61].

4.3. *Inferior colliculus*

Axons of neurons from the CN and SOC project either directly, or via the nucleus of the lateral lemniscus, to the major auditory midbrain nucleus, the inferior colliculus (IC). The IC is an obligatory relay nucleus along the ascending auditory pathway and therefore represents the principal source of ascending inputs to the auditory thalamus [68, 69]. In this way the IC is believed to be key in the reintegration of multiple auditory inputs from the lower brainstem and in the beginning of auditory perception.

Based on cellular architecture, the IC has been divided into three major subdivisions; the central (ICC), dorsal (DC) and lateral (LN) nuclei (Fig. 13). The ICC, which is the major relay center, exhibits a clear tonotopic organization based on electrophysiological and functional mapping studies [*70, 71*]. This tonotopicity is consistent with the laminar organization of the nucleus [*72, 73*], in which frequency ranges are grouped into iso-frequency laminae. However there appears to be partial segregation of ascending inputs, as each brainstem nucleus projects to a localized region rather than the entire ICC. The ICC is a site of convergence and integration of auditory input from multiple nuclei, and complex response properties of these neurons reflects the spatio-temporal integration of both excitatory and inhibitory activity [*58*].

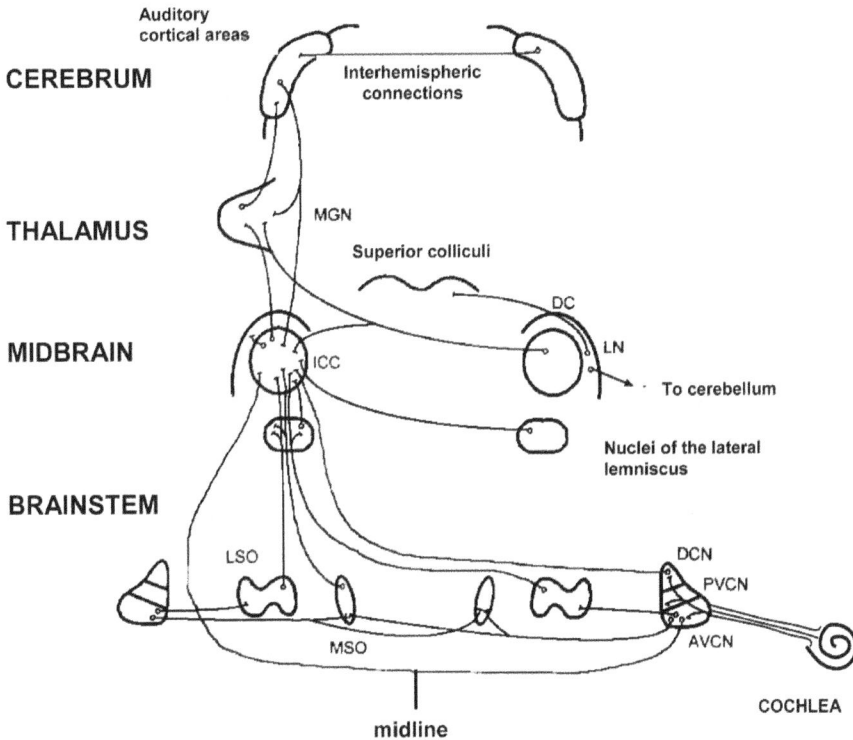

Fig. 13. Schematic diagram of the major ascending auditory pathway from the right cochlea. Note that above the level of the CN, this pathway is predominantly a contralateral one. A number of minor nuclei and projections have been omitted for clarity. AVCN, anteroventral cochlear nucleus; DCN, dorsal cochlear nucleus; DC dorsal cortex of the inferior colliculus; ICC, central nucleus of the inferior colliculus; LN, lateral nucleus of the inferior colliculus; LSO, lateral superior olive; MGN, medial geniculate nucleus; MSO, medial superior olive; PVCN, posteroventral cochlear nucleus. (adapted from [*58*], with permission).

Both DC and LN neurons exhibit broad and often complex tuning characteristics [*58*]. These nuclei make connections with non-auditory structures and are thought to play a role in acousticomotor reflexes and rapid orienting responses (LN), and attention and arousal mechanisms (DC) [*58*].

4.4. *Medial geniculate nucleus*

The medial geniculate nucleus (MGN) is the principal auditory relay nucleus within the thalamus. Ascending afferents come mainly from the ipsilateral IC, projecting to the ventral division of the MGN. This is the largest MGN division and exhibits the most extensive degree of tonotopic organization. Neurons from the ventral MGN project to the ipsilateral primary auditory cortex. The dorsal MGN receives afferents from outside the ICC (including the DC). These neurons are broadly tuned to acoustic stimuli, and project to secondary auditory cortical fields. Finally, the medial MGN receives a variety of afferent inputs including the LN of the IC. Tuning characteristics of these neurons are quite variable. They project widely in all auditory cortical areas and also parts of the somatosensory cortex.

4.5. *Auditory cortex*

Each sensory pathway, including audition, touch and vision, has assigned to it a reasonably specific cortical representation. In all mammalian species studied to date, there is at least one representation of the cochlea within the cerebral cortex known as the primary auditory cortex (AI). Secondary auditory fields have also been identified in many species. These auditory fields are located in the temporal lobe of the cortex, and in most non-primate mammals this area is mainly localized to the lateral surface of the temporal lobe. In contrast, the auditory cortex (AC) in humans lies deep within the sylvian fissue of the transverse temporal gyrus (Heschl's gyrus). This inaccessibility has important implications for the development of auditory prostheses based on electrical stimulation of the AC.

Like other auditory centers, the AC has been characterized using electrophysiological recording techniques together with cellular architecture [59]. The AC, is arranged into six vertical layers of cells located within a 2 mm sheet of neurons on the cortical surface. Each layer is defined on the basis of cell type and cell density.

Major afferent input into the AC comes from the IC (predominantly the ICC, but also the DN and LN) via the MGN. The AI demonstrates clear tonotopic organization in all mammals studied to date [59]. Secondary auditory fields usually surround the primary field, and typically exhibit some degree of tonotopic organization.

Anatomical studies of the AI suggest that it is organized vertically into functional columns of 200–300 μm in diameter that extends through the six cortical layers. Neurons within a column (estimated to be in the order of ~5000) share common traits such as best frequency and binaural responses properties [59]. Each module receives the same thalamic input (predominantly to layer IV), which is then distributed within the module via intrinsic connections. Information is processed within the module before the output is sent to contralateral auditory areas, other cortical modules within the hemisphere, as well as the MGN and the IC.

The neocortex is the most complex structure within the central nervous system. It is therefore not surprising that we remain unsure of the precise role the AC plays in audition. It is known to play an important role in sound localization and is necessary for selective attention to auditory stimuli and short-term auditory memory, and may play an important role in the analysis of complex sounds such as speech [59]. However, relatively little is known of its relationship to cortical areas devoted to long-term auditory memory, speech perception and speech production.

5. Conclusion

This chapter provides an overview of the mammalian auditory system with a particular emphasis on the anatomy and physiology of the cochlea. This background provides important insights into the design and implementation of both cochlear implants and central auditory prostheses.

Acknowledgments

This work was supported by the Garnett Passe and Rodney Williams Memorial Foundation, the National Institute on Deafness and other Communication Disorders (RO1 DC015031-01) and the Australian National Health and Medical Research Council. The Bionics Institute acknowledges the support it receives from the Victorian Government through its Operational Infrastructure Support Program.

References

1. J. Rosowski, L. Carney, T. Lynch III, W. Peake, The effectiveness of external and middle ears in coupling acoustic power into the cochlea, in *Peripheral Auditory Mechanisms,* eds. J. L. H. J. B. Allen, A. Hubbard, S. T. Neely, and A. Tubis, (Springer, Berlin, 1986), pp. 3-12.
2. D. Myers, W. D. Schlosser, R. J. Wolfson, R. A. Winchester, and N. H. Carmel, Otologic diagnosis and the treatment of deafness, *Clin Symp,* **22**, 35-69 (1970).
3. P. Dallos, A. N. Popper, and R. R. Fay, The cochlea, *Springer Handbook of Auditory Research,* eds. R. R. Fay and A. N. Popper (Springer-Verlag, New York, 1996), pp. 1-551.
4. A. C. Lysaght, S.-Y. Kao, J. A. Paulo, S. N. Merchant, H. Steen, and K. M. Stankovic, Proteome of human perilymph, *Journal of Proteome Research,* **10**, 3845-3851 (2011).
5. C. A. Smith, O. H. Lowry, and M. L. Wu, The electrolytes of the labyrinthine fluids, *The Laryngoscope,* **64**, 141-153 (1954).

6. J. Pickles, S. Comis, and M. Osborne, Cross-links between stereocilia in the guinea pig organ of Corti, and their possible relation to sensory transduction, *Hearing Research,* **15**, 103-112 (1984).

7. A. J. Hudspeth, Mechanical amplification of stimuli by hair cells, *Current opinion in neurobiology,* **7**, 480-486 (1997).

8. P. Sellick, R. Patuzzi, and B. Johnstone, Measurement of basilar membrane motion in the guinea pig using the Mössbauer technique, *The Journal of the Acoustical Society of America,* **72**, 131-141 (1982).

9. I. Friedmann and J. C. Ballantyne, *Ultrastructural atlas of the inner ear,* (Butterworth-Heinemann, London) 1984.

10. J. O. Pickles, *An Introduction to the Physiology of Hearing,* (Academic Press, London, 1982).

11. J. B. Nadol, Jr., Patterns of neural degeneration in the human cochlea and auditory nerve: implications for cochlear implantation, *Otolaryngol Head Neck Surg,* **117**, 220-228 (1997).

12. H. Spoendlin, in *Ultrastructural atlas of the inner ear,* eds. I. Friedmann, and J. Ballantyne, (Butterworths, London, 1984), pp. 133-164.

13. R. L. De No, *The primary acoustic nuclei,* (Raven Press, New York, 1981).

14. W. B. Warr and J. J. Guinan, Efferent innervation of the organ of Corti: two separate systems, *Brain Research* **173**, 152-155 (1979).

15. M. C. Brown, A. L. Nuttall, and R. I. Masta, Intracellular recordings from cochlear inner hair cells: effects of stimulation of the crossed olivocochlear efferents, *Science,* **222**, 69-72 (1983).

16. R. Rajan, Centrifugal pathways protect hearing sensitivity at the cochlea in noisy environments that exacerbate the damage induced by loud sound, *The Journal of Neuroscience,* **20**, 6684-6693 (2000).

17. P. W. Flint and C. W. Cummings, *Cummings Otolaryngology - Head and Neck Surgery,* 5th ed. (Elsevier Health Sciences, New York, 2010).

18. G. Von Békésy and E. G. Wever, *Experiments in hearing,* vol. 8 (McGraw-Hill, New York, 1960).

19. P. Dallos, The active cochlea, *Journal of Neuroscience* **12**, 4575-4585 (1992).

20. W. Rhode, in *Basic mechanisms in hearing,* ed. A. R. Moller (Academic Press New York, 1973), pp. 49-67.

21. M. A. Ruggero and N. C. Rich, Application of a commercially-manufactured Doppler-shift laser velocimeter to the measurement of basilar-membrane vibration, *Hearing Research* **51**, 215-230 (1991).

22. P. Dallos, J. Santos-Sacchi and Å. Flock, Cochlear outer hair cells: Intracellular recordings, *Science* **218**, 582-584 (1982).

23. I. Russell and P. Sellick, Intracellular studies of hair cells in the mammalian cochlea, *The Journal of Physiology* **284**, 261-290 (1978).

24. N. Y.-S. Kiang, Discharge Patterns of Single Fibers in the Cat's Auditory Nerve, *Research Monograph 35,* (MIT Press, Cambridge, MA, 1965), pp. 1-154.

25. J. F. Ashmore, A fast motile response in guinea-pig outer hair cells: the cellular basis of the cochlear amplifier, *J Physiol* **388**, 323-347 (1987).

26. W. E. Brownell, C. R. Bader, D. Bertrand, and Y. De Ribaupierre, Evoked mechanical responses of isolated cochlear outer hair cells, *Science* **227**, 194-196 (1985).

27. H. Zenner, U. Zimmermann, and U. Schmitt, Reversible contraction of isolated mammalian cochlear hair cells, *Hearing Research* **18**, 127-133 (1985).

28. B. Johnstone, R. Patuzzi, and G. Yates, Basilar membrane measurements and the travelling wave, *Hearing Research* **22**, 147-153 (1986).

29. P. Dallos, Outer hair cells: the inside story, *The Annals of Otology, Rhinology & Laryngology, Supplement* **168**, 16-22 (1997).

30. D. Oliver *et al.*, Intracellular anions as the voltage sensor of prestin, the outer hair cell motor protein, *Science* **292**, 2340-2343 (2001).

31. J. Zheng, W. Shen, D. Z. He, K. B. Long, L. D. Madison, and P. Dallos, Prestin is the motor protein of cochlear outer hair cells, *Nature* **405**, 149-155 (2000).

32. M. Holley and J. Ashmore, On the mechanism of a high-frequency force generator in outer hair cells isolated from the guinea pig cochlea, *Proceedings of the Royal Society of London B: Biological Sciences* **232**, 413-429 (1988).

33. G. K. Yates, B. M. Johnstone, R. B. Patuzzi, and D. Robertson, Mechanical preprocessing in the mammalian cochlea, *Trends in Neurosciences* **15**, 57-61 (1992).

34. G. von Békésy, DC resting potentials inside the cochlear partition, *The Journal of the Acoustical Society of America* **24**, 72-75 (1952).

35. J. P. McGuirt, and B. A. Schulte, Distribution of immunoreactive alpha-and beta-subunit isoforms of Na, K-ATPase in the gerbil inner ear, *Journal of Histochemistry & Cytochemistry* **42**, 843-853 (1994).

36. S. L. Garetz and J. Schacht, Ototoxicity: of mice and men, in eds. T. R. Van De Water, A. N. Popper, and R. R. Fay, *Clinical Aspects of Hearing*, (Springer, New York, 1996), pp. 116-154.

37. J. Syka, Experimental models of sensorineural hearing loss - effects of noise and ototoxic drugs on hearing, in eds. H. Autrum, E. R. Perl, R. F. Schmidt, H. Shimazu, W. D. Willis, and D. Ottoson, *Progress in Sensory Physiology 9*, (Springer, New York, 1989), pp. 97-170.

38. B. Pan, G. S. Géléoc, Y. Asai, G. C. Horwitz, K. Kurima, K. Ishikawa, Y. Kawashima, A. J. Griffith, and J. R. Holt, TMC1 and TMC2 are components of the mechanotransduction channel in hair cells of the mammalian inner ear, *Neuron* **79**, 504-515 (2013).

39. A. Hudspeth and D. Corey, Sensitivity, polarity, and conductance change in the response of vertebrate hair cells to controlled mechanical stimuli, *Proceedings of the National Academy of Sciences* **74**, 2407-2411 (1977).

40. I. Russell and G. Richardson, The morphology and physiology of hair cells in organotypic cultures of the mouse cochlea, *Hearing Research* **31**, 9-24 (1987).

41. J. M. Appler and L. V. Goodrich, Connecting the ear to the brain: Molecular mechanisms of auditory circuit assembly, *Prog Neurobiol* **93**, 488-508 (2011).

42. A. Brugeaud, M. Tong, L. Luo, and A. S. Edge, Inhibition of repulsive guidance molecule, RGMa, increases afferent synapse formation with auditory hair cells, *Dev Neurobiol* **74**, 457-466 (2014).

43. A. C. Meyer and T. Moser, Structure and function of cochlear afferent innervation, *Current Opinion in Otolaryngology & Head and Neck Surgery* **18**, 441-446 (2010).

44. M. C. Liberman, Single-neuron labeling in the cat auditory nerve, *Science* **216**, 1239-1241 (1982).

45. M. C. Liberman, L. W. Dodds, and S. Pierce, Afferent and efferent innervation of the cat cochlea: quantitative analysis with light and electron microscopy, *Journal of Comparative Neurology* **301**, 443-460 (1990).

46. H. M. Sobkowicz, J. E. Rose, G. E. Scott, and S. M. Slapnick, Ribbon synapses in the developing intact and cultured organ of Corti in the mouse, *The Journal of Neuroscience* **2**, 942-957 (1982).

47. T. Frank, D. Khimich, A. Neef, and T. Moser, Mechanisms contributing to synaptic Ca2+ signals and their heterogeneity in hair cells, *Proceedings of the National Academy of Sciences* **106**, 4483-4488 (2009).

48. A. Merchan-Perez and M. C. Liberman, Ultrastructural differences among afferent synapses on cochlear hair cells: correlations with spontaneous discharge rate, *Journal of Comparative Neurology* **371**, 208-221 (1996).

49. A. C. Furman, S. G. Kujawa, and M. C. Liberman, Noise-induced cochlear neuropathy is selective for fibers with low spontaneous rates, *Journal of Neurophysiology* **110**, 577-586 (2013).

50. L. Liberman and M. C. Liberman, Dynamics of cochlear synaptopathy after acoustic overexposure, *Journal of the Association for Research in Otolaryngology* **16**, 205-219,221 (2015).

51. W. F. Sewell, Neurotransmitters and synaptic transmission, in eds. P. Dallos, A. N. Popper and R. R. Fay, *The Cochlea* (Springer, New York, 1996), pp. 503-533.

52. P. Heil, First-spike latency of auditory neurons revisited, *Current Opinion in Neurobiology* **14**, 461-467 (2004).

53. M. C. Liberman, The cochlear frequency map for the cat: Labeling auditory-nerve fibers of known characteristic frequency, *The Journal of the Acoustical Society of America* **72**, 1441-1449 (1982).

54. J. E. Rose, J. F. Brugge, D. J. Anderson, and J. E. Hind, Phase-locked response to low-frequency tones in single auditory nerve fibers of the squirrel monkey, *Journal of Neurophysiology* **30**, 769-793 (1967).

55. R. J. Harrison, in eds. A. F Jahn and J. Santos-Sacchi, *Physiology of the Ear,* (Raven Press, New York, 1988), pp. 359-384.

56. E. Javel and J. B. Mott, Physiological and psychophysical correlates of temporal processes in hearing, *Hearing Research* **34**, 275-294 (1988).

57. M. C. Liberman, Auditory-nerve response from cats raised in a low-noise chamber, *The Journal of the Acoustical Society of America* **63**, 442-455 (1978).

58. L. Aitkin, *The Auditory Midbrain. Structure and Function in the Central Auditory Pathway,* (Humana Press, Clifton, New Jersey, 1986).

59. L. Aitkin, *The Auditory Cortex. Structural and Functional Bases of Auditory Perception.,* (Chapman and Hall, London, 1990).

60. G. Ehret and R. Romand, *The Central Auditory System,* (Oxford University Press, Oxford, 1996).

61. D. R. F. Irvine, *The Auditory Brainstem,* (Springer, Berlin, 1986).

62. R. Fay, *The Mammalian Auditory Pathway: Neurophysiology,* (Springer, New York, 1992).

63. D. B. Webster and R. R. Fay, *The Mammalian Auditory Pathway: Neuroanatomy,* (Springer, New York, 1992).

64. J. R. Brawer, D. K. Morest, and E. C. Kane, The neuronal architecture of the cochlear nucleus of the cat, *Journal of Comparative Neurology* **155**, 251-300 (1974).

65. K. K. Osen, Cytoarchitecture of the cochlear nuclei in the cat, *The Journal of Comparative Neurology* **136**, 453-484 (1969).

66. T. R. Bourk, J. P. Mielcarz, and B. E. Norris, Tonotopic organization of the anteroventral cochlear nucleus of the cat, *Hearing Research* **4**, 215-241 (1981).

67. W. Webster, J. Serviere, C. Batini, and S. Laplante, Autroradiographic demonstration with 2-[14 C] deoxyglucose of frequency selectivity in the auditory system of cats under conditions of functional activity, *Neuroscience Letters* **10**, 43-48 (1978).

68. E. M. Rouiller, Functional organization of the auditory pathways, in eds. G. Ehret and R. Romand, *The Central Auditory System,* (Oxford University Press, New York, 1997), pp. 3-96.

69. L. M. Aitkin, S. C. Phillips, Is the inferior colliculus an obligatory relay in the cat auditory system? *Neurosci Lett* **44**, 259-264 (1984).

70. M. M. Merzenich and M. D. Reid, Representation of the cochlea within the inferior colliculus of the cat, *Brain research* **77**, 397-415 (1974).

71. J. Servière, W. R. Webster, and M. B. Calford, Isofrequency labelling revealed by a combined [14C]-2-deoxyglucose, electrophysiological, and horseradish peroxidase study of the inferior colliculus of the cat, *Journal of Comparative Neurology* **228**, 463-477 (1984).

72. D. L. Oliver and D. K. Morest, The central nucleus of the inferior colliculus in the cat, *The Journal of Comparative Neurology* **222**, 237-264 (1984).

73. A. Rockel and E. Jones, The neuronal organization of the inferior colliculus of the adult cat. I. The central nucleus. *Journal of Comparative Neurology* **147**, 11-60 (1973).

Neuroplasticity

Pablo A. Celnik[1], Michael J. Makey[2], Esteban Fridman[3] and Leonardo G. Cohen[3]

[1] Department of Physical Medicine and Rehabilitation, Johns Hopkins University
[2] Department of Neurology, University of Maryland Medical System
[3] Human Cortical Physiology Section, NINDS, NIH
celnik@jhmi.edu, cohenl@ninds.nih.gov

In recent years our understanding of the organization of the cerebral cortex has changed. It is now known that the brain is capable of adaptation to environmental challenges (as in learning) and to functional disabilities produced by lesions. The existence of this process, often described as plasticity, stimulated the development of interventions geared to enhance plasticity when it plays a beneficial role and to inhibit it when it is detrimental. This chapter will review the use of transcranial magnetic stimulation, a noninvasive technique used to study and to modulate neuroplasticity in humans.

1. Introduction

The discovery in 1861 by Paul Broca [11] that the left inferior frontal cortex was actively involved in speech production heralded a century of domination by cerebral localizationists [62] Although there were few experimental studies and clinical observations that could have indicated that the central nervous system (CNS) can reorganize, these studies were not pursued because they directly challenged adherence of the cerebral localization dogma [62] The clinical wisdom was that the brain was hardwired with strict localization of function that left no room for reorganization.

In 1965, Hubel and Wiesel showed that visual experience during early life has a profound impact in shaping the responsiveness of individual cortical neurons [43]. This discovery, together with the finding of nerve growth factor (NGP) expressed in the adult brain [58], the demonstration of sprouting in the central nervous system [86,122], and the study of long-term potentiation (LTP) [8] all contributed to initiate an era of intense activity that saw the emergence and acceptance of the concept of brain plasticity, the ability of the brain to reorganize to compensate for lost function or new environmental requirements. This chapter will review some of the basic mechanisms of neuroplasticity in humans.

The cerebral cortex experiences constant remodeling and these changes are shaped by experience. Numerous studies have shown that deafferentation of the retina [19,48,119,121], cochlea [96] and skin [26,27,49,68,69,85] induce cortical reorganization. Cortical modifications have also been identified in the motor system after nerve transection [26-28,103], when limb positions were modified [104], after repetitive stimulation [75], after focal lesions of the motor cortex [77], with training of a small object retrieval [76], and after exercise using a target reaching task [1,71]. Similarly, cortical changes have been detected in the somatosensory system after interruption and reconnection of peripheral nerves [120], when crossing the connections between two peripheral nerves, after fusing different fingers [2], after moving islands of skin to new locations [70], when maintaining finger contact pressure for several seconds for food reward [45], and following training in discrimination of vibratory frequencies [90-93]. Clearly, these studies show that the adult cortex has the ability to reorganize.

2. Technical Considerations for the Study of Plasticity in Humans

The development of techniques such as electroencephalography (EEG), magneto encephalography (MEG), transcranial magnetic stimulation (TMS), functional magnetic resonance imaging (fMRI), and positron emission tomography (PET) have allowed the non-invasive study of brain plasticity in intact humans. Whereas functional neuroimaging methods can demonstrate patterns of activity in cortical and subcortical structures in association with behavior, electrophysiological tools can demonstrate a time correlation between brain activity and behavior.

Currently, one of the most extensively used electrophysiological techniques is transcranial magnetic stimulation (TMS; Fig. 1). In TMS a brief, strong current is passed through a wire (coil). The current passing through the wire induces a magnetic field that readily and painlessly passes through the subject's scalp and skull. The magnetic field in turn evokes electric currents. The magnitude of these currents drops as a function of the distance between the stimulating coil and the target neural structures[3,23,65,99,106]. The strength of the induced current is a function of the rate of change of the magnetic field, which is determined by the rate of change of the current in the coil. Thus, the current passed through the coil must change within few hundred microseconds to generate a current large enough to excite neurons in the brain. The stimulators commonly used today are able to activate cortical neurons at a depth of 1.5 to 2 cm underneath the scalp [30,100].

P. A. Celnik et al.

When applied to the motor cortex, TMS activates pyramidal tract neurons and distant neural structures trans-synaptically [54,82,124].

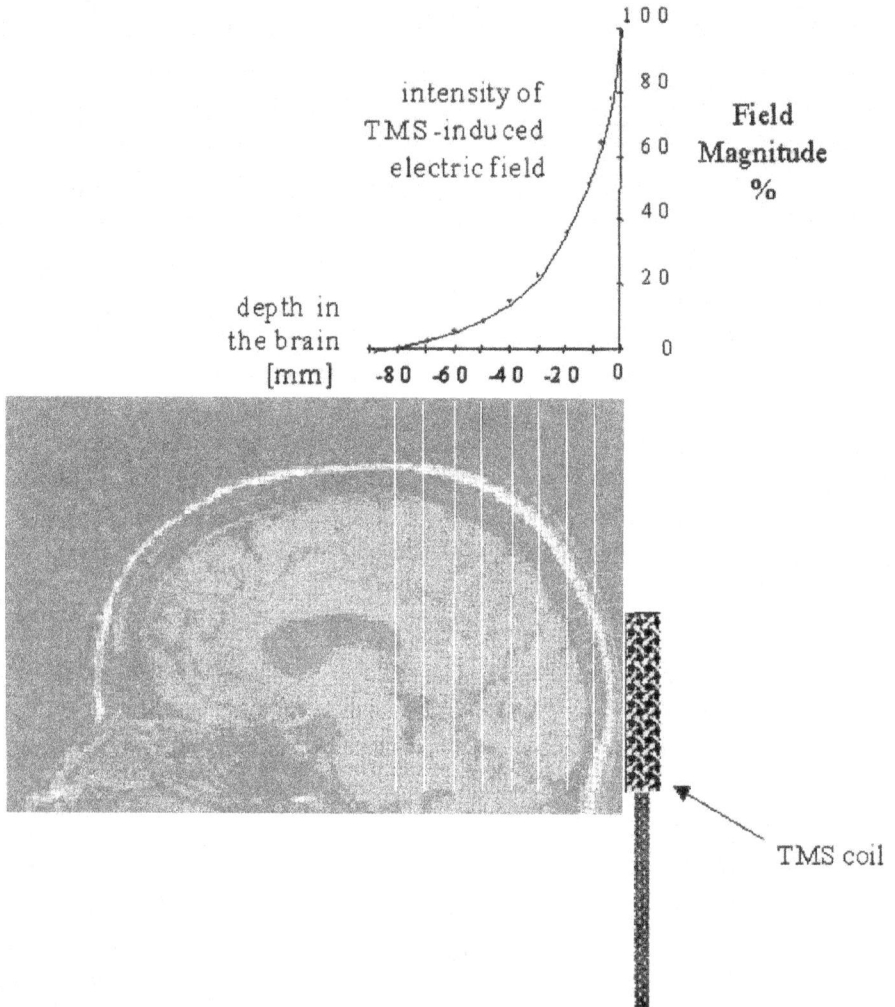

Fig. 1. Sagittal view of the brain by MRI of a normal volunteer. The magnetic coil is positioned over the midoccipital cortex, and the concentric lines represent electric field lines of different field magnitudes. The field magnitudes for each line can be identified in the graph on the top plotted as a function of the depth inside the brain. Note the decline of the magnetic field intensity as a function of the distance from the magnetic coil. Modified from [35].

Available TMS stimulators can deliver single stimuli or trains of pulses. TMS has been utilized to enhance the activity of a brain region or to down-regulate such activity. For example, single TMS pulses applied to the motor cortex elicit a muscle twitch accompanied by a motor evoked response (MEP) in contralateral hand muscles. This response represents a positive effect that resembles normal function [6]. Similarly, stimulation of the occipital cortex can elicit phosphenes [66] (brief perception of flashes or lights). TMS can be used to down regulate activity in one specific area of the brain. This effect has been described as a "virtual lesion" because it results in a transient reversible disruption in the activity of the stimulated area. The purpose of this use is to identify the behavioral consequences of disruption of activity in that region [22]. Single pulse stimuli may lead to inhibitory effects lasting for up to 250 ms [81]. Repetitive TMS allows longer duration of the effect and therefore evaluation of more complex behaviors [22]. In general, it is believed that trains of stimuli are more effective than single stimuli in inducing disruption of cortical activity [42,64,78].

3. Studies of Cortical Reorganization in Intact Humans Using TMS

3.1. *Transient deafferentation*

Transient deafferentation of a limb is a strategy utilized to evaluate cortical reorganization. When ischemic nerve block (INB) is applied by inflating a blood pressure cuff around the forearm above systolic blood pressure, it leads to motor block, measured as disappearance of motor evoked potentials (MEP) from muscles distal to the cuff. Hand deafferentation, in turn, leads to increased excitability of the cortical representation of the muscles proximal to the cuff [9,10,94,132] and to perceptual enhancement of tactile discriminative skills in the non-deafferented handl [25]. In the motor domain, hand deafferentation leads to increased excitability of corticomotor connections targeting the non-deafferented hand [126]. Moreover, the excitability of the cortical representation of muscles proximal to the cuff can be modulated by activity in nearby cortical representations [132]. These studies demonstrate that the human motor cortex is able to rapidly and selectively facilitate the motor outputs immediately above the deafferentation level and even to the non-deafferented hand.

In a different set of experiments, the changes of the cortical representation of the first dorsal interosseus muscle (FDI) were studied when the median and radial nerve were blocked with local anesthetic [98]. In this paradigm the FDI was entirely "enveloped" in the hand region deprived of its cutaneous sensory information, despite maintaining its usual proprioceptive feed-back and strength via the ulnar nerve. Thus, the cortical motor representation of the FDI was reduced in size, while other muscles innervated by the ulnar or median nerve outside the area of anesthesia remained unchanged. Therefore, somatosensory input is capable of rapidly modulating cortical motor output in humans.

The most likely mechanism underlying rapid deafferentation-induced plasticity is unmasking of pre-existing anatomical connections. Changes in neuronal membrane excitability, removal of local inhibition, or various forms of short or long-term synaptic plasticity could possibly lead to this effect. Ziemann et al. [131], using a pharmacological approach combined with application of low-frequency rTMS to the deafferented human motor cortex, found that transient deafferentation by ischemic nerve block (INB) plus rTMS increased the MEP amplitude from the biceps brachii muscle proximal to the cuff. These changes were blocked by pre-medication with a single oral dose of either a GABA agonist (benzodiazepine) or a voltage-gated Na^+ and Ca^{++} channel blocker (lamotrigine). Conversely, a NMDA receptor blocker (dextromethorphan) suppressed the reduction in intracortical inhibition but not the increase in MEP size. These findings are consistent with the involvement of (a) rapid removal of GABA-related cortical inhibition, and (b) short term changes in synaptic efficacy dependent on Na^+ or Ca^{++} channels in this form of plasticity [131].

3.2. *Use-dependent plasticity*

Motor practice consisting of simple, repetitive motions can lead to a form of use-dependent plasticity that encodes the kinematic details of the practiced movements in the primary motor cortex (Fig. 2). Classen et al. [20] used TMS to evoke isolated and directionally consistent thumb movements in healthy volunteers. Subjects then practiced thumb movements in the opposite direction from that induced by TMS. Subsequent magnetic stimulation in the same location came to evoke movements in or near the recently practiced movements for several minutes, before returning to the baseline direction. This experiment suggests that the motor cortex can retain a memory trace of the most recently practiced movements, a phenomenon that may explain the beneficial effects of pre-performance practice in musicians and athletes. This form of plasticity involves NMDA and muscarinic receptor activation and is heavily influenced by GABAergic neurotransmission [14,105].

The acquisition of a motor skill is associated with modulation of the cortical motor outputs to the muscles involved in the task. Human studies using neuroimaging techniques have demonstrated plasticity in primary [51] and non-primary motor cortices [109] associated with learning of complex finger sequences. Pascual-Leone et al. [80] used TMS to study the changes that occur in corticomotoneuronal output of normal subjects who learned a more complex, one-handed, five-finger sequence exercise on a piano over 5 days. During training (2 hours/day) subjects were asked to practice a finger sequence on a piano keyboard paying particular attention to regularity of intervals between individual key presses. Over the course of the five days' practice the playing skills improved significantly and the variability of the intervals between key presses also improved. Concurrent with this behavioral gain, the TMS threshold for activation of finger flexor and extensor muscles in the practicing hand decreased steadily. The magnitude of motor cortical outputs as measured by MEP evoked by TMS increased with practice. These changes were not observed in one control group that did not train nor in a second control group that performed self generated sequences matching the number of key presses but not organized in specific sequences to be learned. Due to the rapid modulation found in this studies, it is likely that the mechanism underlying this process is unmasking of existing connections possibly due to disinhibition.

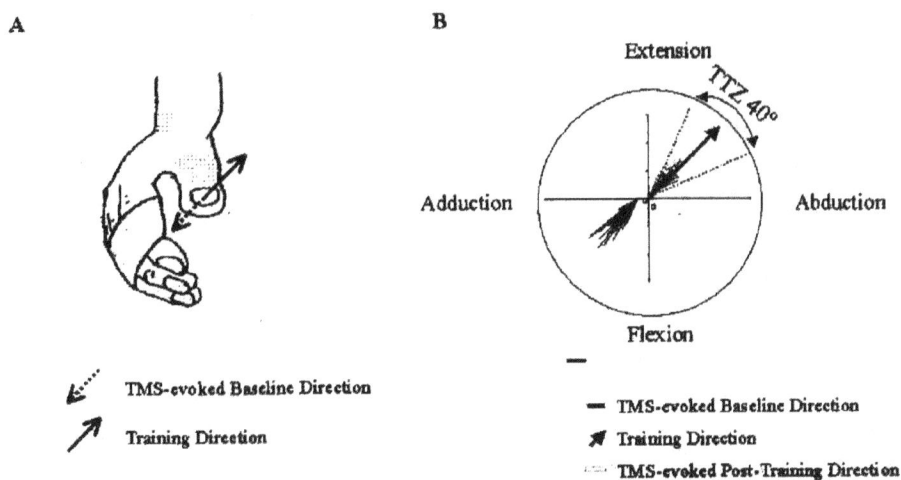

Fig. 2. Representation of the directional change of first peak acceleration vector of movements evoked by transcranial magnetic stimulation (TMS) before and after training. A) This graph represents the direction of TMS-evoked movement at baseline (dashed arrow) and the direction of voluntary movements during training (solid arrow). B) At baseline, TMS evoked predominantly extension and abduction thumb movements (black lines). Training movements were performed in a direction approximately opposite to baseline (solid arrow). During the post-training stimulation the direction of TMS-evoked thumb movements changed from the baseline direction to the trained direction (gray lines). TMS-induced movement directions after training fell mostly within the training target zone (TTZ), near to a 1800 change from baseline direction. Modified from [13].

3.3. *Disuse and plasticity*

Liepert et al., used TMS to study the effects of disuse on motor cortical output. They reported that immobilization of the ankle led to reduced motor cortical output to the tibialis anterior muscle in the immobilized leg relative to the other leg. The reduction in the size of the motor map correlated well with the duration of immobilization and could be quickly reversed by voluntary muscle contraction [61]. Therefore, use is associated with increased corticomotor output to muscles involved in the task, while disuse appears to be associated with reductions in corticomotor output.

3.4. *Procedural learning and plasticity*

Procedural learning may involve implicit and explicit learning [112]. Implicit learning refers to unintentional or non-conscious learning whereas explicit learning requires conscious recollection of previous experiences [107,108]. Implicit and explicit learning can be studied during performance of repeated motor sequences not identified as such in the setting of a serial reaction time task (SRTT) [73,127]. Progressive shortening of reaction times (RT) in the absence of conscious recognition of repetition of the stereotyped sequence involves implicit learning. Explicit learning is acquired when the subject can consciously identify the presence and characteristics of the repeating sequence.

Pascual-Leone et al. [79] studied the changes in excitability of the human motor cortex in the process of acquisition of implicit and explicit knowledge. The cortical representation of the muscles involved in the task was studied with TMS while normal volunteers acquired first implicit and later explicit knowledge of a sequence in a SRTT. TMS mapping showed that the cortical representation of these muscles became progressively larger until explicit knowledge was acquired and then returned to baseline levels. Therefore, there was a correlation between the progressive improvement in RT during implicit learning and the enlargement of the representation of muscles involved in the SRTI. The fact that the motor maps returned to baseline when the motor sequence was explicitly identified suggests that at that point in time other cortical regions assume more active roles in task performance. Thus, learning a complex motor task is associated with fundamental changes in cortical activity. These flexible changes in cortical organization may be important in the acquisition of motor skills and could lead to structural changes as skills become over-learned and automatic. For example, rats that learned new motor skills over a period of 30 days had a greater number of synapses per neuron than those that simply exercised [4].

4. Studies of Cortical Reorganization in Patient Populations Using TMS

4.1. *Amputees*

Numerous reorganizational changes have been described after amputation in the somatosensory and motor cortices. Using magnetic source imaging in humans Elbert et al. [29] showed that the topographic representation of the face in the somatosensory cortex shifted an average of 1.5 cm toward the area that would normally receive input from the amputated hand and fingers. Kew et al. [53] measured regional cerebral blood flow changes associated with vibrotactile stimulation (VS) of the pectoral region ipsilateral and contralateral to an amputated arm. VS ipsilateral to the stump activated a region of the contralateral S1 that extended ventrally to the trunk representation, extending into the hand representation. These results raised the hypothesis that the deafferented digit or hand/arm area had been activated by sensory input from the pectoral region.

In the motor domain, stimulation with TMS over the sensorimotor cortex contralateral to the stump induced sensation of movement in the missing hand or fingers in patients with acquired amputation, but failed to do so in a patient with congenital absence of a limb. Furthermore, the cortical representations of muscles immediately proximal to the stump were larger than those of the homonymous muscles on the intact side [21,37]. These changes could reflect either a true enlargement of the motor cortical representation or an increased excitability of a topographically unchanged motor representation. Later experiments documented plastic modifications at cortical sites [16,34,97]. The mechanisms involved in this form of plasticity are likely to include a combination of changes in GAB A-related disinhibition and changes in neuronal membrane excitability [18].

Phantom limb pain after amputation is characterized by sensations of pain in the missing limb. It is usually more common in the initial stages following the injury [46,47], but in some cases, can be present for many years [111,114]. Relationships between phantom limb pain and neuroplastic changes have also been described. Flor et al. [33] studied subjects with different levels of phantom limb pain, using magnetic source imaging, a technique that allows the non-invasive mapping of the human brain with a spatial resolution high enough to demonstrate somatotopic organization of the somatosensory homunculus. The somatosensory representation of the face expanded medially towards the missing hand representation in patients with phantom pain symptoms relative to the pain-free amputees. Additionally, the magnitude of phantom limb pain correlated with the amount of cortical reorganization. More recently, Karl et al. [50] demonstrated that patients with phantom limb pain also experienced more extensive motor reorganization than those without pain. These findings raised the possibility that in some cases cortical reorganization may be a form of maladaptive plasticity. Finally, Birbaumer et al. [7] studied the functional role of this form of cortical reorganization using brachial plexus block in subjects with phantom pain after amputation. Subjects experienced a reduction of pain in association with reduction in the magnitude of plasticity. These findings were later confirmed in another study where phantom pain reduction with the use of morphine was associated with diminished cortical reorganization [44]. Therefore, contrary to the past belief that neural plastic modifications play only adaptive or compensatory functions, these data indicates that cortical reorganization could be maladaptive and result in undesirable symptoms like pain [52,87,88].

4.2. *Swallowing disorders*

The process of swallowing entails a complex sequence of motions that lead to the transport of food and liquids from the mouth to the stomach while protecting the airway. Dysphagia occurs when there is damage to the swallowing centers or their connections, as in stroke. One-third of stroke patients present with dysphagia [36], however, most of them will recover within few weeks [5]. Recently, Hamdy et al. [40] demonstrated that the cortical representation of esophageal and pharyngeal muscles involved in swallowing function is bilaterally organized with variable degrees of unilateral dominance [40]. This asymmetric hemispheric representation for swallowing could explain why some stroke patients have dysphagia but others don't. Hamdy et al. [38] found that TMS stimulation of the intact motor cortex elicited poorer motor responses from pharyngeal muscles in patients with dysphagia. These results suggest that the hemisphere dominant for swallowing was predominantly affected in the dysphagic patients. In a follow up study, the authors demonstrated that functional recovery of dysphagia correlated with motor cortical reorganization in the intact hemisphere. In the initial evaluation of stroke survivors with dysphagia, they observed that pharyngeal motor maps in the intact hemisphere were smaller in dysphagic than in non-dysphagic patients. At 1 and 3 months following the stroke onset, pharyngeal motor maps increased only in patients who experienced substantial recovery. It was concluded that recovery of dysphagia correlated with a representational change in the esophageal region in the intact motor cortex [39]. These findings also suggest that adaptation to a lesion in the cortical swallowing representation may rely on the presence of an intact projection from the intact hemisphere that can develop increasing control over brainstem centers.

4.3. *Spinal cord injury*

Plastic changes have been described in patients with cervical [59] and thoracic [115] spinal cord injury. TMS in paraplegic patients recruited a larger percentage of the alpha motoneuron pool in muscles immediately proximal to the sensory/motor lesional level when compared to the same muscles in normal controls. These findings suggest that there is an enhanced excitability of motor pathways targeting muscles rostral to the level of a spinal cord injury. Interestingly Topka et al. [115] reported that this form of plasticity was seen only when testing was performed with muscles at rest and was absent when the same recordings were done under slight activation of target muscles. In addition, these changes appear to take place within days after the injury [113].

4.4. *Bell's palsy*

A most striking finding in these patients has been the enlargement of the motor cortical representation of the hand. The enlargement of the hand representation was in part secondary to a lateral expansion into the face representation [95]. Thus, regions of the face representation deprived of output connections may become involved in controlling motor output to the hand. This finding suggests that human motor cortical plasticity can take place across limb representational boundaries, as has been demonstrated in animals [85].

4.5. *Blindness*

Cross-modal plasticity refers to the ability of a cortical region devoted to one sensory modality to process information from a different sensory modality. Much of what is known about this concept originates in experiments performed in the visual cortex. It has been proposed that a cortical region in charge of processing visual information after light deprivation could be recruited to process information from a different sensory modality [55,56,84]. Behavioral studies demonstrated that blind cats are more accurate than sighted cats in localizing sound sources in space [89]. Similarly, blind humans may be able to perform auditory localization tasks better than sighted individuals [72].

Early neuroimaging studies showed that despite early-onset visual deprivation, the cortical areas normally devoted to visual processing retain their macroanatomy and display levels of glucose metabolism that are higher than or similar to those of the visual cortex of sighted individuals with their eyes covered or closed [83,123]. Increased regional cerebral blood flow (rCBF) was also found in the occipital cortex of early-blind subjects [116]. These studies in individuals who became blind at an early age indicated that the deafferented occipital areas of the brain remained active despite the lack of visual input.

In a more recent study using PET, Sadato et al. [102] demonstrated that the occipital cortex is one of the regions activated in a distributed network during Braille reading and tactile discrimination tasks in blind subjects, but not in sighted volunteers. While this study identified the network of regions activated in association with Braille reading, it was not clear what the functional relevance of that activation was in terms of sensory substitution. To address this issue TMS was used to disrupt different cortical areas while early blind individuals read Braille and embossed Roman letters (Fig. 3). Results obtained in the blind group were later compared to those obtained from a group of sighted volunteers reading embossed Roman letters. Five subjects who became blind early in life and who were experienced Braille readers were studied while they read strings of non-word Braille letters. In addition, five sighted volunteers and four of the early blind subjects were studied while performing a tactile discrimination task requiring identification of the same embossed Roman letters. Subjects were asked to identify and read aloud letter-by-letter as fast and accurately as possible. Letters were presented with a specially designed device that showed five letters at a time and permited simultaneous triggering of the TMS train with the initiation of the sweeping motion to read Braille. Phonographic recordings of voice and EMG from hand muscles involved in the reading task were monitored.

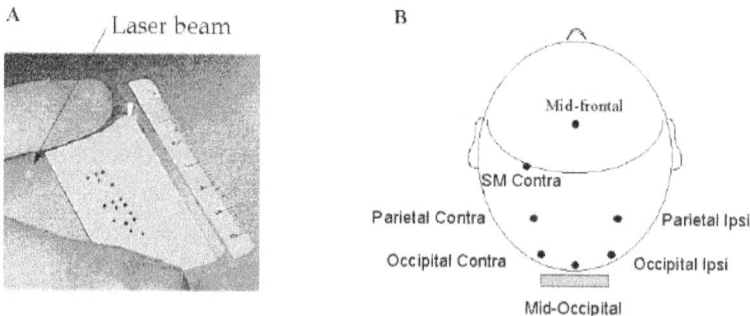

Fig. 3. A) Picture of the device utilized to present Braille letters for tactile discrimination. The index finger is resting on a finger station. As the subject moves the finger to read the first letter, crosses a laser beam which in turn triggers a 3 second train of TMS. B) Schematic representation of the top of the head showing the scalp positions stimulated with TMS. The magnetic coil is shown positioned over the mid-occipital position. S-M: sensorimotor cortex; contra: contralateral; ipsi: ipsilateral. Modified from [22].

Overall accuracy in reading performance before TMS was around 95% in the different groups. In the blind, mid-occipital stimulation induced significantly more errors than the control condition (stimulation in the air). In addition, stimulation of occipital positions occasionally elicited distorted somatosensory perceptions such as negative ("missing dots"), positive ("phantom dots"), and confusing sensations ("dots don't make sense"). Blind and sighted subjects performing the same task (reading embossed Roman letters) showed different effects with TMS. Mid-occipital stimulation induced more errors than control (stimulation in the air) in the blind, but not in sighted volunteers [22]. These results are consistent with the view that the occipital cortex is functionally active despite decades of visual deafferentation [101,110], and that it is actively engaged in meaningful processing of tactile information related to Braille reading and other tactile discrimination tasks.

Interestingly, these effects were only found if blindness started early in life. A follow up study was done on subjects who became blind after age 14 (late onset blind group, LOB) [24]. Eight subjects were studied using a combination of PET and rTMS. The results in patients with late-onset blindness were compared with those obtained from subjects with early-onset blindness [22]• Except for small regions in the right inferior occipital gyrus and lingual gyrus, the occipital cortex was not activated in association with the tactile discrimination task in this late blind group. This finding was clearly in contrast to the activation of most of the visual cortex, including the primary visual regions, in the congenitally blind and the early blind group. In addition, disruption of occipital activity by TMS did not affect the reading task in the LOB group. Therefore, the occipital cortex appears to playa fundamentally different role in LOB subjects compared to the other two groups.

Taken together, neuroimaging and neurophysiological results provide evidence to support the concept of a window of opportunity for this form of functionally relevant cross-modal plasticity [24]• However, some level of tactile processing is known to take place even in sighted individuals. Zangaladze and associates [128] instructed sighted subjects to discriminate the orientation of a grating applied to the right index finger with their eyes closed. When TMS was applied to occipital sites at 180 ms delay it markedly impaired task performance. In contrast, TMS ipsilateral to the hand undergoing the discriminative task had no deleterious effects on performance. In addition, TMS applied during a control task to test whether the disruption of tactile performance by occipital TMS was specific to discrimination of orientation or texture did not affect performance. However, when TMS was applied over the contralateral somatosensory cortex, it blocked discrimination of grating texture as well as orientation. Taken together, these studies suggest that the visual cortex may participate in processing of some tactile tasks even in sighted individuals.

5. Modulation of Plasticity

As we have reviewed, there is ample evidence that the human brain has the inherent capacity for plastic changes during learning or following lesions. Plasticity can play a beneficial role as in blind individuals, or a maladaptive role as in patients with phantom limb pain. Therefore, the development of strategies to modulate human plasticity would be desirable. Ziemann et al. [131] studied the effects of rTMS as a tool to modulate deafferentation-induced plasticity. As discussed previously, deafferentation leads to the enlargement of MEP amplitudes recorded from muscles proximal to the nerve block (see above). Slow rTMS, which by itself does not cause changes in cortical excitability [17], over the deafferented motor cortical representation enhanced this form of plasticity. On the other hand, rTMS applied over the non-deafferented cortex decreased this form of plasticity [130]. Additional experiments were consistent with the idea that this modulation of plasticity is secondary to rapid removal of GABA-related cortical inhibition and short-term changes in synaptic efficacy dependent on Na+ or Ca++ channels [131].

Recent experiments have used pharmacological approaches to enhance motor plasticity. D-amphetamine (AMPH) can enhance the beneficial effects of physical therapy on motor recovery after injury in rats [31] and humans [25,117,118]. In a double blind placebo control design, Bütefisch et al. [13] studied the effects of AMPH over use-dependent plasticity. First, the direction of TMS-evoked thumb movements after stimulation of the contralateral motor cortex was determined (baseline). Then, subjects were asked to practice movements in the opposite direction. Post-training TMS-evoked thumb movement directions were compared relative to baseline. Use-dependent plasticity was defined as the increase in the number of TMS-evoked movements falling in the training direction at the end of the practice period. Normal volunteers pre-medicated with AMPH showed an increase in magnitude, faster development and longer lasting duration of use-dependent plasticity when compared to placebo. These findings demonstrate a facilitatory effect of d-amphetamine on use-dependent plasticity, which has been proposed as a possible mechanism involved in the enhancement of functional recovery after cortical lesions.

6. Mechanisms Involved in Human Plasticity

Various mechanisms could operate in human plasticity. Rapidly developing behavioral gains could involve unmasking of previously existing connections [57], long-term potentiation [12], or long-term depression [129]. Examples of changes that occur on a longer time frame include changes in dendritic arborization [15], receptor density [63], and perhaps even neurogenesis [74]. Different neurotransmitter systems are known to influence plasticity including GABAergic [32,60], muscarinic [41,105] and glutamate [67] receptor function.

7. Conclusions

The CNS experiences constant remodeling. New technical tools including fMRI, PET and TMS permit the non-invasive study of these plastic changes in humans and have led to a greater understanding of these processes. The mechanisms underlying human plasticity are incompletely understood. The future will bring light in this direction, which will in turn have a significant impact on the way plasticity is modulated to enhance functional recovery following brain injury.

References

1. Aizawa, H., Inase, M., Mushiake, H., Shima, K. and Tanji, I. Reorganization of activity in the supplementary motor area associated with motor learning and functional recovery, *Exp. Brain Res.* **84**, 668-671, 1991.
2. Allard, T., Clark, S. A., Jenkins, W. M. and Merzenich, M. M. Reorganization of somatosensory area 3b representations in adult owl monkeys after digital syndactyly, *J. Neurophysiol.* **66**, 1048-1058, 1991.
3. Amassian, V. E., Maccabee, P. J., Cracco, R. Q., Cracco, J. B. , Somasundaram, M., Rothwell, I. C., Eberle, L., Henry, K., and Rudell, A. The polarity of the induced electric field influences magnetic coil inhibition of human visual cortex: implications for the site of excitation, *Electroencephalog. Clin. Neurophysiol.* **93**, 21-26, 1994.
4. Anderson, B. J., Li, X., Alcantara, A. A., Isaacs, K. R., Black, J. E., and Greenough, W. Glial hypertrophy is associated with synaptogenesis following motor-skill learning, but not with angiogenesis following exercise, *Glia* **11**, 73-80, 1994.
5. Barer, D. The natural history and functional consequences of dysphagia after hemispheric stroke, *Journal of Neurology Neurosurgery and Psychiatry*, **52**, 236-241, 1989.
6. Barker, A. T., Jalinous, R., and Freeston, I. Non-invasive magnetic stimulation of human motor cortex, *Lancet* **1**, 1106-1107, 1985.
7. Birbaumer, N., Lutzenberger, W., Montoya, P., Larbig, W., Unertl, K,. Topfner, S., Grodd, W., Taub, E., and Flor, H. Effects of regional anesthesia on phantom limb pain are mirrored in changes in cortical reorganization *J. Neurosci.*, **17**, 5503-5508, 1997.
8. Bliss, T. V., and Gardner, M. A. Long-lasting potentiation of synaptic transmission in the dentate area of the unanaestetized rabbit following stimulation of the perforant path, *J. Physiol. (Lond)*, **232**, 357-374, 1973.
9. Brasil-Neto, J. P., Cohen, L. G., Pascual-Leone, A., Jabir, F. K., Wall, R. T., and Hallett, M. Rapid reversible modulation of human motor outputs after transient deafferentation of the forearm: a study with transcranial magnetic stimulation, *Neurology* **42**, 1302-1306, 1992.

10. Brasil-Neto, J. P., Valls-Sole, J., Pascual-Leone, A., Cammarota, A., Amassian, V. E., Cracco, R., Maccabee, P., Cracco, J., Hallett, M., and Cohen, L. G. Rapid modulation of human cortical motor outputs following ischemic nerve block, *Brain*, **116**, 511-525, 1993.

11. Broca, P. Remarques sur la siege de la faculte du langage articule: suivies d'une observation d'aphemie (perte de la parole), *Bulletins de la Societe Anatomique*, **6**, 330-357, 1861.

12. Brown, T. H., Chapman, P. F., Kairiss, E. W., and Keenan, C. Long-term synaptic potentiation, *Science*, **242**, 724-728, 1988.

13. Bütefisch, C. M., Davis, B. C., Sawaki, L., Waldvogel, D., Classen, J. K. L., and Cohen, L. G. Modulation of use-dependent plasticity by D-amphetamine, *Annals of Neurology*, **51**, 59-68, 2002.

14. Bütefisch, C. M., Davis, B. C., Wise, S. P., Sawaki, L., Kopylev, L., Classen, J., and Cohen, L. G. Mechanisms of use-dependent plasticity in the human motor cortex, *Proc Natl Acad Sci USA*, **97**, 3661-3665, 2000.

15. Caceres, A. O. and Steward, O. Dendritic reorganization in the denervated dentate gyrus of the rat following enthorinal cortical lesions. A Golgi and electron microscopic analysis, *J. Comp. Neurol.*, **214**, 387-403, 1983.

16. Chen, R., Corwell, B., Yaseen, Z., Hallett, M., and Cohen, L. Mechanisms of cortical reorganization in lower-limb amputees, *Journal of Neuroscience*, **18**, 3443-3450, 1998.

17. Chen, R., Classen, J., Gerloff, C., Celnik, P., Wassermann, E. M., Hallett, M. and Cohen, L. G. Expression of motor cortex excitability by low-frequency trans cranial magnetic stimulation, *Neurology*, **48**, 1398-1403, 1997.

18. Chen, R., Corwell, B., Hallett, M. and Cohen, L.G. Mechanisms involved in motor reorganization following lower limb amputation, *Neurology*, **48**, A345, 1997.

19. Chino, Y. M., Kaas, J. H., Smith, E. D., Langston, A. L. and Cheng, H. Rapid reorganization of cortical maps in adult cats following restricted deafferentation in retina, *Vision Res.*, **32**, 789-796, 1992.

20. Classen J., Liepert. J., Wise, S. P., Hallett, M., and Cohen, L. G. Rapid plasticity of human cortical movement representation induced by practice, *J. Neurophysiol.*, **79**, 1117-1123, 1998.

21. Cohen, L., Bandinelli, S., Findley, T. W, and Hallett, M. Motor reorganization after upper limb amputation in man. A study with focal magnetic stimulation, *Brain*, **114**, 615-627, 1991.

22. Cohen, L. G., Celnik, P., Pascual-Leone, A., Corwell, B., Falz, L,. Dambrosia, J., Honda, M., Sadato, N., Gerloff, C., Catala, M. D., and Hallett, M. Functional relevance of cross-modal plasticity in blind humans, *Nature*, **389**, 180-183, 1997.

23. Cohen, L. G., Roth, B. J., Nilsson, J., Dang, N., Panizza, M., Bandinelli, S., Friauf, W. and Hallett, M. Effects of coil design on delivery of focal magnetic stimulation. Technical considerations, *Electroencephalog. Clin, Neurophysiol.*, **75**, 350-357, 1990.

24. Cohen, L. G., Weeks, R. A., Sadato, N., Celnik, P., Ishii, K. and Hallett, M. Period of susceptibility for cross-modal plasticity in the blind, *Ann. Neurol.*, **45**, 451-460, 1999.

25. Crisostomo, E. A., Duncan, P. W., Propst, M., Dawson, D. V. and Davis, I. N. Evidence that amphetamine with physical therapy promotes recovery of motor function in stroke patients, *Ann. Neurol.*, **23**, 94-97, 1988.

26. Donoghue, J. P., Suner, S. and Sanes, J. N. Dynamic organization of primary motor cortex output to target muscles in adult rats. II. Rapid reorganization following motor nerve lesions, *Exp. Brain Res.*, **79**, 492-503, 1990.

27. Donoghue, J. P. and Sanes, J. N. Organization of adult motor cortex representation patterns following neonatal forelimb nerve injury in rats, *J. Neurosci.*, **8**, 3221-3232, 1988.

28. Donoghue, J. P. and Sanes, J. N. Peripheral nerve injury in developing rats reorganizes representation pattern in motor cortex, *Proc. Natl. Acad. Sci. USA*, **84**, 1123-1126, 1987.

29. Elbert, T., Flor, H., Birbaumer, N., Knecht, S., Hampson, S., Larbig, W., and Taub, E. Extensive reorganization of the somatosensory cortex in adult humans after nervous system injury, *Neuroreport*, **5**, 2593-2597, 1994.

30. Epstein, C. M., Schwartzberg, D. G., Davey, K. R. and Sudderth, D. B. Localizing the site of magnetic brain stimulation in humans, *Neurology*, **40**, 666-670, 1990.

31. Feeney, D. M., Gonzalez, A., Law, W, A. Amphetamine, haloperidol, and experience interact to affect rate of recovery after motor cortex injury, *Science*, **217**, 855-857, 1982.

32. Feldman, D. E. Inhibition and plasticity, *Nat. Neurosci.*, **3**, 303-304, 2000.

33. Flor, H., Elbert, T., Knecht, S., Wienbruch, C., Pantev, C., and Larbig, W. Phantom limb pain as a perceptual correlate of massive cortical reorganization in upper extremity amputees, *Nature*, **375**, 482-484, 1995.

34. ,Fuhr P., Cohen, L. G., Dang, N., Findley, T. W., Haghighi, S., Oro, 1., and Hallett, M. Physiological analysis of motor reorganization following lower limb amputation. *Electroencephalography and Clinical Neurophysiology*, **85**, 53-60, 1992.

35. Gerloff, C., Corwell, B., Chen, R., Hallett, M. and Cohen, L. Stimulation over the human supplementary motor area interferes with the organization of future elements in complex motor sequences, *Brain*, **120**, 1587-1602, 1997.

36. Gordon, C., Langton-Hewer, R., and Wade, D. T. Dysphagia in acute stroke, *British Medical Journal*, **295**, 411-414, 1987.

37. Hall, E. I., Flament, D., Fraser, C., and Lemon, R. Non-invasive brain stimulation reveals reorganized cortical outputs in amputees, *Neuroscience Letters*, **116**, 379-386, 1990.

38. Hamdy, S., Aziz, Q., Rothwell, I. C., Crone, R., Hughes, D. G., Tallis, R. C., and Thompson, D. Explaining oro-pharyngeal dysphagia after unilateral hemispheric stroke, *Lancet*, **350**, 686-692, 1997.

39. Hamdy, S., Aziz, Q., Rothwell, I. C., Power, M., Singh, K. D., Nicholson, D. A., Tallis, R. C., and Thompson, D. Recovery of swallowing after dysphagic stroke relates to functional reorganization in the intact motor cortex, *Gastroenterology*, **115**, 1104-1112, 1998.

40. Hamdy, S., Aziz, Q., Rothwell, I. C., Singh, K. D., Barlow, J., Hughes, D. G., Tallis, R. C., and Thompson, D. The cortical topography of human swallowing musculature in health and disease, *Nature Medicine*, **2**, 1217-1224, 1996.

41. Hasselmo, M. Neuromodulation and cortical function: modeling the physiological basis of behavior, *Behav. Brain Res.*, **67**, 1-27, 1995.

42. Henderson, D. C., Evans, 1. R. and Dobelle, W. H. The relationship between stimulus parameters and phosphene threshold brightness during stimulation of human visual cortex, *Trans. Am. Soc. Artif. Intern. Organs*, **25**, 367-371, 1979.

43. Hubel, D. H. and Wiesel, T. N. Binocular interaction in striate cortex of kittens raised with artificial squint, *J. Neurophysiol.*, **28**, 1041-1059, 1965.

44. Huse, E., Larbig ,W., Flor ,H., and Birbaumer, N. The effect of opioids on phantom limb pain and cortical reorganization, *Pain*, **90**, 47-55, 2001.

45. Jenkins, W. M., Merzenich, M. M., Ochs, M. T., Allard, T., and Ouic-Robles, E. J. Functional reorganization of primary somatosensory cortex in adult owl monkeys after behaviorally controlled tactile stimulation, *J. Neurophysiol.*, **63**, 82-104, 1990.

46. Jensen, T. S., Krebs, B., Nielsen, J., and Rasmussen, P. Immediate and long-term phantom limb pain in amputees: incidence, clinical characteristics and relationship to pre-amputation limb pain, *Pain*, **21**, 267-278, 1985.

47. Jensen, T. S., and Rasmussen, P. Phantom limb pain and related phenomena after amputation, In: *Textbook of Pain*, eds. Wall, P. D. and Melzack, R. (Churchill Livingstone, New York) pp. 651-665, 1995.

48. Kaas, J. H., Krubitzer, L. A., Chino, Y. M., Langston, A. L., Polley, E. H. and Blair, N. Reorganization of retinotopic cortical maps in adult mammals after lesions of the retina, *Science*, **248**, 229-231, 1990.

49. Kalaska, J. and Pomeranz, B. Chronic paw denervation causes and age-dependent appearance of novel responses from forearm in "paw cortex" of kittens and adult cats, *J. Neurophysiol.*, **42**, 618-633, 1979.

50. Karl, A., Birbaumer, N., Lutzenberger, W., Cohen, L. G. and Flor, H. Reorganization of motor and somatosensory cortex in upper extremity amputees with phantom limb pain, *J. Neurosci.*, **21**, 3609-3618, 2001.

51. Karni, A., Meyer, G., Jezzard, P., Adams, M. M., Turner, R. and Ungerleider, L. G. Functional MRI evidence for adult motor cortex plasticity during motor skill learning, *Nature*, **377**, 155-158, 1995.

52. Katz, J. Psychophysiological contributions to phantom limbs, *Canadian Journal of Psychiatry*, **37**, 282-298, 1992.

53. Kew, J, J., Halligan, P. W., Marshall, J. C., Passingham, R. E., Rothwell, J. C., Ridding M. C., Marsden, C. D. and Brooks, D. Abnormal access of axial vibrotactile input to deafferented somatosensory cortex in human upper limb amputees, *Journal of Neurophysiology*, **77**, 2753-2764, 1997.

54. Kimbrell, T. A. et al. Regional decreases in glucose metabolism with 1 Hz prefrontal transcranial magnetic stimulation: a new technique for tracing functional networks in the human brain. *Soc. Neurosci. Abstr.*, **23**, 1576, 1997.

55. Kujala, T., Huotilainen, M., Sinkkonen, J., Ahonen, A. I., Alho, K., Hamalainen, M. S., Ilmoniemi, R. J., Kajola, M., Knuutila, J. E. T., Lavikainen, J., Salonen, O., Simola, J., Sandertskjold-Nordenstam, C. G., Tiitinen, H., Tissari, S. O., and Naatanen, R. Visual cortex activation in blind subjects during sound discrimination, *Neuroscience Letters*, **183**, 143-146, 1995.

56. Kujala, T., Alho, K., Huotilainen, M., Ilmoniemi, R. I., Lehtokoski, A., Leinonen, A., Rinne, T., Salonen, O., Sinkkonen, J., Standertskjold-Nordenstam, C. G., and Naatanen, R. Electrophysiological evidence for cross-modal plasticity in humans with early-and late-onset blindness, *Psychophysiology*, **34**, 213-216, 1997.

57. Kullman, D. Amplitude fluctuations of dual-component EPSCs in hippocampal pyramidal cells: implications for long-term potentiation, *Neuron*, **12**, 1111-1120, 1994.

58. Levi-Montalcini, R. and Angeletti, P.U. Nerve growth factor, *Physiol. Rev.*, **48**, 534-569, 1968.

59. Levy, W. J., Amassian, V. E., Traad, M. and Cadwell, J. Focal magnetic coil stimulation reveals motor cortical system reorganized in humans after traumatic quadriplegia, *Brain Research*, **510**, 130-134, 1990.

60. Liao, D., Hessler, N., Malinow, R. Activation of postsynaptically silent synapses during pairing-induced LTP in CAl region of hippocampal slice, *Nature*, **375**, 400-404, 1995.

61. Liepert, J., Tegenthoff, M. and Malin, J. P. Changes of cortical motor area size during immobilization, *Electroencephalog. Clin. Neurophysiol.*, **97**, 382-386, 1995.

62. Payne, B. R. and Lomber, S. G. Reconstructing functional systems after lesions of cerebral cortex, *Nature Reviews Neuroscience*, **2**, 911-919, 2001.

63. Lømø, T. and Rosenthal, J. Control of acetylcholine sensitivity by muscle activity in the rat, *Journal of Physiology*, **221**, 493-513, 1972.

64. Luders, H., Lesser, R. P., Dinner, D. S., Morris, H. H., Hahn, J. F., Friedman, L., Skipper, G., Wyllie, E., and Friedman, D. Commentary: Chronic intracranial recording and stimulation with subdural electrodes. In: *Surgical Treatment of the Epilepsies*, ed. Engel, J. (Raven Press, New York) pp. 297-321, 1987.

65. Maccabee, P. J., Amassian, V. E., Cracco, R. Q., Cracco, J. B., Eberle, L. and Rudell, A. Stimulation of the human nervous system using the magnetic coil, *J. Clin. Neurophysiol.*, **8**, 38-55, 1991.

66. Maccabee, P. J., Amassian, V. E., Cracco, R. Q., Cracco, J. B., Rudell, A. P., Eberle, L. P. and Zemon, V. Magnetic coil stimulation of human visual cortex: studies of perception. *Electroencephalog. Clin. Neurophysiol. Suppl.*, **43**, 111-120, 1991.

67. Malenka, R. C. and Nicoll, R. A. Long-term potentiation--a decade of progress?, *Science*, **285**, 1870-1874, 1999.

68. Merzenich, M. M., Kaas, J. H., Wall, J. T., Sur, M., Nelson, R. J. and Felleman, D. I. Progression of change following median nerve section in the cortical representation of the hand in areas 3b and 1 in adult owl and squirrel monkeys, *Neurosci.*, **10**, 639-665, 1983.

69. Merzenich, M. M., Nelson, R. J., Stryker, M. P., Cynder, M. S., Shoppmann, A. and Zook, J .M. Somatosensory cortical map changes following digit amputation in adult monkeys, *J. Comp. Neurol.*, **224**, 591-605, 1984.

70. Merzenich, M. M., Recanzone, G., Jenkins, W. M., Allard, T. T. and Nudo, R. J. Cortical representational plasticity. In: Neurobiology of Neocortex, eds. Rakic, P. and Singer, W. (John Wiley & Sons Ltd., New York) pp. 41-67, 1988.

71. Mitz, A. R., Godschalk, M. and Wise, S. P. Learning-dependent neuronal activity in the premotor cortex: activity during the acquisition of conditional motor associations, *J. Neurosci.*, **11**, 1855-1872, 1991.

72. Muchnik, C., Efrati, M., Nemeth, E., Malin, M., and Hildesheimer, M. Central auditory skills in blind and sighted subjects, *Scandinavian Audiology*, **20**, 19-23, 1991.

73. Nissen, M. J. and Bullemer, P. Attention requirements of learning: evidence from performance measures, *Cogn. Psychol.*, **19**, 1-32, 1987.

74. Nottebohm, F. Why are some neurons replaced in adult brain?, *J. Neurosci.*, **22**, 624-628, 2002.

75. Nudo, R. J., Jenkins, W. M. and Merzenich, M. M. Repetitive microstimulation alters the cortical representation of movements in adult rats, *Somatosens. Mot. Res.*, **7**, 463-83, 1990.

76. Nudo, R. J., Milliken, G. W., Jenkins, W. M. and Merzenich, M. M. Use-dependent alterations of movement representations in primary motor cortex of adult squirrel monkeys. *J. Neurosci.*, **16**, 785-807, 1996.

77. Nudo, R. J., Wise, B. M. and SiFuentes, F. Neural substrate for effects of rehabilitation on motor recovery following focal ischemic infarct, *Neurosci. Abstr.*, **21**, 517, 1995.

78. Ojemann, G. Brain organization for language from the perspective of electrical stimulation mapping, *Behavioral Brain Science*, **6**, 190-206, 1983.

79. Pascual-Leone, A., Grafman, J. and Hallett, M. Modulation of cortical motor output maps during development of implicit and explicit knowledge, *Science*, **263**, 1287-1289, 1994.

80. Pascual-Leone, A., Nguyet, D., Cohen, L. G., Brasil, N. J., Cammarota, A. and Hallett, M. Modulation of muscle responses evoked by transcranial magnetic stimulation during the acquisition of new fine motor skills, *J. Neurophysiol.*, **74**, 1037 1045, 1995.
81. Pascual-Leone, A., Walsh, V. and Rothwell, J. Transcranial magnetic stimulation in cognitive neuroscience--virtual lesion, chronometry, and functional connectivity, *Curr. Opin. Neurobiol.*, **10**, 232-237, 2000.
82. Paus T., Jech, R., Thompson, C. J., Comeau, R., Peters, T., and Evans, A. C. Transcranial magnetic stimulation during positron emission tomography: a new method for studying connectivity of the human cerebral cortex, *J. Neurosci.*, **17**, 3178-3184, 1997.
83. Phelps, M. E., Mazziotta, J. C., Kuhl, D. E., Nuwer, M., Packwood, J., Metter, J., Engel, J. Jr. Tomographic mapping of human cerebral metabolism visual stimulation and deprivation, *Neurology*, **31**, 517-529, 1981.
84. Pons, T. Novel sensations in the congenitally blind, *Nature*, **380**, 479-480, 1996.
85. Pons, T. P., Garraghty, P. E., Ommaya, A. K., Kaas, J. H., Taub, E. and Mishkin, M. Massive cortical reorganization after sensory deafferentation in adult macaques, *Science*, **252**, 1857-1860, 1991.
86. Raisman, O. and Field, P. M. A quantitative investigation of the development of collateral reinnervation after partial deafferentation of the septal nuclei, *Brain Res.*, **50**, 241-264, 1973.
87. Ramachandran, V. S., Rogers-Ramachandran, D., and Stewart, M. Perceptual correlates of massive cortical reorganization, *Science*, **13**, 1159-1160, 1992.
88. Ramachandran, V. S., Stewart, M., and Rogers-Ramachandran, D. Perceptual correlates of massive cortical reorganization, *Neuroreport*, **3**, 583-586, 1992.
89. Rauschecker, J. P. and Kniepert, U. Auditory localization behaviour in visually deprived cats. *European Journal of Neuroscience*, **6**, 149-160, 1994.
90. Recanzone, G. H., Jenkins, W. M., Hradek, G. T. and Merzenich, M. M. Progressive improvement in discriminative abilities in adult owl monkeys performing a tactile frequency discrimination task, *J. Neurophysiol.*, **67**, 1015-1030, 1992.
91. Recanzone, G. H., Merzenich, M. M. and Jenkins, W. M. Frequency discrimination training engaging a restricted skin surface results in an emergence of a cutaneous response zone in cortical area 3a, *J. Neurophysiol.*, **67**, 1057-1070, 1992.
92. Recanzone, G. H., Merzenich, M. M. and Schreiner, C. E. Changes in the distributed temporal response properties of SI cortical neurons reflect improvements in performance on a temporally based tactile discrimination task, *J. Neurophysiol.*, **67**, 1071-1091, 1992.
93. Recanzone, G. H., Merzenich, M. M., Jenkins, W. M., Grajski, K. A. and Dinse, H. R. Topographic reorganization of the hand representation in cortical area 3b owl monkeys trained in a frequency-discrimination task, *J. Neurophysiol.*, **67**, 1031-1056, 1992.
94. Ridding, M. C. and Rothwell, I. C. Reorganization in human motor cortex, *Can. J. Physiol. Pharmacol.*, **73**, 218-222, 1995.
95. Rijntjes, M., Tegenthoff, M., Liepert, J., Leonhardt, G., Kotterba, S., Muller, S., Kiebel, S., Malin, J.-P., Diener, H.-C. and Weiller, C. Cortical reorganization in patients with facial palsy. *Annals of Neurology*, **41**, 621-630, 1997.
96. Robertson D. and Irvine, D. R. F. Plasticity of frequency organization in auditory cortex of guinea pigs with partial unilateral deafness, *J. Comp. Neurol.*, **282**, 456-471, 1989.
97. Roricht, S., Meyer, B. U., Niehaus, L., and Brandt, S. A. Long-term reorganization of motor cortex outputs after arm amputation, *Neurology*, **53**, 106-111, 1999.

98. Rossini, P. M., Rossi, S., Tecchio, P., Pasqualetti, P., Finazzi-Agro, A. and Sabato, A. Focal brain stimulation in healthy humans: motor maps changes following partial hand sensory deprivation, *Neurosci. Lett.*, **214**, 191-195, 1996.

99. Roth, B. J., Saypol, J. M., Hallett, M. and Cohen, L. G. A theoretical calculation of the electric field induced in the cortex during magnetic stimulation, *Electroencephalog. Clin. Neurophysiol.*, **81**, 47-56, 1991.

100. Rudiak D. and Marg, E. Finding the depth of magnetic brain stimulation: a re-evaluation, *Electroenceph. Clin. Neurophysiol.*, **93**, 358-371, 1994.

101. Rushton, D. N. and Brindley, G. Properties of cortical electrical phosphenes. In: *Frontiers in Visual Science*, eds. Cool, S. J. and Smith, E. L. (Springer-Verlag, New York) 1978, pp. 574-593.

102. Sadato, N., Pascual-Leone, A., Grafmani, J., Iba-ez, V., Deiber, M.-P., Dold, G., and Hallett, M. Activation of the primary visual cortex by Braille reading in blind subjects, *Nature*, **380**, 526-528, 1996.

103. Sanes, J. N., Suner, S. and Donoghue, J. P. Dynamic organization of primary motor cortex output to target muscles in adult rats. I. Long-term patterns of reorganization following motor or mixed peripheral nerve lesions, *Exp. Brain Res.*, **79**, 479-91, 1990.

104. Sanes, J. N., Wang, J. and Donoghue, J. P. Immediate and delayed changes of rat motor cortical output representation with new forelimb configurations, *Cereb. Cortex*, **2**, 141-152, 1992.

105. Sawaki, L., Boroojerdi, B., Kaelin-Lang, A., Burstein, A. H., Butefisch, C. M., Kopylev, L., Davis, B. and Cohen, L. G. Cholinergic influences on use-dependent plasticity, *J. Neurophysiol.*, **87**, 166-171, 2002.

106. Saypol, J. M., Roth, B. J., Cohen, L. G. and Hallett, M. A theoretical comparison of electric and magnetic stimulation of the brain, *Ann. Biomed. Eng.*, **19**, 317-328, 1991.

107. Schacter, D. L. Implicit knowledge: new perspectives on unconscious processes, *Int. Rev. Neurobiol.*, **37**, 271-284, 1994.

108. Schacter, D. L., Chiu, C. Y. and Ochsner, K. N. Implicit memory: a selective review. *Ann. Rev. Neurosci.*, **16**, 159-182, 1993.

109. Schlaug, G., Knorr, U. and Seitz, R. Inter-subject variability of cerebral activations in acquiring a motor skill: a study with positron emission tomography, *Exp. Brain Res.*, **98**, 523-534, 1994.

110. Schmidt, E. M., Bak, M. J., Hambrecht, F. I., Kufta, C. V., O'Rourke, D. K., and Vallabhanath, P. Feasibility of a visual prosthesis for the blind based on intracortical microstimulation of the visual cortex, *Brain*, **119**, 507-522, 1996.

111. Sherman, R. Stump and phantom limb pain, *Neurol. Clin.*, **7**, 249-264, 1989.

112. Squire, L. R. Mechanisms of memory, *Science*, **232**, 1612-1619, 1986.

113. Streletz, L. J., Belevich, J. K., Jones, S. M., Bhushan, A., Shah, S. H. and Herbison, G. J. Transcranial magnetic stimulation: cortical motor maps in acute spinal cord injury, *Brain Topog.*, **7**, 245-250, 1995.

114. Sunderland, S. *Nerves and Nerve Injuries*, (Churchill Livingstone, Edinburgh) 1978.

115. Topka, H., Cohen, L. G., Cole, R. A. and Hallett, M. Reorganization of corticospinal pathways following spinal cord injury, *Neurology*, **41**, 1276-1283, 1991.

116. Uhl, F., Franzen, P., Podreka, I., Steiner, M., and Deecke, L. Increased regional cerebral blood flow in inferior occipital cortex and cerebellum of early blind humans, *Neuroscience Letters*, **19**, 162-164, 1993.

117. Walker-Batson, D., Smith, P., Curtis, S., Unwin, H. and Greenlee, R. Amphetamine paired with physical therapy accelerates motor recovery after stroke. Further evidence, *Stroke*, **26**, 2254-2259, 1995.
118. Walker-Batson, D., Unwin, H., Curtis, S., Allen, E., Wood, M., Smith, P., Devous, Michael D., Reynolds, S., Greenlee, R. G. Use of amphetamine in the treatment of aphasia, *Restor. Neurol. Neurosci.*, **4**, 47-50, 1992.
119. Wall, J. T. Development and maintenance of somatotopic maps of the skin: a mosaic hypothesis based on peripheral and central contiguities, *Brain Behav. Evol.*, **31**, 252-268, 1988.
120. Wall, J. T., Kaas, J. H., Sur, M., Nelson, R. I., Felleman, D. J. and Merzenich, M. M. Functional reorganization in somatosensory cortical areas 3b and 1 of adult monkeys after median nerve repair: possible relationships to sensory recovery in humans, *J. Neurosci.*, **6**, 218-33, 1986.
121. Wall, J. T. and Kaas, J. H. Long-term cortical consequences of reinnervation errors after nerve regeneration in monkeys, *Brain Res.*, **372**, 400-404, 1986.
122. Wall, P. and Egger, M. Formation of new connections in adult rat brains after partial denervation, *Nature*, **232**, 542-545, 1971.
123. Wanet-Defalque, M. C., Veraart, C., De Volder, A., Metz, R., Michel, C., Dooms, G., and Goffinet, A. High metabolic activity in the visual cortex of early blind human subjects, *Brain Research*, **446**, 369-373, 1988.
124. Wassermann, E. M. et al. Local and distant changes in cerebral glucose metabolism during repetitive transcranial magnetic stimulation (rTMS), *Neurology* (abstract), **48**, A107, 1997.
125. Werhahn, K. I., Mortensen, J., Van Boven, R., Zeuner, K. and Cohen, L. Enhanced tactile spatial acuity and cortical processing during acute hand deafferentation, *Nat. Neurosci.*, **5**, 936-938, 2002.
126. Werhahn, K. J., Mortensen, J., Kaelin-Lang, A., Boroojerdi, B. and Cohen, L. G. Cortical excitability changes induced by deafferentation of the contralateral hemisphere, *Brain*, **125**, 1402-1413, 2002.
127. Willingham, D. B., Nissen, M. J. and Bullemer, P. On the development of procedural knowledge, *J. Exp. Psychol. Learn. Mem. Cogn.*, **15**, 1047-1060, 1989.
128. Zangaladze, A., Epstein, C. M., Grafton, S. T., and Sathian, K. Involvement of visual cortex in tactile discrimination of orientation, *Nature*, **401**, 587-590, 1999.
129. Zhuo, M. and Hawkins, R. D. Long-term depression: a learning-related type of synaptic plasticity in the mammalian central nervous system, *Rev. Neurosci.*, **6**, 259-277, 1995.
130. Ziemann, U., Corwell, B., and Cohen, L. G. Modulation of plasticity in human motor cortex after forearm ischemic nerve block, *Journal of Neuroscience*, **18**, 1115-1123, 1998.
131. Ziemann, U., Hallett, M., and Cohen, L. G. Mechanisms of deafferentation-induced plasticity in human motor cortex, *Journal of Neuroscience*, **18**, 7000-7007, 1998.
132. Ziemann, U., Wittenberg, G. F. and Cohen, L. G. Stimulation-induced within-representation and across-representation plasticity in human motor cortex, *J. Neurosci.*, **22**, 5563-5571, 2002.

Section 2

Stimulation and Recording

Chapter 2.1

Passive Models of Excitable Cells

Johannes Jan Struijk

Center for Sensory-Motor Interaction, Aalborg University
Fredrik Bajersvej 7D3, DK-9220 Aalborg, Denmark
jjs@hst.auc.dk

Excitable cells show a strongly nonlinear relationship between the transmembrane potential and the membrane current. In particular, after the membrane potential reaches threshold, the membrane potential follows a stereotyped wave shape called the action potential. Nevertheless, up to about 80% of the threshold level, the membrane potential and current can be described accurately using linear, or passive, models. In this chapter, we focus on the description of biological tissue as a target for electrical stimulation based on the passive properties of excitable cells. We first look at the relevant structure of the excitable cell with regard to electrical activation: the cell membrane, and the presence of ion channels. Then the resting potential is described and, finally, linear models for the response of excitable cells to intracellular and extracellular electrical stimuli are given for various kinds of cells.

1. Introduction

Although the term neuroprosthesis might very well comprise several modes of action, current practice in neuroprosthetic devices leaves a wide area of possibilities untouched. Typically, neuroprosthetic devices restore or support parts of the neuromuscular or neurosensory systems by stimulating muscle or neural tissue electrically. A chemical/pharmacological mode of action, or even a mechanical one, may open up a whole new area within neural prostheses but is beyond the state of the art of the field. Electric current can activate nerve and muscle cells to set off a stereotyped sequence of events mainly taking place at the cell membrane. Cells that exhibit the property of being activated are said to be *excitable*, whereas the process of initiating the cell's electrochemical activity is called *excitation*. The cell's activity can be recorded as a change of potential difference across the cell membrane, a process that actually travels over the cell membrane to other parts of the cell or to other cells. At rest, when the cell is inactive, the *transmembrane potential* of an excitable cell is between -50 and -100 mV, depending on the type of cell. The cell membrane is thus normally *polarized*, where the inside is negative relative to the outside. During excitation the inside first becomes less negative and even slightly positive, after which the resting state is gradually restored. The duration of the whole process, the *depolarization* and *repolarization*, also called the *action potential*, strongly depends on the type of cell. In a typical nerve cell this duration is about 0.5–1 ms, whereas in cardiac muscle cells it may be more than 400 ms, and in smooth muscle the action potential may last even longer[3].

Electric current can be induced in the body through electrodes or by the application of a varying magnetic field. Some examples are pacing and defibrillation of the heart, spinal cord stimulation for pain management, stimulation of nerves and muscles for restoration of functional movement or perception, stimulation of the auditory nerve or its receptors for cochlear prostheses, and electrical stimulation of peripheral nerves for diagnostic purposes to assess parts of the neuromuscular system. The characteristics of the activation depend on 1) the current sources (e.g., the electrical stimulator: amplitude, waveform, repetition rate), 2) the conducting biological tissue between and around the electrodes and the target cells, and 3) the properties of the target cells.

In turn, the electrical or electrochemical activity of muscle and nerve can be measured extracellularly and be used in neuroprosthetic devices as well as in many diagnostic methods in daily clinical practice (electrocardiogram, electromyogram, electroencephalogram, electro-oculogram, electroretinagram, electroneurogram, electronystagmogram, evoked potentials, etc.). In neural prostheses, recorded signals from muscle and nerve will mainly be utilized to control prosthetic devices or to replace sensory perception. The characteristics of the recorded signals depend on 1) the current sources, being at the membranes of the nerve and muscle cells, 2) the conducting biological tissue between and around the active cells and the recording sites, and 3) the way the signals are recorded.

Excitable tissue can thus serve as a target tissue for electrical stimulation or as a current source for recording purposes. In both cases, the tissue is part of a conducting medium. Whether physiologically evoked currents or artificially impressed currents are studied, they all obey the same laws of physics, which can be derived from Maxwell's equations. Because most of the energy of biological signals is always in a frequency band below 10 kHz, it is in general safe to assume that the tissue is purely resistive. However, cell membranes in particular have very low conductivities and, therefore, on a microscopic scale the time-varying term of the current cannot be neglected. Usually, this is taken into account by assigning leaking capacitors to the membranes as soon as a microscopic scale is considered. But on a macroscopic scale the time varying terms in Maxwell's equations can be neglected. Even though in electrical stimulation square pulses are often used and those pulses certainly have higher frequency components than 10 kHz, the energy in those higher frequencies is relatively low, and the response of excitable tissue to those high frequencies is negligible. Therefore, for all practical cases, the low frequency -quasi static- approach can be used in electrical stimulation as well as in recording situations.

For our considerations the relevant Maxwell equation is Ampère's law, which relates the magnetic field strength to the total current density, $\mathbf{J}$, in each point in space. When we take the divergence of Ampère's law it reduces to

$$\nabla \cdot \mathbf{J} = 0 \tag{1}$$

which is the mathematical formulation of the property of resistive materials that the current generated in a certain volume (source current) is equal to the total current flowing out of the volume through the surface enclosing that volume (conduction current). In other words: it is Kirchhoff's current law for volume conductors.

For us the interesting case is the one where $\mathbf{J}$ is the sum of a conduction current, $\mathbf{J}_c$, and a source current (free current, or impressed current) $\mathbf{J}_s$:

$$\mathbf{J} = \mathbf{J}_c + \mathbf{J}_s \tag{2}$$

Here, the source current is the current generated at the membranes of cells or the current through a stimulation electrode. According to Ohm's law the conduction current or ohmic current can be written as:

$$\mathbf{J_c} = \sigma \mathbf{E} \tag{3}$$

where $\mathbf{E}$ is the electric field strength, given in Volt/meter, and σ is the conductivity of the conducting medium, in Siemens/meter, or 1/(Ohm·meter). Instead of working with the electric field it is easier to work with the electric potential, especially because potential differences (voltages) are easy to measure. The electric potential φ is defined as $\mathbf{E} = -\nabla\varphi$, where $\nabla\varphi$ is the gradient of the potential field. Combining this with Eqs. (1—3) gives the potential as a function of the source current:

$$\nabla \cdot \sigma \nabla \varphi = \nabla \cdot \mathbf{J}_s \tag{4}$$

which is a form of Poisson's equation. This equation directly relates the electric potential to the current density of the source and to the conductivity of the tissue. All conduction problems in bioelectricity are contained in this equation, although appropriate boundary conditions are needed to define a unique solution. Above all, Eq. (4) makes clear that to understand the electrical part of neuroprosthetics we must understand the properties of the tissue as a conductor and we must understand either the tissue or the electric stimulator as a current source. In the latter case, the response of the nerve cells or muscle cells to an extracellular field φ has to be understood.

The step from stimulation to movement, or from stimulation to perception is a wholly different area, involving several mechanical, chemical, physiological and psychological processes.

Moreover, the interface between the neuroprosthesis and the living organism is a complicated one, not only in terms of biocompatibility, but the conversion from electronic conduction of electric current (as in the electronic part of the prosthesis) to ionic conduction (in the body or organic parts of the prosthesis) or vice versa, is by no means simple.

2. Properties of Various Excitable Cells

2.1. *Excitable cells*

The excitation of a cell is the result of a stimulus, either physiological or artificial, or it is the result of a cyclic process inside the cell itself. The latter occurs in cardiac or intestinal pacemaker cells or in certain nerve cells that are rhythmically active even if isolated. All excitable cells exhibit some commonalities that make it possible to describe the process of excitation in a general way, but at the same time the number of differences is enormous, leading to a wealth of different cells all with their individual characteristics.

One of the most important commonalities is that all excitable cells have selective ion channels in their cell membrane that make it possible for certain ions to cross the membrane easily whereas for other ions the membrane is an effective barrier. This property of ion selective permeability of the membrane is the basis of the resting potential. However, the membrane permeabilities are not constant. On the contrary, the selective ion channels can open and close, making it respectively possible and impossible for a certain ion species to cross the membrane. This property, together with the resting potential, forms the basis of the action potential. The ion channels thus play a crucial role in the excitation process.

2.2. *Membrane*

The cell membrane of excitable cells has the same basic structure as other cells in the body. Primarily, it consists of a double lipid layer with a total thickness of 5–8 nm. The lipids are phosphoglycerides consisting of heads of phosphoric acids and long glycerid tails (fatty acids). The heads are hydrophilic, whereas the hydrocarbon chains, forming the tails of the glycerids, have a low solubility in water and thus are hydrophobic. The solubility properties form the basis for the double layer structure of the membrane where the phosphoric acids are in contact with the extracellular fluid on one side and with the intracellular fluid on the other side of the membrane. The hydrocarbon tails of these two layers are pointing towards each other.

The membrane is covered on both sides by loosely bound proteins (peripheral proteins), which are water soluble. Non-soluble, so-called integral proteins are embedded in the lipid bilayer and form lipid protein complexes. Some of these proteins cross the membrane completely (transmembrane proteins), being in contact with both the extracellular and intracellular fluids. They are the main transport carriers for ions, but also for water-soluble substrates such as glucose.

At body temperature the lipid bilayer is in a fluid state, like oil, which makes it possible for the proteins to rotate and to move around in a 2D fashion, but not to topple over easily. In principle, the proteins that do not extend through the membrane but are exposed to either the extracellular or the intracellular fluids can move through the membrane from one side to the other (flip-flop), but this mode of transport is very energy inefficient.

Some of the proteins in the cell membrane of excitable cells are passively or actively involved in the maintenance of excitability as well as the excitation process itself. They can be divided into ion transporters and ion channels.

2.3. *Ion channels*

Voltage-controlled and ion-selective variability of the membrane permeability is the key to the action potential. To account for experimentally observed membrane behavior, Hodgkin and Huxley postulated ion channels to be the active components needed to create action potentials and they gave a statistical description of their opening and closing behavior, based on voltage clamp experiments. But until the development of patch-clamp techniques with which the quantitative behavior of single channels was established, the real evidence for the existence of channels was meager. The physical structure of the channels is still an important research topic, although much has been exposed in recent years.

An ion channel is basically a protein consisting of chained helical domains, each of them crossing the membrane. A well studied bacterial K^+ channel consists of four subunits, each consisting of two membrane spanning helices. For other types of K^+ channels each subunit spans the membrane four, six, or seven times. The four subunits together form a water filled pore in the membrane, narrow enough to dehydrate a K^+ ion (strip it from its water mantle) and just wide enough to let the naked ion go through. Larger ions cannot pass the bottle neck, whereas smaller ions, such as Na^+ are too small to be effectively dehydrated by the channel, whereas they are too big in their hydrated state. The ion channel is thus selective for K^+ ions. In the same way, other types of channels can be selective for Na^+ ions, for Cl^- ions, for Ca^{++} ions, etc. [3,8]

An important property of some ion channels is that they can be open or closed. Many types of channels can bind signaling molecules (ligands) to open or close, other channels, especially in receptors, are activated by heat or by mechanical deformation. Another mode of action is electrical: a voltage across the membrane, which gives rise to the so-called voltage-gated ion channels. Although the molecular structure of the voltage-gating part of the channels is far from clear yet, it is known that some of the membrane spanning (helical) domains contain amino acids that are electrically charged. A changing voltage across the membrane then rotates the helix, thereby deforming the protein and thus allowing the channel to open or to close.

The molecular structure of ion channels thus allows for the membrane permeability to be selective for specific ions and to be voltage controlled.

2.4. *Ion transporters*

Ion transporters are divided into pumps and exchangers, but in all cases the duty of the transporter is to move specific ions against their electrochemical gradients in order to maintain a non-equilibrium steady state, such as the resting membrane potential. The required energy is obtained either from the hydrolysis of ATP (adenosine tri-phosphate), as in the case of the important Na-K pump, or from the electrochemical gradients of ions or molecules that are co-transported, as is the case for the Na-Ca exchanger, where the energy released by the downhill transportation of Na^+ is used to transport Ca^{++} against the electrochemical gradient.

The Na-K pump is the best known transporter, but its mode of action is still hypothetical. It is an integral protein, which spans the membrane eleven times. Its function is to move Na^+ ions from inside to outside the cell, and to take K^+ ions in the opposite direction, thus maintaining the concentration gradients across the membrane. In each cycle three Na^+ ions are transported for only two K^+ ions. This means that the pump generates a (small) net current and therefore this kind of transporter is called *electrogenic*. Intracellularly, K^+ is released, whereas Na^+ is bound to a part of the protein. Intracellular phosphorylation of the protein, involving the hydrolysis of ATP, somehow (by deformation of the protein) moves the Na^+ ions through the protein, to be released extracellularly, after which extracellar K^+ is bound in order to be transported into the cell, mediated by intracellular dephosphorylation of the protein.

It is estimated that in the brain approximately 30% of the energy consumption is used to fuel the Na-K pump.

3. Action Potential

When measuring with micro electrodes between the inside and the outside of an excitable cell, i.e., across the cell membrane, a potential difference is observed. When the cell is inactive, or at rest, this potential difference is in the order of -50 to -100 mV, depending on the type of cell. The minus sign in this so-called resting potential appears because the intracellular potential is negative relative to the extracellular potential and convention prescribes that the transmembrane potential be defined as the intracellular potential minus the extracellular potential: $V_m = V_i - V_e$.

Now, when the cell is activated an action potential develops across the cell membrane. Figure 1 shows action potentials for three types of cells: nerve, skeletal muscle and cardiac muscle. Starting at the resting potential the transmembrane potential quickly rises to a slightly positive value after which the polarization of the membrane is restored: relatively quickly in the nerve fiber, where the whole process lasts less than a millisecond, about 1.5 ms in the skeletal muscle fiber, and 200–400 ms in the cardiac fiber. During the action potential and some time after the action potential the cell is not excitable by additional stimuli (absolute refractory period) and less excitable for a further short duration (relative refractory period), up to 2 ms for the nerve cell. The muscle cell in Fig. 1 shows a very slow final return to baseline and stays slightly depolarized for quite a long period (after-depolarization). Instead of after-depolarization, also after-hyperpolarization may occur, in particular in nerve cells.

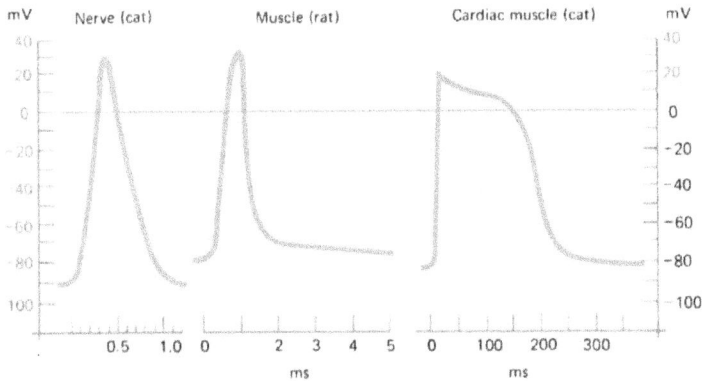

Fig. 1. Transmembrane action potentials of nerve, skeletal muscle, and cardiac muscle. Note the widely varying time scale. (From [10])

4. Resting Potential

The resting potential of an excitable cell is dependent on several factors, the most important of which are: 1) the presence of intracellular charged proteins that cannot pass the cell membrane, 2) the presence of (constant) concentrations of various ion species, 3) the ion selective permeability of the cell membrane, 4) the existence of an active ion pump. These factors will be analysed in the following.

For the purpose of describing the transmembrane resting potential, an excitable cell can roughly be described as a compartment containing charged molecules and ions immersed in water. The extracellular space can similarly be described as a compartment with ions in water. Starting with this point of view we need to consider two driving fields that act on the ions in the compartments:

1. The concentration gradient (giving rise to *diffusion*), and
2. The electric field (giving rise to *migration*).

Both these driving fields give rise to fluxes of charge carriers and thus to electric currents. During rest, the net current has to be zero. It will turn out that this view is insufficient and that a third mechanism has to be included:

3. Active (using energy) transport of ions through the membrane.

First we will consider the effects of diffusion and migration on a single ion species, *k*.

4.1. Diffusion

Fick's first law gives the relationship between the flux of an ion species *k* and its concentration gradient as follows:

$$\mathbf{j}_{diff,k} = -D_k \nabla C_k \tag{5}$$

where $\mathbf{j}_{diff,k}$ is the number of ions that pass a unit area per unit time (mole/m^{2}s), C_k is the concentration (mole/m^3) for ion species *k*, and D_k is Fick's constant (m^2/s) for this ion species in this solvent. This law describes that the movement or flux of ions from a high concentration to a low concentration is proportional to the concentration gradient with a proportionality constant D_k. Fick's constant depends on the size of the ion, including its mantle of water molecules, and the viscosity of the solvent (in this case water). The minus sign arises because the gradient is defined as pointing in the direction from a low value to a high value, whereas the actual flux is "downhill".

4.2. Migration

The flux of ions driven by an electric field is proportional to the electric field, the mobility of the ions, and the concentration of the ions:

$$\mathbf{j}_{migr,k} = -\mu_k \frac{z_k}{|z_k|} C_k \nabla \Phi \tag{6}$$

where $\mathbf{j}_{migr,k}$ is the flux, or the number of ions that pass a unit area per unit time (mole/m^{2}s), μ_k is the mobility (m^2/Vs), which is defined as the velocity achieved under a unit electric field, and z_k is the valence of the ion (the ratio $z_k/|z_k|$ is but the sign of the charge of the ion: $z_k/|z_k|=1$ for a cation and $z_k/|z_k|=-1$ for an anion). $\mathbf{E} =$

-$\nabla\Phi$ is the electric field (V/m), where Φ is the electric potential in Volts. Equation (6) implies that positive ions move from a higher potential to a lower potential (hence the minus sign) and negative ions move from a lower to a higher potential. The mobility depends on the viscosity of the solvent, on the size of the ion and its valence. It is therefore not surprising that Fick's constant and the mobility of an ion species are proportional to each other. The exact relationship was given by Einstein (1905) as:

$$D_k = \frac{RT}{|z_k|F} \mu_k \tag{7}$$

where R is the gas constant (8.3143 J/moleK), F is Faraday's constant (9.64867x10^4 C/mole), and T is the temperature in Kelvin (RT/F=26.7 mV at normal human body temperature (37 °C)).

4.3. Nernst-Planck equation

With Einstein's relation we can arrive at a form of Nernst-Planck equation by writing for the total flux for ion species k: $\mathbf{j}_k = \mathbf{j}_{diff,k} + \mathbf{j}_{migr,k}$, or

$$\mathbf{j}_k = -D_k\left(\nabla C_k + \frac{Fz_kC_k}{RT}\nabla\Phi\right) \tag{8}$$

From ion flux it is a small step to current density. With Fz_k being the charge carried per mole of ions with valence z_k, the current density is $\mathbf{J}_k = \mathbf{j}_k Fz_k$.

When considering a thin membrane (5–8 nm), where thin means thin as compared with the membrane's lateral extent, the gradients within the membrane are safely assumed to have non-vanishing components in the transverse direction only (normal to the membrane). Using x for this transverse dimension, the gradients reduce to simple derivatives $\nabla C_k \rightarrow dC_k/dx$ and $\nabla\Phi \rightarrow d\Phi/dx$. The Nernst-Planck equation for the membrane can then be rewritten after some rearrangement as:

$$\frac{dC_k}{dx}(x) + z_k\frac{F}{RT}\frac{d\Phi}{dx}(x)C_k(x) = -\frac{1}{D_k}j_k(x), \quad \text{for } k=1,\dots,N \tag{9}$$

where now $j_k(x)$ is the flux of ions species k in the x-direction as a function of x inside the membrane, and N is the number of ion species to be considered. Equations (9) are N ordinary differential equations, one for each of the ion species, coupled by the common potential function $\Phi(x)$.

Before giving the solution of this set of equations it is instructive to look at a special case where the membrane is permeable to a single ion species only.

4.4. *Nernst equation*

During rest the membrane has a relatively high permeability for potassium (K^+) ions as compared with other ions. Now consider a cell separated by the cell membrane from the extracellular space. In the two compartments the substance KA is dissolved, but in the intracellular space the concentration is higher than in the extracellular space. The membrane is permeable for cation K^+ but not for the large anion A^-, which could be a large protein. Note that for this initial condition both compartments are electrically neutral.

Since the membrane is permeable for K^+ and we assume that, initially, there is no potential difference between the compartments, there will be a net movement (by diffusion) of K^+ from the intracellular space to the extracellular space, resulting in an increasing potential difference across the membrane, such that the extracellular space becomes positive with respect to the intracellular space. This in turn results in a migration flux, from the extracellular space to the intracellular space. After some time the resulting migration of K^+ ions (from outside to inside) will balance the diffusion flux (from inside to outside). Under this equilibrium condition there is no further net ion flux: $j_{K^+}(x) = 0$, which means that the right hand side in Eq. (9) vanishes. With $C_k = [K^+]$ and $z_k = z_K$ Eq. (9) thus reduces to:

$$\frac{d\Phi}{dx} = -\frac{RT}{z_K F} \frac{1}{[K^+]} \frac{d[K^+]}{dx} \tag{10}$$

Integrating Eq. (10) across the membrane yields:

$$E_K = \Phi_i - \Phi_e = \frac{RT}{z_K F} \ln \frac{[K^+]_e}{[K^+]_i} \tag{11}$$

where $[K^+]_e$ is the extracellular K^+ concentration and $[K^+]_i$ the intracellular K^+ concentration. z_K is the valence for potassium, which is $z_K = 1$. Because the extracellular concentration is lower than the intracellular concentration, E_K is negative.

Equation (11) is known as the Nernst equation and E_K is the Nernst potential. The Nernst equation has to be derived under equilibrium conditions during which the net flux or current of ions is zero [7].

4.5. *Donnan equilibrium*

Now suppose that we do not only have large anions and potassium, but also sodium ions Na^+ and chloride ions Cl^- in the solutions, and suppose that all ions are in equilibrium, i.e., that for each ion species the diffusion current cancels the migration current through the membrane. According to the Nernst equation for potassium, sodium and chloride, this means:

$$E_K = \frac{RT}{F}\ln\left(\frac{[K^+]_e}{[K^+]_i}\right)$$

$$E_{Na} = \frac{RT}{F}\ln\left(\frac{[Na^+]_e}{[Na^+]_i}\right)$$

$$E_{Cl} = \frac{RT}{F}\ln\left(\frac{[Cl^-]_i}{[Cl^-]_e}\right) \tag{12}$$

Because there can be only one potential difference across the membrane these three Nernst potentials must be equal: $E_K=E_{Na}=E_{Cl}$, leading to

$$\frac{[K^+]_e}{[K^+]_i} = \frac{[Na^+]_e}{[Na^+]_i} = \frac{[Cl^-]_i}{[Cl^-]_e} \tag{13}$$

This condition, arising when all permeable ions are in equilibrium, is known as the Donnan equilibrium (see, e.g., [5]).

4.6. *Sodium-potassium pump*

In the cat motoneuron the ratios of the extracellular and the intracellular concentrations for potassium, sodium and chloride were found to be approximately 0.037, 10, and 14, respectively. This is far from the Donnan equilibrium. In general, in excitable cells the Donnan equilibrium does not exist, i.e., the ions are not in equilibrium, not even during the resting condition of the cell.

The reason for this lack of equilibrium is that an active mechanism is disturbing the situation. The sodium-potassium pump (Na-K pump) pumps potassium into the cell and sodium out of the cell at a ratio of 2:3. Other pumps have also been identified, the most important one, after the Na-K pump, being a Na-Ca pump in, for example, cardiac muscle.

4.7. *Goldman's equation*

Under the non-equilibrium condition the $j_k(x)$ in Eq. (9) are not zero, and the set of equations is not solvable unless certain assumptions are adopted. In general, the potential function Φ is implicitly given by Poisson's Equation (4) and depends directly on the charge distributions inside the membrane. A crude assumption, which implies that there are no fixed charges in the membrane (which is definitely wrong) and that the influence of external surface charges is negligible (which may not be true either), is that the electric field $E_x=-d\Phi/dx$ is constant across the membrane (Goldman's assumption). In this case the term $d\Phi/dx$ in Eq. (9) can be written as

$$\frac{d\Phi}{dx} = \frac{V_m}{h} \tag{14}$$

where V_m is the transmembrane potential and h is the membrane thickness.

With this assumption and "a little algebra" the membrane potential can be solved as

$$V_m = -\frac{RT}{F}\ln\frac{P_K[K^+]_e + P_{Na}[Na^+]_e + P_{Cl}[Cl^+]_i}{P_K[K^+]_i + P_{Na}[Na^+]_i + P_{Cl}[Cl^+]_e} \tag{15}$$

where P_K, P_{Na}, and P_{Cl} are the permeabilities for the potassium, sodium and chloride ions.

An additional assumption used to derive Eq. (15) is that, where the individual ion fluxes were not zero, during the resting state we may assume that the total flux of all ions vanishes:

$$j_K + j_{Na} + j_{Cl} = 0 \tag{16}$$

Equation (15) is Goldman's equation, also called the Goldman-Hodgkin-Katz equation[2].

Despite the crudeness of the constant field assumption, Goldman's equation turns out to be a very good approximation of the resting potential given the various concentrations of the ions involved.

Because during rest the permeability for potassium is much greater than for sodium and chloride, the resting membrane potential is close to the Nernst potential for potassium.

During the development of an action potential net current is flowing into (depolarization) and out of (repolarization) the cell. This means that the Goldman equation is not valid during the action potential, except at those points where the net current is (close to) zero. This occurs at the peak of the action potential and, for example, for cardiac muscle fibers, at the plateau phase of the action potential. At the peak of the action potential the permeability of sodium is very high compared with the other permeabilities, which means that at the peak the membrane potential tends towards the Nernst potential for sodium.

5. Subthreshold Phenomena

Subthreshold phenomena may be interesting in themselves, but the active behavior of a nerve or a muscle fiber, seen from a functional point of view, is the most important part of the physiological description of nerve and muscle. However, in the context of bioelectricity, and up to about 80% of the threshold, the neural membrane can be adequately described as a passive RC network. This implies that, even when studying electrical stimulation, where the goal is to activate neurons, study of the passive behavior can give a good insight in the behavior of the neurons and the effect of several stimulus parameters. Roughly speaking, the passive behavior of the cell explains 80% of the phenomena during electrical activation.

5.1. *I-t curve (based on passive model of membrane patch)*

The simplest model of a cell is a spherical passive membrane. If a stimulation electrode, carrying a current, I_s, with duration T, would be placed in the center of such a cell, together with a reference electrode far away from the cell, then the membrane voltage due to the current would be spherically symmetrical. Therefore, this whole cell membrane can be represented by a lumped R_mC_m network (Fig. 2).

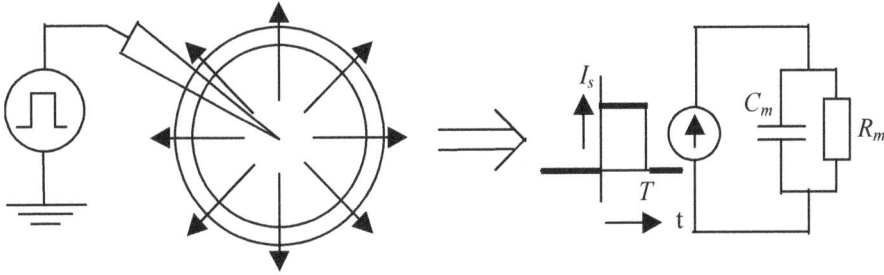

Fig. 2. Left: schematic view of a stimulation electrode in the center of a spherical cell; the arrows indicate the current flow through the cell membrane. Right: RC network as an electric circuit model of the cell.

The total current, I_s, through the membrane is then divided into a capacitive (displacement) current and a current through the membrane resistor (ionic):

$$I_s = I_c + I_i = C_m \frac{dV_m}{dt} + \frac{V_m}{R_m} \tag{17}$$

The membrane potential $V_m=V_m(t)$ can then be solved for the duration of the pulse $(0 \le t \le T)$ as:

$$V_m(t) = I_s R_m \left(1 - e^{-t/\tau_m}\right), 0 \le t \le T \tag{18}$$

where τ_m is the membrane time constant: $\tau_m = R_mC_m$. This function is monotonically increasing with t. Thus, for a pulse with length T, the maximum voltage will be reached at the end of the pulse, $t=T$.

If we assume that the threshold for excitation is simply a constant voltage V_{th}, then the lowest current needed to reach V_{th} will be obtained when the duration of the current pulse is infinitely long.

The minimum current to reach threshold with the infinitely long pulse is called the *rheobase*, I_{rh}.

$$\lim_{t \to \infty} V_m(t) = V_{th} = \lim_{t \to \infty} \left(I_{rh} R_m \left(1 - e^{-t/\tau_m} \right) \right) = I_{rh} R_m \qquad (19)$$

which gives

$$I_{rh} = \frac{V_{th}}{R_m} \qquad (20)$$

Then, for pulse durations $T < \infty$ the threshold V_{th} will be reached at the end of the pulse ($t=T$) when the stimulus current is:

$$I_{s,th} = \frac{I_{rh}}{1 - e^{-T/\tau_m}} \qquad (21)$$

The graph of the threshold current $I_{s,th}$ as a function of the pulse duration, T, is called the *strength-duration curve*, or in short, *I-t curve* (Fig. 3).

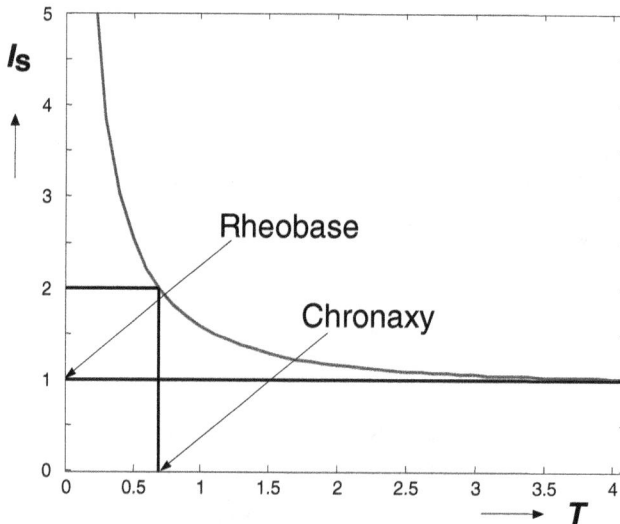

Fig. 3. Strength duration curve for the spherical cell of Fig. 2. Rheobase is defined as the minimum threshold for infinite pulse duration; chronaxy is the minimum pulse duration needed to excite the cell with a current that is twice the rheobase. The Is-axis is normalized to the rheobase, and the membrane time constant $\tau_m=1$.

A useful parameter is the *chronaxy* of the cell. Chronaxy, T_{chr}, is defined as the minimum pulse duration needed to reach threshold if the current is twice the rheobase: $I_{s,th} = 2I_{rh}$. From Eq. (21) it follows directly that

$$T_{chr} = \tau_m \ln 2 \approx 0.69 \tau_m \qquad (22)$$

It is important to note that for a given membrane thickness and membrane material, R_m depends only on the size of the spherical cell: $R_m = c/r^2$, where c is a constant and r is the radius of the cell. According to Eq. (20) the rheobase will then increase with the square of the radius of the cell.

The chronaxy, however, depends on both Rm and Cm. And because Cm=k·r2, with k a constant, we see that the membrane time constant, τ_m, is independent of the size of the cell. With Eq. (22) this means that the chronaxy is independent of the size of the cell. Chronaxy can, therefore, be used to characterize the membrane independent of the size of the cell. We will see later that this is true only for a spherical cell, but not for the general case of stimulation of nervous tissue (even though generally it is true that chronaxy is much less dependent on parameters such as cell size and electrode-tissue distance than rheobase).

The derivation above was made with an electrode in the center of the cell. Because the intracellular fluid has a much higher conductivity than the cell membrane, it is almost irrelevant what the exact location of the electrode inside the cell is. Even if the current source is not an electrode but a synaptic transmission, which can be modeled as a small current injected through the membrane into the cell, the considerations as given above still hold: larger cells have a lower input impedance, which means that the cell needs higher currents (i.e., more synaptic inputs) than smaller cells to be excited.

Note however that a model is just a model. In reality larger cells tend to have higher membrane time constants and smaller cells have lower values for the membrane time constant, which indicates that the constants c and k are not really constant or that the non-spherical shape of the cell plays a role as well.

For practical stimulation purposes, not only current is of interest, but also the charge injection is important. The threshold charge, associated with the threshold current $I_{s,th}$ is given by

$$Q_{th} = T I_{s,th} \qquad (23)$$

From Eqs. (21) and (23) it follows that

$$Q_{th}(T) = \frac{T \cdot I_{rh}}{1 - e^{-T/\tau_m}} \qquad (24)$$

This function has a minimum for $T=0$: $Q_{th}(T=0)=I_{rh}/\tau_m$ which means that short pulses give the best conditions in terms of total injected charge (relatively low charge for short pulses with high currents as compared with the injected charge for longer pulses with lower currents).

The spherical cell as described above serves as a paradigm for other situations. Especially, the nomenclature rheobase, chronaxy, and I-t curve are derived from it.

5.2. Passive axon model (unmyelinated axon)

Whereas the resistance and capacitance of the membrane of a perfectly spherical passive cell in the case of current injection in the center of the cell can be lumped into a single RC network, current injection in an axon demands a more elaborate description of the membrane.

A very popular, highly stylized model of an axon is the description of the membrane as a cable network. Let us first consider the unmyelinated axon. The axon membrane is considered to be a perfect, long cylinder and the electric current and membrane potential are assumed to be perfectly cylindrically symmetrical, as for example, in the case of a point current injection at the axis of the cylinder (Fig. 4) or a long wire electrode at the axis of the axon.

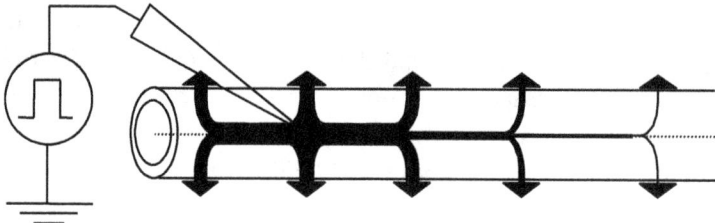

Fig. 4. Current injection in a cylindrical cell. The line thickness of the current flow schematically indicates the current density.

In this case the membrane can be collapsed into a one dimensional cable structure consisting of resistances and capacitances: a resistance times unit length, r_m (Ωm), and a capacitance per unit length, c_m (F/m). The core of the cylinder (the intracellular space) is modeled as a resistive one dimensional medium with a resistance per unit length (r_i, in Ω/m) as is the extracellular space (r_e, in Ω/m) (Fig. 5).

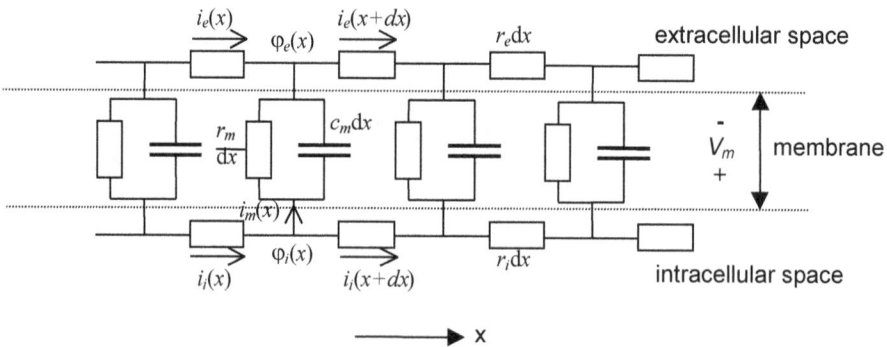

Fig. 5. RC cable model of the cylindrical cell.

The differential equation describing the membrane potential in this cable model is obtained as follows.

$$V_m(x,t) = \varphi_i(x,t) - \varphi_e(x,t) \qquad (25)$$

$$\frac{\partial \varphi_i}{\partial x} = -r_i i_i \tag{26}$$

$$\frac{\partial \varphi_e}{\partial x} = -r_e i_e \tag{27}$$

$$i_m = -\frac{\partial i_i}{\partial x} = \frac{\partial i_e}{\partial x} = \frac{V_m}{r_m} + c_m \frac{\partial V_m}{\partial t} \tag{28}$$

Differentiating Eq. (25) twice with respect to x, and using Eqs. (26) and (27) and subsequently Eq. (28) yields

$$\frac{\partial^2 V_m}{\partial x^2} = \frac{\partial^2}{\partial x^2}(\varphi_i - \varphi_e) = \frac{\partial}{\partial x}(r_e i_e - r_i i_i) = \frac{r_e + r_i}{r_m} V_m + (r_e + r_i)c_m \frac{\partial V_m}{\partial t} \tag{29}$$

or

$$-\lambda^2 \frac{\partial^2 V_m}{\partial x^2} + \tau_m \frac{\partial V_m}{\partial t} + V_m = 0 \tag{30}$$

where $\lambda^2 = \dfrac{r_m}{r_e + r_i}$ is the square of the so-called length constant and

$\tau_m = r_m c_m$ is the time constant of the membrane. The interpretation of the length constant can be highlighted by considering a steady state situation, in which the membrane potential does not change as a function of time. In that case the second term in Eq. (30) vanishes, leaving a simple second order ordinary differential equation. With boundary condition $V_m(0)=V_0$ and a vanishing potential at infinity, the solution then is

$$V_m(x) = V_0 \cdot e^{-|x|/\lambda} \tag{31}$$

In other words: the length constant is the distance from the site $x=0$ of a (steady state) disturbance in the membrane potential to the position where the influence of the disturbance is reduced to $e^{-1} = 0.37$ $(x=\pm\lambda)$.

For an interpretation of the time constant a similar exercise can be made. Assume the membrane potential is independent of x. Then Eq. (30) reduces to

$$\tau_m \frac{\partial V_m}{\partial t} + V_m = 0 \tag{32}$$

which is of the same form as Eq. (17). Without sources, but with the initial condition $Vm(0)=V_0$, we have

$$V_m(t) = V_0 e^{-t/\tau_m} \tag{33}$$

The time constant thus gives an indication of how quickly the membrane potential changes after a disturbance.

These two cases, the membrane potential either being independent of time or independent of the spatial coordinate, have relatively simple solutions. If we do not assume these simplifications, then the solution of Eq. (30) becomes quite complicated indeed. Suppose we have a sudden intracellular current injection in $x=0$ at $t=0$ with a current I_0: $I_s(x,t)=I_0\delta(x,t)$. In this case the solution of Eq. (30) can be obtained as

$$V_{m,I_s=\delta}(x,t) = r_m I_0 \sqrt{\frac{\tau_m/t}{4\pi\lambda^2}} \exp\left(-\frac{\tau_m}{t}\left(\left(\frac{t}{\tau_m}\right)^2 + \left(\frac{x}{2\lambda}\right)^2\right)\right) \quad (34)$$

which shows a rather complicated interaction between t and x.

Because Eq. (34) is the impulse response of the membrane, the membrane potential for an infinitely long fiber, due to a current injection with a different current waveform, $I_s=I_s(x,t)$, in time, t, and a distribution in space, x, can be obtained by a convolution of V_m as given in Eq. (34) with the current $I_s(x,t)$ with respect to both x and t:

$$V_m(x,t) = \int_{\xi=-\infty}^{\infty} \int_{\tau=0}^{\infty} I_s(\xi,\tau) V_{m,I_s=\delta}(x-\xi,t-\tau)\,d\tau d\xi \quad (35)$$

A detailed analysis of Eq. (34) or even more complex situations (Eq. (35)) is beyond the scope of this text, but can be found in [1].

The time constant, $\tau_m = r_m c_m$, is independent of axon diameter since r_m is reciprocal with diameter and c_m is proportional with diameter. The length constant, $\lambda^2 = r_m/(r_i + r_e)$, depends on axon diameter because r_i is reciprocal with diameter squared, whereas r_e is negligible under normal circumstances, where the extracellular space is much larger than the intracellular space. Therefore, λ^2 is linear with fiber diameter: larger fibers have greater length constants. In other words a change in membrane potential in a thick fiber is spread over a longer distance than in a thin fiber. This is the key to understanding why thick unmyelinated fibers have a higher conduction velocity than thin unmyelinated fibers.

Typical length constants are in the order of 0.1–1 mm. Typical time constants are in the order of 1 ms.

5.3. Myelinated axon

The simplest way to model the (passive) myelinated axon is to consider each node of Ranvier as a discrete RC network, the axonal cylinder between adjacent nodes as a single resistor, and the extracellular space between adjacent nodes as a single resistor as well. Labelling the membrane potentials for node of Ranvier number n as $V_{m,n}(t)$, the membrane potential can be written as:

$$-\lambda^2 \left(V_{m,n-1} - 2V_{m,n} + V_{m,n+1}\right) + \tau_m \frac{\partial V_{m,n}}{\partial t} + V_{m,n} = 0 \qquad (36)$$

similar to Eq. (30), but with a second order difference term with respect to the discrete space coordinate n, instead of the second order derivative with respect to the continuous space coordinate x.

$\tau_m = R_m C_m$, and $\lambda^2 = R_m/(R_i + R_e)$, where R_m (Ω) is the nodal membrane resistance (inversely proportional to the axon diameter), C_m (F) is the nodal membrane capacitance (proportional to axon diameter), R_i is the intra-axonal resistance between adjacent nodes (inversely proportional to axon diameter), and R_e, the extracellular resistance is negligible because it represents a much larger space than R_i. The proportionalities mentioned are valid only under the assumptions that the length of the node of Ranvier (1–2 μm) is independent of fiber diameter, and that the distance between adjacent nodes of Ranvier (internodal distance) is proportional to fiber diameter (proportionality constant approximately 100). In that case it turns out that both τ_m and λ are independent of fiber diameter, which implies that Eq. (36), and thus the membrane potential, is independent of fiber diameter. However, experiments show that the conduction velocity is close to linear with fiber diameter and that excitation thresholds for electrical stimulation also have a strong dependence on fiber diameter. The key is that the distance between nodes n and $n+1$ is proportional to fiber diameter, which explains the linearity of conduction velocity with fiber diameter when assuming that the conduction velocity is constant in terms of number of nodes per second.

6. Extracellular stimulation

Within the framework of neuroprostheses we are particularly interested in the situation where the stimulating electrodes are not inside the cell, but at some distance outside the cell, and in the case of nerve stimulation we are often interested in axons rather than cell bodies. If the field is created by external electrodes at some distance from the cell, it is the larger cell, or the larger axon that has the lower threshold, opposite to the situation of intracellular current injection.

6.1. Spherical cells

Consider an extremely simplified spherical cell, with a membrane having a very high resistivity and a plasma having a very high conductivity. If such a cell is placed in a flat electric field E, for example, because of a stimulation electrode at some distance from the cell, then the cell membrane will become depolarized on one side of the cell and hyperpolarized at the other side, with membrane potential[1]:

$$V_m = -\frac{3}{2}Er\cos\theta \qquad (37)$$

where r is the cell's radius and θ is the angle with the field axis as shown in Fig. 6.

The mathematics used to derive Eq. .(37) involves the Laplace equation in polar coordinates with suitable boundary conditions (Eq. (4) with vanishing right hand side) and is beyond the scope of this chapter. The importance of Eq. (37) is that it shows that the membrane potential is linear with the size of the cell. Or, equivalently, that the stimulus threshold is inversely proportional with the cell radius, which is the opposite of the result that we obtained for intracellular stimulation of a spherical cell. In summary:

Intracellular stimulation $\Rightarrow$ stimulus threshold proportional to the square of the cell's radius.

Extracellular stimulation $\Rightarrow$ stimulus threshold inversely proportional to the cell's radius.

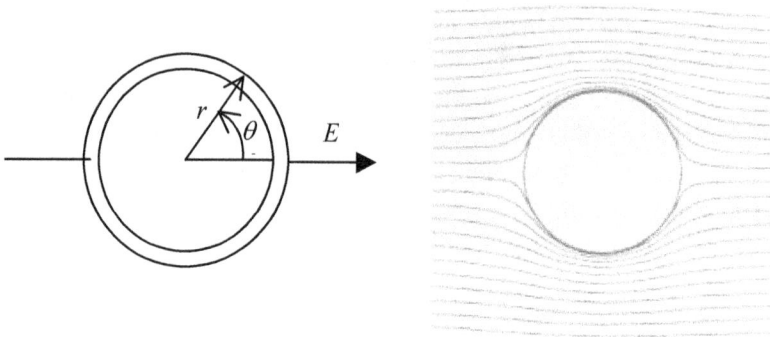

Fig. 6. Left: Spherical cell with the definition of the angle θ relative to the direction of the electric field E. Right: current flow around a spherical cell with very high membrane resistivity (from [1]).

6.2. Nerve fibers

For cylindrical cells, and for a homogeneous field perpendicular to the fiber, the same approach as for the spherical cell could be used, now based on Laplace's equation in cylindrical coordinates, resulting in[4]

$$V_m = -2Er\cos\theta \qquad (38)$$

However, for a cylindrical cell the field along the cylinder can usually not be considered to be homogeneous, but a clear nonhomogeneous potential profile along the fiber will usually exist, together with a longitudinal component of the field. It turns out that the longitudinal component becomes the dominating factor in virtually all cases of interest, making Eq. (38) useless. A different approach has thus to be used.

Moreover, the models for the unmyelinated and myelinated nerve fibers as presented in earlier sections, are difficult to use for the case of electrical stimulation with an electrode at some distance from the fiber. But, for this situation a modification of the models was made by McNeal[6], who used the extracellular potential field V_e, due to electrical stimulation, as the driving source for the membrane potential (Fig. 7). Thus the external potential field at the nodes of Ranvier serve as ideal voltage sources in the cable model.

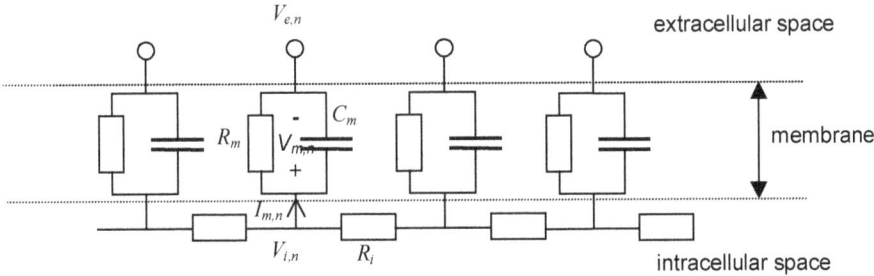

Fig. 7. McNeal's cable model of a myelinated fiber for extracellular stimulation[6].

For the passive model the governing equation for the membrane potential can be derived as follows.

$$V_{m,n} = V_{i,n} - V_{e,n} \tag{39}$$

where $V_{e,n}$ is the known, impressed, extracellular potenital at node n.

$$I_{m,n} = \frac{V_{i,n-1} - V_{i,n}}{R_i} - \frac{V_{i,n} - V_{i,n+1}}{R_i} = \frac{1}{R_i}\left(V_{i,n-1} - 2V_{i,n} + V_{i,n+1}\right) \tag{40}$$

$$I_{m,n} = \frac{1}{R_m}V_{m,n} + C_m\frac{dV_{m,n}}{dt} \tag{41}$$

Combining Eqs. (40) and (41) and subsequently substituting Eq. (39) finally gives:

$$-\lambda^2\left(V_{m,n-1} - 2V_{m,n} + V_{m,n+1}\right) + \tau_m\frac{\partial V_{m,n}}{\partial t} + V_{m,n} = -\lambda^2\left(V_{e,n-1} - 2V_{e,n} + V_{e,n+1}\right) \tag{42}$$

Note that the left hand side of Eq. (42) is identical to Eq. (38), whereas the right hand side now is the second order difference of the extracellular potentials at the nodes of Ranvier.

A similar derivation for the extracellular stimulation of unmyelinated fibers yields:

$$-\lambda^2\frac{\partial^2 V_m}{\partial x^2} + \tau_m\frac{\partial V_m}{\partial t} + V_m = -\lambda^2\frac{\partial^2 V_e}{\partial x^2} \tag{43}$$

which is similar to Eq. (30) but with the right hand side now being the second derivative of the extracellular potential along the fiber.

The right hand side in Eq. (43) was termed "activating function" by Rattay[9], and this activating function is very useful to see what initially happens to the membrane potential when a stimulus pulse is applied. Suppose that a fiber is stimulated with a rectangular stimulus pulse, and that initially the membrane potential $V_m(0)=0$. Then V_e will be constant for the duration of the stimulus pulse, and zero before and after the pulse, and so will $\dfrac{\partial^2 V_m}{\partial x^2}$. Then Eq. (43) reduces to

$$\tau_m \left. \frac{\partial V_m}{\partial t}\right|_{t=0} = -\lambda^2 \frac{\partial^2 V_e}{\partial x^2} \text{ with a solution}$$

$$V_m(t) \approx -\frac{\lambda^2}{\tau_m} \frac{\partial^2 V_e}{\partial x^2}\cdot t , \text{ for small values of } t \text{ (relative to } \tau_m). \qquad (44)$$

Thus, a positive activating function will decrease the membrane potential (hyperpolarize the membrane) and a negative activating function will increase the membrane potential (depolarize the membrane). In other words: if activation of the fiber occurs, it will be there where the activating function is negative

For a long fiber in a large homogeneous medium and a monopolar point electrode in $x=0$ at some distance, h, from the fiber, the extracellular potential at the fiber is given by

$$V_e(x,t) = \frac{I_s(t)}{4\pi\sigma\sqrt{x^2 + h^2}} \qquad (45)$$

The second order derivative with respect to x then is

$$\frac{\partial^2 V_e(x,t)}{\partial x^2} = \frac{I_s(t)}{4\pi\sigma}\cdot\frac{2x^2 - h^2}{\left(x^2 + h^2\right)^{5/2}} \qquad (46)$$

Figure 8 shows the extracellular potential profile along the fiber and the activating function, apart from the constant $-\lambda^2$, for a monopolar cathode at 1 mm from the fiber (normalized to their peak values).

We see that the activating function (including $-\lambda^2$) is negative near the cathode ($x=0$) where the membrane depolarizes, corresponding to an outward current from the fiber towards the negative electrode. The relatively limited region of outward current is flanked by regions of more diffuse inward current, which is shown in the activating function as sidelobes with sidelobe amplitudes that are approximately 20% of the main lobe amplitude.

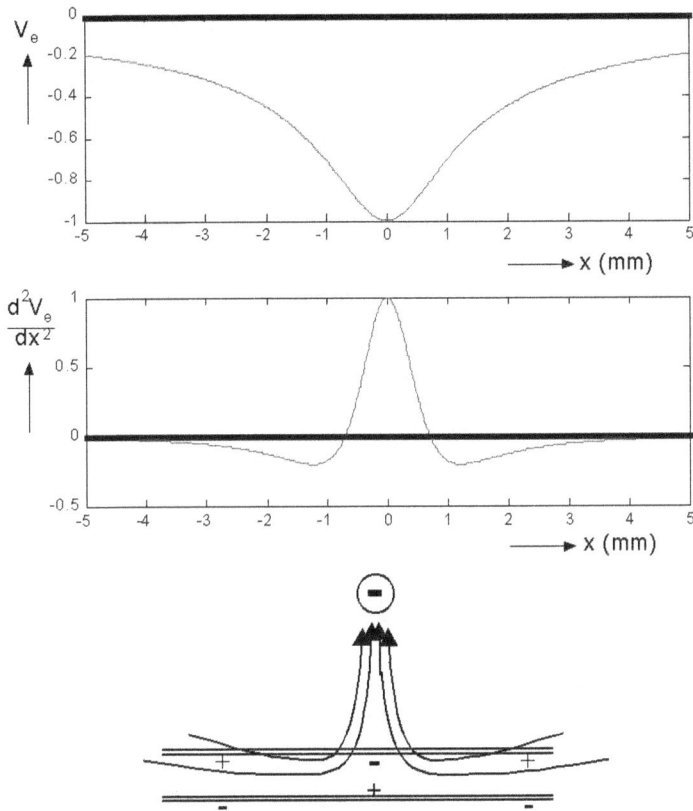

Fig..8. Top: extracellular potential along the nerve fiber. Middle: 2nd order derivative of the extracellular potential. Bottom: schematic drawing of the current flow towards the negative electrode (cathode). The high density current leaves the fiber close to the cathode, strongly depolarizing the membrane, whereas the current is more diffuse where it enters the fiber.

For an anodal electrode the signs of V_e and d^2V_e/dx^2 would be reversed, meaning that close to the electrode there would be a region of hyperpolarization and somewhat away from the electrode there would be regions of depolarization with a much lower amplitude. This is confirmed by experimental data that show that direct anodal stimulation requires higher currents than cathodal stimulation of nerves.

For longer pulses the transmembrane potential becomes a smeared version of the activating function, but even in the steady state case (infinitely long pulse) the activating function is a useful indicator for the transmembrane potential.

The analysis as described in this section can be extended to more complicated situations, such as nerve fibers with collateral branches and curving fibers. For examples see [11,12].

6.3. *Rheobase and chronaxy for the case of external stimulation*

Where for the round cell chronaxy was found to be related to the membrane time constant in a very straightforward way, Eq. (22), for the axon the matter is much more complicated (Table 1). One would not like to do an analysis similar to the one made for the spherical cell, on basis of, for example, Eqs. (34) and (35). Simulations show that for extracellular stimulation of the stylized axon as described above, chronaxy depends on, for example, electrode-fiber distance, in such a way that a point source close to the fiber gives the lowest value for the chronaxy, which monotonically increases by up to a factor two for increasing electrode-fiber distance.

Table 1. Chronaxy values for various tissues.

Tissue	Chronaxy (ms)
Skeletal muscle	0.1–1
Cardiac muscle	1–3
Smooth muscle	100
Myelinated nerve fiber	0.1–0.3

Of course, rheobase values are dependent on the size of the target cell, electrode-cell distance, electrode configuration, surrounding tissue, and cell orientation. The value of the rheobase can vary over several decades of magnitude for different situations. Chronaxy is much less variable, and, even though chronaxy is not completely independent of the stimulation conditions, it makes sense to give chronaxy values to classify various tissues.

Note the importance of chronaxy for the choice of pulse width for electrical stimulation: it doesn't make sense to try to stimulate smooth muscle with 100 μs pulses, whereas for myelinated nerve fibers this would be a perfectly sensible thing to do.

Other important electrical properties of nerve and muscle cells are shown in Table 2.

Table 2. Electrical properties of nerve and muscle cells.

membrane capacitance	$0.05–0.2$ F/m^2
membrane resistivity*	$0.1–1$ Ωm^2
intracellular resistivity*	$0.5–2$ Ωm

* values for nerve are in the lower range, for muscle in the higher values

References

1. Cole, K. S., Membranes Ions and Impulses, (University of California Press, Berkeley, 1968).
2. Goldman, D. E., Potential, impedance, and rectification in membranes, J. Gen. Physiol., 27, 37-60, 1943.
3. Kandel, E. R., Schwartz, J. H., and Jessell, T. M., Principles of Neural Science, (McGraw-Hill Companies, Inc., New York, 2000).
4. Krassowska, W. and Neu, J. C., Response of a single cell to an external electric field, Biophys. J., 66, 1768-1776, 1994.
5. Malmivuo, J. and Plonsey, R., Bioelectromagnetism – Principles and Applications of Bioelectric and Biomagnetic Fields, (Oxford University Press, Inc., Oxford, 1995).
6. McNeal, D. R., Analysis of a model for excitation of myelinated nerve, IEEE Trans. Biomed. Eng., 23, 329-337, 1976.
7. Nernst, W. H., Zur Kinetik der Lösung befindlichen Körper: Theorie der Diffusion, Z. Phys. Chem., 3, 613-637, 1888.
8. Purves, D., Augustine, G. J., Fitzpatrick, D., Katz, L. C., LaMantia, A.-S., McNamara, J. O., and Williams, S. M., Neuroscience, (Sinauer Associates, Inc., Sunderland, MA, 2001).
9. Rattay, F., Analysis of models for external stimulation of axons, IEEE, Trans. Biomed. Eng., 33, 974-977, 1986.
10. Schmidt, R. F., Fundamentals of Neurophysiology, (Springer-Verlag, New York, 1985).
11. Struijk, J. J., Holsheimer, J., Van der Heide, G. G., and Boom, H. B. K, Recruitment of dorsal column fibers in spinal cord stimulation: Influence of collateral branching, IEEE Trans. Biomed. Eng., 39, 903-912, 1992.
12. Struijk, J. J., Holsheimer, J., and Boom, H. B. K, Excitation of dorsal root fibers in spinal cord stimulation: A theoretical study, IEEE Trans. Biomed. Eng., 40, 632-639, 1993.

Chapter 2.2

Conductive and Insulative Materials

Stuart F. Cogan

University of Texas at Dallas
800 West Campbell Road, Dallas, TX, 75080 USA
stuart.cogan@utdallas.edu

Electrically conductive and insulative materials used in the construction of chronically implantable neural devices are reviewed. Metals are used as conductors in leads, as electrodes, and as the material of construction of hermetically sealed implanted pulse generators (IPGs). Metals commonly used in clinical devices, titanium, austenitic stainless steels, NiCoCr and related alloys, and PtIr alloys, are described in terms of applications and material properties. Insulative materials include a variety of polymers and inorganic dielectrics that are used primarily for encapsulation and as a structural element in nerve cuffs and electrode arrays. An overview of polymers typically used in these applications is provided with an emphasis on encapsulation and packaging strategies involving conformal coatings and polymer-based soft encapsulation.

1. Introduction

Conductive and insulative materials in neural prostheses perform a variety of functions that include the material of construction of implanted pulse generators (IPGs), flexible electrical leads that connect the IPG to one or more electrodes, the electrode substrate which might be a nerve cuff, a paddle with extradural spinal cord electrodes, a spiraled linear array for cochlear electrodes, or simply an exposed distal wire typical of intramuscular electrodes. At the active interface with the tissue is the electrode which stimulates or records neural activity. Neural prostheses in current clinical use generally employ a titanium-based IPG, a multi-conductor flexible lead often made of a NiCoCr alloy, and electrodes fabricated from platinum or platinum-iridium (PtIr) alloys. Common examples are the cochlear implant for deafness, deep brain stimulators (DBS) for movement disorders, spinal cord stimulators for pain, and vagus nerve stimulators for epilepsy and depression. There are also emerging clinical applications in retinal stimulation for vision, adaptive stimulation and recording in brain for intractable epilepsy, vagus nerve stimulation for augmenting rehabilitation therapies, and a variety of devices intended to record volitional intent, and in some devices to provide sensory and proprioceptive input to the nervous system. There are of course many other indications for which chronically implanted devices employing electrical stimulation and recording of the nervous system are being considered as a functional substitute or therapy. While the complexity, efficacy, target neural tissue, and size of the devices either in practice or contemplated varies greatly, the functional requirements on the conductive and insulative materials used in their construction are common to most devices. The discussion that follows focuses on those conductors and insulators that are used in neural prostheses employing electrical stimulation and recording and mostly on materials that are tissue contacting. The chapter is organized into two major sections; one on conductive materials and one on insulative materials, with each section subdivided by individual material.

2. Conductive Materials

The discussion of conductive materials is limited to those that are electronically conducting or at least exhibit mixed electronic and ionic conductivity. The properties of individual metallic conductors as stimulation and recording electrodes are briefly discussed. A more in-depth discussion of the electrochemical properties of conductors as electrodes can be found in focused reviews [1,2].

2.1 *Titanium*

Titanium is used almost exclusively in a neural prosthesis as the external casing of an implanted pulse generator (IPG). A commercially pure (CP) grade of titanium is selected because of its excellent *in vivo* corrosion resistance, absence of alloying elements that have the potential to produce toxic ions, the suitability of pure titanium for fabrication into thin-walled enclosures, and the ease with which these enclosures can be hermetically sealed by welding. CP titanium also has a density of 4.5 g/cm^3, which is notably lower than that of the stainless steels, leading to a desirable reduction in weight of the IPG. There are four grades of CP titanium in general use for implantable devices, differentiated primarily by their iron and oxygen content, and the effect of these impurity-level constituents on mechanical properties and ductility [3]. Titanium owes its corrosion resistance to a thin surface oxide that forms spontaneously on exposure to air or body fluids. This oxide layer, often called a passive film, should be differentiated from passive coatings on the stainless steels, in that the passive layer on titanium is a good electronic insulator which allows CP titanium to be anodized to form a comparatively thick oxide coating. The high dielectric constant of titanium oxide led to the investigation of anodized titanium as a charge injection electrode for neural stimulation [4]. However, the need for a large positive voltage bias in the interpulse period during pulsed stimulation, consequent high DC leakage currents, and the difficulty in achieving a high charge injection capacity with microelectrodes prevented the adoption of anodized titanium as a neural stimulation electrode.

Many stimulation devices have the option of delivering stimulus pulses in a monopolar configuration in which the current, during either a controlled voltage or controlled current pulse, is delivered to the stimulation electrode with the return being the case of the IPG. Since the maximum charge/phase in a stimulation pulse is on the order of 5 μC, this amount of charge is usually insufficient to cause polarization of the titanium IPG which has a surface area vastly larger than the stimulation electrode. The charge density, the charge per unit area, on the tissue-exposed surface of the IPG is likely less than 1 $μC/cm^2$ and thus almost entirely capacitive meaning no species are oxidized or reduced at the IPG to support the charge transfer process. For very small IPGs or situations where the IPG may have to sustain direct current, such as with bone growth stimulators or electrodes that are voltage biased in the interpulse period, the titanium may be coated with a thin film of platinum. The platinum, which may cover only a portion of the IPG, limits the polarization to levels that avoid undesirable reactions with biological molecules or oxidation of the titanium as well as lowering the voltage necessary to deliver a stimulation pulse.

2.2 Stainless steels

Stainless steels are iron-based alloys containing various amounts of chromium, nickel and molybdenum. Applications in neural prostheses have been limited to insulated lead wires and charge injection electrodes, primarily for intramuscular stimulation in limb prostheses for paralysis and as extraneural nerve cuff electrodes for stimulation and recording of motor function [5,6]. Only the 316L or 316LVM austenitic stainless steels, referring to the face-centered cubic austenite phase, are used in neural prostheses. These alloys are described in ASTM F138-13a [7]. The stainless steels derive their corrosion resistance from a thin passive film that is comprised primarily of chromium oxide. Corrosion of austenitic stainless steel can occur when this passive film is compromised, either mechanically or chemically. The resulting corrosion is usually highly localized in the form of pitting or crevice corrosion and the loss of passivity and the inability of the passive film to reform are exacerbated by the presence of Cl^- ions. In the absence of electrical stimulation or cyclic loading, the 316-alloys are generally stable in the body and elicit minimal tissue response although the potential for release of Ni and Cr and consequent systemic toxicity is a concern. As a stimulation electrode, 316LVM has a modest charge injection capacity of 20-40

$\mu C/cm^2$ in an 0.1-0.2 ms pulse which is about 25% of the charge injection capacity of a platinum electrode [8,9]. During pulsing studies in physiological saline, nickel is observed to selectively dissolve into solution and metal dissolution is probably an inevitable consequence of using stainless steels as stimulation electrodes [10]. The 316LVM alloy can be used as a lead wire, usually as a polymer insulated multi-strand cable designed to improve flexibility and fatigue resistance. These cables are available commercially in a wide selection of geometries including cables comprised of composite wires having a high electrical conductivity core surrounded by a 316LVM matrix or as a multi-wire strand brazed with silver to improve electrical conductivity [11]. In any case, the advent of high performance cobalt-chromium alloys such as MP35N [12] or 35N LT, with excellent corrosion resistance and superior flexural fatigue properties to 316LVM, has led to the decline in the use of 316LVM for lead applications.

2.3 *High performance alloys*

Non-ferrous high performance alloys used in neural prostheses are limited to nickel-cobalt alloys, primarily MP35N and its derivative 35N LT, containing chromium and molybdenum as secondary alloying elements. These alloys are used as lead conductors in DBS, vagus nerve, and cardiac pacing devices. Similar to the stainless steels, the NiCo-alloys are available as composites with high conductivity metals or as multi-strand cabling brazed with silver. These alloys exhibit excellent corrosion resistance due to the formation of a passive surface film and are generally considered more corrosion resistant than the iron-based stainless steels. Since lead conductors are always polymer insulated, the alloys are not exposed directly to physiological fluids unless the insulation is damaged or the alloy is exposed at an interconnect or electrode site. Interestingly, while MP35N has superior corrosion to stainless steel during static immersion in the absence of electrical stimulation, studies have shown that MP35N undergoes rapid pitting corrosion when used as a stimulation electrode at charge densities of 40 $\mu C/cm^2$ in carbonate-buffered saline [9]. Under the same pulsed conditions, no corrosion was observed on 316LVM stainless steel electrodes. Indirect evidence of the pitting susceptibility of MP35N compared to 316LVM under charge injection conditions was also provided by Lan and coworkers [13].

2.4 *Platinum and gold*

Platinum and platinum-iridium alloys, containing 10-20% iridium, are used extensively as charge injection electrodes in clinical devices. The properties of these noble metal electrodes for neural stimulation have been studied extensively, both *in vivo* and in physiological saline [2,14]. The platinum-based electrodes can support charge densities of 50-150 $\mu C/cm^2$ using typical charge-balanced neural stimulation waveforms, although some platinum dissolution is expected at charge densities above 20 $\mu C/cm^2$ [14]. Protein has been observed to dramatically reduce dissolution and the extent to which Pt dissolution occurs *in vivo* is uncertain, but probably less than observed in saline under identical pulsing conditions [15]. Iridium is alloyed with platinum to increase strength. PtIr alloys in the 10-20% iridium composition range form a solid solution with a corresponding increase in strength and stiffness due to solid-solution hardening. Tensile strength various significantly with prior processing history but is expected to increase from ~150-300 MPa for pure platinum to ~470 MPa for a 10% iridium alloy drawn to wire without annealing. The increased strength of the PtIr alloy allows it to be used as a conductor in the lead wires of cabling between the IPG and electrode array of devices in which the cable does not experience large flexural stresses. A good example of this application of PtIr alloys is the cochlear implant in which the strength and stiffness of the alloy are critical factors in balancing the stiffness of the electrode for implantation and proper positioning in the cochlear [16].

Gold has very limited use in neural prostheses being used primarily as a lead conductor or electrode in research devices. Gold has inadequate mechanical strength for most lead applications and is susceptible to fracture under repeated flexural loading. The charge injection properties of gold are substantially inferior to platinum, with gold electrodes having a maximum charge injection capacity of about one quarter that of an equivalent sized platinum electrode under similar charge injection conditions [17].

3. Insulative Materials

Insulative materials in neural prostheses include polymers, polycrystalline ceramics and thin-film dielectrics. All three classes of materials may be used to protect metallic conductors, discrete electronic components, telemetry coils, and application specific integrated circuits (ASICs) from corrosion by exposure to physiological fluids. Equally, these insulating materials must prevent electrolysis - reduction or oxidation - of biomolecules, dissolved salts, and water. In some cases the insulator may constitute a structural element of the implanted device such as the silicone (polysiloxane) substrate of a multielectrode array for spinal cord stimulation or the ceramic housing of an IPG. Insulative materials may be divided into two classes based on their mode of protection: 1) those that provide an impermeable barrier to ion and water ingress such as polycrystalline alumina or the titanium case of an IPG and 2) those that absorb water but provide corrosion protection by preventing the formation of a corrosive environment at the interface between the encapsulating insulative material and the substrate it protects. In the latter case, maintaining adhesion between the substrate and encapsulant, as well as avoiding hydrolysis or electrolysis of adhesive bonds at the interface, is essential for providing long-term chronic stability of implanted devices. A second major distinction between the different approaches for chronic packaging of implanted devices is whether the packaging strategy involves a container with internal free volume, such as a titanium IPG, or whether there is no internal volume such as with emerging silicone-encapsulated wireless devices. Having free internal volume has the advantage that helium leak rate measurements can be used to determine the hermeticity of package and the disadvantage that outgassing of internal components and undetected leaks could eventually lead to condensation of water in the package and consequent corrosion. The term hermetic refers to a barrier that is gas and water impermeable. Metal and ceramic IPGs are hermetic enclosures. Polymers such as the polysiloxane are not hermetic because they absorb water. These polymers provide a soft, non-hermetic encapsulation with their mode of protection being to prevent formation of a corrosive aqueous environment at the interface between the encapsulant and device rather than to exclude water and ion transport. Edell has provided a detailed review of polymers for implantable devices and their characterization by leakage current measurements in a previous edition of this volume [18].

With the advent of chronically implanted microelectrode devices for recording and stimulation in rehabilitation treatments for stroke, traumatic brain injury, and spinal cord injury, as well as for sensory restoration in vision and hearing, attention has focused on long-term reliability. Studies have shown that the failure of insulating materials is a significant, and perhaps the most significant, limitation on the functional lifetime of some types of implanted microelectrodes devices [19,20]. The need for reliable materials and strategies for encapsulating microelectrode devices is likely to be even more critical if emerging electrical therapies based on stimulation and blocking of the peripheral innervation of end organs becomes a viable treatment option for diseases such as hypertension, diabetes and rheumatoid arthritis [21,22,23].

3.1 *Polysiloxanes*

Silicones are polysiloxanes with the general chemical formula $-[R_1R_2SiO]_n-$ where n is the number of repeat units in the polymer and R_1 and R_2 are side groups attached via a single bond to the Si. These side groups may also be siloxanes that can act as cross-linking elements or have reactive terminal groups that promote adhesion. Siloxane chemistry is very rich and a wide variety of polymers with different physical and chemical properties can be prepared. The important features of siloxanes for neural device encapsulation are the low viscosity and excellent wetting characteristics of uncured polymer which promotes adhesion, the flexibility and elastomeric properties of the cured polymer, the minimal foreign–body response provoked by the polymer, and the observation that siloxanes have provided effective chronic encapsulation of electrically active devices in humans. For example, the Finetech Medical sacral anterior root stimulation (SARS) system for bladder and bowel control in spinal cord injury employs siloxane encapsulation, rather than an IPG, and has worked successfully in a large number of patients [24,25,26]. This device is powered through a wireless link and does not have an implanted battery.

The principles behind the use of siloxanes in neural prostheses have been detailed in a series of papers by P. E. Donaldson beginning in 1976 [27,28,29,30, 31]. The use of siloxanes for the protection of implanted ASICs and methods of lifetime prediction have been reviewed recently by A. Vanhoestenberghe and N. Donaldson [32]. These authors conclude that polysiloxanes can provide effective encapsulation of implantable devices over at least two decades. The primary mode of failure for a siloxane-based encapsulant is the nucleation of liquid water at the junction between the siloxane and the substrate being protected. Water can nucleate at interfacial voids that may arise for several reasons, including: entrapment of air due to poor wetting during application of the uncured elastomer; poor adhesion between the elastomer and substrate due to surface contamination; loss of interfacial adhesion due to thermal stress or flexural loading; loss of interfacial adhesion due to hydrolysis of bonds between the siloxane and substrate, including interfacial bonds formed with an adhesion promoter; and lastly the nucleation of an aqueous electrolyte due to ionic (e.g., salt) contamination on the substrate. In all cases, the ingress or egress of liquid water from voids at the interface or within the polymer encapsulation is driven by osmotic pressure. Osmotic effects are most damaging at ionic contaminants where the high ionic strength of the electrolyte within the void drives the ingress of water and an increase in pressure. The pressure within the void can be high enough to cause delamination or rupture of the polymer encapsulant. These failure mechanisms are shown schematically in Figure 1, which is adapted from Vanhoestenberghe [32] and Osenbach [33]. In the absence of ionic species within the condensed water phase, the osmotic pressure works in the reverse direction opposing the nucleation of liquid water within the encapsulant or at the interface.

When delamination occurs in the presence of a voltage, such as at a wire bond pad, condensed water or solutes in the water are susceptible to electrolysis. Electrolysis reactions can result in large pH changes as well as the generation of gas bubbles. Besides rupture of the encapsulation due to bubble formation, the acidity or alkalinity of the water at the bond pad site can promote corrosion of the metallization, particularly if aluminum is used as the bond pad metal [33].

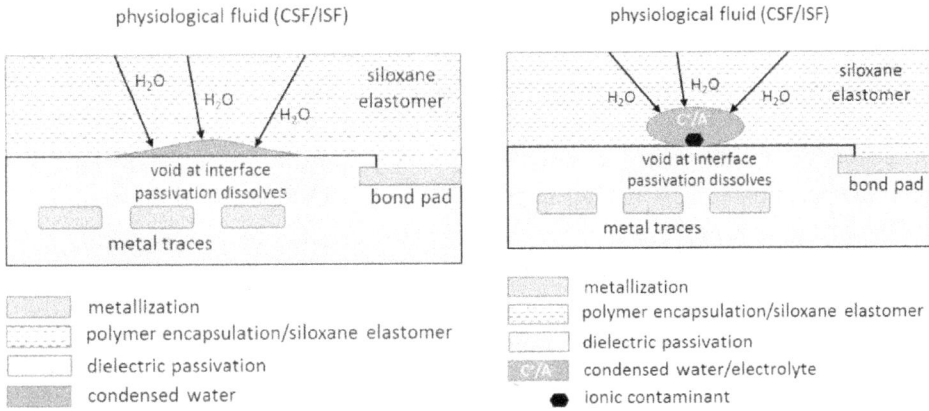

Fig. 1. (left) The nucleation of liquid water at the interface between a metal substrate and a polysiloxane (silicone) elastomer due to the presence of a void. (right) Ionic contaminants can promote ingress of H2O and delamination due to osomotic pressure. (after Vanhoestenberghe [32] and Osenbach [33])

Recent work with polysiloxane encapsulated wireless nerve stimulators has demonstrated the ability of polysiloxanes to provide chronic protection of wire-bonded ASICs without the need for additional encapsulation materials or layers. These devices, shown in Figure 2, employ an array of 16 penetrating iridium oxide stimulation electrodes and are controlled and powered by a wireless link. Two devices implanted on rat sciatic nerve and functioned for 15 months preserving current thresholds for hind limb movement as well the reverse telemetry of voltage waveforms at the electrodes during the constant current pulsing [34].

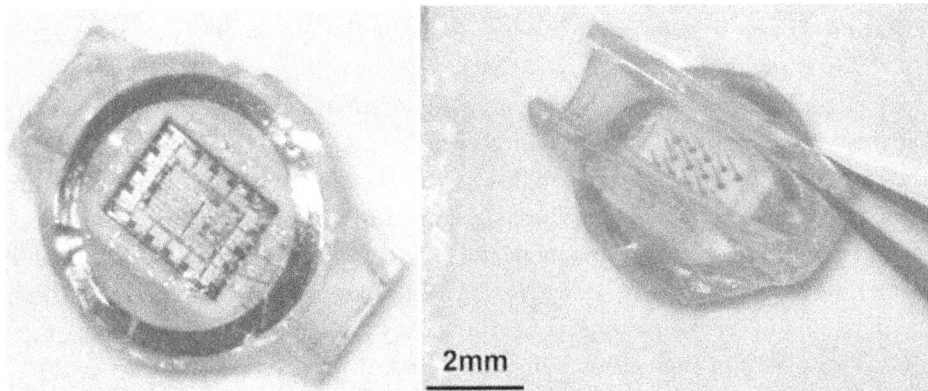

Fig. 2. A 16-channel wireless stimulator with an integrated circuit mounted on a ceramic substrate. (left) The output channels on the integrated circuit are connected to the electrodes by wire bonds to metal tracks on the ceramic substrate. The IC and wire bonds are encapsulated with a polysiloxane only. (right) 16 penetrating microelectrodes are mounted in the alumina substrate and are Parylene-C insulated. Such devices have been operated *in vivo* for 12 months without failure.

3.2 *Polyurethanes*

Polyurethanes are a large class of copolymers based on the formation of urethane linkages (-NHCOO-) between diisocyanates (OCN-R_1-NCO, where R_1 is aliphatic or aromatic) and polyols. The polyol is typically a linear polyether or polyester oligomer terminated at both ends in an –OH group (HO-R_2-OH, a diol in which R_2 is the polyether or polyester). The first step in the preparation of a polyurethane is the synthesis of a copolymer with the structure OCN-(R_1-NHCOO-R_2)-NCO. This copolymer is further polymerized in the presence of a chain extender, usually a short chain diol or diamine containing 2-6 methylene units. Polymerization with the chain extender results in a high molecular weight polymer. An essential feature of the polyurethanes is the formation of a two phase microstructure comprised of nano-sized hard and soft segments. The hard segments are crystalline or glassy and formed from the R_1 segment of the diisocyanates and the chain extenders and act as a reinforcing phase that provides toughness and abrasion resistance. The soft segments derive from the highly flexible R_2 segment of the diol which forms an amorphous phase that has a low glass transition temperature and is thus extensible. The combination of hard and soft phases results in an elastomer that has higher strength, tear resistance, and abrasion resistance than the siloxanes.

In neural prostheses, polyurethanes are used primarily as an outer insulation or jacket in leads, the Medtronic 3387/3389 quadripolar leads for DBS being a typical example. Polyurethanes have lower friction against tissue than siloxanes and better abrasion resistance. For lead applications, polyurethane is not used as a primary insulation for the metal conductors. Typically, the metal wires will be individually insulated with a silicone or fluoropolymer. Since the polyurethanes are usually stiffer than polysiloxanes, they are less desirable in applications where extreme flexibility is required such as in a cochlear implant.

A major difference between polyurethane and polysiloxane elastomers is the thermoplastic nature of the polyurethane. The elastomeric properties of the siloxanes are achieved by cross-linking, and even though these elastomers are often only lightly cross-linked, they are generally not processable by extrusion, injection molding or other methods that involve heating to melt-processable temperatures. Polyurethanes however can be heated to above the glass transition temperature (T_g) or melt temperature of their crystalline or glassy phase and then melt-processed into final shape. On cooling below T_g, the two-phase structure of the polyurethane reforms providing the desirable combination of strength and elastomeric extensibility.

3.3 *Polyimides*

Polyimides have not been used extensively as an insulative material for implanted neural devices. However, the high temperature stability of polyimides and the suitability of polyimide-precursor formulations for fabrication into thin film devices by standard microfabrication processing techniques has led to their extensive use as a substrate for multielectrode arrays, particularly for applications in retinal prostheses [35,36,37]. Thin films of polyimide, on the order of 2-10 μm thick, can be prepared by spin-coating a monomer solution on to a planar substrate and curing at elevated temperature, usually at ~350°C. These polyimides have a high modulus (~8 GPa) and a glass transition temperature of about 350°C. While polyimides are rigid polymers, they are very flexible as thin films and can easily conform to the contours of most target tissues. Previous studies have suggested that polyimides are susceptible to degradation by hydrolysis [18]. Recent studies of polyimides derived from biphenyltetracarboxylic dianhydride and para-phenylenediamine (BPDA-PPD), however, suggest that the BPDA-PPD polyimides may be stable for long term implantation. The results reported by Rubehn and Stielglitz showed no degradation in the mechanical properties of BPDA-PPD polyimides over 20 months in phosphate buffered saline at 60°C [38]. They suggest that the absence of degradation in their studies is due to the selection of a polyimide based on BPDA-PPD and that other polyimides such as Kapton®, which is based on pyromeliticdianhydride (PMDA) and 4-4'-diaminodipheny-lether (ODA), may exhibit a higher water uptake and reduced hydrolytic stability.

The physical and chemical properties of the polyimide depend on the molecular weight and molecular weight distribution of the poly(amic acid). The linear BPDA-PPD polymer chains are rigid, promoting the formation of inter-chain charge transfer complexes and crystallinity, which results in a polymer with a high tensile elastic modulus and low coefficient of thermal expansion. The correspondingly higher packing density of the BPDA-PPD polymer, compared with polyimides based on the more flexible PMDA-ODA chain structure, also results in a higher density, which may contribute the reduced water uptake.

While there is some uncertainty as to the chronic *in vivo* stability of polyimide, the opportunities provided by spin-coatable and photo-definable polyimides for the fabrication of devices with large numbers of electrodes, the ability to mount integrated circuits and other discrete electronic components onto polyimide, and the promising recent results suggest that there will be continued interest in polyimides for implantable neural prostheses.

3.4 Parylene

Parylene is a polymer derived from di-para-xylylene or halogen-substituted di-para-xylylene. Parylene coatings are formed from these dimers in a multi-step process that involves dimer vaporization, high temperature formation of monomer radicals from the dimer, and then *in situ* polymerization on the surface of the part being coated. The polymerization process occurs at ambient temperature and at pressures on the order of 0.1 Torr. The mono-chlorine substituted Parylene, Parylene-C, is most commonly used in implantable neural devices and was first introduced for cortical applications in about 1977 [39]. Since that time, Parylene-C has seen extensive use as insulation on metal electrodes and silicon-based substrates or as a substrate for fabricating thin-film multi-electrode arrays [40,41,42,43]. The many advantages of Parylene-C include its very low moisture absorption, excellent biocompatibility as judged by the minimal adverse foreign body response induced by Parylene coatings, superb conformality of coatings over complex 3-dimensional structures, ambient temperature deposition, and relatively inexpensive deposition equipment for a vacuum coating process.

However, the ability of Parylene-C to provide effective encapsulation of devices implanted chronically for long periods, over one year, remains in question. Several studies of Parylene-encapsulated devices implanted in cortex revealed cracking and delamination with associated changes in electrode impedance and loss of neuronal recordings characterized by a progressive decrease in neural signal amplitude and loss of viable recording channels [19,44]. The decline in ability to record neural signals is accompanied by a decrease in electrode impedance and a decrease in signal-to-noise ratio (SNR). In one study reporting on 78 multielectrode arrays (MEAs) in 27 monkeys, a failure rate of 56% was identified for these devices at one year post implant with a mean time to complete device failure of 332 days [19]. While electrodes on some devices successfully provided neural recordings for almost six years, the mean time to failure of individual electrodes for all reasons was 387 days. The decline in recording performance of these MEAs is multifactorial involving degradation of Parylene insulation and other degradation mechanisms including corrosion at electrode sites and connector failure [20,44]. The observed decrease in electrode impedance combined with a decrease in the amplitude of neural signals is consistent with increased electrode surface area and channel interactions due to leakage of physiological fluids into the device superstructure. SEM analyses of explanted arrays have shown extensive degradation and cracking of Parylene insulation, as shown in Figure 3, for a Parylene-insulated device implanted for 537 days in cat cortex [20]. Fluid ingress through these cracks is presumed to form an electrically conductive path between underlying metallization from different electrodes resulting in an apparent increase in surface area.

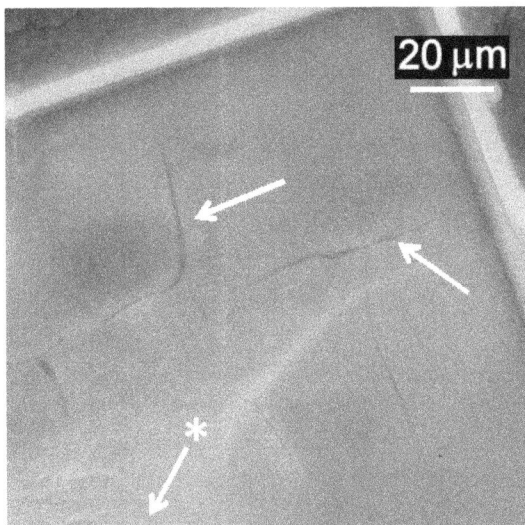

Fig. 3. Cracks in Parylene insulation on a multielectrode array explanted from cat cortex after a 537 day implantation period from Kane [20].

3.5 *Silicon-based inorganic dielectrics*

Inorganic dielectrics based on silicon oxide and silicon nitride deposited by low pressure chemical vapor deposition (LPCVD) have been used as passivation on multielectrode silicon arrays since at least 1985 [45,46]. The fabrication and performance of these devices, often called Michigan probes, has been reported extensively [47,48]. The passivation acts as the primary barrier between the metal or polysilicon traces on the silicon substrate and the physiological environment. This passivation is typically a multilayer structure comprised of $SiO_2/Si_3N_4/SiO_2$ with film thicknesses of about 800 nm for the SiO_2 and 200 nm for the Si_3N_4. The multilayer structure and film thicknesses are selected to minimize bending of the probes from residual stresses due to either intrinsic film stress or to differences in the thermal expansion coefficients of the different layers in the device. LPCVD is a high temperature process, typically higher than 800°C, which limits the utility of LPCVD dielectrics to devices capable of tolerating these temperatures. Studies of the stability of silicon oxide and silicon nitride in physiological saline at 37°C or under accelerated conditions show that silicon nitride, in particular, is susceptible to dissolution, exhibiting a dissolution rate of 0.4 nm/day at 37°C in buffered saline [49]. The dissolution rate of LPCVD SiO_2 is much lower as measured by changes in the Si-O absorption band intensity in infrared spectroscopy measurements. However, the SiO_2 appears to be a less effective barrier to ions and water than Si_3N_4 based on leakage current measurements. Interestingly, the trilayer $SiO_2/Si_3N_4/SiO_2$ stack appears to exhibit better stability than would be predicted from the performance of the individual dielectrics. This improved performance is probably due to the outer SiO$_2$ layer which greatly reduces or prevents dissolution of the underlying Si$_3$N$_4$. The trilayer thus preserves the low dissolution rate of the SiO$_2$ and the good barrier properties of the Si$_3$N$_4$.

More recently, thin films of amorphous silicon carbide (a-SiC) have been evaluated as an inorganic dielectric encapsulation for implanted devices. The a-SiC is deposited by plasma enhanced chemical vapor deposition (PECVD) at a temperature typically between 100°C and 400°C and with a thickness ranging from 200 nm to ~1 μm [49,50]. The higher deposition temperatures lead to higher density films with lower hydrogen content and, consequently, lower intrinsic compressive stress in the film. Compared with LPCVD Si$_3$N$_4$ films, the dissolution rate of a-SiC measured in buffered physiological saline at 87°C is negligible. Changes in film thickness for PECVD a-SiC and LPCVD Si$_3$N$_4$, measured by infrared transmittance spectroscopy of coatings on both sides of double-polished silicon wafers are compared in Figure 4 as a function of soak time at 87°C in saline. The LPCVD Si$_3$N$_4$ exhibits a dissolution rate of 18 nm/hr with a 500 nm film being entirely dissolved in 30 days. The a-SiC thickness remains substantially unchanged over 350 days, demonstrating exceptional stability. Amorphous SiC is also well-tolerated in cortex exhibiting minimal tissue response comparable with that of Parylene-C [49].

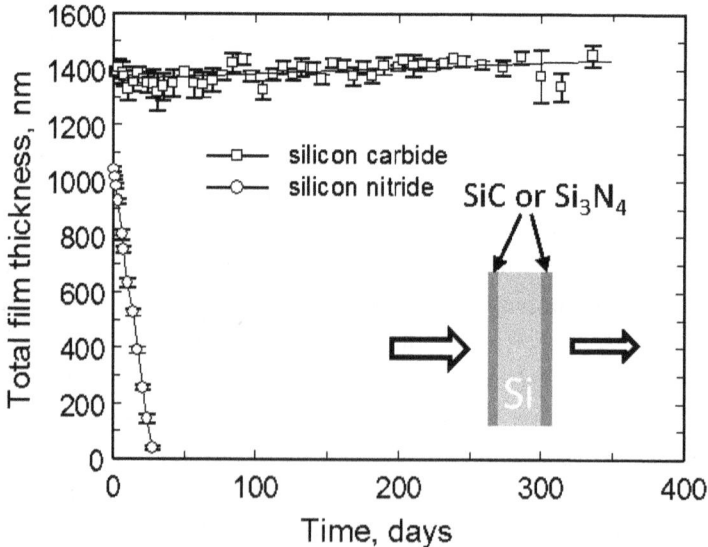

Fig. 4. Dissolution rate of a-SiC and LPCVD silicon nitride in buffered saline at 87°C measured by changes in the absorption band intensity of the Si-C and Si-N stretching modes. The a-SiC showed no evidence of dissolution while the LPCVD Si$_3$N$_4$ dissolution was linear with a rate of 18 nm/day 87°C.

Besides its potential as a tissue-contacting insulating coating for neural implants, a-SiC has also been used as an adhesive interlayer between gold metallization and polyimide in the fabrication of flexible ribbon cables and multielectrode arrays. In these structures the a-SiC has a dual role, providing interlayer adhesion and acting as an ion and water barrier layer. The enhanced stability provided by a-SiC in a polyimide-based multielectrode array is shown by the comparison in Figure 5 of two arrays subjected to accelerated testing by soaking in buffered saline at 87°C. The electrode array with the gold metallization encapsulated in a-SiC tolerated 20 weeks at 87°C with no evidence of interlayer delamination (Fig. 5a) and preservation of the electrochemical properties of the sputtered iridium oxide electrodes (Fig. 5b). The electrode array without a-SiC delaminated at all internal interfaces after four weeks at 87°C (Fig. 5c).

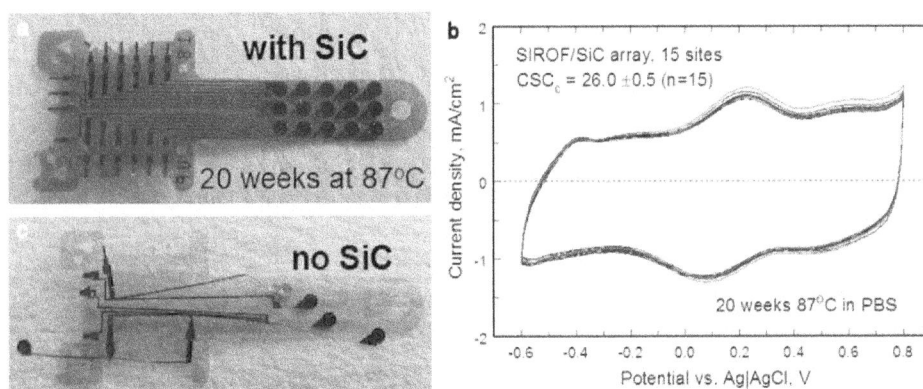

Fig. 5. (a) After 20 weeks soaking in buffered saline at pH 7, polyimide multielectrode arrays shown no evidence of interlayer delamination. (b) Cyclic voltammograms (CVs) of 15 sputtered iridium oxide (SIROF) electrodes on a polyimide multielectrode array with a-SiC after 20 weeks at 87°C in buffered. The CV response is substantially unchanged from that measured prior to accelerated testing. (c) Without a-SiC the arrays completely delaminate at internal interfaces in four weeks at 87°C.

In the electrode arrays shown in Figure 5, a thin layer of titanium is used as an additional adhesion layer between the polyimide and gold or between the SiC and gold. For the devices with a-SiC, the titanium/gold metallization is completely encased in a-SiC which forms a strong bond to the titanium, preventing transport of fluid between the metal and polyimide. This geometry is shown schematically in Figure 6.

There are limitations to the use of any thin-film dielectric as an encapsulation layer. To varying degrees, methods for depositing inorganic coatings such as PECVD, LPCVD, atomic-layer deposition (ALD), and physical vapor deposition (PVD), are limited in their ability to conformally coat devices with challenging surface topography such as narrow vias and structures with reentrant angles. Since future neural devices are likely to have complex three-dimensional structures with micron-sized features that require conformal coatings, careful selection of appropriate deposition methods will be required, as well as long-term accelerated testing to reveal latent defects in coatings.

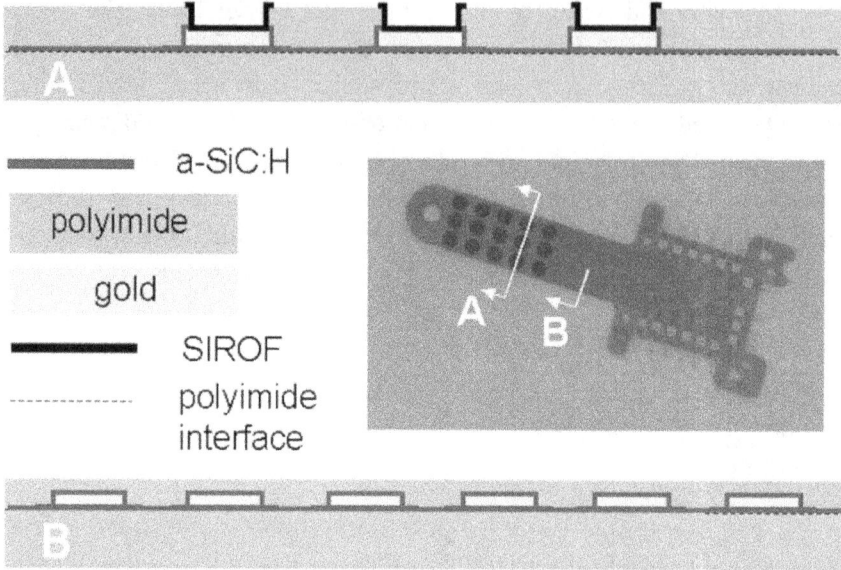

Fig. 6. Schematic diagram showing the "wrapping" of Ti/Au metallization with a-SiC. The a-SiC also acts as an adhesion layer at the interface between the two layers of polyimide used in array construction.

3.6 *Nanocrystalline diamond*

Nanocrystalline diamond films deposited by microwave plasma enhanced chemical vapor deposition have been evaluated as encapsulation for implanted electronics [51]. With appropriate processing conditions, polycrystalline diamond films with a crystallite size on the order of 3-5 nm can be deposited at substrate temperatures as low as 350°C. These films are often referred to as ultrananocrystalline diamond (UNCD). Besides its potential as a barrier layer, UNCD coatings are also permissive to the proliferation of a variety of cell types and are likely well-tolerated chronically [52,53]. The long-term stability of UNCD is yet to be adequately demonstrated in chronic applications, but the intrinsic stability of UNCD combined with the ability to form electronically conducting diamond films by nitrogen doping, and potential use of nitrogen-doped UNCD as a stimulation electrode, ensures continued interest in this material [54].

3.7 *Hybrid coatings*

Hybrid or multilayer coatings comprising two or more different materials offer the possibility of improved encapsulation by having one coating compensate for any inherent weakness of the other coating. An example of this approach is the use of plasma-assisted atomic layer deposition (ALD) of Al_2O_3 in combination with Parylene-C [55]. The Al_2O_3 is deposited first as an adherent and conformal coating with good water barrier properties. However, Al_2O_3 will corrode slowly in water. To minimize dissolution of the Al_2O_3, a layer of Parylene-C is deposited over the alumina to provide an ion and water barrier that greatly reduces the rate at which the alumina will dissolve. The ALD alumina used in these bilayer coatings is thin (~50 nm) but conformal and pinhole free. Accelerated testing of Al_2O_3 (50 nm)/Parylene-C (6 μm) bilayers showed excellent stability as measured by changes in impedance and leakage currents over times exceeding 2000 days for samples immersed in saline at 67°C [56]. A notable advantage of hybrid coatings based on Al_2O_3 and Parylene-C is the low temperature deposition of each material. Hybrid Al_2O_3/Parylene coatings have not been evaluated in long-term chronic implants. However, the hybrid approach offers a potential path to encapsulating implanted devices when very small device size or very large number of electrodes, precludes the use of conventional hermetic encapsulation with IPGs.

4. Summary

Most clinical neural devices employ a predictable range of conductive and insulative materials in which their selection is driven by an established history of use in implantable devices as much as by their materials properties. For this reason, titanium, NiCoCr-alloys, and PtIr dominate as conductors and polysiloxanes and polyurethanes dominate as insulators. However, emerging applications of neural stimulation and recording involving large numbers of electrodes or small tissue targets will require a different approach, particularly for packaging when conventional IPGs are not feasible. Novel materials and packaging approaches will be required to address these more challenging applications and interest in a-SiC, UNCD, new polymers and hybrid encapsulation will continue.

References

1. D. R. Merrill, M. Bikson, and J. G. Jefferys, Electrical stimulation of excitable tissue: design of efficacious and safe protocols, *J Neurosci Methods*, **141**, 171-198, 2005.
2. S. F. Cogan, Neural stimulation and recording electrodes, *Annu Rev Biomed Eng*, **10**, 275-309, 2008.
3. ASTM F67-13, *Standard Specification for Unalloyed Titanium, for Surgical Implant Applications*, (ASTM International, West Conshohocken, PA, 2013).

4. T. L. Rose, E. M. Kelliher, and L. S. Robblee, Assessment of capacitor electrodes for intracortical neural stimulation, *J. Neurosci. Methods,* **12**, 181-193, 1985.

5. P. H. Peckham, E. B. Marsolais and J. T. Mortimer, Restoration of key grip and release in the C6 tetraplegic patient through functional electrical stimulation, *J. Hand Surg*, **5**, 462-469, 1980.

6. G. E. Loeb and R. A. Peck, Cuff electrodes for chronic stimulation and recording of peripheral nerve activity, *J Neurosci. Methods*, **64**, 95-103, 1996.

7. ASTM F138-13a, *Standard Specification for Wrought 18Chromium-14Nickel-2.5Molybdenum Stainless Steel Bar and Wire for Surgical Implants*, (ASTM International, West Conshohocken, PA, 2013).

8. L. S. Robblee and T. L. Rose, Electrochemical guidelines for selection of protocols and electrode materials for neural stimulation, In eds. W. F. Agnew and D. B. McCreery, *Neural Prostheses*, (Prentice Hall, Englewood Cliffs, 1990) pp. 25-67.

9. S. F. Cogan, G. S. Jones, D. V. Hills, J. S. Walter, and L. W. Riedy, Comparison of 316LVM amd MP35M alloys as charge injection electrodes, *J. Biomedical Materials Research*, **28**, 233-240, 1994.

10. L. S. Robblee, S. F. Cogan, and A. G. Kimball, Dissolution of 316LVM stainless steel electrodes during electrical stimulation, *Proc. Annual Conference of the IEEE EMBS San Diego CA*, **15**, 1501-1502, 1993.

11. DFT® (Drawn Filled Tubing) wire, Fort Wayne Wire, Fort Wayne, Indianna, 2016.

12. ASTM F562-13, *Standard Specification for Wrought 35Cobalt-35Nickel-20Chromium-10 Molybdenum Alloy for Surgical Implant Applications*, (ASTM International, West Conshohocken, PA, 2013).

13. N. Lan, M. Daroux, and J. T. Mortimer, Pitting corrosion of high strength alloy stimulation electrodes under dynamic conditions, *J. Electrochem. Soc.*, **136**, 947-954, 1989.

14. L. S. Robblee, J. McHardy, W. F. Agnew, and L. A. Bullara, Electrical stimulation with Pt electrodes. VII. Dissolution of Pt electrodes during electrical stimulation of the cat cerebral cortex, *J. Neurosci. Methods*, **9**, 300-308, 1983.

15. L. S. Robblee, J. McCardy, J. M. Marston, and S. B. Brummer, Electrical stimulation with Pt electrodes. V. The effects of protein on Pt dissolution, *Biomaterials*, **1**, 135-139, 1980.

16. T. Stover and T. Lenarz, Biomaterials in cochlear implants, *GMS Current Topics in Otorhinolaryngology – Head and Neck Surgery*, 8, doc 10, 2009.

17. A. Kanneganti and S. F. Cogan, unpublished results, 2016.

18. D. J. Edell, Insulating biomaterials, in eds. K. W. Horch and G. S. Dhillon, *Neuroprosthetics: Theory and Practice* (World Scientific, New Jersey, 2004).

19. J. C. Barrese, N. Rau, K. Raroo, C. Triebwasser, C. Vargas-Irwin, L. Franquemont, and J. P. Donoghue, Failure mode analysis of silicon-based intracortical microelectrode arrays in non-human primates, *J. Neural Engineering*, **10**, 066014, 2013.

20. S. R. Kane, S. F. Cogan, J. Ehrlich, T. D. Plante, D. B. McCreery, and P. R. Troyk, Electrical performance of penetrating microelectrodes chronically implanted in cat cortex, *IEEE Trans Biomed Eng*, **60**, 2153-2160, 2013.

21. V. A. Pavlov and K. J. Tracey, Neural circuitry and immunity, *Immunol Res*, **63**, 38-57, 2015.

22. E. Sundman and P. S. Olofsson, Neural control of the immune system. *Adv Physiol Educ*, **38**, 135-139, 2014.

23. K. Birmingham, V. Gradinaru, P. Anikeeva, W. M. Grill, V. Pikov, B. McLaughlin, P. Pasricha, D. Weber, K. Ludwig, and K. Famm, Bioelectronic medicines: a research roadmap, *Nat Rev Drug Discov*, 13, 399-400, 2014.

24. Finetech Medical Ltd., Welwyn Garden City, United Kingdom (http://finetech-medical.co.uk/en-gb/home.aspx).

25. G. S. Brindley, The first 500 patients with sacral anterior root stimulator implants: general description, *Paraplegia*, **32**, 795-805, 1994.

26. J. M. Vastenholt, G. J. Snoek, H. P. Buschman, H. E. van der Aa, E. R. Alleman, and M. J. Ijzerman, A 7-year follow-up of sacral anterior root stimulation for bladder control in patients with a spinal cord injury: quality of life and users' experiences, *Spinal Cord*, **41**, 397-402, 2003.

27. P. E. Donaldson, The encapsulation of microelectronic devices for long-term surgical implantation, *IEEE Trans Biomed Eng*, **23**, 281-285, 1976.

28. P. E. Donaldson, Aspects of silicone rubber as an encapsulant for neurological prostheses. Part 1. Osmosis, *Med Biol Eng Comput*, **29**, 34-39, 1991.

29. P. E. Donaldson and B. J. Aylett, Aspects of silicone rubber as encapsulant for neurological prostheses. Part 2: Adhesion to binary oxides, *Med Biol Eng Comput*, **33**, 289-292, 1995.

30. P. E. Donaldson, Aspects of silicone rubber as encapsulant for neurological prostheses. Part 3: Adhesion to mixed oxides, *Med Biol Eng Comput*, **33**, 725-727, 1995.

31. P. E. Donaldson, Aspects of silicone rubber as encapsulant for neurological prostheses. Part 4: Two-part rubbers, *Med Biol Eng Comput*, **35**, 283-286, 1997.

32. A. Vanhoestenberghe and N. Donaldson, Corrosion of silicon integrated circuits and lifetime predictions in implantable electronic devices, *J Neural Eng*, **10**, 031002, 2013.

33. J. W. Osenbach, Water-induced corrosion of materials used for semiconductor passivation, *J. Electrochem. Soc.*, **140**, 3667-3675, 1993.

34. S. Bredeson, A. Kanneganti, F. Deku, S. Cogan, M. Romero-Ortega, and P. Troyk, Chronic in-vivo testing of a 16-channel implantable wireless neural stimulator, *IEEE EMBS Conference, August 26, Milan, Italy*, 2015.

35. H. G. Sachs, T. Schanze, M. Wilms, A. Rentzos, U. Brunner, F. Gekeler, and L. Hesse, Subretinal implantation and testing of polyimide film electrodes in cats, *Graefes Arch Clin Exp Ophthalmol*, **243**, 464-468, 2005.

36. S. K. Kelly, D. B. Shire, J. Chen, P. Doyle, M. D. Gingerich, S. F. Cogan, W. A. Drohan, S. Behan, L. Theogarajan, J. L. Wyatt, and J. F. Rizzo 3rd., A hermetic wireless subretinal neurostimulator for vision prostheses, *IEEE Trans Biomed Eng*, **58**, 3197-3205, 2011.

37. V. B. Kitiratschky, K. Stingl, B. Wilhelm, T. Peters, D. Besch, H. Sachs, F. Gekeler, K. U. Bartz-Schmidt, and E. Zrenner, Safety evaluation of "retina implant alpha IMS"—a prospective clinical trial, *Graefes Arch Clin Exp Ophthalmol*, **253**, 381-387, 2015.

38. B. Rubehn and T. Stieglitz, In vitro evaluation of the long-term stability of polyimide as a material for neural implants, *Biomaterials*, **31**, 3449-3458, 2010.

39. G. E. Loeb, M. J. Bak, M. Salcman, E. M. Schmidt, Parylene as a chronically stable, reproducible microelectrode insulator, *IEEE Trans Biomed Eng*, **24**, 121-8, 1977.

40. E. M. Schmidt, J. S. McIntosh, and M. J. Bak, Long-term implants of Parylene-C coated microelectrodes, *Med Biol Eng Comput*, **26**, 96-101, 1988.

41. A. Sharma, L. Rieth, P. Tathireddy, R. Harrison, H. Oppermann, M. Klein, M. Töpper, E. Jung, R. Normann, G. Clark, and F. Solzbacher, Evaluation of the packaging and encapsulation reliability in fully integrated, fully wireless 100 channel Utah Slant Electrode Array (USEA): Implications for long term functionality, *Sens Actuators A Phys*, **188**, 167-172, 2012.

42. J. M. Hsu, L. Rieth, R. A. Normann, P. Tathireddy, and F. Solzbacher, Encapsulation of an integrated neural interface device with Parylene C, *IEEE Trans Biomed Eng*, **56**, 23-29, 2009.

43. C. Metallo, R. D. White, and B. A. Trimmer, Flexible parylene-based microelectrode arrays for high resolution EMG recordings in freely moving small animals, *J Neurosci Methods*, **195**, 176-184, 2011.

44. J. C. Barrese, J. Aceros, and J. P. Donoghue, Scanning electron microscopy of chronically implanted intracortical microelectrode arrays in non-human primates, *J Neural Eng,* **13**, 026003, 2016.

45. K. Najafi, K. D. Wise, and T. Mochizuki, A high-yield IC-compatible multichannel recording array, *IEEE Trans. Electron. Dev.*, **32**, 1206–1211, 1985.

46. S. L. BeMent, K. D. Wise, D. J. Anderson, K. Najafi, and K. L..Drake, Solid-state electrodes for multichannel multiplexed intracortical neuronal recording, *IEEE Trans Biomed Eng*, **33**, 230-241, 1986.

47. D. J. Anderson, K. Najafi, S. J. Tanghe, D. A. Evans, K. L. Levy, J. F. Hetke, X. L. Xue, J. J. Zappia, and K. D. Wise, Batch-fabricated thin-film electrodes for stimulation of the central auditory system, *IEEE Trans Biomed Eng*, **36**, 693-704, 1989.

48. D. J. Anderson, Penetrating multichannel stimulation and recording electrodes in auditory prosthesis research, *Hear Res*, **242**, 31-41, 2008.

49. S. F. Cogan, D. J. Edell, A. A. Guzelian, Y. Ping Liu, and R. Edell, Plasma-enhanced chemical vapor deposited silicon carbide as an implantable dielectric coating, *J Biomed Mater Res A*, **67**, 856-867, 2003.

50. J. M. Hsu, P. Tathireddy, L. Rieth, R. A. Normann, and F. Solzbacher, Characterization of a-SiC(x):H thin films as an encapsulation material for integrated silicon basedneural interface devices, *Thin Solid Films,* **516**, 34-41, 2007.

51. W. Li, B. Kabius, and O. Auciello, Science and technology of biocompatible thin films for implantable biomedical devices, *Conf Proc IEEE Eng Med Biol Soc 2010*, 6237-6242, 2010.

52. B. Shi, Q. Jin, L. Chen, A. S. Woods, A. J. Schultz, and O. Auciello, Cell growth on different types of ultrananocrystalline diamond thin films, *J Funct Biomater*, **3**, 588-600, 2012.

53. X. Xiao, J. Wang, C. Liu, J. A. Carlisle, B. Mech, R. Greenberg, D. Guven, R. Freda, M. S. Humayun, J. Weiland, and O. Auciello, In vitro and in vivo evaluation of ultrananocrystalline diamond for coating of implantable retinal microchips, *J. Biomed Mater Res B Appl Biomater*, **77**, 273-281, 2006.

54. A. E. Hadjinicolaou, R. T. Leung, D. J. Garrett, K. Ganesan, K. Fox, D. A. Nayagam, M. N. Shivdasani, H. Meffin, M. R. Ibbotson, S. Prawer, and B. J. O'Brien, Electrical stimulation of retinal ganglion cells with diamond and the development of an all diamond retinal prosthesis, *Biomaterials*, **33**, 5812-5820, 2012.

55. X. Xie, L. Rieth, S. Merugu, P. Tathireddy, and F. Solzbacher, Plasma-assisted atomic layer deposition of Al2O3 and Parylene C bi-layer encapsulation for chronic implantable electronics, *Appl. Phys. Lett.*, **101**, 093701, 2012.

56. X. Xie, L. Rieth, R. Caldwell, M. Diwekar, P. Tathireddy, R. Sharma, and F. Solzbacher, Long-term bilayer encapsulation performance of atomic layer deposited Al_2O_3 and Parylene C for biomedical implantable devices, *IEEE Trans Biomed Eng,* **60**, 2943-2951, 2013.

Chapter 2.3

The Biocompatibility of Intracortical Microelectrode Recording Arrays for Brain Machine Interfacing

John L. Skousen and Patrick A. Tresco

Department of Biomedical Engineering, University of Utah,
36 S. Wasatch Drive, Rm. 3100, Salt Lake City UT, 84112
john.skousen@utah.edu, patrick.tresco@utah.edu

The potential of brain machine interfaces (BMI): also called brain computer interfaces, neural interfaces, or neuroprosthetics) provide hope for many suffering from long-term paralysis or amputation.[1] This hope is based on a number of exciting pre-clinical and clinical studies demonstrating that consciously modulated neuronal signaling can be used to control external devices and permit paralyzed and locked-in patients to interact with their environment.[2-6]

With expanding efforts from researchers, clinicians, government agencies and patient volunteers to bring these devices to the clinic, one of the primary questions that must be addressed is how to make these types of biomedical devices more biocompatible. Here the term biocompatibility describes "the ability of an [implant] to perform with an appropriate host response in a specific application."[7, 8] Answering this two-part question is a large component of the broader regulatory requirement that requires developers to provide valid scientific evidence of a device's safety and efficacy prior to receiving approval to go to market for clinical use.[9]

As the first part of the definition of biocompatility centers on device performance, Section 1 will analyze the types, successes and current functional limitations of intracortical recording microelectrode arrays used in BMI applications. Then to provide insight into the second part of the definition, Section 2 will describe what has been learned over the last 70 years from studies of the brain tissue response to recording microelectrode arrays implanted in brain tissue. Section 3 will discuss the progress that has been made to elucidate the connection between the brain tissue response and recording performance. The chapter concludes in Section 4 where we consider what lies ahead.

The primary purpose of this chapter is to present what is known of microelectrode-based BMI biocompatibility to the wide audience involved in this field. By identifying primary failure modes and describing how the host tissue response likely impacts device function and patient health, we hope to direct the field toward strategies that will improve the biocompatibility of existing and next generation intracortical recording devices to extend their usefulness as a basic science tool and in clinical applications.

1. Intracortical Microelectrode Arrays for Brain Machine Interfacing (BMI) Applications

1.1. *Intracortical microelectrode types*

A variety of devices have been created to access consciously modulated neural activity by placing recording sites in close proximity to neuronal cell bodies. Such proximity allows for the capture of not only local field potentials (LFPs) but also spiking activity from individual neurons called single unit activity. Single unit activity is considered the most useful type of information for complex and high-degree of freedom BMI applications.[10] Devices designed for such applications include insulated metal microwire arrays and two types of silicon-based systems including the Michigan microelectrode array (MI) and the Utah electrode array (UEA)). To provide insight into their potential clinical applications, Table 1 provides a summary of important studies conducted on patient volunteers. Other types of devices have been created in research laboratories around the world, however, for the sake of economy we will limit the discussion to the three primary types of microelectrode arrays that are available commercially.

Table 1: Overview of Clinical Studies Examining Microelectrode-Based BMIs.

NCT Identifier	Condition(s)	Intervention*	Primary Outcome Measure	Est. Completion Date	Publications
NCT00912041**	SCI -Tetraplegia / Brain Stem Infarct / Locked in Syndrome / Muscular Dystrophy / ALS	UEA implanted in motor cortex (for recording)	Safety - 1 yr follow up	Sept 2018	Hochberg et al, Nature 2006 / Donoghue et al, J. Physiol 2007 / Simeral et al, J Neural Eng 2011 / Hochberg et al, Nature 2012 / Bacher et al, Neurorehab Neural Rep 2015
NCT01364480	SCI - Tetraplegia	Two UEAs implanted in the motor cortex (for recording)	Safety - 1 yr follow up	Dec. 2016	Woodlinger et al, J Neural Eng 2015 / Collinger et al, Lancet 2013
NCT01849822	SCI - Tetraplegia	Two UEAs implanted in the posterior parietal cortex (for recording)	Efficacy - Task performance / Efficacy - Quality of life inventory / Safety - 1 yr follow up	May 2016	None reported to date
NCT01894802	SCI - Tetraplegia / Brain Stem Stroke	Two UEAs implanted in the motor cortex (for recording) and sensory cortex (for microstimulation)	Safety - 1 yr follow up	Dec. 2016	None reported to date
NCT01958086	SCI - Tetraplegia	Two UEAs implanted in Brodmann's Area 5 in the posterior parietal cortex	Efficacy - Control of a tablet computer / Safety - 1 yr follow up	Sept 2016	None reported to date
NCT01964261	SCI - Tetraplegia	Two Pt tipped UEAs implanted in the posterior parietal cortex (for recording) and one SIROF tippied UEA in the somatosensory cortex (for microstimulation)	Efficacy - Task performance with and without microstimulation / Safety - 1 yr follow up	Oct. 2016	None reported to date

* All studies to date have been perfromed with UEA-based systems produced by BlackRock Microsystems, LLC
** Clinicaltrials.gov lists other publications pertaining to this study

1.1.1. *Microwire arrays*

Microwire recording arrays have contributed greatly to our knowledge of electrophysiology with their use dating back to the 1940s.[11, 12] Such devices are composed of insulated conductors that have at least one exposed recording site that is generally placed at the tip of an extended shank. The composition of the conductor was originally a metal core, which has evolved over the years from more corrosive-prone metals such as Ag/AgCl to more stable metals such as Iridium (Ir), Platinum (Pt) and Pt/Ir alloys.[11, 13, 14] A similar progression has occurred in the insulating materials, with a gradual transition to more stable polymers (e.g. parylene-c, Al_2O_3, and epoxylite).[13, 15, 16] While no microwire arrays are currently approved for BMI applications or testing in humans, they are a very popular choice among the research community with groups conducting ground breaking studies in small animals and non-human primates.[6, 17, 18] Today, a number of companies produce microwire arrays for use in research including Microprobes (Gaithersburg, MD), Tucker Davis Technologies (Alachua, FL), FHC (Bowdin, ME) and Plexon (Dallas, TX).

1.1.2. *Planar Michigan (MI)-style microelectrode arrays*

Using a variety of microfabrication processes, including diffusion-based etch stops, Kensall Wise and colleagues at the University of Michigan developed a planar-silicon microelectrode array in the 1980s.[19, 20] The primary advantage of such planar devices compared to traditional microwire arrays is the ability to position multiple recording sites along a planar shank to record neural activity at various depths. Grids of penetrating shanks also have been fabricated to allow access to larger volumes of neural tissue. To the best of our knowledge, no MI-style microelectrode array has advanced to the stage of human clinical testing, however a variety of devices are under investigation in preclinical models.[21-23] NeuroNexus (Ann Arbor, MI), FHC (Bowdin, ME), and Blackrock Microsystems (Salt Lake City, UT) currently produce planar microelectrode arrays for research applications. For further discussion of the development and history of planar MI-style devices refer to the excellent review by Kensall Wise.[20]

1.1.3. *Utah electrode arrays*

During roughly the same period that the MI-style devices were being developed using thin film processing, Richard Normann and colleagues at the University of Utah were developing an alternative process to create a microelectrode array (referred to as Utah Electrode Array (UEA)) from thicker blocks of silicon.[24]

Specifically, a UEA is created using a series of glass reflow, dicing, chemical etchings and metallization processes.[25-27] A variety of designs have evolved over time, including arrays with varying shaft architectures and/or spacing.[28-31] Unlike microwire arrays and planar MI-style devices, the UEA has received FDA approval and has served as the basis for human clinical trials, including at least six trials in the US (Table 1). Blackrock Microsystems (Salt Lake City, Utah) is currently the sole supplier of the UEA (trade name Neuroprobe) and a number of universities are assessing the technology for a variety of clinical applications.

1.2. *Recording performance*

1.2.1. *Understanding how microelectrode arrays function*

Irrespective of their underlying substrate or individual design, each microelectrode array system creates a similar compound circuit with nearby neurons in order to record the combined spiking activity of groups of neurons or to isolate single unit activity.[32] Studies have demonstrated that the recording site of a microelectrode must be no greater than 150μm from a viable neuronal cell body to detect single unit activity.[33] Beyond this distance, group potentials are primarily detected as the ionic signal from a given neuron experiences sufficient diffusive spread and decay to become indistinguishable from other neurons or background noise. The limited diffusivity of brain tissue also impacts signals generated within the recording range, making it easier to isolate individual signals from neurons nearest to the recording sites.

Besides being close to the recording site, the target neuron must also be active, capable of firing, and properly integrated into functional brain circuits. Moreover, in order to generate an action potential, the extracellular microenvironment surrounding a viable target neuron must be within specific concentration ranges for a variety of ions. Disruption of the local microenvironment can lead to neuronal silencing even if viable neurons are present. In addition, the target neuron must receive sufficient synaptic input from innervating neurons. It is important to note that innervating neurons extend to other portions of the cortical column and distant neural tissue.

Therefore, to perform properly over a long indwelling period, BMIs controlled by an intracortical microelectrode array must maintain the integrity of not only (1) the recording device itself, but (2) the local neural microenvironment surrounding the recording site, as well as (3) the larger volume of neural tissue, extending both vertically along the cortical column and laterally to nearby columns or distant brain regions.

1.2.2. *Microelectrode-based BMIs offer treatment options to a variety of patient populations*

Despite the demanding requirements to record consciously modulated single unit activity from populations of neurons over time, a variety of conditions have been treated with intracortical microelectrode array technology. Perhaps the most celebrated BMI success to date has been the BrainGate clinical trials (NCT00912041) conducted by Hochberg and colleagues. In these landmark studies, volitional control of external devices (including a computer cursor and robotic hand/arm) was controlled by a UEA implanted in a patient's motor cortex.[2, 3, 34-37] Based on these and related findings, it is apparent that researchers have created a technology that can address many of the top priorities of patients with spinal cord injury or other forms of paralysis.[38] For further clinical successes refer to Table 1. From a biocompatibility standpoint, many of the studies listed in Table 1 have successfully recorded adequate information to control a particular BMI application for a significant amount of time in at least one subject.

When considering whether such devices are ready for widespread clinical use, it is important to note that the clinical studies listed in Tables 1 and nearly all preclinical studies in non-human primates have very small sample sizes. Furthermore, as the goal of the majority of these studies was to demonstrate safe and successful execution of a particular BMI application. Important aspects regarding biocompatibility at the tissue level may not have been analyzed.

1.2.3. *Inconsistent performance over clinically relevant timeframes hinders widespread clinical use*

To gain a better understanding of the reliability of such devices, other groups have used animal models as a cost-effective way of achieving a statistically meaningful sample size. Similar to the human BMI feasibility studies, numerous groups have shown that successful single unit recording can be achieved for months and in some cases years after implantation in animals.[21, 39-44]

Available evidence indicates that such successes are not necessarily the rule. For example, Burns et al. showed a progressive decline in recording performance from Pt microwire devices implanted in cat cerebral cortex, with less than 10% of the individual microelectrodes remaining functional 5 months after implantation.[45] Similar results have been reported using each of the primary microelectrode array recording systems across a variety of animal models including mice[46], rats[22, 47-49], and cats[39, 40, 44].

Retrospective examinations of studies in non-human primates perhaps best illustrate the challenge. In 2013 Barrese et al. analyzed historical performance data from 62 UEAs implanted in 27 macaques over 17 years of preclinical studies.[50] Over 50% of devices failed within 150 days of implantation. Moreover, recording performance was inconsistent from session to session, and showed a gradual decline of performance quality (signal-to-noise ratio and number of actively recording channels) over time. Schwartz et al. recorded similar observations in a subsequent retrospective study.[51] Together these studies indicate that inconsistent recording performance and premature device failure over clinically relevant time frames are observed in small animal and non-human primate models.

A review of the literature, indicates that microelectrode array-based recording systems perform better and longer in larger animal models and in humans. While the precise reason for this is unclear, a number of factors may explain such findings, including differences in the foreign body response (FBR) among different species, device differences (e.g., less developed/validated device designs), anatomical differences (e.g., skull thickness for device anchoring, relative size of the brain and cortical structures, and diffusivity of cortical tissue), quality of subject care, variability in the experience of investigative teams, and subject lifespan. Taken together, the available evidence suggests that small animal models should be considered as an accelerated failure model compared to longer lived species. In addition, due to the specific issues that may arise only in large animal brains and humans, early feasibility studies where devices may still be readily modified should be performed in larger animals or patient volunteers prior to moving to pivotal clinical trials where design features become largely unchangeable.[52]

The foregoing discussion is not to say that small animal studies are without value. A similar incidence of recording inconsistency and eventual failure is observed across all animal models, indicating that significantly useful information can be gleaned from statistically-powered, low-cost studies performed in smaller animals. Furthermore, small animal studies are the predominant source of information regarding the FBR as detailed histological studies are rare in non-human primate and human subject based studies. Moreover, the failure rate and inconsistent recording performance seen in non-human primates and human subjects requires that our present generation of devices be improved before widespread clinical translation occurs. Statistically-powered preclinical testing will undoubtedly be performed in smaller animals prior to moving to non-human primate and human subjects for both ethical and financial reasons.

1.2.4. *Potential microelectrode array failure mechanisms*

If we examine the compound circuit that serves to extract consciously modulated neural activity, it becomes apparent that a variety of factors could lead to inconsistent performance and premature recording failure over time.[32] Beginning with the device itself and then moving toward the tissue side of the equation, these factors include:

1. Mechanical breakage of the device, including wires, connector, and the headstage (removal or loosening of the headstage from the skull) [15, 48-50, 53, 54];
2. Recording site corrosion [48, 49, 55, 56];
3. Damage to or degradation of insulating and passivating layers [15, 57-60]; and,
4. Disruption of the neural microenvironment (both local and distant from the recording site).[45, 61-64]

While often considered independently from one another, it is critical to note that many if not all of these failure modes can occur in the same animal over different and overlapping periods of time. Furthermore, many can be traced back to the harsh tissue microenvironment created in response to the implantation and the chronic presence of the device in the biological milieu. For example, breakage of wires as well as breakage, loosening, and/or removal of the headstage are often due to manipulation of the device by the animal in response to inflammatory sequela. In addition, recording site corrosion and degradation of insulating and passivating layers can result from the elevated temperature and harsh environment of mammalian tissue.

2. Host Response to Intracortical Microelectrode Arrays and Associated Hardware

While the recording of neuronal spiking activity by all types of microelectrode arrays is similar, the unique design elements of different types of devices leads to differences in the brain tissue response to a given device type. To understand the biocompatibility concerns of each device it is necessary to understand the impact of specific device features on the evolution of the host response, which for the sake of clarity will be referred to as the foreign body response (FBR).

The FBR is a sterile inflammatory reaction carried out by the innate immune system that accompanies the implantation of any biomaterial or biomedical device anywhere in the body. The term FBR differs from the term biocompatibility in that it is a description of the cellular and molecular events following implantation of a biomaterial or biomedical device over the entire indwelling period, irrespective of whether the implant or device is functional or not. The term biocompatibility, on the other hand, is a conditional term that requires that an implant or device is functioning as intended, and that the FBR is acceptable when weighed against benefits provided by the device. The two terms are frequently misused as synonyms. For the purposes of this chapter the two terms, "biocompatibility and FBR" have different meanings. Notice that by definition the term "biocompatibility" is also conditional in another sense, that is, a particular implant or device may be biocompatible in the early part of its indwelling period and then be less biocompatible with time until it no longer functions. At that point when an implant or device no longer functions as intended it cannot be considered biocompatible.

In this section, we will examine what is known of the FBR to simple devices that cause a single penetrating injury in brain cortex (e.g., single cylindrical microwire and a planar MI-style device) and to more complex devices, including high-density microwire arrays and the UEA, in which every microelectrode shaft causes a penetrating injury upon implantation.

To date over 100 studies have analyzed the FBR to intracortical microelectrode arrays, while only a handful of more recent studies have attempted to study the biocompatibility of such devices, that is, studied the FBR while the device was functioning as intended. The majority of studies have examined the FBR to non-functional single planar MI-style devices and to a lesser extent single cylindrical microwires (Figure 1a).[65] These simple devices offer a number of benefits over high-density recording arrays that have made them the model of choice among researchers for analyzing the FBR. Among these is the fact that the small, single penetrating injury created is more reproducible, enabling robust quantification compared to the complex injury made by higher density devices that inflict multiple, closely spaced penetrating injuries.

Nearly all attempts to study the FBR have been performed in larger-cohorts of small animals (Figure 1a). Of these studies, nearly all have been performed in young adult rats (Figure 1b).[66] This is in contrast to many patient populations that may eventually benefit from a BMI system, including those suffering from paralysis [67] or limb amputation [68], where many individuals acquire their condition later in adulthood and will obviously age over time. Due to increasing evidence that the FBR and immune response may change with age [69], the field needs to investigate the impact of aging on device function and biocompatibility as there is currently a lack of studies in this area.

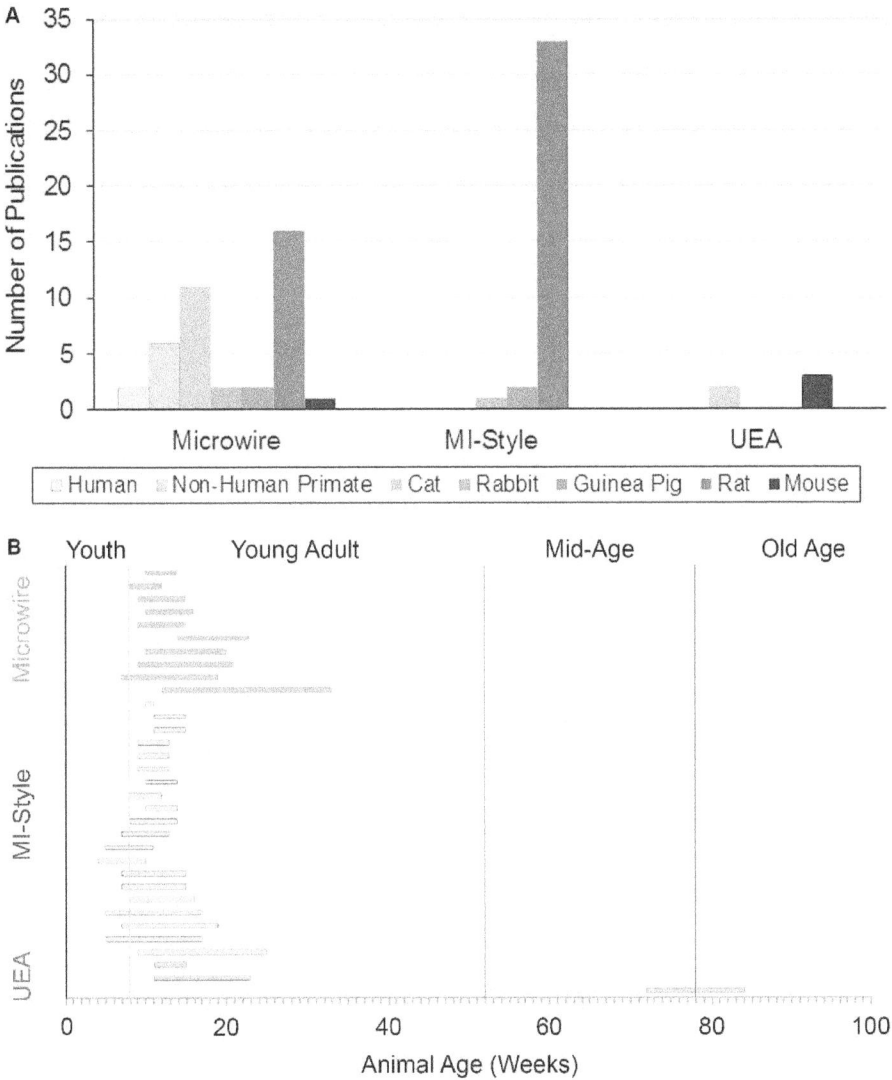

Fig. 1: (A) Number of publications for each major electrode type broken down by type of species the device was implanted into. The majority of FBR studies have focused on MI-style microelectrode arrays implanted into rats. Despite being the only system used in clinical studies there have been very few studies examining the FBR to the UEA. (B) Age of rats used in the rat FBR literature. Bar extends from age of implantation until the age at euthanasia of the oldest animal in the study. Unlike the broad age range for patients that could benefit from a BMI, the majority of such studies have focused on young adult animals.

One of the key pieces of information that is beginning to evolve from the literature is the multi-faceted nature of the FBR. To date the majority of reports have described the FBR as a linear progression of events; one feeding into another.[32, 70, 71] However, based on a number of studies that have examined the impact of design modifications or have used pharmacological agents, there is reason to believe that the sterile immune process involves multiple parallel downstream paths that may affect the histological makeup of the FBR differently. The FBR may be further complicated by the introduction of microorganisms either directly or by planktonic seeding from distant sites anytime in the indwelling period.

2.1. *The FBR to single microwire and MI-style microelectrode arrays*

2.1.1. *Vascular injury is unavoidable during microelectrode implantation*

The cellular density within brain cortical tissue is orders of magnitude higher than in other mammalian soft tissues. Typical cellular density for neurons ranges from 50,000-100,000 neurons/mm^2 in the motor cortex of rodents and small primates, respectively.[72] The density of glial cells (supporting cells within the brain) is also extremely high with newer studies indicating that there is roughly 1 glial cell per neuron in the brain of nearly all primates (including humans).[73] Such cellular density limits small molecule diffusivity and clearance in the cortical extracellular space compared to that in other soft tissues of the body.

To maintain viability of such cell-dense tissue, the cerebral cortex is one of the most highly vascularized tissues in the human body [74]. To meet the metabolic demands of proper brain function, neuronal cell bodies are typically no more than 100μm from the nearest capillary and often much closer. In mammalian cortex there are roughly 400-500 capillary sections/mm^2.[75-80] This network of cortical capillaries receives its input from a dense descending network of larger arterioles and equally dense set of venules.[79] While originally thought to mirror the cortical column organization, recent studies have shown that the number of descending arterioles and ascending venules varies throughout the cortex.[79] These largely vertical vascular arbors in turn connect to larger vessels that laterally span the upper cortical layers and the cortical surface. Figure 2 shows representative images of the vascular arborization in both the healthy unimplanted rat brain and surrounding a MI-style microelectrode implanted in rat cortical tissue.

Due to the high density of both cells and vasculature, it should come as no surprise that the implantation of a microelectrode array into mammalian cortical tissue is a traumatic event that damages cells, extracellular matrix (ECM), and vasculature along the implantation tract.[81] The initial penetrating injury is exacerbated for a short period of time due to the resulting edema and the acute inflammatory response incited by neutrophils dumped into the extracellular space, as well as, the deprivation of oxygen, nutrients and waste elimination to all downstream tissue.

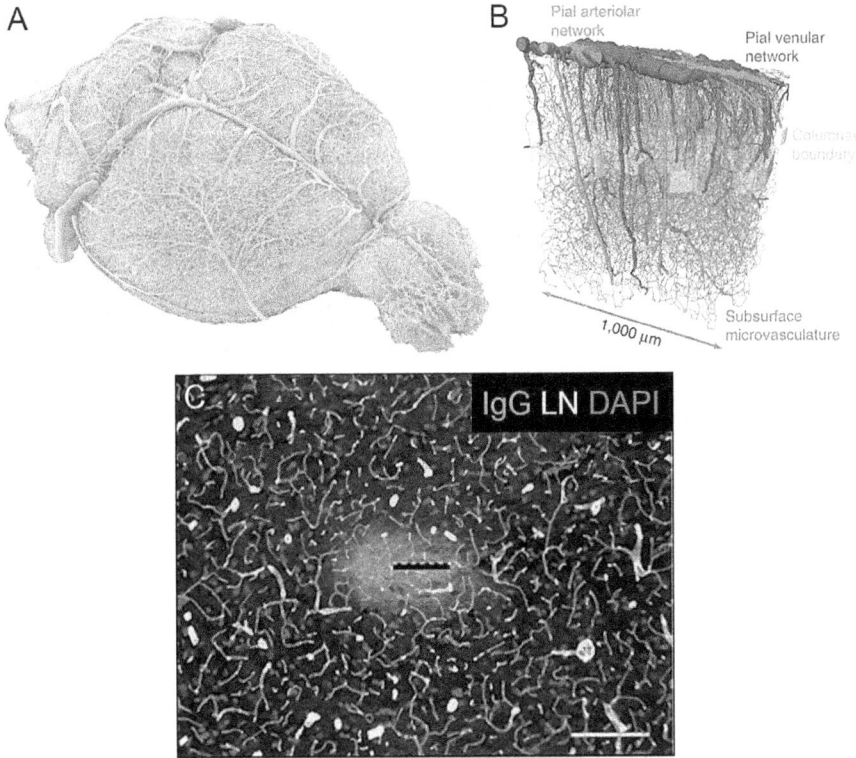

Fig. 2: (A) Vascular cast showing density of blood vessels at surface of rodent brain.[80] (B) 3-D reconstruction of the vascular elements found in a representative 1mm³ block of rodent brain.[79] (C) Horizontal section showing vasculature (LN+ immunoreactivity) and extravasated host IgG surrounding a chronically implanted MI-style microelectrode. Scale bar in C = 100μm. 2A: Adapted by permission from John Wiley & Sons, Inc.: Microscopy Research and Technique, copyright 2006, doi: 10.1002/jemt.20263. 2B Adapted with permission from Macmillan Publishers Ltd: Nature Neuroscience, copyright 2013, doi:10.1038/nn.3426.

2.1.2. *Early events*

Following the initial injury, several critical biological cascades have evolved to (1) induce hemostasis, (2) combat the potential introduction of pathogens, and (3) clean up the debris from blood loss, damaged cells and extracellular matrix. Insertion of the microelectrode array breaks various types of blood vessels, dumping red blood cells, platelets, white blood cells and plasma proteins into the extracellular space of cortical tissue. Hemostasis is restored by a combination of vasoconstriction, platelet activation, and initiation of the coagulation cascade.[82]

Vascular damage also releases plasma proteins into the extracellular space including immunoglobulin and complement molecules that initiate the complement cascade.[83] In the sterile surgical environment, formation of the complement cascade's membrane attack complexes causes indiscriminant cell death along the implantation tract.[84, 85] Neutrophil activation kills additional cells wherever they are distributed. Moreover, alternatively activated complement adsorbed to the microelectrode surface and adjoining extracellular components provides chemotactic signals that recruit immune cells to the site of injury.[84-86]

The recruited cells include tissue specific macrophages and blood borne monocytes that become macrophages as they migrate into tissue. Macrophage phagocytosis of RBC's, platelets, cell and matrix debris as well as clot resorption involves secretion of a variety of matrix metalloproteases and such small reactive species as reactive oxygen intermediates and nitrogen species that continue to damage adjacent neural tissue. These processes must certainly have an impact on the stability and efficacy of biological surface coatings placed on microelectrode arrays. However, this area has not been studied to date. Ultimately the phagocytized cellular debris and matrix is digested in the lysosomal compartment of the recruited macrophages and presented on their cell surface.

At least a portion of the activated and recruited macrophages serve as antigen-presenting cells where they migrate to lymphatic tissue and present their surface antigens to B- and T-cell populations.[87, 88] In order to get to lymphatic tissue macrophages must migrate through neural tissue and reenter the vasculature at post capillary venules, which disrupts the BBB.[89] Such white blood cell trafficking disrupts blood vessel integrity and re-releases plasma proteins (e.g., immunoglobulins, fibrinogen, fibronectin, and complement factors) that diffuse into the implantation tract. Such released plasma proteins likely readsorb to the microelectrode surface and components of the extracellular space. They perpetuate inflammatory cell recruitment and activation throughout the indwelling period. White blood cell trafficking is likely a key mechanistic connection between the acute and chronic phases of the FBR that must be addressed to attenuate the persistent inflammatory component of the FBR.[90]

2.1.3. *Injury at later time points*

It is important to note that injury and initiation of these cascades is likely not isolated to the initial surgical implantation of the microelectrode.[91] BMI researchers often note that animals physically manipulate headstage components, presumably to alleviate the pain and irritation resulting from the implanted hardware. Animals also perform behaviors that can cause rapid accelerations/decelerations of their heads.[50] Such activities likely exacerbate or may cause new injury at the implantation site. While paralyzed human patients are less likely to perform such activities, unforeseen accidents will likely be a residual risk that developers and regulatory personnel must consider.

Beyond these larger movements, researchers have suggested that smaller unavoidable physiologically-related micromotion, due to vascular pulsation- and respiration-related movements, likely contribute to the FBR, especially to devices tethered to the skull.[91-93] Specifically, there is a large group within the field that believe that such micromotion combined with the mismatch in mechanical properties (primarily material stiffness) between brain tissue (10s of MPas) and traditional microelectrodes (100s of GPas) leads to persistent and repetitive stimuli that contributes to the FBR.

A number of in silico and in vitro studies support the theory.[92, 94, 95] Perhaps the most cited in vivo studies in support of this theory are those that show that the FBR is increased when devices are tethered to the skull.[96-99] While device tethering may result in greater relative motions between the brain and skull upon large movements, it is unclear how much the more subtle physiological stresses/strains influence the FBR and whether they can be avoided.

It should be noted that alternative explanations exist to explain why the tethering of implants to the skull increases the FBR. One such explanation focuses on meningeal macrophage migration from the brain surface into cortical tissue. There are differences between the resident macrophage population within the meninges and those found in cortical tissue. Meningeal macrophages are derived from bone marrow whereas the majority of cortical microglia originate from the yolk sac.[100-102] Growing evidence supports the theory that bone-marrow derived cells exhibit a more pronounced inflammatory response compared to their yolk sac derived counterparts as the two cell types respond differently to injury, infection and immune stimuli.[101, 103, 104] In support of this theory, recent findings indicate that sub-meningeal implantation reduces the FBR.[105]

A second set of studies investigating the relationship between mechanical mismatch, micromotion and the FBR are studies comparing the FBR between traditional microelectrode arrays and those made from softer or in situ softening materials. Specifically, work by Harris et al. reported short term-differences in the FBR between a stiff microwire (~400GPa) and an in situ softening probe made from cellulose whiskers embedded in poly(vinyl acetate) (PVAc: ~15-30MPa after implantation), but found no differences in the FBR at chronic time points.[106, 107] Capadona and colleagues recently repeated these experiments and reported that the in situ softening devices reduced the host response compared to silicon control devices coated with a thin layer of PVAc.[108] However, subsequent efforts from the same group while examining two in situ softening devices with or without a short-term dose of resveratrol show no differences compared to the well documented response to traditional stiffer devices including quantitative metrics showing no differences in neuronal loss at chronic time points.[109]

Based on the discrepancies and alternative interpretations, it is still not clear what role brain micromotion and mechanical mismatch have on the FBR. We suspect that the materials that have been created to deal with this issue will likely be useful for reducing injury risks stemming from larger relative movements and unforeseen accidents that may cause rapid accelerations and decelerations of the head. The usefulness of low modulus materials to combat issues arising from larger movements will require controlled intentional movements or sufficiently powered studies to capture these larger-scale but less frequent injury events.

2.1.4. *Persistent neuroinflammation throughout the indwelling period*

The acute phase of the FBR gradually evolves to a more chronic phase of the wound healing response where the focus shifts to tissue remodeling and stabilization. Figures 3 and 4 show the stereotypic architecture of the chronic FBR to a single microwire and a planar MI-style device, respectively. The key feature of the chronic FBR is a persistent sterile inflammatory response at the device/tissue interface. This response occurs regardless of the type of device or where in the cortex the device is implanted as long as the implant or device creates a single penetrating injury.

In neuronal tissue, the neuroinflammatory component likely involves activation of three types of macrophages: (1) blood-born macrophages derived from bone marrow monocytes that enter brain tissue following implantation related injury and as a result of persistent pro-inflammatory recruitment; (2) resident yolk sac derived microglia that colonize the brain in utero, and (3) resident bone-marrow derived macrophages that begin infiltrating the brain shortly after birth. Studies have suggested that both microglia and macrophages are capable of responding to invading pathogens, recognizing extravasated plasma proteins, phagocytizing RBCs, platelets, damaged or dead cells, and in clearing residual cell debris.[110-112] It is unclear at present how these separate populations contribute to the FBR so for the remainder of this chapter we will only use the term macrophages to describe the three classes of cells until studies examining the role of each cell type are more fully defined.

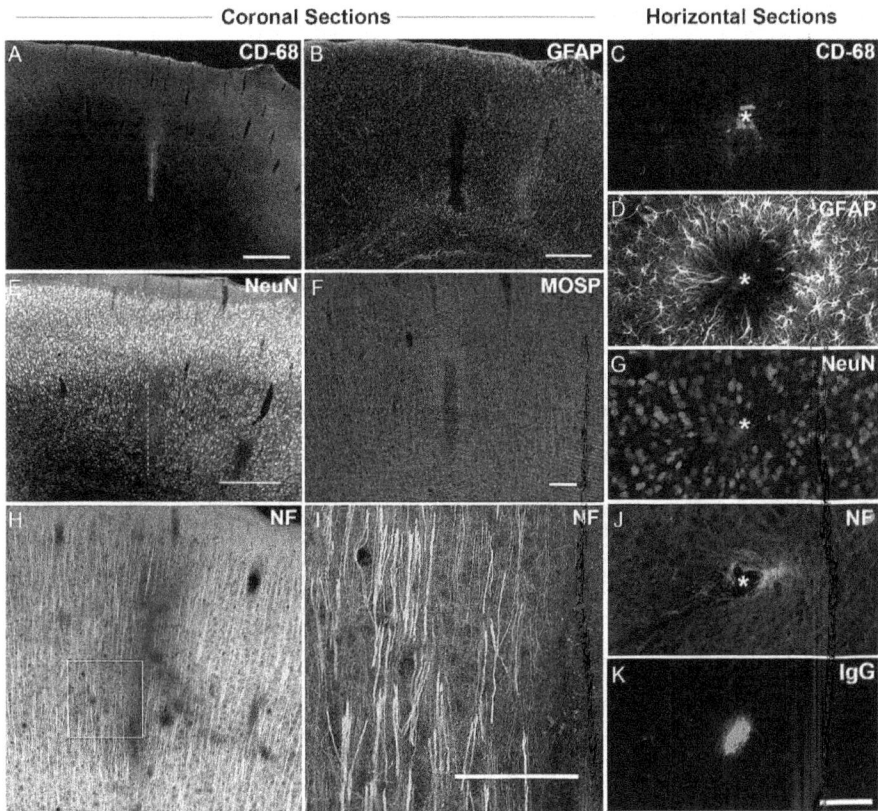

Fig. 3: Representative images showing the FBR to a single 75μm diameter stainless steel microwire (FHC: Bowdoinham, ME).[143] The first two columns show coronal sections adjacent to the implantation track while the third column shows representative horizontal sections. (A & C) Activated macrophages and (B & D) astrogliosis extend the length of the implant. Associated with this region of inflammation and astrogliosis are reductions in (E & G) neuronal cell and (H-J) fiber density, (F) demyelination, (K) BBB leakiness. 2B Scale Bar in A,B,E,F,H = 500μm and scale bar in C,D,G,I,J,K = 100μm. Adapted with permission from Elsevier: Biomaterials, copyright 2010, doi:10.1016/j.biomaterials.2009.11.049

Upon activation, macrophages secrete a variety of pro-inflammatory and potentially cytotoxic soluble factors that can activate and damage healthy bystander cells in the surrounding tissue including astrocytes, neurons, oligodendrocytes and cells associated with the neurovasculature unit. Not surprisingly a number of cytokines have been linked to the neuroinflammatory response to chronically implanted microelectrode arrays. Biran et al. have shown that adherent macrophages on the surface of retrieved microelectrode arrays release both tumor necrosis factor-alpha (TNF-α) and monocyte chemotactic protein-1 (MCP-1).[61] TNF-α is the prototypical cytokine of inflammation and is cytotoxic to neurons and oligodendrocytes. TNF-α is also heavily implicated in a variety of neuroinflammatory diseases.[113-115] The chemokine MCP-1 is heavily involved in recruiting new macrophages to sites of injury and inflammation by disrupting the blood brain barrier and acting as a chemotactic signal.[116-118] Furthermore, Karumbaiah et al. have shown that gene expression for various pro-inflammatory soluble factors (IL-1, 6 and 17 as well as TNF-α) is up-regulated in tissue surrounding poorly performing microelectrode arrays.[64]

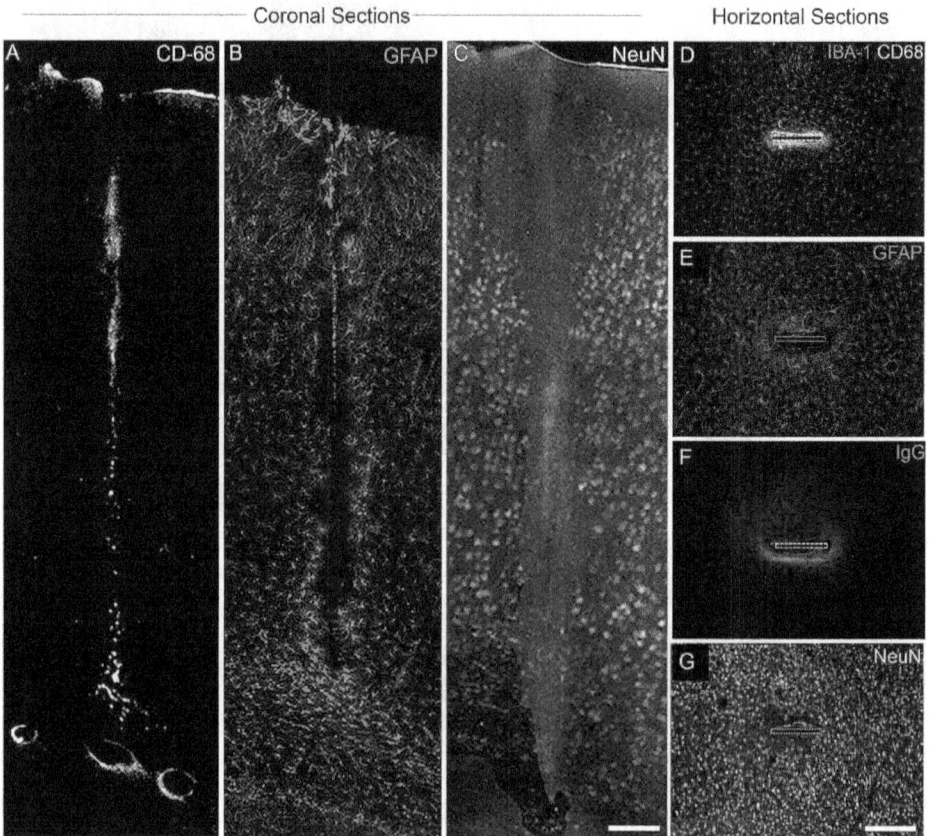

Fig. 4: Representative images showing the FBR to a single MI-style microelectrode array.[142] (A-C) Show coronal sections adjacent to the implantation track while (D-G) shows horizontal sections. (A & D) Activated macrophages and (B & E) astrogliosis extend the length of the implant. Similar to neuroinflammatory diseases, (C & G) neuronal cell density and (F) BBB leakiness has been reported to occur in this region of inflammation and astrogliosis. Scale Bar in A-C = 100μm and scale bar in D-G = 300μm. (A-C) Adapted by permission from Elsevier: Biomaterials, copyright 2010, doi:10.1016/j.biomaterials.2010.05.050. (D-G) Adapted with permission from Elsevier: Biomaterials, copyright 2014, doi:10.1016/j.biomaterials.2014.08.039.

2.1.5. *Astrogliosis and fibrotic encapsulation*

Another hallmark of the chronic FBR to simple devices implanted into the brain is the formation of a largely concentric region of hypertrophic astrocytes surrounding the zone of activated macrophages that persists at the device-tissue interface.[70] Following injury, astrocytes increase in number and enlarge the size of their intermediate cytoskeletal elements; a hallmark of central nervous system (CNS) injury called the glial scar.[61, 70] Immunoreactivity for glial fibrillary acid protein (GFAP), an astrocyte-specific intermediate filament, is the primary means used to visualize astrogliosis (increase in number of astrocytes) and hypertrophy (increase in size of GFAP intermediate filaments within astrocytes). It should be noted that cell-filling experiments indicate that the actual volume taken up by astrocytes is much larger than that seen with the star-like distribution of immunoreactive GFAP.[119, 120] Hypertrophic astrocytes are believed to play a similar role to that of reactive fibroblasts in the FBR in non-neural tissues, creating a denser scar-like layer that limits small molecule diffusivity and volume transmission.[121, 122]

A number of studies have described that hypertrophic astrocytes alter their production of extracellular matrix (ECM). For example, changes in ECM have been reported in both traumatic brain injury and in many neurodegenerative conditions.[123-125] Not surprisingly, similar changes, including up-regulation of chondroitin sulfate proteoglycan (CSPG) expression, has been reported surrounding microelectrode arrays implanted chronically in brain tissue.[126] Such upregulation of CSPG could be the result of continued astrocyte exposure to plasma proteins like fibronectin, which are known activating agents and are present in the extracellular space around leaky vasculature.[127] As CSPGs are generally considered neuroinhibitory it is likely that neuronal regeneration in such areas is affected.[128-132] Furthermore, increased production of charged ECM molecules could further limit small molecule diffusivity and its clearance surrounding implanted microelectrode arrays.[121, 122, 133]

The overall impact of the astroglial component of the foreign body response on recording performance is becoming clearer. Initially it was thought that astrogliosis would limit recording function by reducing small ion transport [134] or pushing neurons away from the recording zone [40, 135]. Nolta et al. have recently shown that the degree of astrogliosis, as indicated by the intensity and spatial distribution of GFAP immunoreactivity, inversely correlates with recording performance of a 4x4 UEA implanted in rat cortex.[62]

The cause of astrogliosis surrounding chronically implanted intracortical microelectrode arrays is an important outstanding question. Increasing evidence indicates that astrogliosis is likely a result of a combination of acute inflammatory events resulting from the initial vascular damage and from chronic neuroinflammation at the device/tissue interface that persists throughout the indwelling period. Specifically, Biran et al. showed that enhanced astrogliosis, unlike other hallmarks of the host response to microelectrodes, was present 4 weeks following a stab injury inflicted with a microelectrode array to the cortex that was subsequently removed shortly after implantation.[61] Other studies support this finding and extend the duration of astrogliosis following stab wound injuries to at least 16 weeks with similar types of microelectrode arrays.[136] Moreover, studies beyond those investigating stab injures also support the notion that astrogliosis results from the initial vascular damage. Specifically, Skousen et al. compared the FBR of a 300μm wide planar MI-style device to a planar lattice style device that produced a similar amount of implantation injury but presented roughly 50% less surface area during the indwelling period.[90] This study found that the lattice devices showed a similar degree of astrogliosis compared to the solid planar devices despite showing a reduction in biomarkers associated with the chronic phase of the FBR including persistent macrophage activation, BBB dysfunction, and neuronal loss.

There is also evidence that targeting the acute period of the FBR may be sufficient to reduce, though not completely suppress, astrogliosis while not impacting other aspects of the FBR. Specifically, delivering a short-term dose of the anti-inflammatory drug dexamethasone from an implanted microelectrode array was sufficient to reduce the level of astrogliosis at both one and four weeks after implantation compared to nondexamethasone-eluting control devices.[126] Systemic delivery had a similar affect, reducing astrogliosis at one and six weeks after implantation.[137] Further studies investigating bioactive protein coatings, which are likely quickly removed from the device surface, also reported reduced astrogliosis at chronic time frames.[138] This is encouraging from a device development standpoint, as it suggests that short-term delivery of anti-inflammatory drugs or other acute strategies may be sufficient to reduce the level of chronic astrogliosis. Whether this is also observed in high-density devices is unclear as such studies have not been reported.

Another important question that needs addressing with respect to the astrogliotic component of the FBR is whether there are any alterations to the many critical functions that astrocytes play in healthy brain tissue, especially given their proximity to a persistent layer of activated macrophages.[139-141] Under normal conditions astrocytes maintain the local microenvironment by sequestering neurotransmitters and ions. Astrocytes are also a critical component of the blood brain barrier that separates the brain microenvironment from that of the supporting vasculature. Local disruption of these functions could have a detrimental impact on the health and function of local neurons.

2.1.6. *Blood-Brain Barrier (BBB) dysfunction and disruption of the ionic environment*

While little work has addressed whether neurotransmitter and ion sequestration is impacted by astrocyte hypertrophy, growing evidence indicates that the BBB surrounding implanted microelectrodes is impaired. Beginning with work by Winslow et al., a number of groups have now documented that IgG can be detected in the extracellular space surrounding microelectrode array implantation tracts following perfusion fixation.[63, 90, 142, 143] Under normal circumstances, many blood borne molecules, such as IgG, are excluded from the extracellular compartment of brain tissue due to their large size. Such large molecules are completely removed from vasculature following the standard tissue perfusion techniques applied while performing traditional histological analysis and are generally not observed a few hundred microns away from devices that create a minimal penetrating injury. However, in areas of neuroinflammation, as seen in many neuroinflammatory diseases or surrounding other types of implanted devices, the BBB is leaky, allowing normally excluded plasma proteins access to the brain extracellular space where they remain following perfusion fixation. Many of these components, including fibrinogen, immunoglobulins and complement molecules, can activate astrocytes and tissue macrophages thus contributing to astrogliosis and the persistence of neuroinflammation.[144, 145] Moreover, altering the local ionic environment by mixing with the different ionic composition of plasma could have a detrimental impact on neuronal recording. In support of this theory Nolta et al. and Saxena et al. recently observed that an increased level of local BBB leakiness correlated with decreases in recording performance of Utah Electrode Arrays (Nolta), Microwires (Saxena) and MI-style Microelectrode arrays (Saxena).[62, 63]

This raises the question of whether BBB dysfunction is a result of altered astrocyte function, neuroinflammation, or a combination of both. To our knowledge there are no studies that have described a reduction in neuroinflammation that have not also described a reduction in BBB leakiness. Therefore, these appear to be coupled processes. Moreover, a number of studies have documented regions of enhanced astrogliosis without observing BBB dysfunction, including those examining stab wound injuries and lattice devices that present less surface area while inducing a significant vascular injury.[61, 90] Therefore, it appears that BBB leakiness observed throughout the indwelling period is primarily a result of persistent neuroinflammation (i.e., macrophage activation) and not simply enhanced astrogliosis.

2.1.7. *Neuronal loss occurs within the critical recording range*

Often considered the most critical component of the host response that could impact recording function, a region of neuronal loss has been observed associated with the zone of persistent macrophage activation. The overall reduction in neuronal density surrounding simple single shank devices is approximately 40-60% within the recording zone. While a significant number of NeuN+ neurons remain, this large degree of loss supports the theory that the local microenvironment may not be adequate to support neurons that function properly.

A number of studies have investigated the cause and evolution of neuronal loss following implantation of devices that create a small penetrating injury. In their paper, Biran et al. observed an ~60% loss of neurons surrounding implanted MI-style microelectrodes at both 2 and 4 weeks following device implantation.[61] However, no neuronal loss was observed in similarly stab-wounded animals. This finding and subsequent supporting studies emphasize the fact that neuronal loss surrounding implants that create a small single penetrating injury (i.e. single microwire and MI-style microelectrodes) requires the presence of a device and is not associated with the implantation injury itself. Furthermore, it is clear that neuron cell body loss occurs early following implantation, as both Biran et al. and Winslow et al. observed no signs of progressive neuronal loss using such devices over time with devices tethered to the skull.[61, 142, 143] However, unlike reducing astrogliosis, it appears that just reducing acute inflammation with drug treatment or other short acting strategies may not be sufficient to protect neurons over the lifetime of the device as, to the best of our knowledge, no such strategy has shown chronic sparing of neurons adjacent to simple single shank microelectrode arrays.[138] Therefore, a more permanent means of reducing the FBR may be needed to maintain sufficient normal neuronal densities in the recording zone or adjacent to the device.

It is also important to note that similar degrees of neuronal loss have been reported in a very large number of studies.[90, 96, 108, 109, 136, 142, 143, 146-149] Therefore, quantified loss surrounding traditional single shank microwire and MI-style microelectrodes outside of this well-established range, while possible, should be considered suspect until reproduced. A limited number of studies have suggested that neuronal density surrounding implanted microelectrodes fluctuates over time.[150, 151] This seems unlikely given the extensive literature describing (1) the low proliferation rate of adult neurons (almost exclusively occurring in neurogenic zones) and (2) the almost irreversible loss of neurons in areas of traumatic injury or disease adjacent to tissue environments typified by neuroinflammation. A more plausible explanation of such discrepancies include use of multiple people during tissue processing and neuronal counting procedures, poor mounting technique causing compaction or stretching of tissue, analysis of tissue derived from different cortical layers during comparisons, and possible infection/endotoxin contamination. To avoid these issues, we suggest the use of (1) the same surgeon across cohorts (and perhaps even studies), (2) batch preparation and histological analysis of devices and tissues that will be compared to each other, (3) use of blinded evaluators regarding device types and conditions wherever possible, and (4) internally verified measurements by having additional evaluators reevaluate critical findings.

2.1.8. *Dendritic loss and demyelination may impact connectivity of remaining neurons*

Beyond neuronal cell bodies themselves, neuronal processes also appear to be impacted by chronic implantation of a microelectrode array. Much of the early documentation of this aspect of the FBR was reported by Biran et al. who observed significant reduction in neurofilament immunoreactivity surrounding microelectrodes implanted in rat cortex for 2 and 4 weeks.[61] In harmony with the loss of neuronal cell bodies, similarities in the reduction of neurofilament immunoreactivity at various time points suggests that the majority of neurofilament loss occurred early after implantation. Other studies that looked later in the indwelling period described changes in the level of dendrites and axons in the cortical column. Specifically, Winslow et al. observed that while there was a general reduction in dendritic processes (MAP-2 immunoreactivity), some animals expressed increased NF-160 immunoreactivity (axonal marker) in deeper cortical layers suggesting that axonal spouting can occur at longer time points near the implantation tract consistent with observations in other brain injury models.[142, 143]

Beyond expanding our understanding of the types of neuronal fibers impacted, Winslow et al. reported that the level of axon myelination was decreased surrounding intracortical microelectrode arrays.[142, 143] Demyelination is a classic hallmark of neuroinflammatory diseases that likely affects neuronal signaling and synaptic stability and is another likely candidate marker of poor recording performance.

Taken together, these findings provide evidence that, while a significant number of NeuN+ neuronal cell bodies remain within the recording range of the device, the connectivity and function of the remaining neurons may be at risk. These findings also indicate that it is likely insufficient to analyze just the number of neuronal cell bodies in the recording zone when trying to understand the impact of the FBR on recording function as neural connectivity, ionic milieu and myelination surrounding the entire microelectrode and any associated hardware may be impacted over long indwelling periods.

2.1.9.   *Combating the host response to small simple devices like single microwire and MI-style microelectrodes*

Based on the findings described above, we hope that it has become clear that a combination of acute and longer persistent neuroinflammatory sequelae likely underlie nearly all elements of the FBR to devices that create a small penetrating injury. Therefore, we believe that the primary target for improving the performance and biocompatibility of such simple intracortical microelectrode arrays should focus on limiting the triggers to both acute and persistent neuroinflammation. The available evidence suggests that a single approach is unlikely to alleviate all components of the FBR to such devices.

To effectively reduce the impact of acute and persistent neuroinflammation at the interface of these devices, the available evidence suggests that next generation device designs should 1) limit the extent of vasculature injury 2) limit the local accumulation of activated macrophages at the device interface, 3) reduce the level of activation of inflammatory cells, and/or 4) directly antagonize the pro-inflammatory and cytotoxic soluble factors released by activated macrophages. A number of techniques have been developed to do this including:

- modifications to classic device architectures to limit vascular injury and the number of adherent macrophages in a given volume of brain tissue;[90, 99, 149]
- use of coatings that are hemostatic to limit blood loss after implantation;
- delivery of soluble anti-inflammatory agents (primarily used to combat acute inflammation);[126, 137, 152]
- addition of immunomodulatory coatings that reduce macrophage activation through haptic signaling;[138, 153, 154]
- increasing device permeability to increase clearance of pro-inflammatory and cytotoxic soluble factors;[136] and
- incorporation of released or surface bound lytic enzymes that actively degrade reactive species.[153]

For further review of the progress of each of these methods refer to the review by Jorfi et al.[32]

2.2. FBR to complex, high density recording array

As described above, the majority of our understanding of the brain FBR to intracortical microelectrode arrays comes from studies analyzing simple devices that cause a single or well isolated, small penetrating injury (i.e. single microwire and MI-style microelectrodes). In contrast, the majority of long-term recording studies in non-human primates as well as clinical feasibility studies in human volunteers have been performed with high density devices, primarily the UEA. To address this lack of knowledge, investigators have begun to extend our knowledge of the FBR to these more complicated devices.

2.2.1. *Initial injury due to implantation of a high density microelectrode*

Due to their increased size and higher number of regularly spaced penetrating elements, high density microelectrode arrays (like the UEA, microwire arrays, or multi-shaft MI-style microelectrode arrays) create significantly greater vasculature injury upon implantation compared to single microwire or MI-style microelectrode arrays. Much of our knowledge of the initial injury caused by these devices stem from very acute studies in humans where devices were inserted into cortical tissue of patients undergoing resection procedures and then removed along with the surrounding tissue.[155, 156] In these studies, it was observed that the implantation of high-density UEAs caused acute subarachnoid hemorrhage associated with each penetrating shaft regardless of the exact technique used to insert the device (Figure 5). Blood loss was limited to within millimeters of each microelectrode track, a distance that is significantly greater than observed surrounding single penetrating microelectrode arrays. Also observed in a number of subjects was extra-arachnoidal and petechial hemorrhage at some distance from the implantation site. In harmony with our understanding of the evolution of the FBR to simpler devices, these studies also noted that device insertion caused rapid activation and recruitment of inflammatory cells.

2.2.2. *Subchronic FBR to a high density microelectrode array*

Unlike the longest-term recording studies and the initial injury response to high-density devices conducted primarily in human patients, all of what we know concerning longer-term aspects of the host response to high-density devices is derived from small animal models (rats and cats). This change in model is due primarily to the ethical and financial constraints of performing longer-term implantation studies followed by tissue resection or animal euthanasia in non-human primates.

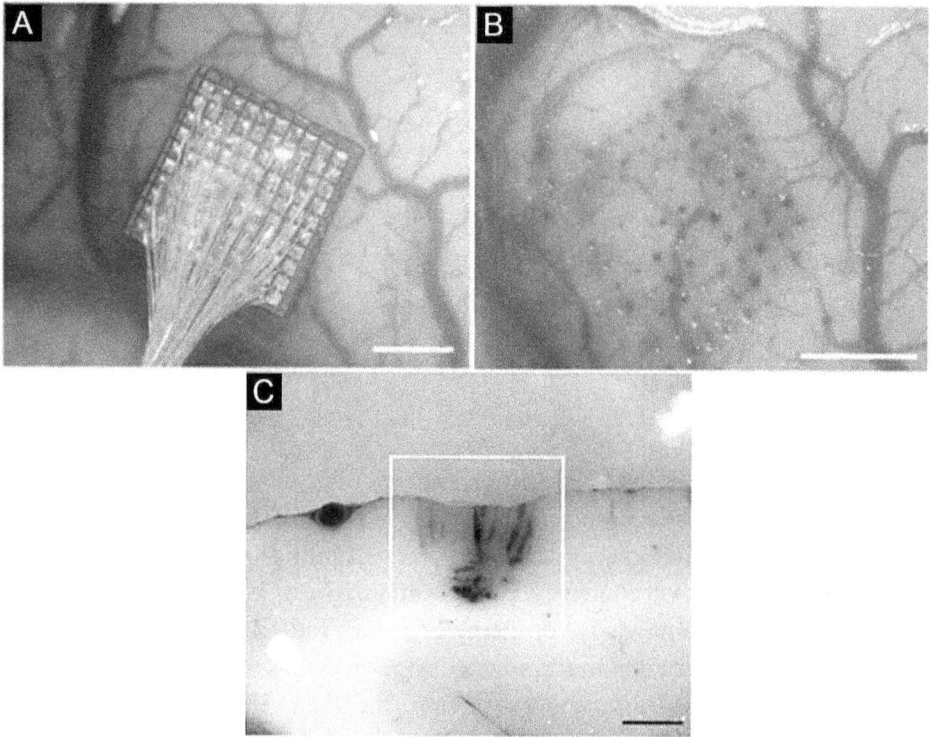

Fig. 5: (A) Photograph of a 10x10 UEA implanted into human temporal cortex.[156] (B) Photograph of cortical surface following UEA removal after a few minutes of implantation (A). Photographic evidence of vasculature damage and microhemmorhage in human cortical tissue after UEA implantation and removal. (C) Section showing the penetration tracks of one row of UEA microelectrode shafts. Blood is visible along the electrode tracks. Petechial hemorrhaging is also visible below the tips of the electrode tracks. Scale Bars = 2mm. Adapted with permission from Frontiers, copyright 2014, dx.doi.org/10.3389/fneng.2014.00024.

To examine the impact of the initial damage versus the chronic neuroinflammatory response to the indwelling device, Nolta et al. examined the FBR to 4x4 UEAs implanted into the cortices of young-adult and elderly rats to aged-matched control animals receiving a sham stab wound.[62] The FBR was analyzed at a variety of time points through a 12-week indwelling period. These statistically powered rat studies found that in some respects the FBR to the UEA was similar to that described for simple microwire and MI-style microelectrode arrays (Figure 6). Similar immunological hallmarks of the FBR were observed including:

- persistent inflammatory cell activation (CD68+ and IBA-1+ immunoreactivity) at the device interface surrounded by;
- astrogliosis and astroglial hypertrophy (upregulated GFAP immunoreactivity);

- blood-brain-barrier leakiness (IgG+ immunoreactivity following perfusion);
- neuronal loss (decreased NeuN+ cell body density); and,
- disrupted neuronal connectivity (reduced neurofilament immunoreactivity).

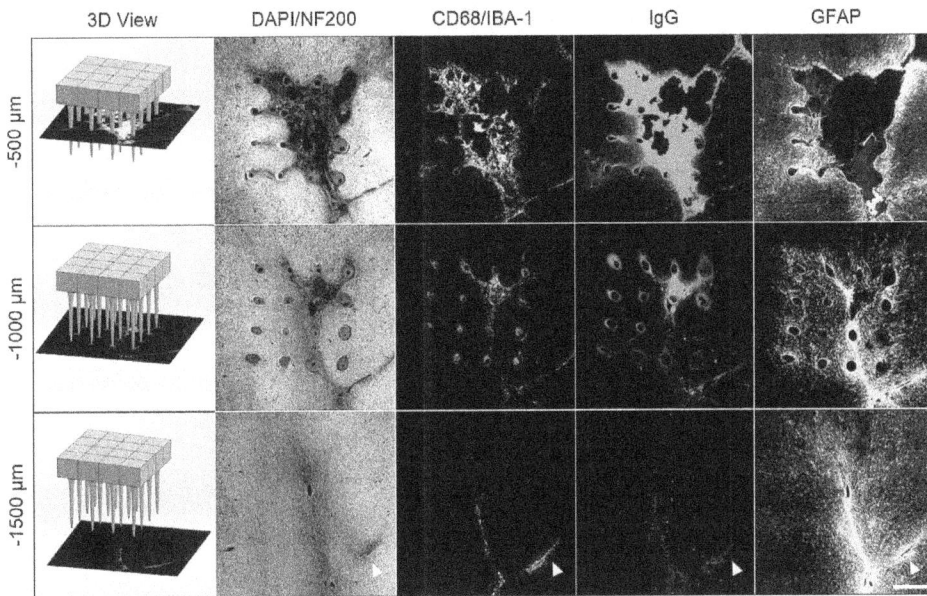

Fig. 6: Representative horizontal sections from rats chronically implanted with a 4x4 UEA.[62] The depth of each row of images from the cortical surface with respect to the base of the UEA is shown in the schematic on the left. Similar to contusion injuries, a pyramidal lesion cavity extending downward from the base of the array was commonly observed at the site of implantation. This lesion cavity contained activated macrophages (CD68/IBA-1) as well as plasma proteins (IgG). Immunoreactivity for GFAP was enhanced at the edge of the lesion cavity and surrounding each microelectrode track. Scale Bar = 400μm. Adapted with permission from Elsevier: Biomaterials, copyright 2015, doi:10.1016/j.biomaterials.2015.02.081.

However, unlike what has been described for simpler, single-shank devices, the researchers observed substantial brain tissue loss and pyramidal lesions devoid of neuronal cell bodies, weeks to months after implantation (Figure 6). The observed tissue loss and lesion formation was greatest in the superficial layers of the cortex beneath the base of the UEA and resembled lesions observed in experimental models of traumatic brain injury. Similar lesions were observed in stab-wounded animals where the UEA was implanted and then withdrawn from the cortex two minutes later. It was noted by the researchers that no tissue was observed on the retrieved blood-coated arrays and the surface of the brain looked like that seen in human patients immediately after stab injury. This finding indicates that the lesions were caused by vascular injury and the resulting acute inflammatory sequelae following implantation and not the result of the FBR.

2.2.3. *Chronic FBR to a high density microelectrode*

Typically, 8-12 weeks has been considered a chronic time frame for studying the FBR to recording devices implanted in rat models.[142, 143] However, based on the extent of injury that develops after implantation it is likely that extensive tissue remodeling occurs throughout the indwelling period. To investigate the FBR at later time points researchers analyzed the FBR to 10x10 UEAs implanted into the cortices of adult-purpose bred cats after a period of 34-73 weeks.[66]

Figure 7 shows images of the chronic response to UEAs implanted in cat cortex. Signs of neural tissue loss and device settling were observed at the implantation site. Upon removal of the device, the tissue under the UEA and surrounding the base exhibited signs of persistent inflammation. Such observations, that can be easily detected with the naked eye, are not normally observed near chronic indwelling single shank recording devices.

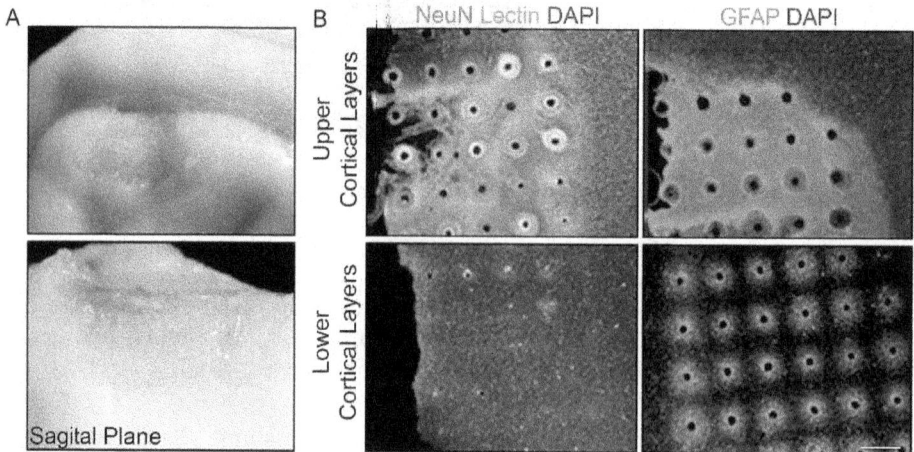

Fig. 7: (A) Photograph of perfused cat cortex implanted with a 10x10 UEA for 511 days. Signs of surface tissue erosion and device settling were visible following removal of the UEA. (B) Representative horizontal sections from the same animal showed significant loss of neuronal cell bodies in the upper cortical layers similar to what was observed in the rat (Fig 6) with significant increases in macrophage (Lectin), and astrocyte (GFAP) biomarker distribution under the array that decreased in intensity toward the microelectrode tips. Scale Bar = 400μm.

Immunohistological examination of the tissue surrounding chronically implanted UEAs in cat cortex showed a similar neural tissue lesion as observed in the rat that decreased in volume as a function of depth from the cortical surface

(Figure 7). Specifically, a large area devoid of neurons was observed spanning the area adjacent to and underneath the base of the array near the superficial cortex. Similar to what was observed in rat, the lesion cavity was filled with activated macrophages, hypertrophic astrocytes and connective tissue. As observed in rodent studies, researchers noted a significantly reduced reaction near the recording tips that was isolated to each microelectrode track and resembled that described for single microwires and MI-style planar microelectrode arrays.

2.2.4. *Understanding the evolution of the host response to high density devices*

Similar to single microwire and MI-style devices, we believe there are a number of distinct yet interconnected processes that occur following implantation of high-density microelectrode arrays. Specifically, the increased initial vascular injury leads to widespread neural cell necrosis in superficial cortical layers. The initial damage coupled with the large inflammatory footprint presented by the base of the microelectrode array leads to tissue loss and eventually device settling over long indwelling periods that is not observed in the shorter 12-week studies conducted in the rat. As the initial lesion is cleared, the device settles and the overall response appears to become dominated by activated macrophages that persist at the device/tissue interface, similar to the chronic FBR to simpler devices.

Based on this explanation we believe that a reduction in the level of vascular damage at the time of implantation coupled to a reduction of inflammatory sequela will likely improve the biocompatibility and recording performance of high-density microelectrode arrays such as the UEA.

2.3. *Host response to BMI associated hardware*

When discussing the biocompatibility of intracortical microelectrode-based BMIs, it is important to consider the impact of associated hardware that comes into contact with biological tissue (e.g., brain, dura, skull, scalp). Such hardware commonly includes head stages, adhesives, acrylic cements and bone screws. The majority of studies to date have focused on describing the FBR to the components of the microelectrode array that interfaces directly with brain tissue and has ignored the response mounted against the other components used to anchor the array to the skull.

Extensive literature indicates that all devices implanted into vascularized tissue elicit a host response characterized by persistent inflammation at the device/tissue interface.[157] Therefore, while still undocumented, it is nearly certain that every component of the BMI system that interfaces with tissue will be persistently colonized by activated macrophages and foreign body giant cells and contribute to the inflammatory burden of the device.

As with the microelectrode itself, the host response to BMI associated hardware can impact adjacent tissue in a number of ways. For example, typical symptoms of inflammation in the skin include heat, irritation and pain. Such inflammatory reactions will likely cause discomfort in implanted patients and animal subjects, resulting in attempts to alleviate the discomfort that will involve device manipulation. Furthermore, persistent inflammation surrounding devices implanted in bone leads to osteolysis and bone resorption over time.[158] A result of this macrophage-induced bone resorption is aseptic loosening of the device over time, which is a common failure mechanism of chronic recording microelectrode arrays.[50] Clearly more basic research needs to be conducted in this area.

3. The FBR and Recording Performance

While potential mechanisms connecting the FBR to recording performance have been suggested for over 40 years [45, 70], detailed, quantitative histological studies using functional devices has only recently been reported in the peer reviewed literature. Traditionally little effort was directed at establishing the connection due to the additional costs and complications associated with the use of functional devices for such studies. Furthermore, most groups lacked either the electrophysiological or quantitative histological expertise to perform such experiments.

Renneker et al. performed the first such study connecting the host response and recording performance.[152] Specifically, this study asked whether systemic delivery of the anti-inflammatory drug minocycline, known to attenuate activated macrophage activity, could improve recording performance of an 8-channel microwire device implanted in cats. Minocycline delivery prior to and following the first few days after implantation improved recording performance (signal to noise ratio and mean number of driven channels) compared to untreated controls.

Tyler and colleagues studied whether increased activation of the host response via administration of the bacterial endotoxin lipopolysaccharide (LPS) would reduce recording performance.[159] LPS is a classic macrophage stimulant known to direct macrophages toward a pro-inflammatory phenotype via TLR-mediated signaling pathways.[160-162] Not surprisingly, they found that LPS administration reduced recording performance. Taken together, the findings indicate that lowering persistent inflammation will likely improve microelectrode recording performance and improve biocompatibility.

Unfortunately, while quality recording metrics were obtained from these studies only limited histological analysis was performed so no direct link to the FBR was established. To overcome these limitations more recent studies have examined and described how individual aspects of the FBR correlate with recording performance. In the first of these more detailed studies, Freire et al., using a 4x8 microwire array, reported a decrease in single units recorded over a six-month period in rats that dropped by 45% at three months followed by a decrease of 85% at 6 months. They found that increased levels of macrophage activation (CD68 immunoreactivity) and neural cell loss correlated with decreased microwire recording performance in rats over a 24 weeks indwelling period.[47] Furthermore, this group noted that neural activity and metabolism was reduced surrounding poorly performing devices.

Two studies by Prasad et al. that examined microwire arrays implanted in rat cortical tissue reported that the initial degree of vascular damage and persistent blood brain barrier dysfunction correlated with reduced levels of recording performance.[48, 49] As described earlier, BBB disruption can have a number of detrimental impacts on the surrounding tissue including inflammatory cell recruitment and neuronal silencing.

In the first of their two papers, Prasad et al. also described that the level of axonal injury (quantified by measuring levels of phosphorylated axonal neurofilament subunit H (pNF-H) in serum and CSF) correlated well with changes in recording performance.[49] This finding supports the idea that both neuronal health at the recording site and its connection to a functional cortical circuit are needed to achieve robust BMI performance.

These studies did not find a correlation between recording performance and the level of macrophage activation (CD68, IBA-1 & OX-6 immunoreactivity). This is not entirely unexpected as such markers are not strong indicators of activation level of these cells. However other findings presented in the study provided evidence for the impact of activated macrophages on recording performance. Beyond the correlation with specific tissue components, Prasad et al. also noted in both of their studies that recording site performance correlated with the level of corrosion and damage at the microelectrode-recording site. While not directly investigated, it is likely that secretion of a variety of reactive molecular species by activated macrophages underlies this finding. Therefore, development of more robust materials as well as strategies to reduce the impact of reactive species secreted by inflammatory cells may be useful for improving microelectrode performance.

To emphasize this theory that macrophage numbers and phagocytic activity may not be sufficient to fully understand the impact of inflammation on recording function, Karumbaiah et al. have shown that gene expression for various proinflammatory soluble factors is upregulated in tissue surrounding poorly performing microelectrode arrays.[64] They showed that high levels of IL-1, IL-6 and IL-17 as well as TNF-α correlated with reduced recording performance. While others cells, such as astrocytes, may secrete these molecules, it has been established that activated macrophages are the primary source of these molecules.[69]

Saxena et al. also showed that other macrophage released soluble factors (MMP-2 and MMP-9) correlate with reduced recording performance and increased BBB dysfunction surrounding implanted microwire and MI-style microelectrode arrays.[63] Matrix metalloproteases (MMPs) are heavily involved in both macrophage migration within tissue as well as macrophage trafficking in and out of vasculature. Saxena's findings further support the idea that BBB disruption due to macrophage trafficking may underlie recording inconsistency over time.

Nolta et al. has shown that individual aspects of the FBR within an array correlate with recording performance changes observed with UEAs implanted in the motor cortex of rats.[62] Specifically, they found that increased levels of BBB leakiness, astrogliosis and cortical tissue loss all correlated with decreased recording performance. Similar to the other studies, statistically based correlations between classic markers of macrophage activation and recording performance were inconclusive. This may stem from the fact that traditional biomarkers are not good indicators of the level of activity of these cells. However, based upon the previously cited work indicating that recording performance can be improved or reduced by limiting or exacerbating inflammation, it seems clear that reducing neuroinflammation is a key piece to improving microelectrode performance and biocompatibility.

Beyond the response to the UEA itself Nolta et al. also observed a large number of failures in young animals due to osteolysis surrounding implanted bone screws and subsequent head stage removal. Similar observations were made by Baresse et al. in their retrospective study examining failure modes of 62 UEA-based systems implanted in non-human primates, indicating that these issues are not isolated to the rodent model.[50] Taken together, these findings suggest that the response to associated hardware (e.g. head stage and bone fixation screws) should be further examined and improved methods for securing the device to the skull be developed.

4. Conclusion

In this chapter we have presented an overview of intracortical recording microelectrode-based BMI biocompatibility. Specifically, we have described the need to improve intracortical recording microelectrode technology so that such devices consistently record high-quality neuronal signals over longer time-frames. Mounting evidence indicates that the FBR to implanted microelectrodes and associated hardware affects single unit recording performance and should be considered when improving existing or developing next generation devices. Understanding how to reduce the FBR will lead to strategies that improve the biocompatibility of recording microelectrode arrays and extend their usefulness as a basic science tool and in clinical applications.

We have described that the FBR involves a series of inflammatory sequelae that are initiated by device implantation into the dense and highly vascularized cortical tissue. These inflammatory sequelae include macrophage activation, astrogliosis, BBB dysfunction, neuronal cell and fiber loss, as well as demyelination. Growing evidence indicates the continual presence of the device causes these inflammatory events to persist for as long as the device is left in place, likely through a self-sustaining cycle of BBB dysfunction, macrophage activation, and white blood cell trafficking. Therefore, strategies for reducing the FBR and improving microelectrode biocompatibility should focus on reducing the initial vascular injury as well as the chronic inflammatory response to intracortical microelectrodes.

As mentioned in the introduction, answering the question of whether microelectrode-based systems are biocompatible will be a large component of determining whether such devices are safe and effective enough for widespread clinical use. We believe that statistically-powered research performed in animals will be a critical step toward answering this question and improving the technology, we also believe that there are likely specific issues that will only be identifiable in early feasibility studies in non-human primates and patients. Due to their therapeutic potential and small size, we do not believe that BMIs should be kept from properly informed patients who consent to participate in clinical trials.

Beyond directly investigating strategies to improve intracortical recording microelectrode array biocompatibility in animal models and human clinical trials, we also believe that their development can be accelerated by turning to other fields. Informatively, the chronic FBR to microelectrode recording arrays shares many features with neuroinflammatory diseases and brain injury caused by trauma. Due to these similarities, we believe that many of the approaches being developed to combat these neuroinflammatory conditions can be applied to improve intracortical microelectrode recording technology and vice versa. Furthermore, we also believe that these neuroinflammatory conditions can also guide us to further understand the evolution and long-term impact of the FBR.

References

1. Nicolelis MA, Brain–machine interfaces to restore motor function and probe neural circuits. *Nature Reviews Neuroscience*, 2003. **4**: p. 417-422.

2. Hochberg LR, Bacher D, Jarosiewicz B, Masse NY, Simeral JD, Vogel J, Haddadin S, Liu J, Cash SS, van der Smagt P, and JP Donoghue, Reach and grasp by people with tetraplegia using a neurally controlled robotic arm. *Nature*, 2012. **485**(7398): p. 372-5.

3. Hochberg LR, Serruya MD, Friehs GM, Mukand JA, Saleh M, Caplan AH, Branner A, Chen D, Penn RD, and JP Donoghue, Neuronal ensemble control of prosthetic devices by a human with tetraplegia. *Nature*, 2006. **442**(7099): p. 164-71.

4. Kennedy PR and RA Bakay, Restoration of neural output from a paralyzed patient by a direct brain connection. *Neuroreport*, 1998. **9**(8): p. 1707-11.

5. Kennedy PR, Kirby MT, Moore MM, King B, and A Mallory, Computer control using human intracortical local field potentials. IEEE *Trans Neural Syst Rehabil Eng*, 2004. **12**(3): p. 339-44.

6. Kruger J, Caruana F, Volta RD, and G Rizzolatti, Seven years of recording from monkey cortex with a chronically implanted multiple microelectrode. *Front Neuroengineering*, 2010. **3**(6): p.1-9

7. Williams DF, On the mechanisms of biocompatibility. *Biomaterials*, 2008. **29**(20): p. 2941-53.

8. Ratner BD, The biocompatibility manifesto: biocompatibility for the twenty-first century. *J Cardiovasc Transl Res*, 2011. **4**(5): p. 523-7.

9. Premarket Approval of Medical Devices, Title 21 Code of Federal Regulations (CFR) 814, 2002.

10. Lebedev MA and MA Nicolelis, Brain-machine interfaces: past, present and future. *Trends Neurosci*, 2006. **29**(9): p. 536-46.

11. Renshaw B, Forbes A, and BR Morison, Activity of isocortex and hippocampus: electrical studies with micro-electrodes. *J Neurophysiol*, 1940. **3**(1): p. 74-105.

12. Grundfest H and B Campbell, Origin, conduction and termination of impulses in the dorsal spino-cerebellar tract of cats. *J Neurophysiol*, 1942. **5**(4): p. 275-94.

13. Salcman M and MJ Bak, Design, fabrication, and in vivo behavior of chronic recording intracortical microelectrodes. *IEEE Trans Biomed Eng*, 1973. **20**(4): p. 253-60.

14. Salcman M and MJ Bak, A new chronic recording intracortical microelectrode. *Med Biol Eng*, 1976. **14**(1): p. 42-50.

15. Schmidt EM, McIntosh JS, and MJ Bak, Long-term implants of Parylene-C coated microelectrodes. *Med Biol Eng Comput*, 1988. **26**(1): p. 96-101.

16. Minnikanti S, Diao G, Pancrazio JJ, Xie X, Rieth L, Solzbacher F, and N Peixoto, Lifetime assessment of atomic-layer-deposited Al2O3-Parylene C bilayer coating for neural interfaces using accelerated age testing and electrochemical characterization. *Acta Biomater*, 2014. **10**(2): p. 960-7.

17. Wessberg J, Stambaugh CR, Kralik JD, Beck PD, Laubach M, Chapin JK, Kim J, Biggs SJ, Srinivasan MA, and MA Nicolelis, Real-time prediction of hand trajectory by ensembles of cortical neurons in primates. *Nature*, 2000. **408**(6810): p. 361-5.

18. Laubach M, J Wessberg, and MA Nicolelis, Cortical ensemble activity increasingly predicts behaviour outcomes during learning of a motor task. *Nature*, 2000. **405**(6786): p. 567-71.

19. BeMent SL, Wise KD, Anderson DJ, Najafi K, and KL Drake, Solid-state electrodes for multichannel multiplexed intracortical neuronal recording. *IEEE Trans Biomed Eng*, 1986. **33**(2): p. 230-41.

20. Wise KD, Silicon microsystems for neuroscience and neural prostheses. *IEEE Eng Med Biol Mag*, 2005. **24**(5): p. 22-9.

21. Kipke DR, Vetter RJ, Williams JC, and JF Hetke, Silicon-substrate intracortical microelectrode arrays for long-term recording of neuronal spike activity in cerebral cortex. *IEEE Trans Neural Syst Rehabil Eng*, 2003. **11**(2): p. 151-5.

22. Vetter RJ, Williams JC, Hetke JF, Nunamaker EA, and DR Kipke, Chronic neural recording using silicon-substrate microelectrode arrays implanted in cerebral cortex. *IEEE Trans Biomed Eng*, 2004. **51**(6): p. 896-904.

23. Ludwig KA, Uram JD, Yang J, Martin DC, and DR Kipke, Chronic neural recordings using silicon microelectrode arrays electrochemically deposited with a poly(3,4-ethylenedioxythiophene) (PEDOT) film. *J Neural Eng*, 2006. **3**(1): p. 59-70.

24. Campbell PK, Jones KE, Huber RJ, Horch KW, and RA Normann, A silicon-based, three-dimensional neural interface: manufacturing processes for an intracortical electrode array. *IEEE Trans Biomed Eng*, 1991. **38**(8): p. 758-68.

25. Negi S, Bhandari R, Rieth L, and F Solzbacher, In vitro comparison of sputtered iridium oxide and platinum-coated neural implantable microelectrode arrays. *Biomed Mater*, 2010. **5**(1): 15007.

26. Hsu JM, Rieth L, Normann RA, Tathireddy P, and F Solzbacher, Encapsulation of an integrated neural interface device with Parylene C. *IEEE Trans Biomed Eng*, 2009. **56**(1): p. 23-9.

27. Bhandari R, Negi S, and F Solzbacher, Wafer-scale fabrication of penetrating neural microelectrode arrays. *Biomed Microdevices*, 2010. **12**(5): p. 797-807.

28. Bhandari R, Negi S, Rieth L, Normann RA, and F Solzbacher, A Novel Method of Fabricating Convoluted Shaped Electrode Arrays for Neural and Retinal Prostheses. *Sens Actuators A Phys*, 2008. **145-146**(1-2): p. 123-130.

29. Bhandari R, Negi S, Rieth L, and F Solzbacher, A Wafer-Scale Etching Technique for High Aspect Ratio Implantable MEMS Structures. *Sens Actuators A Phys*, 2010. **162**(1): p. 130-136.

30. Branner A, Stein RB, Normann RA, Selective stimulation of cat sciatic nerve using an array of varying-length microelectrodes. *J Neurophysiol*, 2001. **85**(4): p. 1585-94.

31. Wark HAC, Sharma R, Mathews KS, Fernandez E, Yoo J, Christensen B, Tresco P, Rieth L, Solzbacher F, Normann RA, and P Tathireddy, A new high-density (25 electrodes/mm2) penetrating microelectrode array for recording and stimulating sub-millimeter neuroanatomical structures. *Journal of Neural Engineering*, 2013. **10**(4).

32. Jorfi M, Skousen JL, Weder C, and JR Capadona, Progress towards biocompatible intracortical microelectrodes for neural interfacing applications. *J Neural Eng*, 2015. **12**(1): 011001.

33. Buzsáki G, Large-scale recording of neuronal ensembles. *Nature Neuroscience*, 2004. **7**(5): p. 446-451.

34. Jarosiewicz B, Sarma AA, Bacher D, Masse NY, Simeral JD, Sorice B, Oakley EM, Blabe C, Pandarinath C, Gilja V, Cash SS, Eskandar EN, Friehs G, Henderson JM, Shenoy KV, Donoghue JP, Hochberg LR, Virtual typing by people with tetraplegia using a self-calibrating intracortical brain-computer interface. *Sci Transl Med*, 2015. **7**(313): 313ra179.

35. Gilja V, Pandarinath C, Blabe CH, Nuyujukian P, Simeral JD, Sarma AA, Sorice BL, Perge JA, Jarosiewicz B, Hochberg LR, Shenoy KV, and JM Henderson, Clinical translation of a high-performance neural prosthesis. *Nat Med*, 2015. **21**(10): p. 1142-5.

36. Perge JA, Zhang S, Malik WQ, Homer ML, Cash S, Friehs G, Eskandar EN, Donoghue JP, and LR Hochberg, Reliability of directional information in unsorted spikes and local field potentials recorded in human motor cortex. *J Neural Eng*, 2014. **11**(4): 046007.

37.   Simeral JD, Kim SP, Black MJ, Donoghue JP, and LR Hochberg, Neural control of cursor trajectory and click by a human with tetraplegia 1000 days after implant of an intracortical microelectrode array. *J Neural Eng*, 2011. **8**(2): 025027.

38.   Collinger JL, Boninger ML, Bruns TM, Curley K, Wang W, and DJ Weber, Functional priorities, assistive technology, and brain-computer interfaces after spinal cord injury. *J Rehabil Res Dev*, 2013. **50**(2): p. 145-60.

39.   Liu X, McCreery DB, Bullara LA, and WF Agnew, Evaluation of the stability of intracortical microelectrode arrays. *IEEE Trans Neural Syst Rehabil Eng*, 2006. **14**(1): p. 91-100.

40.   Liu X, McCreery DB, Carter RR, Bullara LA, Yuen TG, and WF Agnew WF, Stability of the interface between neural tissue and chronically implanted intracortical microelectrodes. *IEEE Trans Rehabil Eng*, 1999. **7**(3): p. 315-26.

41.   Kennedy, P.R., The cone electrode: a long-term electrode that records from neurites grown onto its recording surface. *J Neurosci Methods*, 1989. **29**(3): p. 181-93.

42.   Carter RH and JC Houk, Multiple Single-unit recordings from the CNS using thin-film electrode arrays. *IEEE Trans Rehab Eng*, 1993. **1**: p. 175-184.

43.   Hetke JF, Lund JL, Najafi K, Wise KD, and DJ Anderson, Silicon ribbon cables for chronically implantable microelectrode arrays. *IEEE Trans Biomed Eng*, 1994. **41**(4): p. 314-21.

44.   Rousche PJ and RA Normann, Chronic recording capability of the Utah Intracortical Electrode Array in cat sensory cortex. *J Neurosci Methods*, 1998. **82**(1): p. 1-15.

45.   Burns BD, JP Stean, and AC Webb, Recording for several days from single cortical neurons in completely unrestrained cats. *Electroencephalogr Clin Neurophysiol*, 1974. **36**(3): p. 314-8.

46.   Kozai TD, Du Z, Gugel ZV, Smith MA, Chase SM, Bodily LM, Caparosa EM, Friedlander RM, and XT Cui XT, Comprehensive chronic laminar single-unit, multi-unit, and local field potential recording performance with planar single shank electrode arrays. *J Neurosci Methods*, 2015. **242**: p. 15-40.

47.   Freire MA, Morya E, Faber J, Santos JR, Guimaraes JS, Lemos NA, Sameshima K, Pereira A, Ribeiro S, and MA Nicolelis, Comprehensive analysis of tissue preservation and recording quality from chronic multielectrode implants. *PLoS One*, 2011. **6**(11): e27554.

48.   Prasad A, Xue QS, Dieme R, Sankar V, Mayrand RC, Nishida T, Streit WJ, and JC Sanchez, Abiotic-biotic characterization of Pt/Ir microelectrode arrays in chronic implants. *Front Neuroeng*, 2014. **7**(2).

49.   Prasad A, Xue QS, Sankar V, Nishida T, Shaw G, Streit WJ, and JC Sanchez, Comprehensive characterization and failure modes of tungsten microwire arrays in chronic neural implants. *Journal of Neural Engineering*, 2012. **9**(5): 056015.

50.   Barrese JC, Rao N, Paroo K, Triebwasser C, Vargas-Irwin C, Franquemont L, and JP Donoghue, Failure mode analysis of silicon-based intracortical microelectrode arrays in non¬human primates. *Journal of Neural Engineering*, 2013. **10**(6): 066014.

51.   Schwarz DA, Lebedev MA, Hanson TL, Dimitrov DF, Lehew G, Meloy J, Rajangam S, Subramanian V, Ifft PJ, Li Z, Ramakrishnan A, Tate A, Zhuang KZ, and MA Nicolelis, Chronic, wireless recordings of large-scale brain activity in freely moving rhesus monkeys. *Nat Methods*, 2014. **11**(6): p. 670-6.

52.   US FDA Guidance, Investigational Device Exemptions (IDEs) for Early Feasibility Medical Device Clinical Studies, Including Certain First in Human (FIH) Studies. 2013.

53.   Jiang J, Willett FR, and DM Taylor, Relationship between microelectrode array impedance and chronic recording quality of single units and local field potentials. *Conf Proc IEEE Eng Med Biol Soc*, 2014. **2014**: p. 3045-8.

54. Ward MP, Rajdev P, Ellison C, and PP Irazoqui, Toward a comparison of microelectrodes for acute and chronic recordings. *Brain Research*, 2009. **1282**: p. 183-200.

55. Patrick E, Orazem ME, Sanchez JC, and T Nishida, Corrosion of tungsten microelectrodes used in neural recording applications. *Journal of Neuroscience Methods*, 2011. **198**(2): p. 158-71.

56. Dymond AM, Kaechele LE, Jurist JM, and PH Crandall, Brain tissue reaction to some chronically implanted metals. *J Neurosurg*, 1970. **33**(5): p. 574-80.

57. Wang A, Liang X, McAllister JP 2nd, Li J, Brabant K, Black C, Finlayson P, Cao T, Tang H, Salley SO, Auner GW, and KY Simon NY, Stability of and inflammatory response to silicon coated with a fluoroalkyl self-assembled monolayer in the central nervous system. *J Biomed Mater Res A*, 2007. **81**(2): p. 363-72.

58. Hammerle H, Kobuch K, Kohler K, Nisch W, Sachs H, and M Stelzle, Biostability of micro-photodiode arrays for subretinal implantation. *Biomaterials*, 2002. **23**(3): p. 797-804.

59. Maloney JM, Lipka SA, and SP Baldwin SP, In Vivo Biostability of CVD Silicon Oxide and Silicon Nitride Films. *MRS Proc*, 2005. **872**

60. Schmidt EM, MJ Bak, and JS McIntosh, Long-term chronic recording from cortical neurons. *Exp Neurol*, 1976. **52**(3): p. 496-506.

61. Biran R, Martin DC, and PA Tresco, Neuronal cell loss accompanies the brain tissue response to chronically implanted silicon microelectrode arrays. *Exp Neurol*, 2005. **195**(1): p. 115-26.

62. Nolta NF, Christensen MB, Crane PD, Skousen JL, Tresco PA, BBB leakage, astrogliosis, and tissue loss correlate with silicon microelectrode array recording performance. *Biomaterials*, 2015. **53**: p. 753-62.

63. Saxena T, Karumbaiah L, Gaupp EA, Patkar R, Patil K, Betancur M, Stanley GB, and RV Bellamkonda, The impact of chronic blood-brain barrier breach on intracortical electrode function. *Biomaterials*, 2013. **34**(20): p. 4703-13.

64. Karumbaiah L, Saxena T, Carlson D, Patil K, Patkar R, Gaupp EA, Betancur M, Stanley GB, Carin L, and RV Bellamkonda, Relationship between intracortical electrode design and chronic recording function. *Biomaterials*, 2013. **34**(33): p. 8061-74.

65. Tresco PA and BD Winslow, The challenge of integrating devices into the central nervous system. *Crit Rev Biomed Eng*, 2011. **39**(1): p. 29-44.

66. Nolta NF, Studies Of Intracortical Microelectrode Array Performance And Foreign Body Response In Young And Aged Rats, University of Utah, 2015.

67. National Spinal Cord Injury Statistical Center (NSCISC), Spinal Cord Injury (SCI) Facts and Figures at a Glance, 2015,

68. Ziegler-Graham K, MacKenzie EJ, Ephraim PL, Travison TG, and R Brookmeyer, Estimating the prevalence of limb loss in the United States: 2005 to 2050. *Arch Phys Med Rehabil*, 2008. **89**(3): p. 422-9.

69. Rao A, Avula MN, and DW Grainger, Aging and the Host Response, in *Host Response to Biomaterials*, S.F. Badylak, Editor. 2015, Academic Press: Oxford. p. 269-313.

70. Polikov VS, Tresco PA, and WM Reichert, Response of brain tissue to chronically implanted neural electrodes. *J Neurosci Methods*, 2005. **148**(1): p. 1-18.

71. Grill WM, Norman SE, and RV Bellamkonda, Implanted neural interfaces: biochallenges and engineered solutions. *Annu Rev Biomed Eng*, 2009. **11**: p. 1-24.

72. Young NA, Collins CE, and JH Kaas, Cell and neuron densities in the primary motor cortex of primates. *Front Neural Circuits*, 2013. **7**(30).

73.   Azevedo FA, Carvalho LR, Grinberg LT, Farfel JM, Ferretti RE, Leite RE, Jacob Filho W, Lent R, and S Herculano-Houzel, Equal numbers of neuronal and nonneuronal cells make the human brain an isometrically scaled-up primate brain. *J Comp Neurol*, 2009. **513**(5): p. 532-41.

74.   Cipolla MJ, The Cerebral Circulation, in *The Cerebral Circulation*. 2009: San Rafael (CA).

75.   Klein B, Kuschinsky W, Schröck H, and F Vetterlein, Interdependency of local capillary density, blood flow, and metabolism in rat brains. *Am J Physiol*, 1986. **251**(6 Pt 2): H1333-40.

76.   Cavaglia M, Dombrowski SM, Drazba J, Vasanji A, Bokesch PM, and D Janigro, Regional variation in brain capillary density and vascular response to ischemia. *Brain Res*, 2001. **910**(1-2): p. 81-93.

77.   Gjedde A, Kuwabara H, and AM Hakim, Reduction of functional capillary density in human brain after stroke. *J Cereb Blood Flow Metab*, 1990. **10**(3): p. 317-26.

78.   Wrzolkowa T, Cofta T, and I Lukaszyk, Capillary blood vessels of the brain. I. Vascularisation density in various parts of the cat and rat cerebral cortex. *Neuropatol Pol*, 1984. **22**(1): p. 77-83.

79.   Blinder P, Tsai PS, Kaufhold JP, Knutsen PM, Suhl H, and D Kleinfeld, The cortical angiome: an interconnected vascular network with noncolumnar patterns of blood flow. *Nat Neurosci*, 2013. **16**(7): p. 889-97.

80.   Krucker T, Lang A, and EP Meyer, New polyurethane-based material for vascular corrosion casting with improved physical and imaging characteristics. *Microsc Res Tech*, 2006. **69**(2): p. 138-47.

81.   Kozai TD, Marzullo TC, Hooi F, Langhals NB, Majewska AK, Brown EB, and DR Kipke, Reduction of neurovascular damage resulting from microelectrode insertion into the cerebral cortex using in vivo two-photon mapping. *J Neural Eng*, 2010. **7**(4): 046011.

82.   Smith SA, Travers RJ, and JH Morrissey, How it all starts: Initiation of the clotting cascade. *Crit Rev Biochem Mol Biol*, 2015. **50**(4): p. 326-36.

83.   Markiewski MM, Nilsson B, Ekdahl KN, Mollnes TE, and JD Lambris, Complement and coagulation: strangers or partners in crime? *Trends Immunol*, 2007. **28**(4): p. 184-92.

84.   Ekdahl KN, Hong J, Hamad OA, Larsson R, and B Nilsson, Evaluation of the blood compatibility of materials, cells, and tissues: basic concepts, test models, and practical guidelines. *Adv Exp Med Biol*, 2013. **735**: p. 257-70.

85.   Hein E and P Garred, The Lectin Pathway of Complement and Biocompatibility. *Adv Exp Med Biol*, 2015. **865**: p. 77-92.

86.   Nilsson B, Ekdahl KN, Mollnes TE, and JD Lambris, The role of complement in biomaterial-induced inflammation. *Mol Immunol*, 2007. **44**(1-3): p. 82-94.

87.   Betjes MG, Tuk CW, Struijk DG, Krediet RT, Arisz L, and RH Beelen, Antigen-presenting capacity of macrophages and dendritic cells in the peritoneal cavity of patients treated with peritoneal dialysis. *Clin Exp Immunol*, 1993. **94**(2): p. 377-84.

88.   Poltorak M and WJ Freed, Immunological reactions induced by intracerebral transplantation: evidence that host microglia but not astroglia are the antigen-presenting cells. *Exp Neurol*, 1989. **103**(3): p. 222-33.

89.   Larochelle CA, Alvarez JI, and A Prat, How do immune cells overcome the blood–brain barrier in multiple sclerosis? *Autoimmunity: Rheumatoid Arthritis & Multiple Sclerosis*, 2011. **585**(23): p. 3770-3780.

90.   Skousen J, Merriam SM, Srivannavit O, Perlin G, Wise KD, and PA Tresco, Reducing surface area while maintaining implant penetrating profile lowers the brain foreign body response to

chronically implanted planar silicon microelectrode arrays. *Progress in Brain Research*, 2011. **194C**: p. 167-180.

91. Goldstein SR and M Salcman, Mechanical factors in the design of chronic recording intracortical microelectrodes. *IEEE Trans Biomed Eng*, 1973. **20**(4): p. 260-9.

92. Subbaroyan J, Martin DC, and DR Kipke, A finite-element model of the mechanical effects of implantable microelectrodes in the cerebral cortex. *J Neural Eng*, 2005. **2**(4): p. 103-13.

93. Edell DJ, Toi VV, McNeil VM, and LD Clark, Factors influencing the biocompatibility of insertable silicon microshafts in cerebral cortex. *IEEE Trans Biomed Eng*, 1992. **39**(6): p. 635-43.

94. Lee H, Bellamkonda RV, Sun W, and ME Levenston, Biomechanical analysis of silicon microelectrode-induced strain in the brain. *J Neural Eng*, 2005. **2**(4): p. 81-9.

95. Zhu R, Huang GL, Yoon H, Smith CS, and VK Varadan, Biomechanical Strain Analysis at the Interface of Brain and Nanowire Electrodes on a Neural Probe. *Journal of Nanotechnology in Engineering and Medicine*, 2012. **2**(3).

96. Biran R, Martin DC, and PA Tresco, The brain tissue response to implanted silicon microelectrode arrays is increased when the device is tethered to the skull. *J Biomed Mater Res A*, 2007. **82**(1): p. 169-78.

97. Subbaroyan J and DR Kipke. The role of flexible polymer interconnects in chronic tissue response induced by intracortical microelectrodes--a modeling and an in vivo study. *IEEE Eng Med Biol Soc.* 2006.

98. Kim YT, Hitchcock RW, Bridge MJ, and PA Tresco, Chronic response of adult rat brain tissue to implants anchored to the skull. *Biomaterials*, 2004. **25**(12): p. 2229-37.

99. Thelin J, Jörntell H, Psouni E, Garwicz M, Schouenborg J, Danielsen N, and CE Linsmeier, Implant size and fixation mode strongly influence tissue reactions in the CNS. *PLoS One*, 2011. **6**(1): e16267.

100. Gomez Perdiguero E, Klapproth K, Schulz C, Busch K, Azzoni E, Crozet L, Garner H, Trouillet C, de Bruijn MF, Geissmann F, and HR Rodewald, Tissue-resident macrophages originate from yolk-sac-derived erythro-myeloid progenitors. *Nature*, 2015. **518**(7540): p. 547-51.

101. Polfliet MM, Zwijnenburg PJ, van Furth AM, van der Poll T, Döpp EA, Renardel de Lavalette C, van Kesteren-Hendrikx EM, van Rooijen N, Dijkstra CD, and TK van den Berg, Meningeal and perivascular macrophages of the central nervous system play a protective role during bacterial meningitis. *J Immunol*, 2001. **167**(8): p. 4644-50.

102. Jordan FL and WE Thomas, Brain macrophages: questions of origin and interrelationship. *Brain Res*, 1988. **472**(2): p. 165-78.

103. Evans TA, Barkauskas DS, Myers JT, Hare EG, You JQ, Ransohoff RM, Huang AY, and J Silver, High-resolution intravital imaging reveals that blood-derived macrophages but not resident microglia facilitate secondary axonal dieback in traumatic spinal cord injury. *Exp Neurol*, 2014. **254**: p. 109-20.

104. Prinz M and J Priller, Microglia and brain macrophages in the molecular age: from origin to neuropsychiatric disease. *Nat Rev Neurosci*, 2014. **15**(5): p. 300-12.

105. Markwardt NT, J Stokol, and RL Rennaker, 2nd, Sub-meninges implantation reduces immune response to neural implants. *J Neurosci Methods*, 2013. **214**(2): p. 119-25.

106. Harris JP, Capadona JR, Miller RH, Healy BC, Shanmuganathan K, Rowan SJ, Weder C, and DJ Tyler, Mechanically adaptive intracortical implants improve the proximity of neuronal cell bodies. *J Neural Eng*, 2011. **8**(6): 066011.

107.   Harris JP, Hess AE, Rowan SJ, Weder C, Zorman CA, Tyler DJ, and JR Capadona, In vivo deployment of mechanically adaptive nanocomposites for intracortical microelectrodes. *J Neural Eng*, 2011. **8**(4): 046010.

108.   Nguyen JK, Park DJ, Skousen JL, Hess-Dunning AE, Tyler DJ, Rowan SJ, Weder C, and JR Capadona, Mechanically-compliant intracortical implants reduce the neuroinflammatory response. *J Neural Eng*, 2014. **11**(5): 056014.

109.   Nguyen JK, Jorfi M, Buchanan KL, Park DJ, Foster EJ, Tyler DJ, Rowan SJ, Weder C, and JR Capadona JR, Influence of resveratrol release on the tissue response to mechanically adaptive cortical implants. *Acta Biomater*, 2015. **29**: p. 81-83.

110.   Block ML, L Zecca, and JS Hong, Microglia-mediated neurotoxicity: uncovering the molecular mechanisms. *Nature Reviews Neuroscience*, 2007. **8**(1): p. 57-69.

111.   Hanisch UK and H Kettenmann, Microglia: active sensor and versatile effector cells in the normal and pathologic brain. *Nature neuroscience*, 2007. **10**(11): p. 1387-94.

112.   Mantovani A, Sozzani S, Locati M, Allavena P, and A Sica, Macrophage polarization: tumor-associated macrophages as a paradigm for polarized M2 mononuclear phagocytes. *Trends in immunology*, 2002. **23**(11): p. 549-55.

113.   Clark IA, Alleva LM, and B Vissel, The roles of TNF in brain dysfunction and disease. *Pharmacology & therapeutics*, 2010. **128**(3): p. 519-48.

114.   Feuerstein GZ, Liu T, and FC Barone, Cytokines, inflammation, and brain injury: role of tumor necrosis factor-alpha. *Cerebrovascular and brain metabolism reviews*, 1994. **6**(4): p. 341-60.

115.   Sugama S, Takenouchi T, Cho BP, Joh TH, Hashimoto M, and H Kitani, Possible roles of microglial cells for neurotoxicity in clinical neurodegenerative diseases and experimental animal models. *Inflammation & allergy drug targets*, 2009. **8**(4): p. 277-84.

116.   Yadav A, Saini V, and S Arora, MCP-1: chemoattractant with a role beyond immunity: a review. *Clinica chimica acta; international journal of clinical chemistry*, 2010. **411**(21-22): p. 1570-9.

117.   Stamatovic SM, Keep RF, Kunkel SL, nd AV Andjelkovic, Potential role of MCP-1 in endothelial cell tight junction 'opening': signaling via Rho and Rho kinase. *Journal of cell science*, 2003. **116**(Pt 22): p. 4615-28.

118.   Stamatovic SM, Shakui P, Keep RF, Moore BB, Kunkel SL, Van Rooijen N, and AV Andjelkovic, Monocyte chemoattractant protein-1 regulation of blood-brain barrier permeability. *Journal of cerebral blood flow and metabolism*, 2005. **25**(5): p. 593-606.

119.   Wilhelmsson U, Li L, Pekna M, Berthold CH, Blom S, Eliasson C, Renner O, Bushong E, Ellisman M, Morgan TE, and M Pekny, Absence of glial fibrillary acidic protein and vimentin prevents hypertrophy of astrocytic processes and improves post-traumatic regeneration. *J Neurosci*, 2004. **24**(21): p. 5016-21.

120.   Butt AM and K Colquhoun, Glial cells in transected optic nerves of immature rats. I. An analysis of individual cells by intracellular dye-injection. *J Neurocytol*, 1996. **25**(6): p. 365-80.

121.   Kim YT, MJ Bridge, and PA Tresco, The influence of the foreign body response evoked by fibroblast transplantation on soluble factor diffusion in surrounding brain tissue. *J Control Release*, 2007. **118**(3): p. 340-7.

122.   Kim YT, Hitchcock R, Broadhead KW, Messina DJ, and PA Tresco, A cell encapsulation device for studying soluble factor release from cells transplanted in the rat brain. *J Control Release*, 2005. **102**(1): p. 101-11.

123.   Jones LL, Margolis RU, Tuszynski MH, The chondroitin sulfate proteoglycans neurocan, brevican, phosphacan, and versican are differentially regulated following spinal cord injury. *Exp Neurol*, 2003. **182**(2): p. 399-411.

124. Jones LL, Yamaguchi Y, Stallcup WB, Tuszynski MH, NG2 is a major chondroitin sulfate proteoglycan produced after spinal cord injury and is expressed by macrophages and oligodendrocyte progenitors. *J Neurosci Methods*, 2002. **22**(7): p. 2792-803.

125. Fawcett JW and RA Asher, The glial scar and central nervous system repair. *Brain Research Bulletin*, 1999. **49**(6): p. 377-391.

126. Zhong Y and RV Bellamkonda, Dexamethasone-coated neural probes elicit attenuated inflammatory response and neuronal loss compared to uncoated neural probes. *Brain Res,* 2007. **1148**: p. 15-27.

127. Hsiao TW, Swarup VP, Kuberan B, Tresco PA, and V Hlady , Astrocytes specifically remove surface-adsorbed fibrinogen and locally express chondroitin sulfate proteoglycans. *Acta Biomater*, 2013. **9**(7): p. 7200-8.

128. Friedlander DR, Milev P, Karthikeyan L, Margolis RK, Margolis RU, and M Grumet, The neuronal chondroitin sulfate proteoglycan neurocan binds to the neural cell adhesion molecules Ng-CAM/L1/NILE and N-CAM, and inhibits neuronal adhesion and neurite outgrowth. *J Cell Biol*, 1994. **125**(3): p. 669-80.

129. Gopalakrishnan SM, Teusch N, Imhof C, Bakker MH, Schurdak M, Burns DJ, and U Warrior, Role of Rho kinase pathway in chondroitin sulfate proteoglycan-mediated inhibition of neurite outgrowth in PC12 cells. *J Neurosci Res*, 2008. **86**(10): p. 2214-26.

130. Hynds DL and DM Snow, Neurite outgrowth inhibition by chondroitin sulfate proteoglycan: stalling/stopping exceeds turning in human neuroblastoma growth cones. *Exp Neurol*, 1999. **160**(1): p. 244-55.

131. Kuffler DP, Sosa IJ, and O Reyes, Schwann cell chondroitin sulfate proteoglycan inhibits dorsal root ganglion neuron neurite outgrowth and substrate specificity via a soma and not a growth cone mechanism. *J Neurosci Res*, 2009. **87**(13): p. 2863-71.

132. Yamada H, Fredette B, Shitara K, Hagihara K, Miura R, Ranscht B, Stallcup WB, and Y Yamaguchi, The brain chondroitin sulfate proteoglycan brevican associates with astrocytes ensheathing cerebellar glomeruli and inhibits neurite outgrowth from granule neurons. *The Journal of neuroscience,* 1997. **17**(20): p. 7784-95.

133. Scordilis-Kelly C and JG Osteryoung, Voltammetric Studies of Counterion Transport in Solutions of Chondroitin Sulfate. *J Phys chem* 1996, 1996. **100**: p. 797-804.

134. Schultz RL and TJ Willey, The ultrastructure of the sheath around chronically implanted electrodes in brain. *J Neurocytol*, 1976. **5**(6): p. 621-42.

135. Turner JN, Shain W, Szarowski DH, Andersen M, Martins S, Isaacson M, and H Craighead, Cerebral astrocyte response to micromachined silicon implants. *Exp Neurol*, 1999. **156**(1): p. 33-49.

136. Skousen JL, Bridge MJ, and PA Tresco, A strategy to passively reduce neuroinflammation surrounding devices implanted chronically in brain tissue by manipulating device surface permeability. *Biomaterials*, 2015. **36**: p. 33-43.

137. Spataro, L, Dilgen J, Retterer S, Spence AJ, Isaacson M, Turner JN, Shain W, Dexamethasone treatment reduces astroglia responses to inserted neuroprosthetic devices in rat neocortex. *Exp Neurol*, 2005. **194**(2): p. 289-300.

138. He W, McConnell GC, and RV Bellamkonda, Nanoscale laminin coating modulates cortical scarring response around implanted silicon microelectrode arrays. *J Neural Eng*, 2006. **3**(4): p. 316-26.

139. Abbott NJ, Astrocyte-endothelial interactions and blood-brain barrier permeability. *J Anat*, 2002. **200**(6): p. 629-38.

140.   Andjelkovic AV, Kerkovich D, and JS Pachter, Monocyte:astrocyte interactions regulate MCP-1 expression in both cell types. *J Leukoc Biol*, 2000. **68**(4): p. 545-52.

141.   Goldstein GW, Endothelial cell-astrocyte interactions. A cellular model of the blood-brain barrier. *Ann N Y Acad Sci*, 1988. **529**: p. 31-9.

142.   Winslow BD, Christensen MB, Yang WK, Solzbacher F, Tresco PA, A comparison of the tissue response to chronically implanted Parylene-C-coated and uncoated planar silicon microelectrode arrays in rat cortex. *Biomaterials*, 2010. **31**(35): p. 9163-72.

143.   Winslow BD and PA Tresco, Quantitative analysis of the tissue response to chronically implanted microwire electrodes in rat cortex. *Biomaterials*, 2010. **31**(7): p. 1558-67.

144.   Larochelle C, Alvarez JI, and A Prat, How do immune cells overcome the blood-brain barrier in multiple sclerosis? *FEBS Lett*, 2011. **585**(23): p. 3770-80.

145.   Lassmann H, A dynamic view of the blood-brain barrier in active multiple sclerosis lesions. *Ann Neurol*, 2011. **70**(1): p. 1-2.

146.   Azemi E, Gobbel GT, and XT Cui, Seeding neural progenitor cells on silicon-based neural probes. *J Neurosurg*, 2010. **113**(3): p. 673-81.

147.   Lewitus DY, Smith KL, Shain W, Bolikal D, and J Kohn, The fate of ultrafast degrading polymeric implants in the brain. *Biomaterials*, 2011. **32**(24): p. 5543-5550.

148.   Ravikumar M, Hageman DJ, Tomaszewski WH, Chandra GM, Skousen JL, Capadona JR, The effect of residual bacterial contamination on the neuroinflammatory response to sterilized intracortical microelectrodes. *J Mater Chem B Mater Biol Med*, 2014. **2**(17): p.2517-2529

149.   Seymour JP and DR Kipke, Neural probe design for reduced tissue encapsulation in CNS. *Biomaterials*, 2007. **28**(25): p. 3594-607.

150.   Potter KA, Buck AC, Self WK, and JR Capadona, Stab injury and device implantation within the brain results in inversely multiphasic neuroinflammatory and neurodegenerative responses. *J Neural Eng*, 2012. **9**(4): 046020.

151.   Potter KA, Simon JS, Velagapudi B, and JR Capadona, Reduction of autofluorescence at the microelectrode-cortical tissue interface improves antibody detection. *J Neurosci Methods*, 2012. **203**(1): p. 96-105.

152.   Rennaker RL, Miller J, Tang H, and DA Wilson, Minocycline increases quality and longevity of chronic neural recordings. *Journal of neural engineering*, 2007. **4**(2): p. L1-5.

153.   Potter-Baker KA, Nguyen JK, Kovach KM, Gitomer MM, Srail TW, Stewart WG, Skousen JL, and JR Capadona, Development of Superoxide Dismutase Mimetic Surfaces to Reduce Accumulation of Reactive Oxygen Species for Neural Interfacing Applications. *J Mater Chem B Mater Biol Med*, 2014. **2**(16): p. 2248-2258.

154.   He W and RV Bellamkonda, Nanoscale neuro-integrative coatings for neural implants. *Biomaterials*, 2005. **26**(16): p. 2983-90.

155.   House PA, MacDonald JD, Tresco PA, and RA Normann, Acute microelectrode array implantation into human neocortex: preliminary technique and histological considerations. *Neurosurg Focus*, 2006. **20**(5): E4.

156.   Fernandez E, Greger B, House PA, Aranda I, Botella C, Albisua J, Soto-Sánchez C, Alfaro A, and RA Normann, Acute human brain responses to intracortical microelectrode arrays: challenges and future prospects. *Front Neuroeng*, 2014. **7**: p. 24.

157.   Anderson JM, Rodriguez A, and DT Chang, Foreign body reaction to biomaterials. *Semin Immunol*, 2008. **20**(2): p. 86-100.

158. Trindade R, Albrektsson T, Tengvall P, Wennerberg A, Foreign Body Reaction to Biomaterials: On Mechanisms for Buildup and Breakdown of Osseointegration. *Clin Implant Dent Relat Res*, 2014. **18**(1).

159. Harris JP, The Glia-Neuronal Response to Cortical Electrodes: Interactions with Substrate Stiffness and Electrophysiology, in Department of Biomedical Engineering. Case Western Reserve University, 2011.

160. Dobrovolskaia MA and SN Vogel, Toll receptors, CD14, and macrophage activation and deactivation by LPS. *Microbes and Infection*, 2002. **4**: p. 903-914.

161. Doyle A, Zhang G, Abdel Fattah EA, Eissa NT, and YP Li, Toll-like receptor 4 mediates lipopolysaccharide-induced muscle catabolism via coordinate activation of ubiquitin-proteasome and autophagy-lysosome pathways. *The FASEB journal*, 2011. **25**(1): p. 99-110.

162. Lund S, Christensen KV, Hedtjärn M, Mortensen AL, Hagberg H, Falsig J, Hasseldam H, Schrattenholz A, Pörzgen P, and M Leist, The dynamics of the LPS triggered inflammatory response of murine microglia under different culture and in vivo conditions. *Journal of Neuroimmunology*, 2006. **180**(1-2): p. 71-87.

Chapter 2.4

Peripheral Nerve Stimulation

Dustin J. Tyler

Department of Biomedical Engineering, Case Western Reserve University
10900 Euclid Ave., Cleveland, OH 44106
dustin.tyler@case.edu

The sections of this chapter build from basic principles of neural activation of peripheral nerves to descriptions of the effects of various stimulation energies. The first section describes the bioelectric phenomenon. This includes the origin of the membrane potential and the membrane channels. Peripheral nerve stimulation is essentially manipulation of the state of membrane channels. The second section describes how various energies affect the membrane channels. The third section briefly discusses the factors affecting the physical design of a peripheral nerve stimulation device. The final section provides a non-exhaustive list of example devices that have been developed to stimulate peripheral nerves.

1. Introduction

Activation of the peripheral nervous system can be efferent or afferent. Efferent activation will cause action in end organs, such as muscle, innervated by a nerve. Afferent activation provides information to the central nervous system about the state of the body and environment. For example, stimulation of neurons innervating cutaneous sensory organs, such as the Pacinian corpuscles, provides tactile information. The goal of peripheral nerve stimulation is to activate the neurons with sufficient specificity and accurate patterns of activation to mimic the natural activity of the nerves. Stimulation is essentially applying focal external energy to the peripheral nerves to open or close the ion channels in the cell membrane to affect cell function. Typically, the goal is to generate self-sustaining action potentials. These action potentials are then faithfully transmitted to their end organ or to the central nervous system (CNS). It is also possible to apply energy in such a manner as to inactivate the channels and prevent unwanted activity in a nerve from reaching its target. This can be useful, for example, to block painful sensations to the brain or to stop unwanted spastic muscle activity. This chapter provides a detailed understanding of the neuron's response to several forms of energy and a few examples of devices that have been developed to apply the energy in a focused manner.

Formally, the peripheral nervous system is defined as the portion of the nervous system outside the brain and spinal cord. It includes the lower motor neurons connected directly to muscles. It includes the primary sensory neurons directly connected to the sensory organs of the body that carry information to the spinal cord. The peripheral nervous system can be divided into the somatosensory system and autonomic nervous system (ANS). The somatosensory system is generally part of our conscious sense and control. The autonomic system regulates internal organ function and maintains body stasis. The mechanisms of nerve fiber action that are detailed in this chapter apply to both the somatosensory and autonomic systems, however, there are several anatomical differences that will affect the final design of devices to deliver energy to each system. The existence of many plexuses within the ANS and the small size of the ANS nerves are the most significant. This chapter does not cover or discuss the influence of these elements of the ANS.

The peripheral nerve is the primary input and final output of the nervous system. It is the initial input to and final output from the complex processing circuitry of the CNS. Afferent stimulation takes advantage of all the CNS systems for tasks such as conscious perception, motor control, and reflex responses. Efferent stimulation can directly control end organs.

Three primary aspects need to be considered for achieving maximum benefit from peripheral nerve stimulation. The first is precision of stimulation. This refers to the ability of an interface to stimulate a sufficiently focused and synergistic population of fibers within the peripheral nerve to affect a desired, and only the desired, function or sensation. The factors affecting precision are the form of energy delivered, the physical interaction of the interface with the nerve, the organization within the nerve, and the location of the interface along the peripheral nerve. Typically, peripheral nerves are more functionally organized farther distally. The second aspect is the information content of the stimulation patterns. In efferent stimulation, the complex performance of a task requires proper balance and timing of activity of many muscles. In afferent stimulation, sensory perception is dependent on the correct timing and frequency of action potentials from afferents. The third aspect is the safety of the interface to deliver the energy. The method selected to achieve the first two objectives cannot adversely affect or destroy the nerve that the interface it attempting to activate.

2. Bioelectric Phenomenon

2.1. *The action potential*

Neural stimulation is the activation of one or more axons within the peripheral nerve by an application of external energy. Activation means producing a self-sustained action potential (AP) that will propagate along the activated axons. Once this action potential is generated it will be faithfully propagated in the orthodromic and antidromic directions. Orthodromic propagation means the AP travels in the normal biological direction. For efferent fibers, this would be from the spinal cord to the distal end organ, such as the muscle. For afferent fibers, orthodromic propagation is from distal organs, such as the tactile sensors in the skin, toward the spinal cord.

While the intent is typically to generate orthodromic activity, a typical stimulation peripheral nerve will generate both orthodromically and antidromically propagating Aps. An antidromically propagating AP will collide with orthodromically propagating Aps proximal to the electrode. When two Aps collide, they annihilate each other and cancel any transfer of information. This could be advantageous to cancel negative information, such as spasticity or pain. It could be detrimental if it cancels voluntary action.

2.2. *The membrane potential*

Nernst Potential. The action potential, like all bioelectric phenomena, is a consequence of an ionic imbalance across the semi-permeable cell membrane. A complex system that includes active ion pumping mechanisms maintains an imbalance of ion concentrations between the inside and outside of the cell. The cell is constantly in a state of dynamic equilibrium, not static or lowest energy equilibrium. In terms of dynamic systems, the resting potential of the membrane is a stable node of the system. Perturbation will cause a dynamic fluctuation from the stable point. The trajectory of the fluctuation will depend on the type of perturbation. A small perturbation will cause a small transient shift in membrane potential that quickly returns to equilibrium without a full action potential. When the perturbation is large enough to move the membrane past a threshold point, the system follows a predetermined trajectory representing the action potential. The shape of that trajectory is determined by the non-linear properties of the specific channels in the membrane. While full dynamic systems analysis is beyond the scope of this chapter, it can be insightful to realize that peripheral nerve stimulation can be understood as manipulation of a dynamic system describing the membrane potential. The system has a stable nodal point at rest. Stimulation of the nerve is a manipulation of the nodal points and state of the dynamic system.

Every charged component, including proteins, ion, and molecules, has a Nernst potential across the membrane. The membrane is relatively impermeable to most species on the time-scale and with mechanisms relevant to an AP. However, they may affect the resting equilibrium of the membrane and, hence, the dynamic system behavior.

The main ions contributing to the membrane potential of peripheral nerves are sodium (Na^+) and potassium (K^+). Chlorine (Cl^-) and calcium (Ca^{2+}) also contribute the membrane voltage, but to a lesser extent. At equilibrium, the electrical voltage across the membrane arising from the separation of charge such that the electromotive force exactly balances the chemical diffusion force of the concentration gradient. This equilibrium potential is the Nernst potential for the ion. It is defined as the voltage inside the cell minus the voltage outside the cell.

$$V_{ion} = V_i - V_o = \frac{RT}{zF} \ln \left(\frac{[ion]_{out}}{[ion]_{in}} \right) = 2.303 \frac{RT}{zF} \log_{10} \left(\frac{[ion]_{out}}{[ion]_{in}} \right) \tag{1}$$

where,

> R = gas constant (8.31451 j/mol-K;
> T = temp (K)
> z = valence of ion
> F = Faraday's constant (96485 C/mol).

At T=20° C = 293 K, 2.303·RT/F = 58.1 mV, which is the value used in amphibian studies. At T=37° C = 310 K, or mammalian body temperature, 2.303·RT/F = 61.5 mV. Table 1 shows the typical concentrations of ions for a mammalian nerve and the resulting Nernst potentials.

Table 1. Typical mammalian ion concentrations and resulting Nernst potentials.

ion	$[ion]_{in}$	$[ion]_{out}$	V_{ion} (mV)
K^+	125	5	-86.0
Na^+	12	120	61.5
Cl^-	5	125	-86.0
Ca^{2+}	0.0002	2	123

Total Membrane Potential. Membrane permeability to a specific ion is controlled by ion-specific protein channels that span the membrane. The details of channel behavior leading to changes in permeability are discussed in the following section. First, however, it is important to understand the powerful impact of dynamically changing permeability for specific ions. The total membrane potential from several ions, or the resting potential of the membrane, is determined by the permeability of the membrane to each ion and the concentration difference of the ion. While not strictly true, it is instructive to think of the resting potential as a weighted balance of Nernst potentials. The weighting is based on the ratio of the permeabilities to the different axons. The exact net potential is derived from an analysis of free energy of the membrane [103]. A closed-form solution for the Na^+, K^+, and Cl^- single valent ions only is the Goldman-Hodgkin-Katz (GHK) equation

$$V_{rest} = \frac{RT}{F} \ln \left(\frac{P_{Na}[Na^+]_{out} + P_K[K^+]_{out} + P_{Cl}[Cl^-]_{in}}{P_{Na}[Na^+]_{in} + P_K[K^+]_{in} + P_{Cl}[Cl^-]_{out}} \right)$$

$$= 2.303 \frac{RT}{F} \log \left(\frac{P_{Na}[Na^+]_{out} + P_K[K^+]_{out} + P_{Cl}[Cl^-]_{in}}{P_{Na}[Na^+]_{in} + P_K[K^+]_{in} + P_{Cl}[Cl^-]_{out}} \right) \qquad (2)$$

Notice that the locations of the inside and outside concentrations for the negative valent Cl- ion is opposite of that for the positive ions. Now, consider the impact of the relative permeability of the ions to each other. Near rest, the ratio of the permeabilities $P_K:P_{Na}:P_{Cl}$ is approximately 1:0.03:0.1. Potassium dominants the membrane and V_{rest} = -86.0 mV, which is essentially the Nernst potential of potassium. If, however the relative permeabilities change to $P_K:P_{Na}:P_{Cl}$ = 1:15:0.1, or dominated by sodium, V_{rest} = +46.4 mV. This is nearly the Nernst potential for sodium. Therefore, the membrane potential of the neuron is controlled by the balance of permeability to different ions.

Membrane Channels. The permeability is directly controlled by the state of the membrane channels. The beautiful complexity of the entire bioelectric system is derived from this basic relationship. By integrating a variety of channels in the membrane that are responsive to different cues and signals, the peripheral (and central) nervous system can sense, process, and respond to the myriad of signals in the environment, including chemical, electrical, mechanical, optical, and magnetic. This is the basic mechanism of action throughout the animal kingdom.

Further development of the relationship between the permeability of the cell membrane and integrated channels will provide the full theoretical basis for peripheral nerve stimulation. The permeability of the membrane to a given ion is dependent on the number of ion channels within the membrane and how many of the channels are open.

First, consider a small patch of the neural membrane. Within this patch, there will be several different types of channels. For each channel, there will be a density of channels given by D_{ch}. The total number of channels in an area of membrane is simply, $A_{patch} \cdot D_{ch}$. If the permeability of a single channel, P_{ch}, is known, the permeability of several channels in parallel is the sum of the permeabilities of each channel. Detail electrophysiology experiments have shown that each channel has an identical permeability, and therefore, the total permeability of a patch of membrane for the specific ion is $P_{patch} = A_{patch} \cdot D_{ch} \cdot P_{ch}$. The density of channels and the permeability of each channel need to be determined experimentally for each cell and each channel.

While other approaches exist, this chapter will continue to develop the peripheral nerve stimulation concepts around an electrical model of the nerve. The Nernst and GHK equations give the transformation between chemical and electrical domains. The electrical equivalent behavior of ion channels has been developed through electrophysiology experiments. A channel is either open and allowing ion flow or it is closed and no current flows. When a voltage is applied to a very small patch of membrane with only one active ion channel, small pulses of current are measured. The pulses represent the times that a channel is open and conducting current. This small quantum of current, $I_{quantum}$, is directly related to the applied voltage difference from the Nernst potential, $V_d = V_{Nernst} - V_{applied}$, across the membrane. The conductance of each open channel is then calculated as

$$g'_{ch} = \frac{I_{quantum}}{V_d} \tag{3}$$

The typical conductance per channel is in the range of 10's of pS/ch. The total conductance per a patch of membrane is the channel conductance times the channel density

$$g_{ch} = D_{ch} g'_{ch} \tag{4}$$

Channel densities can range from 2,000 to 17,000 per μm^2 resulting in a conductivity as high as several 1,000 mS/cm². For the moment, the dynamics and channel response to a stimulus has been ignored, but will be considered a few sections later in the development of the dynamic cable equation. Next, the passive or static cable equation is developed to show the behavior of an entire cell and provide the fundamental theory of peripheral nerve stimulation.

2.3. Cable equations

Passive, continuous cable equation. There are many models and each is dependent on assumptions about the membrane and details that are intended to be modeled. Since this chapter is only concerned with peripheral nerve stimulation, only the extended axon of the cell is considered. Central nervous system stimulation must also consider cell bodies, dendrites, and more complex cell geometries. In the peripheral nervous system, it is assumed that the axon is a long tube with constant diameter and channel composition, at least in the region of interest near the stimulation device.

The cable equation [116 - 119] defined for a passive, continuous axon, is

$$\tau \frac{\partial V_m}{\partial t} + V_m - \lambda^2 \frac{\partial^2 V_m}{\partial l^2} = \lambda^2 \frac{\partial^2 V_e}{\partial l^2} \tag{5}$$

Where the components are defined as follows:

$$C_m = \frac{\epsilon_m A_m}{th_m} = \frac{\epsilon_m(\pi d_a \Delta l)}{th_m} = c_m \Delta l, \ c_m = \frac{\pi \epsilon_m d_a}{th_m} \tag{6}$$

$$R_m = \frac{\rho_m th_m}{A_m} = \frac{\rho_m th_m}{\pi d_a \Delta l} = \frac{r_m}{\Delta l}, \ r_m = \frac{\rho_m th_m}{\pi d_a} \tag{7}$$

$$R_a = \frac{\rho_a \Delta l}{\pi d_a^2 / 4} = \frac{4\rho_a \Delta l}{\pi d_a^2} = r_a \Delta l, \ r_a = \frac{4\rho_a}{\pi d_a^2} \tag{8}$$

$$\lambda^2 = \frac{r_m}{r_a} \tag{9}$$

$$\tau = r_m c_m \tag{10}$$

If the axon is myelinated, the myelin can be assumed to be a perfect insulator or in more detailed models, the electrical properties of the cell-myelin and myelin-extracellular space are modeled [88]. For myelinated axons, the spatial derivatives are replaced spatial difference equations over the inter-nodal length, $L = 100D_a = 170d_a$, where D_a is the diameter of the axon including the myelin and d_a is the diameter of the axon without myelin. R_a is calculated as in eq. 8. The membrane capacitance and resistance are calculated over the node of Ranvier, which has a length of about 1 μm, typically. The discrete or myelinated cable equation is given as

$$C_m \frac{dV_m}{dt} + \frac{V_m(n)}{R_m} - \frac{V_m(n-1)+V_m(n+1)-2V_m(n)}{R_a} = \frac{V_e(n-1)+V_e(n+1)-2V_e(n)}{R_a} \tag{11a}$$

$$C_m \frac{dV_m}{dt} + \frac{V_m(n)}{R_m} - \frac{\Delta_2 V_m(n)}{R_a} = \frac{\Delta_2 V_e(n)}{R_a} \tag{11b}$$

where n denotes the node number and Δ_2 is a short-hand notation for the second central difference.

Characteristics of the Passive Cable Equation. Most important elements of peripheral nerve stimulation with electromagnetic fields can be understood by examination of the passive cable equations. The electromagnetic field is described in more detail below, but at this point it is sufficient to understand that it creates an external voltage field, V_e, that drives the membrane voltage. The driving function, i.e., the external potentials on the right-hand side of the equation, is the second difference of the voltage along the length of the axon. While it is an illustrative simplification, the goal of electrical stimulation of a non-myelinated axon is to establish a second spatial derivative along the axon. For myelinated axons, the goal is to establish a second difference of the voltage at the nodes of Ranvier.

In an infinite homogeneous medium, the voltage field from a point source of stimulation decays with a 1/r characteristic. Considering unmyelinated axons, the strength of a field is proportional to λ and λ is proportional to $\sqrt{d_a}$. For myelinated axons, the axoplasmic resistance, R_a, is smaller for large axons and the inter-nodal spacing is bigger. Hence, there is a larger second spatial difference and it is more influential. Therefore, if all other elements are equal, a larger axon in the same electric field will be more likely to activate than a smaller one.

In a realistic peripheral nerve with thousands of axons, however, the nodes of Ranvier are randomly distributed and the axons of various diameters are randomly distributed throughout the nerve. An electrical field centered on a node of Ranvier will be more effective at stimulation than between the nodes. As well, close small axons are more likely to fire than farther away large axons. Therefore, it is not correct to assume electrical stimulation has a strictly large to small recruitment order. Further, more complex field shapes can manipulate the second spatial difference along the nerve and the firing patterns within a nerve structure.

Active cable models. Passive cable models are insufficient to completely understand peripheral nerve stimulation for two reasons. First, a passive cable model does not generate an action potential or capture the non-linear characteristics of stimulation. To understand the stimulation characteristics using non-square stimulation pulses requires addition of models for the channel dynamic behavior. Second, the passive equations only give insight into the response of the axon to electrical fields. Electromagnetic stimulation is an indirect approach that directly changes the membrane potential and the membrane potential that then affects the channels to cause an action potential. There are emerging stimulation approaches that utilize different forms of energy, such as optical, mechanical, and thermal mechanisms for activating axons. These methods, however, manipulate the channels directly. To understand these forms of stimulation, our models need to include dynamic channel properties.

Active models are similar to the passive models, but we add the membrane channels to the model. Every channel adds a branch to the membrane. The behavior of channels are described in the following section. Each channel is responsive to either electrical, optical, chemical, mechanical, etc. energy The addition of batteries with voltages labels as E_{ion} represent the Nerst potentials of the ions associate with each channel. R_{ion} is the stimulus-dependent resistance of the channel, as described below.

The modification of the cable equation is simple. The membrane current now has many different components. These add as parallel branches in the membrane with a resistance component representing the stimulus responsive conductance and a battery representing the Nernst potential for the specific ion of the membrane. The leak channel, R_l, represents the passive resistance of the membrane and is typically a collection of anions, such as Cl^-. Each of the other branches represent the active ions, such as Na^+, K^+, and the many variations in the channels that conduct these ions. The number of branches is not limited and are added to represent all of the channels in a patch of membrane. These can be, but are not limited to, ion channels, ligand channels, optogenetic channels, synaptic channels, and mechanical channels. For each channel there is a formulation of the channel dynamics that is added to the model, such as in the prior section. To model the active channels, the membrane current of the cable equation is modified as

$$i_m = C_m \frac{\partial V_m}{\partial t} + \Sigma_{ions}[G_{ion}(V_m - E_{ion})] = C_m \frac{\partial V_m}{\partial t} + I_{ionic} \qquad (12)$$

where $G_{ion} = \frac{1}{R_{ion}}$.

G_{ion} is a dynamic, non-linear conductance that is based on the equations of the channel describing its conductance in response to an input that it responds to. Inserting equation (12) into the continuous, unmyelinated cable equation results in the contiuous active cable equation

$$\frac{\partial V_m}{\partial t} + \frac{I_{ionic}}{c'_m \pi d_a l} - \frac{d_a}{4c'_m \rho_a} \frac{\partial^2 V_m}{\partial l^2} = \frac{d_a}{4c'_m \rho_a} \frac{\partial^2 V_e}{\partial l^2}, \qquad (13)$$

where $c'_m = \frac{\epsilon_0 \epsilon_r}{th}$.

To get the myelinated version of the cable equation, substituting equation (12) into the membrane components of (11b) gives

$$C_m \frac{dV_m}{dt} + \Sigma_{ions}[G_{ion}(V_m - E_{ion})] - G_a \Delta_2 V_m(n) = G_a \Delta_2 V_e(n) \qquad (14)$$

These cable equation formulations describe the behavior in response to an external voltage field. However, with many neuroscience experiments, currents are injected directly into the cell. This can be simply added to the left-hand side of the equations as another current source into the node. Note that all of the currents are defined as leaving the node in the definition of the cable equations. If the convention is followed, additional current source density can be added to the left-hand side of the continuous equations (5) and (13), or current sources can be added to the left-hand side of the myelinated equations (11a) or (14).

2.4. *Membrane Channel Dynamics*

As indicated previously in discussing the GHK equation, the amazing capabilities of the cell are driven by the protein channels in the cell membrane that change their permeability in response to different signals. In peripheral nerves, channels that respond to changes in the membrane voltage, V_m, are the most common native membrane channels. This chapter develops a channel model that is best thought of as a tube with a number of binary gates. Each channel has a characteristic conductance, g_{ch}. For any patch of membrane with a surface area of A_{surf}, channels with a conductance of g_{ch}; and channel density of D_{ch}, the maximum possible conductance is

$$g_{ch,max} = A_{surf} D_{ch} g_{ch}. \qquad (15)$$

Each gate is either open or closed. When all gates in a channel are open, the channel conducts ions according to the quantized current model discussed earlier. The probability of a gate being open is dependent on the signal the channel detects.

The rest of this development will focus on a mammalian "fast sodium" channel that is sensitive to membrane voltage. The same process would apply to channels sensitive to other signals, such as incident optical irradiance, with appropriate changes in the independent variable. It is also possible that there are modifications and more complex dynamic equations of channel state, but the process is the same. For an example of optical channels, see [8, 42].

First, each channel has one or several gates. In the fast sodium channel, there are four gates. Three of the gates normally have a very low probability of being open and the fourth normally has a high probability of being open. The open probability of the normally closed gates is m and the open probability of the normally open gate is h. Using basic rules of probability, the total probability of the channel being open is then given as the multiple of the individual probabilities, m^3h. Combining this probability with equation (15), the conductance of the membrane channel at any instant is the maximum possible conductance times the probability of a channel being open or

$$G_{ch} = g_{ch,max}m^3h \tag{16}$$

The rates of change in the number of open m-gates and number of h-gates are defined by the rate reactions

$$\frac{dm}{dt} = \alpha_m(1-m) - \beta_m m \qquad \frac{dh}{dt} = \alpha_h(1-h) - \beta_h h \tag{17}$$

where α and β are the rate constant of closed channels going to open channel and open channels going to closed channels, respectively. The rate constants are dependent on the signal to which the channel responds. In the example of the fast sodium channel, the rate constants have been experimentally measured to be best described by the equations

$$\alpha_m = \frac{7.11(V_m+25.4)}{1-e^{\frac{-(V_m+25.4)}{103}}} \qquad \beta_m = \frac{-0.3286(V_m+29.7)}{1-e^{\frac{(V_m+29.7)}{9.16}}}$$

$$\alpha_h = \frac{-0.2053(V_m+118.0)}{1-e^{\frac{-(V_m+118.0)}{11.0}}} \qquad \beta_h = \frac{14.0541}{1+e^{\frac{-(V_m+35.8)}{13.4}}}$$

These equations not give insight to the mechanism of electromagnetic stimulation of the peripheral nerve. The external voltage driving function from the right side of the cable equation will cause a change in the membrane voltage. This in turn changes the rate constants, which changes the conductance of the voltage sensitive channels. If the membrane voltage moves more positive, the probability of the m-gates opening will increase and the membrane will become more permeable to sodium. Recall from equation (2) that an increase in sodium permeability will drive the membrane closer to the sodium Nernst potential, which is more positive, hence continuing the positive increase of the membrane potential. When the membrane reaches a threshold level, the system will generate an action potential. The shape of the potential is completely described by the dynamic equations of all the channels in the membrane. An action potential propagates because the neighbor node is connected through the axoplasmic conductance. This causes a rise in the membrane potentials at the neighbor node. The neuron is exquisitely balanced such that an action potential at one node will cause an action potential at the neighboring node. This process propagates along the entire axon. Diseases such as multiple sclerosis and amyotrophic lateral sclerosis cause changes in the channel dynamics to upset this balance of activity and prevents propagation of the action potential.

Also, note that each of the gate parameters has a different time course of action. The m-gates change rapidly while the h-gates change more slowly. This provides part of the shape of the action potential. In fact, an action potential is possible with a sodium channel only [138]. The rapid m-gates open the sodium channels, moving the membrane to the positive sodium Nernst potential. The h-gate lags, but shortly after begins closing the sodium channel, again reducing the sodium conductance and driving the membrane back to the potassium Nernst potential, which is resting potential. As the potential returns to the resting potential, the h-gate again closes. The h-gate, however, is slower in opening again. It is during the period with the h-gate closed that a neuron is in the absolute refractory period. It is not possible to initiate another action potential. This is understood by understanding the h-gate behavior. If another pulse is applied to increase the membrane voltage, the more positive voltage works to close the h-gate again. No matter how open the m-gates are, the channel will remain closed.

By understanding the dynamics of the channel gates, it is also possible to design time-dependent driving function profiles that can manipulate the channel state. For example, a slowly ramping pulse can close the h-gates before activating the m-gates. If timed appropriately, axons in a strong field will be inactivated to an absolutely refractory-like state without first firing an action potential. Then, a following stronger pulse will active further axons that have not been fully deactivated while the closer fibers will fail to initiate and action potential [47].

3.   Stimulation Methods

Now that the points of affecting a membrane behavior are identified, this section describes several of the techniques that have been implemented to stimulate peripheral nerves. To reiterate the most important point, peripheral nerve stimulation is completely about manipulation of channel permeability by application of external energies. There are several approaches including electrical, magnetic, optical, ultrasound, and heat. Electromagnetic stimulation is the most studied and will be the focus of this chapter. Optical and optogenetic stimulation techniques have been heavily used for experimental procedures and will be introduced. Finally, a survey of other techniques will be presented.

3.1. *Electromagnetic Stimulation*

3.1.1. *General equations of electromagnetic stimulation*

The cable equations development in the prior section focus on the nerve and only introduced the external fields. Now we change focus to the generation of the electromagnetic field. This requires a more detailed look at the right-hand side of the cable equation to define electromagnetic stimulation.

Since our systems operates at filed frequencies well below 10^6 Hz and the physical domain of peripheral nerves, e.g. the body, are significantly smaller than the wavelength of the field, $\lambda = c/f \approx 300$ m at 10^6 Hz, the system can be considered quasi-static in generation of the equations defining the electromagnetic fields within the body and ignore propagating waves and radiation [68]. Unlike most formulations, the following does not directly separate the magnetic and electric potential fields, nor does it assume an axon geometry within the quasi-static electromagnetic field. The following is a general definition of electromagnetic stimulation that can be implemented for any stimulation approach [6]. From fundamental field electromagnetics [25], the following equations can be defined.

Faraday's Law: $\quad \nabla \times E = -\dfrac{\partial B}{\partial t}$

Magnetic Potential Field, A: $\quad B = \nabla \times A$

E is the electric field vector and A is the vector magnetic potential generated by neural interface devices for electrical stimulation. Substituting $\nabla \times A$ for B in Faraday's Law and rearranging gives $\nabla \times \left(E + \dfrac{\partial A}{\partial t} \right) = 0$. Since this means that the vector field $E + \dfrac{\partial A}{\partial t}$ is curl-free and it can be represented by the gradient of the scalar electric potential, V, giving the definition of the gradient of the voltage as

$$\nabla V = -(E + \partial A/\partial t) \tag{18}$$

A slight modification of the continuous passive cable equation (5) to consider the axon moving through an arbitrary path defined as the parameterized vector path, $l(s)$, through an external electrostatic field over distance s along the axon, can be written as follows:

$$\lambda^2 \frac{\partial^2 V_m}{\partial s^2} - V_m - \tau \frac{\partial V_m}{\partial t} = -\lambda^2 \frac{\partial^2 V_e}{\partial s^2} \tag{19}$$

$\dfrac{\partial^2 V_e}{\partial s^2}$ is the second spatial difference of the voltage along the axon path. It is defined as the directional gradient of the directional gradient of the voltage at all points *l(s)*. From equation (18) the generic driving function for a complete electromagnetic field is

$$\frac{\partial^2 V_e}{\partial s^2} = \nabla(\nabla V_e \cdot \hat{l}) \cdot \hat{l} = -\nabla\left(\left(E + \frac{\partial A}{\partial t}\right) \cdot \hat{l}\right) \cdot \hat{l} \tag{20}$$

where $\hat{l}$ is the unit vector pointing in the direction of the axon path at any point, s.

The complete and generic cable equation for a continuous, passive axon over an arbitrary path through a quasi-static electromagnetic field is given by

$$\lambda^2 \frac{\partial^2 V_m}{\partial s^2} - V_m - \tau\frac{\partial V_m}{\partial t} = \lambda^2 \nabla\left(\left(E + \frac{\partial A}{\partial t}\right) \cdot \hat{l}\right) \cdot \hat{l} \tag{21}$$

Applying the same derivation to the continuous, active axon, equation (13) results in

$$\frac{d_a}{4c'_m\rho_a}\frac{\partial^2 V_m}{\partial s^2} - \frac{I_{ionic}}{c'_m\pi\rho_a l} - \frac{\partial V_m}{\partial t} = \frac{d_a}{4c'_m\rho_a}\nabla\left(\left(E + \frac{\partial A}{\partial t}\right) \cdot \hat{l}\right) \cdot \hat{l} \tag{22}$$

The generic driving function derivation for myelinated axons requires a little more consideration. Because the generic field includes both the electric and magnetic fields, the difference in voltage between two point along the axon is not necessarily path independent and we must use the following definition of the potential difference along a path *l(s)* to substitute into the myelinated cable equations [98].

$$\nabla V_e = -\left(E + \frac{\partial A}{\partial t}\right)$$

$$V_e(n-1) - V_e(n) = \int_s^{s-L}(\nabla V_e \cdot \hat{l})ds = -\int_s^{s-L}\left(\left(E + \frac{\partial A}{\partial t}\right) \cdot \hat{l}\right)ds \tag{23}$$

$$V_e(n+1) - V_e(n) = \int_s^{s+L}(\nabla V_e \cdot \hat{l})ds = -\int_s^{s+L}\left(\left(E + \frac{\partial A}{\partial t}\right) \cdot \hat{l}\right)ds \tag{24}$$

Equations (23) and (24) define the current traveling away from the node in the two directions. Substituting them back into equation (14) give the generic form of the active, myelinated axon traveling an arbitrary path through a quasi-static electromagnetic field:

$$C_m\frac{dV_m}{dt} + I_{ionic} - G_a\Delta_2 V_m(n)$$

$$= -G_a\left[\int_s^{s-L}\left(\left(E + \frac{\partial A}{\partial t}\right) \cdot \hat{l}\right)ds + \int_s^{s+L}\left(\left(E + \frac{\partial A}{\partial t}\right) \cdot \hat{l}\right)ds\right] \tag{25}$$

The electric field, E, is created by current sources applied through the tissue, such as by an exposed electrical contact. A is the induced magnetic field created by a time-varying current in a conductor. These two domains are typically implemented separately. Electrical stimulation is more common in peripheral nerve stimulation and magnetic stimulation has been more common in diagnostic and therapeutic trans-cranial stimulation. While both domains cause activation of the nerve by the resulting electric field, stimulation resulting from E is referred to as electrical stimulation and stimulation resulting from $\frac{\partial A}{\partial t}$ is, somewhat misleadingly, referred to as magnetic stimulation.

Before continuing, it is illustrative to consider the relative power requirements of the two different components of the electromagnetic field. First, the threshold strength of the electromagnetic field required for axon activation is on the order of -10 mV/mm. The E field is of the order of $\frac{\rho I}{r}$, where ρ is the tissue resistivity, I is the injected current, and r is the distance between the electrode and the axon. This requires current on the order of milliamps to generate a field of -10 mV/mm. The magnetic potential field is on the order of the permeability, μ_0, or 10^{-8} mV·s/ mm·A. Consequently, the time rate of change of current in a single wire is required to be on the order of 100 A/μsec. This requirement is the primary challenge to design of magnetic stimulation system.

Historically, electric and magnetic stimulation have always been considered separately. Consequently, the following two sections will discuss the properties and aspects of neural stimulation for each separately.

3.1.2. *Electrical stimulation*

Basic equations. In electrical stimulation, the magnetic field is negligible and $\frac{\partial A}{\partial t} \approx$ 0. Note that there is a magnetic field produced by any current traveling in the wire to provide the stimulation current to the tissue. However, this field is approximately six orders of magnitude below the electric field and can be ignored. The generic, continuous, passive cable equation (21) reduces to

$$\lambda^2 \frac{\partial^2 V_m}{\partial s^2} - V_m - \tau \frac{\partial V_m}{\partial t} = \lambda^2 \nabla(\boldsymbol{E} \cdot \hat{\boldsymbol{l}}) \cdot \hat{\boldsymbol{l}}$$

and the generic, continuous, active equation (22) reduces to

$$\frac{d_a}{4c'_m \rho_a} \frac{\partial^2 V_m}{\partial s^2} - \frac{I_{ionic}}{c'_m \pi \rho_a l} - \frac{\partial V_m}{\partial t} = \frac{d_a}{4c'_m \rho_a} \nabla(\boldsymbol{E} \cdot \hat{\boldsymbol{l}}) \cdot \hat{\boldsymbol{l}}$$

and the generic, myelinated, active equation (14) becomes

$$C_m \frac{dV_m}{dt} + I_{ionic} - G_a \Delta_2 V_m(n) = -G_a \left[\int_s^{s-L}(\boldsymbol{E} \cdot \hat{\boldsymbol{l}})ds + \int_s^{s+L}(\boldsymbol{E} \cdot \hat{\boldsymbol{l}})ds \right]$$

If the axon is aligned with the x-axis, then the equations above are further simplified to the more customary forms of

$$\lambda^2 \frac{\partial^2 V_m}{\partial x^2} - V_m - \tau \frac{\partial V_m}{\partial t} = \lambda^2 \frac{\partial E_x}{\partial x}$$

$$\frac{d_a}{4c'_m \rho_a} \frac{\partial^2 V_m}{\partial x^2} - \frac{I_{ionic}}{c'_m \pi \rho_a l} - \frac{\partial V_m}{\partial t} = \frac{d_a}{4c'_m \rho_a} \frac{\partial E_x}{\partial x}$$

$$C_m \frac{dV_m}{dt} + I_{ionic} - G_a \Delta_2 V_m(n) = -G_a \frac{\partial E_x}{\partial x}$$

where E_x is the x-component of the electric potential field.

D. J. Tyler

Current computational ability is sufficient to quickly simulate the general forms of the equations. This can be extremely beneficial in designing electrode configurations [49, 128, 129], optimal waveform shapes [45, 46, 57, 87, 155, 168], and characteristic responses to stimulation paradigms. However, to understand the behavior of many neurons or to optimize stimulation over many dimensions and many electrodes, it is necessary to implement linear approximations to the active neural models. A few linear approximations include [95, 106, 158].

General field shape from a single electrode. In developing peripheral stimulation devices and paradigms, the field produced by a simple case of a point source of current in an infinite homogeneous medium is instructive. More complex and realistic models with anatomically correct models of the peripheral nerve can be solved using FEM techniques [49, 128, 129, 152]. In the point source model, the electric field normal to the surface of a sphere with radius r centered on the source at P with an injected current, I, is given by

$$E = \rho J$$
$$J = \frac{I}{A} = \frac{I}{4\pi r^2}$$
$$E(r) = \frac{\rho I}{4\pi r^2} \widehat{a_n}$$

where ρ is the resistivity of the media, $r = |P - P'|$ and $\widehat{a_n}$ is the unit normal vector on the surface of the sphere and r is the distance from the current source to the point. The voltage, V, at any point P' compared to an infinite reference can be calculated from

$$V(P') = \int_r^\infty \frac{\rho I}{4\pi s^2} ds = -\left(\frac{\rho I}{4\pi s}\right)\Big|_r^\infty = \frac{\rho I}{4\pi r}$$

The general shape of the driving function is triphasic along the axon with a peak centered at the perpendicular bisector of the axon connected to the point source and two side lobe of smaller size and opposite polarity (Figure 1). If the current is negative, the central lobe causes axon depolarization and moves the axon toward activation. The side lobes hyperpolarize the axon at the side lobes. If the depolarization is sufficient, an action potential will fire in the area of the central node. If the depolarization is small enough, the action potential will propagate. By manipulating the size of the central and side lobes, the effect of the stimulation can be modulated.

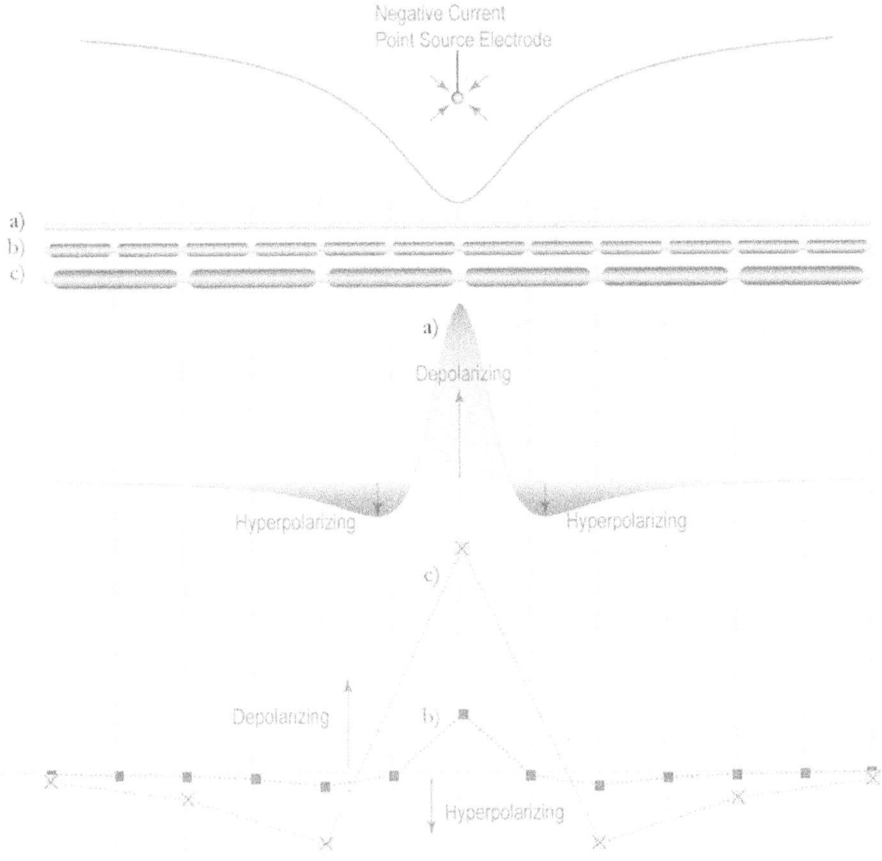

Fig. 1. Triphasic waveform.

A very strong stimulus with large side-lobes will initiate and action potential in the center, but the strong hyperpolarization can be sufficient to block propagation. As discussed earlier, larger fibers are more affected than are smaller fibers. This is true for both depolarizing and hyperpolarizing pulses. Therefore, the hyperpolarizing side-lobes will block propagation from larger fibers before smaller fibers, effectively reversing or changing the recruitment order [38].

The strong hyperpolarizing stimulus, however, can lead to a phenomenon called anodal break. During a strong hyperpolarization the m-gates of the nerve are more fully closed and the h-gates are more fully opened. If the hyperpolarizing pulse is released immediately, as in a square pulse, the faster m-gates will move to their more open state before the slower h-gates return to their closed state. This will result in a polarizing current through the sodium channels. This may be sufficient to initiate an action potential, especially in a charge balanced pulse. In a charge balanced pulse, the pulse direction is reversed in the second phase. The central lobe becomes hyperpolarizing, but the side lobes become depolarizing, which further drives the sodium channel currents. To stop this from occurring, the pulse can be modified from a square pulse to one having a slower decaying trailing edge. The trailing edge can be linear or exponential, depending on the stimulation circuitry and is called a quasi-trapezoidal pulse [38].

Strength Duration relationship. A characteristic relationship exists between the strength of the stimulation and the duration required for that stimulation to bring the axon to activation threshold. This strength-duration (SD) relationship (Figure 2) is characterized by two parameters, rheobase and chronaxie. Rheobase is the stimulus strength below which activation will not occur, even for infinite pulse width. This corresponds to a stimulation strength that cannot sufficiently open the sodium *m*-gates (activation gates) before the *h*-gates (inactivation gates) close.

Chronaxie is the minimum pulse duration required to activate the axon at a stimulus strength of two times the value of rheobase. The SD curve can be considered in as having three "operating" regions. At very short pulse widths, typically 10 µs or less the SD curve is nearly vertical. This means that the response is not particularly sensitive to changes in stimulus strength. Larger changes in strength result in recruitment of only a few additional axons, and hence, greater control of stimulation. Similarly, at very small strengths, the SD curve is nearly horizontal. Consequently, near rheobase, the response is less sensitive to changes in PW, again allowing greater control. In the low pulse amplitude or low pulse width regions, however, stimulation is very sensitive to stimulus strength or stimulus duration, respectively. Small changes will significantly change response. The third region is the rest of the SD curve. The axons are generally equally responsive to both strength and duration.

The charge-duration (QD) relationship is directly derived from the SD curve with Q=strength·duration. The QD plot, however, shows two important regions. First, short pulses require the minimum amount of charge to cause axon activation. Second, past chronaxie the SD curve increases nearly linearly. To minimize the required charge, one should use the minimum pulse width and control stimulation with pulse amplitude modulation. The actual region of stimulation will depend on the stimulator characteristics and electronics. If there is limited resolution in one parameter it should be operated at the minimum possible level and modulate the other.

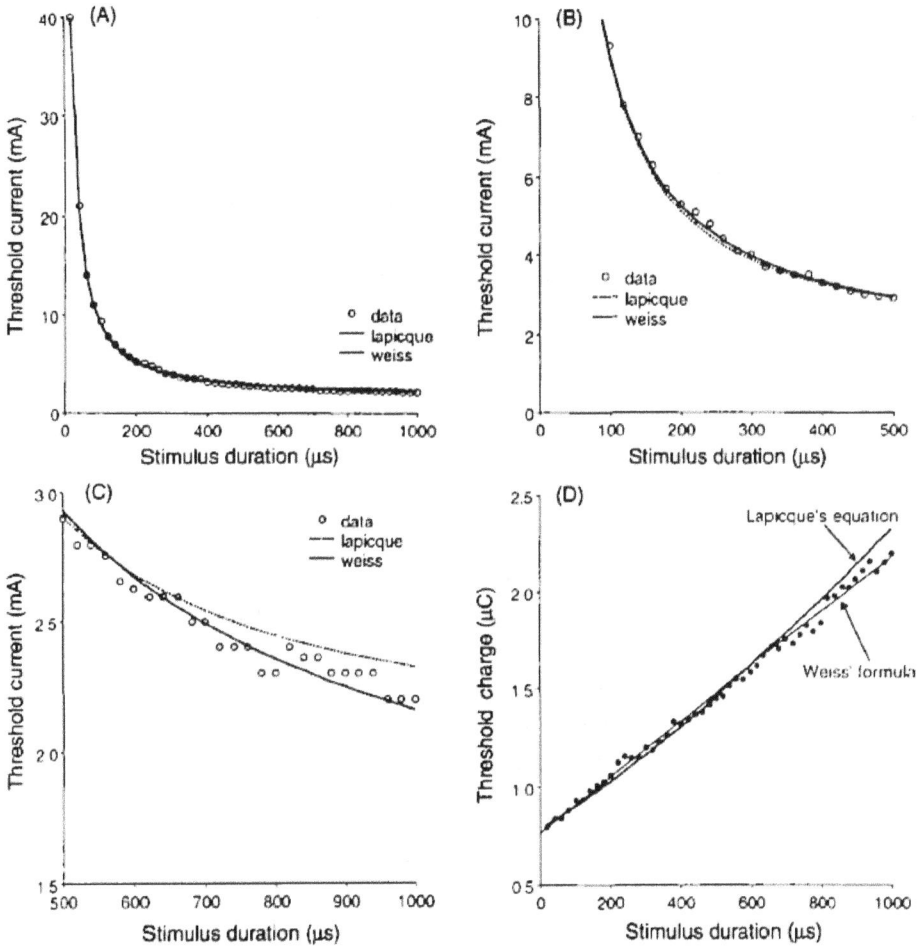

Fig. 2. Strength duration and charge duration relationships. From [96]

Multi-polar stimulation. More complicated fields can be developed to affect the nerve stimulation paradigm. Assuming the tissue is only a resistive media and the capacitive effects can be ignored, the net potential field from multiple electrodes is the linear sum of the fields produced by the individual electrodes

$$E = \sum_i E_i$$

An electrode with positive or anodal stimulation to one side of the axon, for example, will accentuate the hyperpolarization field to that side and can prevent propagation in that direction while the action potential does propagate in the other direction. Many different uses of multi-polar stimulation and field manipulation along the nerve include inverse recruitment order [38], uni-directional propagation [97, 151], collision blocking of nerve activity [137], and size-specific activation [72, 73].

Typically, peripheral nerves consist of thousands of axons distributed around the electrodes. The axons have a distribution of diameters and locations of nodes of Ranvier. The challenge of designing the device that generates the stimulation field is to selectively activate a subset of the neuronal population that goes to a specific organ, such as an individual muscle. Within the nerve, the axons are most organized distally, i.e., axons to the same organ are in the same physical location at the distal end of the nerve. This organization is maintained moving proximally, but spreads and becomes more diffuse. The objective in selective peripheral nerve stimulation is to restrict fields to specific regions of the nerve with functionally similar axons and to control the recruitment within this region to accomplish a functional goal.

Multiple electrical points around or throughout the nerve can refine and localize the field to focus on a smaller population of axons. Addition of fields also effectively increase the capability of an electrode by creating "virtual" stimulation channels.

Pulse shape. As introduced in the *Membrane Channel Dynamics* section, the channel impedances are non-linear and their response is dependent on the temporal shape of the stimulation pulse. The effect on the nerve will be dependent on the composition of channels within the axon and the time constants of the gates within each channel. The anodal break phenomenon already discussed is one such effect of the non-linear channel dynamics. By design of pulse shape and field strength, it is possible to inactivate some fibers prior to causing stimulation of others. This improves control of the size and spatial selectivity of stimulation. A slowly ramping pulse, for example, can inactivate fibers by closing the inactivation sodium channel gate prior to sufficiently opening the activation sodium channel gate. The axons in the stronger field will be more susceptible to this inactivation than those in a weaker field. By immediately following the ramp with a stronger stimulation pulse, the inactive fibers cannot fire while those less affected will. This alters the typical relationship of distance and size of a square pulse to change the recruitment pattern [47]. In addition to changing recruitment order and changing recruitment location, optimization of pulse shapes for optimal energy efficiency have been developed [45, 57, 155].

Blocking stimulation. While electrical stimulation is typically intended to activate axons, it can also be implemented for blocking propagation of action potentials. For example, in cases of pain or spasticity caused by excessive nerve activity, it would be beneficial to block pulses from propagating along the nerve. One approach would be to simply hyperpolarize the nerve with a strong anodal electrode. This is not useful for long-term applications, however, because the electrochemistry (see below) of the electrical interface will produce undesirable reactions that can damage both the electrode and the nerve.

Two methods of blocking nerve propagation include collision block and nerve inactivation. Collision block is based on the absolute refractory period of a nerve following an action potential. If two action potentials traveling in opposite directions meet along the axon, each of the portions of the membrane that just completed an action potential will be in its absolute refractory period and cannot initiate another action potential for about a millisecond. This will prevent the oppositely traveling action potential from propagating, effectively annihilating or blocking the action potential in both directions. Of course, for this to work properly, the electrical stimulation must initiate an antidromically traveling pulse only. Multiple electrodes creating an imbalanced electrical field along the nerve, as discussed earlier, is one approach to creating this affect.

Another approach to blocking action potential propagation is based on manipulating the non-linear conductance of the channels with higher frequency sinusoid electric fields. Note that "higher frequency" still refers to field of a few kilohertz and the quasi-static field assumption remains valid. When a sinusoidally varying electrical field is applied at a frequency that is near the time constants of the membrane gating reactions, it is possible to alter the "resting" potential of the membrane by changing the state of the gates [10, 59]. For a sinusoid waveform at the effective frequency, the membrane voltage is slightly depolarized and a higher portion of the sodium h-gates are closed, making it harder for action potentials to propagate through this region [10, 11].

Surface or transcutaneous electrical stimulation. Electrical stimulation is a "contact" interface. This means that the electrode is in tight approximation and touching the tissue – it requires an electrochemical interface to transform electrical current to ionic current. The electrode can be placed on any part of the body that has a continuous conductive pathway with the nerve. Electrodes on the surface of the skin can stimulate nerves. This is typically farther from the nerve and since voltage falls off inversely with increasing distance, it typically requires higher current. Also, the skin is a highly resistive tissue, and therefore, requires a significantly higher voltage in the stimulation source to generate the needed current for stimulation. Stimulators of 50 to 100 V are typical for surface stimulation. This can be reduced with conductive gels and better surface electrodes that reduce the skin impedance. Most of the resistance is from the outermost layer of skin cells. Slight abrasion of the skin or use of micro-penetrating electrodes can reduce the impedance and voltage requirements.

The second challenge with surface electrodes is that the current going to the nerve first passes through the skin, creating a driving function for the cutaneous nerves that can often be stimulated. This leads to a tingling, or possibly, painful sensation before a functional stimulation of the target nerve is achieved.

Third, even with reduced impedance, the voltage field spreads and decays rapidly. Therefore, focal stimulation, such as a specific nerve, requires complicated electrode designs. Selective stimulation of only parts of a nerve are extremely difficult. Therefore, selective stimulation of small regions of the peripheral nerve typically require invasive procedures to place electrodes directly on or in the nerve.

Electrochemical interface. Current in a metal conductor is carried by free electrons moving through the metal lattice. In the tissue, however, current is carried by the flow of ions. The electrochemical interface is the interface between the metal conductor and the tissue where the electron current is converted to ionic current. Understanding the electrochemical interface is critical to appropriate and safe design of neural stimulation devices [54, 85, 86, 92, 93, 121, 131]. The charge transfer is governed by matching Fermi levels of electrons in the metal with electrochemical reactions in the tissue and available at the surface of the electrode. There are three basic mechanisms of charge transfer. The first is called the double-layer capacitance. Water molecules – the most abundant molecule in the tissue – are polar. When current is applied to an electrode, electrons reach the surface of the metal and accumulate, giving rise to a local buildup of negative charge on the electrode surface. In response, water molecules orient in a common direction on the electrode surface, creating a charge separation, behaving like a capacitor. The double-layer capacitance is approximately 10 to 20 $\mu F/cm^2$.

As the electrons accumulate on the electrode surface, the electric potential and the Fermi energy rise. Species in the tissue that are at the surface of the electrode can accept an electron when the Fermi level reaches the electrochemical potential for the available reaction. This reduction reaction in the tissue forms a new species and transfers the current. When the available reactants are depleted, either by complete consumption from the tissue, or more likely, from a diffusion limitation, then the Fermi level continues to rise again until it is high enough for the next available reaction. This elevation process will continue until the Fermi level reaches the oxidation potential. Water is a universal donor that will not be depleted from the system.

In a mono-phasic stimulation pulse, i.e., stimulation is only in one direction, there is a net distribution of charge into the tissue. Effectively all of the electrochemical products remain in the tissue. Several of these products, such a H_2O_2, are free radicals that can cause tissue damage over long periods of stimulation. Therefore, any chronic form of stimulation must be charge-balanced.

When reactions beyond the double layer charging occur, it is important to know whether the products of the reaction remain at the surface of the electrode or if they diffuse away. During the recharge phase of a charge-balance waveform, species that remained at the surface can participate in the opposite reaction and transfer an electron back into the metal. This essentially balances out the initial reaction and leaves the system in the same state that it was prior to the stimulation. Reactants that diffuse away from the electrode surface or participate in other reactions become unavailable for the reverse reaction. An excessive these products can cause tissue damage. Each electrode material has different surface and electrochemical characteristics and hence different charge carrying capability.

Current-controlled vs. voltage-controlled stimulation source. The interface between the electrical system and the biological system changes the current from free electrons moving through the metal lattice to ions moving in the tissue. This conversion from electron to ion flow is a complicated process described in greater detail elsewhere. It is important, however, to understand that the dynamics of the electrochemical conversion is represented as a capacitive and variable resistance process. Therefore, control of the pulse is by control of either the voltage or the current. Once converted to ionic current flow, the remainder of the tissue can be assumed to be simply resistive and hence the voltage will follow the shape of the injected current. Consequently, understanding of the nerve response is best when applying current-controlled stimulation pulses. Also, if the current pulse is controlled, the exact injected charge can be controlled to improve the safety of the stimulation. Current-controlled stimulation is also less dependent on the resistance of the electrical system and changes in the tissue during tissue reaction to the neural interface. Hence, current-controlled stimulation is generally preferred to voltage-controlled stimulation. The only time that a voltage controlled system is preferred is in stimulation through electrodes attached to the surface of the skin. Because the connection is variable and might have concentrated areas of current flow, the risks of burns is reduced using a voltage controlled stimulation.

3.1.3. *Magnetic stimulation*

The surgical requirements for direct approximation to the nerve for selectivity [31] and the electrochemical requirements of electrical stimulation have motivated development of "non-contact" forms of stimulation that do not require implants, direct tissue contact, or direct electron transfer, such as magnetic stimulation. Referring back to equations (22) and (25), the gradient of the potential field is a combination of both electric potential distribution and a time-varying magnetic potential field.

In magnetic stimulation, it is assumed that the body volume is sufficiently large such that charge separation from the magnetic field can be ignored and the applied electric field is **E** = 0. If there is no relative motion between the coil that creates the magnetic potential and the tissue volume, the magnetic potential field caused by wire carrying a time varying current, $I(t)$, is described by

$$A(P,t) = \frac{\mu_0 \mu_r}{4\pi} I(t) \oint_{C'} \frac{dl'}{R}$$

where C' is the path of the wire, P is the point in the tissue, dl' is a differential portion of the wire, and R is the distance between P and dl'. μ_0 is the permittivity of free space and μ_r is the relative permittivity of tissue, which is $\mu_r = 1$.

The exact field shape depends on many geometric factors, including the coil design, depth in tissue, tissue interfaces – such as bone, skin, and muscle – and nerve geometry. Generally, as with electric fields, FEM simulations are typically implemented to find the magnetic potentials in the tissue.

The above relationship defines the electric field resulting from the magnetic field, not the extracellular potential. Therefore, the equations of activation are as follows for a passive, infinitely long, unmyelinated axon. In the presence of only magnetic fields without charge distribution or injected current, the electric field is **E** = 0 and the generic continuous cable equation becomes

$$\lambda^2 \frac{\partial^2 V_m}{\partial s^2} - V_m - \tau \frac{\partial V_m}{\partial t} = \lambda^2 \nabla \left(\frac{\partial A}{\partial t} \cdot \hat{l} \right) \cdot \hat{l}$$

If, for example, the axon is aligned with the x-direction of the coordinate system, the equation further reduces to

$$\lambda^2 \frac{\partial^2 V_m}{\partial x^2} - V_m - \tau \frac{\partial V_m}{\partial t} = \lambda^2 \frac{\partial}{\partial x} \frac{\partial A_x}{\partial t}$$

where A_x the function describing the x-direction of the magnetic potential vector.

In the case of a myelinated axon, using the compartment model, the equation describing the behavior of the nth node is [6, 98]

$$C_m \frac{dV(n)}{dt} + I_{ionic} - G_a \big(V(n+1) - 2V(n) + V(n-1) \big) =$$
$$-G_a \left(\int_{nL}^{(n+1)L} \frac{\partial A_x}{\partial t}(s)ds - \int_{(n-1)L}^{nL} \frac{\partial A_x}{\partial t}(s)ds \right)$$

If the field is approximately uniform over the length of the node, as is the case with a large coil, the field integrals can be approximated as follows:

$$\int_{nL}^{(n+1)L} \frac{\partial A_x}{\partial t}(s)ds = L \frac{\partial A_x}{\partial t}(n)$$
$$\int_{(n-1)L}^{nL} \frac{\partial A_x}{\partial t}(s)ds = L \frac{\partial A_x}{\partial t}(n-1)$$
$$\int_{nL}^{(n+1)L} \frac{\partial A_x}{\partial t}(s)ds - \int_{(n-1)L}^{nL} \frac{\partial A_x}{\partial t}(s)ds = L \left[\frac{\partial A_x}{\partial t}(n) - \frac{\partial A_x}{\partial t}(n-1) \right]$$

The most important design element of magnetic stimulation is creating a sufficiently localized field for focal neural activation. There are several analyses of generation of the magnetic fields for various scenarios and coil designs to localize stimulation with the greatest efficiency. Two important designs are the figure of 8 and butterfly coils (Figure 3) [26, 122, 123].

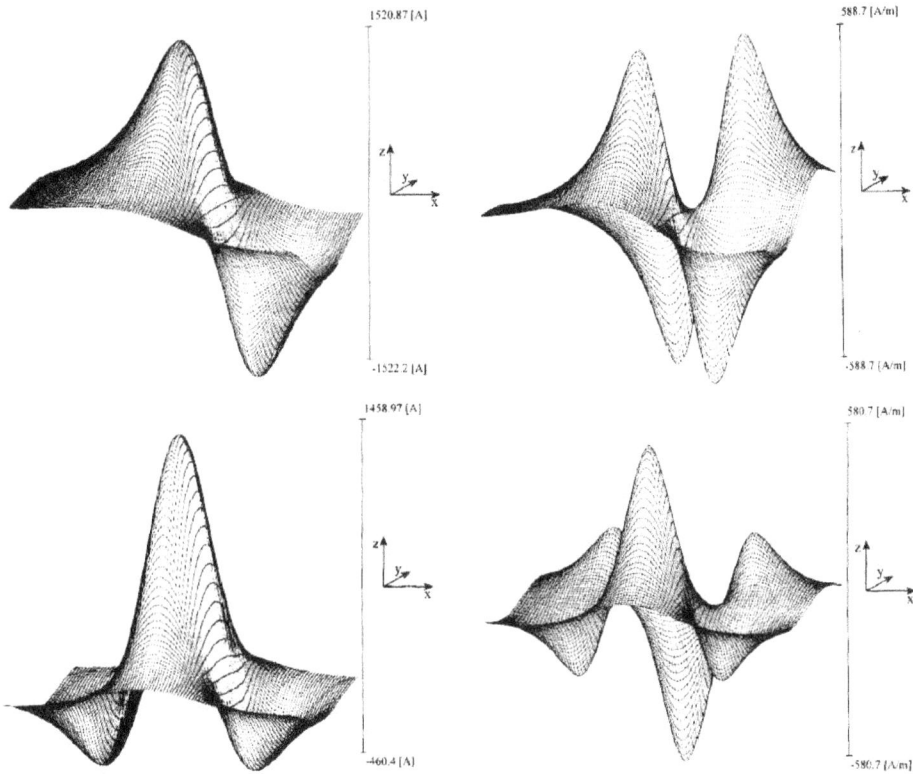

Fig. 3. Electric fields and driving functions for a single coil (top) and "butterfly" (bottom) coil design. From [170].

Magnetic stimulation has made a larger clinical impact in CNS stimulation [37, 71, 113] than in peripheral nerve stimulation. This is due to two main factors. First the selectivity of stimulation with external coils is typically not smaller than a cm^3 volume of tissue, which is not selective of components within the nerve. The second is that is very inefficient. The current requirements are often several 10's to 100's of amps with a charge pump of 100's of volts and current rise on the order of 100 A/μs. This leads to heating of the stimulation coils, large excessive power usage, needs for cooling, and limited rate of stimulus frequency.

There have been a few descriptions and demonstrations of micro-magnetic coils for stimulation within the body. Microcoils have been described [12] and shown to activate cells in the CNS [105]. MEMS-fabricated micro-coil designed for implant around the nerve [2] and CNS [104] have been theoretically proposed.

3.2. *Infrared neural stimulation*

In the visible spectrum, the water absorption coefficient is low, but in biological materials, such as protein, oxygenated and de-oxygenated hemoglobin, and melanin it is high. In the near to mid-infrared (NIR) radiation, $\lambda = 2$ to $10\ \mu m$ water is increasingly absorptive (Figure 4). Activation of peripheral nerves has been observed when wavelengths of 2.1 μm and 4 μm are applied to the nerve through a fiber optic cable positioned immediately within a millimeter of the nerve [120, 164, 165]. As with electromagnetic stimulation, it is the generation of current across the membrane that produces an action potential. The exact mechanisms generating current, however, are not known. The leading hypothesis is localized time dependent change in temperature. There is a balance between the power required to activate the nerve and that which causes heat ablation of the tissue. The advantage of the 2.1 and 4 μm wavelengths is that it is in a local valley of the absorption spectrum, producing the maximum safety factor of about 5 between activation and ablation energy.

Heat has several potential mechanisms of action and the exact mechanism is yet to be determined [120]. One is the heat sensitive TRPv channel [5]. Another is heat-mediated change in membrane thickness [132] which causes a change in the capacitance of the membrane. Development of the traditional cable equation in the electromagnetic development earlier assumes the membrane thickness, and hence the membrane capacitance, is constant. The membrane current through the capacitor is more correctly written as $= \frac{d(CV)}{dt}$. If the capacitance is also time variant the capacitive term of membrane current is actually

$$I = C\frac{d(V)}{dt} + V\frac{d(C)}{dt}$$

Heat, then, causes a current flow across the membrane. This would also explain why the time course of the heating of the tissue appears related to the activation [132]. A slow change in temperature is not sufficient to cause or sustain excitation and a sustained elevation in temperature can block the cell propagation [34]. Other possible mechanisms of action include mechanical stresses in the membrane by either expansion from heat or optical shock [165], transient intracellular calcium release [33], and nanoporation of the cell membrane with changes in internal cell signaling [9].

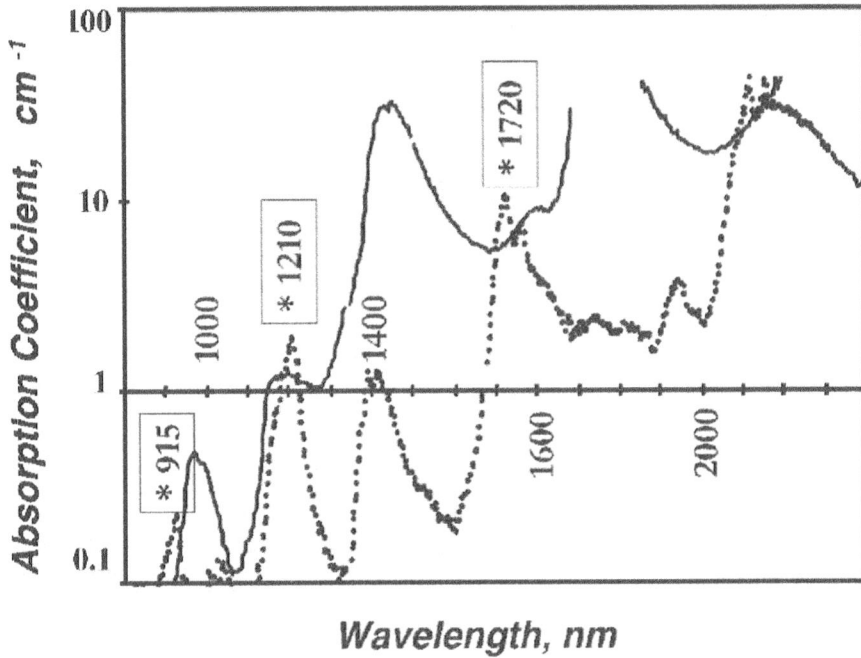

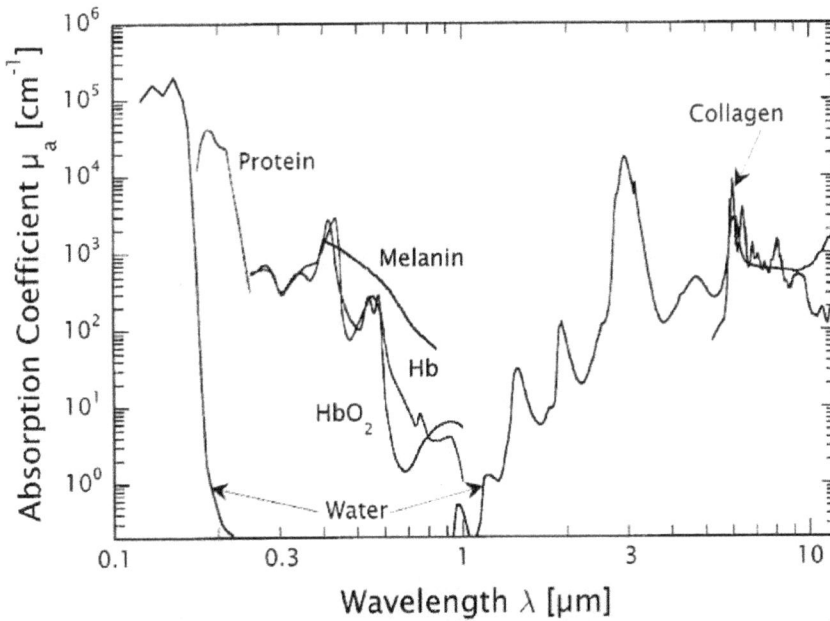

Fig. 4. Absorption spectrum of water (top) and various biological tissues (bottom). From [7, 154].

Each of these mechanisms probably contributes to the membrane behavior and ultimately initiation of an action potential. Also contributing to the membrane behavior is a change in the rate constants of the channel dynamics. According to the Arrhenius relationship, the rate of the channel dynamics is correlated with the temperature of the system. This can be expressed as the Q_{10} relationship of rates,

$$Q_{10} = \left(\frac{R_2}{R_1}\right)^{10/(T_2-T_1)}$$

Q_{10} values for infrared nerve stimulation (INS) have been measured to be around 2.6 for the sodium channel [78]. This is not sufficient alone to cause activation [107], but will contribute to the change in dynamics.

Several applications of optical radiation stimulation have been demonstrated [120] including auditory applications [55, 56, 142], activation of peripheral nerves [108, 164, 166], and modulation of excitation in combined electrical and INS stimulation paradigms [36]. Functional application of INS of the peripheral nervous system, however, is difficult. Experiments in peripheral nerve show about 81% of nerves testing in a series of rabbits are responsive to INS. Of those responding, only a maximum of about 9% muscle activation was possible with INS alone. Models suggest that the penetration depth of the NIR radiation, myelin, and stochastic distribution of nodes of Ranvier affect the efficacy. Studies in unmyelinated fibers in Aplysia show both excitatory and inhibitory effects of INS [34, 35].

3.3. *Optogenetic stimulation*

Infrared neural stimulation is dependent on the optical properties of the tissue and dissipation of energy around the tissue. Optogenetic stimulation [15] is a different approach. Rather than relying of the naturally occurring channels of the neuron, optogenetics first transfects a cell with genes to produce opsin or other optically active channels derived from other organism. The opening and closing of the optically-active channels is dependent on the wavelength and energy of incident light. The cable equation describing the cell behavior is the same as for electromagnetic stimulation, but the I_{ionic} term adds currents for the optically-active channels [8, 42]. The goal is to add non-endogenous switches into the cell that respond to unique signals that are not normally present to the cell. These artificial signals are manipulated to control or modify the cell behavior.

Optogenetics has had a significant impact on neuroscience [81, 157]. Using a library of opsins, each responsive to different wavelengths of light and targeted delivery vectors, different cells can be uniquely labeled with optically responsive channels of various wavelengths. Similarly, several channels, each responsive to different wavelength can be engineered into each cell. Incident laser radiation can be targeted by wavelength to each engineered channel coded into a subset of axons. It is even possible to selectively encode excitatory channels with one wavelength and inhibitory channels with another for selective activation or inhibition, respectively. With optogenetic stimulation (and NIR) there is no electrochemical interface. Thus, unlike electrical stimulation that requires charge-balanced pulses, light can be applied continuously. The potential drawbacks to optical stimulation include the necessity of genetic modification, potential heat-related tissue damage, effects of electroporation, and low total energy efficiency.

Optogenetic techniques are powerful in neuroscience with many studies demonstrating its use in the CNS, typical for modulation of circuit activity focal excitation of small brain regions. In peripheral nerve stimulation for sensation, motor control, or visceral function, the goal is to activate fibers for each target organ selectively. While attention to peripheral nervous system has been far less that CNS, control of motor function of a single muscle has been shown in freely moving animals [144]. The optogenetic technique is more selective for stimulation of a single muscle compared to a single-contact, circumferential electrode and is similar to the selectivity of multi-contact circumferential [76, 140, 147] and penetrating [18, 51, 99, 169] electrodes. When a unique optogenetic channel responsive to unique wavelengths can be inserted into each muscle, then optogenetic techniques may achieve the potential of multiple-channel electrical stimulation interfaces.

3.4. *Ultrasound neuromodulation*

Ultrasound frequency range is from about 0.1 to 3 MHz, corresponding to wavelength between 0.5 and 15 mm. Like all waves, an array of ultrasound waves can be focused via acoustic lenses to place energy on a specific, localized volume of tissue, typically about 5 to 150 mm in diameter. This can be sufficient to focus on a nerve, but not likely to produce small regions of selectivity within the nerve. The mechanisms of activation are not known, but appear to be similar to those of infrared stimulation. Specifically, local heating from absorbed acoustic energy or changes in membrane capacitance associated with ultrasound induced cavitation. Ultrasound is also a non-contact stimulation modality and can be applied externally. With focusing, it is possible to target specific nerves. For a review of ultrasound techniques and theory, see Naor et al., [100].

4. Delivery of Peripheral Nerve Stimulation

The previous sections reported on forms of energy that can cause peripheral nerve stimulation. In this section, approaches to delivery of stimulation energy are presented. Generally, the delivery device is considered the peripheral nerve interface. This section is a survey of the important considerations related to delivering stimulation with illustrative examples of approaches, not an exhaustive treatment of the topic. For a more complete discussion of the basic principles of the neural interface and further examples, see [102, 124, 149].

4.1. *Location selection*

The location of a peripheral interface can range from as close as directly next to axons within the fascicles of the nerve to as far away as the surface of the skin. Factors that affect the choice of interface location include the proximity to the neuron required for neuron activation, the invasiveness that is acceptable by clinician and patient, the risk/benefit ratio of a chosen approach, and available technology to create the interface. The electric field approaches to stimulation are the most developed and will be the focus of this section. Most of the principles of an interface that are presented for electrical stimulation are equally relevant for optical stimulation, but the delivery technology is a fiber optic cable rather than an electrical wire.

Proximity to the neurons. Generally, the closer the interface is to the nerve and axons, the higher the degree of selectivity, the less energy required, and the better the functional performance. Theoretically, multiple stimulating electrodes inside a peripheral nerve fascicle can only be considered unique for stimulation if they are separated by about 250 μm [125] because of the stochastic nature of the distribution of axon diameters and nodes of Ranvier. Optical fibers need to be close to the target fibers to avoid scattering and absorption of the incident optical energy in the surrounding tissue.

There is a trade-off between capability of the electrode and invasiveness. Electrodes external to the body are not likely to interact with individual axons or even individual fascicles. Only in favorable anatomical arrangements with a single nerve close to the surface, such as the common peroneal nerve at the knee, can an external electrode stimulate a single whole nerve selectively. The most significant advantage of external electrodes is that do not require surgery to implement. Consequently, they can be used for a short time, removed, and reapplied for later use.

The other end of invasiveness is to place the electrode directly next to the axons within the fascicles. Placement of the electrode requires penetration of the perineurium and within the protected environment of the endoneurium. The blood nerve barrier, tissue perfusion, chemical and osmotic balances need to be considered and managed in development of these interfaces.

Risk-Benefit Ratio. The risk associated with the interface needs to be balanced with the benefit expected. In general, an electrode should be placed at the least invasive point possible to accomplish the necessary function. For example, if the goal is to activate a single muscle, an electrode on the peripheral nerve or even on the surface of the skin may be a better choice than in the portion of the motor cortex responsible for the motor action. Both the design complexity and risk of the electrode generally increase with increasing levels of invasiveness.

Material and processing technology. There are several interdependent factors to consider when choosing the electrode materials, including electrode size, material mechanical characteristics, electrode durability, number of contacts, connecting leads to the electrode, and electrochemistry. The ideal electrode would approximate the size of the neurons, have mechanical properties equivalent to the neural tissue, function reliably for the remainder of the user's lifetime, have one contact for each neuron, not require any leads external to the electrode, and neither corrode, introduce foreign molecules to the environment, nor cause oxidation or reduction reactions. Unfortunately, the technology to achieve this perfect combination of properties is yet to be realized. Therefore, the balance of the characteristics will be ultimately determined by the application. In general, there are a few guiding principles.

First, electrochemical safety at the interface must be maintained. This becomes more challenging as the surface area of the electrode decreases for smaller electrodes. Second, more invasive electrodes should be smaller, mechanically matched, and durable. Third, the number of connecting leads should be kept to the smallest possible number.

4.2. *Tissue Response*

The tissue response is divided into the conformational changes in the tissue and the cellular and inflammatory response. The conformational changes are induced by the forces applied by the interface to the neural tissue. The cellular and inflammatory response is caused by any device or foreign object placed in the body or any procedure that disturbs the tissues. Similarly, devices remaining in the body will elicit a chronic tissue response. The two most important factors that control the tissue response are the forces applied to the tissue by the interface and the surface chemistry of the materials that contact the tissue, including the molecular and protein attachments to the surface. The interface design should minimize and control the response as much as possible.

In addition to the surface chemistry and molecular modification of the material of the interface, the mechanical design of the interface is important. The mechanical aspects can be divided into macromechanics and micromechanics. Macromechanics refer to the gross effects of forces applied by an interface to the tissue. The interface should avoid or minimize physical damage to the neural tissue, both during implant and during long-term implementation. The interface must not significantly reduce blood flow and tissue perfusion. Blood flow is sensitive to applied forces. The interface should not raise pressure in the tissue above 20 to 60 mmHg. These pressures correspond to the initial reduction and completely restriction of blood flow, respectively [126]. The second design principle is to keep the strain in the tissue below 8 to 15%, which correspond to initial reduction and complete restriction of blood flow, respectively [80].

Micromechanical effects refer to the stress and strain applied directly to the cells. Typically, glia are responsive to the micromechanical perturbation induced by the interface. Small strains in cell membranes cause ion flow, typically Ca^{2+}, in mechnosensitive channels. The influx of calcium, especially if excessive and continuous, up-regulates several of the pro-inflammatory cytokine cascades and promotes continual inflammatory response until the mechanical irritation is minimized or removed. Consequently, to maintain close long-term proximity to neurons or direct connection to neurons, the electrode's mechanical properties should match the tissue's mechanical properties.

4.3.   *Other design considerations*

These are not critical to the success of the interface, but will influence the eventual patient acceptance and clinical application of a given interface if it is intended for human application.

Implant procedure. One of the significant barriers to neuromodulation therapies over traditional pharmacological therapy is the perceived invasiveness and complication of the neuromodulation systems [31]. They require the implantation of at least one neural interface and usually at least one permanent device to deliver the stimulation pulses. The most significant risk of most neuromodulation systems is from the implant procedure, and specifically of the neural interface. The optimal electrode design, therefore, would minimize the invasiveness of the implant procedure.

Removability. Despite years of research and the generally good performance of neural interfaces, a design should consider the potential need to remove the electrode. In particular, the design of an interface should ideally allow for its removal without damage or disruption of the neural tissue with which it was interfaced and for deployment of a replacement interface. This is relatively straightforward with interfaces fabricated from inert materials such as poly(dimethylsiloxane) (PDMS) or poly(perfluoroalyoxyethylene) (PFA). However, as interface research increasingly explores other biomimetic and biointegrated systems designed for direct molecular attachment to and ingrowth of neurons, removal without damage of the neurons becomes difficult or impossible. The effects of this integration need to be considered.

5. Neural Interface Electrode Examples

This is not an exhaustive list of available interfaces. Rather, it demonstrates several interfaces that represent different design choices that balance the design constraints of peripheral nerve stimulation interfaces.

5.1. *Surface electrodes*

Owing to their simplicity and negligible risk, surface electrodes applied to the skin are widely used in many neuromodulation applications and clinical diagnostic procedures, ranging from ECG and EEG measurement to transcutaneous electrical nerve stimulation (TENS) for pain management and physical therapy [83]. Patch electrodes are large surface area electrodes that adhere to the skin and typically have a conductive gel to enhance the ion flow for stimulation, reduce the electrical impedance of the skin, produce uniform current distribution, and help prevent electrical burns that could result from high current concentrations. Since the currents pass through the skin, sensory nerves are also activated and this can cause painful sensation prior to full activation of the muscles. Many uses of patch stimulating electrodes are for short term therapy, such as after a stroke [28, 133, 167] or as a temporary non-invasive neuroprosthesis [23, 52, 114, 115, 134]. Electrodes are placed on the skin, over the nerve entry point (motor point) of the target muscles. High stimulating currents (25 – 100 mA) are required to activate the muscles [115].

Obstacles to widespread use of surface electrodes for peripheral nerve stimulation include poor target selectivity, especially for small or deep targets, inconsistent stimulation due to variations in electrode placement and impractical donning time [84, 160].

5.2. *Organ-based electrodes*

The most distal neural interfaces are located directly at the point where the peripheral nerve innervates the organ of interest. The distal placement virtually guarantees activation of the target organ. Muscle-based interfaces, for example, are placed at the motor points of a muscle to stimulate the nerve, which then activates the muscle. Two common types of muscle-based electrodes are epimysial [44], which are sewn on the surface of the muscle, and intramuscular [4, 90], which are inserted within the muscle (Figure 5A). They must be placed within a few millimeters of the motor point to get effective stimulation with reasonably small stimulation parameters. Typical parameters for stimulation are pulse amplitudes of 2 to 20 mA and pulse widths of 50 to 250 μsec. The challenge for either electrode is a stable anchor to the muscle. The epimysial electrode is typically sewn to the muscle surface. The epimysial electrode implant procedure requires exposure of the muscle, test stimulation of the muscle surface to find the optimal stimulation point, and then surgical stitching of the electrode to the muscle. This typically requires a general anesthesia and open exposure of the muscles. If several muscles are to be implanted, the surgery can be lengthy and it can be challenging to implant on deep or small muscles. Intramuscular electrodes can be implanted via needle. A probe is inserted into the muscle either percutaneously or through a small incision and then manipulated to find the optimal stimulation point (Figure 5B). Then the outer sheath is slid over the probe and the probe is removed. Finally, the electrode is inserted through the sheath to the same location where the probe had been. When the outer sheath is removed, the barbed tip anchors the electrode in the muscle tissue [90].

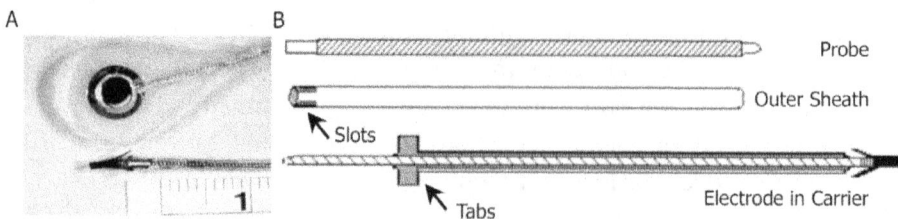

Fig. 5. A: Epimysial and interamuscular electrodes. B: Insertion probes for placing the electrodes.

Many permanent neuroprostheses use implanted muscle-based electrodes connected to an internal stimulator for arm and hand function [27, 58, 60, 61, 89], and standing and walking [30, 62, 145, 150]. Implanted systems eliminate the variability due to day-to-day electrode placement and reduce the number of tasks users must perform prior to the device functioning. Intramuscular electrodes have the potential to be implanted laparoscopically. Minimally invasive surgery is used to implant intramuscular type electrodes for cardiac pacemakers, gastric stimulation [1] and diaphragm pacing in ventilator dependent individuals [32].

Another type of muscle–based electrode that can be implanted minimally invasively is the BION (BIOnic Neuron). The BION integrates the stimulator and the electrode into a single capsule, eliminating the need for leads [24, 79]. The BION has been used clinically to correct footdrop [162] and to treat incontinence [50]. A similar design, the Implantable Myoelectric Sensor (IMES) can record muscle activity for use as a command source [94, 163].

5.3. *Peripheral nerve interfaces*

Peripheral nerve interfaces are classified as either extraneural, interfascicular, intrafascicular, or regeneration depending on their location within the peripheral nerve.

Extraneural. Extraneural electrodes do not penetrate any of the structures of the peripheral nerve. The least invasive extraneural interfaces include electrodes that are placed near the nerve or sewn onto the nerve. These have been referred to as epineural. Examples of this type of interface include an implanted electrode/stimulator placed near the peroneal nerve for treatment of footdrop [135] and a ribbon type electrode that is implanted near the phrenic nerve for diaphragm pacing [43].

Cuff interfaces place contacts as close as possible to the nerve without restricting blood flow to the nerve. The central design parameter for these electrodes related to safety is to keep the intraneural pressure to less than 20 to 40 mmHg [126]. They must account for normal as well as swollen nerves during inflammation. Closed cylinder electrodes, such as the chambered electrode [53] (Figure 6) must allow extra space for nerve swelling and the general design guideline is that the cuff-to-nerve diameter ratio (CNR) is 1.5. The disadvantage of this design is that the contacts may be far from the nerve.

Self-sizing electrodes, such as the spiral [101] or helix [3], allow for swelling by expanding and contracting without increasing intraneural pressure above 20 mmHg (Figure 7). These electrodes maintain tight contact with the nerve and can selectively stimulate small regions of the nerve [45, 46, 48, 136, 139, 140, 153]. Spiral electrodes have demonstrated selective stimulation in the upper extremity of human subjects [91, 111, 112] and have been implemented in standing systems for paraplegic subjects [40, 41, 112, 127, 130]. The chronic effects of these extraneural electrodes are well studied and they have been introduced to several clinical applications [19 – 22, 109, 141, 161].

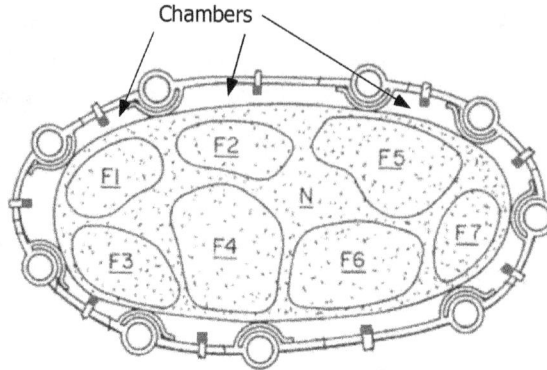

Fig. 6. Chambered extraneural electrode.

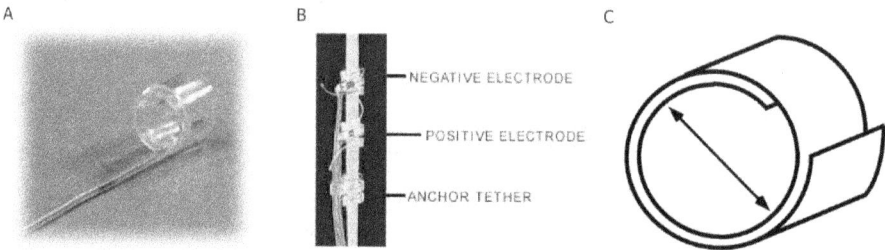

Fig. 7. Spiral and helical self-sizing electrodes.

The cross-section of many peripheral nerves is more oblong than round. Alternate electrode geometries, such as the Flat Interface Nerve Electrode or FINE [76, 147] (Figure 8), optimize the perimeter area, and hence, the interface with the nerve. These interfaces apply small forces to the nerve that are sufficient to change its shape [75, 77, 148], but low enough to not cause nerve damage from occluded blood flow.

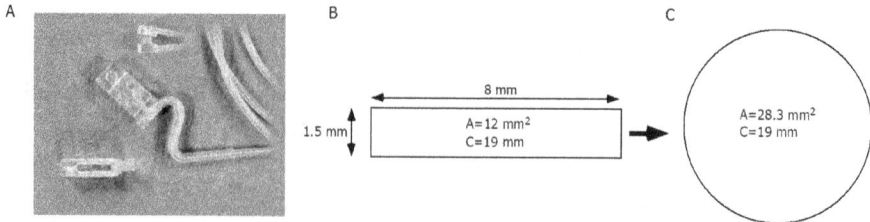

Fig. 8. Flat interface nerve electrode for nerve reshaping.

Placing multiple contacts are placed around and along the nerve enable multipolar electrical stimulation. Multiple contacts along the axon can be implemented to control the second spatial field difference for selective stimulation of small populations of fibers [72 - 74]. Contacts around the nerve active small sections of the cross-section and can be combined to further direct the stimulation field. Micro-magnetic stimulation may be possible by printing circular loops of wire on polyimide based cuff interfaces [2].

Interfascicular. Interfascicular electrodes are designed to gain greater access to the neurons while still not penetrating into the fascicles. The multigroove electrode [63], and the Slowly Penetrating Interfascicular Nerve Electrode (SPINE) [146] are examples of interfascicular electrodes (Figure 9).

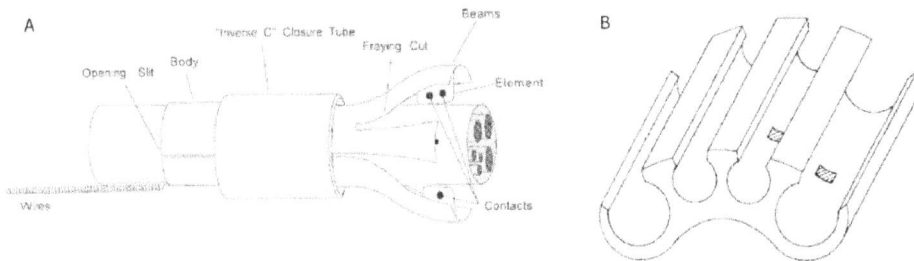

Fig. 9. A: Slowly penetrating nerve electrode. B: Multi-groove electrode.

Intrafascicular. Intrafascicular electrodes place contacts directly inside the fascicle and in contact with the axons. The Longitudinal IntraFascicular Electrode (LIFE) [70, 99, 169] and its variants [69, 82, 143] are essentially very thin wires threaded into a fascicle. The surgeon isolates the fascicles and then inserts each LIFE independently. Thin film (tf-LIFE) arrays [14, 39, 67], have multiple electrodes on a shaft that is inserted through the nerve, placing the contacts into the fascicles (Figure 10A). Similar to the LIFE, the Transverse Intrafascicular Multichannel Electrode (TIME) places a thin array transversely through a fascicle, allowing selective stimulation of subpopulations of axons in the same plane [13]. The Utah Slant Electrode Array (USEA) is an array of up to 100 electrode shanks that can all be inserted simultaneously through the nerve (Figure 10B) [18]. Individual shanks have demonstrated the ability to interact selectively with a small number of axons [17].

Regeneration. The regeneration array [16, 64 - 66] places the ends of a severed nerve on opposite sides of a perpetrated electrode array and allows the axons to regenerate through the array (Figure 11). The array needs to be designed to allow cytokines and soluble factors to communicate between the ends of the nerve. Over time, the chemical signals lead to axon regeneration with some of the axons growing through the holes. Electrodes around the holes then stimulate the individual axons. Axon regeneration has been demonstrated through holes as small as 30 μm in an array with a 30% transparency factor [156].

D. J. Tyler

General Comments. Placement of a peripheral nerve electrode along the length of a nerve is based on the nerve anatomy, surgical accessibility, and selectivity requirements for the neuromodualtion application. To rationally place an electrode and appropriately design its dimensions, a detailed, quantitative, and morphologic knowledge of the peripheral nerve anatomy and fascicular arrangement is required. In general, the nerves are more highly organized more distally. Therefore, as a rule-of-thumb, extraneural electrodes are most effective distally and more proximal locations benefit from more invasive electrodes. The potential benefit of more proximal placement is access to axons to a greater number of muscles using a single electrode. This would imply the need for fewer implant locations and greater function.

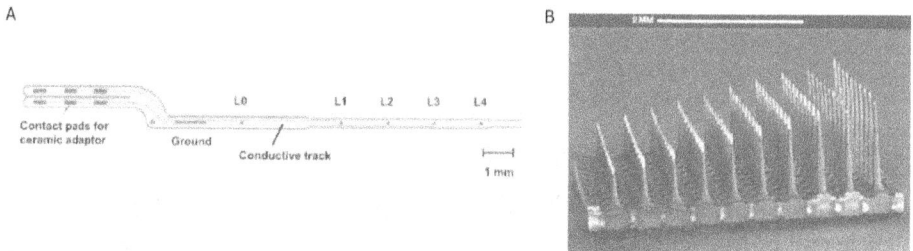

Fig. 10. A: Thin-film longitudinal intrafascicular electrode (tfLIFE). B: Utah slant electrode array (USEA).

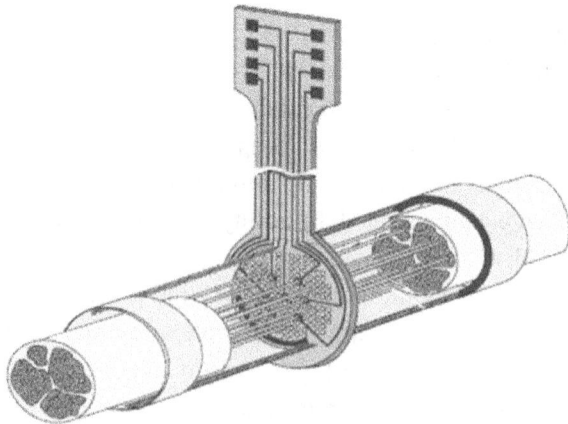

Fig. 11. Regeneration nerve electrode array.

6. Key Points

Bioelectric cells, such as the axons in the peripheral nerve, maintain a membrane potential by a combination of several ionic imbalances across the membrane. The actual membrane voltage is dependent on the permeability of the membrane to each of the ions imbalanced across the membrane.

The permeability is controlled by stimulus responsive protein channels in the membrane. Many types of stimulus responsive channels exist, such as voltage, optical, heat, mechanical, and chemical.

Peripheral nerve stimulation is accomplished by manipulating the channel permeability.

The behavior of a peripheral nerve can be understood by the cable equation.

Electromagnetic stimulation changes the driving function in the cable equation.

Infrared, and possibly ultrasound, stimulation affects mechanically sensitive channels, heat sensitive channels, and changes the capacitance of the membrane.

Optogenetic stimulation, introduces a specifically engineering, non-endogenous channel to the membrane that is responsive to a specific wavelength of light.

Electrical stimulation is the most efficient stimulation approach.

References

1. Abell, T., McCallum, R., Hocking, M., Koch, K., Abrahamsson, H., Leblanc, I., Lindberg, G., Konturek, J., Nowak, T., Quigley, E. M., Tougas, G., and Starkebaum, W. (2003) Gastric electrical stimulation for medically refractory gastroparesis, *Gastroenterology*, **125**(2), 421–428.
2. Accoto, D., Francomano, M. T., Rainer, A., Trombetta, M., Rossini, P. M., and Guglielmelli, E. (2013) An implantable neural interface with electromagnetic stimulation capabilities, *Medical Hypotheses*, **81**(2), 322–327.
3. Agnew, W. F., McCreery, D. B., Yuen, T. G. H., and Bullara, L. A. (1989) Histologic and physiologic evaluation of electrically stimulated peripheral nerve: Considerations for the selection of parameters, *Annals of Biomedical Engineering*, **17**(1), 39–60.
4. Akers, J. M., Peckham, P. H., Keith, M. W., and Merritt, K. (1997) Tissue response to chronically stimulated implanted epimysial and intramuscular electrodes, *IEEE Trans Rehabil Eng*, **5**(2), 207–20.
5. Albert, E. S., Bec, J. M., Desmadryl, G., Chekroud, K., Travo, C., Gaboyard, S., Bardin, F., Marc, I., Dumas, M., Lenaers, G., Hamel, C., Muller, A., and Chabbert, C. (2012) TRPV4 channels mediate the infrared laser-evoked response in sensory neurons, *Journal of Neurophysiology*, **107**(12), 3227–3234.
6. Altman, K. W. and Plonsey, R. (1986) A two-part model for determining the electromagnetic and physiologic behavior of cuff electrode nerve stimulators, *IEEE Transactions on Bio-Medical Engineering*, **33**(3), 285–293.

7. Anderson, R. R., Farinelli, W., Laubach, H., Manstein, D., Yaroslavsky, A. N., Gubeli, J., 3rd, Jordan, K., Nei, G. R., Shinn, M., Chandler, W., Williams, G. P., Benson, S. V., Douglas, D. R., and Dylla, H. F. (2006) Selective photothermolysis of lipid-rich tissues: A free electron laser study, *Lasers in Surgery and Medicine*, **38**(10), 913–919.

8. Arlow, R. L., Foutz, T. J., and McIntyre, C. C. (2013) Theoretical principles underlying optical stimulation of myelinated axons expressing channelrhodopsin-2, *Neuroscience*, **248**, 541–551. http://doi.org/10.1016/j.neuroscience.2013.06.031

9. Beier, H. T., Tolstykh, G. P., Musick, J. D., Thomas, R. J., and Ibey, B. L. (2014) Plasma membrane nanoporation as a possible mechanism behind infrared excitation of cells, *Journal of Neural Engineering*, **11**(6), 66006.

10. Bhadra, N. and Kilgore, K. L. (2005) High-frequency electrical conduction block of mammalian peripheral motor nerve, *Muscle Nerve*, **32**(6), 782–790.

11. Bhadra, N., Lahowetz, E. A., Foldes, S. T., and Kilgore, K. L. (2007) Simulation of high-frequency sinusoidal electrical block of mammalian myelinated axons, *J Comput Neurosci*, **22**(3), 313–326.

12. Bonmassar, G., Lee, S. W., Freeman, D. K., Polasek, M., Fried, S. I., and Gale, J. T. (2012) Microscopic magnetic stimulation of neural tissue, *Nature Communications*, **3**, 921.

13. Boretius, T., Badia, J., Pascual-Font, A., Schuettler, M., Navarro, X., Yoshida, K., and Stieglitz, T. (2010) A transverse intrafascicular multichannel electrode (TIME) to interface with the peripheral nerve. *Biosensors and Bioelectronics*, **26**(1), 62–69.

14. Bossi, S., Kammer, S., Dörge, T., Menciassi, A., Hoffmann, K. P., and Micera, S. (2009) An implantable microactuated intrafascicular electrode for peripheral nerves, *IEEE Transactions on Biomedical Engineering*, **56**(11), 2701–2706.

15. Boyden, E. S., Zhang, F., Bamberg, E., Nagel, G., and Deisseroth, K. (2005) Millisecond-timescale, genetically targeted optical control of neural activity, *Nature Neuroscience*, **8**(9), 1263–1268.

16. Bradley, R. M., Smoke, R. H., Akin, T., and Najafi, K. (1992) Functional regeneration of glossopharyngeal nerve through micromachined sieve electrode arrays, *Brain Research*, **594**(1), 84–90.

17. Branner, A., Stein, R. B., Fernandez, E., Aoyagi, Y., and Normann, R. A. (2004) Long-term stimulation and recording with a penetrating microelectrode array in cat sciatic nerve, *IEEE Transactions on Biomedical Engineering*, **51**(1), 146–157.

18. Branner, A., Stein, R. B., and Normann, R. A. (2001) Selective stimulation of cat sciatic nerve using an array of varying-length microelectrodes, *Journal of Neurophysiology*, **85**(4), 1585–1594.

19. Broniatowski, M., Grundfest-Broniatowski, S., Hadley, A. J., Shah, N. S., Barbu, A. M., Phillipbar, S. A., Strohl, K. P., Tucker, H. M., and Tyler, D. J. (2010) Improvement of respiratory compromise through abductor reinnervation and pacing in a patient with bilateral vocal fold impairment, *Laryngoscope*, **120**(1).

20. Broniatowski, M., Grundfest-Broniatowski, S., Tyler, D. J., Scolieri, P., Abbass, F., Tucker, H. M., and Brodsky, S. (2001) Dynamic laryngotracheal closure for aspiration: a preliminary report, *Laryngoscope*, **111**(11), 2032–2040.

21. Broniatowski, M., Grundfest-Broniatowski, S., Zobenica, N. S., and Tyler, D. J. (2008) Artificial manipulation of voice in the human by an implanted stimulator, *Laryngoscope*, **118**(10), 1889-1893.

22. Broniatowski, M., Moore, N. Z., Grundfest-Broniatowski, S., Tucker, H. M., Lancaster, E., Krival, K., Hadley, A. J., and Tyler, D. J. (2010) Paced glottic closure for controlling aspiration pneumonia in patients with neurologic deficits of various causes, *Annals of Otology, Rhinology and Laryngology*, *119*(3), 141-149.

23. Burridge, J. H., Taylor, P. N., Hagan, S. A., Wood, D. E., and Swain, I. D. (1997) The effects of common peroneal stimulation on the effort and speed of walking: a randomized controlled trial with chronic hemiplegic patients, *Clin Rehabil*, 11(3), 201–210.

24. Carbunaru, R., Whitehurst, T., Jaax, K., Koff, J., and Makous, J. (2004) Rechargeable battery-powered bion/spl reg/microstimulators for neuromudulation, *Proceedings 26th Annual International Conference of the Engineering in Medicine and Biology Society*, 2, 4193–4196.

25. Cheng, D. K. (1989) *Field and Wave Electromagnetics* (2nd ed.), (Addison-Wesley Publishing Company, Reading, MA).

26. Cohen, L. G., Roth, B. J., Nilsson, J., Dang, N., Panizza, M., Bandinelli, S., Friauf, W., and Hallett, M. (1990) Effects of coil design on delivery of focal magnetic stimulation. Technical considerations, *Electroencephalography and Clinical Neurophysiology*, 75(4), 350–357.

27. Crago, P. E., Memberg, W. D., Usey, M. K., Keith, M. W., Kirsch, R. F., Chapman, G. J., Katorgi, M. A., and Perreault, E. J. (1998) An elbow extension neuroprosthesis for individuals with tetraplegia, *IEEE Trans Rehabil Eng*, 6(1), 1–6.

28. Daly, J. J., Hogan, N., Perepezko, E. M., Krebs, H. I., Rogers, J. M., Goyal, K. S., Dohring, M. E., Fredrickson, E., Nethery, J., and Ruff, R. L. (2005) Response to upper-limb robotics and functional neuromuscular stimulation following stroke, *J Rehabil Res Dev*, 42(6), 723–736.

29. Dario, P., Garzella, P., Toro, M., Micera, S., Alavi, M., Meyer, U., Valderrama, E., Sebastiani, L., Ghelarducci, B., Mazzoni, C., and Pastacaldi, P. (1998) Neural interfaces for regenerated nerve stimulation and recording, *IEEE Transactions on Rehabilitation Engineering*, 6(4), 353–363.

30. Davis, J. A., Triolo, R. J., Uhlir, J., Bieri, C., Rohde, L., Lissy, D., and Kukke, S. (2001) Preliminary performance of a surgically implanted neuroprosthesis for standing and transfers-- where do we stand? *J Rehabil Res Dev*, 38(6), 609–617.

31. Di Pino, G., Denaro, L., Vadalà, G., Marinozzi, A., Tombini, M., Ferreri, F., Papalia, R., Accoto, D., Guglielmelli, E., Di Lazzaro, V., and Denaro, V. (2014) Invasive neural interfaces: the perspective of the surgeon, *The Journal of Surgical Research*, 188(1), 77–87.

32. DiMarco, A. F., Onders, R. P., Kowalski, K. E., Miller, M. E., Ferek, S., and Mortimer, J. T. (2002) Phrenic nerve pacing in a tetraplegic patient via intramuscular diaphragm electrodes, *American Journal of Respiratory and Critical Care Medicine*, 166(12 Pt 1), 1604–6.

33. Dittami, G. M., Rajguru, S. M., Lasher, R. A., Hitchcock, R. W., and Rabbitt, R. D. (2011) Intracellular calcium transients evoked by pulsed infrared radiation in neonatal cardiomyocytes, *The Journal of Physiology*, 589(Pt 6), 1295–306.

34. Duke, A. R., Jenkins, M. W., Lu, H., McManus, J. M., Chiel, H. J., and Jansen, E. D. (2013) Transient and selective suppression of neural activity with infrared light, *Scientific Reports*, 3, 2600.

35. Duke, A. R., Lu, H., Jenkins, M. W., Chiel, H. J., and Jansen, E. D. (2012) Spatial and temporal variability in response to hybrid electro-optical stimulation, *Journal of Neural Engineering*, 9(3), 36003.

36. Duke, A. R., Peterson, E., Mackanos, M. A., Atkinson, J., Tyler, D., and Jansen, E. D. (2012) Hybrid electro-optical stimulation of the rat sciatic nerve induces force generation in the plantarflexor muscles, *Journal of Neural Engineering*, 9(6), 66006.

37. Eldaief, M. C., Press, D. Z., and Pascual-Leone, A. (2013) Transcranial magnetic stimulation in neurology A review of established and prospective applications, *Neurology: Clinical Practice*, **3**(6), 519–526.

38. Fang, Z. P. and Mortimer, J. T. (1991) Selective activation of small motor axous by quasitrapezoidal current pulses, *IEEE Trans Biomed Eng*, **38**(2), 168–174.

39. Farina, D., Yoshida, K., Stieglitz, T., and Koch, K. P. (2008) Multichannel thin-film electrode for intramuscular electromyographic recordings, *J Appl Physiol*, **104**(3), 821–827.

40. Fisher, L. E., Tyler, D. J., Anderson, J. S., and Triolo, R. J. (2009) Chronic stability and selectivity of four-contact spiral nerve-cuff electrodes in stimulating the human femoral nerve, *Journal of Neural Engineering*, **6**(4), 46010.

41. Fisher, L. E., Tyler, D. J., and Triolo, R. J. (2013) Optimization of selective stimulation parameters for multi-contact electrodes, *Journal of Neuroengineering and Rehabilitation*, **10**, 25.

42. Foutz, T. J., Arlow, R. L., and McIntyre, C. C. (2012) Theoretical principles underlying optical stimulation of a channelrhodopsin-2 positive pyramidal neuron, *Journal of Neurophysiology*, **107**(12), 3235–3245.

43. Glenn, W. W. and Phelps, M. L. (1985) Diaphragm pacing by electrical stimulation of the phrenic nerve, *Neurosurgery*, **17**(6), 974–984.

44. Grandjean, P. A. and Mortimer, J. T. (1986) Recruitment properties of monopolar and bipolar epimysial electrodes, *Ann Biomed Eng*, **14**(1), 53–66.

45. Grill, W. M. (2015) Model-based analysis and design of waveforms for efficient neural stimulation, in ed. Bestmann, S., *Progress in Brain Research*, vol. 222, (Elsevier, Amsterdam).

46. Grill, W. M., and Mortimer, J. T. (1996) The effect of stimulus pulse duration on selectivity of neural stimulation, *IEEE Transactions on Biomedical Engineering*, **43**(2), 161–166.

47. Grill, W. M., and Mortimer, J. T. (1997) Inversion of the current-distance relationship by transient depolarization, *IEEE Trans Biomed Eng*, **44**(1), 1–9.

48. Grill, W. M., and Mortimer, J. T. (1998) Stability of the input – output properties of nerve cuff stimulating electrodes, *Rehabilitation*, **6**(4), 364–373.

49. Grinberg, Y., Schiefer, M. A., Tyler, D. J., and Gustafson, K. J. (2008) Fascicular perineurium thickness, size, and position affect model predictions of neural excitation, *IEEE Trans Neural Syst Rehabil Eng*, **16**(6), 572–81.

50. Groen, J., Amiel, C., and Bosch, J. L. H. R. (2005) Chronic pudendal nerve neuromodulation in women with idiopathic refractory detrusor overactivity incontinence: results of a pilot study with a novel minimally invasive implantable mini-stimulator, *Neurourology and Urodynamics*, **24**(3), 226–30.

51. Harreby, K. R., Kundu, A., Yoshida, K., Boretius, T., Stieglitz, T., and Jensen, W. (2014) Subchronic stimulation performance of transverse intrafascicular multichannel electrodes in the median nerve of the Göttingen minipig, *Artificial Organs*, **39**(2), E36-48.

52. Hines, A. E., Crago, P. E., and Billian, C. (1995) Hand opening by electrical stimulation in patients with spastic hemiplegia, *IEEE Trans Rehabil Eng*, **3**(2), 193–205.

53. Hoffer, J. A., Chen, Y., Strange, K. D., and Christensen, P. R. (1998) Nerve cuff having one or more isolated chambers, *US Patent* 5,824,027.

54. Hudak, E. M., Mortimer, J. T., Martin, H. B., and al, et. (2010) Platinum for neural stimulation: voltammetry considerations, *Journal of Neural Engineering*, **7**(2), 26005.

55. Izzo, A. D., Suh, E., Pathria, J., Walsh, J. T., Whitlon, D. S., and Richter, C.-P. (2015) Selectivity of neural stimulation in the auditory system: a comparison of optic and electric stimuli, *Journal of Biomedical Optics*, **12**(2), 21008.

56. Izzo, A. D., Walsh, J. T., Jansen, E. D., Bendett, M., Webb, J., Ralph, H., and Richter, C. P. (2007) Optical parameter variability in laser nerve stimulation: A study of pulse duration, repetition rate, and wavelength, *IEEE Transactions on Biomedical Engineering*, **54**(6), 1108–1114.

57. Jezernik, S., Sinkjaer, T., and Morari, M. (2010) Charge and energy minimization in electrical/magnetic stimulation of nervous tissue, *Journal of Neural Engineering*, 7(4), 46004.

58. Keith, M. W., Kilgore, K. L., Peckham, P. H., Wuolle, K. S., Creasey, G., and Lemay, M. (1996) Tendon transfers and functional electrical stimulation for restoration of hand function in spinal cord injury, *J Hand Surg [Am]*, **21**(1), 89–99.

59. Kilgore, K. L., and Bhadra, N. (2004) Nerve conduction block utilising high-frequency alternating current, *Med Biol Eng Comput*, **42**(3), 394–406.

60. Kilgore, K. L., Peckham, P. H., Keith, M. W., Thrope, G. B., Wuolle, K. S., Bryden, A. M., and Hart, R. L. (1997) An implanted upper-extremity neuroprosthesis. Follow-up of five patients, *The Journal of Bone and Joint Surgery. American Volume*, **79**(4), 533–41.

61. Knutson, J. S., Chae, J., Hart, R. L., Keith, M. W., Hoyen, H. A., Harley, M. Y., Hisel, T. Z., Bryden, A. M., Kilgore, K. L., and Peckham, H. (2012) Implanted neuroprosthesis for assisting arm and hand function after stroke: a case study, *Journal of Rehabilitation Research and Development*, **49**(10), 1505–1516.

62. Kobetic, R., Triolo, R. J., Uhlir, J. P., Bieri, C., Wibowo, M., Polando, G., Marsolais, E. B., Davis, J. A., Jr, and Ferguson, K. A. (1999) Implanted functional electrical stimulation system for mobility in paraplegia: a follow-up case report, *IEEE Trans Rehabil Eng*, 7(4), 390–398.

63. Koole, P., Holsheimer, J., Struijk, J. J., and Verloop, A. J. (1997) Recruitment characteristics of nerve fascicles stimulated by a multigroove electrode, *IEEE Trans Rehabil Eng*, **5**(1), 40–50.

64. Kovacs, G. T., Storment, C. W., and Rosen, J. M. (1992) Regeneration microelectrode array for peripheral nerve recording and stimulation, *IEEE Trans Biomed Eng*, **39**(9), 893–902.

65. Lago, N., Ceballos, D., Rodriguez, F. J., Stieglitz, T., and Navarro, X. (2005) Long term assessment of axonal regeneration through polyimide regenerative electrodes to interface the peripheral nerve, *Biomaterials*, **26**(14), 2021–2031.

66. Lago, N., Udina, E., Ramachandran, A., and Navarro, X. (2007) Neurobiological assessment of regenerative electrodes for bidirectional interfacing injured peripheral nerves, *IEEE Trans Biomed Eng*, **54**(6 Pt 1), 1129–1137.

67. Lago, N., Yoshida, K., Koch, K. P., and Navarro, X. (2007) Assessment of biocompatibility of chronically implanted polyimide and platinum intrafascicular electrodes, *IEEE Trans Biomed Eng*, **54**(2), 281–290.

68. Larsson, J. (2007) Electromagnetics from a quasistatic perspective, *American Journal of Physics*, **75**(3), 230.

69. Lawrence, S. M., Dhillon, G. S., and Horch, K. W. (2003) Fabrication and characteristics of an implantable, polymer-based, intrafascicular electrode, *J Neurosci Methods*, **131**(1–2), 9–26.

70. Lefurge, T., Goodall, E., Horch, K., Stensaas, L., and Schoenberg, A. (1991) Chronically implanted intrafascicular recording electrodes, *Ann Biomed Eng*, **19**(2), 197–207.

71. Lepping, P., Schönfeldt-Lecuona, C., Sambhi, R. S., Lanka, S. V. N., Lane, S., Whittington, R., Leucht, S., and Poole, R. (2014) A systematic review of the clinical relevance of repetitive transcranial magnetic stimulation, *Acta Psychiatrica Scandinavica*, **130**(5), 326–341.

72. Lertmanorat, Z. and Durand, D. M. (2004) A novel electrode array for diameter-dependent control of axonal excitability: a Simulation study, *IEEE Transactions on Biomedical Engineering*, **51**(7), 1242–1250.

73. Lertmanorat, Z. and Durand, D. M. (2004) Extracellular voltage profile for reversing the recruitment order of peripheral nerve stimulation: a simulation study, *Journal of Neural Engineering*, **1**(4), 202–211.

74. Lertmanorat, Z., Gustafson, K. J., and Durand, D. M. (2006) Electrode array for reversing the recruitment order of peripheral nerve stimulation: experimental studies, *Annals of Biomedical Engineering*, **34**(1), 152–160.

75. Leventhal, D. K., Cohen, M., and Durand, D. M. (2006) Chronic histological effects of the flat interface nerve electrode, *J Neural Eng*, **3**(2), 102–113.

76. Leventhal, D. K. and Durand, D. M. (2003) Subfascicle stimulation selectivity with the flat interface nerve electrode, *Ann Biomed Eng.*, **31**(6), 643-52.

77. Leventhal, D. K. and Durand, D. M. (2004) Chronic measurement of the stimulation selectivity of the flat interface nerve electrode, *IEEE Transactions on Biomedical Engineering*, **51**(9), 1649–1658.

78. Li, X., Liu, J., Liang, S., Guan, K., An, L., Wu, X., Li, S., and Sun, C. (2013) Temporal modulation of sodium current kinetics in neuron cells by near-infrared laser, *Cell Biochemistry and Biophysics*, **67**(3), 1409–1419.

79. Loeb, G. E., Peck, R. A., Moore, W. H., and Hood, K. (2001) BION system for distributed neural prosthetic interfaces, *Med Eng Phys*, **23**(1), 9–18.

80. Lundborg, G. and Rydevik, B. (1973) Effects of stretching the tibial nerve of the rabbit. A preliminary study of the intraneural circulation and the barrier function of the perineurium, *J Bone Joint Surg Br*, **55**(2), 390–401.

81. Lüscher, C., Pascoli, V., and Creed, M. (2015) Optogenetic dissection of neural circuitry: from synaptic causalities to blue prints for novel treatments of behavioral diseases, *Current Opinion in Neurobiology*, **35**, 95–100.

82. Malmstrom, J. A., McNaughton, T. G., and Horch, K. W. (1998) Recording properties and biocompatibility of chronically implanted polymer-based intrafascicular electrodes, *Annals of Biomedical Engineering*, **26**(6), 1055–1064.

83. Marchand, S., Charest, J., Li, J., Chenard, J. R., Lavignolle, B., and Laurencelle, L. (1993) Is TENS purely a placebo effect? A controlled study on chronic low back pain, *Pain*, **54**(1), 99–106.

84. Marsolais, E. B. and Kobetic, R. (1983) Functional walking in paralyzed patients by means of electrical stimulation, *Clin Orthop Relat Res*, **175**, 30–36.

85. McCreery, D. B., Agnew, W. F., Yuen, T. G. H., and Bullara, L. (1990) Charge density and charge per phase as cofactors in neural injury induced by electrical stimulation, *IEEE Transactions on Biomedical Engineering*, **37**(10), 996–1001.

86. McCreery, D. B., Agnew, W. F., Yuen, T. G. H., and Bullara, L. A. (1992) Damage in peripheral nerve from continuous electrical stimulation: Comparison of two stimulus waveforms, *Medical and Biological Engineering and Computing*, **30**(1), 109–114.

87. McIntyre, C. C. and Grill, W. M. (2002) Extracellular stimulation of central neurons: influence of stimulus waveform and frequency on neuronal output, *J Neurophysiol*, **88**(4), 1592–1604.

88. McIntyre, C. C., Richardson, A. G., and Grill, W. M. (2002) Modeling the excitability of mammalian nerve fibers: influence of afterpotentials on the recovery cycle, *J Neurophysiol*, **87**(2), 995–1006.

89. Memberg, W. D., Crago, P. E., and Keith, M. W. (2003) Restoration of elbow extension via functional electrical stimulation in individuals with tetraplegia, *J Rehabil Res Dev*, **40**(6), 477–486.

90. Memberg, W. D., Peckham, P. H., and Keith, M. W. (1994) A surgically-implanted intramuscular electrode for an implantable neuromuscular stimulation system, *IEEE Trans Neural Syst Rehabil Eng*, **2**(2), 80–91.

91. Memberg, W. D., Polasek, K. H., Hart, R. L., Bryden, A. M., Kilgore, K. L., Nemunaitis, G. A., Hoyen, H. A., Keith, M.W., and Kirsch, R. F. (2014) Implanted neuroprosthesis for restoring arm and hand function in people with high level tetraplegia, *Archives of Physical Medicine and Rehabilitation*, **95**(6), 1201–1211.

92. Merrill, D. R. (2014) Materials considerations of implantable neuroengineering devices for clinical use, *Current Opinion in Solid State and Materials Science*, **18**(6), 329-336

93. Merrill, D. R., Bikson, M., and Jefferys, J. G. R. (2005) Electrical stimulation of excitable tissue: design of efficacious and safe protocols, *Journal of Neuroscience Methods*, **141**(2), 171–198.

94. Merrill, D. R., Lockhard, J., Troyk, P. R., Weir, R. F., and Hankin, D. L. (2011) Development of an implantable myoelectric sensor for advanced prosthesis control, *Artificial Organs*, **35**(3), 249–252.

95. Moffitt, M. A., McIntyre, C. C., and Grill, W. M. (2004) Prediction of myelinated nerve fiber stimulation thresholds: limitations of linear models, *IEEE Trans Biomed Eng*, **51**(2), 229–236.

96. Mogyoros, I., Kiernan, M. C., and Burke, D. (1996) Strength-duration properties of human peripheral nerve, *Brain*, **119**(2), 439–447.

97. Mortimer, J. T. and Bhadra, N. (2004) Peripheral nerve and muscle stimulation, in eds Horch, K. W. and Dhillon, G. S., *Neuroprosthetics: Theory and Practice*, (World Scientific, Singapore).

98. Nagarajan, S. S., Durand, D. M., and Warman, E. N. (1993) Effects of induced electric fields on finite neuronal structures: a stimulation study, *IEEE Trans. Biomed. Eng.*, **40**(92), 1175–1188.

99. Nannini, N. and Horch, K. (1991) Muscle recruitment with intrafascicular electrodes, *IEEE Trans Biomed Eng*, **38**(8), 769–776.

100. Naor, O., Krupa, S., and Shoham, S. (2016) Ultrasonic neuromodulation, *Journal of Neural Engineering*, **13**(3), 31003.

101. Naples, G., Mortimer, J., Scheiner, A., and Sweeney, J. D. (1988) A spiral nerve cuff electrode for peripheral nerve stimulation, *IEEE Trans Biomed Eng*, **35** (11), 905-916.

102. Navarro, X., Krueger, T. B., Lago, N., Micera, S., Stieglitz, T., and Dario, P. (2005) A critical review of interfaces with the peripheral nervous system for the control of neuroprostheses and hybrid bionic systems, *Journal of the Peripheral Nervous System*, **10**(3), 229–258.

103. Nicholls, J. G., Martin, A. R., and Wallace, B. G. (1992) *From Neuron to Brain* (3rd ed.), (Sinauer Associates, Inc., Sunderland, MA).

104. Park, H., Seol, J., Ku, J., and Kim, S. (2015) Computational study on the thermal effects of implantable magnetic stimulation based on planar coils, *IEEE Transactions on Biomedical Engineering*, **63**(1), 1–1.

105. Park, H.-J., Bonmassar, G., Kaltenbach, J. a, Machado, A. G., Manzoor, N. F., and Gale, J. T. (2013) Activation of the central nervous system induced by micro-magnetic stimulation, *Nature Communications*, **4**, 2463.

106. Peterson, E. J., Izad, O., and Tyler, D. J. (2011) Predicting myelinated axon activation using spatial characteristics of the extracellular field, *Journal of Neural Engineering*, **8**(4), 46030.

107. Peterson, E. J. and Tyler, D. J. (2012) Activation using infrared light in a mammalian axon model, In *Proceedings of the Annual International Conference of the IEEE Engineering in Medicine and Biology Society,* **2012**.
108. Peterson, E. J. and Tyler, D. J. (2014) Motor neuron activation in peripheral nerves using infrared neural stimulation, *Journal of Neural Engineering,* **11**(1), 16001.
109. Picaza, J. A., Hunter, S. E., and Cannon, B. W. (1977) Pain suppression by peripheral nerve stimulation. Chronic effects of implanted devices, *Appl Neurophysiol,* **40**(2–4), 223–234.
110. Polasek, K. H., Hoyen, H. A., Keith, M. W., Kirsch, R. F., and Tyler, D. J. (2009) Stimulation stability and selectivity of chronically implanted multicontact nerve cuff electrodes in the human upper extremity, *IEEE Transactions on Neural Systems and Rehabilitation Engineering,* **17**(5), 428–437.
111. Polasek, K. H., Hoyen, H. A., Keith, M. W., and Tyler, D. J. (2007) Human nerve stimulation thresholds and selectivity using a multi-contact nerve cuff electrode, *IEEE Transactions on Neural Systems and Rehabilitation Engineering,* **15**(1), 76–82.
112. Polasek, K. H., Schiefer, M. A., Pinault, G. C. J., Triolo, R. J., and Tyler, D. J. (2009) Intraoperative evaluation of the spiral nerve cuff electrode on the femoral nerve trunk, *Journal of Neural Engineering,* **6**(6), 66005.
113. Pollak, T. A., Nicholson, T. R., Edwards, M. J., and David, A. S. (2014) A systematic review of transcranial magnetic stimulation in the treatment of functional (conversion) neurological symptoms, *Journal of Neurology, Neurosurgery, and Psychiatry,* **85**(2), 191–197.
114. Popovic, D., Stojanovic, A., Pjanovic, A., Radosavljevic, S., Popovic, M., Jovic, S., and Vulovic, D. (1999) Clinical evaluation of the bionic glove, *Arch Phys Med Rehabil,* **80**(3), 299–304.
115. Prochazka, A., Gauthier, M., Wieler, M., and Kenwell, Z. (1997) The bionic glove: an electrical stimulator garment that provides controlled grasp and hand opening in quadriplegia, *Arch Phys Med Rehabil,* **78**(6), 608–14.
116. Rattay, F. (1986) Analysis of models for external stimulation of axons, *IEEE Transactions on Biomedical Engineering,* **33**(10), 974–977.
117. Rattay, F. (1988) Modeling the excitation of fibers under surface electrodes, *IEEE Transactions on Biomedical Engineering,* **35**(3), 199–202.
118. Rattay, F. (1999) The basic mechanism for the electrical stimulation of the nervous system, *Neuroscience,* **89**(2), 335–346.
119. Rattay, F. and Aberham, M. (1993) Modeling axon membranes for functional electrical stimulation, *IEEE Trans Biomed Eng,* **40**(12), 1201–1209.
120. Richter, C.-P., Matic, A. I., Wells, J. D., Jansen, E. D., and Walsh, J. T. (2011) Neural stimulation with optical radiation, *Laser and Photonics Reviews,* **5**(1), 68–80.
121. Robblee, L. S. and T. L. R. (1990) Electrochemical guidelines for selection of protocols and electrode materials for neural stimulation. In eds. Agnew, W. F. and McCreery, D. B., *Neural Prostheses. Fundamental Studies,* (Prentice Hall, Englewood Cliffs, NJ), pp. 25–66.
122. Roth, B. J. and Basser, P. J. (1990) A model of the stimulation of a nerve fiber by electromagnetic induction, *IEEE Transactions on Biomedical Engineering,* **37**(6), 588–597.
123. Ruohonen, J., Ravazzani, P., and Grandori, F. (1998) Functional magnetic stimulation: Theory and coil optimization, *Bioelectrochemistry and Bioenergetics,* **47**(2), 213–219.
124. Rutten, W. L. C. (2002) Selective electrical interfaces with the nervous system, *Annu Rev Biomed Eng,* **4**, 407–452.

125. Rutten, W. L., van Wier, H. J., and Put, J. H. (1991) Sensitivity and selectivity of intraneural stimulation using a silicon electrode array, *IEEE Trans Biomed Eng*, **38**(2), 192–198.

126. Rydevik, B., Lundborg, G., and Bagge, U. (1981) Effects of graded compression on intraneural blood blow. An in vivo study on rabbit tibial nerve, *J Hand Surg [Am]*, **6**(1), 3–12.

127. Schiefer, M. A., Polasek, K. H., Triolo, R. J., Pinault, G. C. J., and Tyler, D. J. (2010) Selective stimulation of the human femoral nerve with a flat interface nerve electrode, *Journal of Neural Engineering*, **7**(2), 26006.

128. Schiefer, M. A., Triolo, R. J., Tyler, D. J., Durand, D. M., and Tyler, D. J. (2006) Models of selective stimulation with a flat interface nerve electrode for standing neuroprosthetic systems, *Annual International Conference of the IEEE Engineering in Medicine and Biology*, **1**, 4639–4642.

129. Schiefer, M. A., Tyler, D. J., and Triolo, R. J. (2011) Probabilistic modeling of selective stimulation of the human sciatic nerve with a flat interface nerve electrode, *Proceedings of the Annual International Conference of the IEEE Engineering in Medicine and Biology Society*, **2011**.

130. Schiefer, M. A., Tyler, D. J., and Triolo, R. J. (2012) Probabilistic modeling of selective stimulation of the human sciatic nerve with a flat interface nerve electrode, *Journal of Computational Neuroscience*, **33**(1), 179-190.

131. Shannon, R. V. (1992) A model of safe levels for electrical stimulation, *IEEE Trans Biomed Eng*, **39**(4), 424–426.

132. Shapiro, M. G., Homma, K., Villarreal, S., Richter, C.-P., and Bezanilla, F. (2012) Infrared light excites cells by changing their electrical capacitance, *Nature Communications*, **3**, 736.

133. Sheffler, L. R., Hennessey, M. T., Naples, G. G., and Chae, J. (2006) Peroneal nerve stimulation versus an ankle foot orthosis for correction of footdrop in stroke: impact on functional ambulation, *Neurorehabil Neural Repair*, **20**(3), 355–360.

134. Snoek, G. J., IJzerman, M. J., in 't Groen, F. A. C. G., Stoffers, T. S., and Zilvold, G. (2000) Use of the NESS Handmaster to restore hand function in tetraplegia: Clinical experiences in ten patients, *Spinal Cord*, **38**, 244–249.

135. Strojnik, P., Acimovic, R., Vavken, E., Simic, V., and Stanic, U. (1987) Treatment of drop foot using an implantable peroneal underknee stimulator, *Scand J Rehabil Med*, **19**(1), 37–43.

136. Sweeney, J. D., Crawford, N. R., and Brandon, T. A. (1995) Neuromuscular stimulation selectivity of multiple-contact nerve cuff electrode arrays, *Med Biol Eng Comput*, **33**(3), 418–425.

137. Sweeney, J. D. and Mortimer, J. T. (1986) An asymmetrie two electrode cuff for generation of unidirectionally propagated action potentials, *IEEE Transactions on Biomedical Engineering*, **33**(6), 541–549.

138. Sweeney, J. D., Mortimer, J. T., and Durand, D. M. (1987) Modeling of mammalian myelinated nerve for functional neuromuscular stimulation, *IEEE 9th Annual Conference of the Engineering in Medicine and Biology Society*, 1577–1578.

139. Tarler, M. D. and Mortimer, J. T. (2003) Comparison of joint torque evoked with monopolar and tripolar-cuff electrodes, *IEEE Trans Neural Syst Rehabil Eng*, **11**(3), 227–235.

140. Tarler, M. D. and Mortimer, J. T. (2004) Selective and independent activation of four motor fascicles using a four contact nerve-cuff electrode, *IEEE Transactions on Neural Systems and Rehabilitation Engineering*, **12**(2), 251–257.

141. Tarver, W. B., George, R. E., Maschino, S. E., Holder, L. K., and Wernicke, J. F. (1992) Clinical experience with a helical bipolar stimulating lead, *Pacing Clin Electrophysiol*, **15**(10 Pt 2), 1545–1556.

142. Teudt, I. U., Maier, H., Richter, C. P., and Kral, A. (2011) Acoustic events and "optophonic" cochlear responses induced by pulsed near-infrared LASER, *IEEE Transactions on Biomedical Engineering*, **58**(6), 1648–1655.

143. Thota, A. K., Kuntaegowdanahalli, S., Starosciak, A. K., Abbas, J. J., Orbay, J., Horch, K. W., and Jung, R. (2015) A system and method to interface with multiple groups of axons in several fascicles of peripheral nerves, *Journal of Neuroscience Methods*, **244**, 78–84.

144. Towne, C., Montgomery, K. L., Iyer, S. M., Deisseroth, K., and Delp, S. L. (2013) Optogenetic control of targeted peripheral axons in freely moving animals, *PLoS ONE*, **8**(8).

145. Triolo, R. J., Liu, M. Q., Kobetic, R., and Uhlir, J. P. (2001) Selectivity of intramuscular stimulating electrodes in the lower limbs, *J Rehabil Res Dev*, **38**(5), 533–44.

146. Tyler, D. J. and Durand, D. M. (1997) A slowly penetrating interfascicular nerve electrode for selective activation of peripheral nerves, *IEEE Transactions on Rehabilitation Engineering*, **5**(1), 51–61.

147. Tyler, D. J. and Durand, D. M. (2002) Functionally selective peripheral nerve stimulation with a flat interface nerve electrode. *IEEE Transactions on Neural Systems Rehabilitation Engineering*, **10**(4), 294–303.

148. Tyler, D. J. and Durand, D. M. (2003) Chronic response of the rat sciatic nerve to the flat interface nerve electrode, *Ann Biomed Eng*, **31**(6), 633–42.

149. Tyler, D. J., and Polasek, K. H. (2009) Electrodes for the neural interface, in eds. Krames, E. S., Peckham, P. H. and Rezai, A. R., *Neuromodulation* (Vol. 1). 2009, (Elsevier, Amsterdam), pp. 181–213.

150. Uhlir, J. P., Triolo, R. J., Davis, J. A., and Bieri, C. (2004) Performance of epimysial stimulating electrodes in the lower extremities of individuals with spinal cord injury, *IEEE Trans Neural Syst Rehabil Eng*, **12**(2), 279–287.

151. Ungar, I. J., Mortimer, J. T., and Sweeney, J. D. (1986) Generation of unidirectionally propagating action-potentials using a monopolar electrode cuff,. *Annals of Biomedical Engineering*, **14**(5), 437–450.

152. Veltink, P. H., van Veen, B. K., Struijk, J. J., Holsheimer, J., and Boom, H. B. (1989) A modeling study of nerve fascicle stimulation, *IEEE Trans Biomed Eng*, **36**(7), 683–692.

153. Veraart, C., Grill, W. M., and Mortimer, J. T. (1993) Selective control of muscle activation with a multipolar nerve cuff electrode, *IEEE Trans Biomed Eng*, **40**(7), 640–653.

154. Vogel, A. and Venugopalan, V. (2003) Mechanisms of pulsed laser ablation of biological tissues, *Chem Rev*, **103**(2), 577-644.

155. Vuckovic, A., Tosato, M., and Struijk, J. J. (2008) A comparative study of three techniques for diameter selective fiber activation in the vagal nerve: anodal block, depolarizing prepulses and slowly rising pulses, *Journal of Neural Engineering*, **5**, 275–286.

156. Wallman, L., Zhang, Y., Laurell, T., and Danielsen, N. (2001) The geometric design of micromachined silicon sieve electrodes influences functional nerve regeneration, *Biomaterials*, **22**(10), 1187–1193.

157. Warden, M. R., Cardin, J. A., and Deisseroth, K. (2014) Optical neural interfaces, *Annu. Rev. Biomed. Eng*, **16**, 103–129.

158. Warman, E. N., Grill, W. M., and Durand, D. (1992) Modeling the effects of electric fields on nerve fibers: determination of excitation thresholds, *IEEE Trans Biomed Eng*, **39**(12), 1244–1254.

159. Grill, W. M. and Mortimer, J. T. (2000) Neural and connective tissue response to long-term implantation of multiple contact nerve cuff electrodes, *Journal of Biomedical Materials Research*, **50**(2), 215–226.

160. Waters, R. L., McNeal, D. R., Faloon, W., and Clifford, B. (1985) Functional electrical stimulation of the peroneal nerve for hemiplegia. Long-term clinical follow-up, *J Bone Joint Surg Am*, **67**(5), 792–793.

161. Waters, R. L., McNeal, D. R., and Perry, J. (1982) Experimental correction of footdrop by electrical stimulation of the peroneal nerve, *J. Bone Joint Surg*, **57A**, 1047–1054.

162. Weber, D. J., Stein, R. B., Chan, K. M., Loeb, G., Richmond, F., Rolf, R., James, K., Chong, S. L. (2005) BIONic WalkAide for correcting foot drop, *IEEE Trans Neural Syst Rehabil Eng*, **13**(2), 242–246.

163. Weir, R. F., Troyk, P. R., DeMichele, G. A., Kerns, D. A., Schorsch, J. F., and Maas, H. (2009) Implantable myoelectric sensors (IMESs) for intramuscular electromyogram recording, *IEEE Trans Biomed Eng*, **56**(1), 159–171.

164. Wells, J., Kao, C., Jansen, E. D., Konrad, P., and Mahadevan-Jansen, A. (2015) Application of infrared light for in vivo neural stimulation, *Journal of Biomedical Optics*, **10**(6), 64003.

165. Wells, J., Kao, C., Konrad, P., Milner, T., Kim, J., Mahadevan-Jansen, A., and Jansen, E. D. (2007) Biophysical mechanisms of transient optical stimulation of peripheral nerve, *Biophysical Journal*, **93**(7), 2567–2580.

166. Wells, J., Konrad, P., Kao, C., Jansen, E. D., and Mahadevan-Jansen, A. (2007) Pulsed laser versus electrical energy for peripheral nerve stimulation, *Journal of Neuroscience Methods*, **163**(2), 326–337.

167. Wieler, M., Stein, R. B., Ladouceur, M., Whittaker, M., Smith, A. W., Naaman, S., Barbeau, H., Bugaresti, J., Aimone, E. (1999) Multicenter evaluation of electrical stimulation systems for walking, *Arch Phys Med Rehabil*, **80**(5), 495–500.

168. Wongsarnpigoon, A. and Grill, W. M. (2010) Energy-efficient waveform shapes for neural stimulation revealed with a genetic algorithm, *Journal of Neural Engineering*, **7**(4), 46009.

169. Yoshida, K. and Horch, K. (1993) Selective stimulation of peripheral nerve fibers using dual intrafascicular electrodes, *IEEE Trans Biomed Eng*, **40**(5), 492–494.

170. Zimmermann, K. P. and Simpson, R. K. (1996) "Slinky" coils for neuromagnetic stimulation, *Electroencephalogr. Clin. Neurophysiol. - Electromyogr. Mot. Control*, **101**, 145–152.

Chapter 2.5

Central Nervous System Stimulation

Andrew S. Koivuniemi[1] and Kevin J. Otto[2]

[1]Department of Neurological Surgery, Indiana University School of Medicine
Indianapolis, IN 46202
akoivuni@umail.iu.edu
[2]J. Crayton Pruitt Department of Biomedical Engineering and the Department of
Neuroscience, University of Florida, Gainesville, FL 32611
kevin.otto@bme.ufl.edu

The application of electrical stimulation to the central nervous system is described. We discuss some of the basic techniques of exciting nervous tissue electrically. A discussion of sensory modulation is provided. Finally, a brief discussion of current progress and future directions is offered.

1. Introduction

Central nervous system (CNS) stimulation is invaluable for basic research, for therapies for neurologic or psychiatric disease, and for the prosthetic replacement of lost sensory function. There are many modalities of CNS stimulation, each having a set of benefits and drawbacks. Mechanisms to stimulate the CNS include, but are not limited to, the following: electrical, mechanical, chemical, and optical. Additionally, genetic manipulation has been used to make cells more receptive to these modalities. A highlight of some of the benefits and limitations of each is shown in Table 1. However, electrical stimulation is by far the most prevalent stimulation modality being the easiest to deploy and the longest studied. Thus, electrical stimulation is currently the most relevant stimulation modality for neuroprosthetics [1]. In this chapter we will provide the basics of electrical CNS stimulation. We will especially focus on the application of electrical CNS stimulation as it pertains to providing sensory information for neuroprosthetics.

Sensory neuroprostheses seek to provide the user with useful information about the local environment. Despite individual successes such as the cochlear implant and deep brain stimulating implant, generally, creation of reliable CNS stimulation providing rich informational bandwidth that faithfully reproduces the complexity and richness of the natural senses remains a significant challenge. Electrical stimulating neuroprostheses can either be superficial (remaining outside of the brain or spinal cord), or penetrating (residing within the CNS tissue). Penetrating central nervous system interfaces persist as the most challenging to realize, but continue to be the most intriguing and promising because of the information bandwidth advantages they provide. This rich information source is essential for achieving next-generation sensory prostheses. The ultimate realization of reliable penetrating neural interfaces will require careful science and engineering approaches incorporating knowledge of the relevant and critical biological, physical, and chemical factors, especially their interrelationship along with a deep appreciation of the subjective experience of the user. The conclusion of this chapter provides a highlight of the future direction of research and development. First, a primer on the biophysics of delivering electrical current to the CNS is warranted.

Table 1. Some benefits and limitations of CNS stimulation modalities.

Modality	Benefit	Limitation
Electrical	• Proven • Existing technology	• Non-specific cellular excitation • Susceptible to encapsulation and rejection
Magnetic	• Enhanced selectivity of inactivation • Enhanced stability of stimulation	• Unproven technology • High power requirements • Difficult to implant
Chemical	• Cell-selective activation	• Transmitter depletion
Optical	• Ability to focus activation	• Mechanism of stimulation unknown • Long-term safety unknown
Genetic	• Ability to target specific cell populations	• Requires modification of genetic material

2. Biophysical fundamentals of electrical neural activation

2.1. *Fundamentals of neural stimulation*

When writing about experiments or treatments involving electrical stimulation of the brain, it is typical to use expressions such as "We stimulated the subthalamic nucleus." While this is an effective description of where in the brain the stimulating electrodes rests, it is not an accurate description of what is actually happening in the brain. Electrical stimulation does not stimulate regions of the brain. It stimulates neurons in the brain. Under some stimulation conditions it depolarizes these neurons and they fire action potentials. The neurons that fire action potentials are governed by a few basic principles, which are explained below. The purpose of the following section is *not* to give the reader a thorough theoretical background of the biophysics of electrical stimulation of the nervous system but to prime the intuition as to what factors influence the stimulation of neurons and why those factors matter for neuroprosthetics.

2.2. *The pulse*

The pulse is the basic unit of stimulation. It represents a brief period of voltage applied to an electrode, the impedance of which determines how much current flows through the electrode and into the neural tissue. The typical purpose of a pulse is to depolarize the membrane of neighboring neurons to the point that they fire an action potential. Theoretically, one can control the voltage in order to sculpt the current flow in the tissue into any arbitrary shape or waveform. However, the vast majority of experiments and clinical applications use a specific pulse where electric current is turned on, the charge flows through the electrode at a fixed rate, and then the current is turned off. This is referred to as a "square wave" as depicted in Figure 1A.

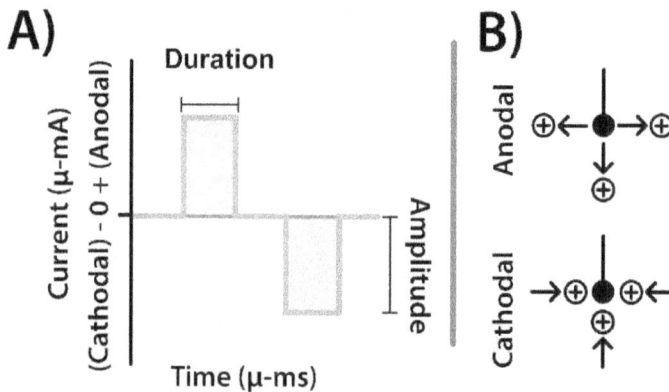

Fig. 1. Fundamental terminology of an electrical stimulation pulse. A) Features of a pulse, B) Direction of current flow.

With an understanding of a few terms one can describe all pulses. The direction of electric current is either into or out of the electrode as schematized in Figure 1B). Current flow is the movement of charge, which in the brain, represents the movement of ions such as sodium, potassium, or chloride – as opposed to electrons in the electrodes wires. By convention, current is positive in the direction of positive ion movement (or opposite the direction of electron movement). When positive charge is flowing away from the electrode the current is positive and is called "*anodal.*" The opposite condition, when positive charge flows to electrode, is called "*cathodal*." The other two terms are the pulse "*duration*" which describes how long the current is on (typically on the order of microseconds to milliseconds) and the pulse "*amplitude*" which is amount of electric current flowing during that time (typically on the order of microamps to milliamps) [2].

The final term to know is "phase". This concept is important for cases where the current flows in both the anodal and cathodal direction during a single pulse. The number of directions in which the current flows is noted by the Greek numeral prefixes – mono, bi, tri, and so on. Thus, a pulse that flows in one direction is called "*monophasic*". If, however, current flowed in the positive (anodal) direction for the first part of the pulse and then switched to the negative direction (cathodal) for the second half it is referred to as a "*biphasic*" (this specific example is "*anode-leading*"). The importance of this distinction will be discussed in the next section.

2.3. *Stimulation safety*

Every central nervous system prosthesis relies on the long term use of electrical stimulation. Thus, all pulses must have a benign influence on the surrounding neural tissue. If done incorrectly, long term stimulation of the nervous system can cause irreversible damage to the neighboring tissue [3, 4]. Two factors are critical in ensuring that pulses can be delivered to the brain without significantly damaging the neurons. The first factor is the shape of the stimulus waveform; it must be biphasic. Based on the original work of John Lilly it was found that stimulation waveforms that have both cathodal and anodal phases that transfer equal amounts of charge into and out of the electrode can be delivered chronically without causing damage to the tissue [5]. So called "charge balancing" is done by ensuring that the product of phase amplitude and the phase duration (the total charge transferred) are equal for both phases of the pulse in order to reverse harmful electrochemical reactions at the electrode surface [6]. Figure 2A) demonstrates a putatively safe, *i.e.*, charge balanced pulse, while Figure 2B) demonstrates an unsafe, *i.e.*, charge unbalanced pulse.

It is important to keep in mind that charge balancing alone is not enough to ensure the safety of chronic neural stimulation. The second factor that determines the safety of a pulse is the charge density. Based on the *in vivo* histology work of McCreery *et al.* [7-10], Shannon derived the following empirical equation that determined safe levels of stimulation [11].

$$\log(CD) = k - \log(Q) \tag{1}$$

where CD stands for charge density (the amount of charge [μC] delivered in one phase of a charge balanced pulse divided by the area of the electrode [cm^2]) and Q stands for charge per phase. The value k was found to be 1.85 (dimensionless) and demarcated a dividing line for simulation parameters that caused histologic tissue damage and those that did not. While this equation might seem unwieldy to some, it captures a simple fundamental intuition: when the electrode site size gets bigger (thus lowing the density of charge – CD) or the amount of charge delivered per phase gets smaller (thus lowering both Q and CD) the effect of the charge on the tissue is more likely to be innocuous. Conversely, as either total charge (Q) or charge density (CD) get larger the likelihood for tissue damage increases.

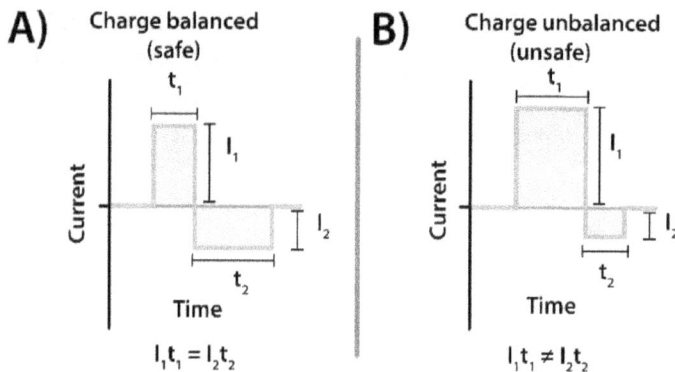

Fig. 2. Graphical representation of A) charge balanced and B) charge unbalanced pulses.

This equation is remarkable by the variables that are absent: voltage and electric current. Though counterintuitive, it is critical to understand when evaluating a pulse for safety that these factors are not essential. Thus, even pulses with very low amplitude currents can still lead to tissue if the duration is long (and therefore the charge per phase is high), while those with very high amplitudes with brief durations can be safe.

2.4. *Stimulation selectivity*

When stimulating the brain, the goal of the experimenter or clinician it to generate action potentials in specifically chosen populations of neurons. The following section quickly details the important factors that influence which neurons in the brain fire action potentials when a given stimulation pulse is delivered to the brain using electrodes that rest outside the cell. A well informed reader on this subject will note that numerous nuances have been glossed over or simply ignored, but we hope s/he would agree that what remains captures the essentials that any one working with electrical stimulation of the brain should appreciate. For those interested in nuances the reviews of Ranck [12] and Tehovnik [13] are excellent starting points.

2.4.1. *Current direction*

As mentioned above, electrical current in the brain comes in two different flavors: anodal (positive current) and cathodal (negative current). In the resting state a neuron has a positively charged outer and a negatively charged inner membrane [14]. The purpose of electrical stimulation is to depolarize the membrane to the point where the voltage gated sodium channels open and generate an action potential. Cathodal current is by far the more efficient current at depolarizing the cell membrane [12]. While Figure 3 does not faithfully represent the true biophysics of this phenomenon, it is meant to demonstrate that a cathodal current will increase negative charge on the positively charged outer membrane. For this reason cathode-leading, biphasic stimulation pulses have lower thresholds for the neurons in the immediate vicinity; anode-leading, biphasic pulses hyperpolarize the membrane initially and have been shown to have significantly higher thresholds [15].

2.4.2. *Current-distance relationship*

The CNS tissue can be modeled as a volume conductor. Volume conductor theory suggests that neurons that are closer to the stimulating electrode require less current to activate than neurons farther away from the electrode. Empirical studies [16] have demonstrated that the relationship between the activation threshold and the distance is as follows:

$$I_{th} = a + cD^2 \tag{2}$$

where I_{th} is the current required to stimulate an action potential for a given pulse duration, a is the stimulation threshold for an electrode directly adjacent to the neuron, c is the current-distance constant, and D is the distance from the neuron to the electrode. It is important to take away two points from the above relationship. First, the threshold increases with distance in a square fashion which helps increase the specificity of stimulation but also means that when trying to stimulate elements farther from the electrode increasing amounts of current to do not linearly increase the range of stimulation. So an increase in stimulation amplitude from 200 to 400 μA represents a much larger increase in the distance from the electrode to the farthest stimulated neuron than an increase from 800 to 1000 μA.

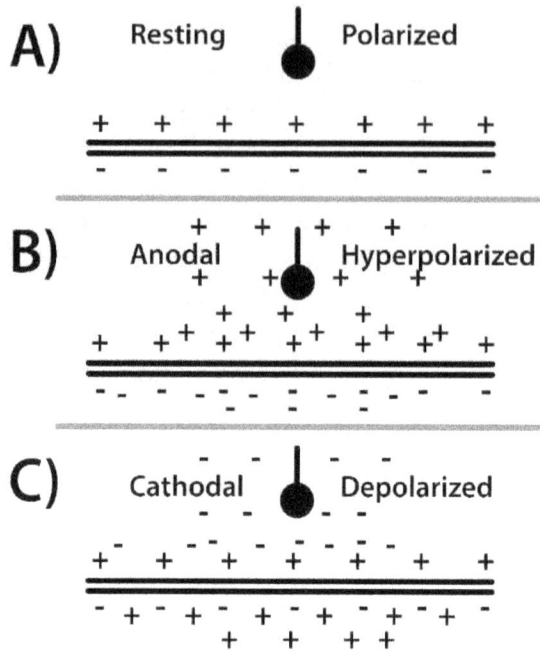

Fig. 3. The direction of current flow in three different stimulation conditions: A) resting, B) anodal, and C) cathodal.

The second take away is the current distance constant c. Due to its position in the equation, c modifies the current distance relationship. The value of c correlates with the type of neuron being stimulated. Smaller diameter fibers, such as C-fibers associated with pain or cortical interneurons, have higher values of c, while larger diameter fibers, such as the pyramidal neurons of the cortical spinal tract in the motor system, have lower values of c [17]. This relationship is graphically represented in Figure 4 (which is adapted from the review by Tehovnik [13]). In other words, if a large fiber neuron and a small fiber neuron are an equal distance from an electrode, then a larger amplitude of current is required to generate an action potential in the small fiber neuron than in the large fiber (or, the large fiber neuron will be excited first). This relationship is also important to remember when considering the specificity of a given stimulation. Small changes in the stimulus amplitude will result in large changes in the number of large fiber neurons that are stimulated, and large changes in amplitude will result in small changes in the number of small fiber neurons that are stimulated.

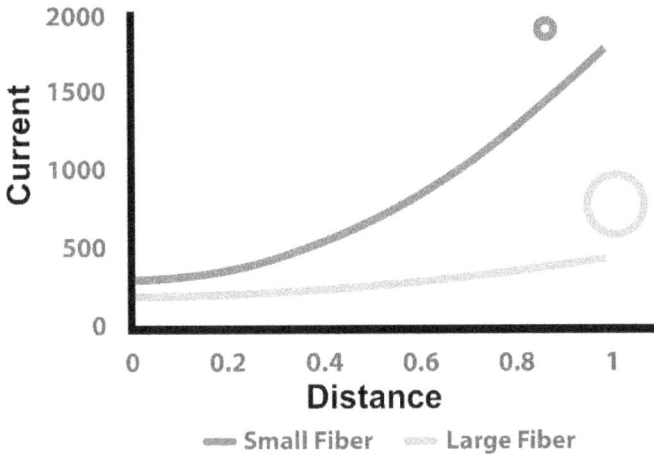

Fig. 4. Current-distance relationship of two arbitrary fibers, one small the other large.

2.4.3. *Strength-duration curve*

The last critical relationship to understand when stimulating the CNS is known as the strength-duration curve, as seen in Figure 5. The basic principle is that for increasing pulse duration there is a decreasing amount of current that is required in order to stimulate the neurons to fire [18]. The equation used to describe this relationship between a neurons activation threshold and the pulse duration is as follows:

$$I_{th} = I_r(1 + C/t) \tag{3}$$

where I_{th} is the current required to stimulate an action potential, I_r is the rheobase current (the amount of current required to stimulate and action potential for an "infinitely" long pulse), C is the chronaxie (the time point on the strength duration curve where the threshold is twice the rheobase current).

It is important to point of that, like c in the current-distance relationship above, the values of the rheobase and chronaxie are a reflection of the type of neuron being stimulated. Larger fibers have lower rheobase currents and shorter chronaxies when compared to smaller fibers [19]. Figure 5 is based on arbitrary values for the rheobase and chronaxie of 1 and 1 for the "large fiber" while the rheobase and chronaxie for the small fiber were set at 4 and 5 respectively. In reality, large myelinated neurons, like A-alpha fibers in the peripheral nervous system, have chronaxies as short as 20 μsec, while the adjacent C fibers have chronaxies as long as 1.5 msec [20] – an even greater contrast than that demonstrated in Figure 5. Again, it is much easier to activate larger fibers using electrical stimulation. Also, when using short pulse durations one can have extremely high specificity for the activation of large fibers. The tradeoff is that stimulation of smaller fibers requires much longer pulse durations.

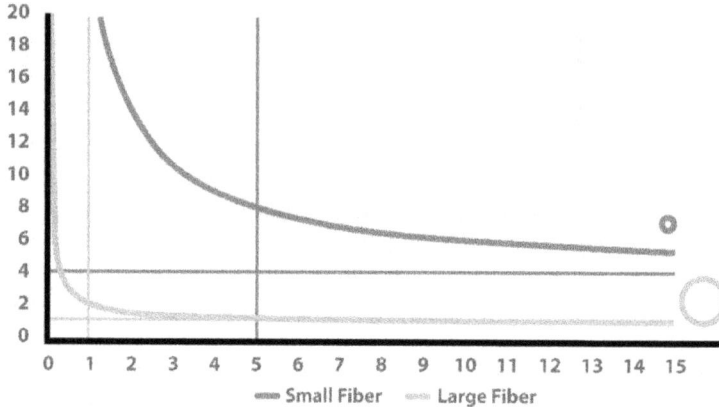

Fig. 5. Strength-duration relationship for a small and large diameter fiber.

2.5. *The pulse train and modulation*

Up to this point, we have concerned ourselves with the individual electrical pulses used to generate action potentials. However, just as a single swallow does not indicate a summer, a single pulse does not make a useful prosthesis. A series of pulses must be sent into the brain, and this series is called a *"pulse train"*. In the context of DBS, the pulse train is set at a constant rate, or frequency, typically greater 100 pulses per second [21]. However, in the context of CNS prosthetics the purpose of stimulation is to provide information about the outside world to the brain. Because the world changes, the stimulation must change in order to represent it.

Changing the stimulation can either change the population of neurons being activated or the rate at which those cells are activated. This is called *"modulation"*. There are 4 fundamental ways that a pulse train can be modulated, three of which are represented in Figure 6. The first, is *"frequency modulation"* in which the timing between pulses changes in order to change the rate at which action potentials are produce from the targeted volume of cells.

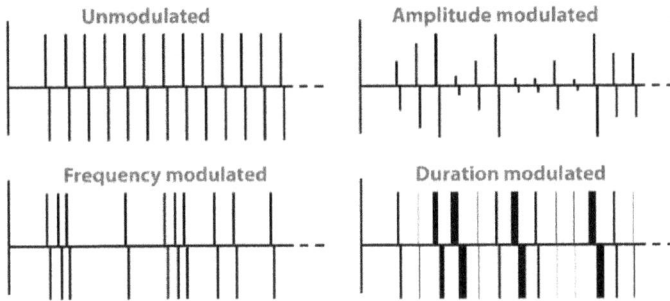

Fig. 6. Modulation strategies.

There are two limitations to frequency modulation alone. The first is that the frequency used must be tuned to the refractory period (the amount of time that must pass before a neuron can fire the next action potential) of the neurons one seeks to stimulate [22]. If pulses are sent in faster than the cells can recover then those pulses do not generate action potentials and result in wasted energy. The second limitation to frequency modulation is that it stimulates approximately a fixed volume of neurons because individual waveforms are identical.

Amplitude modulation, the second form of modulation, overcomes this limitation and varies the volume of cells being stimulation. In amplitude modulation the rate of stimulation remains unchanged but the amount of current delivered for each pulse varies. Amplitude modulation allows one to vary the number of neurons activated with each pulse according the neurons' current distance relationships described in §2.4.2. The main limitation with amplitude modulation is that the type of cells being activated may or may not change, in accordance with the strength-duration relationship described in 2.4.3.

"*Duration modulation*" gives one the chance to not only vary the volume of neurons activated but, to a degree, the type of neurons being activated. By changing the duration of the pulse form one to the next, one moves along positions on the strength duration curve. For example, a pulse duration of 80 µsec will require high currents to activate neurons with chronaxies greater than 400 µsec; however, a pulse width of 600 µsec would easily activate this population of neurons. Thus, duration modulation allows modulating which cell types are being activated.

All of these modulation strategies are fundamentally limited to stimulating the populations of neurons that are near to the electrode being stimulated. The addition of multiple electrodes in different regions of the CNS allows one to spatially modulate the stimulation, and thus completely change the population of neurons being stimulated.

It should be noted of course that none of these stimulation strategies are mutually exclusive and sophisticated stimulation paradigms use multiple strategies simultaneously.

3. Stimulation for sensory modulation

This section summarizes and analyzes what is known about electrical stimulation of the CNS when it is done in order to generate an artificial or prosthetic sensation in an individual. This distinction is important because it excludes deep brain stimulation, which also uses electrical stimulation of the nervous system, but is done in order to treat neurologic or psychiatric illness. It is divided between studies done in humans and animals. However, it could have just as easily been divided by decade since the vast majority of research on CNS stimulation as a prosthetic tool was done in human volunteers from the late 1960's [23] until the 1990's [24] when studies shifted into behaving animal models.

3.1.1. *CNS stimulation-induced perception: human studies*

Use of CNS stimulation in a sensory prosthesis seeks to ameliorate replacement of a lost sensory function. Because CNS stimulation is a subjective experience, truth about the nature of CNS stimulation ultimately rests in the conscious experience of the stimulated individuals. This is what makes anecdotal human experiments so critical. Furthermore, beyond simply generating any sensation, CNS stimulation must provide some cognitive value to the individual, be it sight for the blind, speech recognition and understanding in the deaf, or somatosensory feedback from a paralyzed individual's brain machine interface device. The following sections review the discoveries of three high quality CNS stimulation research groups that studied human volunteers: Penfield, Dobelle, and Schmidt and Bak. The work of these groups is highlighted because they provide both the historical context for the development of sensory prostheses of the central nervous system as well as valuable personal detail of what humans say they experience when different regions of the brain are stimulated.

Early Cortical Mapping - Penfield

The pioneer in studying the effect of CNS stimulation on sensation was the neurosurgeon Wilder Penfield. While Cushing [25] was the first to successfully stimulate sensory cortex in a conscious patient without generating movement, the credit for the first thorough study of somatosensory cortical stimulation belongs to Penfield [26].

Penfield explored the effects of passing electrical current through electrodes on the surface of the brain of subjects who were undergoing surgery for the treatment of epilepsy or to remove brain tumors [26]. While the patient's brain was exposed, Penfield placed electrodes on the brain, applied stimulation and asked the subject what he or she was experiencing. Using this technique, he created the first diagram of the sensory homunculus in which regions of the body are represented in a specific region of the sensory cortex. While the somatotopic detail of the generated map is excellent, the results do not vividly address the subjective quality of the experiences, which were simply described as "sensation," or "pain," or "numbness." However, in the few cases that are described in the patient's words, the expression used most often is "tingling" located in a specific body region.

This lack of qualitative detail is not a feature of Penfield's second CNS stimulation opus in which he explored the effect of auditory cortical stimulation [27]. Almost all stimulation was done on secondary cortical structures along the superior temporal lobe near Heschl's gyrus. Here, Penfield provides full narrative detail in the words of the patients who often claimed the stimulations produced the sensation of voices or music. These auditory hallucinations were occasionally strikingly specific and elaborate, a particular song, such as "White Christmas," or a mother calling a name. Stimulation of regions of the temporal lobe closer to the auditory cortex were more abstract but widely varied. "When the auditory cortex is stimulated, the subject variously describes the sound as ringing, humming, clicking, rushing, chirping, buzzing, knocking, or rumbling." [28]

Cortical surface stimulation neuroprosthetic development

The first major effort to develop a sensory prosthesis came in the 1970's. It was inspired primarily by Brindley and Lewin's [23] demonstration that blind individuals could be chronically implanted with a grid of surface electrodes over the primary visual cortex and that stimulation of these electrodes could produce visual effects in the individual. Previous studies had explored the subjective effects of electrical stimulation of the visual cortex [29]; however, these were only accomplished in acute settings in patients undergoing operations for other reasons and no insight was made into the stimulus parameters necessary to produce an effect.

Brindley and Lewin's study demonstrated the following:

1) Stimulating electrodes could be implanted chronically in humans;

2) Stimulation through those electrodes produces effects for the duration of the study using constant current pulses on the order of 2 to 15 mA;

3) The subjective effect created in the individual was perceived as a circle or bar of white light, termed a "phosphene";

4) The subjective threshold for detecting the stimulus decreased with increased stimulation frequency;

5) The subjective threshold for detecting the stimulus decreased with increasing pulse durations;

6) Rudimentary patterns could be formed by stimulating multiple electrodes simultaneously.

The discovery that patterns of phosphenes could be produced by stimulating multiple electrodes simultaneously inspired a group of biomedical engineers, led by William Dobelle working out of the University of Utah, to try to develop a visual aid for the blind. The result of their effort was published as a case series of 36 patients who were stimulated while undergoing surgery [30]. In all cases, it confirmed Brindley's findings while adding significantly to them as summarized in the following:

1) Useful phosphenes can only be produced in the primary visual cortex;

2) For the large surface electrodes used (1 mm^2 *vs.* 3 mm^2 *vs.* 9 mm^2), size did not appreciably affect the patient's sensation or threshold level;

3) Monophasic vs. biphasic pulses, as well as the direction of the pulses (anodal or cathodal first) did not appreciably affect threshold level or the sensation quality;

4) Pulses of higher amplitude could be detected with shorter stimulus train lengths;

5) The perceived brightness of the pulse increased with the pulse amplitude;

6) Some phosphenes tended to "flicker" while others were constant; the rate of flickering seemed to be independent of the pulse parameters;

7) Phosphenes appeared immediately after stimulation began;

8) Phosphenes typically ended with the stimulation but, on occasion, lasted up to 2 minutes after the end of stimulations;

9) Some phosphenes had distinct colors and sometimes took on complex shapes such as rotating pinwheels; however, they were typically white and circular;

10) Phosphenes produced by different electrodes could typically be discriminated from one another only if the electrodes were at least 3 mm apart.

Using the same protocol and equipment, Dobelle and his team also studied the auditory cortex [31]. The goal was to identify an "audene," an auditory unit of perception that could be used as a conceptual basis for a prosthetic device. These studies were far more limited than the visual cortical studies for two primary reasons: 1) fewer patients met the requirement for the protocol (only eight were studied), and 2) the researchers never gained stimulation access to the primary auditory cortex because it was never exposed during the normal course of surgery and, thus, were forced to stimulate only secondary structures. The subjective effects experienced by individuals were described with words like "buzz," "hum," "knock," "crickets," and "wavering" – similar to those describe by Penfield. These effects were only altered by movement of the stimulating electrode and were unaffected, at least in terms of quality, by alteration in the stimulation parameters. However, the effect was perceived as "louder" when the stimulation amplitude was increased. All other observations were consistent with those made in the visual cortex.

The final major contribution Dobelle made to the field of central stimulation was the chronic implantation of a visual prosthesis in a series of blind patients during the mid-1970's [32, 33]. In 2000, Dobelle detailed the performance of one of these patients [34] who, having been implanted in 1978, still used his device for three hours a day on a nearly daily basis over twenty years later without infection or any other problems. This report serves primarily to demonstrate that surface stimulation produces a subjective effect consistently for the individual. In addition, there was no suggestion that such prolonged stimulation led to any form of seizures or epilepsy which could have been a consequence of overdriving the neural system, as seen in kindling experiments [35-37]. However, it was not clearly demonstrated that such a device could transfer useful visual information to the individual. "With scanning [the subject] can now routinely recognize a 6 inch square 'tumbling E' at five feet...which corresponds to a visual acuity of 20/1200." However, the details about limitations in terms of the cost, the complexity of programming, and the difficulty and slowness of use, when compared with other means for the blind to navigate their world, were not addressed.

Nevertheless, the prosthesis was still working and the location of the phosphenes in subjective space remained constant over two decades. This means that the prolonged stimulation, in this case of surface stimulation, had no degradation of its functional effect on the patient demonstrating good consistency. The next major advance in CNS stimulation for sensory prostheses came nearly a dozen years after the implantation of Dobelle's patient when a team of researchers, based on promising penetrating stimulation studies performed in behaving animal models [38], used these techniques in human subjects.

Penetrating microstimulation

Bak *et al.* in 1990 and Schmidt *et al.* in 1996 [24, 39] produced two indispensable studies for the field of CNS stimulation. Being the only systematic microstimulation experiments conducted either in an acute and or in a chronic fashion in humans they provide unique insight into the value of stimulating through microelectrodes implanted within the cerebral cortex, as opposed to the previous work, which solely used macroelectrodes on the surface of the brain. Both studies richly detail the sensory experiences of the subjects while providing a systematic analysis of how stimulation parameters and conditions influence those experiences.

Bak *et al.* [39] details three case studies. For these studies, the subjects were implanted acutely with pairs of parylene-C coated iridium oxide microwires [40]. The distance between the paired electrode tips was varied between 250 μm and 1000 μm in order to determine the minimum distance the electrodes could be from each other and still generate separate phosphenes.

Before the acute electrodes were implanted, the cortex was mapped with surface stimulation, and the subjects reported detecting phosphenes when the stimulus was higher than 1-2 mA. When the depth electrodes were inserted, the first comment from all three patients was that the phosphenes no longer flickered and instead appeared as crisp delineated points that began and ended with the stimulation train. Second, the depth at which the electrodes demonstrated their lowest thresholds, (20 - 200 μA), was found between 2 and 4 mm below the surface of the cortex, which histologically corresponded to layers 4-6 (this has been later corroborated through animal studies, *e.g.* [41]). Third, at the depth of 2 mm, cathode-leading biphasic pulses had thresholds ~40% lower than anode-leading biphasic pulses. Fourth, stimulation near threshold produced phosphenes of distinct colors, usually blue or yellow. Finally, when stimulated simultaneously with interleaved pulses, electrodes spaced more than 700 μm apart produced novel phosphenes described as "blobs fusing" and "like a teddy bear."

The follow-up study expanded significantly on the findings of the first study, implanting a 42-year old woman with a 22-year history of blindness due to glaucoma, with 38 microelectrode pairs of the same design as the electrodes used in Bak *et al.*, described above. After three days of recovery, the electrodes were stimulated in well controlled experiments for four months. Using this one patient, numerous experiments were performed. What follows is a list of findings selected for their usefulness and their relevance to the parameters and studies described above.

1) Of the 38 electrodes, 34 produced phosphenes. Of the four not producing phosphenes, 2 had broken leads meaning a 90% overall success rate and a 94% success rate for functional electrodes;

2) For cathodal first biphasic pulses of 200 μs/phase (μs/ph.), detection thresholds were as low as 1.9 μA while most were closer to 25 μA;

3) For pulses of 200 μs/ph, the thresholds for cathodal first pulses were always lower than anodal first thresholds, typically by 27%;

4) Observations concerning the effect of pulse stimulation frequency and stimulus duration were fundamentally the same as Dobelle's [30];

5) The introduction of a phase delay of 100 μs lowered the threshold for a 200 μs/ph by 5.4%;

6) Pulses with a 200 μs/ph duration required 51% more current than pulses with a longer phase of 400 μs/ph. These 400 μs/ph pulses had thresholds only 5% higher than pulses with a 600 μs/ph. This information can be used to estimate a behavioral chronaxie of 110 μs, suggesting that the stimulation of large myelinated axons was driving behavior [12, 13, 16];

7) Phosphenes ranged in size from a "pin point" to a nickel held at arm's length;

8) For 17 phosphenes studied, nine decreased in size with increasing stimulus amplitude while the other eight remained the same size or grew slightly during increasing stimulus amplitude;

9) Increasing the pulse train duration always increased the phosphene's size;

10) Phosphenes stimulated near threshold typically took on a distinct color, such as red, blue, or violet; however, increasing the stimulus amplitude turned the phosphene white, yellow or gray;

11) The subject was sensitive to stimulation pauses of >~25 ms. This suggests the possibility of delivering information in amplitude modulated fashion at a rate of 40 Hz;

12) Phosphenes were perceived as being at distances away from the subject, but they were not co-planar. Some seemed close (8 cm from her face) while others were far away (like a 'distant star'). Nonetheless, most were estimated at 60 cm from her face;

13) Phosphenes generated by electrodes separated by distances ≥ 500 μm could be discriminated.

The rest of the paper concerns more complicated effects such as latency, sensation duration, accommodation, perceived brightness, after discharges, multiple phosphenes from a single electrode, and complex interactions between stimulations of electrode pairs.

Summary of Human Experiments

The preceding sub-section was relatively long with minimal citations by design. It was meant to demonstrate the magnitude of useful information that has been gained from a handful of historic studies performed with human subjects. There are many unique patient reports in the Dobelle and Schmidt/Bak studies that the researchers could not have anticipated. For example, one report from Dobelle's 1974 study on visual cortex stimulation is as follows: "On a number of occasions, subjects have reported 'unreal' colors. This was first reported by patient 3, whose best description was 'non-spectral brown' or 'a color from another world" [30]. Schmidt *et al.* also reported many unpredictable findings, but the least intuitive and probably most useful was that "as the experiment progressed, it was found that wide [phase durations] provided a more pleasing percept to the subject" [24]. However, many important questions remain, particularly those involving the microstimulation of auditory and somatosensory cortex which have yet to be systematically mapped in man using penetrating stimulation.

The next section reviews the work that has been done in behaving animal models and delineates how such studies have added to the human studies.

3.1.2. CNS stimulation-induced behavior: non-human studies

Animal studies of the auditory and somatosensory cortex have been the most enlightening in terms of the subjective effects of electrical stimulation. This is because little is known about what humans would experience if stimulated through penetrating electrodes in these regions. While the concept of phosphenes is well established, there is simply no known equivalent "unit of perception" in these cortical structures in humans. However, carefully designed animal behavior studies of stimulation in these cortices offer some clues.

Somatosensory Cortex

In the somatosensory cortex, aside from reports about "tingling" and "numbness" generated with acute surface stimulation [26], there is very little known about what human subjects would feel upon stimulation with depth microelectrodes. However, thanks to the groundbreaking work of Romo et al. [42, 43] there is good evidence of what they might perceive. Romo et al. trained monkeys (*Macaca mulatta*) to discriminate between mechanical flutters of different frequencies delivered to the monkeys' fingers. The monkeys were acutely implanted with microwire electrodes, similar to those used by Schmidt et al. [24]. These electrodes were then stimulated in place of the mechanical stimuli during some of the tasks in a behavioral session. Stated in simplest terms, the finding was that the monkeys could not tell the difference between a mechanical stimulus and electrical stimulus of the same frequency. This would strongly suggest that electrical stimulation of the somatosensory cortex can deliver frequency dependent, *i.e.*, tactile, information aimed at a given site on the sensory homunculus.

This work also demonstrated that the neurophysiology of the stimulated neurons played an important role in determining whether the electrical stimulus would be perceived as a flutter [43]. Electrodes placed among quickly adapting neurons, which are physiologically responsive to the mechanical flutter stimuli, could produce a flutter response in the monkey, while electrodes placed among slow adapting neurons, which do not respond to the mechanical flutter stimuli, could be detected by the monkey but did not elicit any behavior that would suggest that the animal perceived an illusory flutter.

Since the publication of Romo *et al.*'s work, several groups have attempted to further study the effects of stimulation on somatosensory cortexes (for a review see [44]. These include simultaneous stimulation with the electrodes while recording from motor sites [45] in order to develop a bi-directional brain machine interface (BMI) for paralyzed individuals. These types of studies are valuable because they demonstrated and overcame some of the engineering challenges involved with trying to simultaneously stimulate and record useful information from adjacent somatosensory and motor cortical structures respectively. Modelling studies have suggested optimal ways to program these bi-directional interfaces [46].

Other studies have helped to probe the limits of stimulation by evaluating the role of pulse parameters in determining detection thresholds. The work of Butovas and Schwartz [47, 48] generated useful data sets on the effective stimulation parameters for the rat barrel cortex, the part which processes sensory information from the whiskers, and the role of train duration and pulse frequency on threshold levels. In this work they showed that, in spite of a refractory inhibitory state seen in the neural network, increasing pulse train duration and pulse frequency lowers the overall detection threshold for a given stimulus. A separate study performed by a different group demonstrated that activation of single neurons in the barrel cortex of a rat could elicit detection responses from the animal [49]. These, among other studies [50, 51], help to establish a baseline for future human studies.

Auditory Cortex

In the auditory cortex, several microstimulation experiments have been performed in behaving animal models. The first demonstrated that cats could detect electrical stimulation of the auditory cortex [52] with threshold levels roughly equivalent to those reported by Schmidt *et al.* in the visual cortex [24]. The second demonstrated that gerbils could discriminate between electrical stimulation delivered through spatially separated electrodes, as well as between frequency modulated pulse trains [53]. The third study strongly suggested that the electrode's tonotopic location influenced the perceived pitch of the electrically generated sensation [54]. Other studies performed using microstimulation of the auditory cortex help to confirm these findings [54-56].

Taken together, these three complementary studies strongly suggest that the auditory cortex is a viable option for therapeutic intervention for patients who lack cochlear nerves when considered in relation to the cochlear implant [57] and warrants further evaluation in human subjects.

Visual Cortex

Finally, while there has been far more work published on the topic of visual cortical microstimulation, for the most part, it has been largely redundant with the work of Schmidt *et al.* [24], detailed above. Nonetheless, Bartlett *et al.* [58] offers a sweeping review of the role of various stimulus parameters in the detection and discrimination of stimulus pulses. This dense article contains 14 figures all offering enlightening detail on the effect of stimulus parameters and stimulation regimes on detection and discrimination in behaving monkeys (*Macaca nemestrina*). Any researcher interested in this topic should carefully read this article in its entirety.

Because so many findings can be accounted for between Schmidt *et al.* [24] and Bartlett *et al.* [58], the majority of subsequent studies serve primarily to confirm and refine their discoveries. The researchers Tehovnik and Slocum studied CNS stimulation of the monkey visual cortex using the delayed saccade behavior paradigm [59-61]. This technique allowed them to infer the location of the electrically evoked phosphenes in the subject's visual field based on where the monkeys looked immediately after the delivery of electrical stimulation to the visual cortex. What made this work groundbreaking was the demonstration that well-trained monkeys are virtually the same as the human subjects described by Schmidt and Bak [24, 39] in terms of 1) the detection chronaxie (~100-200 μs), 2) the depth of minimum threshold (~2 mm deep), and 3) the ratio of anodal to cathodal threshold level for the most sensitive layers (~1.3). Therefore, the delayed saccade is a valuable paradigm in the prototyping of a visual cortex prosthesis for the blind.

Other studies have contributed insights, albeit with less success than Tehovnik and Slocum. One example is a single monkey that was implanted with 152 microelectrodes in its visual cortex. This monkey was studied over the course of many months and the findings, published in a series of papers [62-66], were largely inconclusive and difficult to interpret based on the performance of the subject and an infection at the site of implantation five months post-operation. The authors felt moderately confident that sensations produced by the CNS stimulation were relatively durable, demonstrating the potential longitudinal efficacy of the device. However, because these electrodes were never stimulated with the high duty cycles that exist in a sensory prosthesis, it is difficult to know whether this optimism is justified.

4. Emergent Needs and Future Directions

The previous sections detailed some of the basic operating principles and findings from electrical microstimulation of the central nervous system. In this section we will highlight a few of the directions that ongoing and future research is addressing to improve CNS stimulation.

4.1. *Performance and failure mechanisms*

Due to the necessity for some level of invasive surgery to implant stimulation devices it is imperative that the stimulation remain efficacious for many years; repeated invasive brain surgery is undesirable. A lofty goal is to achieve stable and effective performance for the lifetime of the patient, potentially 80+ years. While the large deep brain stimulation electrodes have shown chronic stability, microelectrode arrays implanted in the brain are much less reliable. The putative mechanism of failure of the electrode arrays is limited biocompatibility due to the reactive tissue response [67-69]. Biofouling at the electrode tissue interface is often implicated as the failure model of chronically implanted microelectrodes [70-73]. This mechanism likely contributes to the results from chronic microstimulation experiments; specifically, several studies suggest increasing and variable thresholds post-implant [24, 41, 52, 58], which are correlated with electrode impedance changes over this time [74]. However, changes in the neural tissue have been reported to be limited [75]. It may be possible to prevent longitudinal electrode-tissue changes through the use of advanced waveforms. One study found that several waveforms were equally detectable, as long as the waveform was cathode-leading [15].

Macroelectrodes used for DBS exhibit stable performance in essential tremor [76], dystonia [77], and even the neurodegenerative condition of Parkinson's disease [78-81]. It has been shown that DBS electrodes encounter a similar reactive tissue response as microelectrodes [82], but nevertheless are able to perform stably and reliably. It is not clear why DBS is more stable than microelectrode stimulation though it should be noted DBS seeks to functionally produce the same effect as surgical ablation, or lesion of the targeted tissue.

Nonetheless, there is a need to explore the function of stimulation surface area on detection threshold stability. It may be possible to compromise invasiveness by stimulating with electrocorticography (ECoG) [83] or micro-ECoG [84] interfaces. Regardless, in order to maximize information transfer to a given neural area it will be necessary to maximize the number of functionally independent stimulation channels. This argument suggests that we need the densest and smallest possible sites that still result in stable performance.

4.2. *Stimulation channel density*

The sensory threshold for penetrating cortical stimulation has been reported in the µA range [24, 38, 39, 55]. Theoretically, these stimulation amplitudes result in compact stimulation volumes, enabling a large number of non-overlapping channels for a cortical neuroprosthesis. However, Schmidt *et al.* reported that subjects could only discern penetrating stimulation of visual cortex as close as 700 µm [24]. This value is surprisingly large, given volume conductor models and other stimulation recording results [13, 16, 85], which suggest that the stimulation used by Schmidt *et al.* activates a volume of approximately 100-200 µm diameter In contrast, animal experiments using psychophysical techniques have shown significant discriminability of stimuli separated by 250 µm [86] or 400 µm [87], and spatiotemporal stimulation using electrodes separated on a 300 µm pitch [88, 89].

   Multi-channel microelectrode array technologies have been developed largely based on neuroanatomical and electrophysiological observations. For example, site spacing for some devices has been based on cortical column observations [90, 91], the ability to insert the devices [92], or the ability to neurophysiologically record a single unit simultaneously on multiple electrodes [93]. However, none of these devices have been developed specifically for stimulation of independent circuits of neurons. Additionally, reevaluation of the volume conductor model needs to be considered as we learn more details about the actual circuit being excited [94].

4.3. *Stimulation programming and pulse patterning*

An implant technology with sufficient channel density and functional stability will allow programming of the current delivery to increase information transfer. This programming largely seeks to increase the temporal information delivery.

   Inherent in the ability to provide useful information to the user is the carrier frequency of the electrical pulse train. Information theory indicates that higher frequency pulse trains will provide higher bandwidth for information communication [95]; this theory has been directly translated for cochlear implants as improved sampling of speech waveforms [96], and theoretically more natural auditory nerve activation [97, 98]. Furthermore, increased pulse train frequency for cortical stimulation has been shown to lower the threshold for sensation [24, 58, 99]. However, high frequency stimulation of the cochlea (>1000 Hz) can result in significant channel interaction that may be detrimental to prosthesis performance [100]. Even more importantly for the proposed studies, McCreery *et al.* [7, 101] examined stimulation-induced depression of neuronal excitability

(SIDNE) while stimulating in the posteroventral cochlear nucleus and cortex. They found that pulse trains at 500 Hz exhibited SIDNE, while pulse trains at 100 Hz did not. Therefore, further investigation into optimizing the carrier frequency of the CNS stimulation train needs to be conducted.

In typical nervous system stimulation, information content is conveyed not via the presence or absence of stimulation, but rather through modulation of the basic carrier pulse train. This strategy is designed to communicate with the nervous targets in a biomimetic approach. Specifically, sensory areas often encode information through modulation of the rate or timing of the generation of action potentials from single neurons, *i.e.*, frequency modulation [91]. Alternatively, visual [102], somatosensory [103], and auditory [104] areas can phase-lock to amplitude-modulated stimuli, presumably encoding information about the frequency content of the incident stimulus. This behavior of CNS neurons has been utilized by several studies, demonstrating that information can be delivered to awake, behaving animals via modulated electrical stimulation of cortex [42, 53, 88, 89]. Neuroprosthetic systems also depend on modulation: amplitude modulation is used for information transfer in cochlear implants [105, 106], and frequency modulation has been implicated for improved performance of deep brain stimulation [107, 108]. The primary determinate of the efficacy of modulation-based information transfer is the modulation sensitivity [109, 110], though it is not yet clear if populations of neurons are integrating the stimulation trains or detecting the peaks in the modulation [111]. The full efficacy of amplitude or frequency modulation of electrical pulse trains applied via chronically-implanted microelectrodes in the CNS is not yet known.

5. Summary

This chapter provided details about stimulation of the central nervous system, particularly in its potential for sensory neuroprosthetics. Armed with biophysical models and empirical results from human and animal studies researchers are working to develop reliable, high-fidelity neuroprostheses. Ongoing studies are focusing on advancing the implants, programming the stimulation, and even alternative stimulation modalities, including magnetic, chemical, optical, or mechanical. Still, we must continue to develop these next-generation technologies safely and ethically [112]

References

1. Fritsch, G. and E. Hitzig, Ueber die elektrishe Erregarkeit des Grosshims, *The Cerebral Cortex.* Thomas, Springfield, 1870, **101** , 73-96.
2. Merrill, D. R., M. Bikson, and J. G. Jefferys, Electrical stimulation of excitable tissue: design of efficacious and safe protocols, *J Neurosci Methods*, 2005, **141**(2), 171-198.
3. Mortimer, J. T., C. N. Shealy, and C. Wheeler, Experimental nondestructive electrical stimulation of the brain and spinal cord, *Journal of Neurosurgery*, 1970, **32**(5), 553-559.
4. Pudenz, R. H., W. F. Agnew, and L. A. Bullara, Effects of electrical-stimulation of brain - light-microscope and electron-microscope studies, *Brain Behavior and Evolution*, 1977, **14**(1-2), 103-125.
5. Lilly, J. C., J. R. Hughes, E. C. Alvord Jr, and T. W.Galkin, Brief, noninjurious electric waveform for stimulation of the brain, *Science*, 1955, **121**(3144), 468-469.
6. Brummer, S. B. and M. J. Turner, Electrochemical considerations for safe electrical stimulation of the nervous system with platinum electrodes, *IEEE Trans Biomed Eng*, 1977, **24**(1), 59-63.
7. McCreery, D. B., L. A. Bullara, and W. F. Agnew, Neuronal activity evoked by chronically implanted intracortical microelectrodes, *Exp Neurol*, 1986, **92**(1), 147-161.
8. Agnew, W.F., et al., *Histopathologic evaluation of prolonged intracortical electrical stimulation.* Exp Neurol, 1986. **92**(1), 162-185.
9. McCreery, D. B., W. F. Agnew, T. G. Yuen, and L. A. Bullara, Comparison of neural damage induced by electrical stimulation with faradaic and capacitor electrodes, *Annals of Biomedical Engineering*, 1988, **16**(5), 463-481.
10. McCreery, D. B., T. G. Yuen, W. F. Agnew, and L. A. Bullara, Stimulation with chronically implanted microelectrodes in the cochlear nucleus of the cat: histologic and physiologic effects, *Hear Res*, 1992, **62**(1), 42-56.
11. Shannon, R. V., A model of safe levels for electrical stimulation, *IEEE Transactions on Biomedical Engineering*, 1992, **39**(4), 424-426.
12. Ranck, J. J. B., Which elements are excited in electrical stimulation of mammalian central nervous system: A review, *Brain Research*, 1975, **98**(3), 417-440.
13. Tehovnik, E. J., Electrical stimulation of neural tissue to evoke behavioral responses, *Journal of Neuroscience Methods*, 1996, **65**(1), 1-17.
14. Hodgkin, A. L. and A. F. Huxley, A quantitative description of membrane current and its application to conduction and excitation in nerve, *J Physiol*, 1952, **117**(4), 500-44.
15. Koivuniemi, A. S. and K. J. Otto, Asymmetric versus symmetric pulses for cortical microstimulation, *IEEE Trans Neural Syst Rehabil Eng*, 2011, **19**(5), 468-476.
16. Stoney, S. D., W. D. Thompson, and H. Asanuma, Excitation of pyramidal tract cells by intracortical microstimulation: effective extent of stimulating current., *Journal of Neurophysiology*, 1968, **31**(5), 659-69.
17. BeMent, S. L. and J. B. Ranck Jr, A quantitative study of electrical stimulation of central myelinated fibers, *Experimental Neurology*, 1969, **24**(2), 147-170.
18. Lapicque, L., Recherches quantitatives sur l'excitation electrique des nerf traites comme une polarization, *J Physiol*, 1907, **9**, 622-635.
19. West, D. C. and J. H. Wolstencroft, Strength-duration characteristics of myelinated and non-myelinated bulbospinal axons in the cat spinal cord, *The Journal of Physiology*, 1983, **337**(1), 37-50.

20. Li, C. L. and A. Bak, Excitability characteristics of A-fiber and C-fiber in a peripheral-nerve, *Experimental Neurology*, 1976, **50**(1), 67-79.

21. Montgomery Jr, E. B., *Deep Brain Stimulation Programming: Principles and Practice*, (Oxford University Press, Oxford, 2010).

22. Waxman, S. G. and H. A. Swadlow, The conduction properties of axons in central white matter, *Progress in Neurobiology*, 1977, **8**, 297-324.

23. Brindley, G. S. and W. S. Lewin, The sensations produced by electrical stimulation of the visual cortex, *Journal of Physiology*, 1968, **196**(2), 479-93.

24. Schmidt, E. M., M. J. Bak, F. T. Hambrecht, C. V. Kufta, D. K. O'Rourke, and P. Vallabhanath, Feasibility of a visual prosthesis for the blind based on intracortical microstimulation of the visual cortex, *Brain*, 1996, **119 (Pt 2)**, 507-522.

25. Cushing, H., A note upon the faradic stimulation of the postcentral gyrus in conscious patients, *Brain*, 1909, **32**(1), 44-53.

26. Penfield, W. and E. Boldrey, Somatic motor and sensory representation in the cerebral cortex of man as studied by electrical stimulation, *Brain*, 1937, **60**, 389-443.

27. Penfield, W. and P. Perot, The brain's record of auditory and visual experience, *Brain*, 1963, **86**, 595-696.

28. Penfield, W. and L. Roberts, *Speech and Brain Mechanisms* (Princeton University Press, Princeton, NJ, 1959).

29. Foerster, O., Beitrage zur Pathophysiologie der Sehbahn und der Sehsphare, *Journal of Psychology and Neurology, Lpz*, 1929, **39**, 463-485.

30. Dobelle, W. H. and M. G. Mladejovsky, Phosphenes produced by electrical stimulation of human occipital cortex, and their application to the development of a prosthesis for the blind, *Journal of Physiology*, 1974, **243**(2), 553-576.

31. Dobelle, W.H., S. S. Stensaas, M. G. Mladejovsky, and J. B. Smith, A prosthesis for the deaf based on cortical stimulation, *Ann Otol Rhinol Laryngol*, 1973, **82**(4), 445-463.

32. Dobelle, W. H., M. G. Mladejovsky, and J. P. Girvin, Artifical vision for the blind: electrical stimulation of visual cortex offers hope for a functional prosthesis, *Science*, 1974, **183**(123), 440-444.

33. Dobelle, W. H., D. O. Quest, J. L. Antunes, T. S. Roberts, and J. P. Girvin, Artificial vision for the blind by electrical stimulation of the visual cortex, *Neurosurgery*, 1979, **5**(4), 521-527.

34. Dobelle, W. H., Artificial vision for the blind by connecting a television camera to the visual cortex, *ASAIO Journal*, 2000, **46**(1), 3-9.

35. Cavazos, J., I. Das, and T. Sutula, Neuronal loss induced in limbic pathways by kindling: evidence for induction of hippocampal sclerosis by repeated brief seizures, *J. Neurosci.*, 1994, **14**(5), 3106-3121.

36. Wada, J. A., M. Sato, and M. E. Corcoran, Persistent seizure susceptibility and recurrent spontaneous seizures in kindled cats, *Epilepsia*, 1974, **15**(4), 465-478.

37. Blumenfeld, H., A. Lampert, J. P. Klein, J. Mission, M. C. Chen, M. Rivera, S. Dib-Hajj, A. R. Brennan, B. C. Hains, and S. G. Waxman, Role of hippocampal sodium channel Nav1.6 in kindling epileptogenesis. *Epilepsia*, 2009. **50**(1), 44-55.

38. Bartlett, J. R. and R. W. Doty, An exploration of the ability of macaques to detect microstimulation of striate cortex, *Acta Neurobiol Exp (Wars)*, 1980, **40**(4), 713-727.

39. Bak, M.J., J. P. Girvin, F. T. Hambrecht, C. V. Kufta, G. E. Loeb, and E. M. Schmidt, Visual sensations produced by intracortical microstimulation of the human occipital cortex, *Medical & Biological Engineering & Computing*, 1990, **28**(3), 257-259.

40.   Schmidt, E. M., J. S. McIntosh, and M. J. Bak, Long-term implants of Parylene-C coated microelectrodes, *Med Biol Eng Comput*, 1988, **26**(1), 96-101.

41.   Koivuniemi, A., S. J. Wilks, A. J. Woolley, and K. J. Otto, Multimodal, longitudinal assessment of intracortical microstimulation, *Prog Brain Res*, 2011, **194**, 131-144.

42.   Romo, R., A. Hernández, A. Zainos, and E. Salinas, Somatosensory discrimination based on cortical microstimulation, *Nature*, 1998, **392**(6674), 387-390.

43.   Romo, R., A. Hernández, A. Zainos, C. D. Brody, and L. Lemus, Sensing without touching: psychophysical performance based on cortical microstimulation, *Neuron*, 2000, **26**(1), 273-278.

44.   Tabot, G. A., S. S. Kim, J. E. Winberry, and S. J. Bensmaia, Restoring tactile and proprioceptive sensation through a brain interface, *Neurobiol Dis*, 2015, **83**, 191-198.

45.   O'Doherty, J. E., M. A. Lebedev, T. L. Hanson, N. A. Fitzsimmons, and M. A. Nicolelis, A brain-machine interface instructed by direct intracortical microstimulation, *Front Integr Neurosci*, 2009, **3**, 20.

46.   Daly, J., J. Liu, M. Aghagolzadeh, and K. Oweiss, Optimal space-time precoding of artificial sensory feedback through mutichannel microstimulation in bi-directional brain-machine interfaces, *J Neural Eng*, 2012, **9**(6), 065004.

47.   Butovas, S. and C. Schwarz, Detection psychophysics of intracortical microstimulation in rat primary somatosensory cortex, *Eur J Neurosci*, 2007, **25**(7), 2161-2169.

48.   Butovas, S. and C. Schwarz, Spatiotemporal effects of microstimulation in rat neocortex: a parametric study using multielectrode recordings, *Journal of Neurophysiology*, 2003, **90**(5), 3024-3039.

49.   Houweling, A. R. and M. Brecht, Behavioural report of single neuron stimulation in somatosensory cortex, *Nature*, 2008, **451**(7174), 65-68.

50.   London, B. M., L. R. Jordan, C. R. Jackson, and L. E. Miller, Electrical stimulation of the proprioceptive cortex (area 3a) used to instruct a behaving monkey, *IEEE Trans Neural Syst Rehabil Eng*, 2008, **16**(1), 32-36.

51.   Venkatraman, S. and J. M. Carmena, Active sensing of target location encoded by cortical microstimulation, *IEEE Trans Neural Syst Rehabil Eng*, 2011, **19**(3), 317-324.

52.   Rousche, P .J. and R. A. Normann, Chronic intracortical microstimulation (ICMS) of cat sensory cortex using the Utah Intracortical Electrode Array, *IEEE Transactions On Rehabilitation Engineering*, 1999, **7**(1), 56-68.

53.   Scheich, H. and A. Breindl, An animal model of auditory cortex prostheses, *Audiology & Neuro-Otology*, 2002, **7**(3), 191-194.

54.   Otto, K. J., P. J. Rousche, and D. R. Kipke, Cortical microstimulation in auditory cortex of rat elicits best-frequency dependent behaviors, *J Neural Eng*, 2005, **2**(2), 42-51.

55.   Rousche, P. J., K. J. Otto, M. P. Reilly, and D. R. Kipke, Single electrode micro-stimulation of rat auditory cortex: an evaluation of behavioral performance, *Hear Res*, 2003, **179**(1-2), 62-71.

56.   Deliano, M., H. Scheich, and F. W. Ohl, Auditory cortical activity after intracortical microstimulation and its role for sensory processing and learning, *J Neurosci*, 2009, **29**(50), 15898-15909.

57.   Pfingst, B. E., K. H. Franck, L. Xu, E. M. Bauer, and T. A. Zwolan, Effects of electrode configuration and place of stimulation on speech perception with cochlear prostheses, *J Assoc Res Otolaryngol*, 2001, **2**(2), 87-103.

58. Bartlett, J. R., E. A. DeYoe, R. W. Doty, B. B. Lee, J. D. Lewine, N. Negrão, and W. H. Overman Jr., Psychophysics of electrical stimulation of striate cortex in macaques, *J Neurophysiol*, 2005, **94**(5), 3430-3442.

59. Tehovnik, E. J., W. M. Slocum, and P. H. Schiller, Saccadic eye movements evoked by microstimulation of striate cortex, *Eur J Neurosci*, 2003, **17**(4), 870-878.

60. Tehovnik, E. J., W. M. Slocum, C. E. Carvey, and P. H. Schiller, Phosphene induction and the generation of saccadic eye movements by striate cortex, *J Neurophysiol*, 2005, **93**(1), 1-19.

61. Tehovnik, E. J., W. M. Slocum, and P. H. Schiller, Delaying visually guided saccades by microstimulation of macaque V1: spatial properties of delay fields, *Eur J Neurosci*, 2005, **22**(10), 2635-43.

62. Troyk, P.R., et al., Multichannel cortical stimulation for restoration of vision. in *Conf Proc IEEE Eng Med Biol Soc/BMES* 2002.

63. Troyk, P. R., D. Bradley, V. Towle, R. Erickson, D. McCreery, M. Bak, E. Schmidt, C. Kufta, S. Cogan, and J. Berg, Experimental Results of Intracortical Electrode Stimulation in Macaque V1, *Invest. Ophthalmol. Vis. Sci.*, 2003, **44**(13), 4203.

64. Troyk, P., M. Bak, J. Berg, D. Bradley, S. Cogan, R. Erickson, C. Kufta, D. McCreery, E. Schmidt, and V. Towle, A model for intracortical visual prosthesis research, *Artificial Organs*, 2003, **27**(11), 1005-1015.

65. Troyk, P. R., et al., Intracortical visual prosthesis research - approach and progress, *Conf Proc IEEE Eng Med Biol Soc*, 2005, **7**, 7376-7379.

66. Bradley, D. C., P. R. Troyk, J. A. Berg, M. Bak, S. Cogan, R. Erickson, C. Kufta, M. Mascaro, D. McCreery, E. M. Schmidt, V. L. Towle, and H. Xu, Visuotopic mapping through a multichannel stimulating implant in primate V1, *Journal of Neurophysiology*, 2005, **93**(3), 1659-1670.

67. Maynard, E. M., C. T. Nordhausen, and R. A. Normann, The Utah intracortical Electrode Array: a recording structure for potential brain-computer interfaces, *Electroencephalography and Clinical Neurophysiology*, 1997, **102**(3), 228-239.

68. Shain, W., L. Spataro, J. Dilgen, K. Haverstick, S. Retterer, M. Isaacson, M. Saltzman, and J. N. Turner, Controlling cellular reactive responses around neural prosthetic devices using peripheral and local intervention strategies, *IEEE Transactions on Neural Systems and Rehabilitation Engineering*, 2003, **11**(2), 186-188.

69. Stensaas, S. S. and L. J. Stensaas, Histopathological evaluation of materials implanted in cerebral-cortex, *Acta Neuropathologica*, 1978, **41**(2), 145-155.

70. McConnell, G. C., R. J. Butera, and R. V. Bellamkonda, Bioimpedance modeling to monitor astrocytic response to chronically implanted electrodes, *J Neural Eng*, 2009, **6**(5), 055005.

71. McConnell, G. C., H. D. Rees, A. I. Levey, C. A. Gutekunst, R. E. Gross, and R. V. Bellamkonda, Implanted neural electrodes cause chronic, local inflammation that is correlated with local neurodegeneration, *J Neural Eng*, 2009, **6**(5), 056003.

72. Vetter, R. J., J. C, Williams, J. F. Hetke, E. A. Nunamaker, and D. R. Kipke, Chronic neural recording using silicon-substrate microelectrode arrays implanted in cerebral cortex, *IEEE Trans Biomed Eng*, 2004, **51**(6), 896-904.

73. Williams, J. C., J. A. Hippensteel, J. Dilgen, W. Shain, D. R. Kipke, Complex impedance spectroscopy for monitoring tissue responses to inserted neural implants, *J Neural Eng*, 2007, **4**(4), 410-423.

74. Chen, K. H., J. F. Dammann, J. L. Boback, F. V. Tenore, K. J. Otto, R. A. Gaunt, and S. J. Bensmaia, The effect of chronic intracortical microstimulation on the electrode-tissue interface, *J Neural Eng*, 2014, **11**(2), 026004.

75. Rajan, A. T., J. L. Boback, J. F. Dammann, F. V. Tenore, B. A. Wester, K. J. Otto, R. A. Gaunt, S. J. Bensmaia, The effects of chronic intracortical microstimulation on neural tissue and fine motor behavior, *J Neural Eng*, 2015, **12**(6), 066018.

76. Zesiewicz, T. A., R. Elble, E. D. Louis, R. A. Hauser, K. L. Sullivan, R. B. Dewey Jr, W. G. Ondo, G. S. Gronseth, and W. J. Weiner, Practice parameter: therapies for essential tremor: report of the Quality Standards Subcommittee of the American Academy of Neurology, *Neurology*, 2005, **64**(12), 2008-2020.

77. Cif, L., X. Vasques, V. Gonzalez, P. Ravel, B. Biolsi, G. Collod-Beroud, S. Tuffery-Giraud, H. Elfertit, M. Claustres, and P. Coubes, Long-term follow-up of DYT1 dystonia patients treated by deep brain stimulation: an open-label study, *Mov Disord*, 2010, **25**(3), 289-299.

78. Krack, P., A. Batir, N. Van Blercom, S .Chabardes, V. Fraix, C. Ardouin, A. Koudsie, P. D. Limousin, A. Benazzouz, J. F. LeBas, A. L. Benabid, and P. Pollak, Five-year follow-up of bilateral stimulation of the subthalamic nucleus in advanced Parkinson's disease, *N Engl J Med*, 2003, **349**(20), 1925-1934.

79. Rodriguez-Oroz, M. C., I. Zamarbide, J. Guridi, M. R. Palmero, and J. A. Obeso, Efficacy of deep brain stimulation of the subthalamic nucleus in Parkinson's disease 4 years after surgery: double blind and open label evaluation, *J Neurol Neurosurg Psychiatry*, 2004, **75**(10), 1382-1385.

80. Rodriguez-Oroz, M. C., J. A. Obeso, A. E. Lang, J. L. Houeto, P. Pollak, S. Rehncrona, J. Kulisevsky, A. Albanese, J. Volkmann, M. I. Hariz, N. P. Quinn, J. D. Speelman, J. Guridi, I. Zamarbide, A. Gironell, J. Molet, B. Pascual-Sedano, B. Pidoux, A. M. Bonnet, Y. Agid, J. Xie, A. L. Benabid, A. M. Lozano, J. Saint-Cyr, L. Romito, M. F. Contarino, M. Scerrati, V. Fraix, and N. Van Blercom, Bilateral deep brain stimulation in Parkinson's disease: a multicentre study with 4 years follow-up. *Brain*, 2005, **128**(Pt 10), 2240-2249.

81. Schüpbach, W. M., N. Chastan, M. L. Welter, J. L. Houeto, V. Mesnage, A. M. Bonnet, V. Czernecki, D. Maltête, A. Hartmann, L. Mallet, B. Pidoux, D. Dormont, S. Navarro, P. Cornu, A. Mallet, and Y.Agid, Stimulation of the subthalamic nucleus in Parkinson's disease: a 5 year follow up, *J Neurol Neurosurg Psychiatry*, 2005, **76**(12), 1640-1644.

82. Vedam-Mai, V., N. Krock, M. Ullman, K. D. Foote, W. Shain, K. Smith, A. T. Yachnis, D. Steindler, B. Reynolds, S. Merritt, F. Pagan, J. Marjama-Lyons, P. Hogarth, A. S. Resnick, P. Zeilman, M. S. Okun, The national DBS brain tissue network pilot study: need for more tissue and more standardization, *Cell Tissue Bank*, 2011, **12**(3), 219-231.

83. Johnson, L. A., J. D. Wander, D. Sarma, D. K. Su, E. E. Fetz, and J. G. Ojemann, Direct electrical stimulation of the somatosensory cortex in humans using electrocorticography electrodes: a qualitative and quantitative report, *J Neural Eng*, 2013, **10**(3), 036021.

84. Lycke, R.J., et al., *In vivo evaluation of a muECoG array for chronic stimulation.* Conf Proc IEEE Eng Med Biol Soc, 2014. **2014**, 1294-1297.

85. Nunez, P. L., *Electric Fields of the Brain: the Neurophysics of EEG*, (Oxford University Press, New York, 1981).

86. Otto, K. J., P. J. Rousche, and D. R. Kipke, Microstimulation in auditory cortex provides a substrate for detailed behaviors, *Hear Res*, 2005, **210**(1-2), 112-117.

87. Kim, S., T. Callier, G. A. Tabot, F. V. Tenore, S. J. Bensmaia, Sensitivity to microstimulation of somatosensory cortex distributed over multiple electrodes. *Front Syst Neurosci*, 2015, **9**, 47.

88. Fitzsimmons, N. A., W. Drake, T. L. Hanson, M. A. Lebedev, and M. A. Nicolelis, Primate reaching cued by multichannel spatiotemporal cortical microstimulation, *J Neurosci*, 2007, **27**(21), 5593-5602.

89. O'Doherty, J. E., M. A. Lebedev, P. J. Ifft, K. Z. Zhuang, S. Shokur, H. Bleuler, and M. A. Nicolelis, Active tactile exploration using a brain-machine-brain interface, *Nature*, 2011, **479**(7372), 228-231.

90. Campbell, P. K., R. A. Normann, K. W. Horch, and S. S. Stensaas, A chronic intracortical electrode array: preliminary results, *Journal of Biomedical Materials Research*, 1989, **23**(A2 Suppl), 245-259.

91. Mountcastle, V. B., Modality and topographic properties of single neurons of cat's somatic sensory cortex, *J Neurophysiol*, 1957, **20**(4), 408-434.

92. Rousche, P. J. and R. A. Normann, A method for pneumatically inserting an array of penetrating electrodes into cortical tissue, *Annals of Biomedical Engineering*, 1992, **20**(4), 413-422.

93. Gray, C. M., P. E. Maldonado, M. Wilson, and B. McNaughton, Tetrodes markedly improve the reliability and yield of multiple single-unit isolation from multi-unit recordings in cat striate cortex, *J Neurosci Methods*, 1995, **63**(1-2), 43-54.

94. Histed, M. H., V. Bonin, and R. C. Reid, Direct activation of sparse, distributed populations of cortical neurons by electrical microstimulation, *Neuron*, 2009, **63**(4), 508-522.

95. Shannon, C. E., A Mathematical Theory of Communication, *Bell System Technical Journal*, 1948, **27**(3), 379-423.

96. Wilson, B. S., The future of cochlear implants, *British Journal of Audiology*, 1997, **31**(4), 205-225.

97. Litvak, L. M., Z. M. Smith, B. Delgutte, D. K. Eddington, Desynchronization of electrically evoked auditory-nerve activity by high-frequency pulse trains of long duration, *J Acoust Soc Am*, 2003, **114**(4 Pt 1), 2066-2078.

98. Rubinstein, J.T., B. S. Wilson, C. C. Finley, and P. J. Abbas, Pseudospontaneous activity: stochastic independence of auditory nerve fibers with electrical stimulation, *Hearing Research*, 1999, **127**(1-2), 108-118.

99. Kim, S., T. Callier, G. A. Tabot, R. A. Gaunt, F. V. Tenore, S. J. Bensmaia, Behavioral assessment of sensitivity to intracortical microstimulation of primate somatosensory cortex, *Proc Natl Acad Sci U S A*, 2015, **112**(49), 15202-15207.

100. Middlebrooks, J. C., Effects of cochlear-implant pulse rate and inter-channel timing on channel interactions and thresholds, *J Acoust Soc Am*, 2004, **116**(1), 452-468.

101. McCreery, D. B., T. G. Yuen, W. F. Agnew, and L. A. Bullara, A characterization of the effects on neuronal excitability due to prolonged microstimulation with chronically implanted microelectrodes, *IEEE Transactions on Biomedical Engineering*, 1997, **44**(10), 931-939.

102. Williams, P. E., F. Mechler, J. Gordon, R. Shapley, and M. J. Hawken, Entrainment to video displays in primary visual cortex of macaque and humans, *J Neurosci*, 2004, **24**(38), 8278-8288.

103. Ewert, T. A., C. Vahle-Hinz, and A. K. Engel, High-frequency whisker vibration is encoded by phase-locked responses of neurons in the rat's barrel cortex, *J Neurosci*, 2008, **28**(20), 5359-5368.

104. Joris, P. X., C. E. Schreiner, and A. Rees, Neural processing of amplitude-modulated sounds, *Physiol Rev*, 2004, **84**(2), 541-577.

105. Fu, Q. J. and R. V. Shannon, Effects of dynamic range and amplitude mapping on phoneme recognition in Nucleus-22 cochlear implant users, *Ear and Hearing*, 2000, **21**(3), 227-235.

106. Shannon, R. V., F. G. Zeng, V. Kamath, J. Wygonski, and M. Ekelid, Speech recognition with primarily temporal cues, *Science*, 1995, **270**(5234), 303-304.

107. Birdno, M.J ., S. E. Cooper, A. R. Rezai, W. M. Grill, Pulse-to-pulse changes in the frequency of deep brain stimulation affect tremor and modeled neuronal activity, *J Neurophysiol*, 2007, **98**(3), 1675-1684.

108. Quinkert, A. W., N. D. Schiff, and D. W. Pfaff, Temporal patterning of pulses during deep brain stimulation affects central nervous system arousal, *Behav Brain Res*, 2010, **214**(2), 377-85.

109. Busby, P. A., Y. C. Tong, and G. M. Clark, The perception of temporal modulations by cochlear implant patients, *J Acoust Soc Am*, 1993, **94**(1), 124-131.

110. Shannon, R. V., Temporal modulation transfer functions in patients with cochlear implants, *J Acoust Soc Am*, 1992, **91**(4 Pt 1), 2156-2164.

111. Regele, O. B., A. S. Koivuniemi, and K. J. Otto, Constant RMS versus constant peak modulation for the perceptual equivalence of sinusoidal amplitude modulated signals, *Conf Proc IEEE Eng Med Biol Soc, 2013*, 3115-3118.

112. Koivuniemi, A. and K. Otto, When "altering brain function" becomes "mind control", *Front Syst Neurosci*, 2014, **8**, 202.

Chapter 2.6

Peripheral Nerve Recording Electrodes and Techniques

Ken Yoshida, Michael J. Bertram, T.G. Hunter Cox, and Ronald R. Riso

Department of Biomedical Engineering,
Indiana University – Purdue University Indianapolis
Media Lab, Biomechatronics Department,
Massachusetts Institute of Technology
yoshidak@iupui.edu, rriso@media.mit.edu

Functional neuromuscular stimulation (FNS) systems for neuroprostheses often involve implanted peripheral nerve interfaces. The utility of these implanted electrode systems includes stimulation to evoke muscle or other end organ activation but also extends to recording from sensory afferents to provide sensory information for feedback control of the FNS systems. Peripheral nerve recordings can also provide cognitive feedback to the user of the FNS system and obtain user generated volitional commands. This chapter describes these sensory applications and provides a summary of the current state of the art in this field. The narrative begins with an explanation of the concepts and rationale behind recording peripheral nerve signals for FNS systems, followed by a survey of current electrode architectures, including descriptions and illustrations of many devices that researchers have fabricated. This is followed by a presentation of current applications of sensory recording for use with various FNS systems such as apnea monitoring, correction of foot drop and restoration of grasp function. The chapter concludes with a statement of our opinion concerning the trends and future directions in the field. These trends include advances in electrode structure and materials that have increased the likelihood and efficacy of clinical and therapeutic applications.

1. Introduction

1.1 *What place do peripheral nerve electrodes and recordings have in functional neuromuscular stimulation systems?*

To answer this question, we would like to draw an analogy: When we talk about peripheral nerve recording techniques for use within neuroprostheses, we are talking about techniques which are in many ways analogous to wire-tapping an old style copper cable telephone line. In the case of peripheral nerve interfaces, the telephone lines are the peripheral nerve bundles containing many hundreds of independent channels of communication, which either transmit information centrally from the periphery or from the spinal cord to the periphery. The peripheral nerve electrodes and recording techniques for Functional Neuromuscular Stimulation (FNS) are based upon chronically implanted electrode systems, which form the physical wiretap in our analogy. The electrode forms the biological-electronic interface and has the task of intercepting the signals in the nerve without damaging or disrupting the body's communication pathways. Finally, the signals intercepted by the wiretap must be deciphered and interpreted to extract the signal's information before they are passed on to and acted upon by the neuroprosthetic system controller.

   In this chapter, we will discuss different techniques and electrodes used to make the physical wiretap to the peripheral nervous system. Since the kinds of electrodes are highly dependent on their end use and implant location, we discuss the electrodes in the context of their applications in neuroprosthetics.

1.2   *Functional neuromuscular stimulation systems*

Patient and clinical demands for ease of use and cosmesis have driven the development of FNS systems in diametrically opposite directions. They have either become minimally invasive, simple surface systems (such as the WalkAide™ [19] and Tetron Glove™ [109]) or sophisticated, totally implanted systems. Both types of systems employ some kind of controller to translate a command signal to a set of stimulation parameters. Currently, most FNS controllers can also be classified as open loop controllers despite the fact that many of the electrically excitable organs which FNS systems target are non-linear, non-stationary and prone to influences of external non-modeled perturbations. Classically, engineers have tackled similar problems in other systems by incorporating sensors into their systems and devising closed loop controllers. Biomedical engineers working in neuroprosthetics have also applied closed-loop controllers to increase the accuracy and stability of some FNS systems. Peripheral nerve recording is useful to access natural sensors or motor neurons to provide, respectively, feedback or command signals to the FNS controller.

   Electrodes used to electrically activate muscle can be either implanted within the muscle belly or fixed to the muscle surface (epimysal electrodes used by the Freehand or BioPatRec system [102], or by the injectable stimulation device the Bion™ [83] or the iMES system) or on/in the nerve (such as cuff electrodes and intrafascicular electrodes). Note that, when stimulation electrodes are implanted in a muscle, they aim to activate the nerve fibers leading to the neuromuscular junctions rather than directly activating the muscle sarcomere. Two exceptions in which the electrodes do activate the muscles directly are electrodes for cardiac pacemakers and electrodes that activate denervated muscles. Thus, in general, both muscle implanted and nerve implanted electrodes aim to activate nerve fibers. Muscle based recording electrodes are ElectroMyoGram (EMG) electrodes and implanted ElectroCardioGram (ECG) electrodes. The former records the electrical activity of skeletal muscle, while the latter records cardiac muscle activity. Unlike the stimulation case, EMG electrodes strictly record the activity of muscles and not the nerves.

1.3 *Implanted electrodes*

For neural recording, electrodes can be implanted either into or around a nerve. In either case, they can also pick up stray EMG activity from nearby muscles, which is a major source of noise that must be removed by filtering or by the addition of shielding structures. The ability to use peripheral nerve based electrodes to access neural traffic opens up the possibility to monitor natural sensory end organs such as mechanoreceptors and nociceptors and use them for feedback about the state of the body part. Moreover, if the same electrode can be used to stimulate and to record, the number of implants in the patient can be minimized to reduce the surgery duration and risk. Similarly, efferent motor neuron traffic can also be monitored to measure the command signals to the motor end organs, the skeletal muscles. Natural sensor feedback thus presents an alternative to implanting artificial sensors within the body or fixing external sensors onto the body to provide feedback to the FNS controller.

There are several advantages in using natural sensors. Peripheral sensory end organs remain functional after injury to the central nervous system as long as the locus of trauma/injury does not damage the cell bodies and support cells in and around the spinal cord. They are already part of the body and relay a plethora of information about the periphery. The sensors are robust, self-powered, and optimally (through evolution) distributed around the body. Moreover, they are automatically maintained and kept in good repair by the body. The sensors do not become fouled and are not attacked/encapsulated by the body. Finally, the number, type, and distribution of sensors in the body that can be accessed range beyond what can currently be provided using artificial sensors. They can, in theory, access information that cannot be accessed by artificial sensors. By comparison, artificial sensors are large, require external power, and need to be appropriately distributed. Implanted artificial sensors also tend to be less durable, and in the case of failure must be explanted and replaced.

Some disadvantages of using natural sensors are that their signals must be registered by implanted electrodes. The electrodes must not damage the nerve, become displaced or migrate from their implant site, but rather must be accepted by the body and be chronically stable. Given chronic stability of the electrodes, their signals must be coherent or selective enough so that information from specific sensors at specific parts of the body can be resolved. The records from the electrode must have a high degree of selectivity and sufficient signal-to-noise ratio. The degree of recording selectivity that is attainable can be influenced by the electrode active site geometry or the placement of the electrode.

If stable signals are achieved, some basic understanding of how the nervous system encodes the information traveling within the peripheral nervous system must be used to interpret the signal. Moreover, since motor peripheral nerves are mixed, containing both afferent and efferent fibers, the direction of the recorded signal must be ascertained. Neural recording electrodes are more sensitive to changes in the nerve morphology or damage to the nerve than are neural stimulating electrodes. And, generally, the more selective the recording electrode, the more sensitive it is to these changes. Thus, intracellular electrodes are more sensitive than extracellular single unit electrodes, which in turn are more sensitive than extracellular electrodes recording general mass activity. Extrafascicular electrodes, such as the cuff electrode, are generally the least affected by nerve changes.

There are also some support device issues that should be considered. Although neither the natural sensors nor, in general, peripheral nerve based electrodes require external power, the amplifiers and signal transmitting electronics do. Thus, although natural sensors do not need to be maintained, the potential point of failure is shifted to the implanted electrode and support electronics/hardware. To minimize the potential for failure of the implanted device, electrodes should be placed away from areas of high mechanical stress and away from the delicate nervous structures surrounding the peripheral end organ, whenever possible.

1.4   *The peripheral nervous system*

In this chapter, we define the PNS as the nervous tissues lying peripheral to the spinal canal. This includes nerve axons (efferent and afferent) emerging from the spinal nerves, the motor and sensory end organs and the dorsal root ganglia (DRGs). The dorsal root ganglia are located in an intermediate zone between the spinal cord dorsal roots and the peripheral spinal nerves before they emerge from the vertebral bodies. They contain the cell bodies (soma) of the cutaneous and proprioceptive sensory afferent nerve fibers and pain fibers, which project to the dorsal horn of the spinal cord.

We limit our discussion to electrodes implanted in the peripheral nervous system as a means to tap into the communication between the spinal cord and the end-organ (muscle or natural peripheral sensors). The techniques presented can be used to infer information about the state of the periphery interacting with the environment, or the body commands to the periphery — in particular motor commands to muscles. In general, our definition does not include any interneurons or central synapses. With the exception of possible presynaptic inhibition mediated antidromic volleys and action potential collisions in the dorsal root [32], there is very little processing of the rate coded signals in this part of the nervous system. Thus, signals in the peripheral nervous system, in general, can be taken as commands from the spinal cord to the muscles and sensory signals from peripheral sensors to the spinal cord.

1.5 *Methods of recording nerve activity*

There are several ways in which nerve activity records can be obtained: compound, triggered average, and spontaneous.

Compound activity is commonly used when studying spinal reflexes or measuring the conduction properties of the whole nerve. It measures the synchronous superimposed activity of the fibers within the nerve to a large external electrical, magnetic, or mechanical stimulus. Compound action potentials, in the context of FNS systems, are commonly generated as an artifact of electrical stimulation and override the natural activity in the nerve, first by a synchronous compound volley directly generated by the stimulation, second by a silent period related to the distance between the stimulation site and the source of natural activity (natural sensory end organ or motor neuron soma) and the duration of the refractory period, and third by the reflex volley and its associated periods of excitation and inhibition.

Triggered averaging is used to enhance the signal-to-noise ratio and selectivity of the recording. Multiple sweeps or records are synchronized to a trigger signal, commonly a stimulus or a triggerable event and averaged. With averaging, signals buried in the noise can be brought out of the record. Assuming independence between signal and noise, the signal-to-noise ratio of the activity can be improved by a factor of the square root of the number of averaged events by reducing the noise floor of the recording. The technique works only for noise sources that are asynchronous, stochastic, and independent of the trigger, while the event to be detected occurs with a predictable delay following the trigger. The triggered averaging technique is often used in combination with compound action potentials by using the electrical stimulus as the trigger source. Because of the time needed to compute averages, the response to changes is slow and makes this technique inappropriate for most control applications.

Recording of spontaneous activity is the mode most associated with the use of natural sensors for feedback or the use of motor nerve activity for command in FNS systems. Depending upon the electrode used, changes in either the direct firing rate of the axonal units or the overall energy of the signal is measured. These changes are processed to relate the measured signal to changes in a physical input parameter or command level by the interpretation subsystem before being routed to the FNS controller. A variant of the triggered average recording is the averaged spontaneous recording where multiple low noise amplifiers are used in parallel for each electrode, thereby reducing the preamplifier noise of the recording setup. This comes at the expense of a reduction in the input impedance of the preamplifier stage, an increase in the physical size of the circuitry, an increase in the power needs, and an increase in potential points of failure per recording channel.

2.   Electrodes

2.1   The ideal electrode

The purpose of the electrode influences its shape and design, so it is difficult to define an ideal electrode structure. An ideal structure in one part of the nervous system or designed for one purpose is not necessarily ideal for another. The qualities that the ideal peripheral neuro-electronic interface should embody, however, can be defined. They include the ability to independently detect the activity of a sufficient number of nerve fibers in the peripheral nerve to obtain adequate information from the sensory receptors or motor units. Moreover, they must function throughout the human lifespan without failing, damaging the nerve, influencing the nerve activity or evoking an immune response. Real neuro-electric interfaces strive to attain this ideal. Several parameters that can be used to compare electrode designs are described below. These parameters can also indicate the directions of research for peripheral nerve interfaces (Figure 1).

Selectivity describes the size of the population of units the electrode records. The meaning of the term depends upon the philosophy behind the electrode, whether the electrode is designed to record the composite energy of the activity or to resolve the activity of single axons. Ideal electrodes have high selectivity.

Unit selectivity is the ability of the electrode to record the activity from a single unit, or axon, without interference from other units. It is a measure of the independence of the information channel, or conversely, can be thought of as a measure of the absence of crosstalk. If a recorded signal is only due to a single axon firing, the selectivity is high (ideal). If all units in the nerve contribute to a signal, the selectivity is low (absent). Unit selectivity is independent of unit size and unit location.

Size selectivity is the ability of the interface to discriminate activity based on the axonal diameter of the unit. Since axonal diameter is related to the conduction velocity, an electrode with high size selectivity is able to record selectively from units of a specific diameter or conduction velocity range. Size selectivity does not imply unit selectivity. Similarly, unit selectivity does not imply size selectivity, unless the conduction velocity of a particular unit is established *a priori*. In practice, larger diameter nerve fibers produce higher current flow during action potentials making it easier to record from the largest fibers in the nerve. Thus, research to improve size selectivity in electrodes aims to improve their ability to selectively record from the small fibers in the nerve, and size selectivity has often been a measure of the electrode's ability to reject large fiber activity over small fiber activity. Ideal electrodes would be able to resolve unit activity and thus would be able to selectively differentiate units by fiber size established on *a priori* measurements of conduction velocity.

Spatial selectivity is the ability of the interface to record from a specific location within the nerve, regardless of the conduction velocity of the nerve fiber. Many nerves have a topological organization where, for example, nerve fibers innervating adjacent parts of the body travel together down the nerve trunk [141, 145]. Electrodes with high spatial selectivity could take advantage of this anatomical property, to selectively record from specific parts of the nerve and access coherent information from a specific part of the body. Ideal electrodes would have high spatial selectivity and be able to target and resolve unit activity from specific parts of the nerve.

Reach is the ability of the neural interface to measure, transduce or infer the total information contained within the nerve trunk. It is typically inversely related to the selectivity, the ability to measure high resolution information. If we draw a parallel to the idiom "can't see the forest for the trees", using the trees as the information contained in the single nerve fiber and the forest as the information contained in the entire peripheral nerve trunk, then selectivity would be the ability to resolve single trees, while reach would be the ability to see trees at all corners of the forest.

Signal-to-noise ratio is a measure of how much a recorded signal is corrupted by noise. Many different methods have been used to quantify the signal-to-noise ratio including the peak-to-peak voltage, root mean square of the voltage, and ratio of the means of the amplitudes of the power spectral density. The amplitudes from extra-axonal recordings of action potentials are typically small relative to the thermal noise of the electrode interface and pre-amplifier. The noise floor, even when using low noise pre-amplifiers, could be as high as 1 μV peak-to-peak in the raw record. Extracellular action potentials that can be considered to be large might actually be as small as 5 – 10 μV$_{pp}$. In general, signals recorded extracellularly have signal-to-noise ratios which can be as low as ~1. Factors which influence the signal-to-noise ratio include the efficiency of the recording site, the electrode impedance, the amplifier noise and the distance of the electrode recording site to the active tissue. Filtering and other signal processing techniques could be used to improve the signal-to-noise ratio but require extra hardware and computational time, and may change the shape and timing of the signal depending on the process used. Ideally, noise would be zero so ideal electrodes would have infinite signal-to-noise ratios.

Electrode impedance is defined as the complex, frequency-dependent ratio of the voltage drop through the electrode divided by the current passed through the electrode. Being a complex function of frequency, the electrode impedance is a two dimensional function and is often represented as magnitude vs. frequency and phase vs. frequency curves similar to a Bode Plot, or in the case of Cole-Cole plots (Warburg Diagram) as the locus of real vs. imaginary conductances. Electrode impedance is dominated by the impedance of the electrode interface, but also consists of the series impedance of the lead wires and parallel parasitic capacitances. The interfacial impedance is governed by the surface area and charge transfer efficiency of the electro-ionic interface. The interfacial impedance is commonly reported for a frequency of 1 kHz, or the galvanic (DC) impedance is specified, although alternate methods have been suggested [170]. Although it is commonly thought that high impedance electrodes have better recording properties for needle and glass micropipette electrodes, in actuality the key factor is the small size of the recording site. The electrode impedance is high as a consequence of the small recording area, but this reduces the signal-to-noise ratio of the recording and increases the sensitivity of the electrode to line noise contamination. The ideal electrode is one with a small recording area and as low interfacial impedance as possible.

Coherence/Correlation is a measure of the quality of the relationship of the recorded signal to a functional input. It can be thought of as the strength of the mapping from the observed signal to a physical state or level. This is a purely functional measure and does not make any assumptions regarding the selectivity of the recording site. For example, a low selectivity electrode implanted on a nerve which is purely sensory might respond only to cutaneous pressure on one part of the foot. This electrode would have high information coherence/correlation but low selectivity.

Invasiveness indicates how much penetration into the body is required by the implantation procedure. The more invasive the procedure, the more the body's structures are disrupted by the surgical procedure to place the electrode and the number of structures the electrode itself penetrates. Implanted electrodes are invasive by definition, but there exists a wide range in invasiveness between different electrodes depending upon the amount of surgery required to access the implant site, the amount of manipulation to the nerve and nearby tissues for implantation, and the amount of healing time required. Invasiveness of the procedure must be balanced by the benefits gained and the degree of acceptance of the electrode in the body.

Speed and ease of implantation is related to the invasiveness of the electrode and implantation procedure. It has direct implication on the ultimate cost of the FNS system as well as the rate of success, surgical recovery time, and incidence of infection. For the FNS system to be cost effective, the implant procedure should be as easy as possible and the surgical time as short as possible.

Expected lifespan of the implant is critical because the implanted subsystems must have a sufficiently long working lifetime to justify their use. Ideally, the working lifespan should match the human lifespan. Failure of any of the components in the systems would require surgical revision to remove the defective component and replace it, which is costly and in some cases not possible.

Biocompatibility is a multifaceted term related to material properties, acceptance of the implant by the body, and impact of the implant on the body's tissues. Long term impact on the nerve is a specific measure of biocompatibility, and can be quantified by measuring the morphological changes to the nerve as a result of implanting the neural interface.

Chronic recording stability is a measure of the long term performance of the electrode. It is influenced by the biocompatibility of the electrode, integrity of the electrode structure, and changes in the morphology at the implant site. In this chapter, we use this measure as an estimate of the length of time over which useful recordings can be made.

Robustness is a measure of how resistant the electrode structure is to physical manipulation, such as stresses during implantation and during chronic use. It can be a measure of how easy the electrodes are to handle or how many times the electrode can be re-implanted and reused before it wears out. It is also a measure of the resistance of the electrode recording technique to failure and includes measures of the noise immunity and fault tolerance of the neural recording technique.

Cost is a measure of how financially realistic the system is for implementation in a neuroprosthetic device. It can be quantified not only by the cost to produce the electrode, but also by the cost of the support hardware, surgical time, rehabilitation time and duration of training required for the system to be functional.

2.2   *Overview of current electrode technologies*

The recording electrode is the key component in the interface. Peripheral nerve recording electrodes can be classified into four broad groups based upon the location of the electrode's active site: Intracellular, Intraneural, Extraneural Regeneration-based, and Cellular-based. Intracellular electrodes are electrodes which measure the transmembrane potential of the cell. Intraneural electrodes are those in which the electrode recording site is placed in the extraaxonal or extracellular space, but within the endoneurium of the peripheral nerve fascicle or the dorsal root ganglion (DRG) neuropil. Extraneural electrodes place the electrode recording site on the surface of the nerve fascicle or the nerve trunk. Regeneration based nerve interfaces consist of specially designed structures that sprouting fibers from a regenerating transected nerve grow into to form an intimate and stable contact with one or more electrodes. Cellular-based recording systems are electrodes that have had had neural cells or tissues grown onto them to facilitate signal conduction.

We will use the parameters presented above to draw comparisons between the real electrodes presented in this section and the ideal case. The ratings are subjective based upon personal experience and the literature. The comparisons are meant to introduce and illustrate the relative strengths and weaknesses of various electrode technologies currently available or under development. We do not intend to draw any conclusions, leaving this to the reader, but hope to indicate the state of the art and the direction of current research in the field. We first describe the classical electrophysiological techniques from which neuroprosthetic electrodes originated for each of the first three defined electrode types. These range from hook or suction electrodes, used in acute studies to record the general activity of nerve trunks or branches; to needle electrodes, used for recording unit activity (i.e., where the activity of one or more individual nerve fibers can be distinguished from each other among a population of active fibers); to glass micropipette electrodes, used for recording axonal and transmembrane bioelectric potentials.

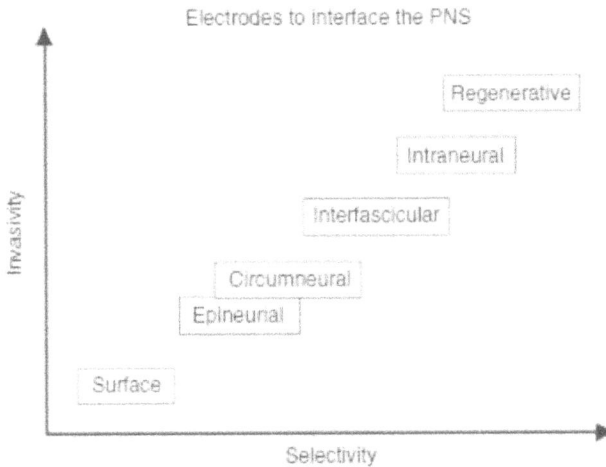

Fig. 1. Visual representation of the trade-off between selectivity and invasiveness that demonstrates the ideal electrode is greatly dependent on the application [99].

2.3 *Intracellular electrodes*

Intracellular electrodes measure the transmembrane potential of the cell. Current designs are unsuited for long term implantation and thus not useful for application in neuroprostheses. They are the antithesis of the ideal neuroprosthetic electrode in all aspects except one: they achieve ideal selectivity. Moreover, intracellular electrodes, when properly applied, record the electrical activity of a single cell and are the only electrodes capable of directly observing the classic action potential waveform described in physiology textbooks, showing a rapid depolarization followed by a rapid repolarization and slow after-hyperpolarization. All other electrodes described in this chapter record extracellular potentials resulting from propagating action potentials in the peripheral nerve. They differ from intracellularly recorded action potentials in that they are either biphasic or triphasic, and are proportional to the first or second temporal derivative of the classic transmembrane action potential.

There are two modern modes of making intracellular recordings, current clamp and voltage clamp (Figure 2) [38, 111]. The techniques used are analogous to current source based and voltage source based electrical impedance characterizations of an unknown electrical system, which should be familiar to electrical engineers. Current clamp measurements are analogous to the current source based characterization of an unknown system. A fixed current is imposed on the unknown system and the potential is free to change in response to this applied stimulus. In the traditional current clamp recording mode, an amplifier with a high input impedance and low bias current is used with the recording electrode to monitor the potential at the recording site relative to an indifferent electrode in the extracellular space. Since there is almost no current passing through the recording electrode into the cell, the test current from the setup is fixed or 'clamped'.

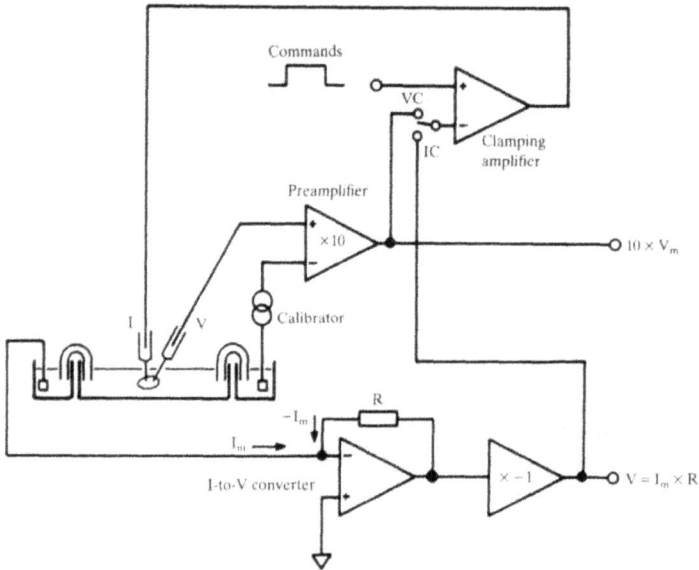

Fig. 2. Schematic of a typical intracellular recording setup for both voltage clamp and current clamp recordings. From [38].

This traditional current clamp, or voltage follower, with the current clamped at zero, is the common method to record the action potential intracellularly and extracellularly. A departure of this generalization, which is only applicable to intracellular recordings, is when non-zero bias currents are imposed on the cell. The ratio of the resulting voltage to the imposed current characterizes the impedance of the cell.

The voltage clamp mode is similar to the voltage source based electrical characterization where a voltage is imposed on the system and the resulting current is monitored. The technique is typically limited in use to intracellular recordings or extracellular tissue impedance characterization. The ratio of the resulting current to the imposed voltage characterizes the conductance of the cell, or more importantly the channels in the cell membrane. The technique was used by Hodgkin and Huxley in the late 1930's to observe the behavior of voltage gated channels in giant squid axon and led to their seminal work - a model describing and predicting the nature and behavior of these channels during the action potential [46].

The method was pioneered with the squid giant axon by threading fine wire electrodes inside the excised axon and making recordings *in vitro*. A refinement to the technique is the use of a glass micropipette electrode. It and its variants, such as the patch micropipette electrode and the double barrel micropipette electrode, have become the standard electrode for basic electrophysiology. Practically speaking, these electrodes are not commonly used in the peripheral nerve for axonal recordings because of the small size of mammalian axons and the extremely tough tissue surrounding them, though with persistence it can be done. They have been used in mammalian DRGs [1] and are commonly used in the spinal cord.

2.3.1 *The glass micropipette electrode*

Glass micropipette electrodes are very fine electrodes constructed by heating glass capillary tubes (~1mm OD) at a temperature above its melting point and drawing them to form a continuous, hollow glass electrically insulating shell with a tip of ~1 μm OD It is a physical property of glass tubes that when they are drawn they retain their wall to lumen (ID) ratio. Thus, it is possible to produce extremely fine insulating and structurally patent hollow shells. Although the electrical insulation value of the glass walls of the electrode varies with the wall thickness, the insulation is continuous and pin-hole free. The shape and profile of the shell depends on the end use of the electrode and the tissue it is meant to penetrate. The shell is filled with a conductive solution, typically 4-M KCl. A piece of chlorided silver wire is threaded inside the stem of the glass shell and is the electrode's electro-ionic interface. The high conductivity salt solution provides a fluid phase conductive path or bridge between the electro-ionic interface and the electrode's recording site at the tip of the micropipette. The sintered Ag/AgCl interface of the silver wire is an electro-ionic interface of the second kind and thus is a non-polarizable electrode capable of transmitting sustained DC currents in solutions containing mobile chloride ions (Figure 3).

The glass micropipette is used to penetrate tissue and impale cells to place the electrode recording site within the cytoplasm of the cell. The electrode is relatively easy to make, easy to reproduce, and inexpensive.

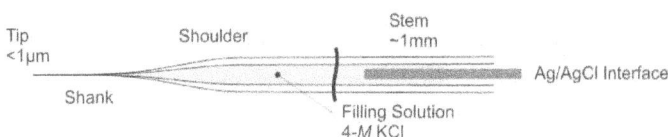

Fig. 3. A glass micropipette electrode for intracellular recording.

Glass micropipette electrodes are used for basic electrophysiological measurements of transmembrane cellular potentials or currents, to record nerve membrane potentials and to stimulate single cells (bacteria/plant/animal). Cells can be within the tissue *in situ*, *in vivo*, or *in vitro*. Use of these electrodes is typically restricted to acute studies in animal preparations, single isolated cells, or cultured cells. They are not suitable for chronic animal, human, or clinical use because of mechanical stability issues and damage to the cells they interrogate. Moreover, since Ag^+ is toxic to cells, chronic use of electrodes using Ag/AgCl interfaces is not appropriate, unless diffusion of the ion to tissue can be prevented by an ionic diffusion barrier (Figure 4).

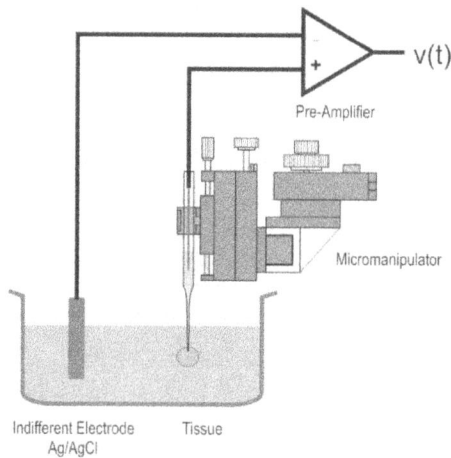

Fig. 4. Drawing (not to scale) of a monopolar *in-vitro* intracellular recording setup.

Micropipette electrodes are slowly advanced into tissue using a microdrive attached to a micromanipulator. Microscopes are used to visualize and assist in impaling nerve cells which may be *in situ* in the tissue or dissociated. They are also used to visualize tip and/or track locations when used in tissue slices or *in situ* where a blind approach is required. Once the electrode has penetrated the cell, the cell membrane must seal around the electrode shaft and relative movement between the electrode and the cell must be limited to less than a few hundred nanometers to prevent rupturing the cell and to allow stable recordings. When the electrode-cell seal is broken, or if the electrode-cell seal does not form, the built up ionic gradients and cytoplasm discharge through the hole in the cell membrane which ultimately kills the cell. This rapid depolarization of the cell results in a characteristic high frequency volley of action potentials, called an injury discharge. An advantage of pipette electrodes is that dyes can be added to the filling solutions, and electrophoretically injected into impaled cells. This labels the cells where recordings are made and allows for their identification with *post hoc* histological examination of the tissue.

2.4 *Intraneural penetrating electrodes*

Intraneural electrodes are those, which penetrate the nerve fascicle and place their active site in the peripheral nerve endoneurium or, in the case of the DRG, within the neuropil. The basic electrophysiological prototype of this electrode is the needle microelectrode, whose fundamental working principle is to place a small recording site as close as possible to the active part of the bioelectrical tissue to try to record from as small a population of fibers as possible. Like the intracellular electrode, basic studies with intraneural electrodes have formed the basis of our understanding of how the nervous system functions. They continue to be used in basic research to extend our understanding.

Unlike the intracellular electrode, various types of intraneural electrodes have made their way into clinical application such as microneurography, and intraoperative guidance for surgery of deep brain structures. They have also been an area of active research in neuroprosthetics as a chronic nerve interface. Placing the active site in close proximity to the active tissue, within the perineurium (which is an electrically insulating membrane), leads to the key advantage of intraneural electrode techniques over extraneural recording techniques: they inherently have higher recording selectivity and better signal-to-noise properties over their extraneural counterparts. The key developmental challenge has been to extend their recording stability, biocompatibility, and robustness. Being early in their development as a FNS neural interface, intraneural penetrating electrodes have not yet made their way into FNS systems as the primary neural interface.

2.4.1 *Needle microelectrodes*

Needle microelectrodes are very fine electrodes constructed out of an electrosharpened metal wire or carbon fiber ranging in diameter from 10 to 500 μm. Electrodes can be between ~1 mm to ~10 cm in length depending on their application. The electrode is insulated with a thin polymer varnish or glass, and the tip exposed by an electric arc [80], heat, laser ablation, or by grinding. Because of their small recording area, they are capable of making highly selectivity recordings of extracellular fields in nervous tissue and muscle fibers, and they can be used for microstimulation of nervous tissue as well. The electrodes are intended for use in recording from and stimulating small populations of cells.

Needle electrodes can be used in central and peripheral nerves as well as in muscle. They are constructed out of a stiff metal (e.g., tungsten or hardened stainless steel) or a carbon fiber core, which forms a strong but rigid structure that is used to push the tip of the electrode through skin, muscle and other soft tissue. The sharpened exposed tip of the electrode helps to penetrate the tissue, and forms the bioelectric interface of the electrode.

Due to its extremely small tip, this interface is selective enough to record single units. The electrode is relatively easy to make, though insulating the electrode can be problematic. Their applications are broad, ranging from basic electrophysiology to clinical use, and from short-term acute to chronic use in animals. Longevity and stability depend on electrode design, which is application dependent. Chronic electrodes require additional stabilization and support. They are mostly used in the brain where the skull can be used to stabilize and anchor the electrode. Clinical techniques using needle electrodes include microneurography, micromyography, and deep brain recording, stimulation, and lesioning.

Although there is no standard method to apply needle electrodes, they are typically advanced slowly through the tissue. Microneurography electrodes are advanced through the skin and towards superficial peripheral nerves. A microdrive system attached to micromanipulators often in combination with a stereotaxic frame is commonly used in animal work, and intraoperatively in deep brain applications. However, manual application of the electrode is common with microneurography in the clinic. In this case, the electrode, once inserted, is left "floating" in the tissue and not attached to an external structure, as a safety precaution to minimize movement of the electrode in the tissue in case the patient moves.

2.4.2 Intrafasicular electrodes

Chronically implanted intraneural penetrating electrodes implanted into a peripheral nerve trunk are classified as intrafascicular electrodes. The electrode active site is located in the endoneural space between axons within the nerve fascicle. The implantation direction of the electrode differentiates two major types of intrafascicular electrodes: Electrodes implanted such that the structural elements containing the active site are parallel to the axis of the nerve are called *Longitudinally Implanted Intrafascicular Electrodes* (LIFE), while those where the structural components are implanted normal to the axis of the nerve are called *Transversely Implanted Intrafascicular Electrodes* (TIME). Finally, a new structure called *Self-Opening Intraneural Peripheral Interface* (SELINE), is implanted like a TIME or LIFE, but seeks to solve the issue of electrode migration after implantation by adding tines to prevent movement inside the nerve trunk (Figure 5).

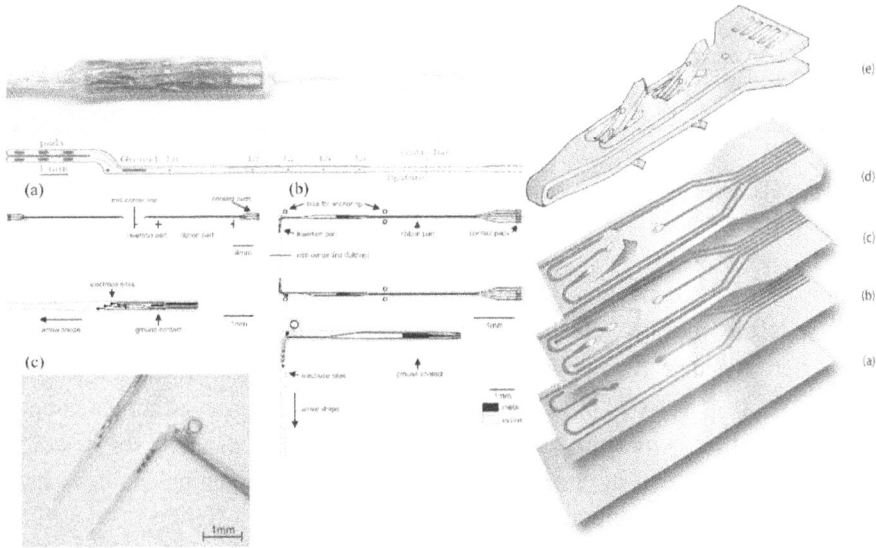

Fig. 5. Schematic and physical representations of: (top left) LIFE structures [91] that would be pulled through the nerve longitudinally via tungsten introduction needle attached to the loop shown above, (bottom left) TIME structures [4] which would be injected through the nerve transversely using a tungsten introducing needle, similar to the LIFE, and (right) SELINE structures [18] which once inserted would use the barbs seen in picture **(e)** to prevent any slippage out of the nerve.

2.4.3 *Microneurography*

TIME and LIFE structures are derived from microneurography electrodes. Microneurography electrodes are long needle electrodes typically made of tungsten or stainless steel; concentric needle electrodes are constructed out of hypodermic needles. The electrode recording site is located at the tip of the needle in the case of needle electrodes or near the tip in the case of concentric needle electrodes. The recording site is percutaneously driven through the skin perpendicular to the surface of the nerve so that their active site and the tip of the electrode structure lie within the endoneural space. Although it is somewhat controversial, there are some who claim that the active site of these electrodes is driven intrafascicularly through the perineurium to make intrafascicular recordings or even through the axonal membrane to make intraneural recordings [37] (Figure 6).

A   B

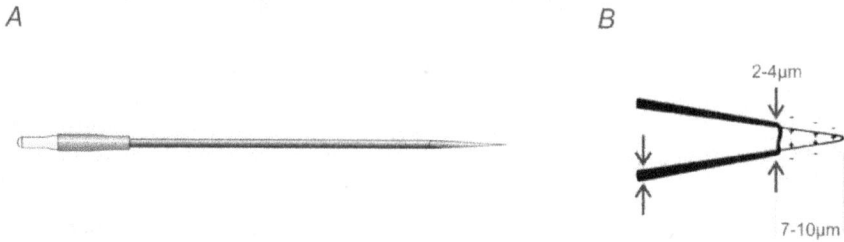

Fig. 6. Microneurography needle electrode. A shows a commercial tungsten needle electrode whose tip geometry is shown in B.

An example of an early, chronically implanted, transverse intrafascicular electrode is the "hatpin" electrode which was implanted in the dorsal roots to record afferent neural activity in chronic animals to investigate basic motor control physiology. This electrode is constructed out of a short, sharpened tungsten needle, with a thin lead-out wire soldered at a right angle to the needle. The solder junction is insulated with a drop of epoxy, which also forms a convenient point to handle the electrode during implantation [80].

Another example is the dorsal root and dorsal root ganglion electrode pioneered by Loeb [80] and Prochazka [108] for use in chronic awake animal experiments. This electrode is constructed using a varnish insulated, 17 μm diameter, PtIr wire. The varnish near the end of the wire is mechanically cracked to deinsulate a zone on the wire by placing a portion near the end of the wire in tension. This zone is then cut at an angle to produce a sharp point which doubles as the recording site. The electrode is implanted by pushing the sharpened point of the wire into the dorsal root ganglion and secured into place with a small drop of cyanoacrylate glue. Signals from the DRG from these electrodes were wirelessly transmitted through a custom built telemeter to enable highly selective recordings of nerve afferent activity from an awake, behaving cat. The electrode has moderate stability but low reach, with recordings from single units lasting from a few minutes to several days, limited by the migration of the tip within the DRG.

2.4.4 Transversely implanted intrafasicular electrodes (TIMEs)

Microneurography electrodes may have been the inspiration for the TIME and LIFE, in that they were designed to achieve microneurography level resolution through insertion, however these large needles had some major design flaws such as the lack of biocompatibility, chronic implantation viability, poor signal to noise ratio, and the limitation of only one recording site per insertion, though Prochazka and colleagues have recently modified the electrode to be used as a chronic electrode for the spinal cord [95].

Multi-contact electrodes based on micropatterned silicon and high-density wire electrode array structures were attempted by Rutten and his colleagues [122]. They were primarily used as a means to determine the optimal electrode density for stimulation to form a one-to-one connection with fibers within the nerve fascicle.

Flexible multicontact electrode arrays constructed from micropatterned polyimide were first reported by González [29]. Relatively large electrodes were constructed and implanted in muscle using a needle introducer or transversely in peripheral nerve using an attached suture. This novel structure was able to record EMG activity; however, no evidence of neural recording was presented. A key advantage of electrode arrays is that multiple high selectivity electrodes are implanted simultaneously. Instead of searching for active units during implantation, arrays are designed to maximize the probability of finding a unit, thereby overcoming some of the disadvantages of the high selectivity electrode by extending the reach of the overall electrode structure introduced with a single implant.

Although not all the electrodes in the array will have a differentiable unit, there is a good chance that at least one will. Simultaneous recording with multiple sites also opens up the possibility of spatial averaging or using the stereotrode/tetrode effect originally applied in cortical and deep brain structures for unit separation [33, 89]. Recently, chronic high-density electrode array structures constructed out of micromachined silicon have been developed by Normann and his colleagues [11]. They have successfully modified a technique used for cortical recording and stimulation, the Utah Array, for use in peripheral nerves and have named their new interface the Utah Slant Array. Branner successfully demonstrated highly selective recordings using this array in acute cats [11]. Harreby et al. [39] were able to demonstrate chronic implantation feasibility by examining the encapsulation of the nerve in large human-sized nerve in the Göttingen Minipig.

2.4.5 *Longitudinally implanted intrafasicular electrodes (LIFEs)*

Longitudinal Intra-Fascicular Electrodes or LIFEs are a family of intrafascicular electrodes which differ from the transversely implanted design in two ways. They are implanted longitudinally, or parallel to the main axis of the peripheral nerve, and the active site of the electrode is not at the tip of the electrode wire. This enables the electrode structure to be pulled or drawn through the nerve and anchored at both the entry and exit points to secure the active site within the nerve at two points. Bowman and Erickson at Rancho Los Amigos Rehabilitation Center first suggested a neural interface consisting of 300 μm coiled stainless steel wire electrodes that are intraneurally implanted using a 30G needle. They tested the concept in the chronic rabbit and cat model to determine stimulation stability and saw no evidence of demyelination or denervation [8].

Horch and Schoenberg at the University of Utah modified the technique to minimize the implant trauma and produce an appropriate recording electrode by replacing the thick stainless steel wire with a much finer 25 μm Teflon insulated, platinum iridium wire. The fine wire was attached to an electrosharpened tungsten needle so that the electrode could be implanted by sewing the fine wire electrode into the nerve. The active site of the electrode was created by de-insulating a small 1 – 2 mm segment of the insulated wire [86]. The technique was further refined by electro-depositing platinum black on the de-insulated platinum wire to reduce the interfacial impedance and thermal noise. Horch's group further went on to demonstrate the recording [78] and stimulation selectivity [96, 171] of metal wire based LIFEs, and the possibility of using other more exotic electrode materials including p-pyrole, carbon fiber, and metallized poly-aramid fibers [90].

Yoshida and Stein at the University of Alberta demonstrated the possibility of using metal wire LIFEs for recording neural activity in chronically implanted awake cats. These studies characterized the effect of electrode spacing for rejecting EMG and stimulus artifact, and explored the possibility of using multichannel recordings for noise reduction. There have also been attempts to use silicon [62] and fine thin-film [173] microfabricated structures implanted longitudinally, with initial reports indicating that highly selective recordings are possible with these structures. This was confirmed in Muceli et al. [94] who were able to sample large populations and selectively record from motor units in humans.

2.4.6 *The self-opening intraneural peripheral interface (SELINE)*

The Self-Opening Intraneural Peripheral Interface (SELINE) class of electrodes is an attempt to solve the mechanical stabilization and selectivity problem without compromising either. Previous iterations of TIME and tf-LIFE electrodes showed that some movement from limb motion and scar tissue can reduce the signal-to-noise ratio. SELINEs are developed to be implanted transversely or obliquely to allow for stimulation and recording from different fascicles by using a main body and two lateral 'wing' structures to reach into other directions for added selectivity.

Micera and Navarro [18] pioneered the SELINE with a silicone wafer for spin-coated polyimide substrate layers. The main body of the SELINE is 360 μm wide, the wings are 150 μm wide and 400 μm long. The length of the total body SELINE varies to fit the diameter of the nerve it is implanted in. The active sites are .0037

mm^2 and are located in specific sensitive regions: one site on the main shaft and two active sites on each wing. The microfabrication of the device follows the standard lithographic techniques established for thin-film electrodes.

The creators of the SELINE discovered that it takes between 5 and 10 times as much force to remove the SELINE from the nerve as a TIME and both recording and stimulating indices are increased. These sub-chronic studies seem promising to helping solve the problem, but further studies are needed to determine its true functionality in human subjects.

2.5   *Extraneural electrodes*

Extraneural electrodes are those in which the active site is placed on the surface of the peripheral nerve (i.e., on the epineurium). The basic prototype is the hook electrode or suction electrode, whose fundamental working principle is to record the general activity of the nerve. Like the previous two electrode types, many extraneural techniques have been and continue to be used in basic electrophysiology studies. Among the neural interfaces discussed in this chapter, extraneural techniques, particularly in the form of cuff electrodes described below, are the least invasive, and were the first to be used in human subjects as an interface to provide feedback from natural sensors to a fully implemented closed loop FNS system. They are the most researched, and most widely used nerve-based neuroprosthetic interface. Their advantages are recording stability, durability, and ease of implementation. Key areas of active research have been to improve their recording selectivity.

2.5.1 *Hook electrodes*

Hook electrodes are general purpose electrodes for peripheral nerve stimulation and recording. They are used in acute animal studies and as an intraoperative tool for nerve identification during reconstructive surgery and FNS electrode implants in humans [168]. The electrode is constructed out of two or more "J" shaped wires, which are soldered to insulated lead wires that are routed through a tube or handle. Peripheral nerves or filaments are draped over these wires to make the nerve-electrode interface. The wires must be stiff enough to support the nerve or nerve filaments without yielding. Typical materials for the electrode are Ag/AgCl, Pt, stainless steel, tungsten, and copper (for use in animal work only). The electrode is extremely easy to make and can be produced at a nominal cost (Figure 7).

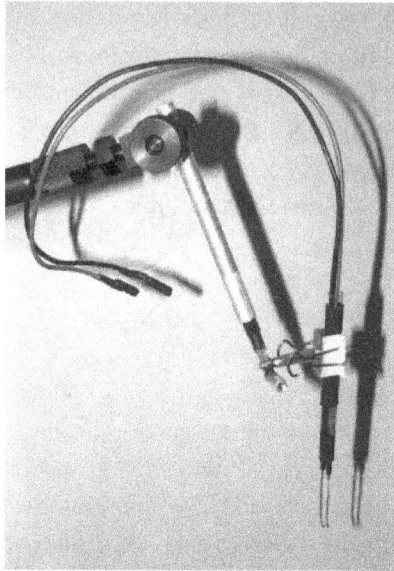

Fig. 7. A bipolar hook electrode for use in animal experiments on large nerves. The electrode is shown attached to ball joint holder and anchoring support.

The hook electrode is a basic tool used in electrophysiology. Although hook electrodes are typically restricted to acute, non-survival animal experiments due to the invasiveness of the protocols in which they are applied, they have made their way into the hospital surgical theater. In these procedures, they have been used as an intraoperative tool for identifying nerve branches in reconstructive nerve surgery or before implant of FNS electrodes.

These electrodes provide general purpose, low selectivity recordings of extracellular potentials from peripheral nerves or peripheral nerve filaments. Hook electrodes can also be used for recording or stimulating small skeletal, cardiac and smooth muscles. To apply hook electrodes, an access is created to the nerve or muscle of interest. The hook electrode is mounted on a support and the nerve or muscle of interest is draped over the end of one or more of the hook electrode's wires. The separation between the electrodes can be adjusted to change the recording/stimulating properties.

To eliminate electrical shunting between the electrode leads through the extracellular fluid, hook electrodes are often used in combination with a paraffin oil pool in acute animal models. An oil pool is created by tying the skin flaps from the surgical incision to a hoop, and filling the access cavity with warm paraffin oil. The electrode hook and the hooked tissue are pulled into the paraffin oil pool during use. In human surgical procedures with hook electrodes, the nerve can be temporarily suspended in air to remove current shunts instead of using an oil pool.

Due to its large interfacial area, this interface is inherently non-selective. Its reach can span the entire nerve trunk, with its sensitivity skewed to large fibers. In acute animal studies, selectivity is often increased by surgically reducing the preparation, and dividing the nerve by physically splitting it. While it isn't possible to dissect a single nerve filament free, the reduction to just a small bundle still allows single unit responses to be recognized in the nerve recordings. This technique for improving selectivity causes considerable damage to the nerve and is not applicable to human or chronic animal work. The exception to this statement may be when sacral root rhizotomy is performed to remove spastic reflexes or exaggerated muscle tone which sometimes interferes with neuroprosthetic function. In the case of FNS systems to produce voiding, the sacral dorsal roots are cut as part of the operating procedure. Further splitting of the cut sacral root may be an option to improve recording selectivity without influencing the benefits of the rhizotomy.

2.5.2 *Circumferential cuff electrodes*

The cuff electrode is currently the most researched and developed recording interface for use in neuroprosthetics. At the time of this writing, it is the only implanted nerve interface being used in humans with spinal cord injury or stroke to provide FNS systems with natural sensory feedback information. As such, it is currently, the most clinically important neuroprosthetic recording electrode for the peripheral nervous system.

The cuff electrode is an advance over the hook electrode and can be thought of as a chronically implantable hook electrode. The predominant structural component of the cuff electrode is a silicone tube or cuff, which is placed around the nerve trunk. This silicone tube is used as a portable paraffin oil bath to constrain the extracellular currents and magnify the electrical fields within it. Thin metal film strips or bared metal wire are laminated against or inlaid into the inner wall of the silicone cuff to form the active sites of the electrode structure. These electrodes sites are sometimes in the form of rings and pick up propagating action potential fields that are confined by the cuff, in the case of recording, or transmit stimulation currents, in the case of stimulation.

Similar to the hook electrode, since the active sites of the cuff electrode are large circumferential conductive rings, they average the signal seen by different parts of the recording site. This results in an electrode with poor topological selectivity, but one which can measure the general electrical activity within a nerve. The axonal size selectivity of the cuff electrode during recording depends on the inter-ring spacing of the electrodes and the width of the contact along the path of the nerve fiber. Large caliber nerve fibers have longer inter-nodal spacings whereas smaller caliber fibers have shorter inter-nodal spacings, and this has led to the suggestion that spatial filtering techniques could be used to design a cuff electrode to selectivity discriminate small fibers verses large fiber activity [147].

The first circumferential cuff electrode used for chronic recording was described by Hoffer [175] and later by Stein et al. [137, 138] as a stable electrode to study cutaneous and muscle afferents, first in animals and later in humans. A major breakthrough in the design was to make a longitudinal slit in the cuff tubing to enable implantation of the electrode without cutting the nerve [139]. Several modeling and in-vivo studies on the impact of the slit on the recording properties of the cuff have been made [3]. Although it enables a less invasive method to implant the electrode, the slit represents a breach of the insulating cuff and forms a leakage pathway for the extracellular action current. These studies showed that the cuff relies on the integrity of the insulating shell to focus the extracellular current, and that this leakage pathway has major consequences in the recording properties of the electrode. Subsequently, new closure methods were developed to minimize the effect. These include the addition of a second cuff over the first cuff with staggered slits, the incorporation of a silicone flap over the slit [3], the use of piano hinge-like closures [63], the use of intraoperative silicone glue to seal the slit, and the development of the self-curling spiral cuff electrode at CWRU [97].

Each of the above methods has advantages and disadvantages. The addition of a second insulating cuff creates an extremely thick and inflexible electrode which is difficult to implant and size properly. The piano hinge structure is an elegant design but requires more skill by the surgeon to close. Furthermore, it was found that the closure does not prevent leakage. The use of intraoperative silicone glues and sealers is not optimal in that the curing of the silicone is not well controlled, nor is the surface it is adhering to clean. Moreover, there is the danger that the glue penetrates the recording electrode to cover the electrode active site. The best closure of a cuff with a slit in it was found to be the use of a silicone flap [3]. The self-spiraling cuff design is another elegant design in which stress is built into the wall of the electrode structure so that it curls on itself to simplify implantation and minimize current leakage [97, 127].

Sizing of the cuff electrode is a critical factor in the performance of the electrode. Both the length of the cuff and the diameter play an important part in the success of the electrode's chronic use. The length of the cuff plays a role in the strength of the signal recorded from the nerve [139]. The number of nodes of Ranvier within the cuff is a key determining parameter of the shape and strength of the recorded signal. Given that the internodal spacing varies with the diameter of the nerve fiber, some discrimination potential exists by manipulating the length of the cuff [3]. There are practical limits to the length of the cuff, however, because long cuffs become difficult to implant, and finding sites to accommodate long cuffs is difficult. Surgical and biological concerns point to shorter cuffs, while theoretical concerns point to cuffs ranging between 20 – 50 mm in length.

The inner diameter of the cuff plays an equally significant role. Snug fitting electrodes, theoretically, limit current leakage and this results in the strongest signals. However, surgical manipulation of the nerve during implantation can result in trauma to the nerve, which can result in acute swelling and ischemia. Chronically, given that the body does not reject the electrode, the electrode becomes encapsulated. While it is most desirable to maintain an intimate contact between the circumferential electrodes and the nerve to achieve the highest amplitude recordings, fixed diameter cuffs must be sized between 10 - 20% larger than the outer diameter of the nerve to accommodate post-surgical expansion of the nerve [75, 92] and encapsulation of the electrode. Self-spiraling cuffs, on the other hand, are designed to be able to adjust their diameter (expand) in the post-surgical period if swelling does occur, and thus, eliminate the need to implant a cuff that is deliberately oversized.

2.5.3 *Multi-contact cuff electrodes*

A substantial advancement in the development of cuff electrodes that can activate different fascicles was first introduced by Veraart et al. [152] who fixed 12 small electrode contacts to the interior surface of a silicone spiral cuff. The contacts were connected as 4 sets of tripoles. This arrangement allowed separate activation of each of the four quadrants around the circumference of the cuffed nerve. While Verrart et al. were principally interested in selective nerve stimulation, the idea of using an array of distributed contacts within a cuff for purposes of obtaining fascicle selective nerve recording has been taken up by others. One design developed and tested by Hoffer et al. [48] places the electrode contacts at the bottom of longitudinal 'grooves' formed on the inside walls of the cuff. Such grooves constrain the feeble neural currents to travel within the channel spaces formed between the nerve surface and the silicone tubing walls where each tripole set of contacts is placed.

2.5.4 Polyimide-silicone hybrid cuff electrodes

A drawback of the early prototypes of the multicontact cuff electrodes developed by Verrart and his colleagues was the increased bulkiness of the cuff due to the additional lead wires and weld joints at each of the contact sites. This situation can be improved by using metalized polyimide sheeting as the carrier for the electrode contacts and intracuff leads. Figure 8 shows a schema for fabricating such a hybrid cuff [133]. The electrode sites consist of thin platinum discs which are accessed by integral conductive traces formed from gold. Both the shape of the polyimide substrate and metalization traces are easily realized by standard microfabrication techniques so that arbitrary designs can be formed with high precision and repeatability and tested for efficacy.

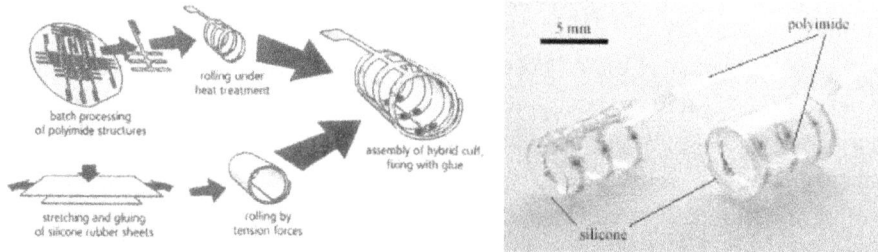

Fig. 8. **Left** - fabrication scheme for a polyimide silicone hybrid cuff having 18 contact sites arranged into 6 tripoles. **Right** - photo of assembled cuffs showing a fixed diameter cuff with a piano hinge closure and a self-coiling spiral structure. (Figure courtesy of M. Schuettler, Fraunhofer Inst. Biomed. Eng. St. Ingbert, Germany)

By using a minimal polyimide carrier laminated to the interior of a self-spiraling silicone cuff, the hybrid design shown in Figure 8 retains the favorable flexibility of a thin walled silicone cuff. Research issues with such cuff designs include obtaining good adherence of the platinum contacts with the polyimide carrier and the inclusion of a multiplexer circuit near the cuff to minimize the number of leads needed to access the cuff sites [133]. Densities of up to 18 contacts (arranged as 6 tripolar channels) have been realized for cuffs of 4 to 6 mm diameter (12 mm length) and tested in studies involving nerve activation for muscle contraction [114, 115]. It is expected that these hybrid cuff designs could be useful for selective fascicular neural recording applications as well.

2.5.5 Electrodes that remodel the shape of the nerve

A major limitation of the 'cuff mounted' multi-contact approach discussed above is that there is little or no access to nerve fascicles that are located deep within the trunk nerve. To circumvent this limitation researchers have set upon an approach that involves coaxing a trunk nerve to remodel itself. Initial studies utilized 'spring loaded' electrodes named SPINE (Slowly Penetrating Interfascicular Electrodes) [149] that inserted themselves into the nerve as depicted in Fig. 9. These studies later shifted toward trying to reshape the nerve into a more planar structure so that there wouldn't be any deep or 'centrally' located fascicles. Essentially, the approach is to apply moderate mechanical pressure to the nerve so that it is forced to change into a more flattened shape [148]. Ideally, the nerve fascicles will then lie alongside each other much like the conductors in a ribbon cable. Planar arrays of electrode contacts should then be able to record from (or stimulate) any of the fascicles as might be desired. Issues with the application of this technique concern being able to apply the electrode and achieve the desired nerve flattening without damaging any of the fascicles. Successes from studies in animals suggest that this is possible.

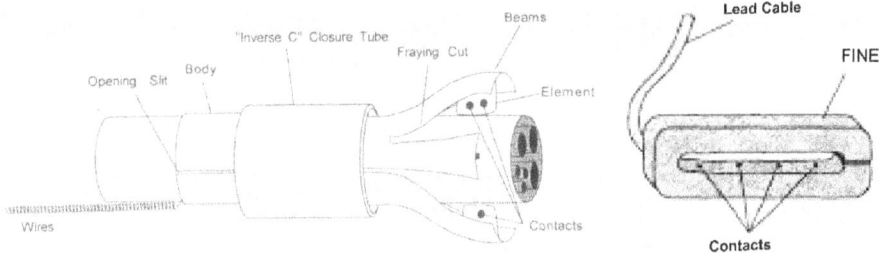

Fig. 9. Cuff electrodes that re-model the nerve. **Left** - SPINE design in which 'spring loaded' beams slowly penetrate the nerve and insinuate themselves between the major fascicles. **Right** - FINE design which aims to flatten the nerve into a planar array of fascicles. (Left and right drawing modified from Tyler [148].)

The FINE design has continued to show further success in studies from Tyler et al [130], where they were able to implant this device successfully around the femoral nerve of a group of seven patients. The goal of this study was to demonstrate the FINEs ability to selectively and independently stimulate individual fibers that innervate individual muscles in the leg. This was successfully verified by taking EMG recordings of the twitch response to stimulation in four of the six muscles innervated by the femoral nerve. From these results it is possible to estimate the parameters needed for restoration of knee extension and hip flexion via FNS. It was determined that in five of the seven patients implanted with a FINE no adverse effects on the nerve was present. Manual Muscle Test (MMT) scores were used to verify this after about a month. Of the remaining two, one subject voluntarily removed himself from the study before implantation, while the other did not participate in post-operative studies due to a schedule conflict.

2.6 *Regeneration based nerve interfaces*

A totally different approach to interfacing with nerves involves the ability of peripheral nerves to regenerate following deliberate or traumatic transection. The basic idea is to provide a bio-compatible structure that outgrowing nerve fibers can grow into or through. In general such nerve interface devices are termed regeneration electrodes. Regeneration electrodes can have different shapes and were first fashioned as thin disks or wafers termed "sieve electrodes" that contained multiple vias which transected nerve fibers would grow through. More recent developments have centered around constructing arrays of microtubes or microchannels which can provide several inherent advantages compared to sieve devices. The principle designs of sieve and microchannel nerve interfaces are described below.

2.6.1 *Sieve electrodes*

A sieve electrode (as the name implies) consists of an array of holes or channels that are formed in a thin substrate that is positioned at the end of a transected nerve. Some or all of the holes are surrounded by an addressable electrode contact for recording or for electrical stimulation. Ideally, the severed axons of the nerve regenerate through the holes of the sieve, and, in so doing, become well anchored to the sieve structure to provide an enduring, stable neural interface.

Using microfabrication techniques to produce slits in a silicon disc, Edell [27] applied the device to the end of the tibial nerve in a behaving rabbit, and first demonstrated the capability to record motor nerve activity from regenerated axons that grew into the sieve channels. If more than a few independent recording or stimulation channels are desired, then the number of lead wires needed to connect to the isolated channels becomes a limiting factor. Typically, sieve devices have been constructed with only modest numbers (e.g., 12) of independently wired channels [27, 70, 124] even though some fabricated structures contain up to several hundred via holes. Sieve electrode designs generally place the recording electrode sites outside of the sieve channel (i.e., on the surface of the structure through which the holes or "channels" pass). This is done for two reasons. First, so that the electrodes do not take up space in the lumen of the channel and thereby obstruct the path through which the nerve must regenerate. Second, because sieve structures can be constructed by forming holes in a flat thin substrate. As such the electrode contacts and conductive interconnects can be fabricated using standard photolithography techniques for planar devices (Figure 10).

Current research issues surrounding the sieve concept include the geometry of the sieve structure, the materials it is fabricated from, the size and density of the via holes and the locations of the electrode contacts, to list just a few.

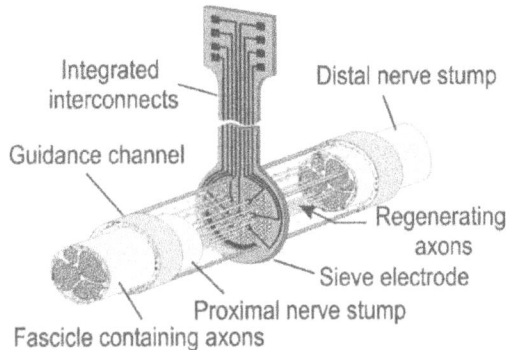

Fig. 10. Schematic of a sieve electrode fabricated from a polyimide substrate, gold conductor traces and platinum electrode contacts. (Drawing courtesy of T. Stieglitz, Fraunhoffer Inst. For Biomed Eng. St. Inbert, Germany).

Research has provided some insight regarding the effects of the hole size on the ability of axons to regenerate into the sieve. In one study, Zhao et al. [174] working with sieve structures fabricated from thin (60 μm) silicon disks, compared 3 different sieve disks containing holes of either 10, 50 or 100 μm diameter. The sieves were mounted within the lumen of a silicone tube that served as a nerve guidance chamber, and the composite structure was introduced between the transected ends of the sciatic nerve in rats. After 16 weeks, the extent of nerve regeneration through the sieves was accessed by measuring the amplitude of the EMG evoked in the medial gastrocnemius muscle by electrical stimulation of the sciatic nerve proximal to the sieve implant. In comparison to the contralateral control limb, the sieves having 10 and 50 μm holes produced an average EMG amplitude only 4.6% of that of the control EMG. The 100 μm hole sieves, however, produced 56.6%. Moreover, histological study of the nerve tissue that grew through each of the sieves showed that the 10 and 50 μm sieves yielded morphologies that were completely abnormal. Thus, it appeared that sieve holes needed to be greater than 50 μm to support functional nerve regeneration.

This conclusion was in contradiction with the work of, for example, Bradley et al. [9] who obtained functional regeneration through sieves having 2 μm diameter holes. Navarro et al. [98] and Kovacs et al. [70] have recommended sizes on the order of 40-65 μm. The explanation for this disparity was discovered to be dependent on another design parameter of the sieves which has been termed the 'transparency factor'. This term is simply the ratio of open space verses closed area that the nerve encounters in trying to grow through the sieve device. The sieve with the 2 μm holes used in the Bradley study had a total of 777 holes with minimal material between adjacent holes, thus giving it a high transparency. In a follow up study by Swedish investigators [155], where sieves having holes of either 30 μm or 90 μm were compared using sieves with transparency factors of either 20% or 30%, it was determined that sieves having 30 μm holes and 30% transparency yielded the best nerve regeneration (38% functional gastrocnemius EMG using their rat sciatic model), and that the sieves with 20% transparency yielded poorer regeneration regardless of whether 30 or 90 μm hole sizes were employed.

2.6.2 Substrates for sieve electrodes

Silicon as a substrate for regeneration electrodes is attractive because of its ability to be shaped with standard microfabrication techniques, and gold or platinum electrode sites can be applied with high spatial precision. Another advantage is that 'on board' circuitry to amplify recorded signals and apply multiplexing, for example, can be made integral with the device.

Sieve structures that utilize a polyimide substrate have also been fabricated and tested. Navarro and his colleagues [14, 98] implanted the transected sciatic nerve in rats and showed that efferent fibers regenerated through the sieve and reconnected to muscle. In those studies, a 12 channel polyimide based device was employed by placing it inside a short length of silicone tubing into which the freshly transected nerve was introduced. Regeneration was successful in 12 of 13 animals and was found to reach a plateau level after about 7 months post implantation. Testing of the average EMG activity that could be evoked in the gastrocnemius muscle to electrical stimulation applied to the regenerated nerve through the polyimide electrode evoked nerve responses similar in amplitude to those evoked by nerve stimulation with hook metal electrodes. The polyimide electrodes were useful for recording nerve action potentials in response to electrical stimulation of the distal regenerated nerve, and in response to functional sensory stimulation of several modalities. The histological contents of a chronically implanted sieve electrode are shown in Figure 11.

A convenient feature of the polyimide material is that the initial portion of the access cable can be integrated with the sieve structure. Another possible advantage of using polyimide over silicon is that polyimide can't be shattered in the event that some trauma occurs at the implantation site.

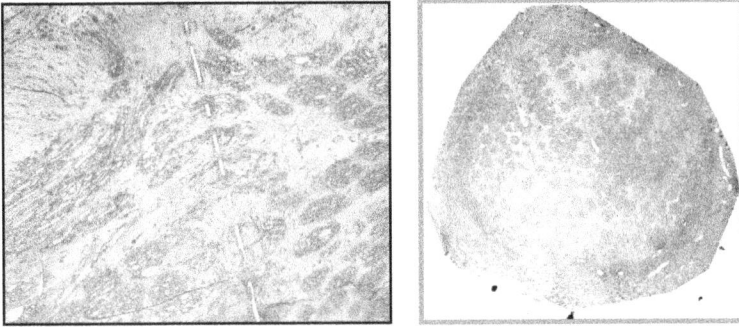

Fig. 11. **Left** - Longitudinal semi-thin section showing regenerated nerve bundles traversing sieve via holes. **Right** - Cross section of regenerated nerve at exit of the sieve device (distal) after 60 days post implantation and showing regenerated fibers organized into mini-fascicles. The sieve device was implanted in the transected sciatic nerve of the rat. (Photomicrographs courtesy of X. Navarro).

2.6.3 *Inherent deficiencies of sieve designs are mitigated with microchannel approaches*

Having the electrode contacts on the sides of the sieve device is not ideal. Of the many modeling and empirical studies that have been performed to elucidate the effects of various parameters of sieve design, the most important may be the effect of the length of the sieve hole and the hole diameter on the recorded signal and noise amplitudes, and also on the ability of transected nerves to grow through the device [176]. In particular, attention must be paid to the thickness of the sieve device since this determines the distance that separates the electrode faces on the front and/or back sides. The feeble extracellular currents that the nerve action potentials generate are strongest at the nodes of Ranvier, and because this electrode separation is substantially less in sieve devices than the intranodal distance of large caliber nerve fibers the probability that many axons will have a node located at the edge of a sieve hole where the electrode is located is low causing much of the activity present in a sieve channel to go unrecorded. This drawback can be mitigated by allowing nerve fibers to regenerate through much longer holes which are generally referred to as "microtubes" or "microchannels" and which physically separate and electrically isolate the fibers in one channel from those in neighboring channels.

A major advantage of the microchannel approach is that electrodes can be located within each channel, and because the action potential currents are constrained to travel within the electrically insulated channels, the recorded signal amplitudes are greatly increased [23, 24, 176]. Also, the amount of signal crosstalk among adjacent channels is substantially reduced in comparison to the case of sieves.

Attempts to evaluate the microtube concept in early studies produced mixed results and may have depended on species differences and features of the particular fiber tracts under study (e.g., peripheral nerve vs. central fiber tracts). Nevertheless, progress in micro-fabrication techniques has produced a resurgence in efforts to develop effective micro-channel based neural interfaces. Several approaches have been described and tested. In one early design a bundle of commercial polyimide microtubes (either 99 μm or 203 μm ID) were inserted into the lumen of a short length of 2 mm ID silicone tubing to form an arrays of either 1, 3 or 5 mm long microchannels. Individual 50 μm diameter platinum-iridium micro-wire electrodes were each inserted by hand into several of the microtubes in the 203 μm diameter arrays to serve as recording or stimulating electrodes for the instrumented channels as depicted in Fig 12. An evaluation study was performed in a rabbit model in which the tibial nerve was isolated and transected and sutured into one end of the microtube array. The distal stump of the transected nerve was similarly sutured to the distal end of the implanted nerve interface array so that regenerating nerve fibers could traverse the channels and reconnect to their former muscle, joint and skin end organs in the lower leg. Results showed good regeneration of the transected nerve thorough the microchannel implant and robust neural activity could be recorded (Fig. 12 and Fig. 13) [23, 51].

Successful neural regeneration through a microchannel interface containing four (75 μm diameter) metal wire electrodes that were inserted into an array consisting of 200 μm microchannels was also demonstrated for the transected sciatic nerve in a rat model. In that study, the microchannel array was used as a conduit bridge between the proximal and distal ends of the transected nerve at the mid-thigh. Following recovery, neural activity evoked during treadmill walking was simultaneously recorded from the four instrumented channels of the array along with EMG activity from the soleus and tibialis anterior muscles. By employing spike triggered averaging, the study showed that among the four wire electrodes, 19 of 38 discernable units could be identified as motor efferents innervating the soleus (2 units) or tibialis anterior (17 units) muscles [31].

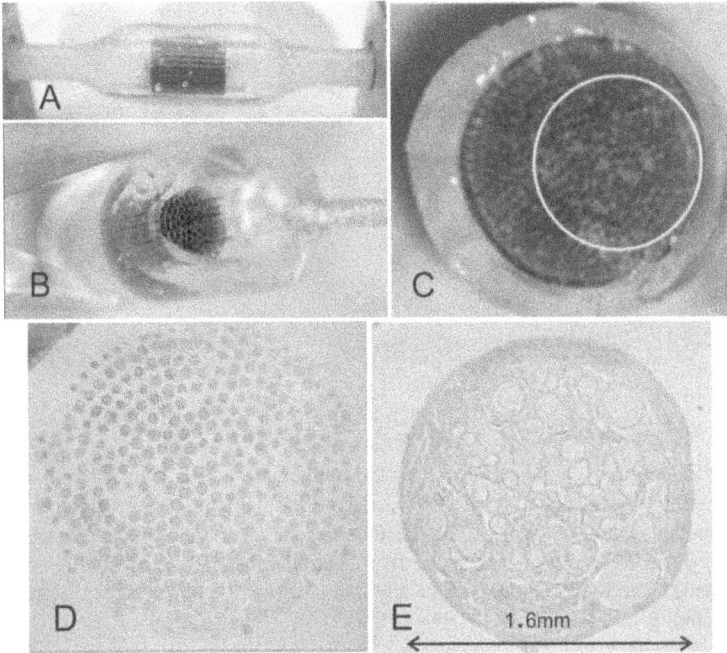

Fig. 12. A) – Photograph of a partially constructed microtube implant containing 3 mm long, 203 μm diameter microtubes. B) Photograph showing placement of 50 μm diameter insulated iridium microelectrode shafts halfway into 12 of the microtubes. The hole visible in the center of the photograph is the port through which the proximal end of the amputated tibial nerve would be introduced during the implantation procedure. Reference electrode coils and nerve cuffs were added to both the entry and exit chambers after this photo was obtained. C) An explanted microtube array fabricated using 1 mm long, 99 μm diameter tubes without electrodes after it was cut open and the regenerated nerve mini-fascicles were pulled out. D) and E) Low and higher power micrographs of the core of neural tissue removed from the area demarcated by the circle in photograph C and then fixed, embedded, sectioned and stained. Examination reveals healthy myelinated axons along with blood capillaries, collagen and fibroblasts that regenerated into the 1 mm long array of 99 μm microtubes shown in C. Modified from Figs. 2 and 3 in [24].

An alternative technique for fabricating a microchannel array was demonstrated by Kim et al. [67] who formed microchannels by stuffing a bundle of 160 μm wires into a silastic tube (1.96 mm OD) then immersing the tube into liquid PDMS and allowing the PDMS to solidify. The structure was then immersed in liquid chloroform which caused the PDMS to swell so that the wires could be pulled out leaving a flexible scaffold that contained an array of microchannels. Electrodes for recording or stimulation were then able to be added by manually inserting 75 μm wires into several of the microchannels (Figure 14).

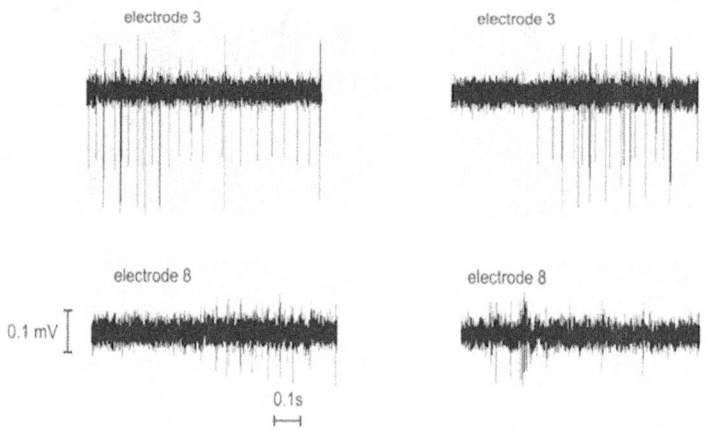

Fig. 13. **Left** - Examples of neural activity recorded simultaneously from two different electrodes (#3 and #8) in a microtube array neural interface. The device was implanted on the tibial nerve in a rabbit regeneration model. **Right** - recordings from another episode of activity from the same study session again showing little correlation between the two electrode channels other than similar timing of general heightened activity. Recordings were acquired 6 weeks post implantation. [Reproduced with permission from Fig. 6 in Edell et al. [24)].

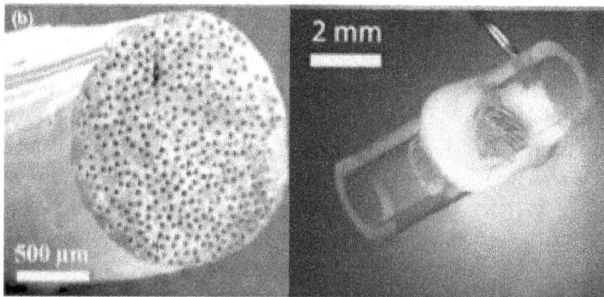

Fig. 14. **Left** – SEM showing a microchannel array formed by casting silicone around a bundle of microwires and then removing the wires. **Right** - Photograph of a fully assembled microchannel implant showing microwires inserted into several microchannels of the array. Adapted from Figs. 2 and 6 in Kim et al. [67]. Reproduced with permission.

3-D Microchannel arrays can also be constructed by first fabricating individual planar structures having a series of parallel vertical walls and then either rolling the device upon itself [6, 146] (e.g., much like a baker produces a "jelly roll" confection) or by stacking the elements on top of each other so that the underside of each successive layer forms the roof of the previous layer and so provides closed channels [74, A. Zorzos, unpublished] (Figures 15, 16).

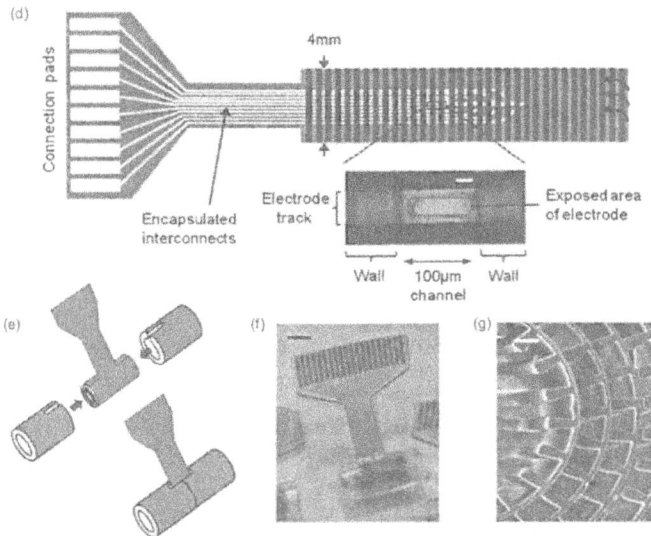

Fig. 15. Modified from Fig. 1 in FitzGerald et al. [25]. Reproduced with permission.

Fig. 16. **Left**: 5 x 4 array of 200 um channels fabricated from SU8 polymer. Each channel contains an individually addressable tripolar electrode array made by vapor depositing titanium and then platinum on the SU8 substrate. **Right**: a typical strategy employed to connect cables to the conductive traces from the electrode sites. (Left image courtesy of A. Zorzos; Right image from Song- et al. [77].)

In either case the electrodes can be formed by metal vapor-deposition onto bio-compatible polymer films such as polyimide, and then laminating those electrode carrying films to a molded or etched backing that contains U shaped channels. Much of this work has utilized molded PDMS (polydimethylsiloxane) or SU8 to form the microchamber device. To further simplify the fabrication steps metal electrode sites and conductive traces can be deposited directly onto an SU8 polymer substrate to eliminate the need for an intermediate electrode carrier that takes up precious real estate within the microchannels. To increase the physical compliance of these implanted devices, investigators are developing techniques to deposit metal electrodes and conductive traces directly onto PDMS, without risks that the metal traces will de-laminate or fracture if the silicone material is stretched modestly [35, Zorzos, unpublished]. In this regard, investigators working with other biocompatible polymeric substrates such as photosensitive polyimides have also stressed the benefits of locating the electrode traces at the center of the device where mechanical stresses caused by flexing of the implant would be minimized [146].

A continuing obstacle to achieving high densities of array channels is that the electrodes within each channel must be "wired out". This can result in a cable that is too bulky to fit into the desired nerve location and also presents a risk of damaging the interfaced nerve due to mechanical trauma from tethering effects. Eventually, signal multiplexing strategies, high speed serial communication and implanted telemetry functions should be able to be integrated with the microchannel devices to mitigate these shortcomings [101, 146]. Also, when dealing with larger trunk nerves, fascicle dissection can be performed in some cases to allow multiple small microchannel implants to be applied to each of the parts of the divided trunk nerve.

A common design that is used to access the electrodes within a stacked microchannel array is illustrated in Fig 16. Basically each layer is designed so that it contains an apron having contact bonding pads that extend at right angles to the nerve axis. The distance that each apron extends away from the microchannels is less for each successive layer so that there isn't any overlap when the layers are assembled by stacking. Incorporating amplifier stages that are integral with each electrode site may also become feasible as has been demonstrated by the development of exceptionally conformable high density electrode arrays for cortical recording in clinical epilepsy studies or EcoG applications [153]. These investigators have fabricated arrays with as many as 350 active electrodes distributed over a 9 x 10 mm area of cortex (yielding a spatial resolution of 500 μm spacing). Moreover, their array integrated circuitry can achieve sampling rates > 10k samples/s and provide for independent channel recording with fewer than 40 lead out wires.

2.6.4 *Modality specificity of individual microchannels following nerve regeneration*

Since most nerves consist of a mixture of different fiber diameters, having different thickness of myelin or no myelin, and since the various fiber types and sizes subserve different functions, it is important to determine what mix of fibers grows through individual microchannels. Histological studies have indicated that where microchannels have allowed functional regeneration, the individual microchannels usually contain a small bundle of axons arranged into one or more mini fascicles [51, 146, 164].

It isn't known yet, however, to what extent such mini fascicles consist of pure sensory or pure motor fibers. To input sensory signals for cognitive tactile feedback from artificial limbs, to take just one example, it would be best if individual cutaneous afferents could be activated on a single fiber basis. This is because the re-creation of natural sensory experiences will not be possible if afferents that subserve different tactile modalities are activated indiscriminately [118]. A common example of this is the vibratory sensation that is felt when a train of electrical pulses is applied to the skin surface. While this stimulation patterning might be adequate to evoke the familiar vibratory experience induced when a tuning fork is held against the skin, it doesn't produce pure sensations of light touch, deep pressure, skin stretch or hot or cold. Some solace can be taken, however, in the knowledge derived from microneurography studies in man [21, 140] that electrical activation of specific cutaneous afferent types in isolation can evoke the familiar sensations of contact and of sustained pressure. To have the best chances of mimicking natural sensory neural codes, researchers would like to be able to establish 'one-to-one' connectivity to the entire pallet of modality specific afferent types. Achieving this level of selectivity with current neural interfaces that are clinically applicable remains a continuing challenge.

Among the most promising strategies to direct the regeneration of different categories of nerve fibers concerns the chemical microenvironment provided by the Schwann cells that accompany motor vs. sensory nerves. Studies have shown that regenerating motor axons, if given an equal choice between traversing a degenerating sensory nerve vs. a motor nerve, will preferentially chose the motor path to reach a muscle target. This action, referred to as PMR "Preferential Motor Regeneration" has been shown to be controlled by differences in the upregulation by Schwann cells of genes that produce specific nerve growth factors that differentially influence the outgrowth of motor vs. sensory fibers. Thus, motor and sensory nerves are served by Schwann cells having distinctly different motor vs. sensory phenotypes. This suggests that the inclusion of specific Schwann cell phenotypes to different microchannels could assist in achieving motor vs. sensory fiber sorting [13, 51, 169]. Possibly, the sorting of different modalities of sensory afferents may be achievable by finding subtle differences among the Schwann cells of sensory nerves as well.

Based upon studies of neurite outgrowth in cell culture and research to develop nerve repair conduits *in-vivo*, other factors which may influence the growth of regenerating fibers differentially through microchannels would include the surface texture of the channel walls and the presence of extracellular matrix molecules such as laminin or collagen [77].

There are likely to be persistent biological constraints such as the need to be accompanied by blood capillaries that discourage single axons to travel in isolation through very fine pore microchannels. That being said, however, studies involving neurons grown in tissue culture showed that individual axons would migrate along grooves as narrow as 5 μm in isolation from their neighboring axons [164] and this has led to attempts to apply these findings to transected nerve fibers regenerating in in-vivo environments as well [142].

2.6.5 Fiber segregation using 3-d bifurcating electrode arrays

Inspired by the results from neuronal cell culture studies that demonstrated that neurons could grow axons into very narrow grooves, researchers Stoyanova et al. [142] commenced a series of in-vivo studies in rats to determine if it would be possible to reduce the number of regenerated axons that populate individual microchannels by imposing a series of bifurcating channels that are designed to become progressively narrower with each succeeding branch point as shown in Figure 17. To test this, microchannel arrays were fabricated that consisted of 2 stages or 3 stages of 3D bifurcating guidance scaffolds and implanted onto the transected sciatic nerve in rats. The results showed that this technique enabled the re-growth of neurites into channels with gradually diminished width (e.g., 70 μm tall by 80, 40 and 20 μm wide, respectively) and that this facilitated the separation of the axonal bundles with 91% success.

2.6.6 Is single fiber accessibility always required?

With regard to recording efferent motor commands from the trunk nerves of the residual limb in upper extremity amputees, it isn't certain to what extent single fiber connectivity would be required. If the axons within a microchannel were all efferents that prior to the nerve transection were targeted to a single muscle, then recording from the nerve fiber population within that microchannel would likely provide superior command information for controlling some limb function because the activity of all of the fibers that were activated to achieve a given function would be more completely sampled than if a limited number of single unit recordings were combined. Unfortunately, however, almost nothing is known about the homogeneity or lack of it regarding the functional types of nerve fibers that may grow into one and the same microchannel. Are the fibers, for example, all efferents, a mixture of cutaneous and muscle afferents, cutaneous afferents from diverse regions of skin, etc.? These are very important questions that must be addressed before microchannel electrode interfaces can be expected to be useful clinically for neuroprostheses.

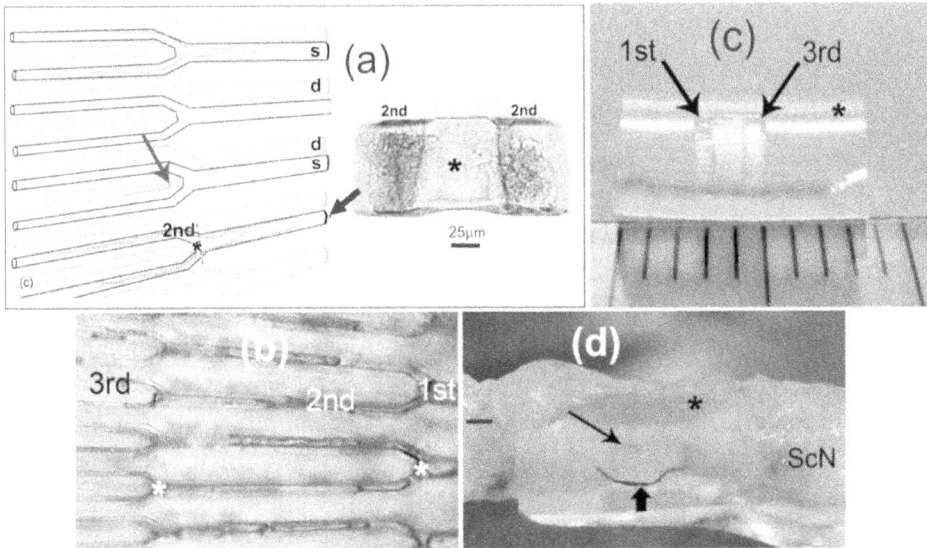

Fig. 17. (a) Hand drawn reconstruction of laser confocal micrographs depicting the ingrowth of neurites in a portion of a scaffold having a superficial and a deep layer (labeled 's' and 'd' respectively. Thin arrow indicates location of a regenerating neurite entering a secondary channel in the deep layer. The micrograph to the right in panel (a) shows a cross section of the scaffold cut just beyond the bifurcation at the position indicated on the sketch by the asterisk and the dashed line. Note that the advancing nerve growth clearly divided at the branch point to populate both of the new channels formed by the bifurcation. (b) Confocal micrograph longitudinal view of another explanted neural interface showing a scaffold having two successive bifurcations as indicated by the asterisks at the sites where the primary (1st) and secondary (2nd) channels divide. (c) photo of fully assembled scaffold having two bifurcations ready for use. Arrows indicate the primary and tertiary microchannels. (d) photo of a scaffold that contained a single bifurcation (thin arrow) and was explanted and fixed with formaldehyde. The device was installed on the transected sciatic nerve using a single silk suture stitch (thick arrow) to secure the proximal and distal nerve stumps to the silicone tubing. (Adapted from Figures 1 and 4 in Stoyanov [142]).

Since the utility of microchannel devices requires adequate nerve regeneration, future research must stress studies to determine not only how to enhance regeneration, but how to 'direct' or control the regeneration so that specificity of the contents of the microchannels can be achieved. Likely, pharmacological agents such as nerve growth factors could be used to promote regeneration, and other neurotropic substances will be discovered that influence which functional types of nerve fibers, beyond the basic separation of motor verses sensory, can be coaxed to grow into particular channels.

Another issue of paramount importance is to determine the long term stability of the nerve fibers once they have successfully regenerated into the microchannel structure. What seems to be crucial is for the regenerated axons that grow into the microchannel device to be able to establish contact with appropriate target end organs, which must be provided or somehow mimicked.

2.7   Cell based nerve interfaces

2.7.1 Neuromuscular hybrid electrode

Presently, EMG control is the main strategy that is employed for commercial powered hands. The major drawback of using EMG is that above the elbow amputees do not have many muscles available from which to obtain EMG signals. Since the trunk nerves are generally still viable in the above elbow amputee, for example, researchers have sought to overcome this problem by employing direct nerve based interfaces such as sieve or intrafasicular electrodes. A disadvantage of using recorded nerve signals is that the signals are very weak (in the range of a few microvolts) so that electrical noise from the environment as well as EMG from neighboring contracting muscles can easily contaminate the recording.

It is possible, however, to surgically connect a motor nerve or a mixed trunk nerve (such as the median and ulnar nerve) from the residual limb to a nearby muscle and allow the efferent nerve fascicles to establish contact with that muscle. The prosthesis user can then contract the newly innervated muscle and the evoked EMG can be used to produce the prosthesis command. The newly innervated muscles acts as a biological amplifier that boosts the weak action potentials into EMG signals in order to be read by a prosthesis.

Kuiken et al [44, 45] have developed this concept for prosthesis control first through cadaver dissections then through a series of planned surgeries involving upper extremity amputee subjects. The goal of these surgeries was to create a system of "myoneurosomes" – muscle segments under voluntary cortical control that are isolatable from other muscles via EMG. It should be noted that the muscle segments involved are only being used as a form of "biological signal amplifier", and not mechanical actuators intended to produce joint motions.

An early example of the application of this technique which is referred to as "Targeted Muscle Reinervation" (TMR) involved an amputee subject who had a shoulder disarticulation. For this surgery, four nerves (musculocutaneous, median, radial, and ulnar) were rerouted to the pectoralis major or minor muscles of the chest (Figure 18, upper). Special care was taken to clear away as much subcutaneous fat as possible so that the nerves were as close as possible to the surface. Doing so ensures the most focal recording from surface electrodes.

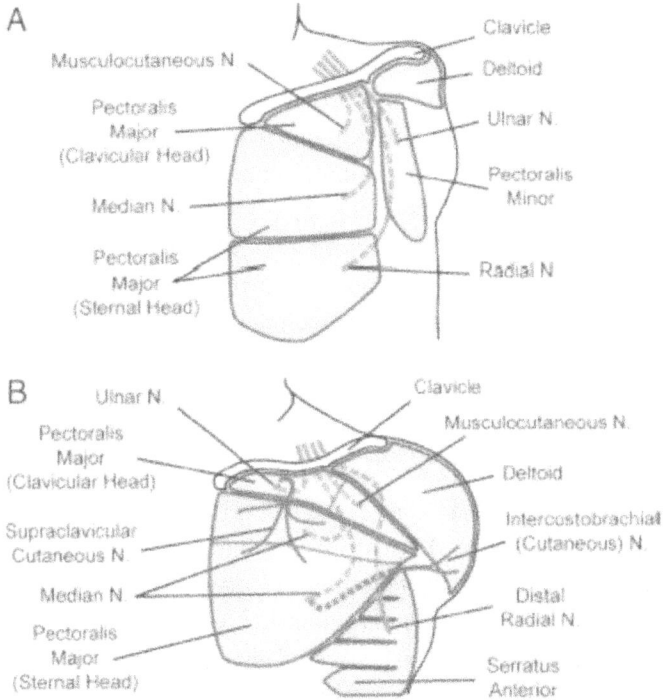

Fig. 18. Cartoon illustrating treatment of two patients who received TMR surgery [72]. (A) This patient had their pectoralis muscles denervated, subcutaneous fat removed, and the remnant 4 arm nerves were sewn to four anatomically distinct muscle segments as shown. (B) In this patient, cutaneous nerves from the trunk were sewn to the proximal remnants of the cutaneous nerves that formerly provided tactile sensation from the hand so that mechanical stimulation of the trunk skin could active the hand nerves and provide substitute tactile sensation that would be perceived as coming from the amputee's "phantom" hand.

After the surgical procedure the patient was trained using a prosthesis custom built for this purpose. To determine the efficacy of the TMR surgeries for prosthesis control, the patient performed the "box-and-blocks" test, where the subject moves a 1-inch-square block from box to box. Post-surgery the patient showed a 246% increase in number of boxes moved with the custom prostheses and TMR controller compared to his performance prior to the surgery. This improvement has been credited, by the patient, to the more natural and intuitive operation of the device as opposed to the standard prostheses with touch pad control that he had previously used.

2.7.2 *Nerve-muscle graft chamber*

The Nerve-Muscle Graft Chamber (NMGC) approach to neural interfacing, as with the TMR technique discussed above, is being developed to derive control signals from an amputee's peripheral limb nerves so that a prosthesis user can command the multiple actuators in a powered artificial limb simultaneously in an entirely intuitive, well-coordinated, and effortless manner. The NMGC technique consists of grafting a viable nerve or portion of a nerve present in an amputee's residual limb onto a small slice of autologous muscle tissue that is located within a surgically implanted device containing one or more electrically isolated compartments. Inspiration for developing the NMGC concept arose from a report by Wells and his associates [160]. Working with rats, they transected the peroneal component of the sciatic nerve and placed it inside of a 2 mm ID silicone tube along with a mobilized strip of isolated gluteus maximus muscle. The nerve segment succeeded in establishing functional connections with the muscle strip as demonstrated by the presence of EMG evoked when the nerve was electrically stimulated proximally.

A NMGC that contains only two compartments is shown in Figure 19. Each compartment contains electrodes that record EMG activity evoked by the neural activity of the grafted nerve. As with TMR, the nerve-muscle unit acts as a biological amplifier that boosts the recordable electrical activity of the nerve fibers by about 1000x (i.e., from a few microvolts for typical nerve recording to 1 or more millivolts for muscle EMG responses). This allows the amputee's volitional nerve activity to be more easily transduced into high quality, reliable prosthesis commands then would be possible using traditional neural recording techniques.

The successful demonstrations of simultaneous control of multiple joints in advanced prosthetic arms depends heavily on being able to derive an independent control signal for each respective joint axis and direction by accessing (interfacing to) the motor nerve which would normally control the muscle that moved that joint in the respective direction. By doing so, the prosthesis user's brain and nervous system is able to coordinate the motions of the various joints that are required to accomplish an intended task. Theoretically, for an upper extremity amputees to control an artificial arm that contained all of the degrees of freedom and matched the dexterity of a human arm and hand, a neural interface would have to be capable of sampling the activity of the motor nerves to every arm and hand muscle independently. To this end, the development of techniques to achieve higher selectivity from neural interface devices is a prominent goal among researchers.

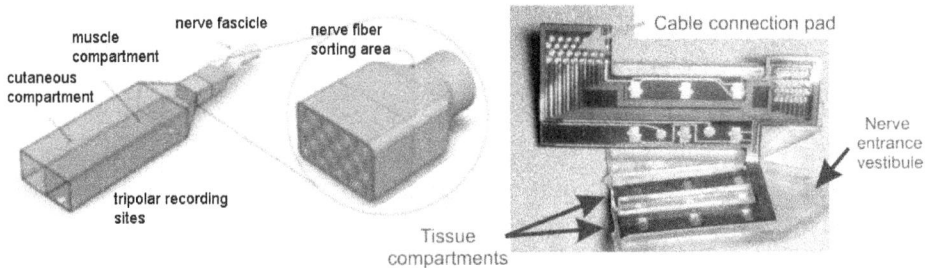

Fig. 19. **Left** -Depicting concept of a Nerve-Muscle Graft Chamber. In this case designed to record from a single muscle sliver that would be innervated by a motor nerve that subserved a single joint movement. A separate compartment is also illustrated that could be filled with de-epithelized cutaneous tissue to provide a target for any cutaneous fibers that might be present with the motor nerve fibers, preventing them from invading the muscle compartment and "stealing" muscle target sites away from the regenerating motor nerve fibers. **Right** – Photograph of a partially assembled NMGC containing 2 compartments and consisting of a polyimide electrode carrier laminated to a silicone molded "clam shell" structure. The gold electrodes are set up for tri-polar recording. Bonding sites visible at the top left and right of the polyimide insert are used to connect fine wire cables leading to a percutaneous connector for chronic in-vivo studies in research animals.

The NMGC represents a step forward in this endeavor as it mitigates several shortcomings associated with classical TMR techniques. For example, a drawback with transferring an amputated nerve stump to a normal muscle is that it sacrifices the original function of the host muscle to create the interface. In addition, depending on the composition of the transferred nerve, the host muscle could become innervated by a mix of nerve fascicles originally targeted at multiple other muscles which may have subserved several different limb or joint motions. To the extent that a multi-fascicule nerve can be surgically divided, by employing a NMGC each divided nerve segment could be directed to a separate compartment within a multi-compartment NMGC. Alternatively, depending on the specific nerves involved and their locations, multiple NMGCs could be implanted. NMGCs can thus be designed in a modular or even fully customized fashion to greatly increase the available number of natural control signal sources available from residual limb nerves without compromising existing healthy muscle.

Another inherent advantage of a NMGC is that the desired EMG activity is recorded using electrodes that are located within an electrically insulated compartment. This design reduces signal crosstalk to neighboring compartments; reduces pick up of unwanted EMG activity from the surrounding muscles within the limb; and provides for a consistent electrode-tissue interface. A final advantage of the NMGC approach with regard to collecting EMG based prosthesis command signals is that (size permitting) the device can be implanted at the site where the targeted nerve is located rather than having to mobilize the nerve possibly over a long distance to graft it to a suitable host muscle. This feature can reduce surgery time and overall invasiveness as well as provide an interface to nerves that would not be candidates for TMR techniques because their size or location prevented them from being brought into close apposition with a host muscle.

Results from an early study [Edell and Riso, unpublished] in which an NMGC having two separate compartments was installed in a rabbit transgenu amputee model are shown in Figure 20. The implanted device was formed by gluing two short lengths of silicon tubing side by side and placing wire electrodes within each in a tripolar recording arrangement. During the implant surgery session, one compartment of the NMGC was packed with a small cylindrical core of lateral gastrocnemius muscle (2 mm diameter x 10 mm length) salvaged from the amputated limb, and the other compartment received a core of tibialis anterior muscle. The tibial and peroneal components of the sciatic nerve were then separated and each was introduced into the compartment that contained a slice of muscle which they formerly innervated. A percutaneous plug was installed at the animal's back to be used to connect to the electrodes during the follow up evaluations of the chronic experiment. Examples of recorded EMG activity from the tibial and peroneal compartments of the implanted NMGC are shown in Fig 20. The activity was evoked by gently rocking the animal's head from side to side to elicit a righting response with the animal lying prone on a table top. While the data in the figure show several instances where there was coactivation of the two nerve-muscle systems, there are clear epochs that show independent activity as well.

In summary, the use of a NMGC may be an attractive addition to the nerve interface tool box and may be clinically useful for prosthesis control. A major challenge which still needs to be addressed, however, since this represents an implanted device, is to develop a suitable telemetry link to recover the recorded EMG signals.

A further nuance to the design of a NMGC is to provide a separate compartment that is filled with cutaneous tissue. The rational for this is to provide a suitable skin target for regenerating sensory cutaneous afferents that are present in many mixed peripheral nerves. In the absence of finding suitable cutaneous end organs, transected cutaneous nerve fibers would compete with the regenerating motor nerve fibers in an attempt to connect to available muscle tissue. While it has also been shown that the motor nerve fibers ultimately retain an advantage in such a competition [Brushart, 1993], any impediment to the robust and timely connectivity between the motor nerve and the limited volume of muscle tissue available could limit the effectiveness of the muscle nerve to evoke well graded, high amplitude EMG signals for prosthesis commands. An additional motivation for the inclusion of a compartment that contains cutaneous tissue, is the possibility to provide cognitive tactile feedback via electrical stimulation of the cutaneous afferents that innervate that compartment.

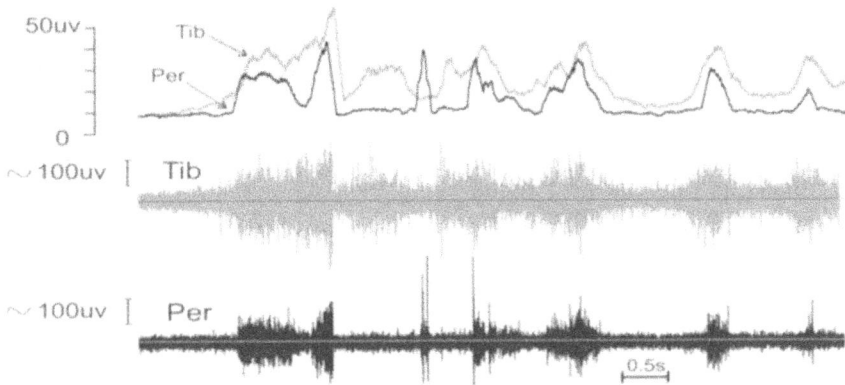

Fig. 20. Simultaneous recordings of EMGs from TIB and PER nerve channels of an NMGC implanted in the thigh area of a transgene amputee rabbit. Upper Traces: Processed EMG consisting of rectification followed by applying a symmetric sliding window averager using +/- 400 samples (i.e., +/- 50 ms). Lower Traces: Raw signals band pass filtered 100 Hz - 1 kHz and sampled at 8 kHz. Note regions of signals that clearly show independent activity within the TIB and PER compartments of the NMGC.

The goal of harnessing the electrical activity that an amputee can generate in the muscles and nerves of the residual limb in order to control advanced prosthetic limbs is being pursued using at least two additional techniques. The first is similar to the NMGC strategy discussed above in that it involves anastomosing a freshly transected viable motor nerve to a denervated muscle so that the nerve can re-innervate the muscle and generate an EMG signal that can be recorded. One implementation that is being studied in the rat femoral nerve model [Langhals, 2014] does not involve placing muscle tissue into an electrically isolative chamber as with NMGC. Instead a whole muscle (extensor digitorum longus) is excised and freely transplanted to the thigh region. The animal's femoral nerve is transected, placed onto the transplanted muscle along with one or more epimesially mounted EMG electrodes. The nerve-muscle-electrode system is then secured in place by first wrapping it with decelluarized gut tissue and then suturing that package to the fascia of the surrounding musculature. The researchers report good success regarding the nerve ingrowth, and the production of evoked EMG, after a period of convalescence. Deficiencies that were noted included mainly mechanical failures that developed over time such as the epimysial electrodes pulling away from the muscle surface and lead breakage on route to the head mounted connector.

2.7.3 Cultured neuron electrodes

An intriguing alternative approach to interface with neural tissue is to grow selected neural cells onto an electrode array structure so that they are captured either in small wells or they are adherent to a substrate having a two dimensional matrix of electrode contacts [84, 85, 104, 113, 122, 123]. The electrode array with its imprisoned cells is then implanted into the neural tissue where the neural communication is ultimately desired. The strategy is to select the appropriate neurons for incorporation into the electrode array and then expect them to grow axon collaterals into the host tissue using their natural mechanisms of axonal guidance to achieve this. Figure 21 shows one implementation of this electrode concept using silicon as a substrate.

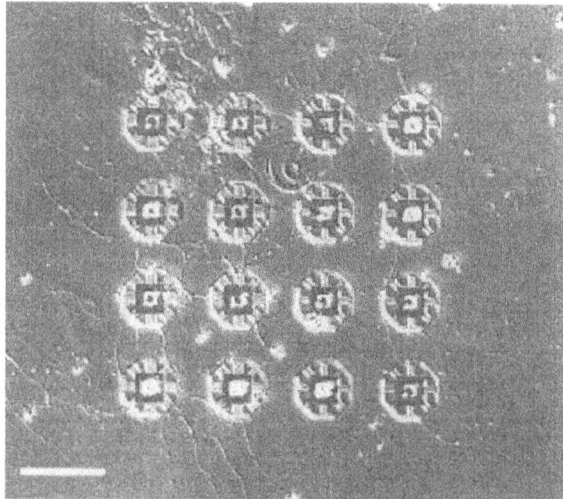

Fig. 21. Photomicrograph showing caged wells formed in a neurochip. Each well was seeded with an immature rat hippocampal neuron eight days prior. Multiple neurites can be seen arising from most of the wells. Scale bar: 100 μm. (From [85]).

Another scheme to produce a cultured probe doesn't use a 'cage' approach. Instead, bioactive substances are employed that are known to promote neuronal attachment and axon outgrowth, or to inhibit neuronal attachment. Regions can then be patterned on a pre-fabricated substrate to control where seeded neurons will adhere, and to restrict the directions and paths along which growing neurites will travel. An illustration of this concept as presented by Rutten and his colleagues [122, 123] is reproduced in Fig 22. Axons from the host tissue are expected to form connections with the implanted neuron colonies (networks) via intrinsic chemotropic means as well as any 'engineered' techniques that future research may develop. A glass cover slip with a layer of glia cells grown on it is placed over the neuron probe structure with the glia facing the neurons to provide nutrients and sustain the neurons.

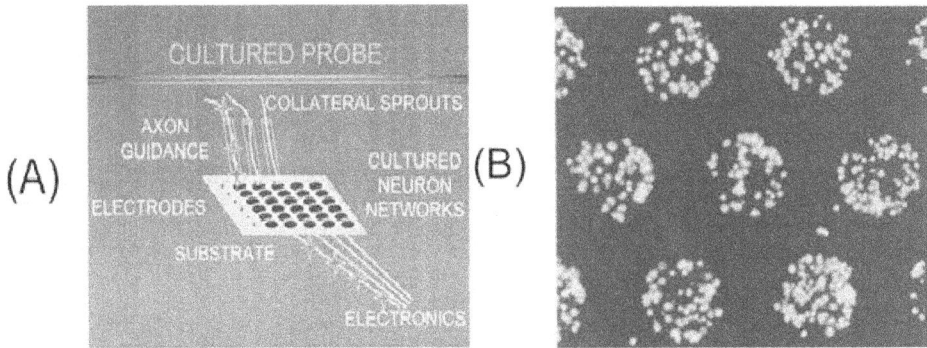

Fig. 22. **(A)** - Schematic for a cultured probe which uses a glass substrate that has electrodes patterned onto it. The networks of cultured neurons are kept separate from each other by adhesive treatment of the substrate. After implantation, the host tissue is expected to form functional connections with the neuronal colonies. **(B)** - Fluorescent micrograph showing viable cortical neuronal colonies growing within polyethylene imine-coated, 150 μm, 'islands'. Live and dead neurons are distinguishable by differential staining using acridine orange (live neurons w/ green fluorescence) and propidium iodide (dead neurons w/ red fluorescence). The dark areas between the circles are regions containing a 'neurophobic' fluorocarbon-coated layer. Part **A** and **B** of the figure are reproduced with permission from [123] (Figures 3 and 17a, respectively), and also appear in [122] (as Figure 23).

3.   Design Considerations

There are many factors which must be taken into account when designing and using nerve recording electrodes. Both the needs of the biology and the needs of the implant must be weighed against one another and balanced. A list of factors for the needs of the biology might include the following:

- The implant uses biocompatible materials;
- The implant is non-toxic, has a small footprint, and is inert to the immune system;
- The implant matches mechanical compliance (flexibility) between implanted material and nervous tissue;
- The implant does not disrupt circulation, nutrient pathways, maintenance pathways, cellular processes, or tissue function;
- The implant does not become a vector for bacterial infection;
- The implant is not a cause for continuous agitation in tissue surrounding the implant;
- The implant is geometrically matched to the implantation region to reduce unnecessary fracture and injury.

The basic technical problem in electrode design is to develop a structure that will place the electrode's active site on or in the peripheral nerve and keep it there in such a way so as not to disturb the nerve yet be strong enough to survive for very long periods of time in the harsh, biochemically and mechanically active, corrosive, saline environment that exists within the body. A list of the needs of the interface might include the following:

- Electrical continuity;
- Interfacial stability;
- Inertness in a saline environment;
- A low electrical impedance pathway insulated from the body between electrode and amplifier;
- A reversible or non-polarizable interface such as a chlorided surface;
- Surgical access for the implantation as simple as possible;
- Electrode interfacial area as large as possible;
- Surgery time minimal;
- Long functional life;
- An interface subsystem able to record during electrical stimulation.

3.1 *Materials*

Electrodes and their lead wires, like all implanted devices, should be constructed so that all components that make physical contact with the physiological fluids are biocompatible. If non-biocompatible materials are implanted, they must be hermetically sealed or passivated with a biocompatible material. Although new biomaterials are constantly being developed, the selection of available biomaterials is restricted to a small subset of the available engineering materials. Commonly used materials for electrode structures and insulation include: glass, silicon, polyimide, silicone, Teflon™, nylon, polypropylene, diamond like carbon, parylene, and certain polyurethanes.

The iono-electric properties and the ionic byproducts must be further considered for the electrically conductive components of the electrode, as they must remain functional not only under passive conditions, but also under an electrical bias. Reversible/non-polarizable electrode materials commonly used in electrochemistry such as Camomel paste cannot be used due to the toxic effects of mercury. Silver-silver chloride electrodes commonly used for ECG, EEG, and reference electrodes cannot be used within the body because of the toxicity of silver ions, especially to nerve tissue. Similarly, ions and oxidation byproducts of commonly used electrical conductors such as copper and aluminum are toxic and should be avoided. Materials such as gold or stainless steels containing nickel, previously thought of as inert, have recently been found to cause allergic reactions when implanted in the body. Commonly used materials for the electrode interface include: low nickel stainless steel, platinum/platinum black, carbon graphite, glassy carbon, and iridium/iridium oxide.

The final barrier limiting the selection of biomaterials is the threat of litigation. Even though a prospective material is electrically and mechanically ideal and all evidence shows it to be biocompatible, the producer of the material may prohibit its use in biomedical applications because of the threat of litigation in case the material proves to be non-biocompatible in the future.

3.2 *Mechanical stabilization*

Mechanical stabilization of an electrode is one of the first challenges facing bioengineers developing electrodes for neuroprostheses. Methods to place and secure the active site of the electrode on or in the nervous tissue, while at the same time minimizing the injury to the tissue and surgical time, must be found. The stability of a recording is partially a function of how well one can physically secure the electrode in place to maintain the electrode's active site relationship to the active nerve fibers. As we saw in discussing the theory of recording, the amplitude of the recorded signal is related to the distance of the electrode active site to the active nerve fiber.

Generally speaking, electrodes tend to preferentially record from the nerve fibers closest to the electrode active site, but at the same time the nerve fibers most susceptible to injury are those closest to the electrode. Injury can occur during implantation or later by mechanical trauma or irritation. For example, micro-movements such as pulsatile vasodilation may contribute to continuous injury at the implant site. It is also possible that everyday normal motion may contribute to continuous irritation if the material properties of the implant mismatch the tissue. Depending on the severity of the injury, the injured fibers may either be repaired by the support cells in the peripheral nerve (such as the Schwann cells) or else they undergo Wallerian degeneration. Glial scaring or foreign body reactions that encapsulate implanted materials tend to form around the electrode structure. This reduces the efficiency of regenerating nerve fibers as it disrupts the path of the nerve sheath which these fibers follow during regeneration [27, 30]. Thus, degenerated fibers do not tend to regenerate near the electrode. The general effect is that the overall distance between the electrode active site and the active nerve fibers increases, resulting in a decrease in the recorded signal amplitude.

In general, nerve recording techniques are more sensitive to changes in the relationship between active site and nerve fiber than stimulating techniques. In the case of stimulation, higher stimulus amplitudes can be employed to recruit fibers more distant from the active site and thus try to achieve a desired level of overall activation. Such changes, however, result in an increase in the stimulation threshold and possibly also a loss of stimulation specificity. Such compensatory techniques do not apply for recording situations - signal amplitudes and specificity are simply degraded without any recourse for recovery.

The challenge of keeping the electrode active site fixed relative to the active nerve fibers is made more difficult by the peripheral nerve being loosely fixed to the surrounding soft tissue in the body. The electrode site must move in tandem with the nerve as the nerve moves within the body. Non-coupled movements or vibrations risk disrupting the electrode double layer at the chemo-electric interface, and can result in movement artifacts and movement related shot noise that can overwhelm the signal. Some examples of how mechanical stability has been achieved are described below.

Glass pipette intracellular electrodes for acute animal work use "the tank" approach. Since the electrode tolerates very little vibration or movement, everything and anything is done to minimize the amount of vibration or mechanical movement of the preparation and electrode. All components are solidly anchored onto a solid structural mass to ensure that there is little to no movement. The anchoring mass or table top is often suspended on an air table to minimize mechanical vibrations coming from the floor. If an animal is used, instead of excised tissue, its body is clamped onto the structural anchor using bone pins and clamps. It may also be advantageous to locate the laboratory in the basement or ground floor to help minimize building vibrations.

Clinical neuroprostheses require chronically implanted electrodes to work in a freely moving person. One nerve interface that is appropriate for this is a nerve cuff. Cuff electrodes use a silicone tube to surround the nerve. Silicone is a biocompatible, non-resorbable, elastomeric, insulating material, which conforms to the outer surface of the nerve. The electrode active sites are incorporated in the inner wall of the elastomer cuff, which holds them in place. The cuff electrode itself is ultimately held in place by connective tissue, which forms around the cuff electrode and the nerve trunk. Intrafascicular electrodes meant for chronic use are, in contrast, fixed into place by physically suturing or gluing the electrode wires onto the nerve trunk.

The fibrotic encapsulation that forms between the inner lumen of a cuff electrode and the nerve trunk moves the active fibers further from the electrode recording sites which acts to reduce the signal-to-noise ratio. However, there is also an advantageous effect of the fibrotic encapsulation. Because the encapsulating tissue is higher in impedance than the physiological fluids within the body, current flow in the extra-axonal space is restricted. This leads to an increase in the extracellular potential due to action currents in the extracellular space and results in an increase in the electrical signal picked up by the electrode recording sites. In addition, the formation of the fibrotic encapsulation can help to chronically anchor the electrode structure to the nerve (note that this requires that the electrode structure has a sufficiently rough surface for the tissue to grab onto).

3.2.1 *Lead-out wiring*

Once the problem of placing and securing the recording site is resolved, one faces the problem of transmitting the signal to the pre-amplifier or interpretation stage of the system. Usually, these components are placed outside of the body because of powering issues, and also to allow for future upgrades to the hardware. The most common technique is to use lead outs with a percutaneous connector. Lead out cables provide a cost effective, low impedance electrical pathway between the electrode and the pre-amplifier, or between the pre-amplifier and interpretation subsystem if an implanted pre-amplifier is used.

Lead out cables can be single stranded, multistranded, multichannel, with or without reinforcement, coiled or uncoiled, etc. They must be flexible, durable and small. There are many commercial manufacturers of bioelectric cabling including Finetech Medical, Cooner Wire, and MedWire. When used in the periphery, lead cables must be able to accommodate elongation without transmitting stresses to the electrode. A commonly used approach in chronic animal work is to implant the electrode so that the wires from the electrode are routed first distally through an additional bight, before routing them proximally toward the connector. The additional of the bight provides slack so that any tugging on the lead out wire takes out the slack in the cable before transmitting the stress to the electrode that is tethered to it. It is important that a bight and not a loop is used since loops become a fixed anchor point which can work against the electrode once the loop is encapsulated. Most bioelectric cables are Teflon^{TM} insulated stainless steel wires. NEC's material scientists have developed bioelectric, low nickel stainless steels [52]. The number of joints used in a cable should be minimized as much as possible because they constitute stress risers, points of corrosive multi-metallic junctions and weak points in the insulation. These effects can cause high electrical resistance at the wire junctions as well as total mechanical failures.

In general, multistranded lead out wires are preferable over single stranded wires for chronic implants, because this allows for multiple points of mechanical failure of single strands, before there is a failure in the overall electrical conduction. Multistrand lead wires sacrifice size to achieve a more robust and often more flexible lead as compared to single conductor wires. Care, however, should be exercised with high impedance electrodes and long leads, because the leads behave like an antenna and can increase line and EM noise pickup. Lead out wires intrinsically have a capacitance between the conductor core and the physiological fluid. Since the physiological fluid is commonly used as a ground or reference point, this capacitance becomes parasitic and can influence the transmission of electric potentials through the cabling and reduce the high frequency components of the signal.

FNS application in the periphery of adolescents or children brings up another cabling issue. The electrode and associated cables must be able to accommodate changes in limb length and girth as the child grows [2, 135]. The problem has been approached in FNS research in cerebral palsy children where excess wire is implanted in the body within a plastic pouch. The pouch prevents encapsulation of the excess wire and allows it to be slowly drawn out as the limb grows.

Care must be taken when using cabling to a percutaneous connector. The connector must be kept as clean as possible. An infection starting at the connector could work its way into the body by tracking along the bioelectric cabling.

3.2.2 Telemetry

Given all of the problems associated with tethering, potential infection, strain relief, potential for mechanical fatigue and failure, wireless techniques, such as those methods used to command stimulators through RF telemetry, are an important adjunct to implanted systems. Telemetry systems require an implanted preamplifier stage to amplify the nerve signal sufficiently before transmission through an RF link. Although fully implanted systems are an attractive solution, current issues of adequate bandwidth, power consumption, size, and cost limit the availability of telemetric devices for transmission of neural signals. Unless the interpretation and controller subsystems are fully implanted, multiple channels may be required to achieve adequate control for many neuroprostheses. Devices developed to date have been implemented with a small number of channels in animal models. Other developments include the two channel telemetry amplifier developed by Prochazka [109] that is used in combination with a percutaneous connector to eliminate external cabling, but may be further developed to an implanted device. Technological challenges to telemetry include finding methods to miniaturize complex analog and digital electronics as well as finding methods to supply the relatively high power requirements of these devices. One such example of a solution to these challenges is the IMES system [159] which is capable of measuring time and frequency related EMG signals and communicate them wirelessly to commercially available clinical EMG systems. This elimination of the need for percutaneous wires is critical to the long term development of fully integrated neuroprostheses.

3.3   *Electrical Considerations*

3.3.1 *Signal characteristics*

Nerve based biopotentials in the peripheral nervous system consist of two potentials, the transmembrane potential and the action potential. The membrane potential generally can only be measured by transmembrane or intracellular recording and cannot be captured with extracellular recording techniques. Both intracellular and extracellular electrodes, however, can detect the action potential. The origin of the neural signal recorded through the interface subsystem is, generally speaking, the action potential. The action potential in itself contains very little information, but by modulating the frequency of action potential trains the nervous system can encode magnitude, for example. The action potential is similar to an electronic transmitter's digital carrier signal which is pulse rate modulated to convey information. Both the magnitude and frequency range of neural signals recorded through the interface is dependent on the electrode used. Magnitudes from intraneural recording can be as large as ~100 mV. Intrafascicularly recorded action potentials can be as large as ~100 µV while extrafascicularly recorded action potentials, in contrast, have amplitudes only in the 1 – 10 µV range.

The frequency content of recorded neural signals has a slight dependence on the recording method used and the electrode used. As a rule of thumb, selective electrodes with small recording sites have a broader bandwidth signal with higher frequency content as compared to electrodes with large recording sites. Similarly, the bipolar and tripolar recording configurations tend to shift the signal content towards higher frequencies, as does decreasing inter-electrode spacing. Intracellularly recorded nerve potentials have both membrane potential and action potential components, with the former having energy down to DC. Extracellularly recorded nerve potentials only contain action potentials which have signal energy between ~100 Hz and ~10 kHz. Being roughly matched to the frequency range of human hearing, the raw neural action potential signal can be recorded and listened to using high fidelity audio equipment. Even with the untrained ear it is possible to listen to the signal during an experiment and qualitatively estimate neural activity levels in the raw recording. The human auditory system is often better at discriminating differences in the neural response than are advanced signal processing techniques and computer algorithms.

3.3.2 Amplifier requirements

The magnitudes of the signals being recorded, especially in the case of extracellular recording electrodes, require very low noise amplifiers with total system gains of the order of 1000x – 100000x. When working with electrode systems, several additional factors must be taken into consideration. For electronic amplifiers to work, there must be at least two points of contact with the biology. One point is the *sensing electrode*, which we described above. Since electrical potentials are not absolute but relative measures, in addition to the sensing point we must establish a common electrical reference point with a *ground* electrode. When placed into an electrolyte solution, electrochemical potentials form at the electrochemical interface between the conductors (electrodes) and solution. These potentials can range from a few millivolts through many volts and are dependent on many factors, including electrode material, size, electrolyte concentration, and temperature. When used in bioelectrical interfaces, they manifest themselves as a large offset voltage on top of the bioelectrical activity. Given a need to amplify the bioelectrical activity by up to 100000 x, one can immediately see that simple amplification would block the amplifier. The bio-amplifier should have some provision to deal with offsets.

One strategy to minimize the electrochemical potential is to add a third sensing point, the indifferent electrode, using an electrode of the same material and size as the sensing electrode, and placed close enough to the sensing electrode that it is in the same environment as the sensing electrode, but far enough away from the sensing electrode that it does not measure any bioelectrical activity. A differential amplifier is used to take the difference between the sensing and indifferent electrode to minimize the offset potential as well as remove common mode noise. A second strategy is to actively or passively high pass filter the measured potential to remove the electrochemical offset potential before it is amplified. Since electrochemical offset potentials are relatively slow in forming and changing, they do not occupy the same part of the spectrum as action potentials and can be removed by high pass filtering. This strategy is not suited for intracellular recordings since the membrane potential is also removed by high pass filtering. In this case, a method of zeroing the interfacial electrochemical potential must be used.

A second key factor in the design of bio-amplifiers is that small DC currents such as bias currents for the amplifier will force reactions to take place at the electrode interface. This can modify the electrode either by plating or corroding the interfacial surface depending on the direction of the current. To minimize this problem, amplifiers with low bias currents should be selected.

There are various ways to physically realize the amplifier, including using monolithic linear active components such as instrumentation amplifiers. However, it should be noted that the differential preamplifier should not be implemented by simply using the differential op-amp configuration.

3.3.3 *Electrode impedance*

A third factor related to amplifier design and selection is the impedance of the electrode. Impedance is related to the electrochemical interface, the electrode insulation and the conductivity of the electrode lead wires among other key parameters. A typical impedance spectrum for a metal electrode is shown in Figure 23.

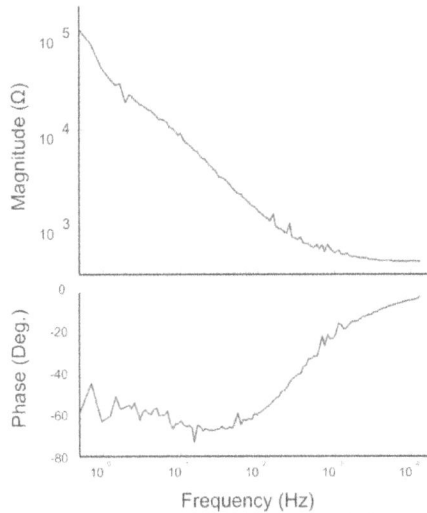

Fig. 23. Typical impedance spectrum as a Bode Plot for a metal electrode.

The impedance of the electrode is often characterized as the magnitude of the impedance at 1 kHz or the magnitude of the impedance at DC. A frequency of 1 kHz is used for neural electrodes since the center of the energy of action potentials is about 1 kHz, making it the most relevant frequency to measure impedance. Typical electrode impedances at 1 kHz can range from a few hundred Ohms for non-selective hook electrodes, to about 1 MΩ for microneurography needle electrodes. The impedance at DC can range between 1 MΩ to tens of Gigaohms. Recording configurations with amplifiers place the electrode in series with the input impedance of the amplifier and, thus, the input impedance of the amplifier must be so that most of the potential is dropped across the amplifier and not the electrode interface. Moreover, the common mode rejection ratio of differential amplifiers is highly sensitive to differences in the total impedance seen at each input terminal to the amplifier. The input impedance of the amplifier should be several orders of magnitude larger than the impedance of the electrode so that the inevitable imbalance in electrode impedance does not degrade the amplifier performance. Because of these issues, low noise amplifiers with FET input stages are commonly used. FET input amplifiers have low bias currents and input impedances > 1 TΩ.

4. Applications of Peripheral Nerve Recording for Feedback Control in FNS Systems

The performance of functional electrical stimulation systems that provide mobility for paralyzed limbs can be enhanced by the provision of closed loop control strategies. In such cases it is desirable to know the position of the joints as well as the forces and moments that the muscles exert during the evoked contractions. This can also be demonstrated in complex lower and upper limb prostheses. FNS systems, such as diaphragm pacing to relieve sleep apnea, cannot function at all without sensory information. Recently, research has demonstrated the wide ranging benefits of Vagal Nerve Stimulation (VNS). Various studies have shown efficacy in humans for endpoints from epilepsy [16, 87, 121] to hypertension [17]. Efforts to extract sensory information from efferent and afferent nerves are discussed below in relation to FNS systems having various applications. This section is divided into somatic and autonomic recordings, with the latter being the forefront of the field.

4.1   Somatic recordings

These applications utilize somatic peripheral nerves in order to control sophisticated limb and hand prostheses that have been developed in the past 10 years. For the most part, older prostheses had few degrees of freedom (DOFs) and often gave little sensory feedback to the user. The next generation of prostheses focus on resolving both of these problems and developing a bidirectional communication between user and device. Use of new surgical techniques like targeted muscle reinnervation (TMR) or osseointegration and advances in more selective electrode types, such as TIME or FINE, have given the user more control. Advances such as these have made prosthetic limb use much more natural and increased the time of usage in amputees.

4.1.1 *Heel strike detection for foot-drop FNS systems*

Liberson [79] is credited with having presented the first demonstration of FNS for motor rehabilitation. By electrically stimulating the peroneal nerve where it passes just under the skin near the posterior-lateral border of the knee, he was able to evoke a contraction in the ankle dorsiflexors to correct for foot-drop in stroke patients. The activation and cessation of the muscle stimulation was synchronized with the user's gait via a pressure switch mounted within the shoe. There later followed a long succession of additional research efforts aimed to improve the controllability, cosmesis and convenience of such devices. This included the use of implanted stimulation components [143], telemetered heel strike information using an insole pressure switch and shoe mounted transmitter (Medtronic Inc. Neuro-Muscular Assist), and accelerometer sensors [165].

More recently, Haugland and Sinkjaer [41] showed that heel strike information could also be obtained by recording directly from the sural nerve (Figure 24). This provides the intrinsic advantage that a foot drop neuroprosthesis can function even when the user is walking barefoot. And because the neural interface is permanent, routine 'tuning' of the stimulation parameters to compensate for electrode positioning errors is unnecessary. Sensor reliability, however, isn't automatically assured. Because the amplitude of the nerve signal is only in the range of a few microvolts, it is necessary to employ special amplifier circuitry to 'block out' the contaminating EMG generated by the FNS pulses [26]. Moreover, some ambiguity can arise in interpreting the neural activity during certain foot placements and because of extraneous neural activity evoked by stretch of the skin during foot motion that is not coincident with a heel strike event. This difficulty has been effectively overcome by applying an adaptive logic network to interpret weak recorded nerve activity [69].

4.1.2 *Natural sensors for determining joint angle in FNS systems*

Perhaps the greatest need to have sensor information to enhance the function of FNS systems is associated with restoring standing and walking in paraplegia. Normal motor function relies heavily on signals from muscle afferents for information about the static and dynamic forces acting about the joints. It might be useful for future FNS systems if control signals could be derived from recordings of this afferent activity, and initial successes in this area by Yoshida and Horch [172] lend support for this effort. Those investigators utilized "dual channel" intrafasicular electrodes placed into the tibial and peroneal nerves in anesthetized and in unanesthetized, decerebrate cats to record the activity of spindle afferents. It was demonstrated that the position of the ankle joint could be made to follow a predefined sinusoidal trajectory using functional electrical stimulation applied to the tibial nerve coupled with ankle joint position information derived from the recorded afferents. Moreover, the control system could reach and maintain a given target position in the face of an applied external joint moment opposing the movement. Success was achieved for joint velocities up to 1 Hz. Figure 25 shows the tracking from a typical movement trial.

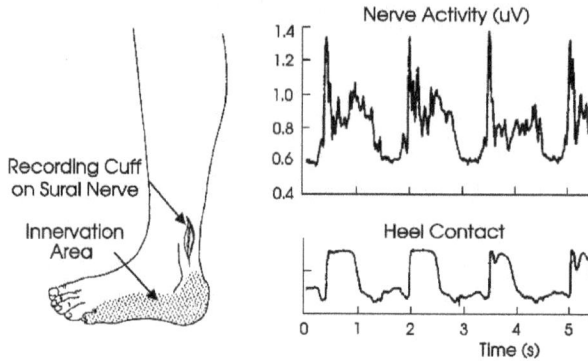

Fig. 24. Use of cutaneous afferent activity for controlling a drop-foot neuroprosthesis. **Left** - a nerve cuff is implanted around the sural nerve to register activity evoked by mechanical stimulation of the foot sole and heel which is included in the innervation territory of this nerve. **Right** - the upper trace shows the rectified and integrated nerve activity as the individual walks. The lower trace represents the output of a controller that further processed the recorded neural activity to determine the heel strike event which served to turn off the stimulation of the dorsiflexors at each stance event. A pre-programmed adjustable delay was used to turn the simulation back on in synchrony with the beginning of the next swing event. This figure is modified from Haugland and Sinkjaer [41].

Based on those positive results, investigators sought to determine if muscle afferent activity recorded using nerve cuffs could also be used for such closed-loop FNS control, with particular regard to neuroprosthetic standing and walking [119]. This would be desirable because cuffs are less invasive than is the case with intrafasicular electrodes.

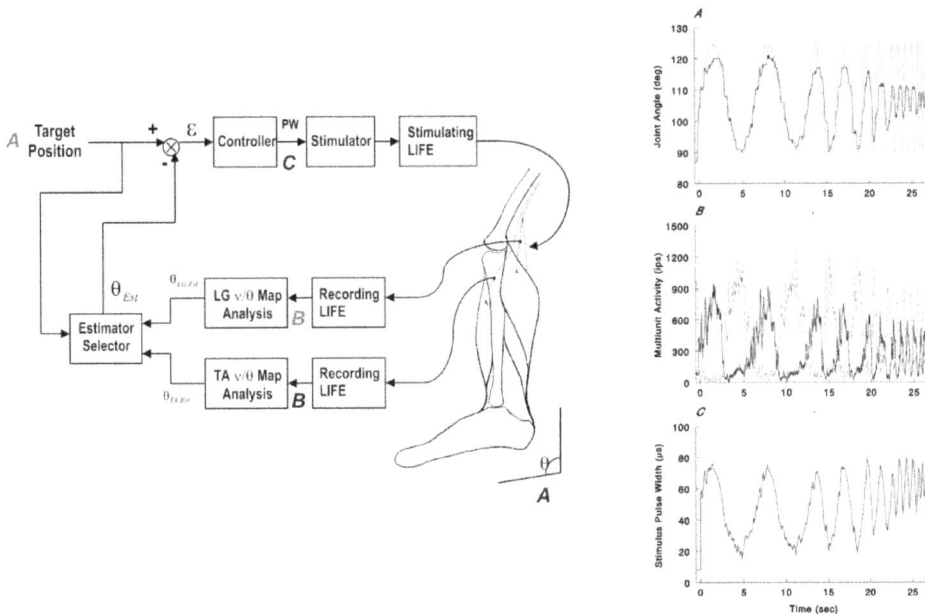

Fig. 25. Closed loop control FNS system based upon neural feedback from natural sensors (muscle afferents). The concept was shown in the anaesthetized and the decerebrate feline model. Sinusoidal tracking of a target ankle angle was possible for frequencies up to ~1Hz. Adapted from Yoshida and Horch [172].

Using an anesthetized rabbit preparation, individual tripolar recording cuffs were applied around the tibial and peroneal divisions of the sciatic nerve. The knee was fixated, and a 'shoe' applied around the hock was coupled to a servo motor that allowed the ankle to be rotated. During rotation in the flexion direction (Figure 26), the ankle extensor muscles were stretched and the tibial nerve cuff recorded a volley of neural activity that originated in the spindle afferents of the stretched extensor muscles. When the motion was halted, the phasic activity decayed and a low level of tonic activity remained. Movement in the opposite direction, towards extension, caused a complementary response from the peroneal muscle afferents since the motion stretched those muscles. At the same time there was an immediate cessation of the tibial afferent activity because those muscles were passively shortened (and their stretch receptors were relaxed). The use of nerve recording cuffs applied to a pair of antagonistic muscles acting over a common joint thus affords a kind of 'push pull' sensor signal. It is relatively straightforward to discern the direction of movement of the ankle at any moment given the paired signals, and because of the dynamic sensitivity of the group Ia spindle receptors, rapid joint rotation is distinguishable from more slow movement because of the increased response.

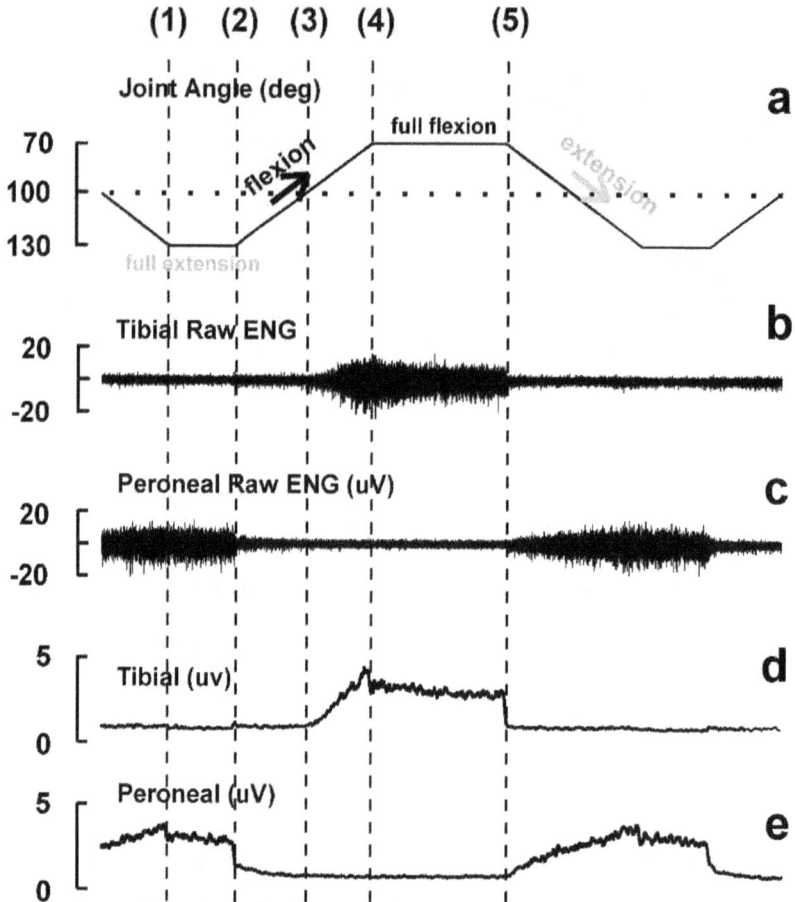

Fig. 26. Cuff recorded afferent responses of the peroneal and tibial nerves in the rabbit to passive motion of the ankle. Traces **a** through **e** as indicated. ENG in **d** and **e** is rectified and integrated. Dorsiflexion movement ('2') stretches the extensor muscles and after a position threshold ('3') is exceeded, evokes vigorous activity in the tibial nerve. At the start of the movement plateau phase ('4') there is a decline in the tibial activity because the dynamic response from the spindle primary afferents ceases, leaving only the spindle secondary (static) afferents discharging and possibly some contribution from the Golgi tendon afferents. At '5' the ankle motion reverses direction toward extension causing the activity in the tibial recording to halt abruptly (since the spindles are relaxed), and in a complimentary manner, the neural activity recorded from the peroneal nerve is seen to increase.

If more detailed position information is desired, then the 'whole nerve' recordings obtained in this manner are not sufficient. It appears unlikely to be able to obtain enduring calibration information for using afferent signals recorded with nerve cuffs, particularly with regard to the dynamic sensitivity, which has been shown to depend strongly on the initial stretch (i.e., it is related to the starting position) of the responding muscles [54, 119]. Thus, a muscle which is already stretched produces higher afferent discharge than when that muscle is passively elongated from a more slackened initial state.

Another complicating factor is that the magnitude of the evoked activity during joint movement is increased if the muscles that are being stretched by the movement are allowed to remain stationary for more than a few minutes prior to the stretch onset [54]. Such effects are in agreement with prior reports of the characteristics of spindle afferents from single unit studies. Based on studies of isolated spindle afferents performed by Proske and Gregory [110], the effect of a stationary period is presumed to be caused by the physiological property of both intra- and extrafusal muscle fibers forming new cross-bridges between the actin and myosin filaments whenever the muscle length is held stationary. This removes any slackness in the muscle so that an applied stretch is immediately effective in exciting the spindle receptors. It should be noted that the rabbit studies described above utilized recordings from passively stretched muscles. This is to avoid additional complications that arise when a muscle which contributes to a recorded afferent signal is subjected to FNS so that it undergoes an active contraction. In the absence of a functioning gamma drive system, its spindles are unloaded [54] and their discharges are halted.

At the same time, however, the Golgi tendon receptors are activated by the contraction. The activity recorded by the cuff represents a summation of these opposing effects. To circumvent these potential problems, it might be possible, in an FNS application, to reserve some muscles from each joint system for passive movement by not applying FNS to them. Thus, afferent control signals would be sought only from passively stretched muscles. In situations where FNS is given to the muscle(s) on one side of a joint at any given time (i.e., co-contraction of antagonistic pairs is avoided) then the muscles opposite the FNS muscle will be passively stretched. In either case, stimulus artifacts from nearby stimulated muscles will still contaminate the cuff recordings, but there will be periods between the artifacts when the neural activity can be analyzed.

4.1.3 *Tactile sensing in grasp neuroprostheses*

An especially useful application for natural sensing in FNS systems involves the need for tactile feedback from the finger tips to provide closed loop control during FNS assisted grasp. It has long been recognized that externally worn sensors placed on the fingers as well as any requisite lead wires are undesirable to the user from a cosmetic perspective and can also interfere with the grasp function.

Experiments involving normal subjects have elucidated the importance of tactile sensing of pressure, skin stretch and object slippage in the normal control of grasp function [162, 163]. When a load is lifted, cutaneous receptors within the fingertip skin monitor the normal (grip) contacting force, the sheer force (skin stretch), and information regarding the frictional properties of the grasped surface. Normally, the application of grasping force is pre-programmed to always be greater (with only a modest safety margin) than that which is necessary to avoid slippage of the grasped object. In the event that the ratio of the grip force to the load presented by trying to move the object is too low so that slippage occurs, a natural reflex is evoked that increases the grip force and arrests the slippage. A similar scheme operates during the control of grip force when active objects are restrained (such as holding an umbrella in the wind) except that in this case information about the pulling load regulates the magnitude of the grasp effort in a feedback control mode [58 - 60].

This principle of detecting slippage and using it to adjust grip force has been partially mimicked for controlling FNS assisted grasp in volunteer subjects [43, 53]. While it isn't yet practical (because of technological shortcomings) to try to 'connect' with individual tactile afferents that might come into contact with a grasped object, it has been possible to implant a nerve recording cuff in the palm around the digital nerve that innervates the lateral border of the index finger. If a lateral grasp is used, then the grasped object will be in contact with the skin region that is within the innervation territory of the cuffed nerve as shown in Figure 28. Any slippage that occurs during manipulation of the grasped object will evoke a robust discharge from the tactile receptors and their activity can be detected in the recorded signal picked up by the cuff electrode. Following the detection of a slippage event, the grip force can be automatically upgraded by an arbitrary amount. To determine the feasibility of implementing this control strategy, the signals recorded from the cuff during grasping activities needed to be well characterized.

The results of the above study have shown that a cuff could return slippage feedback in a non-amputated patient. However, this becomes more interesting when this is applied to an amputated patient. When a limb is amputated, the nerve trunk(s) become transected. They no longer go to the limb, but the brain still sends information down the efferent nerve fibers, and the afferent nerve fibers are still capable of conducting action potentials [20]. Much work has gone into developing a bidirectional communication pathway that allows for two-way signals from user to device and vice versa.

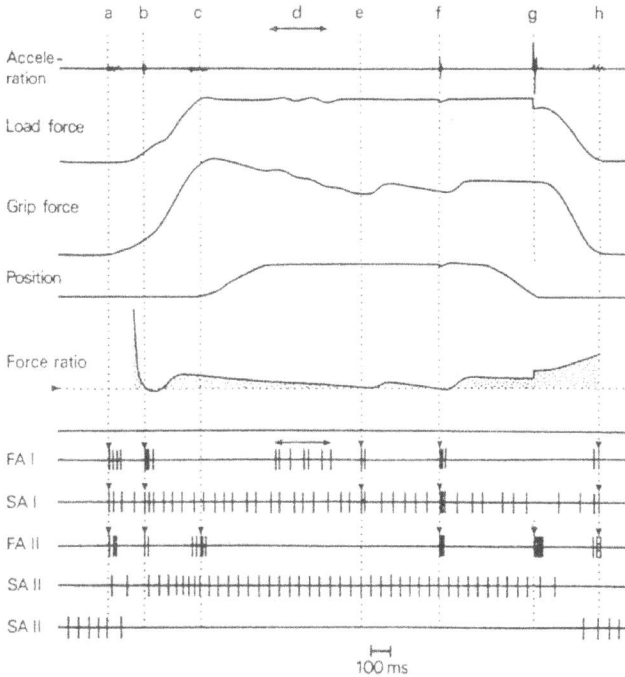

Fig. 27. Schematic illustration of the kinds of responses that may occur among the four types of tactile afferents (FA1, SA1, FA2, and SA2) during lifting using precision grip. Note the parallel increase of the grip and load force during the lift phase and the maintenance of a critical grip/load force ratio. Marked events are: **a** - initial responses in FA1, SA1 and FA2 units; **b** - slip responses in FA1, SA1 and FA2 units during the loading phase; **c** - FA2 discharges at the start of the vertical movement; **d** - FA2 discharges during epoch of pronounced muscular tremor; **e** - localized slip response in FA1 and SA1; **f** - slip responses in FA1, SA1 and FA2 units; **g**- FA2 burst at the time the grasped object was returned to the table; **h**- responses in FA1, SA1 and FA2 units during object release. Note the force upgrades following slips at **e**, **f** and **g**. (Figure is copied with permission from [163]).

One of the biggest obstacles to this research is what Kuiken et al. describe as a "real estate" issue in TMR where there isn't enough space to place all needed electrodes. Mostly this event arises from allowing both parts of the bidirectional communication to occupy the same physical space (the cutaneous area that has been reinnervated). Studies performed by Micera et al [112], attempted to rectify this issue by utilizing more selective electrodes, namely TIME structures. It should be noted that this study did not depend on the TMR surgical procedure, but rather used the natural nerve stumps of the patient. Their approach was similar to TMR, in that they applied surface EMG electrodes to control a complex prosthesis. Rather than using more surface electrodes, Micera et al. implanted TIME structures into the median and ulnar nerve of the patient. Once the implants were placed and the patient healed, they were tasked with performing some 700 trials to verify their ability in both proper grasping and cutaneous response to various physical objects (i.e., rough vs smooth). In order to verify that the patient was only using sensory information from the electrodes, they were visually and acoustically isolated (Figure 29).

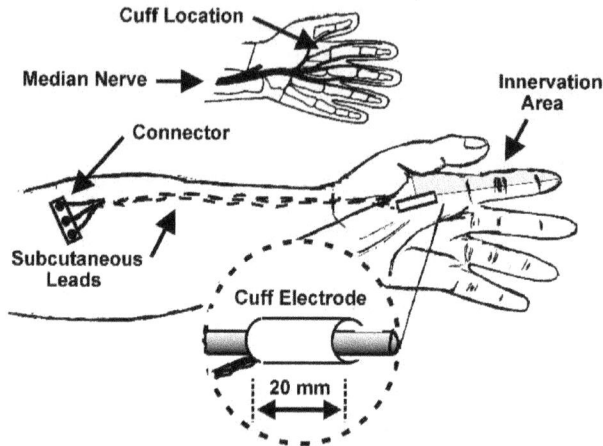

Fig. 28. Location of a tri-polar nerve recording cuff implanted around the palmer digital nerve that innervates the skin along the radial half of the index finger. This skin region is contacted during lateral grasp activities. (Reproduced with permission from Fig. 2 in [117]).

Through proper controls, Micera et al. were able to validate their hypothesis and state their electrodes could restore tactile sensation, resulting in increases in performance not seen in current prosthetics. The patient could reliably control the prosthesis, with only tactile feedback, in a staircase task and outperformed visual only feedback. Along with this proficiency in operation, the patient was able to distinguish between visually dissimilar objects with only tactile sensation, allowing for them to determine a proper grasp for each. In addition, the patient did this in a physically appropriate time frame (< 3 seconds).

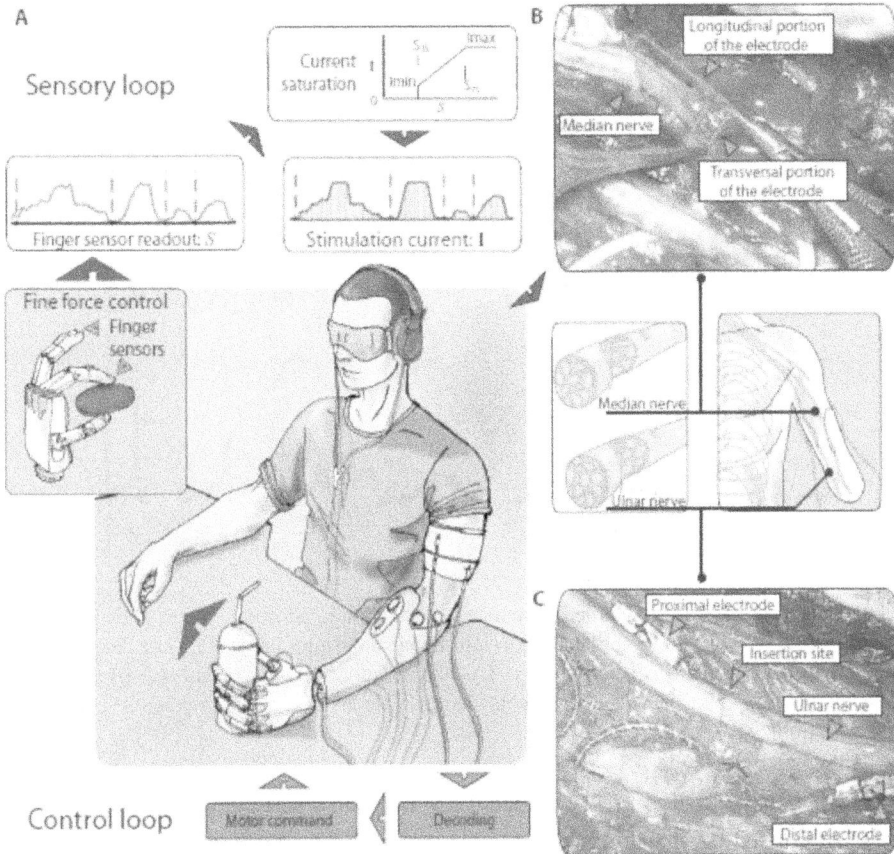

Fig. 29. Illustration of the experimental procedure with the patient. (A) Fine force sensors in the prosthesis were read out and delivered current via TIME electrodes. (B) Two TIME electrodes were implanted into median and ulnar nerves of the patients. (C) The insertion of the TIME electrodes can be seen here.

4.1.4 *Cutaneous responses to contacting objects*

A series of studies were undertaken to characterize the responses of a nerve cuff electrode to tactile events including skin stretch, object slippage and normal contact force systems [117]. Figure 30 shows neural responses to skin stretch obtained from the palmer digital nerve of a volunteer subject who is quadriplegic. A flat contactor (15mm by 30mm) having a smooth surface was applied on the radial side of the (immobilized) index finger between the proximal and distal interphalangial joints. A layer of double faced adhesive tape interposed at the skin interface allowed the skin to be stretched without slippage. A 0.7 N normal force was maintained throughout the movement trials, and servo regulated symmetric trapezoidal ramp profiles were used to deliver shear forces to the skin. The results clearly show a strong phasic discharge during the shear force ramp followed by a modest level of tonic activity during the 'hold' phase of the trapezoidal stimulus. The phasic portion of the response was enhanced linearly when the velocity of the applied shear force was increased.

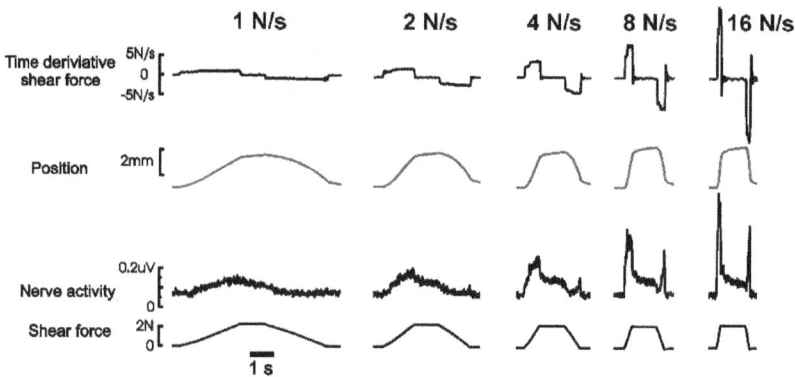

Fig. 30. Cutaneous responses recorded from a nerve cuff applied around a palmer digital nerve in a quadriplegic subject during the application of skin stretch at the rates indicated. Note the presence of phasic and tonic portions of the responses. The neural activity has been full wave rectified and integrated, and each trace displayed represents the ensemble average of ten trials. (Reproduced with permission from [117], Fig. 3).

The responses of the cuff recorded skin afferent discharges to slippage of the contactor consist of brief bursts of phasic activity. The slippage response derives from two sources. One source is a recoiling of the skin when the shear force is abruptly released, and the other contribution comes when (and if) the slippage event subsides and the skin is again stretched. The cycle of release and stretch can be repeated in a 'ratcheting' mode during slippage of an object with the skin. The effect of increasing the rate of sliding is to increase the frequency of the 'stretch-release-stretch' cycles which increases the average afferent activity during the slippage. The effect of friction is that increased friction causes the skin to be stretched to a higher level before the slippage event occurs. This leads to a larger afferent discharge when the slippage occurs. The data shown in Fig. 31 summarize the findings of an experiment where contactors having 3 grades of slipperiness (sandpaper, suede and silk) were moved across the index finger at several different velocities. Again a 0.7 N contact force was maintained throughout the slippage trials, and the contactor was moved at a rate of either 8, 16 or 24mm/s using a position servo system. For each friction condition, the effect of increased velocity is to increase the cutaneous response. This is a useful circumstance because it implies that the corrective action of an FNS feedback controller could be graded by measuring the amplitude of the evoked nerve response. Thus, an object that is slipping faster over the skin could result in a stronger grip force increase than for an object that is slipping more slowly. Similarly, when a grasping activity causes the skin to be stretched at a fast rate there is an increased risk of impending slippage of the object, and this could be more securely averted by a brisk and more intense grip force increase.

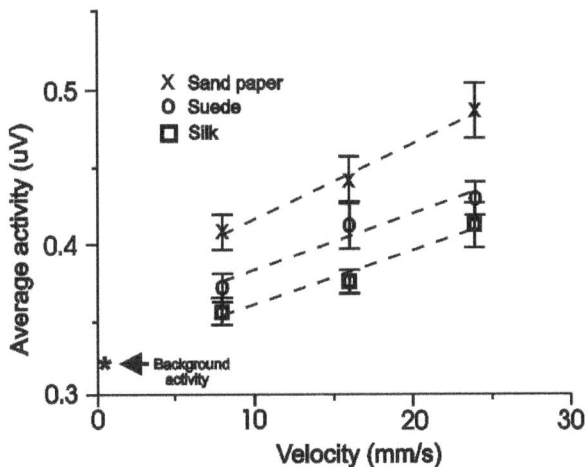

Fig. 31. Cutaneous activity from the index finger in response to a sliding contactor as a function of velocity and surface texture. Each data point is the average of 20 trials. Error bars are +/- 2 std dev. Higher velocity movement evokes a stronger slip response and a more rough texture of the contact surface also produces greater afferent activity during the period when the contactor is sliding over the skin. The neural activity is quantified by rectifying and integrating the cuff recording. (Reproduced with permission from [117], Fig. 5).

The situation with regard to the effect of object texture on the cutaneous slip response is, unfortunately, just opposite to what the control engineer would like to deal with. Namely, an object with a more slippery contact surface (and which is thus most likely to slip from the grasp during manipulation) evokes the weakest neural response in comparison with (higher friction) rougher surfaces.

It was also demonstrated in these studies that the cuff recorded signals from the cutaneous afferents are dominated by phasic responses from the tactile receptors. There is only very poor information available in the recorded signal (owing to the very low signal level) concerning the magnitude of static contact forces on the skin. Because the nerve recording cuff integrates the activity from all types of tactile afferents indiscriminately, it is not possible to separately quantify the components of the response that are caused by the normal (contact) force that monitors the strength of the grasp and the loading force that is applied to move or to restrain the grasped object. Clearly then, if only cuff recordings are available, then the 'natural' grasp control strategies described above cannot be directly applied.

This problem aside, it has still been possible to employ a modified control strategy that has proven to be advantageous in FNS hand grasp control as follows. Instead of attempting to monitor the "grip to load force ratio" during grasping activities, the grip level was increased each time that a slippage event (signaled by a sudden increase in the nerve activity) was detected. It should be pointed out that an increase in the nerve activity will take place due to the increased grasp force. But since this event is expected within a fixed latency following the increased stimulation parameters, it can simply be "edited out".

Another consideration is that while the slippage induced grasp force increases might be effective to arrest slippage, it would not be practical to maintain an elevated level of grip force indefinitely as that could result in unnecessary muscle fatigue. To deal with this difficulty, a fixed rate of grip force relaxation was programmed into the control strategy. Thus, the elevated grasp force level following a slip was allowed to decay slowly, but the higher grip level could be reinstated at any moment by the occurrence of another small slippage event (as determined from the monitored cutaneous nerve activity). Figure 32 shows data obtained during studies with a volunteer subject who used a modified FNS grasp neuroprosthesis that was elaborated around the FreeHand™ System to include this type of slippage based 'artificial reflex' controller strategy [42, 43, 53].

Restoring this cutaneous response to a patient has been proven possible, but greatly plagued by inconsistent operation. A major issue that effects the efficacy and reliability of a prosthetic device is the placement of the electrodes. Their placement is crucial to their signal fidelity over time. With both the TMR and TIME procedures, there is an issue with the placement of the electrodes. In the case of TMR, the patient must don and doff the device daily, changing the position of the electrodes with respect to the reinnervated muscles. This would cause a change in the waveforms that the device depends on for control, as well as the area the electrodes would stimulate for sensory feedback. Eventually, this would cause frustration in the user, leading discontinuation of its use. This problem is not remedied with the TIME structures, either. The body responses to the TIME penetrating the nerve trunk via the foreign body response, eventually encapsulating it and rejecting it. There are also issues due to the micro-movements of the nerve that lead to further injury. To further the problems, there must be some way to transmit the signal out of the body. Normally, wires are fed percutaneously to interface with the outside world, but percutaneous wires often are plagued by infections that can require surgical intervention.

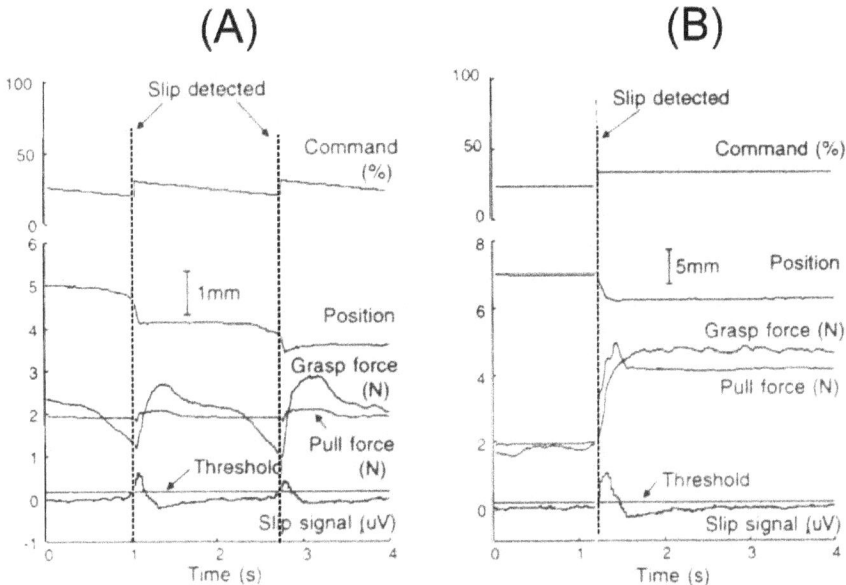

Fig. 32. (A) System reaction and neural activity evoked by slippage of a grasped object caused by slow deliberate relaxation of the grip force. (B) Slippage and system reactions following a sudden increase in the pulling load. Signal processing to detect a slippage event consisted of rectification and integration of the afferent neural activity followed by the application of a threshold. The contact surface of the grasped object was covered with sandpaper for both (A) and (B). (Modified from [43], fig. 3 and reproduced with permission.)

Information transmission to outer circuitry has been a problem not easily remedied. It has been addressed via telemetry with the iMES device [159], however this only allows for a narrow bandwidth of communication that often is not sufficient to transmit the information needed for control of sophisticated prostheses. The need for wired communication is still in high demand. Osseointegrated devices have been a solution for stability for decades and have been shown to be useful in transfemoral prosthetics. A recent 2-year study from OPRA resulted in a 92% success rate of transfemoral prosthetics. Ortiz-Catalan et al [103] manipulated this concept for transhumeral prostheses (Figure 33).

The system consists of an abutment screw that is fixated into the bone, where wires lead to and from epimysial muscle electrodes and a cuff electrode around the ulnar nerve. The epimysial muscle electrodes are very similar to the surface electrodes used with the TIME structures and the TMR paradigm. However, the difference between them is that these epimysial electrodes are sutured into the

targeted muscles so they remain stationary. This removes the variability of position
that plagues the TMR and the TIME applications. Also, the osseointegrated device
uses a nerve cuff, which segregates sensory information from motor, but is less
invasive (and therefore less selective) than the TIME application. In their work,
Ortiz-Catalan et al were able to implant this system into a patient. However, they
were unable to demonstrate the same level of utility as with the TIME application.
Nonetheless, removal and replacement of electrodes is made easy with the stability
of the abutment screw.

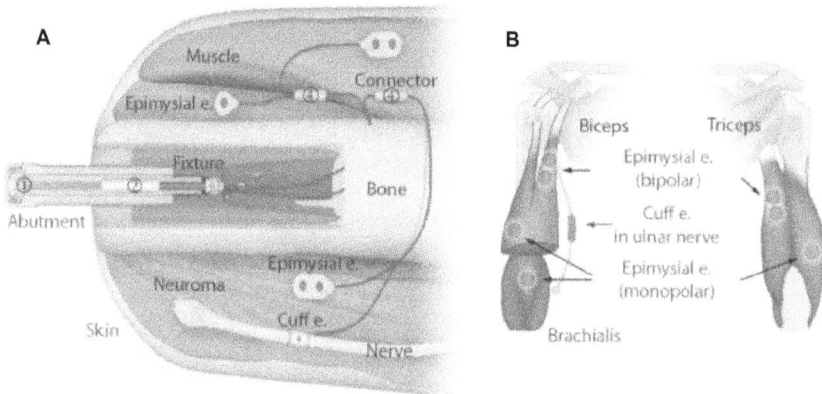

Fig. 33. (A) Depiction of abutment screw interface with the residual bone in cross-section. The lead-
out wires are run through the bone to the target nerves and muscles. (B) Illustration of the placement
of the epimysial electrodes used for pattern recognition.

4.1.5 *Evoked EMG as a sensory control signal in FNS systems*

Another approach to using natural sensor signals for FNS control has been to use
the amplitude of the EMG evoked by the contraction as a measure of the developed
muscle force. In a series of experiments, Popovic and his colleagues [106] used
the rectified and integrated EMG signals from the principal muscles of one leg to
control the timing and amplitude of FNS delivered to the opposite leg while an
awake cat walked on a treadmill.

Further development of this technique in a more sophisticated manner can be
seen in targeted muscle reinnervation (TMR) – as described above. Discovery that
this technique not only allowed for control of a simple prosthetic more intuitively,
but also provided some tactile feedback happened almost serendipitously. In their
pilot study, Kuiken et al. [44, 45], found that their patients could feel sensations
over the area where the nerve had been rerouted. Nervous tissue from the main
nerve trunk had sprouted sensory afferents that reinnervated the patient's skin.
Further studies had shown that not only had large mechanoreceptor fibers

regenerated under the skin, but also smaller pain and temperature receptors, as well. The regrowth allowed the patient the sensation of touch, temperature, pain, and even vibration – in a limb that was no longer there.

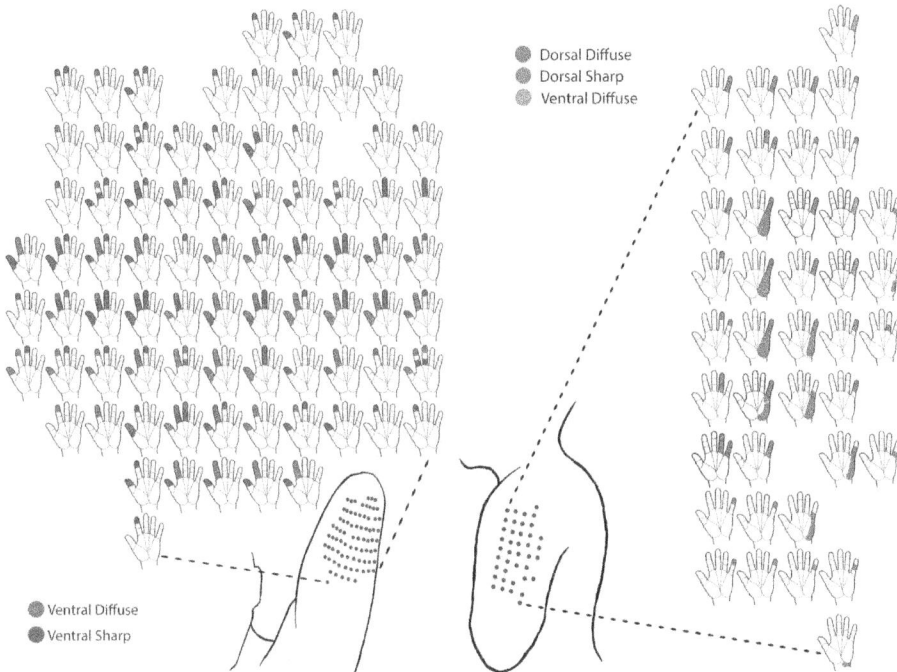

Fig. 34. Left, dots represent a 9x10 cm surface area in corresponding to the T2 intercostobrachial cutaneous nerve. Discrete sensation was abundant and wide spread in this area. This is the territory of the median nerve. Right, the ulnar nerve territory was mapped to this location which corresponds to the axillary nerve cutaneous distribution, measuring 5x9 cm.

There are a few drawbacks to TMR, however. The first being the surgery itself. It is highly invasive and requires quite a bit of healing and rehabilitation time on the part of the patient. This requirement is a heavy toll on the patient, which decreases the likelihood of success of the prosthetic. A bigger issue of TMR for sensory feedback is, as Kuiken puts it, a "real estate issue". The electrodes used to stimulate sensation can take up quite a bit of space. Not to be forgotten, the electrodes for motor control must also be placed in order to make the prosthetic operate. Compounding this issue, the patient must simultaneously contract the newly activated muscle while sensing – which has proven difficult. Kuiken et al. believe they have a technique to mitigate this issue by isolating the sensory fibers and redirecting to a surface skin sensory fiber – which might be further away from the motor intention nerve. Kuiken et al. have shown that this surgical technique alleviates some of the difficulty for the patient. Although TMR has shown promise

448 K. Yoshida et al.

in its ability to provide tactile feedback along with motor control, the tactile leg of
the bidirectional communication has proven to be difficult for the patient to control
and often leads to a phenomena known as sensory gating.

4.1.6 *Obtaining afferent signals from DRG cells*

The DRG (dorsal root ganglia) is an especially appealing location for obtaining
sensory afferent signals using microwire implants [85, 108]. Because the dorsal
root ganglia contain the cell bodies of only afferent neurons, all of the signals that
are recorded are concerned with sensory events. Thus, all of the channels available
from an implanted interface located in the DRG can be dedicated to the acquisition
of sensory information. Because the recordings are from the cell somas, the signal
amplitudes of action potentials are very large (ca. 40 – 70 µv) compared to
extracellular axonal recordings, making it possible to distinguish the activity of
specific afferent neurons.

There is also a bias to record from the largest cells which means that muscle
afferents and cutaneous mechanoreceptors are the most likely sources of any
recorded activity. Another advantage of the DRG location is the fact that each
region of the body projects to only a few adjacent spinal segments and thus a few
DRGs. All of these features help to obtain modality and body location specificity
of the recorded afferent signals. Figure 35 depicts 'state of the art' deployment of
a micromachined electrode array (fabricated at the University of Utah) implanted
into a DRG in chronic experiments with behaving cats. The signals were led out
using percutaneous techniques, and stabile recordings of identified afferent units
were demonstrated for periods up to several weeks [158].

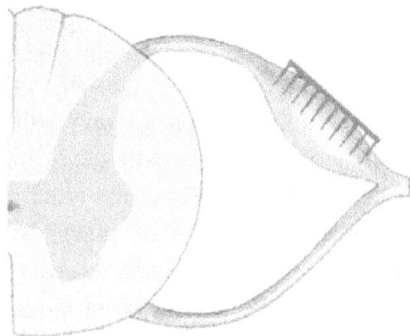

Fig. 35. Use of a micromachined electrode array to obtain chronic recordings from the dorsal root
ganglion cells. (Diagram courtesy of Doug Weber).

4.2   *Autonomic recordings*

Recording and stimulating from the autonomic side of the peripheral nervous system has been somewhat of a forefront. The pharmaceutical company Glaxo-Smith-Klein has recently funded thousands of researchers to investigate and develop a full recording and stimulation device for various autonomic applications, such as incontinence and sleep apnea. Some of these applications have already found their way to clinical use, such as the Inspire therapy from Inspire Medical Systems, Inc. However, GSK's push is not the only one into the autonomic world. Vagal Nerve Stimulation (VNS) has become a very attractive area of research, with applications already showing clinical usefulness in refractory depression and epilepsy. VNS has also shown efficacy in treatment of hypertension. The following section will delve deeper into the history of how these devices have advanced their way to the clinical side and also point to a few frontiers in the area that are showing promise.

4.2.1 *Use of FNS in the correction of sleep apnea*

An example in which only a binary signal is needed for FNS control is in the detection of sleep apnea. Researchers have placed a cuff electrode around the vagal nerve and monitored the cyclical neural activity caused by the efferent volleys to the diaphragm muscles during normal breathing. Any change in the cyclical rhythm of the recorded activity could be an indication of the onset of apnea, and a 'watchdog' controller can be made to respond by applying electrical stimulation to the vagus nerve to contract the diaphragm muscles as needed to ensure that breathing will be restored [128].

Many avenues of stimulation have been pursued – stimulation of the submental nerve, direct stimulation of the genioglossal muscle – but the most efficient mode of stimulation was found to be selective stimulation of the hypoglossal nerve [128]. Most recently, Inspire Medical Systems (Medtronic Inc.) found success in both a feasibility study [66] and a larger clinical study [144]. The goal of their device is to synchronize stimulation of the hypoglossal nerve with the patient's breathing pattern while sleeping. The system consists of a tripole half cuff molded to the hypoglossal nerve, a custom implantable pulse generator implanted subcutaneously, and a respiratory pressure sensor implanted near the patient's midline. Parameters of the device can be altered by the physician and the patient can also switch the device on and off.

4.2.2 Feedback for FNS assisted micturition and continence

In continence restoration systems, it is possible to sense the status of bladder filling from the activity of stretch sensitive mechanoreceptors within the bladder. The behavior of these afferents was shown early on using single fiber studies in cats [36] (see Figure 36), and it has subsequently been demonstrated that similar afferent activity can be recorded using cuff electrodes placed on the sacral dorsal roots or on the pelvic nerve in acute experiments using anesthetized pigs [56] (see Figure 37).

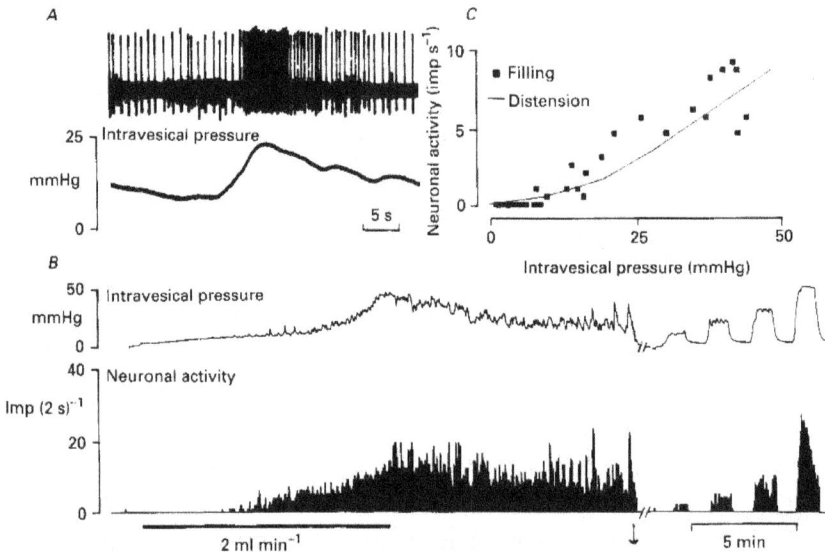

Fig. 36. Responses of an afferent unit during slow filling and distention of the urinary bladder. **A**, specimen record taken during slow filling of the urinary bladder through a urethral catheter at 2 ml·min⁻¹. Upper trace, activity of a single afferent fiber; lower trace, intravesical pressure. **B**, histograms of intravesical pressure and neuronal activity during filling of the bladder (bar) at 2 ml·min⁻¹ and during a series of distention stimuli (right panel). The arrow indicates emptying of the bladder. The afferent unit exhibits no spontaneous activity and does not respond during the first 5 min of slow filling. Thereafter, the increase of intravesical pressure is faithfully encoded. After termination of filling the unit exhibits considerable phasic responses to isovolumetric bladder contractions. **C**, stimulation-response relations of the afferent activity for both stimulation procedures showing a close similarity of the quantitative responses. From [36].

Another use of recordings from bladder afferents is to try to detect spontaneous bladder contractions that can cause incontinence. If such unwanted contractions can be detected early, then electrical stimulation might be applied to tighten the urethral sphincter and prevent the leakage of urine or perhaps the contractions could be blocked or inhibited. The feasibility of detecting spontaneous bladder contractions is supported by data obtained from acute studies in anesthetized cat preparations in which cuff electrodes were applied to the S1 spinal nerve. Using a cumulative summation (CUSUM) algorithm, instead of simply applying a threshold to the rectified and integrated ENG signal, allowed 29 of 30 bladder contractions (across 5 animals) to be detected. One difficulty with this scheme, however, is that the detection of the bladder contractions had an average latency of 6 ± 8 s (s.d.) and ranged between 0.2 and 42 s. Thus, many of the contractions would be detected too late to maintain continence. These researchers suggest that the interval between the contractions could be monitored. Increased frequency of contractions occurs as the bladder fills naturally and could be used to predict when bladder emptying should be performed [56].

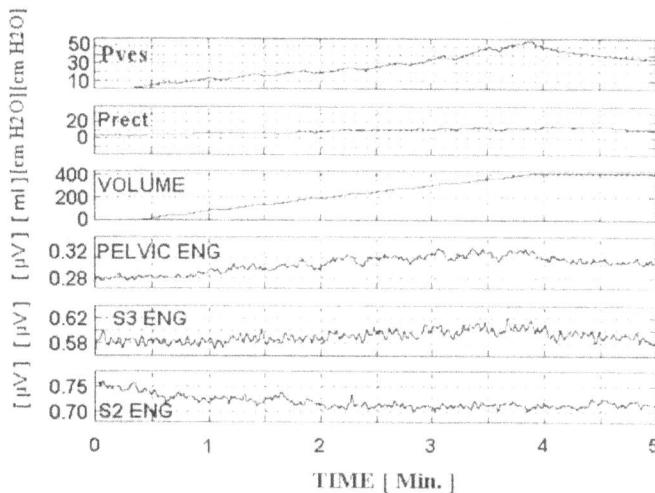

Fig. 37. ENG signals recorded using cuff electrodes applied around the pelvic nerve and 2nd and 3rd spinal sacral root (S2, S3) during the forced filling of the pig urinary bladder at a fast rate of 150 ml/min. Note tracking of S2 and pelvic nerve activity as the bladder volume increases. (Reproduced with permission from [Jesernik, 2000], fig. 5).

Throughout most of the research in which cuffs have been used to detect neural activity, the major shortcoming is the lack of specificity for the type of nerve fibers that contribute to the recorded signal. The cuff recordings from the pelvic nerve or sacral roots, for example, are frequently contaminated with activity from other afferents such as cutaneous and muscle afferents from the pelvic floor, rectum, and anus. Means must be found to separate the activities having different origins.

One strategy that has been proposed [147] is based on a separation according to the conduction velocity (and hence diameter) of the different types of afferents. Because the bladder (detrusor) afferents are comprised of small myelinated fibers in the A-delta class (conduction velocity <16 m/s) it should be possible to separate their activity from the large myelinated muscle and cutaneous afferents which have conduction velocities in the range of 35–120 m/s [5, 36, 58 – 60, 93, 129, 166].

4.2.3 Vagal nerve stimulation

Coming from the Latin word for wandering, the vagus nerve innervates organs in the neck, thorax, abdomen, and reaching as far as the colon. Once thought to be a one way path to change the tone of the viscera, it was found that about 80% of the vagus fibers are afferents [34]. This strongly indicates that this nerve is one of the body's major connection to the CNS. From this, it would follow that stimulation of the vagus would result in changes in cognitive brain regions and autonomic tone in regards to cardiovascular state. Both clinical studies and pilot studies in animals have shown this to be true. In this section, successes in both of these avenues are explored.

4.2.3.1 Psychiatric disorders

Three of the disorders being treated via VNS are anxiety, depression, and epilepsy, with the latter having the most success. Anxiety has been considered a perception of autonomic signals of arousal [34]. In one clinical study [16] patients receiving VNS for epilepsy also reported significantly less anxiety. The findings of this study was further supported in another study looking at more cognitive effects [121], that showed mean improvement in psychic anxiety of 50% and 36% in somatic anxiety.

This same study was not originally designed to monitor the effects of VNS on anxiety, but in fact another disorder – depression. All 30 patients involved in this study had no diagnosis of epilepsy, but did have a positive diagnosis for major depressive disorder. These patients were also particularly unresponsive to normal drug treatment; in other words they were suffering from refractory depression. At the end of a 10 week study period with VNS, 12 of the 30 patients (40%) showed improvement in mood. This study was then extended by another year [87] and found that there is a sustained benefit. The same study also called for larger clinical studies, which resulted in 15 original studies that all pointed towards VNS as beneficial to those with refractory depression [34].

VNS has been shown to be most effective in treating epilepsy. So much so that an entire company, Cyberonics, Inc., has based its research around it. VNS for treatment of epilepsy was first postulated in 1992 by Zabara, where he speculated that stimulation of the vagus nerve would result in termination and suppression of seizure [34]. The efficacy of this idea was analyzed in three clinical studies sponsored by Cyberonics, Inc. Of a total 454 patients, the number of patients seeing 50% or more reduction of seizures increased over three years. This indicates not only that VNS is effective, but its continued use improves its performance. Possibly, the biggest development is the work of Harreby [40] that demonstrated that epileptic seizures in rats could be predicted minutes before onset by monitoring cardiac and respiratory activity in cervical vagus nerves. This is important because with a robust pattern recognition algorithm, the vagal activity could be used to develop a fully closed loop system; rather than a normally paced open loop system that is the current standard.

4.2.3.2 Blood Pressure and Hypertension

Among the many afferents in the vagus nerve, fibers involved with monitoring the stretch of the aortic arch are of interest. These fibers are involved with the baroreflex, which lowers blood pressure in stressful situations, such as injury. However, due to the large number of nerve fibers in the vagus, recording and stimulating these fibers selectively is no trivial matter. However, work conducted by Stieglitz et al. [17] has shown that these fibers can be selectively stimulated using a multichannel tripolar cuff. For closed-loop control, the activity of a few fibers needs to be distinguished from the overall energy of the entire nerve. With the use of a triggered coherent average algorithm using both blood pressure and the R-wave of the EKG, activity of nerve fibers concerned with the stretch of the aortic arch can be discerned.

5. Trends

Neuroprosthetic recording electrodes grew out of efforts begun as early as the start of the 20th century to apply electrophysiological techniques to medically relevant problems. Perhaps the greatest development of neuroprosthetics coincides with the formal beginnings of the field of biomedical engineering, and can be summarized in a series of trends that originated in the late 1960s. The trend from then through the mid 1980's was the progression of recording techniques in animal models from acute anaesthetized studies to acute decerebrate studies and finally towards awake chronic studies. This occurred from the realization that anesthetics have an influence on the spontaneous and evoked neural activity, in some cases even invalidating the results of acute anaesthetized studies. The reliability of the techniques developed for chronic animal work, such as the cuff electrode and the DRG electrode, led to the expansion of their use into the first human implants of nerve based electrodes. Finally from the 80's through the present, there has been a movement to develop clinically relevant rehabilitation devices using, for example, FNS techniques that require chronic reliable and safe neural interfaces. The most common of these has been the nerve cuff which has undergone substantial developmental efforts to improve its functionality; biocompatibility; and longevity.

Many of the techniques used for neuroprostheses originated from basic neuroscience or electrophysiological techniques that were developed and refined for the rigors of use by patients and clinicians. The principles of their operation are grounded on basic electrophysiological research to understand how the body encodes signals and how the CNS achieves control of the body through the peripheral nervous system. Research in neural interfaces is, in fact, in a gray area which straddles the basic (neuroscience) and the applied sciences (neural engineering). Most of the techniques discussed here are still active areas of research and range from early developmental work to proof of concept in clinical trials. At the same time, however, they are also being used as stable chronic recording platforms for further basic research in fields such as motor control physiology.

The current trend in electrode development has been the movement from handmade devices towards electrodes fabricated using microfabrication or MEMS (micro-electro-mechanical systems) techniques originally developed for the microelectronics industry. This has given rise to electrodes based on microfabricated silicon such as the Utah Slant Array [10], Michigan probes [136, 167], and VSAMUEL probes [50, 100], as well as a host of devices fabricated using micropatterned thin polymer films such as thin film sieve electrodes [98], thin film LIFEs [173], and thin film multipolar cuff electrodes [177]. The principal advantages of MEMS techniques are better process control, reproducibility, and flexibility in design at the micro scale. The technique is also better suited for batch processing and mass production, with the potential that the devices could be fabricated at an extremely low per unit cost. This is presently offset, however, by high process setup costs in relation to limited consumer demands. Finally, the electrodes themselves are relatively new devices which presently are being tested in the hands of physiologists and bioengineers. The performance of these devices is approaching and sometimes surpassing their handmade counterparts, and their acceptance in the community is slowly increasing despite their relatively high unit cost to buy and support. The near future points to research to better understand how microfabricated devices interact with the biology, how their performance can be improved, and how to simplify the handling of the devices themselves and the data they produce.

References

1. Abdulla, F. A. and Smith, P. A. (1997) Ectopic alpha2-adrenoceptors couple to N-type Ca2+ channels in axotomized rat sensory neurons, *The Journal of Neuroscience*, **17**(5), 1633–1641.
2. Akers, J. M., Triolo, R. J. and Betz, R. R. (1996) Motor responses to FES electrodes in a growing limb, *IEEE Transactions on Rehabilitation Engineering*, **4**(4), 243–250.
3. Andreasen, L. N., Struijk, J. J., and Lawrence, S. (2000) Measurement of the performance of nerve cuff electrodes for recording, *Medical and Biological Engineering and Computing*, **38**(4), 447–453.
4. Badia, J., Boretius, T., Pascual-Font, A., Udina, E., Stieglitz, T., and Navarro, X. (2011) Biocompatibility of chronically implanted transverse intrafascicular multichannel electrode (TIME) in the rat sciatic nerve, *IEEE Transactions on Bio-Medical Engineering*, **58**(8), 2324–2332.
5. Bahns, E., Halsband, U., and Jänig, W. (1987) Responses of sacral visceral afferents from the lower urinary tract, colon and anus to mechanical stimulation, *Pflügers Archiv*, **410**(3), 296–303.
6. Barrett, R., Benmerah, S., Frommhold, A., and Tarte, E. (2013), Spiral peripheral nerve interface; updated fabrication process of the regenerative implant, *Annual International Conference of the IEEE Engineering in Medicine and Biology Society*, **2013**, 771–774.
7. Berthold, C. H., Lugnegård, H., and Rydmark, M. (1984) Ultrastructural morphometric studies on regeneration of the lateral sural cutaneous nerve in the white rat after transection of the sciatic nerve, *Scandinavian Journal of Plastic and Reconstructive Surgery. Supplementum*, **20**, 1–126.
8. Bowman, B. R. and Erickson, R. C. (1985) Acute and chronic implantation of coiled wire intraneural electrodes during cyclical electrical stimulation, *Annals of Biomedical Engineering*, **13**(1), 75–93.
9. Bradley, R. M., Smoke, R. H., Akin, T., and Najafi, K. (1992) Functional regeneration of glossopharyngeal nerve through micromachined sieve electrode arrays, *Brain Research*, **594**(1), 84–90.
10. Branner, A., and Normann, R. A. (2000) A multielectrode array for intrafascicular recording and stimulation in sciatic nerve of cats, *Brain Research Bulletin*, **51**(4), 293–306.
11. Branner, A., Stein, R. B., and Normann, R. A. (2001) Selective stimulation of cat sciatic nerve using an array of varying-length microelectrodes, *Journal of Neurophysiology*, **85**(4), 1585–1594.
12. Brunelli, G. (1982) Direct neurotization of severely damaged muscles, *The Journal of Hand Surgery*, **7**(6), 572–579.
13. Brushart, T. M. (1993) Motor axons preferentially reinnervate motor pathways, *The Journal of Neuroscience*, **13**(6), 2730–2738.
14. Ceballos, D., Valero-Cabré, A., Valderrama, E., Schüttler, M., Stieglitz, T., and Navarro, X. (2002) Morphologic and functional evaluation of peripheral nerve fibers regenerated through polyimide sieve electrodes over long-term implantation, *Journal of Biomedical Materials Research*, **60**(4), 517–528.

15. Chapin, J. K., and Moxon, K. A. (2000) *Neural Prostheses for Restoration of Sensory and Motor Function,* (CRC Press, Boca Raton, FL).

16. Chavel, S. M., Westerveld, M., and Spencer, S. (2003) Long-term outcome of vagus nerve stimulation for refractory partial epilepsy, *Epilepsy and Behavior,* **4**(3), 302–309.

17. Cota, O. F., Schlösser, M., Schiek, M., Stieglitz, T., Gierthmuehlen, M., and Plachta, D. (2015) iNODE in-vivo testing for selective vagus nerve recording and stimulation, *7th International IEEE/EMBS Conference on Neural Engineering,* pp. 525–528.

18. Cutrone, A., Del Valle, J., Santos, D., Badia, J., Filippeschi, C., Micera, S., Navarro, X., and Bossi S. (2015) A three-dimensional self-opening intraneural peripheral interface (SELINE), *Journal of Neural Engineering,* **12**(1), 016016.

19. Dai, R., Stein, R. B., Andrews, B. J., James, K. B., and Wieler, M. (1996) Application of tilt sensors in functional electrical stimulation, *IEEE Transactions on Rehabilitation Engineering,* **4**(2), 63–72.

20. Dhillon, G. S., Lawrence, S. M., Hutchinson, D. T., and Horch, K. W. (2004) Residual function in peripheral nerve stumps of amputees: implications for neural control of artificial limbs, *J. Hand Surg.* **29A**, 605-615.

21. Dhillon, G. S. and Horch, K. W. (2005) Direct neural sensory feedback and control of a prosthetic arm, *IEEE Transactions on Neural Systems and Rehabilitation Engineering,* **13**(4), 468–472.

22. Edell, D. J. (1986) A peripheral nerve information transducer for amputees: long-term multichannel recordings from rabbit peripheral nerves, *IEEE Transactions on Bio-Medical Engineering,* **33**(2), 203–214.

23. Edell, D. J., Riso, R. R., and Herr, H. (2006) Bi-directional peripheral nerve interface for the control of powered prosthetic limbs, (*No. DARPA Contract N66001-05-C-8030*).

24. Edell, D. J., R. Riso, R., and Herr, H. (2014) Development of micro-channel arrays for peripheral nerve recording, *Proceedings of the 2nd International Congress on Neurotechnology, Electronics and Informatics,* pp. 5–12.

25. FitzGerald, J. J., Lago, N., Benmerah, S., Serra, J., Watling, C. P., Cameron, R. E., Tarte, E., Lacour, S. P., McMahon, S. B., and Fawcett, J. W. (2012) A regenerative microchannel neural interface for recording from and stimulating peripheral axons in vivo. *Journal of Neural Engineering,* **9**(1), 016010.

26. Frigo, C., Ferrarin, M., Frasson, W., Pavan, E., and Thorsen, R. (2000) EMG signals detection and processing for on-line control of functional electrical stimulation, *Journal of Electromyography and Kinesiology,* **10**(5), 351–360.

27. Fu, S. Y. and Gordon, T. (1995) Contributing factors to poor functional recovery after delayed nerve repair: prolonged denervation, *The Journal of Neuroscience,* **15**(5 Pt 2), 3886–3895.

28. Gasson, M., Hutt, B., Goodhew, I., Kyberd, P., and Warwick, K. (2002) Bi-directional human machine interface via direct neural connection, *11th IEEE International Workshop on Robot and Human Interactive Communication,* pp. 265–270.

29. González, C. and Rodríguez, M. (1997) A flexible perforated microelectrode array probe for action potential recording in nerve and muscle tissues, *Journal of Neuroscience Methods,* **72**(2), 189–195.

30. Gordon, T., Gillespie, J., Orozco, R., and Davis, L. (1991) Axotomy-induced changes in rabbit hindlimb nerves and the effects of chronic electrical stimulation, *The Journal of Neuroscience,* **11**(7), 2157–2169.

31. Gore, R. K., Choi, Y., Bellamkonda, R., and English, A. (2015) Functional recordings from awake, behaving rodents through a microchannel based regenerative neural interface, *Journal of Neural Engineering*, **12**(1), 016017.

32. Gossard, J. P., Bouyer, L., and Rossignol, S. (1999) The effects of antidromic discharges on orthodromic firing of primary afferents in the cat, *Brain Research*, **825**(1-2), 132–145.

33. Gray, C. M., Maldonado, P. E., Wilson, M., and McNaughton, B. (1995) Tetrodes markedly improve the reliability and yield of multiple single-unit isolation from multi-unit recordings in cat striate cortex, *Journal of Neuroscience Methods*, **63**(1-2), 43–54.

34. Groves, D. A. and Brown, V. J. (2005) Vagal nerve stimulation: a review of its applications and potential mechanisms that mediate its clinical effects, *Neuroscience and Biobehavioral Reviews*, **29**(3), 493–500.

35. Guo, L., Clements, I. P., Li, D., Bellamkonda, R. V., and DeWeerth, S. P. (2010) A conformable microelectrode array (cMEA) with integrated electronics for peripheral nerve interfacing, *Biomedical Circuits and Systems Conference (BioCAS)*, pp. 194–197.

36. Häbler, H. J., Jänig, W., and Koltzenburg, M. (1993) Myelinated primary afferents of the sacral spinal cord responding to slow filling and distension of the cat urinary bladder, *The Journal of Physiology*, **463**, 449–460.

37. Hallin, R. G., and Wu, G. (1998) Protocol for microneurography with concentric needle electrodes, *Brain Research. Brain Research Protocols*, **2**(2), 120–132.

38. Halliwell, J., Plant, T., and Standen, N. (n.d.) Voltage Clamp Techniques. In *Microelectrode Techniques, the Plymouth Workshop Handbook, 2nd ed.*, (The Company of Biologist Ltd., London), pp. 17–37.

39. Harreby, K. R., Kundu, A., Yoshida, K., Boretius, T., Stieglitz, T., and Jensen, W. (2015) Subchronic stimulation performance of transverse intrafascicular multichannel electrodes in the median nerve of the Göttingen minipig, *Artificial Organs*, **39**(2), E36–48.

40. Harreby, K. R., Sevcencu, C., and Struijk, J. J. (2011) Early seizure detection in rats based on vagus nerve activity, *Medical and Biological Engineering and Computing*, **49**(2), 143–151.

41. Haugland, M. K. and Sinkjaer, T. (1995) Cutaneous whole nerve recordings used for correction of footdrop in hemiplegic man, *IEEE Transactions on Rehabilitation Engineering*, **3**(4), 307–317.

42. Haugland, M., Lickel, A., Haase, J., and Sinkjaer, T. (1999) Control of FES thumb force using slip information obtained from the cutaneous electroneurogram in quadriplegic man, *IEEE Transactions on Rehabilitation Engineering*, **7**(2), 215–227.

43. Haugland, M., Lickel, A., Riso, R., Adamczyk, M. M., Keith, M., Jensen, I. L., Haase, J., and Sinkjaer, T. (1997) Restoration of lateral hand grasp using natural sensors. *Artificial Organs*, *21*(3), 250–253.

44. Hebert, J. S., Olson, J. L., Morhart, M. J., Dawson, M. R., Marasco, P. D., Kuiken, T. A., and Chan, K. M. (2014) Novel targeted sensory reinnervation technique to restore functional hand sensation after transhumeral amputation, *IEEE Transactions on Neural Systems and Rehabilitation Engineering*, **22**(4), 765–773.

45. Hijjawi, J. B., Kuiken, T. A., Lipschutz, R. D., Miller, L. A., Stubblefield, K. A., and Dumanian, G. A. (2006) Improved myoelectric prosthesis control accomplished using multiple nerve transfers, *Plastic and Reconstructive Surgery*, **118**(7), 1573–1578.

46. Hodgkin, A. L., Huxley, A. F., and Katz, B. (1952) Measurement of current-voltage relations in the membrane of the giant axon of <u>Loligo</u>, *The Journal of Physiology*, **116**(4), 424–448.

47. Hoffer, J. (1990) Techniques to Study Spinal-Cord, Peripheral Nerve, and Muscle Activity in Freely Moving Animals. In eds. A. Boulton, G. Baker, and C. Vanderwolf, *Neurophysiological Techniques* (Humana Press, New York), pp. 65–145.

48. Hoffer, J. A., Chen, Y., Strange, K. D., and Christensen, P. R. (1998) Nerve cuff having one or more isolated chambers, *US patent 5824027*.

49. Hoffer, J. A., and Loeb, G. E. (1980) Implantable electrical and mechanical interfaces with nerve and muscle, *Annals of Biomedical Engineering*, **8**(4-6), 351–360.

50. Hofmann, U. G., Folkers, A., Mösch, F., Höhl, D., Kindlundh, M., and Norlin, P. (2002) A 64(128)-channel multisite neuronal recording system, *Biomedizinische Technik. Biomedical Engineering*, **47**(Suppl. 1, Pt. 1), 194–197.

51. Höke, A., Redett, R., Hameed, H., Jari, R., Zhou, C., Li, Z. B., Griffin. J. W., Brushart, T. M. (2006) Schwann cells express motor and sensory phenotypes that regulate axon regeneration, *The Journal of Neuroscience*, **26**(38), 9646–9655.

52. Iguchi, Ohuchi, C., Narushima, T., Watanabe, M., Kinami, T., Nishikawa, T., Hoshimiya, N., and Handa, Y. (2000) Development of implanted bio-materials and application to FES electrodes as the interface between stimulator and nerve, *IFESS Proc.*

53. Inmann, A., Haugland, M., Haase, J., Biering-Sørensen, F., and Sinkjaer, T. (2001) Signals from skin mechanoreceptors used in control of a hand grasp neuroprosthesis, *Neuroreport*, **12**(13), 2817–2820.

54. Jensen, W., Lawrence, S. M., Riso, R. R., and Sinkjaer, T. (2001) Effect of initial joint position on nerve-cuff recordings of muscle afferents in rabbits, *IEEE Transactions on Neural Systems and Rehabilitation Engineering*, **9**(3), 265–273.

55. Jensen, W., Riso, R., and Sinkjaer, T. (2000) Effect of intertrial delay on whole nerve cuff recordings of muscle afferents in rabbits, *Neuromodulation*, **3**(1), 43–53.

56. Jezernik, S., Grill, W. M., and Sinkjaer, T. (2001) Detection and inhibition of hyperreflexia-like bladder contractions in the cat by sacral nerve root recording and electrical stimulation, *Neurourology and Urodynamics*, **20**(2), 215–230.

57. Jezernik, S., Wen, J. G., Rijkhoff, N. J., Djurhuus, J. C., and Sinkjaer, T. (2000) Analysis of bladder related nerve cuff electrode recordings from preganglionic pelvic nerve and sacral roots in pigs, *The Journal of Urology*, **163**(4), 1309–1314.

58. Johansson, R. S., Häger, C., and Riso, R. (1992) Somatosensory control of precision grip during unpredictable pulling loads. II. Changes in load force rate, *Experimental Brain Research*, **89**(1), 192–203.

59. Johansson, R. S., Häger, C., and Bäckström, L. (1992) Somatosensory control of precision grip during unpredictable pulling loads. III. Impairments during digital anesthesia, *Experimental Brain Research*, **89**(1), 204–213.

60. Johansson, R. S., Riso, R., Häger, C., and Bäckström, L. (1992) Somatosensory control of precision grip during unpredictable pulling loads. I. Changes in load force amplitude, *Experimental Brain Research*, **89**(1), 181–191.

61. Johansson, R. S., and Vallbo, Å. B. (1983) Tactile sensory coding in the glabrous skin of the human hand, *Trends in Neurosciences*, **6**, 27–32.

62. Kallesøe, K. (1998) *Implantable Transducers for Neurokinesiological Research and Neural Prostheses [microform]*. Thesis (Ph.D.), Simon Fraser University.

63. Kallesoe, K., Hoffer, J. A., Strange, K., and Valenzuela, I. (1996) Implantable cuff having improved closure, *US patent 5487756*.

64. Kennedy, P. R., Bakay, R. A., Moore, M. M., Adams, K., and Goldwaithe, J. (2000) Direct control of a computer from the human central nervous system, *IEEE Transactions on Rehabilitation Engineering*, **8**(2), 198–202.
65. Kennedy, P. R., Bakay, R. A., and Sharpe, S. M. (1992) Behavioral correlates of action potentials recorded chronically inside the cone electrode, *Neuroreport*, **3**(7), 605–608.
66. Kezirian, E. J., Boudewyns, A., Eisele, D. W., Schwartz, A. R., Smith, P. L., Van de Heyning, P. H., and De Backer, W. A. (2010) Electrical stimulation of the hypoglossal nerve in the treatment of obstructive sleep apnea, *Sleep Medicine Reviews*, **14**(5), 299–305.
67. Kim, B., Reyes, A., Garza, B., and Choi, Y. (2015) A microchannel neural interface with embedded microwires targeting the peripheral nervous system, *Microsystem Technologies*, **21**(7), 1551–1557.
68. Kim, S., Bhandari, R., Klein, M., Negi, S., Rieth, L., Tathireddy, P., Toepper, M., Oppermann, H., and Solzbacher, F. (2009) Integrated wireless neural interface based on the Utah electrode array, *Biomedical Microdevices*, **11**(2), 453–466.
69. Kostov, A., Hansen, M., Haugland, M., and Sinkjaer, T. (1999) Adaptive restriction rules provide functional and safe stimulation pattern for foot drop correction, *Artificial Organs*, **23**(5), 443–446.
70. Kovacs, G. T., Storment, C. W., Halks-Miller, M., Belczynski, C. R., Della Santina, C. C., Lewis, E. R., and Maluf, N. I. (1994) Silicon-substrate microelectrode arrays for parallel recording of neural activity in peripheral and cranial nerves, *IEEE Transactions on Bio-Medical Engineering*, **41**(6), 567–577.
71. Krnjevic, K. (1982) Microelectrode methods for intracellular recording and iontophoresis, *Trends in Neurosciences*, **5**, 133.
72. Kuiken, T. A., Marasco, P. D., Lock, B. A., Harden, R. N., and Dewald, J. P. A. (2007) Redirection of cutaneous sensation from the hand to the chest skin of human amputees with targeted reinnervation, *Proceedings of the National Academy of Sciences of the United States of America*, **104**(50), 20061–20066.
73. Kung, T. A., Langhals, N. B., Martin, D. C., Johnson, P. J., Cederna, P. S., and Urbanchek, M. G. (2014) Regenerative peripheral nerve interface viability and signal transduction with an implanted electrode, *Plastic and Reconstructive Surgery*, **133**(6), 1380–1394.
74. Lacour, S. P., Fitzgerald, J. J., Lago, N., Tarte, E., McMahon, S., and Fawcett, J. (2009) Long micro-channel electrode arrays: a novel type of regenerative peripheral nerve interface, *IEEE Trans Neural Syst Rehabil Eng.*, **17**(5):454-60.
75. Larsen, J. O., Thomsen, M., Haugland, M., and Sinkjaer, T. (1998) Degeneration and regeneration in rabbit peripheral nerve with long-term nerve cuff electrode implant: a stereological study of myelinated and unmyelinated axons, *Acta Neuropathologica*, **96**(4), 365–378.
76. Larson, J. V., Urbanchek, M. G., Moon, J. D., Hunter, D. A., Newton, P., Johnson, P. J., Wood, M. D., Kung, T. A., Cederna, P. S., and Langhals, N. B. (2014) Abstract 17: prototype sensory regenerative peripheral nerve interface for artificial limb somatosensory feedback, *Plastic and Reconstructive Surgery*, **133**(3 Suppl), 26–27.
77. Lee, Y. J., Song, K. I., Kang, J. Y., and Lee, S. H. (2015) Fabrication and characterization of stimulus nerve cuff electrode with highly roughened surface for chronic implant, *Conf Proc IEEE Eng Med Biol Soc*.

78. Lefurge, T., Goodall, E., Horch, K., Stensaas, L., and Schoenberg, A. (1991) Chronically implanted intrafascicular recording electrodes, *Annals of Biomedical Engineering*, **19**(2), 197–207.

79. Liberson, W. T., Holmquest, H. J., Scot, D., and Dow, M. (1961) Functional electrotherapy: stimulation of the peroneal nerve synchronized with the swing phase of the gait of hemiplegic patients, *Archives of Physical Medicine and Rehabilitation*, **42**, 101–105.

80. Loeb, G. E., Bak, M. J., and Duysens, J. (1977) Long-term unit recording from somatosensory neurons in the spinal ganglia of the freely walking cat, *Science*, **197**(4309), 1192–1194.

81. Loeb, G. E., Bak, M. J., Salcman, M., and Schmidt, E. M. (1977) Parylene as a chronically stable, reproducible microelectrode insulator, *IEEE Transactions on Bio-Medical Engineering*, **24**(2), 121–128.

82. Loeb, G. E., Hoffer, J. A., and Pratt, C. A. (1985) Activity of spindle afferents from cat anterior thigh muscles. I. Identification and patterns during normal locomotion, *Journal of Neurophysiology*, **54**(3), 549–564.

83. Loeb, G. E., Peck, R. A., Moore, W. H., and Hood, K. (2001) BION system for distributed neural prosthetic interfaces, *Medical Engineering and Physics*, **23**(1), 9–18.

84. Maher, M. P., Dvorak-Carbone, H., Pine, J., Wright, J. A., and Tai, Y. C. (1999) Microstructures for studies of cultured neural networks, *Medical and Biological Engineering and Computing*, **37**(1), 110–118.

85. Maher, M. P., Pine, J., Wright, J., and Tai, Y. C. (1999) The neurochip: a new multielectrode device for stimulating and recording from cultured neurons, *Journal of Neuroscience Methods*, **87**(1), 45–56.

86. Malagodi, M. S., Horch, K. W., and Schoenberg, A. A. (1989) An intrafascicular electrode for recording of action potentials in peripheral nerves, *Annals of Biomedical Engineering*, **17**(4), 397–410.

87. Marangell, L. B., Rush, A. J., George, M. S., Sackeim, H. A., Johnson, C. R., Husain, M. M., Nahas, Z., and Lisanby, S. H. (2002) Vagus nerve stimulation (VNS) for major depressive episodes: one year outcomes, *Biological Psychiatry*, **51**(4), 280–287.

88. Marks, W. B. and Loeb, G. E. (1976) Action currents, internodal potentials, and extracellular records of myelinated mammalian nerve fibers derived from node potentials, *Biophysical Journal*, **16**(6), 655–668.

89. McNaughton, B. L., O'Keefe, J., and Barnes, C. A. (1983) The stereotrode: a new technique for simultaneous isolation of several single units in the central nervous system from multiple unit records, *Journal of Neuroscience Methods*, **8**(4), 391–397.

90. McNaughton, T. G., and Horch, K. W. (1996) Metallized polymer fibers as leadwires and intrafascicular microelectrodes, *Journal of Neuroscience Methods*, **70**(1), 103–110.

91. Micera, S., Citi, L., Rigosa, J., Carpaneto, J., Raspopovic, S., Pino, G. D., Rossini, L., Yoshida, K., Denaro, L., Dario, P., and Rossini, P. M. (2010) Decoding information from neural signals recorded using intraneural electrodes: toward the development of a neurocontrolled hand prosthesis. *Proceedings of the IEEE*, **98**(3), 407–417.

92. Milner, T. E., and Hoffer, J. A. (1987) Long-term peripheral nerve and muscle recordings from normal and dystrophic mice, *Journal of Neuroscience Methods*, **19**(1), 37–45.

93. Morrison, J., Wen, J., and Kibble, A. (1999) Activation of pelvic afferent nerves from the rat bladder during filling, *Scandinavian Journal of Urology and Nephrology. Supplementum*, **201**, 73–75.

94. Muceli, S., Negro, F., Jensen, W., Yoshida, K., Poppendieck, W., Doerge, T., and Farina, D. (2010) Sampling large populations of motor units in humans with multichannel thin-film electrodes, *Annual Meeting of the Society for Neuroscience*.

95. Mushahwar, V. K., Collins, D. F., and Prochazka, A. (2000) Spinal cord microstimulation generates functional limb movements in chronically implanted cats, *Experimental Neurology*, **163**(2), 422–429.

96. Nannini, N. and Horch, K. (1991) Muscle recruitment with intrafascicular electrodes, *IEEE Transactions on Bio-Medical Engineering*, **38**(8), 769–776.

97. Naples, G. G., Mortimer, J. T., Scheiner, A., and Sweeney, J. D. (1988) A spiral nerve cuff electrode for peripheral nerve stimulation, *IEEE Transactions on Bio-Medical Engineering*, **35**(11), 905–916.

98. Navarro, X., Calvet, S., Rodríguez, F. J., Stieglitz, T., Blau, C., Butí, M., Valderrama, E., and Meyer, J. U. (1998) Stimulation and recording from regenerated peripheral nerves through polyimide sieve electrodes, *Journal of the Peripheral Nervous System*, **3**(2), 91–101.

99. Navarro, X., Krueger, T. B., Lago, N., Micera, S., Stieglitz, T., and Dario, P. (2005) A critical review of interfaces with the peripheral nervous system for the control of neuroprostheses and hybrid bionic systems, *Journal of the Peripheral Nervous System*, **10**(3), 229–258.

100. Norlin, P., Kindlundh, M., Mouroux, A., Yoshida, K., and Hofmann, U. G. (2002) A 32-site neural recording probe fabricated by DRIE of SOI substrates, *Journal of Micromechanics and Microengineering*, **12**(4), 414.

101. Ochoa, J. and Torebjörk, E. (1983) Sensations evoked by intraneural microstimulation of single mechanoreceptor units innervating the human hand. *The Journal of Physiology*, **342**, 633–654.

102. Ortiz-Catalan, M., Brånemark, R., and Håkansson, B. (2013) BioPatRec: A modular research platform for the control of artificial limbs based on pattern recognition algorithms, *Source Code for Biology and Medicine*, **8**(1), 11.

103. Ortiz-Catalan, M., Håkansson, B., and Brånemark, R. (2014) An osseointegrated human-machine gateway for long-term sensory feedback and motor control of artificial limbs, *Science Translational Medicine*, **6**(257), 3008933.

104. Pine, J. (1980) Recording action potentials from cultured neurons with extracellular microcircuit electrodes, *Journal of Neuroscience Methods*, **2**(1), 19–31.

105. Plachta, D. T. T., Gierthmuehlen, M., Cota, O., Espinosa, N., Boeser, F., Herrera, T. C., Stieglitz, T., and Zentner, J. (2014) Blood pressure control with selective vagal nerve stimulation and minimal side effects, *Journal of Neural Engineering*, **11**(3), 036011.

106. Popović, D. B., Stein, R. B., Jovanović, K. L., Dai, R., Kostov, A., and Armstrong, W. W. (1993) Sensory nerve recording for closed-loop control to restore motor functions, *IEEE Transactions on Bio-Medical Engineering*, **40**(10), 1024–1031.

107. Prochazka, A., Gauthier, M., Wieler, M., and Kenwell, Z. (1997) The bionic glove: an electrical stimulator garment that provides controlled grasp and hand opening in quadriplegia, *Archives of Physical Medicine and Rehabilitation*, **78**(6), 608–614.

108. Prochazka, A., Westerman, R. A., and Ziccone, S. P. (1976) Discharges of single hindlimb afferents in the freely moving cat, *Journal of Neurophysiology*, **39**(5), 1090–1104.

109. Prochazka, V. J., Tate, K., Westerman, R. A., and Ziccone, S. P. (1974) Remote monitoring of muscle length and EMG in unrestrained cats, *Electroencephalography and Clinical Neurophysiology*, **37**(6), 649–653.

110. Proske, U. and Gregory, J. E. (1977) The time-course of recovery of the initial burst of primary endings of muscle spindles, *Brain Research*, **121**(2), 358–361.

111. Purves, R. D. (1981) *Microelectrode Methods for Intracellular Recording and Ionophoresis,* (Academic Press, Cambridge, MA).

112. Raspopovic, S., Capogrosso, M., Petrini, F. M., Bonizzato, M., Rigosa, J., Di Pino, G., Carpaneto, J., Controzzi, M., Boretius, T., Fernandez, E., Granata, G., Oddo, C. M., Citi, L., Ciancio, A. L., Cipriani, C., Carrozza, M. C., Jensen, W., Guglielmelli, E., Stieglitz, T., Rossini, P. M., and Micera, S. (2014) Restoring natural sensory feedback in real-time bidirectional hand prostheses, *Science Translational Medicine,* **6**(222), 3006820.

113. Regehr, W. G., Pine, J., and Rutledge, D. B. (1988) A long-term in vitro silicon-based microelectrode-neuron connection, *IEEE Transactions on Bio-Medical Engineering,* **35**(12), 1023–1032.

114. Riso, R., Dalmose, A., Schuettler, M., and Stieglitz, T. (2000) Activation of muscles in the pig forlimb using a large diameter multipolar nerve cuff installed on the radial nerve in the axilla, *Proc. IFESS,* pp. 272-275.

115. Riso, R., Dalmose, A., Stefania, D., and Schuttler, M. (2001) Addition of an intrafascicular electrode at the site of application of a multipolar nerve cuff enhances the opportunity for selective fascicular activation, *Proceedings of the 23rd Annual International Conference of the IEEE Engineering in Medicine and Biology Society,* pp. 711–714.

116. Riso, R. R. (1996) Characterization of the ENG activity from a digital nerve for feedback control in grasp neuroprostheses, in eds. A. Pedotti, M. Ferrarin, Quintern J., and R. Riener, *Neuroprosthetics from Basic Research to Clinical Applications,* (Springer -Verlag, Berlin), pp. 345-357.

117. Riso, R. R. (1998) Perspectives on the role of natural sensors for cognitive feedback in neuromotor prostheses, *Automedica,* **16**, 329-353.

118. Riso, R. R. (1999) Strategies for providing upper extremity amputees with tactile and hand position feedback--moving closer to the bionic arm, *Technology and Health Care,* **7**(6), 401–409.

119. Riso, R. R., Mosallaie, F. K., Jensen, W., and Sinkjaer, T. (2000) Nerve cuff recordings of muscle afferent activity from tibial and peroneal nerves in rabbit during passive ankle motion, *IEEE Transactions on Rehabilitation Engineering,* **8**(2), 244–258.

120. Rodríguez, F. J., Ceballos, D., Schüttler, M., Valero, A., Valderrama, E., Stieglitz, T., and Navarro, X. (2000) Polyimide cuff electrodes for peripheral nerve stimulation, *Journal of Neuroscience Methods,* **98**(2), 105–118.

121. Rush, A. J., George, M. S., Sackeim, H. A., Marangell, L. B., Husain, M. M., Giller, C., Nahas, Z., Haines, S., Simpson, R. K. Jr, and Goodman, R. (2000) Vagus nerve stimulation (VNS) for treatment-resistant depressions: a multicenter study, *Biological Psychiatry,* **47**(4), 276–286.

122. Rutten, W. L. C. (2002) Selective electrical interfaces with the nervous system, *Annual Review of Biomedical Engineering,* **4**, 407–452.

123. Rutten, W. L., Smit, J. P., Frieswijk, T. A., Bielen, J. A., Brouwer, A. L., Buitenweg, J. R., and Heida, C. (1999) Neuro-electronic interfacing with multielectrode arrays, *IEEE Engineering in Medicine and Biology Magazine,* **18**(3), 47–55.

124. Rutten, W. L., van Wier, H. J., and Put, J. H. (1991) Sensitivity and selectivity of intraneural stimulation using a silicon electrode array, *IEEE Transactions on Bio-Medical Engineering,* **38**(2), 192–198.

125. Rutten, W., Mouveroux, J.-M., Buitenweg, J., Heida, C., Ruardij, T., Marani, E., and Lakke, E. (2001) Neuroelectronic interfacing with cultured multielectrode arrays toward a cultured probe, *Proceedings of the IEEE,* **89**(7), 1013–1029.

126. Sahin, M., Durand, D. M., and Haxhiu, M. A. (1999) Chronic recordings of hypoglossal nerve activity in a dog model of upper airway obstruction, *Journal of Applied Physiology*, **87**(6), 2197–2206.

127. Sahin, M., Haxhiu, M. A., Durand, D. M., and Dreshaj, I. A. (1997) Spiral nerve cuff electrode for recordings of respiratory output, *Journal of Applied Physiology*, **83**(1), 317–322.

128. Sahin, M., and Huang, J. (2006) Obstructive sleep apnea: electrical stimulation treatment, In ed. M. Akay, *Wiley Encyclopedia of Biomedical Engineering*, (John Wiley and Sons, Hoboken, NJ).

129. Schalow, G. (1991) Conduction velocities and nerve fibre diameters of touch, pain, urinary bladder and anal canal afferents and alpha and gamma-motoneurons in human dorsal sacral roots, *Electromyography and Clinical Neurophysiology*, **31**(5), 265–296.

130. Schiefer, M. A., Polasek, K. H., Triolo, R. J., Pinault, G. C. J., and Tyler, D. J. (2010) Selective stimulation of the human femoral nerve with a flat interface nerve electrode, *Journal of Neural Engineering*, **7**(2), 026006.

131. Scholvin, J., Zorzos, A., Fonstad, C., and Boyden, E. (2015) Methods and apparatus for three-dimensional microfabricated arrays, *US patent 8939774*.

132. Schuettler, Koch, K. P., Scholz, O., and Stieglitz, T. (2001) Control and performance of a miniature smart electrode multiplexer, *Proceedings of the IFESS*.

133. Schuettler, M., Stieglitz, T., Gross, M., Altpeter, D., Staiger, A., Doerge, T., and Katzenberg, F. (2001) Reducing stiffness and electrical losses of high channel hybrid nerve cuff electrodes, *Proceedings of the 23rd Annual International Conference of the IEEE Engineering in Medicine and Biology Society*, pp. 769–772.

134. Schuettler, and Stieglitz, T. (2000) 18polar hybrid cuff electrodes for stimulation of peripheral nerves, *Proceedings of the IFESS*.

135. Smith, B. T., Mulcahey, M. J., and Betz, R. R. (2001) An implantable upper extremity neuroprosthesis in a growing child with a C5 spinal cord injury, *Spinal Cord*, **39**(2), 118–123.

136. Starr, A., Wise, K. D., and Csongradi, J. (1973) An evaluation of photoengraved microelectrodes for extracellular single-unit recording, *IEEE Transactions on Bio-Medical Engineering*, **20**(4), 291–293.

137. Stein, R. B., Charles, D., Gordon, T., Hoffer, J. A., and Jhamandas, J. (1978) Impedance properties of metal electrodes for chronic recording from mammalian nerves, *IEEE Transactions on Bio-Medical Engineering*, **25**(6), 532–537.

138. Stein, R. B., Charles, D., Hoffer, J. A., Arsenault, J., Davis, L. A., Moorman, S., and Moss, B. (1980) New approaches for the control of powered prostheses particularly by high-level amputees, *Bulletin of Prosthetics Research*, **10-33**, 51–62.

139. Stein, R. B., Nichols, T. R., Jhamandas, J., Davis, L., and Charles, D. (1977) Stable long-term recordings from cat peripheral nerves, *Brain Research*, **128**(1), 21–38.

140. Stein, R. B., Weber, D. J., Aoyagi, Y., Prochazka, A., Wagenaar, J. B. M., Shoham, S., and Normann, R. A. (2004) Coding of position by simultaneously recorded sensory neurones in the cat dorsal root ganglion, *The Journal of Physiology*, **560**(Pt 3), 883–896.

141. Stewart, J. D. (2003) Peripheral nerve fascicles: anatomy and clinical relevance, *Muscle Nerve*, **28**, 525–541.

142. Stoyanova, I. I., van Wezel, R. J. A., and Rutten, W. L. C. (2013) In vivo testing of a 3D bifurcating microchannel scaffold inducing separation of regenerating axon bundles in peripheral nerves, *Journal of Neural Engineering*, **10**(6), 066018.

143. Strojnik, P., Acimovic, R., Vavken, E., Simic, V., and Stanic, U. (1987) Treatment of drop foot using an implantable peroneal underknee stimulator, *Scandinavian Journal of Rehabilitation Medicine*, **19**(1), 37–43.

144. Strollo, P. J. J., Soose, R. J., Maurer, J. T., de Vries, N., Cornelius, J., Froymovich, O., Hanson, R. D., Padhya, T. A., Steward, D. L., Gillespie, M. B., Woodson, B. T., Van de Heyning, P. H., Goetting, M. G., Vanderveken, O. M., Feldman, N., Knaack, L., and Strohl, K. P. (2014) Upper-airway stimulation for obstructive sleep apnea, *New England Journal of Medicine*, **370**(2), 139–149.

145. Sunderland, S. (1978) *Nerves and Nerve Injuries* (Churchill Livingstone New York).

146. Tarte, E. J., FitzGerald, J. J., Lago, N., Benmerah, S., Serra, J., Watling, C. P., Cameron, R. E., Lacour, S. P., McMahon, S. B., and Fawcett, J. W. (2011) The spiral peripheral nerve interface: design, fabrication and performance, in ed. Á. Jobbágy, *5th European Conference of the International Federation for Medical and Biological Engineering*, (Springer, Berlin) pp. 1338–1341.

147. Taylor, J., Donaldson, N., and Winter, J. (2004) Multiple-electrode nerve cuffs for low-velocity and velocity-selective neural recording, *Medical and Biological Engineering and Computing*, **42**(5), 634–643.

148. Tyler, D. J. and Durand, D. M. (1997a) Alteration of neural geometry for selective nerve stimulation, *Proceedings of the 19th Annual International Conference of the IEEE Engineering in Medicine and Biology Society*, pp. 2002–2003.

149. Tyler, D. J. and Durand, D. M. (1997b) A slowly penetrating interfascicular nerve electrode for selective activation of peripheral nerves, *IEEE Transactions on Rehabilitation Engineering*, **5**(1), 51–61.

150. Upshaw, B. J. and Sinkjaer, T. (1997) Natural versus artificial sensors applied in peroneal nerve stimulation, *Artificial Organs*, **21**(3), 227–231.

151. Vallbo, A. B., Olsson, K. A., Westberg, K. G., and Clark, F. J. (1984) Microstimulation of single tactile afferents from the human hand. Sensory attributes related to unit type and properties of receptive fields, *Brain*, **107**(Pt 3), 727–749.

152. Veraart, C., Grill, W. M., and Mortimer, J. T. (1993) Selective control of muscle activation with a multipolar nerve cuff electrode, *IEEE Transactions on Bio-Medical Engineering*, **40**(7), 640–653.

153. Viventi, J., Kim, D.-H., Vigeland, L., Frechette, E. S., Blanco, J. A., Kim, Y.-S., Avrin, A. E., Tiruvadi, V. R., Hwang, S.-W., Vanleer, A. C., Wulsin, D. F., Davis, K., Gelber, C. E., Palmer, L., Van der Spiegel, J., Wu, J., Xiao, J., Huang, Y., Contreras, D., Rogers, J. A., and Litt, B. (2011) Flexible, foldable, actively multiplexed, high-density electrode array for mapping brain activity *in vivo*, *Nature Neuroscience*, **14**(12), 1599–1605.

154. Vrbova, G., Mehra, N., Shanmuganathan, H., Tyreman, N., Schachner, M., and Gordon, T. (2009) Chemical communication between regenerating motor axons and Schwann cells in the growth pathway, *The European Journal of Neuroscience*, **30**(3), 366–375.

155. Wallman, L., Levinsson, A., Schouenborg, J., Holmberg, H., Montelius, L., Danielsen, N., and Laurell, T. (1999) Perforated silicon nerve chips with doped registration electrodes: in vitro performance and in vivo operation, *IEEE Transactions on Bio-Medical Engineering*, **46**(9), 1065–1073.

156. Weber, D. J., London, B. M., Hokanson, J. A., Ayers, C. A., Gaunt, R. A., Torres, R. R., Zaaimi, B., and Miller, L. E. (2011) Limb-state information encoded by peripheral and central

somatosensory neurons: implications for an afferent interface. *IEEE Transactions on Neural Systems and Rehabilitation Engineering*, **19**(5), 501–513.

157. Weber, D. J., Stein, R. B., Everaert, D. G., and Prochazka, A. (2007) Limb-state feedback from ensembles of simultaneously recorded dorsal root ganglion neurons, *Journal of Neural Engineering*, **4**(3), S168–180.

158. Weber, D., Stein, R. B., Aoyagi, Y., and Prochazka, A. (2002) Chronic multiunit recording of sensory neuronal activity in the cat dorsal root ganglion, *Society for Neurosciences Abstracts*, p. 348.7.

159. Weir, R. F. ff, Troyk, P. R., DeMichele, G. A., Kerns, D. A., Schorsch, J. F., and Maas, H. (2009) Implantable myoelectric sensors (IMESs) for intramuscular electromyogram recording, *IEEE Transactions on Bio-Medical Engineering*, **56**(1), 159–171.

160. Wells, M. R., Vaidya, U., Ricci, J. L., and Christie, C. (2001) A neuromuscular platform to extract electrophysiological signals from lesioned nerves: a technical note, *Journal of Rehabilitation Research and Development*, **38**(4), 385–390.

161. Westling, G. (n.d.) Sensorimotor mechanisms during precision grip in man, *Medical Dissertation*, Umea University.

162. Westling, G., and Johansson, R. S. (1984) Factors influencing the force control during precision grip, *Experimental Brain Research*, **53**(2), 277–284.

163. Westling, G., and Johansson, R. S. (1987) Responses in glabrous skin mechanoreceptors during precision grip in humans, *Experimental Brain Research*, **66**(1), 128–140.

164. Wieringa, P. A., Wiertz, R. W. F., Weerd, E. L. de, and Rutten, W. L. C. (2010) *In vitro* verification of a 3-d regenerative neural interface design: Examination of neurite growth and electrical properties within a bifurcating microchannel structure, *Proceedings of the IEEE*, **98**(3), 389–397.

165. Willemsen, A. T., Bloemhof, F., and Boom, H. B. (1990) Automatic stance-swing phase detection from accelerometer data for peroneal nerve stimulation, *IEEE Transactions on Bio-Medical Engineering*, **37**(12), 1201–1208.

166. Winter, D. L. (1971) Receptor characteristics and conduction velocites in bladder afferents, *Journal of Psychiatric Research*, **8**(3), 225–235.

167. Wise, K. D., and Angell, J. B. (1975) A low-capacitance multielectrode probe for use in extracellular neurophysiology, *IEEE Transactions on Bio-Medical Engineering*, **22**(3), 212–219.

168. Woo, P., and Arandia, H. (1992) Intraoperative laryngeal electromyographic assessment of patients with immobile vocal fold, *The Annals of Otology, Rhinology, and Laryngology*, **101**(10), 799–806.

169. Wright, M. C., Mi, R., Connor, E., Reed, N., Vyas, A., Alspalter, M., Coppola, G., Geschwind, D. H., Brushart, T. M., and Höke, A. (2014) Novel roles for osteopontin and clusterin in peripheral motor and sensory axon regeneration. *The Journal of Neuroscience*, **34**(5), 1689–1700.

170. Yoshida, K., Inmann, A., and Haugland, M. K. (1999) Measurement of complex impedance spectra of implanted electrodes, *IFESS 99 Proceedings, Sendai, Japan*, pp. 267–270..

171. Yoshida, K. and Horch, K. (1993) Reduced fatigue in electrically stimulated muscle using dual channel intrafascicular electrodes with interleaved stimulation, *Annals of Biomedical Engineering*, **21**(6), 709–714.

172. Yoshida, K. and Horch, K. (1996) Closed-loop control of ankle position using muscle afferent feedback with functional neuromuscular stimulation. *IEEE Transactions on Bio-Medical Engineering,* **43**(2), 167–176.

173. Yoshida, K., Pellinen, D., Pivin, D., Rousche, P., and Kipke, D. (2000) Development of the thin-film longitudinal intra-fascicular electrode, presented at the Center for Sensory-Motor Interaction (SMI), Department of Health Science and Technology, Aalborg University, *http://vbn.aau.dk/en/publications/development-of-the-thinfilm-longitudinal-intrafascicular-electrode(40effdc0-8ac2-11db-bb3d-000ea68e967b)/export.html*

174. Zhao, Q., Dahlin, L. B., Kanje, M., and Lundborg, G. (1992) Specificity of muscle reinnervation following repair of the transected sciatic nerve. A comparative study of different repair techniques in the rat, *Journal of Hand Surgery (Br.),* **17**(3), 257–261.

175. Hoffer, J.-A. (1975) Long-term Peripheral Nerve Activity during Behaviour in the Rabbit: the Control of Locomotion, Ph.D. Thesis, Dept. Biophysics, Johns Hopkins Univ., Baltimore, Md.

176. Loeb, G. E., Marks, W. B., and Beatty, P. G. (1977) Analysis and microelectronic design of tubular electrode arrays intended for chronic, multiple single-unit recording from captured nerve fibres, *Med. Bio.l Eng. Comput.,* **15**(2), 195-201.

177. Rodríguez, F. J., Ceballos, D., Schüttler, M., Valero, A., Valderrama, E., Stieglitz, T., and Navarro, X. (2000) Polyimide cuff electrodes for peripheral nerve stimulation, *J. Neurosci. Methods,* **98**(2), 105-18.

Chapter 2.7

CNS Recording: Devices and Techniques

Daryl R. Kipke

NeuroNexus Technologies, Inc.
655 Fairfield Court, Ann Arbor, Michigan USA
dkipke@neuronexus.com

This chapter covers the basics of extracellular neural recordings and their application to neuroprosthetic and neuromodulation systems. A generalized instrumentation model of extracellular neural recording is presented, including overviews of the biophysical origins of extracellular signals, the electrode interface, the electronics interface, and neuroanalytics and control. Overall there is a strong scientific rationale for using extracellular neural recording in these application areas, as well as solid technological and engineering foundations for designing and using practical, high-performance recording systems.

1. Introduction

Neural recording in the CNS is an important aspect of neuroprosthetics and neuromodulation. For example, in brain-computer interfaces for motor restoration, neural recordings at several different spatial scales have been shown to provide control signals for the prosthesis [1 - 3]. For neuromodulation systems that deliver small electrical stimulation for targeted therapies, neural recordings have been used to provide feedback signals for stimulation closed-loop control [4, 5] and diagnostics [6].

Extracellular neural recordings using implantable sensors (electrodes) are used in these application areas for several reasons. First, these signals are well grounded in electrophysiology and neuroscience to provide strong scientific rationale for the choice of signals and their use for particular application [7 - 11]. Second, extracellular recording provides a structured approach for monitoring neural activity across many spatial scales—from about 0.01 mm to about 10 mm—at millisecond resolution [12]. And third, the types of devices and systems that are required for extracellular recordings are available and well developed [13 - 17]. Because extracellular neural recording is a fundamental aspect of

467

D. R. Kipke

neurophysiology, the understanding of neural signals and how to record them has grown hand-in-hand with the development of the field [18 - 20].

While extracellular neural recording is well established, it remains a difficult problem and is by no means optimized. In commercial applications as part of active implantable medical devices (AIMDs), some of the significant problems include recording selectivity and stability, system miniaturization, signal processing complexity, and cost. For discovery-based science applications, for example, there is growing interest in being able to record from progressively more neurons—100s to 1,000s of neurons—over long periods of time, which presents challenges to electrode technology, neural signal processing, and analytics [13, 17].

This chapter provides an overview of the basics of extracellular neural recording and its application to neuroprosthetic and neuromodulation systems. Section 2 introduces a generalized instrumentation model of extracellular neural recording. Section 3 highlights the biophysical origins of extracellular neural signals, namely the relationships between neural current sources and extracellular voltage fields and presents a neural recording model. Section 4 describes an electrode interface model and highlights several types of electrodes used for neural recording across several spatial scales. Section 5 discusses primary elements of the electronics interface. Finally, Section 6 introduces the neuroanalytic component and highlights one important neuroanalytic application that relates directly to the importance of a well-designed recording system to match electrodes with the neural signal sources. An appendix provides a guide to reference materials for further study. The focus is on neural recording using implantable electrodes on the brain surface or penetrating into the brain. A discussion of neuroprosthesis-focused EEG recording using non-invasive electrodes can be found elsewhere [21].

2. System model

It is instructive to consider CNS neural recording in the generalized context of instrumentation systems (Fig. 1). The measured signal inputs to the system are extracellular voltages arising from the neural signal sources of interest. For neuroprosthetic and neuromodulation applications, the spatial scale of the signals of interest range over three orders of magnitude from ~0.01 mm to ~10 mm, while the time resolution is ~1 ms. Typically, there are significant sources of both intrinsic noise – e.g., interfering neural signals, interfering biopotentials, instrumentation noise – and extrinsic noise – e.g., electrical stimulation in the measurements.

The electrode is the system sensor that transduces extracellular voltage signals to electronic signals. In electrophysiology, the electrode is variously referred to as a lead or probe. More precisely, a probe or neural probe typically refers to a microelectrode array that penetrates into the CNS paryenchma, whereas a 'lead' typically refers to the sensor used in a clinical neuromodulation system (e.g., 'stimulation lead'). The region surrounding the electrode and the neural targets is referred to as the neural interface region. The site of transduction is referred to as the electrode site or contact. An electrode's structure, material composition, and usage dictate both its electrical characteristics for signal transduction and its impact on the neural interface. Typically, there is an 'observer effect' in extracellular neural recording in which the act of observation changes to some degree the interface itself. Often an array of sensors is used to simultaneously measure extracellular voltages at multiple positions.

The electronics interface, consisting of signal conditioning, signal acquisition, and digital signal processing sub-components, serves to amplify and filter the transduced extracellular voltages and do the initial stages of signal processing to extract desired signals from the raw measurements. The final neuroanalytic and control component serves to further process the signals to result in actionable or interpretive information per application requirements.

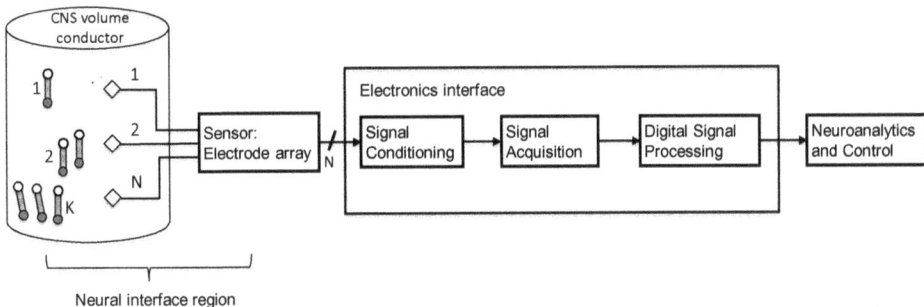

Fig. 1. System diagram for a generalized CNS neural recording system. The illustrated system has K neural signal sources of interest (represented by current sink/source dipoles) in the CNS volume conductor. The three main system components (Electrode, Electronics Interface, Neuroanalytics and Control) combine to sense, process, and analyze extracellular voltages sampled from the extracellular voltage field. The electrode array has N separate electrode sites.

3. Extracellular neural signals

3.1. *Relating current sources to extracellular voltage fields*

Extracellular voltage fields in the CNS are generated by transmembrane currents of neurons. These transmembrane currents are inward (depolarizing) or outward (hyperpolarizing) ionic currents through passive and active channels of the neurons during synaptic inputs, action potentials, and other electrically active events. From an extracellular field perspective, an inward transmembrane current appears as a current sink and an outward current appears as a current source. Because brain tissue is conductive and electroneutral, these current sources and sinks cause ionic currents in the extracellular space. Through Ohms law for volume conductors, this extracellular current in the resistive extracellular medium creates the extracellular voltage fields. The complex spatial and temporal relationships among the aggregated current sources over different spatial scales – from small groups of neurons to neuronal assemblies to entire brain lobes – together with anatomical properties, tissue volume conduction, and the particulars of measuring the extracellular field results in different types of neural signals [22].

Quantitative relationships among current sources and extracellular fields can be developed from fundamental consideration of Maxwell's equations and basic assumptions involving linearity, homogeneity and isotropy of tissue conductivity, and a relatively low frequency (<~10 kHz) regime of interest [12, 23, 24]. For the present discussion, the governing relationship between current sources and extracellular voltage fields is described in terms of Ohms law for linear volume conductors,

$$J = \sigma E \tag{1}$$

where J is the current density in $\mu A/mm^2$, σ is the tissue conductivity Ω^{-1} mm^{-1} of the volume conductor, and E is the electric field ($\mu V/mm$). The electric field is the gradient of the scalar potential field,

$$E = -\nabla \Phi = -\left(\frac{\partial}{\partial x}\Phi + \frac{\partial}{\partial y}\Phi + \frac{\partial}{\partial z}\Phi\right) \tag{2}$$

where ∇ is gradient operator and Φ is the scalar extracellular voltage field relative to a distant (infinite) ground region. Combining equations 1 and 2 gives the basic defining relationship between current sources, J, and the resulting extracellular voltage field, Φ,

$$J = -\sigma \nabla \Phi \tag{3}$$

For a point current source $I(t)$ in μA, the current density, J, at a distance r from the source is the current magnitude divided by the area of a sphere of radius r, or

$$J = \frac{I(t)}{4\pi r^2} a_r \tag{4}$$

where a_r is a unit vector in the outward radial direction. Combining equations 3 and 4 and solving for the extracellular voltage, Φ, results in the expression for an idealized monopole point current source

$$\Phi(r,t) = \frac{I(t)}{4\pi\sigma r} \tag{5}$$

where $\Phi(r, t)$ is the extracellular voltage referenced to a ground region at infinity and r is the distance between the current source and the voltage field point of interest in mm. This expression indicates that current from a point distributes within a spherical region, with the extracellular voltage decreasing with $1/r$ from the source (Fig. 2A). Because of linearity, the net extracellular voltage at a point resulting from multiple point monopole current sources is represented by summing their individual contributions.

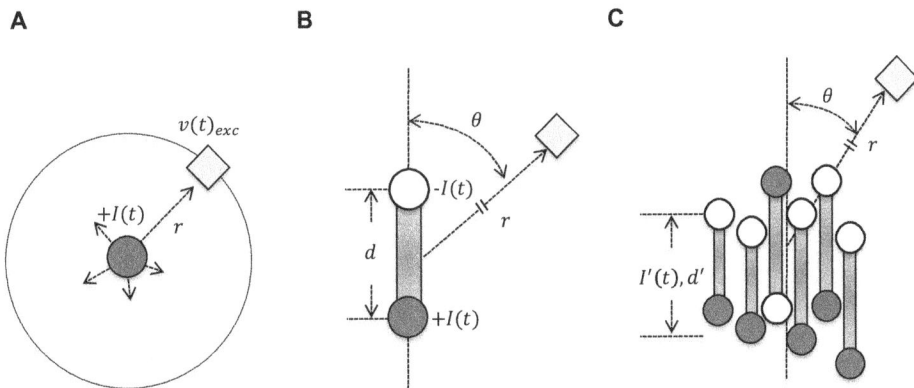

Fig. 2. Current source models. (A) Idealized monopole with point current source, $I(t)$ (dark circle) and corresponding spherical extracellular voltage field contour at radius r. Shaded diamond represents a discrete region over which a measurement is made corresponding to an electrode site. (B) Idealized dipole having approximately equal point current source and sink (dark and open circle, respectively) with separation d (C) Effective dipole, $I'(t)$ with separation d' resulting from closely spaced, spatially organized dipoles.

The idealized dipole point current source is of particular interest because it can represent the balanced current source and sinks of a firing neuron or synchronous, spatially organized neural assembly. The current dipole expression is

$$\Phi(r, t) = \frac{I(t)d \cos \theta}{4\pi\sigma r^2} \qquad [6]$$

where d is the distance between the current source and sink and θ is the angle between vector connecting the dipole axis midpoint to the measurement point (Fig. 2B). Current dipoles provide a reasonable approximation for situations in which the total source and sink are approximately equal and the measurement location is much greater than the effective dipole separation ($r \gg 3d$). The limiting case of $d \rightarrow 0$ represents sources and sinks being about evenly distributed throughout the field, whereby the aggregate dipole becomes small as does the extracellular potential at a distance. An assembly of closely spaced, spatially organized dipoles can be represented in the aggregate as an 'effective dipole' due to its effect on the extracellular voltage field (Fig. 2C).

The relationship between currents and extracellular voltage fields is also useful for considering effects of electrode site size on recording characteristics. An electrode site transduces the extracellular potentials distributed across its conductive surface. If this transduction surface is not well matched to the spatial scale of the differential extracellular field generated by the neural sources of interest, then the intended signals will either be spatially averaged and become buried in noise (if the surface is too large) or missed entirely (if the surface is too small). This spatial relationship underlies the electrode characteristics of selectivity and sensitivity as described in the following section.

3.2. *Extracellular neural recording model*

The quantitative relationship between current sources and extracellular voltages provide the basis for a more elaborated functional model of extracellular neural recording that maps K effective neural current sources of interest to N voltage signals input to the electronics interface (Fig. 3). The first stage of the model represents the extracellular voltage on electrode site n, $v(t)_{exc,n}$, as a function of the summed effective neural current dipoles, $I(t)_k$, within its recording volume, each scaled inversely with its distance from the site, $r_{k,n}$. Two additive noise sources are also included: $I(t)_{ns-neu}$ representing neural activity that is below detectable levels or not of interest and $I(t)_{ns-bio}$ representing interfering biopotentials (e.g., EMG, ECG) or motion artifacts.

The second stage of the model represents the transduction of ion-based extracellular potentials by a lumped-element equivalent circuit (described below) of the electrode interface. The resulting measured voltages on each electrode, $v(t)_{s,n}$, provide the inputs to the first-stage differential amplifier of the electronics interface. The model includes the reference extracellular voltage and associated electrode to indicate how this signal typically provides the common reference for the recording system. The reference signal corresponds to the 'distant ground' that is one of the assumptions in the mathematical description of extracellular voltage fields of the previous section.

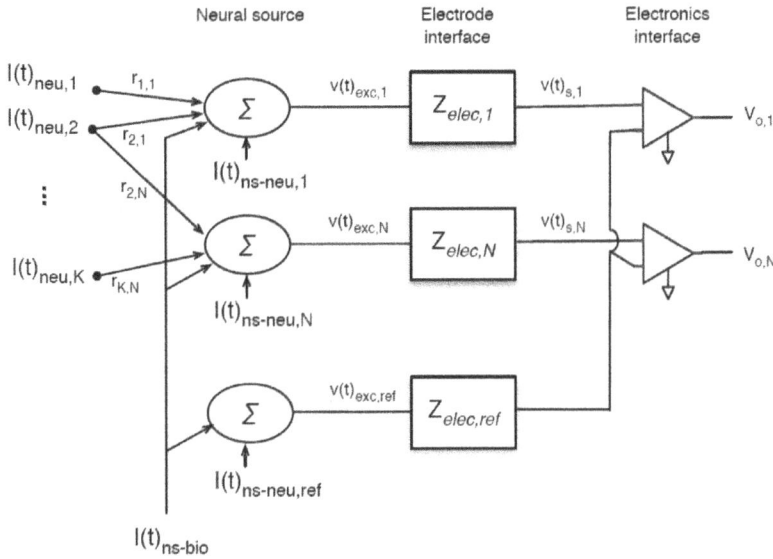

Fig. 3. Extracellular neural recording model. K neural sources are recorded on N electrode sites to result in N signal channels, $v(t)_o$ with three functional stages: (1) neural source, (2) electrode interface, and (3) electronics interface. Each electrode channel is referenced to a separate, common extracellular signal, $v(t)_{exc,ref}$.

3.3. *Extracellular signals of interest*

Across the application range of neuroprosthetic and neuromodulation systems, the primary signals of interest are extracellular action potentials (spike), local field potentials (LFPs), and electrocorticograms (ECoGs). While these signals each have millisecond temporal resolution, they result from aggregate neural activity ranging over spatial scales from ~0.01 mm to ~10 mm. The spatial and temporal relationships among these signals are generally complex and specific to brain region, anatomy, brain state, and details of recording [7, 22].

ECoGs have the largest spatial scale. These signals result primarily from synchronous synaptic currents in neural populations extending up to ~10 mm from the electrode. ECoGs are typically measured from the cortical surface with millimeter sized electrodes placed either subdurally or epidurally. ECoG have amplitudes ranging from ~ 50 μV to 100 μV with bandwidth of ~0.1 Hz to ~500 Hz.

Local field potentials (LFPs) have an intermediate spatial scale. These signals result primarily from synchronous synaptic transmembrane currents in dendrites and somas in neural populations extending up to ~1 mm from the electrode site.

These signals are recorded with penetrating electrodes. LFPs typically have amplitudes ranging from ~10 µV to 1,000 µV and bandwidth of ~1 Hz to 300 Hz. The information bearing components of LFPs are typically spectral components or specific temporal features associated with an event, such as a stimulus pulse or spike time.

Extracellular action potential ('spike') signals are recorded at the smallest spatial scale. These signals result from current dipoles created by transmembrane active currents in firing neurons. Because of the relatively small current sources and the short dipole axis, these signals can typically be recorded up to distances of ~0.2 mm from the electrode site. Extracellular spikes have amplitudes ranging from ~50 µV to 500 µV and bandwidth of ~300 Hz to 5,000 Hz, with the signal characteristics depending on the magnitude of the current sink and the distance and orientation of the dipole relative to the recording electrode site. Depending on application requirements, the desired signal may be the combined spike activity from a small cluster of nearby neurons, often referred to as 'multiunit activity'. Or it may be well-isolated spike activity from individual neurons, referred to as 'single-unit activity'. While spike waveforms are used to identify firing neurons, the spike times are typically the information bearing component of spike signals.

Using sufficiently small penetrating electrodes, an extracellular recording can contain both lower frequency LFPs and higher frequency spike signals in which the two signals are discriminated by appropriate bandpass filtering (Fig. 4).

4. Electrode interface model

The electrode is the sensor that transduces ion-based extracellular voltages to electronic signals that provide the inputs to the electronics interface (Fig. 5). This transduction process occurs at the thin interface of the electrode contact (typically a nonreactive metal) and the tissue via complex electrochemical processes and capacitive displacement currents [26 - 28]. The electrode interface can be functionally well represented with a lumped-element equivalent circuit model (Fig. 5). In this case, the voltage source, E_{hc}, represents the half-cell potential of the electrode-tissue interface. The capacitor, C_{dl}, represents the double layer capacitance. The resistor, R_{ct}, represents the resistance to the transfer of charge that occurs through reversible faradaic (reduction-oxidation) currents. The constant phase element (CPE) impedance represents charge transfer variations resulting from surface morphology of the electrode site and ion diffusion non-linearities in the tissue at the interface. The resistor, R_a, represents the resistance to ion movement in the diffusion region. The capacitor, C_{sh}, and resistor, R_{sh}, represent the shunt or leakage pathways from the insulated electrode traces to the bulk tissue. The resistor, R_t, represents the resistance in the electrode trace from the electrode site to electronics interface. The voltage source, $v_{ns-elec}$ represents the lumped electrode intrinsic noise sources that arise from various biophysical and electrical phenomena.

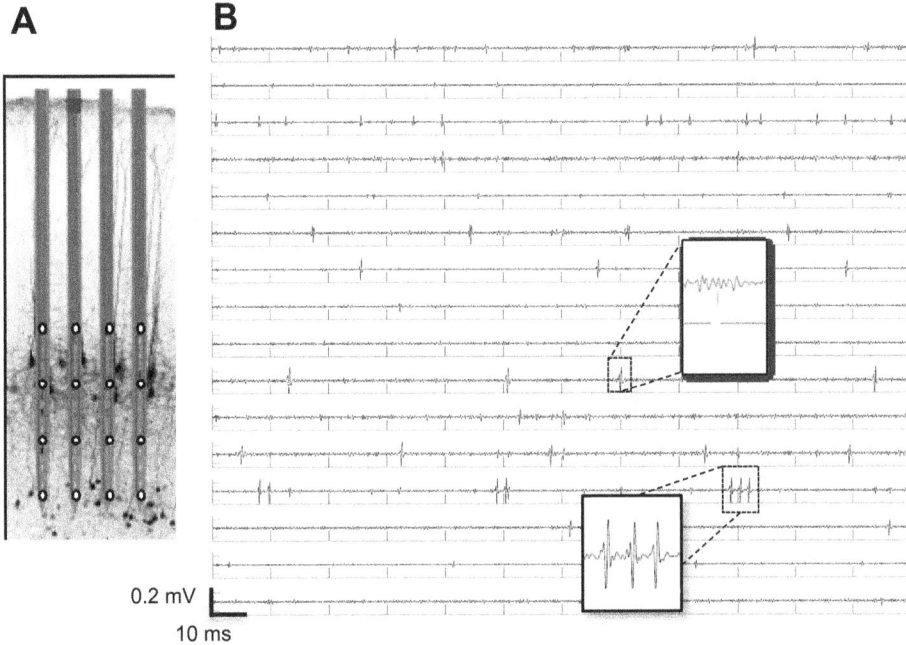

Fig. 4. Neural recordings from a microelectrode array in the brain. (A) Cross-section of stained brain tissue superimposed with a 4-shank silicon neural probe having a total of 16 individual closely spaced recording sites (white circles). (B) Extracellular neural signals bandpass filtered to highlight spike activity (action potentials) recorded on an electrode site. Examples of well isolated spikes are illustrated in the insets.

Extracellular signal transduction has several intrinsic noise components. The primary source is associated with the electrode-tissue interface and caused by Brownian motion of electrons, drift and diffusion of charged ions due to concentration gradients, oxidation/reduction reactions occurring at the electrode-tissue interface [29, 30]. The magnitude of the noise depends on the site material, size, and surface morphology and contamination. Additional sources include random fluctuations and instability in the half-cell potential caused by disturbances of the double layer capacitance and contamination of the electrode surface, thermal noise (also referred to as Johnson or Nyquist noise) due to the random motion of electrons in the electrode trace, and frequency-dependent 1/f noise (also referred to as flicker or pink noise). To a reasonable first approximation, these noise sources can be modeled as thermal (Johnson) noise and represented by the voltage source, $v_{ns-elec} = \sqrt{4kTZ\Delta f}$, where k is Boltzmann's constant, T is Kelvin temperature, Z is electrode magnitude impedance at 1 kHz, and Δf is the frequency range of interest.

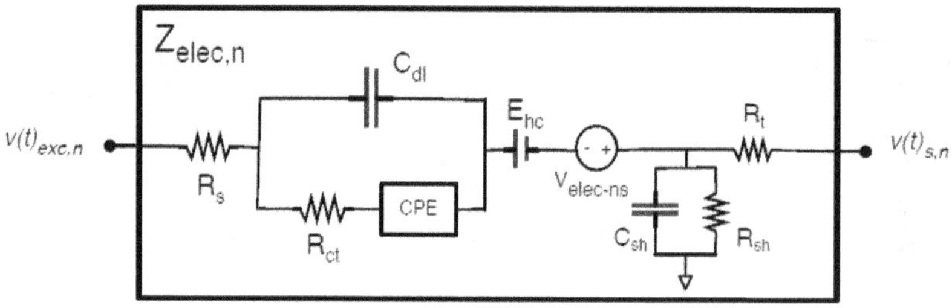

Fig. 5. Equivalent circuit of the electrode interface. $v(t)_{exc,n}$ is the integrated extracellular voltage field that is distributed over electrode site n. $v(t)_{s,n}$ is the voltage signal at the input of the electronics interface. Refer to the text for additional details.

4.1. *Factors that influence neural recording characteristics*

Neural recording fidelity is maximized through the design and use of electrodes that are well matched—in terms of size, position, and electrical properties—to the spatial scale and temporal characteristics of the neural signal sources of interest. Recording sensitivity, selectivity, and stability are useful summary characteristics. Generally, extracellular neural recordings are biased towards larger neural sources over smaller sources, and sources that are closer to electrode sites over sources that are more distant. Electrode arrays having sites spaced sufficiently close to record from overlapping neural signal sources can be important for improving recording characteristics.

Recording sensitivity refers to the degree to which a change in the underlying neural source (e.g., current source amplitude) is reflected in the signal measurement. Sensitivity depends on the match between the size and position of the electrode site relative and the region of the extracellular voltage field with highest signal content. All else being equal, the most sensitive recordings would be obtained with electrode sites encompassing the region of interest and not elsewhere. Electrodes too large or too small or positioned outside this region would have lower sensitivity. Sensitivity is a complicated function of the electrical characteristics of the electrode and electrode-tissue interface, spatial averaging effects of volume conduction, signal attenuation associated with progressive tissue encapsulation, signal shunting in the electrode and resistive losses in the electrode trace.

Recording selectivity refers to the degree to which an electrode preferentially measures neuron signals of interest and rejects interfering signals. Similar to sensitivity, selectivity depends on suitable matching of electrode site size and placement with the spatial and temporal characteristics of the extracellular voltage field of interest. Selectivity generally varies inversely with electrode site size because a larger sensing area will integrate both interfering signals and signals of interest.

Recording stability refers to the degree to which the functional characteristics of the recording system—including both biological components such as tissue encapsulation and device characteristics such as electrode site biofouling—remain largely constant over time. With high-quality, well-designed electrodes that do not appreciably degrade over time and a high quality recording system, recording stability tends to be dominated by biological factors.

In general, extracellular action potential recordings, recorded with microelectrodes positioned within ~0.2 mm of the sources provide the most sensitive and selective resolution recordings. However, these recordings are often less stable than LFPs and ECoGs, because the signal is a function of relatively few neural signal sources over a small region. Any perturbations in this region can lead to significant signal changes or degradation. Conversely, while LFPs and ECoG can be more stable, the size of the recording region limits their sensitivity and selectivity. These considerations and tradeoffs are important in the design of neuroprosthetic and neuromodulation systems.

4.2. *Electrode technologies*

Electrodes are not one size fits all. The broad range of spatial scales underlying neural signals of interest require diverse types of electrodes in order to establish well matched neural interfaces (Fig. 6). ECoGs are acquired using flexible grid electrodes on the cortical surface (either subdural or epidural). Local field potentials and spike recordings are acquired using penetrating electrodes positioned in or near the brain region of interest. In some DBS applications, local field potentials are acquired using relatively large ~1mm diameter penetrating leads.

Amidst these different types of electrodes, there are several common functional elements. First, all electrodes have one or more electrode sites that must be in direct contact with the brain volume conductor. The primary design elements are the site material and the site area, shape, and surface properties. Second, they have conductive traces connecting the electrode sites to the electronics interface that are embedded in insulating materials (dielectrics) to be electrically isolated from the surrounding extracellular fluids. Third, the insulating materials are sufficiently biostable and biocompatible to maintain electrical integrity and elicit minimal host responses over the lifetime of the device, which could be years.

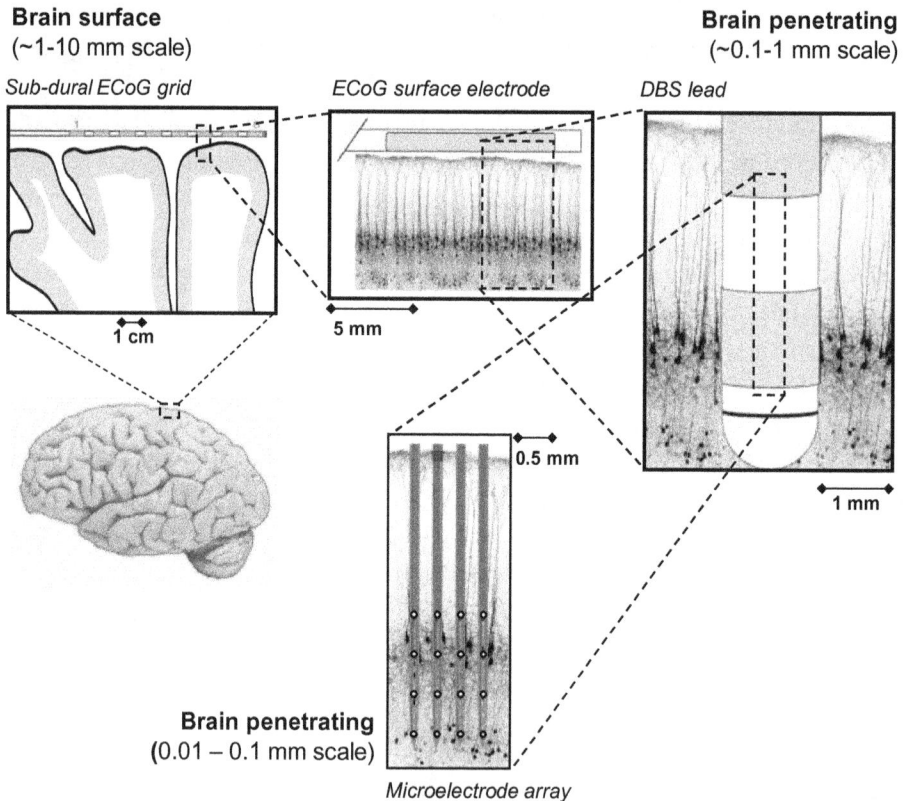

Fig. 6. Neural interfaces at different spatial scales. Brain surface recordings ECoG grid electrodes on the 1-10 mm spatial scale. Brain penetrating recordings are made with intermediate sized electrodes or microelectrodes.

Most neuroprosthetic and neuromodulation applications requiring ECoG recordings have used grid electrodes designed primarily for intracranial neuromonitoring of epilepsy. These grids are typically relatively thin, flexible devices having a multiple disk electrode contacts arranged in either a linear strip having four to six electrodes or rectangular 8x8 grid having 64 electrodes, with spacing of 10 mm. The typical contact is platinum with 2.3 mm diameter (4.16 mm^2 area) [3]. This type of ECoG grid is made using standard neurostimulation lead technology consisting of small gauge wires embedded in medical grade polyurethane or silicone insulating materials. ECoG grids having smaller site sizes and closer spacing for more selective and higher resolution recordings have been developed using thin-film polymer technologies [31, 32]. At the extreme selectivity and spatial resolution of recording from the brain surface, very small and high resolution thin-film grids (10 μm x 10 μm sites) have been used to record extracellular action potentials from superficial cortical layers in the mouse [33].

Microelectrode arrays for spike or LFP recordings have a larger design space and use additional technologies because of more diverse requirements of the microscale neural interfaces and the complexities of penetrating into the brain. One type of microelectrode array is based on microwires that are assembled into wire clusters of various sizes and shapes [34 - 36]. A second type of microelectrode array is based on micro-electro-mechanical systems (MEMS) microfabrication technologies [14 - 16, 37, 38, 39]. MEMS electrode technologies use a broad range of conductive and dielectric materials to make microelectrode arrays in many sizes and architectures and can be fabricated with high precision and consistency. These processes involve detailed sequences of selective deposition or removal of patterned thin films of conductive or dielectric materials on a substrate, and/or bulk micromachining of materials through etching, grinding, or sawing. MEMS thin-film electrode technology has a broad design space that allows designs having precise one-, two-, or three-dimensional layout of electrode sites across one or more planar shanks. This provides a very strong technology platform for making electrode arrays that are precisely matched to their intended neural signals and neural interfaces [40].

5. Electronics interface

The electronics interface is a critical component of every CNS recording system. Even with well-matched and properly positioned electrodes, recording extracellular neural signals is typically complicated by interfering inputs and noise, neural interface variability, and small signal-to-noise levels. Commercial neuroprosthetic and neuromodulation applications are particularly challenging because the recording must be done within the constraints of an active implantable medical device (AIMD), which typically include limited computational capacity, real-time processing requirements, limited power budgets, limited control and communications, stringent safety and reliability requirements, and cost effectiveness. The electronics interface is implemented using a set of well-defined sub-systems for signal conditioning, signal acquisition, and digital signal processing (see Figure 1).

5.1. *Signal conditioning and signal acquisition*

Signal conditioning involves amplification and filtering of the raw analog signals ($v(t)_s$ in Figure 3) to match the input requirements of the subsequent analog-to-digital conversion process in the acquisition stage [41]. Typically, signal conditioning requires a low-noise, high-precision multichannel differential amplifier followed by bandpass filtering configured to reject signal frequencies outside the bandwidth of the neural sources of interest. This amplifier must have high input impedance (typically $>>10$ MΩ) to accommodate high impedance electrodes (the small sites of microelectrodes typically have impedances ranging from 0.2 to 2 MΩ) and sufficient common mode rejection to block interfering biopotentials (e.g., ECG) and common noise sources. These common mode signals can potentially be an order of magnitude higher than neural signals and thus deleterious to system function if not properly blocked. Acquisition requires a high-resolution analog-to-digital converter (typically 16 bits or higher) operating at a sample rate of up to about 30,000 samples per second depending on the bandwidth of the neural signals of interest. In systems that support electrode arrays, the acquisition stage often includes a signal multiplexer to acquiring multiple analog signals into a single digital data stream.

It is generally desirable to digitize the analog neural signals as early as possible and then use digital signal processing techniques to extract desired information. This approach moves neural signal processing into the information technology domain of algorithms, software, and computing hardware.

In most neuroprosthetic and neuromodulation applications, as well as in many high-performance neural recording systems, the signal conditioning and acquisition stages are typically implemented using application-specific integrated circuits (ASIC) chips [4, 16, 42 - 45]. This is critical for CNS recording because it results in miniaturized, high-performance, low-power, and reliable solutions to this technically difficult method.

Signal referencing is an important aspect of signal conditioning to minimize contributions of interfering biological noise. Typically, a relatively large electrode site is positioned in a location having minimal neural activity and is used as a reference to remove correlated noise across channels. This reference electrode signal is connected to the input of differential amplifiers across all channels. The amplifiers themselves are referenced to a separate ground site, which may be the implantable electronics enclosure for an AIMD, or in the case of external electronics, to an externally derived ground terminal.

5.2. *Digital signal processing*

Digital signal processing (DSP) is used in the initial stages of processing the digitized extracellular signals to extract desired signals and data. The specific DSP algorithms and their implementation details are generally application and device dependent. For example, a commercial-grade neuromodulation AIMD that utilizes neural recording for monitoring or feedback control must implement real-time DSP algorithms with embedded software running on microcontrollers in the implantable pulse generator of the system. This puts hard constraints on algorithm structure and complexity, among other things. Alternatively, a system intended for more open-ended discovery or development applications could have DSP algorithms running off-line on a computer workstation far removed from the neural interface and subject.

Digital noise rejection is an example of early stage DSP that is relevant to many applications of neural recording. Using a single reference electrode to provide the signal reference for all electrode channels is sometimes an issue if, for example, it is difficult to identify a good reference signal. A DSP-based alternative is to use a digital common average reference (CAR) algorithm. Common average referencing is commonly used in EEG systems to be able to detect small signals in noisy recordings [46] and was originally implemented with analog signal processing [47]. With the digital CAR algorithm, the signals from all electrode sites are averaged and then subtracted from each individual electrode signal [48]. Through the averaging process, only signal or noise that is common to all sites (correlated) remains on the CAR (e.g., 60-Hz noise or motion artifact). Digital subtraction of the CAR from each electrode signal eliminates the common signal. The digital CAR algorithm is analogous to differential amplification of the corresponding analog signals. Digital common average referencing is computationally efficient and can be implemented using embedded software on microcontrollers for real-time processing.

An additional example of early stage DSP is the process of spike detection in extracellular spike recordings. In this case, amplitude thresholding is used to detect the occurrences of large amplitude, transient waveforms in the raw electrode signals that are the putative extracellular action potentials. Simple thresholding may be sufficient to estimate aggregate spike activity from multiunit clusters per some application requirements [49]. In other cases, this thresholding may be the initial processing stage of more extensive algorithms for detailed spike sorting [50 - 52]. Similarly, applications involving local field potentials and ECoG recordings each have their particular DSP requirements [3, 22, 53, 54]. The salient point is that the signal processing requirements across broad applications can be met with specialized algorithms and software that run on conventional microcontrollers and computing systems, thereby leveraging information technology for cost, performance, and flexibility.

6. Neuroanalytics

The neuroanalytic and control components of a CNS recording system serve to extract actionable or interpretive data from the neural recordings. In general, this process is highly application dependent and encompasses a broad range of statistical signal processing models and algorithms [55, 56]. A general discussion of neuroanalytics is outside the scope of this chapter.

One neuroanalytic application that nicely illustrates the importance of matching the electrode to the neural signals of interest is the process of spike sorting using closely spaced sites on a microelectrode array. Spike sorting refers to the process of using recorded extracellular spike waveforms to estimate the firing times of the individual members of the underlying set of active neurons. Spike sorting is a ubiquitous inverse problem in extracellular electrophysiology that has been well studied [50 - 52].

The magnitude and shape of the extracellular spike waveform of a firing neuron is a function of the neuron's effective current dipole and the position of the electrode site relative to that dipole [8, 9, 57]. The stereotypical extracellular spike waveform is tri-phasic with negative initial phase, but biphasic and even monophasic waveforms are not uncommon. This waveform is considered the 'signature' of the neuron in the extracellular recording; an instance of the spike signature is recorded each time the neuron fires. However, this signature is not unique and it often changes over time due to changes of the current dipole, ion channel dynamics, or small movements of the electrode relative to the neuron. When electrode site spacing is larger than the recording radius for extracellular spike recording (typically about 100 to 200 μm), then each electrode site records the aggregate spike activity from non-overlapping, distinct sets of neurons in the form of brief one-dimensional (voltage vs. time) spike signatures (waveforms).

However, with electrode sites with sufficiently close spacing (typically ~15 to 40 μm), the recording spheres of adjacent sites overlap such that each firing neuron can be simultaneously recorded on multiple sites. This results in a spatiotemporal spike signature (voltage and space vs. time) for each firing neuron across the electrode array. Sophisticated algorithms that are used to detect and classify these spatiotemporal signatures significantly increase the accuracy of spike sorting and the number of well isolated neurons compared with recordings made with electrodes having widely spaced sites.

7. Concluding Remarks

This chapter has covered the basics of CNS extracellular neural recordings and their application to neuroprosthetic and neuromodulation systems. A generalized instrumentation model of extracellular neural recording was presented, along with overviews of the biophysical origins of extracellular signals, electrode interfaces, electronics interfaces, and system analytics and control. There is a strong scientific rationale for using extracellular neural recording in these application areas, as well as solid technological and engineering foundations for designing and using practical, high-performance recording systems.

The primary challenges are not so much about what signals should be recorded, nor where they should be recorded, but rather about extending, improving, and optimizing the recording system to meet the requirements of the overlying neuroprosthetic or neuromodulation system. As such the engineering details of the system become very important. For example, poorly matched electrodes, low quality or inappropriate signal conditioning, or inadequate DSP algorithms may severely limit system performance. Conversely, a well-designed, high quality system typically has outstanding performance and high reliability.

Overall, the progressively more sophisticated and powerful approaches for recording extracellular signals aligns well with emerging application requirements and the ability to process these more complex, information-dense signals. The future looks bright for neuroprostheses and neuromodulation—and neural recording is likely to play an important role in that future.

8. Appendix

This chapter was intended as an introduction or review of CNS neural recording techniques and devices. There is an extensive and diverse body of work spanning the relevant areas of science and technology. The following references may be of particular interest for deeper study:

- Extracellular neural signals: [12, 22, 23]
- Electrode interface and electrode technologies: [13, 27, 40, 58]
- Electronics interface and neuroanalytics: [41, 52, 59]

References

1. J. L. Collinger, B. Wodlinger, J. E. Downey, W. Wang, E. C. Tyler-Kabara, D. J. Weber, A. J. C. McMorland, M. Velliste, M. L. Boninger, and A. B. Schwartz, High-performance

neuroprosthetic control by an individual with tetraplegia, *Lancet*, vol. 381, no. 9866, pp. 557–564, 2013.

2. L. R. Hochberg, D. Bacher, B. Jarosiewicz, N. Y. Masse, J. D. Simeral, J. Vogel, S. Haddadin, J. Liu, S. S. Cash, P. van der Smagt, and J. P. Donoghue, Reach and grasp by people with tetraplegia using a neurally controlled robotic arm, *Nature*, vol. 485, no. 7398, pp. 372–375, 2012.

3. G. Schalk, BCIs that use electrocorticographic activity, in *Brain-computer Interfaces: Principles and Practice*, eds. J. R. Wolpaw and E. W. Wolpaw, (Oxford University Press, New York, 2012).

4. A. G. Rouse, S. R. Stanslaski, P. Cong, R. M. Jensen, P. Afshar, D. Ullestad, R. Gupta, G. F. Molnar, D. W. Moran, and T. J. Denison, A chronic generalized bi-directional brain-machine interface, *J. Neural Eng.*, vol. 8, no. 3, p. 36018, 2011.

5. J. B. Zimmermann and A. Jackson, Closed-loop control of spinal cord stimulation to restore hand function after paralysis, *Front. Neurosci.*, vol. 8, p. 87, 2014.

6. G. E. Gmel, T. J. Hamilton, M. Obradovic, R. B. Gorman, P. S. Single, H. J. Chenery, T. Coyne, and P. A. Silburn, A new biomarker for subthalamic deep brain stimulation for patients with advanced Parkinson ' s disease — a pilot study, *J. Neural Eng.*, vol. 12, no. 6, p. 066013, 2015.

7. C. Gold, D. Henze, C. Koch, and G. Buzsaki, On the origin of the extracellular action potential waveform: A modeling study, *J. Neurophysiol.*, vol. 9, no. 5, pp. 3113-3128, 2006.

8. D. A. Henze, Z. Borhegyi, J. Csicsvari, A. Mamiya, K. D. Harris, and G. Buzsaki, Intracellular features predicted by extracellular recordings in the hippocampus in vivo, *J. Neurophysiol.*, vol. 84, no. 1, pp. 390–400, 2000.

9. D. Johnston and S. M. Wu, *Foundations of Cellular Neurophysiology*, (MIT Press, Cambridge, MA, 1995).

10. A. B. Schwartz, Movement: How the brain communicates with the world, *Cell*, vol. 164, no. 6, pp. 1122–1135, 2016.

11. A. Schwartz, X. Cui, D. Weber, and D. Moran, Brain-controlled interfaces: Movement restoration with neural prosthetics, *Neuron*, vol. 52, no. 1, pp. 205-220, 2006.

12. P. L. Nunez, Electric and magnetic fields produced by the brain, in *Brain-computer Interfaces: Principles and Practice*, eds. J. Wolpaw and E. W. Wolpaw, (Oxford University Press, New York, 2012), pp. 45–63.

13. G. Buzsáki, E. Stark, A. Berényi, D. Khodagholy, D. R. Kipke, E. Yoon, and K. D. Wise, Tools for probing local circuits: high-density silicon probes combined with optogenetics, *Neuron*, vol. 86, no. 1, pp. 92–105, 2015.

14. K. D. Wise, D. J. Anderson, J. F. Hetke, D. R. Kipke, and K. Najafi, Wireless implantable microsystems: High-density electronic interfaces to the nervous system, *Proc. IEEE*, vol. 92, no. 1, pp. 76–97, 2004.

15. K. Wise, A. Sodagar, Y. Yao, M. Gulari, G. Perlin, and K. Najafi, Microelectrodes, microelectronics, and implantable neural microsystems, *Proc. IEEE*, vol. 96, no. 7, pp. 1184–1202, 2008.

16. A. V Nurmikko, J. P. Donoghue, L. R. Hochberg, W. R. Patterson, Y. K. Song, C. W. Bull, D. A. Borton, F. Laiwalla, S. Park, and Y. Ming, Listening to brain microcircuits for interfacing with external world—Progress in wireless implantable microelectronic neuroengineering devices, *Proc. IEEE*, vol. 98, no. 3, pp. 375–388, 2010.

17. A. P. Alivisatos, A. M. Andrews, E. S. Boyden, M. Chun, G. M. Church, K. Deisseroth, J. P. Donoghue, S. E. Fraser, J. Lippincott-Schwartz, L. L. Looger, S. Masmanidis, P. L. McEuen,

A. V. Nurmikko, H. Park, D. S. Peterka, C. Reid, M. L. Roukes, A. Scherer, M. Schnitzer, T. J. Sejnowski, K. L. Shepard, D. Tsao, G. Turrigiano, P. S. Weiss, C. Xu, R. Yuste, and X. Zhuang, Nanotools for neuroscience and brain activity mapping, *ACS Nano*, vol. 7, no. 3, pp. 1850–1866, 2013.

18. F. Strumwasser, Long-term recording from single neurons in brain of unrestrained mammals, *Science*, vol. 127, no. 3296, pp. 469–470, 1958.

19. E. E. Fetz and M. A Baker, Operantly conditioned patterns on precentral unit activity and correlated responses in adjacent cells and contralateral muscles, *J. Neurophysiol.*, vol. 36, no. 2, pp. 179–204, 1973.

20. D. R. Humphrey and E. M. Schmidt, Extracellular single-unit recording methods, eds A. A. Boulton, G. B. Baker, and C. H. Vanderwolf, *Neurophysiological Techniques, Applications to Neural Systems*, (Humana Press, Clifton, New Jersey, 1990), pp. 1–64.

21. R. Srinivasan, Acquiring brain signals from outside the brain, in eds. J. Wolpaw and E. Winter Wolpaw, *Brain–computer interfaces Principles and Practice,* (Oxford Univ. Press, New York, 2012) pp. 105–122.

22. G. Buzsáki, C. A. Anastassiou, and C. Koch, The origin of extracellular fields and currents — EEG, ECoG, LFP and spikes, *Nat. Rev. Neurosci.*, vol. 13, no. 6, pp. 407–420, 2012.

23. P. Nunez, *Electric Fields of the Brain*, (Oxford University Press, New York, 1981).

24. R. Plonsey and R. C. Barr, *Bioelectricity: A quantitative approach*, 2nd ed., (Kluwer Academic, New York, 2000).

25. G. Buzsáki, Large-scale recording of neuronal ensembles, *Nat. Neurosci.*, vol. 7, no. 5, pp. 446–451, 2004.

26. S. Cogan, Neural stimulation and recording electrodes, *Annu. Rev. Biomed. Eng.*, vol. 10, pp. 275-309, 2008.

27. D. R. Merrill, M. Bikson, and J. G. R. Jefferys, Electrical stimulation of excitable tissue: design of efficacious and safe protocols, *J. Neurosci. Methods*, vol. 141, no. 2, pp. 171–198, 2005.

28. K. J. Otto, K. A. Ludwig, and D. R. Kipke, Acquiring signals from within the brain, in eds. J. R. Wolpaw and E. W. Wolpaw, *Brain-computer Interfaces: Principles and Practice*, (Oxford University Press, New York, 2012).

29. A. Hassibi, R. Navid, R. W. Dutton, and T. H. Lee, Comprehensive study of noise processes in electrode electrolyte interfaces, *J. Appl. Phys.*, vol. 96, no. 2, p. 1074, 2004.

30. D. R. Humphrey and E. M. Schmidt, Extracellular single-unit recording methods, in eds. A. A. Boulton, G. B. Baker, and C. H. Vanderwolf, *Neurophysiological Techniques Applications to Neural Systems*, (Springer, New York, 1990), pp. 1–33.

31. M. Piangerelli, M. Ciavarro, A. Paris, S. Marchetti, P. Cristiani, C. Puttilli, N. Torres, A. Benabid, and P. Romanelli, A fully-integrated wireless system for intracranial direct cortical stimulation, real-time electrocorticography data transmission and smart cage for wireless battery recharge, *Front. Neurol.*, vol. 25, no. 5, p. 156, 2014.

32. A. G. Rouse, J. J. Williams, J. J. Wheeler, and D. W. Moran, Cortical adaptation to a chronic micro- electrocorticographic brain computer interface, *J. Neurosci.*, vol. 33, no. 4, pp. 1326–1330, 2013.

33. D. Khodagholy, J. N. Gelinas, T. Thesen, W. Doyle, O. Devinsky, G. G. Malliaras, and G. Buzsaki, NeuroGrid: recording action potentials from the surface of the brain, *Nat Neurosci*, vol. 18, no. 2, pp. 310–315, 2015.

34. J. Williams and R. Rennaker, Long-term neural recording characteristics of wire microelectrode arrays implanted in cerebral cortex, *Brain Res. Protoc.*, vol. 4, no. 3, pp. 303-313, 1999.

35. M. A. L. Nicolelis, D. Dimitrov, J. M. Carmena, R. Crist, G. Lehew, J. D. Kralik, and S. P. Wise, Chronic, multisite, multielectrode recordings in macaque monkeys, *Proc. Natl. Acad. Sci. U. S. A.*, vol. 100, no. 19, pp. 11041–11046, 2003.

36. S. Musallam, M. J. Bak, P. R. Troyk, and R. A. Andersen, A floating metal microelectrode array for chronic implantation, *J. Neurosci. Methods*, vol. 160, no. 1, pp. 122–127, 2007.

37. P. K. Campbell, K. E. Jones, R. J. Huber, K. W. Horch, and R. A. Normann, A silicon-based, three-dimensional neural interface: manufacturing processes for an intracortical electrode array, *IEEE Trans. Biomed. Eng.*, vol. 38, no. 8, pp. 758–768, 1991.

38. R. J. Vetter, R. H. Olsson, J. F. Hetke, J. C. Williams, D. Pellinen, K. D. Wise, and D. R. Kipke, Silicon-substrate intracortical microelectrode arrays with integrated electronics for chronic cortical recording, in *Proceedings of the 25th Annual International Conference of the IEEE Engineering in Medicine and Biology Society*, pp. 2164–2167, 2003.

39. R. Bhandari, S. Negi, and F. Solzbacher, Wafer-scale fabrication of penetrating neural microelectrode arrays, *Biomed. Microdevices*, vol. 12, no. 5, pp. 797–807, 2010.

40. J. F. Hetke and D. J. Anderson, Silicon microelectrodes for extracellular recording, in eds. W. E. Finn and P. G. LoPresti, *Handbook of Neuroprosthetic Methods*, (CRC Press, Boca Raton, FL, 2002), pp. 163–194.

41. R. Harrison, The design of integrated circuits to observe brain activity, *Proc. IEEE*, vol. 96, no. 7, pp. 1203–1216, 2008.

42. *ibid.*

43. A. Csavoy, G. Molnar, and T. Denison, Creating support circuits for the nervous system: Considerations for brain-machine interfacing, *Symp. VLSI Circuits*, vol. 3, pp. 4–7, 2009.

44. P. H. Stypulkowski, S. R. Stanslaski, T. J. Denison, and J. E. Giftakis, Chronic evaluation of a clinical system for deep brain stimulation and recording of neural network activity, *Stereotact. Funct. Neurosurg.*, vol. 91, no. 4, pp. 220–232, 2013.

45. A. Berényi, Z. Somogyvári, A. J. Nagy, L. Roux, J. D. Long, S. Fujisawa, E. Stark, A. Leonardo, T. D. Harris, and G. Buzsáki, Large-scale, high-density (up to 512 channels) recording of local circuits in behaving animals., *J. Neurophysiol.*, vol. 111, no. 5, pp. 1132–49, 2014.

46. R. Cooper, C. Binnie, J. C. Schaw, C. Binnie, R. Cooper, F. Mauguiere, J. W. Osselton, P. F. Prior, and B. M. Tedman, Clinical neurophysiology: EEG, paediatric neurophysiology, special techniques and applications, in ed. C. Binnie, *Handbook of Clinical Neurophysiology. Vol. 10. Transient Disorders in Adults and Children*, (Elsevier Science, Amsterdam, 2012).

47. J. W. Osselton, Acquisition of EEG data by bipolar, unipolar and average reference methods: a theoretical comparison., *Electroencephalogr. Clin. Neurophysiol.*, vol. 19, no. 5, pp. 527–528, 1965.

48. K. A. Ludwig, R. M. Miriani, N. B. Langhals, M. D. Joseph, D. J. Anderson, and D. R. Kipke, Using a common average reference to improve cortical neuron recordings from microelectrode arrays, *J. Neurophysiol.*, vol. 101, no. 3, pp. 1679–1689, 2009.

49. G. W. Fraser, S. M. Chase, A. Whitford, and A. B. Schwartz, Control of a brain-computer interface without spike sorting, *J. Neural Eng.*, vol. 6, no. 5, p. 55004, 2009.

50. C. Rossant, S. N. Kadir, D. F. M. Goodman, J. Schulman, M. L. D. Hunter, A. B. Saleem, A. Grosmark, M. Belluscio, G. H. Denfield, A. S. Ecker, A. S. Tolias, S. Solomon, G. Buzsaki, M. Carandini, and K. D. Harris, Spike sorting for large, dense electrode arrays, *Nat Neurosci*, vol. 19, no. 4, pp. 634–641, 2016.

51. R. Q. Quiroga, Spike sorting., *Curr. Biol.*, vol. 22, no. 2, pp. R45–46, 2012.

52. H. G. Rey, C. Pedreira, and R. Q. Quiroga, Past, present and future of spike sorting techniques, *Brain Res. Bull.*, vol 119(Pt B), pp. 106-117, 2015.

53. J. J. Williams, A. G. Rouse, S. Thongpang, J. C. Williams, and D. W. Moran, Differentiating closed-loop cortical intention from rest: building an asynchronous electrocorticographic BCI, *J. Neural Eng.*, vol. 10, no. 4, p. 046001, 2013.

54. U. Mitzdorf, Current source-density method and application in cat cerebral cortex: investigation of evoked potentials and EEG phenomena, *Physiol. Rev.*, vol. 65, no. 1, pp. 37–100, 1985.

55. R. A. A. Ince, A. Mazzoni, R. S. Petersen, and S. Panzeri, Open source tools for the information theoretic analysis of neural data, *Front. Neurosci.*, vol. 4, pp. 62–70, 2010.

56. C. Magri, K. Whittingstall, V. Singh, N. K. Logothetis, and S. Panzeri, A toolbox for the fast information analysis of multiple-site LFP, EEG and spike train recordings, *BMC Neurosci.*, vol. 10, no. 1, p. 81, 2009.

57. R. Quiroga, What is the real shape of extracellular spikes?, *J. Neurosci. Methods*, vol. 177, no. 1, pp. 194-198, 2009.

58. S. F. Cogan, Neural stimulation and recording electrodes., *Annu. Rev. Biomed. Eng.*, vol. 10, pp. 275–309, 2008.

59. G. Buzsáki, Neural Syntax: Cell assemblies, synapsembles, and readers, *Neuron*, vol. 68, no. 3, pp. 362–385, 2010.

Section 3

Existing Systems

Chapter 3.1

Skeletal Motor Neuroprostheses

Kevin L. Kilgore[1], Robert F. Kirsch[2], and P. Hunter Peckham[1,2]

[1]Department of Orthopaedics and MetroHealth Rehabilitation Institute,
MetroHealth Medical Center
2500 MetroHealth Drive, Cleveland, OH 44109
pxp2@case.edu
[2]Department of Biomedical Engineering, Case Western Reserve University
Cleveland FES Center
Cleveland, OH 44106

Motor neuroprostheses can provide standing, stepping, and walking functions for individuals with hemiplegia or paraplegia; and can provide grasping and reaching functions for individuals with tetraplegia. Motor neuroprostheses are designed to give the user control of the patterned electrical activation of his or her muscles. There are over 30 different clinically-deployed upper or lower extremity neuroprostheses reported in the literature, ranging in complexity from single channel surface stimulators to multi-channel implanted stimulator-telemeter systems. Significant functional gains have been reported for these applications and there are a number of commercially available systems. Motor neuroprostheses provide a tool for improving the independence of disabled individuals in a manner that cannot be achieved through any other means.

1. Introduction

Neuroprostheses have been developed for the restoration of joint movement in central nervous system (CNS) diseases. This includes the coordination of movements in a paralyzed upper extremity to produce grasping and reaching, and in the lower extremity to produce standing, stepping, and walking. The majority of these systems have been implemented in individuals with stroke (primarily in the lower extremity) and spinal cord injury (in both upper and lower extremities), although efforts to provide function in cerebral palsy and multiple sclerosis have received limited attention. Neuroprostheses have not been implemented in diseases that result in damage the peripheral nervous system due to the difficulty in activating muscle directly with safe levels of stimulation.

The first motor neuroprosthetic systems were developed in Ljubljana, Slovenia. In 1961, Lieberson et. al. [76], reported on a single channel peroneal nerve stimulator to provide ankle dorsiflexion during the swing phase of gate. The first upper extremity neuroprosthesis was described by Long and Masciarelli [78]. This system was an orthosis with a spring providing grasp closure and used electrical stimulation of the thumb extensor muscle to release the grasp. Weak muscle response was a major limiting factor in these early systems, and a key breakthrough in motor neuroprostheses was the discovery that electrical exercise of paralyzed muscle resulted in a stronger, more fatigue-resistant muscle [78]. Today, there are many clinicians and researchers pursuing neuroprosthetic applications which provide both upper and lower extremity function. These applications range from simple single channel devices activating a single muscle, to complex multichannel microprocessor controlled devices.

Electrical stimulation of both upper and lower extremities is also used for many therapeutic applications, in addition to the neuroprosthetic applications described in this chapter. In *therapeutic applications*, the goal is to produce a functional benefit that lasts beyond the application of the stimulation itself, such as motor-relearning or functional recovery. In *neuroprosthetic applications*, it is expected that the primary functional benefit is realized while the system is actively stimulating. However, neuroprosthetic systems can provide benefits beyond the stimulation itself, such as increased range of motion and increased muscle bulk. Nevertheless, the primary goal of a neuroprosthesis is to provide a functional benefit through the direct movement of joints achieved by electrically elicited muscle contractions.

The basic components of motor neuroprostheses are shown in Figure 1. Motor neuroprostheses essentially provide a means of bypassing the damaged motor pathways of the CNS, utilizing electrical stimulation to produce muscle contractions. Motor neuroprostheses, in their simplest form, consist of a user-generated command input which initiates the coordinated delivery of electrical stimulation to one or more paralyzed muscles. Feedback can be incorporated into the neuroprosthesis, either internal to the neuroprosthesis, or provided as sensory feedback directly to the user. In this chapter, we will compare and contrast the neuroprosthetic applications providing upper and lower extremity function, as summarized in Table 1.

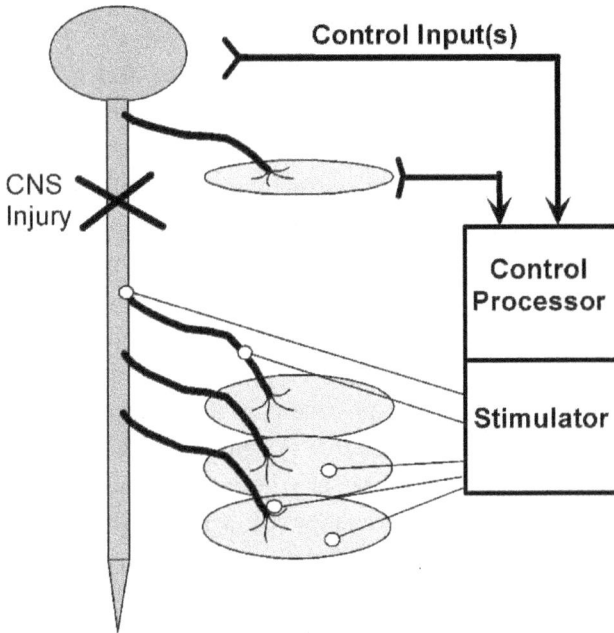

Fig. 1. General motor neuroprosthetic system components. One or more control signals are obtained from the user from above the level of injury. Examples of control signals include the operation of switches, joint motion, myoelectric control, voice control, etc. The signal is processed and used to determine the stimulation levels through a control algorithm, usually implemented electronically or through software in the processing unit. Based on the instructions generated by the processing unit, the stimulator delivers the appropriate stimulus levels to each electrode. Electrodes can be placed within the muscle, on the peripheral nerves or in the spinal cord.

Table 1. Comparison of implanted upper and lower extremity neuroprosthetic systems.

Feature	Upper Extremity	Lower Extremity
Number of electrodes	4 to 20	8 to 50
Stimulation Frequency	12–16 Hz	20–50 Hz
Stimulation Amplitudes	20 mA	20 mA
Stimulation Duration	0–200 µS	0–350 µS
Control Source	Joint Movement, Switches	Finger Switches, Contact Sensors
Control Algorithm	Proportional to Control Input	Time-based Patterns
Feedback	Visual, Auditory, Electrocutaneous	Foot Switches
Bracing	Wrist orthosis when necessary	AFO in most cases, extensive bracing in some cases
Conditioning Regimen	8 hours/day, 7 days/wk	2 hours/day, 3 days/wk
Muscle Fatigue	Minor problem	Major problem
Energy Consumption	Negligible	Considerable

2. Motor Neuroprosthesis Components

Neuroprosthetic motor systems can be categorized according to the location of the various components relative to the skin, as shown in Figure 2. Neuroprostheses can be completely external, in which case no foreign material is introduced into the body and only the stimulating current crosses the skin boundary. When subsystems are implanted (for example, the electrodes and/or stimulus delivery circuitry), communication must be maintained with those parts of the system remaining outside of the body. This can be done by direct percutaneous connection, or via a radio-frequency (RF) transmission. Implanting components of the system requires additional circuitry (RF transmitters and receivers) to complete the communication pathways, and may increase the complexity of the design. In spite of the required surgery, implantable systems offer the advantage of placing the stimulating electrodes in close proximity to neural structures, greatly increasing the selectivity and efficiency of activation while simultaneously reducing the current required. In some configurations, the control input transducer is also implanted inside the body. Until recently, there have been no totally implanted systems due to the lack of an implanted power source capable of generating the power needed for these systems.

The stimulation waveforms used in motor neuroprostheses are based on the well-established parameters of safe nerve and muscle stimulation. All current clinically deployed motor neuroprostheses use cathodic first, charge-balanced biphasic stimuli with safe levels of charge density. Most applications use current-controlled stimuli to allow direct control of the charge delivered to the tissue. Stimulation frequencies range from 12 to 50Hz, with lower extremity systems typically operating in the higher end of this range. The stimulating pulse duration is less than 350 µs. Current amplitudes vary with the type of electrode used for stimulation. Surface electrodes require 50-100 V to overcome the electrode-skin impedance, and can require in excess of 100 mA in order to achieve activation of nerves deep in the tissue. Intramuscular electrodes require 10-20 mA in order to fully activate a large muscle. Electrode-tissue impedances for intramuscular electrodes are 500-1000 Ω, resulting in required stimulator voltages of 20-40 V to insure constant current regulation. Electrodes placed on or around a nerve generally require less than 1 mA for complete activation of the motor fibers within the nerve.

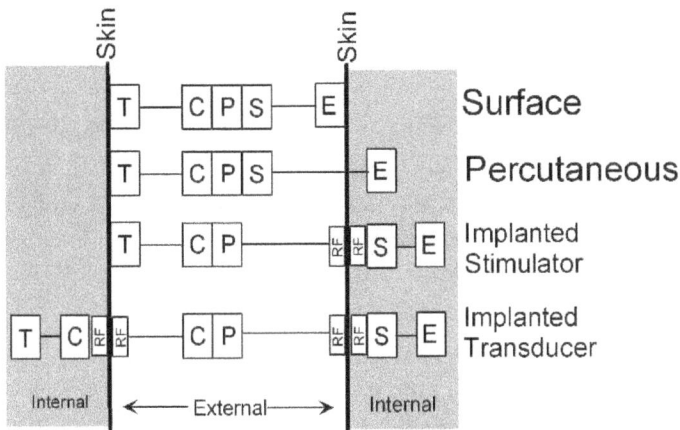

Fig. 2. Classification of motor neuroprostheses based on the relationship of components to the skin. Components are: T= Transducer, C=Control Processing, P=Processor, S=Stimulator, E=Electrodes, RF=RF link. Four types of systems currently exist: 1) surface stimulation systems, in which all components are external, 2) percutaneous systems, in which the electrode is placed within the muscle or on the nerve, with the lead exiting through the skin, 3) implanted stimulator systems, which use RF transmission for control of the implanted stimulator and 4) implanted transducer, where an implanted transducer transmits its signal out of the body through an RF link.

Every neuroprosthesis has an electronic controller/stimulator, often driven by microprocessor circuitry. The controller/stimulator can be divided into four units: 1) a stimulation output stage, 2) a control signal conditioning stage, 3) a processing algorithm to convert the control signal into the necessary stimulus levels, and 4) a power supply and regulator. In some cases the stimulus generator is implanted, but in all applications to date there is an external control unit that contains the power and processing capacity for the system.

3. Clinical Objectives of Motor Neuroprostheses

3.1. *Lower extremity*

The overall objective of applying neuroprostheses in cases of lower extremity disability is to restore mobility. Historically, it was expected that neuroprostheses would replace wheelchairs as the most common mode of mobility restoration. Although this may still be possible in the future, many researchers have focused on more attainable goals, such as standing for wheelchair transfers and reaching tasks, and to provide options for short-duration mobility-related tasks, such as overcoming physical obstacles or architectural barriers in the vicinity of the wheelchair.

Clinical outcome measures for lower extremity systems include standing time, walking distance and walking speed. Percent of body weight supported by the arms is an important outcome measure. Minimizing energy consumption is also a critical factor in lower extremity systems, and energy consumption is often used to compare systems [12]. For systems that primarily provide standing functions, the ability to perform new activities, such as reaching items off of a shelf, is measured. User satisfaction and usage rates are also recorded.

3.2. *Upper extremity*

The objectives of upper extremity neuroprostheses are to reduce the need of individuals to rely on assistance from others, reduce the need for adaptive equipment, reduce the need to wear braces or other orthotic devices, and reduce the time it takes to perform tasks. Basic activities of daily living such as eating, personal hygiene, writing and office tasks are the types of functions provided by the neuroprosthesis. Unlike lower extremity mobility, where the wheelchair is the universally accepted standard treatment, there are no standard alternatives for providing true grasping and reaching functions.

The outcome measures for upper extremity systems include pinch force, grasp and release of standardized objects, and increased independence in daily activities. Function gained with the neuroprosthesis is compared to the function using the best available alternatives, which include orthotics and adaptive equipment. Home use is also recorded as a measure of the neuroprosthesis effectiveness. This can be measured using surveys or through device data logging capabilities [145].

4. Targeted Disabilities and Candidate Selection

4.1. *Lower extremity*

The vast majority of individuals who have utilized lower extremity neuroprostheses are those with hemiplegia due to stroke. This is because only a single limb needs to be controlled with electrical stimulation, and in many cases there still exists some residual function in the impaired limb. Although footdrop in stroke was the first targeted application, there has been considerable work to provide systems for hemiplegic individuals with knee and hip flexion deficits as well.

The other major disability group targeted for lower extremity neuroprostheses is spinal cord injury. Neuroprosthetic systems for individuals with thoracic level injuries have been developed using coordinated stimulation of both lower extremities for standing, walking, and even stair climbing. More recently, systems to provide standing to assist in wheelchair transfers have been applied to spinal cord injury (SCI) individuals as high as C6. Lumbar level injuries are typically excluded from neuroprosthetic application because of the extensive denervation of key lower extremity muscles.

Not all individuals with SCI are candidates for lower extremity neuroprostheses because some clinical presentations contra-indicate the application of electrical currents, joint mobilization, or weight bearing. However, several precautions can be taken to prevent interfering complications from developing, and several other clinical interventions can be identified to address pre-existing medical contra-indications in preparation for standing or walking with neuroprostheses. Several medical conditions need to be identified early when screening potential candidates for lower extremity neuroprostheses programs. The major physical barriers to application of neuroprostheses are summarized below.

Range of motion limitations and soft tissue contractures will significantly limit neuroprostheses use in standing and walking, and should be aggressively prevented and treated.

Spasticity can be troublesome for the patient trying to stand and walk with a neuroprosthesis. Exercise with neuroprostheses appears to result in stronger, but less frequent, involuntary spasms. Medication is recommended for controlling spasticity that may interfere with function. However, neuromuscular blocking agents that may adversely affect the excitability of the peripheral nerve or muscle contractility should be avoided.

High grade *pressure sores* that may require surgery can be contra-indications to the application of neuroprostheses. Certain muscles that might be utilized for standard surgical repairs may be critical for standing or walking with neuroprostheses.

Joint instability appears to be a common problem at the hip among spinal cord individuals [7]. Soft tissue stretching of the adductors and flexors, control of spasticity, and prophylactic abduction bracing will help prevent the contractions and deforming forces that may contribute to subluxation. Should subluxation occur, surgical procedures such as soft-tissue releases and bony supplementation are possible. Early surgical intervention is strongly recommended for established instabilities.

Spinal deformities occur in many patients with spinal cord injury [26] and may compromise standing posture requiring excessive use of the arms for stability during lower extremity neuroprosthetic applications.

Finally, *peripheral denervation* is the most common contraindication for neuroprosthetic application. In the lower extremity, the highest incidence of denervation may be expected to occur in individuals with T12-L3 level injuries.

4.2. *Upper extremity*

The most clinically advanced upper extremity neuroprostheses have been applied to individuals with C5 and C6 motor level complete spinal cord injury. These patients have good control of shoulder motion and strong elbow flexion and may also have voluntary wrist extension. These individuals can move their arm in space and bring their hand to their face, but they do not have the ability to grasp and hold utensils. For these individuals, the provision of grasp opening and closing using electrical stimulation provides a distinct functional benefit. For injuries at the C4 level and higher, control of elbow flexion and shoulder abduction must be provided, greatly increasing the complexity of the system. Neuroprostheses have been applied to a limited extent to these individuals, but there are no clinically deployed systems for this population to date.

The contra-indications for upper extremity applications are similar to those for lower extremity applications. *Joint contractures* must be corrected or the grasp functions will be limited.

Spasticity must be under control, although this is not nearly as much of an issue in the upper extremity as it is in the lower extremity.

For implant systems, problems such as *pressure sores*, persistent urinary tract or other chronic *infections* are contraindications. Neither age nor time post-injury appear to be major factors when considering neuroprosthetic applications.

Peripheral denervation is a significant consideration in upper extremity neuroprostheses because there is almost always some motor horn cell loss that occurs in the spinal segments below the level of function preservation. As a result, individuals with cervical level SCI will almost always have some denervated forearm and hand muscles. Nevertheless, Peckham and Keith [98] found that between 80 and 100% of the muscles necessary for grasp had sufficient innervation intact to generate functional levels of force. In many cases, other paralyzed muscles can be used to substitute for the function that is not available, although this may require surgical intervention [38].

Individuals who are motivated and desire greater independence are the best candidates for neuroprostheses. In addition, most current neuroprostheses still require the user to have assistance in donning the device, so it is necessary for the individual to have good attendant support.

The application of upper extremity neuroprostheses in stroke has been limited to either: 1) systems primarily targeted for therapeutic applications such as motor recovery or improved range of motion or 2) systems limited to research evaluation in a few human subjects. There are two major impediments to the application of neuroprostheses in stroke. First, the spasticity of antagonist muscles makes fine control of grasp difficult to achieve. Second, since the individuals usually have one normally-functioning upper extremity, the potential functional benefits in this population are limited. Unlike the lower extremity, where bilateral function is essential, nearly every functional task using the upper extremity can be performed to some degree with a single functioning arm. Issues such as neglect and cognitive deficits also make upper extremity applications difficult in stroke.

5. Motor System Requirements

5.1. *Lower extremity*

Motor neuroprostheses for footdrop use activation of the tibialis anterior and peroneal muscles to gain ankle dorsiflexion. The simplest systems for walking use a combination of activation of the quadriceps muscle coupled with the triggering of a flexion withdrawal reflex. The withdrawal reflex is triggered by stimulation of the sensory component of the peroneal nerve, and results in hip, knee and ankle flexion. This combination allows walking functions to be generated with as few as two electrodes per leg. When the number of electrodes are minimized, bracing is often used to support joints that are not under active control.

Muscles activated to provide standing and walking motions in SCI can be divided into seven functional groups: 1) hip extensors (gluteus maximus, semi-membranosus, posterior adductor), 2) hip flexors (iliopsoas, sartorius, tensor fasciae latae), 3) hip abductors (gluteus medius), 4) knee extensors (vastus lateralis, vastus intermedius), 5) ankle dorsiflexors (tibialis anterior), 6) ankle plantar flexors (soleus), and 7) trunk extensors (erector spinae). It is not unusual for multiple electrodes to be placed in the same muscle in order to achieve full activation of the muscle.

The most complex systems (in terms of muscle activation), developed by Marsolais and colleagues use up to 48 separate muscles (via a combination of 40 chronically indwelling intramuscular electrodes with percutaneous leads plus eight surface electrodes). Kobetic, et al. [66] compared the walking characteristics of systems utilizing eight versus sixteen electrodes. They demonstrated that the higher number of channels produced higher gait speeds and provided more capacity for functional movements such as side-stepping.

Another approach to activation of lower extremity muscles is to utilize nerve-based electrodes. These electrodes include epineural and nerve cuff electrodes placed on or around motor nerves such as the peroneal nerve [22,53,131,137]. Stimulation of the spinal roots (L2–S2) can be accomplished using intradural electrodes [144]. Nerve electrodes require lower currents than intramuscular electrodes, but may not produce responses that are isolated to single muscles, especially when stimulating at the spinal root level.

Muscle conditioning is an important component of motor neuroprostheses. Electrical stimulation is used to build muscle strength and endurance. Most users of neuroprostheses will need to maintain a conditioning regimen in order to retain functional capacity. The conditioning regimen for lower extremity neuroprostheses typically consists of a patterned stimulation session lasting two hours, with multiple sessions per week. Many spinal cord injured individuals continue to use the neuroprosthesis for muscle conditioning, even if they do not make regular use of it for other functional tasks, because it maintains muscle tone and provides a cardiovascular workout for them [12,123].

5.2. *Upper extremity*

Essentially every muscle in the forearm and hand has been used in upper extremity neuroprostheses, but five muscles are necessary to provide the essential grasping functions: adductor pollicis, extensor pollicis longus, abductor pollicis brevis, extensor digitorum communis, and flexor digitorum superficialis. Since more force is required in flexion than extension, a second thumb and finger flexor are often utilized, usually the flexor pollicis longus and flexor digitorum profundus. Wrist extensors, forearm pronators, and even the finger intrinsic muscles have also been used [73,75,113]. More recently, stimulation of the triceps to provide elbow extension has become common practice [13,17,19,31].

Selectivity is an important characteristic of upper extremity electrodes. A highly selective electrode is one which only recruits fibers from a single muscle even at high stimulus levels. Because the muscles in the upper extremity are small, and the nerves to different groups of muscles lie close to each other in the forearm, it can be difficult to obtain a selective response. Electrode placement is therefore critical to the success of upper extremity motor neuroprostheses.

Because of the importance of selectivity in upper extremity neuroprostheses, nerve based electrodes have not been used. The most distal branches of the motor nerves are too small and difficult to access for nerve cuff electrodes. Proximally, it is difficult to isolate stimulation to a single muscle because this would require activating a single fascicle within the nerve. There have been some attempts to accomplish this with innovative electrode designs and stimulus delivery, but these have not been tested in the upper extremity [33].

Muscle conditioning is also utilized in upper extremity systems just as it is in lower extremity systems. Because the muscle forces are smaller, and the joint movements are not so vigorous, users can sleep during the muscle conditioning session. As a result, users can exercise as much as eight hours per day, seven days per week, while they are sleeping. Typically, however, regular functional users find that they usually only need to exercise every other night (or less) in order to maintain adequate fatigue resistance and strength.

6. Stimulation Patterns

6.1. *Lower extremity*

Lower extremity movements generated by neuroprostheses are always patterned and cycled movements. These patterns are triggered by a user-controlled switch, and the stimulus pattern proceeds to completion at a preprogrammed rate unless it is interrupted by another control input. Therefore, the focus in lower extremity systems is on the development of highly coordinated stimulus patterns. The timing of individual muscle activity is never under continuous control by the user because this would be mentally exhausting and impractical.

The stimulation pattern developed for lower extremity systems describes the relationship between time (relative to an identified event in the gait cycle) and the stimulus intensity delivered to each muscle. The stimulation can be ramped up to a maximum level, and the majority of electrodes are stimulated at their maximum level during some portion of the gait cycle. In all cases to date, trial and error is used to develop and fine-tune the stimulation patterns for each subject. This can be a difficult task, especially when the number of electrodes approaches 50. Multi-joint muscles further complicate the development of stimulus patterns because the action at a single joint cannot be independently optimized. A detailed review of the procedure for developing stimulus patterns in lower extremity neuroprostheses can be found in Kobetic and Marsolais [64] and Kralj et al. [69]

In the simplest systems, standing is achieved by simultaneously activating the quadriceps bilaterally in response to a command input, such as the simultaneous depression of switches on the handles of a rolling walker or crutches. A stride is produced by maintaining activation to the quadriceps of the stance limb while initiating a flexion withdrawal in the contralateral limb via afferent stimulation of the swing limb side. To complete the reaching phase of the stride, activation of the knee extensors on the swinging limb is initiated while the reflex is still active and flexing the hip. The stimulus producing the flexion reflex is then removed, leaving the user in double-limb support once again with bilateral quadriceps stimulation. The user then moves the walker or other supporting aid and repeats the procedure for the opposite limb. Trunk extension is usually achieved passively by adopting a C-curve posture or by activating the gluteal muscles to extend the hips.

The same basic pattern is followed in more complex systems, but each muscle can be independently activated and controlled. Rather than use a flexion withdrawal reflex, individual hip, knee, and ankle flexors are activated. The relative timing of the activation of these muscles can be fine-tuned to provide a smoother gait motion. Trunk extension is achieved by activating the gluteal muscles and the erector spinae muscles. Independent control of each muscle allows alternative patterns, such as stair-climbing and side stepping, to be programmed as well.

6.2. *Upper extremity*

Stimulation patterns in upper extremity systems are developed through trial and error, similar to lower extremity systems. In upper extremity systems, the stimulus patterns describe the relationship between the input proportional command signal and the stimulus level to each electrode. The rate of change is often determined entirely by the user. A rule-based system has been developed to aid in the process of determining the stimulation patterns [58]. Although methods for automating this procedure have been proposed, they have not been utilized clinically, due in large part to the simplicity and relative success of the rule-based methods [55].

Unlike lower extremity systems, the maximum stimulation levels utilized in upper extremity systems are rarely determined by the maximum stimulator output. Instead, the maximum stimulus level is almost always limited by activation of other muscles as the current spreads beyond a single muscle. In addition, it is often undesirable to have extremely high grasp forces because of the tendency to crush objects or squeeze them out of the hand. Therefore, the stimulation level is limited based on the desired functional goals.

Several grasp patterns are generally provided for functional activities. The two primary patterns are lateral pinch and palmar prehension. These are supplemented by additional grasp patterns as the user develops proficiency or wishes to accomplish additional tasks which benefit from other movement patterns. These include power grip and a flat pinch (for grasping objects like sandwiches). Other grasp patterns have been described for use in neuroprostheses, including a "pinch grip" between the index and thumb [94] and "parallel extension grasp" with finger extension and thumb abduction [35].

Lateral pinch is used for holding small utensils such as a fork, spoon, or pencil. In the open phase of this grasp, the fingers and thumb are extended. The fingers are then fully flexed at all joints while the thumb remains extended. The thumb is then flexed against the lateral aspect of the index finger to produce pinch. *Palmar prehension* is used for acquiring large objects. The fingers are extended and the thumb is posted in full abduction. The fingers then flex against the thumb, ideally resulting in contact between the tip of the thumb and the tips of the index and long fingers. Thumb flexion can be added to increase grasp force if needed. *Pinch grip* is a modification of the palmar grasp, where the index finger and thumb make contact, while the other fingers remain extended. This grasp is used for picking up and manipulating small objects. *Parallel extension grasp* involves extension of the fingers and adduction of the thumb. This can be accomplished with stimulation of the ulnar nerve at the wrist, recruiting thumb adductor and finger intrinsic muscles. This grasp is used for holding things in the hand, such as playing cards. Stimulated control of the wrist is sometimes incorporated into the grasp patterns, although most systems use braces to fix the wrist if the patient does not have voluntary control of wrist extension. Without stabilization, stimulation of the finger flexors generates a strong flexion moment about the wrist.

7. User Generated Control Signals

7.1. *Lower extremity*

Since most lower extremity neuroprostheses have been implemented in individuals with normal or near-normal hand function, finger switches are the most common means of allowing users to control the functions of their neuroprosthesis. These switches can be mounted on walkers or in crutches, or can be worn like a ring on the finger. The Cleveland system utilizes a finger-mounted joystick, which allows the user to select from a menu of options to initiate functional patterns [21].

Ideally, gait would be controlled using subconscious cues and would not require continual input from the user. Attempts to identify these cues are described in § 8.1. For the near future, however, finger activated switches are likely to remain as a simple control method for lower extremity neuroprostheses.

7.2. *Upper extremity*

In contrast to lower extremity systems, identifying a method of control for upper extremity systems is probably the biggest challenge currently faced in neuroprosthesis design. Because of their extensive paralysis, quadriplegic individuals have few voluntary movements that can be used as command sources. None of the control methods developed to date are ideal, and the ultimate choice of the control method depends on the user's goals and physical abilities. Even the criteria for an "ideal" control is not well-established for upper extremity neuroprostheses [74,94,114].

Control signals issued by the user are utilized in one of two ways to control grasp: 1) as a proportional command signal or 2) as a state or logic command. For a proportional command, the magnitude of the system response is graded according to the magnitude of the command signal. State command is an on/off or yes/no command, initiating a change in the mode of operation of the system. Many neuroprostheses use a proportional control for grasp opening and closing and use one or more state commands to switch between different grasp patterns or carry out other features.

The simplest form of control is to use large switches that can be operated by the palm or forearm and can be mounted on the wheelchair or some other location within reach of the user. They are simple to use and understand, and provide a reliable and repeatable signal. The major disadvantage of switches is that they require the user to occupy their opposite arm to control their instrumented arm. This usually means that tasks have to be done one handed and the individual must have, at a minimum, voluntary elbow flexion in both arms (C5 SCI or lower bilaterally). It can also be difficult to locate switches where they are always accessible to the patient. For example, switches located on a wheelchair can become inaccessible when the user is working at a table.

Movement of the contralateral shoulder to control grasp opening and closing has been a popular choice for proportional control of neuroprostheses [8,14,35,46,89,120]. Specifically, movement of the contralateral sterno-clavicular joint is used as a proportional control source for grasp opening and closing. The sterno-clavicular angle is determined using a joystick transducer or resistive tube that is taped to the chest. This type of control allows both hands to be free to perform tasks, although there is some interference with two handed movements [46]. The use of shoulder control generally requires that the system have a "lock" feature because it is too difficult to maintain the shoulder in one position in order to hold the grasp closed for a long period of time, such as for writing or eating. The lock enables the user to "disconnect" the grasp from the proportional control source so that the grasp remains at a constant level regardless of shoulder position [46]. The "lock" signal can be triggered by a quick shrug of the shoulder.

The use of wrist extension/flexion to control grasp opening and closing has been another popular choice [40,109,112]. Control of grasp by wrist motion works in coordination with the tenodesis grasp that patients are already trained to use. Wrist extension closes the grasp, wrist flexion (by gravity) opens the grasp. If a lock is necessary, it is usually provided by a switch. Wrist control is much more amenable to bilateral control than shoulder control because the control is derived from the instrumented hand and there is synergy between extension of the wrist (the control signal) and hand grasp (the output). This leads to a more natural relationship between the user's intention and the action.

There are fewer control (command) options for higher level spinal cord injured patients. Head movement or head orientation has been used as both a proportional and logic command [37,103,140]. Respiration control, such as the sip/puff signal used for wheelchair control, has been evaluated as a neuroprosthetic control signal [44]. One major disadvantage of respiration control is that it is difficult to use while eating, which is one of the tasks for which the neuroprosthesis is frequently utilized.

Voice control is a potentially appealing control method because of the ability to generate a wide variety of control signals. However, there are major drawbacks with the implementation of voice control in an upper extremity neuroprosthesis. First, as with respiration control, it is difficult to use while eating or drinking. Secondly, users are self-conscious about having to "talk to their hand" in a public setting. It is also more difficult to implement a proportional control using voice commands. Nevertheless, some systems have been developed using voice commands for testing in the laboratory [36,37,95].

The use of myoelectric signals (MESs) from muscles under voluntary control by the patient provides a great variety of potential signal sources. MESs were used in the earliest implementation of neuroprosthetics to the upper extremity[136]. There are two major difficulties that have to be overcome to use MES control. First, suitable control muscles have to be found. Potential control muscles include those synergistic to the grasp movement, such as wrist extensors and, to a lesser extent, brachioradialis, as well as non-synergists such as sternocleidomastoid and auricularis posterior. Secondly, the MES must be obtained in the presence of stimulus artifacts that are huge in comparison to the signal and tend to saturate the amplifiers. These difficulties have been overcome to various degrees in different implementations [40,103,112,124]. More recently, there has been exploration on the availability of viable MES signals from the lower extremity in people with complete (ASIA A) or motor complete (ASIA B) spinal cord injuries. Surface muscle recordings in up to 12 muscles on each side below the knee have been made in each of 24 subjects, and most have at least one muscle in each extremity, and usually more, that exhibit the features that would most likely be sufficient for viable control signals. This realization potentially provides a significant additional number of control sites possible for MES control [90]. MES control is likely to become the most common form of control for upper extremity neuroprostheses because of its applicability to almost any disabled individual.

Brain computer interface signals have also been explored as control sites for upper extremity neuroprosthesis. A complete discussion of BCI is outside of this chapter (but see chapter 2.7). These demonstrations have consisted of electrodes for recording from the skin surface over the cortex and recording with penetrating electrodes. Early demonstrations of surface recordings for control of stimulated muscles were provided both by Lauer [72] and by Pfurtscheller [92]. These studies demonstrated BCI for controlling grasp and release of an implanted Freehand system, with the BCI substituting for the Freehand's external shoulder control. In both cases, BCI signals were recorded largely without the interference of artifacts of the stimulation pulses, and demonstrated the fundamental concept. More recently, indwelling penetrating electrodes (Blackrock®) have been used. Ajiboye et al. [1] demonstrated complex movement restoration in a subject with C4 injury, showing control of the upper arm, elbow, and hand grasp release with stimulation provided by percutaneous electrodes for stimulation of the peripheral nerves. Bouton et al [10] demonstrated the use of a Blackrock penetrating array to control grasping movement with a surface stimulation matrix placed over the forearm to activate muscles. Functional use of the limb has been demonstrated in both cases.

The lack of an ideal control source is one of the reasons that there are not neuroprostheses implemented for the upper extremity in stroke. For these patients, it would be unacceptable to occupy their non-impaired hand to control their impaired hand. The tolerance for systems that are not "natural" to operate is very low in this patient population.

8. Neuroprosthesis Feedback

8.1. *Lower extremity*

The primary purpose for incorporating feedback into lower extremity neuroprostheses is to free the user from having to manually trigger each step or movement using a finger switch. Feedback could also be used to detect missteps and stumbling. Considerable research has been performed to develop sensors that can be used to detect various stages of the gait cycle and use that information to control the timing and sequencing of stimulation patterns in lower extremity applications. Sensors that have been evaluated include: foot switches, force sensitive resistors, inclinometers, goniometers, gyroscopes, accelerometers, myoelectric signals, and nerve recording signals [97]. None of these sensors been proven to be foolproof in real life situations. For example, foot switches cannot differentiate between foot contact during gait and loading and unloading during weight shifts. Position and movement sensors, such as goniometers, inclinometers and accelerometers, are subject to detection errors when the subject performs non-walking activities. Successful walking is very intolerant of gait cycle detection errors because a single detection error could cause the user to stumble and fall. Researchers have used combinations of sensors to try to improve performance and eliminate errors [97]. This is a continuing area of research, but at present, the only clinically-deployed systems that utilize feedback are the drop foot systems, which utilize foot switches or inclinometers.

Feedback to the neuroprosthesis user consists of readout displays on the external control box. Although electrocutaneous feedback has been proposed as a means of providing information about posture and balance, these systems have not yet been implemented outside of the laboratory.

8.2. *Upper extremity*

Vision is an important feedback component of upper extremity neuroprostheses. In all existing systems, users *must* be able to see the objects they are acquiring. Visual feedback is often supplemented with audio feedback from the neuroprosthesis. Various tones are used to indicate different system states. Electrotactile feedback can be provided by stimulating the skin surface over an area of normal sensation [110]. Electrocutaneous feedback can be provided comfortably, and patients describe the sensation as a buzzing or tapping. Both the stimulus frequency and intensity can be used to encode different types of information. At present, only one clinically-deployed system utilizes electrocutaneous feedback [57], and this feedback only indicates state information about the neuroprosthesis.

Clearly the sense of touch, pressure, temperature, etc. are important functions for which the hands are typically utilized. Although many researchers have proposed methods of recording these sensory modalities and making the patient aware of them, no practical systems have been developed. Among the impediments to implementing true sensory feedback in upper extremity systems is the lack of cosmetically acceptable and durable sensors. Haugland and Hoffer [41] proposed the use of nerve recordings as a means of detecting object contact and slip. These systems have been tested in a few patients using nerve recording cuff electrodes with percutaneous leads [42]. These systems are successful in detecting slip in a controlled environment, but have proven to be difficult to implement in an open environment, and therefore have not yet received application outside of the research setting.

9. Clinically Deployed Motor Neuroprostheses

9.1. *Lower extremity*

There are at least twenty different lower extremity neuroprostheses that have been clinically deployed and reported in the literature, as shown in Table 2. These systems can be divided into three main categories: 1) systems to correct hemiplegic gait deficits (primarily foot drop), 2) bilateral systems for standing and walking and 3) systems that combine electrical stimulation and orthotics (referred to as hybrid systems), as diagrammed in Fig. 3. These systems can be further divided into surface, percutaneous and implanted neuroprostheses. At present, the only commercially available systems are those that correct footdrop; and one surface stimulation system for walking.

Table 2. Lower extremity neuroprostheses

Type / Name or Group	Features	Ref
Hemiplegia Gait Deficit (Foot Drop)		
Footlifter - Elmetec A/S	Surface stimulation, foot switch, over 3,800 implemented	32
Unistim, Walkaide - Neuromotion	Surface stimulation, tilt sensor	141
Medtronic/Rancho Implant	Implanted stimulator, foot switch	86
Ljubljana Implant	Implanted stimulator, epineural electrode	61,128
Aalborg Implant	Nerve recording, surface stimulation	115
Odstock 2	Surface stimulation, randomized clinical trial	15
ETHZ-ParaCare	Surface stimulation, modular component design	108
Enschede Implant	Implanted stimulator, two subepineural electrodes	52,135
Bilateral Standing and Walking		
Ljubljana - hemiplegia	Surface stimulation, hand switches	70
Ljubljana - SCI	Surface stimulation, six channels	69-71
Sigmedics - Parastep	Surface stimulation, four channels, commercial device	12,30
Cleveland - Percutaneous	48 channels of percutaneous stimulation, minimal bracing	66,80
Cleveland - Implant	One or two 8 channel stimulators, multicenter trial	67,84
LARSI	Spinal root stimulation, implanted stimulator	111
Vienna - Epineural	Epineural electrodes, hand switches	53
Praxis24/FES-22 - Neopraxis	Implanted, borrows cochlear technology, 22 channels	22,23
SAUW	16 channel stimulator, epimysial and neural electrodes	137
Hybrid		
LSU-RGO II	Reciprocating gait orthosis, surface stimulation	123
HAS	Active bracing	107
Strathclyde Hybrid	Sensor-based orthosis, surface stimulation	3
Cleveland Hybrid	Percutaneous electrodes, mechanically actuated clutches	81,82,84

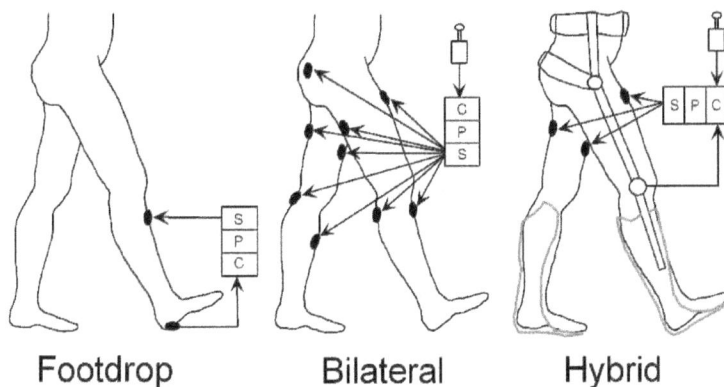

Fig. 3. Diagram of three types of lower extremity motor neuroprostheses. Foot drop systems use one or two channels of stimulation, and both surface and implanted electrode systems have been tested. Bilateral neuroprosthetic systems for standing and walking use two to 48 electrodes. These systems can use surface, percutaneous or implanted electrodes. Hybrid systems combine bracing and electrical stimulation. (C=Control Processor; P=Processor; S=Stimulator)

9.1.1. *Lower extremity neuroprosthetic systems for hemiplegia*

Neuroprostheses can be used to correct a number of gait deficits following stroke. During the swing phase of gait, diminished ankle dorsiflexion, knee flexion, and/or hip flexion can result in the inability to clear the floor with the affected limb. Neuroprostheses can be used to activate the ankle dorsiflexors, allowing the foot to clear the floor. Likewise, diminished control of weight-bearing muscles can result in gait deficits during the stance phase of gait. Gait deficits can include stance phase knee hyper-extension; hyper-flexion of the knee during stance; and deficient weight shifting to the affected limb. Neuroprostheses can be used to retrain weight-bearing muscles and improve stance phase limb control, restoring a more normal appearing gait.

In the 1970s and early 80s a single channel implantable system to correct footdrop was tested and marketed [138,139]. The system utilized an implanted stimulator located in the abdominal region linked by a single cable directly to a nerve electrode in the popliteal area. External components consisted of a heel switch and small telemetry unit that communicated foot-floor contact information to a belt-worn controller. The system successfully provided users with active dorsiflexion and long-term results were generally good. However, the reliability of early versions of the technology, in particular the external heel switch and foot-floor contact transmitter, proved to be a barrier to use. In many cases, similar clinical results could be obtained with a simple and inexpensive flexible molded ankle-foot orthosis (AFO).

Subsequent footdrop systems have sought to correct some of the technological deficits encountered with the early systems. Many researchers have used surface stimulation because of the simplicity in the initial implementation of these systems. Appropriately placed surface electrodes have been used to generate contractions of the tibialis anterior, peroneals and other muscles that, when appropriately timed to the gait cycle, actively dorsiflex the ankle and allow the foot to clear the floor during swing. Timing in this application can be controlled by simple heel switches or automatic timers that can initiate stimulation at heel rise, and continue stimulation to maintain dorsiflexion until heel contact at the end of swing, or shortly thereafter to resist the rapid acceleration of the foot into plantar flexion.

Stanic et al. [126] studied the use of multiple channels of surface stimulation timed with the gait cycle according to the electromyographic activity observed during normal walking. These systems automatically adjusted the stimulation sequences to the preferred cadence of each individual based on the timing of foot-floor contact patterns measured by insole-mounted switches. Significant improvements in the kinematics of gait occurred when electrical stimulation was applied during walking trials in the laboratory.

Commercial systems have now been developed that provide correction of foot drop. These include surface stimulation systems ODFS and ODFS Pace XL, developed in Salisbury, England by Swain and Taylor and sold by Odstock Medical; Walk-Aid, developed by Stein and colleagues in Edmonton, Alberta (Hanger Clinics); and the NESS L300 (Bioness). Implanted systems include the NeuroStep developed Hoffer in Vancouver, BC (Neurostream Technologies) and now owned by Otto Bock and ActiGait, developed by Sinkjaer and Haugland and available from Otto Bock. Recently, Peclin and colleagues reported on their 20 years of experience with an implantable stimulator for correcting drop foot (DF) via stimulation of the common peroneal nerve in a patient with left-sided hemiplegia. Long-term, daily FES was reported to provide functional and reliable recruitment of nerve fibers, thus providing a sufficient dorsal flexion and optimal eversion of the affected foot to sustain unassisted, almost normal gait. This report adds to the accumulating experience in human subjects of the safe performance of the stimulation systems [104]. It is apparent that there is an unmet clinical need in restoring function in the proximal joints of the lower extremity. Techniques and technology to accomplish this have been developed by the Cleveland group for individuals with spinal cord injury, discussed in the following section, and are now being translated to stroke survivors [79].

9.1.2. *Lower extremity neuroprostheses for posture, standing and walking*

Pioneering work in the application of surface stimulation to the restoration of standing and walking function to individuals with complete and incomplete spinal cord injuries was conducted in the 1970's and 1980's in Ljubljana, Slovenia. The techniques developed by Kralj, Bajd and others [6,68,69] continue to be employed in many laboratories and clinics around the world. Using as few as two surface stimulation channels per leg, standing and reciprocal walking is produced through a combination of direct activation of the quadriceps muscles and triggering the flexion withdrawal reflex to obtain hip, knee and ankle flexion. Standing is achieved by simultaneously activating the quadriceps bilaterally in response to a command input, such as the simultaneous depression of switches on the handles of a rolling walker or crutches.

The Slovenian group has fit systems of this type to over 50 patients with several years follow-up, and have developed extensive prescriptive criteria for individuals with various neurological deficits [6]. Patients with incomplete injuries are first evaluated for conventional orthoses alone before adding neuroprostheses. Individuals with high-level injuries are considered for combinations or orthoses and stimulation, and persons with mid- to low-level paraplegia are candidates for the surface neuroprosthesis without orthoses. These systems and implementation procedures have been successfully transferred to clinical practice. Using these principles, a commercially available surface stimulation system for standing and stepping was developed. This system, the Parastep system (Sigmedics, Inc. Northfield, IL) received FDA approval in 1994.

The reflex-based, two electrode system has some limitations. Active flexion forces at the hip are generated by the rectus femoris when the quadriceps are stimulated with surface electrodes, compromising standing stability. Not all patients will exhibit a flexion withdrawal reflex that is strong or repeatable enough to be used for stepping. Reflex stepping tends to be jerky and inconsistent, and habituates with repeated activation, limiting the number of steps that can be taken at one time.

Concentrating exclusively on standing function, rather than walking, allows the command and control structure to be greatly simplified. Jaeger and colleagues [20,45,147] adopted this approach and used techniques similar to those originally developed in Slovenia. Two channels of surface stimulation were applied to the quadriceps bilaterally, and operation consisted of manipulation of a single switch on the stimulator housing. Stimulation for standing was initiated or deactivated by a single switch depression. When activated, the standing system issued an initial audio tone. A time delay enabled the subject to prepare to stand by repositioning the hands and body immediately prior to the onset of the stimulation. A second depression of the control switch reversed the sequence and lowered the user back into the wheelchair. Protocols for implementing these systems clinically have also been developed and published along with results from small-scale clinical trials [45].

Clinicians and researchers in Cleveland, Ohio (Veterans Administration Medical Center and Case Western Reserve University), have been developing systems that utilize implanted electrodes for personal mobility functions such as standing, one-handed reaching, forward, side and back stepping, and stair ascent and descent. The Cleveland approach to lower extremity neuroprostheses has involved individual activation of many muscles via implanted muscle-based electrodes (intramuscular and epimysial), rather than the use of synergistic patterns such as the flexion withdrawal reflex or extensive bracing. Intramuscular electrodes afford access to deep structures, or anatomically adjacent nerves that are difficult to isolate and activate separately from the surface. Marsolais and colleagues have synthesized complex lower extremity motions by activating up to 48 separate muscles under the control of a programmable microprocessor-based external stimulator [64,80]. Access to deep muscles minimizes the need for bracing with the system, and only a freely-articulated ankle-foot orthosis is used to protect the ligaments and structure of the foot and ankle. All components of the system are worn by the user, freeing him or her from cabling to a walker, wheelchair or other assistive device that might interfere with transfers or other daily function.

Users select one of a series of movement patterns by scrolling through a menu of options presented on a liquid-crystal display. Switches on a command ring worn on the index finger are used to activate and deactivate the stimulation patterns. Successive depressions of the switch with the thumb initiated the next step, or insole-mounted pressure sensors can be used to sense foot-floor contact and trigger steps automatically.

Some well trained subjects can walk 300 m repeatedly at 0.5 m/s with this system. By triggering the steps with insole pressure sensors, walking speed can increase to 0.73 m/s with a cadence of 65 steps/min. Double support and swing times can average close to the nominal values of 15 and 40 percent of the gait cycle, respectively [65]. The quality of the motions produced by neuroprostheses with this system depends on the availability, strength, and endurance of paralyzed muscles, the ability of the therapist or engineer to specify patterns of stimulation for ambulation, and the subject's experience with the device [64,134]

In spite of these accomplishments, installing and maintaining systems consisting of large numbers of percutaneous intramuscular electrodes becomes impractical in the clinical setting. For this reason, the Cleveland group has pursued clinical trials of implantable lower extremity systems. Both eight-channel and 16 channel implantable receiver-stimulators developed in Cleveland [116] are being used as the platform for clinical trials of systems to facilitate standing and wheelchair transfers, walking, stair climbing, and trunk control in persons with neurologically complete or incomplete injuries at the C6-T4 levels [84]. Stimulation is delivered via epimysial, intramuscular, and nerve cuff electrodes.

A major desire of individuals with spinal cord injury (SCI) is the ability to maintain a stable trunk while in a seated position. Stability can provide better posture in regular work in the home and office environments, during wheelchair propulsion and in driving. Postural control in SCI has been a major undertaking of the Cleveland group. Systems that have been provided enable both open and closed loop control of posture. Studies include reach and accessible working volume, balance, righting, the mechanics, effort and efficiency in wheelchair propulsion and others. The overall conclusion is that postural control of the trunk with neuroprosthesis can provide both actual and perceived benefits [4,93,132]

Stimulation using the 8-channel implant applied to the knee, hip and trunk extensors can enable sit-to-stand transition and support the body vertically against collapse. Transfers to high surfaces, performing swing-to gait for short distances, and participating in other social, work and personal activities are possible. On average, 90% of body weight was supported by the legs, with light touch with the hands providing balance. System performance and patterns of usage were maintained following discharge for at least one year follow-up. Long term use of neuroprostheses for standing was safe and effective, and had no adverse physiological effects. It would seem apparent from the results of this study that an implanted standing transfer system is ready for further translation [21].

Walking in people with complete (ASIA A) and incomplete thoracic spinal cord injuries has been a major focus of the Cleveland group. Walking is a complex issue requiring generation of sufficient joint torques to provide body weight support, enable coordinated reciprocal action of muscles, weight transfer from one limb to another, postural balance, and many other factors. Walking takes place in a changing environment of ground surfaces and impediments, up and down ramps and steps. All of this must be accomplished in an energy efficient manner that competes with or complements alternate mobility means - primarily the wheelchair - and is safe for the user. Clearly this is a high order challenge.

Walking of up to 100 m has also been achieved with pre-programmed patterns of open-loop stimulation delivered via 8- and 16-channel implanted pulse generators. Stepping cycles can be either continuous, with the upper body adjusting for variations until the pattern is stopped, or with steps triggered sequentially by a ring- or walker-mounted switches or automatically from body-mounted sensors such as inclinometers, accelerometers, gyroscopes or foot/heel switches [67].

Walking for people with incomplete motor injuries requires activation of a smaller number of muscles, and would likely rely on one leg having stronger voluntary function. Walking with stimulation has demonstrated a decreased time in double support phases of gait, and muscles under volitional control could be used as control muscles to activate the gait pattern. Muscles that could be used for control include those active in the gait sequence that are synergists to the muscle to be activated, or weak muscles that would also be activated to provide greater strength. In this way, voluntary activity could be used to modulate the overall gait pattern and provide a means to continuously control the walking characteristics. Gait training with stimulation may also have a therapeutic effect in terms of improvement in walking without the neuroprosthesis. In a single case study, the use of the neuroprosthesis for improving voluntary function resulted in significant volitional improvements in 6 min walking distance and speed, speed during maximum walk, double support time, and 10 m walking speed. With the neuroprosthesis active, additional gains of muscle activation and control were sufficient to enable the subject to advance from household ambulation to limited community ambulation. Additionally, the subject could perform multiple walks per day when using FES-assisted gait, which was impossible with volitional effort alone. It is likely that the use of a neuroprosthetic intervention for walking is going to be for people with incomplete injuries before those for people with complete injuries [5,39].

9.1.3 Hybrid systems for standing and walking

Standing with neuroprostheses alone requires continuous activation of the antigravity muscles, leading to rapid fatigue. Fine control of posture and balance is currently unattainable with the present level of neuroprosthetic technology. As previously noted, activation of the flexion withdrawal reflex and quadriceps with surface stimulation introduces additional complicating factors. One method to overcome the disadvantages of standing and walking systems that rely exclusively on surface stimulation involves combining neuroprostheses with conventional bracing [3,83,122,125]. The advantages of orthotic bracing lie primarily in their ability to constrain the motions of the joints, reduce the degrees of freedom of movement and provide mechanical stability. However, walking with hip-knee-ankle-foot orthoses (HKAFOs) alone can also be prohibitively difficult because of the demands placed on the upper extremities. Combining neuroprostheses and bracing in a *hybrid orthosis* offers an opportunity to take advantage of the positive aspects of each technology and minimize the potential shortcomings.

One method of effectively combining the advantages of orthoses and neuroprostheses is under investigation at Louisiana State University (LSU). Solomonow and colleagues developed a hybrid system that utilized an LSU Reciprocating Gait Orthosis (RGO) and a custom-designed surface stimulator [48,122,125]. The LSU-RGO is a passive mechanical HKAFO with the key feature being a reciprocal coupling between the hip joints which transmits hip extension movements on one side to flexion movements on the contralateral side. This reciprocating mechanism engages automatically when the hips are fully extended upon standing up, and can be disengaged voluntarily to allow the user to return to the seated position. Individuals with complete paraplegia can walk by shifting their weight onto the stance limb, pushing up on a walker with their arms, and letting the swing limb advance as the stance limb extends.

The neuroprosthetic component of the system consists of a four-channel surface stimulator and a flexible copolymer electrode cuff that locates and maintains the surface electrodes over the rectus femoris and hamstrings. Stimulating the hamstrings with the knees locked will extend the hip and flex the contralateral limb through the action of the reciprocating mechanism. Conversely, the rectus femoris is used to flex the hip actively, rather than extend the knee, and assist with contralateral hip extension via the reciprocating mechanism. Rectus femoris and contralateral hamstrings are activated simultaneously to initiate a step upon the depression of a walker-mounted switch. The hybrid system has been fitted to approximately 50 patients to date with complete or incomplete thoracic or low-level cervical injuries at LSU and collaborating centers [48]. Similar systems employing a hip-guidance orthosis or alternative reciprocating mechanism have been devised and tested in various centers in North America and Europe [85].

With the introduction on commercial exoskeletons, it seems likely that hybrid systems utilizing the best features of both electrically stimulated muscles and the external exoskeleton will be evaluated. While the exoskeleton can provide a "platform" for movement, the power requirements for movement are extensive. A substantial potential advantage that electrical stimulation of paralyzed muscles provides, when used in conjunction with the best structural features of the exoskeleton, is that the electrically stimulated muscles requires considerable less energy than do motors to create movement. Thus, a hybrid system would benefit from weight in both batteries and the motors as well as the exoskeleton structure itself. Goldfarb demonstrated this in the hip and knee and showed cooperative control provided repeatable gait motions and reduced torque and power from the exoskeleton motors [34]. Triolo examined the feasibility of using pressurized hydraulic fluid as a source of on-demand assistive power for a hybrid neuroprosthesis, and found sufficient assistive torque needed in exoskeletal devices for walking or stair climbing beyond those possible either volitionally or with electrical stimulation alone [28,63]. While challenges remain in the combination FES-robotic control because of the non-linear behavior of the stimulated muscle and the lack of developments in the field of hybrid control, Moreno reported on an ambulatory hybrid exoskeleton that can balance robotic and FES actuation during walking [27]. Hybrid exoskeletons present a new approach for locomotor intervention for people with spinal cord injury.

9.2. Upper extremity

Clinical application of upper extremity motor neuroprostheses has not been nearly as widespread as lower extremity systems. Only ten systems have been reported, as shown in Table 3, and are categorized as surface, percutaneous or implanted systems, as diagrammed in Fig. 4. At present, there are three commercially available neuroprosthetic systems designed to provide upper extremity function for stroke or spinal cord injured individuals: Handmaster (NESS Ltd., Ra'anana, Israel; Bioness Inc., Valencia, CA), FESMate (NEC Medical Systems, Tokyo, Japan), and Freehand (NeuroControl, Cleveland, USA) [23,32,133].

Table 3. Upper extremity neuroprostheses

Type / Name or Group	Features	Ref
Surface Electrodes		
Handmaster - NESS	Hinged splint housing electrodes, FDA approval	94
Bionic Glove - Neuromotion	Glove housing electrodes, wrist position control	106,109
EZTH-ParaCare	Modular design	108
Miami Project	EMG controlled	112
Percutaneous Electrodes		
Cleveland - Percutaneous	16 channel, shoulder/wrist control, multicenter trial	25,98
FESMate - NEC	30 channels of stimulation, switch control	35
Aalborg - Nerve	Percutaneous nerve recording for slip detection	42,115
Implanted Systems		
Freehand - NeuroControl	8 channel, control by shoulder position, FDA approval	16,24,57,99,116,130
London - Implant	11 channel, joystick control, one patient	105
Cleveland IST-10/IJAT	10 channel, implanted wrist position sensor	9,100
Cleveland IST-12	12 channel, implanted myoelectric control	59
Cleveland NNP	>30channel, fully implanted, trunk and manipulation	54

* **Bold** text indicates systems that are currently being implemented.

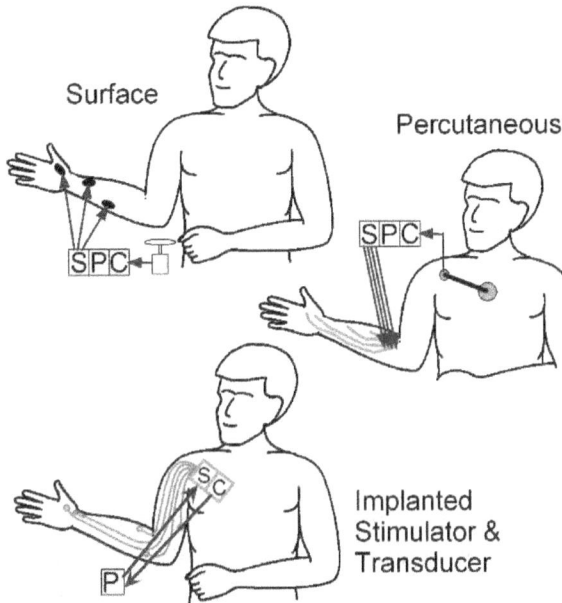

Fig. 4. Diagram of three types of upper extremity motor neuroprostheses. Surface stimulation systems use a glove or splint as a means of more easily locating the electrodes. Control is by switches (as shown) or joint movement. Percutaneous systems use up to 30 electrodes, with a variety of control mechanism, including shoulder motion (as shown). Implanted systems use up to 10 electrodes, with either shoulder or wrist motion control. The most advanced system utilizes an implanted wrist angle transducer (as shown). (C=Control Processor; P=Processor; S=Stimulator)

9.2.1 *Upper extremity surface stimulation systems*

Nathan [95] from BeerSheva, Israel developed a splint which incorporated surface electrodes for grasp called the Handmaster (NESS Ltd, Ra'anana, Israel). The brace fixes the wrist in neutral, making it applicable primarily to C5 level tetraplegic individuals who do not have a tenodesis grasp. It is more widely used for therapeutic applications in stroke. A clinical study of the Handmaster was done by Snoek et al. [121]. Ten C5/C6 quadriplegic individuals were evaluated for fitting of the neuroprosthesis, and four participated in the functional training. Functional performance was assessed in at least four tasks, which included pouring water from a can, opening a jar, opening a bottle and inserting and removing a video tape. The results demonstrated that all four of the subjects could perform at least two tasks independently using the Handmaster that they could not perform without assistance using their hand with a splint. Three of the subjects demonstrated improvement in pouring from a can and opening a bottle. Other improved tasks included shaving, putting on socks, and handling a hammer. However, in this group, only one subject continued to use the Handmaster at home. Evaluation of a similar surface stimulation unit demonstrated a significant therapeutic benefit from the stimulation [106]. The Handmaster has the CE Mark and is approved by the FDA (July, 2001) as a therapeutic device. This system is marketed by Bioness Corporation. Surface stimulation was used in a BCI controlled system for hand grasp in a single user demonstration [10]. A matrix of electrodes was placed over the forearm and stimulation applied to electrically excite the underlying muscles. This enabled the most superficial muscles of that are anatomically located in the forearm to be excited. Further development is ongoing.

9.2.2 *Upper extremity percutaneous stimulation systems*

Percutaneous electrodes allow isolated activation of upper extremity muscles and do not require the repeated donning and doffing of surface electrodes. The stimulated response of these electrodes is consistent from day to day. The use of percutaneous electrodes for motor neuroprostheses was pioneered by Peckham and Mortimer[101]. The implantation is minimally invasive, requiring needle insertion only, with no surgical exposure. The Cleveland percutaneous clinical system was the first upper extremity neuroprosthesis system to undergo multi-center clinical trials [14,50,98]. The system used up to 16 electrodes to provide palmar and lateral grasp for both C5 and C6 complete spinal cord injured individuals. Hand grasp was controlled using a shoulder position transducer. The clinical trials demonstrated significant improvements in both laboratory and home based impairment and disability assessments [91,119,127,142,146]. Percutaneous electrode systems have been implanted for well over ten years in many research subjects [87], with occasional replacement of electrodes needed in the event of an electrode failure. However, for chronic clinical applications, percutaneous systems have been abandoned in favor of implanted systems due to the need for regular upkeep of the percutaneous electrodes and percutaneous sites.

The FESMate system used up to 30 percutaneous electrodes to provide palmar, lateral and parallel extension grasp patterns, and was developed by Handa and colleagues [35-38,43,44] of Sendai, Japan, based on the Cleveland system. Grasp opening and closing was controlled by a switch operated by the opposite arm or by respiration using a sip/puff type of control. This system was primarily used in stroke for therapeutic applications, and is not available commercially.

Percutaneous electrodes are used experimentally for many research applications to demonstrate clinical feasibility of new concepts, and are a powerful tool to investigate new neural interfaces in human volunteers. Examples of these are the hand grasp system that lead to the multiple implantable systems for upper extremity control (elbow and hand) described below, systems for standing and walking, systems for full arm control in SCI using BCI [1], and interfaces for access to implanted nerve cuffs for sensory feedback in upper extremity prostheses [129].

Percutaneous electrodes are also used in commercial products. The NeuRx Diaphragm Pacing System®, manufactured by Synapse Biomedical (Oberlin, Ohio) is approved for respiratory control in spinal cord injury and amyotrophic lateral sclerosis [96]. Smartpatch® is a percutaneous peripheral nerve stimulation system developed by SPR Therapeutics (Cleveland, Ohio) for interventional pain management. Smartpatch is being evaluated in clinical trials to demonstrate its safety and effectiveness in delivering pain relief [143].

9.2.3 *Upper extremity implant stimulation systems in spinal cord injury*

An implanted upper extremity neuroprosthesis was first implanted in 1986 by Peckham, Keith, Kilgore and colleagues in at Case Western Reserve University in Cleveland in individuals with spinal cord injury. Jim Jatich who had sustained a C5 spinal cord injury, was the first pioneer to receive an implanted motor system neuroprosthesis. He used this system for 28 years before his death in 2013 of unrelated medical causes. Jim was well known to the neuroprosthesis community as an educator of the NIH, Congress, and the public. This system was commercialized by NeuroControl Corporation and was known as the Freehand System [16,24,25,51,57,99,130]. Freehand consisted of eight implanted electrodes and an implanted receiver-stimulator unit [116], providing lateral and palmar grasp to persons with C5 and C6 tetraplegia. A radio frequency inductive link provided the communication and power to the implant receiver-stimulator. Proportional control of grasp opening and closing was achieved using shoulder motion which was measured with an externally worn joystick on the chest and shoulder [46]. The Freehand System had FDA approval (August, 1997) and the CE Mark as a neuroprosthesis providing hand function for spinal cord injury, but the company ended distribution of Freehand in October, 2001. Three hundred and twelve patients were reported to have been implanted worldwide. It was successful clinically but not commercially as a venture-backed startup.

A multi-center study was conducted to evaluate the safety, effectiveness, and clinical impact of the Freehand neuroprosthesis on fifty individuals with spinal cord injuries [99]. The results showed that the neuroprosthesis produced increased pinch force in every patient. In a test of grasp and release ability using six objects of different sizes and weights [119], 49 of the 50 participants (98%) moved at least one more object with the neuroprosthesis than they could without it. The direct impact of the neuroprosthesis in the performance of activities of daily living was tested in 28 patients. Each participant was tested in 6 to 15 tasks, which included eating with a fork, drinking from a glass, writing with a pen, dialing a phone, using a computer diskette, and brushing teeth. All 28 (100%) participants improved in independence in at least one task, and 78% were more independent using the neuroprosthesis in at least three of the tested tasks. All (100%) participants preferred to use the neuroprosthesis in at least one task and 27 (96%) preferred to use the neuroprosthesis in at least three tasks. Satisfaction and daily utilization of the neuroprosthesis at home was measured through surveys and device data-logging [145]. More than 90% of the participants were satisfied with the neuroprosthesis, and most used it regularly. Follow-up surveys indicated that usage patterns are maintained at least four years post implant.

A second generation of the Freehand neuroprostheses was developed which incorporates an implanted joint angle sensor [9,47], ten stimulating electrodes, and an implanted stimulator/telemeter [117]. This was developed in response to user requests to have the sensor implanted and to provide more channels of stimulation for control of the finger intrinsic muscles (first and second dorsal interossei). Monopolar epimysial and intramuscular electrodes were used. The sensor provided the control source of grasp-release, forearm pronation, and elbow extension to persons with cervical level spinal cord injury with wrist extension proportionally generating stimulation to provide grasp, and wrist flexion providing finger and thumb extension. This system was implanted four persons with spinal cord injury at C5/C6 [100]. All subjects demonstrated increased grasp strength and range of motion, increased ability to grasp objects, and increased independence in the performance of activities of daily living, and used the systems in daily home use. The importance of this advance was to show the advantage of an implanted control source.

More recently, the second generation of the original Freehand neuroprosthesis was further developed to enable implanted myoelectric control (as an alternative to joint angle control) from two voluntarily controlled muscles and to provide stimulation of 12 paralyzed muscles. The use of myoelectric control enabled the selection of more control sites, one for proportional control and one for toggling functions on and off, and stimulation of additional muscles such as triceps for elbow extension and activation of additional muscle motor units other muscles. Epimysial and intramuscular stimulating electrodes were used, and a bipolar epimysial or intramuscular recording electrode was developed based upon the stimulating electrode design. Myoelectric control also enabled bilateral implantation such that users could control both limbs. This system has been implemented in 10 users in one limb, with the first in 2003. Three of these individuals have both limbs implanted, with the first bilateral implant in 2004.

Their levels of spinal cord injury were high C5 to low C6. As in the earlier generation systems, users similarly increased in activities of daily living, and regularly use these neuroprostheses in their homes [59] The flexible selection of muscles for use in myoelectric control and the availability of multiple channels of stimulation is an important principle that has been learned from the configuration of this systems in patients with voluntary control of considerably different muscles and muscles available for stimulation and surgical intervention.

Restoring functional control in high level (C4 and above) spinal cord injury has proven to be an extremely complex undertaking. Kirsch et al. [88] have implemented the second generation IST system in a single arm in each of two C2/C4 SCI subjects. Spiral nerve cuff electrodes were placed around upper extremity nerves and activated the intended shoulder muscles; intramuscular electrodes were used to activate distal muscles of the forearm and hand. In both individuals, the neuroprosthesis functioned properly for at least 2.5 years post-implant, and wrist, forearm, elbow and shoulder movements were achieved. A mobile arm support was needed to support the mass of the arm during functional activities. One individual was able to perform several activities of daily living with some limitations due to spasticity, while the second individual was able to partially complete two activities of daily living. While these interventions demonstrate feasibility, they also identify the significant impediments that must be overcome. Multiple degrees of freedom (joints movements) must be controlled with a high degree of accuracy, and the muscles may be weak or denervated due to damage of the anterior horn cells from the spinal cord injury. Additionally, the control signal demands require control of a substantial number of degrees of freedom and the control sites and control information are limited with high level injuries. This leads to the intriguing possibility of the brain control interface [88].

9.2.4 *Upper extremity implant stimulation systems in hemilegia*

Loss of arm and hand function is common after stroke. An implantable 12-channel electromyogram (EMG)-controlled functional electrical stimulation neuroprosthesis may be a viable assistive device for upper limb hemiplegia. A case study was done with one individual over a 2.3 yr period. The neuroprosthesis increased active range of finger extension, increased lateral pinch force, increased the number of objects that the participant could grasp and place in a Grasp-Release Test, and increased scores on the Arm Motor Abilities Test. The upper limb Fugl-Meyer score increased from 27 at baseline to 36 by the end of the study. The participant reported using the neuroprosthesis at home 3–4 days/wk, up to 3 hr/day for exercise and household tasks. The effectiveness of the neuroprosthesis to assist with ADL was dependent on the degree of flexor tone, which varied with task and level of fatigue. The EMG-based control strategy was not successfully implemented; button presses were used instead. It was found that stimulated finger extension was reduced if the participant attempted to assist the stimulation or when stimulation followed voluntary flexion. Further advancements in technology to block undesired spasticity are likely to improve ease of use and address limitations caused by muscle spasticity [62]. One such technique for blocking spasticity already developed is electrical nerve block by either high frequency alternating current or by direct current block [60].

10. Recent Advances

Advances in function in people with spinal cord injury have been made in many areas. These include limb function (bilateral use of the paralyzed hands and arms, standing and stepping function); trunk control for postural stability and rolling over; bladder and bowel control; breathing and cough. While surveys of people with spinal cord injuries have indicated the most desired of these functions [2,29], the reality is that people with spinal cord injuries desire all of these functions to be restored. If an effective neuroprosthetic intervention for spinal cord injury is to be made available, it must address these needs and realize that the target regions for intervention are throughout the body (arms, trunk, chest, legs).

The current design of all neuroprostheses is essentially characterized as one device for each function. That is, for example, for bilateral hearing, there are two devices. For bilateral hemispheric deep brain stimulation, only two leads in the same cortical region are available from a single device. Extension of the strategy of using a single device for each function is not infinitely expandable, because of the safety and complexity of having a large number of devices in the body. Furthermore, that strategy is highly unlikely to achieve commercial viability of being cost effective. With the feasibility of functional restoration of multiple organs being demonstrated in individuals with SCI, it became necessary to envision how a single platform device could serve as the technology basis for restoring these multiple functions. Because the nature of spinal cord injury is a multi-system injury that affects multiple organ systems, this new technology strategy must address many or all of the body organs with a single expandable device. A technology platform that would address multiple applications has been a conceived in two substantially different designs: the Bion and the Networked Neuroprosthesis.

The Bion is a pill shaped device that was designed for being implanted in distinctly separated regions of the body. The fundamental concept of this innovative design was a capsule with electrodes at each end of a hermetic enclosure that contains the electronics. Stimulation flowed from one end of the device and the return pathway was to the electrode at the other end. The desire was to have the Bion implanted with a minimal surgical procedure. It was developed in two forms, a RF Bion and a battery powered Bion. In the former, the RF Bion (RFB) was a small rice-sized passive device and would receive power and control information from the antenna (or coil) that had to be placed immediately over the device. The battery powered Bion (BPB) had a rechargeable battery, and would receive information to activate it from an external signal. The development of these devices was led by the team from the Alfred E. Mann Foundation and Advanced Bionics [77]. This design was an exciting contribution, but whose clinical applications have not been successful to date. It has been used in some clinical trials, where it was reported to migrate in the tissue, and even small amount of migration may significantly alter the tissue excitation. The RFB further was limited in the success of transmitting reliably to devices with different orientations and having to locate the transmitting coil over the device.

The network neuroprosthesis (NNP) is a platform technology that provides for closed loop control by a distributed system of sensors and stimulation modules. This design is a modular, scalable, fully implanted reprogrammable design that allows for both recording and stimulation, where the sites for control signal acquisition and stimulation may be remote from one another, and can be located throughout the body. The basic configuration of this device is a central unit that communicates and powers stimulating and control modules that are remotely placed at the target end position in the body. The current design of the remote modules enables two channels of bipolar recording from each sensing module and four channels of monopolar biphasic stimulation from each stimulation module. Each module includes sensors for temperature and 3-axis accelerometers. The electrodes currently used are the epimysial and intramuscular stimulating and recording electrodes described above (allowing use of a reliable neural interface that has demonstrated excellent performance in decades of human use, and upward compatibility to a new NNP for patients implanted with IRS, IST10, or IST12). The design of the circuitry and packaging allows straightforward implementation of alternative circuit designs or electrode technology without redesign of the entire platform.

The NNP is totally implanted, with no external components during use. A rechargeable battery is used for system powering, and can be recharged via a RF source with a coil placed over the implanted power module. This design is expandable to allow a large number of remote modules to be controlled by a single central "power module", which prioritizes traffic on the network. The use of a rechargeable battery enables the system to be fully implanted with no external components during daily use. Ultimately the single component with the rechargeable battery (power module) will require replacement, and the design of the NNP allows the power module to be easily accessed and replaced without disturbing any of the remote modules (similar to replacement of a cardiac pacemaker).

The NNP has received FDA Investigational Device Exemption status for feasibility testing for hand/arm/trunk control, and a first in human implant has been performed. One subject with C5 ASIA A (motor and sensory complete) spinal cord injury was implanted to provide hand manipulation (grasp and release, with several grasping patterns), elbow extension for overhead reach, and trunk control for postural balance. System testing is underway. This procedure was implemented in a single surgical procedure, and included implantation of one power module, 5 stimulation modules, 2 recording modules, and 20 intramuscular stimulating and 4 epimysial recording electrodes [54]. It is anticipated that this system will be expanded to include more functions, as described above. This would be accomplished by adding new modules for stimulation and recording near the target sites.

11. Current Status of Motor Neuroprostheses and Challenges

Motor neuroprostheses have been clearly demonstrated to provide a functional benefit for patients with both upper and lower extremity paralysis. There are no other existing methods of treatment that allow patients the capacity and satisfaction of being able to use their own muscles to accomplish tasks that they could not do otherwise. Many of these systems are just beginning to become available to the clinicians who treat these patients, and it is expected that the use of motor neuroprostheses will become more widespread in the near future.

Despite the measurable increase in independence provided by motor neuroprostheses, these systems are not yet close to restoring *normal* ability. Neuroprosthetic gait requires considerably more energy expenditure than normal gait. Neuroprosthetic grasping functions do not allow dynamic manipulation of objects in the hand. None of the existing systems provide any return of sensation, such as touch or proprioception. These are just some of the areas of considerable challenge for future research.

In light of the limitations of motor neuroprostheses, it is important to recognize the vast array of questions that have been, or are now, being answered. It is now clear that paralyzed muscles can be activated using electrical stimulation as long as the lower motor neuron is intact. Motor neuroprostheses have been implemented in individuals as long as 30 years post-injury, indicating that even chronically paralyzed muscles can be conditioned using stimulation so that they produce functional levels of force. We now know that disuse atrophy can be reversed by an intensive conditioning regimen. Stimulation can be delivered safely through electrodes indwelling in the muscle tissue. In the implanted upper extremity systems, users have gone many years without the need for alterations in their stimulation patterns, indicating excellent long-term stability of the electrode-muscle interface. These electrodes remain in the same location in the body, and are not continuously being further encapsulated by the body, i.e., the tissue response is stable.

The durability of the implanted components is another area in which reliability of components has been demonstrated. Users of implanted neuroprostheses are now approaching 20 to 30 years of use. Initial fears regarding high rates of infection and frequent lead failures have proven to be unfounded [11,21,56,99]. Lead failures are rare, in spite of the fact that the leads must cross multiple joints in the body. Infection rates are extremely low, even when leads exit percutaneously [87,118]. The materials used are well-tolerated by the body. Skin breakdown over the implanted components is also rare and can be avoided by careful placement of these components [99].

Procedures for candidate screening and selection, and neuroprosthetic implementation and training are becoming well-established. As more neuroprosthetic systems are becoming utilized by rehabilitation physicians, therapists, and surgeons in many different countries, it is apparent that, with some effort, these systems can be implemented using commonly understood medical delivery systems. Experience is now being accumulated that may lead to motor neuroprostheses becoming standard clinical treatment for individuals with spinal cord injury and stroke.

12. Commercialization Strategy

The commercialization of neuroprostheses for motor restoration provides several distinct challenges. Only one implantable motor system neuroprosthesis has received regulatory approval from the FDA - the Freehand System. Despite excellent clinical performance for the users, Freehand was taken off the market by the manufacturer primarily because the sales targets were not achieved. It also required a fairly hands-on support of a clinical specialist for clinical sites to be operational, and reimbursement proved challenging, as is the case for all new medical interventions. This experience presents a window to the challenge when introducing new rehabilitation technologies to the marketplace. Not only is the market unproven, but it is not clear the extent to which new technologies will be accepted by either the potential users or the clinician-deployers. Furthermore, the number of potential patients may be limited, thus making the "market size" uncertain. This is because there may be a small "orphan" population affected, there can be a heterogeneous presentation of the same injury, and some "tailoring" of the rehabilitation approach and technology to the individual may be necessary. Such an environment requires innovation to address this market.

One approach that is being explored by the non-profit Institute for Functional Restoration at Case Western Reserve University is to incubate technologies further across the commercialization "gap", where resources for innovation end until the business activities become attractive and viable. The Institute (IFR) will provide enduring access to innovative technologies by providing a commercialization pathway that is less dependent upon the market pressures of achieving large volume sales as the metric of success. Rather, the metric of success is a sustained ability for patients to have access to technologies that provide functional restoration. The IFR, as a non-profit, will perform pivotal clinical trials that bring resources from product sales, public grants, and philanthropy all directed toward the mission of the Institute. It will utilize the principle of "mass customization" of the technology as a fundamental part of the process, in which the technology platform can serve to provide many different functions. This design aspect is inherent in the Networked Neuroprosthesis, in which the modularity and scalability of the technology can be deployed to enable many of the desired functions for people with spinal cord injuries.

Commercialization is always facilitated when researchers employ translatable approaches at the earliest stages of discovery research, since these practices ease the process of translation. Such practices include, but are not limited to, using design controls in technology innovation, principles of good manufacturing practice, and careful study designs that provide clear evidence. This is particularly the case when the challenges of deployment are magnified by the uncertainties described above. Furthermore, researchers who are anticipating that the contributions will be utilized clinically must consider not only the specific aspects of an individual component, but also must consider this in light of the entire system that is to be deployed. That is, any individual component of a system will most likely affect operation in many other parts of the system, and reduction to practice necessitates that all system components operate harmoniously.

Engineers generally are motivated by solving problems. At this stage of development, it has been shown unequivocally that the restoration of function for people with spinal cord injuries is feasible with the use of neuroprostheses that employ stimulation of the peripheral nervous system. To date however, the problem of providing this solution in a sustainable form has not been accomplished. This can come only when a solvent business argument can be established, and this is the current focus. The NNP technology is currently in the process of being transferred into a full quality system, with the intention of having a device master file record established. Feasibility trials, conducted with earlier generations of implantable stimulators, have been conducted, and the outcomes of these trials are outstanding in showing an increase in quantifiable and beneficial clinical outcomes. The current focus is to insure that the current technology performs safely and effectively, and to move toward pivotal trials. At the completion of these trials, we expect to have demonstrated safety, efficacy, and clinical utility for restoration of multiple functions and to have identified reimbursement parameters for neuroprosthetic interventions for people with spinal cord injury. Furthermore, we anticipate that we will have demonstrated a new commercialization strategy that is applicable to bringing new interventions to small markets.

Motor neuroprostheses provide clinicians with a powerful tool for improving the independence of disabled individuals in a manner that cannot be achieved through any other means. The question to be asked regarding motor neuroprostheses is no longer "do they work?" but rather "do they work well enough to warrant widespread clinical deployment?". Issues regarding the impact on quality of life and cost-benefit are now the questions that must be addressed in clinical studies. At the same time, researchers continue to find new ways to improve functional outcomes, further increasing the clinical desirability of motor neuroprostheses.

References

1. Ajiboye, B., F. Willet, D. Young, W. Memberg, B. Murphy, J. Miller, J. Sweet, B. Walter, J. Simeral, L. Hochberg, and R. Kirsch, Functional electrical stimulation arm and hand neuroprosthesis controlled by an intracortical brain-computer-interface, *Society for Neuroscience*, 2015.
2. Anderson, K. D., Targeting recovery: priorities of the spinal cord-injured population, *J Neurotrauma*, **21**(10), 1371-83, 2004.
3. Andrews, B. J., R. H. Baxendale, R. Barnett, G. F. Phillips, T. Yamazaki, J. P. Paul, and P. A. Freeman, Hybrid FES orthosis incorporating closed loop control and sensory feedback, *Journal of Biomedical Engineering*, **10**, 189-195, 1988.
4. Audu, M. L., L. M. Lombardo, J. R. Schnellenberger, K. M. Foglyano, M. E. Miller, and R. J. Triolo, A neuroprosthesis for control of seated balance after spinal cord injury, *J Neuroeng Rehabil*, **12**(8), 1743-0003-12-8, 2015.

5. Bailey, S. N., E. C. Hardin, R. Kobetic, L. M. Boggs, G. Pinault, and R. J. Triolo, Neurotherapeutic and neuroprosthetic effects of implanted functional electrical stimulation for ambulation after incomplete spinal cord injury, *J Rehabil Res Dev*, **47**(1), 7-16, 2010.

6. Bajd, T., A. Kralj, R. Turk, H. Benko, and J. Sega, The use of a four channel electrical stimulator as an ambulatory aid for paraplegic patients, *Phys Ther* **63**(7), 1116-1120, 1983.

7. Betz, R., B. Boden, R. Triolo, M. Mesgarzadeh, E. Gardner, and R. Fife, Effects of functional neuromuscular stimulation on the joints of adolescents with spinal cord injury, *Paraplegia* **34**, 127-136, 1996.

8. Betz, R. R., M. J. Mulcahey, B. T. Smith, R. J. Triolo, A. A. Weiss, M. Moynahan, M. W. Keith, and P. H. Peckham, Bipolar latissimus dorsi transposition and functional FNS to restore elbow flexion in an individual with C4 quadriplegia and C5 denervation, *J American Paraplegia Society*, **15**(4), 220-228, 1992.

9. Bhadra, N., P. H. Peckham, M. W. Keith, K. L. Kilgore, F. W. Montague, M. M. Gazdik, and T. G. Stage, Implementation of an implantable joint angle transducer, *J Rehab Research and Development*, **39**(3), 411-422, 2002.

10. Bouton, C. E., A. Shaikhouni, N. V. Annetta, M. A. Bockbrader, D. A. Friedenberg, D. M. Nielson, G. Sharma, P. B. Sederberg, B. C. Glenn, W. J. Mysiw, A. G .Morgan, M .Deogaonkar, and A. R. Rezai, Restoring cortical control of functional movement in a human with quadriplegia, *Nature*, **533**, 247–250, 2016

11. Brindley, G., The first 500 sacral anterior root stimulators: Implant failures and their repair, *Paraplegia*, **33**, 5-9, 1995.

12. Brissot, R., P. Gallien, M. P. L. Bot, A. Beaubras, D. Laisne, J. Beillot, and J. Dassonville, Clinical experience with functional electrical stimulation -assisted gait with parastep in spinal cord-injured patients, *Spine*, **25**, 501-508, 2000.

13. Bryden, A. M., W. D. Memberg, and P. E. Crago, Electrically stimulated elbow extension in persons with c5/c6 tetraplegia: A functional and physiological evaluation, *Archives of Physical Medicine and Rehabilitation*, **81**, 80-88, 2000.

14. Buckett, J. R., P. H. Peckham, G. B. Thrope, S. D. Braswell, and M. W. Keith, A flexible, portable system for fns in the paralyzed upper extremity, *IEEE Transactions Biomedical Engineering*, **35**(11), 897-904, 1988.

15. Burridge, J. H., P. N. Taylor, S. A. Hagan, D. E. Wood, and I. D. Swain, The effect of common peroneal nerve stimulation on the effort and speed of walking. A randomised controlled trial with chronic hemiplegic patients, *Clinical Rehabilitation*, **11**, 201-210, 1997.

16. Carroll, S., C. Cooper, D. Brown, G. Sormann, S. Flood, and M. Denison, Australian experience with the freehand system for restoring grasp in quadriplegia, *Aust N Z J Surg*, **70**, 563-8, 2000.

17. Carroll, S. G., C. A. Cooper, D. J. Brown, and G. W. Sormann, Electrical activation of triceps brachii using the freehand system: A case report, *Proceedings of the 2nd Annual Conference of the International Functional Electrical Stimulation Society*, 131-132, 1997.

18. Cho W., C. Vidaurre, U. Hoffmann, N. Birbaumer, and A. Ramos-Murguialday, Afferent and efferent activity control in the design of brain computer interfaces for motor rehabilitation, *Conf Proc IEEE Eng Med Biol Soc.*, 2011.

19. Crago, P. E., W. D. Memberg, M. K. Usey, M. W. Keith, R. F. Kirsch, G. J. Chapman, M. A. Katorgi, and E. J. Perreault, An elbow extension neuroprosthesis for individuals with tetraplegia, *IEEE Transactions Rehabilitation Engineering*, **6**, 1-6, 1998.

20. Cybulski, G. R., R. D. Penn, and R. Jaeger, Lower extremity functional neuromuscular stimulation in cases of spinal cord injury, *Neurosurg*, **15**, 132-146, 1985.

21. Davis, J. A., R. J. Triolo, J. Uhlir, C. Bieri, L. Rohde, D. Lissy, and S. Kukke, Preliminary performance of a surgically implanted neuroprosthesis for standing and transfers - where do we stand? *J Rehab Res & Dev,* **38**, 609-617, 2001.

22. Davis, R., J. Kuzma, J. Patrick, J. W. Heller, J. McKendry, R. Eckhouse, and S. E. Emmons, Nucleus FES-22 stimulator for motor function in a paraplegic subject, *Proceedings of the RESNA International '92 Conference,* 228-229, 1992.

23. Davis, R., W. C. Macfarland, and S. E. Emmons, Initial results of the nucleus FES-22 implanted system for limb movement in paraplegia, *Stereotactic and Functional Neurosurgery,* **63**, 192-197, 1994.

24. Davis, S. E., M. J. Mulcahey, B. T. Smith, and R. R. Betz, Self-reported use of an implanted fes hand system by adolescents with tetraplegia, *J Spinal Cord Med,* **21**, 220-226, 1998.

25. Davis, S. E., M. J. Mulcahey, B. T. Smith, and R. R. Betz, Outcome of functional electrical stimulation in the rehabilitation of a child with c-5 tetraplegia, *J Spinal Cord Med,* **22**, 107-113, 1999.

26. Dearolf, W. W., R. R. Betz, L. C. Vogel, J. Levin, M. Clancy, and H. Steel, Scoliosis in spinal injured patients, *J Ped Orthop,* **10**, 214-218, 1990.

27. del-Ama, A. J., A. Gil-Agudo, J. L. Pons, and J. C. Moreno, Hybrid FES-robot cooperative control of ambulatory gait rehabilitation exoskeleton, J *Neuroeng Rehabil.,* **11**, 27, 2014.

28. Foglyano, K. M., R. Kobetic, C. S. To, T. C. Bulea, J. R. Schnellenberger, M. L. Audu, M. J. Nandor, R. D. Quinn, and R. J. Triolo, Feasibility of a hydraulic power assist system for use in hybrid neuroprostheses, *Appl Bionics Biomech,* **2015**, 205104, 2015.

29. French, J. S., K. D. Anderson-Erisman, and M. Sutter, What do spinal cord injury consumers want? A review of spinal cord injury consumer priorities and neuroprosthesis from the 2008 neural interfaces conference, *Neuromodulation,* **13**(3), 229-231, 2010

30. Graupe, D., and K. H. Kohn, Transcutaneous functional neuromuscular stimulation of certain traumatic complete thoracic paraplegics for independent short-distance ambulation, *Neurological Research,* **19**, 323-333, 1997.

31. Grill, J. H., and P. H. Peckham, Functional neuromuscular stimulation for combined control of elbow extension and hand grasp in c5 and c6 quadriplegics, *IEEE Transactions Rehabilitation Engineering,* **6**, 190-199, 1998.

32. Grill, W. M., and R. F. Kirsch, Neuroprosthetic applications of electrical stimulation, *Assist Technol,* **12**, 6-20, 2000.

33. Grill, W. M., and J. T. Mortimer, Quantification of recruitment properties of multiple contact cuff electrodes, *IEEE Transactions Rehabilitation Engineering,* **4**(2), 49-62, 1996.

34. Ha, K. H., S. A. Murray, and M. Goldfarb, An approach for the cooperative control of FES with a powered exoskeleton during level walking for persons with paraplegia, *IEEE Trans Neural Syst Rehabil Eng,* **24**(4), 455-466, 2016

35. Handa, Y., T. Handa, M. Ichie, H. Murakami, N. Hoshimiya, S. Ishikawa, and K. Ohkubo, Functional electrical stimulation (FNS) systems for restoration of motor function of paralyzed muscles - versatile systems and a portable system, *Frontiers Med Biol Eng,* **4**(4), 214-255, 1992.

36. Handa, Y., T. Handa, Y. Nakatsuchi, R. Yagi, and N. Hoshimiya, A voice controlled functional electrical stimulation system for the paralyzed hand, *Japanese J Medical Electronics and Biological Engineering,* **23**(5), 292-298, 1985.

37. Handa, Y., and N. Hoshimiya, Functional electrical stimulation for the control of the upper extremities, *Medical Progress through Technology,* **12**, 51-63, 1987.

38. Handa, Y., K. Ohkubo, and N. Hoshimiya, A portable multi-channel FNS system for restoration of motor function of the paralyzed extremities, *Automedica,* **11**, 221-231, 1989.

39. Hardin, E., R. Kobetic, L. Murray, M. Corado-Ahmed, G. Pinault, J. Sakai, S. N. Bailey, C. Ho, and R. J. Triolo, Walking after incomplete spinal cord injury using an implanted FES system: a case report, *J Rehabil Res Dev,* **44**(3), 333-346, 2007.

40. Hart, R. L., K. L. Kilgore, and P. H. Peckham, A comparison between control methods for implanted FES hand grasp systems, *IEEE Transactions Rehabilitation Engineering,* **6**, 1-11, 1998.

41. Haugland, M. K. and J. A. Hoffer, Slip information provided by nerve cuff signals: Application in closed-loop control of functional electrical stimulation, *IEEE Transactions Rehabilitation Engineering,* **2**, 29-36, 1994.

42. Haugland, M. K., A. Lickel, R. Riso, M. A. Adamczyk, M. W. Keith, I. L. Jensen, J. Haase, and T. Sinkjaer, Restoration of lateral hand grasp using natural sensors, *Artificial Organs,* **21**, 250-253, 1997.

43. Hoshimiya, N. and Y. Handa, A master-slave type multichannel functional electrical stimulation (FNS) system for the control of the paralyzed upper extremities, *Automedica,* **11**, 209-220, 1989.

44. Hoshimiya, N., A. Naito, M. Yajima, and Y. Handa, A multichannel FNS system for the restoration of motor functions in high spinal cord injury patients: A respiration-controlled system for multijoint upper extremity, *IEEE Transactions Biomedical Engineering,* **36**(7), 754-760, 1989.

45. Jaeger, R., G. Yarkony, and R. Smith, Standing the spinal cord injured patient by electrical stimulation: Refinement of a protocol for clinical use, *IEEE Transactions Biomedical Engineering,* **36**(7), 720-728, 1989.

46. Johnson, M. W. and P. H. Peckham, Evaluation of shoulder movement as a command control source, *IEEE Transactions Biomedical Engineering,* **37**, 876-885, 1990.

47. Johnson, M. W., P. H. Peckham, N. Bhadra, K. L. Kilgore, M. Gazdik, M. W. Keith, and P. Strojnik, Implantable transducer for two-degree of freedom joint angle sensing, *IEEE Transactions Rehabilitation Engineering,* **7**, 349-359, 1999.

48. Kantor, C., B. J. Andrews, E. B. Marsolais, M. Solomonow, R. D. Lew, and K. T. Ragnarsson, Report on a conference on motor prostheses for workplace mobility of paraplegic patients in North America, *Paraplegia,* **31**, 439-456, 1993.

49. Keith, M. W., K. L. Kilgore, P. H. Peckham, K. S. Wuolle, G. Creasey, and M. Lemay, Tendon transfers and functional electrical stimulation for restoration of hand function in spinal cord injury, *J Hand Surgery,* **21A**, 89-99, 1996.

50. Keith, M. W., P. H. Peckham, G. B. Thrope, J. R. Buckett, K. C. Stroh, and V. Menger, Functional FNS neuroprostheses for the tetraplegic hand, *Clin Orthop Rel Res,* **233**, 25-33, 1988.

51. Keith, M. W., P. H. Peckham, G. B. Thrope, K. C. Stroh, B. Smith, J. R. Buckett, K. L. Kilgore, and J. W. Jatich, Implantable functional fns in the tetraplegic hand, *Journal of Hand Surgery,* **14A**, 524-530, 1989.

52. Kenney, L., G. Bultstra, R. Buschman, P. Taylor, G. Mann, H. Hermans, J. Holsheimer, A. Nene, M. Tenniglo, H. V. D. Aa, and J. Hobby, An implantable two channel drop foot stimulator: Initial clinical results, *Artificial Organs,* **26**, 267-270, 2002.

53. Kern, H., M. Frey, J. Holle, W. Mayr, G. Schwanda, H. Stohr, and H. Thoma, Functional electrostimulation of paraplegic patients - 1 year's practical application. Results in patients and experiences, *Zeitschrift fur Orthopadie udn Ihre Grenzgebiete,* **123**, 1-12, 1985.

54. Kilgore, K. L., H. A. Hoyen, M. W. Keith, R. J. Triolo, A. M. Bryden, L. Lombardo, R. L .Hart, M. Miller, G. A. Nemunaitis, and P. H. Peckham, Implanted network for motor function in cervical SCI, *American Spinal Cord Injury Association Annual Meeting*, Philadelphia, PA, 2016.

55. Kilgore, K. L. and P. H. Peckham, Grasp synthesis for upper-extremity FNS: Part 1 an automated method for synthesizing the stimulus map for upper extremity FNS, *Medical and Biological Engineering and Computing,* **31**, 607-614, 1993.

56. Kilgore, K. L., P. H. Peckham, and M. W. Keith, The durability of implanted electrodes and leads, *Proceedings of the 7th Annual Conference of the International Functional Electrical Stimulation Society*, 193-195, 2002.

57. Kilgore, K. L., P. H. Peckham, M.W. Keith, G.B. Thrope, K.S. Wuolle, A.M. Bryden, and R. L. Hart, An implanted upper-extremity neuroprosthesis, *J Bone Joint Surg,* **79-A**(4), 533-541, 1997.

58. Kilgore, K. L., P. H. Peckham, G. B. Thrope, M. W. Keith, and K. A. Gallaher-Stone, Synthesis of hand grasp using functional neuromuscular stimulation, *IEEE Transactions Biomedical Engineering,* **36**(7), 761-770, 1989.

59. Kilgore K. L., H. A. Hoyen, A. M. Bryden, R. L. Hart, M. W. Keith, and P. H. Peckham, An implanted upper-extremity neuroprosthesis using myoelectric control, *J Hand Surg Am,* **33**(4), 539-550, 2008

60. Kilgore K. L. and N. Bhadra, Reversible nerve conduction block using kilohertz frequency alternating current, *Neuromodulation,* **17**(3), 242-254, 2014.

61. Kljajic, M., M. Malezic, R. Acimovic, E. Vavken, U. Stanic, B. Pangrsic, and J. Rozman, Gait evaluation in hemiparetic patients using subcutaneous peroneal electrical stimulation, *Scandinavian Journal of Rehabilitation Medicine,* **24**, 121-126, 1992.

62. Knutson J. S., J. Chae, R. L. Hart, M. W. Keith, H. A. Hoyen, M. Y. Harley, T. Z. Hisel, A. M. Bryden, K. L. Kilgore, and H. Peckham, Implanted neuroprosthesis for assisting arm and hand function after stroke: a case study, *J Rehabil Res Dev,* **49**(10), 1505-1516, 2012

63. Kobetic R., C. S. To, J. R. Schnellenberger, M. L. Audu, T. C. Bulea, R. Gaudio, G. Pinault, S. Tashman, and R. J. Triolo, Development of hybrid orthosis for standing, walking, and stair climbing after spinal cord injury, *J Rehabil Res Dev,* **46**(3), 447-462, 2009.

64. Kobetic, R. and E. B. Marsolais, Synthesis of paraplegic gait with multi-channel functional neuromuscular stimulation, *IEEE Transactions Rehabilitation Engineering,* **2**(2), 66-79, 1994.

65. Kobetic, R., E. B. Marsolais, P. Samame, and G. Borges, The next step: Artificial walking, in eds. J. Rose and J. G. Gamble, *Human Walking. Second Edition*, (Williams & Wilkins, Baltimore, MD, 1994), pp. 225-252.

66. Kobetic, R., R. J. Triolo, and E. B. Marsolais, Muscle selection and walking performance of multichannel FES systems for ambulation in paraplegia, *IEEE Transactions Rehabilitation Engineering,* **5**, 23-29, 1997.

67. Kobetic, R., R. J. Triolo, J. P. Uhlir, C. Bieri, M. Wibowo, G. Polando, E. B. Marsolais, and J. A. Davis, Implanted functional electrical stimulation system for mobility in paraplegia: A follow-up case report, *IEEE Transactions Rehabilitation Engineering,* **7**, 390-398, 1999.

68. Kralj, A. and T. Bajd, *Functional Electrical Stimulation: Standing and Walking After Spinal Cord Injury*, (CRC Press, Boca Raton, FL, 1989).

69. Kralj, A., T. Bajd, R. Turk, and H. Benko, Gait restoration in paraplegic patients: A feasibility demonstration using multichannel surface electrode FES, *Journal of Rehabilitation Research and Development,* **20**, 3-20, 1983.

70. Kralj, A. R., T. Bajd, M. Munih, and R. Turk, FES gait restoration and balance control in spinal cord-injured patients, *Progress Brain Res,* **97**, 387-396, 1993.
71. Kuzelicki, J., R. Kamnik, T. Bajd, P. Obreza, and H. Benko, Paraplegics standing up using multichannel fes and arm support, *J Med Eng Technol,* **26**, 106-110, 2002.
72. Lauer R. T., P. H. Peckham, and K. L. Kilgore, EEG-based control of a hand grasp neuroprosthesis, *Neuroreport,* **10**(8), 1767-1771, 1999.
73. Lauer, R. T., K. L. Kilgore, P. H. Peckham, N. Bhadra, and M. W. Keith, The function of the finger intrinsic muscles in response to electrical stimulation, *IEEE Transactions Rehabilitation Engineering,* **7**, 19-26, 1999.
74. Lauer, R. T., P. H. Peckham, K. L. Kilgore, and W. J. Heetderks, Applications of cortical signals to neuroprosthetic control: A critical review, *IEEE Transactions Rehabilitation Engineering,* **6**, 205-208, 2000.
75. Lemay, M. A. and P. E. Crago, Restoration of pronosupination control by FNS in tetraplegia: Experimental and biomechanical evaluation of feasibility, *J Biomechanics,* **29**, 435-442, 1996.
76. Lieberson, W. T., H. J. Holmquest, D. Scot, and M. Dow, Functional electrotherapy: Stimulation of the peroneal nerve synchronized with the swing phase of the gait of hemiplegic patients, *Archives of Physical Medicine and Rehabilitation,* **42**, 101-105, 1961.
77. Loeb, G. E., F. J. R. Richmond, and L. L. Baker, The BION devices: injectable interfaces with peripheral nerves and muscles, *Neurosurgical Focus,* **20**(5), 1-9, 2006
78. Long, C. and V. Masciarelli, An electrophysiologic splint for the hand, *Arch Phys Med,* **44**, 499-503, 1963.
79. Makowski, N. S., R. Kobetic, L. M. Lombardo, K. M. Foglyano, G. Pinault, S. M. Selkirk, and R. J. Triolo, Improving walking with an implanted neuroprosthesis for hip, knee, and ankle control after stroke, *American Journal of Physical Medicine and Rehabilitation,* (in press).
80. Marsolais, E. B. and R. Kobetic, Functional walking in paralyzed patients by means of electrical stimulation, *Clinical Orthopaedics,* **175**, 30-36, 1983.
81. Marsolais, E. B. and R. Kobetic, Implantation techniques and experience with percutaneous intramuscular electrodes in the lower extremities, *Journal of Rehabilitation Research and Development,* **23**, 1-8, 1986.
82. Marsolais, E. B. and R. Kobetic, Development of a practical electrical stimulation system for restoring gait in the paralyzed patient, *Clinical Orthopaedics and Related Research,* **233**, 64-74, 1988.
83. Marsolais, E. B., R. Kobetic, J. H. Chizek, and J. L. Jacobs, Orthoses and electrical stimulation for walking in complete paraplegia, *J Neuro Rehab,* **5**, 13-22, 1991.
84. Marsolais, E. B., A. Scheiner, P. C. Miller, R. Kobetic, and J. Daly, Augmentation of transfers for a quadriplegic patient using an implanted fns system. Case report, *Paraplegia,* **32**, 573-579, 1994.
85. McClelland, M., B. J. Andrews, J. H. Patrick, and P. A. Freeman, Augmentation of the Oswestry parawalker orthosis by means of surface electrical stimulation: Gait analysis of three patients, *Paraplegia,* **25**(1), 32-38, 1987.
86. McNeal, D. R., R. Waters, and J. B. Reswick, Medtronic implanted system in 31 subjects, *Neurosurgery,* **1**, 228-229, 1977.
87. Memberg, W. D., P. H. Peckham, G. B. Thrope, M. W. Keith, and T. P. Kicher, An analysis of the reliability of percutaneous intramuscular electrodes in upper extremity FNS applications, *IEEE Transactions Rehabilitation Engineering,* **1**, 126-132, 1993.

88. Memberg, W. D., K. .H Polasek, R. L. Hart, A. M. Bryden, K. L. Kilgore, G. A. Nemunaitis, H. A. Hoyen, M. W. Keith, and R. F. Kirsch, Implanted neuroprosthesis for restoring arm and hand function in people with high level tetraplegia, *Arch Phys Med Rehabil*, **95**(6), 1201-1211, 2014.

89. Mortimer, J. T., D. M. Bayer, R. H. Lord, and J. W. Swanker, Shoulder position transduction for proportional two axis control of orthotic/prosthetic systems, in eds. P. Heberts, R. Kadefors, R. Magnusson and I. Petersen, *The Control of Upper-Extremity Prostheses and Orthoses*, (Charles C Thomas, Springfield, Illinois, 1974), pp. 131-145.

90. Moss, C. W., K. L. Kilgore, and P. H. Peckham, A novel command signal for motor neuroprosthetic control, *Neurorehabil Neural Repair*, **25**(9), 847-854, 2011.

91. Mulcahey, M. J., B. T. Smith, R. R. Betz, R. J. Triolo, and P. H. Peckham, Functional fns: Outcomes in young people with tetraplegia, *J American Paraplegia Society*, **17**(1), 20-35, 1994.

92. Müller-Putz, G. R., R. Scherer, G. Pfurtscheller, and R. Rupp, EEG-based neuroprosthesis control: a step towards clinical practice, *Neurosci Lett*, **382**(1-2), 169-174, 2005.

93. Murphy, J. O., M. L. Audu, L. M. Lombardo, K. M. Foglyano, and R. J. Triolo, Feasibility of closed-loop controller for righting seated posture after spinal cord injury, *J Rehabil Res Dev*, **51**(5), 747-60, 2014.

94. Nathan, R. H., Control strategies in FNS systems for the upper extremities, *Critical Reviews in Biomedical Engineering*, **21**(6), 485-568, 1993.

95. Nathan, R. H. and A. Ohry, Upper limb functions regained in quadriplegia: A hybrid computerized fns system, *Archives of Physical Medicine and Rehabilitation*, **71**, 415-42, 1990.

96. Onders, R. P., M. Elmo, S. Khansarinia, B. Bowman, J. Yee, J. Road, B. Bass, B. Dunkin, P. E. Ingvarsson, and M. Oddsdóttir, Complete worldwide operative experience in laparoscopic diaphragm pacing: results and differences in spinal cord injured patients and amyotrophic lateral sclerosis patients, *Surg Endosc*, **23**(7), 1433-1440, 2009.

97. Pappas, I. P., M. R. Popovic, T. Keller, V. Dietz, and M. Morari, A reliable gait phase detection system, *IEEE Trans Neural Syst Rehabil Eng*, **9**, 113-125, 2001.

98. Peckham, P. H. and M. W. Keith, Motor prostheses for restoration of upper extremity function, in eds. R. B. Stein, P. H. Peckham and D. B. Popovic, *Neural Prostheses: Replacing Motor Function After Disease or Disability*, (Oxford University Press, New York, 1992), pp. 162-190.

99. Peckham, P. H., M. W. Keith, K. L. Kilgore, J. H. Grill, K. S. Wuolle, G. B. Thrope, P. Gorman, J. Hobby, M. J. Mulcahey, S. Carroll, V. Hentz, and A. Wiegner, Efficacy of an implanted neuroprosthesis for restoring hand grasp in tetraplegia: A multicenter study, *Arch Physical Medicine and Rehabilitation*, **82**, 1380-1388, 2001.

100. Peckham, P. H., K. L. Kilgore, M. W. Keith, A. M. Bryden, N. Bhadra, and F. W. Montague, An advanced neuroprosthesis for restoration of hand and upper arm control employing an implantable controller, *J Hand Surgery*, **27A**(2), 265-276, 2002.

101. Peckham, P. H. and J. T. Mortimer, Restoration of hand function in the quadriplegic through electrical stimulation, in eds. J. B. Reswick and F. T. Hambrecht, *Functional Electrical Stimulation: Applications in Neural Prosthesis*, (Marcel Dekker, New York, 1977), pp. 83-95.

102. Peckham, P. H., J. T. Mortimer, and E. B. Marsolais, Alteration in the force and fatigability of skeletal muscle in quadriplegic humans following exercise induced by chronic electrical stimulation, *Clinical Orthopaedics*, **114**, 326-334, 1976.

103. Peckham, P. H., J. T. Mortimer, and E. B. Marsolais, Controlled prehension and release in the C5 quadriplegic elicited by functional electrical stimulation of the paralyzed forearm musculature, *Annals of Biomedical Engineering*, **8**, 369-388, 1980.

104. Pečlin, P., J. Rozman, J. Krajnik, and S. Ribarič, Evaluation of the efficacy and robustness of a second generation implantable stimulator in a patient with hemiplegia during 20 years of functional electrical stimulation of the common peroneal nerve, *Artif Organs,* in press, 2016.

105. Perkins, T. A., G. S. Brindley, N. N. Donaldson, C. E. Polkey, and D. N. Rushton, Implant provision of key, pinch and power grips in a c6 tetraplegic, *Medical and Biological Engineering and Computing,* **32**, 367-372, 1994.

106. Popovic, D., A. Stojanovic, A. Pjanovic, S. Radosavljevic, M. Popovic, S. Jovic, and D. Vulovic, Clinical evaluation of the bionic glove, *Archives of Physical Medicine and Rehabilitation,* **80**, 299-304, 1999.

107. Popovic, D., R. Tomovic, and R. Schwirtlich, Hybrid assistive system: The motor neuroprosthesis, *IEEE Transactions Biomedical Engineering,* **36**, 729-737, 1989.

108. Popovic, M. R., T. Keller, I. P. I. Pappas, V. Dietz, and M. Morari, Surface-stimulation technology for grasping and walking neuroprostheses, *IEEE Eng Med Biol,* **20**, 82-93, 2001.

109. Prochazka, A., M. Gauthier, M. Wieler, and Z. Kenwell, The bionic glove: An electrical stimulator garment that provides controlled grasp and hand opening in quadriplegia, *Archives of Physical Medicine and Rehabilitation,* **78**, 608-614, 1997.

110. Riso, R. R., A. R. Ignagni, and M. W. Keith, Cognitive feedback for use with FES upper extremity neuroprostheses, *IEEE Transactions Biomedical Engineering,* **38**, 29-38, 1991.

111. Rushton, D. N., N. D. Donaldson, F. M. Barr, V. J. Harper, T. A. Perkins, P. N. Taylor, and A. M. Tromans, Lumbar root stimulation for restoring leg functions: Results in paraplegia, *Artificial Organs,* **21**, 180-182, 1997.

112. Saxena, A., S. Nikolic, and D. Popovic, An EMG-controlled grasping system for tetraplegics, *Journal of Rehabilitation Research and Development,* **32**(1), 17-24, 1995.

113. Scott, T. R. D., L Atmore, J. M. Heasman, R. Y. Flynn, V. A. Vare, and C. Gschwind, Synergistic control of stimulated pronosupination with the stimulated grasp of persons with tetraplegia, *IEEE Trans Neural Syst Rehabil Eng,* **9**, 258-264, 2001.

114. Scott, T. R. D., P. H. Peckham, and M. W. Keith, Upper extremity neuroprostheses using functional electrical stimulation, in eds. G. S. Brindley and D. N. Rushton, *Bailliere's Clinical Neurology,* (Bailliere Tindall, London, 1995), pp. 57-75.

115. Sinkjaer, T., M. K. Haugland, and J. Haase, Natural neural sensing and artificial muscle control in man, *Experimental Brain Research,* **98**, 542-545, 1994.

116. Smith, B., J. R. Buckett, P. H. Peckham, M. W. Keith, and D. D. Roscoe, An externally powered, multichannel, implantable stimulator for versatile control of paralyzed muscle, *IEEE Transactions Biomedical Engineering,* **34**, 499-508, 1987.

117. Smith, B., Z. Tang, M. W. Johnson, S. Pourmehdi, M. Gazdik, J. R. Buckett, and P. Peckham, An externally powered, multichannel, implantable stimulator-telemeter for control of paralyzed muscle, *IEEE Transactions Biomedical Engineering,* **45**, 463-475, 1998.

118. Smith, B. T., R. R. Betz, M. J. Mulcahey, and R. J. Triolo, Reliability of percutaneous intramuscular electrodes for upper extremity functional neuromuscular stimulation in adolescents with C5 tetraplegia, *Archives of Physical Medicine and Rehabilitation,* **75**, 939-945, 1994.

119. Smith, B. T., M. J. Mulcahey, and R. R. Betz, Quantitative comparison of grasp and release abilities with and without functional fns in adolescents with tetraplegia, *Paraplegia,* **34**, 16-23, 1996.

120. Smith, B. T., M. J. Mulcahey, R. J. Triolo, and R. R. Betz, The application of a modified neuroprosthetic hand system in a child with a C7 spinal cord injury, case report, *Paraplegia*, **30**, 598-606, 1992.

121. Snoek, G. J., M. J. Ijzerman, F. A. C. G. in 't Groen, T. S. Stoffers, and G. Zilvold, Use of the NESS handmaster to restore handfunction in tetraplegia: Clinical experiences in ten patients, *Spinal Cord*, **38**, 244-249, 2000.

122. Solomonow, M., Biomechanics and physiology of a practical functional neuromuscular stimulation powered walking orthosis for paraplegics, in eds. R. B. Stein, P. H. Peckham and D. P. Popovic, *Neural Prostheses: Replacing Motor Function After Disease or Disability*, (Oxford University Press, New York, 1992), pp. 202-232.

123. Solomonow, M., E. Aguilar, E. Reisin, R. V. Baratta, R. Best, T. Coetzee, and R. D'Ambrosia, Reciprocating gait orthosis powered with electrical muscle stimulation (RGO II). Part I: Performance evaluation of 70 paraplegic patients, *Orthopedics*, **20**, 315-324, 1997.

124. Solomonow, M., R. Baratta, H. Shoji, and R. D. D'Ambrosia, The myoelectric signal of electrically stimulated muscle during recruitment: An inherent feedback parameter for a closed-loop control scheme, *IEEE Transactions Biomedical Engineering*, **33**(8), 735-745, 1986.

125. Solomonow, M., R. V. Baratta, and S. Hirokawa, The RGO generation II: Muscle stimulation powered orthosis as a practical walking system for paraplegics, *Orthopaedics*, **12**, 1309-1315, 1989.

126. Stanic, U., R. Acimovic-Janezic, N. Gros, A. Trnkocsy, T. Bajd, and M. Kljajic, Multichannel electrical stimulation for correction of hemiplegic gait, *Scan J Rehab Med*, **56**, 507-513, 1975.

127. Stroh-Wuolle, K., C. L. Van Doren, G. B. Thrope, M. W. Keith, and P. H. Peckham, Development of a quantitative hand grasp and release test for patients with tetraplegia using a hand neuroprosthesis, *J Hand Surgery*, **19A**, 209-218, 1994.

128. Strojnik, P., R. Acimovic, E. Vavken, V. Simic, and U. Stanic, Treatment of drop foot using an implantable peroneal underknee stimulator, *Scandinavian Journal of Rehabilitation Medicine*, **19**, 37-43, 1987.

129. Tan, D. W., M. A. Schiefer, M. W. Keith, J. R. Anderson, J. Tyler, and D. J. Tyler, A neural interface provides long-term stable natural touch perception, *Sci Transl Med*, **6**(257), 257ra138, 2014.

130. Taylor, P., J. Esnouf, and J. Hobby, The functional impact of the freehand system on tetraplegic hand function. Clinical results, *Spinal Cord*, **40**, 560-566, 2002.

131. Thoma, H., M. Grey, J. Holle, H. Kern, W. Mayr, G. Schwanda, and H. Stoehr, Functional neurostimulation to substitute locomotion in paraplegia patients, in ed. J. D. Andrade, *Artificial Organs*, (VCH Publishers, New York, 1987), pp. 515-529.

132. Triolo, R. J., S. N. Bailey, M. E. Miller, L. M. Lombardo, and M. L. Audu Effects of stimulating hip and trunk muscles on seated stability, posture, and reach after spinal cord injury, *Arch Phys Med Rehabil*, **94**(9), 1766-1775, 2013.

133. Triolo, R., R. H. Nathan, Y. Handa, M. W. Keith, R. Betz, S. Carroll, and C. Kantor, Challenges to clinical deployment of upper limb neuroprostheses, *Journal of Rehabilitation Research and Development*, **33**(2), 111-122, 1996.

134. Triolo, R. J., R. Kobetic, and R. R. Betz, Standing and walking with FNS: Technical and clinical challenges, in eds. G. F. Harris and P. A. Smith, *Human Motion Analysis: Current Applications and Future Directions*, (IEEE Press, New York, 1996), pp. 318-350.

135. Van Der Aa, H. E., G. Bultstra, A. J. Verloop, L. Kenney, J. Holsheimer, A. Nene, H. J. Hermens, G. Zilvold, and H. P. J. Buschman, Application of a dual channel peroneal nerve stimulator in a patient with a "central" drop foot, *Acta Neurochir Suppl*, **79**, 105-107, 2001.

136. Vodovnik, L., C. Long, J. Reswick, A. Lippay, and D. Starbuck, Myo-electric control of paralyzed muscles, *IEEE Transactions Biomedical Engineering*, **12**, 169-172, 1965.

137. Von Wild, K., P. Rabischong, G. Brunelli, M. Benichou, and K. Krishnan, Computer added locomotion by implanted electrical stimulation in paraplegic patients (SUAW), *Acta Neurochir Suppl*, **79**, 99-104, 2002.

138. Waters, R., D. McNeal, W. Faloon, and B. Clifford, Functional electrical stimulation of peroneal nerve for hemiplegia, *J Bone Joint Surg*, **67**, 792-793, 1985.

139. Waters, R., D. McNeal, and J. Perry, Experimental correction of footdrop by electrical stimulation of the peroneal nerve, *J Bone Joint Surg*, **57-A**(8), 1047-1054, 1975.

140. Weiss, M., J. Kiwerski, and R. Pasniczek, An electronic hybrid device for the control of hand functions by electrical stimulation methods, in ed. A. Morecki, *International Series on Biomechanics*, (University Park Press, Baltimore, 1981), pp. 397-404.

141. Wieler, M., R. B. Stein, M. Ladouceur, M. Whittaker, A. W. Smith, S. Naaman, H. Barbeau, J. Bugaresti, and E. Aimone, Multicenter evaluation of electrical stimulation systems for walking, *Archives of Physical Medicine and Rehabilitation*, **80**, 495-500, 1999.

142. Wijman, C. A., K. C. Stroh, C. L. Van Doren, G. B. Thrope, P. H. Peckham, and M. W. Keith, Functional evaluation of quadriplegic patients using a hand neuroprosthesis, *Archives of Physical Medicine and Rehabilitation*, **71**, 1053-1057, 1990.

143. Wilson, R. D., D. D. Gunzler, M. E. Bennett, and J. Chae, Peripheral nerve stimulation compared with usual care for pain relief of hemiplegic shoulder pain: a randomized controlled trial, *Am J Phys Med Rehabil*, **93**(1), 17-28, 2014.

144. Wood, D. E., N. D. Donaldson, C. McFadden, T. A. Perkins, D. N. Rushton, and A. M. Tromans, Is paraplegic standing by root stimulation a practical option? - Conclusions from the larsi project, *Proceedings of the 6th Annual Conference of the International Functional Electrical Stimulation Society*, 13-15, 2001.

145. Wuolle, K. S., C. L. Van Doren, A. M. Bryden, P. H. Peckham, M. W. Keith, and K. L. Kilgore, Satisfaction and usage of a hand neuroprosthesis, *Archives of Physical Medicine and Rehabilitation*, **80**, 206-213, 1999.

146. Wuolle, K. S., C. L. Van Doren, G. B. Thrope, M. W. Keith, and P. H. Peckham, Development of a quantitative hand grasp and release test for patients with tetraplegia using a hand neuroprosthesis, *J Hand Surgery*, **19A**, 209-218, 1994.

147. Yarkony, G. M., R. Jaeger, E. Roth, A. Kralj, and J. Quintern, Functional neuromuscular stimulation for standing after spinal cord injury, *Archives of Physical Medicine and Rehabilitation*, **70**(3), 201-206, 1990.

Chapter 3.2

Neuroprosthetic Control of Lower Urinary Tract Function

James A. Hokanson, Cindy L. Amundsen and Warren M. Grill

Departments of Biomedical Engineering (JAH, WMG), Obstetrics and Gynecology and Surgery (CLA), Electrical and Computer Engineering (WMG), Neurobiology (WMG), and Surgery (WMG)
Duke University, Durham, NC 27708
jim.hokanson@duke.edu, cindy.amundsen@duke.edu, warren.grill@duke.edu

Lower urinary tract dysfunction is highly prevalent, leads to a decreased quality of life, and is associated with a high economic burden. In the past decade electrical stimulation has emerged as a valid treatment modality for those with lower urinary tract dysfunction who have failed more conservative medical approaches. This chapter reviews three techniques: sacral neuromodulation; posterior tibial nerve stimulation; and sacral anterior root stimulation. Their history, usage, and efficacy are discussed.

1. Introduction

Lower urinary tract dysfunction (LUTD) is common in both men and women, and the incidence and prevalence increase with age. LUTD includes urinary incontinence and voiding dysfunction/urinary retention, as well as bladder pain. These conditions have negative social, mental health and physical health effects. The financial burden of LUTD is expected to increase dramatically as the population ages.

First line treatments for lower urinary tract dysfunction often include medications and/or catheterization. Anticholinergics, historically the standard treatment for overactive bladder, as well as for neurogenic detrusor overactivity, have 2 year continuation rates of less than 10% [20], likely due to the combination of limited effectiveness and side effects [6]. Catheterization to treat urinary retention, although effective, can be unpleasant, often leads to urinary tract infections, and can be difficult to self-administer for certain populations (e.g., spinal cord injury) [9].

Electrical stimulation is an alternative therapeutic approach for refractory LUTD and is a promising alternative to current methods of treating neurogenic lower urinary tract dysfunction (NLUTD) resulting from spinal cord injury (SCI). For idiopathic LUTD, electrical stimulation has supplanted major invasive surgical procedures such as augmentation cystoplasty, detrusor myectomy and urinary diversion.

In the following sections, we examine three different stimulation approaches that are in relatively widespread clinical use. Before examining these approaches we briefly review various clinical diagnoses that would warrant such therapies.

2. Clinical Diagnoses

Following is a brief overview of various conditions related to lower urinary tract dysfunction.

2.1. *Overactive bladder*

The overactive bladder is a symptom complex defined by urinary urgency, with or without urge incontinence, usually with frequency and nocturia, in the absence of an infection or other obvious pathology [1]. Urgency is the sudden need to pass urine, which is difficult to defer, and can lead to urge incontinence. Urgency differs from stress incontinence, which occurs in response to some physical event, such as coughing or sneezing. Frequency means voiding often in the day. Although more than 8 voids per day is often considered abnormal, this depends heavily on fluid intake and many physicians use voiding diaries that record fluid intake and output to determine whether the frequency is due to excessive fluid intake. Overactive bladder is a highly prevalent LUT condition that impacts 1 in 6 adults [52] and costs the United States an estimated $36.5 billion dollars per year [68].

2.2. *Chronic retention of urine (urinary retention)*

Chronic retention of urine is defined as a non-painful bladder which remains palpable or percussible (in other words, retains a significant amount of urine) after the patient has passed urine [1]. Such patients may be incontinent, and often experience frequent voiding and recurrent urinary tract infections. This symptom is also commonly referred to as urinary retention, although this term can also be used to describe acute retention (e.g., following surgery). Clinically, if a patient is able to void at all, then a urodynamic evaluation is used to help determine if the inefficient emptying is due to bladder outlet obstruction (e.g., enlarged prostate, vaginal prolapse, obstructive incontinence procedure, or non-relaxing pelvic floor) or due to underactive detrusor function. In obstructive cases treatment is guided towards rectifying the cause, rather than trying to improve bladder contractility.

2.3. *Neurogenic bladder*

Neurogenic bladder is used to describe patients who have known neurological issues that influence lower urinary tract function. Examples include multiple sclerosis, Parkinson's disease, and spinal cord injury. People without clear neurological insult are considered to have idiopathic bladder dysfunction. However, these two groups are treated with similar therapies.

3. Sacral Neuromodulation

In a departure from previous work in nerve stimulation to treat lower urinary tract dysfunction, the clinical use of sacral nerve stimulation did not attempt to directly stimulate muscles responsible for continence (urethra) or micturition (bladder). This departure led to the use of the term "neuromodulation" to describe the effect of stimulation. Sacral neuromodulation thus refers to electrical stimulation of sacral level spinal nerves (generally the S3 nerve in humans) to "modulate" or change neural activity so as to reduce or eliminate voiding dysfunction.

3.1. *History*

Notable work on sacral nerve stimulation started at the department of Urology at the University of California, San Francisco in the 1970s [39, 81] as part of the Neural Prosthesis Program at NINCDS led by Dr. F. Terry Hambrecht. Most, if not all, of this initial work, however, was oriented toward the eventual treatment of persons with spinal cord injury.

In 1981 clinical testing was started [79], and testing expanded from persons with spinal cord injury to treating those with non-neurogenic voiding dysfunction (e.g., urge incontinence, urinary retention) (see 80). The results of this work were promising [79, 95].

In the early 1990's, Medtronic took over previously stalled commercialization efforts of a sacral nerve stimulation device [80]. They undertook a multi-center, international clinical trial for persons with urinary retention, urge incontinence, and urgency/frequency [82]. Again, the results were promising [38, 89], as were other non-Medtronic sponsored clinical trials conducted around this time [11, 23, 101].

Sacral neuromodulation, marketed by Medtronic as the InterStim system, is FDA approved for treatment of urge urinary incontinence (1997), urgency-frequency (1999), non-obstructive urinary retention (1999), and fecal incontinence (2011). Today the InterStim system has been implanted in over 175,000 patients (http://www.medtronic.com/patients/overactive-bladder/about-therapy/questions-answers/index.htm).

3.2. Therapy candidates

Sacral neuromodulation is used to treat overactive bladder symptoms, urinary retention, and fecal incontinence. Patients with these symptoms that do not respond to more conservative approaches, such as behavioral therapy, physical therapy, or medications, are candidates for sacral neuromodulation. Additional therapeutic approaches include botulinum toxin injected into the bladder (for urgency urinary incontinence), posterior tibial nerve stimulation (next section), and invasive reconstructive surgery.

3.2.1. Predicative factors

Several studies examined whether there are factors that are predicative of success of sacral neuromodulation therapy. In a study of 100 patients with lower urinary tract dysfunction, gender, age, history, and diagnosis were not predictors of success [50]. However, the patient population was very diverse and the study was likely underpowered. A similar lack of predictability was observed by Janknegt et al. [41], who commented that gender, age, and pretreatment variables were not predictors of success in 96 treated patients for urge incontinence.

The lack of impact of age in the previous studies appears to contradict the findings of Amundsen et al. [3] who found that persons 55 and older were less likely to be cured of urgency incontinence than those under the age of 55 (n = 55 patients). One possible explanation for these results is the difference in outcome measures (i.e., cured versus clinical success). Clinical success is typically defined as a reduction by 50% in the number of urgency urinary incontinent episodes, while cure implies no incontinent episodes. The predictive power of age on cure rate is seemingly at odds with the results from Janknegt et al. [41] and Koldewijn et al. [50]. However in the latter cases they were examining the predictive power of age on the success rate. Collectively, these studies suggest that older patients disproportionally experience clinical success but less so cure.

Other factors that may indicate that someone will not respond to sacral nerve stimulation for the treatment of urge incontinence include having three or more chronic conditions [3] and an inability to voluntarily contract pelvic floor muscles [85]. The latter indicator is one of the few physiological factors that may predict outcomes. Urodynamics, including evidence of detrusor overactivity [35, 30], are not predictive of success.

Goh and Diokno [33] examined 29 patients with urinary retention for factors that predicted successful initial screening test (as opposed to success following a permanent implant). While age had no impact, positive predictive factors included the ability to void voluntarily and the duration of retention (*i.e.*, those in retention longer were more likely to have a successful screening).

3.2.2. *Other medical conditions*

There are other conditions for which sacral neuromodulation has been tested but is not currently FDA approved for use [27]. These include constipation [44, 45, for review see 96], interstitial cystitis/bladder pain syndrome [22, 24, 57, 59, 75, 87, for review see 19], and lower urinary tract dysfunction of clear neurogenic origin [10, 58, 99]. Despite these reports with positive outcomes, these studies tend to have few patients, limited long-term follow-up, and are poorly controlled for potential physician and patient bias.

3.3. *Implantation and usage*

The implant procedure has changed numerous times since human studies began in the early 1980s. What has remained relatively constant is the placement of an electrode into the S3 foramen. Surgical details are omitted here and can be found in the following reviews [83, 88, 92].

3.3.1. *Initial testing*

Prior to receiving a full implant, candidates undergo an initial testing period to evaluate whether or not they are responsive to this mode of therapy. This is necessary since, as described above, it is not clear who will respond to sacral nerve stimulation, and the risks and high cost of the full implant are not warranted if the patient is unlikely to benefit from to the therapy.

There are currently two forms of the initial testing procedure. The first type of testing is performed in the office and is referred to as PNE (percutaneous or peripheral nerve evaluation). A temporary wire with a single contact electrode is placed adjacent to the sacral nerve (typically S3) for up to 7 days of testing. The other approach, known as a stage 1, involves placement of a permanent tined lead with 4 electrodes. The tined lead is placed in the operating room via fluoroscopy and under conscious sedation or general anesthesia. Since the tines anchor the lead into the surrounding subcutaneous tissue, the lead is less prone to movement during the initial testing phase which can last up to 14 days (and sometimes longer based on physician preference). For both forms of testing, the lead/wire are externalized and connected to a pulse generator. Placement of the test lead prior to anchoring is shown in Figure 1.

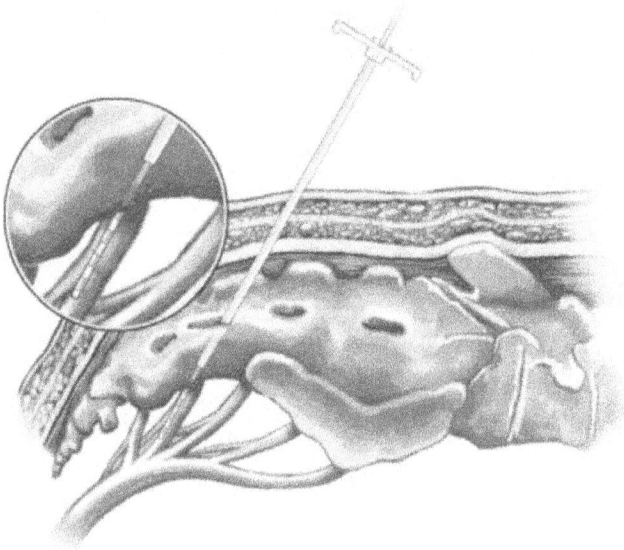

Fig. 1. Placement of the permanent tined lead in the S3 foramen prior to retraction of the introducer sheath. (Reproduced from [92] with permission)

Success criteria of the initial testing phase are remarkably consistent across various studies during the past three decades. Generally, ≥50% improvement in symptoms is considered a success. Siddiqui et al. [86] summarized various studies that performed both PNE and stage 1 screening and 20-52% of patients undergoing PNE progressed to full implant (permanent lead and neurostimulator) while 67-88% of patients undergoing stage 1 lead placement progressed to neurostimulator placement. For those patients who do not respond to the initial testing period, the lead is removed.

3.3.2. *Permanent implant*

Depending upon the type of initial testing, the permanent implant surgery requires placement of only the pulse generator (second stage of the two-stage implant) or both the permanent electrode and the pulse generator (when PNE was done initially). The pulse generator is typically placed into the upper buttock region.

3.3.3. *Stimulation programming and usage*

The output of the implanted stimulator is set with an external programmer. The stimulation amplitude is specified in volts with a 10.5 V max (InterStim) or 8.5 V max (InterStim II) and 0.1 V increments (InterStim Model 8870 Programming Guide for Software Version B). An option of using 0.05 V increments is also available in which case the maximum for both pulse generators is 6.35 V. Low amplitude settings are preferable as these will extend the life expectancy of the (battery-powered) neurostimulator. Placement of the lead intraoperatively is guided by motor and/or sensory responses. A comfortable response should be achieved at amplitudes < 4V. Stimulus pulses are biphasic. The pulse width can be adjusted and the recommended range is 180 – 240 μs. The stimulation rate can be adjusted with a recommended range of 10 – 14 Hz. The stimulator is able to cycle on and off so as to preserve battery life, with the expectation that the therapeutic effect persists for some period post-stimulation. Each epoch, on or off, can be programmed to last for durations of 0.1 s to 24 hours. Additionally, since the onset of stimulation can be unpleasant, a "soft" start (and stop) can be enabled in which the amplitude ramps up (or down) between 0 V and the specified amplitude.

Active electrode locations can also be programmed. Each of the four electrodes can be an anode or cathode, and the implantable pulse generator (IPG) case can be programmed to be an anode. When the IPG case is made an anode there can be no other anodes and this is referred to as the "unipolar" configuration. Any other configuration (which does not use the IPG case) is referred to as "bipolar." Multiple electrodes can be anodes ("bipolar" only) or cathodes ('unipolar" and "bipolar").

The patient receives a personal control device that they can take home and use as needed. This device allows them to turn the stimulation on and off, as well as adjust the stimulation amplitude (within limits set by the clinician). Additionally, newer controllers allow the patient to select between one of four different stimulation programs, which can each have unique settings (*e.g.*, voltage, pulse width, etc.).

3.4. *Improvements to sacral neuromodulation therapy*

The technology for sacral neuromodulation has been FDA approved for nearly two decades with improvements made to both the device and on surgical technique (for review see [92]), despite many unknowns regarding the underlying mechanisms of action and the neural interface.

3.4.1. *Development of the tined lead*

In the initial PNE testing phase a wire is implanted adjacent to the sacral nerve and sutured to the skin. In many studies lead migration was suspected when initial successful stimulation led to no improvement on the subsequent testing days. Per protocol, this failure meant that the patients were not candidates for a permanent implant, even though they had initially responded.

To investigate the impact of lead migration, Janknegt et al. [42] placed a permanent lead in 10 people who were selected because they had failed PNE testing but had shown promise in the initial days of the PNE test. In eight of these 10 patients, who had previously failed the initial testing, permanent fixation of the lead to the sacrum was associated with success in the initial testing phase. This work suggested that sacral neuromodulation was not being applied chronically to all those would benefit from it, due to failure of PNE testing from wire migration.

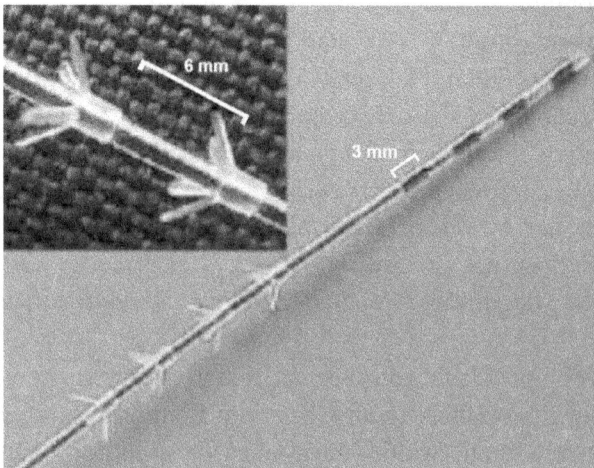

Fig. 2. View of a four-contact electrode with tines. A close-up of the tines is shown in the inset (Adapted from [92] with permission)

The addition of tines to the lead brought about a less invasive approach to placement while also reducing lead migration and is now the standard. [91]. When allowed to expand, these tines grab into tissue and reduce movement of the lead. The implant can also be performed under conscious sedation anesthesia allowing for patient feedback regarding sensations from stimulation, which can be useful for guiding placement. For those who fail the initial testing period, minor surgery under conscious sedation is performed to remove the lead. Fig. 2 shows the four contact electrodes with anchoring tines.

3.4.2. *Pulse generator placement*

Another relatively simple but important change was the movement of the implantable pulse generator (IPG) from the anterior abdomen to the buttock. Pain at the site of the IPG was a major reason for re-operation. In one study 29% of patients (12 of 42) reported pain at the implant site, accounting for 42% of adverse events [101]. In a 2001 study of 39 patients, 10% reported pain from the implant site, which was lower than the group average of 15% calculated from other studies [77]. Importantly, the level of discomfort experienced by the patients was such that a re-operation was not needed. Given that this approach also simplifies the surgery (fewer incisions, no patient movement) it has become the standard surgical practice.

3.4.3. *InterStim II*

Furthermore, with the introduction of the InterStim II (IPG), FDA approved in 2006, there were further reductions in surgical revisions due to pain from the implant site. The InterStim II is about half the size and weight of the original InterStim IPG, can be implanted without lead extensions, and also supports user-switching between four stimulation programs. The new IPG simplifies the surgical procedure and may also reduce discomfort from the indwelling device. However, the smaller size has a reduced battery capacity (1.3 Ah vs. 2.7 Ah) as well a higher cost [2]. The new IPG is also approved for a 1.5 T head MRI, but it is not approved for body MRIs, one of the remaining limitations of the technology.

3.4.4. *Verify evaluation system*

In 2013 Medtronic introduced the Verify system for the initial testing phase [60]. Unlike the previous device, the Verify system physically decoupled the stimulator from the control unit that controlled the stimulator (now linked wirelessly). Without an attached control system the new external stimulator is much smaller and more discreet. The control unit has a touchscreen interface instead of the small switches and knobs on the old stimulator. This digital interface allows the clinician to set pre-defined programs (like the implanted system) as well as access usage data (previously not logged). It is expected that this change will allow the user to more fully and accurately explore the therapeutic potential of the system.

3.5. *Efficacy*

Assessment of efficacy is hampered by a number of factors. Many early reports appeared to use the same patient data. More current studies differ in patient populations, primary outcome measures, and results are not always differentiated by symptom type or severity of symptoms. Lastly, surgical techniques and technology have evolved over time, making efficacy a moving target.

In a prospective randomized trial of 155 patients, Schmidt et al. [82] reported a success rate (≥ 50 % improvement) for urge incontinence of 75 % and a cure rate of 47% at 6 months, of those that had received an implant (63 % of those screened). In a case series of 105 patients with urge incontinence, Amundsen et al. [3] reported a cure rate of 45 % (mean time since implant was 29 months). This cure rate however differed for older (37 % cure rate) and younger (65 % cure rate) age groups. Success rates of permanent implants were not reported in that study. In a case series (FDA post-approval study) van Kerrebroeck et al. [46] reported success rates of 68 % (urgency incontinence), 56 % (urgency-frequency), and 71 % (urinary retention). Cure rates were not provided in that study.

Overall rates are dependent on the number of patients that pass initial testing. With the tined lead this appears to be about 75 %, based on references provided in Siddiqui et al. [86]. If we assume average success and cure rates of approximately 70 % and 50 % for those that receive a permanent implant for urinary urge incontinence, this would mean overall success and cure rates of about 52 % (*e.g.,* 75 % of 70 %) and 38 % respectively for all urgency urinary incontinence. What remains unclear is whether there are subtypes/phenotypes who may respond more favorably to this therapy than others.

In a review of implants between 1996 and 2010, Peeters et al. [71] observed success and cure rates of 73 % and 57 % (Fowler's and non-Fowler's combined) for idiopathic retention. Average follow-up time for all patients (not just those with urinary retention) was 47 months. An implantation rate of 57% was reported, however, many of the patients underwent initial testing with PNE. A more accurate implantation rate is difficult to estimate as most published studies used PNE rather than the stage 1 screening [36].

3.6. *Mechanisms of action*

The mechanism(s) of action of sacral neuromodulation is unclear. This lack of knowledge complicates patient selection, since it is not known whether or not someone will respond to stimulation. It is also possible that methodological improvements could be made if the mechanism of action were better understood.

Although a full discussion of the mechanism of action is outside of the scope of this chapter, there are some useful comments that can be made regarding various theories, and what is known and unknown.

The consensus is that sacral neuromodulation works via activation of neural afferents that modulate reflex pathways. This statement's implication that sacral neuromodulation does not work via activation of efferent neural pathways does not seem to be based on any studies showing that activation of motor pathways *cannot* treat dysfunction, but rather on evidence showing that activation of sensory pathways *can* treat dysfunction.

This distinction is not just semantics. Motor activation may lead to improved tissue properties, such as increased sphincter tone (*i.e.,* from stimulation induced exercise) [78]. Additionally, motor activation can reflexively activate sensory pathways, and may be an efficient and natural way of recruiting sensory axons (termed re-afference [104]). Although motor activation may not be therapeutic, its unknown contribution highlights the many opportunities still remaining for further exploration of mechanisms of action.

Occasionally mechanisms of action of sacral neuromodulation are explained from the perspective of pudendal nerve activation. Before exploring the implications of this association, it is first useful to clarify some anatomy. Stimulation of a sacral nerve is not equivalent to stimulation of the pudendal nerve, as the sacral nerves contribute to both the pelvic and pudendal nerves, as well as sciatic. In children undergoing posterior rhizotomy, pudendal afferent activity was present in the S1 nerve in 21%, S2 nerve in 84%, and S3 nerve in 62% [40]. Put another way, the S3 nerve did not contribute to the pudendal nerve in 38% of the patients. Schmidt [79] also indicates that stimulation of the S2 nerve is typically necessary to activate the urethral sphincter (the anal sphincter receives projections from S2 and S3). This evidence suggests that S2 stimulation may be more similar to pudendal nerve stimulation than S3 would be.

However, the mechanisms of bladder inhibition by pudendal nerve stimulation may provide some insight into the mechanisms of sacral neuromodulation. Bladder inhibition from pudendal afferent stimulation is believed to act via activation of sympathetic outflow [54] as well as central inhibition of parasympathetic neurons via a GABAergic mechanism [62, 103].

In addition to inhibiting the bladder, pudendal afferent stimulation can facilitate micturition, depending on the stimulation rate [8], location [102], and amplitude [72]. Differences in stimulation rates may differentially impact excitatory and inhibitory interneurons in the lumbosacral spinal cord, leading to excitation or inhibition of the bladder [63]. Although it is conceivable that these differences may explain the ability of sacral neuromodulation to treat seemingly disparate patient populations, it is unclear whether or not the stimulation parameters used differ when treating urgency urinary incontinence versus urinary retention.

4. Percutaneous Tibial Nerve Stimulation

Percutaneous tibial nerve stimulation, commonly referred to as PTNS, aims to reduce or eliminate overactive bladder symptoms through stimulation of the tibial nerve. Like sacral neuromodulation, stimulation of the tibial nerve is thought to modulate neural activity as it does not directly stimulate the bladder or urethral sphincter(s). Unlike sacral neuromodulation, PTNS is currently not an implanted system, and, rather than stimulation being applied continuously, PTNS is delivered for short periods (30 minutes) in repeated dosing sessions.

4.1. *History*

Percutaneous tibial nerve stimulation was introduced as an alternative treatment for overactive bladder via electrical stimulation of the tibial nerve. With the growing acceptance of sacral neuromodulation as a therapy for overactive bladder, clinicians have advocated for PTNS as being a lower-cost, less-invasive alternative to InterStim [25, 56, 61], but long term efficacy studies are lacking and therefore the true cost effectiveness is yet to be established.

Tibial nerve stimulation to treat overactive bladder symptoms was first introduced by McGuire et al. [64] and Nakamura et al. [67]. This approach was motivated by Chinese acupuncture:

> "Indeed, the acupuncture points for inhibition of bladder activity are over the common peroneal and posterior tibial nerves. This traditional Chinese practice was the source of our idea to use transcutaneous stimulation at those points." [64]

Although results were promising from both groups - described as "astonishingly good" by McGuire et al. - this approach did not immediately take off. We found only one other published study on tibial nerve stimulation [31] between the first studies in 1983 and a resurgence that began in 2000 [34, 49, see 25 for review]. The lack of pursuit of this approach is likely indicative of the relative level of distrust of electrical stimulation for therapy; something that has diminished, although perhaps not completely [56], since the introduction and use of InterStim (as well as other successful electrical stimulation therapies).

In 1987 Dr. Marshall Stoller at UCSF started a decade long endeavor to test percutaneous tibial nerve stimulation in patients with urinary frequency, incontinence, and pelvic pain. A total of 98 patients were eventually treated by

Stoller using the Stoller Afferent Nerve Stimulator or SANS. Among 22 patients who complained primarily of urgency continence, 80% had at least a 75% reduction in urgency incontinence, and 45% were completely dry [25]. These results were only presented in abstract form, but this success prompted the first prospective multi-center clinical trial by Govier et al. [34] to determine the safety and efficacy of tibial nerve stimulation. PTNS received FDA approval in 2000 to treat overactive bladder symptoms.

Unlike sacral neuromodulation, which Medtronic exclusively controlled throughout its commercial history [80], the commercialization of tibial nerve stimulation involved multiple companies. Initial commercialization of the "percutaneous SANS" device was pursued by UroSurge [34]. In 2000 UroSurge obtained FDA approval for their device but also went bankrupt. In 2002 CystoMedix acquired UroSurge assets related to the SANS device and renamed the device the "Urgent PC" in 2003. In 2005 Uroplasty signed a licensing agreement with CystoMedix to commercialize Urgent PC in the United States. In 2007 Uroplasty acquired Urgent PC assets from CystoMedix, making Uroplasty the sole manufacturer of a commercial PTNS system. In 2015 Uroplasty merged with another company to become Cogentix Medical, the current commercial provider of Urgent PC.

4.2. *Implantation and usage*

A 34-gauge needle electrode is inserted approximately 5 cm cephalad (approximately 3 finger widths) to the medial malleolus. The needle is advanced approximately 3 to 4 cm posterior to the tibia. A return surface electrode is placed at the base of the foot, generally on the medial aspect of the calcaneus [34, 93]. The setup is shown in Figure 3.

Correct placement can be verified through electrical stimulation evoked flexion of the big toe. Stimulation amplitude is set to the highest level tolerated by the patient. A 200 μs pulse width and 20 Hz stimulation rate are used. A standard single stimulation session lasts for 30 minutes. Sessions are typically performed once a week for 10 – 12 weeks [29]. If symptoms haven't fully resolved after 12 weeks, then patients may elect to try botulinum toxin treatment or sacral neuromodulation.

For patients who experience successful treatment, maintenance treatment is needed [55]. Appropriate scheduling of maintenance treatments is an ongoing research question [74].

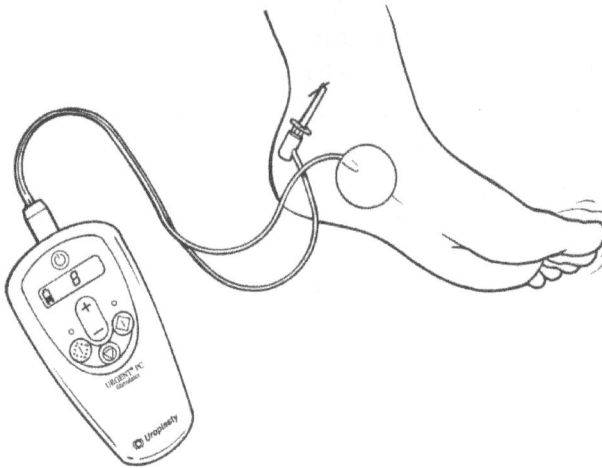

Fig. 3. Tibial nerve stimulation setup (Reprinted with permission from [93])

4.3. *Patient population*

Tibial nerve stimulation is an option for those with overactive bladder symptoms who are refractory to standard medical treatment. Insurance reimbursement can currently be obtained for treatment of urgency-incontinence, mixed-incontinence, and urgency-frequency syndromes if patients have failed two medications (anticholingerics and/or beta adrenergic agonists).

Like sacral neuromodulation, there are no agreed upon predictors of success or failure of PTNS. In a study of patients with overactive bladder symptoms (n = 46), cystometric capacity, volume at which detrusor overactivity occurred (if any), and detrusor pressure during overactivity were not significant predictors of subjective success [98]. However, patients with lack of detrusor overactivity prior to treatment were 1.75 times more likely to experience success. Similar lack of predictive power of urodynamics was found in patients with urinary retention (n = 39) [97]. Both studies however had relatively small numbers of patients.

Van Balken et al. [5] also observed that poor mental health as assessed by the SF-36 MCS questionnaire [100] led to poorer objective responses in a population with mixed symptoms.

4.4. *Efficacy*

4.4.1. *General performance*

There are several systematic reviews of PTNS for overactive bladder symptoms as well as for urinary retention, pelvic pain, fecal incontinence, and neurogenic bladder [7, 21, 29, 53, 66]. All studies found PTNS to be effective for these conditions to varying degrees (different levels of evidence). All reviews recommended further studies to clarify the range of therapeutic effects, usefulness in non-OAB conditions, patient selection criteria, and long-term therapeutic benefit.

4.4.2. *Long term performance*

McGuire et al. [64] noted that repeated episodes of stimulation were needed to maintain continence. Geirsson et al. [31] had patients receive electrical stimulation for 30 minutes each day. By the time of Stoller [94] the frequency of stimulation had been reduced to one 20 – 30 minute session per week. This prolonged approach likely resulted from the considerable amount of work that had been done on maximal electrical stimulation, a technique typically involving anal, vaginal, or pelvic floor electrical stimulation at high stimulus amplitudes for short sessions separated by many days or weeks [30, 32, 65, 76].

Peters et al. [74] followed PTNS patients through three years of treatment. A total of 50 patients enrolled in the study out of 60 total eligible patients that had shown success with PTNS in a previous study [73]. Nearly all of the patients that completed the study met the primary efficacy goals (28 of 29). Accounting for estimated success that occurred from early withdrawal patients, the authors suggest that the success rate was 76% (38 of 50). If one accounts for the previous study, and splits any failed enrollment (n = 10 [74]) or completion (n = 7 [73]) into equal failure and success groups, then the overall success rate for this mixed overactive bladder group would be 42% (46.5 out of 110).

4.4.3. *Comparison to sacral neuromodulation*

No head to head comparison of performance has been done between sacral neuromodulation and PTNS. The opinion of Dr. Steven Siegel [56] most likely matches the opinion of many physicians when he mentioned that he thinks of PTNS as "neuromodulation lite." However, it is possible that PTNS could be not only be more cost-effective for patients [61, 93] but could also work just as well if not better [69] for a specific population of patients. This uncertainty highlights the need for a better understanding of mechanisms of action of both stimulation modalities as well as better patient characterization.

4.5. Mechanisms of action

Like sacral neuromodulation, the mechanisms of action of PTNS are unclear. Various observations regarding PTNS are made in the systematic review by Gaziev et al. [29], with the main conclusion being that there is evidence that the effect could be from changes at the end organ, spinal cord, and supraspinal locations.

4.6. Future directions

4.6.1. Permanent implant

A permanent PTNS implant has potential advantages over the present repeated sessions of percutaneous stimulation, presumably with an increase in initial cost and risk. With the implant, the patient would not need to visit the clinic to receive treatment. Depending on the cost of the surgery and equipment, it is possible that over the long-term the implanted system would be less expensive than the numerous visits to the clinic over the patient's lifetime.

Van der Pal and colleagues [70] published results from 8 patients that received tibial nerve stimulation through the combination of a subcutaneous implant and an external stimulator known as the Urgent SQ. All patients had been successfully treated (>= 50% reduction of the number of incontinence episodes and/or voids on bladder diary – the primary objective) previously with PTNS. At the 12 month follow-up, four met the primary outcome.

Despite the relative success of the implant there have been no new developments regarding an implantable system. In 2013, a 9-year follow-up study was presented examining safety and efficacy of the implants [43]. No major safety concerns were reported and three of the patients still used their device.

4.6.2. Transcutaneous stimulation

An alternative approach to an implant or percutaneous stimulation is the use of electrodes on the surface of the skin. Like an implant, this approach may allow the patient to control their own therapy as well as reduce cost. Both McGuire et al. [64] and Geirsson et al. [31] used surface electrodes for stimulation with positive results. A study in 2010 used transcutaneous PTNS with the current therapeutic regimen (i.e., 12 weekly sessions of 30 minute duration) to treat older women (age

≥ 60 years) with urgency urinary incontinence [84]. The average number of incontinent episodes over a 72 hour period was reduced by 6.3 ± 5.3 (mean $\pm$ SD) versus a reduction of only 1.3 ± 1.6 in a control group. These results suggest that positive outcomes using transcutaneous PTNS are possible, although it is still unclear how these results would compare to a percutaneous approach.

The uncertainty surrounding the transcutaneous approach highlights the importance of neural recruitment at the site of the tibial nerve. It is not known if, or to what degree, performance varies as a function of the number and type of tibial nerve fibers activated by electrical stimulation. Assuming that performance does indeed depend on the complement of nerve fibers activated, it is not clear what pattern of activation is produced by either percutaneous or transcutaneous stimulation.

5. Sacral Anterior Root Stimulation for Spinal Cord Injury

Bladder dysfunction secondary to spinal cord injury significantly impacts quality of life [4]. Lack of sensation often leads to reflex incontinence in which the lower urinary tract reflexively voids without a person being able to prepare appropriately. At the same time, this voiding is often inefficient and can lead to urinary retention, a significant problem that can lead to damage to the upper urinary tract and the bladder.

Clean intermittent catheterization is typically recommended for treatment. An effective alternative is the use of a sacral anterior root stimulator (SARS). Electrical stimulation is performed at a location that is proximal to the site of sacral neuromodulation and is targeted to the anterior (ventral) roots that contain the preganglionic parasympathetic nerve fibers innervating the bladder as well as the somatic nerve fibers innervating the striated external urethral sphincter. Due to lack of commercial support in the United States as well as the need to perform an irreversible posterior rhizotomy, market penetrance is quite low given the reported efficacy of this technique.

5.1. *History*

Work towards what would become the SARS stimulator was started in 1969 by Dr. Giles Brindley, who directed the Medical Research Council (Britain's NIH) Neurological Prosthesis Unit. Much of the early work on bladder emptying via electrical stimulation focused on direct bladder stimulation (*i.e.*, placement of electrodes on the bladder) [12, 13, 37]. Brindley instead focused on stimulation of sacral nerve roots.

Initial studies were performed in baboons [14]. In 1982 Brindley published a report of having implanted 11 patients with traumatic spinal cord lesions [17]. In the same year the Finetech-Brindley bladder controller (Fintech Ltd.) became commercially available (http://finetech-medical.co.uk/en-gb/aboutus.aspx). By 1992 there were 500 patients implanted with the device across Europe [16].

CE Mark for the stimulator was achieved in 1996. A Human-Device Exemption was granted by the FDA in 1998 to NeuroControl Corporation to market the device (branded as VOCARE in the United States). Unfortunately, in 2007 NeuroControl went out of business, limiting US access to the device. To some extent this illustrates the difficult commercial environment for products addressing spinal cord injury due to the relatively small market (~10,000 new injuries in the United States per year).

The Finetech-Bradley sacral anterior root stimulator is still commercially available from Finetech Medical. Their website estimates that nearly 4000 people have received the implant (http://finetech-medical.co.uk/en-gb/aboutus.aspx).

5.2. *Implantation Procedure*

Sacral nerve roots are exposed via a laminectomy. The anterior (ventral, motor) and posterior (dorsal, sensory) roots are mechanically separated. The anterior roots are placed in electrodes, known as books due to their shape (see Fig. 4). Wires from the electrode are routed to a radio receiver block which is placed subcutaneously in the abdominal wall. Unlike the InterStim system which uses a battery-powered IPG, the Finetech-Brindley implant is passive, and the external controller sends power and control signals wirelessly via induction. The stimulator equipment can be seen in Figure 5. Further descriptions of the surgical procedures can be found elsewhere [28, 47]. Additionally, in some cases extradural electrodes may be used [105].

In addition to placing the anterior roots inside an electrode, a posterior rhizotomy is also performed as part of the procedure. As discussed by Brindley [15], posterior rhizotomy is thought to treat reflex incontinence, improve bladder compliance, and abolish detrusor-sphincter dyssynergia. This sensory nerve transection, however, eliminates any residual sensation as well as reflex erection and ejaculation, making this approach an unattractive option for some individuals.

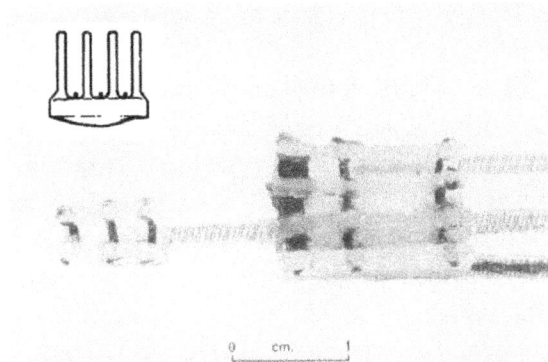

Fig. 4. Example electrodes with leads. Anterior sacral roots are placed in each individual slot. A cover (not shown) is then placed over the electrode to hold the roots in place. In the configuration shown S4 roots are placed in the individual slot (left) and the S2 and S3 roots are placed in the grouped slots (right). Each slot contains three electrodes, a cathode in the center and two anodes at the ends to avoid stimulation of unwanted structures. The inset shows a transverse view of an electrode. (Adapted from [17])

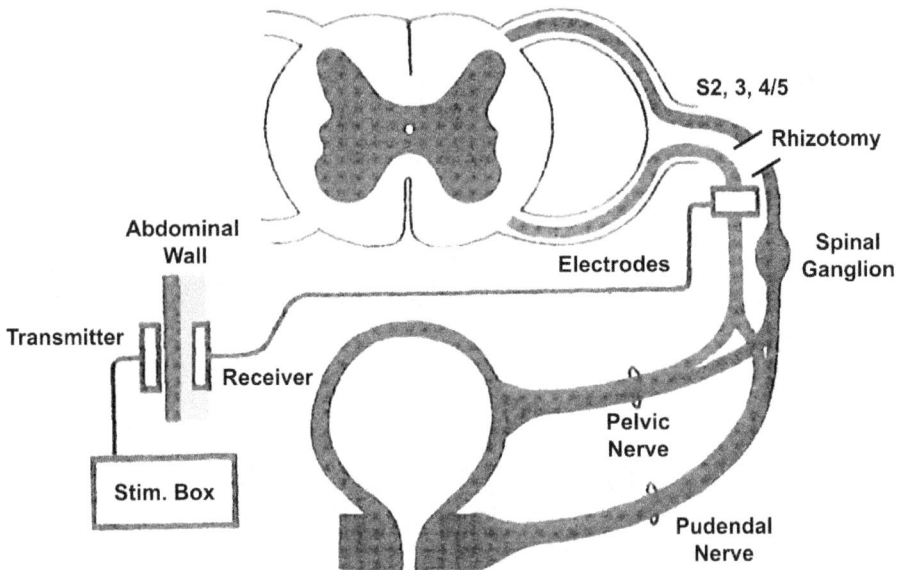

Fig. 5. Schematic of the Finetech-Brindley system.

5.3. *Stimulation paradigm and usage*

Unlike sacral neuromodulation, sacral anterior root stimulation is not applied continuously. Using the external controller, a patient can typically select from up

J. A. Hokanson et al.

to three programs. The primary program (in this context) is to empty the bladder on demand. Secondary programs can be used to trigger defecation as well as erection or vaginal lubrication [15].

Although a rhizotomy eliminates spontaneous detrusor-sphincter dyssnergia, electrical stimulation of the anterior roots still causes simultaneous activation of the striated sphincter muscle along with a bladder contraction. This is because neurons innervating the striated muscle have larger diameter axons and are thus recruited by electrical stimulation at a lower amplitude than the smaller diameter axons innervating the bladder. Put another way, it is not possible using standard electrical stimulation paradigms to activate only nerve fibers that innervate the bladder, so as to cause voiding without increasing urethral outlet resistance.

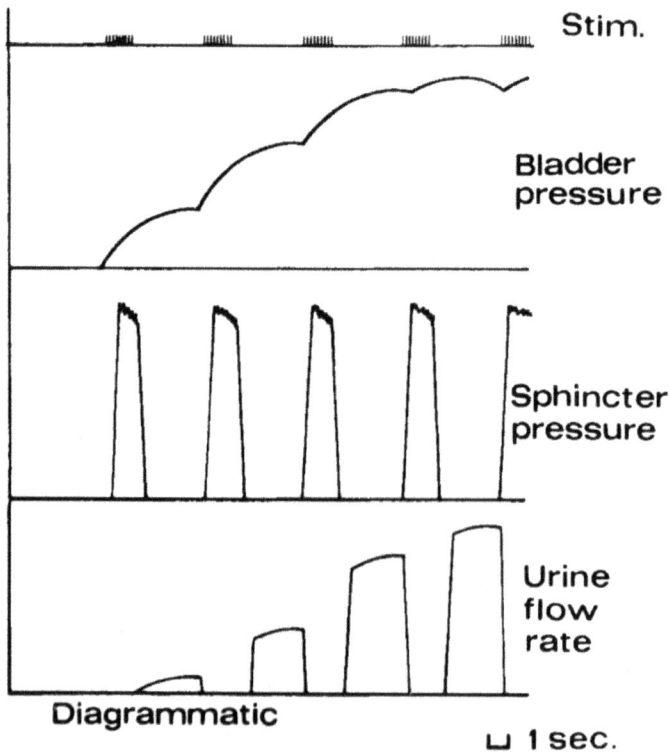

Stim.

Bladder pressure

Sphincter pressure

Urine flow rate

Diagrammatic

⊔ 1 sec.

Fig. 6. Diagram illustrating voiding between bursts of stimulation. Stimulation increases both urethral sphincter pressure and bladder pressure. When stimulation is not occurring the sphincter quickly relaxes, allowing the built up bladder pressure to expel fluid. Optimal burst duration and rest interval vary between patients. (Reproduced from [17] with permission)

To overcome this obstacle, stimulation is performed with a series of stimulus pulses followed by a non-stimulation epoch. Since the striated sphincter muscle relaxes more rapidly than the smooth muscle of the bladder, adequate pressure to cause voiding is maintained during the non-stimulation period. This process of stimulation followed by a non-stimulation period is repeated multiple times to fully empty the bladder. This process is illustrated in Figure 6.

5.4. *Efficacy*

The percentage of patients using their sacral root stimulators after many years is high. Egon et al. [28] reported that 89 % of patients (83 of 93) still used their implant for micturition (mean follow-up 5.4 years for males and 5.8 years for females). A similar result of 92 % (170 of 184) was reported by van Kerrebroeck [48] (follow-up time unspecified). Krasmik et al. [51] reported a slightly lower success rate of 78 % (107 of 137) although their mean follow-up time was 14.8 years. Krasmik et al. noted that this long-term success rate was in spite of a substantial long-term complication rate, with 54 patients requiring a total of 83 surgical revisions.

Use of the stimulator decreased residual volume after voiding. Creasey et al. [26] reported that 81 % patients (17 of 21) achieved residuals of less than 50 ml. Similarly, van Kerrebroeck et al. [48] reported that 88 % of patients (161/184) had residual volumes less than 60 ml.

Following stimulator implant there was also a reduction in the severity and frequency of incontinent episodes. These changes are likely mostly due to the dorsal rhizotomy as opposed to the use of the stimulator. Reported percentages of patients that were continent following implant were 61 % [51], 86 % [48] and 88 % [28]. Creasey et al. [26] reported that only 6 of 17 patients were continent (35 %) but that incontinence had been reduced in 12 of 17 (71 %) of patients, often to a level that was easily managed with pads.

Use of the stimulator led to a decrease in the number of urinary tract infections (UTIs). Presumably these changes come from a decrease in residual volume and the reduction or elimination of incontinent episodes. Creasey et al. [26] reported that 18 of 23 patients reported fewer UTIs. van Kerrebroeck et al. [48] reported that 119 patients did not have UTIs, up from 17 preoperatively.

The stimulator can also be used to assist defecation or cause (and maintain) an erection. Usage rates for defecation were 55 % [28], 56 % [18], and 70 % [48]. Stimulation was used by patients to cause an erection in 68 % [28], 41 % [18], and 56 % [48] of cases. Although stimulation of the sacral roots can cause vaginal lubrication [15], we could not find any reported rates of this occurring in the literature.

6. Conclusions

Electrical stimulation for treatment of lower urinary tract dysfunction is now well established when more conservative measures fail. Sacral neuromodulation is effective across multiple symptoms of LUT dysfunction, although there are many patients that do not benefit from this therapy. Posterior tibial nerve stimulation appears to be a therapeutic option after failing first line therapy, although much work remains to identify who will benefit most from this therapy, and how treatment works in the long term. Sacral anterior root stimulation works extremely well in the spinal cord injured patient, but requires a posterior rhizotomy in order to facilitate proper bladder filling and emptying.

As was evident from the history of these devices, moving out of the lab and gaining clinical traction required strong commercial backing. After over a decade of small clinical trials, Medtronic's commercialization of sacral neuromodulation was certainly instrumental in advancing the therapy. Similarly, after nearly a decade of small scale clinical testing, commercial interests secured FDA approval for percutaneous tibial nerve stimulation. Finetech (now Finetech Medical) was there from the start to produce stimulators for sacral anterior root stimulation. The commercial failure of this device in the United States has hindered its subsequent clinical use.

Mechanisms of action remain largely unknown for both sacral neuromodulation and PTNS. This translates into a poor ability to identify patients that will benefit from these therapies. Instead, a "try it and see" approach seems to prevail, in which the therapy is tried and continued if successful. This approach however is neither cost effective nor efficient. Additionally, the lack of well understood mechanisms of action makes it difficult to improve the therapy.

It is beneficial to identify patient characteristics that are predictive factors of success to guide treatment. Although there have been some efforts to do this, statistical power has been lacking, and overall characterization has been minimal. There is currently a NIDDK led effort known as the Symptoms of Lower Urinary Tract Dysfunction Research Network (LURN) to develop and qualify symptom-based instruments to measure early, late, transient, and persistent symptoms in both men and women, as well as to define phenotypes of men and women with symptoms of lower urinary tract dysfunction. Results from this study could have a significant impact on identifying patients that will respond well to treatment.

Acknowledgements

NIH K12-DK100024 and NIH R01 NS050514.

References

1. Abrams, P., Cardozo, L., Fall, M., Griffiths, D. J., Rosier, P., Ulmsten, U., van Kerrebroeck, P. E. V., Victor, A. and Wein, A. (2002). The standardisation of terminology of lower urinary tract function: Report from the standardisation sub-committee of the international continence society, *Am J Obstet Gynecol* **187**, 116–126.

2. Amend, B., Khalil, M., Kessler, T. M. and Sievert, K. (2011). How does sacral modulation work best? Placement and programming techniques to maximize efficacy, *Curr Urol Rep* **12**, 327–335.

3. Amundsen, C. L., Romero, A. A., Jamison, M. G. and Webster, G. D. (2005). Sacral neuromodulation for intractable urge incontinence: are there factors associated with cure? *Urology* **66**, 746–750.

4. Anderson, K. D. (2004). Targeting recovery: priorities of the spinal cord-injured population, *J Neurotrauma* **21**, 1371–1383.

5. van Balken, M. R., Vergunst, H. and Bemelmans, B. L. H. (2006). Prognostic factors for successful percutaneous tibial nerve stimulation, *Eur Urol* **49**, 360–365.

6. Benner, J. S., Nichol, M. B., Rovner, E. S., Jumadilova, Z., Alvir, J., Hussein, M., Fanning, K., Trocio, J. N. and Brubaker, L. (2010). Patient-reported reasons for discontinuing overactive bladder medication, *BJU Int* **105**, 1276–1282.

7. Biemans, J. M. and van Balken, M. R. (2013). Efficacy and effectiveness of percutaneous tibial nerve stimulation in the treatment of pelvic organ disorders: a systematic review, *Neuromodulation* **16**, 25–34.

8. Boggs, J. W., Wenzel, B. J., Gustafson, K. J. and Grill, W. M. (2006). Frequency-dependent selection of reflexes by pudendal afferents in the cat, *J Physiol* **577**, 115–126.

9. Bolinger, R. and Engberg, S. (2012). Barriers, complications, adherence, and self-reported quality of life for people using clean intermittent catheterization, *J Wound Ostomy Continence Nurs* **40**, 1–7.

10. Bosch, J. L. H. R. and Groen, J. (1996). Treatment of refractory urge urinary incontinence with sacral spinal nerve stimulation in multiple sclerosis patients, *Lancet* **348**, 717–719.

11. Bosch, J. L. H. R. and Groen, J. (2000). Sacral nerve neuromodulation in the treatment of patients with refractory motor urge incontinence: long-term results of a prospective longitudinal study, *J Urol* **163**, 1219–1222.

12. Boyce, W. H., Lathem, J. E. and Hunt, L. D. (1964). Research related to the development of an artificial electrical stimulator for the paralyzed human bladder: a review, *J Urol* **91**, 41–51.

13. Bradley, W. E., Wittmers, L. E., Chou, S. N. and French, L. A. (1962). Use of a radio transmitter receiver unit for the treatment of neurogenic bladder. A preliminary report, *J Neurosurg* **19**, 782–786.

14. Brindley, G. S. (1977). An implant to empty the bladder or close the urethra, *J Neurol Neurosurg Psychiatry* **40**, 358–369.

15. Brindley, G. S. (1988). The Ferrier lecture, 1986. The actions of parasympathetic and sympathetic nerves in human micturition, erection and seminal emission, and their restoration in paraplegic patients by implanted electrical stimulators, *Proc R Soc London Ser B, Biol Sci* **235**, 111–120.

16. Brindley, G. S. (1994). The first 500 patients with sacral anterior root stimulator implants: general description, *Paraplegia* **32**, 795–805.

17. Brindley, G. S., Polkey, C. E. and Rushton, D. N. (1982). Sacral anterior root stimulators for bladder control in paraplegia, *Paraplegia* **20**, 365–381.

18. Brindley, G. S. and Rushton, D. N. (1990). Long-term follow-up of patients with sacral anterior root stimulator implants, *Paraplegia* **28**, 469–475.

19. Brookoff, D. and Bennett, D. S. (2006). Neuromodulation in intractable interstitial cystitis and related pelvic pain syndromes, *Pain Med* **7**, S166–S184.

20. Brostrøm, S. and Hallas, J. (2009). Persistence of antimuscarinic drug use, *Eur J Clin Pharmacol* **65**, 309–314.

21. Burton, C., Sajja, A. and Latthe, P.M. (2012). Effectiveness of percutaneous posterior tibial nerve stimulation for overactive bladder: a systematic review and meta-analysis, *Neurourol Urodyn* **31**, 1206–1216.

22. Chai, T. C., Zhang, C.-O., Warren, J. W. and Keay, S. (2000). Percutaneous sacral third nerve root neurostimulation improves symptoms and normalizes urinary HB-EGF levels and antiproliferative activity in patients with interstitial cystitis, *Urology* **55**, 643–646.

23. Chartier-Kastler, E. J., Ruud Bosch, J. L., Perrigot, M., Chancellor, M. B., Richard, F. and Denys, P. (2000). Long-term results of sacral nerve stimulation (S3) for the treatment of neurogenic refractory urge incontinence related to detrusor hyperreflexia, *J Urol* **164**, 1476–1480.

24. Comiter, C. V. (2003). Sacral neuromodulation for the symptomatic treatment of refractory interstitial cystitis: a prospective study, *J Urol* **169**, 1369–1373.

25. Cooperberg, M. R. and Stoller, M. L. (2005). Percutaneous neuromodulation, *Urol Clin North Am* **32**, 71–78, vii.

26. Creasey, G. H., Grill, J. H., Korsten, M., Betz, R., Anderson, R. and Walter, J. (2001). An implantable neuroprosthesis for restoring bladder and bowel control to patients with spinal cord injuries: A multicenter trial, *Arch Phys Med Rehabil* **82**, 1512–1519.

27. Dudding, T. C. (2011). Future indications for sacral nerve stimulation, *Colorectal Dis* **13 Suppl 2**, 23–28.

28. Egon, G., Barat, M., Colombel, P., Visentin, C., Isambert, J. L. and Guerin, J. (1998). Implantation of anterior sacral root stimulators combined with posterior sacral rhizotomy in spinal injury patients, *World J Urol* **16**, 342–349.

29. Gaziev, G., Topazio, L., Iacovelli, V., Asimakopoulos, A., Di Santo, A., De Nunzio, C. & Finazzi-Agrò, E. (2013). Percutaneous Tibial Nerve Stimulation (PTNS) efficacy in the treatment of lower urinary tract dysfunctions: a systematic review, *BMC Urol* **13**, 61.

30. Geirsson, G. and Fall, M. (1997). Maximal functional electrical stimulation in routine practice, *Neurourol Urodyn* **16**, 559–565.

31. Geirsson, G., Wang, Y. H., Lindström, S. and Fall, M. (1993). Traditional acupuncture and electrical stimulation of the posterior tibial nerve. A trial in chronic interstitial cystitis, *Scand J Urol Nephrol* **27**, 67–70.

32. Godec, C. and Cass, A. (1978). Acute electrical stimulation for urinary incontinence, *Urology* **12**, 340–341.

33. Goh, M. and Diokno, A. C. (2007). Sacral neuromodulation for nonobstructive urinary retention--is success predictable? *J Urol* **178**, 197–199; discussion 199.

34. Govier, F. E., Litwiller, S., Nitti, V., Kreder, K. J. and Rosenblatt, P. (2001). Percutaneous afferent neuromodulation for the refractory overactive bladder: results of a multicenter study, *J Urol* **165**, 1193–1198.

35. Groenendijk, P. M., Lycklama à Nyeholt, A. A. B., Heesakkers, J. P. F. A., van Kerrebroeck, P. E. V., Hassouna, M. M., Gajewski, J. B., Cappellano, F., Siegel, S. W., Fall, M., Dijkema, H. E., Jonas, U. and van den Hombergh, U. (2008). Urodynamic evaluation of sacral neuromodulation for urge urinary incontinence, *BJU Int* **101**, 325–329.

36. Gross, C., Habli, M., Lindsell, C. and South, M. (2010). Sacral neuromodulation for nonobstructive urinary retention: a meta-analysis, *Female Pelvic Med Reconstr Surg* **16**, 249–253.

37. Habib, H. N. (1967). Experience and recent contributions in sacral nerve stimulation for voiding in both human and animal, *Br J Urol* **39**, 73–83.

38. Hassouna, M. M., Siegel, S. W., Nÿeholt, A. A., Elhilali, M. M., van Kerrebroeck, P. E. V., Das, A. K., Gajewski, J. B., Janknegt, R. A., Rivas, D. A., Dijkema, H., Milam, D. F., Oleson, K. A. and Schmidt, R. A. (2000). Sacral neuromodulation in the treatment of urgency-frequency symptoms: a multicenter study on efficacy and safety, *J Urol* **163**, 1849–1854.

39. Heine, J. P., Schmidt, R. A. and Tanagho, E. A. (1977). Intraspinal sacral root stimulation for controlled micturition, *Invest Urol* **15**, 78–82.

40. Huang, J. C., Deletis, V., Vodušek, D. B. and Abbott, R. (1997). Preservation of pudendal afferents in sacral rhizotomies, *Neurosurgery* **41**, 411–415.

41. Janknegt, R. A., Hassouna, M. M., Siegel, S. W., Schmidt, R. A., Gajewski, J. B., Rivas, D. A., Elhilali, M. M., Milam, D. C., van Kerrebroeck, P. E. V. A., Dijkema, H. E., Lycklama a Nyeholt, A. A., Fall, M., Jonas, U., Catanzaro, F., Fowler, C. J. and Oleson, K. A. (2001). Long-term effectiveness of sacral nerve stimulation for refractory urge incontinence, *Eur Urol* **39**, 101–106.

42. Janknegt, R. A., Weil, E. H. and Eerdmans, P. H. (1997). Improving neuromodulation technique for refractory voiding dysfunctions: two-stage implant, *Urology* **49**, 358–362.

43. Janssen, D. A., Farag, F. and Heesakkers, J. P. (2013). Urgent-SQ implant in treatment of overactive bladder syndrome: 9-year follow-up study, *Neurourol Urodyn* **32**, 472–475.

44. Kamm, M. A., Dudding, T. C., Melenhorst, J., Jarrett, M., Wang, Z., Buntzen, S., Johansson, C., Laurberg, S., Rosen, H., Vaizey, C. J., Matzel, K. and Baeten, C. (2010). Sacral nerve stimulation for intractable constipation, *Gut* **59**, 333–340.

45. Kenefick, N. J., Vaizey, C. J., Cohen, C. R. G., Nicholls, R. J. and Kamm, M. A. (2002). Double-blind placebo-controlled crossover study of sacral nerve stimulation for idiopathic constipation, *Br J Surg* **89**, 1570–1571.

46. van Kerrebroeck, P. E. V., van Voskuilen, A. C., Heesakkers, J. P. F. A., Lycklama á Nijholt, A. A. B., Siegel, S. W., Jonas, U., Fowler, C. J., Fall, M., Gajewski, J. B., Hassouna, M. M., Cappellano, F., Elhilali, M. M., Milam, D. F., Das, A. K., Dijkema, H. E. and van den Hombergh, U. (2007). Results of sacral neuromodulation therapy for urinary voiding dysfunction: outcomes of a prospective, worldwide clinical study, *J Urol* **178**, 2029–2034.

47. van Kerrebroeck, P. E. V. A., Koldewijn, E., Wijkstra, H. and Debruyne, F. M. (1991). Intradural sacral rhizotomies and implantation of an anterior sacral root stimulator in the treatment of neurogenic bladder dysfunction after spinal cord injury - Surgical technique and complications, *World J Urol* **9**, 126–132.

48. van Kerrebroeck, P. E. V. A., Koldewijn, E. L. and Debruyne, F. M. (1993). Worldwide experience with the Finetech-Brindley sacral anterior root stimulator, *Neurourol Urodyn* **12**, 497–503.

49. Klingler, H. C., Pycha, A., Schmidbauer, J. and Marberger, M. (2000). Use of peripheral neuromodulation of the S3 region for treatment of detrusor overactivity: a urodynamic-based study, *Urology* **56**, 776–777.

50. Koldewijn, E. L., Rosier, P. F., Meuleman, E. J., Koster, A. M., Debruyne, F. M. and van Kerrebroeck, P. E. (1994). Predictors of success with neuromodulation in lower urinary tract dysfunction: results of trial stimulation in 100 patients, *J Urol* **152**, 2071–2075.

51. Krasmik, D., Krebs, J., van Ophoven, A. and Pannek, J (2014). Urodynamic results, clinical efficacy, and complication rates of sacral intradural deafferentation and sacral anterior root stimulation in patients with neurogenic lower urinary tract dysfunction resulting from complete spinal cord injury, *Neurourol Urodyn* **33**, 1202–1206.

52. Latini, J. M. and Giannantoni, A. (2011). Pharmacotherapy of overactive bladder: epidemiology and pathophysiology of overactive bladder, *Expert Opin Pharmacother* **12**, 1017–1027.

53. Levin, P. J., Wu, J. M., Kawasaki, A., Weidner, A. C. and Amundsen, C. L. (2012). The efficacy of posterior tibial nerve stimulation for the treatment of overactive bladder in women: a systematic review, *Int Urogynecol J* **23**, 1591–1597.

54. Lindström, S., Fall, M., Carlsson, C. A. and Erlandson, B. E. (1983). The neurophysiological basis of bladder inhibition in response to intravaginal electrical stimulation, *J Urol* **129**, 405–410.

55. MacDiarmid, S. A., Peters, K. M., Shobeiri, S. A., Wooldridge, L. S., Rovner, E. S., Leong, F. C., Siegel, S. W., Tate, S. B. and Feagins, B. A. (2010). Long-term durability of percutaneous tibial nerve stimulation for the treatment of overactive bladder, *J Urol* **183**, 234–240.

56. MacDiarmid, S. A. and Siegel, S. W. (2014). Posterior tibial nerve stimulation before a trial of sacral nerve stimulation for refractory urge incontinence, *J Urol* **191**, 1652–1654.

57. Maher, C. F., Carey, M. P., Dwyer, P. L. and Schluter, P. L. (2001). Percutaneous sacral nerve root neuromodulation for intractable interstitial cystitis, *J Urol* **165**, 884–886.

58. Marinkovic, S. P. and Gillen, L. M. (2010). Sacral neuromodulation for multiple sclerosis patients with urinary retention and clean intermittent catheterization, *Int Urogynecol J* **21**, 223–228.

59. Marinkovic, S. P., Gillen, L. M. and Marinkovic, C. M. (2011). Minimum 6-year outcomes for interstitial cystitis treated with sacral neuromodulation, *Int Urogynecol J* **22**, 407–412.

60. Martellucci, J. (2015). The technique of sacral nerve modulation, *Colorectal Dis* **17**, O88–O94.

61. Martinson, M., MacDiarmid, S. and Black, E. (2013). Cost of neuromodulation therapies for overactive bladder: percutaneous tibial nerve stimulation versus sacral nerve stimulation, *J Urol* **189**, 210–216.

62. McGee, M. J., Danziger, Z. C., Bamford, J. A. and Grill, W. M. (2014). A spinal GABAergic mechanism is necessary for bladder inhibition by pudendal afferent stimulation, *Am J Physiol Renal Physiol* **307**, F921–F930.

63. McGee, M. J. and Grill, W. M. (2015). Temporal pattern of stimulation modulates reflex bladder activation by pudendal nerve stimulation, *Neurourol Urodyn* **35**, n/a – n/a.

64. McGuire, E. J., Zhang, S. C., Horwinski, E. R. and Lytton, B. (1983). Treatment of motor and sensory detrusor instability by electrical stimulation, *J Urol* **129**, 78–79.

65. Moore, T. and Schofield, P. F. (1967). Treatment of stress incontinence by maximum perineal electrical stimulation, *Br Med J* **3**, 150–151.

66. Moossdorff-Steinhauser, H. F. A. and Berghmans, B. (2013). Effects of percutaneous tibial nerve stimulation on adult patients with overactive bladder syndrome: a systematic review, *Neurourol Urodyn* **32**, 206–214.

67. Nakamura, M., Sakurai, T., Tsujimoto, Y. and Tada, Y. (1983). [Transcutaneous electrical stimulation for the control of frequency and urge incontinence], *Hinyokika Kiyo* **29**, 1053–1059.

68. Onukwugha, E., Zuckerman, I. H., McNally, D., Coyne, K. S., Vats, V. and Mullins, C. D. (2009). The total economic burden of overactive bladder in the United States: a disease-specific approach, *Am J Manag Care* **15**, S90–S97.

69. van der Pal, F., van Balken, M. R., Heesakkers, J. P. F. A., Debruyne, F. M. J. and Bemelmans, B. L. H. (2006). Percutaneous tibial nerve stimulation in the treatment of refractory overactive bladder syndrome: Is maintenance treatment necessary? *BJU Int* **97**, 547–550.

70. van der Pal, F., van Balken, M. R., Heesakkers, J. P. F. A., Debruyne, F. M. J. and Bemelmans, B. L. H. (2006). Implant-driven tibial nerve stimulation in the treatment of refractory overactive bladder syndrome: 12-month follow-up, *Neuromodulation* **9**, 163–171.

71. Peeters, K., Sahai, A., de Ridder, D. and van der Aa, F. (2014). Long-term follow-up of sacral neuromodulation for lower urinary tract dysfunction, *BJU Int* **113**, 789–794.

72. Peng, C.-W., Chen, J.-J. J., Cheng, C.-L. and Grill, W. M. (2008). Improved bladder emptying in urinary retention by electrical stimulation of pudendal afferents, *J Neural Eng* **5**, 144–154.

73. Peters, K. M., Carrico, D. J., Perez-Marrero, R. A., Khan, A. U., Wooldridge, L. S., Davis, G. L. and MacDiarmid, S. A. (2010). Randomized trial of percutaneous tibial nerve stimulation versus Sham efficacy in the treatment of overactive bladder syndrome: results from the SUmiT trial, *J Urol* **183**, 1438–1443.

74. Peters, K. M., Carrico, D. J., Wooldridge, L. S., Miller, C. J. and MacDiarmid, S. A. (2013). Percutaneous tibial nerve stimulation for the long-term treatment of overactive bladder: 3-year results of the STEP study, *J Urol* **189**, 2194–2201.

75. Peters, K. M. and Konstandt, D. (2004). Sacral neuromodulation decreases narcotic requirements in refractory interstitial cystitis, *BJU Int* **93**, 777–779.

76. Plevnik, S. and Janez, J. (1979). Maximal electrical stimulation for urinary incontinence: report of 98 cases, *Urology* **14**, 638–645.

77. Scheepens, W. A., Weil, E.H., van Koeveringe, G. A., Rohrmann, D., Hedlund, H. E., Schurch, B., Ostardo, E., Pastorello, M., Ratto, C., Nordling, J. and van Kerrebroeck, P. E. (2001). Buttock placement of the implantable pulse generator: a new implantation technique for sacral neuromodulation--a multicenter study, *Eur Urol* **40**, 434–438.

78. Schmidt, R. A. (1983). Neural prostheses and bladder control, *Eng Med Biol Mag* **2**, 31–36.

79. Schmidt, R. A. (1988). Applications of neurostimulation in urology, *Neurourol Urodyn* **7**, 585–592.

80. Schmidt, R. A. (2010). The winding path to sacral foramen neural modulation: a historic chronology. *Int Urogynecol J* **21** Suppl 2, S431–S438.

81. Schmidt, R. A., Bruschini, H. and Tanagho, E. A. (1979). Urinary bladder and sphincter responses to stimulation of dorsal and ventral sacral roots. *Invest Urol* **16**, 300–304.

82. Schmidt, R. A., Jonas, U., Oleson, K. A., Janknegt, R. A., Hassouna, M. M., Siegel, S. W. and van Kerrebroeck, P. E. V. (1999). Sacral nerve stimulation for treatment of refractory urinary urge incontinence. Sacral Nerve Stimulation Study Group, *J Urol* **162**, 352–357.

83. Schmidt, R. A., Senn, E. and Tanagho, E. A. (1990). Functional evaluation of sacral nerve root integrity. Report of a technique, *Urology* **35**, 388–392.

84. Schreiner, L., dos Santos, T. G., Knorst, M. R. and da Silva Filho, I. G. (2010). Randomized trial of transcutaneous tibial nerve stimulation to treat urge urinary incontinence in older women, *Int Urogynecol J* **21**, 1065–1070.

85. Sherman, N. D., Jamison, M. G., Webster, G. D. and Amundsen, C. L. (2005). Sacral neuromodulation for the treatment of refractory urinary urge incontinence after stress incontinence surgery, *Am J Obstet Gynecol* **193**, 2083–2087.

86. Siddiqui, N. Y., Wu, J. M. and Amundsen, C. L. (2010). Efficacy and adverse events of sacral nerve stimulation for overactive bladder: A systematic review, *Neurourol Urodyn* **29 Suppl 1**, S18–S23.

87. Siegel, S., Paszkiewicz ,E., Kirkpatrick, C., Hinkel, B. and Oleson, K. (2001). Sacral nerve stimulation in patients with chronic intractable pelvic pain, *J Urol* **166**, 1742–1745.

88. Siegel SW (1992). Management of voiding dysfunction with an implantable neuroprosthesis, *Urol Clin North Am* **19**, 163-70.

89. Siegel, S. W., Catanzaro, F., Dijkema, H. E., Elhilali, M. M., Fowler, C.J., Gajewski, J. B., Hassouna, M. M., Janknegt, R. A., Jonas, U., van Kerrebroeck, P. E. V., Lycklama a Nijeholt, A. A. B., Oleson, K. A. and Schmidt, R. A. (2000). Long-term results of a multicenter study on sacral nerve stimulation for treatment of urinary urge incontinence, urgency-frequency, and retention, *Urology* **56**, 87–91.

90. South, M. M. T., Romero, A. A., Jamison, M. G., Webster, G. D. and Amundsen, C. L. (2007). Detrusor overactivity does not predict outcome of sacral neuromodulation test stimulation. *Int Urogynecol J Pelvic Floor Dysfunct* **18**, 1395–1398.

91. Spinelli, M., Giardiello, G., Gerber, M., Arduini, A., van den Hombergh, U. and Malaguti, S. (2003). New sacral neuromodulation lead for percutaneous implantation using local anesthesia: description and first experience, *J Urol* **170**, 1905–1907.

92. Spinelli, M. and Sievert, K. (2008). Latest technologic and surgical developments in using interstim therapy for sacral neuromodulation: impact on treatment success and safety, *Eur Urol* **54**, 1287–1296.

93. Staskin, D. R., Peters, K. M., MacDiarmid, S., Shore, N. and de Groat, W. C. (2012). Percutaneous tibial nerve stimulation: a clinically and cost effective addition to the overactive bladder algorithm of care, *Curr Urol Rep* **13**, 327–334.

94. Stoller, M. L. (1999). Afferent nerve stimulation for pelvic floor dysfunction, *Eur Urol* **35**, 16.

95. Tanagho, E. A. and Schmidt, R. A. (1988). Electrical stimulation in the clinical management of the neurogenic bladder, *J Urol* **140**, 1331–1339.

96. Thomas, G. P., Dudding, T. C., Rahbour, G., Nicholls, R. J. and Vaizey, C. J. (2013). Sacral nerve stimulation for constipation, *Br J Surg* **100**, 174–181.

97. Vandoninck, V., van Balken, M. R., Finazzi Agrò, E., Heesakkers, J. P. F. A., Debruyne, F. M. J., Kiemeney, L. A. L. M. and Bemelmans, B. L. H. (2004). Posterior tibial nerve stimulation in the treatment of voiding dysfunction: urodynamic data, *Neurourol Urodyn* **23**, 246–251.

98. Vandoninck, V., van Balken, M. R., Finazzi Agrò, E., Petta, F., Micali, F., Heesakkers, J. P. F. A., Debruyne, F. M. J., Kiemeney, L. A. L. M and Bemelmans, B. L. H. (2003). Percutaneous tibial nerve stimulation in the treatment of overactive bladder: urodynamic data, *Neurourol Urodyn* **22**, 227–232.

99. Wallace, P. A., Lane, F. L. and Noblett, K. L. (2007). Sacral nerve neuromodulation in patients with underlying neurologic disease, *Am J Obstet Gynecol* **197**, 1–5.

100. Ware, J. E. and Sherbourne, C. D. (1992). The MOS 36-item short-form health survey (SF-36). I. Conceptual framework and item selection, *Med Care* **30**, 473–483.

101. Weil, E. H., Ruiz-Cerdá, J. L., Eerdmans, P. H., Janknegt, R. A., Bemelmans, B.L. and van Kerrebroeck, P. E. V. (2000). Sacral root neuromodulation in the treatment of refractory urinary urge incontinence: a prospective randomized clinical trial, *Eur Urol* **37**, 161–171.

102. Woock, J. P., Yoo, P. B. and Grill, W. M. (2009). Intraurethral stimulation evokes bladder responses via 2 distinct reflex pathways, *J Urol* **182**, 366–373.

103. Woock, J. P., Yoo, P. B. and Grill, W. M. (2011). Mechanisms of reflex bladder activation by pudendal afferents, *Am J Physiol Regul Integr Comp Physiol* **300**, R398–R407.

104. Yoo, P. B., Woock, J. P. and Grill, W. M. (2008). Bladder activation by selective stimulation of pudendal nerve afferents in the cat, *Exp Neurol* **212**, 218–225.

105. Martens, F. M. J. and Heesakkers, J. P. F. A. (2011) Clinical results of a Brindley procedure: sacral anterior root stimulation in combination with a rhizotomy of the dorsal roots, *Adv. Urol.*, **2011**, 709708.

Chapter 3.3

Neuroprosthetic Control of Respiratory Muscles

Anthony F. DiMarco and Graham H. Creasey

Professor of Physical Medicine and Rehabilitation, Physiology and Biophysics, Case Western Reserve University Rammelkamp Research Center, MetroHealth Medical Center, Cleveland, Ohio 44109
and
Paralyzed Veterans of America Professor of Spinal Cord Injury Medicine, Department of Neurosurgery, Stanford University School of Medicine, Stanford, California 94305
gcreasey@stanford.edu

Neuroprosthetic control of respiratory muscles has been used for nearly half a century to restore effective inspiration long term, mainly to people with upper motor neuron injury from high spinal cord injury or with central alveolar hypoventilation. This has primarily been achieved by stimulation of the phrenic nerves via an implanted receiver-stimulator powered and controlled by radio transmission to produce diaphragm contraction and active inspiration, with passive expiration occurring after each burst of stimulation. Diaphragm contraction can also be produced by inserting fine wire electrodes into the diaphragm via laparoscopy and connecting them to a stimulator outside the body. Intercostal muscles can be activated by electrodes on the surface of the spinal cord and this has been used in a few patients to supplement diaphragm contraction. In experimental animal studies, high frequency spinal cord stimulation has been shown to produce coordinated activation of both the diaphragm and inspiratory intercostal muscles and may provide more physiological inspiration in the future. Expiratory intercostal and abdominal muscles can be activated by electrodes on the surface of the skin, high frequency magnetic stimulation or spinal cord stimulation. The latter can restore effective coughing, clear secretions, and reduce the incidence of respiratory infection and dependence on caregivers.

1. Introduction

As a result of inspiratory muscle paralysis, 15-20% of patients with acute cervical spinal cord injury (SCI) suffer from respiratory insufficiency on initial presentation

[1]. Fortunately, many of these patients experience subsequent improvement in respiratory muscle function and eventually are able to breathe spontaneously. Based upon data compiled by the National Spinal Cord Injury Statistical Center, Carter [2] estimated that 4.2% of patients who suffer SCI will develop chronic respiratory insufficiency and will require some form of mechanical ventilatory support. Since the average age at time of injury is 32 years and ventilator dependent patients can be expected to live well into their sixth decade (assuming they survive the first year), these patients are generally maintained on mechanical ventilation for 20-25 years or longer [3-5].

Unfortunately, mechanical ventilation is associated with substantial morbidity, mortality, inconvenience and social stigma. Some of the handicaps experienced by these patients include: significant patient and caregiver anxiety associated with machine dependence, physical discomfort, fear of disconnection, difficulty with speech, reduced mobility, and embarrassment associated with the ventilator and attached tubing. Artificial respiration by phrenic nerve pacing, in contrast, eliminates many of these problems and provides a more natural form of artificial ventilation, more closely mimicking spontaneous breathing.

The development of phrenic nerve stimulation as a clinical tool has a rich and long history. More than two centuries ago, Caldani first noted that movement of the diaphragm could be achieved by electrical stimulation of the phrenic nerve [6]. In the early 19th century, Ure noted strong diaphragmatic contractions during application of electricity to the phrenic nerve of a recently hung criminal [7]. In the latter half of the 19th century, Duchenne established phrenic nerve stimulation as the best method of producing natural respiration. This technique became an accepted method of restoring ventilation by the placement of moistened sponges over the phrenic nerves at the outer borders of the sternocleidomastoid muscles [8-12]. When methods for negative and positive pressure ventilation became available in the beginning of the 20th century, the technique of phrenic nerve stimulation was largely abandoned. In 1948, however, Sarnoff rekindled interest in phrenic nerve stimulation by demonstrating in acute animal experiments and in patients with poliomyelitis that adequate alveolar ventilation could be maintained continuously in the acute setting [13-14]. Since implantable stimulators were not available however, the potential of utility of long-term phrenic nerve stimulation was not evaluated.

The pioneering work of Glenn and associates at Yale University in the 1960s led to the development of phrenic nerve pacing as a standard technique for the management of chronic respiratory failure [15]. Through a serious of meticulous experiments, they made significant advances in surgical technique and equipment. They developed a small implantable electrode and receiver, which could be activated by radiofrequency waves generated by a power source external to the body. Moreover, they defined appropriate patient selection criteria, pre-operative evaluation methods, surgical methods to minimize phrenic nerve trauma while achieving optimal electrode placement, and appropriate stimulation parameters resulting in optimal transformation of the deconditioned diaphragm. Using radiofrequency stimulation to activate the phrenic nerves, these investigators first demonstrated that long-term ventilatory support could be provided safely in patients with SCI. Further refinements by these investigators [16-20] and others [21] led to the development of the phrenic nerve stimulation devices available today.

Table 1. Potential Advantages of Phrenic Nerve Pacing

Improved Sense of Well Being and Overall Health
    Sensation of more normal breathing
    Reduction of the volume of respiratory secretions
    Reduction in the incidence of respiratory tract infections
Improved Speech
Increased Mobility
    Easier transfers from bed to chair
    Easier transport to occupational and recreational activities outside the home
Reduced Anxiety and Embarrassment
    Elimination of fear of ventilator disconnection by individual and caregiver
    Elimination of ventilator tubing
    Elimination of ventilator noise
    Possible closure of tracheostomy
Improved Comfort Level
    Elimination of the pull of ventilator tubing
    Elimination of the discomfort associated with positive pressure breathing
Reduction in the Level of Required Nursing Care
Reduction in Overall Costs
    Reduction and/or elimination of ventilator supplies

Phrenic nerve pacing has now been applied in well over 2000 patients worldwide and has become a clinically accepted technique to provide artificial ventilatory support in patients with trauma induced ventilator dependent tetraplegia [17, 21-24]. As described in Table 1, phrenic nerve pacing provides numerous benefits when compared to mechanical ventilation. Although there may be significant patient variability, most patients describe much better speech, improved level of comfort, reduced anxiety and embarrassment, increased mobility and greater sense of well being and overall health as most important [5, 25-29]. In one prospective study comparing outcomes of patients dependent upon mechanical ventilation versus those using phrenic nerve pacing, there was a significantly lower rate of respiratory infections, better speech, and improved quality of life [30]. A separate study demonstrated improved sense of smell and secondary improved quality of life in patients using phrenic nerve pacing [31].

2. Clinical Techniques

2.1. *General comments*

Currently, there are four different phrenic nerve stimulation devices that are commercially available. Three involve placement of electrodes around the phrenic nerve and employ radiofrequency induction using an implantable receiver-electrode assembly with an external power supply and transmitter. A fourth system involves electrodes implanted directly in the diaphragm near the phrenic nerve motor points. With this latter system, wires are tunneled subcutaneously and exit from the skin over the upper chest wall where they are directly connected to an external stimulator. Each of these systems allows for easy adjustment of the multiple stimulation parameters necessary to provide electrically induced ventilation. Moreover, the implanted materials should theoretically never require operative replacement since the power supply is renewed externally.

The three manufacturers that use radiofrequency induction have very similar basic configurations (Fig. 1).

With each system, the stimulating electrodes, radiofrequency receivers, and attached wiring comprise the internal components. A radiofrequency transmitter (which can be powered with a small battery), wires and antenna comprise the external components. The stimulating electrodes are implanted on each phrenic nerve either in the cervical or thoracic regions (see Surgical Implantation). Small wires tunneled subcutaneously connect the electrodes to radiofrequency receivers, which are implanted in an easily accessible area over the anterior portion of the thorax. External circular rubberized antennas connect to the transmitter. During normal operation, each antenna must be positioned directly over each of the receivers on the body surface and taped in place to prevent any movement in relation to the receivers. The transmitter generates a radiofrequency signal, which is inductively coupled to the implanted receivers. The signal is demodulated by the receivers, converting it to electrical signals, which are delivered to the stimulating electrodes in contact with the phrenic nerves.

The most recently developed system involves placement of two electrodes within the muscular body of each hemi-diaphragm near the point where the phrenic nerve rootlets innervate the diaphragm (Fig. 2). The electrodes are connected to wires exiting the skin and attached to connectors. The connectors and stimulator, which is also powered by a small battery, comprise the external components. It is important to note that this system is another form of phrenic nerve stimulation, requiring intact phrenic nerve function, and does not stimulate the diaphragm directly.

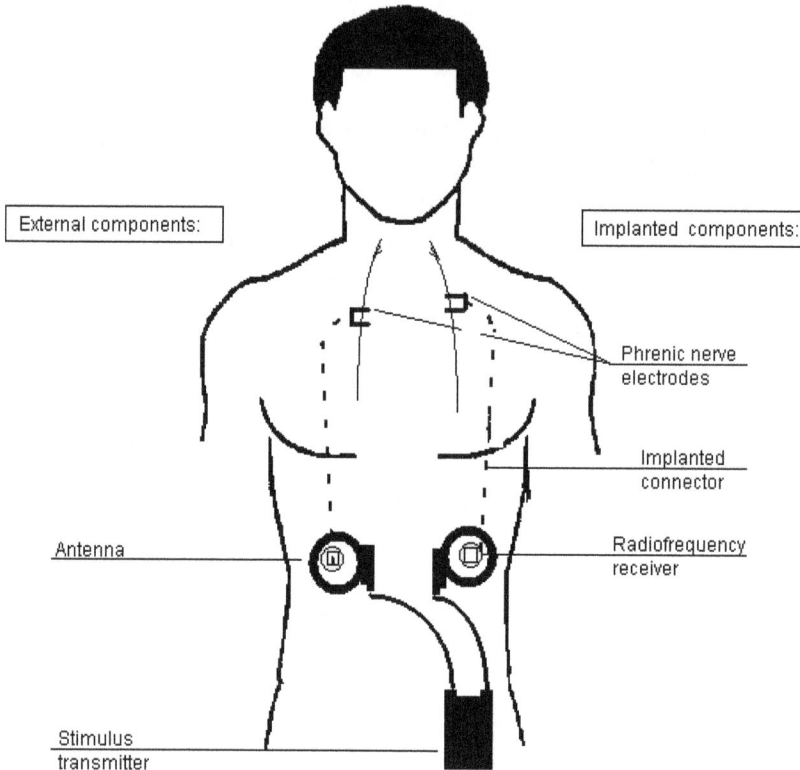

Fig. 1. Bilateral phrenic nerve pacing system.

Bilateral phrenic nerve stimulation results in descent of the diaphragm and a fall in intrathoracic pressure resulting in inspiratory airflow. Diaphragm contraction also results in expansion of the lower rib cage through a direct insertional action and outward movement of the abdominal wall via an increase in intra-abdominal pressure. In fact, palpation of the lower rib cage and abdominal wall are useful physical findings which can be used to assess both the presence and extent of diaphragm contraction. Cessation of stimulation results in diaphragm relaxation, an increase in intrathoracic pressure due to elastic recoil, and passive exhalation. To provide a normal level of ventilation, this pattern is repeated 8-14 times/min. Stimulus amplitude and frequency, and train rate can be adjusted by the operator to alter inspired volume and respiratory rate, respectively. Inspiratory time and inspiratory flow rate can be varied, in tandem, by changing stimulation on-time.

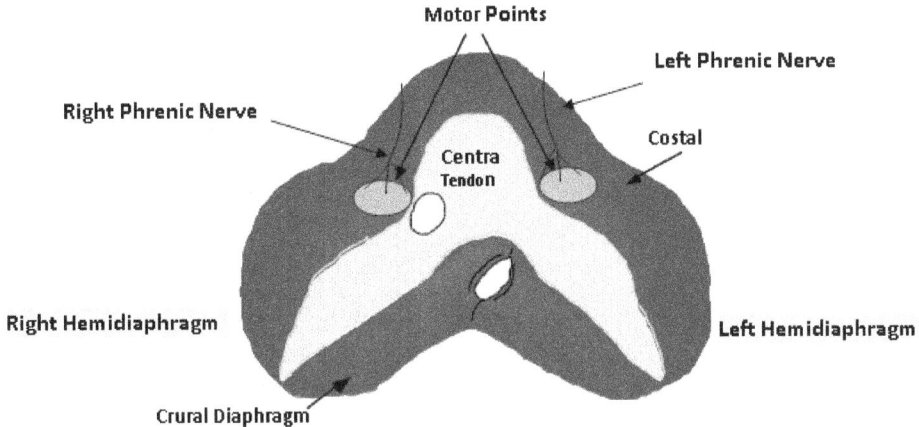

Fig. 2. Abdominal surface of diaphragm showing phrenic nerve motor points.

Phrenic nerve pacing is an expensive undertaking. The cost of the devices alone range between US$50,000-60,000 for the devices using radiofrequency transmission and US$20,000-25,000 for the system using percutaneous wires. The cost of the surgical procedure, hospitalization and medical follow-up can add an additional US$20,000 to the final cost. The cost of phrenic nerve pacing, however, is likely to be less than mechanical ventilation when averaged over time [8]. In some instances, for example, patients can be transferred to less expensive care settings resulting in a marked reduction in the cost of patient care. Moreover, in contrast to mechanical ventilators, pacing systems do not require expensive maintenance or supplies. Currently manufactured systems are designed for lifetime use and lifetime technical support is usually included in the purchase price. Most private and government insurance plans now cover both the costs of these devices and subsequent expenses related to their implantation.

2.2. *Commercially available devices*

The specific characteristics of the four different commercially available phrenic nerve pacing systems are described below. The Avery and Synapse Biomedical systems are available worldwide whereas the Atrotech Oy and MedImplant systems are only available in Europe. The technical characteristics of these devices are presented in Table 2. It should be noted that detailed operational, maintenance and troubleshooting instructions are provided by each of these suppliers.

Table 2. Technical Features of Implantable Phrenic Nerve Stimulation Systems

Device \ Manufacturer	Avery Labolatories Inc., USA		Atrotech OY, Finland	Medimplant Inc, Austria
Transmitter (stimulus generator)	S-232G	Mark IV	PX 244	Medimplant 8-channel stimulator
Size (mm)	178 x 114 x 97	146 x 140 x 26	185 x 88 x 28	170 x 130 x 51
Transmitter/battery weight (kg)	3.6	0.54	0.45 + 0.6 (12V) 0.45 + 0.045 (9V)	1.42
Rate (breaths/min)	10 - 50	6 - 24	8 - 35	5 - 60
Pulse width (us)	150	150	200	100 - 1000
Battery life (hr)	150	400	160 - 320 (12V) 8 (9V)	24
Sigh possible	yes	yes	yes	yes
Antenna	902A	902A	TC 27-260/80	RF transmission coil
Receiver Size (mm)	Model I -107A 46 (diam) x 16	Model I -110A 30 (diam) x 8	RX 44-27-2 49 (diam) x 8.5	implantable receiver 56 x 53 x 14
Electrodes	Monopolar, bipolar	Monopolar, bipolar	Quadripolar	Quadripolar
No. of receivers to stimulate both hemidiaphragm	2	2	2	1

The **Synapse NeuRx Diaphragm Pacing System** has a non-implantable stimulus generator measuring 152x76x33 mm and weighing 12 oz that provides pulses of width 10-200us via percutaneous wires to monopolar electrodes inserted into the diaphragm at laparoscopy to produce 8-18 breaths/minute.

Avery Laboratories Inc. (Commack, NY, USA). The technology and expertise acquired by Dr. William Glenn and co-workers at Yale University led to the development and commercial application of the first available phrenic nerve pacing systems by Avery Laboratories. The Avery system was the first to be developed, has a long history of reliability and is commercially available worldwide. Of note, this is the only system with full PMA approval by the US Food and Drug Administration (FDA). Monopolar electrodes are used most commonly but bipolar electrodes are also available and recommended in patients with cardiac pacemakers. The electrode consists of a semicircular platinum-iridium ribbon embedded in molded silicone rubber. The nerve is placed in a trough in the electrode, which must be fixed to surrounding tissues with sutures. Two different transmitters are available (S-232G and Mark IV). These transmitters are portable and provide considerable flexibility in terms of control of respiratory rate, inspiratory time, stimulus amplitude and pulse interval. The original Avery diaphragm pacing system (available between 1971 and 1991) employed a large receiver (model I-107A) and transmitter with a fixed pulse width of 0.15 ms. This receiver required periodic replacement every 3-5 years. The currently available systems, in contrast, are warranted for at least 10 years and are expected to last the lifetime of the patient. Patients can be upgraded from the old system to the latest model Mark IV/I-110A system since connectors are compatible. The transmitter of the most recently developed Mark IV model (approved by the FDA in 1998) is significantly lighter compared to the S-232G model. The Mark IV transmitter, for which the stimulus parameters can be easily modified, may also provide a significant advantage for specific patients who require high stimulus amplitudes to achieve complete phrenic nerve activation and adequate inspired volume generation. The Mark IV system is also unique in that it allows biofeedback control from pulse oximetry and CO_2 monitoring, via an optional interface. Each of the currently available systems allow sigh breaths to be provided at a fixed rate by altering stimulation frequency. These systems are powered by 9V batteries. With the S-232G model, each transmitter requires a single battery, with an estimated life of 160 hours. Each transmitter of the Mark IV system requires 2 batteries with an estimated life of more than 400 hours. Trans-telephonic monitoring is also available allowing the pacers electronic output and phrenic nerve/diaphragm neurophysiologic response to be monitored by telephone.

Atrotech OY (Tampere, Finland). This system has been in use since 1980 and employs a quadripolar electrode developed at Tampere University of Technology in Finland [32]. This device is commercially available in most developed countries. While initially available in the US under an Investigational Device Exemption, FDA approval has since lapsed. Patients previously implanted however can obtain replacement parts directly from the manufacturer. The major difference between this system and that of the Avery Laboratories device relates to developments in electrode technology. The Atrostim device is a four-pole electrode system that divides the nerve equally into four stimulation compartments. In theory, each quadrant of the nerve, which supplies a specific set of diaphragm motor units, is stimulated sequentially during the inspiratory phase at a stimulus frequency of 5-6 Hz. A smooth contraction of the diaphragm results from the combined stimulation of all quadrants of the nerve at its fusion frequency of 20-25 Hz. This method reduces the stimulation frequency of individual axons to about one fourth of that with unipolar stimulation, allowing greater time for recovery, and as a consequence lessening the risk of fatigue [19]. Compared to unipolar stimulation, the slower frequency of the four-pole sequential stimulation system should enhance the transformation of muscle fibers into slow-twitch, fatigue-resistant fibers and shorten the reconditioning process. The Atrotech electrode consists of two identical strips made from Teflon fabric. Two platinum buttons are mounted into each strip. One strip is placed above and the other behind the nerve. The buttons are positioned symmetrically around the nerve along its long axis. In sequential fashion, one pole acts as a cathode and the pole on the opposite side as the anode. The stimulus receiver is also quite thin, but its diameter is somewhat larger than the Avery system. The transmitter (Stimulus Controller) allows adjustment of respiratory rate and of tidal volume to low, normal and high settings to accommodate changing patient needs e.g. cough efforts, respiratory tract infection or changes in posture. Sigh breaths can also be provided independently at various intervals. The transmitter is powered by two types of batteries: a 12V, which is the main power source, and a back-up 9V NiCd which are rechargeable. The main battery has a capacity for 1-2 weeks and the back-up for about 8 hours of continuous use. This transmitter is also relatively small and quite flexible allowing for adjustments in stimulus amplitude, frequency, inspiratory time and ramp size. Pulse width is fixed at 0.2 ms. Parameter adjustments require the attachment of an external programming unit.

MedImplant Biotechnisches Labor (Vienna, Austria). This system, introduced in 1984, has limited availability, predominantly in Austria and Germany and is not available in the U.S. This system utilizes a unique electrode array requiring a complex microsurgical technique for implantation. Four electrode leads are positioned around each nerve. The electrodes are sutured to the epineurium of the phrenic nerve. The nerve tissue between each electrode lead provides different stimulating compartments. Only one of these compartments is stimulated during any given inspiration, functioning similarly to the bipolar Avery electrode. The various compartments are stimulated in sequence during subsequent inspirations. The control unit generates the stimulating sequence for both phrenic nerves. As many as 16 different electrode combinations can be adjusted individually for each nerve. As with the Atrotech device, only a portion of the nerve is stimulated, and consequently, only a portion of the diaphragm is activated at any given time. This form of sequential stimulation, referred to as carousel stimulation, is also thought to reduce the incidence of fatigue since there is greater time for recovery for the phrenic nerve and diaphragm when compared to conventional monopolar stimulation (Avery device). As with the other devices, stimulus amplitude, pulse interval, respiratory rate, and inspiratory time can be independently adjusted allowing for adequate flexibility. Battery life is 24 hours.

Synapse Biomedical (Oberlin, OH, USA). Conventional placement of phrenic nerve electrodes, as in the previously described systems, carries some risk of phrenic nerve injury and generally requires a thoracotomy, a major surgical procedure with associated risk, required in-patient hospital stay and high cost. These disadvantages have limited the number of patients undergoing this procedure and have been a significant obstacle to those patients undertaking diaphragm pacing. Phrenic nerve activation can also be achieved by stimulation via electrodes placed directly into the body of the diaphragm [33-34]. When placed near the motor point, intramuscular diaphragm stimulation results in virtually the same inspired volume production as that resulting from direct phrenic nerve stimulation. Dr. Thomas Mortimer at Case Western Reserve University pioneered the developed of the specific intramuscular electrodes in use today. The advantages of intramuscular electrodes are that a) the electrodes are not placed directly on the phrenic nerve virtually eliminating the risk of phrenic nerve injury and b) these electrodes can be placed via laparoscopy, a minimally invasive procedure generally performed on an out-patient basis or overnight hospital stay thereby reducing overall cost. In recent years, this latter advantage is somewhat reduced however by the fact that phrenic nerve electrodes for diaphragm pacing can also be successfully placed by minimally invasive video assisted thoracic surgery (VATS; 35].

Intra-muscular electrode placement requires a laparoscopic mapping procedure to locate the phrenic nerve motor points on the abdominal surface of the diaphragm, i.e., where the phrenic nerve motor rootlets innervate the diaphragm [33-34]. Two electrodes are implanted in this region, within the muscular portion of each hemi-diaphragm. The wires are tunneled subcutaneously and typically exit the skin over the upper chest wall where they are connected to a four-channel external stimulator. Diaphragm motion and intra-abdominal pressure can be assessed intra-operatively to evaluate optimal placement. A separate anode is placed in the subcutaneous tissue of the chest wall. While only about 1mA is required to activate each hemi-diaphragm using conventional phrenic nerve pacing, intramuscular phrenic nerve pacing requires about 20 mA delivered to each electrode site. The long-term success of phrenic nerve pacing by this method appears to be comparable to that achieved with intra-thoracic phrenic nerve stimulation.

2.3. *Patient evaluation and assessment*

The degree of respiratory insufficiency consequent to cervical SCI is related to the exact location and degree of spinal cord damage. Injuries above the C3 level result in complete paralysis of the major inspiratory muscles and acute respiratory failure. Injuries involving the C3-C5 level often result in acute respiratory failure as well, due to damage of the phrenic motoneurons pools and /or phrenic nerves directly. In some cases, however, a significant pool of phrenic motoneurons may be viable. Since diaphragm function alone is sufficient to maintain spontaneous breathing, some of these patients may be able to breathe spontaneously or require only partial ventilatory support. Damage to the spinal cord below the C6 level does not result in injury to the phrenic motorneurons or phrenic nerves; these patients therefore can breathe spontaneously but usually require an abdominal binder when assuming the upright posture. In those patients who remain ventilator dependent, the success of phrenic nerve pacing is highly dependent upon bilateral intact phrenic nerve and diaphragm function, as determined by phrenic nerve testing (see below). Most patients with coincident damage to either the phrenic motoneuron pools in the cervical spinal cord and/or to the phrenic nerves directly cannot be offered this modality.

Candidates for phrenic nerve pacing must be free of significant lung disease or primary muscle disease, as these factors will also preclude successful long term pacing. It is also important to note that patients with intact phrenic nerve function who are considered candidates for this technique should be fully informed of all the risks and potential benefits. Implantation of the device requires a surgical procedure with associated potential complications. After careful evaluation, some patients with sufficient inspiratory muscle strength may be better suited for noninvasive means of ventilatory assistance. In these patients, intermittent mouth positive pressure ventilation may be an effective alternative to conventional mechanical ventilation.

Bilateral measurement of phrenic nerve function by experienced personnel is mandatory for all potential candidates of phrenic nerve pacing. Phrenic nerve integrity can be assessed by measurement of nerve conduction time. This test is performed by monitoring diaphragmatic action potentials following application of electrical stimulation transcutaneously in the neck. The phrenic nerve can be stimulated either with surface electrodes or monopolar needle electrodes at the posterior border of the sternocleidomastoid muscle at the level of the cricoid cartilage. The diaphragmatic EMG is monitored with a surface electrode placed between the seventh and ninth intercostal space in the anterior axillary line. A separate ground electrode is usually placed on the skin surface over the sternum. Using the needle technique, the needle is advanced toward the midline so that the tip lies within a few millimeters of the phrenic nerve. With either surface or needle techniques, electrical current is applied with single pulses of gradually increasing intensity until a supramaximal M-wave is observed. Through trial and error, multiple positions may need to be tested to determine the optimal stimulus location. With normal function, there will be visible contraction of the diaphragm as manifested by outward movement of the anterior abdominal wall and lateral expansion of the lower rib cage. By measuring the time interval between the applied stimulus and onset of the muscle compound action potential (CAP), the nerve conduction time can be determined. In adults (age range: 18-74 yrs), mean onset latency is 7.5 ± 0.6 ms with an upper limit of 9.0 ms.. In children, latencies are different; they decrease from birth (mean 2.6 ± 0.3 ms) to about 6 months of age (2.2 ± 2.2 ms) because of maturation of the nerve, and then increase (4.2 ms between 5 and 11 years of age) due to growing length. Successful pacing in adults has been achieved with mild prolongation of conduction velocity up to 14 ms.

The magnitude of the muscle CAP is dependent upon the amount of tissue between the recording electrode and diaphragm. In addition, ventilator dependent patients may have a component of diaphragm atrophy that may also reduce the magnitude of the muscle CAP. For these reasons, the amplitude of the diaphragm CAP is considered a less reliable indicator of phrenic nerve function than conduction time.

While this method has been the gold standard of phrenic nerve functionality for decades, it has been called into question by recent studies indicating significant numbers of both false positive and false negative phrenic nerve conduction tests. These authors suggested that the only certain method of evaluating nerve function was direct intra-operative phrenic nerve stimulation [36-38].

Adequate phrenic nerve function can also be assessed by monitoring the degree of diaphragm descent during transcutaneous phrenic nerve stimulation. Based upon previous work and our own experience, the diaphragm should descend at least 3-4 cm as visualized by fluoroscopy during supramaximal tetanic stimulation. With normal phrenic nerve function, there is marked diaphragm descent exceeding 5 cm.

Diaphragm function can also be assessed by measurements of the pressure difference across the diaphragm, i.e., trans-diaphragmatic pressure. This test requires the placement of small balloon-tipped catheters into the esophagus and stomach to determine intra-thoracic and intra-abdominal pressures, respectively. Single shock stimulation to either phrenic nerve usually results in transdiaphragmatic pressures of approximately 10 cm H_2O.

While the success of phrenic nerve pacing depends upon technical considerations, patient psychosocial conditions are equally important. Prior to any technical assessment, therefore, a critical evaluation of the motivation of both the patient and family members is mandatory. Phrenic nerve pacing is most likely to be successful in home situations in which the patient and family members are anxious to improve the overall health, mobility, social interaction and occupational potential of the patient. The patient should also have a clear understanding of the potential benefits to be achieved (Table I).

2.4. *Surgical implantation*

Phrenic nerve electrodes may be positioned either in the cervical region or within the thorax [17-18, 22-23]. The thoracic approach requires either a thoracotomy or placement via a VATS procedure. A thoracotomy has significant associated risks including hemothorax and pneumothorax, requires chest tube placement and intensive postoperative care. Placement by the minimally invasive VATS procedure therefore is the preferred method. While the cervical approach is a much simpler procedure from a surgical standpoint, there are several disadvantages to this approach. Most importantly, Glenn and co-investigators have shown that the cervical portion of the phrenic nerve is not complete and that one or more additional rootlets join the main trunk of the nerve within the thorax [17]. Activation of the phrenic nerve in the neck therefore, may result in only partial diaphragm activation and suboptimal inspired volume generation. Secondly, other nerves in close vicinity to the electrode in the cervical region may be inadvertently activated resulting in pain and/or movement of the neck or shoulder. Lastly, most tetraplegics have voluntary control of their neck musculature. Excessive neck movement may place the nerve/electrode system under considerable mechanical stress. This may result in poor electrode contact and ineffective stimulation and/or scar formation with resultant nerve injury. The thoracic approach therefore is the preferred method of electrode placement.

While there are a number of acceptable surgical approaches for thoracic electrode placement, the second intercostal space is most commonly used [18, 39-41] for both the thoracotomy and VATS procedures. At the discretion of the thoracic surgeon, the 3rd interspace via an axillary incision or median sternotomy may be preferred. Both electrodes are often placed bilaterally during a single surgical procedure [18]. However, some centers prefer to place each electrode in two separate procedures. Single electrode placement requires a shorter procedure which may reduce the incidence of infection compared to the longer one required for bilateral electrode placement. With either approach, strict aseptic technique is mandatory to prevent the development of infection; prophylactic antibiotics are generally recommended [18, 39-40]. Surveillance cultures should be taken prior to surgery since these patients usually have chronic tracheostomies and urinary catheters and may be colonized with pathogenic bacteria or fungi.

Iatrogenic injury to the phrenic nerve has been a common cause of pacemaker failure in the past [16]. One of the major causes of pacemaker failure is trauma to the phrenic nerve either directly during the surgical procedure or from subsequent injury secondary to tension on the nerve from the electrode itself and/or scar tissue formation. During surgery, it is critical that the electrodes are handled with extreme care to avoid stretching or placement of undue tension on the nerve. It is also extremely important that the network of blood vessels within the perineurium be preserved to prevent ischemic injury. In the past this has been one source of phrenic nerve injury related to the use of bipolar cuff electrodes, which have considerable contact with the nerve. The present use of electrodes which do not encircle the nerve has markedly reduced the incidence of injury at the time of surgery and also subsequent injury as a result of nerve entrapment from scar formation.

Wires from the electrode are connected to a radiofrequency receiver positioned in a subcutaneous pocket on the anterior chest wall. A segment of redundant wire is placed within the thorax to prevent undue tension on the electrode. It is important that the site of receiver placement be selected carefully. The receiver must be placed superficially and be easily accessible. We prefer to place the receivers in the region of the lower anterior rib cage just above the costal margin. This provides a firm surface upon which the receivers can be palpated and the antennas taped in place. In thin people, however, the anterior abdominal wall may be preferable to avoid pressure injury. If the patient gains significant weight, however, the receivers may be difficult to locate for optimal placement of antennas. For both the Avery and Atrotech systems, which require two receivers, they should be placed at least 15 cm apart.

The pacing system should be tested prior to closure of the surgical incisions. This is usually done by placing a sterilized coil over the receiver in the operating room. Threshold currents of each electrode should be determined by gradually increasing stimulus amplitude until a diaphragm twitch is observed. Threshold current should range between 0.1 and 2.0 mA. Suprathreshold current should result in a forceful, smooth diaphragm contraction. With the Atrotech and MedImplant devices, threshold and suprathreshold current should be assessed for each lead combination. If threshold values are high or the difference between the lowest and highest thresholds among leads exceeds 1 mA, the electrode leads may need to be re-positioned around the phrenic nerve. Both the Avery and Atrotech manufacturers provide onsite technical support during the implantation procedure.

2.5. *Pacing schedules*

It is important to note that phrenic nerve pacing is a life support system and must be instituted carefully to avoid complications. Consequently, a gradual switch from mechanical ventilation to phrenic nerve pacing should be performed under the supervision of experienced physicians and respiratory therapists to provide optimal results.

Pacing is usually started approximately 2 weeks following surgery to allow adequate time for all surgical wounds to begin healing and for inflammation and edema round the electrode site to resolve [40]. Several parameters should be assessed when pacing is first initiated. These include stimulation thresholds (minimum stimulus amplitude which results in visible or palpable diaphragm contraction), maximal stimulus amplitudes (values just sufficient to result in maximum inspired volume production) and inspired volume. Changes in airway pressure development during airway occlusion are also a useful indicator of diaphragm force generation. With the development of airway secretions or atelectasis, inspired volume production may fall whereas airway pressure generation will be maintained. With the Atrotech and MedImplant systems, threshold and maximal amplitudes, inspired volumes and pressure development must be determined for each lead combination. Inspired volume and pressure measurements should be made in both the supine and sitting postures. Diaphragm excursions will be less in the sitting posture due to the higher lung volume and shorter diaphragm length, resulting in smaller inspired volumes.

It is important to note that many tetraplegics are maintained in a hyperventilated state with relatively large tidal volumes while on mechanical ventilation. This results in a reduction of bicarbonate stores. Consequently, when initially switching patients to the pacing system, which is designed to maintain eucapnea, an acidosis may develop secondary to the rise in pCO_2 into the normal range. Secondary to the acidosis, patients may experience significant dyspnea suggesting insufficient inspired volume generation during pacing to maintain ventilatory support. This problem can be averted by the gradual adjustment of ventilator parameters to allow pCO_2 to rise to near normal levels prior to the initiation of phrenic nerve pacing. Both tidal volume and respiratory rate on the ventilator should be adjusted to values expected during pacing to allow as smooth a transition as possible. pCO_2 values should be monitored therefore while patients are on mechanical ventilation with either arterial blood gases or capnography.

Full-time ventilatory support cannot be achieved immediately following implantation of the pacing system since the diaphragm has undergone atrophic changes in ventilator dependent tetraplegics. The initiation of pacing is likely to be associated with the development of muscle weakness and fatigue. The diaphragm must be gradually reconditioned to improve strength and endurance. During the initial trials of phrenic nerve pacing, minute ventilation necessary to maintain normal values of pCO_2 (35-45 mm Hg) over 5-10 min periods should be determined. This is best evaluated by continuous monitoring of end-tidal pCO_2 with capnography. Respiratory rate is usually set at 8-12 breaths/min; tidal volume is adjusted by altering stimulation frequency to maintain the desired level of ventilation.

There are no definitive guidelines in terms of pacing schedules to achieve full-time ventilatory support. Specific pacing schedules must be individualized for each patient. General recommendations are to provide phrenic nerve pacing for 10-15 min each hour initially and to gradually increase this time, as tolerated. While the conditioning phase may take 8-10 weeks or longer, it is possible to bring some patients up to full-time support within 3-4 weeks. The approach suggested by Atrotech is initially to provide continuous bilateral phrenic nerve stimulation until the point of CO2 retention, to determine the maximum time tolerated off mechanical ventilatory support. The patient is then stimulated for this time period several times each day. For example, if the patient is able to tolerate only 20 minutes, he is paced for 20 minutes each hour for 10-12 hours/day. At the beginning of each week, the tolerable stimulation time is re-determined and the patient is stimulated for this new time period every hour. After full-time pacing is achieved during waking hours, pacing is provided during sleep and gradually increased until full-time pacing is achieved. During the conditioning phase, the patient must be carefully monitored for signs of fatigue, which is usually manifested by the patient's complaint of shortness of breath. Objective evidence of fatigue including reductions in inspired volume and increased patient effort are usually present, as well. It is advisable to monitor oxygen saturation with pulse oximetry throughout the reconditioning process.

Since the diaphragm must contract 8-15 times/min. for life, this muscle must have high endurance characteristics and be fatigue resistant. Glenn et al. have clearly demonstrated that chronic stimulation with high frequencies is associated with diaphragm myopathic changes in animal studies and reduced diaphragm contraction in humans. In contrast, low frequency electrical stimulation causes favorable biochemical, structural and physiologic alterations. While the normal diaphragm consists of nearly equal populations of both Type I and Type II fibers, low frequency stimulation results in the transformation of the Type II fibers which are fast, fatigue sensitive into highly oxidative, slow-twitch, fatigue-resistant Type I fibers. Consequently, the conditioning phase should be applied with chronic low frequency stimulation. Phrenic nerve pacing is often associated initially with some vibration during contraction due to electrical stimulation below the fusion frequency [19]. However, as the conditioning process progresses, vibrating contractions are gradually replaced by smooth coordinated contractions due to reductions in the fusion frequency and fiber type transformation. This process usually requires several weeks. With the application of low frequency stimulation at low respiratory rates, the total number of diaphragm contractions per respiratory cycle is less, resulting in a lower propensity for the development of fatigue.

With the Avery system, stimulation frequencies of 10-12 Hz are used initially (although higher stimulation frequencies may be necessary due to unpleasant vibratory contractions), with respiratory rates in the range of 8-12 breaths/min. As the conditioning process progresses, stimulation frequencies and respiratory rates are gradually reduced into the 7-9 Hz range and respiratory rates to 6-12 breaths/min while the patient is supine. With the Atrotech device, less adjustment of stimulus frequency is required due to the initial application of low stimulation frequencies via sequential nerve stimulation. The sequential nerve stimulation methodology is designed to mimic the natural activation of skeletal muscle, allowing individual nerve-muscle compartments to be stimulated at low frequencies and providing time for recovery even during muscle contraction. Talonen et al. has argued therefore that the conditioning phase is shortened and muscle fatigue is delayed when compared to unipolar phrenic nerve stimulation [32]. There have been no controlled trials however to compare these different methods of nerve stimulation. Our own experience, however, suggests that full-time pacing with the quadripolar stimulation system can be achieved in 6-8 weeks, which compares favorably with the previously reported 12-16 week conditioning phase with the unipolar stimulation systems. With the Synapse system, initial stimulus frequencies are in the range of 20 Hz and gradually reduced, as tolerated. Once full-time pacing has been achieved, current intensity, stimulus frequency and respiratory rate should always be set to the lowest level that provides adequate ventilation.

With each system, higher levels of stimulation may be required in the sitting compared to the supine posture; assumption of the sitting posture results in a shorter diaphragm length and consequent greater stimulus requirement to generate the same inspired volume. This can be alleviated to a significant degree, however, by the use of a snug fitting abdominal binder, which reduces the change in abdominal girth and secondarily diaphragm length which occurs when patients assume the sitting posture. The Atrotech system has low, normal and high settings, which allow for convenient changes in stimulus parameters, which may also be necessary to accommodate for posture change.

2.6. *Complications*

While a number of complications have been reported since phrenic nerve pacing was first introduced (Table 3), technical developments and patient experience have markedly reduced their incidence [26,16]. With careful patient selection, appropriate use of stimulus parameters, adequate patient monitoring, and involvement of experienced professionals, the incidence of complications should be very low. Nonetheless, complications do arise and appropriate precautions must be taken and remedial action instituted promptly, when necessary.

Phrenic nerve pacing systems may fail to provide adequate ventilatory support due to a variety of factors. As with any life support system, therefore, careful monitoring of the phrenic nerve pacing system is also required. Inspired volume generation should be checked on a routine basis to ensure adequate minute ventilation. Most patients are able to perceive small decrements in inspired volume generation and alert their caregivers to troubleshoot potential problems. Since this sensation may be somewhat less intense during sleep, some manufacturers have recommended continuous pulse oximetry as a monitoring system during the night. Since pacemaker systems do not have internal alarms to monitor inspired volume, all patients should have easy access to a patient triggered alarm system and caregiver attendance. All patients should have a readily accessible alternative method of providing ventilator support.

Table 3. Complications/Side Effects of Phrenic Nerve Pacing

Technical Malfunction
External Components
• battery failure
• breakage of antenna wires
Implanted Components
• receiver failure
• electrode malfunction
• breakage of implanted connecting wires
Infection
• receiver site
• electrode site
Mechanical injury to the phrenic nerve
• iatrogenic injury at the time of surgery
• late injury due to scar formation and/or tension on the nerve
Reduction in ventilation due to altered respiratory system mechanics
• increases in airway resistance
• reduction in lung compliance
Upper airway obstruction following tracheostomy closure
Paradoxical movement of the upper rib cage, particularly in children

There are a number of technical problems that can cause malfunction of the pacing system resulting in reductions in inspired volume generation. One of the most common causes of mechanical failure is battery failure which is easily prevented by regular battery changes and/or recharging schedules. Some systems are equipped with a low battery alarm system to alert patients and caregivers. With the radiofrequency activated systems, another common cause of mechanical failure is breakage of the antenna wires. This usually occurs at stress points, either near the connection to the transmitter or connection to the receivers. Receiver failure was a common occurrence with older systems in which body fluids could seep into the receiver capsule and result in system failure, but this is much less common with current systems due to improvement in housing materials. Iatrogenic injury to the phrenic nerve may occur at the time of electrode implantation. This complication is preventable by meticulous dissection technique, which minimizes manipulation of the nerve. Malfunction can also occur at the nerve-electrode interface, due to tissue reaction around the electrode developing either early or late following implantation. This development may result in gradual reduction in inspired volume production and, in some instances, vibration during diaphragm contraction [16]. The development of scar tissue at the electrode site may also be manifested by changes in stimulus threshold values.

With the Synapse system having wires emanating from the skin, superficial wound infections, skin irritation and wire breakage have been noted. Discomfort during stimulation has also been observed but usually relieved by reducing stimulus amplitude. It is recommended that the wire exit site be kept dry.

Increases in airway resistance or decrements in respiratory system compliance will also result in reductions in inspired volume generation. Due to their inability to cough, most ventilator dependent tetraplegics have tracheostomies in place and require routine evacuation of their secretions by suctioning or other means. The accumulation of airway secretions is a common cause of increased airway resistance and reduced inspired volumes. Most patients are able to perceive the need for suctioning and alert their caregivers. Removal of secretions either by suctioning or other means usually results in prompt improvement in respiratory system mechanics. The development of atelectasis may also reduce lung compliance and thereby reduce inspired volumes. Atelectasis often develops secondary to retained secretions, as well, and can usually be relieved by removal of secretions.

A more serious, but fortunately less common complication, is the development of infection of the implanted materials. As mentioned above, infection is a risk factor with any implanted foreign body [18]. While most infections are manifested soon after implantation, there is a small risk of late infections occurring years after implantation. Infection at the receiver site is usually manifested by local swelling, redness, warmth and/or skin breakdown at the receiver site. The development of infection usually necessitates removal of all implanted components [27,42].

Diaphragm contraction without coincident contraction of the upper airway muscles results in collapse of the upper airway or obstructive apneas. This complication is completely preventable by maintaining a patent tracheostomy. In patients who choose to close the tracheostomy stoma, however, the risk of upper airway obstruction is significant. This is not usually problematic while patients are awake, allowing most patients to cap their tracheostomy tube during the day. During sleep, however, there is a greater tendency toward asynchronous upper airway muscle contraction and the development of obstructive apneas. Most patients therefore are maintained with a patent tracheostomy stoma for nocturnal use. The tracheostomy is also useful for patient suctioning and easy application of mechanical ventilatory support, in the event of pacemaker failure or serious intercurrent infection. However, Tetraplegics treated by the MedImplant group closed their tracheostomies without adverse effects. It should be noted, though, that these patients first underwent a training program to maintain spontaneous breathing for a minimum of 20 minutes without external assistance. One significant advantage of tracheostomy closure was a significant reduction in the volume of respiratory secretions. It is likely that tracheostomy closure would also result in a reduction in the incidence of infection. While it is possible that many patients undergoing phrenic nerve pacing could tolerate tracheostomy closure, strict selection criteria and monitoring systems must first be developed. In this regard, studies have been performed to coordinate diaphragm contraction with upper airway muscle contraction by using the signal from one of the upper airway muscles to trigger the diaphragm pacing system. From a practical standpoint, however, these systems have not met with much success.

Strong magnetic fields, as with magnetic resonance imaging, can override the electronic circuitry of some phrenic pacing systems. Substantial amounts of energy could be transmitted to the electrode resulting in phrenic nerve injury. The manufacturer of the specific pacing system should be consulted prior to the performance of an MRI. Exposure to electrotherapeutic devices, which generate strong radiofrequency fields, should also be avoided since they could interfere with pacing device.

In children, there may be substantial paradoxical motion of the rib cage due to its high compliance, resulting in reduced inspired volume generation. Since compliance gradually decreases between 10 and 15 years of age, the performance of the pacing system can be expected to improve over time [16]. Since the diaphragm has a very small percentage of Type I, fatigue resistant fibers in small children, a much longer period of conditioning may be required to achieve full-time ventilatory support compared to adults [23].

2.7. *Patient outcomes and conclusions*

In patients with ventilator dependent tetraplegia who have intact phrenic nerve function, phrenic nerve pacing is clearly an effective means of providing ventilatory support with significant advantages over mechanical ventilation [23]. It should be noted, however, that previous analyses of large patient groups describe significant numbers of individuals in whom successful ventilatory support could not be achieved. Glenn et al. has reported on the largest series of patients but these included a large miscellaneous group who had pacers implanted prior to 1985 [23]. Data was available on 165 of 477 patients who had pacers implanted.

Approximately 50% of these patients had cervical SCI. There was one operative death. Phrenic nerve pacing was considered successful in providing adequate ventilatory support in only about half of the patients. Although no statistical analyses could be performed, they surmised that reduced lung and chest wall compliance may reduce the effectiveness of diaphragm pacing in the elderly. In a retrospective analysis, approximately 50% of the patients who were deemed failures should not have been selected for phrenic nerve pacing. It is important to note that this study and others were performed at a time when the technology of phrenic nerve pacing and patient-selection methods were not fully developed. Unfortunately, there are few recent analyses of modern day success rates and incidence of side effects and complications. Long term follow-up of 14 tetraplegics who used bilateral low frequency stimulation recorded using the device successfully for as long as 15 years with a mean use of 7.6 years. Moreover, threshold and amplitude of stimulation required for maximum excursion of the diaphragm and tidal volume were unchanged over the period of follow-up. Analyses of the available pathologic specimens demonstrated no evidence of nerve or diaphragm muscle injury [16].

There is some evidence that improved electrode and receiver design is associated with a low incidence of pacer malfunction and high success rates when applied in appropriate candidates. The outcome of 64 patients (45 tetraplegics) who underwent phrenic nerve pacing with the Atrotech system since 1990 was evaluated [42]. The duration of pacing averaged 2 years. The incidence of electrode and receiver failure was quite low at 3.1% and 5.9%, respectively. These values are lower than those previously reported with monopolar-bipolar systems. Failure of one or more of the four leads of the quadripolar system in a given patient was more common, but this occurrence usually did not interfere with successful pacing. In this group, four patients developed infections but none occurred in the tetraplegic group.

A recent publication (2009) of results of patients using the Synapse system (average follow-up of 2 years following implantation) indicated that over 50% of the patients had utilized the diaphragm pacing for over 24 continuous hours and 96% for greater than 4 continuous hours.

The overall results of phrenic nerve pacing indicate that despite careful prescreening of patients, about 50% of patients have inadequate inspired volume generation to maintain full-time ventilatory support [42]. There are also many patients who are not candidates for pacing due to inadequate phrenic nerve function. The majority of ventilator-dependent tetraplegic subjects therefore still require the use of mechanical ventilation. Several factors may account for inadequate inspired volume production during phrenic nerve pacing including incomplete diaphragm activation due to the high thresholds of some axons, reduction in diaphragm strength due to conversion of the diaphragm to predominantly Type 1 muscle fibers which have greater endurance but less strength, and lack of co-incident intercostal activation which may account for 35-40% of the vital capacity. On-going analyses, perhaps in the form of an international registry, are needed to track the incidence of side effects, complications and true success rate of phrenic nerve pacing.

Although there are no controlled studies, it is conceivable that phrenic nerve pacing may improve life expectancy in patients with tetraplegia. Carter, for example, reported only 63% survival at 9 years in patients on positive pressure ventilation [2]. In contrast, all 12 tetraplegic patients who completed the Yale phrenic nerve pacing protocol were alive after 9 years. It is possible that mechanical ventilation is associated with a higher incidence of respiratory tract infections, as noted above, and/or mechanical problems related to the mechanical ventilator, tubing and tracheostomy.

3. Experimental Techniques

3.1. *Intercostal muscle activation to provide ventilatory support*

Since many patients with ventilator dependent tetraplegia cannot be offered phrenic nerve pacing due to phrenic nerve injury, studies have also been performed to evaluate electrical stimulation of the intercostal muscles as an alternative method to provide ventilatory support. While the diaphragm is clearly the major inspiratory muscle, the intercostal muscles also contribute approximately 35-40% to the vital capacity. Synchronous activation of this muscle group also may therefore provide sufficient inspired volume to maintain ventilatory support [43-44]. Activation of the intercostal muscles however is much more complex compared to phrenic nerve stimulation. Whereas two relatively accessible nerves innervate the diaphragm, twelve pairs of intercostal nerves located beneath the lower border of each rib innervate the intercostal muscles. Moreover, each of these nerves innervates both the internal and external intercostal muscles. Investigations in animals however have demonstrated that the application of electrical current with a single electrode positioned on the ventral epidural surface of the upper thoracic spinal cord (T2 level) results in large inspired volumes [45-46]. While stimulation in this region results in diffuse activation of the intercostal muscles of only the upper and mid rib cage musculature, the magnitude of inspired volume production is in the range of 35-40% of the vital capacity [45]. This is not entirely surprising since the major bulk of the inspiratory intercostal musculature lies in the upper six interspaces.

The utility of intercostal muscle pacing alone to provide ventilatory support has been assessed in five ventilator dependent tetraplegics [43, 47]. These patients had phrenic nerve damage and therefore were not candidates for phrenic nerve pacing alone. During an initial surgical procedure, a quadripolar epidural disc electrode (Medtronic Corp., Minneapolis, MN), was positioned on the ventral surface of the upper thoracic spinal cord via a hemi-laminectomy. The electrode was subsequently connected to a radiofrequency receiver implanted subcutaneously over the anterior rib cage in a separate procedure. A two-channel radiofrequency transmitter (Medtronic model #7520) delivered signals through the skin.

In the 4 of 5 patients, initial intercostal muscle stimulation resulted in inspired volumes between 150-240 ml. Following a reconditioning program, maximum inspired volume production increased in 3 of 4 patients to 470-850 ml. Unfortunately, the maximum duration that ventilation could be sustained by low frequency intercostal pacing (12-14 Hz) ranged between 20 min. and 2.75 hours. Intercostal stimulation was not associated with any untoward hemodynamic side effects. During stimulation, each patient had mild flexion of both hands and contraction of the muscles of the upper torso. These findings indicated that intercostal pacing is generally well tolerated but does not result in sufficient inspired volume production to support ventilation for prolonged time periods in humans [47]. These results strongly suggested however, that intercostal pacing may be a useful adjunct to enhance tidal volume production in patients with suboptimal inspired volume production via phrenic nerve pacing alone.

In a separate study, therefore, the utility of combined unilateral phrenic nerve stimulation and intercostal pacing was evaluated in four subjects [44]. Each of the subjects had only unilateral phrenic nerve function and therefore was not a candidate for conventional phrenic nerve pacing. The first subject had a functional unilateral Avery diaphragm pacing system which did not provide sufficient inspired volume to maintain ventilatory support but was used for bed to chair transfers. In this individual, a Medtronic spinal cord electrode was placed for intercostal muscle pacing (as above). A link-up circuit was used to synchronize diaphragm and intercostal muscle stimulation. In the other three subjects, an Atrotech spinal cord electrode which was similar in design to the Medtronic electrode, was employed. This lead has 3 disc shaped electrodes, each of which could be stimulated independently. The Atrotech electrode was connected to an Atrotech intercostal radiofrequency receiver, which was implanted subcutaneously on the anterior surface of the chest wall (Fig. 3). The embedded software was altered to provide a greater amplitude range (0-18 mA) but was otherwise similar to the standard phrenic nerve system hardware. A standard Atrotech quadripolar electrode was implanted on the viable phrenic nerve. A single transmitter provided independent control of the phrenic and intercostal pacing parameters. The phrenic controller triggers the intercostal controller with each inspiration such that stimulation of the intercostal muscles and diaphragm is virtually simultaneous. Following reconditioning of the intercostal muscles and diaphragm, inspired volumes ranged between 250-700 ml. and 260-960 ml, respectively. Combined intercostal and diaphragm pacing resulted in inspired volumes approximating the sum of values obtained during intercostal and diaphragm stimulation alone. Combined intercostal and diaphragm activation resulted in maximum inspired volumes of 600-1300 ml (Table 4). Two of the four subjects achieved full-time pacing while each of the others were comfortably maintained off mechanical ventilatory support for 12-16 hours per day. These patients experienced similar benefits as that reported previously with bilateral phrenic nerve pacing. These preliminary results suggest that combined intercostal and unilateral diaphragm pacing is a useful therapeutic modality capable of maintaining full-time ventilatory support in patients with partial phrenic nerve function.

3.2. *Intercostal and diaphragm muscle activation by high-frequency spinal cord stimulation*

High frequency spinal cord stimulation (HF-SCS) is a novel and potentially more physiologic method of inspiratory muscle activation, which involves the application of high-frequency (~300 Hz) stimulation to the ventral surface of the spinal cord in the upper thoracic region (T2) with low stimulus amplitudes [48]. In animal studies [48-50], HF-SCS results in the activation of both the diaphragm and inspiratory intercostal muscles in concert, and the generation of large inspired volumes. Unlike phrenic nerve pacing, the pattern of EMG during HF-SCS closely resembles that observed during spontaneous breathing (Fig. 4). Moreover, the mean maximum firing frequencies of motor units in the parasternal, external intercostal and diaphragm muscles were ~10-12 Hz and not significantly different from those occurring during spontaneous breathing at comparable inspired volumes (Fig. 5) [48-50].

Maximum inspired volume generation by this method was 0.93 liters, which approximates the inspiratory capacity of these animals [48]. Importantly, ventilation can be maintained on a chronic basis without evidence of fatigue for 6 hours (stimulus parameters: 300 Hz, 0.5 mA, 0.2 ms, 7 breaths/min). Chronic ventilation could also be maintained for 6 hours following bilateral phrenic nerve section, with modestly increased stimulus amplitudes, indicating that this method has the potential to provide artificial ventilation to individuals with SCI who are not candidates for phrenic nerve pacing [50]. Presumably, HF-SCS results in activation of spinal cord tracts that synapse with the inspiratory motoneuron pools, allowing processing of the stimulus and consequent physiologic activation of the inspiratory muscles.

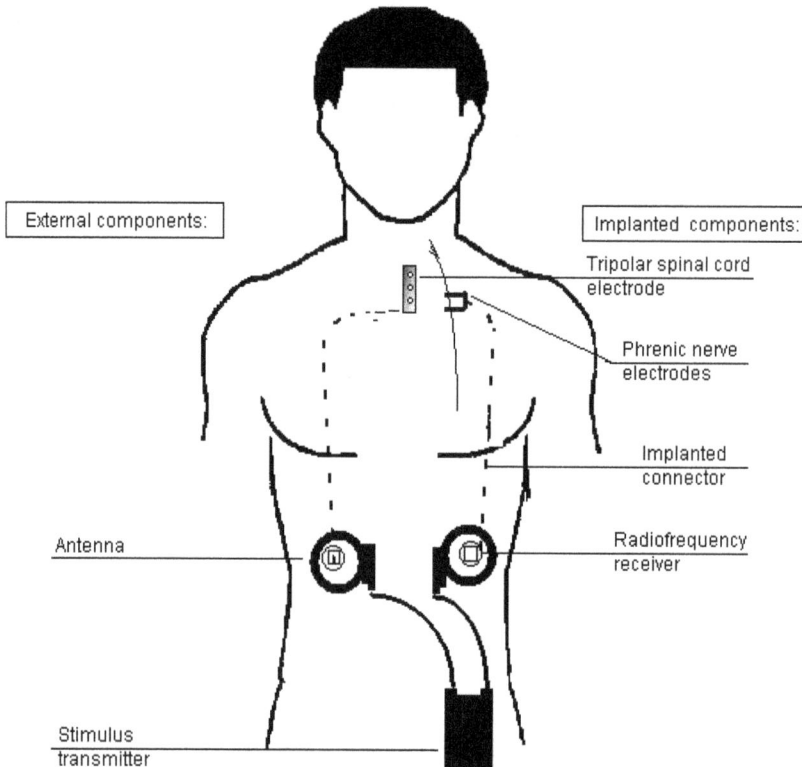

Fig. 3. Combined intercostal and diaphragm pacing system.

This method is likely to be more successful compared to conventional phrenic nerve pacing since a) both the intercostal muscles and diaphragm are activated in concert resulting in larger tidal volumes and b) the pattern of activation should not result in fiber type transformation, resulting in inspiratory muscles with greater strength and therefore the potential for larger inspired volume generation. Future evaluation in clinical trials is necessary to confirm these exciting results found in animal studies. If successful, it is likely that this form of inspiratory muscle pacing could be offered to a significantly higher proportion of the spinal cord injured population with respiratory failure.

Table 4. Effects of combined diaphragm and intercostal pacing on maximum time off ventilatory support, inspired volume and negative inspiratory pressure.

Patient	Pacing Duration (Max Achieved) (h)	Inspired Volume (Chronic) (ml)	Inspired Volume (Maximum) (ml)	Negative Inspiratory Pressure (Maximum) (ml)
GR	24	700	1300	-80
DB	12	350	600	-20
DN	24	500	950	-30
KC	16	850	1070	-53

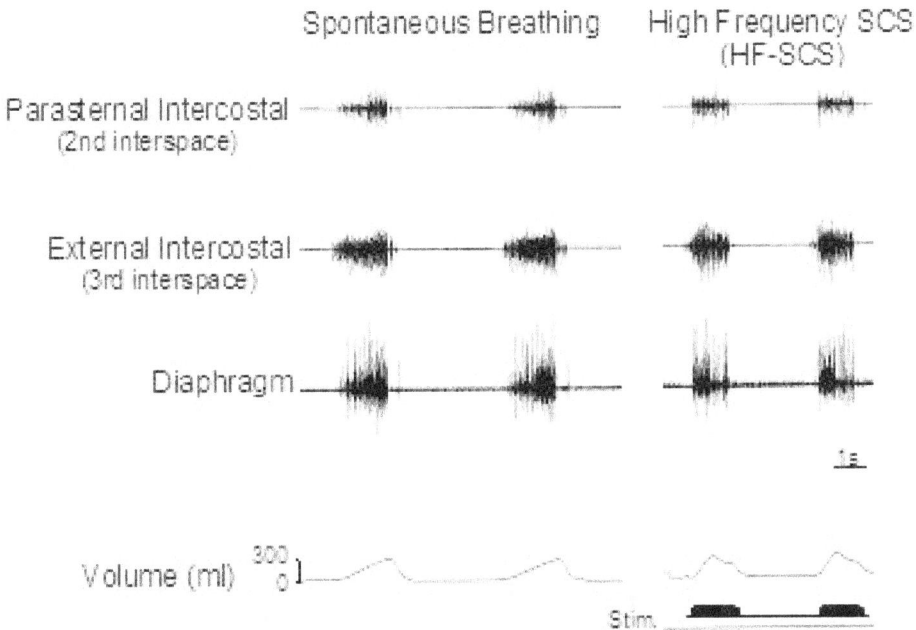

Fig. 4. Multiunit EMGs of the parasternal intercostal muscle, external intercostal muscle and diaphragm during spontaneous breathing (left) and during HF-SCS (right) at comparable inspired volumes. As with spontaneous breathing, HF-SCS results in an asynchronous EMG pattern.

3.3. *Expiratory muscle activation to restore cough*

While restoration of inspiratory muscle function to restore breathing in ventilator dependent subjects is an important goal, the potential for restoration of expiratory muscle function may be even more important. Due to expiratory muscle paralysis and secondary loss of the ability to cough, patients with SCI have difficulty clearing airway secretions. This results in physical discomfort, inconvenience and the development of atelectasis and recurrent respiratory tract infections [2, 51]. Patients are therefore dependent upon caregiver assistance for the application of manual suctioning and various assisted coughing techniques. Despite use of these techniques, respiratory tract infections remain a major cause of morbidity and mortality in the SCI population.

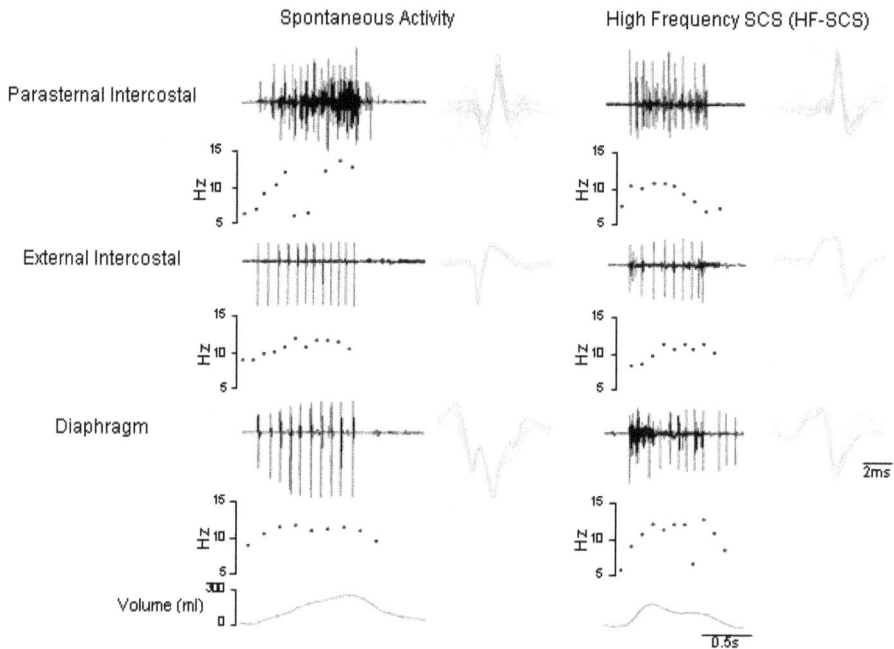

Fig 5. Single motor unit activities recorded from the parasternal intercostal muscle, external intercostal muscle and diaphragm during spontaneous breathing (left) and during HF-SCS (right) in a single animal. Instantaneous motor unit discharge frequencies during HF-SCS were very similar to that occurring during spontaneous breathing suggesting physiological activation of the inspiratory muscles during HF-SCS.

Several techniques have been proposed to activate the expiratory muscles including high frequency magnetic stimulation, surface abdominal muscle stimulation and spinal cord stimulation [52-53].

Magnetic stimulation of the expiratory muscles requires the placement of a stimulating coil over the back at the T10 spinal level [54-56]. This method results in the generation of large positive airway pressures in healthy subjects. In subjects with tetraplegia, however, much lower pressures and airflow rates could be generated [57]. One major advantage of this method is that is can be applied non-invasively. Clinical application is limited by significant disadvantages including the requirement of a bulky and expensive device requiring an external power source, need for caregiver assistance for precise coil placement and the potential for thermal injury. The potential benefit of this device has never been evaluated in clinical trials.

Previous studies using large surface electrodes positioned over the posterolateral portion of the abdominal wall have demonstrated, in healthy subjects, twitch pressures comparable to those achieved with magnetic stimulation [53]. In more recent studies in subjects with SCI, esophageal and gastric pressure, peak expiratory flow and expiratory volume were measured as subjects coughed voluntarily with the simultaneous delivery of trains of electrical stimuli (50 Hz, 1s duration) [58-59]. Stimulus current ranged between 120 and 360 mA. In each individual, a plateau in peak expiratory cough flow was achieved indicating dynamic airway compression, suggesting that the evoked cough would be effective in creating turbulent flow and the expectoration of secretions. While also non-invasive, this method also has significant disadvantages including the fact that repeated application of the electrodes to the skin surface is likely to be very tedious and cumbersome and may lead to skin irritation and breakdown, a common problem in patients with SCI. Also, this method may be less effective in obese subjects due to the high electrical resistance of adipose tissue. The potential benefit of this device has also not been evaluated in clinical trials.

Based upon extensive studies in animals [46, 60-63], a clinical trial was undertaken to evaluate the safety and efficacy of spinal cord stimulation (SCS) to restore an effective cough mechanism [64-65]. This method involves the placement of electrodes in the dorsal epidural space at the T9, T11 and L1 levels via partial hemilaminectomies (Fig. 6).

In a clinical trial involving 9 patients, 4 mm disc electrodes were positioned in these locations, in addition to a ground electrode, and then connected to a radiofrequency receiver (Finetech Medical) implanted subcutaneously on the anterior chest wall. Stimulation was achieved by activating a small portable external control box connected to a rubberized transmitter placed directly over the implanted receiver. Stimulation at each individual site alone resulted in high peak airflow rates and large airway pressures in the range of 6.1 to 6.9 L/s and 94 and 105 cmH$_2$O respectively, at total lung capacity (TLC). Combination of any 2 electrodes resulted in substantially greater values in the range of 7.8 to 8.8 L/sec and 124 to 150 cm H$_2$O at TLC. Stimulation at all 3 sites did not result in any further increases in airflow rate or airway pressure generation. These studies indicate that lower thoracic SCS results in the generation of large peak airflow rates and airway pressures, which in several subjects approach values observed during a maximum cough effort in healthy persons [64-65]. In several patients there was evidence of mild autonomic dysreflexia following the initial application of SCS. These occurrences were asymptomatic but characterized by hypertension and bradycardia. With continued stimulation over several weeks however, signs of this complication abated completely in each subject [64-65]. It is important to mention that this method can only be applied in individuals with absent sensation in the region of the lower chest and abdominal wall as the high stimulus currents would activate sensory fibers resulting in significant discomfort.

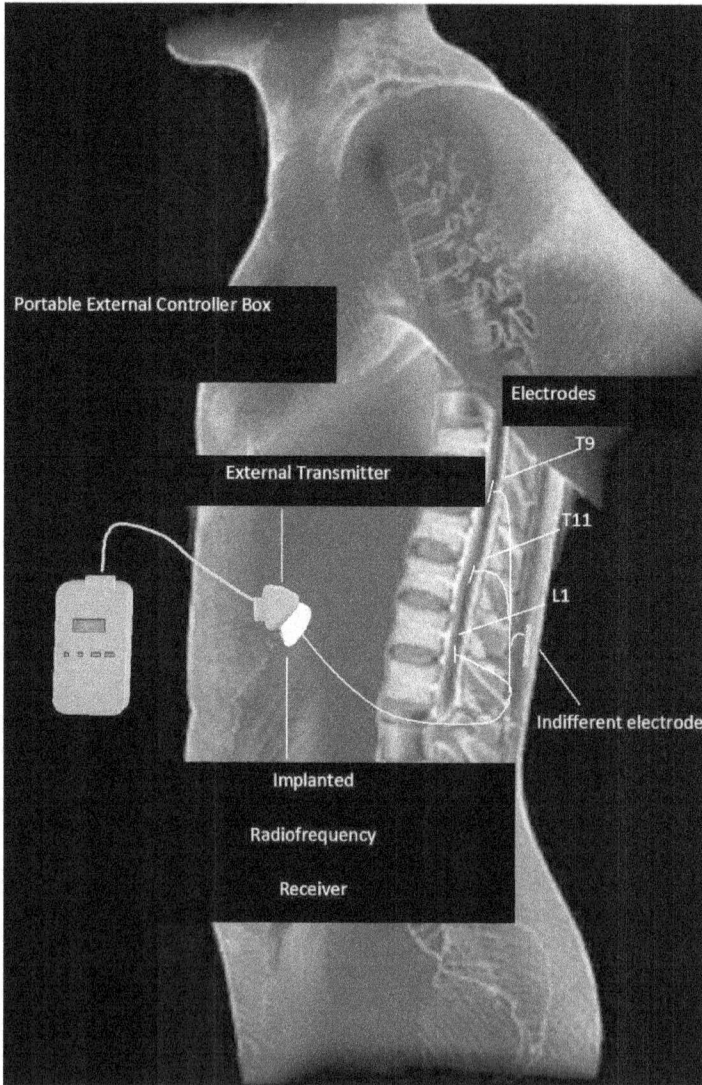

Fig. 6. Spinal cord stimulation system with external transmitter and implanted stimulator-receiver attached to epidural electrodes.

Since initial publication, the clinical trial was extended to 17 patients and in each subject the degree of difficulty in raising secretions improved markedly and the need for alternative methods of secretion removal was virtually eliminated. Subjects also reported greater control of breathing issues and enhanced mobility, resulting in improvements in life quality. Importantly, the incidence of acute respiratory tract infections fell significantly and the level of trained caregiver support related to secretion management decreased significantly.

In a subsequent follow-up study [66], the clinical parameters related to use of the cough system in subjects who had the implant for a minimum of 2 years (mean 4.6 years) was evaluated. Each subject continued to use the device on a regular daily basis. Maximum pressure generation during SCS remained in the same range compared to the 1-year follow-up. The improvements in each of the measures related to airway clearance persisted and alternative methods of secretion removal were unnecessary. The need for trained caregivers to provide other means of secretion management and the incidence of respiratory tract infections remained significantly below pre-implant levels. All subjects reported reduced anxiety and embarrassment related to secretion clearance, greater mobility and consequent improvement in social interaction and improvement in life quality.

It is possible that this method has the potential to reduce the morbidity and mortality associated with recurrent respiratory tract infections in the SCI population. Future studies are planned to evaluate this technique using wire electrodes, which can be placed employing minimally invasive techniques.

4. Future Developments

As described above, inspiratory muscle pacing devices can provide important health and lifestyle benefits compared to mechanical ventilation. Existing systems, however, do have significant limitations and still require further refinement. For example, coordination of paced breaths with the subject's spontaneous respiratory drive would improve speech cadence, match ventilation with metabolic demand and eliminate the need for tracheostomy in many patients. In addition, the development of a fully implantable system would eliminate the need for the application of devices on the body surface and the risk of decoupling between the transmitter and receiver.

Expiratory muscle activation using electrodes in the dorsal epidural space over the thoracolumbar spinal cord can restore effective cough, clear pulmonary secretions, reduce respiratory infection and dependence on caregivers, and improve quality of life. Future developments may allow this to become a minimally invasive technique that is more widely available.

References

1. National Spinal Cord Injury Statistical Center, University of Alabama at Birmingham, *Annual Statistical Report,* (University of Alabama, Birmingham, AL, 1997).
2. Carter, R. E., Donovan W. H., Halstead, L., and Wilkerson, M. A., Comparative study of electrophrenic nerve stimulation and mechanical ventilatory support in traumatic spinal cord injury, *Paraplegia,* **25**, 86-91, 1987.
3. DeVivo, M. J. and Ivie, C. S. III, Life expectancy of ventilator-dependent persons with spinal cord injuries, *Chest,* **108**, 226-232, 1995.
4. Esclarin, A., Bravo, P., Arroyo, O., Mazaira, J., Garrido, H., and Alcaraz, M. A., Tracheostomy ventilation versus diaphragmatic pacemaker ventilation in high spinal cord injury, *Paraplegia,* **32**, 687-693, 1994.
5. Whiteneck, G. G, Charlifue, S. W., Frankel, H. L., Fraser, M. H., Gardner, B. P., Gerhart, K. A., Krishnan, K. R., Menter, R. R., Nuseibeh, I., Short, D. J., et al., Mortality, morbidity, and psychosocial outcomes of persons spinal cord injured more than 20 years ago, *Paraplegia,* **30**, 617-630, 1992
6. Caldani, L. M. A, Institutiones physiologicae, Venezia, 1786, cited by Schechter, D. C., Application of electrotherapy to noncardiac thoracic disorders, *Bull NY Acad Med,* **46**, 932, 1970.
7. Ure, A., Experiments made on the body of criminal immediately after execution, with physiological and philosophical observations, *J Sci Arts,* **12**, 1, 1818, cited by Schechter, D. C., Application of electrotherapy to noncardiac thoracic disorders, *Bull NY Acad Med,* **46**, 932, 1970.
8. Bach, J. F. and Alba, A. S., Noninvasive options for ventilatory support of the traumatic high level quadriplegic, *Chest,* **98**, 613-619, 1990.
9. Baer, G. A., Talonen, P. P., Shneerson, J. M., Markkula, H., Exner, G., and Wells, F. C., Phrenic nerve stimulation for central ventilatory failure with bipolar and four-pole electrode systems, *PACE,* **19**, 1061-1072, 1990.
10. Beard, G. M. and Rockwell, A. D., *A Practical Treatise on the Medical & Surgical Uses of Electricity, Including Localized and General Faradization; Localized and Central Galvanization: Electrolysis and Galvano-Cautery,* (William Wood & Co, New York, 1875) p. 663.
11. Ferguson, cited by Schechter, D. C., Application of electrotherapy to noncardiac thoracic disorders, *Bull NY Acad Med,* **46**, 932, 1970
12. Hufeland, C. W.,: De usu vis electricae in asphyxia experimentis illustrato. Inauguraldissert, Gottingae, 1873, cited by Schechter, D. C., Application of electrotherapy to noncardiac thoracic disorders, *Bull NY Acad Med,* **46**, 932, 1970
13. Sarnoff, S. J., Hardenberg, E., and Whittenberger, J. L., Electrophrenic respiration, *Am J Physiol,* **155**, 1-9, 1948
14. Whittenberger, J. L., Sarnoff, S. J., and Hardenberg, E., Electrophrenic respiration II. Its use in man, *J Clin Invest,* **28**, 124-128, 1949.
15. Glenn, W. W. L., Hageman, J. H., Mauro, A., Eisenberg, L., Flanigan, S., and Harvard, M., Electrical stimulation of excitable tissue by radiofrequency transmission, *Ann Surg,* **160**, 338-350, 1964.

16. Glenn, W. W. L., Brouillette, R. T., and Dents, B., Fundamental considerations in pacing of the diaphragm for chronic ventilatory insufficiency: a multi-center study, *PACE*, **11**, 2121-2127, 1988.

17. Glenn, W. W. L., Hogan, J. F., and Phelps, M. L., Ventilatory support of the quadriplegic patient with respiratory paralysis by diaphragm pacing, *Surg Clin North Am*, **60**, 1055-1078, 1980.

18. Glenn, W. W. L., Holcomb, W. G., Hogan, J., Matano, I., Gee, J. B., Motoyama, E. K., Kim, C. S., Poirier, R. S., and Forbes, G., Diaphragm pacing by radiofrequency transmission in the treatment of chronic ventilatory insufficiency: Present status, *J Thorac Cardiovasc Surg*, **66**, 505-520 1973.

19. Oda, T., Glenn, W. W. L., Fukuda, Y., Hogan, J. F., and Gorfien, J., Evaluation of electrical parameters for diaphragm pacing: an experimental study, *J Surg Res*, **30**, 142-153, 1981.

20. Shaw, R. K., Glenn, W. W. L., Hogan, J. F., and Phelps, M. L., Electrophysiological evaluation of phrenic nerve function in candidates for diaphragm pacing, *J Neurosurg*, **53**, 345-354, 1980.

21. Hunt, C. E., Brouillette, R. T., Weese-Mayer, D. E., Morrow, A., and Ilbawi, M. N., Diaphragm pacing in infants and children, *PACE*, **11**, 2135-2141, 1988.

22. Glenn, W. W. L., Hogan, J. F., Loke, J. S., Ciesielski, T. E., Phelps, M. L., and Rowedder, R., Ventilatory support by pacing of the conditioned diaphragm in quadriplegia, *N Engl J Med*, **310**, 1150-1155, 1984.

23. Glenn, W. W. L. and Sairenji, H., Diaphragm pacing in the treatment of chronic ventilatory insufficiency, in eds. Roussos, C. and Macklem, P. T., *The Thorax: Lung Biology in Health and Disease. Vol 29*, (Marcel Dekker, New York, NY, 1985) p. 1407.

24. Thoma, H., Gerner, H., Holle, J., Kluger, P., Mayr, W., Meister, B., Schwanda, G., and Stöhr, H., The phrenic pacemaker: substitution of paralyzed functions in tetraplegia, *Trans Am Soc Artif Intern Organs*, **33**, 472-479, 1987.

25. Chen, C. F., Lien, I. N., Spinal cord injures in Taipei, Taiwan, 1978-1981, *Paraplegia*, **23**, 364-370, 1985.

26. Dobelle, W. H., D'Angelo, M. S., Goetz, B. F., Kiefer, D. G., Lallier, T. J., Lamb, J. I., and Yazwinsky, J. S., 200 cases with a new breathing pacemaker dispel myths about diaphragm pacing, *Trans Am Soc Artif Intern Organs*, **40**, M244-252, 1994.

27. Glenn, W. W. L., Phelps, M. L., Elefteriades, J. A., Dentz, B., and Hogan, J. F., Twenty years experience in phrenic nerve stimulation to pace the diaphragm, *PACE*, **9**, 781-784, 1986.

28. Hackler, R. H., A 25-year prospective mortality study in the spinal cord injured patient: comparison with the long-term living paraplegic, *J Urol*, **117**, 486-488, 1977.

29. Ilbawi MN, Idriss FS, Hunt CE, Brouillette, and R. T, DeLeon, S. Y., Diaphragmatic pacing in infants. Techniques and results, *Ann Thoracic Surg*, **40**, 323-329, 1985.

30. Hirschfeld, S., Exner, G., Luukkaala, T., and Baer, G. A., Mechanical ventilation or phrenic nerve stimulation for treatment of spinal cord injury-induced respiratory insufficiency, *Spinal Cord*, **46**, 738-742, 2008.

31. Adler, D., Gonzalez-Bermejo, J. E., Duguet, A., Demoule, A., Le Pimpec-Barthes, F., Hurbault, A., Morélot-Panzini, C., and Similowski, T., Diaphragm pacing restores olfaction in tetraplegia, *Eur Respir J*, **34**, 365-370, 2009.

32. Talonen, P. P., Baer, G. A,. Hakkinen, V., and Ojala, J. K., Neurophysiological and technical considerations for the design of an implantable phrenic nerve stimulator, *Med Biol Eng Comput*, **28**, 31-371990.

33. DiMarco, A. F., Onders, R. P., Ignagni, A., Kowalski, K. E., and Mortimer, J. T., Phrenic nerve pacing via intramuscular diaphragm electrodes in tetraplegic subjects, *Chest*, **127**, 671-678, 2005.

34. DiMarco, A. F., Onders, R. P., Kowalski, K. E., Miller, M. E., Ferek, S., and Mortimer, J. T., Phrenic nerve pacing in a tetraplegic patient via intramuscular diaphragm electrodes, *Am J Respir Crit Care Med*, **166**, 1604-1606, 2002.

35. Le Pimpec-Barthes, F., Gonzalez-Bermejo, J., Hubsch, J. P., Duguet, A., Morélot-Panzini, C., Riquet, M., and Similowski, T., Intrathoracic phrenic pacing: a 10-year experience in France, *J Thorac Cardiovasc Surg*, **142**, 378-383, 2011.

36. Onders, R. P., DiMarco, A. F., Ignagni, A. R., Aiyar, H., and Mortimer, J. T., Mapping the phrenic nerve motor point: The key to a successful laparoscopic diaphragm pacing system in the first human series, *Surgery*, **136**, 819-826, 2004.

37. Onders, R. P., DiMarco, A. F., Ignagni, A. R., and Mortimer, J. T., The learning curve for investigational surgery: lessons learned from laparoscopic diaphragm pacing for chronic ventilator dependence, *Surg Endosc*, **19**, 633-637, 2005.

38. Onders, R. P., Elmo, M., Kaplan, C., Katirji, B., and Schilz, R., Extended use of diaphragm pacing in patients with unilateral or bilateral diaphragm dysfunction: A new therapeutic option, *Surgery*, **156**, 776-786, 2014.

39. Glenn, W. W. L. and Hogan, J. F., Technique of transthoracic placement of phrenic nerve electrodes for diaphragm pacing, *American College of Surgeons Film Library*, Chicago, 1982.

40. Glenn, W. W. L. and Phelps, M. L., Diaphragmatic pacing by electrical stimulation of the phrenic nerve, *Neurosurgery*, **17**, 974-984, 1985.

41. Le Pimpec-Barthes, F., Gonzalez-Bermejo, J., Hubsch, J. P., Duguet, A., Morélot-Panzini, C., Riquet, M., and Similowski, T., Intrathoracic phrenic pacing: a 10-year experience in France, *J Thorac Cardiovasc Surg*, **142**, 378-383, 2011.

42. Weese-Mayer, D. E., Silvestri, J. M., Kenny, A. S., Ilbawi, M. N., Hauptman, S. A., Lipton, J. W., Talonen, P. P., Garcia, H. G., Watt, J. W., Exner, G., Baer, G. A., Elefteriades, J. A., Peruzzi, W. T., Alex, C. G., Harlid, R., Vincken, W., Davis, G. M., Decramer, M., Kuenzle, C,. Saeterhaug, A., and Schöber, J. G., Diaphragm pacing with quadripolar phrenic nerve electrode: an international study, *PACE*, **19**, 1311-1319, 1996.

43. DiMarco, A. F., Supinski, G. S., Petro, J., and Takaoka, Y., Evaluation of intercostal pacing to provide artificial ventilation in quadriplegics, *Am J Respir Crit Care Med*, **150**, 934-940, 1994.

44. DiMarco, A. F., Takaoka, Y., and Kowalski, K. E., Combined intercostal and diaphragm pacing to provide artificial ventilation in patients with tetraplegia, *Arch Phys Med Rehabil*, **86**, 1200-1207, 2005.

45. DiMarco, A. F., Budzinska, K., and Supinski, G. S., Artificial ventilation of intercostal/-accessory muscles alone in anesthetized dogs, *Am Rev Respir Dis*, **139**, 961-967, 1989.

46. DiMarco, A. F. and Kowalski, K. E., Effects of chronic electrical stimulation on paralyzed expiratory muscles, *J Appl Physiol*, **104**, 1634-1640, 2008.

47. DiMarco, A. F., Supinski, G. S., Petro, J., and Takaoka, Y., Artificial respiration via combined intercostal and diaphragm pacing in a quadriplegic patient, *Am Rev Respir Dis*, **149**, A135, 1994.

48. DiMarco, A. F. and Kowalski, K. E., High frequency spinal cord stimulation of inspiratory muscles in dogs: a new method of inspiratory muscle pacing, *J Appl Physiol*, **107**, 662-669, 2009.

49. DiMarco, A. F. and Kowalski, K. E., Intercostal muscle pacing with high frequency spinal cord stimulation in dogs, *Respir Physiol Neurobiol*, **171**, 218-224, 2010.

50. DiMarco, A. F. and Kowalski, K. E., Distribution of electrical activation to the external intercostal muscles during high frequency spinal cord stimulation in dogs, *J Physiol*, **589**, 1383-1395, 2011.

51. Brown, R., DiMarco, A. F., Hoit, J. D., and Garshick, E., Respiratory dysfunction and management in spinal cord injury, *Respir Care*, **51**, 853-870, 2006.

52. Linder, S. H., Functional electrical stimulation to enhance cough in quadriplegia, *Chest*, **103**, 166-169, 1993.

53. Lim, J., Gorman, R. B., Saboisky, J. P., Gandevia, S. C., and Butler, J. E., Optimal electrode placement for noninvasive electrical stimulation of human abdominal muscles, J Appl Physiol, 102, 1612-1617, 2007.

54. Kyroussis, D., Polkey, M. I., Mills, G. H., Hughes, P. D., Moxham, J., and Green, M.. Simulation of cough in man by magnetic stimulation of the thoracic nerve roots. *Am J Respir Crit Care Med*, **156**, 1696-1699, 1997.

55. Lin, V. W., Hsieh, C., Hsiao, I. N., and Canfield, J., Functional magnetic stimulation of expiratory muscles: a noninvasive and new method for restoring cough, *J Appl Physiol*, **84**, 1144-1150, 1998.

56. Lin, V. W., Romaniuk, J. R., and DiMarco, A. F., Functional magnetic stimulation of the respiratory muscles in dogs, *Muscle Nerve*, **21**, 1048-1057, 1998.

57. Lin, V. W., Singh, H., Chitkara, R. K., and Perkash, I.. Functional magnetic stimulation for restoring cough in patients with tetraplegia, *Arch Phys Med Rehabil*, **79**, 517-522, 1998.

58. Butler, J. E., Lim, J., Gorman, R. B., Boswell-Ruys, C., Saboisky, J. P., Lee, B. B., and Gandevia, S. C., Posterolateral surface electrical stimulation of abdominal expiratory muscles to enhance cough in spinal cord injury, *Neurorehabil Neural Repair*, **25**, 158-167, 2011.

59. McBain, R. A., Boswell-Ruys, C. L., Lee, B. B., Gandevia, S. C., and Butler, J. E., Electrical stimulation of abdominal muscles to produce cough in spinal cord injury: effect of stimulus intensity, *Neurorehabil Neural Repair*, **29**, 362-369, 2015.

60. DiMarco, A. F., Kowalski, K. E., Geertman, R. T., and Hromyak, D. R., Spinal cord stimulation: a new method to produce cough in patients with spinal cord injury, *Am J Respir Crit Care Med*, **173**, 1386-1389, 2006.

61. DiMarco, A. F., Kowalski, K. E., Supinski, G., and Romaniuk, J. R., Mechanism of expiratory muscle activation during lower thoracic spinal cord stimulation, *J Appl Physiol*, **92**, 2341-2346, 2002.

62. DiMarco, A. F., Romaniuk, J. R., Kowalski, K. E., and Supinski, G., Pattern of expiratory muscle activation during lower thoracic spinal cord stimulation, *J Appl Physiol*, **86**, 1881-1889, 1999.

63. DiMarco, A. F., Romaniuk, J. R., and Supinski, G. S., Electrical activation of the expiratory muscles to restore cough, *Am J Respir Crit Care Med*, **151**, 1466-1471, 1995.

64. DiMarco, A. F., Kowalski, K. E., Geertman, R. T., and Hromyak, D. R., Lower thoracic spinal cord stimulation to restore cough in patients with spinal cord injury: results of a National Institutes of Health-sponsored clinical trial. Part I: methodology and effectiveness of expiratory muscle activation, *Arch Phys Med Rehabil*, **90**, 717-725, 2009.

65. DiMarco, A. F., Kowalski, K. E., Geertman, R. T., Hromyak, D. R., Frost, F. S., Creasey, G. H., and Nemunaitis, G. A., Lower thoracic spinal cord stimulation to restore cough in patients with spinal cord injury: results of a National Institutes of Health-sponsored clinical trial. Part II: clinical outcomes, *Arch Phys Med Rehabil*, **90**, 726-732, 2009.

66. DiMarco, A. F., Kowalski, K. E., Hromyak, D. R., Geertman, R. T., Long-term follow-up of spinal cord stimulation (SCS) to restore cough in subjects with spinal cord injury, *J Spinal Cord Med*, **37**, 380-388, 2013.

Chapter 3.4

Vagus Nerve Stimulation: Therapeutic Applications for Cardiac Disease

Ray W. Chui[1-3]*, Pradeep S. Rajendran[1-3]*, Una Buckley[1-2], Kalyanam Shivkumar[1-3] and Jeffrey L. Ardell[1-3]

[1]University of California – Los Angeles (UCLA) Cardiac Arrhythmia Center, David Geffen School of Medicine, Los Angeles, CA, USA
[2]UCLA Neurocardiology Research Center of Excellence, David Geffen School of Medicine, Los Angeles, CA, USA
[3]Molecular, Cellular & Integrative Physiology Program, UCLA, Los Angeles, CA, USA
jardell@mednet.ucla.edu
* These authors contributed equally.

Cardiac control is mediated via nested neural networks involving thoracic autonomic ganglia, spinal cord, brainstem and higher centers. Each of these processing centers contains afferent, efferent and interneurons which interact locally and in an interdependent fashion with the other levels to coordinate regional cardiac function. It is now recognized that autonomic dysregulation is central to the evolution of heart failure and arrhythmias. Autonomic Regulation Therapy (ART) is an emerging modality in the management of acute and chronic cardiac pathologies; vagus nerve stimulation (VNS) being one of the primary modes of delivery. VNS has the potential to counteract autonomic dysregulation, doing so by targeting select reflex possessing points of the neural hierarchy and ultimately in modulating the neural outflow to heart muscle. Understanding the anatomical and physiological basis for such control is necessary to implement effectively novel neuromodulation therapies. This chapter reviews critical structure/function aspects of the cardiac nervous system, how VNS impacts these control systems, and emerging therapeutic indications for VNS including arrhythmias and heart failure.

1. Introduction

Bioelectric therapy is an emerging field for site-specific therapeutics, with the vagus nerve representing one of the primary targets for electrical stimulation. This is a mixed nerve, containing both ascending (afferent) and descending (efferent) axonal projections [1, 2]. As such, electrical activation has the potential to modulate central neural processing, peripheral neural reflexes and ultimately impact target organ function via these neural pathways [2, 3]. The therapeutic efficacy of vagus nerve stimulation (VNS) is currently being evaluated for disorders of the central nervous system (e.g., epilepsy, depression) [4, 5, 6], cardiovascular system (e.g., arrhythmias, heart failure) [7, 8, 9], and digestive system (e.g., obesity) [10]. Other potential indications include pain, asthma and inflammation [11]. The focus of this chapter will be on cardiovascular applications for VNS, specifically as related to Autonomic Regulation Therapy (ART) and its impact on cardiac electrical and mechanical function. VNS will be considered as applied in normal conditions and then during progressive cardiac pathology.

2. Structure/Anatomy of Vagus Nerve

2.1. *Structure/function of the vagus nerve*

The vagus nerve (from the Latin for "wandering"), also known as cranial nerve X, has a role in direct control of cardiac and visceral function (cardiovascular, respiratory and gastrointestinal systems) [11, 12]. It likewise affects body homeostasis by modulating immune and endocrine function [1, 11]. The vagus nerve is bilateral and contains a mixture of afferent and efferent (parasympathetic and sympathetic) projecting axons [13, 14, 15]. Vagal afferent neurites transduce a number of modalities, including pain, stretch, pressure, temperature, chemical milieu, and osmolarity [11, 16, 17]. These afferent fibers relay this information to multiple brain regions [18, 19], from which preganglionic activity is reflexly controlled and projected back to ganglia on cardiac and visceral organs [20, 21, 22, 23]. The peripheral autonomic ganglia function as the end-stage processors for control of organ function [24, 25, 26].

The vagus nerve embryologically represents the nerve of the 4th branchial arch. It arises from the medulla oblongata as 8 to 10 rootlets, which form a single trunk and exit the cranium via the jugular foramen. The vagus forms two sensory ganglia, one within the jugular foramen (called the jugular or superior ganglion) and one below (nodose or inferior ganglion) [20]. The superior ganglion gives off the auricular branch of the vagus. Upon exit from the jugular foramen, the vagus continues down the neck within the carotid sheath (between the carotid artery and internal jugular vein). At the level of the nodose, the vagus branches off into the superior laryngeal nerve and pharyngeal branches, which join with branches of the glossopharyngeal nerve and superior cervical ganglion [16, 20, 27]. Once the vagus enters the thorax at the base of the neck, the right and left nerves differ anatomically. The right vagus follows the origin of the subclavian artery, with one branch becoming the recurrent (inferior) laryngeal nerve, and the main trunk traversing behind the main bronchus and posterior aspect of the esophagus [16, 20, 27]. On the left side, the nerve enters the thorax between the left common carotid and subclavian arteries, passes anterior to the aortic arch, with one branch coming off as the recurrent laryngeal nerve. The cardiac branches, on the left side, arise only from the recurrent nerve [16, 20, 26, 27]. At the heart level, preganglionic projections innervate multiple intrinsic cardiac ganglia, with subsequent post-ganglionic projections to all four cardiac chambers (atrial and ventricular) [24, 28]. Exiting the thorax through the esophageal hiatus of the diaphragm, the vagus then terminates at various abdominal organs, including the liver, spleen, stomach, pancreas, kidney and bowels [16, 20, 27]. Cervical and thoracic projections also contain substantial contributions from sympathetic fibers that arise from interconnections with the paravertebral chain [29, 30, 31]. This nerve is a mixed vago-sympathetic efferent nerve with major afferent cardio-visceral components [11, 14].

2.2. *Fiber types and general anatomy of the vagus*

Brainstem vagal preganglionic somata originate in the nucleus ambiguous (NA) and dorsal motor nucleus (DMN) [20, 21, 32]. Efferent projections to cardiac and visceral organs traverse the 10th cranial nerve [18, 31]. Vagal efferent projections account for 20% of the fibers contained within the cervical vagosympathetic trunk, the remainder being afferents [33, 34]. According to the classification system of Erlanger and Gasser, the vagus nerve contains A-, B- and C-fibers [11]. Myelinated A-fibers reflect somatic afferent and parasympathetic preganglionic efferent projections, with the smaller A-fibers transmitting visceral afferent information. Small myelinated B-fibers are primarily post-ganglionic sympathetic and preganglionic parasympathetic efferent projections. Unmyelinated C-fibers transmit visceral afferent information [11, 16, 20].

2.3. *Phenotypical organization*

Parasympathetic efferent fibers utilize acetylcholine (ACh) as their mediator neurotransmitter (NT) [35]. Preganglionic neurons release ACh which in turn bind to nicotinic ACh receptors on intrinsic cardiac postganglionic parasympathetic neurons [36, 37, 38]. These neurons are contained within discrete ganglia located on atrial and ventricular tissues, each with specific spheres of influence (e.g., control of heart rate, speed of cardiac conduction) [28, 39, 40]. Histological studies have shown a complex network of acetylcholine containing nerves throughout the endocardium and epicardium on both the left and right ventricles [41, 42]. ACh binds muscarinic (M_2) receptors on cardiac myocytes, inducing decreases in heart rate, speed of electrical conduction and force of cardiac contraction [35, 42, 43]. Besides the expected post-ganglionic parasympathetic neurons, intrinsic cardiac ganglia also contain afferent somata and a major population of local circuit neurons LCN's [24, 28, 44], the latter sub-serving information processing within and between intrathoracic autonomic ganglia [24].

3. Structure/Function of the Cardiac Nervous System

The autonomic nervous system (ANS) modulates cardiac electrical and mechanical indices on a beat-to-beat basis [24, 28, 43, 45]. Classically, peripheral autonomic ganglia were considered passive relay stations [12]. Recent data demonstrates that the cardiac nervous system is an intelligent neural network consisting of nested feedback loops, involving both peripheral and central nervous system neural circuits [24, 28, 45]. As schematically represented in Figure 1, these feedback loops include the intrinsic cardiac ganglia, extracardiac intrathoracic ganglia, spinal cord, brainstem and higher centers [24, 28]. The basic components of the neural circuitry at each nexus point of this hierarchy include sensory neurons, autonomic motor neurons, and local circuit neural processors [24]. The more peripheral of the control loops (intrinsic cardiac and extracardiac intrathoracic) are primarily concerned with cardio-cardiac reflexes [24, 46, 47, 48]. Central nervous system neural circuits (spinal cord, brainstem and above) exert major effects on cardiac function and peripheral blood flow distribution [19, 49, 50]. To understand the functional manifestations for integrated cardiac control, it is critical that one first evaluates the constituent parts.

3.1. *Structure/function of cardiac sensory neurons*

Cardiac afferent neurons transduce the chemical and/or mechanical milieu of myocardial tissue [17]. The cell bodies of afferent neurons are located primarily in the nodose and dorsal root ganglia (DRG) [17]. Bipolar neurons in the nodose have peripheral projections to sensory neurites in all regions of the heart and central projections to second-order neurons in the nucleus tractus solitarii of the medulla [18, 19]. These second-order neurons modulate the activity of efferent parasympathetic neurons located in the NA and DMN of the medulla [18, 21, 22, 32]. They likewise can impact sympathetic outflow via the brainstem reticular formation and reticulospinal projections to sympathetic preganglionic fibers contained within the intermediolateral (IML) cell column of the spinal cord [51,

52]. Bipolar neurons in the DRG have peripheral projections to the neurites throughout the heart and central projecting axons to second-order neurons in the dorsal horn of the spinal cord [51, 52]. These second-order neurons modulate the activity of efferent sympathetic neurons in the IML cell column of the spinal cord [51] with secondary effects mediated by spinal reticular projections to brainstem cardiovascular control sites including the nucleus of the tractus solitarii [18, 19, 52, 53]. While the nodose and DRG are the predominant locations of cardiac afferent neurons, afferent neurons have also been identified in the intrinsic cardiac and extracardiac intrathoracic ganglia [17, 24, 48, 54]. This afferent input can mediate reflex control of regional cardiac function independent of the central nervous system [24, 28].

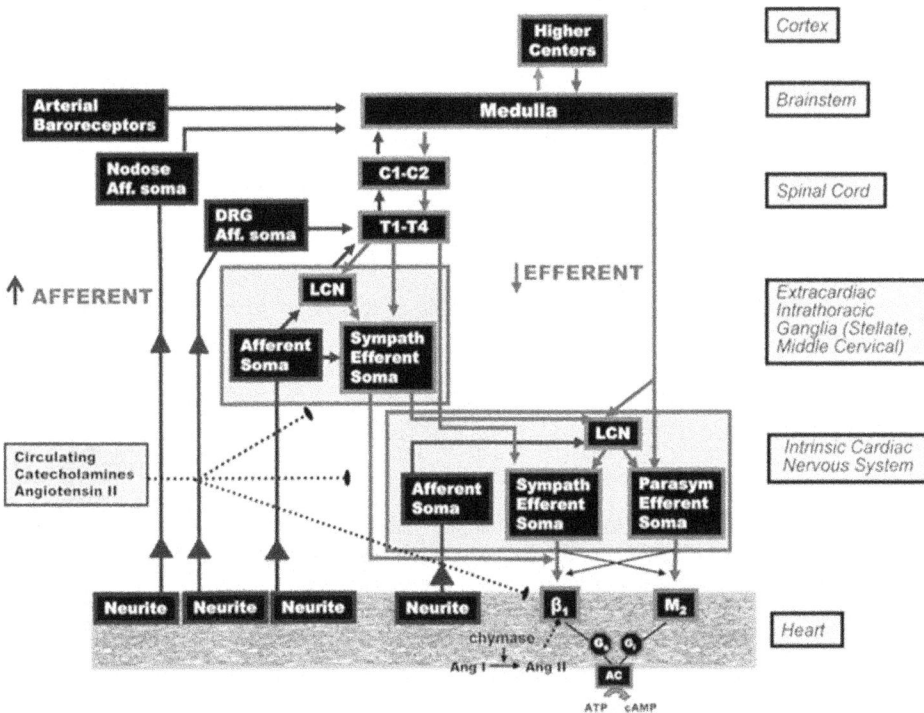

Fig. 1: Neurohumoral control and anatomical organization of cardiac innervation. This schematic illustrates the various levels of organization and the neurotransmitters involved in control of cardiac indices. http://www.ncbi.nlm.nih.gov/pubmed/26044253

3.2. *Structure/function of cardiac parasympathetic neurons*

Cardiac parasympathetic preganglionic neurons originate in the NA and DMN and project to postganglionic neurons located in the intrinsic cardiac nervous system (ICNS) [21, 22, 32, 51]. The ICNS is a distributed network of neuronal aggregates termed ganglionated plexi that are located in atrial and ventricular epicardial tissue [44, 55, 56]. Postganglionic soma from the ICNS send axonal projections to the all heart regions [24, 39, 57]. Figure 2 illustrates a typical response to cervical VNS. Note the suppression in heart rate, left ventricular pressure (LVP), rate of change of LVP (dp/dt) and blood pressure. Under physiological conditions, these various pathways are coordinated such that changes in rate are matched by changes in conduction such that the potential for heart block is minimized [37, 40, 58]. In general, unilateral stimulation of preganglionic inputs leads to similar cardiac effects on both sides of the heart (Figure 3) and between endo- and epicardium (Figure 4). This divergence of control is a manifestation of characteristics of the efferent input and the coupling of activity between the separate aggregates of intrinsic cardiac ganglia via interganglionic interconnections mediated by the local circuit neurons [24].

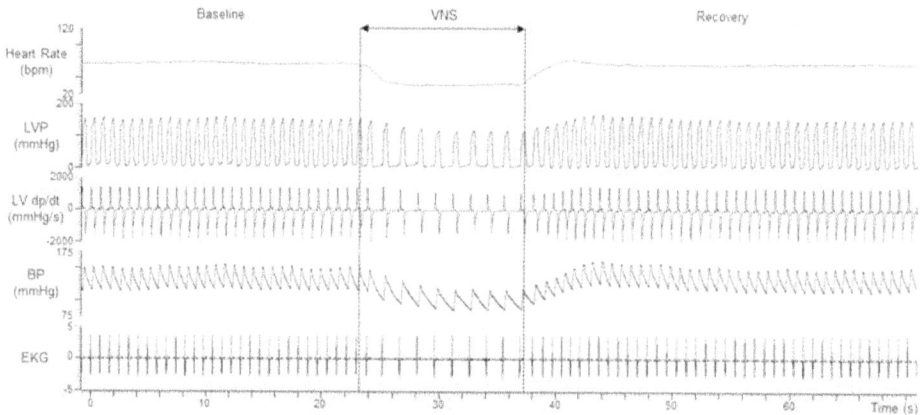

Fig. 2: Hemodynamic response to VNS stimulation. The right cervical vagus was stimulated in an alpha-chloralose-anesthetized mongrel, with intact vagus nerves, with the following parameters: 10 Hz, 500 μs pulse width and 2.50 mA for 14 s. LVP: left ventricular pressure; LV dp/dt: left ventricular contractility (1st derivative of LVP); BP: blood pressure; EKG: lead II electrocardiogram. http://www.ncbi.nlm.nih.gov/pubmed/26371171

The evoked response to cervical vagosympathetic bioelectric stimuli reflects the interdependent interaction mediated within neural hierarchy for cardiac control. As demonstrated by Figure 5, low-level VNS results in augmentations in regional cardiac function, primarily as the result of withdrawal of central parasympathetic drive [2]. Transection of the vagus rostral to stimulation eliminates the VNS-induced augmentation in cardiac function; bilateral transection markedly enhances the functional control manifest by VNS [2, 3]. Figure 6 summarizes the primary impact for VNS on the cardiac nervous system, with afferents engaged before efferent [2]. The point at which afferent mediated withdrawal is balanced against the direct activation of parasympathetic efferent projects is defined at the neural fulcrum [2]. Extending VNS intensities past that point results in suppression of regional cardiac function (Figure 5), with a rebound effect during the immediate time after VNS offset (Figure 2). VNS, delivered at the neural fulcrum, engages the cardiac nervous system without major disruptions in cardiac control [2].

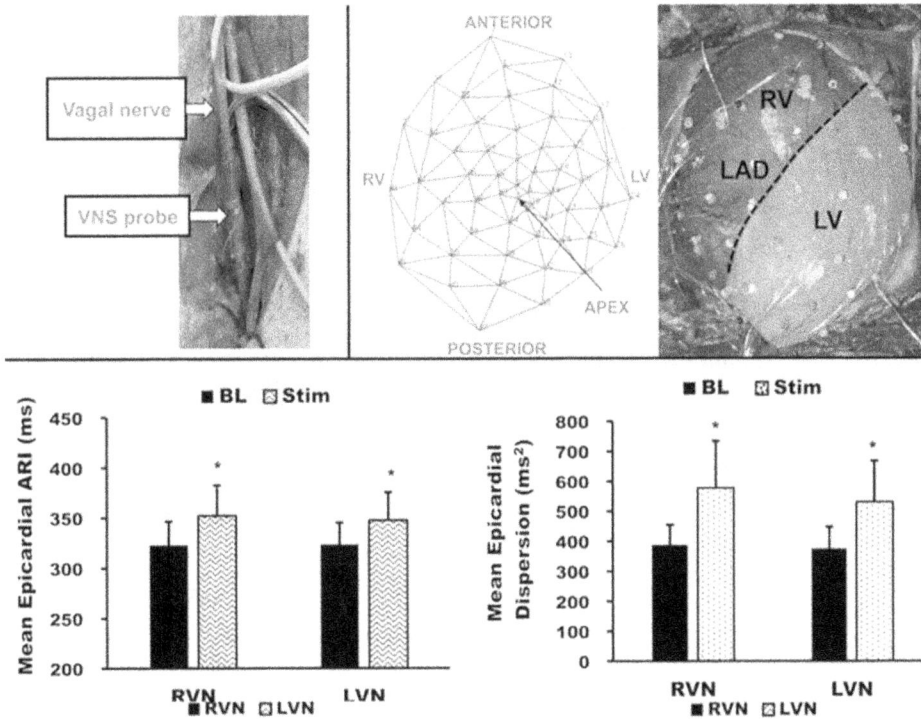

Fig. 3: Global epicardial activation recovery interval (ARI) responses to vagal stimulation in an alpha-chloralose-anesthetized Yorkshire pig. *Top panel (from left to right):* isolation of vagus nerve and bipolar stimulation electrode; locations of the electrodes on the sock; and the sock electrode on the heart. *Bottom panel:* mean epicardial ARI (left) and dispersion of repolarization (DOR, right). Significant differents were noted between BL and stim, but no significant differences were observed between right and left VNS. Data are mean ±SE. * p < 0.01 vs. BL. Stimulation parameters: 10-20 Hz, 0.5-1 ms, variable current to decrease heart rate by 10-20%. RV: right ventricle; RVN: right vagus nerve; LAD: left anterior descending artery; LV: left ventricle; LVN: left vagus nerve; BL: baseline; Stim: during stimulation. http://www.ncbi.nlm.nih.gov/pubmed/25015962

3.3. *Structure/function of cardiac sympathetic neurons*

Cardiac sympathetic preganglionic neurons originate in the intermediolateral (IML) cell column of the thoracic T1 through T5 segments of the spinal cord and project to postganglionic neurons located in the stellate [59], middle cervical [60], mediastinal ganglia [61] and intrinsic cardiac ganglia [24]. Activation of sympathetic projections to the heart results in increases in heart rate, speed of electrical conduction and force of contraction of the heart [31, 62, 63]. There is stratification in sympathetic projections, with unilateral predominance, but with the potential for bilateral control of all regions of the heart [29, 43, 62]. Importantly, the intrinsic cardiac ganglia sub-serve major sympathetic/ parasympathetic interactions to compliment the well-recognized pre- and post-junctional interactions mediated at the neural-myocyte interface (Figure 1) [36, 37, 38].

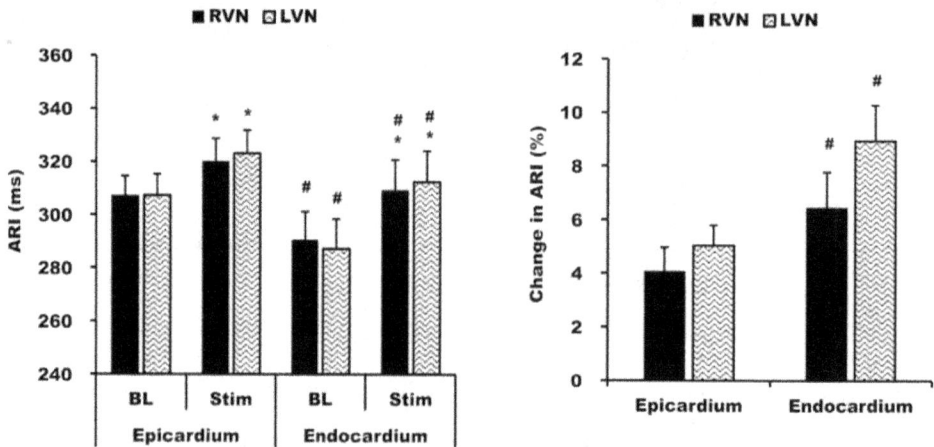

Fig. 4: Epicardial and endocardial ARI changes during right and left VNS in an alpha-chloralose-anesthetized Yorkshire pig. Data are mean ±SE. * $p < 0.01$ vs. BL; # $p < 0.05$ vs the epicardium. Stimulation parameters: 10-20 Hz, 0.5-1 ms, variable current to decrease heart rate by 10-20%. RVN: right vagus nerve; LVN: left vagus nerve; BL: baseline; Stim: during stimulation. http://www.ncbi.nlm.nih.gov/pubmed/25015962

3.4. Structure/function of local circuit neurons

For the cardiac nervous system, local circuit neurons contained within the intrathoracic ganglia are the primary integrating sites for processing of afferent and efferent inputs [24]. They are stratified as afferent LCN's and efferent LCN's if they process second order inputs of afferent or efferent (sympathetic and/or parasympathetic) inputs [24, 64, 65]. They are classified as convergent LCN's if they respond at least one autonomic efferent input and at least one modality of sensory input [64, 65]. Such inputs can enhance or suppress neural activity [24, 64, 65]. Importantly, this subclass of neurons are primary targets for neuromodulation therapy [66], including but not limited to spinal cord stimulation and vagal nerve stimulation [67].

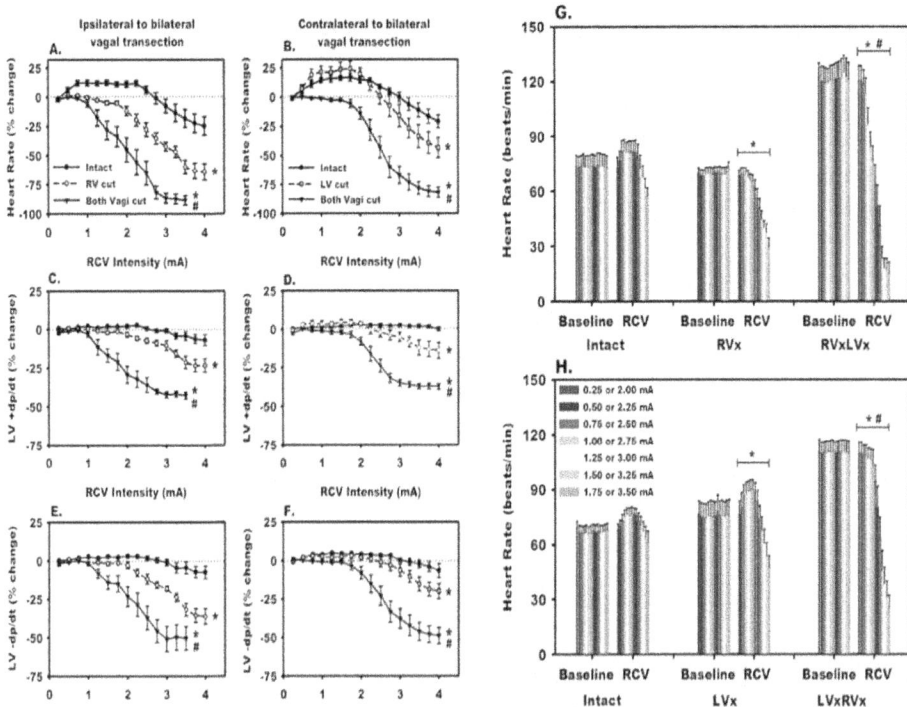

Fig. 5: Right VNS evoked changes in chronotropy (A, B), left ventricular inotropy (C, D) and lusitropy (E, F) in the intact state and following unilateral and bilateral cervical vagotomy (G, H). Vagus nerves were cut rostral to the stimulating electrode. For panels A – F, * $p < 0.004$ vs. intact. # $p < 0.0001$, unilateral vs. bilateral vagus transection. For panels G and H, * $p < 0.001$ vs. intact. # $p < 0.005$, unilateral vs. bilateral vagus transection. http://www.ncbi.nlm.nih.gov/pubmed/26371171

4. History and Development of VNS

4.1. *Historical background*

In the 1880's, James Leonard Corning created the carotid fork for carotid artery compression to terminate epileptic seizures. Later, he would combine carotid compression with transcutaneous electrical stimulation of the cervical vagosympathetic trunk, observing for the first time off-target side effects that including bradycardia, dizziness and syncope [68]. Since the late 1930's, a number of groups have evaluated the effect of vagal afferent stimulation on the cortex, ultimately resulting in the demonstration of the ability to reduce seizures in various animal models, including the "encéphale isolé" cats and the strychnine canine status epilepsy model [69, 70, 71, 72]. Chase et al. [73] used vagal stimulation to show that cortical synchronization and desynchronization were induced by afferent signaling, mediated by rapidly conducted vagal potentials (>15 m/sec) and those conducted at approximately 15 m/sec. It was determined that nature of the EEG response was due to the type of vagal afferent fiber activated and not stimulation frequency [73]. VNS for epilepsy continues to be a standard of care for specific sub-populations of patients [74].

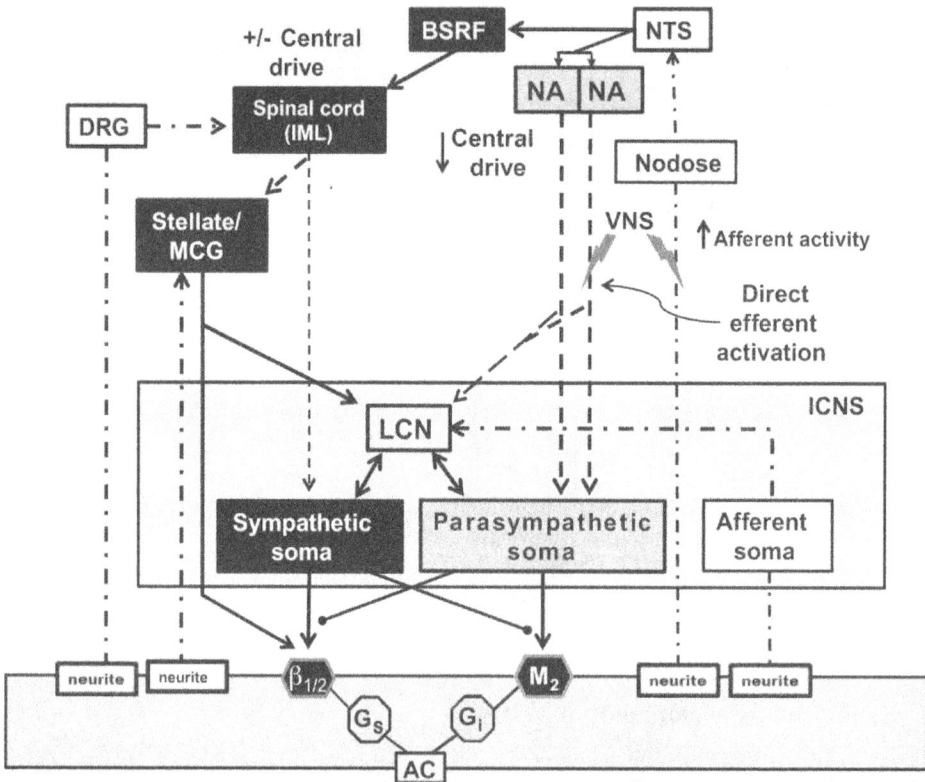

Fig. 6: Schematic summarizing neural interactions mediated by VNS in cardiac control. Dashed lines, preganglionic projections; dotted-dashed lines, afferent projections. NTS, nucleus tractus solitarius; NA, nucleus ambiguus; BSRF, brain stem reticular formation; IML, intermediolateral cell column; DRG, dorsal root ganglion; MCG, middle cervical ganglion; LCN, local circuit neuron; β, β-adrenergic receptor; M2, muscarinic receptor; Gs and Gi, G-coupled proteins; AC, adenylate cyclase. http://www.ncbi.nlm.nih.gov/pubmed/26371171

4.2. Emerging indications

At the current time, a search of active clinical trials (www.clinicaltrials.gov) yields more than 30 active VNS studies, covering disorders such as irritable bowel syndrome, motion sickness, inflammation, arthritis, headache, migraine, diabetes, obesity, appetite suppression, seizure, pain, syncope, heart failure, among others.

4.3. *VNS implementation*

In general terms, these systems can be stratified into implantable vs. transcutaneous devices. For implantable systems, most rely on a modification of a wrap-around helical electrode to form the interface with the vagosympathetic trunk. These leads are connected to an implantable programmable generator (IPG). Critical elements for effective bioelectric control of the cervical vagus include frequency, pulse width, intensity, with a secondary contribution of bipolar orientation [2, 75, 76]. Both continuous and intermittent stimulus paradigms have been utilized with most working in the 20-30% duty cycle range. It is highly likely that optimum stimulus paradigms are target organ specific. For example, while 20-30 Hz is the standard of care for epilepsy [77], cardiovascular indications are well treated in the 2-10 Hz range [7], and VNS efficacy for immune system modulation may require only short-periods of stimulus delivery [78]. One take home from these data is that the effects of VNS can outlive the active phase; this is a reflection of memory within the neural circuits being impacted by VNS [79]. Finally, while VNS is primarily delivered in the open-loop configuration, important strides are being made to close the loop using biomarkers such as heart rate [7].

Emerging technologies for VNS now include non-invasive approaches. These technologies can be suitable for screening for potential efficacy to VNS, or as an adjunct intermittent situational therapy. These devices include trans-auricular and trans-cervical methodologies [80]. A recent study evaluated respiratory-gated auricular vagal afferent nerve stimulation (RAVANS) in patients with chronic pelvic pain due to endometriosis. RAVANS reduced pain intensity, temporal summation of mechanical pain and decreased anxiety [81]. Bilateral tragus (auricular branch of the vagus nerve) stimulation has also be reported to attenuate LV remodeling in conscious dogs with healed MI [82] and suppress of atrial fibrillation (AF) in a rapid atrial pacing canine model [83]. Auricular stimulation likewise exerted an anti-arrhythmic effect in patients with paroxysmal AF [84]. The therapeutic efficacy of VNS is likely dependent on its ability to shift autonomic control from sympathetic towards parasympathetic predominance [85].

5. VNS in Heart Failure

Heart failure (HF) is a complex disorder that manifests itself as impaired ventricular filling or ejection [86]. HF can result from issues with the pericardium, various regions of the heart (myocardium, endocardium, valves, coronary vessels) or from certain metabolic abnormalities [87]. HF patients can be classified roughly into one of two groups: i) HF with reduced ejection fraction (≤40%, HFrEF); or ii)

HF with preserved ejection fraction ($\geq$50%, HFpEF) [87]. At the present time, in the United States, it is estimated that HF afflicts 5.1 million people ($\geq$20 years), with projections that the prevalence will increase 46% by 2030, to an estimated 8 million people [88]. The costs associated with this are $30.7 billion; that number is expected to grow to $69.7 billion by 2030 [89]. Even with improving treatments, morbidity and mortality remain high, with median survival times of 1.7 years in men and 3.2 years in women. The 5-year survival rate is 25% and 38%, in men and women, respectively [90].

5.1. *VNS for HF: Preclinical data*

Over the course of the past century, it has been known vagal efferent nerve activity can modulate cardiac function, even in states of progressive cardiac disease. In mouse models with chronic myocardial infarction (MI), VNS modulates cardiac redox state, decreases adrenergic drive and suppresses free radical generation [91]. Li et al. showed in rat models with chronic MI that 6 weeks of VNS therapy cardiac pump function improved and survival [92]. Even short term (e.g. 3 days) VNS delivered 3 weeks after coronary artery ligation in rat model mitigated cardiac remodeling and improved cardiac excitation-contraction coupling [93]. In canine models of HF, VNS improved left ventricular function and various other cardiac indices in response to the stress of high rate ventricular pacing [94], intracoronary microembolizations [95], and chronic mitral regurgitation [96]. Recent data has suggested that even low level VNS stimulation (inducing minimal HR changes) using invasive [97] and non-invasive (bilateral transcutaneous stimulation of the auricular branch) [98] methods can be efficacious in reducing disease burden in HF [97, 99]. These data have provided critical insights from which clinical trials are now evolving.

5.2. *VNS for HF: Clinical data*

Abnormal autonomic balance has been recognized as a factor in increased mortality in myocardial infarction and heart failure [100]. In general, the progression of HF is associated with a hyper-dynamic sympathetic response with a corresponding decrease in centrally mediated parasympathetic activity [50, 101]. In moderate to severe chronic HF, decreased sensitivity of vagal reflexes is significantly associated with poor outcome [102]. Furthermore, the Autonomic Tone and Reflexes After Myocardial Infarction study (ATRAMI) and the Cardiac Insufficiency Bisprolol Study II (CIBIS II) showed that reduction in vagal activity was one of the predictors for increased mortality [103, 104]. By restoring biomimetic parasympathetic activity with VNS, excessive sympatho-excitation is blunted and myocytes rendered stress-resistant [97, 99, 105, 106]. Results from recent trials of VNS for HF have been equivocal, likely reflecting in part stimulation paradigms and patient selection.

Table 1. Summary of VNS clinical trials in heart failure.

	CardioFit	NECTAR-HF	ANTHEM-HF	INOVATE-HF
Sponsor	BioControl Medical	Boston Scientific	Cyberonics	BioControl Medical
Patient Population	NYHA Class II-III, EF <35%	NYHA Class II-III, EF <35%	NYHA Class II-III, EF <40%	NYHA Class III, EF <40%
Patients Size	32	96 (63 VNS)	60	650 (3:2 design, ~390)
Stimulation Frequency	1-2 Hz	20 Hz	10 Hz	1-2 Hz
Study Design	Open label	Double blind, sham controlled	Open label, randomized	Randomized, no VNS control
Left/Right Vagus	Right	Right	Left and Right	Right
Open/Closed Loop	Closed loop, R-wave	Open loop	Open loop	Closed loop, R-wave
Final Stimulation Amplitude	4.1 ± 1.2 mA	1.42 ± 0.80 mA	2.0 ± 0.6 mA	TBD
Duty Cycle	21 ± 5%	16.7%	17.5%	TBD
Primary Endpoints	LVEF, LVESVI	LVESD	LVEF, LVESV	Time to all-cause mortality, HF hospitalization
Follow-up Duration	12 months	18 months	12 months	18 months
SAEs, Therapy	7 (22%)	9 (14.3%)	1 (1.7%)	TBD
Safety	None	None	None	TBD
Efficacy	Improvement (NYHA, QoL, 6MWT, LVEF)	No improvement (LV endpoints, NT-proBNP); Improvement (NYHA, QoL)	Improvement (LVEF, NYHA, 6MWT, QoL); reduced arrhythmogenic potential, increased HRV at 1 year	TBD
References	De Ferrari et al, 2011	Castoro et al, 2011	Dicarlo et al, 2013	Hauptman et al, 2012
	De Ferrari et al, 2014	De Ferrari et al, 2014	Premchand et al, 2014	
		Zannad et al, 2015	Premchand et al, 2015	
			Libbus et al, 2015	

CardioFit Trial was a Phase II feasibility study conducted using the CardioFit system, an implantable system that is coupled to the R wave. The lead is an asymmetric bipolar stimulating cuff with electrodes for on-phase partial anodal block and a cardiac lead for R wave detection [9, 107]. An initial study with 8 patients (left ventricular ejection fraction (LVEF) <35%, New York Heart Association (NYHA) class II-III) were implanted. Follow-up showed improvement in NYHA class, quality of life, left ventricular end-systolic volume and a trend towards reduction of left ventricular end-diastolic volume [107]. A subsequent larger study was conducted as an open-label Phase II pilot study to assess safety and tolerability of right cervical VNS using the CardioFit system. This study involved patients (n=32) with NYHA class II-IV patients and reduced ejection fraction HF (LVEF 23 ±8%) [9, 108]. Most patients improved at least one NYHA class at 3 (18/32 patients) and 6 months (19/32 patients). Quality of life evaluations and 6-minute walk tests showed similar improvements. These results suggested that chronic VNS was feasible in patients with severe systolic HF and warranted further clinical investigation [9, 108].

Increase of Vagal TonE in Heart Failure (INOVATE-HF) evolved from the Cardiofit trial. The primary efficacy endpoint was defined as whether VNS increases the time to first event defined by all-cause mortality or unplanned HF hospitalization. The trial proposed to enroll 650 symptomatic HF patients NYHA class III, LVEF <40% [109]. This study was initiated in February 2011 with an estimated conclusion by December 2016 (clinicaltrials.gov site). As of fall 2015, The independent Data Safety Monitoring Board for the INOVATE-HF trial completed a pre-specified interim analysis of the data and recommended the discontinuation of the INOVATE-HF trial due to statistical futility in the primary efficacy endpoint. The Steering Committee concurs with this decision and subgroup analysis is now underway. From this analysis is should become clearer if specific subgroups of HF patients may benefit from VNS.

NEural Cardiac TherApy foR Heart Failure (NECTAR-HF) was a double-blind, multi-center randomized control study to evaluate safety and efficacy in patients, with NYHA class II-III symptoms and LVEF ≤ 35% [110]. The VNS system consisted of a bipolar cuff lead placed around the right cervical vagus nerve and an implantable pulse generator. LV end systolic diameter (LVESD), echocardiographic parameters and N-terminal brain natriuretic peptide (NT-proBNP) failed to show significant differences from the control group. However, quality of life, NYHA classification and health surveys showed significant improvement [111]. These findings were unexpected based on previous trials and preclinical data. However, off-target effects evoked during the on-phase (20 Hz) stimulation limited current delivery and may have placed these patients at sub-therapeutic levels [111].

Autonomic Neural regulation Therapy to Enhance Myocardial function in Heart Failure (ANTHEM-HF) was a feasibility study to assess safety and efficacy of the bipolar VNS delivered to the right or left cervical vagus. Patients had NYHA class II-III and LVEF ≤ 40% [112]. Stimulation was unrelated to the cardiac cycle (open loop). After 6 months of VNS therapy, LVEF (both sides) improved significantly (4.5%), but LVESV was not statistically significant. NYHA, 6-minute walk and quality of life all showed significant improvements. There were no statistical differences between right and left VNS [113]. Forty nine patients participated in an extended follow-up (to 1 year) that showed maintenance of results from the 6-month time point, with LVESV now achieving significance from baseline [8]. In these same patients, VNS reduced peak T-wave alternans levels, HR and non-sustained ventricular tachycardias (VT). HR turbulence slope, high frequency power and HR variability all increased [114]. For ANTHEM-HF, the VNS protocol was based on the neural fulcrum approach as outlined above [2].

6. VNS Control of Cardiac Arrhythmias

It is estimated that sudden cardiac death (SCD) accounts for 4 to 5 million cases per year, worldwide, with anywhere from 180 000 to 456 000 deaths in the US annually [115, 116]. SCD can be broadly categorized into electrical and nonelectrical in nature. With respect to electrical causes of SCD, the majority is associated with ventricular tachyarrhythmias, including ventricular fibrillation, and lesser amounts reflecting bradyarrhythmias [117]. Disruptions in autonomic control, superimposed on an altered cardiac myocyte substrate, are fundamental to the induction of cardiac arrhythmias [45, 118]. As a corollary, targeting neural aspects of the cardiac nervous system is an emerging field in anti-arrhythmic therapeutics [7, 30].

6.1. *VNS for atrial fibrillation (AF)*

Bioelectric stimulation, delivered to various elements of the cardiac nervous system, has the potential to increase or decrease atrial arrhythmogenesis [119, 120, 121]. Simultaneous sympathetic and parasympathetic nerve stimulation can trigger rapid firing within canine pulmonary veins, frequently a precursor to AF [122]. Conversely, VNS has been shown to alter the electrophysiological properties of the atrium in the rat [123], improving left atrial (LA) function and suppressing LA fibrosis in a canine tachy-pacing model [124]. While specifics of the neurotransmitters released during neurally-induced AF remains ill-defined, adrenergic, cholinergic and peptinergic receptors are likely involved [120, 125, 126]. Of the neuropeptides involved, VNS-induced release vasoactive intestinal polypeptide (VIP) is one potential candidate [127]. In contradistinction to arrhythmia control by ablating one or more intrinsic cardiac ganglia, VNS can engage multiple ganglia targets on the heart simultaneously [64, 65]. For example, VNS can prevent AF in canines triggered from both PV and non-PV sites [128]. It likely does so by exerted anti-adrenergic effects and by stabilizing reflex processing within peripheral autonomic ganglia [37, 38, 66, 79].

6.2. *VNS for ventricular arrhythmias*

Ventricular arrhythmias, especially ventricular tachycardia, are potentially life threatening. Ventricular fibrillation not converted within minutes is fatal. VNS has been shown to impact ventricular function and prevent severe arrhythmias in a number of preclinical models. Right and left vagi project to both ventricles in a similar manner, on both the endocardial and epicardial surfaces [129]. The literature regarding VNS efficacy on ventricular arrhythmias is mixed, undoubtedly a function of the type of preclinical model and the mode of stimulation delivery [7].

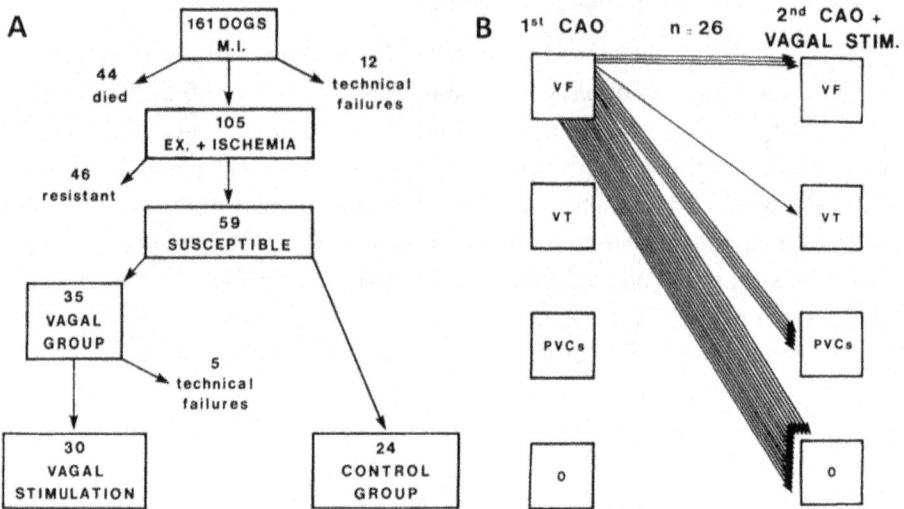

Fig. 7: VNS and prevention of sudden death in conscious mongrels with healed myocardial infarction (MI). 161 mongrel dogs were subjected to MI by occlusion of left anterior descending coronary artery, just above the first diagonal branch. Panel A shows the experimental protocol (EX.: exercise). Animals that completed 17 min of exercise or heart rate reached 210 beats/min, the left circumflex coronary artery was occluded for 2 min. The ones that showed ventricular fibrillation (VF) during control exercise of ischemia test were assigned to either control or vagal stimulation groups and tested again a few days later. Panel B shows the effect of VNS on incidence of ventricular arrhythmias during coronary artery occlusion (CAO). Each arrow represents one animal. VF: ventricular fibrillation; VT: ventricular tachycardia; PVCs: premature ventricular contractions; 0: no ventricular arrhythmias. http://www.ncbi.nlm.nih.gov/pubmed/2019002

The anti-fibrillatory effects of VNS have a long-standing clinical history. Einbrodt, in 1859, demonstrated that VF was harder to induce in a dog while stimulating the vagus [42, 130]. Studies by Scherlag et al. [131], Goldstein et al. [132], Myers et al. [133], among others, supported Einbrodt's early findings. Work by Kolman et al. [134] demonstrated that VNS cardioprotection was due in part to modulation of sympathetic-parasympathetic interactions. Recent studies have shown that pre-emptive VNS limits infarct size in pigs with transient myocardial ischemia [135] and increase the ventricular fibrillation threshold in canines even in models with hyper-dynamic sympathetic activity induced by stellate stimulation [101]. VNS can suppress ventricular tachycardia (VT)/fibrillation (VF) in chronic MI, even when subjected to the high level stress of dynamic exercise with a second ischemic event (Figure 7) [136]. In rats with healed MI, VNS likewise suppressed the incidence of premature ventricular contractions (PVC) and increased the high frequency component of HRV [137]. VNS can exert its cardioprotection, even when delivered with an intermittent duty cycle. For example, Shinlapawittayatorn et al. [105] demonstrated the intermittent VNS significantly reduced infarct size and incidence of VF episodes, improved ventricular function, and attenuated free radical creation in a porcine model of ischemia-reperfusion injury. A follow-up study showed that VNS initiated late in ischemia was effective in cardioprotection, but had no effect after reperfusion (Figure 8) [106]. Recent studies have highlighted the importance of remodeling of peripheral ganglia in response VNS and the fundamental links to preservation of cardiac mechanical and electrical function [95, 97, 99]. Other studies have suggested that VNS induced changes in myocyte function, either directly or indirectly related via its anti-adrenergic effects, are important factors in cardioprotection [97, 105, 106, 120, 138]. Putative neurotransmitters that may be involved in such cardio-protection include galanin [139], neuropeptide-Y [139], and nitric oxide [140, 141]. A potential link to the α-7 nicotinic anti-inflammatory pathway also exists [142, 143]. While the anti-arrhythmic effects of VNS are evident, future studies are essential to optimize efficacy, to determine precise sites of stimulus delivery, and what patient populations are likely to benefit for such autonomic regulation therapy.

6.3. *VNS for arrhythmias – clinical relevance*

VNS can either increase or suppress the potential for cardiac arrhythmias. Some arrhythmia types are triggered by parasympathetic activity, including early repolarization syndrome [144], subgroups of idiopathic VT [145], Brugada [146], and LQT3 [7, 147]. Non-invasive VNS (auricular branch) may serve as an effective screening to determine efficacy prior to implant. In healthy humans, trans-cutaneous VNS causes shift in autonomic balance towards parasympathetic predominance [85]. In patients with coronary artery disease, auricular VNS reduced sympathetic outflow to the heart and improved LV contractility [148]. In patients with drug-resistant focal epilepsy, VNS reduces levels of T-wave alternans and low frequency HRV components, signaling a reduction in electrical instability and a shift in favor of parasympathetic tone [149]. In patients with refractory epilepsy, a significant increase in the high frequency component and reduction in low frequency was noted [150].

7. **Perspectives and Significance**

Delivery of bioelectric medicine must be evaluated in term of its direct and indirect effects for control of thoracic and visceral organ function. Multiple levels of the cardiac neuraxis are impacted with VNS. The vagus nerve, which contains both ascending afferent and descending efferent nerve fibers, is an important pathway for communication between central and peripheral aspects of this cardiac ANS. At the level of the heart, for instance, parasympathetic preganglionic axons in the vagus not only project on parasympathetic postganglionic neurons but also modulate the activity of local circuit neurons [2, 64]. Direct cardiac control via activation of efferent projections can dampen sympathoexcitation [151, 152] and provide cardioprotection [101, 124, 153]. Recruitment of afferent fibers can trigger the involvement of higher centers that control both sympathetic and parasympathetic efferents to impact cardiac function [39, 154]. Going forward, there remains much work to do with respect to elucidating optimal stimulation methods as it pertains to specific cardiovascular issues, approaches for VNS delivery and understanding how VNS can impact cardiac function, interactions with different neuronal populations of the cardiac ANS and reduce disease pathology.

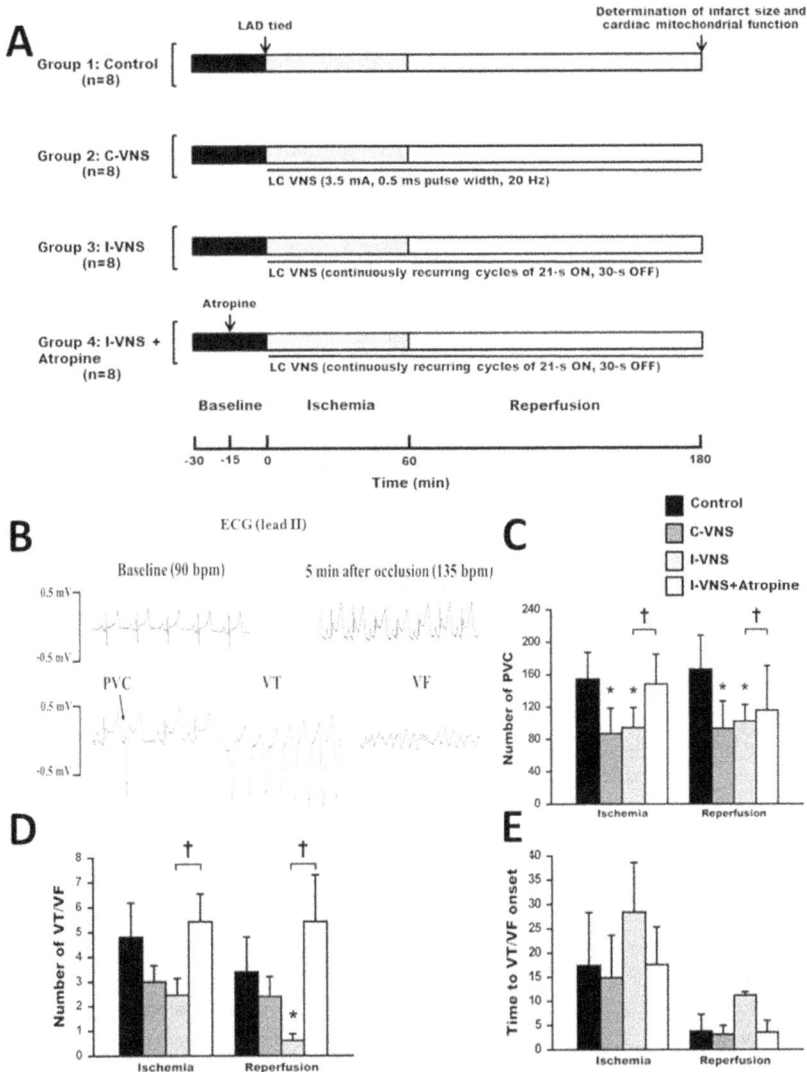

Fig. 8: Low amplitude, left VNS significantly attenuates ventricular arrhythmias in an anesthetized porcine model of acute ischemia-reperfusion injury. Panel A shows the study protocol. Ischemia was induced by complete ligation of the left anterior descending (LAD) coronary artery (60 min), followed by a 120 min reperfusion period. C-VNS: continuous VNS, 3.5 mA, 500 μs pulse duration, 20 Hz). I-VNS: intermittent VNS, 21 s ON, 30 s OFF. LC: left cervical. Panel B – E shows the occurrence of ventricular arrhythmias during ischemia-reperfusion injury. B: lead II ECG recorded before and after LAD occlusion with examples of the arrhythmias observed. C: decreased PVC burden following C- and I-VNS, with attenuation in the presence of atropine. D: VT/VF episodes, with only the I-VNS group showing significant reduction in this endpoint during the reperfusion period. E: Time to VT/VF onset was not significantly different between treatment groups. Data are mean ±SD. * p < 0.05 vs. control. † p < 0.05 vs. I-VNS. PVC: premature ventricular contraction; VF: ventricular fibrillation; VT: ventricular tachycardia.

http://www.ncbi.nlm.nih.gov/pubmed/23933295

References

1. Janig, W., Autonomic nervous system and inflammation, *Autonomic Neuroscience : Basic and Clinical,* **182**, 1-3 (2014).
2. Ardell, J. L., Rajendran, P. S., Nier, H. A., KenKnight, B. H. and Armour, J. A., Central-peripheral neural network interactions evoked by vagus nerve stimulation: functional consequences on control of cardiac function, *American Journal of Physiology. Heart and Circulatory Physiology,* **309**, H1740-1752 (2015).
3. Yamakawa, K., Rajendran, P.S., Takamiya, T., Yagishita, D., So, E. L., Mahajan, A., Shivkumar, K. and Vaseghi, M., Vagal nerve stimulation activates vagal afferent fibers that reduce cardiac efferent parasympathetic effects, *American Journal of Physiology. Heart and Circulatory Physiology,* **309**, H1579-1590 (2015).
4. Morris, G. L., 3rd, Gloss, D., Buchhalter, J., Mack, K.J., Nickels, K. and Harden, C., Evidence-based guideline update: vagus nerve stimulation for the treatment of epilepsy: report of the Guideline Development Subcommittee of the American Academy of Neurology, *Neurology,* **81**, 1453-1459 (2013).
5. Grimonprez, A., Raedt, R., Baeken, C., Boon, P. and Vonck, K., The antidepressant mechanism of action of vagus nerve stimulation: Evidence from preclinical studies, *Neuroscience and Biobehavioral Reviews,* **56**, 26-34 (2015).
6. Rizvi, S. J., Donovan, M., Giacobbe, P., Placenza, F., Rotzinger, S. and Kennedy, S. H., Neurostimulation therapies for treatment resistant depression: a focus on vagus nerve stimulation and deep brain stimulation, *International Review of Psychiatry,* **23**, 424-436 (2011).
7. Huang, W. A., Shivkumar, K. and Vaseghi, M., Device-based autonomic modulation in arrhythmia patients: the role of vagal nerve stimulation, *Current Treatment Options in Cardiovascular Medicine,* **17**, 379 (2015).
8. Premchand, R. K., Sharma, K., Mittal, S., Monteiro, R., Dixit, S., Libbus, I., DiCarlo, L. A., Ardell, J. L., Rector, T. S., Amurthur, B., KenKnight, B. H. and Anand, I. S., Extended follow-up of patients with heart failure receiving autonomic regulation therapy in the ANTHEM-HF study, *Journal of Cardiac Failure,* (2015).
9. De Ferrari, G. M, Vagal stimulation in heart failure. *Journal of cardiovascular Translational Research,* **7**, 310-320 (2014).
10. McClelland, J., Bozhilova, N., Campbell, I. and Schmidt, U., A systematic review of the effects of neuromodulation on eating and body weight: evidence from human and animal studies, *Eur Eat Disord Rev,* **21**, 436-455 (2013).
11. Yuan, H. and Silberstein, S. D., Vagus nerve and vagus nerve stimulation, a comprehensive review: Part I., *Headache,* **56**, 71-78 (2015).
12. Langley, G. *The Autonomic Nervous System.* Cambridge University Press: Cambridge, UK, 1921.
13. Randall, W. C., Priola, D. V. and Pace, J. B., Responses of individual cardiac chambers to stimulation of the cervical vagosympathetic trunk in atropinized dogs, *Circulation Research,* **20**, 534-544 (1967).
14. Seki, A., Green, H. R., Lee, T. D., Hong, L., Tan, J., Vinters, H. V., Chen, P. S. and Fishbein, M. C., Sympathetic nerve fibers in human cervical and thoracic vagus nerves, *Heart Rhythm,* **11**, 1411-1417 (2014).
15. Paintal, A. S., Vagal afferent fibres, *Ergebnisse der Physiologie, Biologischen Chemie und Experimentellen Pharmakologie,* **52**, 74-156 (1963).

16. Berthoud, H. R. and Neuhuber, W. L., Functional and chemical anatomy of the afferent vagal system, *Autonomic Neuroscience : Basic and Clinical*, **85**, 1-17 (2000).
17. Armour, J. A. and Kember, G., Cardiac sensory neurons. in eds. Armour, J. A. and Ardell, J. L., *Basic and Clinical Neurocardiology*, (Oxford University Press, New York, 2004), pp 79-117.
18. Waxman, S. G., *Clinical Neuroanatomy*, 27th edn., (McGraw-Hill, New York, 2013).
19. Andresen, M. C., Kunze, D. L. and Mendelowitz, D., Central nervous system regulation of the heart, in eds. Armour, J. A. and Ardell, J. L., *Basic and Clincial Neurocardiology*, (Oxford University Press, New York), 2004, pp 187-219.
20. Ruffoli, R., Giorgi, F.S., Pizzanelli, C., Murri, L., Paparelli, A. and Fornai, F., The chemical neuroanatomy of vagus nerve stimulation, *Journal of Chemical Neuroanatomy*, **42**, 288-296 (2011).
21. Massari, V. J., Johnson, T. A. and Gatti, P. J., Cardiotopic organization of the nucleus ambiguus? An anatomical and physiological analysis of neurons regulating atrioventricular conduction, *Brain Research*, **679**, 227-240 (1995).
22. Gray, A. L., Johnson, T. A., Lauenstein, J. M., Newton, S. S., Ardell, J. L. and Massari, V. J., Parasympathetic control of the heart. III. Neuropeptide Y-immunoreactive nerve terminals synapse on three populations of negative chronotropic vagal preganglionic neurons, *Journal of Applied Physiology*, **96**, 2279-2287 (2004).
23. Geis, G.S. and Wurster, R.D., Horseradish peroxidase localization of cardiac vagal preganglionic somata, *Brain Research*, **182**, 19-30 (1980).
24. Armour, J.A., Potential clinical relevance of the 'little brain' on the mammalian heart, *Experimental Physiology*, **93**, 165-176 (2008).
25. Armour, J. A., Functional anatomy of intrathoracic neurons innervating the atria and ventricles, *Heart Rhythm*, **7**, 994-996 (2010).
26. Randall, W. C., Ardell, J. L. and Becker, D. M., Differential responses accompanying sequential stimulation and ablation of vagal branches to dog heart, *The American Journal of Physiology*, **249**, H133-140 (1985).
27. Jinkins, J. R., *Atlas of neuroradiologic embryology, anatomy, and variants*, (Lippincott Williams and Wilkins, Philadelphia, 2000).
28. Ardell, J. L., Intrathoracic neuronal regulation of cardiac function, in eds. Armour, J. A. and Ardell, J. L., *Basic and Clinical Neurocardiology*, (Oxford University Press, New York, 2004), pp 118-152.
29. Ardell, J. L., Randall, W. C., Cannon, W. J., Schmacht, D. C. and Tasdemiroglu, E., Differential sympathetic regulation of automatic, conductile, and contractile tissue in dog heart, *The American Journal of Physiology*, **255**, H1050-1059 (1988).
30. Buckley, U., Yamakawa, K., Takamiya, T., Armour, J. A., Shivkumar, K. and Ardell, J. L. Targeted stellate decentralization: implications for sympathetic control of ventricular electrophysiology, *Heart rhythm*, (2015).
31. Randall, W. C. and Armour, J. A., Regional vagosympathetic control of the heart, *The American Journal of Physiology*, **227**, 444-452 (1974).
32. Geis, G. S. and Wurster, R. D., Cardiac responses during stimulation of the dorsal motor nucleus and nucleus ambiguus in the cat, *Circulation Research*, **46**, 606-611 (1980).
33. Agostini, E., Chinnock, J. E., De Burgh Daly, M. and Murray, J. G., Functional and histological studies of the vagus nerve and its branches to the heart, lungs and abdominal viscera in the cat, *The Journal of Physiology*, **135**, 182-205 (1957).

34. Foley, J. O. and DuBois, F. S., Quantitative studies of the vagus nerve in the cat. I. The ratio of sensory to motor fibers, *The Journal of Comparative Neurology,* **67**, 49-67 (1937).

35. Levy, M. N. and Martin, P. J., Neural control of the heart, In ed. Berne, R. M., *Handbook of Physiology: Section 2: The Cardiovascular System, Volume 1: The Heart,* (The American Physiological Society, Bethesda, 1979), pp 581-620.

36. Furukawa, Y., Hoyano, Y. and Chiba, S. Parasympathetic inhibition of sympathetic effects on sinus rate in anesthetized dogs, *The American Journal of Physiology,* **271**, H44-50 (1996).

37. McGuirt, A. S., Schmacht, D. C. and Ardell, J. L., Autonomic interactions for control of atrial rate are maintained after SA nodal parasympathectomy, *The American Journal of Physiology,* **272**, H2525-2533 (1997).

38. Randall, D. C., Brown, D. R., McGuirt, A. S., Thompson, G. W., Armour, J. A. and Ardell, J. L., Interactions within the intrinsic cardiac nervous system contribute to chronotropic regulation, *American Journal of Physiology. Regulatory, Integrative and Comparative Physiology,* **285**, R1066-1075 (2003).

39. Cardinal, R., Page, P., Vermeulen, M., Ardell, J. L. and Armour, J. A., Spatially divergent cardiac responses to nicotinic stimulation of ganglionated plexus neurons in the canine heart, *Autonomic Neuroscience: Basic and Clinical,* **145**, 55-62 (2009).

40. Randall, W. C., Ardell, J. L., O'Toole, M. F. and Wurster, R. D., Differential autonomic control of SAN and AVN regions of the canine heart: structure and function, *Progress in Clinical and Biological Research,* **275**, 15-31 (1988).

41. Dhein, S., van Koppen, C. J. and Brodde, O. E. Muscarinic receptors in the mammalian heart, *Pharmacological Research,* **44**, 161-182 (2001).

42. Brack, K. E., Winter, J. and Ng, G. A., Mechanisms underlying the autonomic modulation of ventricular fibrillation initiation--tentative prophylactic properties of vagus nerve stimulation on malignant arrhythmias in heart failure, *Heart Failure Reviews,* **18**, 389-408 (2013).

43. Levy, M. N. Sympathetic-parasympathetic interactions in the heart, *Circulation Research,* **29**, 437-445 (1971).

44. Armour, J. A., Murphy, D. A., Yuan, B. X., Macdonald, S. and Hopkins, D. A., Gross and microscopic anatomy of the human intrinsic cardiac nervous system, *The Anatomical Record,* **247**, 289-298 (1997).

45. Fukuda, K., Kanazawa, H., Aizawa, Y., Ardell, J. L. and Shivkumar, K., Cardiac innervation and sudden cardiac death, *Circulation Research,* **116**, 2005-2019 (2015).

46. Armour, J. A., Instant to instant reflex cardiac regulation, *Cardiology,* **61**, 309-328 (1976).

47. Armour, J. A., Synaptic transmission in the chronically decentralized middle cervical and stellate ganglia of the dog, *Canadian Journal of Physiology and Pharmacology,* **61**, 1149-1155 (1983).

48. Ardell, J. L., Butler, C. K., Smith, F. M., Hopkins, D. A. and Armour, J. A., Activity of in vivo atrial and ventricular neurons in chronically decentralized canine hearts, *The American Journal of Physiology,* **260**, H713-721 (1991).

49. Kember, G., Armour, J. A. and Zamir, M., Neural control hierarchy of the heart has not evolved to deal with myocardial ischemia. *Physiological Genomics,* **45**, 638-644 (2013).

50. Zucker, I. H., Patel, K. P. and Schultz, H. D., Neurohumoral stimulation., *Heart Failure Clinics,* **8**, 87-99 (2012).

51. Jänig, W., *The Integrative Action of the Autonomic Nervous System: Neurobiology of Homeostasis,* (Cambridge University Press, New York, 2006).

52. Foreman, R. D. Mechanisms of cardiac pain, *Annual Review of Physiology,* **61**, 143-167 (1999).

53. Foreman, R. D. and Linderoth, B., Neural mechanisms of spinal cord stimulation, *International Review of Neurobiology,* **107**, 87-119 (2012).

54. Armour, J. A. Neuronal activity recorded extracellularly in chronically decentralized in situ canine middle cervical ganglia, *Canadian Journal of Physiology and Pharmacology,* **64**, 1038-1046 (1986).

55. Yuan, B. X., Ardell, J. L., Hopkins, D. A., Losier, A. M. and Armour, J. A., Gross and microscopic anatomy of the canine intrinsic cardiac nervous system, *The Anatomical Record,* **239**, 75-87 (1994).

56. Arora, R. C., Waldmann, M., Hopkins, D. A. and Armour, J. A., Porcine intrinsic cardiac ganglia, *The Anatomical Record. Part A, Discoveries in Molecular, Cellular, and Evolutionary Biology,* **271**, 249-258 (2003).

57. Ardell, J. L., Structure and function of mammalian intrinsic cardiac neurons, in eds. Armour, J. A. and Ardell, J. L., *Neurocardiology,* (Oxford University Press, New York, 1994), pp 95-114.

58. O'Toole, M. F., Ardell, J. L. and Randall, W. C., Functional interdependence of discrete vagal projections to SA and AV nodes, *The American Journal of Physiology,* **251**, H398-404 (1986).

59. Kuntz, A., *The Autonomic Nervous System,* (Lea and Febiger, Philadelphia, 1934).

60. Armour, J. A., Activity of in situ middle cervical ganglion neurons in dogs, using extracellular recording techniques, *Canadian Journal of Physiology and Pharmacology,* **63**, 704-716 (1985).

61. Armour, J. A. and Janes, R. D., Neuronal activity recorded extracellularly from in situ canine mediastinal ganglia, *Canadian Journal of Physiology and Pharmacology,* **66**, 119-127 (1988).

62. Vaseghi, M., Yamakawa, K., Sinha, A., So, E. L., Zhou, W., Ajijola, O. A., Lux, R. L., Laks, M., Shivkumar, K. and Mahajan, A., Modulation of regional dispersion of repolarization and T-peak to T-end interval by the right and left stellate ganglia, *American Journal of Physiology. Heart and Circulatory Physiology,* **305**, H1020-1030 (2013).

63. Randall, W. C., Efferent sympathetic innervation of the heart. in eds. Armour, J. A. and Ardell, J. L., *Neurocardiology,* (Oxford University Press, New York, 1994), pp 77-94.

64. Beaumont, E., Salavatian, S., Southerland, E. M., Vinet, A., Jacquemet, V., Armour, J. A. and Ardell, J. L., Network interactions within the canine intrinsic cardiac nervous system: implications for reflex control of regional cardiac function, *The Journal of Physiology,* **591**, 4515-4533 (2013).

65. Rajendran, P. S., Nakamura, K., Ajijola, O. A., Vaseghi, M., Armour, J. A., Ardell, J. L. and Shivkumar, K., Myocardial infarction induces structural and functional remodelling of the intrinsic cardiac nervous system, *J Physiol-London,* **594**, 321-341 (2016).

66. Gibbons, D. D., Southerland, E. M., Hoover, D. B., Beaumont, E., Armour, J. A. and Ardell, J. L., Neuromodulation targets intrinsic cardiac neurons to attenuate neuronally mediated atrial arrhythmias, *American Journal of Physiology. Regulatory, Integrative and Comparative Physiology,* **302**, R357-364 (2012).

67. Ardell, J. L., Cardinal, R., Beaumont, E., Vermeulen, M., Smith, F. M. and Andrew Armour, J., Chronic spinal cord stimulation modifies intrinsic cardiac synaptic efficacy in the suppression of atrial fibrillation, *Autonomic Neuroscience: Basic and Clinica,* **186**, 38-44 (2014).

68. Lanska, D. J. J. L., Corning and vagal nerve stimulation for seizures in the 1880s, *Neurology,* **58**, 452-459 (2002).

69. Zanchetti, A., Wang, S.C. and Moruzzi, G., The effect of vagal afferent stimulation on the EEG pattern of the cat, *Electroencephalography and Clinical Neurophysiology,* **4**, 357-361 (1952).

70. Zabara, J., Inhibition of experimental seizures in canines by repetitive vagal stimulation, *Epilepsia,* **33**, 1005-1012 (1992).

71. Aalbers, M., Vles, J., Klinkenberg, S., Hoogland, G., Majoie, M. and Rijkers, K., Animal models for vagus nerve stimulation in epilepsy, *Experimental Neurology,* **230**, 167-175 (2011).

72. Bailey, P. and Bremer, F., A sensory cortical representation of the vagus nerve, *Journal of Neurophysiology,* **1**, 405-412 (1938).

73. Chase, M. H., Nakamura, Y., Clemente, C. D. and Sterman, M. B., Afferent vagal stimulation: neurographic correlates of induced EEG synchronization and desynchronization, *Brain Research,* **5**, 236-249 (1967).

74. Orosz, I., McCormick, D., Zamponi, N., Varadkar, S., Feucht, M., Parain, D., Griens, R., Vallee, L., Boon, P., Rittey, C., Jayewardene, A. K., Bunker, M., Arzimanoglou, A. and Lagae, L., Vagus nerve stimulation for drug-resistant epilepsy: a European long-term study up to 24 months in 347 children, *Epilepsia,* **55**, 1576-1584 (2014).

75. Rousselet, L., Le Rolle, V., Ojeda, D., Guiraud, D., Hagege, A., Bel, A., Bonnet, J. L., Mabo, P., Carrault, G. and Hernandez, A. I., Influence of vagus nerve stimulation parameters on chronotropism and inotropism in heart failure, *Annual International Conference of the IEEE Engineering in Medicine and Biology Society,* **2014**, 526-529 (2014).

76. Yoo, P.B., Liu, H., Hincapie, J.G., Ruble, S. B., Hamann, J. J. and Grill, W. M., Modulation of heart rate by temporally patterned vagus nerve stimulation in the anesthetized dog, *Physiological Reports,* **4**, (2016).

77. Labiner, D. M. and Ahern, G. L., Vagus nerve stimulation therapy in depression and epilepsy: therapeutic parameter settings, *Acta neurologica Scandinavica,* **115**, 23-33 (2007).

78. Sundman, E. and Olofsson, P. S., Neural control of the immune system, *Advances in Physiology Education,* **38**, 135-139 (2014).

79. Kember, G., Ardell, J. L., Armour, J. A. and Zamir, M., Vagal nerve stimulation therapy: what is being stimulated? *PloS one,* **9**, e114498 (2014).

80. Ben-Menachem, E., Revesz, D., Simon, B. J. and Silberstein, S., Surgically implanted and non-invasive vagus nerve stimulation: a review of efficacy, safety and tolerability, *European Journal of Neurology,* **22**, 1260-1268 (2015).

81. Napadow, V., Edwards, R. R., Cahalan, C. M., Mensing, G., Greenbaum, S., Valovska, A., Li, A., Kim, J., Maeda, Y., Park, K. and Wasan, A. D., Evoked pain analgesia in chronic pelvic pain patients using respiratory-gated auricular vagal afferent nerve stimulation, *Pain Medicine,* **13**, 777-789 (2012).

82. Wang, Z., Yu, L., Wang, S., Huang, B., Liao, K., Saren, G., Tan, T. and Jiang, H., Chronic intermittent low-level transcutaneous electrical stimulation of auricular branch of vagus nerve improves left ventricular remodeling in conscious dogs with healed myocardial infarction, *Circulation. Heart Failure,* **7**, 1014-1021 (2014).

83. Yu, L., Scherlag, B. J., Li, S., Fan, Y., Dyer, J., Male, S., Varma, V., Sha, Y., Stavrakis, S. and Po, S. S., Low-level transcutaneous electrical stimulation of the auricular branch of the vagus nerve: a noninvasive approach to treat the initial phase of atrial fibrillation, *Heart Rhythm,* **10**, 428-435 (2013).

84. Stavrakis, S., Humphrey, M. B., Scherlag, B. J., Hu, Y., Jackman, W. M., Nakagawa, H., Lockwood, D., Lazzara, R. and Po, S. S., Low-level transcutaneous electrical vagus nerve stimulation suppresses atrial fibrillation, *Journal of the American College of Cardiology,* **65**, 867-875 (2015).

85. Clancy, J. A., Mary, D. A., Witte, K. K., Greenwood, J. P., Deuchars, S. A. and Deuchars, J., Non-invasive vagus nerve stimulation in healthy humans reduces sympathetic nerve activity, *Brain Stimulation*, **7**, 871-877 (2014).

86. Ziaeian, B. and Fonarow, G. C., Epidemiology and aetiology of heart failure, *Nature Reviews. Cardiology*, (2016).

87. Yancy, C. W., Jessup, M., Bozkurt, B., Butler, J., Casey, D. E., Jr., Drazner, M. H., Fonarow, G. C., Geraci, S. A., Horwich, T., Januzzi, J.L., Johnson, M. R., Kasper, E. K., Levy, W. C., Masoudi, F. A., McBride, P. E., McMurray, J. J., Mitchell, J. E., Peterson, P. N., Riegel, B., Sam, F., Stevenson, L. W., Tang, W. H., Tsai, E. J., Wilkoff, B. L., American College of Cardiology Foundation, and American Heart Association Task Force on Practice Guidelines, 2013 ACCF/AHA guideline for the management of heart failure: a report of the American College of Cardiology Foundation/American Heart Association Task Force on Practice Guidelines, *Journal of the American College of Cardiology*, **62**, e147-239 (2013).

88. Go, A. S., Mozaffarian, D., Roger, V. L., Benjamin, E. J., Berry, J. D., Blaha, M. J., Dai, S., Ford, E. S., Fox, C. S., Franco, S., Fullerton, H. J., Gillespie, C., Hailpern, S. M., Heit, J. A., Howard, V. J., Huffman, M. D., Judd, S. E., Kissela, B. M., Kittner, S. J., Lackland, D. T., Lichtman, J. H., Lisabeth, L. D., Mackey, R. H., Magid, D. J., Marcus, G. M., Marelli, A., Matchar, D. B., McGuire, D. K., Mohler, E. R., 3rd, Moy, C. S., Mussolino, M. E., Neumar, R. W., Nichol, G., Pandey, D. K., Paynter, N. P., Reeves, M. J., Sorlie, P. D., Stein, J., Towfighi, A., Turan, T. N., Virani, S. S., Wong, N. D., Woo, D., Turner, M.B., American Heart Association Statistics Committee and Stroke Statistics Subcommittee. Heart disease and stroke statistics--2014 update: a report from the American Heart Association, *Circulation*, **129**, e28-e292 (2014).

89. Heidenreich, P. A., Albert, N. M., Allen, L. A., Bluemke, D. A., Butler, J., Fonarow, G. C., Ikonomidis, J. S., Khavjou, O., Konstam, M. A., Maddox, T. M., Nichol, G., Pham, M., Pina, I. L., Trogdon, J. G., American Heart Association Advocacy Coordinating Committee, Council on Arteriosclerosis, Thrombosis and Vascular Biology, Council on Cardiovascular Radiology and Intervention, Council on Clinical Cardiology, Council on Epidemiology and Prevention, and Stroke Council, Forecasting the impact of heart failure in the United States: a policy statement from the American Heart Association, *Circulation. Heart failure*, **6**, 606-619 (2013).

90. Ho, K. K., Pinsky, J. L., Kannel, W. B. and Levy, D., The epidemiology of heart failure: the Framingham Study, *Journal of the American College of Cardiology*, **22**, 6A-13A (1993).

91. Tsutsumi, T., Ide, T., Yamato, M., Kudou, W., Andou, M., Hirooka, Y., Utsumi, H., Tsutsui, H. and Sunagawa, K., Modulation of the myocardial redox state by vagal nerve stimulation after experimental myocardial infarction, *Cardiovascular Research*, **77**, 713-721 (2008).

92. Li, M., Zheng, C., Sato, T., Kawada, T., Sugimachi, M. and Sunagawa, K., Vagal nerve stimulation markedly improves long-term survival after chronic heart failure in rats, *Circulation*, **109**, 120-124 (2004).

93. Li, Y., Xuan, Y. H., Liu, S. S., Dong, J., Luo, J. Y. and Sun, Z. J., Shortterm vagal nerve stimulation improves left ventricular function following chronic heart failure in rats, *Molecular Medicine Reports*, **12**, 1709-1716 (2015).

94. Zhang, Y., Popovic, Z. B., Bibevski, S., Fakhry, I., Sica, D. A., Van Wagoner, D. R. and Mazgalev, T. N., Chronic vagus nerve stimulation improves autonomic control and attenuates systemic inflammation and heart failure progression in a canine high-rate pacing model, *Circulation. Heart Failure*, **2**, 692-699 (2009).

95. Hamann, J. J., Ruble, S. B., Stolen, C., Wang, M., Gupta, R. C., Rastogi, S. and Sabbah, H. N., Vagus nerve stimulation improves left ventricular function in a canine model of chronic heart failure, *European Journal of Heart Failure,* **15**, 1319-1326 (2013).

96. Yu, H., Tang, M., Yu, J., Zhou, X., Zeng, L. and Zhang, S., Chronic vagus nerve stimulation improves left ventricular function in a canine model of chronic mitral regurgitation, *Journal of Translational Medicine,* **12**, 302 (2014).

97. Beaumont, E., Wright, G. L., Southerland, E. M., Li, Y., Chui, R. W., KenKnight, B. H., Armour, J. A. and Ardell, J. L., Vagus nerve stimulation mitigates intrinsic cardiac neuronal remodeling and cardiac hypertrophy induced by chronic pressure overload in guinea pig, *American Journal of Physiology. Heart and Circulatory Physiology,* ajpheart 00939 02015 (2016).

98. Wang, Z., Yu, L., Chen, M., Wang, S. and Jiang, H., Transcutaneous electrical stimulation of auricular branch of vagus nerve: a noninvasive therapeutic approach for post-ischemic heart failure, *International Journal of Cardiology,* **177**, 676-677 (2014).

99. Beaumont, E., Southerland, E. M., Hardwick, J. C., Wright, G. L., Ryan, S., Li, Y., KenKnight, B. H., Armour, J. A. and Ardell, J. L., Vagus nerve stimulation mitigates intrinsic cardiac neuronal and adverse myocyte remodeling postmyocardial infarction, *American Journal of Physiology. Heart and Circulatory Physiology,* **309**, H1198-1206 (2015).

100. Frenneaux, M. P. Autonomic changes in patients with heart failure and in post-myocardial infarction patients, *Heart,* **90**, 1248-1255 (2004).

101. Huang, J., Qian, J., Yao, W., Wang, N., Zhang, Z., Cao, C., Song, B. and Zhang, Z., Vagus nerve stimulation reverses ventricular electrophysiological changes induced by hypersympathetic nerve activity, *Experimental Physiology,* **100**, 239-248 (2015).

102. Mortara, A., La Rovere, M. T., Pinna, G. D., Parziale, P., Maestri, R., Capomolla, S., Opasich, C., Cobelli, F. and Tavazzi, L., Depressed arterial baroreflex sensitivity and not reduced heart rate variability identifies patients with chronic heart failure and nonsustained ventricular tachycardia: the effect of high ventricular filling pressure, *American Heart Journal,* **134**, 879-888 (1997).

103. La Rovere, M. T., Bigger, J. T., Jr., Marcus, F. I., Mortara, A., Schwartz, P. J., and for the ATRAMI (Autonomic Tone and Reflexes After Myocardial Infarction) Investigators, Baroreflex sensitivity and heart-rate variability in prediction of total cardiac mortality after myocardial infarction, *Lance,t* **351**, 478-484 (1998).

104. Lechat, P., Hulot, J. S., Escolano, S., Mallet, A., Leizorovicz, A., Werhlen-Grandjean, M., Pochmalicki, G. and Dargie, H., Heart rate and cardiac rhythm relationships with bisoprolol benefit in chronic heart failure in CIBIS II trial, *Circulation,* **103**, 1428-1433 (2001).

105. Shinlapawittayatorn, K., Chinda, K., Palee, S., Surinkaew, S., Thunsiri, K., Weerateerangkul, P., Chattipakorn, S., KenKnight, B. H. and Chattipakorn, N., Low-amplitude, left vagus nerve stimulation significantly attenuates ventricular dysfunction and infarct size through prevention of mitochondrial dysfunction during acute ischemia-reperfusion injury, *Heart rhythm,* **10**, 1700-1707 (2013).

106. Shinlapawittayatorn, K., Chinda, K., Palee, S., Surinkaew, S., Kumfu, S., Kumphune, S., Chattipakorn, S., KenKnight, B. H. and Chattipakorn, N., Vagus nerve stimulation initiated late during ischemia, but not reperfusion, exerts cardioprotection via amelioration of cardiac mitochondrial dysfunction, *Heart rhythm,* **11**, 2278-2287 (2014).

107. Schwartz, P. J., De Ferrari, G. M., Sanzo, A., Landolina, M., Rordorf, R., Raineri, C., Campana, C., Revera, M., Ajmone-Marsan, N., Tavazzi, L. and Odero, A., Long term vagal stimulation in patients with advanced heart failure: first experience in man, *European Journal of Heart Failure,* **10**, 884-891 (2008).

108. De Ferrari, G. M., Crijns, H. J., Borggrefe, M., Milasinovic, G., Smid, J., Zabel, M., Gavazzi, A., Sanzo, A., Dennert, R., Kuschyk, J., Raspopovic, S., Klein, H., Swedberg, K., Schwartz, P. J. and CardioFit Multicenter Trial Investigators, Chronic vagus nerve stimulation: a new and promising therapeutic approach for chronic heart failure, *European Heart Journa,l* **32**, 847-855 (2011).

109. Hauptman, P. J., Schwartz, P. J., Gold, M. R., Borggrefe, M., Van Veldhuisen, D. J., Starling, R. C. and Mann, D. L., Rationale and study design of the increase of vagal tone in heart failure study: INOVATE-HF, *American Heart Journal,* **163**, 954-962 e951 (2012).

110. De Ferrari, G. M., Tuinenburg, A. E., Ruble, S., Brugada, J., Klein, H., Butter, C., Wright, D. J., Schubert, B., Solomon, S., Meyer, S., Stein, K., Ramuzat, A. and Zannad, F., Rationale and study design of the NEuroCardiac TherApy foR Heart Failure Study: NECTAR-HF, *European Journal of Heart Failure,* **16**, 692-699 (2014).

111. Zannad, F., De Ferrari, G. M., Tuinenburg, A. E., Wright, D., Brugada, J., Butter, C., Klein, H., Stolen, C., Meyer, S., Stein, K.M., Ramuzat, A., Schubert, B., Daum, D., Neuzil, P., Botman, C., Castel, M. A., D'Onofrio, A., Solomon, S. D., Wold, N. and Ruble, S. B., Chronic vagal stimulation for the treatment of low ejection fraction heart failure: results of the NEural Cardiac TherApy foR Heart Failure (NECTAR-HF) randomized controlled trial, *European Heart Journa,l* **36**, 425-433 (2015).

112. Dicarlo, L., Libbus, I., Amurthur, B., Kenknight, B. H. and Anand, I. S., Autonomic regulation therapy for the improvement of left ventricular function and heart failure symptoms: the ANTHEM-HF study, *Journal of Cardiac Failure,* **19**, 655-660 (2013).

113. Premchand, R. K., Sharma, K., Mittal, S., Monteiro, R., Dixit, S., Libbus, I., DiCarlo, L. A., Ardell, J. L., Rector, T. S., Amurthur, B., KenKnight, B. H. and Anand, I. S., Autonomic regulation therapy via left or right cervical vagus nerve stimulation in patients with chronic heart failure: Results of the ANTHEM-HF Trial, *Journal of Cardiac Failure,* **20**, 808-816 (2014).

114. Libbus, I., Nearing, B. D., Amurthur, B., KenKnight, B. H. and Verrier, R. L., Autonomic regulation therapy suppresses quantitative T-wave alternans and improves baroreflex sensitivity in patients with heart failure enrolled in the ANTHEM-HF study, *Heart Rhythm,* **13**, 721-728 (2016).

115. Chugh, S. S., Reinier, K., Teodorescu, C., Evanado, A., Kehr, E., Al Samara, M., Mariani, R., Gunson, K. and Jui, J., Epidemiology of sudden cardiac death: clinical and research implications, *Progress in Cardiovascular Diseases,* **51**, 213-228 (2008).

116. Zheng, Z. J., Croft, J. B., Giles, W. H. and Mensah, G. A., Sudden cardiac death in the United States, 1989 to 1998, *Circulation,* **104**, 2158-2163 (2001).

117. Bayes de Luna, A., Coumel, P. and Leclercq, J. F., Ambulatory sudden cardiac death: mechanisms of production of fatal arrhythmia on the basis of data from 157 cases, *American Heart Journal,* **117**, 151-159 (1989).

118. Vaseghi, M. and Shivkumar, K., The role of the autonomic nervous system in sudden cardiac death, *Progress in Cardiovascular Diseases,* **50**, 404-419 (2008).

119. Nadeau, R., Cardinal, R., Armour, J. A., Kus, T., Richer, L. P., Vermeulen, M., Yin, Y. and Page, P., Cervical vagosympathetic and mediastinal nerves activation effects on atrial arrhythmia formation, *Anatolian Journal of Cardiology,* **7 Suppl 1**, 34-36 (2007).

120. Chen, P. S., Chen, L. S., Fishbein, M. C., Lin, S. F. and Nattel, S., Role of the autonomic nervous system in atrial fibrillation: pathophysiology and therapy, *Circulation research*, **114**, 1500-1515 (2014).

121. Lee, S., Sahadevan, J., Khrestian, C. M., Durand, D. M. and Waldo, A. L., High density mapping of atrial fibrillation during vagal nerve stimulation in the canine heart: restudying the Moe hypothesis, *Journal of Cardiovascular Electrophysiology*, **24**, 328-335 (2013).

122. Patterson, E., Po, S. S., Scherlag, B. J. and Lazzara, R., Triggered firing in pulmonary veins initiated by in vitro autonomic nerve stimulation, *Heart rhythm*, **2**, 624-631 (2005).

123. Xueyi, X., Lee, S. W., Johnson, C., Ippolito, J., KenKnight, B. H. and Tolkacheva, E. G., Intermittent vagal nerve stimulation alters the electrophysiological properties of atrium in the myocardial infarction rat model, *Annual International Conference of the IEEE Engineering in Medicine and Biology Society*, **2014**, 1575-1578 (2014).

124. Kusunose, K., Zhang, Y., Mazgalev, T. N., Van Wagoner, D. R., Thomas, J. D. and Popovic, Z. B., Impact of vagal nerve stimulation on left atrial structure and function in a canine high-rate pacing model, *Circulation. Heart Failure*, **7**, 320-326 (2014).

125. Armour, J. A., Richer, L. P., Page, P., Vinet, A., Kus, T., Vermeulen, M., Nadeau, R. and Cardinal, R., Origin and pharmacological response of atrial tachyarrhythmias induced by activation of mediastinal nerves in canines, *Autonomic Neuroscience: Basic and Clinical*, **118**, 68-78 (2005).

126. Richer, L. P., Vinet, A., Kus, T., Cardinal, R., Ardell, J. L. and Armour, J. A., Alpha-adrenoceptor blockade modifies neurally induced atrial arrhythmias, *American Journal of Physiology. Regulatory, Integrative and Comparative Physiology*, **295**, R1175-1180 (2008).

127. Yang, D., Xi, Y., Ai, T., Wu, G., Sun, J., Razavi, M., Delapasse, S., Shurail, M., Gao, L., Mathuria, N., Elayda, M. and Cheng, J., Vagal stimulation promotes atrial electrical remodeling induced by rapid atrial pacing in dogs: evidence of a noncholinergic effect, *Pacing and Clinical Electrophysiology*, **34**, 1092-1099 (2011).

128. Li, S., Scherlag, B. J., Yu, L., Sheng, X., Zhang, Y., Ali, R., Dong, Y., Ghias, M. and Po, S. S., Low-level vagosympathetic stimulation: a paradox and potential new modality for the treatment of focal atrial fibrillation, *Circulation. Arrhythmia and Electrophysiology*, **2**, 645-651 (2009).

129. Yamakawa, K., So, E. L., Rajendran, P. S., Hoang, J. D., Makkar, N., Mahajan, A., Shivkumar, K. and Vaseghi, M., Electrophysiological effects of right and left vagal nerve stimulation on the ventricular myocardium, *American Journal of Physiology. Heart and Circulatory Physiology*, **307**, H722-731 (2014).

130. Einbrodt, P., Über Herzreizung und ihr Verhaeltnis zum Blutdruck, *Akademie der Wissenschaften (Vienna) Sitzungsberichte*, **38**, 345 (1859).

131. Scherlag, B. J., Helfant, R. H., Haft, J. I. and Damato, A. N., Electrophysiology underlying ventricular arrhythmias due to coronary ligation, *The American Journal of Physiology*, **219**, 1665-1671 (1970).

132. Goldstein, R. E., Karsh, R. B., Smith, E. R., Orlando, M., Norman, D., Farnham, G., Redwood, D. R. and Epstein, S. E., Influence of atropine and of vagally mediated bradycardia on the occurrence of ventricular arrhythmias following acute coronary occlusion in closed-chest dogs, *Circulation*, **47**, 1180-1190 (1973).

133. Myers, R. W., Pearlman, A. S., Hyman, R. M., Goldstein, R. A., Kent, K. M., Goldstein, R. E. and Epstein, S. E., Beneficial effects of vagal stimulation and bradycardia during experimental acute myocardial ischemia, *Circulation*, **49**, 943-947 (1974).

134. Kolman, B. S., Verrier, R. L. and Lown, B., The effect of vagus nerve stimulation upon vulnerability of the canine ventricle: role of sympathetic-parasympathetic interactions, *Circulation*, **52**, 578-585 (1975).

135. Uitterdijk, A., Yetgin, T., te Lintel Hekkert, M., Sneep, S., Krabbendam-Peters, I., van Beusekom, H. M., Fischer, T. M., Cornelussen, R. N., Manintveld, O. C., Merkus, D. and Duncker, D. J., Vagal nerve stimulation started just prior to reperfusion limits infarct size and no-reflow, *Basic Research in Cardiology*, **110**, 508 (2015).

136. Vanoli, E., De Ferrari, G. M., Stramba-Badiale, M., Hull, S. S., Jr., Foreman, R. D. and Schwartz, P. J., Vagal stimulation and prevention of sudden death in conscious dogs with a healed myocardial infarction, *Circulation Research*, **68**, 1471-1481 (1991).

137. Zheng, C., Li, M., Inagaki, M., Kawada, T., Sunagawa, K. and Sugimachi, M., Vagal stimulation markedly suppresses arrhythmias in conscious rats with chronic heart failure after myocardial infarction, *Annual International Conference of the IEEE Engineering in Medicine and Biology Society*, **7**, 7072-7075 (2005).

138. Scherlag, B. J., Nakagawa, H., Jackman, W. M., Lazzara, R. and Po, S. S. Non-pharmacological, non-ablative approaches for the treatment of atrial fibrillation: experimental evidence and potential clinical implications, *Journal of Cardiovascular Translational Research*, **4**, 35-41 (2011).

139. Herring, N., Cranley, J., Lokale, M. N., Li, D., Shanks, J., Alston, E. N., Girard, B. M., Carter, E., Parsons, R. L., Habecker, B. A. and Paterson, D. J., The cardiac sympathetic co-transmitter galanin reduces acetylcholine release and vagal bradycardia: implications for neural control of cardiac excitability, *Journal of Molecular and Cellular Cardiology*, **52**, 667-676 (2012).

140. Annoni, E. M., Xie, X., Lee, S. W., Libbus, I., KenKnight, B. H., Osborn, J. W. and Tolkacheva, E. G., Intermittent electrical stimulation of the right cervical vagus nerve in salt-sensitive hypertensive rats: effects on blood pressure, arrhythmias, and ventricular electrophysiology, *Physiological Reports*, **3**, e12476 (2015).

141. Brack, K. E., Patel, V. H., Coote, J. H. and Ng, G. A., Nitric oxide mediates the vagal protective effect on ventricular fibrillation via effects on action potential duration restitution in the rabbit heart, *The Journal of Physiology*, **583**, 695-704 (2007).

142. Calvillo, L., Vanoli, E., Andreoli, E., Besana, A., Omodeo, E., Gnecchi, M., Zerbi, P., Vago, G., Busca, G. and Schwartz, P. J., Vagal stimulation, through its nicotinic action, limits infarct size and the inflammatory response to myocardial ischemia and reperfusion, *Journal of Cardiovascular Pharmacology*, **58**, 500-507 (2011).

143. Pavlov, V. A. and Tracey, K. J., The cholinergic anti-inflammatory pathway, *Brain, Behavior, and Immunity*, **19**, 493-499 (2005).

144. Koncz, I., Gurabi, Z., Patocskai, B., Panama, B.K., Szel, T., Hu, D., Barajas-Martinez, H. and Antzelevitch, C., Mechanisms underlying the development of the electrocardiographic and arrhythmic manifestations of early repolarization syndrome, *Journal of Molecular and Cellular Cardiology*, **68**, 20-28 (2014).

145. Kasanuki, H., Ohnishi, S., Ohtuka, M., Matsuda, N., Nirei, T., Isogai, R., Shoda, M., Toyoshima, Y. and Hosoda, S., Idiopathic ventricular fibrillation induced with vagal activity in patients without obvious heart disease, *Circulation*, **95**, 2277-2285 (1997).

146. Antzelevitch, C., Brugada syndrome, *Pacing and Clinical Electrophysiology*, **29**, 1130-1159 (2006).

147. Flaim, S. N. and McCulloch, A. D., Acetylcholine-induced shortening of the epicardial action potential duration may increase repolarization gradients and LQT3 arrhythmic risk, *Journal of Electrocardiology*, **40**, S66-69 (2007).

148. Zamotrinsky, A. V., Kondratiev, B. and de Jong, J. W., Vagal neurostimulation in patients with coronary artery disease, *Autonomic Neuroscience: Basic and Clinical*, **88**, 109-116 (2001).

149. Schomer, A. C., Nearing, B. D., Schachter, S. C. and Verrier, R. L., Vagus nerve stimulation reduces cardiac electrical instability assessed by quantitative T-wave alternans analysis in patients with drug-resistant focal epilepsy, *Epilepsia*, **55**, 1996-2002 (2014).

150. Cadeddu, C., Deidda, M., Mercuro, G., Tuveri, A., Muroni, A., Nocco, S., Puligheddu, M., Maleci, A. and Marrosu, F., Cardiovascular modulation during vagus nerve stimulation therapy in patients with refractory epilepsy, *Epilepsy Research*, **92**, 145-152 (2010).

151. Ajijola, O. A., Yagishita, D., Reddy, N. K., Yamakawa, K., Vaseghi, M., Downs, A. M., Hoover, D. B., Ardell, J. L. and Shivkumar, K., Remodeling of stellate ganglion neurons after spatially targeted myocardial infarction: Neuropeptide and morphologic changes, *Heart Rhythm*, **12**, 1027-1035 (2015).

152. Kanazawa, H., Ieda, M., Kimura, K., Arai, T., Kawaguchi-Manabe, H., Matsuhashi, T., Endo, J., Sano, M., Kawakami, T., Kimura, T., Monkawa, T., Hayashi, M., Iwanami, A., Okano, H., Okada, Y., Ishibashi-Ueda, H., Ogawa, S. and Fukuda, K., Heart failure causes cholinergic transdifferentiation of cardiac sympathetic nerves via gp130-signaling cytokines in rodents, *The Journal of Clinical Investigation*, **120**, 408-421 (2010).

153. Zhou, S., Chen, L. S., Miyauchi, Y., Miyauchi, M., Kar, S., Kangavari, S., Fishbein, M. C., Sharifi, B. and Chen, P. S., Mechanisms of cardiac nerve sprouting after myocardial infarction in dogs, *Circulation Research*, **95**, 76-83 (2004).

154. Yu, L., Scherlag, B. J., Li, S., Sheng, X., Lu, Z., Nakagawa, H., Zhang, Y., Jackman, W. M., Lazzara, R., Jiang, H. and Po, S. S., Low-level vagosympathetic nerve stimulation inhibits atrial fibrillation inducibility: direct evidence by neural recordings from intrinsic cardiac ganglia, *Journal of Cardiovascular Electrophysiology*, **22**, 455-463 (2011).

Chapter 3.5

Visual Prostheses

Boshuo Wang[1] and James. D Weiland[2]

[1]*Duke University, Durham, NC, USA*

[2]*University of Southern California, Los Angeles, CA, USA.*

jweiland@med.usc.edu

A significant milestone in the history of bioelectrical visual prostheses has been reached as retinal prosthetic devices have become commercially available in the second decade of the 21st century [1]. In this long-lasting effort to restore vision to the blind [1 - 7], humankind has substituted electrical current for light as the source of stimuli to activate neurons in the visual system in order to create a perception of vision. Prosthesis users are now able to perceive light and perform simple tasks. With the current development in technology, optimistic projections suggest that facial recognition and fairly fluent reading will become feasible in next generation retinal prostheses with resolution of a thousand electrodes. However, continuous research and development is needed to overcome the many challenges to reach this goal.

1. History of the Visual Prostheses—From Cortex to Retina

The neural effects of electrical stimulation have been known from very early on in recorded history, and treatments with electricity have been explored as early as mid-1700s [9] for various purposes. Among these efforts, Charles LeRoy, a French chemist and physician, most likely documented the first account of visual phosphene—light perception without actual light stimuli to the retina—perceived by a blind subject, when a Layden jar was discharged to a coil wrapped around the subject's head and the subject reported seeing a flame rapidly descend before his eyes [10].

Attempts for artificial vision through electrical stimulation succeeded only in the modern era of the 20th century. In 1929, Otfrid Foerster, a German neurosurgeon, placed a stimulating electrode over the visual cortex (posterior pole of the occipital cortex) of a healthy subject under local anesthesia. When electrical stimulation was applied, the subject reported a light spot whose location was dependent on the electrode's placement over the cortex [11]. Similar results were soon reported in a blind patient who lost vision eight years prior to the experiment [12].

These early attempts demonstrated that cortical electrical stimulation can successfully evoke light perception, and such perceptions have a spatially-specific mapping in the cortex. Also vital to the concept of visual prostheses is that blind patients retain the ability to perceive light perception from electrical stimulation, as long as certain neuronal circuits remain intact. Now it is known that this capability persists for decades [13 - 15].

The first chronic prosthetic visual implant was developed in the late 1960s. This device consisted of an electrode array of 80 platinum electrodes, and was placed over the surface of the visual cortex of a blind woman (Fig. 1) [16]. Half the electrodes elicited phosphenes, and the device was still working to a certain extent after 6 years (Karny, 1975). In 1972, a second implantation in a blind patient with retinitis pigmentosa was performed bilaterally. The patient could read Braille letters with little training at a rate of 8.5 characters per minute (Karny, 1975). In the 1970s, William Dobelle designed a visual cortex prosthesis that allowed patients to recognize simple patterns [13]. Electrical signals were converted from images recorded by a television camera and delivered to the medial occipital cortex by electrodes. These attempts yielded impressive results; however they were far from becoming feasible medical devices. The large electrode sizes (around 1 mm^2) led to crosstalk which limited the patients from seeing distinct phosphenes when adjacent electrodes were simultaneously activated. The surface electrode position led to large currents needed for phosphene generation, which had the side effect of evoking seizures [17]. Thus, this prosthesis architecture was impractical [13].

Visual prostheses had a major development milestone when researchers discovered that intracortical stimulation has much lower stimulation thresholds compared to surface stimulation, and the spatial resolution for individual phosphenes was possible for two electrodes placed as close as 700 μm [18]. High density arrays with small electrode sizes also became feasible as fabrication technology advanced [2, 19]. And in the meantime, the success of cochlear implants showed promise for commercial neural prostheses and produced technical advances in hermetic packaging and microelectronics, which could be applied to other electronic implants. All these factors accelerated the development of modern-day visual prostheses.

Although cortical stimulation had been investigated early on and showed promise, the visual cortex is not the only part of the visual system that can be targeted for electrical activation. Actually, its complex functional specialization such as color, orientation, and shape etc. [7], spatial organization, and location inside the skull create numerous challenges. Other locations along the visual pathway, namely the optic nerve [20 - 22] and retina [23], have been proposed and investigated, and the retina stood out as a suitable target due to several reasons. The natural retinotopic projection of the visual field means that patterned stimulation could be performed easily. And stimulating the earliest part of the visual pathway also allows the implant to utilize the early visual processing in the retina, which remains somewhat viable even in degenerate retinas. Finally, the relative ease of accessibility to the retina compared to the later parts in the visual processing pathway results in less complicated surgical procedures. Therefore the retinal prostheses have received the most attention recently and are furthest along the development pathway.

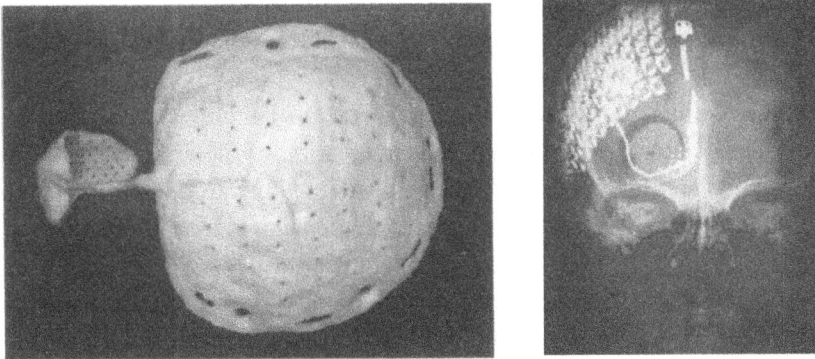

Fig. 1. The cortical implant created by Brindley and Lewin [16]. Left: The electrode array is shown on the left, while the larger receiver array is to the right. Right: X-ray image of the device post implantation. The receiver array was placed beneath the pericranium and secured to the skull. The intracranial electrode array lies between the medial surface of the occipital pole of the right hemisphere and the falx cerebri. (Reprinted from Journal of Physiology, 196/2, G. S. Brindley,W. S. Lewin, The sensations produced by electrical stimulation of the visual cortex, Plates 2 & Plate 3 Fig.1, with permission from John Wiley and Sons.)

2. Retinal Prostheses

Depending on the location of the electrode array, retinal prosthesis could be divided into epiretinal, subretinal and suprachoroidal implants [1, 2]. First, a brief overview of these three types of prostheses is given. The common components and safety concerns of retinal prostheses are then presented. Clinical trial and commercialization efforts of several prosthetic devices are introduced. And finally challenges that the current technology face are discussed.

2.1. *Types of retinal prosthesis*

2.1.1. *Epiretinal prosthesis*

In the epiretinal prosthesis, the electrode array is located on the inner surface of the retina (the inner limiting membrane), with the electrodes being closest to the ganglion cell layer. This configuration provides direct access to the RGCs—the output layer of the retina, while stimulation of the deeper bipolar cell is still possible [25]. On one hand, this is advantageous because it results in the lowest stimulation threshold [26]; and ganglion cell are spiking neurons, thus short latency response to direct stimulation of ganglion cells could be reliably reproduced at high frequency without adaptation [27]. On the other hand, the close proximity between the stimulating electrodes and ganglion cell axons can cause axonal activation, which creates irregular phosphene shapes and degrades the spatial resolution [28, 29].

For the epiretinal prostheses, a tight placement of the electrode array on the retinal surface is a challenge for both the engineering of the array and the clinical procedure. In some devices such as the Argus II, the electrode array is tacked to the retina and necessarily creates limited retinal damage at the tack site [30]. If not positioned correctly, the retinal activation threshold on some electrodes could become too high for safe and effective stimulation, rendering them non-functional and degrading the overall resolution [31, 32]. Some experimental devices are exploring protruding electrodes to improve contact with retina [33], or using 3-D electrodes with one design even aiming to penetrate into the bipolar cell layer from the epiretinal side [34].

The electronics of the epiretinal implants are placed in the orbit of the eye and/or the vitreous humor. The relatively large space is beneficial for avoiding heat and mechanical damage from the electronics [35]. Also, a majority of the electronics of the device can be incorporated into the associated external components, allowing for a smaller implant and upgrades without additional modification to the implanted components [6].

2.1.2. *Subretinal prostheses*

In the subretinal prosthesis, the electrode array is inserted in the subretinal space between the RPE/choroid layer and sensory retina, in the place of the absent photoreceptors [36]. The implantation is achieved typically through an incision of the sclera, choroid and RPE (*ab externo*) but could also be done using an incision on the retina (*ab interno*) [6]. The electrodes are closest with the bipolar cells, and could stimulate any remaining photoreceptors. This could work in favor of the device by accessing the remaining neural networks, but could also be a challenge due to the remodeling of degenerated retina. Some subretinal prostheses utilize a microphotodiode array (MPDA) to convert the incoming light into electrical stimulation, therefore mimicking the function of photoreceptors.

Subretinal stimulation targets bipolar cells. This utilizes some of the neural processing of the inner retina, and avoids activation of ganglion cells axon bundles which could create irregular phosphene shapes. The position of the array in the subretinal space eliminates the necessity to secure the array by mechanical methods (such as a tack); however, the design has to considered thermal damage to the retina by the electronics [6], and the size limitation on the implant. Possible complications include the risk of retinal detachment due to the surgical procedure to insert the array in place and the long-term presence of the array under the retina.

2.1.3. *Suprachoroidal retinal prosthesis*

The suprachoroidal retinal prosthesis has an electrode array located in the suprachoroidal space between the choroid and sclera [37]. The mode of operation is sometimes known as suprachoroidal transretinal stimulation (STS) as the electrical current is passing through the entire retina to a return electrode inserted into the vitreous humor [38]. The electrode array's location can be easily accessed by surgery, therefore simplifying the implantation procedure [37]. The choroid and sclera are more robust and less prone to mechanical disturbance compared to the retina. The only intraocular component (if any) is the return electrode, therefore reducing the risk related with inserting complex components into the eye. Although the choroid layer thins in RP patients [39], the distance between the electrode array and its stimulation targets, whether bipolar cells or RGCs, is larger compared to epiretinal or subretinal implants. This increases the threshold of stimulation and therefore power consumption; Focal stimulation, which is required for high resolution artificial vision, is a challenge due to the wider spread of electrical field and current at those distances [6].

2.2. *Common components of retinal prostheses*

Due to the variable configuration, different types of prostheses don't necessarily share all the same components. The most common components are discussed in the context of the applicable type of devices.

2.2.1. *Multielectrode array (MEA)*

The electrode array is the direct interface between the device and the retina that delivers the electrical stimulation. It may be placed on the inner side of the retina (epiretinal), in the subretinal space, or outside the choroid (suprachoroidal). Considerations for each type of placement have been mentioned in the previous section for the different types of retinal prostheses, and will be further discussed here.

Compared to older implants such as cochlear implants and deep brain stimulators, retinal prostheses demonstrated a significant advancement in electrode technology. Instead of hand-made electrodes, electrode arrays in retinal prostheses utilize microfabrication and photolithography techniques from the integrated circuit (IC) industry to achieve small electrode feature size and high contact density (Fig. 2) [2]. Protruding electrodes have been designed or utilized [38, 40], and complex shape and geometry may become possible for future designs.

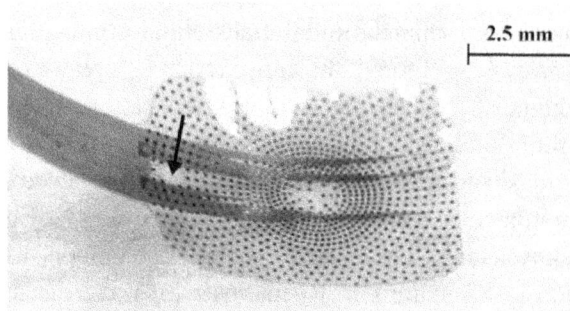

Fig. 2. Heat molded and annealed retinal electrode array with retained spherical curvature [41]. (Reprinted from Sensors and Actuators B: Chemical, 132/2, D. C. Rodger et al., Flexible parylene-based multielectrode array technology for high-density neural stimulation and recording, page 453, Copyright (2008), with permission from Elsevier.)

For epiretinal and suprachoroidal prostheses, which have the electrode array separate from the implant electronics, the array is fabricated of flexible materials—polymers such as silicone, polyimide, or parylene [42]. For subretinal prostheses that utilize photodiodes as the signal source, the electrodes are fabricated on the surface of the chip that contains the photodiodes and relevant electronics [43].

2.2.2. *Electrical stimulator, integrated circuits, and packaging*

The electrical stimulator refers to the electronic components that generate the current/voltage pulse delivered to the electrodes. While often referred to as a chip, which implies a single integrated circuit, even modern retinal prostheses require multiple electronic components to perform all the required functions while maintaining a small volume. The stimulator must produce high voltage to inject suprathreshold current across the electrode-tissue interface to the neuronal targets, and should provide certain programmability in the pulse parameters (pulse rate, pulse width, interphase gap, etc.). The design also needs to trade-off between stimulation efficiency, power consumption, and size [2, 6].

For retinal prostheses without implanted light detectors, the stimulator needs to receive stimulation data, control signals, and power from other components. This has been achieved through radio frequency and infrared wireless links. The stimulator component is implanted, and therefore must be hermetically sealed to avoid malfunctioning and destruction due to the leakage of conductive bodily fluid into the system [44]. The leads pass through the packing via feedthroughs to connect to the electrodes, and achieving high density feedthrough remains a limiting factor for size of the implant [2] and is an active research area [45]. For intraocular implantation, the vitreous humor also serves as a heat sink for the electronics [46], while device located in the orbit of the eye also has efficient heat dissipation due to the relatively large space.

In subretinal prostheses utilizing photodiodes, the stimulators integrated with photodiodes are co-localized with their electrodes. This provides a major advantage because the stimulation units are locally grouped with their respective signal source (the photodiodes); hence there is no need for external signal transmission and wiring of leads from electrodes to a central implanted signal processing unit, allowing a high density of stimulation sites. However, hermetic packaging is a challenge, and polymer coating have not been able to protect the electronics for long periods of use [47]. Also, completely passive photodiodes can't produce enough photocurrent for stimulation as shown in previous studies[40], and active amplification is needed. Therefore power and control signal transmission from outside is still needed, while stimulation amplitude for each channel is controlled by incoming light.

2.2.3. *Power and signal telemetry*

Commercial retinal prostheses avoid direct electrical connection across the sclera or skin, since this is a path for infection. Therefore wireless transmission is necessary to deliver the visual data (if the camera is external), control signals, and power from external unit to the implanted electrical stimulator. This mechanism also provides additional safety to the device, as the implanted component does not contain elements of high energy density and the implanted device can be de-powered rapidly by removing the external source.

Inductive coupling using radio frequency (RF) between two coils is one solution. One coil is on the outside of the body and the other is with the electrical stimulator *in vivo* and in close proximity with the first one. A magnetic field is created as AC flow through the external (primary) coil, and this induces a voltage on the internal (secondary) coil. The rate and efficiency of transmission should be sufficient for delivering the data and power. This could become challenging as the number of individual channels increases with large electrode arrays and more electrodes in the future. Dual frequency bands were designed to achieve optimal transmission for both power and data [49]. Including backward telemetry [50] allows feedback of information about the implant's internal operation.

Infrared (IR) light is another method of transmission of data, and it utilizes the natural optic system of the eye. A light source on the outside, for example on a pair of glasses, projects modulated infrared light through the pupil onto the retina where the stimulator is located. For either epi- or subretinal implants, photodiodes convert the infrared light into electrical signals. One advantage is that the transmission is interrupted by eyelid closing, mimicking the normal situation where no light perception is present during eye closure. Since passive implants cannot generate enough stimulation current through photodiodes, active amplification is required and inductive coupling is used for power telemetry. Still, the power of infrared transmission has to be carefully limited, so that the heat effect doesn't cause any damage to the eye.

2.2.4. *Camera and image processing*

An external camera is used to capture the visual input for the device. The video camera is incorporated on the frame of a pair of glasses for the patient to wear. Miniature cameras have become a fairly mature technology and sufficiently small for the prosthesis purpose, so off-the-shelf cameras can be used with little modification. The resolution of the camera is not a limitation as the number of electrodes of the prosthesis is now far less than the pixel count of the camera (million pixels for smartphones), and will stay so for the foreseeable future. An external camera is not required only when an implanted microphotodiode array is used to directly convert incoming natural light into stimulation currents.

Mounting the camera on the glasses requires the patient to move the head to scan the environment or an object of interest. Although it helps with integrating information from the limited channels, this is an unnatural behavior that requires learning and adaptation by the patient, and it slows the performance of patient using the device [51]. For next generation of prostheses, miniature intraocular cameras are under development [20, 51]. These devices are small enough to be implanted in the lens of the eyeball, and therefore will allow natural target tracking using coordinated eye and head movement. A wide field camera together with eye tracking to select regions of interest from the scenes is another possible solution.

The image processing unit receives visual input from the camera, and processes it before sending the stimulation pattern to the stimulator. The image processing unit is usually part of the external components, which also serve as the general control unit for the entire device; however it could become part of the internal electronics as future devices become fully implanted [52].

The imaging processing as a minimum involves down sampling and compressing the information in the image to match the limited electrode numbers. Gray-scaling, contrast enhancement, edge and motion detection are among the many features that can be implemented. Computer vision can provide optimization [53, 54] and many additional features for patient users (Fig. 3). Information analysis can reduce redundant information in the pixelized image [55]. Saliency-based cues have shown to improve mobility and search task in simulated prosthetic vision [56].

As many prostheses stimulate the ganglion cells and bipolar cells, image processing that mimic retinal processing could improve stimulation. Models have been developed to predict the pattern of action potentials that RGCs fire in response to any light stimulus [57 - 59]. Applying these models, sophisticated image processing could be implemented to create natural stimulation pattern delivered to ganglion cells. Theoretically, this method will provide the best visual percepts for patient users if it is implemented with high resolution electrode arrays and good fidelity.

2.3. *Safety concerns*

Many safety issues have to be considered for an implanted device with active electrical stimulation. For a retinal prosthesis, a safe implantation surgery without complications is only the first step for the use of many years to come. Biological safety is a major consideration for the device to work properly without harming the patients. On the other hand, the device itself needs to stay functional for a long time; and for this purpose, the electrochemical safety and packaging is a major consideration for the implant. Many of the challenges and requirements for safety are similar to other neural implants, such as using biocompatible materials for the electrodes and substrate, improving electrode materials and designing input waveforms to avoid tissue damage due to excess charge/current injection and electrochemical byproducts, and using novel materials to improve the chemical and mechanical stability for the longevity of the device.

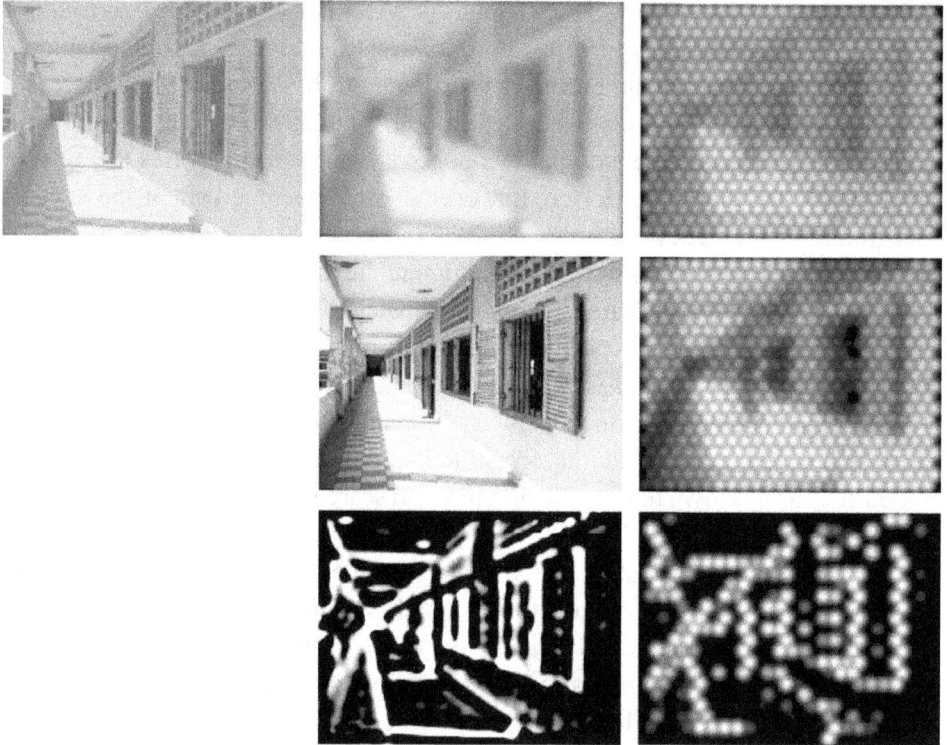

Fig. 3. Example of simulated prosthetic vision showing original image in top left, processed image in the middle column, and corresponding phosphenized output on the right [53]. From top to bottom, the image was processed with filtering, histogram equalization, and edge detection, respectively. (Reprinted from Vision Research, 49/12, S. C. Spencer et al., Simulating prosthetic vision: I. Visual models of phosphenes, page 1501, Copyright (2009), with permission from Elsevier.)

Mechanical damage to the retina and eye is possible, if the electrode exerts mechanical pressure on the retina [65, 66], or if the substrate materials are too rigid. The need to detach the retina for subretinal implants is a consideration that limits the size of the array, as large area of detachment have severe consequences for the health of the retinal tissue. Epiretinal implants are constrained by size of the incisions that can be safely performed on the eye wall during the surgical procedure, and the placement of the retinal tack for securing the array should be carefully performed for minimal tissue damage. Thermal damage is another safety concern, as heat dissipated by the electronics could potentially injure neural tissue. For retinal prostheses, locating the electronics further away from the retina allows a larger electronics case and a greater power budget, since heat can be dissipated over a larger surface (case surface) and heat effects on the retina are minimal because of the distance. [67]

3. Clinical Trials and Commercialization

Among the many efforts for visual prostheses (there are two online sources that maintain a listing of visual prostheses research efforts: http://www.eye-tuebingen.de/zrenner/retimplantlist/ and http://www.io.mei.titech.ac.jp/ research/ retina/index.html#Links) over the past decades [34], a few retinal prosthetic devices have entered/finished clinical trials [2], and two have received regulatory market approval [1]. This section introduces the clinical trials and commercialization of some of these devices (Fig. 4). With the current research and development momentum, it can be expected that more products will enter clinical testing and become available on the market in coming decades.

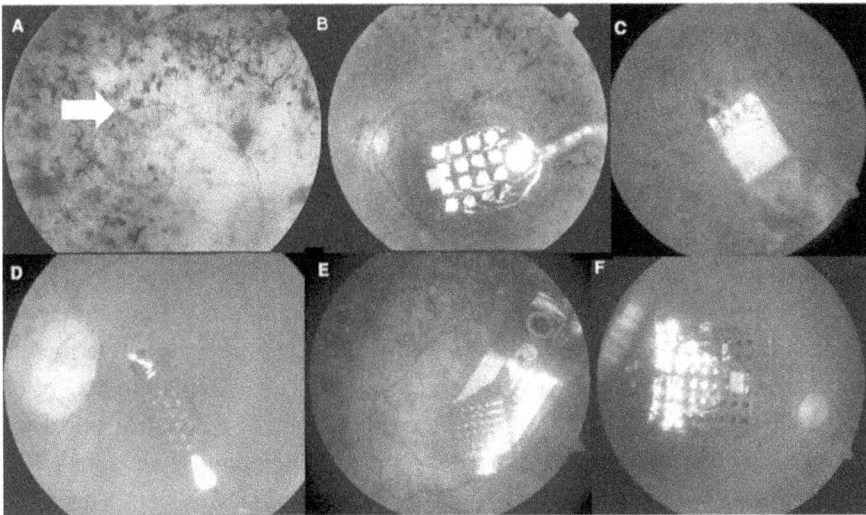

Fig. 4. Fundus photographs of 6 retinal prostheses ([5]). Image from the following prosthesis groups: A. Artificial Silicon Retina (White arrow) (Optobionics, Inc.). B. Argus I (Second Sight Medical Products, Inc.). C. Active subretinal device (Retina Implant, GmbH). D. Epi-Ret 25 electrode device (EpiRet, GmbH). E. Forty-nine electrode epiretinal device (Intelligent Medical Implants). F. Argus II (Second Sight Medical Products, Inc.). (Reprinted from Ophthalmology, 118/11, J. D. Weiland et al., Retinal Prostheses: Current Clinical Results and Future Needs, Pages 2230, Copyright (2011), with permission from Elsevier.)

3.1. *Epiretinal prostheses*

Epiretinal prostheses that have been investigated in clinical trials include devices from Second Sight Medical Products, Inc. (SSMP, Sylmar, CA, USA), Intelligent Medical Implants GmbH (IMI Intelligent Medical Implants GmbH, Bonn, Germany) and EpiRet (EpiRet GmbH, Gießen, Germany). IMI has been recently reformed as Pixium Vision.

A schematic of SSMP epiretinal prosthesis is shown in Fig. 5. A camera mounted on a pair of glasses records the visual information from the environment, which is sent to the implanted electronics through wireless telemetry after being processed by a video processing unit (VPU). The stimulator then generates current pulses, which are delivered to the electrodes on the epiretinal array.

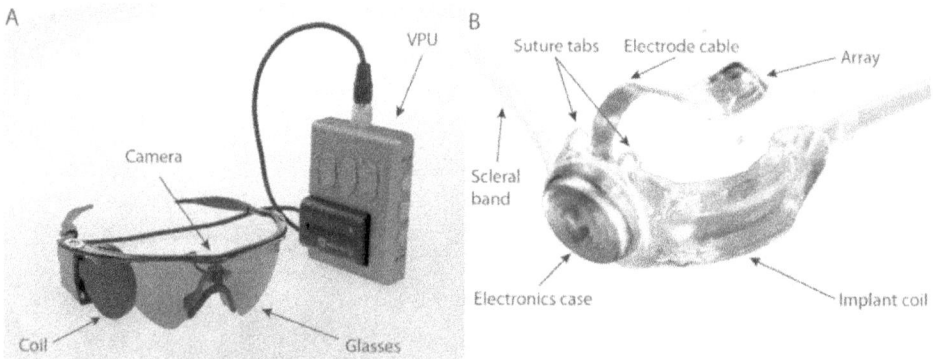

Fig. 5. The external (A) and implanted (B) components of the Argus II device [32].

The first generation device from SSMP, the Argus I implant was tested in 6 subjects with RP between 2002 and 2004 in the United States [2, 31]. The extraocular electronics were implanted in the temporal skull behind the ear in a way similar to cochlear implants [91]. A cable ran along the temple into the orbit, terminating at the intraocular MEA which had a 4×4 grid of 16 platinum electrodes of 260 μm or 520 μm diameters. The device enabled the first demonstration of the safety of long-term retinal stimulation in humans. The stimulation thresholds of most electrodes were within safety limit of platinum [31]. Subjects were able to perceive light, detect and discriminate objects from a small set, and detect motion of a moving bar [92]. The phosphenes produced from single electrodes were in general small and circular shaped [31, 93], although irregular, elongated phosphenes have also been reported [94]. Increases in stimulus amplitude tended to increase the brightness and size [31, 91, 95]. The best possible visual acuity given the electrode spacing of Argus I is 2.21 logMAR (20/3240), which was measured in one subject [96]. Threshold, electrode impedance, and electrode-retina distance were measured, and threshold was correlated only to proximity of the electrode and the retina, and not with other factors [31]. Therefore, maintaining a tight position of the array is critical. A long term follow-up study of up to ten years in one patient demonstrated the stability and durability of the device [97], which is also promising evidence of longevity for the next generation implant.

The second generation device built by SSMP is Argus II, which has an array of 60 electrodes (200 μm diameter and 525 μm pitch), covering a visual field of approximately 20 degrees diagonally [98]. The electronics are implanted in the orbit in a hermetic package, with the epiretinal electrode array connected by a transscleral cable.

The multi-center international clinical trial on the Argus II device is the largest one so far on any retinal prosthesis. The trial showed encouraging results, reporting a total of 45.6 cumulative subject years when the interim results were published in 2012 [32]. Thirty subjects were implanted between 2007 and 2009. Comprehensive studies were tested on 28 subjects, with one device removed due to recurrent conjunctival erosion and one subject was unavailable for testing [32, 99, 2]. All subjects perceived light during electrical stimulation, and the best visual acuity achieved was 20/1260. Object localization, motion detection, and letter reading were tested: With the device on, 27 out of 28 subjects performed better in locating and touching a white square on a computer screen [100], 16 out of 28 subjects performed better at identifying the direction of a moving bar on a computer screen, and 22 subjects could correctly identify a set of eight high-contrast letters with 72.6% success rate, versus 16.8% when the device was off. Subjects were allowed to take time to identify the letters and reading speed was slow, however it improved somewhat with practice [101]. Patients continued to use the device at home.

The Argus II device demonstrated safety and the true feasibility of high-resolution prosthetic vision. It received CE mark in March 2011 and FDA approval in February 2013, becoming the first commercially available retinal prosthesis in the world. As a high-tech medical device, Argus II is relative expensive (about $100,000 for device and surgery, as of 2014), however, simulation studies have shown that it is a cost-effective treatment for RP in the long term [102].

The IMI device is similar to Argus II in terms of external components and their placement, like the camera and telemetry components mounted on a pair eyeglasses, processing unit carried on a waist belt, and the epiretinal location of an array of 49 iridium oxide electrodes [64]. It uses inductive coupling for power transmission, but infrared light for visual information. The IMI device uses an image processing algorithm, Retina Encoder, to predict firing pattern of ganglion cells, and produces stimulation to imitate this pattern. After acute clinical testing in 20 RP patients [103], a chronic implant study started in 2005 with 7 subjects [2, 5]. No external camera was used and the device was only activated in clinical settings. Patients were able to identify phosphenes and patterns created by different electrodes. The thresholds were within safety limits, and the device was stable and well tolerated. The IMI company has been acquired by Pixium Vision, and the IMI device has become IRIS® [34]. According to the company website, the current version of 49 electrodes is under clinical testing, and a product with a 150-electrode array is planned for commercialization in Europe (retrieved Oct. 2015: http://www.pixium-vision.com/en/technology-1/iris-vision-restoration-system).

The latest EpiRet device, EpiRet3, is an epiretinal prosthesis with a hexagonal array of 25 electrodes [104]. The implanted electronics components are miniaturized to fit entirely inside the eye; while the camera and the image processor would be outside the body mounted on a pair of glasses. Inductive wireless telemetry is used for power transmission. The electrodes were fabricated from gold and covered with iridium oxide. The electrodes had a 3D design of 100μm in diameter and 25 μm height, which improved contact with the retina and lowered perceptual thresholds. The intraocular implantation eliminated the use of a transscleral cable for the connection to electronics The device has been implanted in 6 patients in 2006 for a semi-chronic (4 weeks) implantation study [33]. Experimental signal transfer was used instead of a camera for the study. Thresholds were low and within safety limits of electrical stimulation, and subjects could discriminate between unique pairs of electrodes and identify simple shapes. However the company has ceased operation [34].

3.2. *Subretinal prostheses*

Two subretinal prostheses have been tested in clinical trials by Optobionics, Inc. (Glen Ellyn, IL, USA) and Retina Implant AG (RI, Reutlingen, Germany). Both of the implants were microphotodiode arrays (MPDA), however the first was passive and the second is an active device. A brief introduction is also given to two subretinal prostheses in preclinical stage.

Optobionics' device, the Artificial Silicon Retina (ASR), is a chip of 3 mm diameter. Its microphotodiode array contains about 3500 units, with no external power supply [43]. The device was implanted in 30 RP subjects, and safety was demonstrated [5]. The passive photodiodes produced electrical currents on the level of nanoamperes, which are thousands times below thresholds sufficient for neural stimulation [40]. Improvement in visual perception was reported by some patients; however, animal studies show that this was a neurotrophic effect due to the presence of the device [105, 106]. The focus of device development has shifted from eliciting phosphenes to neurotrophic rescuing retinal and visual functions [107, 108].The original company was closed as the ASR was not able to demonstrated efficacy and its future remains uncertain.

Retina Implant developed an active MPDA with 1500 units (Fig. 6). Each unit has a photodiode, an amplifier, and a 70 μm titanium-nitride electrode. External power is transmitted to amplify the photocurrent produced by the photodiodes. This was achieved via a percutaneous cable for the experimental device in the pilot study, and by inductive telemetry for the commercial device (Alpha IMS). The array is about 3 mm in diameter and covers about 15 degree of the visual field [47, 109, 110]. An algorithm that calculates optimal implant position has also been developed, improving the device–tissue interface [111].

The experimental device has been implanted in 11 patients [1]. It has several direct stimulation electrodes besides the photodiode array for testing, and these electrodes demonstrated feasibility of visual perception in 8 of the 11 subjects. Problems with hardware reliability and hermetic packaging led to failure in the early implants, and the MPDA was tested in detail only in the last 3 of the 12 subjects who received an improved device with longer lifetime [110]. Subjects could perform several visual tasks such as identifying and locating objects, and one subject could recognize letters.

The wireless Alpha IMS implant has been tested in 9 subjects [47]. Eight out of nine (8/9) patients could perceive light, detect and identify objects. Light localization (7/9), motion detection (5/9), and grating acuity measurement (6/9) were measured. Three subjects could read letters spontaneously and one could after some training. Best Snellen visual acuity was measured up to 20/546 for one patient. Mechanical stress on the intraocular cable resulted in functional failure in three subjects after three to nine months implantation, which was solved to prevent further cable breaks in the remaining patients. Hermetic sealing was another issue that led to device failure in 3 different subjects after about 250 days post-implantation [47]. This proves to be a challenge as the MPDA requires a thin transparent package that maximizes the light intensity transmitted. The device received CE mark in mid-2013, and a multicenter trial with 19 RP patients is ongoing [1].

A subretinal prosthesis has been developed by the Boston Retina Implant Project [24], which uses a MEA instead of MPDA. This device has only been tested in animals; however a human-grade device with 256 channels of protruding iridium oxide electrode is under development for clinical testing [112]. Another subretinal implant with MPDA approach started in Stanford (now as Prima$^©$ under Pixium Vision, [34]) which also explored the use of penetrating electrodes. This novel approach provides good proximity to bipolar and/or ganglion cells, and therefore should result in lower stimulation thresholds and more focused spatial activation ([113]). However, the risk of tissue damage and the clinical feasibility must be addressed for such method to become practical.

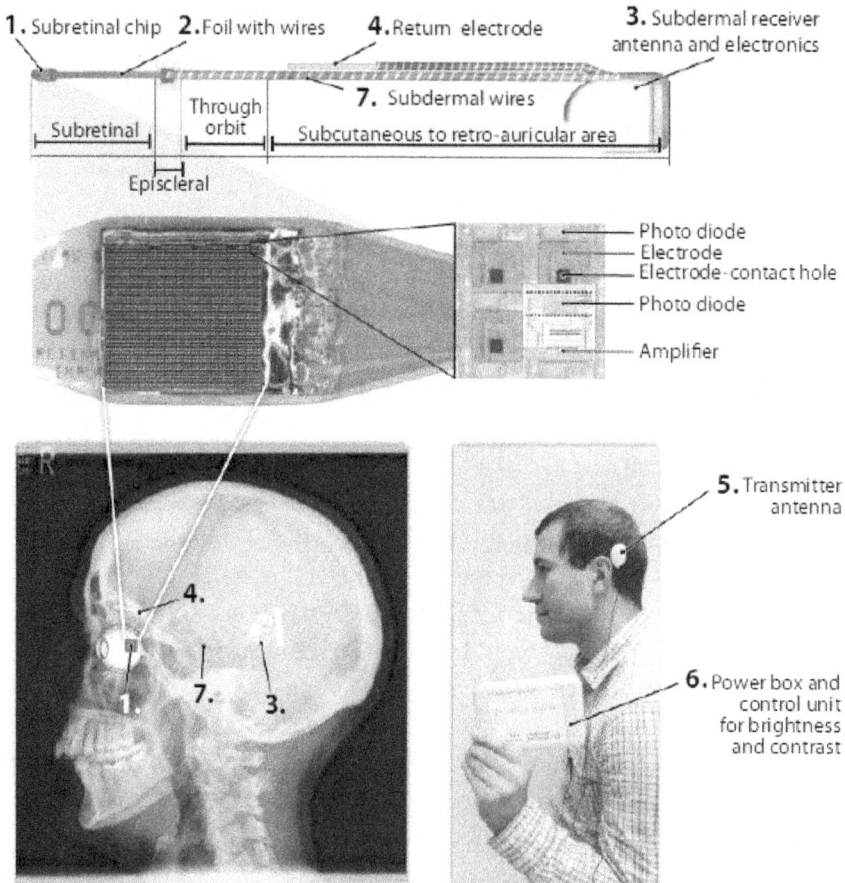

Fig. 6. The Alpha IMS prosthesis from Retina Implant [1]. The implanted part of the device is shown in the top panel, with description of the individual components and their locations *in vivo*. A detailed view of the MPDA is shown in the middle panel. The lower left shows an X-ray illustration of where the individual components are located, and the lower right shows the external components of the device.

3.3. *Suprachoroidal retinal prosthesis*

A suprachoroidal retinal prosthesis has been tested in humans for a limited time (4 weeks) [38, 114]. The implant consists of a 49 channel platinum electrode array with 9 active electrodes, each 0.5 mm in diameter and 0.5 mm in height protruding from the silicon base. The array was inserted into a scleral pocket, and the return electrode was inserted in the vitreous cavity. Two RP patients were implanted, and showed better than chance performs in object detection, object discrimination. Object grasping and touch panel tasks were tested on the second subjects, showing success rate of 90% for object grasping, and accuracy rate increasing up to 70% percent for touch panel with repeated testing. It was also shown that 20 Hz stimulation shows brighter phosphenes than 10 or 50 Hz for the same current level.

The Bionic Vision Australia group has been developing suprachoroidal retinal prostheses [115], and preclinical testing has shown the feasibility of long-term implantation in animals [116, 117]. A pilot clinical trial has been completed for initial safety and efficacy evaluation of the prototype in human (clintrial.gov NCT01603576). The preliminary results from three subjects with end-stage RP showed long-term stability over 18 months; all subjects could perceive phosphenes, and performed better with device on versus off for laboratory based visual function tests [118].

4. Research Areas and Challenges in (Epi-) Retinal Prostheses

This section will address some of the challenges faced by retinal prostheses, with the main focus on epiretinal implants. These challenges include findings from the aforementioned clinical trials and also implications from preclinical device testing and animal studies.

4.1. *Electrode-tissue interface and electric field distributions*

The electrical activation of retinal neurons requires an electrical field to be established in the tissue. The electrode-tissue interface is the first step in this process, and influences the performance of prosthetic devices and the properties of the stimulation. To form useful visual perception, multiple electrodes need to be activated on the electrode array, either simultaneously or within short time intervals. With simultaneous stimulation, the electric field generated by each electrode will overlap spatially and temporally to contribute to the activation of retinal neurons. Electrode crosstalk therefore increases the spatial distribution of activation and limits resolution [119, 120]. Temporal interactions between neighboring electrodes can also impede the resolution of multielectrode stimulation [121, 122]. Besides cross-talk, electrochemistry and heating also limit phosphene density as a function of distance from the electrode surface [40]. Maintaining good contact and small distance between the electrode array and the retina is also important for the proper functioning of epiretinal electrodes. The Argus device sometimes suffers from reduced resolution in patients because not all electrodes may reliably and safely produce a phosphene due to increased distance to the retina after the implantation [32]. Additional crosstalk via the highly conductive vitreous (or the saline that replaced it) could be significant [123].

The distribution of current and potential from the electrical stimulation by the electrodes of the prosthesis is a critical factor determining the response of retinal neurons. So far, no direct study has addressed this distribution, but simulations have been performed based on the physical models of the eye tissue [124, 125]. The resistivity of retinal layers has been estimated [126 - 128] and are used in these models. However, the previous studies have several shortcomings: (1) The studies were, with one exception, carried out in amphibians or birds, whose retinal structure differs from mammals; (2) The current flow was not well controlled; (3) Only one ocular location was measured, but the sclera thickness varies from 0.3 to 0.8 mm and the density of retinal cells changes dependent on eccentricity; and (4) The retinal prosthesis will interface with a diseased retina—in RP the retina may be half the thickness of a normal retina [129], and tissue impedance may be significantly different. Our lab has recently published a study of impedance measurements in the eye [77, 130]. The data show a clear increase in impedance when the electrode is in close proximity to the retina versus in the vitreous cavity, suggesting a change in current flow for electrodes close to the retina. The analyses of these data lumped retina, sclera, RPE, and choroid into a single impedance, while they most likely have different properties.

4.2. *Visual acuity*

High visual acuity is necessary for restoring central vision in tasks like reading and facial recognition. Each electrode can be considered as a pixel of the artificial vision. Although the relationship between each electrode and the phosphene it might create is variable (size, shape, color, etc., see later sections), the number and size of the electrodes on the array is an important factor for the spatial resolution and visual acuity [27]. For example, Argus I, the first epiretinal implant in clinical trial, had only a 4×4 array of 16 electrodes with 260 μm or 520 μm diameter and the second generation has a higher resolution with an array of 10×6 electrodes with 200 μm diameter [2]. In the three extensively tested retina implants, higher visual acuity has been consistent with more closely spaced electrodes. Future generations aim at orders of magnitude more electrodes [131, 132]. As technological development makes it feasible for larger arrays with smaller electrodes and electronics with more channels [2], the number of electrodes and electrode density required for useful vision is a critical question for retinal prostheses.

Investigation with animal models can provide *prima facie* evidence of the spatial resolution of electrical stimulation of the retina. Calcium fluorescence imaging studies with *in vitro* salamander retina found that the smallest activation area by a single electrode was 150 μm in diameter (corresponding to 20/660), regardless of electrode size as small as 10 μm [28]. This suggests that electrode size was not the limiting factor for achieving high visual acuity. In other studies with monkey retina, however, it was found that single RGCs could be stimulated with 10 μm electrodes [133, 134], inducing single spikes with sub-millisecond timing precision; also spatially patterned stimulation could further enhance the spatial resolution [135].

Simulations of prosthetic vision can also provide prediction of the achievable visual acuity (Fig. 7). Pixelized/phosphenized vision experiments have shown that an electrode density of 625 electrodes per square centimeter in the foveal region could achieve a visual acuity of approximately 20/30, and is sufficient for reading and guided mobility [136 - 138]. And a 20/80 visual acuity has been suggested as the target of visual prosthesis which corresponds to 20 μm pixel/phosphene sizes [40]. However, subjects in clinical trials have used head movement to scan the camera of the prosthesis across their environment, and use the integrated visual information to compensate for the limitation of the electrode numbers [139 - 141]; this could be the underlying reason for the hyperacuity beyond the theoretical limit in the Argus II trial [132]. Simulations have also shown that reliable face recognition with crude pixelized grids can be learned [140]. Therefore functional criteria are more useful to patients for determining the effectiveness of the device, which should be clinically evaluated for different visual tasks.

From both animal studies and simulations, spatial resolution and visual acuity can be expected to improve for future prosthesis users. However, issues such as electrode interaction, axonal stimulation, and retinal degeneration still need to be addressed. Another limiting factor is the foveal region, which has the highest neuronal density. Approximately half of the primary visual cortex is dedicated to processing visual information from the fovea [143], and it is responsible for our best visual acuity. Whereas location-dependent image processing [40] and biomimetic inhomogeneous electrode distribution [41, 144] may improve the performance of the prostheses by utilizing the spatial properties of the fovea, selective stimulation is extremely difficult due to the stacking of RGCs in this area. Therefore, it is possible that the acuity of prosthetic vision for patients can only be restored to a certain limit.

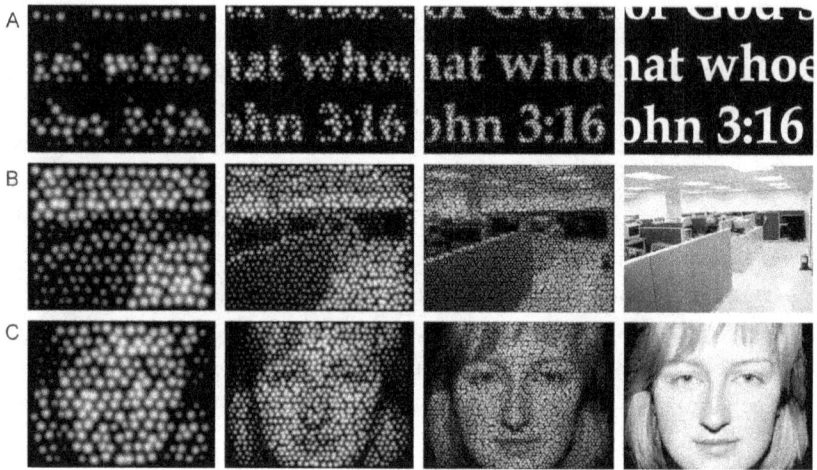

Fig. 7. Simulated vision of text (A), office scene (B), and face (C), with doubling of spatial detail from left to right, and the original image on the right [142]. (Reprinted from Vision Research, 49/19, S. C. Chen et al., Simulating prosthetic vision: II. Measuring functional capacity, Pages 2336, Copyright (2009), with permission from Elsevier.)

4.3. *Visual field*

Visual field is another equally important consideration for the spatial distribution of prosthetic vision. While current prostheses mostly focus on the central visual field, a larger visual field can cover the peripheral retina for better mobility and interaction with the environment, which also reduces the need of head scanning. Subretinal implants span less than 10 degrees of visual angle, due to the aforementioned risk of detaching the retina; current epiretinal devices cover up to 20 degrees of visual field, but size is limited by the incisions on the eye wall; suprachoroidal prosthesis have less surgical limitations, but still need to conform with the curvature of the eyeball.

To increase the visual field, wide field arrays (Fig. 8) for epiretinal prosthesis have been developed and tested in dummy and animal models [41, 144, 145]. Foldable arrays made of flexible polymer substrates can be inserted through the eye wall and then expand when in the eye. A visual field of approximately 35-40 degrees could be covered. Considering the different roles of center versus peripheral vision, the electrode sizes and densities in these two areas could be designed differently to accommodate engineering limitation of the device.

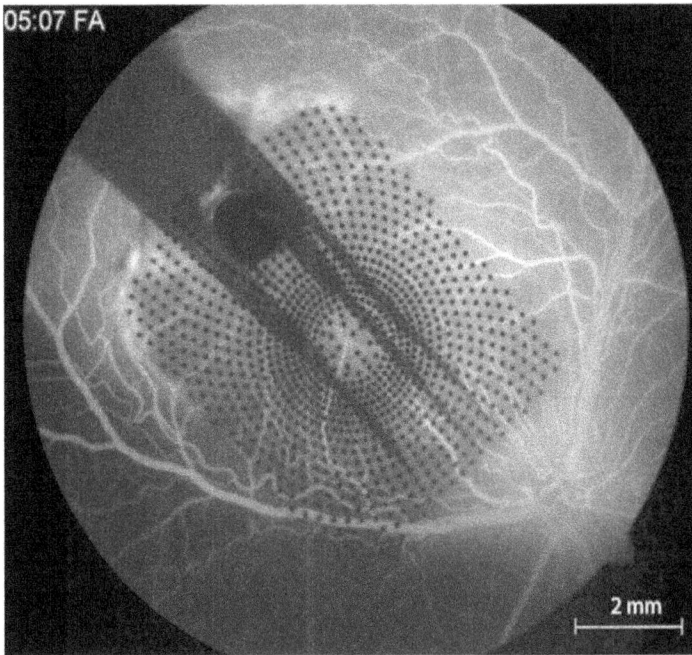

Fig. 8. A fundus image of a wide field array with biomimetic electrode spacing matching the local RGC density [41]. (Reprinted from Sensors and Actuators B: Chemical, 132/2, D. C. Rodger et al., Flexible parylene-based multielectrode array technology for high-density neural stimulation and recording, Pages 454, Copyright (2008), with permission from Elsevier.)

4.4. *Spatial and temporal activation patterns of retinal ganglion cells*

Electrical activation of the retina could recruit various cell types and result in different patterns of visual perception. RGCs could be directly stimulated via activation of their soma or axon, or indirectly activated by the synaptic connection of the inner retina (bipolar cells and amacrine cells). Direct activation of the RGC usually results in one action potential per stimulus pulse, which is time-locked with short (milliseconds) latency [27, 133, 134, 146]. Indirect stimulation via presynaptic retinal neurons generally results in a burst of spikes with longer (tens of milliseconds) and jittery latencies [146 - 150], resembling the response to light stimuli. Both types of activation come with their advantages and disadvantages.

RGCs can follow direct stimulation pulses at fairly high rates (200 Hz up to 500 Hz) with one action potential per pulse [146, 151 - 153], and therefore natural response may be evoked by encoding stimulus pulses to have the same temporal pattern as natural firing [57 - 59].

However, direct stimulation often results in axonal activation for epiretinal stimulation, as the axons are located between the ganglion cell body layer and the epiretinal electrode array. The activated axons convey information to the higher visual processing centers, which perceive them as if they originated from the ganglion cell somas further upstream (farther from the optic disk) of the stimulation site and results in irregular phosphenes shape [154, 155]. A model of ganglion cell axon layout on the fundus [156] and threshold measurements of ganglion cell somas and axons [25, 157] support this conclusion. And indeed, clinical studies with the Argus epiretinal prosthesis reveal that the phosphenes sometimes have irregular elongated shape instead of the ideal round ones depending on stimulation amplitude and electrode location (Fig. 9) [156]. This poses a challenge to provide the patients with a consistent good quality image of high resolution, especially for later generation devices with higher number of electrodes.

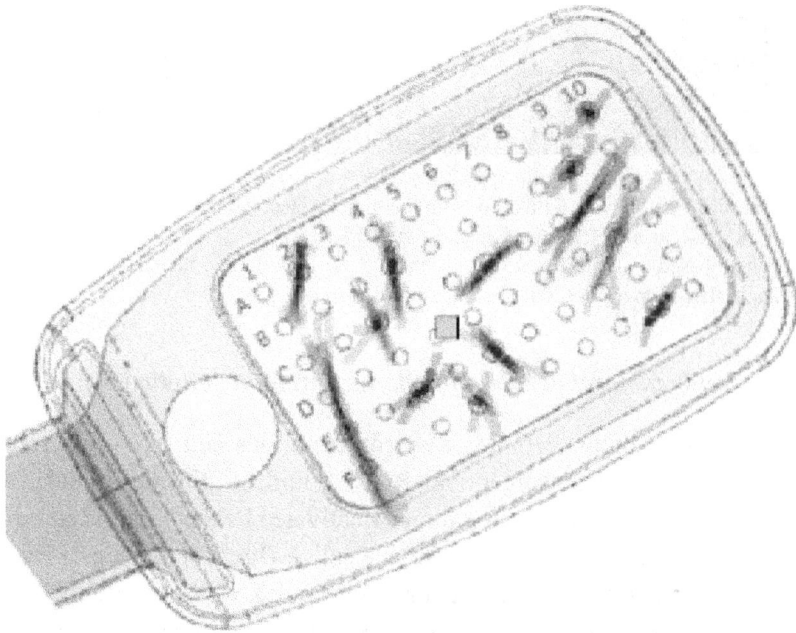

Fig. 9. Phosphenes (black shades) drawn by one Argus II subject, superimposed over the corresponding stimulation electrodes (circles) [156]. Many phosphenes are long streaks, while only a few have a relative round shapes. The square marks the approximate location of the fovea.

Indirect activation recruits some of the remaining neural processing mechanism in the inner retina, and therefore generates spiking pattern in RGCs that might better represent visual information. It reduces the burden to reproduce the natural responses directly in ganglion cells, and may produce better spatial resolution as the bipolar cell recruit only RGCs with direct connection and avoids the diffuse activation due to axonal stimulation.

However, indirect activation favor longer pulse widths and only follows lower frequency stimulation (< 10 Hz) as a result of different dynamic properties of cell membrane, synaptic transmission and ion channels in bipolar cells [25, 158, 159]. Therefore, indirect activation usually has a larger charge threshold as longer pulses typically require [25, 159, 160]. Also, indirect activation desensitizes with repetitive stimulation, for example starting when paired pulses are less than 400 ms apart and become significant when rate of pulse trains increase beyond 10 pulse/seconds [148, 151 - 153, 161]. This phenomenon is attributed to inhibition from amacrine cells and other unknown mechanisms. The desensitization limits the temporal resolution for indirect activation [27], and is thought to be the underlying reason for phosphene fading in human subjects such as those demonstrated by Argus II subjects [162]. Animal experiments [148] revealed two components to the fading—a fast component lasting hundreds of milliseconds, and a slow component lasting several seconds—and the results are in agreement with those observed in human subjects. In subretinal implants the natural micro-saccades of the eye prevent fading to some extent [110]. For epiretinal implants, fading of images can be counteracted by head movements, and the development of an intraocular camera for epiretinal prosthesis will allow saccadic eye movement to mitigate percept fading. Another approach to overcoming desensitization is to vary the stimulus from pulse to pulse, for example by varying the pulse width. Therefore the retina is exposed to a new type of stimulus for each pulse, and different neuron populations are recruited [163].

Direct and indirect response often co-exist, and epiretinal stimulation most likely activates RGCs and the inner retina simultaneously. Separating the two types of response can increase the selectivity of the stimulation, with a tradeoff between spatial and temporal properties of activation. Low frequency sinusoidal stimuli have been shown to preferentially activate the inner retina [164], and different pulse widths have been explored as a factor for avoiding axonal stimulation. Threshold maps of RGCs obtained by calcium fluorescence imaging of *in vitro* rat retinal preparation have shown that the threshold relationship of ganglion cell soma activation versus axonal activation differs with pulse width [25]. Longer stimulation pulse widths (over 16 milliseconds) activate the inner retina only, and are suggested as a potential solution to axonal stimulation.

The temporal resolution of a healthy human eye can range from about 15 Hz (rod-mediated scotopic vision) up to 50 Hz (cone-mediated photopic vision), depending on factors such as illumination, amplitude, adaption, and wavelength, etc. [165]. The temporal resolution in prosthetic implants is usually much lower (e.g. 5 to 20 Hz) compared to these numbers due to two factors. The electrical stimulation mediates membrane potentials of retinal neurons in a different manner compared to neurotransmitter release, and high amplitude stimulation may render retinal neurons unresponsive for a certain period of time. Also, repetitive electrical stimulation is required in order to form a meaningful visual stream in prosthesis users and to compensate for higher thresholds due to retinal degeneration as well.

4.5. *Color vision*

Given the relative large size of electrodes in contrast with the very small dimensions of the three types of cones and their associated color pathways, selective activation of specific color components is not possible with the current devices. In subretinal and suprachoroidal stimulation, each electrode will stimulate a large number of bipolar cells and rods (if there are any remaining), and patients typically report shades of gray [1].

In epiretinal prostheses, the electrode's proximity to the ganglion cells will result in stimulation of color-specific ganglion cell subtypes. Due to the processing of the inner retina to maximize information transmission to cortex, color presentation at the ganglion cell layer consists of opponent hues (red versus green and blue versus yellow). Therefore direct activation of ganglion cells could result in color sensation. Most of the phosphene colors reported by Argus II subjects were yellow or white, likely due to activation of many ganglion cells by a single electrode. However some Argus II subjects were able to perceive colored phosphenes including red, orange, yellow, green, blue, pink, gray, and white. The perceived color depended on the electrode activated, and stimulation parameters used, but results were repeatable [166]. Different colors could be perceived simultaneously [167], and phosphenes could appear darker than background [93, 162]. In the clinical study of the IMI prosthesis, phosphenes appeared in a wide range of colors [64]. White, yellow, and blue were the predominant ones, and red and green were rare. This could be a result of specific neuronal microcircuitry of blue-yellow ganglion cells [168].

While subjects sometimes could perceive color due to random factors in use, explicit color vision will remain a challenge for prosthetic vision.

4.6. *Effects of retinal degeneration*

Retinal degeneration causes significant change in retinal structure, cell density, morphology and physiology. Therefore, it is expected that the performance of the prosthesis is affected by the specific condition of each patient, such as type of RD and disease progression. In agreement with studies in human subjects [169, 170], most animal studies report that RD results in higher stimulation thresholds. For example, rat models of RD have revealed that as the density of surviving retinal neurons decreases, stimulation threshold increases and becomes higher than normal [171]. Results in mice show consistent increase in threshold [172, 173]. A recent study, however, found no significant difference between thresholds of RGCs in RD and normal rat retinas [174]. The use of small electrodes and explicit direct stimulation of RGC in this study suggests direct activation threshold of RGCs is not altered during RD, while threshold increase observed in earlier studies was due to threshold changes of the indirect stimulation via bipolar cells. Threshold mappings via calcium imaging have arrived at a similar conclusion [25]. Therefore, good coupling between the electrode and the retina and selective direct activation of RGCs could lower the stimulation threshold in prosthetic devices.

5. Conclusion

The past two decades have witnessed how retinal prostheses progressed from early concepts and translated from laboratory research through clinical trials to commercial approval. This great success of restoring partial vision through artificial means has demonstrated a feasible treatment for the blind affected by outer retinal degeneration. Hundreds to thousands of patients are expected to benefit with improved mobility and object localization in the near future.

Despite these great achievements, a great many of challenges remain to be solved. The research and development of retinal prostheses has been and will continue to be a highly interdisciplinary effort. At this time, a major goal is to improve the acuity and resolution of prosthetic vision, which is very limited and far from comparable with normal vision. Both acuity and resolution are expected to improve with relentless engineering improvement, which will allow a larger number of smaller and more tightly spaced stimulation electrodes. Also, smarter stimulation strategies based on research in neural electrophysiology will provide more focal and selective activation of the retina without invoking temporal desensitization.

Although there might be an ultimate limit of how much vision can be restored due to the retinal and cortical remodeling of the degenerative diseases, further improvements building on the encouraging achievements of current generation prosthetic devices should allow future patients to read readily and recognize faces and details of objects. With such optimistic and realistic projections, retinal prostheses have the potential to restore sufficient vision to blind patients allowing them to regain independence in their everyday lives.

References

1. E. Zrenner, Fighting blindness with microelectronics, *Sci. Transl. Med.*, **5**, no. 210, pp. 210ps16, 2013.

2. J. D. Weiland and M. S. Humayun, Retinalprosthesis, *IEEE Trans. Biomed. Eng.*, **61**, no. 5, pp. 1412–1424, 2014.

3. A. C. Weitz and J. D. Weiland, Visual prostheses, in *Neural Computation, Neural Devices, and Neural Prosthesis*, ed. Z. Yang (Springer, New York) 2014, pp. 157–188.

4. G. Dagnelie, Retinal implants: emergence of a multidisciplinary field, *Curr. Opin. Neurol.*, **25**, no. 1, pp. 67–75, 2012.

5. J. D. Weiland, A. K. Cho, and M. S. Humayun, Retinal prostheses: Current clinical results and future needs, *Ophthalmology*, **118**, no. 11, pp. 2227–2237, 2011.

6. J. D. Weiland, W. Liu, and M. S. Humayun, Retinal prosthesis, *Annu. Rev. Biomed. Eng.*, **7**, no. 1, pp. 361–401, 2005.

7. E. Margalit, M. Maia, J. D. Weiland, R. J. Greenberg, G. Y. Fujii, G. Torres, D. V. Piyathaisere, T. M. O'Hearn, W. Liu, G. Lazzi, G. Dagnelie, D. A. Scribner, E. de Juan, Jr., and M. S. Humayun, Retinal prosthesis for the blind, *Surv. Ophthalmol.*, **47**, no. 4, pp. 335–356, 2002.

8. L. Galvani, *De viribus electricitatis in motu musculari commentarius*. Bononiæ (Bologna): Ex Typographia Instituti Scientiarum, 1791.

9. G. Veratti, *Osservazioni fisico-mediche intorno alla elettricità*. Bologna: Lelio dalla Volpe, 1748.

10. C. LeRoy, O`u l'on rend compte de quelques tentatives que l'on a faites pour gu´erir plusieurs maladies par l'´electricit´e, *Hist Acad Roy Sci. Paris M´emoires Math Phys*, **60**, pp. 87–95, 1755.

11. O. Foerster, Beiträge zur pathophysiologie der sehbahn und der spehsphare, *J. Psychol. Neurol.*, pp. 435–363, 1929.

12. F. Krause and H. Schum, Die epileptischen Erkrankungen, *Neue Dtsch. Chir.*, **49**, pp. 482–486, 1931.

13. W. H. Dobelle, M. G. Mladejovsky, and J. P. Girvin, Artificial vision for the blind: electrical stimulation of visual cortex offers hope for a functional prosthesis, *Science*, **183**, no. 4123, pp. 440–444, 1974.

14. H. Karny, Clinical and physiological aspects of the cortical visual prosthesis, *Surv. Ophthalmol.*, **20**, no. 1, pp. 47–58, 1975.

15. E. M. Schmidt, M. J. Bak, F. T. Hambrecht, C. V. Kufta, D. K. O'Rourke, and P. Vallabhanath, Feasibility of a visual prosthesis for the blind based on intracortical micro stimulation of the visual cortex, *Brain*, **119**, no. 2, pp. 507–522, 1996.

16. G. S. Brindley and W. S. Lewin, The sensations produced by electrical stimulation of the visual cortex, *J. Physiol.*, **196**, no. 2, pp. 479–493, 1968.

17. S. Kotler, Vision Quest, *WIRED*, **10**, Sep. 2002.

18. M. Bak, J. P. Girvin, F. T. Hambrecht, C. V. Kufta, G. E. Loeb, and E. M. Schmidt, Visual sensations produced by intracortical microstimulation of the human occipital cortex, *Med. Biol. Eng. Comput.*, **28**, no. 3, pp. 257–259, 1990.

19. E. M. Maynard, Visual prostheses, *Annu. Rev. Biomed. Eng.*, **3**, no. 1, pp. 145–168, 2001.

20. X. Chai, L. Li, K. Wu, C. Zhou, P. Cao, and Q. Ren, C-Sight Visual prostheses for the blind, *IEEE Eng. Med. Biol. Mag.*, **27**, no. 5, pp. 20–28, 2008.

21. X. Fang, H. Sakaguchi, T. Fujikado, M. Osanai, Y. Ikuno, M. Kamei, M. Ohji, T. Yagi, and Y. Tano, Electrophysiological and histological studies of chronically implanted intrapapillary

microelectrodes in rabbit eyes, *Graefes Arch. Clin. Exp. Ophthalmol.*, **244**, no. 3, pp. 364–375, 2006.

22. C. Veraart, C. Raftopoulos, J. T. Mortimer, J. Delbeke, D. Pins, G. Michaux, A. Vanlierde, S. Parrini, and M.-C. Wanet-Defalque, Visual sensations produced by optic nerve stimulation using an implanted self-sizing spiral cuff electrode, *Brain Res.*, **813**, no. 1, pp. 181–186, 1998.

23. G. E. Tassicker, Retinal stimulator, US Patent 2,760,483, 28-Aug-1956.

24. J. F. Rizzo, D. B. Shire, S. K. Kelly, P. Troyk, M. Gingerich, B. McKee, A. Priplata, J. Chen, W. Drohan, P. Doyle, O. Mendoza, L. Theogarajan, S. F. Cogan, and J. L. Wyatt, Development of the boston retinal prosthesis, in *Engineering in Medicine and Biology Society, EMBC, 2011 Annual International Conference of the IEEE*, Boston, MA, 2011, pp. 7492–7495.

25. A. C. Weitz, D. Nanduri, M. R. Behrend, A. Gonzalez-Calle, R. J. Greenberg, M. S. Humayun, R. H. Chow, and J. D. Weiland, Improving the spatial resolution of epiretinal implants by increasing stimulus pulse duration, *Sci. Transl. Med.*, **7**, no. 318, pp. 318ra203, 2015.

26. S. I. Fried and R. J. Jensen, The response of retinal neurons to electrical stimulation: A summary of in vitro and in vivo animal studies, in *Visual Prosthetics*, ed. G. Dagnelie, (Springer US, New York) 2011, pp. 229–258.

27. D. K. Freeman, J. F. Rizzo, III, and S. I. Fried, Encoding visual information in retinal ganglion cells with prosthetic stimulation, *J. Neural Eng.*, **8**, no. 3, p. 035005, 2011.

28. M. R. Behrend, A. K. Ahuja, M. S. Humayun, R. H. Chow, and J. D. Weiland, Resolution of the epiretinal prosthesis is not limited by electrode size, *IEEE Trans. Neural Syst. Rehabil. Eng.*, **19**, no. 4, pp. 436–442, 2011.

29. D. Nanduri, I. Fine, A. Horsager, G. M. Boynton, M. S. Humayun, R. J. Greenberg, and J. D. Weiland, Frequency and amplitude modulation have different effects on the percepts elicited by retinal stimulation, *Invest. Ophthalmol. Vis. Sci.*, **53**, no. 1, pp. 205–214, 2012.

30. B. C. Basinger, A. P. Rowley, K. Chen, M. S. Humayun, and J. D. Weiland, Finite element modeling of retinal prosthesis mechanics, *J. Neural Eng.*, **6**, no. 5, p. 055006, 2009.

31. C. de Balthasar, S. Patel, A. Roy, R. Freda, S. Greenwald, A. Horsager, M. Mahadevappa, D. Yanai, M. J. McMahon, M. S. Humayun, R. J. Greenberg, J. D. Weiland, and I. Fine, Factors affecting perceptual thresholds in epiretinal prostheses, *Invest. Ophthalmol. Vis. Sci.*, **49**, no. 6, pp. 2303–2314, 2008.

32. M. S. Humayun, J. D. Dorn, L. da Cruz, G. Dagnelie, J.-A. Sahel, P. E. Stanga, A. V. Cideciyan, J. L. Duncan, D. Eliott, E. Filley, A. C. Ho, A. Santos, A. B. Safran, A. Arditi, L. V. Del Priore, and R. J. Greenberg, Interim results from the international trial of second sight's visual prosthesis, *Ophthalmology*, **119**, no. 4, pp. 779–788, 2012.

33. G. Rössler, T. Laube, C. Brockmann, T. Kirschkamp, B. Mazinani, M. Goertz, C. Koch, I. Krisch, B. Sellhaus, H. K. Trieu, J. Weis, N. Bornfeld, H. Röthgen, A. Messner, W. Mokwa, and P. Walter, Implantation and explantation of a wireless epiretinal retina implant device: Observations during the EPIRET3 prospective clinical trial, *Invest. Ophthalmol. Vis. Sci.*, **50**, no. 6, pp. 3003–3008, 2009.

34. E. Zrenner, List of retinal implants: Developments in electronic visual prosthetics (as of 05-12-2013). Institute for Ophthalmic Research Tuebingen (http://www.eye-tuebingen.de/zrenner/retimplantlist/), 2013.

35. R. R. Lakhanpal, D. Yanai, J. D. Weiland, G. Y. Fujii, S. Caffey, R. J. Greenberg, E. de Juan, and M. S. Humayun, Advances in the development of visual prostheses, *Curr. Opin. Ophthalmol.*, **14**, no. 3, pp. 122–127, 2003.

36. E. Zrenner, A. Stett, S. Weiss, R. B. Aramant, E. Guenther, K. Kohler, K.-D. Miliczek, M. J. Seiler, and H. Haemmerle, Can subretinal microphotodiodes successfully replace degenerated photoreceptors?, *Vision Res.*, **39**, no. 15, pp. 2555–2567, 1999.

37. H. Sakaguchi, T. Fujikado, X. Fang, H. Kanda, M. Osanai, K. Nakauchi, Y. Ikuno, M. Kamei, T. Yagi, S. Nishimura, M. Ohji, T. Yagi, and Y. Tano, Transretinal electrical stimulation with a suprachoroidal multichannel electrode in rabbit eyes, *Jpn. J. Ophthalmol.*, **48**, no. 3, pp. 256–261, 2004.

38. T. Fujikado, M. Kamei, H. Sakaguchi, H. Kanda, T. Morimoto, Y. Ikuno, K. Nishida, H. Kishima, T. Maruo, K. Konoma, M. Ozawa, and K. Nishida, Testing of semichronically implanted retinal prosthesis by suprachoroidal-transretinal stimulation in patients with retinitis pigmentosa, *Invest. Ophthalmol. Vis. Sci.*, **52**, no. 7, pp. 4726–4733, 2011.

39. L. N. Ayton, R. H. Guymer, and C. D. Luu, Choroidal thickness profiles in retinitis pigmentosa, *Clin. Experiment. Ophthalmol.*, **41**, no. 4, pp. 396–403, 2013.

40. D. Palanker, A. Vankov, P. Huie, and S. Baccus, Design of a high-resolution optoelectronic retinal prosthesis, *J. Neural Eng.*, **2**, no. 1, pp. S105–S120, 2005.

41. D. C. Rodger, A. J. Fong, W. Li, H. Ameri, A. K. Ahuja, C. Gutierrez, I. Lavrov, H. Zhong, P. R. Menon, E. Meng, J. W. Burdick, R. R. Roy, V. R. Edgerton, J. D. Weiland, M. S. Humayun, and Y.-C. Tai, Flexible parylene-based multielectrode array technology for high-density neural stimulation and recording, *Sens. Actuators B Chem.*, **132**, no. 2, pp. 449–460, 2008.

42. D. D. Zhou and R. J. Greenberg, Microelectronic visual prostheses, in *Implantable Neural Prostheses 1*, eds. E. Greenbaum and D. Zhou, (Springer, New York), 2009, pp. 1–42.

43. A. Y. Chow, V. Y. Chow, K. H. Packo, J. S. Pollack, G. A. Peyman, and R. Schuchard, The artificial silicon retina microchip for the treatment of vision loss from retinitis pigmentosa, *Arch. Ophthalmol.*, **122**, no. 4, pp. 460–469, 2004.

44. G. Jiang and D. D. Zhou, Technology advances and challenges in hermetic packaging for implantable medical devices, in *Implantable Neural Prostheses 2*, eds. D. Zhou and E. Greenbaum, (Springer, New York), 2009, pp. 27–61.

45. E. C. Gill, J. Antalek, F. M. Kimock, P. J. Nasiatka, B. P. McIntosh, A. R. J. Tanguay, and J. D. Weiland, High-density feedthrough technology for hermetic biomedical micropackaging, in *Symposium SS – Bioelectronics—Materials, Interfaces and Applications*, 2013, 1572.

46. D. V. Piyathaisere, E. Margalit, S.-J. Chen, J.-S. Shyu, S. A. D'Anna, J. D. Weiland, R. R. Grebe, L. Grebe, G. Fujii, S. Y. Kim, R. J. Greenberg, E. De Juan, and M. S. Humayun, Heat effects on the retina, *Ophthalmic Surg. Lasers Imaging*, **34**, no. 2, pp. 114–20, 2003.

47. K. Stingl, K. U. Bartz-Schmidt, D. Besch, A. Braun, A. Bruckmann, F. Gekeler, U. Greppmaier, S. Hipp, G. Hörtdörfer, C. Kernstock, A. Koitschev, A. Kusnyerik, H. Sachs, A. Schatz, K. T. Stingl, T. Peters, B. Wilhelm, and E. Zrenner, Artificial vision with wirelessly powered subretinal electronic implant alpha-IMS, *Proc. R. Soc. B Biol. Sci.*, **280**, no. 1757, p. 20130077, 2013.

48. J. F. Rizzo, L. Snebold, and M. Kenney, Development of a visual prosthesis - a review of the field and an overview of the boston retinal implant project, in *Visual Prosthesis and Ophthalmic Devices: New Hope in Sight*, eds. J. Tombran-Tink, C. J. Barnstable, and J. F. Rizzo, (Springer, New York) 2007, pp. 71–93.

49. K. Chen, Z. Yang, L. Hoang, J. Weiland, M. Humayun, and W. Liu, An integrated 256-channel epiretinal prosthesis, *IEEE J. Solid-State Circuits*, **45**, no. 9, pp. 1946–1956, 2010.

50. N. Tran, S. Bai, J. Yang, H. Chun, O. Kavehei, Y. Yang, V. Muktamath, D. Ng, H. Meffin, M. Halpern, and E. Skafidas, A complete 256-electrode retinal prosthesis chip, *IEEE J. Solid-State Circuits*, **49**, no. 3, pp. 751–765, 2014.

51. N. R. B. Stiles, B. P. McIntosh, P. J. Nasiatka, M. C. Hauer, J. D. Weiland, M. S. Humayun, and A. R. Tanguay, Jr., An intraocular camera for retinal prostheses: Restoring sight to the blind., in *Optical Processes In Microparticles And Nanostructures: A Festschrift Dedicated to Richard Kounai Chang on His Retirement from Yale University*, 6, eds. A. Serpengüzel and A. W. Poon (World Scientific Publishing Co. Pte. Ltd., Singapore) 2011, pp. 385–429.

52. M. S. Humayun, J. D. Weiland, B. Justus, C. Merrit, John J. Whalen, D. V. Piyathaisere, S. J. Chen, E. Margalit, G. Y. Fujii, R. J. Greenberg, E. de Juan, Jr., D. Scribner, and W. Liu, Towards a completely implantable, light-sensitive intraocular retinal prosthesis, in *Engineering in Medicine and Biology Society, 2001. Proceedings of the 23rd Annual International Conference of the IEEE*, Istanbul, Turkey, 2001, 4, pp. 3422–3425.

53. S. C. Chen, G. J. Suaning, J. W. Morley, and N. H. Lovell, Simulating prosthetic vision: I. Visual models of phosphenes, *Vision Res.*, **49**, no. 12, pp. 1493–1506, 2009.

54. J. J. van Rheede, C. Kennard, and S. L. Hicks, Simulating prosthetic vision: Optimizing the information content of a limited visual display, *J. Vis.*, **10**, no. 14, pp. 32, 1–15, 2010.

55. L. E. Hallum, S. L. Cloherty, and N. H. Lovell, Image analysis for microelectronic retinal prosthesis, *IEEE Trans. Biomed. Eng.*, **55**, no. 1, pp. 344–346, 2008.

56. N. Parikh, L. Itti, M. S. Humayun, and J. D. Weiland, Performance of visually guided tasks using simulated prosthetic vision and saliency-based cues, *J. Neural Eng.*, **10**, no. 2, p. 026017, 2013.

57. R. Eckmiller, D. Neumann, and O. Baruth, Tunable retina encoders for retina implants: why and how, *J. Neural Eng.*, **2**, no. 1, pp. S91–S104, 2005.

58. L. H. Jepson, P. Hottowy, G. A. Weiner, W. Dabrowski, A. M. Litke, and E. J. Chichilnisky, High-fidelity reproduction of spatiotemporal visual signals for retinal prosthesis, *Neuron*, **83**, no. 1, pp. 87–92, 2014.

59. S. Nirenberg and C. Pandarinath, Retinal prosthetic strategy with the capacity to restore normal vision, *Proc. Natl. Acad. Sci.*, **109**, no. 37, pp. 15012–15017, 2012.

60. D. R. Merrill, M. Bikson, and J. G. R. Jefferys, Electrical stimulation of excitable tissue: design of efficacious and safe protocols, *J. Neurosci. Methods*, **141**, no. 2, pp. 171–198, 2005.

61. D. McCreery, A. Lossinsky, V. Pikov, and X. Liu, Microelectrode array for chronic deep-brain microstimulation and recording, *IEEE Trans. Biomed. Eng.*, **53**, no. 4, pp. 726–737, 2006.

62. M. Schaldach, M. Hubmann, A. Weikl, and R. Hardt, Sputter-deposited TiN electrode coatings for superior sensing and pacing performance, *Pacing Clin. Electrophysiol.*, **13**, no. 12, pp. 1891–1895, 1990.

63. X. T. Cui and D. D. Zhou, Poly (3,4-Ethylenedioxythiophene) for chronic neural stimulation, *IEEE Trans. Neural Syst. Rehabil. Eng.*, **15**, no. 4, pp. 502–508, 2007.

64. R. Hornig, T. Zehnder, M. Velikay-Parel, T. Laube, M. Feucht, and G. Richard, The IMI retinal implant system, in *Artificial Sight: Basic Research, Biomedical Engineering, and Clinical Advances*, eds. M. S. Humayun, J. D. Weiland, G. Chader, E. Greenbaum, (Springer, New York) 2007, pp. 111–128.

65. L. Colodetti, J. D. Weiland, S. Colodetti, A. Ray, M. J. Seiler, D. R. Hinton, and M. S. Humayun, Pathology of damaging electrical stimulation in the retina, *Exp. Eye Res.*, **85**, no. 1, pp. 23–33, 2007.

66. A. Ray, L. Colodetti, J. D. Weiland, D. R. Hinton, M. S. Humayun, and E.-J. Lee, Immunocytochemical analysis of retinal neurons under electrical stimulation, *Brain Res.*, **1255**, pp. 89–97, 2009.

67. D. V. Piyathaisere, E. Margalit, S. J. Chen, J.-S. Shyu, S. A. D'Anna, M. S. Humayun, J. D. Weiland, R. R. Grebe, L. Grebe, and S. Y. Kim, Effects of short-term exposure to heat on the retina, *Invest. Ophthalmol. Vis. Sci.*, **42**, no. 2, p. S814, 2001.

68. D. B. McCreery, W. F. Agnew, T. G. H. Yuen, and L. Bullara, Charge density and charge per phase as cofactors in neural injury induced by electrical stimulation, *IEEE Trans. Biomed. Eng.*, **37**, no. 10, pp. 996–1001, 1990.

69. R. V. Shannon, A model of safe levels for electrical stimulation, *IEEE Trans. Biomed. Eng.*, **39**, no. 4, pp. 424–426, 1992.

70. A. Petrossians, J. J. Whalen, J. D. Weiland, and F. Mansfeld, Electrodeposition and characterization of thin-film platinum-iridium alloys for biological interfaces, *J. Electrochem. Soc.*, **158**, no. 5, pp. D269–D276, 2011.

71. A. Petrossians, N. Davuluri, J. J. Whalen, F. Mansfeld, and J. D. Weiland, Improved biphasic pulsing power efficiency with Pt-Ir coated microelectrodes, *MRS Proc.*, **1621**, pp. 249–257, 2014.

72. B. Wessling, W. Mokwa, and U. Schnakenberg, Sputtered Ir films evaluated for electrochemical performance I. Experimental results, *J. Electrochem. Soc.*, **155**, no. 5, pp. F61–F65, 2008.

73. J. C. Lilly, Injury and excitation by electric currents, in *Electrical Stimulation of the Brain*, (University of Texas Press ,Austin), 1961, pp. 60–64.

74. J.-J. Sit and R. Sarpeshkar, A low-power blocking-capacitor-free charge-balanced electrode-stimulator chip with less than 6 nA DC error for 1-mA full-scale stimulation, *IEEE Trans. Biomed. Circuits Syst.*, **1**, no. 3, pp. 172–183, 2007.

75. A. Krishnan and S. K. Kelly, On the cause and control of residual voltage generated by electrical stimulation of neural tissue, in *Engineering in Medicine and Biology Society (EMBC), 2012 Annual International Conference of the IEEE*, San Diego, CA, USA, 2012, pp. 3899–3902.

76. L. Teixeira, C. Rodrigues, and C. Prior, A charge-redistribution based controller for keeping charge balance in neural stimulation, in *2015 IEEE 58th International Midwest Symposium on Circuits and Systems (MWSCAS)*, 2015, pp. 1–4.

77. A. Ray, L. L. H. Chan, A. Gonzalez, M. S. Humayun, and J. D. Weiland, Impedance as a method to sense proximity at the electrode-retina interface, *IEEE Trans. Neural Syst. Rehabil. Eng.*, 19, no. 6, pp. 696–699, Dec. 2011.

78. A. Mercanzini, P. Colin, J.-C. Bensadoun, A. Bertsch, and P. Renaud, In vivo electrical impedance spectroscopy of tissue reaction to microelectrode arrays, *IEEE Trans. Biomed. Eng.*, **56**, no. 7, pp. 1909–1918, 2009.

79. A. C. Weitz, M. R. Behrend, M. S. Humayun, R. H. Chow, and J. D. Weiland, Interphase gap decreases electrical stimulation threshold of retinal ganglion cells, in *Engineering in Medicine and Biology Society, EMBC, 2011 Annual International Conference of the IEEE*, Boston, MA, 2011, pp. 6725–6728.

80. D. R. Cantrell and J. B. Troy, Extracellular stimulation of mouse retinal ganglion cells with non-rectangular voltage-controlled waveforms, in *Engineering in Medicine and Biology Society, 2009. EMBC 2009. Annual International Conference of the IEEE*, Minneapolis, MN, USA, 2009, pp. 642–645.

81. T. J. Foutz and C. C. McIntyre, Evaluation of novel stimulus waveforms for deep brain stimulation, *J. Neural Eng.*, **7**, no. 6, p. 066008, 2010.

82. A. Wongsarnpigoon, J. P. Woock, and W. M. Grill, Efficiency analysis of waveform shape for electrical excitation of nerve fibers, *IEEE Trans. Neural Syst. Rehabil. Eng.*, **18**, no. 3, pp. 319–328, 2010.

83. W. M. Grill and J. T. Mortimer, Inversion of the current-distance relationship by transient depolarization, *IEEE Trans. Biomed. Eng.*, **44**, no. 1, pp. 1–9, 1997.

84. G. Jiang, D. Mishler, R. Davis, J. P. Mobley, and J. H. Schulman, Zirconia to Ti-6Al-4V braze joint for implantable biomedical device, *J. Biomed. Mater. Res. B Appl. Biomater.*, **72B**, no. 2, pp. 316–321, 2005.

85. J. Ordonez, P. Dautel, M. Schuettler, and T. Stieglitz, Hermetic glass soldered micro-packages for a vision prosthesis, in *Engineering in Medicine and Biology Society (EMBC), 2012 Annual International Conference of the IEEE*, San Diego, CA, USA, 2012, pp. 2784–2787.

86. J. D. Weiland, F. M. Kimock, J. E. Yehoda, E. Gill, B. P. McIntosh, P. J. Nasiatka, and A. R. Tanguay, Chip-scale packaging for bioelectronic implants, in *2013 6th International IEEE/EMBS Conference on Neural Engineering (NER)*, 2013, pp. 931–936.

87. A. E. Hadjinicolaou, R. T. Leung, D. J. Garrett, K. Ganesan, K. Fox, D. A. X. Nayagam, M. N. Shivdasani, H. Meffin, M. R. Ibbotson, S. Prawer, and B. J. O'Brien, Electrical stimulation of retinal ganglion cells with diamond and the development of an all diamond retinal prosthesis, *Biomaterials*, **33**, no. 24, pp. 5812–5820, 2012.

88. X. Xiao, J. Wang, C. Liu, J. A. Carlisle, B. Mech, R. Greenberg, D. Guven, R. Freda, M. S. Humayun, J. D. Weiland, and O. Auciello, In vitro and in vivo evaluation of ultrananocrystalline diamond for coating of implantable retinal microchips, *J. Biomed. Mater. Res. B Appl. Biomater.*, **77B**, no. 2, pp. 273–281, 2006.

89. S. F. Cogan, D. J. Edell, A. A. Guzelian, Y. Ping Liu, and R. Edell, Plasma-enhanced chemical vapor deposited silicon carbide as an implantable dielectric coating, *J. Biomed. Mater. Res. A*, **67A**, no. 3, pp. 856–867, 2003.

90. A. Sharma, L. Rieth, P. Tathireddy, R. Harrison, H. Oppermann, M. Klein, M. Töpper, E. Jung, R. Normann, G. Clark, and F. Solzbacher, Evaluation of the packaging and encapsulation reliability in fully integrated, fully wireless 100 channel Utah Slant Electrode Array (USEA): Implications for long term functionality, *Sens. Actuators Phys.*, **188**, pp. 167–172, 2012.

91. M. S. Humayun, J. D. Weiland, G. Y. Fujii, R. Greenberg, R. Williamson, J. Little, B. Mech, V. Cimmarusti, G. Van Boemel, G. Dagnelie, and E. de Juan, Jr., Visual perception in a blind subject with a chronic microelectronic retinal prosthesis, *Vision Res.*, **43**, no. 24, pp. 2573–2581, 2003.

92. D. Yanai, J. D. Weiland, M. Mahadevappa, R. J. Greenberg, I. Fine, and M. S. Humayun, Visual performance using a retinal prosthesis in three subjects with retinitis pigmentosa, *Am. J. Ophthalmol.*, **143**, no. 5, pp. 820–827.e2, 2007.

93. A. Horsager, S. H. Greenwald, J. D. Weiland, M. S. Humayun, R. J. Greenberg, M. J. McMahon, G. M. Boynton, and I. Fine, Predicting visual sensitivity in retinal prosthesis patients, *Invest. Ophthalmol. Vis. Sci.*, **50**, no. 4, pp. 1483–1491, 2009.

94. D. Nanduri, M. S. Humayun, R. J. Greenberg, M. J. McMahon, and J. D. Weiland, Retinal prosthesis phosphene shape analysis, in *Engineering in Medicine and Biology Society, 2008. EMBS 2008. 30th Annual International Conference of the IEEE*, Vancouver, Canada, 2008, pp. 1785–1788.

95. S. H. Greenwald, A. Horsager, M. S. Humayun, R. J. Greenberg, M. J. McMahon, and I. Fine, Brightness as a function of current amplitude in human retinal electrical stimulation, *Invest. Ophthalmol. Vis. Sci.*, **50**, no. 11, pp. 5017–5025, 2009.

96. A. Capsi, J. D. Dorn, K. H. McClure, M. S. Humayun, R. J. Greenberg, and M. J. McMahon, Feasibility study of a retinal prosthesis: Spatial vision with a 16-electrode implant, *Arch. Ophthalmol.*, **127**, no. 4, pp. 398–401, 2009.

97. L. Yue, P. Falabella, P. Christopher, V. Wuyyuru, J. Dorn, P. Schor, R. J. Greenberg, J. D. Weiland, and M. S. Humayun, Ten-year follow-up of a blind patient chronically implanted with epiretinal prosthesis Argus I, *Ophthalmology*, in press.

98. D. D. Zhou, J. D. Dorn, and R. J. Greenberg, The Argus® II retinal prosthesis system: An overview, in *Multimedia and Expo Workshops (ICMEW), 2013 IEEE International Conference on*, San Jose, CA , USA, 2013, pp. 1–6.

99. J. D. Dorn, A. K. Ahuja, A. Caspi, L. da Cruz, G. Dagnelie, J. A. Sahel, R. J. Greenberg, M. J. McMahon, and Argus II Study Group, The detection of motion by blind subjects with the epiretinal 60-electrode (Argus II) retinal prosthesis, *JAMA Ophthalmol.*, **131**, no. 2, pp. 183–189, 2013.

100. A. K. Ahuja, J. D. Dorn, A. Caspi, M. J. McMahon, G. Dagnelie, L. DaCruz, P. E. Stanga, M. S. Humayun, R. J. Greenberg, and Argus II Study Group, Blind subjects implanted with the Argus II retinal prosthesis are able to improve performance in a spatial-motor task, *Br. J. Ophthalmol.*, **95**, no. 4, pp. 539–543, 2011.

101. L. da Cruz, B. F. Coley, J. Dorn, F. Merlini, E. Filley, P. Christopher, F. K. Chen, V. Wuyyuru, J. Sahel, P. Stanga, M. Humayun, R. J. Greenberg, and G. Dagnelie, The Argus II epiretinal prosthesis system allows letter and word reading and long-term function in patients with profound vision loss, *Br. J. Ophthalmol.*, **97**, pp. 632-636, 2013.

102. A. Vaidya, E. Borgonovi, R. S. Taylor, J.-A. Sahel, S. Rizzo, P. E. Stanga, A. Kukreja, and P. Walter, The cost-effectiveness of the Argus II retinal prosthesis in Retinitis Pigmentosa patients, *BMC Ophthalmol.*, **14**, p. 49, 2014.

103. M. Keserü, M. Feucht, N. Bornfeld, T. Laube, P. Walter, G. Rössler, M. Velikay-Parel, R. Hornig, and G. Richard, Acute electrical stimulation of the human retina with an epiretinal electrode array, *Acta Ophthalmol. (Copenh.)*, **90**, no. 1, pp. e1–e8, 2012.

104. S. Klauke, M. Goertz, S. Rein, D. Hoehl, U. Thomas, R. Eckhorn, F. Bremmer, and T. Wachtler, Stimulation with a wireless intraocular epiretinal implant elicits visual percepts in blind humans, *Invest. Ophthalmol. Vis. Sci.*, **52**, no. 1, pp. 449–455, 2011.

105. P. J. DeMarco, G. L. Yarbrough, C. W. Yee, G. Y. McLean, B. T. Sagdullaev, S. L. Ball, and M. A. McCall, Stimulation via a subretinally placed prosthetic elicits central activity and induces a trophic effect on visual responses, *Invest. Ophthalmol. Vis. Sci.*, **48**, no. 2, pp. 916–926, 2007.

106. M. T. Pardue, M. J. Phillips, H. Yin, A. Fernandes, Y. Cheng, A. Y. Chow, and S. L. Ball, Possible sources of neuroprotection following subretinal silicon chip implantation in RCS rats, *J. Neural Eng.*, **2**, no. 1, pp. S39–S47, 2005.

107. A. Y. Chow, Retinal prostheses Development in retinitis pigmentosa patients—progress and comparison, *Asia-Pac. J. Ophthalmol.*, **2**, no. 4, pp. 253–268, 2013.

108. A. Y. Chow, A. K. Bittner, and M. T. Pardue, The artificial silicon retina in retinitis pigmentosa patients, *Trans. Am. Ophthalmol. Soc.*, **108**, p. 120, 2010.

109. D. Besch, H. Sachs, P. Szurman, D. Gülicher, R. Wilke, S. Reinert, E. Zrenner, K. U. Bartz-Schmidt, and F. Gekeler, Extraocular surgery for implantation of an active subretinal visual prosthesis with external connections: feasibility and outcome in seven patients, *Br. J. Ophthalmol.*, **92**, no. 10, pp. 1361–1368, 2008.

110. E. Zrenner, K. U. Bartz-Schmidt, H. Benav, D. Besch, A. Bruckmann, V.-P. Gabel, F. Gekeler, U. Greppmaier, A. Harscher, S. Kibbel, J. Koch, A. Kusnyerik, T. Peters, K. Stingl, H. Sachs, A. Stett, P. Szurman, B. Wilhelm, and R. Wilke, Subretinal electronic chips allow blind patients to read letters and combine them to words, *Proc. R. Soc. B Biol. Sci.*, **278**, no. 1711, pp. 1489–1497, 2011.

111. A. Kusnyerik, U. Greppmaier, R. Wilke, F. Gekeler, B. Wilhelm, H. G. Sachs, K. U. Bartz-Schmidt, U. Klose, K. Stingl, M. D. Resch, A. Hekmat, A. Bruckmann, K. Karacs, J. Nemeth, I. Suveges, and E. Zrenner, Positioning of electronic subretinal implants in blind retinitis pigmentosa patients through multimodal assessment of retinal structures, *Invest. Ophthalmol. Vis. Sci.*, **53**, no. 7, pp. 3748–3755, 2012.

112. S. K. Kelly, D. B. Shire, J. Chen, M. D. Gingerich, S. F. Cogan, W. A. Drohan, W. Ellersick, A. Krishnan, S. Behan, J. L. Wyatt, and J. F. Rizzo, III, Developments on the Boston 256-channel retinal implant, in *Multimedia and Expo Workshops (ICMEW), 2013 IEEE International Conference on*, San Jose, CA , USA, 2013, pp. 1–6.

113. D. Palanker, A. Vankov, P. Huie, A. Butterwick, I. Chan, M. F. Marmor, and M. S. Blumenkranz, High-resolution opto-electronic retinal prosthesis: physical limitations and design, in *Artificial Sight*, eds. M. S. Humayun, J. D. Weiland, G. Chader, and E. Greenbaum, (Springer New York), 2007, pp. 255–277.

114. T. Fujikado, M. Kamei, H. Sakaguchi, H. Kanda, T. Morimoto, Y. Ikuno, K. Nishida, H. Kishima, T. Maruo, H. Sawai, T. Miyoshi, K. Osawa, and M. Ozawa, Clinical trial of chronic implantation of suprachoroidal-transretinal stimulation system for retinal prosthesis, *Sens. Mater.*, **24**, no. 4, pp. 181–187, 2012.

115. J. Villalobos, P. J. Allen, M. F. McCombe, M. Ulaganathan, E. Zamir, D. C. Ng, R. K. Shepherd, and C. E. Williams, Development of a surgical approach for a wide-view suprachoroidal retinal prosthesis: evaluation of implantation trauma, *Graefes Arch. Clin. Exp. Ophthalmol.*, **250**, no. 3, pp. 399–407, 2012.

116. J. Villalobos, D. A. X. Nayagam, P. J. Allen, P. McKelvie, C. D. Luu, L. N. Ayton, A. L. Freemantle, M. McPhedran, M. Basa, C. C. McGowan, R. K. Shepherd, and C. E. Williams, A wide-field suprachoroidal retinal prosthesis is stable and well tolerated following chronic implantation, *Invest. Ophthalmol. Vis. Sci.*, **54**, no. 5, pp. 3751–3762, 2013.

117. D. A. X. Nayagam, R. A. Williams, P. J. Allen, M. N. Shivdasani, C. D. Luu, C. M. Salinas-LaRosa, S. Finch, L. N. Ayton, A. L. Saunders, M. McPhedran, C. McGowan, J. Villalobos, J. B. Fallon, A. K. Wise, J. Yeoh, J. Xu, H. Feng, R. Millard, M. McWade, P. C. Thien, C. E. Williams, and R. K. Shepherd, Chronic electrical stimulation with a suprachoroidal retinal prosthesis: A preclinical safety and efficacy study, *PLoS ONE*, **9**, no. 5, p. e97182, 2014.

118. L. N. Ayton, P. J. Blamey, N. C. Sinclair, M. N. Shivdasani, M. A. Petoe, C. McCarthy, N. Barnes, P. J. Allen, C. D. Luu, and R. H. Guymer, Preliminary results of the bionic vision australia suprachoroidal visual prosthesis pilot trial, *Invest. Ophthalmol. Vis. Sci.*, **55**, no. 13, pp. 1813–1813, 2014.

119. R. Wilke, V.-P. Gabel, H. Sachs, K.-U. B. Schmidt, F. Gekeler, D. Besch, P. Szurman, A. Stett, B. Wilhelm, T. Peters, A. Harscher, U. Greppmaier, S. Kibbel, H. Benav, A. Bruckmann, K. Stingl, A. Kusnyerik, and E. Zrenner, Spatial resolution and perception of patterns mediated by a subretinal 16-electrode array in patients blinded by hereditary retinal dystrophies, *Invest. Ophthalmol. Vis. Sci.*, **52**, no. 8, pp. 5995–6003, 2011.

120. R. G. H. Wilke, G. K. Moghadam, N. H. Lovell, G. J. Suaning, and S. Dokos, Electric crosstalk impairs spatial resolution of multi-electrode arrays in retinal implants, *J. Neural Eng.*, **8**, no. 4, p. 046016, 2011.

121. A. Horsager, R. J. Greenberg, and I. Fine, Spatiotemporal interactions in retinal prosthesis subjects, *Invest. Ophthalmol. Vis. Sci.*, **51**, no. 2, pp. 1223–1233, 2010.

122. A. Horsager, G. M. Boynton, R. J. Greenberg, and I. Fine, Temporal interactions during paired-electrode stimulation in two retinal prosthesis subjects, *Invest. Ophthalmol. Vis. Sci.*, **52**, no. 1, pp. 549–557, 2011.

123. N. Tran, M. Halpern, S. Bai, and E. Skafidas, Crosstalk current measurements using multi-electrode arrays in saline, in *Engineering in Medicine and Biology Society (EMBC), 2012 Annual International Conference of the IEEE*, San Diego, CA, USA, 2012, pp. 3021–3024.

124. H. Kasi, A. Bertsch, J.-L. Guyomard, B. Kolomiets, S. Picaud, M. Pelizzone, and P. Renaud, Simulations to study spatial extent of stimulation and effect of electrode–tissue gap in subretinal implants, *Med. Eng. Phys.*, **33**, no. 6, pp. 755–763, 2011.

125. H. Kasi, W. Hasenkamp, G. Cosendai, A. Bertsch, and P. Renaud, Simulation of epiretinal prostheses - Evaluation of geometrical factors affecting stimulation thresholds, *J. NeuroEngineering Rehabil.*, **8**, no. 1, p. 44, 2011.

126. G. S. Brindley, The passive electrical properties of the frog's retina, choroid and sclera for radial fields and currents, *J. Physiol.*, **134**, no. 2, pp. 339–352, 1956.

127. H. Heynen and D. van Norren, Origin of the electroretinogram in the intact macaque eye—II: Current source-density analysis, *Vision Res.*, **25**, no. 5, pp. 709–715, 1985.

128. T. E. Ogden and H. Ito, Avian retina. II. An evaluation of retinal electrical anisotropy, *J. Neurophysiol.*, **34**, no. 3, pp. 367–373, 1971.

129. E. L. Berson, Retinitis pigmentosa. The Friedenwald Lecture, *Invest. Ophthalmol. Vis. Sci.*, **34**, no. 5, pp. 1659–1676, 1993.

130. S. Shah, A. Hines, D. Zhou, R. J. Greenberg, M. S. Humayun, and J. D. Weiland, Electrical properties of retinal–electrode interface, *J. Neural Eng.*, **4**, no. 1, pp. S24–S29, 2007.

131. G. J. Chader, J. D. Weiland, M. S. Humayun, J. Verhaagen, E. M. Hol, I. Huitenga, J. Wijnholds, A. B. Bergen, Gerald J. Boer, and D. F. Swaab, Artificial vision: needs, functioning, and testing of a retinal electronic prosthesis, in *Progress in Brain Research*, **175**, Elsevier, 2009, pp. 317–332.

132. H. C. Stronks and G. Dagnelie, The functional performance of the Argus II retinal prosthesis, *Expert Rev. Med. Devices*, **11**, no. 1, pp. 23–30, 2014.

133. L. H. Jepson, P. Hottowy, K. Mathieson, D. E. Gunning, W. Dąbrowski, A. M. Litke, and E. J. Chichilnisky, Focal electrical stimulation of major ganglion cell types in the primate retina for the design of visual prostheses, *J. Neurosci.*, **33**, no. 17, pp. 7194–7205, 2013.

134. C. Sekirnjak, P. Hottowy, A. Sher, W. Dabrowski, A. M. Litke, and E. J. Chichilnisky, High-resolution electrical stimulation of primate retina for epiretinal implant design, *J. Neurosci.*, **28**, no. 17, pp. 4446–4456, 2008.

135. L. H. Jepson, P. Hottowy, K. Mathieson, D. E. Gunning, W. Dąbrowski, A. M. Litke, and E. J. Chichilnisky, Spatially patterned electrical stimulation to enhance resolution of retinal prostheses, *J. Neurosci.*, **34**, no. 14, pp. 4871–4881, 2014.

136. K. Cha, K. W. Horch, and R. A. Normann, Mobility performance with a pixelized vision system, *Vision Res.*, **32**, no. 7, pp. 1367–1372, 1992.

137. K. Cha, K. W. Horch, and R. A. Normann, Simulation of a phosphene-based visual field: Visual acuity in a pixelized vision system, *Ann. Biomed. Eng.*, **20**, no. 4, pp. 439–449, 1992.

138. K. Cha, K. W. Horch, R. A. Normann, and D. K. Boman, Reading speed with a pixelized vision system, *J. Opt. Soc. Am. A*, **9**, no. 5, pp. 673–677, 1992.

139. J. S. Hayes, V. T. Yin, D. Piyathaisere, J. D. Weiland, M. S. Humayun, and G. Dagnelie, Visually guided performance of simple tasks using simulated prosthetic vision, *Artif. Organs*, **27**, no. 11, pp. 1016–1028, 2003.

140. R. W. Thompson, G. D. Barnett, M. S. Humayun, and G. Dagnelie, Facial recognition using simulated prosthetic pixelized vision, *Invest. Ophthalmol. Vis. Sci.*, **44**, no. 11, pp. 5035–5042, 2003.

141. G. Dagnelie, P. Keane, V. Narla, L. Yang, J. Weiland, and M. S. Humayun, Real and virtual mobility performance in simulated prosthetic vision, *J. Neural Eng.*, **4**, no. 1, pp. S92–S101, 2007.

142. S. C. Chen, G. J. Suaning, J. W. Morley, and N. H. Lovell, Simulating prosthetic vision: II. Measuring functional capacity, *Vision Res.*, **49**, no. 19, pp. 2329–2343, 2009.

143. R. W. Rodieck, *The First Steps In Seeing*, (Sinauer Associates, Sunderland, MA), 1998.

144. F. Waschkowski, S. Hesse, A. C. Rieck, T. Lohmann, C. Brockmann, T. Laube, N. Bornfeld, G. Thumann, P. Walter, W. Mokwa, S. Johnen, and G. Roessler, Development of very large electrode arrays for epiretinal stimulation (VLARS), *Biomed. Eng. Online*, **13**, no. 1, p. 11, 2014.

145. H. Ameri, T. Ratanapakorn, S. Ufer, H. Eckhardt, M. S. Humayun, and J. D. Weiland, Toward a wide-field retinal prosthesis, *J. Neural Eng.*, **6**, no. 3, p. 035002, 2009.

146. S. I. Fried, H. A. Hsueh, and F. S. Werblin, A method for generating precise temporal patterns of retinal spiking using prosthetic stimulation, *J. Neurophysiol.*, **95**, no. 2, pp. 970–978, 2006.

147. D. Freeman, Electric stimulation with sinusoids and white noise for neural prostheses, *Front. Neurosci.*, neuro.20.001.2010, 2010.

148. D. K. Freeman and S. I. Fried, Multiple components of ganglion cell desensitization in response to prosthetic stimulation, *J. Neural Eng.*, **8**, no. 1, p. 016008, 2011.

149. R. J. Jensen, O. R. Ziv, and J. F. Rizzo, III, Responses of rabbit retinal ganglion cells to electrical stimulation with an epiretinal electrode, *J. Neural Eng.*, **2**, no. 1, p. S16, 2005.

150. S. W. Lee, D. K. Eddington, and S. I. Fried, Responses to pulsatile subretinal electric stimulation: effects of amplitude and duration, *J. Neurophysiol.*, **109**, no. 7, pp. 1954–1968, 2013.

151. A. K. Ahuja, M. R. Behrend, M. Kuroda, M. S. Humayun, and J. D. Weiland, An in vitro model of a retinal prosthesis, *IEEE Trans. Biomed. Eng.*, **55**, no. 6, pp. 1744–1753, 2008.

152. R. J. Jensen and J. F. Rizzo, Responses of ganglion cells to repetitive electrical stimulation of the retina, *J. Neural Eng.*, **4**, no. 1, pp. S1–S6, 2007.

153. C. Sekirnjak, P. Hottowy, A. Sher, W. Dabrowski, A. M. Litke, and E. J. Chichilnisky, Electrical stimulation of mammalian retinal ganglion cells with multielectrode arrays, *J. Neurophysiol.*, **95**, no. 6, pp. 3311–3327, 2006.

154. R. J. Greenberg, T. J. Velte, M. S. Humayun, G. N. Scarlatis, and E. de Juan, Jr., A computational model of electrical stimulation of the retinal ganglion cell, *IEEE Trans. Biomed. Eng.*, **46**, no. 5, pp. 505–514, 1999.

155. M. A. Schiefer and W. M. Grill, Sites of neuronal excitation by epiretinal electrical stimulation, *IEEE Trans. Neural Syst. Rehabil. Eng.*, **14**, no. 1, pp. 5–13, 2006.

156. D. Nanduri, Prosthetic vision in blind human patients: Predicting the percepts of epiretinal stimulation, Ph.D. Thesis, University of Southern California, Los Angeles, CA, USA, 2011.

B. Wang & J. Weiland

157. S. I. Fried, A. C. W. Lasker, N. J. Desai, D. K. Eddington, and J. F. Rizzo, III, Axonal sodium-channel bands shape the response to electric stimulation in retinal ganglion cells, *J. Neurophysiol.*, **101**, no. 4, pp. 1972–1987, 2009.

158. D. K. Freeman, J. S. Jeng, S. K. Kelly, E. Hartveit, and S. I. Fried, Calcium channel dynamics limit synaptic release in response to prosthetic stimulation with sinusoidal waveforms, *J. Neural Eng.*, **8**, no. 4, p. 046005, 2011.

159. R. J. Jensen, O. R. Ziv, and J. F. Rizzo, Thresholds for activation of rabbit retinal ganglion cells with relatively large, extracellular microelectrodes, *Invest. Ophthalmol. Vis. Sci.*, **46**, no. 4, pp. 1486–1496, 2005.

160. L. A. Geddes, Accuracy limitations of chronaxie values, *IEEE Trans. Biomed. Eng.*, **51**, no. 1, pp. 176–181, 2004.

161. S. B. Ryu, J. H. Ye, J. S. Lee, Y. S. Goo, C. H. Kim, and K. H. Kim, Electrically-evoked neural activities of rd1 mice retinal ganglion cells by repetitive pulse stimulation, *Korean J. Physiol. Pharmacol.*, **13**, no. 6, p. 443, 2009.

162. A. Pérez Fornos, J. Sommerhalder, L. da Cruz, J. A. Sahel, S. Mohand-Said, F. Hafezi, and M. Pelizzone, Temporal properties of visual perception on electrical stimulation of the retina, *Invest. Ophthalmol. Vis. Sci.*, **53**, no. 6, pp. 2720–2731, 2012.

163. N. S. Davuluri and J. D. Weiland, Time-varying pulse trains limit retinal desensitization caused by continuous electrical stimulation, in *2014 36th Annual International Conference of the IEEE Engineering in Medicine and Biology Society (EMBC)*, 2014, pp. 414–417.

164. D. K. Freeman, D. K. Eddington, J. F. Rizzo, III, and S. I. Fried, Selective activation of neuronal targets with sinusoidal electric stimulation, *J. Neurophysiol.*, **104**, no. 5, pp. 2778–2791, 2010.

165. W. M. Hart, The temporal responsiveness of vision, in *Adler's Physiology of the Eye*, eds. R. A. Moses and W. M. Hart, (The C. V. Mosby Company, St. Louis), 1987.

166. P. E. Stanga, F. Hafezi, J.-A. Sahel, L. da Cruz, F. Merlini, B. Coley, and R. J. Greenberg, Patients blinded by outer retinal dystrophies are able to perceive color using the Argus II Retinal Prosthesis, in *ARVO 2011*, 2011.

167. P. E. Stanga, J. Jose A. Sahel, L. daCruz, F. Hafezi, F. Merlini, B. Coley, R. J. Greenberg, and A. I. S. Group, Patients blinded by outer retinal dystrophies are able to perceive simultaneous colors using the Argus® II Retinal Prosthesis System, *Invest. Ophthalmol. Vis. Sci.*, **53**, no. 14, pp. 6952–6952, 2012.

168. D. J. Calkins, Y. Tsukamoto, and P. Sterling, Microcircuitry and mosaic of a blue–yellow ganglion cell in the primate retina, *J. Neurosci.*, **18**, no. 9, pp. 3373–3385, 1998.

169. M. S. Humayun, E. de Juan, Jr., J. D. Weiland, G. Dagnelie, S. Katona, R. Greenberg, and S. Suzuki, Pattern electrical stimulation of the human retina, *Vision Res.*, **39**, no. 15, pp. 2569–2576, 1999.

170. R. J. Jensen, J. F. Rizzo, III, O. R. Ziv, A. Grumet, and J. Wyatt, Thresholds for activation of rabbit retinal ganglion cells with an ultrafine, extracellular microelectrode, *Invest. Ophthalmol. Vis. Sci.*, **44**, no. 8, pp. 3533–3543, 2003.

171. L. L. H. Chan, E.-J. Lee, M. S. Humayun, and J. D. Weiland, Both electrical stimulation thresholds and SMI-32-immunoreactive retinal ganglion cell density correlate with age in S334ter line 3 rat retina, *J. Neurophysiol.*, **105**, no. 6, pp. 2687–2697, 2011.

172. R. J. Jensen and J. F. Rizzo, Activation of retinal ganglion cells in wild-type and rd1 mice through electrical stimulation of the retinal neural network, *Vision Res.*, **48**, no. 14, pp. 1562–1568, 2008.

173. R. J. Jensen and J. F. Rizzo, Activation of ganglion cells in wild-type and rd1 mouse retinas with monophasic and biphasic current pulses, *J. Neural Eng.*, **6**, no. 3, p. 035004, 2009.

174. C. Sekirnjak, C. Hulse, L. H. Jepson, P. Hottowy, A. Sher, W. Dabrowski, A. M. Litke, and E. J. Chichilnisky, Loss of responses to visual but not electrical stimulation in ganglion cells of rats with severe photoreceptor degeneration, *J. Neurophysiol.*, **102**, no. 6, pp. 3260–3269, 2009.

Restoring Hearing with Neural Prostheses:
Current Status and Future Directions

Hubert H. Lim, Meredith E. Adams, Peggy B. Nelson, and Andrew J. Oxenham

Center for Applied and Translational Sensory Science (CATSS)
University of Minnesota – Twin Cities, Minnea Polis, USA
hlim@umn.edu

This chapter provides a brief history and description of the cochlear implant, which is considered one of the most successful neural prostheses to date. Although the cochlear implant can provide good speech perception in many patients with severe to profound hearing loss, its performance degrades dramatically in noisy environments and for more complex inputs such as music and multiple talkers. The successes and challenges faced by the cochlear implant over the past few decades are presented in this chapter, along with several encouraging opportunities for significantly improving hearing performance with cochlear implants and more central auditory prostheses. The chapter concludes with several novel approaches for pushing the field of auditory prostheses towards more natural hearing.

1. Introduction

Neural prostheses for hearing restoration, particularly the cochlear implant (CI), have achieved immense success beyond original expectations. Many deaf patients implanted with a CI obtain speech understanding and the ability to converse over the telephone without the need for lip-reading cues [1-3]. Children and infants less than one year of age who have been diagnosed with severe to profound hearing loss have been implanted with a CI and have achieved hearing development sufficient to integrate into mainstream schools and society. The CI's success has instilled optimism towards the pursuit of other types of neural prostheses for restoring sensory and motor function [4, 5]. Yet, this success did not occur overnight. Several key clinicians and researchers pushed forward the concept and development of the CI against criticism and doubt by many leaders in the auditory field. They were also faced with the challenge of finding ways to safely implant a foreign device into the human head and to transmit sufficient information to the brain to restore speech perception. Overcoming these challenges and developing a medical device that can now restore intelligible hearing for people with deafness or severe hearing loss is truly a remarkable story [6-9].

The catalyst for the CI field has been attributed to the initial work by the French team of neurophysiologist André Djourno and otolaryngologist Charles Eyriès who were the first to implant an electrode intra-auricularly in a human patient on February 25, 1957. They were performing surgery on this deaf patient for a facial nerve graft and could place an electrode on a remaining portion of the auditory nerve, providing electrical stimulation to induce sound sensations. Although they did not implant electrodes directly into the cochlea, they reported the potential for electrical hearing by cochlear stimulation, which in turn initiated interest by many others in the auditory field, including the American otologist William House from the House Clinic in California. Intrigued by the concept of a cochlear stimulator, Dr. House teamed up with neurosurgeon John Doyle and electronics engineer Jim Doyle (John's brother) to implant an electrode into the scala tympani of the cochlea in a deaf patient on January 9, 1961, which was the first report of a CI in humans and opened the doors for the emerging field of CIs.

There were many scientists, clinicians, and engineers that joined the CI movement to help transform the concept of a single electrode CI into the multi-channel devices that are currently used in hundreds of thousands of children and adults. In the early 1960s, there were efforts by German researchers, including otologist Fritz Zöllner, and American researchers, including otolaryngologist Blair Simmons and Robert White who implanted the first multi-channel CI. In Australia, otologist Graeme Clark became interested in the CI in 1967 and was convinced that a multi-channel CI would be necessary to achieve sufficient hearing. Through animal research and device development, Dr. Clark and his team were able to successfully develop and implant a multi-channel CI in a patient in 1978. The 1970s were filled with exciting developments and research by multiple groups worldwide towards developing and improving the CI. Further details on the history of CIs are provided in Refs. [6-9].

The modern multi-channel CI is now developed by multiple companies, including Cochlear, Advanced Bionics, MED-EL, Oticon Medical, and Neurotron. The design and implementation of the CI are generally similar across devices, consisting of a behind-the-ear processor with a microphone, an inductive wireless interface that allows the processor to communicate with a fully implanted stimulator on the skull underneath the skin, and an electrode array implanted into the cochlea that is connected to the stimulator. An example system developed by Cochlear is shown in Figure 1. Note that the dimensions and number of electrode contacts (12 to 24) of the electrode array vary across companies. The lengths of the electrode array carrier can also vary depending on the application or target population, such as shorter arrays for preserving residual hearing in lower frequency regions of the cochlea.

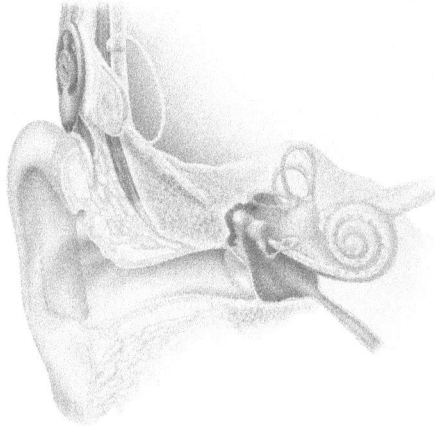

Fig. 1. Image of a behind-the-ear CI system developed by Cochlear (Australia). It consists of a small processor that fits behind the ear with a microphone located near the white tip (not shown). The processor is connected to the receiver-stimulator implanted in a bony bed in the skull beneath the skin surface through a telemetry interface (coil). The ground ball electrode connected to the receiver-stimulator is placed underneath the temporalis muscle while the electrode array is positioned within the cochlea with the 22 electrodes aligned along its tonotopic (frequency) gradient. The electrodes are designed to stimulate the remaining nerve fibers that exit to the right of the image. Image printed with permission from Cochlear.

The general concept behind a multi-channel CI is to position an electrode array into the cochlea and align electrode sites along the length of the cochlea, as shown in Figure 1. In a normal auditory system, sound enters the ear and vibrates the ear drum (tympanic membrane) and middle ear bones (ossicles) that interface with the oval window membrane of the cochlea (i.e., where the horseshoe component is shown in the middle ear cavity in Figure 1). These vibrations cause fluid within the cochlea to move back and forth, which in turn deflect the basilar membrane and hair cells within the cochlea. The hair cells convert the mechanical deflections into neural impulses sent along the auditory nerve fibers to the brain. The cochlea acts as a Fourier analyzer in which sound is decomposed into different frequency components in a spatially ordered manner along the cochlea. High frequency components activate hair cells and nerve fibers in the basal region (closest to the oval window) and lower frequency components activate those neural cells in more apical regions, resulting in a tonotopic activation pattern. Therefore, the spectral information is processed via a place code along the cochlea. The temporal information of sound is coded by the timing of spike activity of the auditory nerve fibers. Placing electrodes along the cochlea and presenting electrical pulses with varying temporal patterns enable transmission of spectral and temporal cues to the brain that has been sufficient to restore speech perception in quiet environments for many deaf individuals.

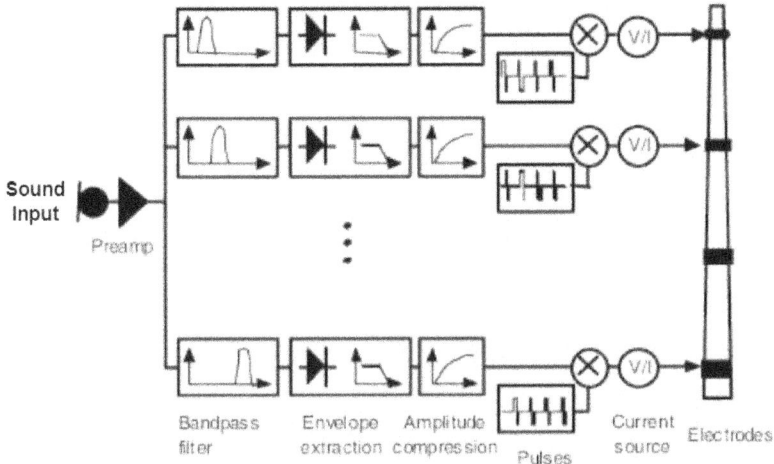

Fig. 2. Block diagram of a typical signal processing strategy used in CIs, known as continuous-interleaved-sampling (CIS) strategy. Image taken from Ref. [2] with permission from IEEE.

A typical stimulation strategy can be represented with a block diagram as shown in Figure 2. The sound input is recorded with a microphone, processed through a preamplifier, and then filtered into different frequency components. The temporal envelope (few hundreds of hertz) from each bandpass filtered component or channel is extracted using half- or full-wave rectification or a Hilbert transform [2]. The temporal envelope values must be logarithmically compressed to match the narrow dynamic range possible with electrical stimulation (e.g., >80 dB SPL acoustic dynamic range down to <20 dB electric dynamic range). Pulse trains with a given pulse rate (e.g., 250 Hz up to several thousand hertz) are presented to each electrode site in which the amplitude of the pulses are modulated by the envelope of each corresponding frequency channel. The pulses are interleaved across electrode sites to minimize channel interaction or interference. The processing strategy shown in Figure 2 is known as the continuous-interleaved-stimulation (CIS) strategy. CI companies have implemented different variations of the CIS strategy. For example, one strategy can identify a subset of frequency channels with the greatest energy and only stimulate those channels for a given time period to minimize channel interaction or over-activation. Another strategy attempts to stimulate a given channel with much higher rates or by varying the pulse rate across channels to attempt to add back finer temporal information, known as temporal fine structure. Further details are provided later in Section 2.1.

At least for speech understanding in quiet environments, these types of strategies have achieved remarkable results, even with just three to four channels of information [10, 11]. For speech understanding in noisy environments and for more complex inputs such as music, studies have shown that a greater number of frequency channels is needed, likely beyond 30 to 40 channels [12-14]. Unfortunately, CI devices appear to achieve less than ten frequency channels of information (i.e., increasing the number of electrodes along the cochlea doesn't necessarily increase the number of actual frequency channels). One major challenge for CIs is the limited bandwidth caused by the poor electrode-neural interface. The CI electrode array is inserted into the cochlea and current must travel from each electrode across the bony cochlear wall to reach the target nerve fibers on the other side. Current flows through the path of least resistance, and thus it does not necessarily reach nerve fibers in the desired tonotopic location. Furthermore, the patients are deaf or have severe hearing loss that has resulted in significant loss of nerve fibers and an inhomogeneous distribution of remaining nerve fibers that can be activated by a CI. Significant research efforts in the auditory prosthesis field seek to improve this electrode-neural interface and increase the number of frequency channels of information, in addition to transmitting finer temporal information across channels.

The journey towards the modern CI is truly an inspiring story. CIs have drastically improved the options for persons with severe and profound hearing loss. More than 300,000 persons have been implanted worldwide. However, there are still challenges faced by the CI, such as significant performance variability across patients and limited performance in noisy environments or for more complex inputs (e.g., music or multiple talkers). Ultimately, the long-term vision is to achieve near natural hearing with neural prostheses. This chapter will describe the current status of the CI and the challenges still faced by current devices. In keeping with the inspiration provided by the CI, several new directions for improving hearing with the CI or with more central auditory prostheses will be highlighted. Finally, the chapter will conclude with an optimistic outlook for the future of implantable auditory prostheses.

2. Current Status of Cochlear Implants

2.1. *Typical cochlear implant configurations*

CI manufacturers have pursued somewhat different approaches in their implementations, but some basic features are common to most currently available implants. These include the division of the spectrum into frequency subbands (channels), the extraction of the temporal envelope within each channel, and the presentation of each envelope via biphasic electrical pulses to electrodes along the array in a tonotopic manner, with the information from the lowest-frequency channel presented to the most apical electrode and information from the highest-frequency channel presented to the most basal electrode (example schematic shown in Figure 2). Some choices of stimulation differ between different implant models and manufacturers. In general, the outcomes of the current devices are comparable, with no one implant type producing clearly better outcomes than any other. Some of the choices available in implementing a CI algorithm are presented below.

2.1.1. *Number of channels*

The number of channels corresponds to the number of electrodes and this ranges from 12 to 24, depending on the manufacturer and the model. A landmark paper by Shannon et al. [15] used acoustic simulations of CI processing in normal-hearing listeners to show that good speech intelligibility could be achieved even when the spectrum was very coarsely represented in four contiguous spectral channels. Since then it has been shown that more channels are required to understand speech in a background of noise [e.g., 16]. Although in theory a larger number of channels provides better spectral resolution and a closer simulation of the frequency resolution in the normal cochlea, in practice various factors limit the benefit of increasing number of channels. Friesen et al. [17] showed that normal-hearing listeners demonstrated continual improvement in speech recognition with increasing number of channels from 2 to 20. However, in actual CI users, performance generally plateaued at around 7 to 10 channels, even in cases where 20 channels were available. This plateau in performance is thought to be due to two main factors: (i) spread of current within the cochlea, leading to overlap between the neural populations excited by each electrode and reduced channel independence, and (ii) regions of poor neural survival or poor electrode-neural interface leading to some ineffective channels. Both these issues, and some potential remedies, are discussed later in this chapter.

2.1.2. *Stimulation strategy*

Various stimulation strategies have been tried in CIs since their inception. These include schemes as simple as filtered analog representations of the acoustic waveform to more complicated schemes that extracted features, such as fundamental frequency (F0) and formant frequencies, from the acoustic stimulus, in order to provide a more simplified signal to the implant that nonetheless included the most relevant features of the stimulus. In general, improvements in speech perception could be achieved by adding more speech features, including higher spectral peaks, and in using sequential stimulation to avoid electrode interactions as used in the Nucleus 22 CI.

A breakthrough in stimulation strategy was achieved with the introduction of the continuous interleaved sampling (CIS) strategy in 1991 [18]. This strategy involved stimulating each electrode in succession with brief biphasic pulses again in such a way that the stimuli from each electrode never overlapped in time (see Figure 2). The lack of overlap of the pulses, and the subsequent reduction in interference between electrodes, led to immediate improvements in the performance of the CI subjects tested. Essentially all major CI manufacturers adopted a version of this CIS strategy.

In many cases, CIS is implemented after envelope extraction in each channel independently. However, some schemes, such as SPEAK, use an "n-of-m" strategy, whereby in a given time frame only a subset of the electrodes (e.g., 8 of 22) are activated, usually based on which channels have the highest intensity or energy within that time frame.

A final variant in some current CI models involves coding the stimulus periodicity in the temporal fine structure (normally discarded when only the temporal envelope is extracted) in the most apical (low-frequency) channels, by synchronizing the pulse presentation time with the zero crossings in the sub-band waveform. This provides for a variable pulse rate that potentially transmits more information that would be provided by the temporal envelope. Unfortunately, so far there is very little evidence for an improvement in performance with this strategy [19].

2.1.3. *Pulse rate*

The rate at which electrical biphasic pulses are presented in each channel can vary considerably across different devices and between individual users, based on the choices made by the user and their audiologist. At low pulse rates (less than 300 pulses per second) changes in pulse rate are perceived by most users as a change in pitch [20-22]. At higher rates, a change in pitch is not normally perceived, although some listeners are able to discriminate changes at higher rates [23], and it appears that the upper limit of pulse rates that evoke a change in pitch may be increased somewhat with training [24].

One attempt to improve the transmission of information through a CI has been to use very high pulse rates, with the rationale that such high rates could lead to more stochastic (and hence more natural) neural responses [25, 26]. Unfortunately, the use of very high pulse rates has not been found to result in improved speech perception, although (as is often the case) there are individual differences, with some CI users showing improvements and others showing degradation in performance with increasing pulse rate [e.g., 27, 28]. In current implants, typical pulse rates are between 900 and 2000 pulses per second per electrode.

2.2. *Remaining challenges for cochlear implants*

Three developments in CI technology can be singled out has having led to dramatic improvements in performance: 1) the shift in the 1980s from single-channel implants to multi-channel systems [e.g., 29, 30], 2) the introduction of higher stimulation rates (e.g., SPEAK to ACE was 250 pps per electrode to 900 pps per electrode), and 3) the development of continuous interleaved sampling in the early 1990s [18]. Since then, improvements have continued to be made in CI design and technology; however, no single innovation has led to consistent and substantial improvements in the performance of CIs. Some of the remaining challenges faced by people with CIs are outlined in this section.

2.2.1. *Speech perception in noise*

Background noise of any type remains a significant and limiting issue for speech understanding by CI users. Listeners with normal hearing can understand a good majority of speech even when background is at the same overall level as the speech (a signal-to-noise ratio, SNR, of 0 dB), or even a little higher. Listeners who use hearing aids typically require somewhat better SNRs, of up to about +5 dB, for example [e.g., 31]. In contrast, listeners with CIs often require much more favorable conditions to understand a message, often needing SNRs of +10 to +15 dB to understand more than 50% of words in sentence recognition tests [e.g., 32]. Many common environments, such as schools and restaurants, do not meet these listening requirements, and so CI users find themselves at a communication disadvantage in daily situations.

Another difference between CI and normal acoustic speech perception in noise is the effect of different types of noise backgrounds. Normal-hearing listeners are able to understand speech better when the background noise is non-stationary, e.g., when it fluctuates in amplitude over time [31]. Hearing-impaired listeners typically receive less benefit in such situations [e.g., 31, 33], whereas CI users often receive no benefit or even a decrement in speech understanding in a fluctuating noise background [34]. The fact that a similar loss of benefit occurs in acoustic simulations of implant processing, even with relatively high numbers of channels (up to 22), suggests that masking release is highly susceptible to the reduction of spectro-temporal resolution produced by the limited number of channels for CIs and the loss of spectro-temporal fine structure within those channels [35].

Typically, robust and redundant speech cues (both spectral and temporal) help normal-hearing listeners to segregate relevant speech signals out of a noise mixture and to integrate the signals into a continuous perceptual stream. However, when spectral cues are reduced via a CI processor, a broadband modulated noise might seem perceptually quite similar to the speech. In other words, its frequency components are overlapped with those of speech, and the rate of fluctuation of noise and speech are similar. Without fine-grained spectral information in speech, listeners might rely more on temporal cues to process consonants and vowels. In the presence of modulated noise, such temporal information in speech is obscured by the noise modulations, and CI listeners may experience more modulation interference rather than (or in addition to) masking release [32, 36].

2.2.2. Pitch perception

CIs were designed to transmit speech information. It is therefore perhaps not surprising that the perception of music and pitch are generally quite poor in CI users. However, as speech perception in quiet has improved, demands have become higher, and a high priority for CI researchers and companies has been to improve pitch perception for CI users. Even in normal-hearing listeners, the mechanisms by which pitch information is extracted from the cochlea are not fully understood [37]. However, theories of pitch can be divided into three broad categories: place, time, and place-time. Place theories of pitch postulate that the pitch of a complex harmonic sound (such as a musical note or a voiced speech sound) is based on the spatial pattern of excitation generated along the basilar membrane of the cochlea [38-40]. Time theories of pitch postulate that pitch is extracted via the stimulus-driven timing of action potentials, or spikes, in the auditory nerve [41-43]. Place-time theories postulate that it requires the interaction of time-synchronous activity at specific places along the basilar membrane to elicit strong pitch percepts; these theories rely on phase dispersion along the basilar membrane to introduce delays between various places along the basilar membrane, which are then exploited to extract the underlying periodicities within the stimulus [44-46].

Unfortunately, regardless of which coding mechanism is revealed as being the correct one, CIs have major disadvantages. In terms of the place code, the limited number of channels, and the spread of excitation produced by each channel, means that the place code of pitch would be much coarser, and highly distorted, relative to normal hearing. In terms of the timing code, the lack of sensitivity to changes in pulse rate beyond about 300 Hz means that only a limited range of fundamental frequencies, and almost no upper harmonics, which are relevant to music are accurately encoded by CIs. In terms of the place-time code, electrode locations are generally not well matched with the acoustical best frequency along the cochlea, and the rapid phase transitions produced along the basilar membrane by the cochlea's traveling wave are not reproduced at all in CIs. This mismatch between place and time information has led Loeb [45] to postulate that CI users suffer from "perceptual dissonance".

Most CI users do, in fact, report pitch changes with changes in the stimulated electrode number, with the pitch generally increasing as the stimulated electrode moves from the apex towards the base of the cochlea [e.g., 47]. However, it is not clear if the percepts elicited by a change in place of stimulation can be compared to the pitch perceived by normal-hearing listeners, or whether it is more like the change in "brightness" or "sharpness" associated with a shift in the spectral centroid of a sound under normal-hearing conditions [48]. Changes in the pulse rate, or changes in the rate of amplitude modulation of high-rate pulse trains, also lead to changes in reported pitch by CI users, at least up to about 300 Hz. Research suggests pitch percepts elicited by electrode position and pulse rate are to some extent orthogonal and independent [49, 50], in line with what would be expected based on results from normal-hearing listeners, suggesting that pitch based on envelope repetition rate and pitch (or brightness) based on spectral centroid are somewhat independent, even though the two dimensions can interfere with one another [51].

The type of pitch that has not yet been elicited via CIs is the strong tonal pitch sensation produced in normal-hearing listeners by harmonic complexes with low-numbered harmonics. This type of pitch, which is critical to music perception and the perception of multiple simultaneous pitches, is thought to require good spectral resolution (much better than is currently available in CIs) and harmonics that are presented to the "correct" place along the cochlea [52-54]. As it is, when listening to electrical pulse trains, CI users seem to experience the same kind of much weaker pitch sensation that is produced in normal-hearing listeners by amplitude modulation of a narrowband stimulus or by bandpass filtering a low-rate acoustic pulse train [55, 56]. This kind of pitch perception is weak and much more susceptible to interference than the stronger pitch produced by lower-numbered spectral harmonics [57, 58].

The poor representation of pitch is not only an issue for music perception. Pitch plays an important role in speech perception, assisting speaker and gender identification [59], conveying prosodic and emotional information in non-tone languages, such as English [60], and conveying important lexical information in tonal languages such as Chinese [61, 62]. In addition, pitch is believed to play an important role in our ability to segregate simultaneous competing sound sources [63].

2.2.3. *Auditory scene analysis and stream segregation*

Auditory stream segregation (also referred to as auditory streaming) occurs naturally in daily life, such as when listening to a talker at a party or when following a melody played by an instrument in an orchestra. Listeners with normal hearing interpret a mixture of ongoing sounds in such a way that sounds from different sources are allocated to individual sound generators that are perceptually concurrent. Both spectral and temporal differences have been documented as cues that can elicit stream segregation in normal-hearing listeners.

Fewer studies of auditory streaming have been carried out in CI users but, as would be expected based on their poorer spectral resolution, perceptual segregation of two sources is generally weaker in CI users than in normal-hearing listeners under comparable listening conditions [64-67].

2.2.4. *Spatial hearing*

An important role of hearing is to orient us to sounds in our environment. Much of the important information about a sound's location relative to our head is gleaned by comparing the signals at the two ears [68]. Traditionally, CIs were only provided to one ear, effectively ruling out good sound localization. More recently, it has become more common to implant people bilaterally, meaning that the brain has input from two CIs and so could, in principle, compare the incoming signals to extract relevant spatial information. Although some timing information may be extracted under ideal conditions [69], in practice any localization tends to be based on interaural level differences and localization skill may be limited to being able to tell left from right [70]. Nevertheless, CI uses can obtain daily benefit from these localization cues, and the hope is that greater synchronization between devices bilaterally could provide further improvements in hearing.

3. Approaches Towards Improving Auditory Implants

As described above, one major challenge that continues to face CIs is the inability to increase the number of effective frequency channels of information that could greatly improve hearing in noise, pitch and music perception, and stream segregation. Therefore, considerable effort has gone into improving the spectral resolution in CIs.

One attempt has been to alter the current stimulation field to reduce the spread of current from individual electrodes, so that each electrode stimulates a more limited population of auditory neurons. Most current systems use monopolar stimulation, with the active electrode along the array, and the ground or reference electrode placed remotely, often outside the cochlea. Attempts to narrow the current field have used bipolar, tripolar, or quadrupolar stimulation, whereby the neighboring electrodes become the return for the active electrode. Physiological studies have confirmed that more focused stimulation can indeed produce narrower excitation patterns [71]. Perceptual studies in humans have so far found relatively limited benefit for speech perception by using more focused stimulation techniques [72].

Another approach has been to increase the number of effective channels in CIs by creating "virtual channels" through the simultaneous stimulation of neighboring electrode pairs, and steering the focus of the current by adjusting the relative amplitudes of the current at the two electrode locations [73]. Virtual channels can also be created beyond the electrode array itself, thereby extending the range of stimulation to slightly more apical (low-frequency) regions [74]. Although these methods provide some promise in enhancing spectral resolution, none have so far offered the promise of restoring normal-like pitch perception to CI users.

Further complicating these attempts at improving frequency resolution has been the significant variability in stimulation effects observed across CI patients. Being able to explain and predict this variability remains an ongoing challenge. One approach has been to harness imaging techniques to assess the location of the electrodes within the cochlea and to assess their distance from auditory neurons. Another approach is to develop new behavioral methods to identify particularly poor electrodes, which are perhaps too far away from surviving auditory neurons to deliver useful information, and so may be more beneficial turned off than on [75-77].

The modest improvements in performance provided by the different attempts described above reveal a fundamental bottleneck faced by CIs, the poor electrode-neural interface. This interface can be significantly variable across patients. If the patient has a poor interface, then implementing different stimulation approaches, even ones that are customized to each patient, achieve insufficient activation. Therefore, the ability to increase hearing performance with auditory implants heavily depends on preserving or improving this electrode-neural interface. Currently, there are two approaches that could significantly improve this electrode-neural interface: (1) less damaging and more consistent peri-modiolar surgical placement of an electrode array into the cochlea, and (2) implantation of electrode arrays into central brain structures for direct interfacing with neurons.

3.1. *Improving surgeries and cochlear implant placement*

Surgical technique and electrode array design govern several factors that impact CI performance and patient outcomes. After reviewing the surgical technique, this section explains the importance of atraumatic placement of the CI electrode in order to preserve cochlear structure and function and of precise positioning of electrodes to direct stimulation current toward neural elements with specificity. Strategies for optimization of surgical technique and device design are presented with the goal of catalyzing future innovation. The typical anatomic location of a CI is depicted in Figure 3.

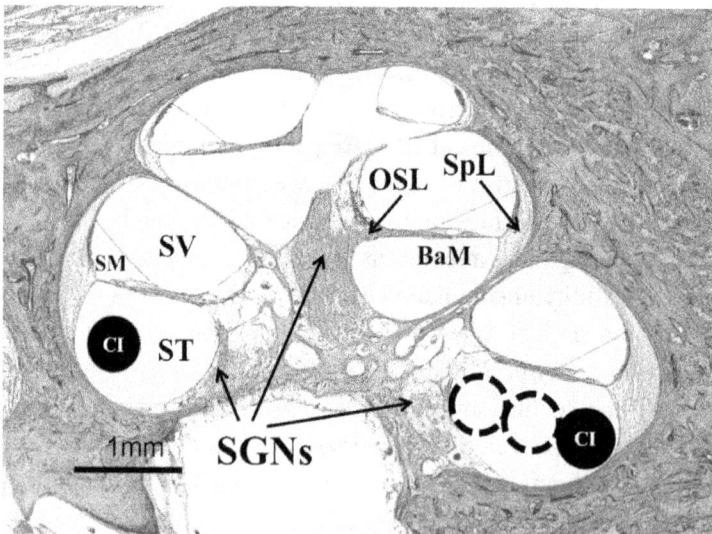

Fig. 3. Photomicrograph of the cochlea, in mid-modiolar cross section. The black filled circle (CI) represents a cochlear implant electrode in the typical position assumed by a straight electrode. Dotted circles represent peri-modiolar and mid-scalar locations. BaM: Basilar membrane; CI: cochlear implant; OSL: osseos spiral lamina; SGNs: spiral ganglion neurons in the modiolus; SM: scala media; SpL: spiral ligament; ST: scala tympani; SV: scala vestibule. Photomicrograph courtesy of the Paparella Otopathology Laboratory, University of Minnesota.

3.1.1. *Surgical technique for cochlear implantation*

Placement of a CI involves 3 main steps: 1) the approach to the cochlea; 2) opening of the cochlea; and 3) electrode insertion [78]. The surgery is typically performed under general anesthesia as an outpatient procedure.

The cochlea is most commonly approached through a mastoidectomy. A curvilinear incision is made in the skin behind the ear and the underlying soft tissues are elevated to expose the mastoid bone and to make a pocket for the receiver-stimulator shown on the skull above the ear in Figure 1. The outer cortex and underlying honeycomb-like air cells of the mastoid bone are removed using a high-speed, hand-held drill under microscopic visualization. The cochlea is located anterior to the mastoid and medial to the tympanic membrane, where it forms part of the innermost wall of the air-containing middle ear space. Its curvature is oriented such that the round window membrane that seals off the scala tympani in the basal turn points posteriorly. To access the cochlea from the mastoid, bone is removed between the chorda tympani (taste) nerve that runs underneath the tympanic membrane and the facial (movement) nerve. Working through this narrow (2-3mm) recess [79], the scala tympani in the basal turn is opened by incising the round window membrane or by drilling an aperture (cochleostomy) either in the cochlear promontory or at the margin of the round window. The receiver-stimulator is secured in the tissue pocket behind the ear and the attached electrode array is inserted into the cochlea manually using forceps or other tools in order to achieve a position shown in Figure 1. The cochleostomy is sealed with soft tissue. The surgical site is closed with sutures and allowed to heal before initial implant activation.

Alternative mastoid-sparing approaches have been developed, including the suprameatal approach, which involves creating a tunnel posterior and parallel to the ear canal for the electrode and accessing the cochlea in the middle ear by elevating the tympanic membrane (thus minimizing risk to the facial nerve) [80, 81]. Minimally invasive approaches that utilize mounted microstereotactic frames and image-guidance to direct cochlear access and insertion with or without robotic assistance are also in development [82, 83].

3.1.2. *Factors that impact CI performance and patient outcomes*

3.1.2.1 Preservation of cochlear structure and function

In the early CI era, complete electrode insertion was emphasized over preservation of cochlear structure and function. Recipients were expected to lose any remaining acoustic hearing at the time of implantation. Subsequent studies demonstrated multiple ways in which CI electrode insertion causes trauma to the delicate cochlear neurosensory architecture [84]. After entering the scala tympani in the basal turn, the electrode may contact the modiolus (the central axis of the cochlea) or impinge on the lateral wall as it makes the first ascending turn [85]. When insertion forces are applied after such contact, the electrode tip or body may displace the basilar membrane and spiral ligament that support the sensory organ of Corti and may penetrate through them into the scala media and scala vestibuli. Such disruption creates a toxic mixture of inner ear fluids, sensory cell death, and loss of acoustic hearing [86]. The electrode may also fracture the modiolus and osseous spiral lamina that contain the spiral ganglion neurons (SGNs) and their dendrites, respectively, resulting in irreversible degeneration of the targets of CI electrode stimulation [86]. Additionally, insertion trauma incites varying degrees of intra-cochlear inflammation, fibrosis (connective tissue scarring) and neoosteogenesis (new bone formation), which further compromise the substrates of natural hearing and occlude the cochlear lumen (Figure 4) [87]. Even without direct mechanical injury, CI insertion initiates molecular events that contribute to sensory cell and neuronal death, including generation of reactive oxygen species and activation of pro-apoptotic pathways [88].

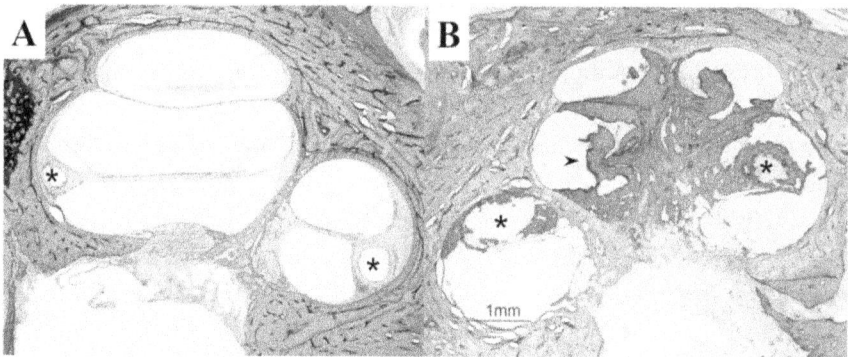

Fig. 4. Photomicrographs of human cochlea that underwent electrode implantation. * indicates the position of the electrode, since removed for bone sectioning. **A** The electrode contacted the lateral cochlear wall in scala tympani, disrupting the spiral ligament. Fibrous tissue encompasses the electrode track. **B** This electrode coursed through scala vestibule. Dense neoossification (arrow head) is observed. Photomicrograph courtesy of the Paparella Otopathology Laboratory, University of Minnesota.

The field has moved strongly towards development of devices and techniques to insert electrodes without injury (i.e., "soft surgery"). The expansion of CI candidacy criteria and the recognition that acoustic hearing can be preserved following implantation are the main drivers of this shift. New technologies have improved post-implantation speech perception outcomes such that patients with residual hearing are eligible for CIs [89]. Now, 80% of CI candidates have some bilateral low-frequency residual hearing [90]. Despite having severe to profound high frequency hearing loss that precludes word understanding with and effective use of conventional hearing aids, a subset of these patients receives significant benefit from the residual low frequency hearing. Surgery and electrodes specifically designed for low frequency hearing preservation allow the same ear to receive simultaneous electrical stimulation with a CI for high frequencies and acoustic stimulation with a hearing aid for low frequencies (i.e., electric-acoustic stimulation (EAS)) [88]. Outcomes of EAS are superior to those of electrical stimulation alone, including hearing in quiet and noise, music appreciation, pitch perception, spectral discrimination, and quality of life [91-95]. Unfortunately, 20 to 50% of patients lose their residual hearing months to years following implantation at rates faster than expected for natural progression [96, 97]. The cause of deterioration is unclear, but may be related to tissue injury, wound remodeling, or afferent neuron injury from high charge electrical stimulation [96, 98, 99].

Research is underway to determine if minimization of cochlear trauma and preservation of residual hearing improve outcomes in traditional CI candidates implanted with conventional electrodes. Performance with a CI alone was not improved by the preservation of residual hearing in several studies that included patients who maintained severe to profound low frequency thresholds [100-102]. But, speech perception was better when recipients maintained milder degrees of low frequency hearing loss and/or when they used hearing aids despite not meeting typical criteria for EAS [84, 90]. Either way, there are additional compelling reasons to attempt atraumatic insertion of conventional electrodes. When an electrode array takes an errant course, the tip may fold over on itself to point backwards and the base may buckle, leading to incomplete insertion and inefficient or aberrant SGN stimulation [86, 103, 104]. It is also intuitively desirable to prevent trauma-related neuronal death in order to maintain the dynamic range and complexity of neural stimulation (although, the minimum number of SGNs necessary for speech performance with a CI remains undefined) [100]. Prevention of injury may lessen cochlear fibrosis and neo-ossification, not only reducing cell death but also simplifying CI revision and re-implantation for device failures and upgrades and permitting application of future therapies (e.g., cellular regeneration) [84, 100].

3.1.2.2 Electrode position

Aspects of intra-cochlear electrode position that contribute to CI performance include scalar location, mediolateral positioning, and depth of insertion [105].

The scala tympani (ST) is the favored intracochlear compartment for CIs (Figure 3). An electrode in ST is in closer proximity to the SGNs in the modiolus than one in scala vestibuli (SV) [106]. Therefore, electrodes in ST are more likely to stimulate SGNs in their immediate scalar turn. Electrodes in the more apically located SV may stimulate SGNs in both the immediate turn and the next, more-apical turn, leading to pitch-confusion and diminished speech understanding [105, 107]. The ST may also be more resistant to electrode trauma because it has a larger cross-sectional area and is reinforced superiorly by the basilar membrane and osseous spiral lamina [106, 108]. Electrodes that traverse from ST to SV penetrate the osseous spiral lamina and basilar membrane, imperiling efforts to preserve cochlear health and hearing [109]. In clinical practice, word understanding scores are indeed worse among CI recipients who have electrodes within SV; performance improves as more electrodes are located within ST compared to SV, reinforcing ST as the target for electrode location [105, 107, 110, 111].

Open-set speech perception can also be improved by using electrodes that rest closer to the modiolus [105, 112]. Compared to lateral wall hugging arrays, perimodiolar electrodes may stimulate a more specific SGN population that corresponds to a particular tonotopic region of the cochlea, promoting better discrimination between electrodes [112]. An array that more tightly hugs the modiolus will span a greater length of the cochlear duct when fully inserted, potentially better approximating normal frequency to place mapping. Placing electrodes closer to their SGN targets also lowers thresholds of stimulation, thus decreasing power consumption and prolonging battery life [113].

Electrode arrays need to reach an appropriate depth of insertion within the cochlea to achieve optimal performance. The ideal insertion depth and the appropriate electrode array length remain matters of investigation. For a given CI system, deeper insertions of apical electrodes appear to result in improved speech perception performance when recipients rely on the CI alone [114-116]. However, when arrays are over-inserted (past the intended design depth), they are more likely to buckle, traumatizing the basilar membrane or osseous spiral lamina [109, 117], and performance may be degraded because the basal-most electrodes bypass high-frequency detecting proximal SGNs [105, 107]. Conversely, short or shallowly inserted electrodes promote hearing preservation by causing less trauma to the cochlear apex, and are thus employed in many EAS strategies. But, since they may fail to stimulate low-frequency detecting apical SGNs, performance degradation from poor tonotopic matching and frequency confusion can occur in CI-only conditions [109, 114].

3.1.3. *Strategies to improve surgery and cochlear implant placement*

3.1.3.1 Electrode design

CI electrodes in clinical use are either *pre-curved*, designed to coil into a perimodiolar or midscalar position in an "average" cochlea, or *straight*, intended to track with the lateral wall of ST (Figure 3) [78]. Pre-curved electrodes contain a stylet (stiff wire) that keeps them straight for initial insertion; the surgeon retracts the stylet as the electrode is introduced into the cochlea so that it regains its preformed curvature [78, 86]. The advance-off-stylet (AOS) technique reduces the force (and trauma) applied to the outer cochlear wall [113]. Compared to other models, perimodiolar arrays have the aforementioned advantages of being closer to the SGNs but are generally larger in diameter and stiffer (due to the stylet housing), and more likely to injure the modiolus [78, 118]. A very thin perimodiolar array that relies on a sheath rather than a stylet is under development [119]. There are also numerous smaller diameter straight arrays designed with modified tip shapes and soft and highly flexible materials to minimize lateral wall trauma, albeit while placing electrodes farther from the SGNs. When thin straight arrays are placed by experienced surgeons, initial hearing is preserved with ~50% of conventional electrodes and >90% of EAS electrodes [95, 96, 120, 121]. As an alternative, a pre-curved midscalar array was introduced that assumes a position in the middle of scala tympani in order to reduce risk to the modiolus and lateral wall while still maintaining stimulus proximity [122]. Initial hearing preservation rates appear to be similar to those achieved with conventional straight arrays [123]. Regardless of shape, hearing preservation and complete hearing loss have been observed, albeit at different rates, with use of the full range of electrode lengths (short to long) and insertion depths [90].

If we are to achieve more reliable and atraumatic CI placement, future designs may need to move beyond refinements in electrode shape, length and materials aimed at the average cochlea to account for the significant intersubject variation in cochlear dimensions and curvature [124]. To this end, prototype "steerable" electrodes have been created for investigation. Intra-cochlear shape changes are induced in these electrodes during insertion by incorporating shape-memory alloys (e.g., nickel-titanium) or actuators that change the implant contour in response to electrical resistance heating or fluid pressure [78, 125, 126]. When combined with robot-assistance, automated insertion tools, and pre- or intraoperative imaging, such active arrays may afford controllable and individually optimized CI insertion [78].

3.1.3.2 Surgical approach and cochlear access

Surgeons influence the trajectory taken by a CI electrode through the cochlea by varying the axis and insertion angle of the array. These features are largely determined by the approach to the cochlea (e.g., transmastoid, suprameatal, transcanal, or minimally invasive) and the location of the cochlear opening (e.g., round window, extended round window or promontory cochleostomy) [78].

The round window membrane is a concave thin soft tissue barrier between the basal-most end of the scala tympani and middle ear, hidden from view by a notoriously variable overhanging ledge of bone that forms its niche [86]. The round window was used in the early CI era. It allows electrodes to access the basal-most SGNs and can be accessed without damaging the cochlear architecture. However, surgeons found visualization challenging and the stiff electrodes of the time had difficulty navigating the hook-like turn that occurs immediately after round window entry. The round window was thus supplanted by the promontory cochleostomy, an opening drilled in the bone anterior and inferior to the round window, that allows surgeons to see down the cochlear lumen and access the basal turn in a straight fashion for the first 8 to 10 mm [106]. Over time, with new electrode designs and hearing preservation goals, the pendulum has swung between the two approaches and a hybrid of the two, the extended round window cochleostomy, is being used. Typical insertion angles, trajectories and sites of electrode trauma associated with each opening have been characterized and vary by person and electrode type [106, 127]. It now appears that similar insertion depths and acceptable rates of hearing preservation can be achieved with either cochleostomy or round window approaches, giving us an opportunity to adapt cochlear access as needed [128, 129].

Regardless of the location selected, the cochlear opening needs to be created in a precise manner to achieve an appropriate size match between the cocheostomy and the electrode, and to avoid disruption of the attachments of the basilar membrane. Technology created for minimally invasive and robotic approaches may allow us to determine, and then execute, an ideal cochleostomy target and insertion trajectory based on pre- or intraoperative imaging [82, 83].

Soft surgery calls for minimization of drill trauma when removing the round window niche overhang (to prevent fracture of the osseous spiral lamina or acoustic trauma) and, especially, while forming a cochleostomy. Ideally, bone is removed until the periosteal lining is exposed but not violated with the drill in order to avoid periosteal injury and introduction of inflammatory bone dust; the periosteum is sharply incised before implant insertion. A better technique would not require bone removal. Accordingly, methods for accomplishing a chemical cohleostomy are being explored [130].

3.1.3.3 Surgical insertion: force, monitoring, and drug delivery

CI arrays are commonly inserted manually, aided by forceps that alternately push and guide the trajectory of the electrode. Surgeons may appreciate tactile feedback when an electrode meets resistance, allowing for course correction during insertion. However, surgeons vary in this perception as well as in accuracy and tremor during placement. It can also be difficult to insert an electrode with one smooth movement. Starts and stops during insertion create multiple, potentially injurious, pressure peaks [131].

Several strategies have been developed that successfully limit insertion forces, including application of lubricants, such as sodium hyaluronate [132], and very slow insertion speeds (~15mm/minute) [133]. Insertion tools containing guide shafts now permit smooth insertion with one hand, thus decreasing overall insertion forces and limiting pressure peaks [131]. Motorized tools hold additional promise and may be combined with minimally invasive access [131].

Intraoperative electrophysiologic measures might also offer real-time feedback on cochlear health during insertion. In patients with residual hearing, cochlear responses to acoustic stimuli can be recorded either directly or through the CI using the technique of electrocochleography. The clinical utility of this approach is an area of active research [134, 135].

Even with a perfect mechanical insertion, post-implantation inflammation, oxidative stress and apoptosis imperil cochlear health. Physical access to the cochlear lumen at the time of implant insertion raises the possibility of providing pharmacologic neuroprotection, either by drug application at the time of insertion or via drug-eluting electrodes. Encouraging levels of hearing preservation have been demonstrated in early trials of topical and parenteral corticosteroids [136, 137]. Other compounds under investigation include neuroprotective growth factors and free radical scavengers [88].

3.2. *Improving central auditory prostheses*

In thinking about the future of auditory prostheses, the question arises as to how hearing performance can be further improved beyond what is possible with current devices, not only for those who are implanted with a CI but also for those who do not have a functional auditory nerve or implantable cochlea. There are exciting efforts towards improving the design and implantation of CIs as described in the previous sections. However, there have also been extensive efforts and progress over the past 30 to 40 years in the development of central auditory prostheses, particularly devices that have been implanted into the brainstem or midbrain areas of deaf patients who cannot sufficiently benefit from a CI. As discussed previously, a major limitation in achieving higher performance with CIs appears to be the limited number of independent information channels available through cochlear stimulation [13]. The CI sends current through a bony modiolar wall of the cochlea with scattered flow of electrical charge to a variable distribution and reduced number of auditory neurons associated with deafness. Therefore, central auditory prostheses may provide a way for achieving more specific activation of a greater number of frequency channels of information than is currently possible with CIs.

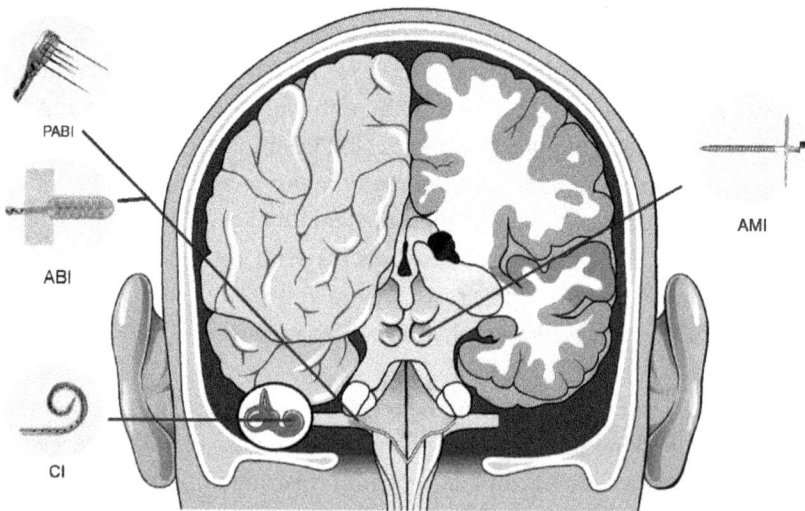

Fig. 5. Different auditory neural prosthetics used in patients for hearing restoration. CI: Cochlear Implant, which consists of an electrode array that is implanted into the cochlea and used for auditory nerve stimulation. ABI: Auditory Brainstem Implant that is used for surface stimulation of the cochlear nucleus. PABI: Penetrating Auditory Brainstem Implant that is used for penetrating stimulation of the cochlear nucleus. AMI: Auditory Midbrain Implant that is used for penetrating stimulation of the auditory midbrain (i.e., the inferior colliculus). There are several companies that build these types of implant devices. The examples shown in this figure are developed by Cochlear Limited (Australia). Figure was taken from Ref. [139] and reprinted with permission from Lippincott Williams & Wilkins.

There are currently two types of central auditory prostheses being implanted into deaf patients, an auditory brainstem implant (ABI) or an auditory midbrain implant (AMI), as shown in Figure 5. Ongoing developments and opportunities for these two types of hearing implants will be described in the following sections. History finds a way of repeating itself. Similar to the CI, there has been doubt surrounding these central auditory prostheses and whether they can be safely implanted into humans and achieve sufficient hearing performance. Yet, recent successes with the ABI and AMI have once again revealed a critical lesson in not underestimating the ability of these neural implants to safely restore useful hearing to deaf patients beyond what could have been expected 35 years ago [138].

3.2.1. *Auditory brainstem implants*

3.2.1.1 History of ABI

For deaf patients without a functional auditory nerve (e.g., due to a head injury or tumor removal surgery, or being born without a nerve) or without an implantable cochlea to enable array insertion (e.g., due to ossification or head trauma), the CI is ineffective and the only hearing option is a central auditory implant. The first central auditory implant was the ABI implanted in 1979 at the House Ear Institute in Los Angeles, California by William Hitselberger and William House. It consisted of two ball electrodes with a fabric backing that was built in collaboration with Douglass McCreery from the Huntington Medical Research Institutes in Pasadena, California. The ABI was positioned onto the surface of the cochlear nucleus. Further details of the development of the first ABIs are provided in [140, 141]. The ABI was initially designed and justified for patients with a genetic disease known as neurofibromatosis type 2 (NF2), which is usually associated with bilateral acoustic neuromas. Due to removal of these tumors and complete damage of the auditory nerves, the patients became bilaterally deaf and unable to benefit from CIs. Since the cochlear nucleus was already approached during tumor removal, it was then possible to place the electrodes on its surface with minimal added surgical risk. A total of 25 patients were implanted with an ABI by 1992 [141]. Since 1992, the single channel ABI has been developed into a multi-site surface array (Figure 6) by several implant companies (i.e., Advanced Bionics Corporation, USA; Cochlear Limited, Australia; MED-EL Company, Austria; MXM Digisonic/Oticon Medical, France) and implanted in over 1200 patients worldwide with etiologies no longer limited to NF2 (e.g., those with nerve aplasia/avulsion or cochlear ossification).

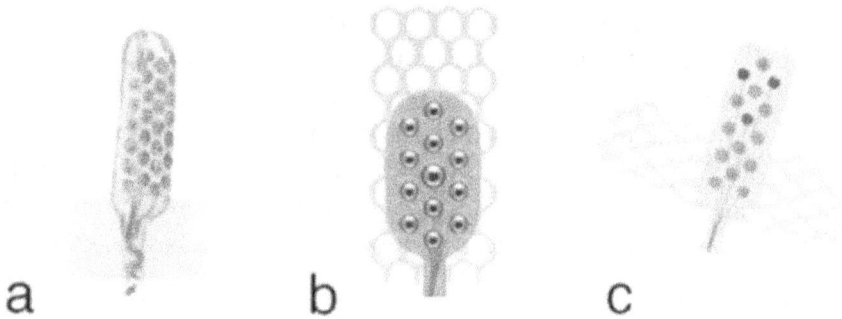

Fig. 6. Three examples of different ABI electrode arrays produced by several companies (**a**: Cochlear Limited, **b**: MED-EL Company, **c**: Oticon Medical). Each array has a different number of electrodes and configuration, in which all have a Dacron mesh/grid that helps secure the array to the brain surface. Image was taken from Ref. [142] and reprinted with permission from Wiley Periodicals, Inc.

3.2.1.2 Good speech understanding is possible with the ABI

The past decade of the ABI has been filled with exciting discoveries, reviving our optimism for the use of central auditory implants for hearing restoration in deaf patients. From 1979 to about 2003, the ABI was viewed as a device that could improve lip-reading capabilities and environmental awareness but generally provided only limited open-set speech perception. Even with this limited performance, clinicians continued to implant the ABI in NF2 deaf patients because they had no other hearing option and the array could be implanted with only incremental risk after tumor removal surgery. Around the early 2000's, clinicians began to implant patients with deafness caused by conditions other than NF2, initially led by the pioneering efforts of Vittorio Colletti and his colleagues from the University of Verona in Italy.

In 2004, they reported on their experiences in implanting the ABI in patients (5 adults and 1 child) with posttraumatic cochlear nerve avulsion [143]. It was the first evidence that ABI patients could potentially achieve good speech perception and even the ability to converse over the phone. Initially these results were received with skepticism. However, Vittorio Colletti and his team, including collaboration with Robert Shannon from House Ear Institute, continued to push forward with implanting the ABI in non-tumor patients and eventually observed open-set speech perception in a larger cohort of patients [144]. Furthermore, they proposed specific subsets of nontumor adult patients that seemed to achieve good speech perception. Patients who lost their auditory nerves from head trauma or severe ossification appeared to achieve better performance than those with neurological disorders, neuropathy, and cochlear malformations, in which the latter groups had performance levels closer to NF2 patients. In children with labyrinthine and cochlear aplasia and auditory nerve aplasia, there were also encouraging findings that they could achieve hearing benefits with the ABI with some achieving performance levels within the range of similarly-aged CI patients [140, 145].

In terms of the safety of the ABI, a meeting was convened by the Hacettepe Cochlear Implant Group on September 18, 2009 that gathered leading health care professionals and scientists involved with the ABI and prepared a consensus statement based on their discussions [146], which was further elaborated by a following meeting in 2013. It was concluded that the ABI, even in children and non-tumor patients, is considered safe in the hands of skilled surgeons with none of the main ABI centers worldwide reporting any permanent serious complications. Another recent report concluded that the percentages of complications for ABI surgeries not requiring tumor removal were surprisingly quite similar to those observed for the CI [147]. Considering the relative safety of the ABI by skilled implant surgeons and its potential for restoring speech perception, multiple clinics worldwide, including within USA, are now implanting the ABI in nontumor patients and even children younger than two years of age.

Another unexpected yet encouraging twist to the ABI story has occurred within the last few years. Since about 2004 to 2010, it was generally thought that the ABI could provide good hearing performance in some subset of nontumor patients but not in NF2 patients. Several hundred NF2 patients had been implanted with the ABI at House Ear Institute by the pioneers of the ABI, and none had achieved high levels of open-set speech perception comparable to CI patients. Most of these ABI patients achieved no or limited speech understanding [141]. Similar results were generally observed across different clinics [140, 148-150]. One hypothesis for this limited performance is that the NF2 tumor growth and/or its removal may be damaging crucial structures in the brainstem required for speech perception using the ABI [151]. In support of this hypothesis, one study [144] showed that over half of the 48 non-tumor patients implanted with the ABI achieved good open-set speech perception with a few reaching levels comparable to the top CI patients. These non-tumor ABI patients obtained an average score of 59% on an open-set speech test compared to an average score of 10% across 32 NF2 ABI patients. Considering that similar devices, stimulation strategies, and surgical approaches were used for both patient groups in the same clinic, these findings supported the hypothesis that the limited performance observed in NF2 patients is caused by damage to the cochlear nucleus related to the tumor and/or its removal.

The unexpected twist came about through findings by the ABI team at Würzburg Hospital in Germany, which included Joachim Müller and Cordula Matthies as well as Robert Behr from Fulda Hospital. Their team demonstrated in several NF2 patients that the ABI could restore high levels of speech understanding approaching that of top CI patients [152, 153]. There were few previous reports suggesting that the ABI may be able to restore good speech perception in NF2 patients [140, 154-156] but they were generally received with skepticism from the auditory implant community considering that several hundred NF2 patients were implanted with an ABI at House Ear Institute by the pioneers of the ABI and none achieved performance levels comparable to the top CI patients [141]. The Würzburg team has suggested that the use of careful microsurgery to minimize damage to the cochlear nucleus and its microvascular supply may be one key factor in enabling better hearing outcomes. These encouraging findings revive our optimism for the ABI in NF2 patients with the hope that similar findings can be replicated in other implant centers.

3.2.1.3 Improving ABI to surpass CI performance?

It is impressive that even with a surface array placed on the cochlear nucleus and broad activation of neurons, especially those within deeper regions of the cochlear nucleus that are the main neurons ascending to higher auditory centers, ABI patients can still achieve reasonable hearing performance in which some achieve performance levels comparable to the top CI patients. The findings described above strongly suggest that minimizing damage to the cochlear nucleus, especially during tumor removal surgery in NF2 patients and electrode array implantation, can lead to much better hearing results with the ABI. However, to eventually achieve more natural hearing capabilities for deaf patients, beyond what is possible with current CI systems, we need more stimulation channels of information [10, 13, 14, 157].

Consistent with this idea and starting in 2003, 10 NF2 patients were implanted with the penetrating ABI (PABI shown in Figure 5) to stimulate deeper regions of the cochlear nucleus along its tonotopic gradient and achieve more localized, frequency-specific activation [158, 159]. The PABI achieved some of these goals by enabling lower activation thresholds, less interference across sites, and a wider pitch range compared to the ABI. However, the performance didn't exceed those of typical ABI patients. One major limitation was that most of the PABI sites were not positioned into the auditory portion of the brainstem and produced significant side effects. It is expected that performance would improve if sites can be better positioned near appropriate neurons and they can correctly activate the neurons with improved stimulation strategies. Surgical approaches to deep brain structures are becoming more accurate and safer through technological advances in other neurological and psychiatric fields, in addition to improved techniques in the ABI field itself. Therefore, there are real opportunities through new types of PABI devices and a better understanding of stimulation coding within the cochlear nucleus to improve hearing performance with auditory brainstem devices.

3.2.2. *Auditory midbrain implants*

3.2.2.1 Rationale for the AMI

The initial motivation for the AMI is to provide an alternative hearing option to the ABI in NF2 deaf patients. AMI research and development began around 2000. Thomas Lenarz and Minoo Lenarz initiated AMI developments at Hannover Medical School in Germany with Jim Patrick and his team from Cochlear Limited in Australia, developing a human single-shank electrode array (Figure 7). They collaborated with Hubert Lim and David Anderson at University of Michigan in U.S. to validate this technology in animal studies, eventually obtaining sufficient evidence and approvals to begin the first clinical trial in 2006-2009 in which five NF2 deaf patients were implanted with the device. At the start of the AMI research, the ABI had not yet shown the ability to achieve good speech perception in NF2 patients. The AMI was developed to address the hypotheses described above, particularly in bypassing the damaged brainstem region in NF2 patients and in achieving more localized, frequency-specific activation. The first generation AMI device consists of a single shank array with 20 linearly spaced sites for alignment along the tonotopic gradient of the ICC (Figure 7). Although the ICC is higher up along the ascending pathway, there are several features that make it a potentially favorable target for an auditory implant.

Unlike the brainstem, the midbrain is directly visible during surgery and is not surrounded by distorted or damaged brain structures caused by a NF2 tumor and/or its removal. Further details of the surgical approach are provided in Refs. [160-162]. Surrounding the brainstem, there are also lower cranial nerves involved with critical functions such as breathing and swallowing that may not be easily visible during surgery. The trochlear nerve is the only nerve near the midbrain and is directly visible during surgery. In terms of function, the ICC has a well-defined tonotopic organization [163-167], which is favorable for implementing an auditory prosthesis [14, 157]. The IC is also the initial converging center of the central auditory system [168, 169]. Once the sound information is transmitted from the auditory nerve to the brain, it gets processed across multiple structures within the brainstem through several diverging pathways [170]. The ascending sound information and pathways then converge, for the most part, into the ICC en route to the thalamus and cortex. In other words, whichever neural pathways through the brainstem are involved with transmission of speech information to higher perceptual centers, it should be possible to implant electrode sites within specific regions of the ICC to access and stimulate those pathways. Whether artificial electrical stimulation of those pathways can restore sufficient speech perception needs to be assessed in future AMI patients.

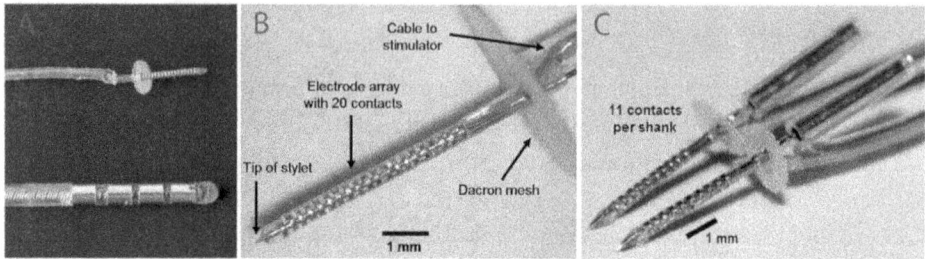

Fig. 7. AMI arrays developed by Cochlear Limited (Australia). **A** (top) and **B** show the first generation AMI array currently implanted into humans with 20 ring sites (200 μm spacing, 200 μm thickness, 400 μm diameter) along a silicone carrier. Dacron mesh prevents over-insertion of the array into the midbrain and tethers it to the brain. The AMI array is much smaller than current deep brain stimulation arrays used for various neurological and psychiatric disorders in which **A** (bottom) shows an example array developed by Medtronic (U.S.). **C** shows the second generation two-shank AMI array that will be implanted into deaf patients in a second clinical trial. Each shank consists of 11 ring sites along a silicone carrier (300 μm site spacing except for one site positioned closer to the Dacron mesh for tinnitus treatment; thus 10 sites to be positioned into the ICC). Images in **A** and **B** were taken from Refs. [139, 160] and reprinted with permission from Lippincott Williams & Wilkins.

3.2.2.2 Progress with the AMI

Prior to the clinical trial, animals studies showed that ICC stimulation achieves low threshold and frequency-specific auditory activation in animals that was better or comparable to CI stimulation [171, 172]. Studies in a cat model further demonstrated that long-term implantation and stimulation of the AMI device was safe without any major side effects and induced minimal tissue damage that was comparable to other clinically approved brain implants [173]. In terms of sound coding, multiple studies have shown that ICC neurons are capable of following the temporal modulations of acoustic stimuli up to or beyond 100 Hz and the ICC has a well-defined tonotopic organization [163, 164, 174-178]. Considering that speech perception, at least in quiet backgrounds, is possible with temporal modulations as low as ~50 Hz with just ~4-8 frequency channels [11, 13, 179], it was expected that the AMI would be able to restore reasonable speech perception using a CI-based strategy. In particular, each electrode site in a specific frequency region of the ICC would be presented with an amplitude modulated pulse train following the bandpass-filtered envelope extracted for the corresponding frequency channel.

After obtaining the necessary approvals, five patients were implanted with the AMI and provided with a CI-based strategy. Encouragingly, the AMI has proven to be safe in all five patients for over seven years and has provided improvements in lip-reading capabilities and environmental awareness with some speech perception, comparable to the range of performance achieved by most ABI NF2 patients [140, 141, 180, 181]. Unfortunately, only one of the five patients had the electrode array ideally aligned along the tonotopic gradient of the ICC, due to the difficulties in inserting the array into the midbrain with the appropriate angles during surgery. Nevertheless, this one patient exhibited good frequency-place coding as expected for the well-defined tonotopic organization within the ICC and also exhibited continuous improvements in hearing performance over time, reaching speech perception levels in the top range of performance across ABI patients at Hannover Medical School. These findings demonstrate that the AMI can be safely implanted and stimulated within the midbrain, different electrodes can access neurons across the tonotopic gradient of the ICC, and the AMI can achieve performance levels in the top range of ABI performance if the array can be aligned along the tonotopic gradient of the ICC.

3.2.2.3 Improving AMI to surpass CI performance?

The ICC is a three-dimensional structure with two-dimensional isofrequency laminae that have shown to code for varying temporal features of sound across different neurons [163, 176]. Unlike stimulation along the length of the cochlea, stimulation of a single site within a given frequency lamina in the ICC may not sufficiently activate higher centers using repeated electrical pulses. Although stimulation of different electrodes can access different frequency regions of the ICC to transmit spectral information, multi-site stimulation within a lamina may be needed to achieve sufficient temporal coding abilities for speech perception. Through additional animal and human studies [182-189], it was discovered that electrical stimulation with a single-shank AMI array with only one electrode in each two-dimensional ICC lamina caused massive suppressive effects in which one pulse significantly reduced the activity to proceeding pulses, which in turn would limit temporal coding capabilities. Encouragingly, these studies showed that a two-shank AMI array with at least two sites within each ICC lamina could greatly improve activation of the auditory system and potentially lead to better hearing performance.

Based on the encouraging animal and human findings and several improvements in the surgical approach, a second generation AMI device with a two-shank array was developed in collaboration with Cochlear Limited and is currently being investigated in a clinical trial through a collaboration with the University of Minnesota and Hannover Medical School that is funded by the National Institutes of Health (Figure 7) [162]. The initial objective of this clinical trial is to demonstrate better speech perception performance than typical ABI NF2 patients. However, the hope is that with the two-shank AMI design and the direct electrode interfacing with auditory neurons, hearing performance would reach the performance levels achieved by CI patients. Note that there are only 10 electrodes per AMI shank that will be positioned into the ICC due to limitations of the commercially approved stimulator by Cochlear Limited. Success with this clinical trial will open up opportunities to design new electrode arrays with a greater number of closely spaced electrodes to significantly increase the number of frequency channels of information and potentially exceed performance levels of the CI, assuming the appropriate stimulation strategies are developed for the ICC.

4. Conclusion

The CI has achieved a level of success beyond what could have been imagined 50 years ago. Many people who have severe to profound hearing loss can be implanted with a CI and obtain sufficient hearing to integrate into society. However, CI performance is still far from normal hearing and it suffers greatly in noisy environments and for more complex inputs such as music and multiple sources. Although extensive research over the past 20 years have attempted to significantly improve the CI, one critical bottleneck is the poor electrode-neural interface between the electrode array and auditory nerve fibers (i.e., SGNs), which limits the total number of independent frequency channels of information necessary to achieve more natural hearing. As described in this chapter, there are two encouraging approaches for improving the electrode-neural interface: (1) achieving better surgical placement of the electrode array into the cochlea to minimize damage and position electrodes closer to the target neural elements, and (2) implanting an electrode array into the brain to achieve direct contact of many sites with auditory neurons.

There are other exciting developments for auditory prostheses that have not yet been implemented in patients. One approach is to directly implant a multi-site array into the auditory nerve to improve specificity and increase the number of independent frequency channels of information. There have been encouraging animal and cadaver studies by several research groups for an auditory nerve implant [190-194] and it is expected that a clinical trial will occur in the near future. Another approach is to use laser stimulation as a new type of CI in order to achieve more focused activation of SGNs. This approach can use infrared laser stimulation to directly activate the neural elements [195, 196] or the neurons can be genetically modified to become sensitive to different types of laser wavelengths (known as optogenetics) for more specific activation [197, 198]. Several groups are also pursuing optogenetics to achieve more focused activation of the brainstem or midbrain [199-201], which could potentially enable a greater number of channels of information than possible with current ABI and AMI devices. Beyond the ABI and AMI, there are also research efforts to directly stimulate the auditory thalamus or auditory cortex for hearing restoration [202-205].

There are concerns regarding the risks for implanting electrode arrays or fiber bundles into the head and in genetically altering neurons to be sensitive to different laser wavelengths. Surgical and health concerns were also faced by the CI over 50 years ago and no one could have imagined that such a device could be safely implanted into humans and restore useful hearing. In looking towards the next 50 years, there should be a sense of optimism in the auditory field due to the success of the CI. This optimism is what should propel us forward with these new approaches to eventually achieve near normal hearing with auditory implants.

References

1. Wilson, B. S. and M. F. Dorman, Cochlear implants: a remarkable past and a brilliant future, *Hear Res*, **242**, pp. 3-21, 2008.
2. Zeng, F. G., S. Rebscher, W. Harrison, X. Sun, and H. Feng, Cochlear implants: system design, integration, and evaluation, *IEEE Rev Biomed Eng*, **1**, pp. 115-42, 2008.
3. Adams, J. S., M. S. Hasenstab, G. W. Pippin, and A. Sismanis, Telephone use and understanding in patients with cochlear implants, *Ear Nose Throat J*, **83**, pp. 96-103, 2004.
4. Weber, D. J., R. Friesen, and L. E. Miller, Interfacing the somatosensory system to restore touch and proprioception: essential considerations, *J Mot Behav*, **44**, pp. 403-418, 2012.
5. Weiland, J. D., A. K. Cho, and M. S. Humayun, Retinal prostheses: current clinical results and future needs, *Ophthalmology*, **118**, pp. 2227-2237, 2011.
6. Mudry, A. and M. Mills, The early history of the cochlear implant: a retrospective, *JAMA Otolaryngol Head Neck Surg*, 139, pp. 446-453, 2013.
7. Eisen, M. D., Djourno, Eyries, and the first implanted electrical neural stimulator to restore hearing, *Otol Neurotol*, **24**, pp. 500-506, 2003.
8. Eisenberg, L. S., The contributions of William F. House to the field of implantable auditory devices, *Hear Res*, **322**, pp. 52-56, 2015.
9. Lasker Foundatiion, Lasker~DeBakey Clinical Medical Research Award, *http://www.laskerfoundation.org/awards/show/modern-cochlear-implant*, 2013.
10. Nie, K., A. Barco, and F. G. Zeng, Spectral and temporal cues in cochlear implant speech perception, *Ear Hear*, **27**, pp. 208-217, 2006.

11. Shannon, R. V., F. G. Zeng, V. Kamath, J. Wygonski, and M. Ekelid, Speech recognition with primarily temporal cues, *Science*, **270**, pp. 303-304, 1995.

12. Smith, Z. M., B. Delgutte, and A. J. Oxenham, Chimaeric sounds reveal dichotomies in auditory perception, *Nature*, **416**, pp. 87-90, 2002.

13. Friesen, L. M., R. V. Shannon, D. Baskent, and X. Wang, Speech recognition in noise as a function of the number of spectral channels: comparison of acoustic hearing and cochlear implants, *J Acoust Soc Am*, **110**, pp. 1150-1163, 2001.

14. Shannon, R. V., Q. J. Fu, and J. Galvin, 3rd, The number of spectral channels required for speech recognition depends on the difficulty of the listening situation, *Acta Otolaryngol*, **Suppl 552**, pp. 50-54, 2004.

15. Shannon, R. V., F. G. Zeng, V. Kamath, J. Wygonski, and M. Ekelid, Speech recognition with primarily temporal cues, *Science*, **270**, pp. 303-304, 1995.

16. Dorman, M. F., P. C. Loizou, J. Fitzke, and Z. Tu, The recognition of sentences in noise by normal-hearing listeners using simulations of cochlear-implant signal processors with 6-20 channels, *J. Acoust. Soc. Am.*, **104**, pp. 3583-3585, 1998.

17. Friesen, L. M., R. V. Shannon, D. Baskent, and X. Wang, Speech recognition in noise as a function of the number of spectral channels: comparison of acoustic hearing and cochlear implants, *J Acoust Soc Am*, **110**, pp. 1150-1163, 2001.

18. Wilson, B. S., C. C. Finley, D. T. Lawson, R. D. Wolford, D. K. Eddington, and W. M. Rabinowitz, Better speech recognition with cochlear implants, *Nature*, **352**, pp. 236-238, 1991.

19. Riss, D., J. S. Hamzavi, M. Blineder, C. Honeder, I. Ehrenreich, A. Kaider, W. D. Baumgartner, W. Gstoettner, and C. Arnoldner, FS4, FS4-p, and FSP: a 4-month crossover study of 3 fine structure sound-coding strategies, *Ear and Hearing*, **35**, pp. e272-e281, 2014.

20. Tong, Y. C., G. M. Clark, P. J. Blamey, P. A. Busby, and R. C. Dowell, Psychophysical studies for two multiple-channel cochlear implant patients, *J Acoust Soc Am*, **71**, pp. 153-60, 1982.

21. Shannon, R. V., Multichannel electrical stimulation of the auditory nerve in man: I. Basic psychophysics, *Hear. Res.*, **11**, pp. 157-189, 1983.

22. Carlyon, R. P., J. M. Deeks, and C. M. McKay, The upper limit of temporal pitch for cochlear-implant listeners: stimulus duration, conditioner pulses, and the number of electrodes stimulated, *J Acoust Soc Am*, **127**, pp. 1469-1478, 2010.

23. Kong, Y. Y. and R. P. Carlyon, Temporal pitch perception at high rates in cochlear implants, *J Acoust Soc Am*, **127**, pp. 3114-3123, 2010.

24. Goldsworthy, R. L. and R. V. Shannon, Training improves cochlear implant rate discrimination on a psychophysical task, *J Acoust Soc Am*, **135**, pp. 334-341, 2014.

25. Rubinstein, J. T., B. S. Wilson, C. C. Finley, and P. J. Abbas, Pseudospontaneous activity: Stochastic independence of auditory nerve fibers with electrical stimulation, *Hear. Res.*, **127**, pp. 108-118, 1999.

26. Litvak, L. M., Z. M. Smith, B. Delgutte, and D. K. Eddington, Desynchronization of electrically evoked auditory-nerve activity by high-frequency pulse trains of long duration, *J Acoust Soc Am*, **114**, pp. 2066-2078, 2003.

27. Bonnet, R. M., P. P. Boermans, O. F. Avenarius, J. J. Briaire, and J. H. Frijns, Effects of pulse width, pulse rate and paired electrode stimulation on psychophysical measures of dynamic range and speech recognition in cochlear implants, *Ear Hear*, **33**, pp. 489-496, 2012.

28. Friesen, L. M., R. V. Shannon, and R. J. Cruz, Effects of stimulation rate on speech recognition with cochlear implants, *Audiol Neurootol*, **10**, pp. 169-84, 2005.

29. Chouard, C. H., C. Fugain, B. Meyer, and H. Lacombe, Long-term results of the multichannel cochlear implant, *Ann N Y Acad Sci*, **405**, pp. 387-411, 1983.

30. Dowell, R. C., G. M. Clark, P. M. Seligman, A. M. Brown, Perception of connected speech without lipreading, using a multi-channel hearing prosthesis, *Acta Otolaryngol*, **102**, pp. 7-11, 1986.

31. Festen, J. M. and R. Plomp, Effects of fluctuating noise and interfering speech on the speech-reception threshold for impaired and normal hearing, *J. Acoust. Soc. Am.*, **88**, pp. 1725-1736, 1990.

32. Oxenham, A. J. and H. A. Kreft, Speech perception in tones and noise via cochlear implants reveals influence of spectral resolution on temporal processing, *Trends Hear*, **18**, p. 2331216514553783, 2014.

33. Gregan, M. J., P. B. Nelson, and A. J. Oxenham, Behavioral measures of cochlear compression and temporal resolution as predictors of speech masking release in hearing-impaired listeners, *J Acoust Soc Am*, **134**, pp. 2895-2912, 2013.

34. Nelson, P. B., S. H. Jin, A. E. Carney, and D. A. Nelson, Understanding speech in modulated interference: Cochlear implant users and normal-hearing listeners, *J. Acoust. Soc. Am.*, **113**, pp. 961-968, 2003.

35. Qin, M. K. and A. J. Oxenham, Effects of simulated cochlear-implant processing on speech reception in fluctuating maskers, *J. Acoust. Soc. Am.*, **114**, pp. 446-454, 2003.

36. Stone, M. A. and B. C. J. Moore, On the near non-existence of "pure" energetic masking release for speech, J. Acoust. Soc. Am., **135**, pp. 1967-1977, 2014.

37. Oxenham, A. J., Pitch perception, *J Neurosci*, **32**, pp. 13335-13338, 2012.

38. Wightman, F. L., The pattern-transformation model of pitch, *J. Acoust. Soc. Am.*, **54**, pp. 407-416, 1973.

39. Goldstein, J. L., An optimum processor theory for the central formation of the pitch of complex tones, *J. Acoust. Soc. Am.*, **54**, pp. 1496-1516, 1973.

40. Terhardt, E., Pitch, consonance, and harmony, *J. Acoust. Soc. Am.*, **55**, pp. 1061-1069, 1974.

41. Licklider, J. C. R., A duplex theory of pitch perception, *Experientia*, **7**, p. 128-133, 1951.

42. Schouten, J. F., The residue and the mechanism of hearing, *Proc. Kon. Akad. Wetenschap.*, **43**, pp. 991-999, 1940.

43. Meddis, R. and L. O'Mard, A unitary model of pitch perception, *J. Acoust. Soc. Am.*, **102**, pp. 1811-1820, 1997.

44. Loeb, G. E., M. W. White, and M. M. Merzenich, Spatial cross correlation: A proposed mechanism for acoustic pitch perception, *Biol. Cybern.*, **47**, pp. 149-163, 1983.

45. Loeb, G. E., Are cochlear implant patients suffering from perceptual dissonance? *Ear Hear*, **26**, pp. 435-450, 2005.

46. Shamma, S. and D. Klein, The case of the missing pitch templates: How harmonic templates emerge in the early auditory system, *J. Acoust. Soc. Am.*, **107**, pp. 2631-2644, 2000.

47. Townshend, B., N .Cotter, D. Van Compernolle, and R. L. White, Pitch perception by cochlear implant subjects, *J. Acoust. Soc. Am.*, **82**, pp. 106-115, 1987.

48. von Bismark, G., Sharpness as an attribute of the timbre of steady sounds, *Acustica*, **30**, pp. 159-172, 1974.

49. McKay, C. M., H. J. McDermott, and R. P. Carlyon, Place and temporal cues in pitch perception: Are they truly independent? *Acoust. Res. Lett. Online*, 1, pp. 25-30, 2000.

50. Tong, Y. C., P. J Blamey, R. C. Dowell, and G. M.Clark, Psychophysical studies evaluating the feasibility of a speech processing strategy for a multiple-channel cochlear implant, *J. Acoust. Soc. Am.*, **74**, pp. 73-80, 1983.
51. Allen, E. J. and A. J. Oxenham, Symmetric interactions and interference between pitch and timbre, *J Acoust Soc Am*, **135**, pp. 1371-1379, 2014.
52. Bernstein, J. G. and A. J. Oxenham, The relationship between frequency selectivity and pitch discrimination: Sensorineural hearing loss, *J. Acoust. Soc. Am.*, **120**, pp. 3929-3945, 2006.
53. Bernstein, J. G. and A. J. Oxenham, The relationship between frequency selectivity and pitch discrimination: Effects of stimulus level, *J. Acoust. Soc. Am.*, **120**, pp. 3916-3928, 2006.
54. Oxenham, A. J., J. G. W. Bernstein, and H. Penagos, Correct tonotopic representation is necessary for complex pitch perception, *Proc Natl Acad Sci U S A*, **101**, pp. 1421-1425, 2004.
55. Carlyon, R. P., A .van Wieringen, C. J. Long, J. M. Deeks, and J. Wouters, Temporal pitch mechanisms in acoustic and electric hearing, *J Acoust Soc Am*, **112**, pp. 621-633, 2002.
56. Kreft, H. A., D. A. Nelson, and A. J. Oxenham, Modulation frequency discrimination with modulated and unmodulated interference in normal hearing and in cochlear-implant users, *J Assoc Res Otolaryngol*, **14**, p. 591-601, 2013.
57. Carlyon, R. P., Encoding the fundamental frequency of a complex tone in the presence of a spectrally overlapping masker, *J. Acoust. Soc. Am.*, **99**, pp. 517-524, 1996.
58. Micheyl, C., M. V. Keebler, and A. J. Oxenham, Pitch perception for mixtures of spectrally overlapping harmonic complex tones, *J Acoust Soc Am*, **128**, pp. 257-269, 2010.
59. Fu, Q.J., S. Chinchilla, G. Nogaki, and J. J. Galvin 3rd., Voice gender identification by cochlear implant users: the role of spectral and temporal resolution, *J Acoust Soc Am*, **118**, pp. 1711-1718, 2005.
60. Chatterjee, M., D. J. Zion, M. L. Deroche, B. A. Burianek, C. J. Limb, A. P. Goren, A. M. Kulkarni, and J. A. Christensen, Voice emotion recognition by cochlear-implanted children and their normally-hearing peers, *Hearing Research*, **322**, pp. 151-162, 2015.
61. Fu, Q. J., C. J. Hsu, and M. J. Horng, Effects of speech processing strategy on Chinese tone recognition by nucleus-24 cochlear implant users, *Ear and Hearing*, **25**, pp. 501-508, 2004.
62. Tao, D., R. Deng, Y. Jiang, J. J. Galvin 3rd, Q. J. Fu, and B. Chen, Melodic pitch perception and lexical tone perception in Mandarin-speaking cochlear implant users, *Ear and Hearing*, **36**, pp. 102-110, 2015.
63. Carlyon, R. P., How the brain separates sounds, *Trends Cogn Sci*, **8**, pp. 465-471, 2004.
64. Hong, R. S. and C. W. Turner, Pure-tone auditory stream segregation and speech perception in noise in cochlear implant recipients, *J Acoust Soc Am*, **120**, pp. 360-374, 2006.
65. Hong, R. S. and C. W. Turner, Sequential stream segregation using temporal periodicity cues in cochlear implant recipients, *J Acoust Soc Am*, **126**, pp. 291-299, 2009.
66. Cooper, H. R. and B. Roberts, Auditory stream segregation of tone sequences in cochlear implant listeners, *Hearing Research*, **225**, pp. 11-24, 2007.
67. Cooper, H. R. and B. Roberts, Auditory stream segregation in cochlear implant listeners: measures based on temporal discrimination and interleaved melody recognition, *Journal of the Acoustical Society of America*, **126**, pp. 1975-1987, 2009.
68. Blauert, J., *Spatial Hearing: The Psychophysics of Human Sound Localization*, (MIT Press, Cambridge, 1997).
69. Long, C. J., R. P. Carlyon, R. Y. Litovsky, and D. H. Downs, Binaural unmasking with bilateral cochlear implants, *J Assoc Res Otolaryngol*, **7**, pp. 352-360, 2006.

70. Seeber, B. U. and H. Fastl, Localization cues with bilateral cochlear implants, *J Acoust Soc Am*, **123**, pp. 1030-1042, 2008.

71. Bierer, J. A. and J. C. Middlebrooks, Cortical responses to cochlear implant stimulation: channel interactions, *J Assoc Res Otolaryngol*, **5**, pp. 32-48, 2004.

72. Srinivasan, A. G., M. Padilla, R. V. Shannon, and D. M. Landsberger, Improving speech perception in noise with current focusing in cochlear implant users, *Hear Res*, **299**, pp. 29-36, 2013.

73. Saoji, A. A. and L. M. Litvak, Use of "phantom electrode" technique to extend the range of pitches available through a cochlear implant, *Ear and Hearing*, **31**, pp. 693-701, 2010.

74. Nogueira, W., L. M. Litvak, A. A. Saoji, and A. Büchner, Design and evaluation of a cochlear implant strategy based on a "Phantom" channel, *PLoS One*, **10**, p. e0120148. 2015.

75. Pfingst, B. E., R. A. Burkholder-Juhasz, T. A. Zwolan, and L. Xu, Psychophysical assessment of stimulation sites in auditory prosthesis electrode arrays, *Hear Res*, **242**, pp. 172-183, 2008.

76. Zhou, N. and B. E. Pfingst, Psychophysically based site selection coupled with dichotic stimulation improves speech recognition in noise with bilateral cochlear implants, *Journal of the Acoustical Society of America*, **132**, pp. 994-1008, 2012.

77. Garadat, S. N., T. A. Zwolan, and B. E. Pfingst, Using temporal modulation sensitivity to select stimulation sites for processor MAPs in cochlear implant listeners, *Audiology and Neuro-Otology*, **18**, pp. 247-60, 2013.

78. Rau, T. S., T. Lenarz, and O. Majdani, Individual optimization of the insertion of a preformed cochlear implant electrode array, *Int J Otolaryngol*, **2015**, p. 724703, 2015.

79. Bielamowicz, S. A., N. J. Coker, H. A. Jenkins, and M. Igarashi, Surgical dimensions of the facial recess in adults and children, *Arch Otolaryngol Head Neck Surg*, **114**, pp. 534-537, 1988.

80. Kronenberg, J., L. Migirov, and T. Dagan, Suprameatal approach: new surgical approach for cochlear implantation, *J Laryngol Otol*, **115**, pp. 283-285, 2001.

81. Bruijnzeel, H., K. Draaisma, R. van Grootel, I. Stegeman, V. Topsakal, and W. Grolman, Systematic review on surgical outcomes and hearing preservation for cochlear implantation in children and adults, *Otolaryngol Head Neck Surg*, in press, p. 0194599815627146, 2016.

82. Labadie, R. F., R. Balachandran, J. H. Noble, G. S. Blachon, J. E. Mitchell, F. A. Reda, B. M. Dawant, and J. M. Fitzpatrick, Minimally invasive image-guided cochlear implantation surgery: first report of clinical implementation, *Laryngoscope*, **124**, pp. 1915-1922, 2014.

83. Wimmer, W., F. Venail, T. Williamson, M. Akkari, N. Gerber, S. Weber, M. Caversaccio, A. Uziel, and B. Bell, Semiautomatic cochleostomy target and insertion trajectory planning for minimally invasive cochlear implantation, *Biomed Res Int*, **2014**, p. 596498, 2014.

84. Carlson, M. L., C. L. Driscoll, R. H. Gifford, G. J. Service, N. M. Tombers, B. J. Hughes-Borst, B. A. Neff, and C. W. Beatty, Implications of minimizing trauma during conventional cochlear implantation, *Otol Neurotol*, **32**, pp. 962-968, 2011.

85. Wanna, G. B., J. H. Noble, M. L. Carlson, R. H. Gifford, M. S. Dietrich, D. S. Haynes, B. M. Dawant, and R. F. Labadie, Impact of electrode design and surgical approach on scalar location and cochlear implant outcomes, *Laryngoscope*, **124 Suppl 6**, pp. S1-S7, 2014.

86. Roland, P. S. and C. G. Wright, Surgical aspects of cochlear implantation: mechanisms of insertional trauma, *Adv Otorhinolaryngol*, **64**, pp. 11-30, 2006.

87. Nadol, J. B. Jr. and D. K. Eddington, Histopathology of the inner ear relevant to cochlear implantation, *Adv Otorhinolaryngol*, **64**, pp. 31-49, 2006.

88. Roche, J. P. and M. R. Hansen, On the horizon: Cochlear implant technology, *Otolaryngol Clin North Am*, **48**, pp. 1097-1116, 2015.

89. Nordfalk, K. F., K. Rasmussen, E. Hopp, M. Bunne, J. T. Silvola, and G. E. Jablonski, Insertion depth in cochlear implantation and outcome in residual hearing and vestibular function, *Ear Hear*, **37**, pp. e129-e137, 2016.

90. Sheffield, S. W., K. Jahn, and R. H. Gifford, Preserved acoustic hearing in cochlear implantation improves speech perception, *J Am Acad Audiol*, **26**, pp. 145-154, 2015.

91. Gantz, B. J., M. R. Hansen, C. W. Turner, J. J. Oleson, L. A. Reiss, and A. J. Parkinson, Hybrid 10 clinical trial: preliminary results, *Audiol Neurootol*, **14 Suppl 1**, pp. 32-38, 2009.

92. Turner, C. W., B. J. Gantz, S. Karsten, J. Fowler, L. A. Reiss, Impact of hair cell preservation in cochlear implantation: combined electric and acoustic hearing, *Otol Neurotol*, **31**, pp. 1227-1232. 2010.

93. Golub, J. S., J. H. Won, W. R. Drennan, T. D. Worman, and J. T. Rubinstein, Spectral and temporal measures in hybrid cochlear implant users: on the mechanism of electroacoustic hearing benefits, *Otol Neurotol*, **33**, pp. 147-153, 2012.

94. Lenarz, T., T. Stöver, A. Buechner, A. Lesinski-Schiedat, J. Patrick, and J. Pesch, Hearing conservation surgery using the Hybrid-L electrode. Results from the first clinical trial at the Medical University of Hannover, *Audiol Neurootol*, **14 Suppl 1**, pp. 22-31, 2009.

95. Gantz, B. J., C. Dunn, J. Oleson, M. Hansen, A. Parkinson, and C. Turner, Multicenter clinical trial of the Nucleus Hybrid S8 cochlear implant: Final outcomes, *Laryngoscope*, **126**, pp. 962-973, 2016.

96. Santa Maria, P. L., C. Domville-Lewis, C. M. Sucher, R. Chester-Browne, and M. D. Atlas, Hearing preservation surgery for cochlear implantation--hearing and quality of life after 2 years, **Otol Neurotol**, **34**, pp. 526-531, 2013.

97. Mowry, S. E., E. Woodson, and B.J. Gantz, New frontiers in cochlear implantation: acoustic plus electric hearing, hearing preservation, and more, *Otolaryngol Clin North Am*, **45**, pp. 187-203, 2012.

98. Quesnel, A. M., H. H. Nakajima, J. J. Rosowski, M. R. Hansen, B. J. Gantz, and J. B. Nadol Jr., Delayed loss of hearing after hearing preservation cochlear implantation: Human temporal bone pathology and implications for etiology, *Hear Res*, **333**, pp. 225-234, 2015.

99. Kopelovich, J. C., L. A Reiss, C. P. Etler, L. Xu, J. T. Bertroche, B. J. Gantz, and M. R. Hansen, Hearing loss after activation of hearing preservation cochlear implants might be related to afferent cochlear innervation injury, *Otol Neurotol*, **36**, pp. 1035-1044, 2015.

100. Cosetti, M. K., D. R. Friedmann, B. Z. Zhu, S. E. Heman-Ackah, Y. Fang, R. G. Keller, W. H. Shapiro, J. T. Roland Jr, and S. B. Waltzman, The effects of residual hearing in traditional cochlear implant candidates after implantation with a conventional electrode, *Otol Neurotol*, **34**, pp. 516-521, 2013.

101. Balkany, T. J., S. S. Connell, A. V. Hodges, S. L. Payne, F. F. Telischi, A. A. Eshraghi, S. I. Angeli, R. Germani, S. Messiah, and K. L. Arheart, Conservation of residual acoustic hearing after cochlear implantation, *Otol Neurotol*, **27**, pp. 1083-1088, 2006.

102. D'Elia, A., R. Bartoli, F. Giagnotti, and N. Quaranta, The role of hearing preservation on electrical thresholds and speech performances in cochlear implantation, *Otol Neurotol*, **33**, pp. 343-347, 2012.

103. Wardrop, P., D. Whinney, S. J. Rebscher, J. T. Roland Jr, W. Luxford, P. A. Leake, A temporal bone study of insertion trauma and intracochlear position of cochlear implant electrodes. I: Comparison of Nucleus banded and Nucleus Contour electrodes, *Hear Res*, **203**, pp. 54-67, 2005.

104. Ketten, D. R., M. W. Skinner, G. Wang, M. W. Vannier, G. A. Gates, and J. G. Neely, In vivo measures of cochlear length and insertion depth of nucleus cochlear implant electrode arrays, *Ann Otol Rhinol Laryngol Suppl*, **175**, pp. 11-16, 1998.

105. Holden, L. K., C. C. Finley, J. B. Firszt, T. A. Holden, C. Brenner, L. G. Potts, B. D. Gotter, S. S. Vanderhoof, K. Mispagel, G. Heydebrand, M. W. Skinner, Factors affecting open-set word recognition in adults with cochlear implants, *Ear Hear*, **34**, pp. 342-360, 2013.

106. Adunka, O. F., A. Radeloff, W. K. Gstoettner, H. C. Pillsbury, and C. A. Buchman, Scala tympani cochleostomy II: topography and histology, *Laryngoscope*, **117**, pp. 2195-2200, 2007.

107. Finley, C. C., T. A. Holden, L. K. Holden, B. R. Whiting, R. A. Chole, G. J. Neely, T. E. Hullar, and M. W. Skinner, Role of electrode placement as a contributor to variability in cochlear implant outcomes, *Otol Neurotol*, **29**, pp. 920-928, 2008.

108. Shepherd, R. K., S. Hatsushika, and G. M. Clark, Electrical stimulation of the auditory nerve: the effect of electrode position on neural excitation, *Hear Res*, **66**, pp. 108-120, 1993.

109. Zhou, L., D. R. Friedmann, C. Treaba, R. Peng, and J. T. Roland Jr., Does cochleostomy location influence electrode trajectory and intracochlear trauma? *Laryngoscope*, **125**, pp. 966-971, 2015.

110. Aschendorff, A., J. Kromeier, T. Klenzner, and R. Laszig, Quality control after insertion of the nucleus contour and contour advance electrode in adults, *Ear Hear*, **28 Suppl**, pp. 75S-79S, 2007.

111. Skinner, M. W., T. A. Holden, B. R. Whiting, A. H. Voie, B. Brunsden, J. G. Neely, E. A. Saxon, T. E. Hullar, and C. C. Finley, In vivo estimates of the position of advanced bionics electrode arrays in the human cochlea, *Ann Otol Rhinol Laryngol Suppl*, **197**, pp. 22-24. 2007.

112. van der Beek, F. B., P. P. Boermans, B. M. Verbist, J. J. Briaire, and J. H. Frijns, Clinical evaluation of the Clarion CII HiFocus 1 with and without positioner, *Ear Hear*, **26**, pp. 577-592, 2005.

113. Waltzman, S. B. and J. T. Roland, *Cochlear implants, 3rd ed.*, (Thieme, New York, 2013), xii, 256 pages.

114. Buchman, C. A., M. T. Dillon, E. R. King, M. C. Adunka, O. F. Adunka, and H. C. Pillsbury, Influence of cochlear implant insertion depth on performance: a prospective randomized trial, *Otol Neurotol*, **35**, pp. 1773-1779, 2014.

115. Skinner, M. W., D. R. Ketten, L. K. Holden, G. W. Harding, P. G. Smith, G. A. Gates, J. G. Neely, G. R. Kletzker, B. Brunsden, and B. Blocker, CT-derived estimation of cochlear morphology and electrode array position in relation to word recognition in Nucleus-22 recipients, *J Assoc Res Otolaryngol*, **3**, pp. 332-350, 2002.

116. Yukawa, K., L. Cohen, P. Blamey, B. Pyman, V. Tungvachirakul, and S. O'Leary, Effects of insertion depth of cochlear implant electrodes upon speech perception, *Audiol Neurootol*, **9**, pp. 163-72, 2004.

117. Adunka, O. and J. Kiefer, Impact of electrode insertion depth on intracochlear trauma, *Otolaryngol Head Neck Surg*, 135, pp. 374-382, 2006.

118. Leake, P. A., G. T. Hradek, and R. L. Snyder, Chronic electrical stimulation by a cochlear implant promotes survival of spiral ganglion neurons after neonatal deafness, *J Comp Neurol*, **412**, pp. 543-562, 1999.

119. Briggs, R. J., M. Tykocinski, R. Lazsig, A. Aschendorff, T. Lenarz, T. Stöver, B. Fraysse, M. Marx, J. T. Roland Jr, P. S. Roland, C. G. Wright, B. J. Gantz, J. F. Patrick, F. Risi, Development and evaluation of the modiolar research array--multi-centre collaborative study in human temporal bones, *Cochlear Implants Int*, **12**, pp. 129-139, 2011.

120. Jurawitz, M. C., A. Büchner, T. Harpel, M. Schüssler, O. Majdani, A. Lesinski-Schiedat, and T. Lenarz, Hearing preservation outcomes with different cochlear implant electrodes: Nucleus(R) Hybrid-L24 and Nucleus Freedom CI422, *Audiol Neurootol*, **19**, pp. 293-309, 2014.

121. Van Abel, K. M., C. C. Dunn, D. P. Sladen, J. J. Oleson, C. W. Beatty, B. A. Neff, M. Hansen, B. J. Gantz, and C. L. Driscoll, Hearing preservation among patients undergoing cochlear implantation, *Otol Neurotol*, **36**, pp. 416-421, 2015.

122. Hassepass, F., S. Bulla, W. Maier, R. Laszig, S. Arndt, R. Beck, L. Traser, and A. Aschendorff, The new mid-scala electrode array: a radiologic and histologic study in human temporal bones, *Otol Neurotol*, **35**, pp. 1415-1420, 2014.

123. Hunter, J. B., R. H. Gifford, G. B. Wanna, R. F. Labadie, M. L. Bennett, D. S. Haynes, and A. Rivas, Hearing preservation outcomes with a mid-scala electrode in cochlear implantation, *Otol Neurotol*, **37**, pp. 235-240, 2016.

124. Singla, A., D. Sahni, A. K. Gupta, A. Aggarwal, and T. Gupta, Surgical anatomy of the basal turn of the human cochlea as pertaining to cochlear implantation, *Otol Neurotol*, **36**, pp. 323-328, 2015.

125. Zhang, J., W. Wei, J. Ding, J. T. Roland Jr, S. Manolidis, and N. Simaan, Inroads toward robot-assisted cochlear implant surgery using steerable electrode arrays, *Otol Neurotol*, **31**, pp. 1199-1206, 2010.

126. Majdani, O., T. Lenarz, N. Pawsey, F. Risi, G. Sedlmayr, and T. Rau, First results with a prototype of a new cochlear implant electrode featuring shape memory effect, *Biomed Tech (Berl)*, **58 (Suppl. 1)**, 2013.

127. Richard, C., J. N. Fayad, J. Doherty, F. H. Linthicum Jr., Round window versus cochleostomy technique in cochlear implantation: histologic findings, *Otol Neurotol*, **33**, pp. 1181-1187, 2012.

128. Hassepass, F., A. Aschendorff, S. Bulla, S. Arndt, W. Maier, R. Laszig, and R. Beck, Radiologic results and hearing preservation with a straight narrow electrode via round window versus cochleostomy approach at initial activation, *Otol Neurotol*, **36**, pp. 993-1000, 2015.

129. Havenith, S., S. Havenith, M. J. Lammers, R. A. Tange, F. Trabalzini, A. della Volpe, G. J. van der Heijden, and W. Grolman, Hearing preservation surgery: cochleostomy or round window approach? A systematic review, *Otol Neurotol*, **34**, pp. 667-674, 2013.

130. Alyono, J. C., C. E. Corrales, M. E. Huth, N. H. Blevins, and A. J. Ricci, Development and characterization of chemical cochleostomy in the Guinea pig, *Otolaryngol Head Neck Surg*, **152**, pp. 1113-1118, 2015.

131. Majdani, O., D. Schurzig, A. Hussong, T. Rau, J. Wittkopf, T. Lenarz, and R. F. Labadie, Force measurement of insertion of cochlear implant electrode arrays in vitro: comparison of surgeon to automated insertion tool, *Acta Otolaryngol*, **130**, pp. 31-36, 2010.

132. Kontorinis, G., G. Paasche, T. Lenarz, and T. Stöver, The effect of different lubricants on cochlear implant electrode insertion forces, *Otol Neurotol*, **32**, pp. 1050-1056, 2011.

133. Rajan, G. P., G. Kontorinis, and J. Kuthubutheen, The effects of insertion speed on inner ear function during cochlear implantation: a comparison study, *Audiol Neurootol*, **18**, pp. 17-22, 2013.

134. Campbell, L., A. Kaicer, R. Briggs, and S. O'Leary, Cochlear response telemetry: intracochlear electrocochleography via cochlear implant neural response telemetry pilot study results, *Otol Neurotol*, 36, pp. 399-405, 2015.

135. Adunka, O. F., C. K. Giardina, E. J. Formeister, B. Choudhury, C. A. Buchman, and D. C. Fitzpatrick, Round window electrocochleography before and after cochlear implant electrode insertion, *Laryngoscope*, lary.25602, 2015.

136. Sweeney, A. D., M. L. Carlson, M. G. Zuniga, M. L. Bennett, G. B. Wanna, D. S. Haynes, and A. Rivas, Impact of perioperative oral steroid use on low-frequency hearing preservation after cochlear implantation, *Otol Neurotol*, **36**, pp. 1480-1485, 2015.

137. Bas, E., J. Bohorquez, S. Goncalves, E. Perez, C. T. Dinh, C. Garnham, R. Hessler, A. A. Eshraghi, and T. R. van de Water, Electrode array-eluted dexamethasone protects against electrode insertion trauma induced hearing and hair cell losses, damage to neural elements, increases in impedance and fibrosis: A dose response study, *Hear Res*, 2016.

138. Lim, H. H. and R. V. Shannon, Two Laskers and counting: learning from the past enables future innovations with central neural prostheses, *Brain Stimul*, 8, pp. 439-441, 2015.

139. Lenarz, T., H. H. Lim, G. Reuter, J. F. Patrick, and M. Lenarz, The auditory midbrain implant: a new auditory prosthesis for neural deafness-concept and device description, *Otol Neurotol*, **27**, pp. 838-843, 2006.

140. Sennaroglu, L. and I. Ziyal, Auditory brainstem implantation, *Auris Nasus Larynx*, **39**, pp. 439-450, 2012.

141. Schwartz, M. S., S. R. Otto, R. V. Shannon, W. E. Hitselberger, and D. E. Brackmann, Auditory brainstem implants, *Neurotherapeutics*, **5**, pp. 128-136, 2008.

142. Vincent, C., Auditory brainstem implants: how do they work? *Anat Rec*, **295**, pp. 1981-1986, 2012.

143. Colletti, V., M. Carner, V. Miorelli, L. Colletti, M. Guida, and F. Fiorino, Auditory brainstem implant in posttraumatic cochlear nerve avulsion, *Audiol Neurootol*, **9**, pp. 247-255, 2004

144. Colletti, V., R. Shannon, M. Carner, S. Veronese, and L. Colletti, Outcomes in nontumor adults fitted with the auditory brainstem implant: 10 years' experience, *Otol Neurotol*, **30**, pp. 614-618, 2009.

145. Colletti, V., M. Carner, V. Miorelli, M. Guida, L. Colletti, and F. Fiorino, Auditory brainstem implant (ABI): new frontiers in adults and children, Otolaryngology, **133**, pp. 126-138, 2005.

146. Sennaroglu, L., V. Colletti, M. Manrique, R. Laszig, E. Offeciers, S. Saeed, R. Ramsden, S. Sarac, S. Freeman, H. R. Andersen, A. Zarowski, I. Ziyal, W. P. Sollmann, J. Kaminsky, B. Bejarano, A. Atas, G. Sennaroglu, E. Yucel, S. Sevinc, L. Colletti, A. Huarte, L. Henderson, T. Wesarg, and K. Konradsson, Auditory brainstem implantation in children and non-neurofibromatosis type 2 patients: a consensus statement, *Otol Neurotol*, **32**, pp. 187-191, 2011.

147. Colletti, V., R. V. Shannon, M. Carner, S. Veronese, and L. Colletti, Complications in auditory brainstem implant surgery in adults and children, *Otol Neurotol*, **31**, pp. 558-564, 2010.

148. Lenarz, M., C. Matthies, A. Lesinski-Schiedat, C. Frohne, U. Rost, A. Illg, R. D. Battmer, M. Samii, and T. Lenarz, Auditory brainstem implant part II: subjective assessment of functional outcome, *Otol Neurotol*, **23**, pp. 694-697, 2002.

149. Nevison, B., R. Laszig, W. P. Sollmann, T. Lenarz, O. Sterkers, R. Ramsden, B. Fraysse, M. Manrique, H. Rask-Andersen, E. Garcia-Ibanez, V. Colletti, and E. von Wallenberg, Results from a European clinical investigation of the Nucleus multichannel auditory brainstem implant, *Ear Hear*, **23**, pp. 170-183, 2002.

150. Kanowitz, S. J., W. H. Shapiro, J. G. Golfinos, N. L. Cohen, J. T. Roland Jr., Auditory brainstem implantation in patients with neurofibromatosis type 2, *Laryngoscope*, **114**, pp. 2135-2146, 2004.

151. Colletti, V. and R. V. Shannon, Open set speech perception with auditory brainstem implant? *Laryngoscope*, **115**, pp. 1974-1978, 2005.

152. Matthies, C., S. Brill, C. Varallyay, L. Solymosi, G. Gelbrich, K. Roosen, R. I. Ernestus, J. Helms, R. Hagen, R. Mlynski, W. Shehata-Dieler, and J. Müller, Auditory brainstem implants

in neurofibromatosis Type 2: is open speech perception feasible? *J Neurosurg*, **120**, pp. 546-558, 2014.

153. Colletti, L., R. Shannon, and V. Colletti, Auditory brainstem implants for neurofibromatosis type 2. *Curr Opin Otolaryngol Head Neck Surg*, **20**, pp. 353-357, 2012.

154. Skarzynski, H., J. Szuchnik, A. Lorens, and R. Zawadzki, First auditory brainstem implantation in Poland: auditory perception results over 12 months, *J Laryngol Otol Suppl*, **27**, pp. 44-45, 2000.

155. Behr, R., J. Müller, W. Shehata-Dieler, H. P. Schlake, J. Helms, K. Roosen, N. Klug, B. Hölper, and A. Lorens, The high rate CIS Auditory Brainstem Implant for Restoration of Hearing in NF-2 patients, *Skull Base*, **17**, pp. 91-107, 2007.

156. Matthies, C., S. Brill, K. Kaga, A. Morita, K. Kumakawa, H. Skarzynski, A. Claassen, Y. Hui, C. Chiong, J. Müller, and R. Behr, Auditory brainstem implantation improves speech recognition in neurofibromatosis type II patients, *ORL J Otorhinolaryngol Relat Spec*, **75**, pp. 282-295, 2013.

157. Xu, L. and B. E. Pfingst, Spectral and temporal cues for speech recognition: implications for auditory prostheses, *Hear Res*, **242**, pp. 132-140, 2008.

158. McCreery, D. B., Cochlear nucleus auditory prostheses, *Hear Res*, **242**, pp. 64-73, 2008.

159. Otto, S. R., R. V Shannon, E. P. Wilkinson, W. E. Hitselberger, D. B. McCreery, J. K. Moore, and D. E. Brackmann, Audiologic outcomes with the penetrating electrode auditory brainstem implant, *Otol Neurotol*, **29**, pp. 1147-1154, 2008.

160. Samii, A., M. Lenarz, O. Majdani, H. H. Lim, M. Samii, and T. Lenarz, Auditory midbrain implant: a combined approach for vestibular schwannoma surgery and device implantation, *Otol Neurotol*, **28**, pp. 31-38, 2007.

161. Vince, G. H., C. Herbold, J. Coburger, T. Westermaier, D. Drenckhahn, A. Schuetz, E. Kunze, L. Solymosi, K. Roosen, and C. Matthies, An anatomical assessment of the supracerebellar midline and paramedian approaches to the inferior colliculus for auditory midbrain implants using a neuronavigation model on cadaveric specimens, *J Clin Neurosci*, **17**, pp. 107-112, 2010.

162. Lim, H. H. and T. Lenarz, Auditory midbrain implant: research and development towards a second clinical trial, *Hear Res*, **322**, pp. 212-223, 2015.

163. Oliver, D. L., Neuronal organization in the inferior colliculus, in eds. J. A. Winer and C.E. Schreiner, *The Inferior Colliculus*, (Springer, New York, 2005) pp. 69-114.

164. Schreiner, C. E. and G. Langner, Laminar fine structure of frequency organization in auditory midbrain, *Nature*, **388**, pp. 383-386, 1997.

165. De Martino, F., M. Moerel, P. F. van de Moortele, K. Ugurbil, R. Goebel, E. Yacoub, and E. Formisano, Spatial organization of frequency preference and selectivity in the human inferior colliculus, *Nat Commun*, **4**, p. 1386, 2013.

166. Lim, H. H., M. Lenarz, G. Joseph, and T. Lenarz, Frequency representation within the human brain: Stability versus plasticity, *Sci Rep*, **3**, p. 1474, 2013.

167. Ress, D. and B. Chandrasekaran, Tonotopic organization in the depth of human inferior colliculus, *Front Hum Neurosci*, **7**, p. 586, 2013.

168. Casseday, J. H., T. Fremouw, and E. Covey, The inferior colliculus: A hub for the central auditory system, in eds. D. Oertel, R. R. Fay, and A. N. Popper, *Springer Handbook of Auditory Research: Integrative Functions in the Mammalian Auditory Pathway (Vol. 15)*, (Springer-Verlag, New York, 2002) pp. 238-318.

169. Ehret, G., The auditory midbrain, a "shunting yard" of acoustical information processing, in eds. G. Ehret and R. Romand ,*The Central Auditory System*, (Oxford University Press, New York,1997), pp. 259-316.

170. Cant, N. B. and C. G. Benson, Parallel auditory pathways: projection patterns of the different neuronal populations in the dorsal and ventral cochlear nuclei, *Brain Res Bull*, **60**, pp. 457-474, 2003.

171. Lim, H. H. and D. J. Anderson, Auditory cortical responses to electrical stimulation of the inferior colliculus: implications for an auditory midbrain implant, *J Neurophysiol*, **96**, pp. 975-988, 2006.

172. Lenarz, M., J. F. Patrick, D. J. Anderson, and T. Lenarz, Electrophysiological validation of a human prototype auditory midbrain implant in a guinea pig model, *J Assoc Res Otolaryngol*, **7**, pp. 383-398, 2006.

173. Lenarz, M., H. H. Lim, T. Lenarz, U. Reich, N. Marquardt, M. N. Klingberg, G. Paasche, G. Reuter, and A. C. Stan, Auditory midbrain implant: histomorphologic effects of long-term implantation and electric stimulation of a new deep brain stimulation array, *Otol Neurotol*, **28**, pp. 1045-1052, 2007.

174. Joris, P. X., C. E. Schreiner, and A. Rees, Neural processing of amplitude-modulated sounds, *Physiol Rev*, **84**, pp. 541-577, 2004.

175. Langner, G., M. Albert, and T. Briede, Temporal and spatial coding of periodicity information in the inferior colliculus of awake chinchilla (Chinchilla laniger), *Hear Res*, **168**, pp. 110-130, 2002.

176. Rees, A. and G. Langner, Temporal coding in the auditory midbrain, in eds. J.A. Winer and C.E. Schreiner, *The Inferior Colliculus*, (Springer, New York, 2005), pp. 346-376.

177. Geniec, P. and D. K. Morest, The neuronal architecture of the human posterior colliculus. A study with the Golgi method, *Acta Otolaryngol Suppl*, **295**, pp. 1-33, 1971.

178. Rode, T., T. Hartmann, P. Hubka, V. Scheper, M. Lenarz, T. Lenarz, A. Kral, and H. H. Lim, Neural representation in the auditory midbrain of the envelope of vocalizations based on a peripheral ear model, *Front Neural Circuits*, **7**, p. 166, 2013.

179. Zeng, F. G., Trends in cochlear implants, *Trends Amplif*, **8**, pp. 1-34, 2004.

180. Lim, H. H., M. Lenarz, and T. Lenarz, Midbrain Auditory Prostheses, in eds. F. G. Zeng, R. R. Fay, and A. N. Popper, *Auditory Prostheses: New Horizons*,(Springer, New York, 2011). pp. 207-232.

181. Lim, H. H., M. Lenarz, and T. Lenarz, Auditory midbrain implant: a review, *Trends Amplif*, **13**, pp. 149-180, 2009.

182. Lim, H. H., T. Lenarz, G. Joseph, R. D. Battmer, J. F. Patrick, and M. Lenarz, Effects of phase duration and pulse rate on loudness and pitch percepts in the first auditory midbrain implant patients: Comparison to cochlear implant and auditory brainstem implant results, *Neuroscience*, **154**, pp. 370-380, 2008.

183. McKay, C. M., H. H. Lim, and T. Lenarz, Temporal processing in the auditory system : insights from cochlear and auditory midbrain implantees, *J Assoc Res Otolaryngol*, **14**, pp. 103-124, 2013.

184. Straka, M. M., M. McMahon, C. D. Markovitz and H. H. Lim, Effects of location and timing of co-activated neurons in the auditory midbrain on cortical activity: implications for a new central auditory prosthesis, *J Neural Eng*, **11**, p. 046021, 2014.

185. Straka, M. M., D. Schendel, and H. H. Lim, Neural integration and enhancement from the inferior colliculus up to different layers of auditory cortex, J Neurophysiol, **110**, pp. 1009-1020, 2013.

186. Straka, M. M., S. Schmitz, and H. H. Lim, Response features across the auditory midbrain reveal an organization consistent with a dual lemniscal pathway, *J Neurophysiol*, **112**, pp. 981-998, 2014.

187. Calixto, R., M. Lenarz, A. Neuheiser, V. Scheper, T. Lenarz, H. H. Lim, Coactivation of different neurons within an isofrequency lamina of the inferior colliculus elicits enhanced auditory cortical activation, *J Neurophysiol*, **108**, pp. 1199-1210, 2012.

188. Neuheiser, A., M. Lenarz, G. Reuter, R. Calixto, I. Nolte, T. Lenarz, and H. H. Lim, Effects of pulse phase duration and location of stimulation within the inferior colliculus on auditory cortical evoked potentials in a guinea pig model, *J Assoc Res Otolaryngol*, **11**, pp. 689-708, 2010.

189. Lim, H. H. and D. J. Anderson, Spatially distinct functional output regions within the central nucleus of the inferior colliculus: Implications for an auditory midbrain implant, *J Neurosci*, **27**, pp. 8733-8743, 2007.

190. Middlebrooks, J. C. and R. L. Snyder, Selective electrical stimulation of the auditory nerve activates a pathway specialized for high temporal acuity, *J Neurosci*, **30**, pp. 1937-1946, 2010.

191. Middlebrooks, J. C. and R. L. Snyder, Auditory prosthesis with a penetrating nerve array, *J Assoc Res Otolaryngol*, **8**, pp. 258-279, 2007.

192. Kim, S. J., A. N. Badi, and R. A. Normann, Selective activation of cat primary auditory cortex by way of direct intraneural auditory nerve stimulation, *Laryngoscope*, **117**, pp. 1053-1062, 2007.

193. Hillman, T., A. N. Badi, R. A. Normann, T. Kertesz, and C. Shelton, Cochlear nerve stimulation with a 3-dimensional penetrating electrode array, *Otol Neurotol*, **24**, pp. 764-768, 2003.

194. Arts, H. A., D. A. Jones, and D. J. Anderson, Prosthetic stimulation of the auditory system with intraneural electrodes, *Ann Otol Rhinol Laryngol Suppl*, **191**, pp. 20-25, 2003.

195. Young, H. K., X. Tan, N. Xia, and C. P. Richter, Target structures for cochlear infrared neural stimulation, *Neurophotonics*, **2**, p. 025002, 2015.

196. Rajguru, S. M., A. I. Matic, A. M. Robinson, A. J. Fishman, L.E. Moreno, A. Bradley, I. Vujanovic, J. Breen, J. D. Wells, M. Bendett, and C. P. Richter, Optical cochlear implants: evaluation of surgical approach and laser parameters in cats, *Hear Res*, **269**, pp. 102-111, 2010.

197. Jeschke, M. and T. Moser, Considering optogenetic stimulation for cochlear implants, *Hear Res*, **322**, pp. 224-234, 2015.

198. Hernandez, V. H., A. Gehrt, Z. Jing, G. Hoch, M. Jeschke, N. Strenzke, and T. Moser, Optogenetic stimulation of the auditory nerve, *J Vis Exp*, **92**, p. e52069, 2014

199. Guo, W., A. E. Hight, J. X. Chen, N. C. Klapoetke, K. E. Hancock, B. G. Shinn-Cunningham, E. S. Boyden, D. J. Lee, and D. B. Polley, Hearing the light: neural and perceptual encoding of optogenetic stimulation in the central auditory pathway, *Sci Rep*, **5**, p. 10319, 2015.

200. Hight, A.E., E. D. Kozin, K. Darrow, A. Lehmann, E. Boyden, M. C. Brown, D. J. Lee, Superior temporal resolution of Chronos versus channelrhodopsin-2 in an optogenetic model of the auditory brainstem implant, *Hear Res*, **322**, pp. 235-241, 2015.

201. Darrow, K.N., M. C. Slama, E. D. Kozin, M. Owoc, K. Hancock, J. Kempfle, A. Edge, S. Lacour, E. Boyden, D. Polley, M. C. Brown, and D. J. Lee, Optogenetic stimulation of the cochlear nucleus using channelrhodopsin-2 evokes activity in the central auditory pathways, *Brain Res*, **1599**, pp. 44-56, 2015.

202. Atencio, C.A., J. Y. Shih, C. E. Schreiner, and S. W. Cheung, Primary auditory cortical responses to electrical stimulation of the thalamus, *J Neurophysiol*, **111**, pp. 1077-1087, 2014.

203. Otto, K. J., P. J. Rousche, and D. R. Kipke, Microstimulation in auditory cortex provides a substrate for detailed behaviors, *Hear Res*, **210**, pp. 112-117, 2005.

204. Smith, E., S. Kellis, P. House, and B. Greger, Decoding stimulus identity from multi-unit activity and local field potentials along the ventral auditory stream in the awake primate: implications for cortical neural prostheses, *J Neural Eng*, **10**, p. 016010, 2013.

205. Dobelle, W.H., S. S. Stensaas, M. G. Mladejovsky, and J. B. Smith, A prosthesis for the deaf based on cortical stimulation, *Ann Otol Rhinol Laryngol*, **82**, pp. 445-463, 1973.

Chapter 3.7

Spinal Cord Stimulation for Pain Control

John L. Parker

Saluda Medical Pty Ltd, Lvl1 407 Pacific Highway, Artarmon, NSW, 2064, Australia
john.parker@saludamedical.com

Spinal cord stimulation (SCS) has been used to provide relief from chronic intractable pain for over thirty years and recently significant improvements in efficacy have been reported. A description of devices, procedures for use and clinical results are provided along with a review of studies relevant to a discussion of the mechanism of action. Data from electrically evoked compound action potentials are used to define the electrophysiological responses of the dorsal column fibers and the implications for stimulation parameter setting are discussed. The concept of an SCS therapeutic window is introduced and how this relates to both conventional SCS and the rationale for newly developed closed loop SCS are presented.

1. Introduction

Shealy performed the first spinal cord stimulation (SCS) procedure for pain in 1967 [1]. The recipient, a terminally ill cancer patient, reported effective pain relief for a period of one and a half days before he died suddenly of bacterial endocarditis. Shealy was motivated by the recent publication of the gate theory of a pain by Melzack and Wall [2]. This suggested that activation of mechano-sensory fibers would, via a dorsal horn "gate", ameliorate pain symptoms. Indeed, it appeared to work and the last 40 years has seen the development of an industry supplying spinal cord stimulators, which in 2012 produced revenues of 1.4b USD.

Commercial development has certainly out-paced the technical and scientific development of the therapy. The mechanisms of action for SCS are still not well understood and devices have changed little since inception. Assessment of performance is based on subjective measures and there have been very few randomized control trials and even fewer sham-controlled trials. This is in part due to the fact that, until recently, stimulation produces a sensation which makes it impossible to blind a subject to receipt of therapy.

Spinal cord stimulation involves the implantation of electrodes in the epidural space above the dorsal column. The electrode array is connected to a pulse generator, which generates a stimulus, which in turn produces activity in the spinal cord. This induced spinal cord activity is responsible for the therapeutic effect, but exactly how is still the subject of debate and research. SCS is indicated for the treatment of chronic, intractable pain of the trunk and/or limbs. Chronic pain is different from acute pain and persists well after the initial insult, injury or illness which produced the initial pain has healed. The International Association for the Study of Pain (IASP) has defined chronic pain as pain that lasts more than six months beyond the normal time of healing.

The origin of the initial pain is often used as a means of classification. This includes: failed back surgery syndrome (FBSS), low back and leg pain, complex regional pain syndrome (CRPS) I and II, and ischemic pain. Surveys indicate 30.7% of the US adult population have experienced chronic pain [3] and the prevalence increases with age. Chronic pain impairs all aspects of an individual's life and often results in mental health issues. In addition to the physical and emotional burden it brings, the financial cost to society is tremendous. In the US alone it is estimated to cost in the order of $560 to $635 billion per year [4] with an added loss of productivity in the range of $299 to $335 billion. Gaskin and Richard concluded that the annual cost of chronic pain is greater than the annual cost of heart disease, cancer, and diabetes combined [4].

Conventional medical management for pain disorders begins with least invasive therapies prescribed first. First line treatment strategies are generally conservative including: exercise programs, rehabilitation programs (physical therapy, occupational therapy, or massage therapy), cognitive and behavioral modifications, transcutaneous electrical nerve stimulation (TENS), biofeedback, and over-the-counter pain medications. Second line treatments are more invasive and involve the use of interventional techniques such as nerve blocks (local anesthetic or steroids) and spinal injections. They can also include more powerful pain medications such as systemic opioids. The last line of treatment involves more advanced therapies that require surgical interventions. These include surgery to repair an anatomical issue responsible for the pain, surgical techniques that permanently block pathways to the brain such as cordotomy, rhizotomy and thalamotomy, and implantation of systems such as intrathecal drug pumps or spinal cord stimulators.

Spinal cord stimulation therapy has a number of distinct advantages over alternative treatments. There are no drug related side effects and unlike surgical revision and neuroablation it is reversible. Over the last 30 years there have been many advances in SCS therapy, including a better understanding of the target patient population and improvements in device technology and reliability. The technology has evolved from large profile, single channel, non-rechargeable implantable pulse generators (IPG) and monopolar leads, to smaller profile, multichannel, rechargeable IPGs and multiple contact leads with various types of electrode arrays.

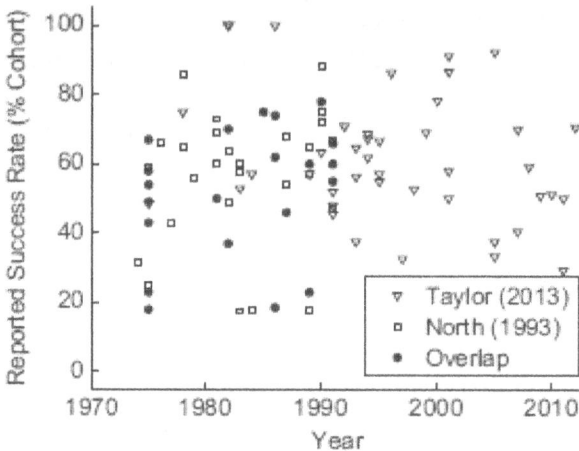

Fig. 1. Scatter plot of the success rates for spinal cord stimulation clinical trials.

Despite the effort in development of technology the reported success rates for the therapy did not improve in the period from 1970 to 2013 (Figure 1). Data from the meta-analysis of Taylor [5] and North [6] were combined and analyzed by Zhang et. al. [7] who concluded that only 58% of individuals gain 50% or more pain reduction with the therapy. They also observed that there was no correlation between the success of therapy with the year the study was conducted (R =0.09, p =0.4 t-test) indicating no improvement in pain reduction over the four decades considered. Despite the lack of improvement in therapeutic outcomes the technological advances have resulted in a significant reduction in the number and severity of complications. More recently a number of trial results have been reported which have shifted the trend toward better performance. High frequency stimulation and dorsal root ganglion stimulation trials have both demonstrated superiority to conventional stimulation. High frequency stimulation was compared with conventional stimulation in a randomized controlled trial which found 84.5% of subjects who received high frequency stimulation were responders (achieved >50% VAS pain reduction) for back pain compared with 43.8% of subjects who received stimulation at conventional frequencies [8]. A responder is conventionally defined as an individual who receives 50% or more pain relief. The high frequency subjects also reported improved pain relief (67% decrease in back pain versus 44%).

The therapy can be life-changing for people when it works, it has no drug related side effects and is completely reversible. Its infrequent use is a result of two complications: invasiveness of the procedure and the inability to predict an outcome. Patients also to have to cope with other complications such as device charging and management of stimulation levels and programs via a remote controller. Perhaps the most severe of these is the need to undergo a trial stimulation period prior to implantation of the full system. This procedure involves the implantation of an epidural lead where the end of the lead is externalized and connected to a body worn stimulator. The patient is then sent home for a number of days to evaluate the stimulation and assess the level of pain relief. The need for this is obvious – when the clinical results demonstrate 58% of patients enjoy 50% relief of pain, a significant number of patients are non-responders to SCS therapy, and so the trial is conducted to reduce the number and cost of procedures performed which result in no benefit. The trial to permanent ratio has been reported to be as low as 50% and as high as 80%. The reason for trial failure is not well understood; some patients will achieve pain relief but are intolerant of the sensations produced by stimulation. Other patients achieve a technical success with the procedure, complete coverage of their painful area but fail to get any pain relief. A further complication is that nociceptive pain, the experience of encoding and processing of harmful stimuli, is not alleviated with SCS. It is not apparent why this should be the case and in fact theories of mechanism have struggled to explain why. A differential diagnosis of nociceptive pain and neuropathic pain can be difficult; in fact many patients have both nociceptive and neuropathic components to their pain. The only way to determine if SCS is effective enough for an individual to endure the complications associated with it is via the trial process.

2. Devices

SCS systems consist of a number of components including an implantable pulse generator (IPG), an electrode array, a patient controller, a programming system and surgical tools for implantation of the device. Two key specifications, the number of electrode contacts and the source of power for the device determine the size of modern IPGs. The electrode needs to be separable from the IPG and therefore implantation requires implantable connectors. The number of electrode contacts defines the size of the header and the number of implantable connector contacts required.

Three methods have been used to power SCS devices: transcutaneous links, primary cell batteries and rechargeable cell batteries. Early devices delivered power to the implant via a transcutaneous inductive link. In this architecture, two coupled coils, one in the implant and the other external aligned and opposed to the internal coil form a transformer. Energizing the external coil induces current flow in the internal coil and powers the implant. A modern version of this technique has been developed and tested which relies on microwave energy (915 MHz) [9] and a device which relies on a similar form of power transduction is currently being commercialized [10]. This approach allows all the IPG components to be embedded in the lead such that the entire device can be implanted via a needle. Devices powered by transcutaneous links can be small but suffer the disadvantage that the patient must wear an external device to power the implant at all times the implant is operational.

Primary cell batteries are a convenient source of power for SCS devices. Batteries are available which have the capacity to provide power to the implant circuits and maintain stimulation for 5 or more years, and which are small enough to be incorporated into an IPG. When the battery is depleted the IPG is explanted and replaced with a new device with a fresh battery. The implantable connector in the header allows disconnection of the lead from the old IPG and reconnection to the new device. IPGs are also available which employ a rechargeable battery and a transcutaneous link for charging the device on a periodic basis (typically 1 week of use between charges). These devices can have much longer operating lifetimes than non-rechargeable devices but will eventually also need replacement as the number of charging cycles is limited.

The mechanical construction of an IPG is simple; a sealed biocompatible titanium box houses the electronics and power sources, and a feedthrough conducts the stimulus from inside the hermetic barrier to outside. The electrodes connect to the device via a header which houses an implantable connector. The connector allows the electrode array to be disconnected when the IPG needs replacement due to battery depletion (Figure 2).

A modern SCS device has a large number of parameters which need to be adjusted to optimize the pain treatment. These adjustments are accomplished during programming sessions where an external programmer is connected to the implant via a radio link. Devices are also capable of measuring the impedance of the electrode and reporting this back via the link. The impedance is particularly useful in assessing if all the contacts on the electrode array are connected properly and the electrode is in the epidural space.

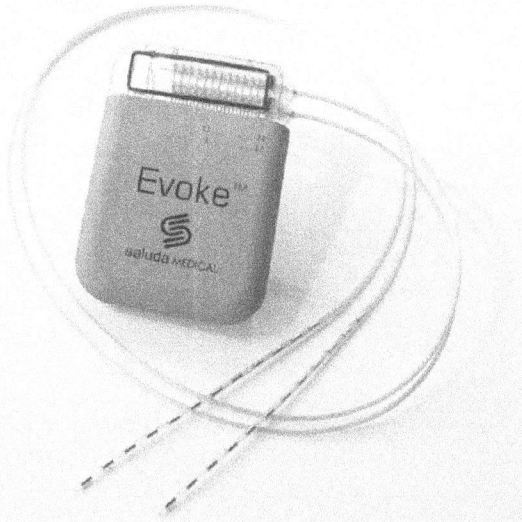

Fig. 2. An example implantable SCS device manufactured by Saluda Medical. This device is similar to other devices which are marketed in that it consists of a hermetic titanium implant which contains battery and electronics and this is connected to electrode arrays.

The cathodic phase of a stimulus generates the action potentials in the range of stimulation currents used during SCS. However, charge recovery is required in order to ensure patient safety. The need to ensure charge recovery is discussed elsewhere in this volume. Charge recovery in SCS has been achieved via both passive and active methods. Passive methods employ a series capacitor connected to each electrode and the devices can output monophasic pulses. A decaying exponential voltage results after the cathodic pulse from the charge stored on the capacitor and the net charge is balanced. The frequency of stimulation for passive charge recovery is limited by the length of time to recover charge. Active charge recovery employs a biphasic pulse where current is driven into the electrode in two phases, anodic and cathodic, and charge balance is obtained in this manner.

The stimulus generation circuit can be connected to the electrode in a number of different ways. There can be multiple sources (stimulating electrodes) and multiple sinks (return electrodes) for the current. Where the sink or return electrode is outside the epidural space, for instance the case of the IPG, this mode is referred to as monopolar. Monopolar stimulation is more power efficient but the electric field is spread much wider. Bipolar stimulation refers to stimulation where the current is passed from one electrode to another in the electrode array, and multipolar stimulation refers to the situation where the stimulation current is passed from one or more electrodes to one or more others. In tripolar stimulation the current is passed from one central contact to two adjacent contacts. Devices with multiple current sources can configure multiple cathodes and anodes in each phase and effectively steer the current to create virtual electrodes where the excitatory field is spread between the electrodes. Multiple pain areas can be covered with different electrodes (or virtual electrodes) and the programs interleaved so that consecutive pulses are devoted to alternate pain areas.

Table 1. Summary of parameters employed

Stimulation Paradigm	Frequency (Hz)	Pulse Width	Notes
Tonic	30-120	<1ms	Voltage, current and passive charge recovery have all been used
HF10	10000	35μS	Charge balanced biphasic
Burst Stimulation	40	1ms	5 x1ms pulses with 1ms gaps followed by 5ms anodic pulse
High Density	1200	200μs	Amplitude adjusted for 90% of paresthesia threshold [11]

The configuration of the electrodes and the stimulation parameters, a choice of pulse widths, amplitudes, frequencies and patterns of stimulation, constitutes a vast search space. Publically available guidelines do not exist for SCS programming and parameter selection. For some devices the methods used are proprietary; for others, effective programming is based on programmer experience and subjective feed back from patients. The lack of an understanding of the basic mechanisms of action and the impact of the device settings on the electrophysiological responses of the dorsal column has been the greatest impediment to improvement of SCS devices and improvement of outcomes for device recipients (Table 1).

Tonic stimulation outputs stimuli at a fixed amplitude and fixed frequency, where a range of 50–80 Hz is considered optimal for clinical SCS [12]. However, recently high frequency stimulation has also been approved for use in humans by regulators. In these systems biphasic stimuli are output at high frequency (10 kHz) and sub-threshold for paresthesia generation.

Burst stimulation employs a train of cathodic pulses followed by a charge recovery phase [13]. The various stimulation modes and patterns so far explored are simple variations in stimulation parameters. The stimulation frequency is increased or the duty cycle, i.e., the amount of time a depolarising stimulus is presented has been explored. What is known of the rationale for these changes will explored in the following sections on device programming and parameter selection.

The mechanisms of action for all forms of stimulation are unclear and this author's perspectives on what is known are presented later; however the new stimulation parameter sets which are being employed all have the feature that they are below the perception threshold, i.e., the amplitude of stimulation is adjusted such that no paresthesia sensations are generated by the stimulation. It is convenient to regard the efficacy of these therapies as prima facie evidence that it is possible to generate action potentials in dorsal columns without producing sensation. The alternative is to contemplate that these therapies have an effect through alternate mechanisms.

The desire to develop paresthesia-free stimulation techniques is to eliminate the unwanted side effects which are the result of the concomitant over stimulation and the variability of sensation which is caused by movement and changes in dorsal column excitability. This variability results in patients needing to interact with their devices constantly to adjust the stimulation levels as they change posture. This has prompted the inclusion of accelerometers in IPGs to detect changes in posture and change stimulation programs depending on the position of the patient. Sensor driven SCS [14] improves patient convenience and reduces the number of interactions that patients have with their devices.

2.1. *Electrodes*

The electrodes used for SCS are designed to be inserted above the dura in the epidural space. This space is filled with epidural fat and varies in size from vertebra to vertebra. There are two types of leads which are commonly employed. Percutaneous leads are designed for percutaneous placement via a Touhey needle and used for both trials and for permanent implant. Surgical paddle leads are placed in the epidural space with surgical access via a partial or full laminectomy. Paddle leads have electrode contacts exposed on one face of the paddle directed toward the spinal cord and insulated on the back surfaces. Paddle leads provide more consistent coverage of the painful areas with paresthesia with reduced power consumption [15]. Paddle leads also have been shown to be more clinically effective and to reduce long-term stimulation related side-effects [16] compared with percutaneous leads. Paddle lead implantation is surgically more invasive and results in a significantly higher postoperative complication rate (3.5% versus 2.2%) [17].

Leads have also been developed which are hybrids between the two; paddle leads which are designed for insertion by customized percutaneous insertion needles. Kinfe et al. reported similar significant pain reduction (VAS pre/post: paddle: 8.8/3.7; cylindrical: 8.5/3.8) comparing percutaneous paddle and cylindrical leads but higher migration and infection rates for the cylindrical group (14% and 10%, respectively) than for the paddle group (6% and 2%, respectively) [18]. There is no consensus on the type of lead most appropriate for each patient group. The surgical paddle leads require a more invasive procedure and longer recovery times but provide some clinical advantages via a much wider range of programing options.

There are a large variety of paddle and percutaneous lead designs available. The key parameters which differentiates leads are the spacing between the electrodes and electrode size. The larger the electrode the lower the impedance to tissue and hence the lower the power consumption, but larger electrodes create broader electric fields and a loss of specificity with targeting stimulation. The spacing between electrodes affects the shape of the electric field. The amplitude of the second derivative of this field sets the threshold for depolarisation. Models [19] of bipolar and tripolar stimulation produce curves of threshold voltage for activation of fibres as a function of electrode spacing that have a minimum at 7 mm spacing. For bipolar stimulation a change in the separation between the electrodes changes the extent of overlap of the cathodic and anodic activating functions. The activating function of the cathode has a positive (depolarising) peak and a smaller negative (hyperpolarising) peak on either side, whereas the anodal activating function has the same shape but opposite sign. The stimulation is most efficient, defined by the largest second derivative of the electric field, when the positive peaks of the anodic and cathodic activating functions are aligned. The most efficient electrode separation depends on the CSF thickness. At 2 mm thickness this corresponds to a 7mm separation between.

2.2. *Dorsal root ganglion stimulation*

The epidural space provides an ideal location to position an electrode for spinal cord stimulation, it is safely accessed via a Touhy needle and leads can be placed with relative ease. However the epidural space with a relatively thick layer of CSF results in a significant amount of current spread and loss of spatial resolution for stimulation. As a result highly localized pain can be difficult to treat and certain areas of the body such as the feet can be difficult to stimulate. Electrodes have been developed for placement on the dorsal root ganglia (DRG). The DRG provides an ideal target for stimulation. The DRG contains the cell bodies of the pseudounipolar sensory neurons, whose axon processes bifurcate with one branch extending toward the periphery and the other branch heading toward the grey matter of the spinal cord.

The mechanosensory Aβ fibres axons envelope the surface of the DRG which is contained in the intervertebral foramen. The space between the bony wall of the foramen and the dura surrounding the DRG is much smaller than the epidural space, the CSF thickness is smaller and so lower stimulation currents are required, and the recruitment as evidenced by variation in paresthesia is more stable [20].

3. Procedures and Use

The patient journey through assessment to receiving an implant can be complex and costly. The variability in outcomes combined with the cost of the intervention forces physicians and patients to carefully weigh the benefit with the risks and burden of complexity for the patient. The primary benefit, the degree of pain relief, may be insufficient to support the secondary benefits, return to work or medication reduction. There are significant complexities for patients in living with an implanted SCS device which include recharging (for rechargeable devices), reprogramming, risk of loss of therapeutic effect and risks and costs of the surgical procedure. There is significant variation in the stimulation intensity with different postures and as a result patients are constantly adjusting their devices and carry their remote controls for their devices at all times. Some are reluctant to or incapable of doing this and so SCS therapy is unsuitable for them [21]. The psychological state of the recipient is thought to be an important factor in the outcome of SCS [22] and results of a psychological assessment are often is used in selection of patients.

Trial stimulation involves implantation of externalized leads and assessment of the response of the patient to stimulation. Typically the patient would be sent home for a few days, after which their change in pain score and tolerance for stimulation would be assessed and a decision made to proceed to permanent implant. The leads are often explanted and patient allowed to heal for four weeks until permanent leads can be implanted. An alternative to this clinical workflow is to implant the trial lead and a buried extension lead which connects with an implantable connector to the lead. The end of the extension lead is externalized and connected to the trial stimulator. To subsequently implant the stimulator the extension lead is removed and new extension used to connect the IPG to the lead. The value of conducting a trial has been questioned with reports indicating that a poor trial outcome is not necessarily prognostic for long-term outcome with implantation [23].

Intra-operative mapping of paraesthesia to bodily location is carried out during many SCS procedures. This requires the patient to be awake so that they can respond to questions regarding the location of sensations produced by the stimulator. This is done to verify that the lead is in the correct location to maximize the chance that stimulation will provide coverage in post-operative programming. Where devices are designed to produce no sensation this step is skipped and the patient can be fully sedated for the procedure.

4. Mechanisms of Action

4.1. *Neuroanatomy and pain*

SCS relies on generation of action potentials in the spinal cord dorsal columns. The fibres of the dorsal column are somatotopically mapped; there is a point-for-point correspondence of an area of the body to a specific point on the surface of the dorsal column. The column is divided into the fasciculi gracilis and cuneatus. The fasciculus gracilis consists of ascending fibres from the lower body and is located medially. This tract exists at all levels of the spinal cord and contains afferent fibers from the sacral, lumbar, and thoracic segments T6—T12. Fibres from the upper body are located in the more lateral in fasciculus cuneatus. A schematic diagram showing the course of the fibres from the periphery to the somatosensory cortex is shown in Figure 3.

The ascending fibres of the first order sensory ganglia ascend ipsilaterally (on the same side of the cord) and terminate on second order neurons in the nucleus gracilis in the medulla (brain stem). The cell bodies of dorsal column fibres are located in the dorsal root ganglion. The peripheral processes of these cells terminate in the skin innervating Pacinian corpuscles (tactile and vibratory sensors), Meissner's corpuscles (touch sensors) and proprioceptors (sensors of movement and body position).

The second order neurons in the nucleus gracilis cross the midline to form the medial lemniscus which travels through the medulla, pons and mid brain to reach their third order neural targets, located in the contralateral, ventral, posterolateral nucleus of the thalamus. Axons from these neurons terminate in the medial aspect of the sensorimotor cortex.

The spinal cord ascending fibres of the pain pathway are third order neurons whereas the ascending fibres of the mechanosensory pathway are first order neurons. Pain inhibition by SCS is thought to be achieved via inhibition of the second order neurons in the spinal cord. Pain is experienced in the primary sensory cortex where the pain signal is relayed from the thalamus via 3rd third order neurons from second order neurons of the spinal cord. The primary first order neurons carry pain signals from the periphery.

The second order neurons are located in the dorsal horn which serves as a relay station for noxious information and is an important site in the modulation and integration of pain signals. There are two main classes of second order neurons, the first are the nociceptive –high threshold neurons and these are contained in the superficial lamina (I,II) of the dorsal horn. These neurons only respond to noxious stimuli. The second class of neurons are the wide dynamic range (WDR) neurons.

Located deeper in the dorsal horn (lamina V), these neurons respond to both noxious and non-noxious stimuli. These neurons are believed to be the major culprit in the production of the unrelenting pain signals that characterize neuropathic pain.

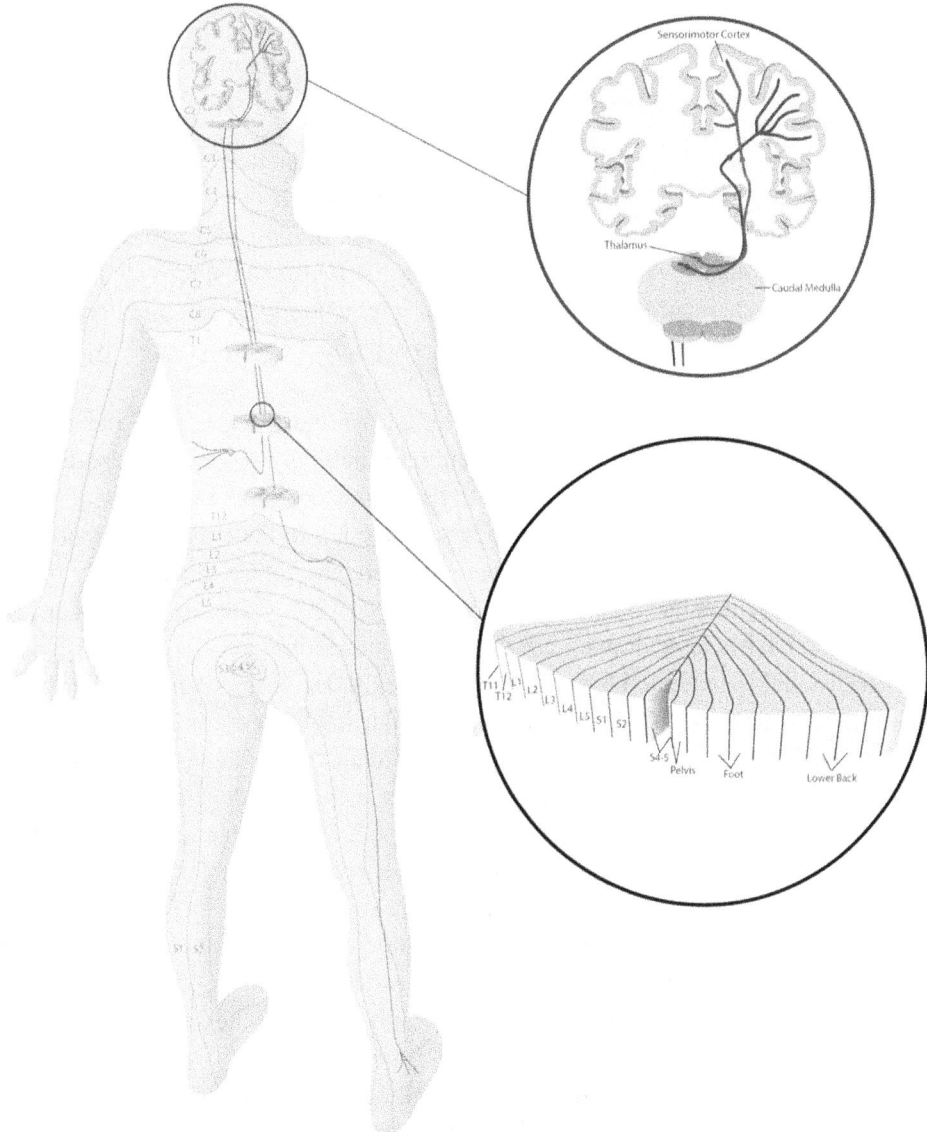

Fig. 3. Schematic diagram illustrating the passage of tactile sensory fibres from the periphery through the spinal cord to the brain. Fasciculus gracilis consists of ascending fibres from the lower body and is located medially in the dorsal column. Upper body fibres are located in fasciculus cuneatus. Pathway to the sensory cortex is shown.

Nerve injury in the periphery results in erratic noxious stimuli which induces a prolonged state of dorsal horn hyperexcitability. The hyperexcitability amplifies pain signals, converts innocuous stimuli to noxious and the result is unremitting pain [24,25]. The second order WDR neurons are the transmission neurons in the gate control theory. They are easily wound up to a hyperexcitable state and it has been shown that SCS suppresses the hyperexcitable state in neuropathic rats [26].

4.2. *Dorsal column electrical stimulation*

Spinal cord stimulators produce electric fields which generate action potentials in dorsal column axons. The shape of the field depends on the arrangement of the electrodes and choices for relative position of the anodes and cathodes. Finite element calculations [27] of the electrical field distribution have provided the only insight into the shape of these fields and their interaction with the spinal cord. The electrode positioned in the epidural space is separated from the cord by several layers of tissue.

Struijk et. al. [28] demonstrated the effect of the thickness of the highly conductive CSF layer concluding that doubling the thickness led to 30% drop in the field potential and activating functions of the dorsal column. The current spreading and the relatively high impedance have led to the conclusion that only the first 300 μm of the dorsal columns are recruited during SCS and that only fibres with a diameter greater than 9.4 μm are activated [29]. Other researchers using similar approaches have drawn very different conclusions

Electric fields generated from the electrodes will depolarize an axon. The shape of the zone of depolarization has been calculated using finite element analysis. The well-ordered somatotopic map of the dorsal column combined with the ability to precisely control the electric field generated at the electrode should allow very precise steering of the pain relieving effect of SCS. At a high enough level all of the fibres from the dermatomes below that level are available for stimulation. In practice it is not so predictable and straight forward.

The Aβ fibres enter the spinal cord via the dorsal root entry zone and send projections rostral a few segments as well as caudal. Recruiting the fibres which project in the rostral direction would result in paresthesia generation in dermatomes which are represented below the stimulation site.

Holsheimer and Barolat studied the probability of paresthesia generation in 106 subjects and concluded that the probability of producing paresthesia in a specific dermatome was highest when the cathode was placed at the corresponding vertebral segment except for the trunk areas. The maximum probability of achieving paresthesia in the low back is half the maximum achievable in the leg and the result is that treating low back pain with SCS is difficult (Figure 4).

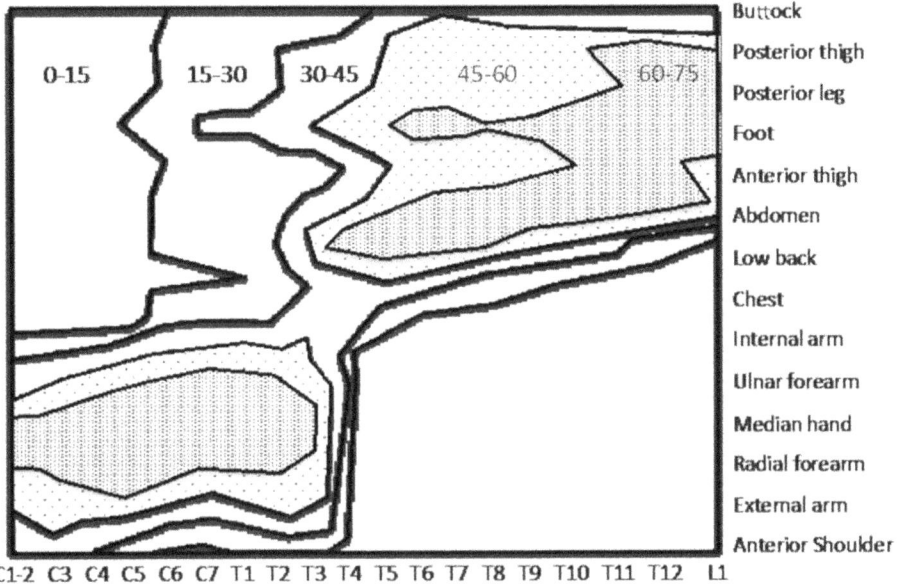

Fig. 4. Probability of generating paresthesia in a particular dermatome with stimulation at the corresponding verterbral level.

Computer simulations have illustrated the effect of cerebral spinal fluid (CSF) layer thickness on the therapeutic window for SCS. The CSF spreads the electric field and Holshiemer and co-workers have estimated that where the CSF layer is thick (>2 mm) the threshold for dorsal root activation is below the threshold for dorsal column activation [30]. This is a result of relatively high conductivity CSF concentrating the field at the dorsal roots. The perception threshold, the minimum stimulus intensity perceptible, correlates with the CSF thickness for stimulating electrodes along the midline of the cord. The CSF thickness varies considerably along the cord length and varies considerably from individual to individual. The thickness of CSF also changes depending on the posture of the patient. Holshiemer et. al. concluded that the thickness of the dorsal CSF layer is the main factor determining the perception threshold and paresthesia coverage in spinal cord stimulation; modeling suggests that a lateral asymmetry of less than 1 mm gives a significant reduction of perception threshold. A small shift in position lateral position can result in unilateral paresthesiae (Figure 5).

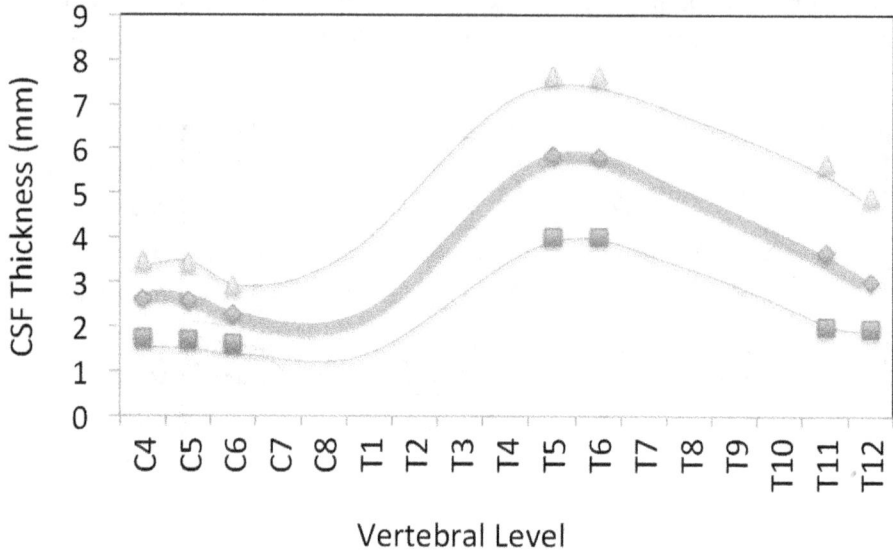

Fig. 5. Cerebral spinal fluid thickness determined from MRI measurements at a number of vertebral levels (data from [31]). Mean value (thickest line) +/- 1s.d.

The choice of electrode stimulating position is a complex trade-off of geometric factors. There is evidence that stimulation over the cord at the corresponding vertebral level for the targeted dermatome is more effective [32], however this is the position where fibres are at the lateral edges of the column and at the closest position to the dorsal roots. As the fibre ascends the dorsal column it moves to a more medial position as each new lamina is added to the column. Hence the target fibers move away from the dorsal roots closer to the midline of the cord and so a larger gap between the stimulating threshold for these fibers and dorsal root fibres results. Activation of dorsal roots sets the upper boundary for stimulation intensity and represents the top of the therapeutic window for electrical stimulation targeting the dorsal column. Stimulating more medial fibres sets the stimulation level further away from the DR stimulation threshold and creates a wider therapeutic window. This is schematically illustrated in Figure 6, where the left side of the figure shows a projection of the path of the fibres for L1 moving more medially as they ascend the cord. The benefit of avoiding the dorsal roots by moving the stimulating site more rostral occurs at a cost of higher stimulation thresholds and reduced selectivity because of the increasing thickness of the CSF layer, and closer arrangement of fibres from different dermatomes, respectively. The CSF thickness and threshold increase as a function of position along the cord by a factor of 2 (illustrated in Figure 5).

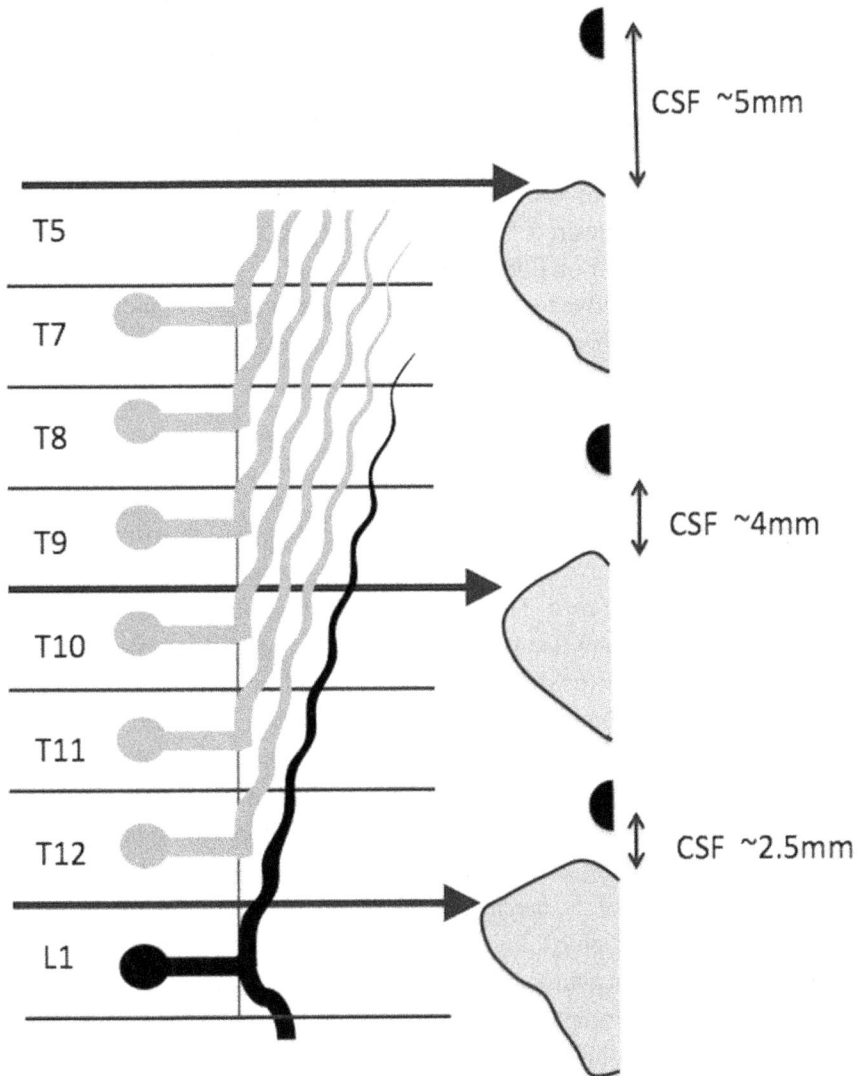

Fig. 6. Schematic illustration of the passage of a nerve fibre from the L1 dermatome as it ascends the spinal cord. The number of ascending fibres reduces as the bundle ascends caudal to rostral (represented by the width of the line) and the fibres move to a more medial location on the column. The CSF layer thickness increases from L1 to T5.

The compromise often chosen for low back L1 coverage is to place the electrode at T8-T9 which is 4 to 5 segments above the L1 entry zone The fibres are more medial, the CSF thickness is larger and the number of fibres available for stimulation are reduced by comparison with the more caudal segments. Less than 25% of the ascending DC fibres reach the dorsal column nuclei [33], 20% of dorsal column fibres leave the DC within 2 to 3 segments from where they enter and others ascend between 4 to 12 segments before they terminate. To avoid DR stimulation, placement of the electrode contacts above the entry zone for the targeted dermatome is desired, but this is at the cost of increased CSF thickness and a smaller population of fibres available to stimulate. The range of available stimulation currents between threshold and comfortable stimulation levels is dependent on the number of vertebral segments, CSF thickness layer and the neuroanatomy of the cord itself.

4.3. *Pain sensation inhibition*

Generation of action potentials in the dorsal column is the first step in SCS mediated pain relief, however inhibition of pain occurs via mechanisms in the dorsal horn of the spinal cord. The first SCS implantations [34] were motivated by the publication of the gate theory of pain [2]. This theory suggested the presence of a gate in the dorsal horn which could be switched by activation of Aβ fibers of the dorsal column. Stimulating myelinated Aβ fiber collaterals in the dorsal columns activates inhibitory interneurons in the dorsal horn that suppress the transmission of nociceptive information from wide-dynamic range (WDR) spinal projection neurons to the brain. For the switch, inhibitory interneurons and WDR neurons are activated by Aβ activity. This simple idea is still considered a reasonable description of the mechanism of action of SCS [35] and is supported by a large amount of neurophysiological evidence that Aβ fibre activation results in inhibition of dorsal horn neurons. This inhibition appears to be mediated by GABA release in the inter-neuronal pool. Increases in spinal GABA and associated decreases in release of glutamate and aspartate have been measured in animals that responded well to SCS analgesia [36,37]. Furthermore both inhibition of animal pain behaviour and WDR neuronal hyperexcitability were closely associated with elevated GABA levels in the dorsal horn after SCS. The involvement of GABA is supported by the observation that bicuculline, a GABA antagonist, reduces the effect of SCS [38] and administration of GABA agonists muscimol and baclofen reduce hyperalgesia and allodynia in animal models of neuropathic pain [39].

SCS appears to function through a shift in balance of spinal cord inhibitory and excitatory neurotransmitters which is more complex than idea of a simple on-off dorsal horn gate. Indeed, gate theory fails to explain why Aβ activation does not effect the perception of acute pain in areas where paresthesia is generated. The gate control theory makes no distinction between the origin of pain and as a result continual Aβ stimulation should mask all pain including nociceptive pain. Gate theory also fails to explain why some patients experience pain relief for periods after the device is switched off and why Aβ fiber tactile or electrical stimulation directly at the site of pain produces allodynia [40] while SCS that produces paresthesia over the region including and surrounding the site of pain provides pain relief.

Elevated GABA levels persist after switch off of SCS [41] and this may be the explanation for the "switch off effect" which is often observed clinically. The length of the switch off effect reported can vary enormously from patient to patient, from none to several hours and even longer. The observation of the correlation between elevated GABA levels and animal responses leads to the inference that SCS is responsible for the elevation and the switch off effect is the result of sustained pain relief due to the time course wash out and return to pre-SCS levels of spinal cord GABA. The clear link between GABA release and SCS has led to the testing of combination therapies of SCS with baclofen [42,43]. This drug is a GABA receptor agonist and the fact that patients who don't receive effective pain relief with SCS alone can be rescued by increasing spinal cord GABA levels by administration of GABA agonist supports the critical role of GABA in SCS mediated pain relief.

Other neurotransmitters have also been implicated in the mechanism of action of SCS. Studies have revealed a role for spinal 5-hydroxytryptamine (5HT) receptors in SCS analgesia under different pain conditions. These serotonin receptors mediate both excitatory and inhibitory neurotransmission. SCS has been shown to increase endogenous serotonin [44] and to activate 5-HT2A,3,4 receptors in the dorsal horn and this may lead to changes in neuronal excitability. Finally acetylcholine and noradrenaline [45,46] are also ingredients in the biochemical soup which is forms the molecular response to SCS.

The observation that multiple SCS sessions can prolong the switch off period has lead some to speculate that the SCS switch off effect may also have a spinal cord neuro-plastic component. The sustained release of inhibitory neuro-transmitters may also reduce the excitability of WDR neurons and reverse the underlying pathophysiological response and central sensitisation, which implies a neuroplastic component to the effect. SCS has been shown not only to block increases in WDR excitability but also to prevent further wind-up [26]. Temporal summation of noxious stimuli in individuals has been shown to be a predictor of response rate to pre-gabalin [47] therapy and is also affected by SCS indicating that SCS may have a direct affect on central sensitization [48,49].

Any description of the mechanism of action of SCS has to consider the changes which occur to dorsal horn pain processing which accompany the neuropathic pain state. Changes which have been observed can be profound.

1. Aberrant sprouting of myelinated fibres in the dorsal horn follows peripheral nerve injury;
2. Sensitization of nociceptive neurons [50,51];
3. Developing hypersensitivity to thermal and mechanical stimuli appears to follow the development and extent of abnormal sprouting; and
4. Expression of synaptic receptors associated with excitation (AMPA,NMDA, NK1).

There is a great deal of evidence from animal models suggesting that sprouting results in the formation of excitatory inputs or loss of inhibitory inputs in the superficial dorsal horn and there appears to be a relationship between this and the abnormal perception of pain. The increase in excitatory input appears to be accompanied by a loss of inhibitory mechanisms. This is supported by the observation that Aβ fibre mediated inhibition is reduced following peripheral nerve injury [52]. The understanding of the development of central sensitisation and changes in spinal cord processing is key to developing a more complete understanding of the mechanism of SCS.

It even may be the case that it is not the direct inhibitory effect of Aβ stimulation on the WDR range neurons but rather a centre-surround inhibitory effect that may best represent the mode of action of SCS [7] Aβ fibre mediated inhibition of C fibre input to WDR neurons is effective when applied via dorsal column but stimulation of Aβ fibres in the peripheral nerve innervating the receptive field of the same WDR neurons and at the same frequency is ineffective [53]. Further there is an expansion of receptive fields of dorsal horn projection neurons following nerve injury [52] and there are connections between GABAergic neurons which extend several spinal segements [54]. This all suggests that pain relief may be afforded via a centre surround inhibition and could explain why the level of coverage of the painful area with paresthesia is the only, albeit poor, prognostic indicator of outcome with conventional SCS.

The gate control theory paradoxes have lead to development of more complex spinal cord pain processing circuit models and a recent attempt has been successful in explaining why neuropathic but not nociceptive pain is ameliorated by SCS [55]. There is a clear need for a more detailed understanding of the pain circuits of the spinal cord. The segmental affects are complex and SCS mechanisms of action may ultimately rely on network modulation and surround inhibition.

To further complicate an understanding of the mechanism of action of SCS the supra-spinal loop appears to play an important role. In rats the analgesic effect of SCS is halved when the dorsal columns are lesioned rostral to the stimulation site [56]. Blocking ascending Aβ action potentials with a lesion presumably removes any descending inhibitory input returning from the brain. SCS in spared nerve injury animals produced neural activity as revealed by C-fos staining low frequencies of stimulation (4Hz) in rostral ventromedial medulla but no increase activity was seen after 60Hz stimulation suggesting that a supraspinal mechanism may have a frequency dependence [57].

SCS has also been shown to reduce glial activity in a frequency dependent manner [58]. Despite the critical role which spinal cord glia play in the production and maintenance of pain and emergence of glia as active participants in neural signaling [59] little work has been done to understand their role in SCS analgesia.

5. Indications and Outcomes

Spinal cord stimulation has been used to treat a number of chronic pain conditions. The current approved indications are broadly defined as; "chronic intractable pain of the trunk and or limbs". Few randomized controlled trials have been conducted and much of the evidence for effectiveness has been obtained from cases series and prospective studies, for a review of results and indications see [60].

The most common presenting etiology is failed back surgery syndrome FBSS and this accounts for ~60% of patients who receive a spinal cord stimulation system. FBSS is defined as persistent or recurrent pain, mainly involving the lower back and/or legs, even after previous anatomically successful spinal surgery. Because this is the largest treatment group for patients the clinical evidence for efficacy for this etiology will be briefly reviewed.

Taylor et. al. recently updated [5] their systematic review and meta analysis [1] of outcomes data for SCS for leg and chronic back pain. The original work reviewed 78 studies, the update tightened the authors inclusion criteria, removed 21 studies from the original data set and added a further 18 studies which were reported prior to 2012: four were randomized controlled trials (RCTS), two were comparative studies with non randomized designs and the remainder were case series. Their conclusion from the analysis did not change with additional studies and tighter inclusion criteria: 62% of patients achieve 50% or more pain relief (95% confidence interval 56% to 69%) with a mean duration of follow up of 26 months. The only correlation with success rate extracted from the data was a negative association with the mean duration of pain. Individuals who were in pain for longer did not do as well as those who were in pain for shorter periods prior to receiving SCS treatment. This finding is supported by Kumar et al. who studied the success or failure of SCS as function of the duration of pain and showed that poorer outcomes are experienced by patients who have long durations of pain [61].

Simpson et. al. conducted a health economic assessment [62] of SCS which included neuropathic pain and ischemic pain. They reviewed data up until 2007 and concluded that SCS was more successful than conventional medical management or reoperation in terms of pain relief. SCS resulted in a greater reduction in use of opiates than reoperation and was more effective in improving functional ability. North et. al. conducted a randomized controlled trial comparing SCS to reoperation in FBSS with 45 patients (90%) available for follow-up. SCS was more successful than reoperation (9 of 19 patients versus 3 of 26 patients, p = 0.01). There is clear evidence that SCS is effective in relieving pain in FBSS patients.

Two significant trials have recently been conducted which demonstrate improved results over conventional SCS. The Senza trial compared HF10, 10 kHz stimulation, with conventional stimulation frequency devices. More than 80% of the HF10 arm achieved 50% or better back and leg pain scores which is a significant improvement in responder rate compared with previous studies of 62% of individuals receiving 50% pain relief. Mean back pain VAS decreased by 67% over 12 months with 10kHz stimulation compared with a 44% decrease for traditional SCS and mean leg pain 70% decrease versus a 49% decrease with traditional SCS.

Dorsal root ganglion stimulation has also recently been shown to be superior to conventional stimulation. At a 12 month follow 74.2% of patients achieved 50% or greater pain reduction compared with traditional stimulation 53%.

SCS has been used to treat a variety of painful conditions. Perhaps one of the worst pain conditions that can afflict an individual is complex regional pain syndrome (CRPS) and SCS has been shown to be effective in treating this condition [55,56,57]. Refractory angina pectoris is caused by coronary insufficiency in the presence of coronary artery disease. In some individuals the pain cannot be adequately controlled by a combination of medical therapy, angioplasty, and coronary artery surgery. SCS has been shown to significantly reduce angina attacks (68 subjects) [63] and a multi center study is currently under-way to asses the cost effectiveness of SCS for angina [64]. SCS is know to improve peripheral circulation and has been used to treat peripheral vascular disease [55]. Occipital nerve stimulation is used to treat chronic migraine and these nerves can be targeted with stimulation leads placed in the high cervical region [65,66,67, 68,69,70]. There are continuing expanding indications for spinal cord stimulation and its use is being extended beyond the treatment of painful conditions.

5.1. *Complications*

A recent retrospective study has reported the overall complication rate for SCS at 34.6% [71] with 25.6% related to hardware complications. IPG discomfort or migration constituted 11.1%, and lead migration 8.5%. Lead fracture (4.3%) constituted the largest physical failure of system component and IPG malfunction was 1.7%. These numbers were obtained from an analysis of 345 cases over a 7 year period from 2006 and are similar to complication rates reported elsewhere [72,73,74]. The complication rates are high in comparison to other active implantable medical devices and there is a clear need to drive the complication rates down.

5.2. *New indications*

SCS has been used to treat angina pain but has also more recently been trialed for heart failure. For this application the leads are implanted at the T1-T4 vertebral level and normal SCS stimulation parameters are used. One study has produced no measureable affect [75] but another study concluded that high thoracic SCS is both safe and feasible and potentially can improve symptoms, functional status, and left ventricular function and promotes remodeling in patients with severe, symptomatic systolic heart failure [76]. Spinal cord stimulation has also been shown to suppress atrial fibrillation by autonomic remodeling [77].

One of the most exciting spinal cord stimulation developments to be reported in recent years has been the observation of functional recovery in patients with spinal cord injuries. These patients were diagnosed with a motor and sensory complete lesions and are paraplegic. A report from a single individual [78] and experience with a further four [79] has led to the conclusion that restoration of voluntary movement in these paralysed individuals is a result of increasing the excitability of lumbosacral spinal networks via neuromodulation. Normal SCS paddle electrodes were implanted over L1, S1 and the stimulation applied at 25 to 30 Hz with electrodes selected on the basis of the muscle groups which were activated.

Spinal cord stimulation has also been found to affect symptoms related to Parkinson's disease in both animals [80] and man [81]. Pain is often associated with advanced Parkinson's disease and individuals who have been implanted for pain management have shown postural stability, motor improvements and significant improvements in gait [82]. These applications extend the use of SCS beyond the treatment of pain to treat other neurological conditions. The modulation of inhibitory GABA in the dorsal horn may prove to have many applications beyond the treatment of pain.

6. Device Programing and Parameter Selection

6.1. *Stimulation frequency*

Regulators have approved for use in humans a number of new stimulation strategies developed with the aim of providing SCS without generation of paresthesia sensations. All the strategies have in common an increase in the duty cycle of stimulation, i.e., stimulation is on for a larger amount of time. One way to achieve an increase in duty cycle is to increase the stimulation frequency. The frequency of electrical stimulation significantly affects the frequency of action potential generation and hence neurotransmitter release and neural modulation. However, the most effective parameters for SCS have not been systematically investigated. The choice of stimulation frequency is made to produce the most comfortable sensations for patients at a reasonable power consumption. The power consumption and hence the expected lifetime of the implanted device is dependent on the total charge delivered overtime which is also dependent on the stimulation frequency. There are two broad range of stimulation frequencies which have been used clinically. With the advent of HF10 10 kHz, high frequency stimulation has come to imply 10 kHz stimulation frequency and low frequency is anything below 500 Hz. A much more useful definition is to rely on the properties of the dorsal column fibres and define the stimulation frequency as either above the frequency at which the fibres entrain to the stimulus or frequencies below which the fibres entrain. In this context entrainment refers to a one to one correspondence between stimulus and action potential generation, i.e., every stimulus produces an action potential. At higher frequencies, where stimuli are presented within the refractory period of the previous stimuli the one to one correspondence is no longer true. We explore the refractory behavior of dorsal column fibres later but the absolute refractory period is ~700 μs corresponding to a frequency of ~1.4 kHz. Here we define to frequency bands those below the MEF (maximal entrainment frequency) and those above where MEF = 1.4 kHz

There has been little systematic study of the effect of frequency on the efficacy of stimulation below MEF. Conventional stimulation frequencies are usually set at under 100 Hz and adjusted to provide comfortable stimulation. Very low frequencies (4 Hz) have been shown to be as effective in animal models as 60 Hz [83]. Higher frequencies (500 Hz) have been shown to improve peripheral blood flow [84] and so ideal stimulation frequency may depend on the application.

The long term safety of higher stimulation frequencies has yet to be fully assessed and there is evidence of the need for caution. Cellular level changes have been reported for stimulation rates as low as 200 Hz where paranodal myelin retraction at the nodes of Ranvier have been observed [85]. In this study retraction began minutes after the onset of stimulation and continued for up to 10 min after stimulation was ceased. The retraction reversed after a 2 h recovery period. Xray diffraction studies have led to the hypothesis that repetitive propagation of action potentials induced by 200 Hz stimulation could modify the ionic compositions at either the sub-myelin space or the paranodal axoglial junction complexes. A computational model has demonstrated a diminishment of the amplitude of the action potential and a slowing of conduction velocity to 40% of original when the length of the node is increased [86].

6.2. *Frequencies greater than MEF*

Stimulation at 10 kHz has been shown to be effective for relief from back and leg pain. A randomized study [8] demonstrated superiority for stimulation at 10 kHz against conventional (sub MEF) stimulation frequencies. The amplitude of the stimulation for 10 kHz stimulation arm of this study was set to sub paresthetic perception level. Biphasic stimulation with short pulse widths (<40 µS) and very short interphase and inter stimulus gaps was used. The strength duration relates the intensity of the stimulation required to the pulse width, shorter pulse widths require a higher stimulation intensity to depolarize an axon when compared with longer pulse widths.

The strength duration curve shows the firing threshold for a stimulus as a function of the pulse width (Figure 7). From this it is apparent that a stimulus current of <5 mA with a pulse with of less than 40µS is well below the firing threshold and no dorsal column recruitment can occur. The strength duration curve is measured using a single biphasic stimulus. When multiple stimuli are presented within the absolute refractory period of the fibre the membrane potential does not have time to recover between the stimuli and is not at equilibrium. The strength duration for a train multiple biphasic stimuli is not the same as for an isolated stimulus. The single stimulus overestimates the current required. The threshold current for a train of stimuli is presented at frequency of 10 kHz is shown in Figure 8, where the number of stimuli in the train is plotted against threshold. This model of a 10 µm diameter fibre demonstrates a decrease with increasing number of stimuli presented and asymptotes to a value 26% lower than the current for a single stimuli.

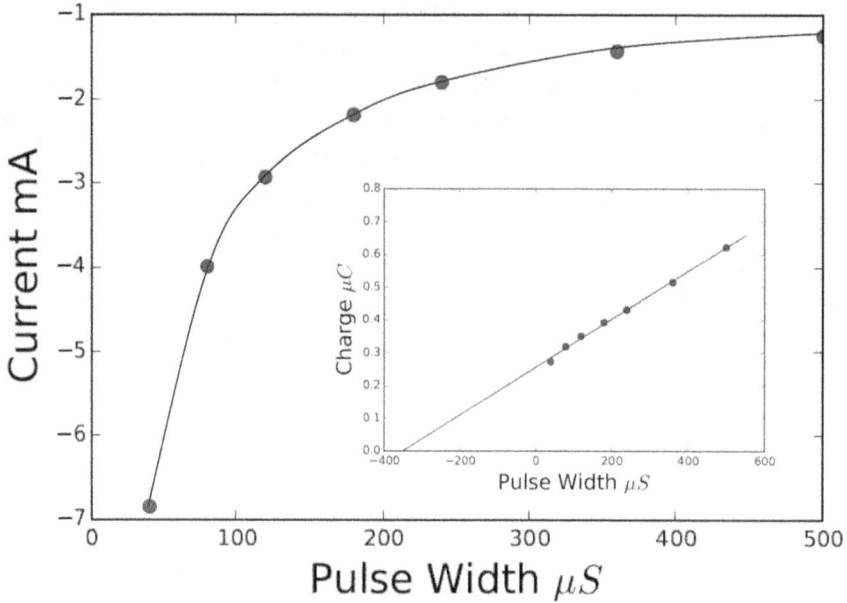

Fig.7. Strength duration curve for a 10µm diameter fibre sited 3mm away from a stimulating electrode. The stimulus was bipolar and biphasic with the return electrode 7mm from the stimulation electrode with a 10µs interphase gap.

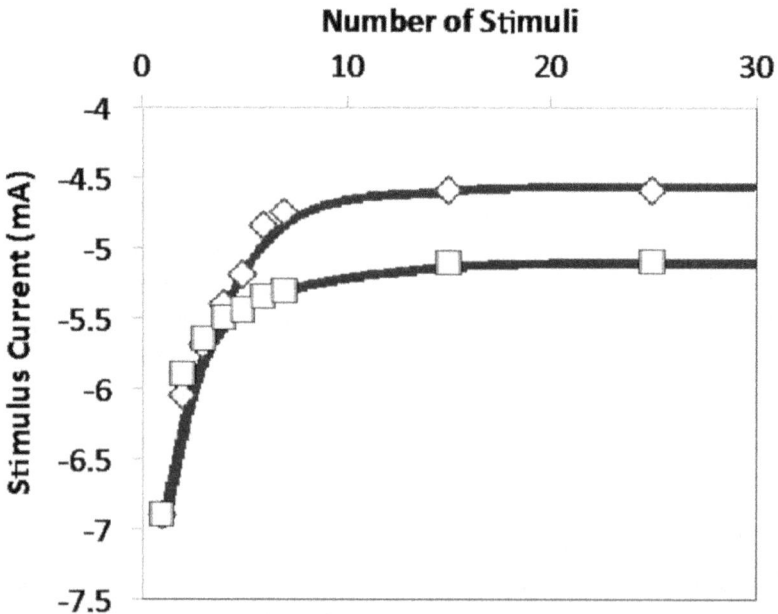

Fig. 8. Threshold current for 40 µS stimuli with 10 µS interphase gap for a number of stimuli . The squares are calculated thresholds with a 10 µS inter-stimulus interval and the diamonds calculated with no inter-stimulus interval.

Multiple stimuli placed closely together, as is the case in 10 kHz stimulation, has a different strength duration relationship when compared with a single stimuli presented at low frequencies. The decrease in threshold is a result of integration of the stimulus charge in the membrane and plateaus after 7 stimuli. The extra cellular potential for a train of 7 stimuli and the membrane voltage is shown in Figure 9. The current is adjusted to be with in 0.05 mA of the threshold current, and no action potential is initiated until the 7th stimuli, the first 6 stimuli are failed initiations but depolarize the membrane pushing it towards threshold for AP generation. The membrane potential doesn't return the resting state with the anodic charge balancing pulses because of the membrane capacitance and voltage gated non linear conductance of the ion channels in the membrane. The neuronal excitability is increased with each subsequent cycle similar result is shown in Figure 6 B [87].

Riely et. al. have shown that a sinusoidal stimulus that is sub-threshold for a single cycle will cause the neuron to fire when it is repeated several times [88]. Similarly, continuous stimulation at 10 kHz below threshold for AP generation reduces the threshold for firing of a test pulse by 50% when the HF stimulus is 30% lower than threshold for AP generation from the HF stimulus [87]. At higher HF stimulation amplitudes neural block occurs. Onset of stimulation produces an initial action potential but subsequent blockade occurs and no further AP's are generated. The amplitude of high frequency stimulation required to generate nerve block depends on the diameter of the fibre, larger diameter fibres will undergo conduction block at lower threshold currents [89]. High frequency stimulation at high stimulation amplitudes is used to produce neural blockade of peripheral nerves for the treatment of phantom limb pain. There is rich literature on the subject of high frequency nerve block and a review of this is beyond the present scope [90,91,91].

The mechanism by which high frequency stimulation affords superior pain relief when compared to < 100 Hz stimulation frequency remains unclear. What is known and described above can be summarized as follows.

1. Higher frequency stimulation reduces firing threshold for stimulation due to membrane integration effects;
2. Super threshold high frequency stimulation leads to neural blockade; and
3. Threshold for blockade is dependent on the fibre diameter.

This has led to the proposal that the mechanism of action of 10 kHz stimulation may be a result of block of the larger diameter dorsal column fibres and recruitment of the smaller diameter fibres. Recall that only a fraction of the DC fibres travel to the DCN and smaller diameter fibres ascend a few segments and terminate and so selective recruitment of these fibres may have the effect of providing pain relief without sensation.

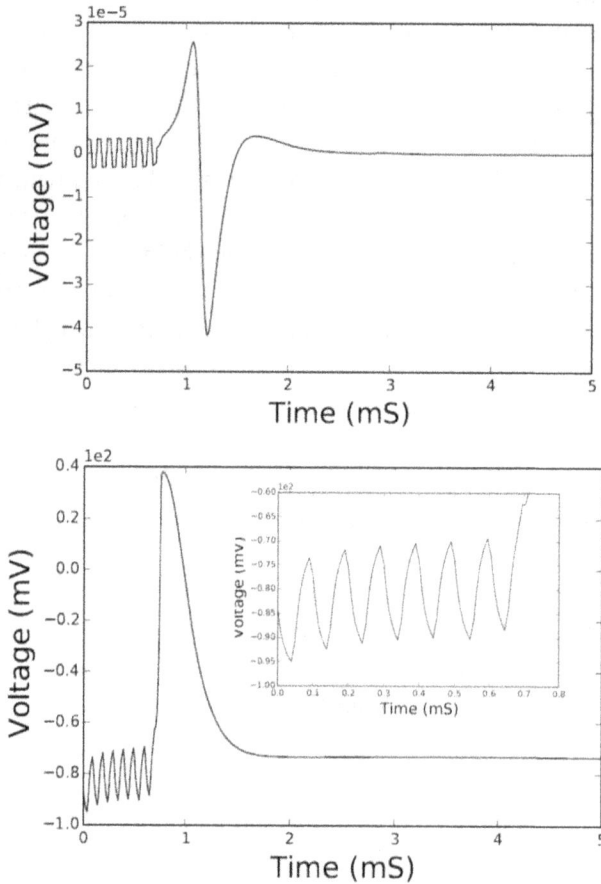

Fig. 9. The extracellular potential (top) and membrane potential (bottom) for model of a 10 μm diameter fibre exposed to 10 kHz train of biphasic stimuli. The amplitude of the stimulus was adjusted so that an action potential is generated on the seventh pulse. The bottom insert shows membrane potential prior to AP generation.

There have been relatively few animal studies comparing the effect of stimulation frequency on the efficacy of spinal cord stimulation. A direct comparison between 50 Hz, 1 kHz 10 kHz and sham on paw withdrawal threshold in a nerve injured rat neuropathic pain model revealed an intensity dependent effect for all three stimulation frequencies [92]. The stimulation levels were set as a percentage of motor threshold and a comparison between the maximal paw withdrawal thresholds which were measured (data from fig. 1, ref 38) reveals that the effect is proportional to stimulation level and not frequency. Further all frequencies had the same threshold. The 50 Hz results showed epoch to epoch improvements and may have improved further with longer exposure and the stimulus PW used for 50 Hz was 24 µS which is much shorter than normally clinically used.

The similarity in threshold and the consistent response between all frequencies was observed by Song et al. [93] who concluded that 50 Hz stimulation had a stronger effect than other frequencies. Recordings of single unit activity in the gracile nucleus showed striking differences between 10 kHz SCS and 50 Hz with the later showing a ~25 Hz discharge rate and the former showing a discharge rate near base line. This indicates that 10 kHz SCS does not have a supra spinal component to its mechanism of action. Further, the authors concluded that the mechanism did not involve a significant component of conduction block because gracile nucleus activity in response to von Frey filament activity was unaffected by 10 kHz stimulation. The stimulation thresholds were set below a level where any behavioral changes were observed in the animals, correspondeding to a level of 40-50% of motor threshold, and the lack of induced gracile nucleus activity suggests that this stimulation level is sub perceptual for the animal under study.

The notion that 10 kHz stimulation frequency produces a conduction block but allows recruitment of smaller diameter fibers which ascend only a few segments is appealing and fits with some but not all the experimental observations namely the lack of observable conduction block effects.

Despite the fact that subparesthetic sensation stimulation allows the conduct of randomized blinded and sham controlled studies, only one such study has been conducted. A comparison between 5 kHz stimulation with sham in humans showed no statistically significant difference in 33 subjects but a highly significant difference in the "period effect" [94]. The patients in this study preferred whichever treatment they received first, sham or 5 KHz.

6.3. *Burst and high density*

Burst stimulation [13] applies five stimuli in a pattern. It has been found that the parameters used for burst stimulation have a strong influence on dorsal horn firing after noxious stimuli [95]. The most effective burst SCS paradigm was found when using parameter settings of seven pulses at 500 Hz and 1000 µs width repeated at a rate of 40 Hz and at amplitude of 90% of motor threshold. Burst and tonic SCS both reduce allodynia [96], however tonic SCS increases serum GABA back to normal from the injury induced decrease, but GABA remains decreased during burst SCS.

A patient's lack of perception of the stimulation is not due to the intrinsic nature of the pulse sequence and both burst and 10 kHz stimulation have a psychophysiological threshold for perception. These algorithms are paresthesia free because the amplitude of stimulation is adjusted to below the perception level not because they intrinsically do not produce paresthesias. Figure 10 shows the perceptual threshold and the maximum tolerable threshold for an individual undergoing trial for SCS as a function of the stimulation frequency.

The data indicates that at higher stimulation frequencies the psychophysical threshold occurs at a lower stimulation amplitude (in current) than at 100 Hz by about 20%. Both threshold and maximum tolerable stimulation levels follow the same trend. The pulse width (40 μs) was held constant for the measurements and so the increase in sensitivity is a result of the membrane integration effects discussed previously. The trend observed in the clinical data is reproduced in a computational model which shows a reduction in threshold by 20%. If the amplitude of stimulation for 10 kHz is set at less than 80% of the psychophysical threshold for paresthesia generation for the same pulse width but at sub-MEF frequencies then it is unlikely to result in recruitment of dorsal column fibres.

6.4. *Compound action potentials*

Improvements in patient outcomes have been achieved via trial-and-error approaches to development. This is the only course available with the current lack of detailed understanding of mechanisms and the subjective nature of the assessment of benefit of the therapy. Recently new techniques have been developed which promise to overcome some of these hurdles. The electrically evoked compound action potential (ECAP) is a measurement of the response the dorsal columns to stimulation and provides a direct a quantifiable measure of the response of the dorsal columns to electrical stimulation [97,98].

ECAPS are a measure of the extracellular potential produced by the population of neurons which respond to the stimulation. The potential arises from the ion currents produced at the nodes of Ranvier of the axon as it is depolarized. The ECAP is the sum of the voltages produced by those currents across a length of the fibre and across all the responding fibres. ECAPS have been measured using the unused contacts of the electrode array as the measurement electrodes. The potential measured at therapeutic levels of stimulation is of the order of 10's of μvolts and voltage required to deliver mAmps of current into the impedance of the tissue can be 20 V. There is 6 orders of magnitude difference between the stimulation potential and the ECAP potential and this makes the measurement a significant challenge.

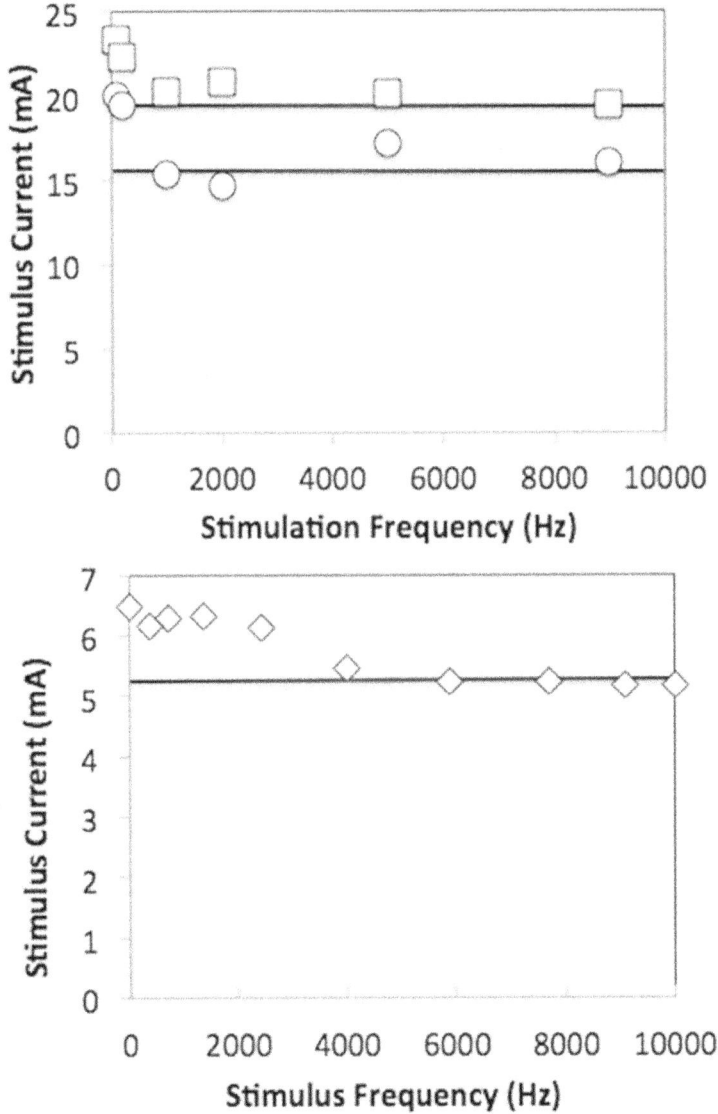

Fig. 10. Threshold and maximal tolerable stimulation levels for an individual patient at different stimulation frequencies (100-9000Hz) in a trial SCS patient (upper plot) and calculation of the threshold of a 10 μm diameter fibre as a function of the stimulation frequency (lower plot).

The ECAP for a dorsal column response is a triphasic potential consisting of P1, N1, and P2 peaks which propagate along the dorsal column. Measuring ECAPS reveals a great deal about the electrophysiology of the fibres which respond to SCS. For instance, the ECAP position at multiple electrodes allows the conduction velocity of the fibres to be estimated. The ECAP is the sum of the single fibre action potentials and its amplitude grows as the stimulation current is increased and more fibres are recruited. At low stimulation currents only the most excitable fibres are recruited and these have the largest fibre diameters, as the stimulus current is increased then it would be expected that there would be contributions from smaller diameter less excitable fibres. The amplitude of the ECAP as measured by the difference between P2 and N1 grows from a threshold value to 2 times threshold almost linearly proportional to the current. The response starts to flatten out and displays a saturation characteristic at 3 to 4 times threshold but in clinical practice SCS devices are set within a range of current from threshold to under 1.5 times threshold and so the plateau region is never reached in clinical applications (Figure 11).

The latency of the N1 peak increases with the propagation distance. With a knowledge of the separation between the electrodes and the timing of the N1 peak the velocity of the fibres can be estimated. The N1 peak latency is shortest close to the stimulation threshold current and increases slightly as the stimulation current is increased (in the range between 1x and 2x threshold). At very high stimulation currents (>2.5 mA in Figure 11D) the latency reduces indicating the recruitment of additional larger diameter fibres which may be more lateral in the dorsal column. The field not only penetrates the cord with increasing current but also increases in area. The total variation in the conduction velocity is between 98 and 101 ms^{-1} from 1x to 2x threshold. This is only a 3% difference from the highest to lowest currents which are clinically relevant. The observation that the velocity change over this range of stimulation currents is so low indicates that there is very little variation in the velocity distribution of fibres over the range of stimulation currents except very close to threshold. These basic measurements indicate that dorsal column recruitment is proportional to the stimulation current and that as the current is increased the fibres with same properties are recruited but their number increases.

The excitability of dorsal column fibres can be directly determined with ECAP measurements from strength duration curves. Here a measure of the threshold is obtain by measuring growth curves at a number of different pulse widths. A plot of the charge delivered versus the pulse width yields a straight line with whose slope is the chronaxie. This is a direct measurement of the properties of the membrane of axon and is used to identify the neural elements which respond to stimulation. The chronaxie is determined by the membrane excitability, surface to volume ratio and the physical parameters of the membrane. The site of activation of a neuronal element can be determined directly from the chronaxie, large myelinated axons ($\sim$30–200 μs), small axons ($\sim$200–700 μs) and cell bodies and dendrites ($\sim$1–10 ms). This technique has been used to identify the neuronal elements excited during DBS [99]. Yearwood reports an average value of 295 μs measured in 19 subjects using psychophysical perception threshold as threshold. We have also measured chronaxie using compound action potential growth curves and objectively measuring the electrophysiological threshold and have found a large variability from patient to patient (150 to 600 μS) but nonetheless both methods lead to the conclusion that it is axons and not other neuronal elements which are recruited during SCS (Table 2).

The dynamic properties of dorsal column fibres can also be determined with more complex stimulation paradigms. The excitability of the axon is determined by both the static and dynamic properties of the cell and both hyperexcitable and hypo-excitable periods occur post action potential generation. During the period immediately post action potential propagation the axon is hypoexcitable, generation of additional action potentials is impossible as a result of the inactivation of the voltage gated Na^+ ion channels. These channels remain open until the membrane hyperpolarizes and its potential returns to the value where they close.

The absolute and relative refractory periods can be determined with compound action potential measurements with a paired pulse experiments. Here a stimulus is applied to produce an action potential and then closely followed by a second stimulus. The amplitude of the ECAP is determined in response to the 2nd stimulus. When the 2nd stimulus is applied within the absolute refractory period of the fibres it elicits no response as all the fibres are still with in their refractory period from the first response (Figure 12).

This period sets the upper limit for stimulation frequency, any stimulus presented at inter-stimulus intervals shorter than the refractory period will elicit no action potentials. For human dorsal column fibres this time is 700 μs. For stimulation with biphasic stimuli with pulse width of 125 μs and interphase gap of 50 μs the upper limit for stimulus frequency is 1 kHz. (250 μs for anodic and cathodic + interphase gap 50 μs + 700 μs results in 1ms total duration). There is no penalty for stimulation at higher rates other than the energy consumed in generation of the stimulus. Dorsal column fibres are simply incapable of generation action potentials at faster rates (dependant of course on the PW of the stimulus).

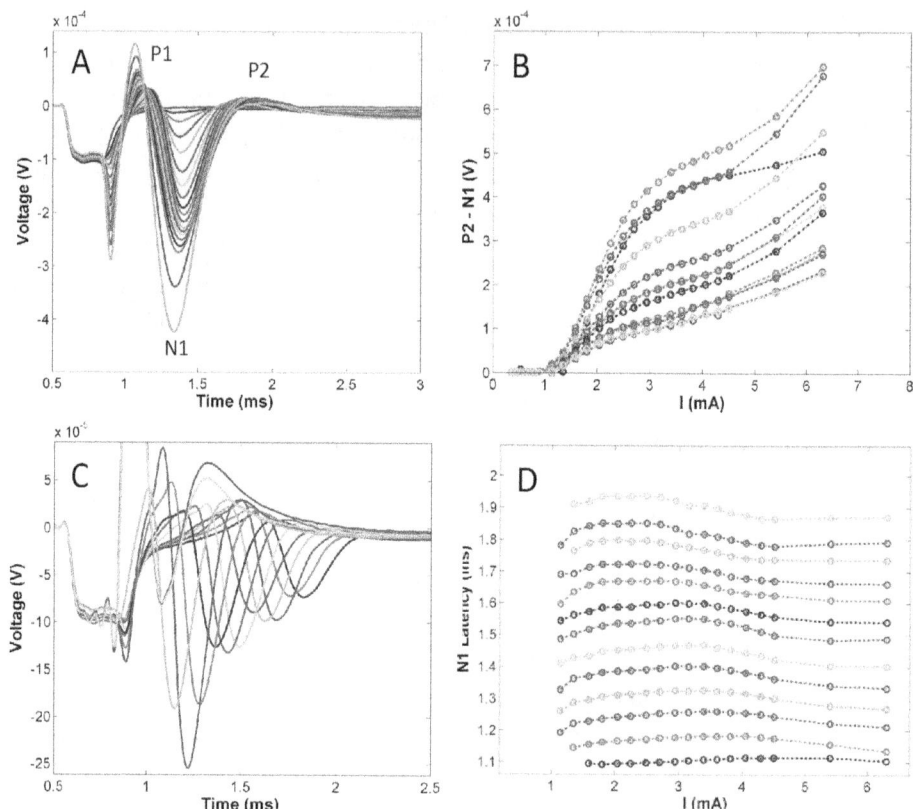

Fig. 11. Example of ECAPS measured for the sheep dorsal column with a 16 channel (2x eight channel electrodes sited on the anatomical midline). ECAPS measured in response to increasing the stimulation amplitude shown in A, and the amplitude of the ECAP (P2-N1) as a function of current for all measurement electrodes in B. The propagating response at a fixed stimulation current for all electrodes C and the latency of the N1 peak as a function of stimulation current for all measurement electrodes D.

Table. 2. Dorsal Column Electrophysiological Parameters Determined from ECAP Measurements

Electrophysiological Property	Value	Notes
Conduction Velocity		Fibre diameters
Refractory Period	Absolute 700 µs	
	Relative 1500 µs	
Chronaxie	150 to 600 µs	Data from 7 subjects
	(average 390, σ=171)	

The basic electrophysiological responses indicate that it is the Aβ fibre axons of the dorsal column respond to SCS during stimulation. In routine clinical use these basic electrophysiological measurements may provide diagnostic and prognostic indications for chronic pain sufferers. The ECAP is a result of the ion channel conductances which occur during action potential generation and so provides a direct measure of any pathological alterations in channel conductance. For instance, the repetitive discharge that develops ectopically in injured sensory neurons after nerve trauma is thought to contribute significantly to chronic neuropathic dysesthesias and pain [100]. This ectopic discharge is a result of altered neuronal excitability and this can be directly measured via ECAPS. Further, neuropathic pain has been associated with increased nodal persistent Na^+ currents in human diabetic neuropathy [101] and nerve injury models have demonstrated a host morphological and electrophysiological changes including [102]:

1. Increased percentages of C-, Aδ-, and Aβ-nociceptors and cutaneous Aα/β-low-threshold mechanoreceptors with ongoing/spontaneous firing;

2. Spontaneous firing in C-nociceptors that originated peripherally in nerve injured animals;

3. Decreased electrical thresholds in A-nociceptors after nerve injury;

4. Hyperpolarised membrane potentials in A-nociceptors and Aα/β-low-threshold-mechanoreceptors after nerve injury but not C-nociceptors;

5. decreased somatic action potential rise times in C- and A-nociceptors, not Aα/β-low-threshold-mechanoreceptors.

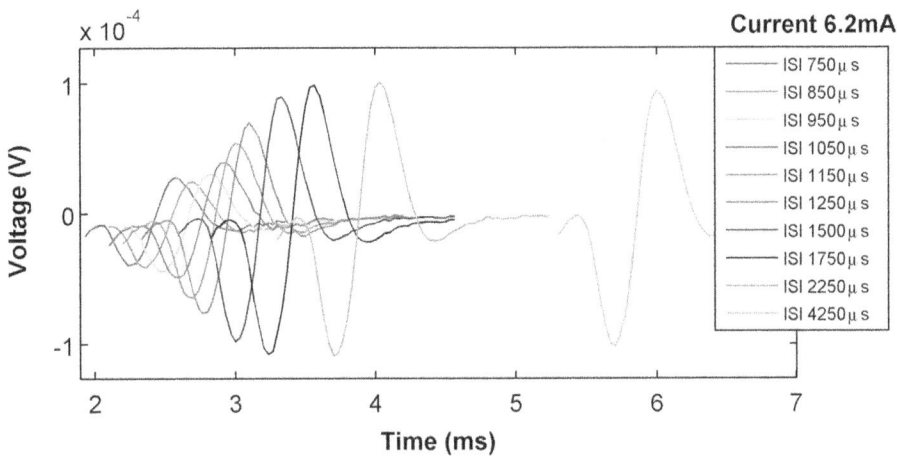

Fig. 12. Example of attenuation of amplitude of the response from the 2nd stimulus in a paired pulse paradigm experiment. ECAPS are shown for responses with different interstimulus intervals (ISI) as indicated in the legend. The relative refractory period at 1500 μs is apparent in the reduction of the amplitude of the response at ISI of 1500 μs.

The compound action potential provides a means to observe some of these effects that have been studied in animals in neuropathic humans. For instance recordings from human dorsal columns have different morphologies.

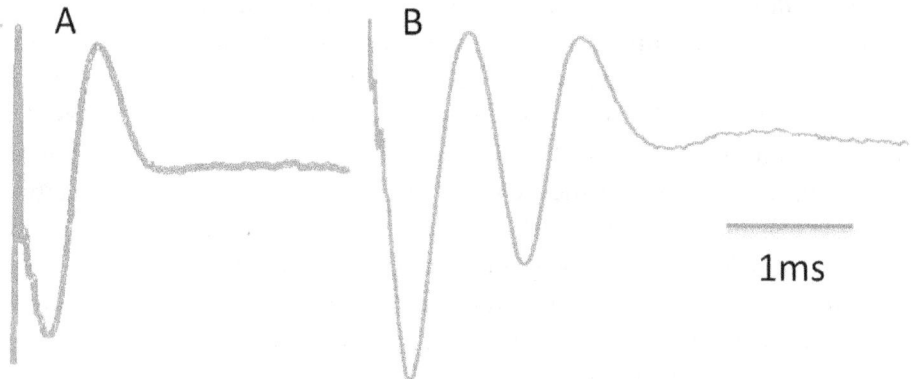

Fig.13. Examples of two different ECAP morphologies recorded from human dorsal columns.

Figure 13 shows recordings from two different subjects, 13A has a normal response but 13B shows a doublet response where the dorsal column fibres are producing multiple action potentials for a single stimulus. Similar responses can be produced by stretching a fibre, and electrical stimulation at the periphery in nerve injured animals produces spontaneous activity in DRG neurons [103]. A reasonable hypothesis for observations of this type of aberrant ECAP response in humans is that it is a direct measure of ectopic firing. It remains to be seen if the collection of large numbers of recordings across a large number of pain aetiologies will produce a diagnostic and prognostic for neuropathic pain treatment.

So far we have considered the Aβ short latency responses observed in the compound action potential measured from the dorsal column. At higher stimulation amplitudes additional responses appear with longer latencies than the initial Aβ responses. In sheep these responses have a latency of 3 ms and are accompanied by an EMG response from the dermatome which is innervated by fibres from the DRG at the spinal segment of stimulation.

These long latency responses are characteristic of spinal cord reflex response. Such responses to L1, S1 stimulation have been characterized in awake rats and consist of multiple components, an early (3.2±0.3 ms), middle (5.3±0.2 ms) and late (9.0±1.4 ms) response [104]. The authors concluded that the early response is a direct motor response and that the middle response showed the neurophysiological properties of a monosynaptic reflex (H-reflex). The responses measured from the epidural space in the sheep shown in Figure 14 correspond to the middle responses observed characterised in the rat. Any early response would be buried in the large dorsal column Aβ potential which is recorded.

Long latency responses are also observed during epidural spinal cord stimulation in humans. Dorsal root activation is uncomfortable and can be painful for recipients of spinal cord stimulation. ECAPS provide a direct means to quantify the threshold for dorsal root activation and set the upper boundary for stimulation current (Figure 15).

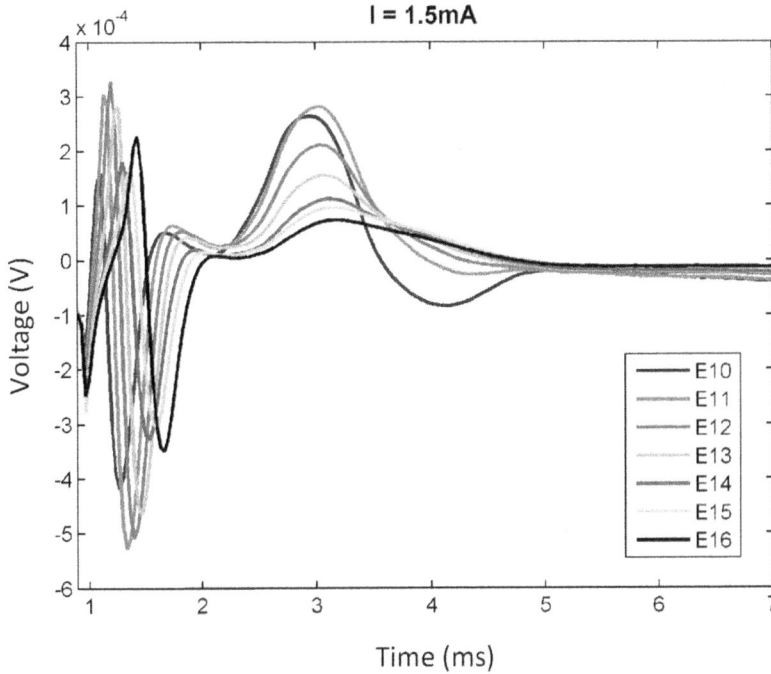

Fig.14. Longer latency responses measured during epidural spinal cord stimulation in anaesthetized sheep.

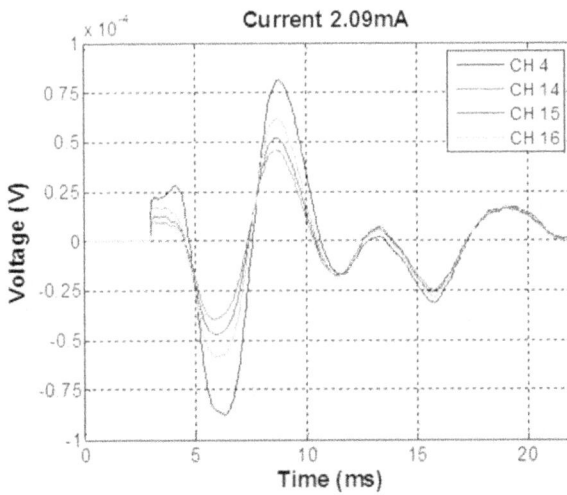

Fig.15. Long latency responses measured from human epidural space above the dorsal column.

In humans, percutaneous electrical stimulation of the S1–S2 dorsal roots can elicit an H-reflex in the soleus muscle [105]. This approach has been used to assess the functional state of the dorsal roots. It has not routinely used in neurophysiological studies mainly because percutaneous dorsal root stimulation is rather painful presumably due to the high intensity of stimulation needed to elicit a response and yet this response is common side effect of SCS stimulation. The goal of adjustment of therapy parameters for spinal cord stimulation is to avoid dorsal root stimulation which is uncomfortable for recipients but at the same time provide sufficient stimulation to produce effective pain relief.

6.5. *Closed loop control*

We have seen that there is no simple relationship between the recruitment of the dorsal column fibres and the stimulation parameters, which are clinically employed. A further profound complication exists as a result of the constant physiological and mechanical changes which occur in the spine, spinal cord and related tissue. A patient's posture has a profound effect on the separation between the dorsal column and the electrode in the epidural space and this change can have a dramatic effect on the threshold for stimulation.

The threshold for stimulation for supine posture (lying on the back) can be 4 times lower for the same patient than when prone (lying on the stomach). When supine, the CSF drains from between the cord and dura and the cord drops and lies against the electrode with the patient on their back and the converse is true when prone. The net result is that a stimulus level which is sub threshold for dorsal column activation in one posture can produce a painful over stimulus and dorsal root stimulation in another (Figure 16).

Posture changes are relatively slow (occurring over time periods of seconds) and the only means patients with fixed stimulation amplitude devices can cope with these changes is by manually adjusting the stimulation level with their remote. Attempts have been made to automate this procedure with addition of accelerometers and clinical studies have shown that these devices have reduced the interaction of the patient with the device [14]. Even these devices can't eliminate all the postural effects but roughly halve the number of interactions a patient has with their device per day (Figure 17).

The electrical evoked compound action potential can be used to asses the amount of dorsal column recruitment which results from a given stimulus. A plot of the amplitude of the ECAP as patient moves shows a more than 5x variation in amplitude from the level when they adjust the stimulation for comfort in a seated position. The slow postural effects are also accompanied by rapid transient changes such as when a patient coughs during which the amplitude of the response is more than six times the amplitude which the patient desires for pain relief. These large amplitudes are almost always accompanied by dorsal root activation and uncomfortable sensation for the patient.

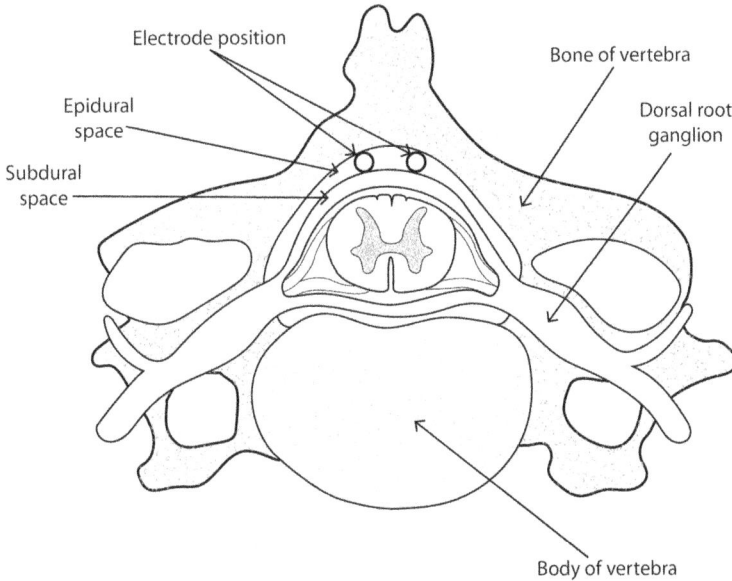

Fig.16. A cross section of the spinal cord illustrated the position of the electrodes is indicated in the epidural space. In this instance two leads are implanted one on either side of the midline. A change in the thickness of the subdural space and consequent change in the separation of the electrode from the surface of the dorsal column leads to changes in threshold current.

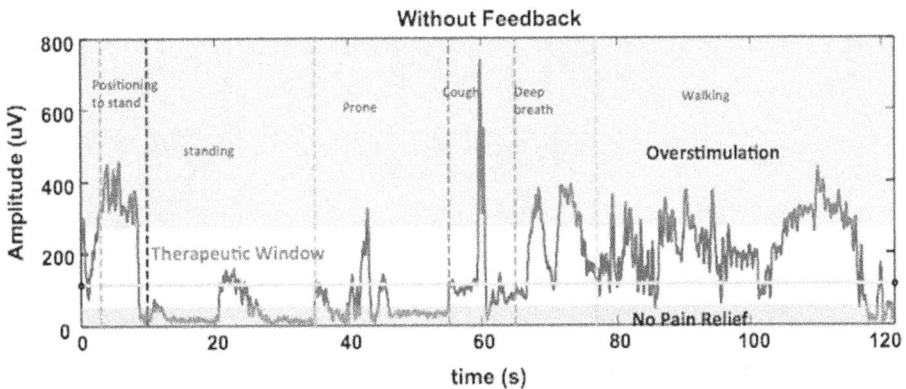

Fig.17. A continuous recording of Aβ dorsal column recruitment as determined by the amplitude of the electrically evoked compound action potential during SCS at constant stimulus amplitude in a human during the labelled movements.

Both fast and slow mechanical changes are superimposed on physiological changes which also affect the excitability of the dorsal columns. The amplitude of the ECAP varies with heart beat. Two effects contribute to these changes, one is the mechanical swelling and contraction (pulse) of the cord with the change in blood pressure and the other is shift in the impedance of the tissue due to the inflow and out flow of blood. Some patients describe the paresthesia sensation as pulsing, it is their own heartbeat which gives rise to this. We have observed patients where this effect is such that between beats there is no dorsal column recruitment and is above comfort level when systolic pressure is highest. Figure 18 shows responses for a patient where the amplitude of the ECAP changes by a factor of 5 with each heartbeat.

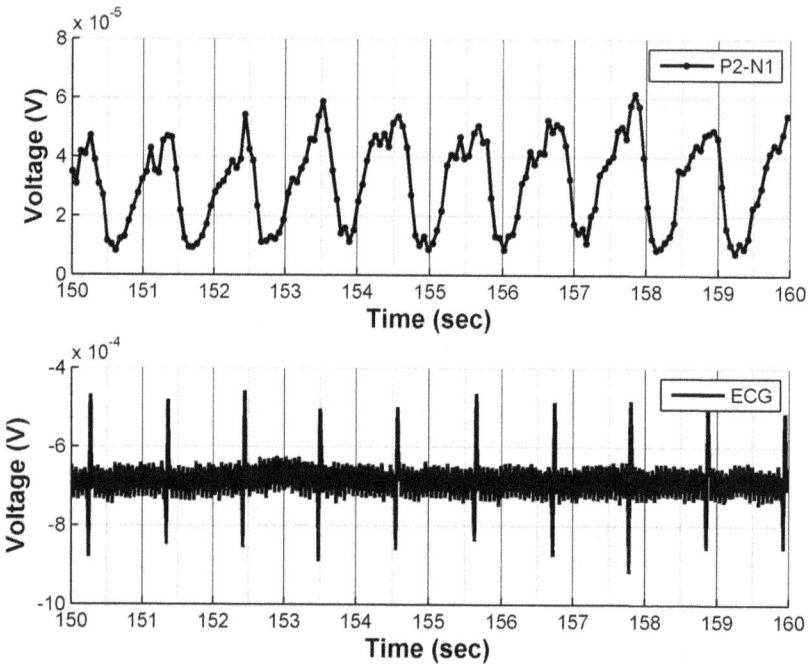

Fig. 18. The amplitude of the compound action potential (P2-N1) amplitude and ECG showing the coincidence of the peaks in ECG with peaks in amplitude of the ECAP.

The only means to ensure stable stimulation which accounts for all the mechanical and physiological changes to excitability is with closed loop control. The amplitude of the Aβ response is used as a control target in a feedback loop and a stimulus parameter, amplitude or pulse width, is adjusted in real time based on the measured ECAP. A fixed target ECAP can be selected or one modulated over time. We have developed such a system where the magnitude of the response is determined for a stimulus and then compared to a set point in a feedback algorithm which calculates a new stimulus amplitude to present. This process is repeated for every stimulus and the net result is that the current is continuously adjusted in order to maintain constant ECAP amplitude. Constant ECAP amplitude is not constant neural recruitment; the amplitude of the ECAP signal varies as a function of the distance between the fibres and the electrode contact due the resistivity of the media and the length of the fibre which is being excited. At the electrode fibre separations and fibre conduction velocities typical in SCS the relationship is $\sim 1/D^2$. Despite this a closed loop system which targets constant ECAP amplitude achieves constant recruitment with $\sim 20\%$ error which is a considerable improvement over the open loop state error of 400% (Figure 19).

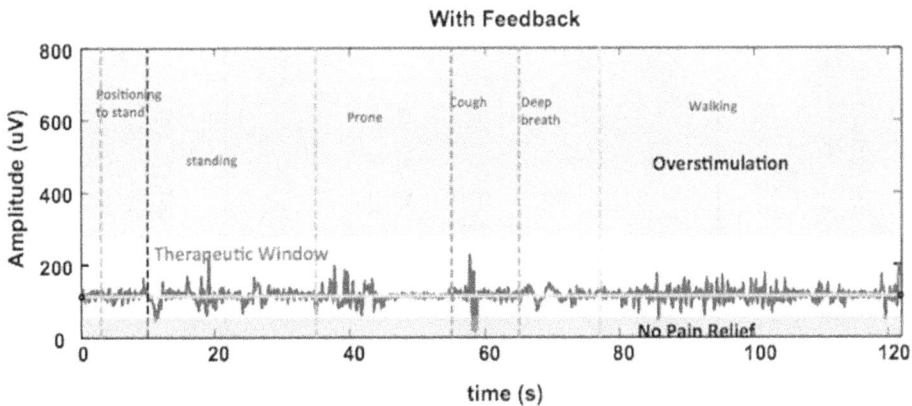

Fig. 19. The Aβ amplitude measured during closed loop feedback control for a similar range of movements as shown in Figure 17.

A randomised double blinded cross over study compared results of closed loop with open loop control. In this study patients were trialled for a 10 day periods with open loop (patient controlled) and then 10 days with closed loop controlled stimulation (or opposite order depending on randomisation) and comparison was made between the trial arms. This study with 22 subjects demonstrated that a 90% subjective preference for closed loop control. It met its primary end points and demonstrated improved pain relief and reduction in side effects [106].

6.6. *Therapeutic window*

The ultimate goal of medical intervention is to reverse the underlying pathophysiological cause of disease and return the subject to normal healthy living. The underlying causes of neuropathic pain are complex, reduction of WDR hyper-excitability even if it takes place in some patients may be wound back up again by aberrant peripheral input from an untreated injured nerve. Nonetheless it is instructive to hypothesize the conditions required to reliably achieve the goal of reversal of central sensitization in routine clinical practice and in so doing highlight gaps in knowledge and investigations required to fill those gaps.

We understand that SCS produces a release of inhibitory neuro-transmitters in the dorsal horn which reduces the excitability of WDR neurons. In this sense SCS could be considered to be a drug, the electrically excited neuronal activity changes the concentration of inhibitory neurotransmitters. It is instructive to contemplate a dose response curve for the electrically stimulated release of these substances .

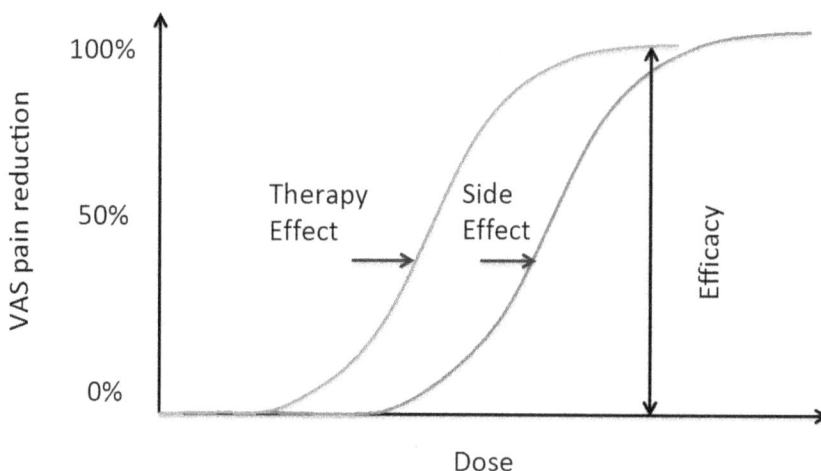

Fig. 20. General illustration of a dose response curve.

The dose response curve for SCS is unknown and until recently defining the dose in terms of neural activity has been impossible. If such a curve could be defined it would provide a relationship between the dorsal column concentrations of inhibitory neurotransmitters and the level of pain relief, and in turn the relationship between the electrical stimulus, number and frequency of axon potentials There would also be similar curve for side effects and a detailed understanding of these curves would provide direct, objective indication of the most effective stimulation conditions.

There is a practical operating window for stimulation. As discussed earlier stimulation at high amplitudes can produce dorsal root stimulation which can be highly uncomfortable for patients. The threshold for this stimulation could be considered used to define the side effect curve illustrated in Figure 20 and the upper limit to therapeutic window. The lower limit for the therapeutic window is harder to define, clearly failure to generate action potentials in the dorsal column would set the lowest limit of the therapeutic window. The Aβ amplitude is related to the area of coverage. When the ECAP amplitude falls to less than half the valu that the ECAP amplitude is adjusted to in order to achieve good pain relief in closed loop conditions, this equates to coverage of less than half the painful area and could be considered the lower boundary of the therapeutic window. The therapeutic window can be objectively defined by the measurement of ECAPs.

A significant number of individuals implanted with SCS devices experience significant pain relief at first and then the therapy looses effectiveness over time and the patient becomes a non-responder. This can take several years and the cause is unknown. This loss of therapeutic benefit may be a result of continuous overstimulation which is an unavoidable consequence of SCS without feedback control. Dorsal column stimulation at very high amplitudes may result in further wind up of the pathophysiological state. It is well understood that short high intensity pulses trains applied to the periphery will wind up WDR neurons, in fact it is a experimental technique used to study the phenomena (12 conditioning stimuli, 0.5 ms duration, three times the threshold for excitation of C-fibers and at a frequency of 0.5 Hz are the parameters used experimentally [107]). This stimulation amplitude is extremely high and unlikely to be reached during SCS. Stimulation of C fibres in a peripheral nerve requires a stimulus which is 75 times the strength required for Aβ fibres and 22 times the strength for Aδ fibres [108]. The relative thresholds for stimulation of the nociceptor fibres to Aβ fibres from dorsal column stimulation is unknown, however the large difference in threshold measured at the periphery makes direct stimulation of smaller diameter C fibres unlikely. Despite this, open loop spinal cord stimulation during a patient's cough produces Aβ responses up to 10 times the amplitude required for therapeutic effect, this is a result of the rapid drop in threshold due to spinal cord movement. Only very short durations and a small number of stimuli are required to produce wind up and with current knowledge, wind up via direct nociceptor stimulation cannot be ruled out from occurring during the frequent over stimulations.

There is, however, a considerable amount of evidence for the presence of large Aβ fibre nociceptors (for a review see [109]). These fibres have approximately double the electrical threshold for Aβ low threshold mechanosensitive fibres. Myelinated primary afferents, perhaps Aβ fibers, have been implicated in signaling the hyperalgesic pain in causalgia [110]. These fibers may be sensitized Aβ nociceptors or low-threshold mechanoreceptors. It has even been suggested that ectopic discharge in Aβ fibres play a key role in the generation and maintenance of central sensitization [111].

A link has also been demonstrated between repetitive stimulation of A-fibre primary afferents and enhancement of spinal excitability which is very similar to the excitability increases evoked by C-fibres. Enhanced ventral root responses, changes in NK1 receptor expression, may contribute to central sensitization and may be directly related to the behavioral hyperalgesia [112]. There is also evidence for cross coupling between afferent A- and C-neurons in dorsal root ganglia [113] which provides a mechanism by which Aβ fibre activity can directly affect C fibres. SCS alone has also been reported to excite WDR neurons and has also been shown to excite and inhibit the same neuron [114,115].

The emerging evidence paints a much more complex picture of the mechanism of action for SCS and suggests that there is complex interplay between excitatory and inhibitory effects and understanding the balance between these is the key to developing more effective therapy. There are mechanisms by which Aβ fibre stimulation can exacerbate the centrally sensitized neuropathopysiological state. With conventional stimulation there is a level of stimulation that an individual can tolerate before it becomes uncomfortable but it is not clear if this level is above or below the pathology-inducing level. A patient's report of the intensity of stimulation is not a reliable indicator of the recruitment level in the spinal cord as evidenced by the fact that patients will tolerate huge transients in stimulation reflected in the evoked responses measured during tonic stimulation. These events are often accompanied by dorsal root excitation and the size of the ECAPs recorded indicate a large number of fibres with high thresholds for excitation are recruited. Loss of stimulation efficacy over time is still not understood, exacerbation of the underlying spinal cord neuropathology by frequent over stimulation via the windup mechanisms may be the culprit in the mystery.

A comparison of the distribution of the Aβ compound action potential amplitudes for patients undergoing SCS with closed loop control and in the same patient with open loop control provides some insight into the role of paresthesia and level of pain relief for SCS. The plot in Figure 21 shows a histogram of Aβ potentials recorded over an extended period with closed loop control and with open loop. The control loop keeps the amplitude of the ECAP centered around ~40 μV and achieves this response for 25% of the stimuli which are presented. Open loop stimulation achieves this amplitude less than a few percent of the time and yet the qualitative sensation intensity reported by the patients is the same.

The ECAP amplitude is proportional to the area of coverage and closed loop control provides a substantial increase in the percentage of stimuli which achieve the desired area of coverage. That pain relief is achieved with open loop SCS, where desired coverage is achieved with such a small percentage of the stimuli presented and the intensity of paresthesia experienced by the patient is very similar, simply indicates that paresthesia sensation is a very poor indicator of the capacity of SCS to produce pain relief. Clinically this is well understood and hence the reason for trial stimulation. There are patients which appear to be ideal SCS candidates, achieve adequate coverage during trial stimulation and tolerate paresthesia but achieve no pain relief.

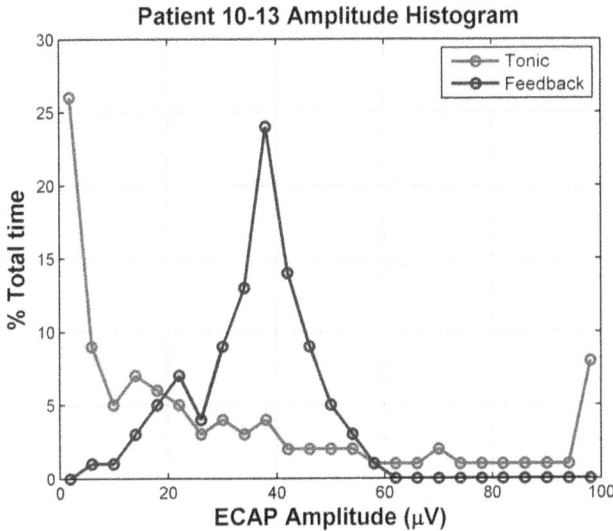

Fig. 21. Comparison of the distribution of the ECAP amplitudes for an individual during open loop and closed loop stimulation.

The data shown in Figure 21 indicates that ideal stimulation dose is not achieved as frequently as the stimulation rate. The lower boundary of the therapeutic window can be defined in terms of the ECAP amplitude which is directly related to the area of coverage. If the center surround hypothesis is found to be true, then anything other than completely surrounding the painful area maybe found to be ineffective. The frequency at which ECAP potential reaches the desired level to provide effective pain relief may be very much lower than the stimulation frequency. The stimulation frequency is adjusted to control the paresthesia sensation and the lack of correlation with effective pain relief discussed for high frequency stimulation persists at lower frequencies. The data shown in Figure 21 with feedback loop off indicates a substantial number of over stimulations, ~8% of the stimulations result in an ECAP amplitude >100 μV. The patient has control of the stimulation amplitude and for open loop stimulation the amplitude is adjusted to minimize this % and still maintain some stimulation which produces recruitments in the therapeutic window. In some patients an adequate comprise is impossible to achieve and all forms of open loop stimulation are likely to fail with these patients.

7. Concluding Remarks

There are a significant number of challenges which still need to be overcome before neuromodulation for pain relief moves up the treatment order. This is despite the strong evidence suggesting that early treatment is important. The improved reliability of modern systems, improved pain relief results and demonstrated cost effectiveness show significant progress in this direction. However, it is clear that a detailed understanding of the mechanisms of action will allow design of systems and therapies with improved outcomes with a much greater speed of development.

References

1. Shealy, C. N., Taslitz, N., Mortimer, J. T. and Becker, D. P., Electrical inhibition of pain: experimental evaluation, *Anesth. Analg.,* **46,** 299–305 (1967).
2. Melzack, R. and Wall, P. D., Pain mechanisms: a new theory, *Science* **150,** 971–979 (1965).
3. Johannes, C. B., Le, T. K., Zhou, X., Johnston, J. A. and Dworkin, R. H., The prevalence of chronic pain in United States adults: Results of an internet-based survey, *J. Pain* **11,** 1230–1239 (2010).
4. Gaskin, D. J. and Richard, P., The economic costs of pain in the United States, *J. Pain* **13,** 715–724 (2012).
5. Taylor, R. S., Desai, M. J., Rigoard, P. and Taylor, R. J., Predictors of pain relief following spinal cord stimulation in chronic back and leg pain and failed back surgery syndrome: A systematic review and meta-regression analysis, *Pain Pract.* **14,** 489–505 (2014).
6. North, R. B., Kidd, D. H., Zahurak, M., James, C. S. and Long, D. M., Spinal cord stimulation for chronic, intractable pain: experience over two decades, *Neurosurgery* **32,** 384-94–5 (1993).
7. Zhang, T. C., Janik, J. J. and Grill, W. M., Mechanisms and models of spinal cord stimulation for the treatment of neuropathic pain, *Brain Res.* **1569,** 19–31 (2014).
8. Kapural, L., Yu, C., Doust, M. W., Gliner, B. E., Vallejo, R., Sitzman, B. T., Amirdelfan, K., Morgan, D., Brown, L. L., Yearwood, T. L., Bundschu, R., Burton, A. W., Yang, T., Benyamin, R., Burgher, A. H., Novel 10-kHz high-frequency therapy (HF10 therapy) is superior to traditional low-frequency spinal cord stimulation for the treatment of chronic back and leg pain: the SENZA-RCT randomized controlled trial, *Anesthesiology* **123,** 851–860 (2015).
9. Towe, B. C., Larson, P. J. and Gulick, D. W., A microwave powered injectable neural stimulator, in *2012 Annual International Conference of the IEEE Engineering in Medicine and Biology Society,* 5006–5009 (2012).
10. Tyler Perryman, L., Speck, B., Montes Garcia, C. and Rashbaum, R., Injectable spinal cord stimulator system: Pilot study, *Tech. Reg. Anesth. Pain Manag.* **16,** 102–105 (2012).

11. Sweet, J., Badjatiya, A., Tan, D. and Miller, J., Paresthesia-free high-density spinal cord stimulation for postlaminectomy syndrome in a prescreened population: a prospective case series, *Neuromodulation Technol. Neural Interface* (2015). doi:10.1111/ner.12357

12. Oakley, J. C. and Prager, J. P., Spinal cord stimulation: mechanisms of action, *Spine* **27**, 2574–2583 (2002).

13. De Ridder, D., Vanneste, S., Plazier, M., van der Loo, E. and Menovsky, T., Burst spinal cord stimulation, *Neurosurgery* **66**, 986–990 (2010).

14. Schultz, D. M. *et al.* Sensor-driven position-adaptive spinal cord stimulation for chronic pain, *Pain Physician* **15**, 1–12 (2012).

15. North, R. B., Kidd, D. H., Olin, J. C. and Sieracki, J. M., Spinal cord stimulation electrode design: prospective, randomized, controlled trial comparing percutaneous and laminectomy electrodes-part I: technical outcomes, *Neurosurgery* **51**, 381-389-390 (2002).

16. North, R. B., Lanning, A., Hessels, R. and Cutchis, P. N., Spinal cord stimulation with percutaneous and plate electrodes: side effects and quantitative comparisons, *Neurosurg. Focus* **2**, E5 (1997).

17. Babu, R., Hazzard, M. A., Huang, K. T., Ugiliweneza, B., Patil, C. G., Boakye, M. and Lad, S. P., Outcomes of percutaneous and paddle lead implantation for spinal cord stimulation: a comparative analysis of complications, reoperation rates, and health-care costs, *Neuromodulation Technol. Neural Interface* **16**, 418–427 (2013).

18. Kinfe, T. M., Quack, F., Wille, C., Schu, S. and Vesper, J., Paddle versus cylindrical leads for percutaneous implantation in spinal cord stimulation for failed back surgery syndrome: a single-center trial, *J. Neurol. Surg. Part Cent. Eur. Neurosurg.* **75**, 467–473 (2014).

19. Holsheimer, J., Struijk, J. J. and Tas, N. R., Effects of electrode geometry and combination on nerve fibre selectivity in spinal cord stimulation, *Med. Biol. Eng. Comput.* **33**, 676–82 (1995).

20. Kramer, J., Liem, L., Russo, M., Smet, I., Van Buyten, J.-P. and Huygen, F., Lack of body positional effects on paresthesias when stimulating the dorsal root ganglion (drg) in the treatment of chronic pain, *Neuromodulation Technol. Neural Interface* **18**, 50-57 (2015).

21. Ross, E. and Abejón, D., Improving patient experience with spinal cord stimulation: implications of position-related changes in neurostimulation, *Neuromodulation Technol. Neural Interface* **17**, 36–41 (2014).

22. Sparkes, E., Raphael, J. H., Duarte, R. V., LeMarchand, K., Jackson, C., and Ashford, R. L., A systematic literature review of psychological characteristics as determinants of outcome for spinal cord stimulation therapy, *Pain* **150**, 284–289 (2010).

23. Oakley, J. C., Krames, E. S., Stamatos, J. and Foster, A. M., Successful long-term outcomes of spinal cord stimulation despite limited pain relief during temporary trialing, *Neuromodulation* **11**, 66–73 (2008).

24. Woolf, C. J., Central sensitization: implications for the diagnosis and treatment of pain, *Pain* **152**, S2-15 (2011).

25. Yan, L.-H., Hou, J.-F., Liu, M.-G., Li, M.-M., Cui, X.-Y. Lu, Z.-M., Zhang, F.-K., An, Y.-Y., Shi, L., and Chen, J., Imbalance between excitatory and inhibitory amino acids at spinal level is associated with maintenance of persistent pain-related behaviors, *Pharmacol. Res.* **59**, 290–299 (2009).

26. Guan, Y., Wacnik, P. W., Yang, F., Carteret, A. F., Chung, C.-Y., Meyer, R. A., and Raja, S. N., Spinal cord stimulation-induced analgesia, *Anesthesiology* **113**, 1392–1405 (2010).

27. Coburn, B. and Sin, W. K., A theoretical study of epidural electrical stimulation of the spinal cord--Part I: Finite element analysis of stimulus fields, *IEEE Trans. Biomed. Eng.* **32**, 971–977 (1985).

28. Struijk, J. J., Holsheimer, J., van Veen, B. K. and Boom, H. B., Epidural spinal cord stimulation: calculation of field potentials with special reference to dorsal column nerve fibers, *IEEE Trans. Biomed. Eng.* **38**, 104–10 (1991).

29. Holsheimer, J., Which neuronal elements are activated directly by spinal cord stimulation, *Neuromodulation* **5**, 25–31 (2002).

30. Holsheimer, J., Effectiveness of spinal cord stimulation in the management of chronic pain: analysis of technical drawbacks and solutions, *Neurosurg.* **40**, 990–999 (1997).

31. He, J., Barolat, G., Holsheimer, J. and Struijk, J. J., Perception threshold and electrode position for spinal cord stimulation, *Pain* **59**, 55–63 (1994).

32. Smits, H., van Kleef, M. and Joosten, E. A., Spinal cord stimulation of dorsal columns in a rat model of neuropathic pain: Evidence for a segmental spinal mechanism of pain relief, *PAIN* **153**, 177–183 (2012).

33. Davidoff, R. A., The dorsal columns, *Neurology* **39**, 1377–1385 (1989).

34. Shealy, C. N., Mortimer, J. T. and Reswick, J. B., Electrical inhibition of pain by stimulation of the dorsal columns: preliminary clinical report, *Anesth. Analg.* **46**, 489–491 (1967).

35. Guan, Y., Spinal cord stimulation: neurophysiological and neurochemical mechanisms of action, *Curr. Pain Headache Rep.* **16**, 217–225 (2012).

36. Linderoth, B., Stiller, C.-O., Gunasekera, L., O'Connor, W. T., Ungerstedt, U. Brodin, E., Gamma-aminobutyric acid is released in the dorsal horn by electrical spinal cord stimulation: an in vivo microdialysis study in the rat, *Neurosurgery* **34**, 484-489 (1994).

37. Stiller, C. O. Cui, J. G., O'Connor, W. T., Brodin, E., Meyerson, B. A., and Linderoth, B., Release of gamma-aminobutyric acid in the dorsal horn and suppression of tactile allodynia by spinal cord stimulation in mononeuropathic rats, *Neurosurgery* **39**, 367-374-375 (1996).

38. Duggan, A. W. and Foong, F. W., Bicuculline and spinal inhibition produced by dorsal column stimulation in the cat, *Pain* **22**, 249–259 (1985).

39. Hwang, J. H. and Yaksh, T. L., The effect of spinal GABA receptor agonists on tactile allodynia in a surgically-induced neuropathic pain model in the rat, *Pain* **70**, 15–22 (1997).

40. Campbell, J. N. and Meyer, R. A., Mechanisms of neuropathic pain, *Neuron* **52**, 77–92 (2006).

41. Cui, J. G., O'Connor, W. T., Ungerstedt, U., Linderoth, B. and Meyerson, B. A., Spinal cord stimulation attenuates augmented dorsal horn release of excitatory amino acids in mononeuropathy via a GABAergic mechanism, *Pain* **73**, 87–95 (1997).

42. Lind, G., Schechtmann, G., Winter, J., Meyerson, B. A. and Linderoth, B., Baclofen-enhanced spinal cord stimulation and intrathecal baclofen alone for neuropathic pain: Long-term outcome of a pilot study, *Eur. J. Pain Lond. Engl.* **12**, 132–6 (2008).

43. Lind, G., Meyerson, B. A., Winter, J. and Linderoth, B., Intrathecal baclofen as adjuvant therapy to enhance the effect of spinal cord stimulation in neuropathic pain: a pilot study, *Eur. J. Pain Lond. Engl.* **8**, 377–83 (2004).

44. Linderoth, B., Gazelius, B., Franck, J. and Brodin, E., Dorsal column stimulation induces release of serotonin and substance P in the cat dorsal horn, *Neurosurgery* **31**, 289-96-7 (1992).

45. Schechtmann, G., Song, Z., Ultenius, C., Meyerson, B. A. and Linderoth, B., Cholinergic mechanisms involved in the pain relieving effect of spinal cord stimulation in a model of neuropathy, *Pain* **139**, 136–145 (2008).

46. Levin, B. E. and Hubschmann, O. R., Dorsal column stimulation: Effect on human cerebrospinal fluid and plasma catecholamines, *Neurology* **30,** 65–71 (1980).

47. Olesen, S. S., Graversen, C., Bouwense, S. A. W., van Goor, H., Wilder-Smith, O. H. G., Drewes, A. M., Quantitative sensory testing predicts pregabalin efficacy in painful chronic pancreatitis, *PLoS ONE* **8,** e57963 (2013).

48. Marchand, S., Spinal cord stimulation analgesia: substantiating the mechanisms for neuropathic pain treatment, *PAIN* **156,** 364–365 (2015).

49. Eisenberg, E., Burstein, Y., Suzan, E., Treister, R. and Aviram, J., Spinal cord stimulation attenuates temporal summation in patients with neuropathic pain, *Pain* **156,** 381–385 (2015).

50. Kawamata, M., Koshizaki, M., Shimada, S. G., Narimatsu, E., Kozuka, Y., Takahashi, T., Namiki, A., Collins, J. G., Changes in response properties and receptive fields of spinal dorsal horn neurons in rats after surgical incision in hairy skin, *Anesthesiol.* **102,** 141–151 (2005).

51. von Hehn, C. A., Baron, R. and Woolf, C. J., Deconstructing the neuropathic pain phenotype to reveal neural mechanisms, *Neuron* **73,** 638–652 (2012).

52. Woolf, C. J. and Wall, P. D., Chronic peripheral nerve section diminishes the primary afferent A-fibre mediated inhibition of rat dorsal horn neurones, *Brain Res.* **242,** 77–85 (1982).

53. Yang, F., Xu, Q., Cheong, Y.-K., Shechter, R., Sdrulla, A., He, S.-Q., Tiwari, V., Dong, X., Wacnik, P. W., Meyer, R., Raja, S. N. and Guan, Y., Comparison of intensity-dependent inhibition of spinal wide-dynamic range neurons by dorsal column and peripheral nerve stimulation in a rat model of neuropathic pain, *Eur. J. Pain* **18,** 978–988 (2014).

54. Todd, A. J., Neuronal circuitry for pain processing in the dorsal horn, *Nat. Rev. Neurosci.* **11,** 823–836 (2010).

55. Arle, J. E., Carlson, K. W., Mei, L., Iftimia, N. and Shils, J. L., Mechanism of dorsal column stimulation to treat neuropathic but not nociceptive pain: Analysis with a computational model, *Neuromodulation Technol. Neural Interface* **17,** 642–655 (2014).

56. Barchini, J., Tchachaghian, S., Shamaa, F., Jabbur, S. J., Meyerson, B. A., Song, Z., Linderoth, B., Saadé, N. E., Spinal segmental and supraspinal mechanisms underlying the pain-relieving effects of spinal cord stimulation: An experimental study in a rat model of neuropathy, *Neuroscience* **215,** 196–208 (2012).

57. Maeda, Y., Ikeuchi, M., Wacnik, P. and Sluka, K. A., Increased c-fos immunoreactivity in the spinal cord and brain following spinal cord stimulation is frequency-dependent, *Brain Res.* **1259,** 40–50 (2009).

58. Sato, K. L., Johanek, L. M., Sanada, L. S. and Sluka, K. A., Spinal cord stimulation reduces mechanical hyperalgesia and glial cell activation in animals with neuropathic pain, *Anesth. Analg.* **118,** 464–472 (2014).

59. Haydon, P. G., GLIA: listening and talking to the synapse, *Nat. Rev. Neurosci.* **2,** 185–193 (2001).

60. Lee, A. W. and Pilitsis, J. G., Spinal cord stimulation: indications and outcomes, *Neurosurg. Focus* **21,** 1–6 (2006).

61. Kumar, K. and Wilson, J. R., Factors affecting spinal cord stimulation outcome in chronic benign pain with suggestions to improve success rate, *Acta Neurochir. Suppl.* **97,** 91–9 (2007).

62. Simpson, E. L., Duenas, A., Holmes, M. W., Papaioannou, D. and Chilcott, J., Spinal cord stimulation for chronic pain of neuropathic or ischaemic origin: systematic review and economic evaluation, *Health Technol. Assess. Winch. Engl.* **13**(17), 1-154 (2009).

63. Zipes, D. P., Svorkdal, N., Berman, D., Boortz-Marx, R., Henry, T., Lerman, A., Ross, E., Turner, M. and Irwin, C., Spinal cord stimulation therapy for patients with refractory angina

who are not candidates for revascularization, *Neuromodulation Technol. Neural Interface* **15,** 550–559 (2012).

64. Eldabe, S., Raphael, J., Thomson, S., Manca, A., de Belder, M., Aggarwal, R., Banks, M., Brookes, M., Merotra, S., Adeniba, R., Davies, E. and Taylor, R. S., The effectiveness and cost-effectiveness of spinal cord stimulation for refractory angina (RASCAL study): study protocol for a pilot randomized controlled trial, *Trials* **14,** 57 (2013).

65. Daousi, C., Benbow, S. J. and MacFarlane, I. A., Electrical spinal cord stimulation in the long-term treatment of chronic painful diabetic neuropathy, *Diabet. Med.* **22,** 393–398 (2005).

66. de Vos, C. C., Meier, K., Zaalberg, P. B., Nijhuis, H. J. A., Duyvendak, W., Vesper, J., Enggaard, T. P., and Lenders, Mathieu W.P.M., Spinal cord stimulation in patients with painful diabetic neuropathy: A multicentre randomized clinical trial, *PAIN®* **155,** 2426-2431 (2014).

67. McGreevy, K. and Williams, K. A., Contemporary insights into painful diabetic neuropathy and treatment with spinal cord stimulation, *Curr. Pain Headache Rep.* **16,** 43–49 (2012).

68. Pluijms, W. A., Slangen R., Joosten, E. A., Kessels, A. G., Merkies, I. S. J., Schaper, N. C., Faber, C. G., and van Kleef, M., Electrical spinal cord stimulation in painful diabetic polyneuropathy, a systematic review on treatment efficacy and safety, *Eur. J. Pain* **15,** 783–788 (2011).

69. Slangen, R., Schaper, N. C., Faber, C. G., Joosten, E. A., Dirksen, C. D., van Dongen, R. T., Kessels, A. G. and van Kleef, M., Spinal cord stimulation and pain relief in painful diabetic peripheral neuropathy: a prospective two-center randomized controlled trial, *Diabetes Care* **37,** 3016-3024 (2014).

70. Tesfaye, S., Watt, J., Benbow, S. J., Pang, K. A., Miles, J., MacFarlane, I. A., Electrical spinal-cord stimulation for painful diabetic peripheral neuropathy, *Lancet* **348,** 1698–1701 (1996).

71. Hayek, S. M., Veizi, E. and Hanes, M., Treatment-limiting complications of percutaneous spinal cord stimulator implants: a review of eight years of experience from an academic center database, *Neuromodulation Technol. Neural Interface* **18,** 603–609 (2015).

72. Turner, J. A., Loeser, J. D., Deyo, R. A. and Sanders, S. B., Spinal cord stimulation for patients with failed back surgery syndrome or complex regional pain syndrome: a systematic review of effectiveness and complications, *Pain* **108,** 137–147 (2004).

73. Kumar, K., Buchser, E., Linderoth, B., Meglio, M. and Van Buyten, J.-P., Avoiding complications from spinal cord stimulation: practical recommendations from an international panel of experts, *Neuromodulation* **10,** 24–33 (2007).

74. Rosenow, J. M., Stanton-Hicks, M., Rezai, A. R. and Henderson, J. M., Failure modes of spinal cord stimulation hardware, *J. Neurosurg. Spine* **5,** 183–190 (2006).

75. Zipes, D. P., Neuzil, P., Theres, H., Caraway, D., Mann, D. L., Mannheimer, C., Van Buren, P., Linde, C., Linderoth, B., Kueffer, F., Sarazin, S. A., and DeJongste, M. J., Ventricular functional response to spinal cord stimulation for advanced heart failure: primary results of the randomized Defeat-HF trial, *Circulation* **130,** 2114–2115 (2014).

76. Tse, H.-F., Turner, S., Sanders, P., Okuyama, Y., Fujiu, K., Cheung, C. W., Russo, M., Green, M. D., Yiu, K. H., Chen, P., Shuto, C., Lau, E. O., and Siu, C. W., Thoracic spinal cord stimulation for heart failure as a restorative treatment (SCS HEART study): first-in-man experience, *Heart Rhythm* **12,** 588–595 (2015).

77. Wang, S., Zhou, X., Huang, B., Wang, Z., Zhou, L., Chen, M., Yu, L., and Jiang, H., Spinal cord stimulation suppresses atrial fibrillation by inhibiting autonomic remodeling, *Heart Rhythm* **13,** 274–281 (2016).

78. Harkema, S., Gerasimenko, Y., Hodes, J., Burdick, J., Angeli, C., Chen, Y., Ferreira, C., Willhite, A., Rejc, E., Grossman, R., Edgerton, V. R., Effect of epidural stimulation of the lumbosacral spinal cord on voluntary movement, standing, and assisted stepping after motor complete paraplegia: a case study, *The Lancet* **377,** 1938–1947 (2011).
79. Angeli, C. A., Edgerton, V. R., Gerasimenko, Y. P. and Harkema, S. J., Altering spinal cord excitability enables voluntary movements after chronic complete paralysis in humans, *Brain* **137,** 1394–1409 (2014).
80. Fuentes, R., Petersson, P., Siesser, W. B., Caron, M. G. and Nicolelis, M. A. L., Spinal cord stimulation restores locomotion in animal models of Parkinson's disease, *Science* **323,** 1578–1582 (2009).
81. Hassan, S., Amer, S., Alwaki, A. and Elborno, A., A patient with Parkinson's disease benefits from spinal cord stimulation, *J. Clin. Neurosci.* **20,** 1155–1156 (2013).
82. Agari, T. and Date, I., Spinal cord stimulation for the treatment of abnormal posture and gait disorder in patients with Parkinson's disease, *Neurol. Med. Chir. (Tokyo)* **52,** 470–474 (2012).
83. Maeda, Y., Wacnik, P. W. and Sluka, K. A., Low frequencies, but not high frequencies of bipolar spinal cord stimulation reduce cutaneous and muscle hyperalgesia induced by nerve injury, *Pain* **138,** 143–152 (2008).
84. Gao, J., Wu, M., Li, L., Qin, C., Farber, J. P., Linderoth, B., and Foreman, R. D., Effects of spinal cord stimulation with 'standard clinical' and higher frequencies on peripheral blood flow in rats, *Brain Res.* **1313,** 53–61 (2010).
85. Huff, T. B., Shi, Y., Sun, W., Wu, W., Shi, R., and Cheng, J.-X., Real-time CARS imaging reveals a calpain-dependent pathway for paranodal myelin retraction during high-frequency stimulation, *PLoS ONE* **6,** e17176 (2011).
86. Babbs, C. F. and Shi, R., Subtle paranodal injury slows impulse conduction in a mathematical model of myelinated axons. *PLoS ONE* **8,** 0067767 (2013).
87. Liu, H., Roppolo, J. R., de Groat, W. C. and Tai, C., Modulation of axonal excitability by high-frequency biphasic electrical current, *IEEE Trans. Biomed. Eng.* **56,** 2167 (2009).
88. Reilly, J. P., Freeman, V. T. and Larkin, W. D., Sensory effects of transient electrical stimulation - evaluation with a neuroelectric model, *IEEE Trans. Biomed. Eng.* **BME-32,** 1001–1011 (1985).
89. Tai, C., de Groat, W. C. and Roppolo, J. R., Simulation analysis of conduction block in unmyelinated axons induced by high frequency biphasic electrical currents, *IEEE Trans. Biomed. Eng.* **52,** 1323 (2005).
90. Kilgore, K. and Bhadra, N., Nerve conduction block utilising high-frequency alternating current, *Med. Biol. Eng. Comput.* **42,** 394–406 (2004).
91. Ackermann, D. M., Bhadra, N., Foldes, E. L. and Kilgore, K. L., Conduction block of whole nerve without onset firing using combined high frequency and direct current, *Med. Biol. Eng. Comput.* **49,** 241–251 (2010).
92. Shechter, R., Yang, F., Xu, Q., Cheong, Y.-K., He, S.-Q., Sdrulla, A., Carteret, A. F., Wacnik, P. W., Dong, X., Meyer, R. A., Raja, S. N., and Guan, Y., Conventional and kilohertz-frequency spinal cord stimulation produces intensity- and frequency-dependent inhibition of mechanical hypersensitivity in a rat model of neuropathic pain, *Anesthesiology* **119,** 422–432 (2013).
93. Song, Z., Viisanen, H., Meyerson, B. A., Pertovaara, A. and Linderoth, B., Efficacy of kilohertz-frequency and conventional spinal cord stimulation in rat models of different pain conditions, *Neuromodulation Technol. Neural Interface* **17,** 226–235 (2014).

94. Perruchoud, C., Eldabe, S., Batterham, A. M., Madzinga, G., Brookes, M., Durrer, A., Rosato, M., Bovet, N., West, S., Bovy, M., Rutschmann, B., Gulve, A., Garner, F. and Buchser, E., Analgesic efficacy of high-frequency spinal cord stimulation: a randomized double-blind placebo-controlled study. *Neuromodulation Technol. Neural Interface* **16**, 363–369 (2013).
95. Crosby, N. D., Goodman Keiser, M. D., Smith, J. R., Zeeman, M. E. and Winkelstein, B. A., Stimulation parameters define the effectiveness of burst spinal cord stimulation in a rat model of neuropathic pain, *Neuromodulation Technol. Neural Interface* **18**, 1–8 (2015).
96. Crosby, N., Weisshaar, C. L., Smith, J. R., Zeeman, M. E., Goodman-Keiser, M. D., and Winkelstein, B. A., Burst and tonic spinal cord stimulation differentially activate GABAergic mechanisms to attenuate pain in a rat model of cervical radiculopathy, *IEEE Trans. Biomed. Eng.* **62**, 1604-1613 (2015).
97. Parker, J. L., Karantonis, D. M., Single, P. S., Obradovic, M. and Cousins, M. J., Compound action potentials recorded in the human spinal cord during neurostimulation for pain relief, *Pain* **153**, 593–601 (2012).
98. Parker, J. L., Karantonis, D. M., Single, P. S., Obradovic, M., Laird, J., Gorman, R. B., Ladd, L. A and Cousins, M. J., Electrically evoked compound action potentials recorded from the sheep spinal cord, *Neuromodulation Technol. Neural Interface* **16**, 295–303 (2013).
99. Holsheimer, J., Demeulemeester, H., Nuttin, B. and De Sutter, P., Identification of the target neuronal elements in electrical deep brain stimulation, *Eur. J. Neurosci.* **12**, 4573–4577 (2000).
100. Devor, M., Ectopic discharge in Aβ afferents as a source of neuropathic pain, *Experimental Brain Research* **196**, 115-128 (2009).
101. Misawa, S., Sakurai, K., Shibuya, K., Isose, S., Kanai, K., Ogino, J., Ishikawa, K. and Kuwabara, S., Neuropathic pain is associated with increased nodal persistent Na(+) currents in human diabetic neuropathy, *J. Peripher. Nerv. Syst.* **14**, 279–284 (2009).
102. Djouhri, L., Fang, X., Koutsikou, S. and Lawson, S. N., Partial nerve injury induces electrophysiological changes in conducting (uninjured) nociceptive and nonnociceptive DRG neurons: Possible relationships to aspects of peripheral neuropathic pain and paresthesias, *PAIN* **153**, 1824–1836 (2012).
103. Zhang, J.-M., Song, X.-J. and LaMotte, R. H., Enhanced excitability of sensory neurons in rats with cutaneous hyperalgesia produced by chronic compression of the dorsal root ganglion, *J. Neurophysiol.* **82**, 3359–3366 (1999).
104. Gerasimenko, Y. P., Lavrov, I. A., Courtine, G., Ichiyama, R. M., Dy, C. J., Zhong, H., Roy, R. R., and Edgerton, V. R., Spinal cord reflexes induced by epidural spinal cord stimulation in normal awake rats, *J. Neurosci. Methods* **157**, 253–63 (2006).
105. de Noordhout, A. M., Rothwell, J. C., Thompson, P. D., Day, B. L. and Marsden, C. D., Percutaneous electrical stimulation of lumbosacral roots in man, *J. Neurol. Neurosurg. Psychiatry* **51**, 174–181 (1988).
106. Rosen, S. *et al.,* Randomized double-blind crossover study examining the safety and effectiveness of closed-loop control in spinal cord stimulation, in *19th Annual Meeting, North American Neuromodulation Society* (2015).
107. Li, J., Simone, D. A. and Larson, A. A., Windup leads to characteristics of central sensitization, *Pain* **79**, 75–82 (1999).
108. Li, C. L. and Bak, A. ,Excitability characteristics of the A- and C-fibers in a peripheral nerve, *Exp. Neurol.* **50**, 67–79 (1976).

109. Djouhri, L. and Lawson, S. N., A [beta]-fiber nociceptive primary afferent neurons: a review of incidence and properties in relation to other afferent A-fiber neurons in mammals, *Brain Res. Rev.* **46,** 131–145 (2004).

110. Campbell, J. N., Raja, S. N., Meyer, R. A. and Mackinnon, S. E., Myelinated afferents signal the hyperalgesia associated with nerve injury, *Pain* **32,** 89–94 (1988).

111. Sukhotinsky, I., Ben-Dor, E., Raber, P. and Devor, M., Key role of the dorsal root ganglion in neuropathic tactile hypersensibility, *Eur. J. Pain* **8,** 135–143 (2004).

112. Thompson, S. W., Dray, A. and Urban, L., Injury-induced plasticity of spinal reflex activity: NK1 neurokinin receptor activation and enhanced A-and C-fiber mediated responses in the rat spinal cord in vitro, *J. Neurosci.* **14,** 3672 (1994).

113. Amir, R. and Devor, M., Functional cross-excitation between afferent A- and C-neurons in dorsal root ganglia, *Neuroscience* **95,** 189–195 (1999).

114. Foreman, R. D., Beall, J. E., Coulter, J. D. and Willis, W. D., Effects of dorsal column stimulation on primate spinothalamic tract neurons, *J. Neurophysiol.* **39,** 534–546 (1976).

115. Dubuisson, D., Effect of dorsal-column stimulation on gelatinosa and marginal neurons of cat spinal cord, *J. Neurosurg.* **70,** 257–265 (1989).

Chapter 3.8

Deep Brain Stimulation

Julia P. Slopsema and Matthew D. Johnson

University of Minnesota, Department of Biomedical Engineering
Minneapolis, MN 55455, USA
john5101@umn.edu

Deep Brain Stimulation (DBS) is a chronic neurosurgical intervention for the treatment of brain disorders. Most notably, DBS is used to treat movement disorders and more recently epilepsy and psychological disorders. The historical roots of DBS therapy stem from ablative procedures in which the removal of key nodal structures within the brain resulted in relief of symptoms, such as reduction in tremor after lesioning the cerebello–thalamocortical pathway. DBS targets these same pathways but uses a high frequency electrical pulse train that can be tuned post-operatively to minimize a patient's symptoms. This chapter explores the current state of the field in terms of the technological components of a DBS system, clinical indications targeted by DBS therapy, and physiological mechanisms underlying effective treatment. Finally, this chapter also explores new directions in the field, such as improving the spatial resolution of DBS for modulating pathways within the brain, leveraging synaptic plasticity in the programming algorithms, and using behavioral and neurophysiological feedback to tailor the therapy to a given patient's symptoms.

1. Introduction

1.1. *Surgical lesions*

Prior to the development of DBS, surgical brain lesions were frequently used as a treatment for medication–refractory neurological disorders such as epilepsy and essential tremor. For treatment of epilepsy, lesions were created by surgically resecting or ablating regions of brain tissue identified as the sources of seizure activity. In these cases, surgical lesions are often effective in decreasing or eliminating seizures; however, the procedure is irreversible and carries risks of inadvertent damage to surrounding tissue.

An alternative to traditional lesioning uses a non-invasive Gamma Knife to apply focused beams of gamma radiation that precisely ablate structures within the brain. Gamma knife thalamotomy has been shown to be an effective non-invasive treatment of essential tremor [1]. MR-guided focused ultrasound can also be used to noninvasively lesion tissue. This technique employs magnetic resonance imaging to determine the precise location of a target structure with respect to a stereotactic frame. Focused ultrasound is then applied to the targeted tissue to create a thermal lesion, while MRI can be used to monitor the dimensions of the focal lesion [2].

Non-invasive lesioning techniques greatly reduce the risks associated with surgical removal of tissue, however any form of lesioning is irreversible. Deep Brain Stimulation (DBS) provides an alternative to lesioning as a treatment for brain disorders via the implantation of electrodes into deep brain structures. Current is applied through one or more electrode contacts to modulate neural activity adjacent to the active contacts, which indirectly modulates neural activity throughout the network associated with the stimulated location. A distinctive benefit of DBS is the adjustability of stimulation parameters which provides control of the volume of tissue activated and can be customized to provide the maximum therapeutic benefit for each patient, while limiting the emergence of stimulation-induced side effects.

1.2. *The DBS system*

A DBS system is composed of three standard components: a battery-powered pulse generator placed in the chest of the patient, a lead containing an array of electrodes implanted into a target structure within the brain, and an extension cable to connect the pulse generator to the lead. The MRI image in Figure 1 shows a standard trajectory for a DBS array targeting the subthalamic nucleus (STN). Commercially available DBS leads are cylindrical with diameters ranging from 1.27 to 1.4 mm and contain 4–8 electrode contacts spaced 0.5 to 1.5 mm apart along the lead. The pulse generator, which is similar in principle to a cardiac pacemaker, contains 4–16 channels to control 1–2 leads implanted in the brain. The pulse generator houses a battery that is either rechargeable or lasts approximately 2–6 years before replacement, depending upon use.

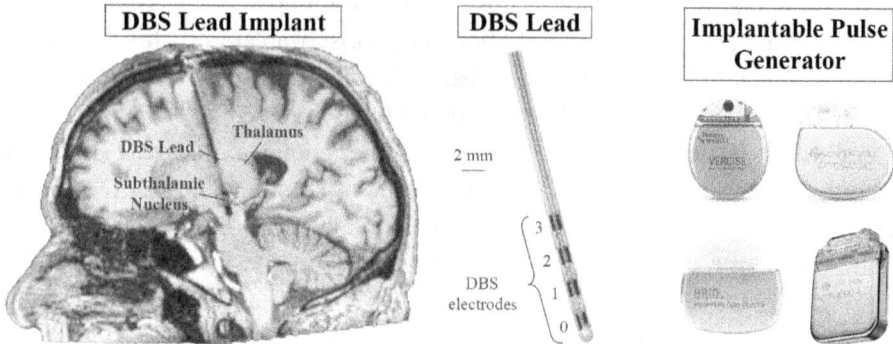

Fig. 1. DBS System. An oblique MR image showing the shadowing artifact of a DBS lead implanted in the subthalamic nucleus. A DBS system typically consists of three primary components: (1) a lead of electrodes that is implanted into a subcortical brain region with stereotactic neurosurgical navigation, (2) an extension cable that tunnels beneath the skin and connects the lead electrodes to (3) an implantable pulse generator that is surgically placed beneath the skin in the subclavicular region of the chest.

1.3. *Implantation and programming*

A DBS system is implanted in several stages. The first stage is the insertion of the DBS lead into the target structure of the brain. Prior to surgery, a stereotactic frame is attached to the skull and surgeons use a combination of MRI and CT scans to localize the target structure relative to the stereotactic frame. Once the target coordinates are obtained, an incision is made in the skin followed by a burr hole through the skull to expose the surface of the brain. A cannula is then inserted through the burr hole to a location slightly above the brain volume of interest. The patient is alert as microelectrodes are advanced through the cannula and into the brain to map the borders of the target structure based on differences in firing rate and pattern of neuronal activity along the insertion tracks. Microstimulation may also be applied through the microelectrodes to identify regions of therapy and regions that when stimulated elicit side effects for the patient. Side effects are monitored based on the patient's behavior, such as muscle twitches, paresthesias, and speech impairments. Surgeons use intraoperative CT and fluoroscopy to monitor microelectrode and lead location throughout the surgery. The specific target location, based on the microelectrode recordings and testing is then used to place the DBS lead. Once implanted, the DBS lead is tested for proper placement and ability to alleviate symptoms in the patient before being secured to the skull. The lead cable is coiled beneath the skin and the patient is given at least a week to recover.

Frameless and MRI-guided approaches to DBS lead implantation have been developed to improve the lead placement accuracy and decrease patient discomfort due to the stereotactic frame. For a frameless approach, bone fiducial markers are attached to the skull, followed by imaging to localize DBS targets relative to the bone markers. A head cradle is used to minimize head movement during surgery and a stereotactic frame is attached to the head cradle rather than the skull for implantation. Imaging is used throughout implantation to localize the structural target relative to the bone markers. This frameless approach showed no decrease in targeting accuracy when compared to the traditional stereotactic frame method [3]. Interventional MRI-guided DBS lead implantation is performed within an MRI machine using imaging throughout the procedure to guide the trajectory of the DBS lead, eliminating the need for microelectrode recording and allowing patients to be under general anesthesia throughout the procedure. The real-time imaging in MRI-guided implantation also allows the surgeon to account for shifting of the brain throughout the procedure. Studies show improved therapy results using MRI-guided implantation when compared to traditional implantation approaches [4].

Once the patient has sufficiently recovered from implantation of the lead, the pulse generator and extension cable are inserted in the second stage of implantation of a DBS system. The patient is placed under general anesthesia while the pulse generator is implanted in the chest below the clavicle and the extension cable is routed percutaneously beneath the skin from the skull to the pulse generator. The DBS system is now operational and the stimulus parameters are customized to the individual patient's symptoms in the third and final stage. Post-implantation, stimulus settings are determined by varying the pulse width, amplitude, and frequency of the stimulus with the goal of obtaining maximum therapeutic benefit while minimizing adverse effects and power consumption. Initially, patients return regularly for fine tuning of the stimulus settings, but over time patients return less frequently for adjustment as the settings are optimized.

2. Clinical Indications

Deep brain stimulation is considered an established therapy for several movement disorders, and is being investigated as a treatment for additional motor and cognitive brain disorders (Table 1). The first FDA approved applications for DBS were treatment of essential tremor and Parkinson's disease. In randomized controlled trials, DBS was found to significantly improve motor signs of both disorders for targets that include the subthalamic nucleus and the internal globus pallidus (GPi).

Table 1: Clinical Indications for Deep Brain Stimulation. Level of approval currently obtained for each clinical indication target: Food and Drug Administration (FDA), European Conformity (CE Mark), Humanitarian Device Exemption (HDE), and Investigational.

	Indication	Primary DBS Target(s) and Symptoms Treated
CE, FDA	Parkinson's Disease	*Subthalamic Nucleus: cardinal motor signs [5] *Internal Globus Pallidus: dyskinesia, cardinal motor signs [5] *Ventral Intermediate Nucleus of the Thalamus: tremor [5]
	Essential Tremor	*Ventral Intermediate Nucleus of the Thalamus: tremor [5]
CE, HDE	Dystonia	*Internal Globus Pallidus: involuntary sustained muscle contractions [5]
	Obsessive Compulsive Disorder	+Anterior Limb of the Internal Capsule: depression and anxiety [5]
CE	Epilepsy	*Anterior Thalamic Nuclei: seizure frequency and severity [5]
INVESTIGATIONAL	Tourette's Syndrome	+Anterior Limb of the Internal Capsule: motor tics [5] *Internal Globus Pallidus: phonic tics, motor tics, and compulsions [5] *Ventromedial Thalamic Nucleus: vocal and motor tics [5]
	Parkinson's Disease	*Pedunculopontine Nucleus: gait abnormalities and postural instability [5]
	Alzheimer's Disease	+Fornix: progressive dementia [6]
	Tinnitus	*Ventral Intermediate Nucleus of the Thalamus: ringing or buzzing in ears [6]
	Depression	+*Subgenual Cingulate: withdrawn, apathy, sadness [5] +Anterior Limb of the Internal Capsule: mood [5]
	Obesity	*Lateral Hypothalamus: feeding behavior [6]
	Addiction	*Nucleus Accumbens: dependence on alcohol, nicotine, or heroine [6]
	Cluster Headache	*Posterior Hypothalamus: periorbital (tissue surrounding the eye) pain [5]
	Chronic Pain	*Ventral Posterior Medial/Lateral nuclei of the thalamus: pain from various origins [6]
	Minimally Conscious State	*Central Thalamus: behavioral responsiveness [7]

* indicates grey matter target,
+ indicates white matter target

The efficacy of DBS for disorders such as dystonia and obsessive compulsive disorder has also been demonstrated with CE Mark and Humanitarian Device Exemption status for each. Epilepsy, characterized by frequent and sometimes severe seizures, remains under investigation but does have CE Mark approval in Europe. Additionally, DBS is emerging as a potential therapy for psychological disorders such as depression, addiction, and Alzheimer's disease. Two of the greatest challenges to applying DBS to established clinical indications, in which the target is more or less known, are in the surgical precision of placement of the DBS lead and the identification of stimulation parameters to selectively activate that target region. For emerging indications of DBS, two of the greatest challenges are identifying the pathway(s) that when stimulated generate a therapeutic effect and also identifying the clinical subtypes of a given brain disorder that best respond to DBS therapy.

3. Mechanisms of DBS

Deep brain stimulation has been accepted as an efficacious treatment for a variety of brain disorders; however, the mechanisms by which DBS specifically mediates symptom reduction remain a focus of DBS research. DBS interacts with the brain at two principle levels: DBS modulates the firing patterns of neurons within a target structure, and more broadly, DBS modifies firing rates and patterns in interconnected circuits and pathways throughout the nervous system.

3.1. *Neuron scale*

At the cellular level, electrical stimulation modulates the firing rates and patterns of neurons within a target nucleus. Stimulation within a nucleus does not necessarily induce facilitation or suppression for all neurons, but rather is dependent on individual neuronal properties (inhibitory versus excitatory) and local network connections. Studies in brain slices led to the theory of depolarization block by which high-frequency stimulation (HFS) causes a reduction in spontaneous spike activity within a stimulated nucleus due to the depression of voltage-gated currents through sodium and calcium channels [8]. However, in vivo, electrophysiological studies have found a complex set of changes in firing rate and pattern, where complete block of activity is rare [9, 10].

More recently, the theory of synaptic modulation has been proposed in which HFS elicits axonal action potentials that result in both orthodromic and antidromic propagation of spike activity to the axonal terminals and cell body, respectively. Indeed, activation of axons, or in other words eliciting action potentials within an axon, is thought to occur at lower stimulation thresholds than direct activation of the soma of a neuron [11]. Depending on the type of axonal terminal, one can observe inhibition or excitation of nuclei innervated by the stimulated axons. This theory is supported, for example, by a study showing that HFS of the GPi elicited transient inhibition of spike activity within the GPi immediately after a stimulation pulse, suggesting HFS drove GABAergic (inhibitory) afferents that synapse onto GPi neurons [12]. This theory also applies to effects downstream of the stimulated cell population. For example, stimulation of STN projection neurons, which are characterized by glutamatergic (excitatory) axon terminal output, resulted in increased release of the excitatory neurotransmitter glutamate in the globus pallidus and substantia nigra [13]. In addition to downstream neurotransmitter release, stimulation of the STN led to latent excitation and inhibition in the GPi and external globus pallidus (GPe) indicating HFS of the STN generates changes in the temporal firing pattern of downstream neurons in addition to changes in firing rate (see Figure 2) [14].

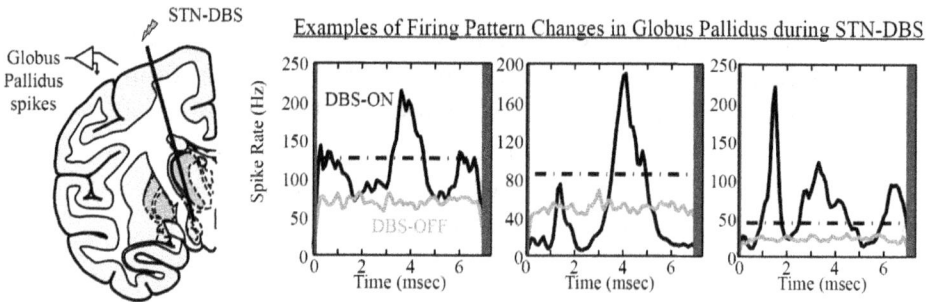

Fig. 2. Physiological mechanisms of DBS: Firing Patterns. Therapeutic DBS is known to modulate the pattern of spike activity, as shown for three cells recorded in the globus pallidus during STN-DBS. These peri-stimulus time histograms reflect the average activity between stimulus pulses, which in this case was approximately 7.4 ms (or 135 Hz). Adapted from Agnesi et al., [15] with permission.

Along with modulation of axonal efferent output, HFS can also lead to synaptic depression. This was confirmed by a study showing external capsule HFS resulted in depression of excitatory postsynaptic neurons in the primary motor cortex, potentially due to neurotransmitter depletion [16]. In the nucleus of stimulation, a range of different changes in synaptic signaling are known to occur. For example, in one study HFS in the STN resulted in STN neuronal activity exhibiting short-term and long-term potentiation as well as long-term depression [17].

Thus, at the cellular level, DBS is likely modulating both afferent and efferent neuronal activity, which can lead to alterations in neuronal firing patterns throughout the network encompassing the stimulated brain region. It is important to note, however, that the mechanisms of DBS at the neuronal level are highly dependent on the local environment, local connections, neuron subtypes, and most likely the internal disease state of the stimulated cells. In this context, the mechanisms of DBS are likely different amongst the various clinical targets and clinical indications shown in Table 1.

3.2. *Population scale*

3.2.1. *Neuromodulator release*

At the neuron population level, DBS can induce release of neuromodulators including dopamine, serotonin, noradrenaline, and adenosine among others. Stimulation in the STN, for instance, showed dopamine release in the substantia nigra that was time-locked to the stimulus pulses and was dependent on both the intensity and frequency of stimulation [18]. Serotonin and noradrenaline are known to be released in the medial and orbital frontal cortex, respectively, during nucleus accumbens DBS for the investigational treatment of obsessive compulsive disorder [19]. Another neuromodulator that can be released during thalamic DBS is adenosine, which was shown to mediate the reduction in pharmacologically-induced tremor [20]. The neurochemical release and their effects may not necessarily be limited to neurons. Glutamate release is also modulated during STN DBS, and the source of this release has been hypothesized to stem from both excitatory afferents in STN as well as astrocytes within STN [21].

3.2.2. *Oscillation disruption*

Deep brain stimulation therapy may also be explained by the disruption of synchronized pathological oscillations at both the single neuron and neuron population levels. Studies have shown that such oscillations are present in patients and animal models of Parkinson's disease, for example. In this case, HFS of the STN can disrupt synchronized pathological beta oscillations (~15–30 Hz) in the STN and more broadly in the basal ganglia–cortex circuit (see Figure 3). The reduction in beta oscillations during stimulation correlated to improved motor task performance in Parkinson's disease patients [22].

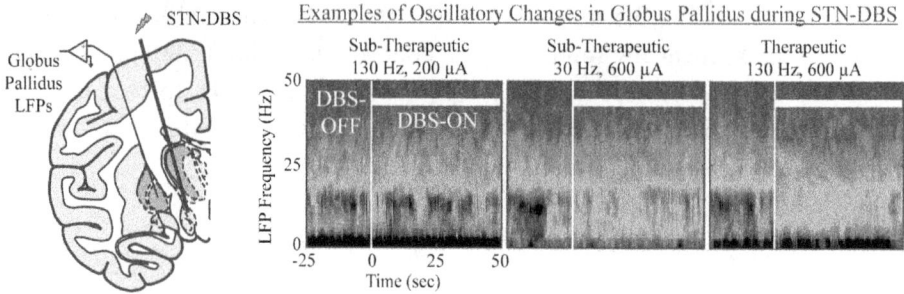

Fig. 3. Physiological mechanisms of DBS: Oscillations. Therapeutic DBS is known to modulate spectral features of local field potential activity, as shown herein with beta oscillations recorded in the globus pallidus during STN-DBS in a parkinsonian primate [23].

3.2.3. *Pathways involved in therapy*

The physiological mechanisms underlying DBS therapy have been shown to be regional or even pathway specific. In the case of essential tremor, for example, a study of the motor network involved in essential tremor found that as the functional connection between the cerebellum and the thalamus is strengthened, tremor severity increases [24]. Not surprisingly, when stimulating the cerebellar–receiving area of motor thalamus or the cerebello–thalamic tract directly, tremor can be abolished [25]. Many DBS targets are within white matter tracts, and those that are not may actually be driving white matter tracts adjacent to the targeted nucleus. For instance, a study by Butson and colleagues found that the most therapeutic targets for reducing bradykinesia and muscle rigidity with STN DBS were regions outside of the STN (Figure 4A,B) [26]. For the treatment of medication-refractory depression, clinically effective DBS of the subcallosal cingulate white matter region was shown to require activation of three tracts: the bilateral forceps minor, the bilateral cingulum bundles, and the medial frontal branch of the uncinate fasciculus (Figure 4C) [27]. Patients showed the greatest improvement in depression symptoms when all three tracts were activated compared to patients with only one or two of these pathways stimulated.

DBS for Parkinson's Disease

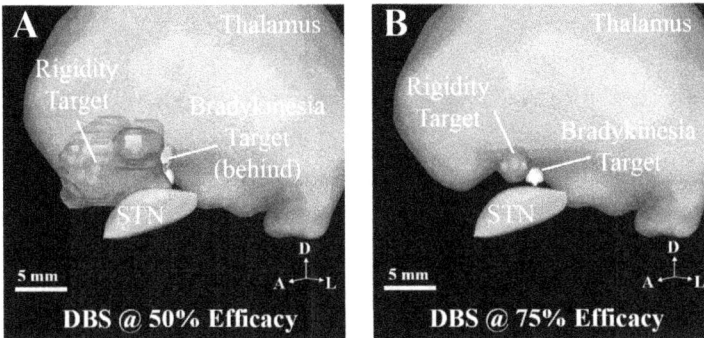

DBS for Treatment-Resistant Depression

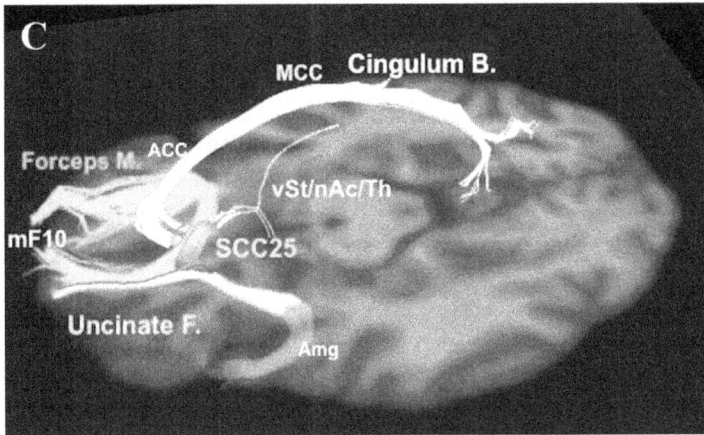

Fig. 4. Probabilistic targets of DBS therapy. Model-based activation volume predictions for improving parkinsonian rigidity and bradykinesia with DBS about the STN at (A) 50% and (B) 75% improvement levels. The combined activation volume results across a series of six patients with Parkinson's disease showed that the therapeutic hot spots are dorsomedial to the STN, and the optimal activation volume for rigidity was slightly lateral to that for bradykinesia. Adapted from Butson *et al.* [26], with permission. (C) Responders to subcallosal cingulate white matter (SCC) DBS, which improved symptoms of their treatment–resistant depression, had activation of the forceps minor and uncinate fasciculus (projecting to the medial frontal cortex), cingulum bundle (dorsal and rostral cingulate cortex), and frontal–striatal fibers. Adapted from Riva-Posse *et al.* [27], with permission.

3.2.4. *Information lesion*

One of the early hypotheses on the physiological mechanisms of DBS was that DBS acts like a surgical lesion in which pathological information in the form of abnormal spike patterns related to the brain disorder is blocked [28,29]. Modeling studies support this hypothesis that HFS, specifically frequencies above the natural firing rate of the stimulated neuron populations, masks pathological firing of a target structure effectively removing the pathological information through the network. DBS may reduce information transmission in several ways. First, stimulation causes bidirectional activation of axons, antidromic spikes travel opposite the natural direction of an axon toward the soma, colliding with the lower frequency information-encoding spikes from the soma. Second, antidromic spikes that reach the soma may induce a refractory state within the soma, preventing further action potential generation. Finally, stimulation induces orthodromic high-frequency action potentials that cannot be interpreted by downstream nuclei because the relevant behavioral information is encoded by lower frequency spike trains [28]. Primate studies showed that stimulation does indeed block information transmission both within and downstream of the stimulated nucleus (Figure 5) and this effect was stronger for stimulation settings that were found to be therapeutic for parkinsonian motor signs [29]. However, DBS did not necessarily completely mask information content within the stimulated and downstream nuclei, suggesting that DBS may create partial informational lesions that allow some information to still flow through the circuit. Thus, DBS mechanisms may be an amalgam of mechanisms found in drug therapies and in surgical lesion-based therapies.

3.3. *Long-term effects of DBS*

3.3.1. *Synaptic plasticity*

In most cases, deep brain stimulation results in nearly instantaneous changes in firing rate, firing pattern, or oscillatory activity as described above. However, DBS also causes long term changes in brain networks through synaptic plasticity and modulation of functional topography. Long-term potentiation and long-term depression in STN neurons were shown to persist for at least 40 min after cessation of stimulation within the STN indicating DBS can induce synaptic plasticity within the stimulated nucleus [17]. Additionally, stimulation of the GPi in dystonia patients causes potentiation of inhibitory synapses that persists following stimulation, the length of prolonged potentiation is frequency dependent and increases with higher frequencies [30].

3.3.2. *Modulation of functional topography*

At the synaptic level, DBS can change the excitability of synapses, but DBS can also lead to changes in functional topography. This is illustrated in a study where stimulation of the nucleus basalis was paired with auditory stimuli. The receptive field for an auditory tone with a given frequency can be nearly doubled when paired with stimulation, confirming that stimulation can lead to reorganization of the primary auditory cortex [31]. This phenomenon has also been seen in dystonia where DBS of the GPi does not result in immediate improvement, but requires weeks or longer for gradual reduction in symptoms, before improvement eventually plateaus [32]. What remains unclear is where and to what extent synaptic plasticity including growth or pruning of connections occurs and how this relates to changes in the functional topography within the brain.

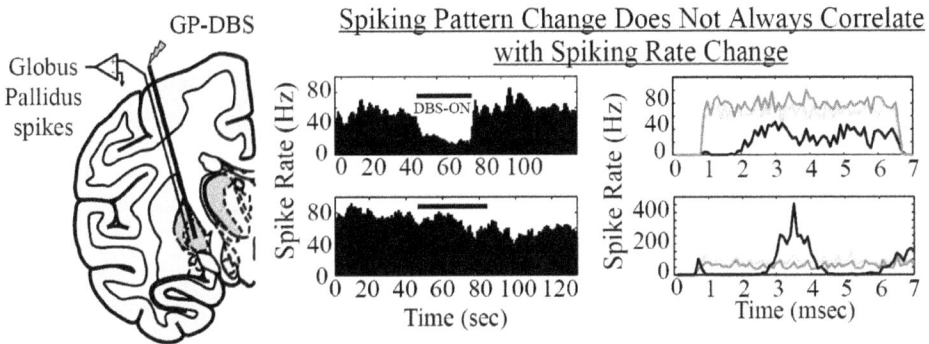

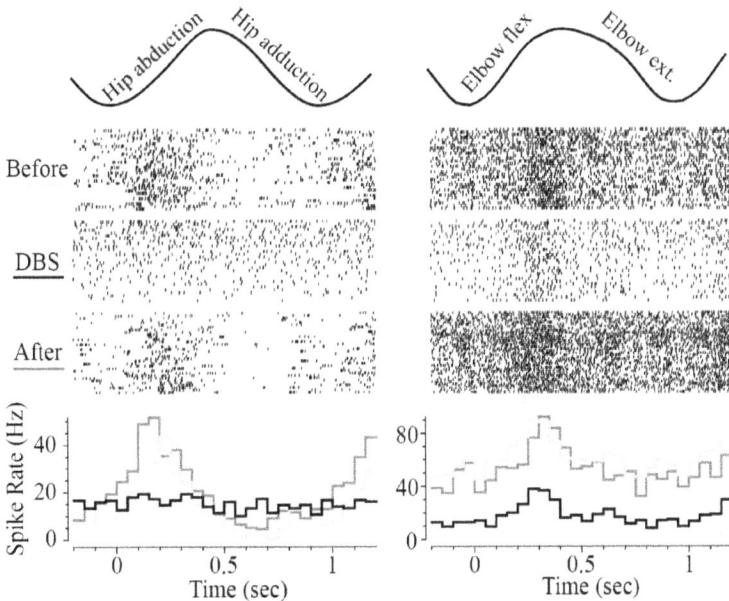

Fig. 5. Physiological mechanisms of DBS: Information. DBS can also affect the rate of spike activity, though the rate and pattern of activity are not always equally modulated. Such modulation in spike activity often results in informational lesions, as shown for kinematic movement encoding in the globus pallidus during DBS in the same nucleus. Adapted from Agnesi *et al.* [9], with permission.

3.3.3. *Adaptation and compensation*

Brain disorders do not necessarily have a sudden onset, but are often characterized by a slow onset of symptoms. As a neurodegenerative disorder progresses or after a brain lesions occurs, broader brain networks can compensate for the disrupted pathways through overactivation of alternative pathways to both suppress symptoms and execute functions that were formerly generated by the now damaged pathway. For example, when the basal ganglia–frontal cortex circuit is damaged by Parkinson's disease, the lateral premotor circuit becomes overactive and may compensate for the loss of dopaminergic and other input to the basal ganglia circuit [33]. Thus, DBS may alleviate symptoms not only by interrupting pathological signals within the stimulated pathways, but also by allowing compensatory pathways to dominate behavioral function [34].

3.4. *Summary of mechanisms*

In conclusion, there are multiple physiological mechanisms of action involved in the clinical efficacy of DBS. The mechanisms depend on the clinical indication as well as the circuitry of targeted structures and upstream and downstream connections. DBS can induce both short-term and long-term changes in the brain in the form of modulation of neuronal firing rates and patterns as well as neuronal plasticity and alterations in functional topography. Finally, similar to a surgical lesion, DBS may enable other circuits to adapt and compensate for loss of information through the stimulated circuit. The benefit of DBS over a surgical lesion, however, is that there is a lower risk for permanent damage and the therapy is adjustable and reversible. Studies investigating the physiological mechanisms of DBS will continue to be important, especially because the mechanisms are likely to be slightly different amongst disorders and targets of DBS. Moreover, as described in the next section, gaining a better understanding of these mechanisms is important to drive innovative developments in the hardware and software of DBS systems.

4. Novel Targeting Approaches

A major challenge when applying DBS is achieving activation of the desired therapy volume without current spreading to neighboring regions resulting in evoked side effects. For example, stimulation of the ventral intermediate nucleus (VIM) of the thalamus for treatment of essential tremor can lead to side effects including mild gait ataxia and dysarthria (difficult speech articulation) [35]. When applying DBS to the STN, activation of the corticobulbar tract on the anterior border of the STN can lead to speech impairment, while activation of the corticospinal tract on the lateral border of the STN can induce sustained muscle contractions on the contralateral side of the body [36]. In addition, DBS lead implantation often results in small deviations from target coordinates. Advanced targeting techniques using high density arrays, modeling, and current steering could correct for lead placement errors post-implantation by steering current around and along the DBS lead.

4.1. *High-density arrays*

One avenue to improve targeting is the development of high spatial resolution electrode arrays. Several investigational DBS leads with high-density array designs are shown in Figure 6. A segmented lead with 32 disc electrodes arranged in 8 rows distributed along a cylindrical lead can supply selective-directional activation of tissue in non-human primates [37,23], with increased thresholds for side effects on columns opposite the side effect region shown in humans [38]. In addition, arrays have been developed with a combination of ring electrodes and segmented rings providing directional control of tissue activation in humans [39]. High-density arrays provide an interface to improve DBS targeting and widen the therapeutic range between therapy and side effect thresholds. However, high-density arrays pose programming challenges with a multitude of potential electrode combinations and stimulation parameters, which will require innovative computational and neurophysiological algorithms to make the programming process practical in a clinical setting.

4.2. *Computational modeling*

As more complicated electrode arrays are developed, computational modeling has become instrumental for evaluation of the efficacy of new designs and stimulation patterns as well as retrospective identification of the therapeutic pathways to stimulate. High-field MRI has been used to develop anatomical patient–specific 3D models of brain structures. These models are used as a base for finite element modeling to evaluate current spread around a DBS lead which is used to calculate the volume of tissue activated (VTA). The VTA is dependent on the electrode contact dimensions and the conductive properties of the surrounding tissue [40]. The VTA can also be used along with patient data to determine specific locations around a DBS lead responsible for improvement in symptoms, as shown in Figure

4A,B where regions around the STN were identified for treatment of rigidity and bradykinesia in patients implanted with DBS for Parkinson's disease.

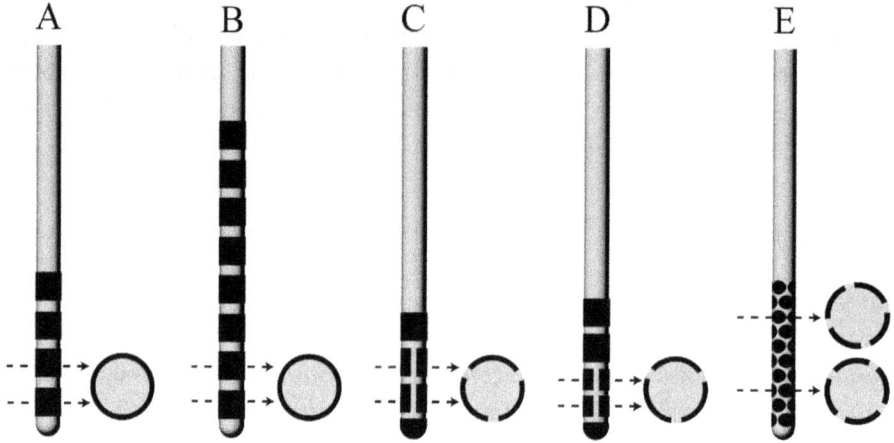

Fig. 6. DBS lead contact configurations: (A) Classic 4–contact lead composed of 4 ring electrodes (Medtronic); (B) 8–ring electrode array (Boston Scientific); (C) 8–contact directional lead composed of a tip electrode, two rows with 3 independent contacts, and a ring electrode (Boston Scientific); (D) 9–contact lead with a tip electrode, 2 rows segmented into 3 contacts each, and 2 ring electrodes (Aleva Neurotherapeutics); (E) high-density 40–disc electrode array (developed by Sapiens SBS, now part of Medtronic).

Along with analyzing the VTA for nuclei targets, probabilistic tractography based on diffusion-weighted imaging has been used to develop models predicting activation of fiber tracts through the brain [41]. This approach then can be used to identify the therapeutic pathways involved in DBS treatment. For example, the tractography activation model in Figure 4C was used to study DBS of the subcallosal cingulate targeted for treatment of depression, in which three therapeutic pathways were identified.

5. Stimulation Parameters

5.1. *Standard parameters*

Once a DBS system is implanted and the patient has been given time to recover, the pulse generator is programmed through telemetry by adjusting the stimulation parameters to balance the maximization of therapeutic benefit with the minimization of side effects and battery consumption. The amplitude, pulse width, and frequency of the pulse are modified with ranges of 0–10.5 V, 0–25.5 mA, 50–500 µs, and 2–250 Hz. Standard stimulation is monopolar, in which the pulse generator can is used as a return, except when side effects are present in which case bipolar settings are employed to constrict the activation volume and reduce the spread of current to side effect regions. Typically, stimulation is cathodic and parameters used for effective therapy are 1–3.6 V, 60 µs, and 130 Hz. Pulse width and voltage thresholds for both therapeutic benefit and side effects follow strength-duration threshold curves specific to each patient, with pulse width and voltage inversely related as shown in Figure 7A. The parameter space between the threshold curves for therapeutic effects and side effects is the known as the therapeutic window, which can be observed in Figure 7B,C. This window is explored to find the optimal parameters for each patient [42]. Recent studies have revealed that the therapeutic window could be widened by decreasing the pulse width below 60 µs leading to improved efficacy due to a wider parameter space between stimulation amplitudes that generate therapy versus side effects [43]. Moreover, the narrower pulse widths were also shown to increase efficiency, thereby reducing overall battery consumption.

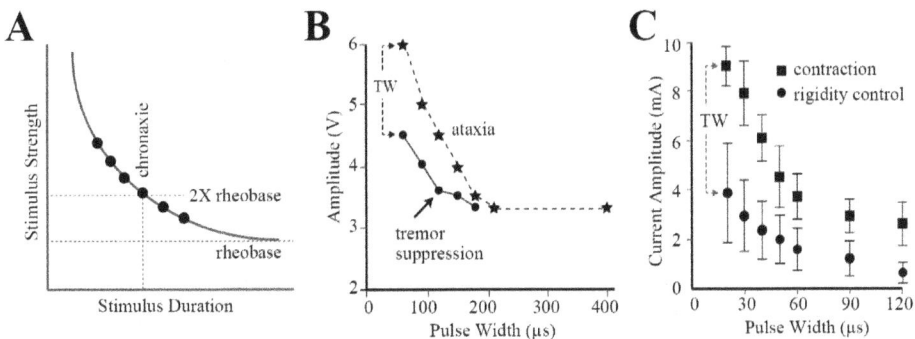

Fig. 7. Strength-Duration Curves. (A) Strength-duration curves of DBS therapy provide a means to characterize the stimulation parameter distance to loss of therapy and side effects. Narrow pulse widths have been shown to extend the therapeutic window (TW), as shown for (B) treating essential tremor with VIM–DBS (adapted from Volkmann *et al.* [42], with permission) and (C) treating parkinsonian rigidity with STN–DBS (adapted from Reich *et al.* [43], with permission).

5.2. *Pulse regularity*

In addition to setting the amplitude, pulse width, and isochronal frequency of stimulation, recent studies have also investigated the necessity for isochronal or fixed frequency DBS. The regularity of stimulation pulses has been explored using temporally non-regular DBS by varying the interstimulus intervals, or intervals between consecutive stimulus pulses. For some targets and clinical indications, the decreased regularity of the DBS pulse train resulted in either decreasing efficacy or worsening of the symptom being treated. For instance, short pauses (≤ 50 ms) in the DBS pulse train can cause increases in tremor [66], and stimulation using irregular patterns was not as effective as isochronal stimulation for reduction of tremor [44]. On the other hand, new stimulation patterns have also been developed to improve DBS efficacy as was shown for treating bradykinesia or a slowness of movement in patients with Parkinson's disease [45]. Thus, the therapeutic effects of DBS are sensitive to the frequency and regularity of the stimulus pulse train being delivered.

5.3. *Coordinated reset*

Therapeutic effects of stimulation can also be improved using a coordinated reset method [46]. In this approach, stimulation is applied to disrupt abnormal synchronization amongst populations of neurons that are thought to underlie the manifestation of symptoms. Coordinated reset desynchronizes these neuronal populations by applying high-frequency bursts of stimulation pulses through multiple electrode contacts on a DBS lead with varied onsets among the contacts. Figure 8 illustrates a computational simulation of coordinated reset, showing that after six synchronized subpopulations of neurons receive stimulation through six contacts with varied polarity and onset, the subpopulations become desynchronized. Modeling studies have suggested that moderately increasing the number of contacts used with coordinated reset can improve the desynchronizing effect of coordinated reset [47]. Coordinated reset has been shown to reduce beta band activity and associated tremor in Parkinson's patients [48] and results in prolonged after-effects when stimulation is discontinued in parkinsonian monkeys [49]. The after-effects of coordinated reset were dependent on the number of sessions in which coordinated reset is applied over a series of days [48], and models predict the after-effects are also dependent on the duration of stimulation within a session [49,50]. The implication of these lasting after-effects is not only a reduction in battery consumption, but also the potential to limit stimulation-induced side effects that may occur coincident with therapy in the case of continuous DBS. Another approach similar to coordinated reset, as shown in a computational network model of STN DBS for treating Parkinson's disease, posits that high-frequency, low intensity periodic stimulation can disrupt oscillations in the globus pallidus through a chaotic desynchronization mechanism [51].

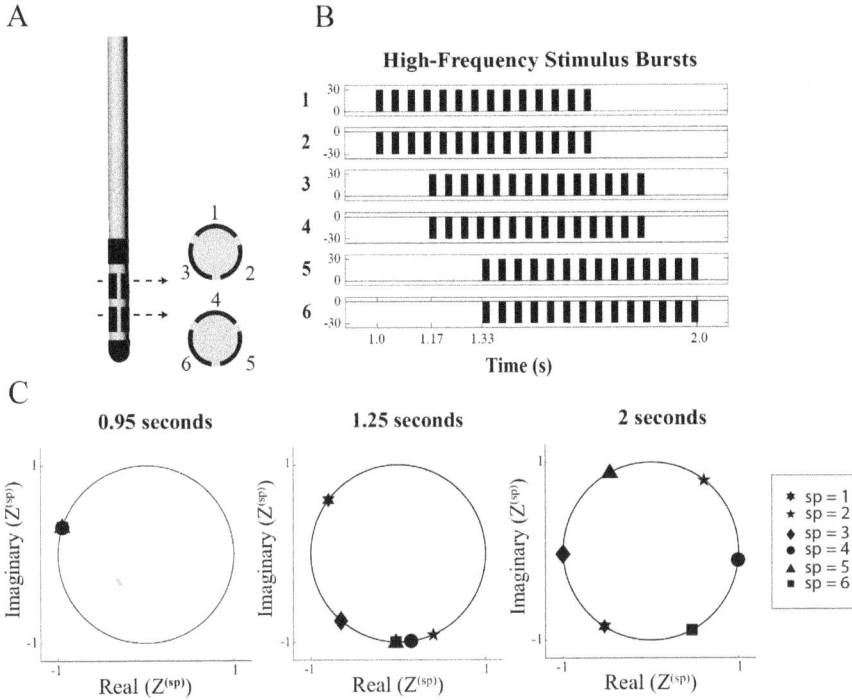

Fig. 8. Coordinated Reset. (A) Segmented DBS lead (Boston Scientific) with 6 labeled contacts used for stimulation. (B) Stimulation pattern through contacts 1 through 6 in part (A) with a pulse durations of 0.02 sec, inter-pulses of 0.03 sec, and onset timing of 1, 1.17, and 1.33 sec. for electrode pairings 1–2, 3–4, and 5–6, respectively. (C) Cluster–variable plots depicting the synchronization of 6 subpopulations (sp) of neurons at three time points: prior to stimulation (0.95 seconds), during stimulation through contacts 1–4 (1.25 seconds), and at the end of the stimulation (2 seconds). Z is the in-phase synchronization of each subpopulation. If Z is a distance of 1 from the origin (on the circle), a subpopulation is internally synchronized, if the subpopulations are on top of each other on the phase plot, the subpopulations are synchronized with each other. Data are generated using the modeling approach described in Tass 2003 [46].

5.4. *Advanced algorithms: Current steering*

Advanced programming algorithms have been developed to steer current around a DBS lead. Current steering can be used to control traditional 4–contact leads with independent current sources by selectively stimulating through multiple electrodes to control the activation volume along the lead [52]. High-density electrode arrays have been developed, and activating subsets of electrodes on a segmented lead allows current steering in a preferred direction to more precisely activate a therapeutic volume while simultaneously avoiding side effect regions. For example, using the 32–contact array in Figure 6E, stimulation through electrodes in one column could be used to direct activation to one side of the array, thereby minimizing the likelihood of activating a side effect region on the opposite side of the lead. Current steering can also be used to correct for implantation errors when an electrode is offset to one side of a target structure or when the target volume consists of a complex geometry. However, the stimulation parameter space for a high-density arrays is much larger than that for a 4–contact array, which may create logistical challenges in the clinic when trying to program patients with high-density arrays. One solution may be using advanced programming techniques that rely on patient-specific computational models to predict the ideal combination of electrodes and stimulation pulse train parameters that will simultaneously maximize activation of the therapeutic zone, minimize activation of side effect regions, and minimize battery consumption. Another approach, as described in the next section, may be to use closed-loop algorithms in which the electrophysiological or behavioral response to DBS for a given patient is used to adapt and optimize stimulation settings.

6. Adaptive DBS Approaches

Traditionally, DBS consists of constant pulsatile stimulation with pulse train parameters that are adjusted periodically based on clinical visits or minor stimulation amplitude adjustments that the patient can make on his or her own. A closed-loop system could optimize DBS more frequently by adapting stimulation parameters to better control fluctuating symptoms that may vary over the course of minutes to hours to days depending on the brain disorder and patient. Optimization in this context has potential to not only treat the brain disorder more consistently and with fewer side effects, but also to decrease the duty cycle, amplitude, or other DBS parameter, thereby reducing overall battery consumption.

The conceptual view of a closed-loop DBS system involves recording one or more physiological and/or behavioral variables and input of the variable(s) into a controller which generates stimulation parameters to adjust the system to a desired set point. In practice, closed-loop DBS requires the isolation of a reliable predictor variable to measure a patient's symptomatic state over time. The variable could be behavioral such as an accelerometer to measure tremor, or neurophysiological using temporal spike patterns recorded from a microelectrode, local field potentials (LFPs) recorded from the DBS lead, or neurochemical markers measured by a neurochemical sensor (Figure 9). An example of behavioral closed-loop stimulation used EMG recordings of bicep muscle activity to detect voluntary movement and trigger DBS to reduce intention tremor when a subject wished to initiate a movement [54]. Modeling studies have also suggested the feasibility of simultaneously recording LFPs and stimulating through multiple contacts on a DBS lead in the VIM thalamus as part of a closed-loop system to regulate the power spectrum of LFPs and therefore reduce tremor [55]. Alternatively, LFP beta oscillations in the STN have been used as a neurophysiological indicator for closed-loop DBS for Parkinson's disease and suppression of these oscillations have corresponded to a decrease in symptoms [56]. In another study with Parkinson's disease patients, adjustment of the duty cycle of STN DBS using a closed-loop system based on the power of beta oscillations recorded from the STN DBS lead showed increased efficacy over continuous stimulation and significant reduction in battery consumption [53]. Closed-loop DBS has also been effective using time-locked stimulation with a set delay between activity recorded from the GPi and motor cortex, and stimulation in the GPi [57].

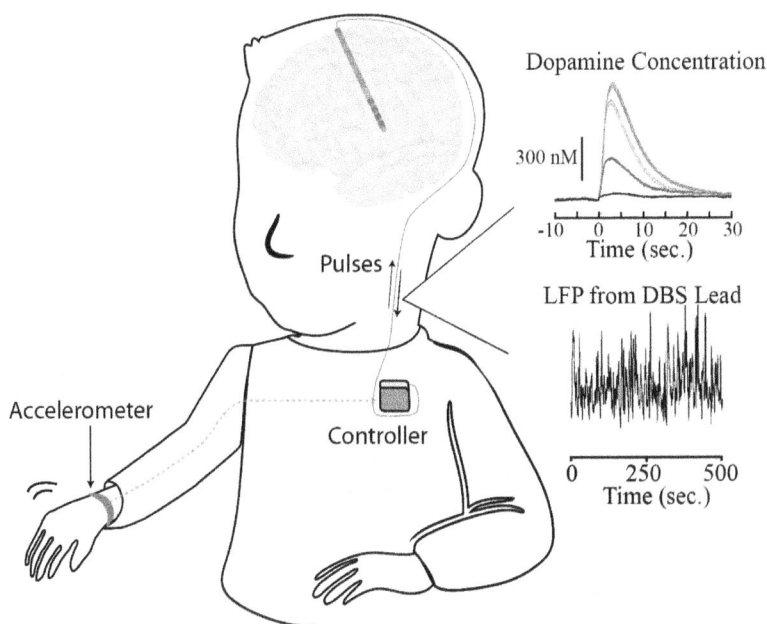

Fig. 9. Behaviorally and neurophysiologically-based closed-loop DBS. (1) Examples of closed-loop stimulation include, for example, an accelerometer to record tremor, transmit the information wirelessly to a controller, and apply stimulation through the DBS lead based on the signal power from the accelerometer. (2) Closed-loop DBS may also consist of sensors recording local field potential (LFP) signals through contacts along the DBS lead, process that information through the controller, and stimulate through other contacts on the DBS lead. (filtered, rectified LFP signal adapted from Little *et al.* [53], with permission) (3) Closed-loop stimulation can also leverage neurochemical concentration due to DBS, such as transient dopamine efflux.

The concept of closed-loop stimulation has made large strides in the treatment of epilepsy. NeuroPace has FDA approval for a product that measures intracranial EEG in or over one or more seizure foci, uses algorithms to detect the onset of seizures, and trigger stimulation to suppress the seizure from occurring. Published results indicate that the closed-loop system reduced the frequency of seizures by 66% after six years [58]. Thus, the algorithms for seizure prediction are effective, but there is room for improvement. In the coming years, there is likely to be an explosion of behaviorally and physiologically-based closed-loop DBS applications, which will be especially important for clinical indications in which symptoms are intermittent (e.g., cues for addiction) or continuously fluctuating (e.g., depression, tinnitus, etc.). Following the lead from rate-responsive cardiac pacemakers that utilize a blending of sensor input, it is likely that practical implementation of closed-loop DBS will also require a blending of multiple behavioral and physiological sensor input.

7. Next Generation

7.1. *Focused ultrasound*

One of the drawbacks of deep brain stimulation is the invasiveness of the surgical procedure and the requirement for a chronically implanted system. Non-invasive neuromodulation techniques, including transcranial electrical stimulation (TES) and transcranial magnetic stimulation (TMS), can in principle modulate subcortical brain activity, but in so doing also strongly modulate cortical activity directly beneath the electrode(s) or magnetic coil(s). Ultrasound is another modality, often used for biomedical imaging applications, that when applied at kilohertz to low-megahertz frequencies can have more selective modulatory effects on neural tissue deep within the brain.

While the mechanisms of low-intensity ultrasound neuromodulation are not established, there are several hypotheses based on mechanical perturbations to the cell membrane and the fluid surrounding the membrane. These include stable cavitation and acoustic streaming, acoustic radiation forces, shear stress, Bernoulli effects, and acoustic impedance mismatches across the membrane bilayers [59]. The net result of these perturbations is thought to affect ion channel dynamics and leakage through the phospholipid bilayer, which together causes a change in membrane potential that alters neuronal activity [60].

One challenge with ultrasound neuromodulation is focusing the energy within a specific volume of tissue. Two approaches have been developed to address this challenge: single ultrasound transducers with concave aperture openings and phased arrays. Phased arrays use a set of transducers with varied phase delays such that the ultrasound waves are out of phase directly below the transducer array, but converge at a deep tissue target in order to modulate a deep brain target without activation of cortical tissue. Neuromodulation via focused ultrasound is a promising alternative to current DBS methods as it does not require invasive surgery, and has no implanted equipment failure or battery consumption concerns.

7.2. *Transcranial magnetic stimulation*

A second approach to non-invasively modulate neural activity employs transcranial magnetic stimulation (TMS). Electric coils produce a magnetic field that passes through the skin and skull and induces current flow through conductive neural tissue. Depending on the orientation of neurons with respect to the induced current, neurons either depolarize or hyperpolarize. The application of TMS to deep brain stimulation poses two primary challenges: focality of activation and penetration of current to deep structures of the brain. A single circular TMS coil induces maximum current below the perimeter of the coil, therefore coil diameter controls the focality of stimulation, however circular coil designs cannot be downsized due to overheating of the coils and Lorentz forces or the mechanical force induced by the coil that can damage the coil casing.

Advanced coil designs may be able to produce focal stimulation of the cortex, however the challenge remains to produce penetrating current to modulate deep brain structures. A surface conductor placed on the scalp can act as a shield when applying TMS using an iron core stimulator, reducing activation of the cortex and causing deeper penetration of current. Widening the angle of an iron core stimulator can also lead to deeper penetration. Both of these method provide activation of deep structures in the brain; however, widespread activation is still a factor as these methods lack the focality seen in modulation of cortical structures [61]. TMS is effective for modulation of cortical activity, however it has proven difficult to focally modulate deep brain structures without widespread activation of cortical regions, leading to adverse side effects including the potential for seizures [62].

7.3. *Optogenetics*

Deep brain stimulation using a DBS lead can activate specific structures in the brain; however, electrical stimulation is largely non-selective to different cell types within the vicinity of the implanted DBS lead. Optogenetics, on the other hand, is a rapidly growing technique for selective modulation of neuron subpopulations. In this approach, neurons are genetically modified by viral vectors containing opsin genes with cell-type specific promoters. The opsin genes cause the targeted neurons to express wavelength-specific light-sensitive rhodopsin ion channel proteins in the cell membrane. An optical fiber is implanted and a light source is used to activate the light-sensitive channels leading to depolarize or hyperpolarization of the membrane depending on the channel type.

For treatment of epilepsy, a halorhodopsin chloride channel can be expressed in glutamatergic neurons. When activated, chloride flows into the neuron causing hyperpolarization and suppression of seizure activity [63]. Optogenetics provide great promise for selective activation of subpopulations of cells in deep brain structures. However, challenges include the delivery of viral vectors, chronic delivery of light to the stimulation site, and scattering of light through brain tissue.

7.4. *Genetic encoding for non-invasive stimulation*

Ultrasound and transcranial magnetic stimulation show promise as non-invasive neuromodulation techniques; however, these approaches lack the neuron population-specificity provided by optogenetics. Recent studies have begun to apply genetic manipulation to these fields. Magnetothermal stimulation is an emerging technique that uses viral vectors containing genes for the membrane expression of the thermo-sensitive cation channel TRPV1. Magnetic nanoparticles that produce heat when exposed to an alternating magnetic field are inserted into the same region in the brain as the viral vectors making a specific population of neurons within the brain sensitive to an external magnetic field [64]. Similarly, mechanosensitive ion channels such as TRP-4 cation channels cause sensitization of neurons to mechanical agitation. Low-intensity ultrasound, for example, could be applied to activate TRP-4 channels leading to sensitization of neurons to ultrasound neuromodulation [65]. Genetic encoding for both TMS and ultrasound may provide subpopulation specific neuromodulation, however both approaches will require further study regarding the safety, efficacy, and longevity of their application.

7.5. *Advanced imaging*

In addition to new avenues of genetic encoding for DBS, in the coming years, traditional electrical DBS therapy is moving towards tailoring the stimulation settings to each patient's symptoms and anatomy using advanced imaging techniques. Computational modeling for DBS relies heavily on high-resolution MRIs to develop anatomically accurate renderings of deep brain structures that are used to predict activation volumes and perform tractography analysis. These patient-specific models may be used for both placement of DBS leads and postoperative analysis of lead placement with respect to therapeutic and side effect regions for optimal programming of stimulation parameters. Patient-specific models will also become important as high-density arrays are developed with a large parameter space, programmers will be able to make informed decisions based on patient-specific anatomy, lead placement, and predicted activation volumes. Barriers to the immediate implementation of patient-specific computational models include the widespread availability of high-resolution MRI systems that are not presently standard in the clinical setting, and the computational intensity and time required to develop computational models, the process will need to be streamlined and automated before becoming clinically feasible.

8. Summary

This chapter provided an overview of the DBS field from its history in lesion therapy to recent technological advances that improve the efficacy and efficiency of therapy as well as extend the therapy to additional clinical indications. In order to truly harness the potential of DBS, the mechanisms behind its efficacy must continue to be explored to drive more effective treatment of brain disorders. The DBS field will continue to evolve as high-density arrays, advanced programming algorithms, and closed-loop approaches are developed. These recent advancements are pushing the field toward the customization of DBS to specific clinical indications and individual patient anatomy and symptomatology.

References

1. C. Loiselle and R. Young, Gamma knife: A useful tool for treatment of essential tremor *Transl. Cancer Res.* **3**(4), 338–341, (2014).
2. N. Lipsman, M. L. Schwartz, Y. Huang, L. Lee, T. Sankar, M. Chapman, K. Hynynen, and A. M. Lozano, MR-guided focused ultrasound thalamotomy for essential tremor: a proof-of-concept study *Lancet Neurol.* **12**(5), 462–468, (2013).
3. K. L. Holloway, S. E. Gaede, P. A. Starr, J. M. Rosenow, V. Ramakrishnan, and J. M. Henderson, Frameless stereotaxy using bone fiducial markers for deep brain stimulation *J. Neurosurg.* **103**(3), 404–413, (2005).
4. J. L. Ostrem, N. B. Galifianakis, L. C. Markun, J. K. Grace, A. J. Martin, P. A. Starr, and P. S. Larson, Clinical outcomes of PD patients having bilateral STN DBS using high-field interventional MR-imaging for lead placement *Clin. Neurol. Neurosurg.* **115**(6), 708–712, (2013).
5. E. A. Pereira, A. L. Green, D. Nandi, and T. Z. Aziz, Deep brain stimulation: indications and evidence *Expert Rev. Med. Devices* **4**(5), 591–603, (2007).

6. M. Hariz, P. Blomstedt, and L. Zrinzo, Future of brain stimulation: New targets, new indications, new technology: Future of Brain Stimulation *Mov. Disord.* **28**(13), 1784–1792, (2013).

7. N. D. Schiff, J. T. Giacino, K. Kalmar, J. D. Victor, K. Baker, M. Gerber, B. Fritz, B. Eisenberg, J. O'Connor, E. J. Kobylarz, S. Farris, A. Machado, C. McCagg, F. Plum, J. J. Fins and A. R. Rezai, Behavioural improvements with thalamic stimulation after severe traumatic brain injury *Nature* **448**(7153), 600–603, (2007).

8. C. Beurrier, B. Bioulac, J. Audin, and C. Hammond, High-frequency stimulation produces a transient blockade of voltage-gated currents in subthalamic neurons *J. Neurophysiol.* **85**(4), 1351–1356, (2001).

9. F. Agnesi, A. T. Connolly, K. B. Baker, J. L. Vitek, and M. D. Johnson, Deep brain stimulation imposes complex informational lesions *PLoS ONE* **8**(8), e74462, (2013).

10. I. Bar-Gad, Complex locking rather than complete cessation of neuronal activity in the globus pallidus of a 1-Methyl-4-Phenyl-1,2,3,6-Tetrahydropyridine-treated primate in response to pallidal microstimulation *J. Neurosci.* **24**(33), 7410–7419, (2004).

11. J. B. Ranck, Which elements are excited in electrical stimulation of mammalian central nervous system: a review *Brain Res.* **98**(3), 417–440, (1975).

12. J. O. Dostrovsky, R. Levy, J. P. Wu, W. D. Hutchison, R. R. Tasker, and A. M. Lozano, Microstimulation-induced inhibition of neuronal firing in human globus pallidus *J. Neurophysiol.* **84**(1), 570–574, (2000).

13. F. Windels, N. Bruet, A. Poupard, C. Feuerstein, A. Bertrand, and M. Savasta, Influence of the frequency parameter on extracellular glutamate and γ-aminobutyric acid in substantia nigra and globus pallidus during electrical stimulation of subthalamic nucleus in rats *J. Neurosci. Res.* **72**(2), 259–267, (2003).

14. T. Hashimoto, C. M. Elder, M. S. Okun, S. K. Patrick, and J. L. Vitek, Stimulation of the subthalamic nucleus changes the firing pattern of pallidal neurons *J. Neurosci.* **23**(5), 1916–1923, (2003).

15. F. Agnesi, A. Muralidharan, K. B. Baker, J. L. Vitek, and M. D. Johnson, Fidelity of frequency and phase entrainment of circuit-level spike activity during DBS *J. Neurophysiol.* **114**(2), 825–834, (2015).

16. K. J. Iremonger, Cellular mechanisms preventing sustained activation of cortex during subcortical high-frequency stimulation *J. Neurophysiol.* **96**(2), 613–621, (2006).

17. K.-Z. Shen, Z.-T. Zhu, A. Munhall, and S. W. Johnson, Synaptic plasticity in rat subthalamic nucleus induced by high-frequency stimulation *Synapse* **50**(4), 314–319, (2003).

18. Y.-M. Shon, K. H. Lee, S. J. Goerss, I. Y. Kim, C. Kimble, J. J. Van Gompel, K. Bennet, C. D. Blaha, and S.-Y. Chang, High frequency stimulation of the subthalamic nucleus evokes striatal dopamine release in a large animal model of human DBS neurosurgery *Neurosci. Lett.* **475**(3), 136–140, (2010).

19. A. van Dijk, A. A. Klompmakers, M. G. P. Feenstra, and D. Denys, Deep brain stimulation of the accumbens increases dopamine, serotonin, and noradrenaline in the prefrontal cortex *J. Neurochem.* **123**(6), 897–903, (2012).

20. L. Bekar, W. Libionka, G.-F. Tian, Q. Xu, A. Torres, X. Wang, D. Lovatt, E. Williams, T. Takano, J. Schnermann, R. Bakos and M. Nedergaard, Adenosine is crucial for deep brain stimulation–mediated attenuation of tremor *Nat. Med.* **14**(1), 75–80, (2008).

21. K. H. Lee, K. Kristic, R. van Hoff, F. L. Hitti, C. Blaha, B. Harris, D. W. Roberts, and J. C. Leiter, High-frequency stimulation of the subthalamic nucleus increases glutamate in the

subthalamic nucleus of rats as demonstrated by in vivo enzyme-linked glutamate sensor *Brain Res.* **1162**121–129, (2007).

22. A. A. Kuhn, F. Kempf, C. Brucke, L. Gaynor Doyle, I. Martinez-Torres, A. Pogosyan, T. Trottenberg, A. Kupsch, G.-H. Schneider, M. I. Hariz, W. Vandenberghe, B. Nuttin, and P. Brown, High-frequency stimulation of the subthalamic nucleus suppresses oscillatory activity in patients with Parkinson's disease in parallel with improvement in motor performance *J. Neurosci.* **28**(24), 6165–6173, (2008).

23. A. T. Connolly, R. J. Vetter, J. F. Hetke, B. A. Teplitzky, D. R. Kipke, D. S. Pellinen, D. J. Anderson, K. B. Baker, J. L. Vitek, and M. D. Johnson, A novel lead design for modulation and sensing of deep brain structures *IEEE Trans. Biomed. Eng.* **63**(1), 148–157, (2016).

24. A. W. G. Buijink, A. M. M. van der Stouwe, M. Broersma, S. Sharifi, P. F. C. Groot, J. D. Speelman, N. M. Maurits, and A.-F. van Rootselaar, Motor network disruption in essential tremor: a functional and effective connectivity study *Brain* **138**(10), 2934–2947, (2015).

25. P. Blomstedt, U. Sandvik, and S. Tisch, Deep brain stimulation in the posterior subthalamic area in the treatment of essential tremor: DBS in the PSA in the Treatment of ET *Mov. Disord.* **25**(10), 1350–1356, (2010).

26. C. R. Butson, S. E. Cooper, J. M. Henderson, B. Wolgamuth, and C. C. McIntyre, Probabilistic analysis of activation volumes generated during deep brain stimulation *NeuroImage* **54**(3), 2096–2104, (2011).

27. P. Riva-Posse, K. S. Choi, P. E. Holtzheimer, C. C. McIntyre, R. E. Gross, A. Chaturvedi, A. L. Crowell, S. J. Garlow, J. K. Rajendra, and H. S. Mayberg, Defining critical white matter pathways mediating successful subcallosal cingulate deep brain stimulation for treatment-resistant depression *Biol. Psychiatry* **76**(12), 963–969, (2014).

28. W. M. Grill, A. N. Snyder, and S. Miocinovic, Deep brain stimulation creates an informational lesion of the stimulated nucleus *NeuroReport* **15**(7), 1137–1140, (2004).

29. A. D. Dorval, G. S. Russo, T. Hashimoto, W. Xu, W. M. Grill, and J. L. Vitek, Deep brain stimulation reduces neuronal entropy in the MPTP-primate model of Parkinson's disease *J. Neurophysiol.* **100**(5), 2807–2818, (2008).

30. L. D. Liu, I. A. Prescott, J. O. Dostrovsky, M. Hodaie, A. M. Lozano, and W. D. Hutchison, Frequency-dependent effects of electrical stimulation in the globus pallidus of dystonia patients *J. Neurophysiol.* **108**(1), 5–17, (2012).

31. M. P. Kilgard and M. M. Merzenich, Cortical map reorganization enabled by nucleus basalis activity *Science* **279**(5357), 1714–1718, (1998).

32. S. Tisch, J. C. Rothwell, P. Limousin, M. I. Hariz, and D. M. Corcos, The physiological effects of pallidal deep brain stimulation in dystonia *IEEE Trans. Neural Syst. Rehabil. Eng.* **15**(2), 166–172, (2007).

33. A. O. Ceballos-Baumann, Functional imaging in Parkinson's disease: activation studies with PET, fMRI and SPECT *J. Neurol.* **250**(S1), i15–i23, (2003).

34. I. Valalik, M. Emri, Z. Lengyel, P. Mikecz, L. Tron, A. Csokay, and T. Marian, Pallidal Deep Brain Stimulation and L-Dopa Effect on PET Motor Activation in Advanced Parkinson's Disease *J Neuroimaging* (2008).

35. J. F. Baizabal-Carvallo, M. N. Kagnoff, J. Jimenez-Shahed, R. Fekete, and J. Jankovic, The safety and efficacy of thalamic deep brain stimulation in essential tremor: 10 years and beyond *J. Neurol. Neurosurg. Psychiatry* **85**(5), 567–572, (2014).

36. P. Krack, V. Fraix, A. Mendes, A.-L. Benabid, and P. Pollak, Postoperative management of subthalamic nucleus stimulation for Parkinson's disease *Mov. Disord.* **17**(S3), S188–S197, (2002).

37. H. C. F. Martens, E. Toader, M. M. J. Decré, D. J. Anderson, R. Vetter, D. R. Kipke, K. B. Baker, M. D. Johnson, and J. L. Vitek, Spatial steering of deep brain stimulation volumes using a novel lead design *Clin. Neurophysiol.* **122**(3), 558–566, (2011).

38. M. F. Contarino, L. J. Bour, R. Verhagen, M. A. J. Lourens, R. M. A. de Bie, P. van den Munckhof, and P. R. Schuurman, Directional steering: A novel approach to deep brain stimulation *Neurology* **83**(13), 1163–1169, (2014).

39. C. Pollo, A. Kaelin-Lang, M. F. Oertel, L. Stieglitz, E. Taub, P. Fuhr, A. M. Lozano, A. Raabe, and M. Schüpbach, Directional deep brain stimulation: an intraoperative double-blind pilot study *Brain* **137**(7), 2015–2026, (2014).

40. C. R. Butson and C. C. McIntyre, Role of electrode design on the volume of tissue activated during deep brain stimulation *J. Neural Eng.* **3**(1), 1–8, (2006).

41. J. L. Lujan, A. Chaturvedi, K. S. Choi, P. E. Holtzheimer, R. E. Gross, H. S. Mayberg, and C. C. McIntyre, Tractography-activation models applied to subcallosal cingulate deep brain stimulation *Brain Stimulat.* **6**(5), 737–739, (2013).

42. J. Volkmann, J. Herzog, F. Kopper, and G. Deuschl, Introduction to the programming of deep brain stimulators *Mov. Disord.* **17**(S3), S181–S187, (2002).

43. M. M. Reich, F. Steigerwald, A. D. Sawalhe, R. Reese, K. Gunalan, S. Johannes, R. Nickl, C. Matthies, C. C. McIntyre and J. Volkmann, Short pulse width widens the therapeutic window of subthalamic neurostimulation *Ann. Clin. Transl. Neurol.* **2**(4), 427–432, (2015).

44. M. J. Birdno and W. M. Grill, Mechanisms of deep brain stimulation in movement disorders as revealed by changes in stimulus frequency *Neurotherapeutics* **5**(1), 14–25, (2008).

45. D. T. Brocker, B. D. Swan, D. A. Turner, R. E. Gross, S. B. Tatter, M. Miller Koop, H. Bronte-Stewart, and W. M. Grill, Improved efficacy of temporally non-regular deep brain stimulation in Parkinson's disease *Exp. Neurol.* **239**60–67, (2013).

46. P. A. Tass, A model of desynchronizing deep brain stimulation with a demand-controlled coordinated reset of neural subpopulations *Biol. Cybern.* **89**(2), 81–88, (2003).

47. B. Lysyansky, O. V. Popovych, and P. A. Tass, Optimal number of stimulation contacts for coordinated reset neuromodulation *Front. Neuroengineering* **6** (2013).

48. I. Adamchic, C. Hauptmann, U. B. Barnikol, N. Pawelczyk, O. Popovych, T. T. Barnikol, A. Silchenko, J. Volkmann, G. Deuschl, W. G Meissner, M. Maarouf, V. Sturm, H.-J. Freund and P. A. Tass, Coordinated reset neuromodulation for Parkinson's disease: Proof-of-concept study *Mov. Disord.* **29**(13), 1679–1684, (2014).

49. P. A. Tass, L. Qin, C. Hauptmann, S. Dovero, E. Bezard, T. Boraud, and W. G. Meissner, Coordinated reset has sustained aftereffects in Parkinsonian monkeys *Ann. Neurol.* **72**(5), 816–820, (2012).

50. L. Lücken, S. Yanchuk, O. V. Popovych, and P. A. Tass, Desynchronization boost by non-uniform coordinated reset stimulation in ensembles of pulse-coupled neurons *Front. Comput. Neurosci.* **7** (2013).

51. C. J. Wilson, B. Beverlin, and T. Netoff, Chaotic desynchronization as the therapeutic mechanism of deep brain stimulation *Front. Syst. Neurosci.* **5** (2011).

52. C. R. Butson and C. C. McIntyre, Current steering to control the volume of tissue activated during deep brain stimulation *Brain Stimulat.* **1**(1), 7–15, (2008).

53. S. Little, A. Pogosyan, S. Neal, B. Zavala, L. Zrinzo, M. Hariz, T. Foltynie, P. Limousin, K. Ashkan, J. FitzGerald, A. L. Green, T. Z. Aziz and P. Brown, Adaptive deep brain stimulation in advanced Parkinson disease: Adaptive DBS in PD *Ann. Neurol.* **74**(3), 449–457, (2013).

54. T. Yamamoto, Y. Katayama, J. Ushiba, H. Yoshino, T. Obuchi, K. Kobayashi, H. Oshima, and C. Fukaya, On-demand control system for deep brain stimulation for treatment of intention tremor: On-demand control system for DBS *Neuromodulation Technol. Neural Interface* **16**(3), 230–235, (2013).

55. S. Santaniello, G. Fiengo, L. Glielmo, and W. M. Grill, Closed-loop control of deep brain stimulation: A simulation study *IEEE Trans. Neural Syst. Rehabil. Eng.* **19**(1), 15–24, (2011).

56. A. Priori, G. Foffani, L. Rossi, and S. Marceglia, Adaptive deep brain stimulation (aDBS) controlled by local field potential oscillations *Exp. Neurol.* **245**77–86, (2013).

57. B. Rosin, M. Slovik, R. Mitelman, M. Rivlin-Etzion, S. N. Haber, Z. Israel, E. Vaadia, and H. Bergman, Closed-loop deep brain stimulation is superior in ameliorating Parkinsonism *Neuron* **72**(2), 370–384, (2011).

58. G. K. Bergey, M. J. Morrell, E. M. Mizrahi, A. Goldman, D. King-Stephens, D. Nair, S. Srinivasan, B. Jobst, R. E. Gross, D. C. Shields, G. Barkley, V. Salanova, P. Olejniczak, A. Cole, S. S. Cash, K. Noe, R. Wharen, G. Worrell, A. M. Murro, J. Edwards, M. Duchowny, D. Spencer, M. Smith, E. Geller, R. Gwinn, C. Skidmore, S. Eisenschenk, M. Berg, C. Heck, P. Van Ness, N. Fountain, P. Rutecki, A. Massey, C. O'Donovan, D. Labar, R. B. Duckrow, L. J. Hirsch, T. Courtney, F. T. Sun, and C. G. Seale, Long-term treatment with responsive brain stimulation in adults with refractory partial seizures *Neurology* **84**(8), 810–817, (2015).

59. W. J. Tyler, Noninvasive neuromodulation with ultrasound? A continuum mechanics hypothesis *The Neuroscientist* **17**(1), 25–36, (2011).

60. A. Bystritsky and A. S. Korb, A review of low-intensity transcranial focused ultrasound for clinical applications *Curr. Behav. Neurosci. Rep.* **2**(2), 60–66, (2015).

61. E. Wassermann, C. Epstein, and U. Ziemann, *Oxford Handbook of Transcranial Stimulation*. (Oxford University Press, 2008).

62. Z.-D. Deng, A. V. Peterchev, and S. H. Lisanby, Coil design considerations for deep-brain transcranial magnetic stimulation (dTMS); pp. 5675–5679 in, *Eng. Med. Biol. Soc. 2008 EMBS 2008 30th Annu. Int. Conf. IEEE.* IEEE, 2008.

63. J. N. Bentley, C. Chestek, W. C. Stacey, and P. G. Patil, Optogenetics in epilepsy *Neurosurg. Focus* **34**(6), E4, (2013).

64. R. Chen, G. Romero, M. G. Christiansen, A. Mohr, and P. Anikeeva, Wireless magnetothermal deep brain stimulation *Science* **347**(6229), 1477–1480, (2015).

65. S. Ibsen, A. Tong, C. Schutt, S. Esener, and S. H. Chalasani, Sonogenetics is a non-invasive approach to activating neurons in Caenorhabditis elegans *Nat. Commun.* **6**8264, (2015).

66. B. D. Swan, D. T. Brocker, J. D. Hilliard, S. B. Tatter, R. E. Gross, D. A. Turner, and W. M. Grill, Short pauses in thalamic deep brain stimulation promote tremor and neuronal bursting *Clin. Neurophysiol.* **127**(2), 1551-1559, (2015).

Section 4

Future Systems

Chapter 4.1

Prosthetic Limbs

Sanford G. Meek

Department of Mechanical Engineering, University of Utah, Salt Lake City UT, 84112
meek@mech.utah.edu

There have been great advances in the development of prosthetic limbs in the past decade. Prosthetic hands with multiple degrees of freedom are available to the amputees. Systems and methods for controlling multiple motions are on the market. Implanted electromyographic and neural sensors have increased the accessible control sites, providing more possibilities of control. Micro-processor controlled legs can adapt to changing gait speeds and different terrains. Sensory feedback of touch and proprioception has been shown to improve the control of prostheses. Osseointegrated attachments are eliminating the greatest complaint of amputees – comfort and tissue problems of the residual limb. What lies in the future? An integrated prosthesis system with efferent and afferent communications providing natural control and natural sensation of touch and proprioception is the next stage of prosthetic technology to come.

To quote Niels Bohr, "Prediction is very difficult, especially if it's about the future."

1. Introduction

In the 11 years since the first edition of the book, many of the predictions of the future of neuroprosthetic limbs have come to be, at least in the laboratory if not clinically. In this chapter, we will review these briefly and then look at the next few years.

A prosthesis must successfully incorporate communication between the user and the device as well as have robust hardware to provide a reliable system for the amputee. Both afferent and efferent signals are needed and provide as natural as possible control and sensation for the amputee.

The communication from the amputee must provide the intent in an accurate and intuitive manner. This has met with a great deal of research with varying levels of success. The most common efferent signal for control is the electromyographic (EMG) signal. A great deal of work has gone into how to get multiple degree of freedom (MDOF) control from a limited number of cutaneous EMGs. The typical approach has been the use of pattern recognition. This has met with limited clinical application, though systems are being marketed [59,72].

The afferent communication to the amputee must give the user sensory and proprioceptive information from the device in a natural manner. The primary methods are by the use of tactors to stimulate the skin with vibrations or pressure, or the use of peripheral nerve stimulation.

Lastly, the other area that has met with a great deal of work is in providing hardware with multiple powered degrees of freedom.

2. Recent Research

A look at recent research can hint at what the future may hold in clinically available prostheses. The great challenge is the human-machine connection. This connection involves both mechanical (sockets, electrodes), and communication (determining the amputees intent) issues for control and providing the amputee with proprioceptive and tactile sensation for closing the loop.

A brief review of recent research results is presented. This is by no means a detailed review, but a summary that pertains to the future trends. As far as the communication between the amputee and the prosthesis there are the afferent, sensory feedback and the efferent, control signals. Finally, a look at the current state of hardware will be presented.

2.1. Sensory feedback

One of the most significant recent results for upper extremity prostheses is that of providing sensory feedback to amputee user of the prosthesis [1,2,24,45,53]. The use of tactors, devices that stimulate the skin through vibration or pressure are not invasive and do improve control but do not provide a natural sensation [62] with most amputees. Significantly better control of grip has been achieved when peripheral nerve stimulation provided touch and proprioception even when coupled with conventional antagonist EMG control [24,42,43,52,55]. This has been proven in several acute laboratory experiments and has been shown to be viable for chronic, clinical tests [29,38,45,64,66].

Two methods can provide a natural sensation to the amputee: Targeted Muscle Reinervation (TMR) and peripheral nerve stimulation.

2.1.1. *Targeted Muscle Reinnervation (TMR)*

Subjects who have had Targeted Muscle Reinervation surgery have often developed sensation referred to their missing limbs as sensory neurons grow into the reinervated tissue. This can provide a non-invasive means of providing the sensory feedback as tactors can push on the reinervated skin to provide the sensation [29,38,45]. This has been very successful in those subjects. The limitation is that the surgery is complex and thus far limited to a small population of amputees. There are approximately 300 amputees world-wide with successful TMR surgery [30].

2.1.2. *Peripheral nerve stimulation*

Peripheral nerve stimulation involves a simpler surgery but does involve permanent implanted devices. Sensory and proprioceptive feedback is best done by stimulating the peripheral nerves. The advantage of peripheral nerve stimulation over central nervous system stimulation is that the neural 'wiring' is in place between the brain and the missing limb. By stimulating a sensory neuron, the brain encodes that as coming from the original source in the missing limb.

There have been several designs for peripheral nerve electrodes. They can be generally classified as penetrating or non-penetrating.

It has been shown that the stimulation of the sensory neurons produces a natural sensation of the missing limb and improves the control in grasping objects [1,10,14,15,20,24,26,31,43,44,47,52,55]. Probably most important is the general acceptance by the amputees and enthusiasm for the sensation and improved control of the prostheses.

2.1.2.1 Penetrating electrodes

There are two general categories of penetrating electrodes: flexible with single or multiple electrode sites and rigid usually with a high number of electrodes. A concern of penetrating electrodes is the risk of tissue damage. Long term use has been demonstrated in animal experiments [32,33,47,48,608] with minimal tissue problems. The advantage of penetrating electrodes is the ability of high selectivity of the sensation and low stimulation levels.

2.1.2.1.1 Longitudinal IntraFascicular Electrodes - LIFEs

Longitudinal Intrafascicular Electrodes (LIFEs) have been used successfully both to record from motoneurons [14] and to stimulate sensory neurons in the peripheral nerves [15,24]. They have the advantage of relatively large electrode area in order to reduce the current density and are flexible to move with the soft tissues of the limb. A disadvantage is that the number of channels is limited when compared to the rigid multi-electrode arrays. Each electrode must be inserted individually into the nerve.

Experiments in Utah and in Italy have demonstrated hand prosthesis control with sensory feedback to the amputee. In the Utah experiments, the subjects were able to discriminate between different size objects as well as relative stiffness of objects. This was done with only 2 proportional channels - one proprioception and one touch [22].

2.1.2.1.2 Transverse Intrafascicular Multichannel Electrodes – TIMEs

An interesting design that helps overcome the limitations of the problem of inserting individual LIFEs into the nerve is the Transverse Intrafascicular Multichannel Electrode (TIME). These are flexible arrays with 5 electrodes that can be inserted into the fascicle. The TIMEs have been shown to have stable long-term performance with minimal problems in animals [7].

Experiments in human subjects have shown improved grip control on multiple degree of freedom hands [41,42,43,44,52,55].

2.1.2.1.3 Utah Slant Electrode Array - USEA

The Utah array consists of 100 penetrating electrodes that can be used for stimulation and recording. They are in a single device so the complexity of inserting individual electrodes as with the other systems is minimized. A disadvantage is that the device is rigid which can cause potential damage to the nerve tissue. USEAs have been used chronically in animal models with minimal problems. Recently, USEAs have been used to control two degrees of freedom of a virtual hand while simultaneously stimulating sensory neurons providing a closed loop control [10].

2.1.2.2 Non-penetrating electrodes

Non penetrating electrodes have the advantage of minimal tissue damage but the disadvantage of less selectivity of stimulation and recording.

2.1.2.2.1 Flat Interface Nerve Electrodes - FINEs

Flat Interface Nerve Electrodes (FINEs) are cuff electrodes than flatten the nerve allowing a closer distance for the stimulating electrodes and providing greater selectivity than conventional electrodes [64,66]. They have been successfully used in human for more than 2 years with continual stimulation capabilities [66].

2.1.2.2.2 Cuff

The least invasive method of neural stimulation and recording is the use of cuff electrodes. These have been shown usable with minimal nerve damage in long term experiments [54,64,66]. They are the least selective and require the highest stimulation levels to evoke responses [47].

2.1.2.2.3 Regenerative

The third method of peripheral nerve interfacing is to have the neurons to grow through micro-channels containing electrodes [31,32,33]. This enables very selective recording and stimulation as well as very stable connections. The disadvantage is that it is very invasive on the nerve and requires that the neurons grow properly through the channels. These methods have only been used in animal models to date.

2.2. *Multi-degree of freedom control*

One of the most difficult problems is determining the users intent, especially when trying to control complex multi-degree of freedom motions. The use of electromyographic (EMG) signals has been the primary focus of work. Surface EMG signals are typically used. EMGs are easy to detect, are non-invasive, and monitor the muscle activity directly. If the muscles that naturally control a motion, say biceps and triceps for elbow control, are used then those motions can be directly and proportional controlled. If those muscles are not available, then indirect control can be done. Simultaneous, proportional control of multiple motions is difficult with simple cutaneous signals [25,39]. The limitations are in the number of signals available and reliably usable on a day-to-day basis. There are several approaches to solving this problem. Pattern recognition and state machine methods are the most common methods that have been tried for MDOF control with varying levels of success [59,68,72]. Problems in consistent placement, changes in the signals due to fatigue and other muscle changes tend to limit the reliability of pattern recognition. The lack of proportional control of each motion in many of the methods has been also a limitation. Recent advancements have led to proportional control of several degrees of freedom and recalibration methods allow for electrode placement changes and muscle characteristics changes. Pattern recognition systems are now being marketed [72].

Implanted myoelectric sensors are clinically available [40,65,76]. These enable more stable positioning and the ability to detect muscle activity from deep muscle that are inaccessible for surface electrodes. These have enabled direct, proportional control of several simultaneous motions.

798   S. Meek

There is still a fundamental limitation with the use of muscle signals. With higher amputations, there are fewer muscles available and the muscles that are available are not those normally directly controlling the desired distal motions.

The obvious solution to the limitations of EMG signals is to detect the activity of the motor neurons that used to activate the missing muscles of the amputee. Recordings of peripheral nerves and prosthesis control have been done in acute laboratory [7,10,14,15,20,24,26,31,32,41,43,44,47,52,54,55,60] and some cases on a chronic basis [64,66].

2.2.1. *EMG*

2.2.1.1 Direct control

With the advent of implantable EMG sensors, muscles that were difficult or impossible to monitor cutaneously can be used for control. This allows for more degrees of freedom to be directly controlled. There is a great advantage to control a motion with the muscle that originally controlled the motion. With more natural control, less learning is required by the user.

2.2.1.2 Antagonistic

Controlling a motion with an antagonist pair of group of muscles results in a simple, reliable, and proportional control. This is the most common type of EMG control and will remain so for in the near future. With implanted EMG electrodes, MDOF control will become more prevalent.

2.2.1.3 Targeted Muscle Reinnervation (TMR)

TMR is essentially a form of direct control in that EMGs from the reinervated muscles control each motion. The muscle has a new activity as seen by the amputee. As the amputee tries to activate say a finger motion, the reinervation stimulates a portion of a different muscle. As far as the amputee is concerned, they activated the original but missing muscle. A limitation is the extensive and complex surgery. TMR has not been used on a wide spread basis, though, it is extremely useful especially for high amputees such as shoulder disarticulation amputation. As the method is refined, the use will no doubt increase and provide amputees with MDOF control using surface EMGs and sensory feedback with non-invasive tactors.

2.2.1.4 Pattern recognition

Pattern recognition methods have been investigated since the 1970s [68]. There is now a system that is commercially available [70]. The basic idea is to derive more information from fewer sites by using signal processing methods to determine changes in the EMG signal related to different hand and arm motions [59]. The problems that have limited the use of pattern recognition have been in the calibration of the patterns and the stability of the recognition due to changes in muscle activity and electrode placement. Efficient re-calibration methods have alleviated many of the issues and a system is now available clinically [72].

2.2.1.5 Principal component control

An interesting approach developed by Segil and Weir [61] is to map the EMGs of several muscles and sort them according to the principal component groupings. This weights the activity to produce control signals for different DOFs. The idea is derived from studies done by Santello et al [56,57,58] of hand postures of subjects performing tool and object manipulation. This approach has the potential to provide stable MDOF control with simple computation in the prosthesis.

This idea has some similarities to an old idea of Jacobsen's [25] Vector Myogram (VMG) control of MDOFs

2.2.1.6 Vector Myogram control (VMG)

It maybe time to resurrect Jacobsen's VMG method. The VMG is a linear array of EMG input to torque output relationships [25,39]. The relationships were made by simultaneously measuring joint torques and multiple EMGs. A multivalent regression was used to find the relationship. Since the EMG activity of different muscles is highly correlated, ridge regression and principal component regression methods were used, resulting in very high predictions of the torques - 95 to 98 percent correlation. The method was not used clinically because to the large number of EMG signals that are needed. With the use of cutaneous electrodes this was impractical. However, with new implantable electrodes this impediment is lessened.

2.2.2. *Neural*

The monitoring of motor neurons in peripheral nerves to control a prosthesis has been shown effective in the laboratory setting [10,14,15,20]. It has not been clinically viable because of the lack of chronically implanted electrodes. It has the benefit of detecting efferent signals that no longer connect to muscles to produce and EMG signal. This will be especially important to above elbow amputees where the muscle that control the hand are missing but the motor neurons are still active. The surgery for electrode implantation is simpler and less invasive than TMR.

2.2.3. *Shared control*

Shared control is beginning to be investigated and implemented in both upper and lower extremity devices. This eases the control for the human by having the device compensate for some disturbances and undesirable behavior of the mechanisms. Examples of these are slip control in hands [9,13,51], gravity compensation in elbow control [16,17], and coordinated control of a MDOF arm [53]. Currently, prosthesis control methods require that the amputee control all of the joint motions either directly or through a pattern recognition system. Any compensation for disturbances, changes in loading of the prosthesis such as held objects must be done by the amputee usually without the ability to sense these effects. Shared control helps compensate for these problems potentially decreasing the cognitive load on the amputee.

2.2.3.1 Hand control

Slip control uses sensors to detect object slip and readjusts the grip typically by increasing the grip force. Otto Bock has implemented a system in their SensorHand. It has met with mixed results. Some amputees do not like the prosthesis doing things that they did not command.

   Another area that might be considered shared control is putting control systems in the hand to help overcome the undesirable characteristics inherent in most prostheses. Since small motors are used in order to fit into the space constraints of the hand but high torques are required to grip objects reliably, high gear ratio transmissions are used. These high ratio transmissions have two undesirable characteristics, high friction and high effective inertia. The effects of these characteristics are the requirement of a high input signal to start the motion due to the friction and a difficulty in stopping the motion due to the high effective inertia. Nonlinear controllers such as sliding mode controller have been some to alleviate these problems. User prefer them over the conventional open-loop control and the ability to grasp such things as delicate objects in greatly improved [18,19]. Such controllers do require internal position, velocity, and force or joint torque sensors in the prosthesis that, unfortunately, are not usually used in clinical prosthetic hands.

2.2.3.2 Arm control

In above elbow prostheses, some motions such as reaching high is difficult if not impossible. The reasons are two fold. One, the socket can restrict the humeral motion and two, the control is difficult because of destabilizing gravity torques.

Better sockets or eliminating the socket (osseointgration) will alleviate the first problem and gravity and dynamic controllers can alleviate the second problem.

Gravity compensation is a standard method in robotics compensating for the torque effects of gravity in the controller allowing for smoother trajectory control. This has not been used in prostheses until recently. Gravity compensation requires the knowledge of the complete position of the limb and the direction of the gravity vector on all limb segments. The problem in prosthetic systems is knowing the kinematic state of the natural part of the system, the human. This requires sensing the amputee's residual limb and body positions and velocities. This can be done in the lab with goniometers or other sensors. These are not practical for clinical arm. With the advent of reliable and inexpensive IMUs, kinematic sensing can be done. Preliminary experiments using a non-drifting inclinometer [50] to sense the kinematics and a simple gravity compensator has shown increased controllability and increased user satisfaction in reaching tasks [16,17].

2.2.4 Lower extremity control

While most of the discussion in this chapter concerns upper-extremity prosthetics, this is not due to any lack of progress in lower-extremity prosthetics but rather due to the bias of the author in his research in upper-extremity prosthetics. Much progress has occurred in lower-extremity prosthetics. There are some different issues between upper- and lower-extremity prosthetics. Upper-extremity devices do not need the same strength and torque capabilities as the natural limb. This is not the case of a lower-extremity device. It must be able to support the weight of the person and have sufficient torques to lift the person up stairs and sit-to-stand motions. Powered lower-extremity prostheses have been slow in coming because of these issues. There are powered ankle/feet and knees now on the market [70,74], though the great majority of prostheses are passive with controllable damping of the joints. The control of lower-extremity devices also differs from the control of upper-extremity devices. Lower-extremity systems can benefit from the somewhat regular gait cycle of walking, whereas upper-extremity control is essentially random with no set patterns. The regularity of the gait does not hold when starting and stopping or when beginning to step up stairs or over uneven terrain.

Better control has been demonstrated in lower extremity prosthesis. Controlled damping prostheses have been shown to improve the gait but not in the cognitive load of the user [23,27].

The control of powered legs differs from the control of hands and arms in that direct control from the EMGs or other direct user commands are not usually used, but rather indirect signals such as the kinematics of the user are used to actuate the joints [21,34,35,36,70,74]. Lenzi et al. [34,35,36] have demonstrated a controller that can provide smooth transitions to stairs and the ability to step over objects.

2.3. *Prosthetic hardware*

There have been many advances in prosthetic hardware as well. Multiple degree of freedom hands are now available   [4,11,61,73,77]. Battery technology has provided higher energy density and lighter weights [80]. Efficient, brushless DC motors are now cheap enough to be used [75,80]. With the advent of inexpensive inertial measurement units (IMUs) and inexpensive but powerful microcontrollers, smart control of lower extremity prostheses continues to provide more natural and efficient gaits [21,23,27,34,35,36,74,75]. Several powered lower extremity prostheses are now clinically available including powered ankles and powered knees [34,70,74].

Robust touch and force sensors are being implemented on hands [13,51,67,75,78]. These can provide signals for sensory feedback to the amputee as well as provide signals for shared controllers for slip control or nonlinear controllers such as sliding-mode controllers that reduce the adverse effects of internal friction and high effective inertias of the motor-drive mechanisms of the prostheses.

3. Current Problems Limiting Prosthetics

There are still problems that have not been satisfactorily solved. The ability to control multiple degree of freedom prostheses lags that of the mechanical design. The mechanical design still suffers from continuing problems of efficiency, weight, and robustness. Touch and position/velocity sensors are not put on most prosthetic hands.

Most prosthetic control requires the amputee to control all aspects of the motion of the prosthesis. This greatly increases the cognitive load of the amputee, interfering with ease of use and control [23,53,69]. Methods of shared control and smart prostheses should help decrease the cognitive load on the user and, hopefully increase the controllability and utility of the prostheses.

Neural stimulation systems require transcutaneous power and signal transmission. Peripheral nerves are flexible and reside in soft tissues. This presents a daunting problem for the mechanical design of electrodes, connectors, and electronic packaging.

The greatest complaint from amputees is and has been that of comfort with the sockets and the weight of the prostheses. The best solution is to eliminate the socket. Osseointegrated attachments have been used for several years in Europe [49] and are now being implemented in the US.

4. What Next?

In spite of the advances in the last several years, the most commonly used prostheses are body-powered devices of a hundred year old design or, in the case of many upper-extremity amputees, no prosthesis. Will this change in the near future? For most amputees, the answer is probably no. The next generation prosthesis will, however, incorporate many of the results of the research of the past ten years. These include multi-degree-of-freedom control, sensory feedback, and shared control.

4.1. *Osseointegration*

The greatest complaint is still comfort with the sockets. The logical step is to use an osseointegrated attachment for both lower and upper extremities. While this does not involve neuro-systems, the implant can solve another problem of implanted myoelectric and neural electrodes, that of powering and transmitting signals transcutaneously. The efficiency of the transmission of power transcutaneously is low. The bandwidth of communication is also limited. A direct wired connection would alleviate these issues. The wires would be Implanted myoelectric sensors will wired to the prosthesis via the implanted connection [49].

4.2. *Control*

Implanted myoelectric sensors also allow for direct control of many prosthesis motions. For transradial and transtibial prosthesis control, most of the muscle are available and EMG signals provide the most direct control signal and implanted electrodes enable access to the deeper muscles. As most muscles are multi-articulate and muscle groups work in synergy to perform motions, the question is how to sort out the signals to provide a natural, proportional control of the prosthesis. Pattern recognition methods attempt to do this using a variety of signal processing methods. Most methods are very sensitive to variations in electrode placement, and day-to-day variations of the muscle [18,63]. A promising method is being developed by Segil and Weir [61]. They are using groupings of signals with principal components methods to provide proportional control of several degrees of freedom. The development of implantable electrodes accessing virtually every muscle in the residual limb opens the possibility of direct control of many degrees of freedom. This would enable a natural control with little relearning or high calibration requirements. All of which will lead to more reliable and robust control.

4.3. *Shared control*

Most control methods require the amputee to control all of the motions of the prosthesis directly. This requires that the user compensate for all disturbances such as grasped objects with unknown weight, or the changing gravity vector in different positions of the remnant limb and prosthesis. This increases the cognitive load of the user [23,69]. There have been several methods to alleviate the problem. Automatic grip control to adjust the grip when slip is detected as been shown to decrease the cognitive load [9,38]. There is evidence in human slip control that the reaction times are so fast as to suggest that it is more a reflex than a higher brain control [2,6,12,22]. This suggests that a shared control system should be used as an artificial reflex.

4.3.1. *Coordinated control*

Coordinated control of several degrees of freedom is the natural control for a human. This type of control is a standard in robotic control. Current control schemes do not incorporate a coordinated control but rather require the user to control each motion. Recent work has incorporated a coordinated control with success. End-point control which has been used in robotics control has met with approval in work on the DEKA arm [53].

4.3.2. *Kinematics/dynamic control*

We have looked at using measurements of the remnant limb motions along with knowledge of the prosthetic limb positions to provide a gravity compensation control of a prosthetic elbow. When doing reaching motions with an arm, the gravity torques of the prosthesis can change from a stabilizing torque when the humerus is vertical (down) to a destabilizing torque when the humerus is extended at 90 degrees - the prosthesis is essentially an inverted pendulum in this position. The use of a simple compensation to remove the gravity torques in these positions has been shown to increase the controllability and increase the ease of the control [16,17]. The remnant limb kinematics were measured using a non- integrating inclinometer attached to the humerus [50].

4.3.3. *Electrode materials*

A problem with current electrode materials is the mismatch between the mechanical properties of the electrode and the mechanical properties of the nerve. Stiff materials are needed to penetrate the epineurium of the nerve, However, flexible materials are needed to match the modulus of the fascicle to prevent damage and motion between the electrode and the neuron.

Several researchers are investigating materials that change their stiffness in time [3,28,32]. If successful, these ideas will solve a major problem with intrafascicular electrodes.

4.3.4. *Transcutaneous power and communications*

Both power and signals must be transmitted from the surface of the skin to implanted electronics. Radio frequency signals have been used for this but the efficiency is low. Improvements are being developed and should be tested clinically in the near future [5,8].

4.4. *The new state of the art prosthesis*

The ideal prosthesis should seamlessly incorporate peripheral nerve stimulation for touch and proprioception and hybrid control from the detection of motor neurons the missing muscles along with implanted EMG of remaining muscles. Complex methods such as pattern recognition would not be needed as sufficient signals would be available for direct control. If sensory feedback is not possible for the detection of slip of objects, then a shared controller would be used to replace this reflex. The load on the limb is detected by the strain on the muscles in the natural arm. Since these muscles are missing or not connected to the load, this sensation must be replaced by nerve stimulation otherwise a shared control should be used to provide gravity compensation or dynamic compensation.

Here is a prediction of the next stage of the art prosthesis - both upper and lower extremity. It will have:

1. Osseointegration to eliminate the socket and also to eliminate the transcutaeous transmission of power and signals to neural and imbedded EMG sensors and electrodes;
2. Multiple subcutaneous EMG electrodes to monitor all of the muscles;
3. Direct control of the MDOF motions using the multiple EMG signals;
4. Sensing of the motor neurons of the missing muscle. These will be combined with the EMG signals for a hybrid proportional control;
5. Variable stiffness electrodes that allow for easy insertion in the nerve bundles which then soften to allow compliance with the nerve;
6. Permanent peripheral nerve stimulation for haptic and proprioceptive sensation;
7. Sensors in the prosthesis to detect slip to provide a shared control of the grasp;

8.   Sensors to measure the kinematics of the amputee - position, velocity, and acceleration of the remnant limb and motion of the body to compensate for disturbances such as destabilizing gravity and other torques.

When will this happen? In the 11 years since the first edition of the book, the primary upper-extremity arms and hands are still the Otto Bock hands and the Motion Control Utah Arms and hands with simple grasps and few degrees of freedom. Multi-degree of freedom hands are on the market and are beginning to become more wide-spread. Micro-controller legs are in common usage as well as powered ankles. But in spite of all of this, the most commonly used systems are body powered or passive. A major challenge is how to make advanced systems available to the majority of amputees.

To quote Eugene Ionesco, "You can only predict things after they have happened."

References

1.   C. Antfolk, M. D'Alonzo, B. Rosén, G. Lundborg, F. Sebelius and C. Cipriani, Sensory feedback in upper limb prosthetics, *Expert Review of Medical Devices*, **10**(1), pp. 45-54 (2013).
2.   A.-S. Augurelle, A. M. Smith, T. Lejeune, and J.-L. Thonnard, Importance of cutaneous feedback in maintaining a secure grip during manipulation of hand-held objects, *J. Neurophysiol.*, **89**, pp. 665-671, (2003).
3.   R.V. Bellamkonda, S. B. Pai, and P. Renaud, Materials for neural interfaces, *MRS Bulletin* **37**(06), pp. 557-561 (2012).
4.   J. T. Belter, J. L. Segil, A. M. Dollar, and R. F. Weir, Mechanical design and performance specifications of anthropomorphic prosthetic hands: A review. *J. Rehabil. Res. Dev.* 50(5), pp. 599-618 (2013).
5.   H. Bhamra, Y.-J. Kim, J. Joseph, J. Lynch, O. Z. Gall, H. Mei, C. Meng, J.-W. Tsai, and P. Irazoqui, A 24 μW, batteryless, crystal-free, multinode synchronized SoC bionode for wireless prosthesis control. *IEEE Journal of Solid-State Circuits,* **50**(11), pp. 2714-2727 (2015).
6.   I. Birznieks, M. K. O. Burstedt, B. B. Edin, and R. S. Johansson, Mechanisms for force adjustments to unpredictable frictional changes at individual digits during two-fingered manipulation, *J. Neurophysiol.*, **80**, pp. 1989-2002 (1998).
7.   T. Boretius, J. Badia, A. Pascual-Font, M. Schuettler, X. Navarro, K. Yoshida, and Thomas Stieglitz, A transverse intrafascicular multichannel electrode (TIME) to interface with the peripheral nerve, *Biosensors and Bioelectronics*, **26**(1), pp. 62-69 (2010).
8.   E. Y Chow, A. Kahn, and Pedro P. Irazoqui, High data-rate 6.7 Ghz wireless asic transmitter for neural prostheses, *29th Annual International Conference of the Engineering in Medicine and Biology Society, 2007.*
9.   C. Cipriani, F. Zaccone, S. Micera, and M. C. Carrozza, On the shared control of an EMG-controlled prosthetic hand: analysis of user–prosthesis interaction. *IEEE Transactions on Robotics,* **24**(1), pp. 170-184 (2008).

10. G. Clark et al., Using multiple high-count electrode arrays in human median and ulnar nerves to restore sensorimotor function after previous transradial amputation of the hand, *36th Annual International Conference of the Engineering in Medicine and Biology Society, 2014*.

11. R. G. E. Clement, K. E. Bugler, and C. W. Oliver, Bionic prosthetic hands: A review of present technology and future aspirations, *The Surgeon*, **9**(6), pp. 336-340 (2011).

12. K. J. Cole and J. H. Abbs, Grip force adjustments evoked by load force perturbations of a grasped object, *J. Neurophysiol.* **60**(4), pp. 1513-1522 (1988).

13. D. P. J. Cotton, P. H. Chappell, A. Cranny, N. M. White and S. P. Beeby, A novel thick-film piezoelectric slip sensor for a prosthetic hand, *IEEE Sensors Journal*, **7**(5), pp. 752-761 (2007).

14. G. S. Dhillon, S. M. Lawrence, D. T. Hutchinson, and K. W. Horch, Residual function in peripheral nerve stumps of amputees: implications for neural control of artificial limbs, *The Journal of Hand Surgery*, **29**(4), pp. 605-615 (2004).

15. G. S. Dhillon, and K. W. Horch, Direct neural sensory feedback and control of a prosthetic arm, *IEEE Transactions on Neural Systems and Rehabilitation Engineering*, **13**(4), pp. 468-472 (2005).

16. J. M. Dotterweich and S. G. Meek, Gravity compensation of an above-elbow prosthetic arm, *36th Annual International Conference of the Engineering in Medicine and Biology Society, 2014*.

17. J. M. Dotterweich, Control improvement of an above elbow prosthetic limb utilizing torque compensation and reaching test analysis, *Dissertation*, The University of Utah, 2015.

18. E. D. Engeberg and S. G. Meek, Adaptive sliding mode control for prosthetic hands to simultaneously prevent slip and minimize deformation of grasped objects, *IEEE/ASME Transactions on Mechatronics*, **18**(1), pp. 376-385 (2013).

19. E. D. Engeberg, S. G. Meek, and M. A. Minor, Hybrid force–velocity sliding mode control of a prosthetic hand. *IEEE Transactions on Biomedical Engineering*, **55**(5), pp. 1572-1581 (2008).

20. M. Gasson, B. Hutt, I. Goodhew, P. Kyberd and K. Warwick, Invasive neural prosthesis for neural signal detection and nerve stimulation, *International Journal of Adaptive Control and Signal Processing*, **19**(5) pp. 365-375 (2005).

21. Geeroms, Joost, et al. Ankle-knee prosthesis with powered ankle and energy transfer for CYBERLEGs α-prototype, *2013 IEEE International Conference on Rehabilitation Robotics*.

22. L. M. Harrison, M. J. Mayston, and R. S. Johansson, Reactive control of precision grip does not depend on fast transcortical reflex pathways in X-linked Kallmann subjects, *Journal of Physiology*, **527**(3), pp. 641-652 (2000).

23. B. W. Heller, D. Datta, and J. Howitt, A pilot study comparing the cognitive demand of walking for transfemoral amputees using the Intelligent Prosthesis with that using conventionally damped knees, *Clinical Rehabilitation*, **14**(5), pp. 518-522 (2000).

24. K. Horch, S. Meek, T. G. Taylor, and D. T. Hutchinson, Object discrimination with an artificial hand using electrical stimulation of peripheral tactile and proprioceptive pathways with intrafascicular electrodes, *IEEE Transactions on Neural Systems and Rehabilitation Engineering*, **19**(5), pp. 483-489 (2011).

25. R. B. Jerard, and S. C. Jacobsen, Laboratory evaluation of a unified theory for simultaneous multiple axis artificial arm control, *Journal of Biomechanical Engineering*, **102**(3), pp. 199-207 (1980).

26. X. Jia, M. A. Koenig, X. Zhang, J. Zhang, T. Chen, and Z. Chen, Residual motor signal in long-term human severed peripheral nerves and feasibility of neural signal-controlled artificial limb, *The Journal of Hand Surgery*, **32**(5), pp. 657-666 (2007).

27. J. L. Johansson, D. M. Sherrill, P. O. Riley, P, Bonato, and H. Herr, A clinical comparison of variable-damping and mechanically passive prosthetic knee devices, *American Journal of Physical Medicine & Rehabilitation*, **84**(8), pp. 563-575 (2005).

28. D.-H. Kim, J. Viventi, J. J. Amsden, J. Xiao, L. Vigeland, Y.-S. Kim, J. A. Blanco, B. Panilaitis, E. S. Frechette, D. Contreras, D. L. Kaplan, F. G. Omenetto, Y. Huang, K.-C. Hwang, M. R. Zakin, B. Litt and J. A. Rogers, Dissolvable films of silk fibroin for ultrathin conformal bio-integrated electronics, *Nature Materials* **9**(6), pp. 511-517 (2010).

29. T. A. Kuiken, G. Li, B. A. Lock, R. D. Lipschutz, L. A. Miller, K. A. Stubblefield, and K. B. Englehart, Targeted muscle reinnervation for real-time myoelectric control of multifunction artificial arms, *JAMA* **301**, (6), pp. 619-628 (2009).

30. T. A. Kuiken, Estimation of the world-wide number of TMR procedures, *Personal Communication,* (2016).

31. S. P. Lacour, J. J. Fitzgerald, N. Lago, E. Tarte, S. McMahon, and J. Fawcett, Long micro-channel electrode arrays: a novel type of regenerative peripheral nerve interface, *IEEE Transactions on Neural Systems and Rehabilitation Engineering,* **17**(5), pp. 454-460 (2009).

32. N. Lago, K. Yoshida, K. P. Koch, and X. Navarro, Assessment of biocompatibility of chronically implanted polyimide and platinum intrafascicular electrodes, *IEEE Transactions on Biomedical Engineering,* **54**(2), pp. 281-290 (2007).

33. N. Lago, D. Ceballos, F. J Rodríguez, T. Stieglitz, and X. Navarro, Long term assessment of axonal regeneration through polyimide regenerative electrodes to interface the peripheral nerve, *Biomaterials,* **26**(14), pp. 2021-2031 (2005).

34. T. Lenzi et al., Design and preliminary testing of the RIC hybrid knee prosthesis, *37th Annual International Conference of the Engineering in Medicine and Biology Society*, 2015.

35. T. Lenzi, L. J. Hargrove, and J. W. Sensinger, Minimum jerk swing control allows variable cadence in powered transfemoral prostheses, *Annual International Conference of the IEEE Engineering in Medicine and Biology Society,* 2014.

36. T. Lenzi, L. J. Hargrove, and J. W. Sensinger, Preliminary evaluation of a new control approach to achieve speed adaptation in robotic transfemoral prostheses, *IEEE/RSJ International Conference on Intelligent Robots and Systems*, 2014.

37. G. Lind, C. E. Linsmeier, J. Thelin and J. S., Gelatine-embedded electrodes—a novel biocompatible vehicle allowing implantation of highly flexible microelectrodes, *Journal of Neural Engineering,* **7**(4), art. 046005 (2010).

38. P. D. Marasco, K. Kim, J. E. Colgate, M. A. Peshkin, and T. A. Kuiken, Robotic touch shifts perception of embodiment to a prosthesis in targeted reinnervation amputees, *Brain,* **134**(3), pp. 747-758 (2011).

39. S. G. Meek, J. E. Wood, and S. C. Jacobsen, Model-based, multi-muscle EMG control of upper-extremity prostheses, In: *Multiple muscle systems*, eds. J. M. Winters and S. L.-Y. Woo, (Springer, New York), 1990, pp. 360-376.

40. D. R. Merrill, J. Lockhart, P. R. Troyk, R. F. Weir and D. L. Hankin, Development of an implantable myoelectric sensor for advanced prosthesis control, *Artificial Organs,* **35**(3), pp. 249-252 (2011).

41. S. Micera, L. Citi, J. Rigosa, J. Carpaneto, S. Raspopovic, G. Di Pino, L. Rossini, K. Yoshida, L. Denaro, P. Dario, and P. M. Rossini, Decoding information from neural signals recorded using intraneural electrodes: toward the development of a neurocontrolled hand prosthesis, *Proceedings of the IEEE,* **98**(3), pp. 407-417 (2010).

42. S. Micera, M. Carrozza, L. Beccai, F. Vecchi, and P. Dario, Hybrid bionic systems for the replacement of hand function, *Proceedings of the IEEE*, **94**(9), pp. 1752-1762 (2006).

43. S. Micera, X. Navarro, J. Carpaneto, L. Citi, O. Tonet, P. M. Rossini, M. C. Carrozza, K. P. Hoffmann, M. Vivo, K. Yoshida, and P. Dario, On the use of longitudinal intrafascicular peripheral interfaces for the control of cybernetic hand prostheses in amputees, *IEEE Transactions on Neural Systems and Rehabilitation Engineering*, **16**(5), pp. 453-472 (2008).

44. S. Micera, J. Carpaneto, and S. Raspopovic, Control of hand prostheses using peripheral information, *IEEE Reviews in Biomedical Engineering*, **3**, pp. 48-68 (2010).

45. L. A. Miller, K. A. Stubblefield, R. D. Lipschutz, B. A. Lock, and T. A. Kuiken, Improved myoelectric prosthesis control using targeted reinnervation surgery: a case series, *IEEE Transactions on Neural Systems and Rehabilitation Engineering*, **16**(1), pp. 46-50 (2008).

46. A. Mingrino, A. Bucci, R. Magni, and P. Dario, Slippage control in hand prostheses by sensing grasping forces and sliding motion, *Proc. IEEE Int. Conf. Intell. Robots Syst.*, **3**, pp. 1803–1809 (1994).

47. X. Navarro, T. B. Krueger, N. Lago, S. Micera, T. Stieglitz and P. Dario, A critical review of interfaces with the peripheral nervous system for the control of neuroprostheses and hybrid bionic systems, *Journal of the Peripheral Nervous System*, **10**(3), pp. 229-258 (2005).

48. K. Ohnishi, R. F. Weir, and T. A. Kuiken, Neural machine interfaces for controlling multifunctional powered upper-limb prostheses, *Expert Review of Medical Devices*, **4**(1), pp. 43-53 (2007).

49. M. Ortiz-Catalan, B. Håkansson, and R. Brånemark, An osseointegrated human-machine gateway for long-term sensory feedback and motor control of artificial limbs, *Science Translational Medicine*, **6** art. 257re6 (2014).

50. A. J.Petruska and S. G. Meek, Non-drifting limb angle measurement relative to the gravitational vector during dynamic motions using accelerometers and rate gyros, *IEEE/RSJ International Conference on Intelligent Robots and Systems*, 2011.

51. G. Puchammer, The Tactile Slip Sensor: Integration of a miniaturized sensory device on a myoelectric hand, Otto Bock Austria, Kaiserstr. 39, 1070 Wien, Austria.

52. S. Raspopovic, M. Capogrosso, F. M. Petrini, M. Bonizzato, J. Rigosa, G. Di Pino, J. Carpaneto, M. Controzzi, T. Boretius, E. Fernandez, G. Granata, C. M. Oddo, L. Citi, A. L. Ciancio, C. Cipriani, M. C. Carrozza, W. Jensen, E. Guglielmelli, T. Stieglitz, P. M. Rossini, and S. Micera, Restoring natural sensory feedback in real-time bidirectional hand prostheses, *Science Translational Medicine* **6**(222), art. 222ra19 (2014):.

53. L. Resnik, S. L. Klinger, and K. Etter, User and clinician perspectives on DEKA Arm: Results of VA study to optimize DEKA Arm, *J. Rehabil. Res. Dev.*, **51**(1), pp. 27-38 (2014).

54. F. J. Rodríguez, D. Ceballos, M. Schüttler, A. Valero, E. Valderrama, T. Stieglitz, and X. Navarro, Polyimide cuff electrodes for peripheral nerve stimulation, *Journal of Neuroscience Methods*, **98**(2), pp. 105-118 (2000).

55. P. M. Rossini, S. Micera, A. Benvenuto, J. Carpaneto, G. Cavallo, L. Citi, C. Cipriani, L. Denaro, V. Denaro, G. Di Pino, F. Ferreri, E. Guglielmelli, K.-P. Hoffmann, S. Raspopovic, J. Rigosa, L. Rossini, M. Tombini, and P. Dario, Double nerve intraneural interface implant on a human amputee for robotic hand control, *Clinical Neurophysiology*, **121**(5), pp. 777-783 (2010).

56. M. Santello and J. F. Soechting, Force synergies for multifingered grasping, *Experimental Brain Research*, **133**(4), pp. 457-467 (2000).

57. M. Santello, M. Flanders, and J. F. Soechting, Patterns of hand motion during grasping and the influence of sensory guidance, *The Journal of Neuroscience*, **22**(4), pp. 1426-1435 (2002).

58. M. Santello, M. Flanders, and J. F. Soechting, Postural hand synergies for tool use, *The Journal of Neuroscience*, **18**(23), pp. 10105-10115 (1998).

59. E. Scheme and K. Englehar, Electromyogram pattern recognition for control of powered upper-limb prostheses: State of the art and challenges for clinical use, *Journal of Rehabilitation Research and Development*, **48**(6), pp. 643 (2011).

60. A. E. Schultz and T. A. Kuiken, Neural interfaces for control of upper limb prostheses: the state of the art and future possibilities, *PM&R* **3**(1), pp. 55-67 (2011).

61. J. L. Segil and R. F. ff Weir, Design and validation of a morphing myoelectric hand posture controller based on principal component analysis of human grasping, *IEEE Transactions on Neural Systems and Rehabilitation Engineering*, **22**(2), pp. 249-257 (2014).

62. C. E. Stepp and Y. Matsuoka, Relative to direct haptic feedback, remote vibrotactile feedback improves but slows object manipulation, *2010 Annual International Conference of the IEEE Engineering in Medicine and Biology Society*.

63. Z. Su, J. A. Fishel1, T. Yamamoto, and G. E. Loeb, Use of tactile feedback to control exploratory movements to characterize object compliance, *Front. Neurorobot.*, **26**, doi 10.3389/fnbot.2012.00007 (2012).

64. D. W. Tan, M. A. Schiefer, M. W. Keith, J. R. Anderson and D. J Tyler, Stability and selectivity of a chronic, multi-contact cuff electrode for sensory stimulation in human amputees, *Journal of Neural Engineering*, **12**(2), art. 026002 (2015).

65. R. F. ff Weir, P. R. Troyk, G. A. DeMichele, D. A. Kerns, J. F. Schorsch, and H. Maas, Implantable myoelectric sensors (IMESs) for intramuscular electromyogram recording, *IEEE Transactions on Biomedical Engineering*, **56**(1), pp. 159-171 (2009).

66. D. J. Tyler, Neural interfaces for somatosensory feedback: bringing life to a prosthesis, *Current Opinion in Neurology*, **28**(6), pp. 574-581 (2015).

67. N. Wettels et al., Biomimetic tactile sensor for control of grip, *IEEE 10th International Conference on Rehabilitation Robotics*, 2007.

68. R. W. Wirta, D. R. Taylor, and F. R. Finley, Pattern-recognition arm prosthesis: a historical perspective-a final report, *Bull. Prosthet. Res.*, **10**(30), pp. 8-35 (1978).

69. P. Wright, Cognitive overheads and prostheses: Some issues in evaluating hypertexts, *Proceedings of the third annual ACM conference on Hypertext*, 1991.

70. www.bionxmed.com/

71. www.blackrockmicro.com/

72. www.coaptengineering.com

73. www.dekaresearch.com/

74. www.ossur.com

75. www.ottobock.com/

76. www.rippleneuro.com/

77. www.rslsteeper.com/

78. www.syntouchllc.com/

79. www.touchbionics.com/

80. www.utaharm.com/

Chapter 4.2

Stimulation of the Spinal Cord for the Control of Walking

Ashley N. Dalrymple[1,2] and Vivian K. Mushahwar[1,2]

[1]*Neuroscience and Mental Health Institute, University of Alberta*
[2]*Division of Physical Medicine and Rehabilitation, Department of Medicine, Faculty of Medicine and Dentistry, University of Alberta*
5005 Katz Group Rexall Centre, Edmonton, Alberta T6G 2E1, Canada
adalrymp@ualberta.ca, vivian.mushahwar@ualberta.ca

This chapter surveys the different control methods developed for spinal cord stimulation to restore walking after neural injury or disease. We start by exploring the networks within the spinal cord that control or modulate walking. Next we introduce the different modes of stimulating the spinal cord: intraspinal microstimulation, epidural spinal cord stimulation, and magnetic spinal cord stimulation. Finally, we delve into the control strategies developed for these spinal cord stimulation methods to generate walking. Many of the control methods were inspired by the locomotor central pattern generator. Others took a more traditional control engineering approach by implementing non-linear control methods such as fuzzy logic and sliding mode control. The ultimate goal is to achieve effortless and natural walking that is adaptable and personalized to the user. Although this goal is a few years away from being realized, the integration of engineering, neuroscience, and rehabilitation is certainly the right approach.

1. Introduction

Functional electrical stimulation (FES) is a rehabilitative intervention that activates remaining neural tissue to restore a lost function after injuries of the central nervous system. FES may be a promising approach to restoring function, especially in combination with traditional rehabilitation and pharmacological intervention. In this chapter, we discuss FES approaches that target the spinal cord, as well as the control strategies that have been developed in order to restore walking using these modalities.

2. Natural Spinal Control of Walking

Before we discuss the different control methods used to generate walking by stimulating the spinal cord, we first discuss natural control mechanisms for locomotion that exist within the spinal cord. The spinal cord is not simply a passive cable that carries commands from the brain to the muscles. There are inherent cellular networks within the spinal cord that are capable of generating and modulating locomotor movements. In this section, we will look into the concepts of the central pattern generator, movement primitives, and spinal reflexes, in the context of locomotion control.

2.1. *Central pattern generator*

A locomotion central pattern generator (CPG) is defined as a neural network that is capable of producing coordinated and rhythmic alternation of flexor and extensor motoneurons in the absence of descending drive or afferent input [54, 98]. It resides in the spinal cord, and has been localized in vertebrates such as the lamprey [53], and is thought to exist in humans as well [34]. Over the past century, various models of the CPG network have been theorized, stemming from experiments performed most frequently in cats. In this section, we will only highlight a few of the more commonly discussed models, and limit the descriptions to basic overall function. The more complex models for the mammalian CPG have yet to be confirmed, nonetheless, they can be very useful in terms of control. As we shall see in a later section, the concepts and models of CPGs are often incorporated into the control paradigms used in spinal cord stimulation to produce walking.

2.1.1. *Half-centre model*

The half-centre model was proposed by T. Graham Brown in the early 1900s. He demonstrated that basic stepping movements could be produced by the spinal cord in the absence of descending motor control and afferent feedback in spinalized, decerebrate cats [25]. The half-centre model is the most basic description of flexion-extension alternation. In this model, neurons directly activate either flexion or extension motoneurons, and through inhibitory interneurons, suppress the motoneurons of the opposite function (Figure 1a) [26].

Suppose we want activation of extensors for the stance phase in the gait cycle. To achieve this, neurons would have to excite the motoneuron pools of extensor muscles, as well as inhibit the flexor muscles. This reciprocal inhibition is accomplished through two mechanisms: first by inhibiting the flexor motoneuron pools directly, and second, by inhibiting the neurons that directly activate flexor motoneuron pools. Switching from extension to flexion was thought to occur through a fatigue mechanism [26], whereby the drive from the extension neurons would slowly decrease, or fatigue. Once below a threshold, the inhibition of the flexors would cease and the flexors would now be active, and inhibit the extensors. The exact mechanism of alternation has been debated [54, 102], and still remains to be determined.

The description above discusses the alternation between flexion and extension of a single limb. There is also alternation between the two hind-limbs (assuming we are talking only about bipeds or the hind-limbs of quadrupeds). However, for simplicity, we will only mention the actions of a single-limb CPG.

2.1.2. Unit burst generators

The idea behind unit burst generators builds upon the half-centre model. It was developed in an effort to explain why some motoneuron pools were active during both flexion and extension phases of the gait cycle [138]. Unit burst generators are separate modules made of oscillators (half-centres) that control subsets of motoneurons, and the modules are coupled together to produce more complex patterns [51]. In this scheme, each joint has its own module, and the modules communicate through excitatory and inhibitory synapses (Figure 1b). A modification to the single-layer unit burst generator model was later made to separate a rhythm generator network from the units to accommodate observations from experiments called deletions [84, 140]. A rhythm generator behaves much like a clock timer function, and is responsible for the alternation between flexion and extension. This model allows for individual control of the joints as needed, in accordance with a desired rhythm.

2.1.3. Two-layer model

Various two-layer models have been proposed by numerous research groups [73, 80, 82, 123, 98, 99, 140, 141, 151]. The difference between these models lies in the number of interneurons and their connections between the layers. In each case, the top layer is the rhythm generator network as described above. The second layer is the pattern formation network, which is responsible for the selection of the motoneuron pools. Burke [28] had proposed a 3-layer CPG where the third layer includes last-order interneurons before synapsing onto the motoneurons. Rybak and McCrea [98, 139] proposed a hierarchical two-layer model. The rhythm generator and pattern formation networks receive inputs from peripheral afferents

(Ia and Ib sensory fibers), as well as descending drive from the mesencephalic locomotor region in the brainstem and other cortical areas (Figure 1c). These inputs can modify the timing and/or the pattern of walking, such as changing the speed of locomotion or when walking on ice. The pattern formation network makes connections with a motoneuron level, which consists of Ia inhibitory interneurons and Renshaw cells, in addition to flexor and extensor motoneurons. This local neural network also has afferent feedback mechanisms and is involved in reciprocal and non-reciprocal interactions between the antagonist muscles.

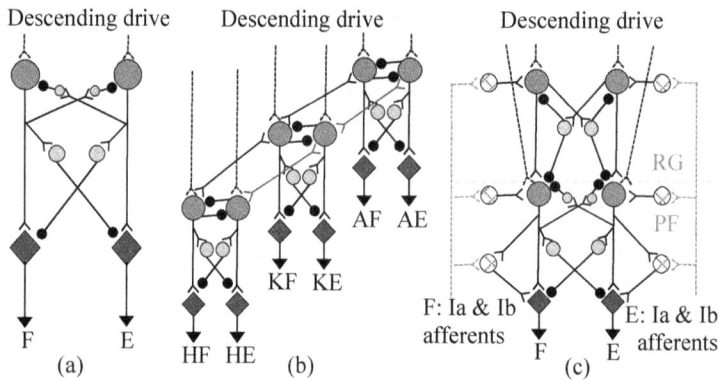

Fig. 1. Models proposed for the central pattern generator. Motoneurons are diamonds; interneurons are gray-scaled circles; neurons receiving sensory input have crisscrosses; excitatory synapses are arrow-like heads; inhibitory synapses are black circles; descending drive is darker hashed lines; sensory input is lighter hashed lines. (a) Half-centre model proposed by Brown [25, 26]. The interneurons are responsible for mutual inhibition to produce alternating flexion and extension movements. (b) Unit burst generator proposed by Grillner [51]. Each joint has its own half-centre. The units for flexion or extension are excitatory with one another, and mutually inhibit the other. (c) Simplified two-layer model proposed by Rybak and McCrea [98]. The top portion is the rhythm generator (RG) layer responsible for flexion-extension alternation, and the bottom is the pattern formation (PF) network responsible for limb movements to the motoneurons. Both layers receive descending drive and inputs from Ia and Ib sensory afferents.

2.2. Movement primitives

Movement primitives can be thought of as the building blocks, or modules, of motor behaviors [21, 44, 46]. It is thought that more complex movements are generated by combining movement primitives that lie in the intermediate gray matter of the lumbar spinal cord (lamina VII) [21, 19, 20, 43, 46]. Early experiments used intraspinal stimulation in decerebrate or spinalized frogs [21, 46]. The motor responses from the stimulation were characterized as force fields that converged to an equilibrium point [19, 46]. Moreover, the force fields were almost identical to the behaviors elicited from mechanical cutaneous stimulation

[162]. Chemical stimulation by applying focal NMDA iontophoresis into the spinal cord revealed seven different muscle synergies [144]. When pairs of sites were simultaneously electrically stimulated, the response was a vectorial summation of the responses seen in the two individual sites [89, 120]. These experiments led to the hypothesis that in the spinal cord lies circuitry that defines certain motor behaviors, or movement primitives, that can be summated to make more complex motor patterns [21, 120]. Recordings of neurons in the frog spinal cord revealed that cutaneous and intermediate zone neurons are related to premotor drive [62].

It has been shown; however, that there are some inconsistencies with the movements generated by stimulating in the intermediate gray matter. For example, if the limb is placed in a particular location in space and stimulation is applied, the movement generated is different from the movement produced if the limb was initially placed in a different starting location [21]. It has also been reported that increasing the stimulation amplitude ($>12\mu A$) changes the response generated [4, 46, 89, 112, 152], possibly due to current spread in the tissue to other nearby networks. In chronically spinalized rats, the majority of responses moved the limb towards the body [161]. Frequently after cessation of the stimulation, the movements continued, sometimes changing magnitude or direction [88, 90, 161]. A study by Mushahwar and colleagues [112] tested the movement primitives hypothesis in cats under varying conditions of descending drive: anesthetized, decerebrate, and spinalized. They noted that under anesthesia the movements generated were similar to those generated by the nearby motoneuron pools. Additionally, acute decerebration and spinalization drastically changed the evoked responses, particularly the direction of the movements. There is also a lack of vectorial summation of responses in the decerebrate cat [90]. Instead of producing a response that is a combination of the two sites stimulated, the response generated was the same as one or the other of the sties.

For a neural prosthesis, electrically-evoked responses have to be consistent and predictable, not only for reliability but also for safety and acceptability of the device. Stimulation in the intermediate gray matter may be a good tool for investigating spinal mechanisms and circuitry, but may not be suitable for a neural prosthesis. However, combining intermediate spinal cord stimulation with other methods of spinal cord stimulation that are more rhythmic (like a CPG) could be used for generating basic gait patterns [45]. The notion of movement primitives and hierarchical activation may also be a useful control technique that could be adopted by a neuroprosthesis [124].

2.3. *Spinal reflexes*

Spinal reflexes can play a role in the modification of locomotion. Their influence is state-dependent, meaning that the reaction produced by the reflex can be different for the different phases of the gait cycle. First, we will describe each spinal reflex, and follow with their relevance to locomotion.

2.3.1. *The stretch reflex*

The stretch reflex, also known as the myotatic reflex, is a monosynaptic spinal reflex [27, 131, 143]. Its purpose is to regulate muscle length. When a muscle is stretched, such as when a person is holding an object, the intrafusal muscle fibers are also stretched, activating type Ia muscle spindle afferents. These afferents travel to the spinal cord, where they make direct excitatory synapses onto the α-motoneurons of the same (homonymous) muscle. The Ia afferents also make a polysynaptic connection to the α -motoneurons of the antagonist muscles via reciprocal inhibition. The result is a contraction of the stretched muscle, and relaxation of the antagonist muscle.

2.3.2. *The Golgi tendon reflex*

The Golgi tendon reflex serves the purpose of protecting the muscles from extreme loads that could cause damage or tearing of the muscle fibers [27, 131, 143]. Its actions are the reverse of the stretch reflex. When a muscle contracts, such as when a load is applied, the tendons in series with the muscle experience tensile force, which is detected by Golgi tendon organs. The Ib afferents from the Golgi tendon organs travel to the spinal cord where they synapse onto Ib inhibitory interneurons, that then synapse onto the homonymous muscles' α-motoneurons, ultimately inhibiting the muscles. The afferents also cause indirect excitation of the antagonist muscles' α-motoneurons. This mechanism is useful when the muscle is generating extremely large forces, such as when a person is lifting an exceptionally heavy object, as it inhibits the muscle before serious damage can be done. It is interesting to note that during instances of smaller levels of loading, the Golgi tendon reflex helps maintain constant muscle force by counteracting small changes in tension.

2.3.3. *Flexor-withdrawal reflex*

The flexor-withdrawal reflex is a polysynaptic reflex that is activated in response to a painful stimulus [27, 131, 143]. Imagine what happens when you unexpectedly touch a hot surface. Your first reaction is to quickly pull your arm away from the surface. This reaction is due to the flexor-withdrawal reflex, which causes activation of the flexor muscles, and reciprocal inhibition of the extensor muscles. It is yet another protective reflex, since by traversing directly through spinal pathways, it can cause a fast escape from the painful stimulus. It is shortly after this reflex response that you experience the pain associated with the stimulus, as this requires the stimulus to travel via longer, cortical pathways.

2.3.4. *Flexion-crossed extension reflex*

The flexion-crossed extension reflex is an expansion of the above described flexor-withdrawal stimulus. In reaction to a painful stimulus, such as stepping on a sharp object, the flexor-withdrawal reflex is triggered in that leg. Specifically, the ipsilateral flexor muscles are activated, and the extensor muscles are inhibited [27, 131, 143]. This reaction is paired with the opposite activation pattern in the contralateral leg, where the extensor muscles are activated, and the flexor muscles are inhibited. Hence the name flexion-crossed extension reflex. The end result is the limb that has experienced the painful stimulus is retracted from said stimulus, and postural support is maintained by transitioning the body's weight onto the contralateral limb that is extended.

2.3.5. *Reflexes and locomotion*

Sherrington proposed in that spinal reflexes were responsible for producing gait [147]. Specifically, he suggested that proprioceptive stimuli are responsible for an alternating reflex composed of flexion and extension, and that alternation is achieved through a refractory period of the responses. He believed that the flexion phase was equivalent to the nociceptive-induced flexor withdrawal response and the contralateral limb's extension phase equivalent to the crossed-extension part of the reflex. However, stronger evidence supporting the existence of inherent spinal circuitry for locomotion led to the pursuit of the CPG [52, 91, 184].

There is evidence for spinal reflexes playing important roles during locomotion, either to facilitate loading and posture during certain states, or to provide a corrective response to perturbations during locomotion. For instance, the stretch reflex has been shown to assist weight-bearing during the stance phase of gait in cats [2] and humans [29]. Ib afferents from the Golgi tendon organs have been shown to reverse their role of inhibition to excitation during locomotion in the cat [126] and humans [153], suggesting that the Ib afferents in extensor muscles largely contribute to weight support and postural responses during stance [178]. Moreover, the Golgi tendon organ reflex can regulate and modify the timing and rhythm of the step cycle [125]. Electrical stimulation of Ib afferents in a decerebrate cat's extensor nerves resulted in a prolonged stance phase during treadmill locomotion [176].

Forssberg [40] was the first to assess the functional role of cutaneous reflexes during locomotion by combining kinematics and neural responses. He electrically and mechanically stimulated the dorsum of a cat's paw during the swing phase of locomotion, and observed a stumbling corrective response, where the perturbed limb continued past the obstacle in order to maintain stability. Prochazka [130] and Wand [174] demonstrated that the origin of the response is cutaneous afferents. This response was also elicited in people by stimulating the superficial peroneal nerve [170, 179]. Zehr and colleagues [179, 180] went further to investigate the role of cutaneous reflexes on locomotion by electrically stimulating various nerves in order to activate cutaneous afferents of the foot in humans. They found that during the stance to swing transition, tibial nerve stimulation elicited a withdrawal response, which allowed for the continuance of the intended swing phase. However, during late swing, the same stimulus generated a placing response, ensuring stability during the weight-transfer. During early swing, stimulation of the superficial peroneal nerve generated a stumble corrective response characterized by knee flexion, as if the limb was clearing an obstacle that made contact with the dorsum of the foot. Stimulation of the sural nerve has different effects for the swing and stance phases of gait. During swing, a withdrawal of the foot occurs through knee flexion and ankle dorsiflexion for an avoidance movement, whereas during stance the withdrawal is characterized by hip and knee flexion and ankle dorsiflexion, transferring the body weight to the unperturbed limb.

Reflexes during locomotion seem to make necessary adjustments to ensure stability, and may elicit different reactions for different phases of the gait cycle. From this we can say that reflexive reactions during locomotion are state-dependent. Reflexes are capable of optimizing reactions in a state-dependent manner, a fact that could be useful when designing a controller to restore walking using spinal cord stimulation.

3. Spinal Cord Stimulation

Spinal cord stimulation is a type of FES, and can be achieved through several different modalities, varying in their targets and location with respect to the spinal cord. Specifically, spinal cord stimulation can be achieved by placing electrodes intraspinally or epidurally, or more recently, using magnetic stimulation over the lower back (Figure 2). Each modality functions through different mechanisms, hence the control methods for each differs. We will first discuss intraspinal microstimulation, followed by epidural electrical stimulation, and finally, magnetic spinal cord stimulation.

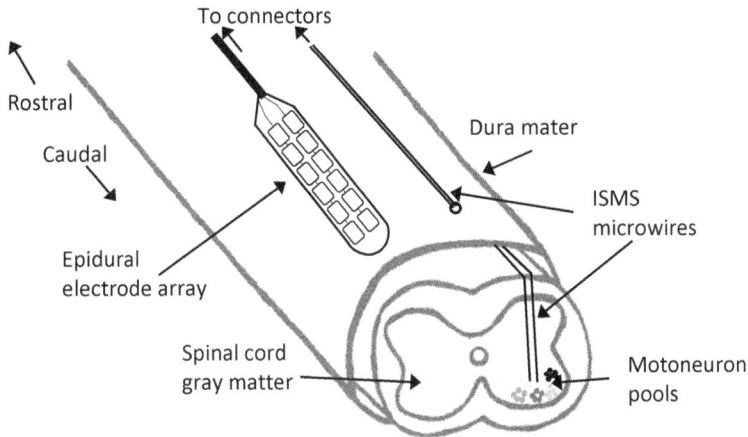

Fig. 2. Cross-section of the lumbosacral enlargement of the spinal cord. An epidural electrode array lies on the dorsal surface of the dura mater. The electrodes are the rectangular pads on the paddle. Intraspinal microwires (50μm) penetrate the spinal cord and target lamina IX of the gray matter, where the motoneuron pools are in close proximity (gray-colored dots). Anatomy and stimulation devices are not to scale.

3.1. *Intraspinal microstimulation*

Intraspinal microstimulation (ISMS) originated as a research tool to study spinal networks. Renshaw [134] stimulated in the spinal cord to measure the synaptic delay in reflex pathways. Later, mapping experiments were performed to investigate the connections between interneurons mediating reciprocal inhibition [71]. ISMS in cats showed that motoneurons can be activated directly if the tip of the electrode was adjacent to the initial segment of the motoneuron axon, or the soma itself [57]. As previously described, ISMS was used by Bizzi [21], Giszter [46], and colleagues to study the organization of spinal circuitry in the intermediate gray matter of bull frogs. More recently, ISMS in the ventral horn of the spinal cord gray matter has been explored as a possible intervention to restore walking after injury or disease. ISMS has been tested in various animal models, including but not limited to rats, cats, pigs, and monkeys. The majority of work investigating the use of ISMS to produce walking has been tested in cat and rat models.

3.1.1. Mechanism of intraspinal microstimulation

ISMS can selectively generate movements in muscles of the hind limbs necessary
for walking [111] using very small current (less than 150 µA) [66, 108, 142].
Selective activation of muscle groups is possible because the electrodes are
implanted into lamina IX of the ventral horn of the lumbosacral enlargement in the
spinal cord (Figure 2). Motoneuron pools for the lower limb muscles are in lamina
IX. Despite the close proximity to the motoneuron pools, ISMS likely activates
them indirectly through networks of afferent projections, propriospinal, and other
interneuronal pathways [10, 41, 115, 116]. Through these networks, ISMS can
selectively produce movements in individual muscles or multi-joint synergies with
a single electrode [66, 108, 113, 142].

3.1.2. Advantages of intraspinal microstimulation

By producing large forces, FES to date has provided the most promising restoration
of movements after neural injury or disease. FES can also improve bone and
muscle health [15], reduce spasticity [3, 22, 105, 149, 150], increase circulatory
function, and restore functions including respiration [157], bladder evacuation [23,
24, 100, 158], standing [7, 164], and even walking [36, 56, 60, 77, 83, 93, 154,
172, 175].

    There are three main advantages of ISMS over peripheral FES systems: The
ISMS implant is distant from moving muscles; the ISMS implant is small, and
contained within a localized region; and ISMS preferentially recruits fatigue-
resistant muscle fibers. Details of these advantages are as follows.

    The ISMS implant is distant from moving muscles [109]. Peripheral FES
systems involve activating peripheral nerve axons by stimulating through surface
or implanted electrodes. The electrodes can target nerves at the nerve trunk, motor
point, or at the muscle belly. An example of a surface peripheral FES system is the
Parastep (Sigmedics, Inc., Northfield, IL, USA) [30], which is the only FDA
approved walking FES system, and is primarily targeted to individuals with a
complete spinal cord injury (SCI). The Parastep activates knee and hip extensors
for the stance phase, and peroneal nerves to induce the flexor withdrawal reflex for
the swing phase. Peripheral FES systems that use implanted electrodes were
developed for use in people with both complete [56, 77] and incomplete [36, 60]
SCIs. Each system uses between 8 and 16 channels, distributed throughout the legs
and trunk muscles for stability. Results demonstrated standing times between 3-40
minutes [32] and walking up to 100 m [56] and 300 m [60] for complete and
incomplete SCI, respectively. Dutta and colleagues [36] added surface
electromyographic (EMG) recordings as feedback signals to trigger the stimulation

to restore walking. However, a study done by the Triolo group [164] involving 15 subjects found that their system was used primarily for exercise.

Surface peripheral FES systems require much effort donning and doffing the electrodes, while implanted systems are susceptible to lead breakage and dislodgement or shifting from the implant site due to the contractions of the muscles surrounding them [76]. However, an intraspinal implant, which is contained in the spinal cord, is not susceptible to dislodgement or lead breakage because it is distant from contracting muscles and moving joints [113]. There is the possibility of some shifting of the electrode locations due to extreme trunk movements and the relative motion between the spinal cord and the fixation point on the vertebral body; however, this possibility can be avoided by using strain-relief mechanisms such as coiling of the lead wires [160]. Thus, the possibility of ISMS electrodes being removed or broken due to physiological movements is substantially less than for peripheral FES systems.

The ISMS implant is small, and contained within a localized region of the spinal cord. The lumbar enlargement in cats is only 3 cm long, and 5 cm in humans. Therefore, the implant itself need only be 3-5 cm long in addition to a small connector that fixes the implant to a spinous process just rostral to the lumbosacral enlargement [142]. The number of implanted electrodes required to produce walking movements can be as few as four [142]; however, it is advantageous to implant more electrodes to achieve redundancy in responses, higher selectivity [66], and to deliver the stimulation in an interleaved manner [11, 12, 85, 110]. Interleaved stimulation entails stimulating through two electrodes targeting the same function at half of the desired frequency such that the combined frequency will be the desired frequency. For example, suppose there are two electrodes that target the quadriceps muscles to produce knee extension. Instead of stimulating through both electrodes at 50Hz, one could stimulate through each electrode at 25Hz, alternating between the two electrodes for a combined frequency of 50Hz. This has the advantage of recruiting different motor units at a lower frequency, thereby reducing fatigue of the muscles.

The entire ISMS system is implantable. Specifically, implantable wireless stimulators have been developed that can be fixed onto the same spinous process that the electrode lead wires are adhered to [48, 165]. They communicate and receive power via radio frequency to an external coil that lies on the surface of the skin over the implant area. Additionally, ISMS control strategies have been successfully implemented on an implantable microchip [96] that was used *in vivo* to produce walking [95].

ISMS preferentially recruits fatigue-resistant muscle fibers. ISMS has been shown to activate motor units in a near-normal recruitment order [10] to produce graded responses [142], largely due being located within the central nervous system and through trans-synaptic activation of motor units [41, 116]. Particularly at higher stimulation amplitudes, ISMS activates fatigue-resistant motor units [10], adhering to Henneman's size principle [63]. Because ISMS recruits motor units in a near-natural physiological order, it is capable of gradually generating force in the muscles as stimulation amplitude is increased. Force recruitment curves demonstrated that peripheral FES at the femoral nerve had a slope that was 4.9 times steeper than that obtained from ISMS targeting the quadriceps motoneuron pool [10].

Despite the tremendous outcomes of peripheral FES systems, people who use them experience rapid fatigue of their muscles and plateaus in strength [49, 77, 92]; thus limiting the use of these systems to exercise tools [164]. The fatigue in the stimulated muscles is due to an unnatural recruitment order of motor units [35, 92, 183, 163] that has been characterized as disorderly and synchronous with limited spatial-activation and favoring of fast fatigable motor units [16, 49, 92]. The functional consequences of fatigue can be seen by comparing standing times and distances walked using FES versus ISMS. For example, an 8-channel implanted peripheral FES system to produce standing in spinal cord injured subjects [32] achieved a range of 3-40 minutes of standing. In a cat model, ISMS produced an average of 20 minutes and up to 40 minutes of standing [85]. Note that the people had an assistive device available to unload some weight onto their upper body. Walking after complete and incomplete SCI using an FES system in people has accomplished up to 100 m [56] and 300 m [60], respectively. Conversely, ISMS produced nearly a kilometer of walking in a cat model [67]. For a person, this could mean walking to the grocery store and back. However, ISMS is limited by only having been tested in an animal model, yet the potential extrapolation from the accomplishments in the animal model to humans could mean an increase in functional capabilities for longer distances.

3.1.3. Stability of an intraspinal implant

With any implanted neuroprosthesis, it is imperative to consider the tissue's response to the implant, as well as to the delivery of electrical stimulation. The body has a natural tendency to reject foreign bodies, such as electrodes, largely due to mechanical mis-match between the tissue and the electrode [9]. The central nervous system reacts to a foreign body through an inflammatory response [50]. Acutely, capillaries and extracellular matrix are damaged from the mechanical insertion of the electrode [50, 128], and microglia are activated and surround the electrode [50, 97]. Chronically, astrocytes encapsulate the electrode [50, 156], ultimately increasing the impedance of the electrode-tissue interface [50, 166]. There is also some migration of neurons away from the electrode implantation site [17, 18]. This remains a challenge for any implanted device, and investigations are underway by many groups to reduce or inhibit the tissue's inflammatory response [for a review see 50].

However, up to 70 months after implanting deep brain stimulation electrodes, only mild gliosis along the track was observed [58], demonstrating that ongoing electrical stimulation in the nervous tissue did not induce an ongoing inflammatory response. Rats with a complete SCI received ISMS for 4 hours per day for 30 days developed a glial scar in the electrode tracks, and no decrease in neuron density near the electrode [12]. Furthermore, cats that had an ISMS implant for 6 months and stimulation 2-3 times per week had no lasting inflammation around the tracks, and no damage to nearby motoneurons [129]. The small inflammatory response seen after an ISMS implant could be due to the small diameter of the electrodes, the current injected is within safe limits [100, 101], and the electrodes are free-floating, as compared to tethered electrodes which can cause an increased tissue response [8, 9, 18].

Implant stability can also be indicated by the functional consistency of responses with a chronic implant, and after a SCI. Functional consistency refers to the movements produced by stimulating through individual electrodes, consistent force recruitment, and stabilization of the stimulation threshold. The movements produced by ISMS have been shown to be relatively consistent throughout a 6-month implantation period, where at least 67% (average of 80%) of the electrodes maintained the same responses [113] in intact awake cats. Thirty days following the implant, ISMS was still able to produce forces in a graded manner [12]. Shortly after implantation of the electrodes, the stimulation threshold has been shown to either increase (in cats) [113] or decrease (in rats) [12]. Although this seems contradictory, it is hypothesized that these differences are due to the different stimulation protocols performed in each study [8]. Whether the stimulation threshold increased or decreased after the implantation, responses steadied over time [113], and the stimulation amplitudes required to produced functional movements were always within safe limits [100, 101]. A cat with a chronic SCI and an ISMS implant maintained stimulation threshold throughout a 6-month period, and following the spinal shock, demonstrated consistent stimulation-evoked movements [117].

Taken together, chronic ISMS implants are safe, and can produce consistent responses throughout the implantation period, even after a SCI [9]. Although this technique is more invasive as it requires a laminectomy over the implant region, spinal surgery not uncommon following a SCI [39].

3.2. *Epidural spinal cord stimulation*

Epidural spinal cord stimulation (SCS) entails delivering electrical pulses to the dorsal surface of the spinal cord through electrodes that are implanted exterior to the dura mater (Figure 2). It was originally developed for the treatment of chronic pain [146], and is now a widely used clinical neuromodulation tool to treat pain [132, 159]. It has also been explored as a possible treatment for spasticity [13, 14, 33, 127, 135], with variable results [14].

3.2.1. *Investigations in animal models and humans*

A study by Iwahara and colleagues [70] demonstrated that epidural SCS in the decerebrate cat could elicit locomotion over a moving treadmill. Specifically, stimulation over the cervical enlargement elicited stepping in all four limbs, and stimulation of the lumbosacral enlargement elicited stepping in the hindlimbs only. Locomotor activity over a moving treadmill in the chronically spinalized cat was demonstrated using epidural SCS between the L4 and L5 spinal segments [42, 43]. In spinalized rats, rhythmic activity could be elicited, but typically only in a single limb for a short duration of time (<10 s), and required at least 5% of body weight support [69]. After an acute SCI only weak rhythmic movements that were not weight-bearing were generated in cats [118]. Similar results were seen in the acute spinalized rat [86], where stepping could only be achieved 3 weeks after the injury, and improved up to 6 weeks post-injury.

Dimitrijevic and colleagues [34] demonstrated that epidural SCS over the lumbar enlargement could generate rhythmic flexion and extension muscle activity in individuals with a chronic complete SCI in the prone position. Similar results were repeated using epidural SCS in other subjects with a chronic incomplete SCI during partial body-weight bearing therapy [64, 68], as well as in subjects with a chronic complete SCI in the prone position [43] and during manually-assisted treadmill stepping [103 - 104].

Recently, studies in human subjects with a motor complete SCI have shown remarkable results where, after training with epidural SCS, some voluntary function returns. A subject with an injury classified as AISA-B (motor complete, sensory incomplete) underwent 7 months of stand training in combination with epidural SCS [61]. At the end of the 7-month period, the subject was able to stand with minimal assistance for at least 4 minutes, and had recovered the ability to perform some toe extension, and ankle and hip flexion. This led to follow-up studies with additional participants (1 ASIA B, 2 ASIA A) [3, 133]. All participants underwent at least 80 locomotor training sessions before receiving an implant, then underwent standing followed by step training with epidural SCS after receiving the implant [3]. By the end of training, 3 out of 4 subjects were able to oscillate their leg between flexion and extension, and modulate the force produced during leg movement (one individual could not perform these tasks due to severe clonus). All subjects achieved full weight-bearing with minimal assistance [133]. Interestingly, the ASIA A subjects required less assistance for standing than the ASIA B participants (holding onto horizontal bars for balance versus elastic bands attached to a frame for assistance with hip extension). Stimulation parameters required for standing ranged from 25-60 Hz at 1-9 V, depending on the participant. Each participant's stimulation settings were non-transferrable to other participants.

3.2.2. *Epidural spinal cord stimulation combined with pharmacological activation*

Recent studies in completely spinalized rats have demonstrated that training combined with epidural SCS and pharmacological agents such as amine agonists can restore weight-bearing stepping over a treadmill in the presence of stimulation [31, 119]. Rats with staggered hemisection SCIs that were trained using a transition from treadmill stepping to intentional over-ground stepping in addition to the electrical and chemical stimulation regained full weight-bearing bipedal locomotion after 5 to 6 weeks [169]. Furthermore, an additional 2 to 3 weeks of training, the rats were able to avoid obstacles and climb stairs in the presence of stimulation.

3.2.3. *Mechanism of epidural spinal cord stimulation*

The precise mechanisms of epidural SCS have yet to be elucidated; however, many theories have been proposed, primarily based on the concept that the stimulation increases the excitability of the spinal cord. Many studies agree that epidural SCS could be activating intrinsic spinal networks, such as a CPG for locomotion [31, 34, 42, 43, 68, 70, 103] or for standing [133]. It has also been proposed that the stimulation enhances the response of spinal networks to sensory input associated with weight-bearing [69], especially proprioceptive feedback [103, 119] to control stepping-like patterns. Lavrov [86] suggested that after an acute SCI, epidural SCS assisted with the return of spinal reflexes, and only then could stepping be initiated. It is also possible that the increased spinal excitability in combination with training reactivates spared neural networks and enhances plasticity [61, 64]. In fact, remodeling of corticospinal projections and the formation of intraspinal and supraspinal relays that detoured an injury were identified after a dual hemisection SCI and volitional effort-based training [169]. These are promising results in the field of spinal cord regeneration and rehabilitation; however, this method of spinal cord stimulation offers little capacity for selectivity and control of spinal circuits needed to achieve weight-bearing over-ground locomotion.

3.3. *Magnetic spinal cord stimulation*

Recently, a non-invasive approach to stimulating the spinal cord to produce walking has emerged. Magnetic stimulation over the lumbar vertebrae, in combination with surface electrical stimulation of the sural nerve, has been shown to produce walking movements in healthy subjects [145]. EMG activity recorded from either the posterior deltoid during arm swing or the first dorsal interosseous during hand grip were used to control the frequency of the magnetic pulses delivered to the spinal cord as well as the frequency and amplitude of the sural nerve stimulation. The participants showed variation in the optimal stimulation site over the vertebrae: T12-L1, L1-L2, or over L2-L3. The reason for individual differences is unknown at this time, and is of interest since these subjects had an intact nervous system. The authors speculate that it may be due to differences in the subjects' posture or gait strategy.

The mechanism of magnetic spinal cord stimulation has yet to be elucidated; however, the authors propose that it likely activates spinal circuits in addition to non-selective activation of afferents in the dorsal roots through eddy currents. Specifically, they believe that large diameter propriospinal and cutaneous afferents are activated and drive the locomotor CPG. Stimulating the sural nerve activates the flexor-crossed extension reflex to enhance the walking movements.

4. Control of Walking using Spinal Cord Stimulation

This section describes the control methods that have been used to produce locomotor movements by stimulating the spinal cord. Also included are the control methods that were developed and tested using other stimulation modalities, such as surface or intramuscular stimulation (IMS), but were either intended to be used or led up to the control strategies for spinal cord stimulation. Some of the control strategies employed do not comply with traditional engineering control methods. Rather, they are physiologically-inspired, attempting to mimic the function of the CPG. We will start with the simplest control strategies, and work our way to more complex approaches.

4.1. *Feed-forward control*

Feed-forward control entails delivering stimulation in a pre-timed pattern with pre-set amplitudes to produce the desired movements. This is much like the concept of the CPG without sensory feedback, where there is an inherent timing mechanism that drives a pattern of movements of the limbs.

The simplest way to implement feed-forward control is to alternate between flexion and extension movements, which act as the swing and stance phases, respectively [55, 114, 142]. This alternation between flexion and extension can be thought of as the half-centre model of the CPG described above. This control strategy has been accomplished using IMS in cats [55] as well as using ISMS with as little as 2 electrodes per side of the spinal cord in intact cats [114] and 4 electrodes per side in spinalized cats [142]. The time spent in swing and stance for a single limb is 60% and 40% of the gait cycle, respectively [55, 59, 142]. Using this simple control method with very few electrodes, full weight bearing (ground reaction forces equivalent to 1.6 kg [142] and 3.71 kg [114]) and ample foot clearance (4.8 cm [114]) were achieved using ISMS. However, during IMS, maximum forces produced only reached 10-12% of the animals' body weight [55], which is insufficient for weight-bearing. Reasons for insufficient force include slipping and fatigue.

Another method of feed-forward control involves dividing the walking cycle for cats into 4 phases: F, E1, E2, and E3 [38, 47], which correspond to lift off to early swing, late swing to touch down, touch down to mid-stance, and mid-stance to push-off, respectively [177], and constitute 20%, 20%, 20%, and 40% of the step cycle, respectively (Figure 3).

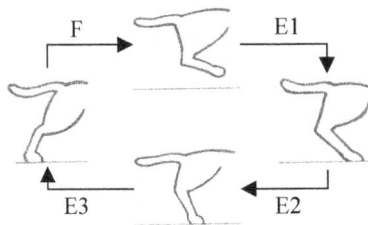

Fig. 3. The phases of the cat gait cycle with the proportion of time spent in each phase. Phases F (20%), E1 (20%), E2 (20%), and E3 (40%) correspond to lift off to early swing, late swing to touch down, touch down to mid-stance, and mid-stance to push-off, respectively.

Breaking down the gait cycle in this way is similar to the two-level CPG model, where there is still an inherent timing mechanism but the pattern of movements is separately produced. Each phase of the gait cycle can be produced separately by stimulating through a combination of ISMS electrodes, depending on their function. For example, E1 includes hip flexion, knee extension, and dorsiflexion, and can be accomplished by simultaneously stimulating through the electrodes that individually perform these movements. Once each phase is put together, they can be concatenated in a cyclical manner to produce a gait cycle.

However, this is only half of the story. Each limb needs to traverse the gait cycle, and the limbs need to alternate with each other while maintaining limb loading during weight transfer. Combining the 4 phases for each limb to achieve successful alternation of the limbs is accomplished by creating 8 states [66, 67, 94] (Figure 4). As shown in the figure, the proportion of time spent in each phase for an individual limb is maintained, with more time spent in the stance phases. Using ISMS [66], 5 of 12 walking trials were successful, as defined by traversing 55% of the walkway (2.5 m). The average sum of the ground reaction forces achieved were equivalent to 10.2% of the cat's body weight, attributed to peak forces that were sufficient for body weight support but periods of very little (4.1%) ground reaction force during weight transfer between the limbs. When this control strategy was implemented using IMS [94], 49% of the steps taken had sufficient body weight support (>12.5% body weight) and a step length less than 20 cm. The authors noted regions of hyperextension during the push-off phase. Since this is a feed-forward controller, it is not possible to make adaptations to the stimulation output to correct this. As we will see later section, adding sensory feedback can correct for hyperextension in real-time.

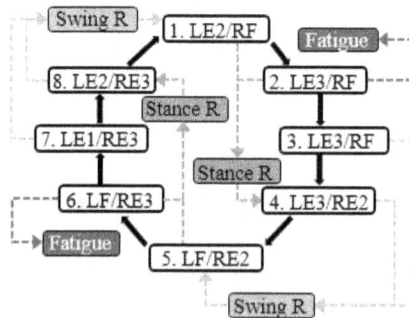

Fig. 4. The states of the gait cycle for the combined feed-forward and feedback controller. Feed-forward states are numbered in the white boxes. The phases shown are F: early swing, E1: late swing, E2: mid-stance, and E3: propulsion. Feedback can trigger safety rules that modify the timing of the state transitions: fatigue compensation rule (dark gray box-Fatigue), swing-to-stance rule (medium gray box-Stance R), and stance-to-swing rule (light gray box-Swing R).

4.2. *Feedback control*

A disadvantage of a feed-forward control system is that it is unable to respond to perturbations or changes within the system. Feedback from sensors allows for such modifications to the output. Different control strategies developed for ISMS have allocated different roles for sensory feedback. In this section, we will outline the pure sensory-based controller. By sensory-based, we mean that the transitions between the states of the step cycle only occur when particular sensory signals cross a threshold. Guevremont and colleagues [55] implemented two IF-THEN rules to accomplish state transitions in cats using information from force plates and accelerometers:

Stance-to-swing transition:

IF	ipsilateral limb is extended
AND	ipsilateral limb is unloaded
AND	contralateral limb is loaded
THEN	initiate swing in ipsilateral limb

Swing-to-stance transition:

IF	ipsilateral limb is flexed
THEN	initiate stance in ipsilateral limb

Criteria to indicate a successful walking trial included the ability to traverse 75% of the distance of the walkway, which was 3 m long, while maintaining appropriate range of motion and paw traction. Out of 157 trials using the sensory-driven controller, only 18 (11.5%) were successful. Reasons for failure included slips and misses that resulted in the paw losing traction with the walkway, double-unloaded stance where both limbs were fully extended behind the animal, standing, stepping in place (no forward progression), and poor limb movements. This controller was highly sensitive to parameter selection, especially since sensor thresholds were used to control state transitions. It is interesting to note that the intrinsically-timed controller only had a 15.5% success rate (15/97 successful trials), largely due to slips and misses, in-place stepping, and poor limb movements.

In another study, a neuromorphic silicon chip was developed to mimic the function of the half-center CPG [173]. It utilized four silicon neurons: one each for the left extensor, the left flexor, the right extensor, and the right flexor. Sensory inputs conveying information about the cats' hip angle and limb loading were relayed to the CPG network, and were used to initiate transitions between the swing and stance states. Many of the trials in these experiments failed due to the same reasons described above [55]. The authors also reported that the walking differed from normal walking. Specifically, the swing-stance ratio was much smaller than in normal walking, and because there were only flexion and extension states, the timing of the onset of different muscles was different from normal walking. Nonetheless, the stimulation was still able to propel the animal across the walkway. In the next section, we shall see that supplementing the intrinsically-timed feed-forward controller with sensory feedback results in more robust walking.

4.3. *Combined feed-forward and feedback control*

Mammals are constantly processing sensory information to accommodate their gait. Moreover, the CPG, which by itself is a feed-forward system, integrates sensory information from proprioceptive and cutaneous afferents, as well as descending information from visual centers and the cerebellum, to adjust the timing and pattern of walking. Therefore, it is logical to replicate physiological control mechanisms to control walking using ISMS. Guevremont and colleagues [55] proposed and tested this concept initially using IMS, and it was further developed and tested in simulation [96] as well as using both IMS [94] and ISMS [65 - 67] in cats. Each controller implemented a feed-forward control by generating intrinsically-timed walking. Feedback signals from force plates, gyroscopes, and accelerometers were then used to monitor the walking using various IF-THEN rules that interrupt and modify the feed-forward control. These rules are outlined below, and include rules that both adjust the transition times between the phases of the step cycle, as well as adapt the stimulation output to ensure sufficient weight-bearing.

Ground Reaction Force Rule: [55]

    IF   stance leg becomes unloaded

    THEN   terminate swing in contralateral leg

Rolling Rule: [55]

    IF   forward progression stops

    THEN   position each leg under body, stand, and push until start moving forward again

Safety Rule: [66]

    IF   insufficient load bearing

    THEN   hold leg in stance while other leg cycles through gait cycle until regain loading

Swing/Swing-to-Stance Rule: [66, 67, 94, 96]

    IF   hip is flexed forward beyond threshold

    THEN   transition limb to stance (E1 to E2)

Slip/Stance-to-Swing Rule: [66, 67, 94, 96]
    IF   hip hyperextends
    THEN   transition limb to swing (E3 to F)
Fatigue Compensation: [66, 67, 94]
    IF   force in propulsion is reduced
    THEN   increase stimulation amplitude next stance phase

A visual representation of the combined feed-forward and feedback control featuring some of the more widely used rules described above is shown in Figure 4. As the control strategies evolved, the rules became more fine-tuned for use in an ISMS neuroprosthesis. Although they are not often triggered, it is imperative to ensure safety and full weight bearing while maintaining efficiency of the walking.

Earlier we said that the rules used feedback from various external sensors; however, there is an exception. Holinski and colleagues [65] used feedback recorded from an implant in the dorsal root ganglia (DRG) at the L6 and L7 spinal levels to adapt ISMS-controlled unilateral stepping. A training phase consisted of matching information from external sensors to recorded neural afferent data from the DRG. The testing phase entailed interpreting the spikes from the DRG neurons as predictions for external sensor signals on-line in real-time. They found that the gyroscope could be predicted most accurately from the neural data, achieving a variance accounted for of 73±8%. In terms of successful rule triggering, the prediction of force yielded the highest number of successful activations (96.3%). This study demonstrates that an adaptable control system for ISMS to produce walking can be fully implanted (i.e., no need for external sensors on limbs).

4.4. *Volitional feedback control*

To control magnetic spinal cord stimulation, subjects used voluntary contractions of upper body muscles to adjust the frequency of the cord stimulation and the frequency and amplitude of stimulation to the sural nerve [145]. Healthy subjects were positioned on their side with the legs suspended. The EMG-controlled stimulation produced alternating EMG activity in the hip flexor and extensor muscles and walking-like movements that could be enhanced by adding stimulation of the sural nerve. Interestingly, continuous magnetic stimulation failed to produce walking movements in 8 of the 10 subjects. Three subjects were also held upright in a partial body weight support walking frame. At 47% body weight support, the subjects moved forward using walking-like movements. This study demonstrated that magnetic stimulation of the spinal cord could be controlled volitionally using EMG activity from any residual muscle. However, there are a few technological advances needed before this can be implemented as a take-home system, such as miniaturization of the magnetic coil. This could also be used as a rehabilitation tool after neural injury or disease.

4.5. *Non-linear control*

Fuzzy logic control and sliding mode control have been tested to restore movements using ISMS. First we will give an overview of fuzzy logic and sliding mode control methods, followed by how they were used and adapted to generate limb movements.

4.5.1. *Introduction to fuzzy logic control*

Fuzzy logic is a method of using values ranging between 0 and 1 as logical probabilities, depicting the inexact way of the world, making it closer to human thinking. In the context of control, fuzzy logic can incorporate expert knowledge [81, 87]. There are four main components to fuzzy logic control: fuzzification, fuzzy rules, implication, and defuzzification [137]. Fuzzification entails modifying the inputs by converting them from a numerical value into a linguistic value by association with a membership function so that they can be interpreted in the rule base. The fuzzy rules are a set of IF-THEN rules, and this is where the prior knowledge is stored. Fuzzy implication uses an inference engine to decide which rules are currently relevant and what the input should be. Defuzzification converts the fuzzy decisions to control actions.

4.5.2. *Fuzzy logic control and intraspinal microstimulation*

Fuzzy logic control has been used to control the ankle joint using ISMS in a rat model, with separate fuzzy controllers for dorsiflexion and plantarflexion [136, 137] aimed to track a target trajectory. Each controller controlled two electrodes, for a total of four electrodes controlling ankle movements measured by a motion tracking system. The average root mean square (RMS) tracking error using fuzzy logic control was 6.3° [136], with trajectory convergence in less than 1 s. The authors noted a 200 ms time delay in the neuromusckuloskeletal response to the stimulation in the spinal cord. To improve the transient response of the controller, a lag compensator was incorporated into the fuzzy logic control system [137], resulting in an average RMS error of 6.4°.

4.5.3. *Introduction to sliding mode control*

Sliding mode control (SMC) is a non-linear control method known for its accuracy, robustness to uncertainty, perturbation rejection, and simple implementation [168]. The goal of the control system is to track a desired trajectory or target by driving the system states onto a surface in the state space, known as the sliding surface [171]. Once the states reach the sliding surface, SMC forces the states to stay within a boundary along the sliding surface. Two steps are required to design a sliding mode controller: design of a sliding surface and selection of a control law that forces the system to track a desired state [167, 171]. The sliding surface depends on the tracking error along with some of its derivatives. The function defining the sliding surface is driven to zero, and in doing so should give rise to a stable differential equation. The sliding manifold is often in the form:

$$s = e^{(k)} + \sum_{i=0}^{k-1} c_i e^{(i)} \tag{1}$$

where k denotes the number of derivatives to be included, and should be $k = r - 1$, where r is the relative degrees of freedom of the input and output and c_i are positive constants. By steering s to zero, the error and its derivatives disappear in the exponential [79].

The next step is to select a control law that forces the state trajectory to the sliding surface and keep it in the vicinity of that surface by switching. For first-order SMC, the control is defined as:

$$u = -\kappa \cdot sgn(s) \tag{2}$$

where κ is the controller gain, and sgn is the sign function. The gain of the switching control must be sufficiently large in order to reject any uncertainties or perturbations in the system. However, this results in high-frequency switching across the surface. This phenomenon of oscillating about the surface is known as chattering [1, 148, 171] (Figure 5). It is undesirable because it causes excitation of the unmodeled high-frequency control components, which can lead to poor system performance or instability. One possible solution to solve the chattering problem is to replace the discontinuous *sgn* function with an approximation such as the continuous *sat* (saturation) or *tanh* (hyperbolic tangent) functions [171]. Unfortunately, these approximations can prevent the system from reaching convergence [1,78].

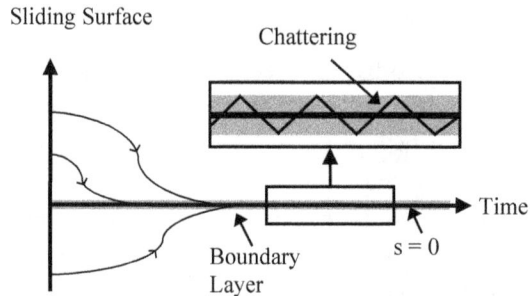

Fig. 5. The sliding surface s converges to zero from multiple initial conditions. Chattering is seen within the boundary layer.

4.5.4. *Sliding mode control and surface electrical stimulation*

Initial control strategies utilizing SMC were tested using surface electrical stimulation over leg muscles at the level of a single joint [1, 78, 121] for standing [79] and to produce walking [122]. Only later was it tested using ISMS [5, 6] and epidural SCS [75] stimulation.

SMC was chosen as a suitable control method for controlling electrical stimulation of muscle because stimulated muscle is non-linear and is subject to fatigue and other time-varying properties [1]. A neuroprosthesis needs to be reliable and stable with the changing conditions of the muscle. Control of the knee-joint angle was achieved by stimulating over the quadriceps muscles. In order to decrease chattering caused by the large controller gain, the authors sought to decrease the gain by decreasing the system uncertainty using an accurate model of the system. They proposed three modules to model the knee joint dynamics. The first module uses prior knowledge to represent the passive knee-joint dynamics. The second module represents the active component of the muscle dynamics. Finally, the third module represents the unmodeled dynamics. The uncertainties were modeled using a neural network, whose parameters were adjusted using gradient descent. Furthermore, they utilized a single-neuron controller instead of a saturation function to reduce chattering. By combining the outputs from the sliding mode controller and the neural controller, control of the knee joint was successful. This control method was tested in intact subjects and subjects with a complete SCI. Using a goniometer to feed-back the knee joint angle, they reported accurate tracking and reduced chattering in all subjects. Furthermore, the controller compensated for fatigue by adapting the stimulation output as needed.

Other variations of SMC were used to control the ankle joint angle by switching between stimulating the tibialis anterior and the soleus and gastrocnemius muscles

[78, 121]. To reduce chattering, both approaches used adaptive robust control to change the boundary around the sliding surface. The system uncertainties were modeled and tuned online based on Lyapunov stability analysis using measurements from input signals. Fuzzy logic was used to approximate the unknown non-linear functions used in the SMC. Kobravi and Erfanian [78] took a decentralized approach by using two different controllers for flexion and extension movements in order to reach a joint angle target. This approach was proposed because in order to coordinate several muscles in a task such as walking, the complexity of the control may be reduced by implementing a set of individual controllers. The interactions between the sub-controllers are simply taken as external disturbances to each isolated controller. This approach was tested in intact and paraplegic subjects. Tracking convergence was achieved after approximately 2 s. For a range of motion of 42°, the average RMS errors for over 90 trials for intact and paraplegic subjects were 3.2° and 3.4°, respectively. Nekoukar and Erfanian [121] did not use a decentralized control scheme, rather they used adaptive terminal SMC to adjust the ankle angle, which is known to achieve stability with a faster convergence rate. This system was tested in two paraplegic subjects. Tracking convergence was achieved after about 2s, with a RMS of 1.3°. Chattering was eliminated using this control strategy. Both strategies were able to track the ankle joint angle target in the presence of fatigue as well as external disturbances applied to the foot, maintaining an RMS error of less than 8° in both cases.

The decentralized adaptive controller developed by Kobravi and Erfanian [78] was used to control ankle joint movement in paraplegic subjects during quiet standing using surface stimulation [79]. The goal of this work was to replicate the ankle strategy used to maintain posture in intact individuals, thereby eliminating the need for the paraplegic subjects to hold on to an assistive device and freeing their arms for other tasks. The subjects were placed in a body brace to lock the joints above the ankles, and were suspended in a harness system for safety. The body's inclination angle was measured by placing a motion tracking sensor over the 3rd lumbar vertebrae, and was used as a feedback signal for the controller. Centre of pressure was also measured and used as for stability analysis. During independent quiet standing, the controller rapidly switched stimulation between ankle flexors and extensors to correct for body sway, maintaining a safe centre of pressure. An average RMS error of less than 2° for inclination angle and 10° for centre of pressure were maintained even with external disturbances induced by subjects lifting weights forward and backward during standing. Fatigue was, again, compensated for. After a few trials, subjects were able to stand for about 10 minutes before falling.

As seen with approaches such as the Parastep [30] and the implanted IMS walking systems [164] discussed above, users rely on their upper body for support and fatigue quickly. This motivated the development of new closed-loop control strategies for controlling the legs during walker-assisted FES [122], whereby the walking pattern follows a target trajectory to minimize the effort exerted on the upper body. A decentralized approach was used with two modules. Module 1 adjusted hip flexion and extension and knee extension using three controllers: one to control the joint angle trajectories, one to minimize the effort exerted by the upper body using a measure of handle reaction force, and the third to regulate the stimulation amplitude using fuzzy logic. The first two controllers used adaptive terminal SMC as described above for fast convergence and reduced chattering. Module 2 produced dorsiflexion or plantarflexion using two fuzzy logic controllers to modulate stimulation pulse width and amplitude. A walking reference for trunk, hip, knee, and ankle trajectories were obtained from a healthy male subject that walked slowly with the walker. The controllers were tested in complete SCI subjects. Surface electrodes were placed over the quadriceps, gluteus maximus/minimus, soleus and gastrocnemius, and iliacus muscles as well as over the common peroneal nerve. Feedback measurements included trunk, hip, knee, and ankle joint angles, ground reaction force, and handle reaction force for a single hand. Trajectory matching was aimed to be within one standard deviation of the reference joint angles. For all three subjects, the average RMS tracking errors for the hip, knee, and ankle joints were less than 7°. During swing there was ample foot clearance. The subjects only exerted an average of 12.05% of their body weight on the walker for stability, and could walk at approximately 0.55 m/s (the target speed).

4.5.5. *Sliding mode control and spinal cord stimulation*

Control of knee and ankle joints using ISMS in rats was realized using a combination of approaches discussed above [6]. Specifically, the system uncertainties of the system were obtained online using an adaptive law based on Lyapunov stability theory with fuzzy logic approximation of the non-linear plant functions. Chattering was further reduced using a neural sliding mode controller. The ISMS implant targeted knee and ankle flexors and extensors. Joint targeting was accomplished individually and coincidentally. Multi-joint control was accomplished using decentralized controllers; however, the authors noted that there was an interaction between the responses at the joints when more than one motoneuron pool was targeted as compared to individual responses. Nonetheless, the trajectory tracking for each joint during multi-site stimulation was robust, attaining average RMS errors of 1.8° and 2.8° for knee and ankle joints, respectively. Furthermore, longer trials of 7 min demonstrated robustness of the tracking to fatigue by adjusting the stimulation amplitudes accordingly (average RMS error = 1.9°). This controller was further tested using ISMS in the intermediate spinal cord of the rat to target movement primitives [5]. Although RMS error was not reported in this study, the tracking was not as accurate as with ISMS in the ventral horn of the gray matter.

SMC-based controllers have been shown to be extremely accurate in tracking joint trajectories using surface stimulation, ISMS, and epidural SCS. They are also robust to external disturbances as well as to muscle fatigue. However, this control method requires that a target trajectory to be known and available. This could be difficult to implement clinically since each individual would need a reference from a person that is of similar height and weight. Additionally, the users would need to have goniometers and possibly other sensors placed on their legs to provide feedback to the controllers.

4.6. *Intraspinal microstimulation in the cervical enlargement*

Although this chapter discusses the use of ISMS to control walking, this technique is now being investigated in the cervical enlargement to restore reaching and grasping after a SCI in both rat [74, 155] and non-human primate models [107, 181, 182]. Zimmerman and Jackson [181] induced hand paralysis by injecting a temporary paralytic muscimol in the primary motor cortex, and used signals from an implant located in the ventral pre-motor area to control the rate of stimulation delivered to the spinal cord to achieve a grasping task. In some cases, the muscimol did not fully paralyze the hand muscles, mimicking an incomplete SCI. In those cases, residual voluntary muscle activity was used to control the stimulation. Kasten and colleagues [74] demonstrated that cervical ISMS improved motor function, with benefits lasting beyond the stimulation trial. Cervical ISMS after incomplete SCI may promote long-term recovery of function, possibly attributed to axonal growth and elongation regulated by neural activity, synaptogenesis, and dendrite stability [106].

5. Conclusion

Various stimulation modalities targeting the spinal cord have been utilized. The modalities differ in both stimulation technique (magnetic or electrical) and target (surface, epidural, intraspinal). Many control methods have been proposed, ranging from simple open loop systems, feedback control, central pattern generator-inspired control, to non-linear control methods such as fuzzy logic and sliding mode control. All of these studies have the same goal: to target the spinal cord's remaining circuitry in order to restore walking after neural injury or disease. The control methods being developed for these stimulation modalities are all moving towards adaptability, personalization, and miniaturization, with great strides.

Acknowledgements

Work on intraspinal microstimulation was funded by the National Institutes of Health, Canadian Institutes of Health Research, Canada Foundation for Innovation and the US Department of Defense. AND was supported by a Queen Elizabeth II Graduate Scholarship and VKM was an Alberta Heritage Foundation for Medical Research Senior Scholar. The authors thank Jae Young Lee for helpful discussions on sliding mode control.

References

1. Ajoudani, A. and Erfanian, A. (2007) Neuro-sliding mode control with modular models for control of knee-joint angle using quadriceps electrical stimulation, *Conf. Proc. IEEE Eng. Med. Biol. Soc.*, 2424-2427.
2. Akazawa, K., Aldridge, J. W., Steeves, J. D. and Stein, R. B. (1982) Modulation of stretch reflexes during locomotion in the mesencephalic cat, *J. Physiol.*, **329**, 553-567.
3. Angeli, C., Edgerton, V. R., Gerasimenko, Y. P., and Harkema, S. J. (2014) Altering spinal cord excitability enables voluntary movements after chronic complete paralysis in humans, *Brain*, **137**(Pt5), 1394-1409.
4. Aoyagi, Y. Mushahwar, V. K., Stein, R. B., and Prochazka, A. (2004) Movements elicited by electrical stimulation of muscles, nerves, intermediate spinal cord, and spinal roots in anesthetized and decerebrate cats, *IEEE Trans. Neural Syst. Rehabil. Eng.*, **12**(1), 1-11.
5. Asadi, A. (2014) Inducing stepping-like movements by controlling movement primitive blocks using intraspinal microstimulation, *Intl. J. Soft. Comput. Eng.*, **4**(2), 2231-2307.
6. Asadi, A. R. and Erfanian, A. (2012) Adaptive neuro-fuzzy sliding mode control of multi-joint movement using intraspinal microstimulation, *IEEE Trans. Neural Syst. Rehabil. Eng.*, **20**(4), 499-509.
7. Bajd, T., Kralj, A., Sega, J., Turk, R., Benko, H., and Strojnik, P. (1981) Use of a two-channel functional electrical stimulator to stand paraplegic patients, *Phys. Ther.*, **61**(4), 526–527.
8. Bamford, J. A. and Mushahwar, V. K. (2011b) Intraspinal microstimulation for the recovery of function following spinal cord injury, *Prog. Brain Res.*, **194**, 227-239.
9. Bamford, J. A., Lebel, R., Parseyan, K., and Mushahwar, V. K. (2016) The fabrication, implantation, and stability of intraspinal microwire arrays in the spinal cord of cat and rat, *IEEE Trans. Neural Syst. Rehabil. Eng.*, [In Press].

10. Bamford, J. A., Putman, C. T., and Mushahwar, V. K. (2005) Intraspinal microstimulation preferentially recruits fatigue-resistant muscle fibres and generates gradual force in rat, *J. Physiol.*, **569**(3), 873–884.

11. Bamford, J. A., Putman, C. T., and Mushahwar, V. K. (2011a) Muscle plasticity in rat following spinal transection and chronic intraspinal microstimulation, *IEEE Trans. Neural Syst. Rehabil. Eng.*, **19**(1), 79-83.

12. Bamford, J. A., Todd, K. G., and Mushahwar, V. K. (2010) The effects of intraspinal microstimulation in the spinal cord tissue in the rat, *Biomaterials*, **31**(21), 5552-5563.

13. Barolat, G. (1988) Surgical management of spasticity and spasms in spinal cord injury: an overview, *J. Am. Paraplegia Soc.*, **11**(1), 9–13.

14. Barolat, G., Myklebust, J. B., and Wenninger, W. (1988) Effects of spinal cord stimulation on spasticity and spasms secondary to myelopathy, *Appl. Neurophysiol.*, **51**(1), 29–44.

15. Belanger, M., Stein, R. B., Wheeler, G. D., Gordon, T. and Leduc, B. (2000) Electrical stimulation: can it increase muscle strength and reverse osteopenia in spinal cord injured individuals?, *Arch. Phys. Med. Rehabil.*, **81**(8), 1090-1098.

16. Bickel, C. S., Gregory, C. M., and Dean, J. C. (2011) Motor unit recruitment during neuromuscular electrical stimulation: a critical appraisal, *Eur. J. Appl. Physiol.*, **111**(10), 2399–2407.

17. Biran, R., Martin, D. C., and Tresco, P. A. (2005) Neuronal cell loss accompanies the brain tissue response to chronically implanted silicon microelectrode arrays, *Exp. Neurol.*, **195**(1), 115-126.

18. Biran, R., Martin, D. C., and Tresco, P. A. (2007) The brain tissue response to implanted silicon microelectrode arrays is increased when the device is tethered to the skull., *J. Biomed. Mater. Res. A*, **82**(1), 169-178.

19. Bizzi, E., Cheung, V. C., d'Avella, A., Saltiel, P., and Tresch, M. (2008) Combining modules for movement, *Brain Res. Rev.*, **57**(1), 125-133.

20. Bizzi, E., d'Avella, A., Saltiel, P., and Tresch, M. (2002) Modular organization of spinal motor systems, *Neuroscientist*, **8**(5), 437-442.

21. Bizzi, E., Mussa-Ivaldi, F. A., and Giszter, S. F. (1991) Computations underlying the execution of movement: a biological perspective, *Science*, **253**(5017), 287-291.

22. Braun, Z., Mizrahi, J., Najenson, T., and Graupe, D. (1985) Activation of paraplegic patients by functional electrical stimulation: training and biomechanical evaluation, *Scand. J. Rehabil. Med. Suppl.*, **12**, 93-101.

23. Brindley, G. S. (1977) An implant to empty the bladder or close the urethra, *J. Neurol. Neurosurg. Psychiatry*, **40**(4), 358-369.

24. Brindley, G. S., Polkey, C. E., and Rushton, D. N. (1982) Sacral anterior root stimulators for bladder control in paraplegia, *Paraplegia*, **20**(6), 365-381.

25. Brown, T. G. (1911) The intrinsic factors in the act of progression in the mammal, *Proc. Royal Soc. Lond. (B)*, **84**, 308-319.

26. Brown, T. G. (1914) On the fundamental activity of the nervous centres: together with an analysis of the conditioning of rhythmic activity in progression, and a theory of the evolution of function in the nervous system, *J. Physiol.*, **48**, 18-41.

27. Burke, D. and Pierrot-Deseilligny, E. (2012) *The Circuitry of the Human Spinal Cord: Spinal and Corticospinal Mechanisms of Movement*, 2nd Ed. (Cambridge University Press, UK).

28. Burke, R. E., Degtyarenko, A. M., and Simon, E. S. (2001) Patterns of locomotor drive to motoneurons and last-order interneurons: clues to the structure of the CPG, *J. Neurophysio.*, **86**(1), 447-462.

29. Capaday, C. and Stein, R. B. (1986) Amplitude modulation of the soleus H-reflex in the human during walking and standing, *J. Neurosci.*, **6**(5), 1308-1313.

30. Chaplin, E. (1996) Functional neuromuscular stimulation for mobility in people with spinal cord injuries. The Parastep I System, *J. Spinal Cord Med.*, **19**(2), 99-105.

31. Courtine, G., Gerasimenko, Y. P., van den Brand, R., Yew, A., Musienko, P. E., Zhong, H., Song, B., Ao, Y., Ichiyama, R. M., Lavrov, I., Roy, R. R., Sofroniew, M. V., and Edgerton, V. R. (2009) Transformation of nonfunctional spinal circuits into functional states after the loss of brain input, *Nat. Neurosci.*, **12**(10), 1333-1342.

32. Davis, J. A., Triolo, R. J., Uhlir, J., Bieri, C., Rohde, L., Lissy, D., and Kukke, S. (2001) Preliminary performance of a surgically implanted neuroprosthesis for standing and transfers— where do we stand?, *J. Rehabil. Res. Dev.*, **38**(6), 609–617.

33. Dekopov, A. V., Shabalov, V. A., Tomsky, A. A., Hit, M. V., and Salova, E. M. (2015) Chronic spinal cord stimulation in the treatment of cerebral and spinal spasticity, *Stereotact. Funct. Neurosurg.*, **93**(2), 133–139.

34. Dimitrijevic, M. R., Gerasimenko, Y., and Pinter, M. M. (1998) Evidence for a spinal central pattern generator in humans, *Ann. NY. Acad. Sci.*, **860**, 360-376.

35. Doucet, B. M., Lam, A., and Griffin, L. (2012) Neuromuscular electrical stimulation for skeletal muscle function, *Yale J. Biol. Med.*, **85**(2), 201-215.

36. Dutta, A., Kobetic, R., Triolo, R. J. (2007) Ambulation after incomplete spinal cord injury with EMG-triggered FES, *IEEE Trans. Biomed. Eng.*, **55**(2), pp.791-794.

37. Elbasiouny, S. M., Moroz, D., Bakr, M. M., and Mushahwar, V. K. (2010) Management of spasticity after spinal cord injury: current techniques and future directions, *Neurorehabil. Neural Repair*, **24**(1), 23-33.

38. Engberg, I. and Lundberg, A. (1969) An electromyographic analysis of muscular activity in the hindlimb of the cat during unrestrained locomotion, *Acta. Physiol. Scand.*, **75**(4), 614–630.

39. Fehlings, M. G. and Perrin, R. G. (2006) The timing of surgical intervention in the treatment of spinal cord injury: a systematic review of recent clinical evidence, *Spine*, **31**(11 Suppl.), S28-35.

40. Forssberg, H. (1979) Stumbling corrective reaction: a phase-dependent compensatory reaction during locomotion, *J. Neurophysiol.*, **42**(4), 936-953.

41. Gaunt, R. A., Prochazka, A., Mushahwar, V. K., Guevremont, L. G., Ellaway, P. H. (2006) Intraspinal microstimulation excites multisegmental sensory afferents at lower stimulus levels than local α-motoneuron responses, *J. Neurophysiol.*, **96**(6), 2995-3005.

42. Gerasimenko, Y. P., Avelev, V. D., Nikitin, O. A., Lavrov, I. A., (2003) Initiation of locomotor activity in spinal cats by epidural stimulation of the spinal cord, *Neurosci. Behav. Physiol.*, **33**(3), 247–254.

43. Gerasimenko, Y. P., Makarovskii, A., Nikitin, O. A. (2002) Control of locomotor activity in humans and animals in the absence of supraspinal influences, *Neurosci. Behav. Physiol.*, **32**(4), 417–423.

44. Giszter, S. F. (2015a) Motor primitives – new data and future directions, *Curr. Opin. Neurobiol.*, **33**, 156-165.

45. Giszter, S. F. (2015b) Spinal primitives and intra-spinal micro-stimulation (ISMS) based prostheses: a neurobiological perspective on the "known unknowns" in ISMS and future prospects, *Front. Neurosci.,* **9**(72), 1-16.

46. Giszter, S. F., Mussa-Ivaldi, F. A., and Bizzi, E. (1993) Convergent force fields organized in the frog's spinal cord, *J. Neurosci.,* **13**(2), 467-491.

47. Goslow, G. E. Jr., Reinking, R. M., and Stuart, D. G. (1973) The cat step cycle: hind limb joint angles and muscle lengths during unrestrained locomotion, *J. Morphol.,* **141**(1), 1-41.

48. Grahn, P. J., Lee, K. H., Kasasbeh, A., Mallory, G. W., Hachmann, J. T., Dube, J. R., Kimble, C. J., Lobel, D. A., Bieber, A., Jeong, J. H., Bennet, K. E., Lujan, J. L. (2015) Wireless control of intraspinal microstimulation in a rodent model of paralysis, *J. Neurosurg.,* **123**(1), 232-242.

49. Gregory, C. M. and Bickel, C.S. (2005) Recruitment patterns in human skeletal muscle during electrical stimulation, *Phys. Ther.,* **85**(4), 358-364.

50. Grill, W. M., Norman, S. E., and Bellamkonda, R. V. (2009) Implanted neural interfaces: biochallenges and engineered solutions, *Annu. Rev. Biomed. Eng.,* **11**, 1-24.

51. Grillner, S. (1981) Control of locomotion in bipeds, tetrapods, and fish, in eds. J. M. Brookhart and V. B. Mountcastle, Handbook of Physiology. Section 1: The Nervous System, ed. V. B Brooks, Vol II. Motor Control, Part 2, (American Physiological Society, Bethesda, MD) 1179-1236.

52. Grillner, S. (1985) Neurobiological bases of rhythmic motor acts in vertebrates, *Science,* **228**, 143–149.

53. Grillner, S. (2006) Neuronal networks in motion from ion channels to behavior, *Ann. R. Acad. Nac. Med. (Madr).,* **123**, 297-298.

54. Guertin, P. A. (2009) The mammalian central pattern generator for locomotion, *Brain Res. Rev.,* **62**, 45-56.

55. Guevremont, L., Norton, J. A., and Mushahwar, V. K. (2007), Physiologically based controller for generating overground locomotion using functional electrical stimulation, *J. Neurophysiol.,* **97**(3), 2499-2510.

56. Guiraud, D., Stieglitz, T., Koch, K. P., Divoux, J. L., and Rabischong, P. (2006) An implantable neuroprosthesis for standing and walking in paraplegia: 5-year patient follow-up, *J. Neural Eng.,* **3**(4), 268-275.

57. Gustafsson, B. and Jankowska, E. (1976) Direct and indirect activation of nerve cells by electrical pulses applied extracellularly, *J. Physiol.,* **258**(1), 33-61.

58. Haberler, C., Alesch, F., Mazal, P. R., Pilz, P., Jellinger, K., Pinter, M. M., Hainfellner, J. A., and Budka, H. (2000) No tissue damage by chronic deep brain stimulation in Parkinson's disease, *Ann. Neurol.,* **48**(3), 372-376.

59. Halbertsma, J. M. (1983) The stride cycle of the cat: the modelling of locomotion by computerized analysis of automatic recordings, *Acta. Physiol. Scand. Suppl.,* **521**, 1-75.

60. Hardin, E., Kobetic, R., Murray, L., Corado-Ahmed, M., Pinault, G., Sakai, J., Bailey, S. N., Ho, C., Triolo, R. J. (2007) Walking after incomplete spinal cord injury using an implanted FES system: a case report, *J. Rehabil. Res. Dev.,* **44**(3), 333-346.

61. Harkema, S., Gerasimenko, Y., Hodes, J., Burdick, J., Angeli, C., Chen, Y., Ferreira, C., Willhite, A., Rejc, E., Grossman, R. G., and Edgerton, V. R. (2011) Effect of epidural stimulation of the lumbosacral spinal cord on voluntary movement, standing, and assisted stepping after motor complete paraplegia: a case study, *Lancet,* **377**(9781), 1938–1947.

62. Hart, C. B. and Giszter, S. F. (2010) A neural basis for motor primitives in the spinal cord, *J. Neurosci.,* **30**(4), 1322-1336.

63. Henneman, E., Somjen, G., and Carpenter, D. O., (1965) Functional significance of cell size in spinal motoneurons, *J. Neurophysiol.*, **28**, 560-580.

64. Herman, R., J. He, S. D'Luzansky, W. Willis, and S. Dilli. (2002) Spinal cord stimulation facilitates functional walking in a chronic, incomplete spinal cord injured, *Spinal Cord*, **40**(2), 65–68.

65. Holinski, B. J., Everaert, D. G., Mushahwar, V. K., and Stein, R. B. (2013) Real-time control of walking using recordings from dorsal root ganglia, *J. Neural Eng.*, **10**(5), 1-31.

66. Holinski, B. J., Mazurek, K. A., Everaert, D. G., Stein, R. B., and Mushahwar, V. K. (2011) Restoring stepping after spinal cord injury using intraspinal microstimulation and novel control strategies, *Conf. Proc. IEEE Eng. Med. Biol. Soc.*, 5798-5801.

67. Holinski, B. J., Mazurek, K. A., Everaert, D. G., Toossi, A., Lucas-Osma, A. M., Troyk, P., Etienne-Cummings, R., Stein, R. B., and Mushahwar, V. K. (2016) Intraspinal microstimulation produces functional over-ground walking, *J. Neural Eng.* [In Revision].

68. Huang, H., He, J., Herman, R., and Carhart, M. R. (2006) Modulation effects of epidural spinal cord stimulation on muscle activities during walking, *IEEE Trans. Neural Syst. Rehabil. Eng.*, **14**(1), 14–23.

69. Ichiyama, R. M., Gerasimenko, Y. P., Zhong, H., Roy, R. R., Edgerton, V. R. (2005) Hindlimb stepping movements in complete spinal rats induced by epidural spinal cord stimulation, *Neurosci. Lett.*, **383**(3), 339–344.

70. Iwahara, T., Atsuta, Y., Garcia-Rill, E. and Skinner, R. D. (1992) Spinal cord stimulation-induced locomotion in the adult cat, *Brain Res. Bull.*, **28**(1), 99–105.

71. Jankowska, E. and Roberts, W. J. (1972) An electrophysiological demonstration of the axonal projections of single spinal interneurons in the cat, *J. Physiol.*, **222**(3), 5977-622.

72. Jankowska, E., Jukes, M. G., Lund, S., and Lundberg, A. (1976) The effect of DOPA on the spinal cord. 6. Half-centre organization of interneurones transmitting effects from the flexor reflex afferents, *Acta. Physiol. Scand.*, **70**(3), 389-402.

73. Jordan, L. M. (1991) Brainstem and spinal cord mechanisms for the initiation of locomotion, in eds. Shimamura, M., Grillner, S., and Edgerton, V. R., *Neurobiological Basis of Human Locomotion*, (Japan Scientific Societies Press, Tokyo) 3-20.

74. Kasten, M. R., Sunshine, M. D., Secrist, E. S., Horner, P. J., and Moritz, C. T. (2013) Therapeutic intraspinal microstimulation improves forelimb function after cervical contusion injury, *J. Neural Eng.*, **10**(4), 1-17.

75. Khazaei, M. and Erfanian, A. (2016) Adaptive fuzzy neuro sliding mode control of the hindlimb movement generated by epidural spinal cord stimulation in cat, *Intl. Funct. Electric. Stim. Soc.* (La Grande Motte, France), 1-4.

76. Kilgore, K. L., Peckham, P. H., Keith, M. W., Montague, F. W., Hart, R. L., Gazdik, M. M., Bryden, A. M., Snyder, S. A., and Stage T. G. (2003) Durability of implanted electrodes and leads in an upper-limb neuroprosthesis, *J. Rehabil. Res. Dev.*, **40**(6), 457–468.

77. Kobetic, R., Triolo, R. J., Uhlir, J. P., Bieri, C., Wibowo, M., Polando, G., Marsolais, E. B., Davis, J. A Jr, and Ferguson, K. A. (1999) Implanted functional electrical stimulation system for mobility in paraplegia: a follow-up case report, *IEEE Trans. Rehabil. Eng.*, **7**(4), 390-398.

78. Kobravi, H. R. and Erfanian, A. (2009) Decentralized adaptive robust control based on sliding mode and nonlinear compensator for the control of ankle movement using functional electrical stimulation of agonist-antagonist muscles, *J. Neural Eng.*, **6**(4), 1-10.

79. Kobravi, H. R. and Erfanian, A. (2012) A decentralized adaptive fuzzy robust strategy for control of upright standing posture in paraplegia using functional electrical stimulation, *Med. Eng. Phys.*, **34**(1), 28-37.

80. Koshland, G. F. and Smith, J. L. (1989) Mutable and immutable features of paw-shake responses after hindlimb deaffernation in the cat, *J. Neurophysiol.*, **62**(1), 162-173.

81. Kovacic, Z. and Bogdan, S. (2006) *Fuzzy Controller Design: Theory and Applications*, (CRC/Taylor & Francis Group, New York), 1-416.

82. Kriellaars, D. J., Brownstone, R. M., Noga, B. R., and Jordan, L. M. (1994) Mechanical entrainment of fictive locomotion in the decerebrate cat, *J. Neurophysiol.*, **71**(6), 2074-2086.

83. Kuzelicki, J., Kamnik, R., Bajd, T., Obreza, P., and Benko, H. (2002) Paraplegics standing up using multichannel FES and arm support, *J. Med. Eng. Technol.*, **26**(3), 106–110.

84. Lafreniere-Roula, M. and McCrea, D. A. (2005) Deletions of rhythmic motoneuron activity during fictive locomotion and scratch provide clues to the organization of the mammalian central pattern generator, *J. Neurophysiol.*, **94**(2), 1120–1132.

85. Lau, B., Gueveremont, L., and Mushahwar, V. K. (2007) Strategies for generating prolonged functional standing using intramuscular stimulation or intraspinal microstimulation, *IEEE Trans. Neural Syst. Rehabil. Eng.*, **15**(2), 273-285.

86. Lavrov, I., Gerasimenko, Y. P., Ichiyama, R. M., Courtine, G., Zhong, H., Roy, R. R., and Edgerton, V.R., (2006) Plasticity of spinal cord reflexes after a complete transection in adult rats: Relationship to stepping ability, *J. Neurophysiol.*, **96**(4), 1699–1710.

87. Lee, C. C. (1990) Fuzzy logic in control systems: fuzzy logic controller – part I, *IEEE Trans. Syst., Man, Cybern.*, **20**(2), 404-418.

88. Lemay, M. A. and Grill, W. M. (2004) Modularity of motor output evoked by intraspinal microstimulation in cats, *J. Neurophysiol.*, **91**(1), 502-514.

89. Lemay, M. A., Galagan, J. E., Hogan, N., and Bizzi, E. (2001) Modulation and vectorial summation of the spinalized frog's hindlimb end-point force produced by intraspinal electrical stimulation of the cord, *IEEE Trans. Neural Syst. Rehabil. Eng.*, **9**(1), 12-23.

90. Lemay, M. A., Grasse, D., and Grill, W. M. (2009) Hindlimb endpoint forces predict movement direction evoked by intraspinal microstimulation in cats, *IEEE Trans. Neural Syst. Rehabil. Eng.*, **17**(4), 379-389.

91. Lundberg, A. (1965) Interactions entre voies reflexes spinales (interaction between the spinal reflex pathways), *Neurophysiol.* (Paris), **16**, 121-137.

92. Maffiuletti, N. A. (2010) Physiological and methodological considerations for the use of neuromuscular electrical stimulation, *Eur. J. Appl. Physiol.*, **110**(2), 223-234.

93. Marsolais, E. B. and Kobetic, R. (1983) Functional walking in paralyzed patients by means of electrical stimulation, *Clin. Orthop. Rel. Res.*, **175**, 30-36.

94. Mazurek, K. A., Holinski, B. J., Everaert, D. G., Stein, R. B., Etienne-Cummings, R., and Mushahwar, V. K. (2012) Feed forward and feedback control for over-ground locomotion in anaesthetized cats, *J. Neural Eng.*, **9**(2), 1-28.

95. Mazurek, K. A., Holinski, B. J., Everaert, D. G., Mushahwar, V. K., and Etienne-Cummings, R. (2016) A mixed-signal VLSI system for producing temporally adapting intraspinal microstimulation patterns for locomotion, *IEEE Trans. Biomed. Circuits Syst.*, epub., 1-10.

96. Mazurek, K. A., Holinski, B.J., Everaert, D. G., Stein, R. B., Mushahwar, V. K., and Etienne-Cummings, R. (2010) Locomotion processing unit, *IEEE Biomed. Circuits Syst. Conf. (BioCAS)*, 286-289.

97. McConnell, G. C., Schneider, T. M., Owens, D. J., and Bellamkonda, R. V. (2007) Extraction force and cortical tissue reaction of silicon microelectrode arrays implanted in the rat brain, *IEEE Trans. Biomed. Eng.,* **54**(6 Pt 1), 1097–107.

98. McCrea, D. A. and Rybak, I. A. (2008) Organization of mammalian locomotor rhythm and pattern generation, *Brain Res. Rev.,* **57**(1), 134-146.

99. McCrea, D. A., Rybak, I. A. (2007) Modeling the mammalian locomotor CPG: insights from mistakes and perturbations, *Prog. Brain Res.,* **165**, 235-253.

100. McCreery, D., Pikov, V., Lossinsky, A., Bullara, L., and Agnew, W. (2004) Arrays for chronic functional microstimulation of the lumbosacral spinal cord, *IEEE Trans. Neural Syst. Rehabil. Eng.,* **12**(2), 195-207.

101. McCreery, D. B., Agnew, W.F., Yuen, T.G., and Bullara, L. (1990) Charge density and charge per phase as cofactors in neural injury induced by electrical stimulation, *IEEE Trans. Biomed. Eng.,* **37**(10), 996-1001.

102. Miller, S. and Scott, P. D. (1977) The spinal locomotor generator, *Exp. Brain Res.,* **30**, 387-403.

103. Minassian, K., Persy, I., Rattay, F., Pinter, M. M., Kern, H., and Dimitrijevic, M. R. (2007) Human lumbar cord circuitries can be activated by extrinsic tonic input to generate locomotor-like activity, *Hum. Mov. Sci.,* **26**(2), 275-295.

104. Minassian. K., Persy, I., Rattay, F., and Dimitrijevic, M. R. (2005) Peripheral and central afferent input to the lumbar cord, *Biocybern. Biomed. Eng.,* **25**(3), 11–29.

105. Mirbagheri, M. M., Ladouceur, M., Barbeau, H., and Kearney, R. E. (2002) The effects of long-term FES assisted walking on intrinsic and reflex dynamic stiffness in spastic spinal cord injured subjects, *IEEE Trans. Neural Syst. Rehabil. Eng.,* **10**(4), 280-289.

106. Mondello, S. E., Kasten, M. R., Horner, P. J. and Moritz, C. T. (2014) Therapeutic intraspinal stimulation to generate activity and promote long-term recovery, *Front Neurosci.,* **8**(21), 1-7.

107. Moritz, C. T., Lucas, T. H., Perlmutter, S. I., Fetz, E. E. (2007) Forelimb movements and muscle responses evoked by microstimulation of cervical spinal cord in sedated monkeys, *J. Neurophysiol.,* **97**(1), 110-120.

108. Mushahwar, V. K. and Horch, K. W. (1998) Selective activation and graded recruitment of functional muscle groups through spinal cord stimulation, *Ann. NY. Acad. Sci.,* **860**, 531–535.

109. Mushahwar, V. K. and Horch, K. W. (1993) Selective activation of functional muscle groups through stimulation of spinal motor pools, *Proc. 15th Ann. Intl. Conf. IEEE Eng. Med. Biol. Soc.,* 1196-1197.

110. Mushahwar, V. K. and Horch, K. W. (1997) Interleaved dual-channel stimulation of the ventral lumbo-sacral spinal cord reduces muscle fatigue, *Proc. 2nd Annu. Intl. Funct. Elect. Stim.Soc., 5th Triennial Neuroprosth.: Motor Syst. V,* (Burnaby, B.C., Canada).

111. Mushahwar, V. K. and Horch, K. W. (2000a) Selective activation of muscle groups in the feline hindlimb through electrical microstimulation of the ventral lumbo-sacral spinal cord, *IEEE Trans. Rehabil. Eng.,* **8**(1), 11-21.

112. Mushahwar, V. K., Aoyagi, Y., Stein, R. B., and Prochazka, A. (2004a) Movements generated by intraspinal microstimulation in the intermediate gray matter of the anesthetized, decerebrate, and spinal cat, *Can. J. Physiol. Pharmacol.,* **82**(8-9), 702-714.

113. Mushahwar, V. K., Collins, D. F., and Prochazka, A. (2000b) Spinal cord microstimulation generates functional limb movements in chronically implanted cats, *Exp. Neurol.,* **163**(2), 422-429.

114. Mushahwar, V. K., Gillard, D. M., Gauthier, M. J., and Prochazka, A. (2002), Intraspinal micro stimulation generates locomotor-like and feedback-controlled movements, *IEEE Trans. Neural Syst. Rehabil. Eng.*, **10**(1), 68-81.

115. Mushahwar, V. K., Jacobs, P. L., Normann, R. A., Triolo, R. J., and Kleitman, N. (2007) New functional electrical stimulation approaches to standing and walking, *J. Neural Eng.*, **4**(3), 181-197.

116. Mushahwar, V. K., Prochazka, A., Ellaway, P. H., Guevremont, L. G., and Gaunt, R. A. (2003) Microstimulation in CNS excites axons before neuronal cell bodies, *Soc. for Neurosci.: Abstract 276.6.*, Washington, DC.

117. Mushahwar, V. K., Saigal, R., Bamford, J., Guevremont, L. G., and Norton, J. A., (2004b) Efficacy of intraspinal microstimulation in restoring stepping after spinal cord injury, *9th Ann. Conf. Intl. Func. Electric. Stim. Soc.* (Bournemouth, UK).

118. Musienko, P. E., Bogacheva, I. N., and Gerasimenko, Y. P., (2007) Significance of peripheral feedback in the generation of stepping movements during epidural stimulation of the spinal cord, *Neurosci. Behav. Physiol.*, **37**(2), 181-190.

119. Musienko, P. E., Heutschi, J., Friedli, L., van den Brand, R., and Courtine, G. (2012) Multi-system neurorehabilitative strategies to restore motor functions following severe spinal cord injury, *Exp. Neurol.*, **235**(1), 100-109.

120. Mussa-Ivaldi, F. A., Giszter, S. F., and Bizzi, E. (1994) Linear combinations of primitives in vertebrate motor control, *Proc. Natl. Acad. Sci. USA*, **91**(16), 7534-7538.

121. Nekoukar, V. and Erfanian, A. (2010) Adaptive terminal sliding mode control of ankle movement using functional electrical stimulation of agonist-antagonist muscles, *Conf. Proc. IEEE Eng. Med. Biol. Soc.*, 5448-5451.

122. Nekoukar, V. and Erfanian, A. (2012) A decentralized modular control framework for robust control of FES-activated walker-assisted paraplegic walking using terminal sliding mode control and fuzzy logic control, *IEEE Trans. Biomed. Eng.*, **59**(10), 2818-2827.

123. Orsal, D., Cabelguen, J. M., and Perret, C. (1990) Interlimb coordination during fictive locomotion in the thalamic cat, *Exp. Brain Res.*, **82**(3), 536-546.

124. Overduin, S. A., d'Avella, A., Roh, J., Carmena, J. M., and Bizzi, E. (2015) Representation of muscle synergies in the primate brain, *J. Neurosci.*, **35**(37), 12615-12624.

125. Pearson, K. G. (1995) Proprioceptive regulation of locomotion, *Curr. Opin. Neurobiol.*, **5**(6), 786-791.

126. Pearson, K. G. and Collins, D. F. (1993) Reversal of the influence of group Ib afferents from plantaris on activity in medial gastrocnemius muscle during locomotor activity, *J. Neurophysiol.*, **70**(3), 1009-1017.

127. Pinter, M. M., Gerstenbrand, F., and Dimitrijevic, M. R. (2000) Epidural electrical stimulation of posterior structures of the human lumbosacral cord: 3. Control of spasticity, *Spinal Cord*, **38**(9), 524–531.

128. Polikov, V. S., Tresco, P. A., and Reichert, W. M. (2005) Response of brain tissue to chronically implanted neural electrodes, *J. Neurosci. Methods*, **148**(1), 1–18.

129. Prochazka, A., Mushahwar, V. K., and McCreery, D. B. (2001) Neural prostheses, *J. Physiol.*, **533**(Pt 1), 99–109.

130. Prochazka, A., Sontag, K. H., and Wand, P. (1978) Motor reactions to perturbations of gait: proprioceptive and somesthetic involvement, *Neurosci. Lett.*, **7**(1), 35-39.

131. Purves, D., Augustine, D. F., Hall, W. C., LaMantia, A. S., and White, L. E. (2012) *Neuroscience*, 5th Ed. (Sinauer Associates, Inc., USA).

132. Raslan, A. M., McCartney, S., and Burchiel, K. J. (2007) Management of chronic severe pain: spinal neuromodulatory and neuroablative approaches, *Acta. Neurochir. Suppl.,* **97**(Pt 1), 33–41.

133. Rejc, E., Angeli, C., and Harkema. S. (2015) Effects of lumbosacral spinal cord epidural stimulation for standing after chronic complete paralysis in humans, *PLoS One,* **10**(7), e0133998.

134. Renshaw, B. (1940) Activity in the simplest spinal reflex pathways, *J. Neurophysiol.,* **3**(5), 373-387.

135. Richardson, R. R. and McLone, D. G. (1978) Percutaneous epidural neurostimulation for paraplegic spasticity, *Surg. Neurol.,* **9**(3), 153–155.

136. Roshani, A. and Erfanian, A. (2013a) Fuzzy logic control of ankle movement using multi-electrode intraspinal microstimulation, *Conf. Proc. IEEE Eng. Med. Biol. Soc.,* 5642-5645.

137. Roshani, A. and Erfanian, A. (2013b) Restoring motor functions in paralyzed limbs through intraspinal multielectrode microstimulation using fuzzy logic control and lag compensator, *Basic Clin. Neurosci.,* **4**(3), 232-243.

138. Rossignol, S. (1996) Neural control of stereotypic limb movements, in eds. Rowell, L., and Shephard, J., *Handbook of Physiology. Section 12, Exercise: Regulation and Integration of Multiple Systems,* (The American Physiological Society, New York) 173-216.

139. Rybak, I. A., Dougherty, K. J., and Shevtsova, N. A. (2015) Organization of the mammalian locomotor CPG: review of computational model and circuit architectures based on genetically identified spinal interneurons (1, 2, 3), *eNeuro.* **2**(5), 1-21.

140. Rybak, I. A., Shevtsova, N. A., Lafreniere-Roula, M., and McCrea, D. A. (2006a) Modelling spinal circuitry involved in locomotor pattern generation: insights from deletions during fictive locomotion, *J. Physiol.,* **577**, 617-639.

141. Rybak, I. A., Stecina, K., Shevtsova, N. A., McCrea, D. A. (2006b) Modelling spinal circuitry involved in locomotor pattern generation: insights from the effects of afferent stimulation, *J. Physiol.,* **577**, 641-658.

142. Saigal, R., Renzi, C., and Mushahwar, V. K. (2004) Intraspinal Microstimulation Generates Functional Movements after Spinal Cord Injury, *IEEE Trans. Neural Syst. Rehabil. Eng.,* **12**(4), 430-440.

143. Saladin, K. S. (2015) *Anatomy and Physiology: The Unity of Form and Function,* 7th Ed. (McGraw Hill Education, USA).

144. Saltiel, P., Wyler-Duda, K., d'Avella, A., Tresch, M. C., and Bizzi, E. (2001) Muscle synergies encoded within the spinal cord: evidence from focal intraspinal NMDA iontophoresis in the frog, *J. Neurophysiol.,* **85**(2), 605-619.

145. Sasada, S., Kato, K., Kadowaki, S., Groiss, S. J., Ugawa, Y., Komiyama, T., and Nishimura, Y. (2014) Volitional walking via upper limb muscle-controlled stimulation of the lumbar locomotor center in man, *J. Neurosci.,* **34**(33), 11131-11142.

146. Shealy, C. N., Mortimer, J. T., and Reswick, J. B. (1967) Electrical inhibition of pain by stimulation of the dorsal columns: preliminary clinical report, *Anesth. Analg.,* **46**(4), 489–491.

147. Sherrington, C. S. (1910) Flexion-reflex of the limb, crossed-extension-reflex, and reflex stepping and standing, *J. Phyisol. (Lond.),* **40**, 28-121.

148. Shtessel, Y., Edwards, C., Fridman, L., and Levant, A. (2014) *Sliding Mode Control and Observation,* (Springer New York) 1-42.

149. Stefanovska, A., Gros, N., Vodovnik, L., Rebersek, S., and Acimovic-Janezic, R. (1988) Chronic electrical stimulation for the modification of spasticity in hemiplegic patients, *Scand. J. Rehabil. Med. Suppl.*, **17**, 115-121.

150. Stefanovska, A., Vodovnik, L., Gros, N., Rebersek, S., and Acimovic-Janezic, R. (1989) FES and spasticity, *IEEE Trans. Biomed. Eng.*, **36**(7), 738-745.

151. Stein, P. S. G. and Smith, J. L. (1997) Neural and biomechanical control strategies for different forms of vertebrate hindlimb motor tasks, in eds. Stein, P. G. S., Grillner, S., Selverston, A. I., and Stuart, D. G., *Neurons, Networks, and Motor Behavior*, (MIT Press, Cambridge, Massachusetts) 61-73.

152. Stein, R. B., Aoyagi, Y., Mushahwar, V. K., and Prochazka, A. (2002) Limb movements generated by stimulating muscle, nerve and spinal cord, *Arch. Ital. Biol.*, **140**(4), 273-281.

153. Stephens, M. J. and Yang, J. F. (1996) Short latency, non-reciprocal group I inhibition is reduced during the stance phase of walking in humans, *Brain Res.*, **743**(1-2), 24-31.

154. Strojnik, P., Acimovic, R., Vavken, E., Simic, V., and Stanic, U. (1987) Treatment of drop foot using an implantable peroneal underknee stimulator, *Scand. J. Rehabil. Med.*, **19**(1), 37-43.

155. Sunshine, M. D., Cho, F. S., Lockwood, D. R., Fechko, A. S., Kasten, M. R., Moritz, C. T. (2013) Cervical intraspinal microstimulation evokes robust forelimb movements before and after injury, *J. Neural Eng.*, **10**(4), 1-11.

156. Szarowski, D. H., Andersen, M. D., Retterer, S., Spence, A.J., Isaacson, M., Craighead, H. G., Turner, J. N., and Shain, W. (2003) Brain responses to micromachined silicon devices, *Brain Res.*, **983**(1-2), 23–35.

157. Talonen, P., Malmivuo, J., Baer, G. Markkula, H. and Hakkinen, V. (1983) Transcutaneous, dual channel phrenic nerve stimulator for diaphragm pacing, *Med.Biol. Eng. Comput.*, **21**(1), 21-30.

158. Tanagho, E. A., Schmidt, R. A., and Orvis, B. R. (1989) Neural stimulation for control of voiding dysfunction: a preliminary report in 22 patients with serious neuropathic voiding disorders, *J. Urol.*, **142**(2 Pt 1), 340-345.

159. Tator, C. H., Minassian, K. and Mushahwar, V. K. (2012) Spinal cord stimulation: therapeutic benefits benefits and movement generation after spinal cord injury, *Handb. Clin. Neurol.*, **109**, 283-296.

160. Toossi, A., Everaert, D. G., Azar, A. Dennison, C. R. and Mushahwar, V. K. (2016) Mechanically stable intraspinal microstimulation implants for human translation, *J. Annals. Biomed. Eng.* [In Revision].

161. Tresch, M. C. and Bizzi, E. (1999) Responses to spinal microstimulation in the chronically spinalized rat and their relationship to spinal systems activated by low threshold cutaneous stimulation, *Exp. Brain Res.*, **129**(3), 401-416.

162. Tresch, M. C., Saltiel, P., and Bizzi, E. (1999) The construction of movement by the spinal cord, *Nat. Neurosci.*, **2**(2), 162-167.

163. Trimble, M. H. and Enoka, R. M. (1991) Mechanisms underlying the training effects associated with neuromuscular electrical stimulation, *Phys. Ther.*, **71**(4), 273–280.

164. Triolo, R. J., Bailey, S. N., Miller, M. E., Rohde, L. M., Anderson, J. S., Davis, J. A., Abbas, J. J., DiPonio, L. A., Forrest, G. P., Gater, D. R. Jr, and Yang, L. J. (2012) Longitudinal performance of a surgically implanted neuroprosthesis for lower-extremity exercise, standing, and transfers after spinal cord injury, *Arch. Phys. Med. Rehabil.*, **93**(5), 896-904.

165. Troyk, P. R., Mushahwar, V. K., Stein, R. B., Suh, S., Everaert, D., Holinski, B., Hu, Z., DeMichele, G., Kerns, D., Kayvani, K. (2012) An implantable neural stimulator for intraspinal microstimulation, *34th Ann Intl. Conf. IEEE EMBS* (San Diego, California, USA), 900-903.

166. Turner, J. N., Shain, W., Szarowski, D. H., Andersen, M., Martins, S., Isaacson, M. and Craighead, H. (1999) Cerebral astrocyte response to micromachined silicon implants, *Exp. Neurol.*, **156**(1), 33–49.

167. Utkin, V. (1977) Variable structure systems with sliding modes, *IEEE Trans. Autom. Control*, **22**(2), 212-222.

168. Utkin, V. (2009) Sliding mode control, in ed. Unbehauen, H., *Control Systems, Robotics, and Automation. Nonlinear, Distributed, and Time Delay Systems II*, Chapter 21, (Encyclopedia of Life Support Systems) 130-152.

169. van den Brand, R., Heutschi, J., Barraud, Q., DiGiovanna, J., Bartholdi, K., Huerlimann, M., Friedli, L., Vollenweider, I., Moraud, E. M., Duis, S., Dominici, N., Micera, S., Musienko, P., and Courtine, G. (2012) Restoring voluntary control of locomotion after paralyzing spinal cord injury, *Science*, **336**(6085), 1182-1185.

170. van Wezel, B. M., Ottenhoff, F. A., and Duysens, J. (1997) Dynamic control of location-specific information in tactile cutaneous reflexes from the foot during human walking, *J. Neurosci.*, **17**(10), 3804-3814.

171. Vecchio, C. (2008) Sliding mode control: theoretical developments and applications to uncertain mechanical systems, Thesis: *Universita Degli Studi di Pavia, Dipartimento di Informatica e Sistemistica*, 1-250.

172. Vodovnik, L. Bajd, T., Kralj, A., Gracanin, F., and Strojnik, P. (1981) Functional electrical stimulation for control of locomotor systems, *Crit. Rev. Bioeng.*, **6**(2), 63-131.

173. Vogelstein, R. J., Tenore, F., Guevremont, L., Etienne-Cummings, R., and Mushahwar, V. K. (2008) A silicon central pattern generator controls locomotion in vivo, *IEEE Trans. Biomed. Circuits Syst.*, **2**(3), 212-222.

174. Wand, P., Prochazka, A. and Sontag, K.-H. (1980) Neuromuscular responses to gait perturbations in freely moving cats, *Exp. Brain Res.*, **38**(1), 109-114.

175. Waters, R. L., McNeal, D. R., Faloon, W., and Clifford, B. (1985) Functional electrical stimulation of the peroneal nerve for hemiplegia: long-term clinical follow-up, *J. Bone Joint Surg. Am.*, **67**(5), 792-793.

176. Whelan, P. J., Hiebert, G. H., and Pearson, K. G. (1995) Stimulation of the group I extensor afferents prolongs the stance phase in walking cats, *Exp. Brain Res.*, **103**(1), 20-30.

177. Yang, J. F. and Winter, D. A. (1985) Surface EMG profiles during different walking cadences in humans, *Electroencephalogr. Clin. Neurophysiol.*, **60**(6), 485-491.

178. Zehr, E. P. and Stein, R. B. (1999) What functions do reflexes serve during human locomotion? *Prog. Neurobiol.*, **58**(2), 185-205.

179. Zehr, E. P., Komiyama, T., and Stein, R. B. (1997) Cutaneous reflexes during human gait: electromyographic and kinematic responses to electrical stimulation, *J. Neurophysiol.*, **77**(6), 3310-3325.

180. Zehr, E. P., Stein, R. B., and Komiyama, T. (1998) Function of sural nerve reflexes during human walking, *J. Physiol.*, **507**(1), 305-314.

181. Zimmerman, J. B., Jackson, A. (2014) Closed-loop control of spinal cord stimulation to restore hand function after paralysis, *Front. Neurosci.*, **8**(87), 1-8.

182. Zimmerman, J. B., Seki, K., Jackson, A. (2011) Reanimating the arm and hand with intraspinal microstimulation, *J. Neural Eng.*, **8**(5), 1-14.

183. Bickel, C. S., Gregory, C. M., and Azuero, A. (2012) Matching initial torque with different stimulation parameters influences skeletal muscle fatigue, *J. Rehabil. Res. Dev.*, 49(2), 323-331.
184. Jankowska, E., Jukes, M. G., Lund, S., and Lundberg, A. (1965) Reciprocal innervation through interneuronal inhibition, Nature, 206(980), 198-199.

Chapter 4.3

Brain Computer Interfaces

Dan Moran

Dept. Biomedical Engineering
Washington University
St. Louis, MO 63130
dmoran@wustl.edu

The goal of brain computer interface (BCI) technology is to decode human intent from brain activity alone in order to create an alternate communication channel for people with severe motor impairments.

1. Introduction

What does the brain do? From a neuroscience point of view, this rather simple question has a rather complex - and to a certain degree unknown - answer. However, from an engineering point of view, this question has an equally simple answer. If one were to treat the brain, or rather the central nervous system, as a black box and determine its inputs, they would see that the brain receives information from senses such as taste, touch, sight, sound and smell. These inputs influence very complicated ongoing internal dynamical processing (e.g., memory, motivation, etc.) within the brain. However, once a course of action is processed, the brain only has two outputs: it can release hormones and move muscles. Release of hormonal chemical messengers into the bloodstream is not an ideal method to communicate with the world. In general, a person can release all the hormones they wish and no one will notice – other than perhaps excessive sweat on their forehead or a flushed face. This leaves muscle movement as the primary output channel that allows the brain to communicate with the world. Everything we do to interact with our environment ultimately requires muscle movement: laughing, crying, walking, talking, gesturing, etc.

Losing our ability to control muscles due neurological disease (such as Amyotrophic Lateral Sclerosis – ALS) or neurological damage (such as spinal cord injury) limits our ability to interact and communicate with the world. In many cases, sensory awareness and intellect remain intact. It is the loss of the output channel of the brain – muscle movement – that limits these individuals from fully expressing their desired behavior. The goal of brain computer interface (BCI) technology is to decode human intent from brain activity alone in order to create an alternate communication channel for people with severe motor impairments [1]. In order for a BCI technology to decode brain activity, one must first know how movement information is encoded in the brain. One of the most studied movements by biomechanists and neuroscientists over the last century is voluntary visuomotor reaching tasks. The results of these studies laid the foundation for neural engineers to develop BCI technology.

2. Musculoskeletal Models

There has been much research as well as debate as to how the central nervous system (CNS) controls voluntary arm movements. When reaching for an object in space, the visual system must first identify the location and orientation of the object. These coordinates must then be transformed into a series of joint movements that will allow the arm to transport and orientate from its current coordinates to the desired object coordinates. In the primate arm, this is a redundant system since there are more degrees of freedom in the arm (>7) than coordinates to specify object location (3) and orientation (3) [2]. Once a desired kinematic path is determined, the CNS must determine the appropriate combinations of muscle activations to satisfy its desired kinematic path [3]. Given the large redundancy of muscles in the primate arm (> 38), another optimization must be performed by the CNS [4]. As Bernstein noted over 80 years ago, there is not a unique and unambiguous relationship between muscle excitation and arm movement kinematics [5].

While the relationship between muscle activation and arm movement is neither unique nor simple, it can be modeled using Newtonian/Lagrangian mechanics. Mathematically, arm dynamics can be modeled as:

$$\vec{M}_{nxn}[\vec{\theta}]\ddot{\vec{\theta}}_{nx1} = \vec{T}_{nx1}[\vec{A},\vec{\theta},\dot{\vec{\theta}}] + \vec{V}_{nx1}[\vec{\theta},\dot{\vec{\theta}}] + \vec{G}_{nx1}[\vec{\theta}] + \vec{E}_{nx1} \tag{1}$$

where n is the number of degrees of freedom in the arm; $\theta, \dot{\theta}, \ddot{\theta}$ are $nx1$ vectors of joint angle, angular velocity and angular acceleration, respectively; M is the mass matrix of the arm that varies with joint angle; T is the joint torque vector that varies with muscle activation (A), joint angle and joint angular velocity; V is the vector of inertial torques (*e.g,.* Coriolis forces, *etc.*); G is the gravity induced torque vector; and E is a torque vector representing the external forces and torques applied to the system [4, 5, 6]. Equation 1 is a coupled, second-order, non-linear differential equation that relates arm orientation to muscle activation. For a seven degree of freedom (n=7) arm model, the equations of motion are quite large (>

25,000 terms and products – most of which include trigonometric functions). The CNS must be able to compute Equation 1 in order to accurately control the hand. Given its large distributed processing structure, the CNS is well suited to task.

The key to controlling a dynamic system such as the musculoskeletal system is to have information on the states of system at all times. Equation 1 is quite complex but its structure is the same as the Newtonian mechanics for a point mass:

$$\vec{F} = m\vec{A} = m\frac{d^2\vec{p}}{dt^2} \tag{2}$$

where F is the force applied to the object, m is the object's mass and A is its acceleration. Equation 2 is also a second order differential equation since acceleration is the second time derivate of position (p). The states of Equation 2 are position and velocity. In order to calculate the movement of a point mass in space given the forces acting on it, you first must know both the current position and velocity of the point mass. Likewise, in order for the CNS to accurately control the musculoskeletal system, it must have current knowledge of both limb position and velocity. In the CNS, the two senses that measure these limb states are proprioception, where muscles spindles measure muscle length and lengthening velocity, and vision (e.g., area MT in cortex). These two senses act as redundant systems independently measuring the states of the limb during movement. Should one system fail, such as in patients with large-fiber myopathy (i.e., lack of spindle proprioception), reasonably accurate reaching movements are still possible in the presence of vision [7]. The key observation in analyzing Equation 1 is that knowledge of limb position and velocity are critical for control; thus, it is highly likely that these parameters will be encoded in the motor areas of the CNS. Furthermore, if the CNS were to model musculoskeletal mechanics in a manner similar to Newtonian/Lagrangian/Hamiltonian mechanics, one would expect these parameters to be encoded in trigonometric functions as well (e.g., cosines).

3. Motor Cortical Areas

The dominant cortical target of all brain computer interface technology has been primary motor cortex (M1). There are several reasons for this. First primary motor cortex accounts for about a third of all corticospinal projections from the brain down the spinal cord and through a series of spinal interneurons that eventually synapse on alpha motor neurons that control arm musculature [8]. Second, over half of the primary motor cortex (rostral M1) is located on a gyrus that is easily accessible by both invasive and non-invasive recording technology. Both dorsal and ventral premotor cortices also have nice gyral locations and contain 17% of corticospinal projections to the primate arm making them ideal targets for BCI.

The other key motor areas having significant corticospinal projections are cingulate sulcus (27%) and supplementary motor area (19%). However, both of these areas are buried on the interhemispheric wall making them very difficult areas to target given current BCI technology.

Initial neurophysiologic studies into primary motor cortex assumed that cell bodies in M1 were merely upper motor neurons and that their axons synapsed directly onto alpha motor neurons in the spinal cord. Therefore, many of the early studies tried to correlate M1 activity during simple one degree of freedom wrist movements with muscle activity or force [9, 10]. In reality, only a small percentage of corticospinal axons in primates synapse directly onto alpha motor neurons. Likewise, these direct projections all originate from caudal M1 deep in the bank of the central sulcus [11] making them a non-ideal targets for current BCI technology. Since most BCI recording technology targets rostral M1 and premotor areas which do not have direct connections to alpha motor neurons, it is unlikely that neurons in these cortical areas represent fully processed muscle activity.

In the 1980's Georgopoulos and colleagues began studying freely reaching monkeys and correlated 3D movement parameters with single unit activity in M1. In their seminal article in *Science* they showed how motor cortical activity is cosine tuned to movement direction [12]. Figure 1 shows an example of a primary motor cortical neuron's activity during a 2D reaching movement (center out task). As seen in the figure, whenever the subject moved its hand to the left, the neuron fired maximally. Whenever it moved to the right, it fired minimally. The neuron is "tuned" for movements to the left and its "preferred direction" would be a vector pointing to the left. Each neuron has its own distinct preferred direction and among the population of neurons they vary throughout all possible movement directions.

Hand direction is just one component of hand velocity. Later studies in the 1990s by Schwartz and colleagues went on to show how both hand direction and hand speed were encoded by a single motor cortical neuron [13, 14]. Figure 2 shows how varying hand speed during reaching modulates the directional tuning curve. As a subject reaches faster to a target, the motor cortical firing rate increases, regardless of which direction the reach is relative to the preferred direction of the neuron. This increase in modulation is both additive (DC shift across all directions) and multiplicative (larger increases in firing rate when moving in the neuron's preferred direction). Similarly, neuroscientists have determined that a single motor cortical neuron can concurrently encode hand position in addition to hand velocity [15, 16]. An encoding model that relates single unit activity (spikes/second) to upcoming hand kinematics (velocity and position) can be written as:

$$f(t) = b_0 + b_n \left\| \vec{V}(t + \tau_v) \right\| + \vec{B}_v \cdot \vec{V}(t + \tau_v) + \vec{B}_p \cdot \vec{P}(t + \tau_p) \tag{3}$$

where f is the instantaneous neural activity at any time t, and b_0 is the baseline activity of a single neuron. B_v, B_p, V, and P are all 3D vectors. B_v is the preferred direction (PD) of a neuron, and B_p is the positional gradient (PG) of the same neuron. The magnitudes of B_p and B_v are the depths of modulation for position and velocity, respectively. V is the hand velocity, and P is the hand position. τ_p is the time delay between neural representation of hand position and actual hand position, while τ_v is the delay for the hand velocity. The cosine tuning seen in Figure 1 is represented by the dot product shown in Equation 3. Both hand velocity and hand position are encoded using cosine functions which, as we will see in the decoding section later, is key to the vector mathematics that will be used to predict desired movement velocity and position from cortical activity.

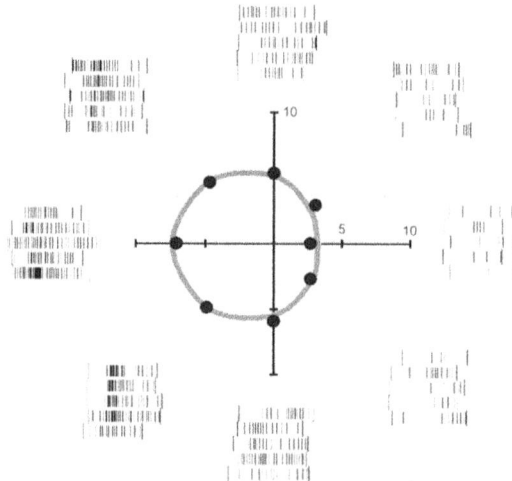

Fig. 1. Primary motor cortical neuron encoding the direction of hand movement during a 2D reaching task in a non-human primate. The subject made repeated reaching movements from a central target to each of eight radially spaced targets (2D center out task). The outer spike rasters illustrate the activity of neuron during five repeated reaches to each target. The central plot shows average firing rate to each target (●) after square root transform. A cosine function was regressed to the data (gray line). The units in the central plot are in square root of spikes/s. Adapted from [13].

Not all neurons in primary motor cortex encode both position and velocity concurrently. In fact only about 25% of the neurons encode both parameters. Overall, about a third of neurons encode position and about 55% encode velocity with 36% of neurons encoding neither kinematic variable [16]. When analyzing the relative depth of modulations between of the two variables (B_p and B_v), velocity is much more dominant. So while both hand position and velocity are encoded in primary motor cortex, they are not represented equally: velocity dominates primary motor cortical activity.

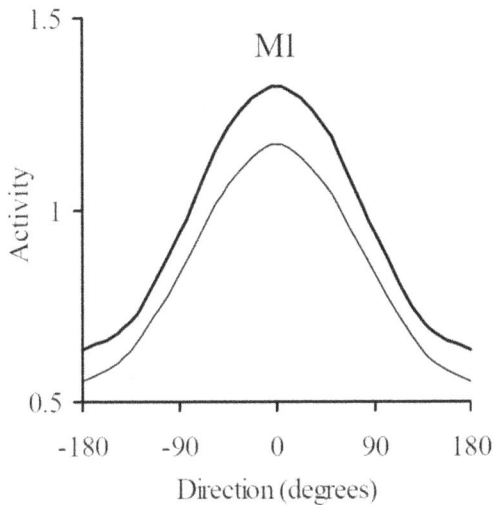

Fig. 2. Velocity encoding in motor cortex. Subjects performed 2D reaching movements at two different speeds: 35 cm/s (thick line) and 25 cm/s (thin line). The preferred direction is 0 degrees and directional variation in activity is well modeled by a cosine function. The speed of movement shifts the tuning curve with faster speed yielding higher cortical activity.

Premotor cortical areas likewise encode both hand velocity [13, 17, 18] and position [19, 20] but can also encode more abstract kinematic properties such as target location[21, 22, 23]. Premotor areas are active during the planning phase of movement [24] which means they can be active well before the subject wishes to move. If there is a desired delay between planning a movement and its execution, premotor areas might not be the ideal source for a BCI signal. However, premotor cortex's ability to encode desired target location can also significantly speed up BCI performance by jumping immediately to the end target rather relying on a velocity signal that must be integrated over a movement period [25].

In order to perform common acts of daily living (i.e., put a key in lock) we must not only have precise control of hand translation (to transport the key to the lock) but also precise control of hand orientation (yaw, pitch and roll) order to align the key with the lock before moving the key into the tumbler. So in addition to encoding 3D hand position and 3D velocity, motor cortical regions should modulate their activity with hand orientation and orientation velocity yielding a total of 12 state variables. The first hint of motor cortical representation of hand orientation came from a study by Strick and colleagues [26]. In this experiment, monkeys performed a 2D center out task with wrist movements only. The 2D task was repeated for three different forearm postures (pronation, neutral, and supination) and the goal was to disassociate movement kinematics and muscle activity (kinetics). If hand translation were the only kinematic variable encoded, then the experiment properly disassociated kinematics from kinetics. However, it turned out that 2/3 of neurons encoding hand translation modulated their baseline activity with forearm posture in that study. Although not discussed in the original study [26], forearm posture co-varied with hand roll suggesting that those neurons are likely encoding hand orientation.

A study done a decade later [27] directly investigated whether hand orientation velocity was encoded in motor cortex. In this study, monkeys performed a modified version of the standard center out task [12] where the target required precise control of hand roll in addition to precise control of 3D location. This center-out with rotation task required monkeys to reach to the same location while concurrently rotating their forearms. Roughly 65% of the motor cortical neurons recorded during the task were modulated by hand kinematics: 55% were modulated by translational velocity, 41% were modulated by hand roll velocity and 33% were modulated by both. Figure 3 below shows the average modulation to both translation and rotation for the 33% of motor cortical neurons encoding both.

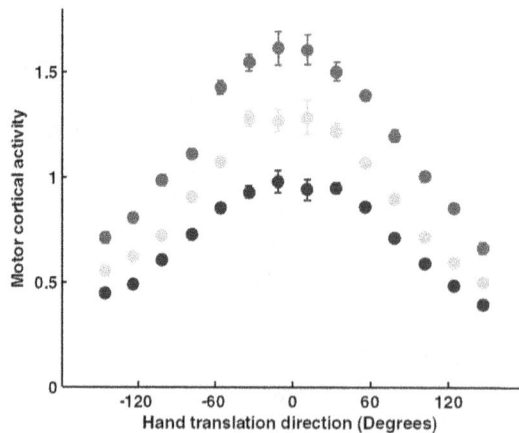

Fig. 3. Generalized tuning curves were made by normalizing the firing rate data of individual neurons and averaging across all neurons modulated to both translation and rotation. Top, middle, and lower shaded dots correspond to rotation conditions with the strongest, medium, and the weakest neuronal responses, respectively. The translation preferred direction is at 0 degrees. Rotational velocity shifts and scales the translational cosine tuning curve in a similar fashion to hand speed. Modified from [27].

Although the study generating Figure 3 only looked at one dimension of hand rotational velocity (i.e., hand roll), one could predict that both hand yaw and pitch would similarly be simultaneously encoded in a subset of motor cortical neurons. Likewise, the cosine tuning seen in 3D translation encoding could also be valid for 3D rotational encoding. This suggests a more generalized motor cortical encoding model where all 12 state variables are represented as follows:

$$ f(t) = \left(b_{0,T} + \vec{B}_T \bullet \vec{T}(t + \tau_T)\right)\left(b_{0,R} + \vec{B}_R \bullet \vec{R}(t + \tau_R)\right) \tag{4} $$

where f is the total neural activity; $b_{0,T}$ is the average neural activity related to hand translation and $b_{0,R}$ is the average neural activity related to hand rotation; $\vec{B}_T$ is a 6x1 vector representing both the preferred direction and preferred positional gradient of the neuron; $\vec{T}$ is 6x1 vector representing both the translational velocity and position of the hand in space (i.e. $[\dot{x}, \dot{y}, \dot{z}, x, y, z]$); $\vec{B}_R$ is a 6x1 vector representing both the preferred rotation and preferred orientation gradient of the neuron; and $\vec{R}$ is 6x1 vector representing both the rotational velocity and orientation of the hand in space (i.e. $[\dot{\theta}, \dot{\phi}, \dot{\psi}, \theta, \phi, \psi]$).

4. Decoding single unit activity

While the investigations into how motor cortical neurons encoded movement kinematics (position and velocity) didn't begin in earnest until the 1980s, this didn't stop neuroscientists from trying to use cortical activity to control artificial devices. In the 1970's Fetz and colleagues were able to isolate single motor cortical neurons for a few hours in an acute recording preparation and operantly train monkeys to modulate their firing rate independent of the movement parameters (e.g., EMG activity) [28]. These results lead Kennedy and colleagues to develop a stable electrode for chronic recording of single unit activity and develop the first fully implantable brain computer interface in humans [29, 30, 31]. These early studies used single unit activity from one to a few neurons to control a single degree of freedom (DOF). Basically, the neurons firing rate activity was directly mapped to the DOF under control and the subjects used biofeedback to obtain and improve control.

As BCI goals evolved from controlling a single DOF to controlling a multi-DOF prosthetic limb, more elegant methods for decoding movement intent from single unit activity was needed. The first of these decoding algorithms was the population vector method proposed by Georgopoulos and colleagues [12]. The population vector algorithm scales each individual neuron's encoding vector ($\vec{T}$

and $\vec{R}$ in Eq. 4) by its normalized instantaneous firing rate and sums the activity over all neurons to get an estimate of either hand position, velocity, orientation and/or orientation velocity. To decode 3D hand velocity, a summation for each of the three Cartesian coordinates (x, y, z) would be needed. As an example, the population vector estimate for the y-component of desired hand velocity would be:

$$PV_y(t) = \sum_{i=1}^{num\ cells} \frac{f_i(t)-b_{i,0}}{M_i} * \frac{B_{y,i}}{M_i}$$ Eq 5

where $PV_y(t)$ is the y-component of the population vector (predicted velocity component) at time t, $b_{i,0}$ is the bias term which centers the firing rate about zero, M_i is the maximum firing rate of the neuron, and $B_{y,i}$ is the y-component of the preferred direction for neuron i. The *num cells* above the summation is all the recorded neurons that have significant encoding of hand velocity. Since hand direction is cosine tuned, Eq. 5 is essentially a simple vector summation that accurately decodes 3D hand direction from motor cortical activity. Where speed modulates directional tuning (Fig. 2), the population vector algorithm can decode speed as well [13].

Decoding hand velocity from motor cortical activity using the population vector algorithm (PVA) is very robust and has been used to decode both reaching and drawing movements [13, 14, 32, 33]. Likewise, almost every invasive single-unit BCI study to date that decoded multiple degrees of freedom has used some form of the population vector algorithm to estimate and then integrate a velocity based control signal [34, 35, 36, 37]. Velocity is a dominant parameter encoded in motor cortical activity so it is easily and accurately decoded using this simple vector addition algorithm. However, care must be taken when decoding other kinematic parameters that are not so robustly represented in cortical activity. One of the assumptions of the PVA algorithm is that the encoding vectors are independent of each other. When decoding hand velocity using neurons with significant velocity tuning, roughly half those neurons will also contain significant positional tuning. As long as a neuron's encoding vector for velocity (i.e., preferred direction) is not correlated to its encoding vector for position (i.e., positional gradient), an accurate estimate will be made. Unfortunately, a neuron's preferred direction is correlated to its positional gradient [16]. This is very evident when trying to decode position from motor cortical activity using the PVA, the dominant and correlated velocity encoding skews the position estimation [16].

The optimal linear estimator algorithm (OLE) is another vector based method (i.e., it assumes cosine tuning) that can accurately decode multiple kinematic variables that are correlated [38]. The OLE method uses the covariance between encoding vectors to scale the decoding weights in order to optimally decode the desired variable (e.g., position) while cancelling the influence of others (e.g., velocity or orientation).

Using single unit recording arrays and vector based decoding methods, Schwartz and colleagues have been able to decode 3D hand translation, 3D hand rotation and hand grasping in an anthropomorphic prosthetic arm in realtime in human patients [39, 40]. In less than two decades, the BCI field has gone from controlling a single dimension or DOF in humans [30] to controlling a 10 dimensional prosthetic arm using single unit activity [40]. Chronic single-unit recordings are the definite gold standard for BCI control; however, they do have current limitations that prevent them from becoming the most pragmatic BCI solution in the clinic. In order to record single unit activity, penetrating microelectrodes have to be invasively implanted into the brain parenchyma. Large layer V pyramidal neurons are the primary target neurons for BCI. These pyramidal cells have long apical dendrites that align perpendicular to the cortical surface. During the peak of an action potential, large extracellular current flows into the axon hillock at the base of the cell body and flows up internally through the apical dendrites and back out into the extracellular matrix. Interestingly, the largest extracellular potential generated in these types of layer V pyramidal cells is not near the cell body but rather midway between the apical dendrites and cell body (i.e., layer III). This allows electrode arrays like the Utah electrode array (UEA), which was originally designed to deliver stimulating current above layer IV sensory neurons, to optimally record layer V pyramidal cells from layer III. Typically, the tips of these electrodes must be within 200 microns lateral to the dendritic arbor making long-term stability an issue [41, 42].

The human brain is a very pliable and almost gelatinous structure that is capable of large deformations relative to the skull under minor accelerations [43]. For microarrays that typically mount to the skull (e.g., Michigan probes, microwire arrays, etc.) these large deflections can cause serious stability problems in humans. To counteract this motion, some microelectrodes (e.g., Utah probes) are designed to sit on top of the brain and float with the relative motion, rather than anchor to the skull. More than likely, however, the subdural implantation of floating arrays induces a reactive immune response that causes the dura to fuse to the underlying cortex via scar tissue. Whether the microarrays are anchored to the skull or fused via dural scaring, they still must penetrate into the brain parenchyma where they cause local neural and vascular damage [44]. Secondly, microarrays are much stiffer mechanically than cortical tissue which results in a mechanical impedance mismatch. This leads to irritation of the surrounding tissue and initiates a cascade of reactive cell responses, typically characterized by activation and migration of microglia and astrocytes towards the implant site [44]. Continued presence of the microelectrode promotes formation of a gliotic sheath composed partly of these reactive astrocytes and microglia that can have numerous deleterious effects, including neural cell death and an increased tissue resistance that electrically isolates the device from the surrounding neural tissue [45]. So, while single unit activity is the gold standard for BCI control, the penetrating microarrays used to measure their activity limit their long-term chronic reliability.

5. Other BCI Modalities

Single unit activity recorded from penetrating microelectrodes is not the only BCI recording modality. As shown in Fig. 4 below, there are a number of electrophysiological signals that can be recorded from the brain. The main recording modalities are electroencephalography (EEG), electrocorticography (ECoG), local field potentials (LFP) and the previously described single unit activity (SUA). The source for all these microvolt-level signals are extracellular currents generated by cortical neurons. The differences between these modalities comes down to how many individual neurons are averaged together to generate the signal as well as the signal bandwidth (i.e., frequency range) of interest. In general, the more invasive the recording modality becomes the higher the spatial and spectral frequency of the signal.

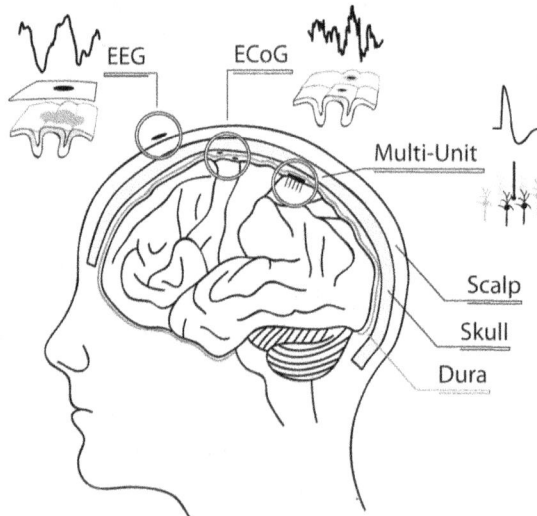

Fig. 4. BCI Modalities. Multi single-unit activity is the most invasive method where microelectrodes penetrate the brain parenchyma and record activity from single neurons within a few hundred microns of the electrode. EEG is non-invasive and records the average cortical activity over a large area from a distance 2-3 cm above the cortex. ECoG recordings can be taken either epidural (2-3 mm above cortex) or subdural (on cortex). In both EEG and ECoG, recordings are the averaged neural activity from the gyral neurons (gray shaded area).

5.1 *EEG*

For SUA recordings of large pyramidal neurons, the apical dendrites and their cell body approximate a dipole oriented perpendicular to the cortical surface. Small microelectrodes with 20 μm tips are placed within a couple hundred microns of this the dipole axis in order to record SUA in the 50-500 μV range. The frequency content of interest for discriminating single unit activity is 300 – 10 kHz. When recording this potential from surface of the scalp (2-3 cm above cortex), this signal would be reduced to around 25 picovolts (electric potential of a dipole falls off at $1/r^2$ of distance). Therefore, in order to record a viable EEG signal ($\sim$ 7μV) from the surface of the scalp, a large population of neurons must synchronize their synaptic and/or spiking activity such the potentials from their individual aligned dipoles can constructively sum. For single trial EEG activity, it has been estimated that around 6 cm^2 of cortical tissue (gray area under EEG electrode in Fig. 4) must be synchronized in order to produce a measurable scalp potential [46, 47]. In the brain, there is a correlation between spectral and spatial frequency. The larger the area that is averaged together, the lower the spectral power of the signal. For that reason, the EEG spectrum is limited to around 40 Hz for single trial recordings. Although it is due to different physics, one can think of the process like a car stereo. As the car gets farther away, you only hear lower frequencies (i.e., bass). As an electrode gets farther away from the cortex, only the lower frequencies constructively add to generate a signal.

Due to its non-invasive nature, EEG has always been a dominant player in human BCI research. One of the earliest methods measured visually evoked potentials over the parietal cortex [48]. The BCI system would rapidly flash letters on a computer monitor in front of the subject. When the letter the subject wished to add to a word she was trying to spell appeared, a significant peak in the EEG time domain waveform occurred 300 ms later over parietal cortex (P300 wave). By incorporating an automatic peak detector, individuals could spell out various words and/or sentences [49, 50]. Slow cortical potentials (SCP) is another EEG BCI technique where low frequency (< 1 Hz) signals recorded over the vertex of the head are used for control [51]. Unfortunately, both SCP and P300 are slowly evolving signals (i.e., low frequency content) and are not ideal for controlling prosthetic arms in realtime. Sensorimotor rhythms [52], where the power in both mu (8-12 Hz) and beta bands (18-25 Hz) of the EEG signal have been used for realtime BCI control of computer cursor via motor imagery [53], have the necessary frequency content for prosthetic control. During imagined movement, these two frequency bands show a significant decrease in power over baseline activity even in patients with severe motor disabilities [54]. Patients with spinal cord injury and ALS have successfully learned to modulate these rhythms for one, two and three dimensional BCI control [55, 56, 57]. For the multidimensional control, the subjects used two different frequency bands on the same electrode for two independent control signals. Unfortunately, given the low spatial frequency content in EEG recordings, finding multiple independent electrode sites for high dimensional prosthetic control seems unlikely.

5.2 *LFP*

Local field potentials use the same recording technology and cortical locations as SUA but analyze a lower spectrum (< 300 Hz) of the recorded potential. In primary motor cortex, the neurons have a loosely columnar organization where adjacent cells are more likely than not to have a similar preferred directions [58, 59, 60]. While adjacent neurons can encode the same movement direction, they do not necessarily fire synchronously. Since the main peak of an action potential has a time course on the order of 1 ms and motor cortical neurons have an average firing rate of only 13 Hz, the chance of even randomly synchronizing their peaks is low. However, the spectral power of an action potential has significant frequency components down into the mid frequency range (60-300 Hz). These mid-frequency components will increase in power with increased firing rate and sum across the local area. Since motor cortex is columnar, LFP signals should be cosine tuned to movement direction. As predicted, several groups have confirmed that gamma band activity in the 70-150 Hz range is directionally tuned to movement direction [61, 62] and correlated with single unit activity [62]. Since the mid-frequency LFP is generated by a group of correlated neurons, recording it should be less affected by encapsulation. Just like the summation of low frequency cortical activity can be seen penetrating the skull (EEG), the summation of mid frequency LFPs should easily penetrate any gliotic sheath encapsulating the electrode making it a potentially more durable signal modality for chronic BCI applications.

5.3 *ECoG*

As shown in Fig. 4, electrocorticography is an intermediate recording technology where electrophysiological recordings are taken either from the surface of the brain (subdural) or from the surface of the dura mater (epidural). Subdural ECoG recordings are routinely taken in human patients for the treatment of epilepsy which provided a clinical window to test the effectiveness of ECoG BCI. Since ECoG activity is recorded below the skull, the electrodes are much closer to the brain and sum activity over a much small area than EEG electrodes. The main advantage is that ECoG signals have significant frequency content up into the high gamma band (> 150 Hz) while EEG is limited to a maximum of around 40 Hz. Like LFP recordings, gamma band activity in ECoG signals are correlated to the underlying single unit activity [63]. The first closed loop ECoG-based BCI study used gamma band activity over motor regions and Broca's speech area to control a computer cursor [64]. Since ECoG BCI studies in human epilepsy patients are based on a clinical procedure, the researchers do not have control over which cortical areas the electrodes will be placed. This has led researchers to test non-motor areas of cortex in BCI tasks. For instance, researchers have used auditory cortex for BCI control [65]. The subject would imagine notes played on a piano which, in turn, would modulate gamma band activity on distinct electrodes to control a cursor. Unfortunately the standard clinical ECoG electrodes used for seizure monitoring in patients have diameters on the order of a few mm. This is a larger diameter than a typical cortical column, so the clinical epilepsy-monitoring ECoG arrays are probably not optimal for BCI control.

As mentioned earlier, there is significant relative motion between the brain and skull [43]. This relative motion is buffered by the three layers of the meninges (dura, arachnoid, and pia). The dura is attached to the skull and the pia is attached to the brain which leaves the intermediate arachnoid layer to buffer relative motion. In epilepsy monitoring, the surgeon will open the dura mater and place the electrodes into the arachnoid space. This allows the surgeon to slide the electrodes to reach cortical areas in the middle of the brain. Furthermore, the end goal of epilepsy monitoring is to find the problem area within the brain that is initiating the seizures and then surgically resect the tissue; therefore, opening of the dura mater is inevitable. For long term BCI applications, opening of the dura mater is probably not an optimal situation. Subdural electrodes placed chronically on the surface of the pia and routed out through the dura mater to the skull interferes with the natural buffering system of the meninges and will lead to scar formation. Furthermore, subdural electrodes placed inside the CNS provide a path for infection (e.g., encephalitis) if their leads are tunneled out to through skull. One solution to these issues is to place the ECoG electrodes on the surface of the dura which will allow the construct to anchor to the skull/dura complex alleviating the irritating effects of brain/skull motion. Using epidural electrodes will move the recording sites a few mm further away from the brain but since dural electrical conductivity is similar cerebral spinal fluid (i.e., low resistivity), epidural recordings will be very similar to subdural recordings for medium sized electrode diameters (e.g., 500 um) [66].

The first studies using epidural ECoG were applied in non-human primates [67, 68, 69]. In these experiments, electrodes were randomly assigned to control the velocity of a computer cursor. The subjects quickly learned control a computer screen by modifying the power in the 65 -100 Hz band. The randomly chosen electrodes were not initially directionally tuned, rather the monkey had to learn this mapping through biofeedback and neural plasticity. As shown in previous single unit studies, neural plasticity plays a huge role in BCI performance improvement [34, 70]. Not only were monkeys able to determine which electrodes within a large ECoG array were assigned for control, they were able identify and modify the specific frequency band used for control [67].

More recent studies have looked at using multiple frequency bands on each electrode [71] for BCI control. As shown in Figure 5, the raw ECoG trace can be split into multiple frequency bands of interest and processed in realtime using DSP hardware. Each electrode has five independent frequency bands or features that the subject can modulate for control. A 32 channel ECoG array will have 160 features that can be regressed to movement kinematics (note that regression assumes that all frequency bands encode movement parameters using cosine tuning). In the initial block, the monkey just sits and watches the computer on the screen (Fig. 6) while the computer controls the movement of the cursor. The animal watches as the computer moves the cursor to each of the targets. When the cursor touches the target, the animal receives a reward (e.g., juice).

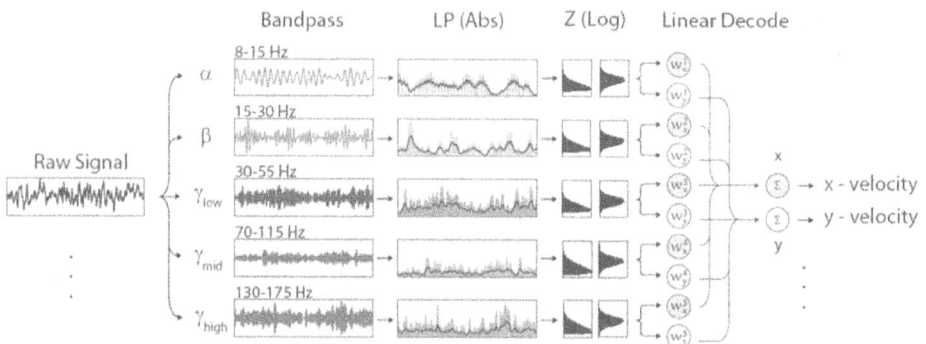

Fig. 5. Decoding multi-band activity from ECoG activity. The raw signal on the left is band-passed filtered into five bands of interest. Once filtered, the signals are rectified (Abs = absolute value) and then low-passed filtered (LP) to get an estimate of band power. The resulting power signal is log transformed to normalize its distribution (Log) and z-scored (subtract mean and divide by standard deviation) to normalize its magnitude. The resulting signal can then be assigned appropriate linear decoding weights and summed across both channels and bands to calculate a velocity control signal.

Assisted Learning Paradigm

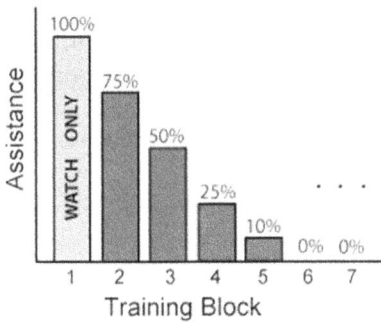

Desired Movement Direction

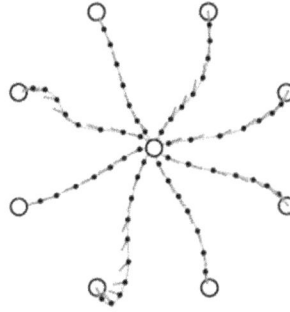

Fig. 6. Using an assistive learning paradigm to enhance co-adaptive learning in BCI task. In the first block of trials, subjects just watch as the computer moves the cursor to the target. After completing the first block, the cortical activity during the "watch task" is regressed against movement direction. In the next block of trials, the computer controls 75% of the cursor and the individual controls 25% through BCI. This allows variation in the movement of the cursor; resulting in the desired movement direction to the target to vary throughout the reach. Regressing on an instant by instant basis throughout the movements allows for much faster co-adaptation. After each training block, the amount of assistance is reduced until the subject is using 100% brain control (6th block).

Rewarding the animal during the initial watch task is key as it causes the subject to pay close attention to the cursor which in turn modulates cortical activity which can be regressed against movement direction. During the next training block, the animal is given partial control of the cursor via the recently regressed encoding vectors. After each block of trials, a new regression is performed and the animal is given more control over the cursor. This coadaptive algorithm allowed the subjects to rapidly learn the BCI task. A BCI naïve animal that had two electrodes and one frequency band (2 features) assigned to cursor velocity would take two months to become competent in 2D BCI control. A BCI naïve animal that was allowed to use all 32 channels and five frequency bands (160 features) in an assisted learning paradigm took 40 minutes to become competent in 2D BCI control.

References

1. J. R. Wolpaw, N. Birbaumer, D. J. McFarland, G. Pfurtscheller, and T. M. Vaughan, Brain-computer interfaces for communication and control, *Clin. Neurophysiol.*, **113**(6), pp. 767–791, 2002.

2. E. Y. Chao and K. N. An, Graphical interpretation of the solution to the redundant problem in biomechanics, *J. Biomech. Eng.*, **100**(3), pp. 159–167, 1978.
3. J. F. Soechting and M. Flanders, Moving in three-dimensional space: frames of reference, vectors, and coordinate systems, *Annu. Rev. Neurosci.*, **15**, pp. 167–191, 1992.
4. S. S. Chan and D. W. Moran, Computational model of a primate arm: from hand position to joint angles, joint torques and muscle forces, *J. Neural Eng.*, **3**(4), pp. 327–337, 2006.
5. N. Bernstein, The problem of the interrelation of coordination and localization, *Arch Biol Sci*, **38**, pp. 1–35, 1935.
6. F. E. Zajac, Muscle and tendon: properties, models, scaling, and application to biomechanics and motor control, *Crit. Rev. Biomed. Eng.*, **17**(4), pp. 359–411, 1989.
7. R. L. Sainburg, H. Poizner, and C. Ghez, Loss of proprioception produces deficits in interjoint coordination, *J. Neurophysiol.*, **70**(5), pp. 2136–2147, 1993.
8. R. Porter and R. Lemon, *Corticospinal function and voluntary movement*, (Clarendon Press, Oxford, 1993).
9. E. V. Evarts, Relation of pyramidal tract activity to force exerted during voluntary movement, *J. Neurophysiol.*, **31**(1), pp. 14–27, 1968.
10. W. T. Thach, Correlation of neural discharge with pattern and force of muscular activity, joint position, and direction of intended next movement in motor cortex and cerebellum, *J. Neurophysiol.*, **41**(3), pp. 654–676, 1978.
11. J.-A. Rathelot and P. L. Strick, Muscle representation in the macaque motor cortex: an anatomical perspective, *Proc. Natl. Acad. Sci. U. S. A.*, **103**(21), pp. 8257–8262, 2006.
12. A. P. Georgopoulos, A. B. Schwartz, and R. E. Kettner, Neuronal population coding of movement direction, *Science*, **233**(4771), pp. 1416–1419, 1986.
13. D. W. Moran and A. B. Schwartz, Motor cortical representation of speed and direction during reaching, *J. Neurophysiol.*, **82**(5), pp. 2676–2692, 1999.
14. A. B. Schwartz, Direct cortical representation of drawing, *Science*, **265**(5171), pp. 540–542, 1994.
15. R. E. Kettner, A. B. Schwartz, and A. P. Georgopoulos, Primate motor cortex and free arm movements to visual targets in three-dimensional space. III. Positional gradients and population coding of movement direction from various movement origins, *J. Neurosci.*, **8**(8), pp. 2938–2947, 1988.
16. W. Wang, S. S. Chan, D. A. Heldman, and D. W. Moran, Motor cortical representation of position and velocity during reaching, *J. Neurophysiol.*, **97**(6), pp. 4258–4270, 2007.
17. A. B. Schwartz, D. W. Moran, and G. A. Reina, Differential representation of perception and action in the frontal cortex, *Science*, **303**(5656), pp. 380–383, 2004.
18. P. Cisek and J. F. Kalaska, Neural correlates of reaching decisions in dorsal premotor cortex: specification of multiple direction choices and final selection of action, *Neuron*, **45**(5), pp. 801–814, 2005.
19. B. Pesaran, M. J. Nelson, and R. A. Andersen, Dorsal premotor neurons encode the relative position of the hand, eye, and goal during reach planning, *Neuron*, **51**(1), pp. 125–134, 2006.
20. T. M. Pearce and D. W. Moran, Strategy-dependent encoding of planned arm movements in the dorsal premotor cortex, *Science*, **337**(6097), pp. 984–988, 2012.
21. L. Shen and G. E. Alexander, Preferential representation of instructed target location versus limb trajectory in dorsal premotor area, *J. Neurophysiol.*, **77**(3), pp. 1195–1212, 1997.
22. T. Ochiai, H. Mushiake, and J. Tanji, Effects of image motion in the dorsal premotor cortex during planning of an arm movement, *J. Neurophysiol.*, **88**(4), pp. 2167–2171, 2002.

23. A. P. Batista, G. Santhanam, B. M. Yu, S. I. Ryu, A. Afshar, and K. V. Shenoy, Reference frames for reach planning in macaque dorsal premotor cortex, *J. Neurophysiol.*, **98**(2), pp. 966–983, 2007.

24. M. Weinrich and S. P. Wise, The premotor cortex of the monkey, *J. Neurosci.*, **2**(9), pp. 1329–1345, 1982.

25. G. Santhanam, S. I. Ryu, B. M. Yu, A. Afshar, and K. V. Shenoy, A high-performance brain-computer interface, *Nature*, **442**(7099), pp. 195–198, 2006.

26. S. Kakei, D. S. Hoffman, and P. L. Strick, Muscle and movement representations in the primary motor cortex, *Science*, **285**(5436), pp. 2136–2139, 1999.

27. W. Wang, S. S. Chan, D. A. Heldman, and D. W. Moran, Motor cortical representation of hand translation and rotation during reaching, *J Neurosci*, **30**(3), pp. 958–962, 2010.

28. E. E. Fetz and D. V. Finocchio, Operant conditioning of specific patterns of neural and muscular activity, *Science*, **174**(7), pp. 431–435, 1971.

29. P. R. Kennedy, The cone electrode: a long-term electrode that records from neurites grown onto its recording surface, *J. Neurosci. Methods*, **29**(3), pp. 181–193, 1989.

30. P. R. Kennedy and R. A. Bakay, Restoration of neural output from a paralyzed patient by a direct brain connection, *Neuroreport*, **9**(8), pp. 1707–1711, 1998.

31. P. R. Kennedy, R. A. Bakay, M. M. Moore, K. Adams, and J. Goldwaithe, Direct control of a computer from the human central nervous system, *IEEE Trans. Rehabil. Eng.*, **8**(2), pp. 198–202, 2000.

32. D. W. Moran and A. B. Schwartz, Motor cortical activity during drawing movements: population representation during spiral tracing, *J. Neurophysiol.*, **82**(5), p. 2693-2704, 1999.

33. A. B. Schwartz and D. W. Moran, Motor cortical activity during drawing movements: population representation during lemniscate tracing, *J. Neurophysiol.*, **82**(5), p. 2705-2718, 1999.

34. D. M. Taylor, S. I. H. Tillery, and A. B. Schwartz, Direct cortical control of 3D neuroprosthetic devices, *Science*, **296**(5574), pp. 1829–1832, 2002.

35. M. D. Serruya, N. G. Hatsopoulos, L. Paninski, M. R. Fellows, and J. P. Donoghue, Brain-machine interface: Instant neural control of a movement signal, *Nature*, **416**(6877), pp. 141–142, 2002.

36. S. P. Kim, J. D. Simeral, L. R. Hochberg, J. P. Donoghue, and M. J. Black, Neural control of computer cursor velocity by decoding motor cortical spiking activity in humans with tetraplegia, *J Neural Eng*, **5**(4), pp. 455–476, 2008.

37. M. Velliste, S. Perel, M. C. Spalding, A. S. Whitford, and A. B. Schwartz, Cortical control of a prosthetic arm for self-feeding, *Nature*, **453**(7198), pp. 1098–1101, 2008.

38. E. Salinas and L. F. Abbott, Vector reconstruction from firing rates, *J. Comput. Neurosci.*, **1**(1–2), pp. 89–107, 1994.

39. J. L. Collinger, B. Wodlinger, J. E. Downey, W. Wang, E. C. Tyler-Kabara, D. J. Weber, A. J. C. McMorland, M. Velliste, M. L. Boninger, and A. B. Schwartz, High-performance neuroprosthetic control by an individual with tetraplegia, *Lancet*, **381**(9866), pp. 557–564, 2013.

40. B. Wodlinger, J. E. Downey, E. C. Tyler-Kabara, A. B. Schwartz, M. L. Boninger, and J. L. Collinger, Ten-dimensional anthropomorphic arm control in a human brain-machine interface: difficulties, solutions, and limitations, *J. Neural Eng.*, **12**(1), p. 16011, 2015.

41. I. V. Bondar, D. A. Leopold, B. J. Richmond, J. D. Victor, and N. K. Logothetis, Long-term stability of visual pattern selective responses of monkey temporal lobe neurons, *PLoS ONE*, **4**(12), p. e8222, 2009.

42. A. S. Dickey, A. Suminski, Y. Amit, and N. G. Hatsopoulos, Single-unit stability using chronically implanted multielectrode arrays, *J. Neurophysiol.*, **102**(2), pp. 1331–1339, 2009.

43. P. V. Bayly, T. S. Cohen, E. P. Leister, D. Ajo, E. C. Leuthardt, and G. M. Genin, Deformation of the human brain induced by mild acceleration, *J. Neurotrauma*, **22**(8), pp. 845–856, 2005.

44. C. S. Bjornsson, S. J. Oh, Y. A. Al-Kofahi, Y. J. Lim, K. L. Smith, J. N. Turner, S. De, B. Roysam, W. Shain, and S. J. Kim, Effects of insertion conditions on tissue strain and vascular damage during neuroprosthetic device insertion, *J. Neural Eng.*, **3**, p. 196-207, 2006.

45. J. C. Williams, J. A. Hippensteel, J. Dilgen, W. Shain, and D. R. Kipke, Complex impedance spectroscopy for monitoring tissue responses to inserted neural implants, *J. Neural Eng.*, **4**, p. 410-424, 2007.

46. R. Cooper, A. . Winter, H. . Crow, and W. G. Walter, Comparison of subcortical, cortical and scalp activity using chronically indwelling electrodes in man, *Electroencephalogr. Clin. Neurophysiol.*, **18**(3), pp. 217–228, 1965.

47. P. L. Nunez and R. Srinivasan, *Electric fields of the brain: the neurophysics of EEG*, (Oxford University Press, New York, 2006).

48. E. Donchin and D. B. Smith, The contingent negative variation and the late positive wave of the average evoked potential, *Electroencephalogr. Clin. Neurophysiol.*, **29**(2), pp. 201–203, 1970.

49. E. Donchin, K. M. Spencer, and R. Wijesinghe, The mental prosthesis: assessing the speed of a P300-based brain-computer interface, *IEEE Trans. Rehabil. Eng.*, **8**(2), pp. 174–179, 2000.

50. E. W. Sellers and E. Donchin, A P300-based brain-computer interface: initial tests by ALS patients, *Clin. Neurophysiol*, **117**(3), pp. 538–548, 2006.

51. T. Elbert, B. Rockstroh, W. Lutzenberger, and N. Birbaumer, Biofeedback of slow cortical potentials. I, *Electroencephalogr. Clin. Neurophysiol.*, **48**(3), pp. 293–301, 1980.

52. E. Niedermeyer and F. H. L. da Silva, *Electroencephalography: Basic Principles, Clinical Applications, and Related Fields*, (Williams & Wilkins, Philadelphia, 1999).

53. D. J. McFarland, L. A. Miner, T. M. Vaughan, and J. R. Wolpaw, Mu and beta rhythm topographies during motor imagery and actual movements, *Brain Topogr.*, **12**(3), pp. 177–186, 2000.

54. G. Pfurtscheller and C. Neuper, Motor imagery activates primary sensorimotor area in humans, *Neurosci. Lett.*, **239**(2–3), pp. 65–68, 1997.

55. J. R. Wolpaw and D. J. McFarland, Control of a two-dimensional movement signal by a noninvasive brain-computer interface in humans, *Proc. Natl. Acad. Sci. U. S. A.*, **101**(51), pp. 17849–17854, 2004.

56. A. Kübler, F. Nijboer, J. Mellinger, T. M. Vaughan, H. Pawelzik, G. Schalk, D. J. McFarland, N. Birbaumer, and J. R. Wolpaw, Patients with ALS can use sensorimotor rhythms to operate a brain-computer interface, *Neurology*, **64**(10), pp. 1775–1777, 2005.

57. D. J. McFarland, W. A. Sarnacki, and J. R. Wolpaw, Electroencephalographic (EEG) control of three-dimensional movement, *J. Neural Eng.*, **7**(3), p. 36007, 2010.

58. B. Amirikian and A. P. Georgopoulos, Modular organization of directionally tuned cells in the motor cortex: Is there a short-range order?, *Proc. Natl. Acad. Sci. U. S. A.*, **100**(21), p. 12474, 2003.

59. E. Stark, R. Drori, and M. Abeles, Motor cortical activity related to movement kinematics exhibits local spatial organization, *Cortex*, **45**(3), pp. 418–431, 2009.

60. N. G. Hatsopoulos, Columnar organization in the motor cortex, *Cortex*, **46**(2), pp. 270–271, 2010.

61. J. Rickert, S. C. de Oliveira, E. Vaadia, A. Aertsen, S. Rotter, and C. Mehring, Encoding of movement direction in different frequency ranges of motor cortical local field potentials, *J. Neurosci.*, **25**(39), p. 8815-8824, 2005.

62. D. A. Heldman, W. Wang, S. S. Chan, and D. W. Moran, Local field potential spectral tuning in motor cortex during reaching, *IEEE Trans. Neural Syst. Rehabil. Eng.*, **14**(2), pp. 180–183, 2006.

63. K. J. Miller, Broadband spectral change: evidence for a macroscale correlate of population firing rate?, *J Neurosci*, **30**(19), pp. 6477–6479, 2010.

64. E. C. Leuthardt, G. Schalk, J. R. Wolpaw, J. G. Ojemann, and D. W. Moran, A brain–computer interface using electrocorticographic signals in humans, *J. Neural Eng.*, **1**, p. 63-71, 2004.

65. E. A. Felton, J. A. Wilson, J. C. Williams, and P. C. Garell, Electrocorticographically controlled brain–computer interfaces using motor and sensory imagery in patients with temporary subdural electrode implants, *J. Neurosurg. Pediatr.*, **106**(3), pp. 495–500, 2007.

66. D. T. Bundy, E. Zellmer, C. M. Gaona, M. Sharma, N. Szrama, C. Hacker, Z. V. Freudenburg, A. Daitch, D. W. Moran, and E. C. Leuthardt, Characterization of the effects of the human dura on macro- and micro-electrocorticographic recordings, *J. Neural Eng.*, **11**(1), p. 16006, 2014.

67. A. G. Rouse and D. W. Moran, Neural adaptation of epidural electrocorticographic (EECoG) signals during closed-loop brain computer interface (BCI) tasks, in *Engineering in Medicine and Biology Society Annual International Conference*, 2009, pp. 5514–5517.

68. A. G. Rouse, S. R. Stanslaski, P. Cong, R. M. Jensen, P. Afshar, D. Ullestad, R. Gupta, G. F. Molnar, D. W. Moran, and T. J. Denison, A chronic generalized bi-directional brain–machine interface, *J. Neural Eng.*, **8**(3), p. 36018, 2011.

69. A. G. Rouse, J. J. Williams, J. J. Wheeler, and D. W. Moran, Cortical adaptation to a chronic micro-electrocorticographic brain computer interface, *J. Neurosci.*, **33**(4), pp. 1326–1330, 2013.

70. B. Jarosiewicz, S. M. Chase, G. W. Fraser, M. Velliste, R. E. Kass, and A. B. Schwartz, Functional network reorganization during learning in a brain-computer interface paradigm, *Proc Natl Acad Sci USA*, **105**(49), pp. 19486–19491, 2008.

71. J. J. Williams, A. G. Rouse, S. Thongpang, J. C. Williams, and D. W. Moran, Differentiating closed-loop cortical intention from rest: building an asynchronous electrocorticographic BCI, *J. Neural Eng.*, **10**(4), p. 46001, 2013.

Chapter 4.4

Gastric and Cardio-Vascular Muscle Stimulation

Amirali Toossi[1], Bethany R. Kondiles[2] and Vivian K. Mushahwar[1,3]

[1]Neuroscience and Mental Health Institute, University of Alberta
[2]Department of Physiology and Biophysics, University of Washington
[3]Department of Medicine, University of Alberta
5-005 Katz Group Centre, 116 St. and 85 Avenue, Edmonton, Alberta, Canada, T6G 2E1
vivian.mushahwar@ualberta.ca

This chapter discusses pathologies of gastric and cardio-vascular smooth muscles that may benefit from electrical stimulation.

1. Introduction

Advances in knowledge about the physiology and pathophysiology of smooth muscles have led to the discovery of multiple elements that are involved in the regulation and initiation of smooth muscle contraction as well as multiple potential sources of dysfunction. Dysfunction can be innate or acquired and the source of dysfunction can span the spectrum from protein mutations to neural irregularities. In recent years, technological developments have introduced possibilities for therapeutic application of neural prosthetic devices as treatments for pathological conditions and disorders associated with smooth muscles. This chapter presents two examples of therapeutic neuroprostheses for the control of smooth muscles after injuries or diseases. The potential mechanism of action of these neuroprostheses are discussed along with examples of the preclinical and clinical results obtained to date.

2. Electrical Stimulation of the Gastrointestinal Tract

Electrical stimulation techniques have been applied to different parts of the GI tract for treatment of GI disorders such as refractory gastroparesis [54], fecal incontinence [41] and constipation [63, 79]. Gastric stimulation is also under investigation for treatment of obesity [21, 22, 99]. This section focuses on the use of electrical stimulation for the treatment of gastroparesis.

Gastroparesis is a condition in which stomach motility is absent or slowed down. Gastroparesis can develop as a sequel to a wide range of conditions including vagal nerve injury [90], thyroid disease [43], diabetes mellitus [68], spinal cord injury [45], and tumors [91]. Gastroparesis can also develop as a side effect of prescription medications (e.g., L-dopa [36]) or idiopathically. Upper abdominal surgery can also lead to gastroparesis [25], perhaps due to iatrogenic vagal nerve injuries.

Disrupted motility can lead to reduced absorption of fluids and nutrients from ingested food as well as reduced absorptions of oral medications [40]. If left untreated, severe gastroparesis can also lead to other complications such as hospitalization for extreme dehydration and malnutrition, abdominal pain and functional dyspepsia, gastroesophageal reflux disease, and formation of obstructive bezoar from the undigested food in the stomach [12, 44, 48, 83, 95].

The general treatment guidelines for gastroparesis address decreased absorption of fluid and nutrients, the symptoms of gastroparesis, and the underlying cause. Patients may be able to elevate fluid and nutrient levels by changing their diet to compensate for the lack of absorption. Symptoms, such as nausea, vomiting and bloating are treated by medications such as antiemetic and prokinetic agents [80]. Finally, the suspected cause of gastroparesis must be addressed to prevent its recurrence. Nonetheless, in people with *refractory* gastroparesis, these treatments are not successful. One of the treatment options for managing refractory gastroparesis is gastrointestinal electrical stimulation (GES).

2.1. *Mechanism of action of GES*

Smooth muscles of the stomach participate in well-coordinated movements called peristalsis that help break down food and transfer its contents to the small intestines. These coordinated movements are driven by the ICC, which are also known as gastric pacemaker cells [2, 84]. Hinder and Kelly [37] found that stomach pacemaker cells in humans are directly responsible for rhythmic oscillations occurring 5-7 cm aborad of the junction of the esophagus and stomach. Pacemaker cells in the stomach produce a basic electrical rhythm (BER) (also known as "slow waves") with a frequency of approximately 3 cycles per minute [37, 49, 73]. Slow waves travel at an aborad velocity of 0.3-0.8 cm/s [37, 49] and these oscillations in membrane potential can create action potentials and contractions of the smooth muscles in their path.

Gastroparesis can result from disruptions in the generation and transport of slow waves [9], from impairments in the innervation of the smooth muscles or from impairments in the muscles themselves [8]. For instance, degeneration or lack of

ICC pacemaker cells might be one of the causative factors in the development of idiopathic and type 1 diabetic gastroparesis [100]. In this respect, Grover et al. [33] extracted biopsy samples from the stomach of 40 patients with gastroparesis (50% idiopathic and 50% diabetic) and 20 control subjects. Histological analysis demonstrated a reduction (of at least 25%) in the number of ICC cells in 50% of patients with diabetic gastroparesis and 50% of patients with idiopathic gastroparesis. Similar findings have also been reported in animal studies [77]. In addition to loss of ICC cells, diabetic gastroparesis may be caused by hyperglycemia [32] and diabetic neuropathies affecting the vagal nerve[18].

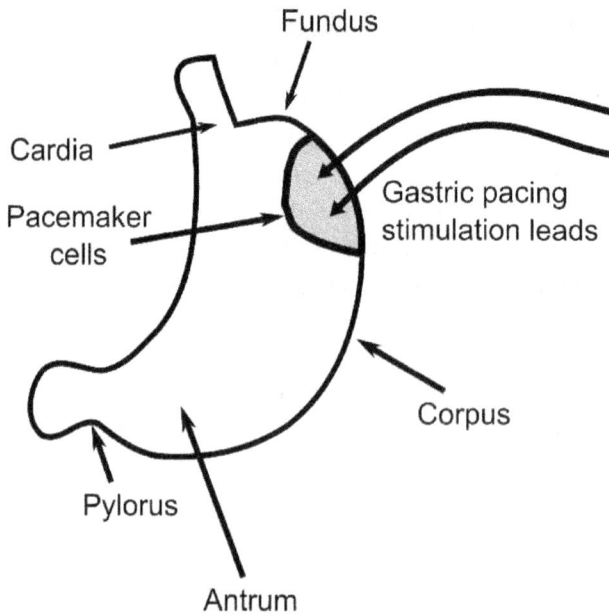

Fig. 1. Implantation target of the gastric pacing GES systems placed by Hocking et al. [39]

A typical GES system consists of an electrical stimulator and one or multiple leads that deliver the stimulus to the target locations of the GI tract. Clinicians may place the electrodes at different locations in the stomach, depending on the type of the GES intervention. An example of a GES system is illustrated in Figure 1.

The effect of electrical stimulation and its mechanism of action can be divided into three main categories based on stimulation frequency [8, 71].

2.1.1. Low stimulation frequencies near the BER (gastric pacing, low frequency–high energy stimulation):

One of the main goals of this low frequency stimulation paradigm is to treat gastric arrhythmias by producing rhythmic slow-waves near the mid-corpus of the stomach [52]. The low frequency–high energy (LF-HE) paradigm attempts to recreate the normal pace of oscillations, and is commonly referred to as "gastric pacing." Because the BER of the stomach in humans is approximately 3 cycles per minute, the gastric pacing technique delivers electrical stimulation at frequencies slightly higher than the BER and lower than ~4.7 cycles per minute, which is the maximal stomach entrainment frequency in humans, to produce slow waves which travel in both orad and aborad directions [8]. This frequency range is chosen because, for unknown reasons, stimulation at the exact frequency of BER has been ineffective in producing gastric entrainment in humans [20] and dogs [6]. The existence of a maximal entrainment frequency for the stomach is thought to be due to the long refractory period of the smooth muscles of the stomach [11, 85, 94]. Other standard parameters of gastric pacing include long pulse durations ranging from 30 to 500 ms and stimulation amplitudes ranging between 2 and 4 mA. The slow frequency and long pulses of stimulation are what give this technique its name of LF-HE [7, 8, 52, 54].

One of the practical challenges of this technique is its high power and battery requirements, which are important considerations for implantable devices [8]. Therefore, many clinical studies so far have utilized external stimulators and transcutaneous leads to deliver stimulation for gastric pacing [20, 53, 65].

2.1.2. *Stimulation frequencies higher than 4.8 cycles per minute but less than 5 per second (High Frequency–Low Energy stimulation):*

This stimulation paradigm involves the delivery of 300 μs long pulses with amplitudes ranging from 2 to 5 mA [7, 28, 29]. Since the duration of the pulse is much shorter than in the LF-HE protocol, this paradigm is comparatively referred to as "high frequency-low energy (HF-LE)." HF-LE stimulation is a potential treatment for the symptoms of gastroparesis such as vomiting, but may not directly affect gastric emptying [29, 55, 67, 76].

The exact mechanism of action of this paradigm is not well known [7, 8]. Since stimulation frequencies for the HF-LE stimulation paradigm are higher than the maximal stomach entrainment frequency that can normally produce slow waves (~4.7 cycles per minute in humans), in most cases it does not affect or interfere with the existing slow waves produced by the stomach [7, 8, 76]. Tougas et al. [97] suggested that improvements in the symptoms of gastroparesis may be due to modulations of the sensory pathways. Indeed, it has been demonstrated that HF-LE stimulation in rats [56] and dogs [19] activates vagal afferents. However, studies in humans demonstrate that the benefits of HF-LE stimulation are present even in patients with vagotomy [67]. Therefore, if vagal pathways are involved, they are not the only mechanism by which HF-LE stimulation affects gastroparesis in humans.

Tang et al. [96] found that the activity of sub-populations of periventricular neurons of the hypothalamus, which sense stomach wall distension, are inhibited during HF-LE GES in rats. This inhibition may contribute to the reduction of symptoms such as nausea and vomiting due to the lack of input regarding distension. Interestingly, they also found that GES paradigms used for treatment of obesity have an opposite effect on these neurons.

2.1.3. Stimulation frequencies higher than 5 per second (neural GES):

The goal of this type of GES is to produce muscle contractions that propagate circumferentially in the aborad direction [8]. This stimulation paradigm has been effective in improving gastric emptying significantly in animal models [71].

Mintchev et al. [71] demonstrated that stomach contractions produced with GES frequencies higher than 5 Hz can be eliminated by the drug atropine (an acetylcholine antagonist). Therefore, contractions produced by these GES paradigms are thought to be mediated by cholinergic axons. Hence, this stimulation paradigm is also called "neural GES."

Since the stimulation frequency of neural GES is higher than the maximal frequency for production of the slow-waves, multiple electrodes need to be placed circumferentially and longitudinally around the stomach to produce coordinated movements similar to natural propagating contractions [8, 71]. For instance, Mintchev et al. [71] used 16 electrodes around the stomach (4 groups separated longitudinally) in dogs and delivered stimulation in the form of trains of pulses (4 second-long, 50 Hz-frequency) in a coordinated fashion, simulating the natural longitudinal propagation of contractions. Using this technique, gastric emptying improved significantly [71]. Neural GES is an emerging research focus [42] and is under ongoing investigation in animal models [8].

2.2. Clinical Results

Various forms of GES have been extensively studied in animal models and in humans. A few clinical studies that demonstrate the efficacy and limitations of GES as a treatment for gastroparesis are highlighted here. Though neural GES may be a promising future avenue, there are currently no published clinical studies detailing its use in humans.

2.2.1. Gastric Pacing:

Miedema et al. [70] conducted experiments wherein electrodes for gastric pacing were implanted in 10 patients undergoing gallbladder removal surgery. The experimenters demonstrated that gastric pacing with stimulation at a frequency of 4.3 cycles per minute (4 V amplitude, 60 ms pulse width) successfully achieved entrainment of gastric rhythms in 90% of the patients one day post-surgery. Potential effects of gastric pacing on stomach emptying were not investigated.

Hocking et al. [39] also investigated the efficacy of gastric pacing in the entrainment of stomach and gastric emptying in human patients. In their study, 17 patients who were at risk of developing gastroparesis were recruited for implantation of a gastric pacing stimulator. Frequencies of stimulation ranged from 0.3 to 1.6 cycles per minute faster than the BER established for each patient. Other stimulation parameters included pulse amplitudes of 2 mA and pulse widths of 300 ms. Gastric entrainment was successful in 63% of the cases. However, gastric emptying of solid contents was not improved. The fact that patients with gastric arrhythmias showed significant entrainment, yet no improvement in gastric emptying, led the authors to suggest that gastric arrhythmias are not the main cause for the development of gastroparesis after gastric surgeries [39].

To study the effects of chronic gastric pacing, Mccallum et al. [65] conducted a study lasting 90 days in 9 patients. They demonstrated that gastric pacing not only was successful in producing gastric entrainment, but it also resulted in significant improvements in gastric emptying by the end of the treatment period. The effect of gastric pacing on gastroparesis symptoms was also investigated by evaluating the patients' daily symptom severity scores. Symptom severity scores were derived from a questionnaire filled out by the patients which associated a score of 0 to 4 (higher score for more severe symptoms) to four of the gastroparesis symptoms (nausea, bloating, pain and vomiting). The numerical average of the individual daily scores was called the daily symptom severity score. Mccallum et al. [65] reported a significant reduction in the daily symptom severity scores after 4 weeks of gastric pacing. Similar results of efficacy in both entrainment and gastric emptying with chronic gastric pacing stimulation have also been reported by Forster et al. [31] and Lin et al. [53].

Recent studies have focused on developing computer models of gastric pacing in order to improve the understanding of its mechanism of action as well as optimize the stimulation parameters [14, 27, 86].

2.2.2. High Frequency – Low Energy stimulation (<5 Hz):

Many clinical studies have demonstrated the efficacy of HF-LE GES for treatment of gastroparesis symptoms, and as a result, the United States Food and Drug Administration (FDA) has approved a humanitarian device exemption (HDE) for an implantable HF-LE GES device called Enterra (produced by Medtronic Co., Dublin, Ireland) [92]. The Enterra system delivers trains of 14 Hz at a repetition rate of 12 cycles per minute. Each pulse has an amplitude of 5 mA and pulse width of 330 μs [64].

Abell et al. [1] conducted a one month long double-blind randomized controlled clinical trial (RCT) on 33 patients with idiopathic and diabetic gastroparesis at 11 centers in Europe and North America. All participants underwent GES implantation and were randomized to either a stimulation (continuously) ON group or a stimulation OFF group. The stimulation parameters were the same as the parameters for Enterra. At the end of the one month period, vomiting frequency was significantly reduced in the stimulation ON vs. the stimulation OFF group. However, the changes in vomiting frequency were not significant for either of the sub-groups of patients with idiopathic and diabetic gastroparesis. The authors suggested that the lack of statistical significance in sub-groups might have been due to the small sample size or limited duration of the study.

In another set of studies, McCallum et al. [64, 66] conducted a double-blind RCT at 8 centres in the US. They implanted Enterra systems in 55 patients with diabetic gastroparesis [66] and 32 patients with idiopathic gastroparesis [64] to study the efficacy and safety of this intervention. The stimulation was turned on for 6 weeks post-surgery in all patients. After the initial period of stimulation, participants were randomly divided into two groups of 1) stimulation ON (3 months) then stimulation OFF (3 months) or 2) stimulation OFF (3 months) then stimulation ON (3 months). They found that after the initial 6 weeks, HF-LE GES significantly reduced the vomiting frequency compared to baseline. However, no statistically significant changes were observed in vomiting frequency between the ON and OFF groups during the second phase of the study. The authors suggested that a long carry-over effect from the initial phase of this trial may have washed out any effects during the second phase.

A recent meta-analysis of the results obtained from the total of 5 RCTs of HF-LE GES to date (three of which are mentioned above) concluded that the change in vomiting frequency in patients with gastroparesis enrolled in stimulation ON and stimulation OFF groups were not significantly different [51]. Similar results were found for symptom severity scores.

2.3. *Summary and Future Directions*

The use of GES for treatment of various types of gastroparesis has been widely investigated in animal and clinical studies. Clinical results obtained so far show promise for treatment of gastric arrhythmia and gastric emptying using gastric pacing. However, high power requirements and the need for external stimulators are barriers for widespread clinical adoption [8]. Continued advances in battery technologies [8, 75] as well as emerging computer modelling studies with the goal of optimizing stimulation parameters may provide a more practical technological solution for gastric pacing techniques in the future.

HF-LE GES clinical studies (using the clinically available Enterra system) have also demonstrated promising results in the treatment of symptoms of gastroparesis such as vomiting and nausea. Nonetheless, the clinical results obtained so far have not been able to rule out placebo effects, and more well designed blinded RCT trials are required to address this question more thoroughly. Furthermore, HF-LE GES has only shown promise for symptoms of gastroparesis and does not appear to produce significant improvements in gastric emptying.

Considering the advantages of low frequency and high frequency GES, Liu et al. [57] suggested a "dual-pulse" stimulation paradigm to maximize the benefits of GES. In this paradigm, each stimulation pulse is replaced with two pulses: a long duration pulse (similar to gastric pacing) followed by a short duration pulse (similar to HF-LE GES). They demonstrated that this type of GES can achieve both the benefits of entraining the stomach and reducing the symptoms of gastroparesis in dogs. This promising technique is an ongoing subject of GES research in animal models [50, 93]. However, this dual system is still subject to the technological limitations of the gastric pacing technique discussed previously.

Preclinical studies of neural GES have shown encouraging results for gastric emptying. Considering the low power requirements of this stimulation paradigm, this technique may provide a more effective and practical solution for refractory gastroparesis in the future [8].

3. Electrical Stimulation for Control of Cardiovascular Vessels

An emerging area of research is the use of electrical stimulation techniques to control blood flow in the vessels by inducing vasoconstriction or thrombosis [78]. Preclinical studies thus far have focused on reducing blood flow to targeted tissues for two potential applications. The first is the occlusion of blood supply to cancerous tissue by localized coagulation of blood vessels [78, 89]. The second is the management of internal bleeding (e.g., in the liver [59, 60]) caused by trauma.

Hemorrhage is one of the main causes of mortality in the first 24 hours after trauma [46]. Electrical stimulation can be used to completely occlude (thrombosis) or reduce blood flow (vasoconstriction) either to cancerous tissue or to hemorrhaging areas. Because the same principles apply for both applications, the ensuing description focuses only on cancerous tissue.

In the case of thrombosis, complete halting of blood flow to cancerous tissue is induced to produce hypoxia-related cell death. Denekamp et al. [24] demonstrated that 8 hours of no blood supply can result in more than 50% reduction in tumor cell viability. Reduction of blood flow to the tumor (as opposed to a complete occlusion) by pulsed electrical stimulation is also a beneficial mechanism in another cancer treatment technique called electrochemotherapy [88]. Electrochemotherapy is a technique that uses electrical pulses to increase the permeability of tumor cells and therefore increases their exposure to administered pharmacological drugs [98]. This stimulation paradigm not only increases the permeability of the tumor cells (electroporation), but also transiently reduces the blood flow to these cells [72, 82]. When timed properly with respect to the administration of the drug, this effect can increase the length of time that cells are exposed to the chemotherapy agents, further enhancing their effect [72].

There are multiple advantages to using pulsed electrical stimulation approaches for reducing blood supply to the cancerous tissue. Pulsed electrical stimulation is rapid, localized, selective and highly tractable [78]. This is in contrast with other available techniques for disrupting blood flow, such as electrocautery [23] and electrosurgery [58] that are based on temperature increase to achieve vascular coagulation. The selectivity and localizability of these techniques are limited by the damage produced in the neighboring heat-affected zone of the tissue [78].

3.1. *Methods and mechanism of action*

Electrical stimulation for localized control of the blood flow is commonly delivered to the target tissue by two electrodes (working and return electrodes). These electrodes are placed in close proximity or in direct contact with their target tissue. For instance, Raeisi et al. [82] placed two planar stainless steel electrodes in contact with the skin directly on top of tumors in rats. Alternatively, for hemorrhage management, Mandel et al. [60] placed copper electrodes directly in contact with the liver in rats, which was the source of bleeding.

Local thrombosis induced by electrical stimulation may be mediated by damage in the endothelial cells of the blood vessels and is therefore irreversible [60]. This mechanism has been consistent with observations in multiple studies [60, 78]. Palanker et al. [78] experimentally characterized the stimulation intensity threshold for thrombosis in veins and arteries with different diameters. Other stimulation parameters used in these experiments were: 1 µs pulse width, repetition rate of 1 Hz and stimulation duration of 30 minutes. They found that the threshold for thrombosis is higher for vessels with larger diameter. Similarly, using higher stimulation intensities in the same vessel size can increase the speed of thrombosis [78].

Vasoconstriction as a result of electrical stimulation is most commonly caused by activation of sympathetic axons innervating the smooth muscle of cardiovascular vessels [3, 30, 47]. Nonetheless, in capillaries especially in the central nervous system, activation of pericytes by electrical stimulation leads to constriction [5, 35, 81]. Pericytes are one of the cell types that surround the capillaries and control their blood flow due to the cells' contractile properties [4].

Similar to thrombosis, Palanker et al. [78] also characterized the stimulation parameters required for the onset of reversible vasoconstriction without damage. Based on their experiments, many sets of stimulation parameters can successfully produce partial or full vasoconstriction depending on the intensity of the electrical field, stimulation frequency, duration of stimulation and the size of the target vessel. With stimulation amplitudes higher than threshold, the extent and speed of reversible vasoconstriction can be achieved (up to full vasoconstriction, and as fast as 1 minute for ~100 µm vessels) [78]. Vasoconstriction by electrical stimulation was also effective for larger vessels such as rat's femoral artery [60]. Taken collectively, the stimulation thresholds for vasoconstriction are lower than the stimulation thresholds for thrombosis [78].

3.2. *Pre-clinical results*

The application of electrical stimulation for thrombosis was first demonstrated in the form of direct current (DC) stimulation by Hladovec [38] and Bourgain et al. [10] in the 1970s. Guarini [34] developed this technique further to produce a reliable animal model for arterial thrombosis. He demonstrated that application of DC stimulation for 5 minutes at an amplitude of 2 mA when the blood flow has been mechanically stopped can lead to thrombotic lesions. Nonetheless, the application of DC stimulation to the tissue can lead to temperature increase [74] and unintended damage (e.g., production of gas bubbles [10]) to the tissue surrounding the site of stimulation [69, 87]. Therefore, the application of DC stimulation for the management of hemorrhage was ultimately deemed unsuitable [78].

Palanker et al. [78] investigated the pulsed electrical stimulation parameters required for thrombosis of vessels up to 100 µm in diameter in chicken embryos.

They were able to cause thrombosis after 30 minutes of stimulation at 1 Hz frequency with pulse widths of 500 ns. With these parameters the temperature increase was limited to less than 0.1°C.

They also investigated the stimulation parameters required for achieving full vasoconstriction in these vessels. Full constriction was achieved within 3-5 minutes of applying electrical stimulation at a repetition rate of 0.1 Hz (pulse width smaller than 5 μs). The vasoconstriction threshold was higher for arteries compared with veins of the same size [78]. Histological analysis did not show any damage resulting from the full vasoconstriction process [78].

In another study, Sersa et al. [89] demonstrated the use of stimulation pulses for the reduction of blood perfusion to cancerous tissue in mice. They showed that delivery of trains of eight pulses with a pulse width of 100 μs (frequency of 10 kHz, train duration of 0.8 ms) at a repetition rate of 1 Hz with an amplitude of 1040 V to the cancerous tissue results in approximately 30% reduction in its blood perfusion after 1 hour. Similar stimulation parameters have also been shown to result in electroporation, and therefore can be used for electrochemotherapy [82, 88].

Mandel et al. [61, 62] used pulsed electrical stimulation to manage bleeding from larger and more critical vessels following traumatic hemorrhage in rats [26]. They demonstrated that using stimulation pulses with an amplitude of 150 V, pulse width of 100 μs and repetition rate of 1 Hz on the cut femoral artery caused constriction by 80% leading to a significant reduction in blood loss. A constriction of 75% was also achieved for mesenteric vessels by using pulses with an amplitude of 40 V, pulse width of 100 μs and repetition rate of 1 Hz. A complete relationship between the intensity of the vasoconstriction in these vessels and the stimulation parameters was obtained experimentally [61, 62]. Accordingly, increasing the pulse width, amplitude and repetition rates of stimulation pulses results in an increase in the extent of the vasoconstriction [61, 62]. Under the most extreme stimulation parameters tested in this study, the temperature increase was estimated by finite element modeling to not increase more than 3 °C.

Electrical stimulation for hemorrhage control has also been applied to the liver in rats and rabbits [59, 60]. In these experiments, 200 stimulation pulses with 25 μs pulse width (40 kHz frequency, train duration of 5 ms), 1250 V amplitude and 1 Hz repetition rate were delivered to the liver in rats and rabbits and successfully reduced the volume of lost blood by 60% and 44%, respectively [60]. A finite element simulation of this process predicted an increase in the temperature of less than 1 °C for these parameters [60]. Histological analysis showed signs of endothelial cell damage which may indicate that both vasoconstriction and thrombosis mechanisms were involved in the reduction of blood loss [60].

3.3. *Summary and Future Directions*

Recent preclinical studies have demonstrated the feasibility and potential of pulsed electrical stimulation for fast and localized control of blood flow. The results obtained so far show promise for multiple applications such as the management of traumatic internal hemorrhage and localized treatment of cancerous tissue. One of the main advantages of electrical stimulation with short pulses is that small portable stimulators can manage the power requirements. These advantages for the prevention of internal bleeding may be critically important, especially since up to 56% of prehospital trauma mortalities are caused by hemorrhage [46]. Indeed, a recent study by Brinton et al. [13] has shown in rats the feasibility of using portable stimulators for this purpose.

Nonetheless, these studies are still at an early stage and further investigations in larger animal models are required to simulate the clinical conditions more closely. Mandel et al. [60] suggested that future studies in this area may also investigate non-invasive application of electrical stimulation for internal hemorrhage management.

4. Conclusions

Two applications of electrical stimulation for the control of smooth muscles have been reviewed: treatment of gastroparesis in the gastrointestinal tract and changing blood flow in cardiovascular vessels to control bleeding or deprive tumors of blood. In recent years, research and clinical interest in the treatment of disorders associated with smooth muscle using neuroprosthetic approaches has rapidly grown. Future efforts will focus on further optimization and customization of existing neuroprosthetic systems, research and translation of promising preclinical techniques, and development of novel approaches for a wider range of disorders.

Acknowledgements

AT was supported by an Alberta Innovates – Health Solutions Graduate Studentship and a Vanier Canada Graduate Scholarship, BRK was supported by the Guy Tribble and Susan Barnes Graduate Discovery Fellowship from the University of Washington School of Medicine and VKM was an Alberta Heritage Foundation for Medical Research Senior Scholar.

References

1. Abell, T., R. McCallum, M. Hocking, K. Koch, H. Abrahamsson, I. LeBlanc, G. Lindberg, J. Konturek, T. Nowak, E. M. M. Quigley, G. Tougas, and W. Starkebaum (2003) Gastric electrical stimulation for medically refractory gastroparesis, *Gastroenterology*, **125**(2), 421–428.

2. Al-Shboul, O. A. (2013) The importance of interstitial cells of Cajal in the gastrointestinal tract, *Saudi J. Gastroenterol.*, **19**(1), 3–15.

3. Atkinson, J., N. Boillat, A. K. Fouda, H. Guillain, M. Sautel, and M. Sonnay (1987) Noradrenaline inhibits vasoconstriction induced by electrical stimulation, *Gen. Pharmacol. Vasc. Syst.*, **18**(3), 219–223.

4. Attwell, D., A. Mishra, C. N. Hall, F. M. O'Farrell, and T. Dalkara (2016) What is a pericyte?, *J. Cereb. Blood Flow Metab.*, **36**(2), 451–455.

5. Bandopadhyay, R., C. Orte, J. G. Lawrenson, A. R. Reid, S. D. Silva, and G. Allt (2001) Contractile proteins in pericytes at the blood-brain and blood-retinal barriers, *J. Neurocytol.*, **30**(1), 35–44.

6. Bellahsène, B. E., C. D. Lind, B. D. Schirmer, O. L. Updike, and R. W. McCallum (1992) Acceleration of gastric emptying with electrical stimulation in a canine model of gastroparesis, *Am. J. Physiol.*, **262**(5 Pt 1), G826–834.

7. Bortolotti, M. (2002) The 'electrical way' to cure gastroparesis, *Am. J. Gastroenterol.*, **97**(8), 1874–1883.

8. Bortolotti, M. (2011) Gastric electrical stimulation for gastroparesis: A goal greatly pursued, but not yet attained, *World J. Gastroenterol.*, **17**(3), 273–282.

9. Bortolotti, M., P. Sarti, L. Barbara, and F. Brunelli (1990) Gastric myoelectric activity in patients with chronic idiopathic gastroparesis, *Neurogastroenterol. Motil.*, **2**(2), 104–108.

10. Bourgain, R. H. and F. Six (1974) A continuous registration method in experimental arterial thrombosis in the rat, *Thromb. Res.*, **4**(4), 599–607.

11. Bozler, E. (1945) The action potentials of the stomach, *Am. J. Physiol.*, **144**(5), 693–700.

12. Briley, L. C., S. P. Harrell, A. Woosley, J. Eversmann, and J. M. Wo (2011) National survey of physicians' perception of the cause, complications, and management of gastroparesis, *South. Med. J.*, **104**(6), 412–417.

13. Brinton, M. R., Y. Mandel, R. Dalal, and D. Palanker (2014) Miniature electrical stimulator for hemorrhage control, *IEEE Trans. Biomed. Eng.*, **61**(6), 1765–1771.

14. Buist, M. L., A. Corrias, and Y. C. Poh (2010) A model of slow wave propagation and entrainment along the stomach, *Ann. Biomed. Eng.*, **38**(9), 3022–3030.

15. Buller, A. J., J. C. Eccles, and R. M. Eccles (1960) Interactions between motoneurons and muscles in respect of the characteristic speeds of their responses, *Journal of Physiology*, **150**, 417-439.

16. Burke, R. E., D. N. Levine, P. Tsairis, and F. E. Zajac (1973) Physiological types and histochemical profiles of motor units in the cat gastrocnemius, *Journal of Physiology*, **234**, 723-748.

17. Butler-Browne, G. S., P. O. Eriksson, C. Laurent, and L. E. Thornell (1988) Adult human masseter muscle fibers express myosin isozymes characteristic of development, *Muscle and Nerve*, **11**, 610-620.

18. Camilleri, M. (2007) Diabetic gastroparesis, *N. Engl. J. Med.*, **356**(8), 820–829.

19. Chen, J. D. Z., L. Qian, H. Ouyang, and J. Yin (2003) Gastric electrical stimulation with short pulses reduces vomiting but not dysrhythmias in dogs, *Gastroenterology*, **124**(2), 401–409.

20. Chen, J. D., B. D. Schirmer, and R. W. McCallum (1994) Serosal and cutaneous recordings of gastric myoelectrical activity in patients with gastroparesis, *Am. J. Physiol.*, **266**(1 Pt 1), G90–98.

21. Cigaina, V. (2014) Gastric pacing as therapy for morbid obesity: Preliminary results, *Obes. Surg.*, **12**(1), S12–S16.

22. Cigaina, V. (2014) Long-term follow-up of gastric stimulation for obesity: The Mestre 8-year experience, *Obes. Surg.*, **14**(1), S14–S22.

23. Cordón, C., R. Fajardo, J. Ramírez, and M. F. Herrera (2005) A randomized, prospective, parallel group study comparing the Harmonic Scalpel to electrocautery in thyroidectomy, *Surgery*, **137**(3), 337–341.

24. Denekamp, J., S. A. Hill, and B. Hobson (1983) Vascular occlusion and tumour cell death, *Eur. J. Cancer Clin. Oncol.*, **19**(2), 271–275.

25. Dong, K., X. J. Yu, B. Li, E. G. Wen, W. Xiong, and Q. L. Guan (2006) Advances in mechanisms of postsurgical gastroparesis syndrome and its diagnosis and treatment, *Chin. J. Dig. Dis.*, **7**(2), 76–82.

26. Drapanas, T., R. L. Hewitt, R. F. Weichert, and A. D. Smith (1970) Civilian vascular injuries: a critical appraisal of three decades of management, *Ann. Surg.*, **172**(3), 351–360.

27. Du, P., G. O'Grady, S. J. Gibbons, R. Yassi, R. Lees-Green, G. Farrugia, L. K. Cheng, and A. J. Pullan (2010) Tissue-specific mathematical models of slow wave entrainment in wild-type and 5-HT(2B) knockout mice with altered interstitial cells of Cajal networks, *Biophys. J.*, **98**(9), 1772–1781.

28. Familoni, B. O., T. L. Abell, D. Nemoto, G. Voeller, and B. Johnson (1997) Efficacy of electrical stimulation at frequencies higher than basal rate in canine stomach, *Dig. Dis. Sci.*, **42**(5), 892–897.

29. Familoni, B. O., T. L. Abell, G. Voeller, A. Salem, and O. Gaber (1997) Electrical stimulation at a frequency higher than basal rate in human stomach, *Dig. Dis. Sci.*, **42**(5), 885–891.

30. Ferrell, W. R. and A. Khoshbaten (1990) Responses of blood vessels in the rabbit knee to electrical stimulation of the joint capsule, *J. Physiol.*, **423**(1), 569–578.

31. Forster, J., I. Sarosiek, R. Delcore, Z. Lin, G. S. Raju, and R. W. McCallum (2001) Gastric pacing is a new surgical treatment for gastroparesis, *Am. J. Surg.*, **182**(6), 676–681.

32. Fraser, R. J., M. Horowitz, A. F. Maddox, P. E. Harding, B. E. Chatterton, and J. Dent (1990) Hyperglycaemia slows gastric emptying in type 1 (insulin-dependent) diabetes mellitus, *Diabetologia*, **33**(11), 675–680.

33. Grover, M., G. Farrugia, M. S. Lurken, C. E. Bernard, M. S. Faussone–Pellegrini, T. C. Smyrk, H. P. Parkman, T. L. Abell, W. J. Snape, W. L. Hasler, A. Ünalp–Arida, L. Nguyen, K. L. Koch, J. Calles, L. Lee, J. Tonascia, F. A. Hamilton, and P. J. Pasricha (2011) Cellular changes in diabetic and idiopathic gastroparesis, *Gastroenterology*, **140**(5), 1575–1585.

34. Guarini, S. (1996) A highly reproducible model of arterial thrombosis in rats, *J. Pharmacol. Toxicol. Methods*, **35**(2), 101–105.

35. Hamilton, N. B., D. Attwell, and C. N. Hall (2010) Pericyte-mediated regulation of capillary diameter: A component of neurovascular coupling in health and disease, *Front. Neuroenergetics*, **2**, 5.

36. Heetun, Z. S. and E. M. M. Quigley (2012) Gastroparesis and Parkinson's disease: A systematic review, *Parkinsonism Relat. Disord.*, **18**(5), 433–440.

37. Hinder, R. A. and K. A. Kelly (1977) Human gastric pacesetter potential. Site of origin, spread, and response to gastric transection and proximal gastric vagotomy, *Am. J. Surg.*, **133**(1), 29–33.

38. Hladovec, J. (1971) Experimental arterial thrombosis in rats with continuous registration, *Thromb. Diath. Haemorrh.*, **26**(2), 407–410.

39. Hocking, M. P., S. B. Vogel, and C. A. Sninsky (1992) Human gastric myoelectric activity and gastric emptying following gastric surgery and with pacing, *Gastroenterology*, **103**(6), 1811–1816.

40. Horowitz, M., Y.-C. Su, C. K. Rayner, and K. L. Jones (2001) Gastroparesis: prevalence, clinical significance and treatment, *Can. J. Gastroenterol. Hepatol.*, **15**(12), 805–813.

41. Hosker, G., J. D. Cody, and C. C. Norton (2007) Electrical stimulation for faecal incontinence in adults, *Cochrane Database Syst. Rev.*, **3**, CD001310.

42. Jalilian, E., D. Onen, E. Neshev, and M. P. Mintchev (2007) Implantable neural electrical stimulator for external control of gastrointestinal motility, *Med. Eng. Phys.*, **29**(2), 238–252.

43. Kahraman, H., N. Kaya, A. Demirçali, I. Bernay, and F. Tanyeri (1997) Gastric emptying time in patients with primary hypothyroidism, *Eur. J. Gastroenterol. Hepatol.*, **9**(9), 901–904.

44. Kahrilas, P. J. (2008) Gastroesophageal reflux disease, *N. Engl. J. Med.*, **359**(16), 1700–1707.

45. Kao, C.-H., Y.-J. Ho, S.-P. Changlai, and H.-J. Ding (1999) Gastric emptying in spinal cord injury patients, *Dig. Dis. Sci.*, **44**(8), 1512–1515.

46. Kauvar, D. S., R. Lefering, and C. E. Wade (2006) Impact of hemorrhage on trauma outcome: an overview of epidemiology, clinical presentations, and therapeutic considerations, *J. Trauma*, **60**(6 Suppl), S3–11.

47. Khoshbaten, A. and W. R. Ferrell (1993) Nerve-mediated responses of blood vessels in the rabbit knee joint, *J. Vasc. Res.*, **30**(2), 102–107.

48. Kramer, M. D. and M. B. Pochapin (2012) Gastric phytobezoar dissolution with ingestion of diet coke and cellulase, *Gastroenterology & Hepatology*, **8**(11), 770-778.

49. Kwong, N. K., B. H. Brown, G. E. Whittaker, and H. L. Duthie (1970) Electrical activity of the gastric antrum in man, *Br. J. Surg.*, **57**(12), 913–916.

50. Lei, Y. and J. D. Z. Chen (2009) Effects of dual pulse gastric electrical stimulation on gastric tone and compliance in dogs, *Dig. Liver Dis.*, **41**(4), 277–282.

51. Levinthal, D. J. and K. Bielefeldt (2016) Systematic review and meta-analysis: Gastric electrical stimulation for gastroparesis, *Auton. Neurosci. Basic Clin.*, in press.

52. Lin, Z., I. Sarosiek, and R. W. McCallum (2007) Gastrointestinal electrical stimulation for treatment of gastrointestinal disorders: gastroparesis, obesity, fecal incontinence, and constipation, *Gastroenterol. Clin. North Am.*, **36**(3), 713–734.

53. Lin, Z., I. Sarosiek, J. Forster, R. A. Ross, J. D. Z. Chen, and R. W. McCallum (2011) Two-channel gastric pacing in patients with diabetic gastroparesis, *Neurogastroenterol. Motil.*, **23**(10), 912–e396.

54. Lin, Z., J. Forster, I. Sarosiek, and R. W. McCallum (2003) Treatment of gastroparesis with electrical stimulation, *Dig. Dis. Sci.*, **48**(5), 837–848.

55. Lin, Z., J. Forster, I. Sarosiek, and R. W. McCallum (2004) Treatment of Diabetic Gastroparesis by High-Frequency Gastric Electrical Stimulation, *Diabetes Care*, **27**(5), 1071–1076.

56. Liu, J., X. Qiao, and J. D. Z. Chen (2004) Vagal afferent is involved in short-pulse gastric electrical stimulation in rats, *Dig. Dis. Sci.*, **49**(5), 729–737.

57. Liu, J., X. Qiao, and J. D. Z. Chen (2006) Therapeutic potentials of a novel method of dual-pulse gastric electrical stimulation for gastric dysrhythmia and symptoms of nausea and vomiting, *Am. J. Surg.*, **191**(2), 255–261.

58. Malis, L. I. (1996) Electrosurgery, *J. Neurosurg.*, **85**(5), 970–975.
59. Malki, G., O. Barnea, and Y. Mandel (2012) Hemorrhage control by short electrical pulses #x2014; In vivo experiments, *IEEE 27th Convention of Electrical Electronics Engineers in Israel*, 1–5.
60. Mandel, Y., G. Malki, E. Adawi, E. Glassberg, A. Afek, M. Zagetzki, and O. Barnea (2013) Hemorrhage control of liver injury by short electrical pulses, *PloS One*, **8**(1), e49852.
61. Mandel, Y., R. Manivanh, R. Dalal, P. Huie, J. Wang, M. Brinton, and D. Palanker (2013a) Hemorrhage control by microsecond electrical pulses, *Proc. SPIE*, **8585**, 12.2002303.
62. Mandel, Y., R. Manivanh, R. Dalal, P. Huie, J. Wang, M. Brinton, and D. Palanker (2013b) Vasoconstriction by electrical stimulation: New approach to control of non-compressible hemorrhage, *Sci. Rep.*, **3**, 2111.
63. Martellucci, J. and A. Valeri (2014) Colonic electrical stimulation for the treatment of slow-transit constipation: a preliminary pilot study, *Surg. Endosc.*, **28**(2), 691–697.
64. McCallum, R. W., I. Sarosiek, H. P. Parkman, W. Snape, F. Brody, J. Wo, and T. Nowak (2013) Gastric electrical stimulation with Enterra therapy improves symptoms of idiopathic gastroparesis, *Neurogastroenterol. Motil.*, **25**(10), 815–e636.
65. McCallum, R. W., J. D. Z. Chen, Z. Lin, B. D. Schirmer, R. D. Williams, and R. A. Ross (1998) Gastric pacing improves emptying and symptoms in patients with gastroparesis, *Gastroenterology*, **114**(3), 456–461.
66. McCallum, R. W., W. Snape, F. Brody, J. Wo, H. P. Parkman, and T. Nowak (2010) Gastric electrical stimulation with Enterra therapy improves symptoms from diabetic gastroparesis in a prospective study, *Clin. Gastroenterol. Hepatol.*, **8**(11), 947–954.
67. McCallum, R., Z. Lin, P. Wetzel, I. Sarosiek, and J. Forster (2005) Clinical response to gastric electrical stimulation in patients with postsurgical gastroparesis, *Clin. Gastroenterol. Hepatol.*, **3**(1), 49–54.
68. Mearin, F and J. R. Malagelada (1995) Gastroparesis and dyspepsia in patients with diabetes mellitus., *Eur. J. Gastroenterol. Hepatol.*, **7**(8), 717–723.
69. Merrill, D. R., M. Bikson, and J. G. R. Jefferys (2005) Electrical stimulation of excitable tissue: design of efficacious and safe protocols, *J. Neurosci. Methods*, **141**(2), 171–198.
70. Miedema, B. W., M. G. Sarr, and K. A. Kelly (1990) Pacing the human stomach, *Gastroenterology*, 99(4), 1217.
71. Mintchev, M. P., C. P. Sanmiguel, S. J. Otto, and K. L. Bowes (1998) Microprocessor controlled movement of liquid gastric content using sequential neural electrical stimulation, *Gut*, **43**(5), 607–611.
72. Mir, L. M. and S. Orlowski (1999) Mechanisms of electrochemotherapy, *Adv. Drug Deliv. Rev.*, **35**(1), 107–118.
73. Monges, H. and J. Salducci (1971) Electrical activity of the gastric antrum in normal human subjects, *Am. J. Dig. Dis.*, **16**(7), 623–627.
74. Munro, M. G. (2012) Fundamentals of electrosurgery Part I: Principles of radiofrequency energy for surgery, in: eds. L. Feldman, P. Fuchshuber, and D. B. Jones, *The SAGES Manual on the Fundamental Use of Surgical Energy (FUSE)*, (Springer, New York), 15–59.
75. Nathan, M. (2010) Microbattery technologies for miniaturized implantable medical devices, *Curr. Pharm. Biotechnol.*, **11**(4), 404–410.
76. O'Grady, G., J. U. Egbuji, P. Du, L. K. Cheng, A. J. Pullan, and J. A. Windsor (2009) High-frequency gastric electrical stimulation for the treatment of gastroparesis: a meta-analysis, *World J. Surg.*, **33**(8), 1693–1701.

77. Ordög, T., I. Takayama, W. K. Cheung, S. M. Ward, and K. M. Sanders (2000) Remodeling of networks of interstitial cells of Cajal in a murine model of diabetic gastroparesis, *Diabetes,* **49**(10), 1731–1739.

78. Palanker, D., A. Vankov, Y. Freyvert, and P. Huie (2008) Pulsed electrical stimulation for control of vasculature: temporary vasoconstriction and permanent thrombosis, *Bioelectromagnetics,* **29**(2), 100–107.

79. Park, M. I. (2013) Can electrical stimulation therapy be helpful for patients with chronic constipation refractory to biofeedback therapy?, *J. Neurogastroenterol. Motil.,* **19**(3), 279–280.

80. Parkman, H. P., W. L. Hasler, and R. S. Fisher (2004) American Gastroenterological Association technical review on the diagnosis and treatment of gastroparesis, *Gastroenterology,* **127**(5), 1592–1622.

81. Peppiatt, C. M., C. Howarth, P. Mobbs, and D. Attwell (2006) Bidirectional control of CNS capillary diameter by pericytes, *Nature,* **443**(7112), 700–704.

82. Raeisi, E., S. M. P. Firoozabadi, S. Hajizadeh, H. Rajabi, and Z. M. Hassan (2010) The effect of high-frequency electric pulses on tumor blood flow in vivo, *J. Membr. Biol.,* **236**(1), 163–166.

83. Robles, R., P. Parrilla, C. Escamilla, J. A. Lujan, J. A. Torralba, R. Liron, and A. Moreno (1994) Gastrointestinal bezoars, *Br. J. Surg.,* **81**(7), 1000–1001.

84. Sanders, K. M., S. D. Koh, and S. M. Ward (2006) Interstitial cells of cajal as pacemakers in the gastrointestinal tract, *Annu. Rev. Physiol.,* **68**, 307–343,.

85. Sarna, S. K. and E. E. Daniel (1973) Electrical stimulation of gastric electrical control activity, *Am. J. Physiol.,* **225**(1), 125–131.

86. Sathar, S., M. L. Trew, P. Du, G. O'Grady, and L. K. Cheng (2013) A biophysically based finite-state machine model for analyzing gastric experimental entrainment and pacing recordings, *Ann. Biomed. Eng.,* **42**(4), 858–870.

87. Scheiner, A., J. T. Mortimer, and U. Roessmann (1990) Imbalanced biphasic electrical stimulation: muscle tissue damage, *Ann. Biomed. Eng.,* **18**(4), 407–425.

88. Sersa, G., D. Miklavcic, M. Cemazar, Z. Rudolf, G. Pucihar, and M. Snoj (2008) Electrochemotherapy in treatment of tumours, *Eur. J. Surg. Oncol.,* **34**(2), 232–240.

89. Sersa, G., M. Cemazar, C. S. Parkins, and D. J. Chaplin (1999) Tumour blood flow changes induced by application of electric pulses, *Eur. J. Cancer,* **35**(4), 672–677.

90. Shafi, M. A. and P. J. Pasricha (2007) Post-surgical and obstructive gastroparesis, *Curr. Gastroenterol. Rep.,* **9**(4), 280–285.

91. Sikora, S. S., B. R. Mital, K. R. Prasad, B. K. Das, and S. P. Kaushik (1995) Functional gastric impairment in carcinoma of the pancreas, *Br. J. Surg.,* **82**(8), 1112–1113.

92. Soffer, E., T. Abell, Z. Lin, A. Lorincz, R. McCallum, H. Parkman, S. Policker, and T. Ordog (2009) Review article: gastric electrical stimulation for gastroparesis--physiological foundations, technical aspects and clinical implications, *Aliment. Pharmacol. Ther.,* **30**(7), 681–694.

93. Song, G.-Q., X. Hou, B. Yang, Y. Sun, W. Qian, and J. D. Z. Chen (2008) A novel method of 2-channel dual-pulse gastric electrical stimulation improves solid gastric emptying in dogs, *Surgery,* **143**(1), 72–78.

94. Stoddard, C. J., R. H. Smallwood, and H. L. Duthie (1981) Electrical arrhythmias in the human stomach, *Gut,* **22**(9), 705–712.

95. Talley, N. J. and A. C. Ford (2015) Functional dyspepsia, *N. Engl. J. Med.,* **373**(19), 1853–1863.

96. Tang, M., J. Zhang, and J. D. Z. Chen (2006) Central mechanisms of gastric electrical stimulation involving neurons in the paraventricular nucleus of the hypothalamus in rats, *Obes. Surg.*, **16**(3), 344–352.

97. Tougas, G. and J. D. Huizinga (1998) Gastric pacing as a treatment for intractable gastroparesis: Shocking news?, *Gastroenterology*, **114**(3), 598–601.

98. Weaver, J. C. and Y. A. Chizmadzhev (1996) Theory of electroporation: A review, *Bioelectrochem. Bioenerg.*, **41**(2), 135–160.

99. Yao, S., M. Ke, Z. Wang, D. Xu, Y. Zhang, and J. D. Z. Chen (2005) Retrograde gastric pacing reduces food intake and delays gastric emptying in humans: A potential therapy for obesity?, *Dig. Dis. Sci.*, **50**(9), 1569–1575.

100. Zárate, N., F. Mearin, X.-Y. Wang, B. Hewlett, J. D. Huizinga, and J.-R. Malagelada (2003) Severe idiopathic gastroparesis due to neuronal and interstitial cells of Cajal degeneration: pathological findings and management, *Gut*, **52**(7), 966–970.

Section 5
Regulatory

Chapter 5.1

**Medical Device Regulations and Biocompatibility Testing Requirements
Focus on Neuroprotheses**

Jeffery R. Nelson and Jerry R. Nelson

Nelson Laboratories, Inc.
6280 S. Redwood Road
PO Box 17557
Salt Lake City, UT 84117-0557
jrnelson@nelsonlabs.com

This chapter presents a brief treatise of biocompatibility concepts, test procedures and their interpretation, including material selection, chemical characterization, design and sterilization, with a foray into the history, rules and regulations one must understand and follow to register a neuroprosthetic medical device before commercialization is presented. An overview of the process that guides selection of the regulatory route is summarized with the basics of the investigational device exemptions, pre-market notification, and pre-market approval process also included.

1. Introduction

This chapter covers basic background and information needed to work with regulatory guidances. Documents addressing the topic are 'guidance' and the reader is expected to have precedent knowledge. Thus, this chapter is intended for an introduction and not inclusive statement on the topic. Nevertheless, a serious effort has been made to explain and outline the process, with some decision points noted. Some background on the submission and approval process is included. Each of the categories of biocompatibility are explained and the results expected for approval of a neuroprosthesis. Also some helpful additional sources of information are provided in an attempt to assist the novice.

2. History

The Federal Food, Drug and Cosmetic Act [1] (FFDCA) became law in 1962. The Medical Device Amendments to the FFDCA were formalized on 28 May 1976. The new amendment defined a medical device in section 201(h) as "...an instrument, apparatus, implement, machine, contrivance, implant, in vitro reagent, or other similar or related article, including a component, part, or accessory, which is recognized in the official National Formulary, or the United States Pharmacopeia (USP), or any supplement to them, intended for use in the diagnosis of disease or other conditions, or in the cure, mitigation, treatment, or prevention of disease, in man or other animals, or intended to affect the structure or any function of the body of man or other animals, and which does not achieve any of its primary intended purposes through chemical action within or on the body of man or other animals and which is not dependent upon being metabolized for the achievement of any of its primary intended purposes."

This law directed the United States Food and Drug Administration (USFDA or FDA) to issue regulations and classify all medical devices in use at the time into three categories with escalating regulatory controls. The three classes (I, II, & III) were based on the degree of regulation thought appropriate to assure reasonable safety and effectiveness of the products when used on humans. The purpose of the new program was to: 1) identify devices that represented new technology and place them into Class III and, thereby, require them to undergo premarket approval (PMA) before going to market; 2) classify new devices— a device without a predicate would be Class III because it represented new technology and a substantially equivalent device would be the same as the class of the predicate device to which it was found equivalent; and 3) achieve marketing equity by requiring manufacturers of new medical devices that are substantially equivalent to pre-amendment devices to have the same regulatory burdens that were faced by the manufacturers of the previously approved products (pre-28 May 1976).

The FDA regulates the marketing of medical devices in the US. The legal basis for this includes:

- The Food, Drug and Cosmetic Act [1] (FFDCA);
- The Medical Device Amendments (1976) to FFDCA;
- The Safe Medical Device Act [2];
- The Quality System Regulation [3];
- Medical Device Amendments of 1992 to FFDCA;
- Food and Drug Administration Modernization Act of 1997 [4];
- Guidance documents published by FDA (examples are included in the bibliography).

The FDA has classified approximately 1,700 different generic types of devices and grouped them into 16 medical specialties referred to as panels. Each type is also assigned to one of three regulatory classes based on the level of control believed to be appropriate to assure the safe and effective use of the device. These three classes and the requirements which apply to them are:

Class I, General Controls; Class II, General Controls and Special Controls; and Class III, General Controls and Premarket Approval.

The U.S. has some of the safest medical devices in the world, and the FDA has played a critical role in this success. It is also important to understand that the FDA will not normally approve devices when unanswered questions or concerns exist, regardless of the potential benefits. There is no incentive to approve devices—but there are consequences for approving bad ones. This can cause delays if it is not understood. Companies who submit products must read and understand the regulations and, if they are interested in rapid and successful review, address all of the safety and efficacy issues in the initial submission.

The FDA has many concerns for the safety and effectiveness of medical devices. They have articulated some of the major ones:

- Mis-use, unintended use or not following label instructions;
- Device failure (components or device);
- Adverse biological effects of the device materials (including extractable/leachable chemicals from the materials or process residuals).

Significant effort should be directed at each of these concerns. It is important to not only have simple, easy to follow instructions, but to understand how the product might be misused. It is also important to *know* how the device is or will be used and counter or stop off-label or unintended use(s) of a device. An example would be labeling a product for use for less than 30 days when there is knowledge or expectation of longer use. This creates issues with labeling instructions because this is an off-label use, and increases the risk for adverse biological effects since most biocompatibility tests are selected based on labeled patient contact time. The safe approach is to perform biocompatibility tests for at least the expected contact time, instruct sales staff to not give tacit or verbal approval for longer use, and to assure any physical or performance tests include effects of longer contact times.

New medical devices manufactured for use in the U.S. must first undergo critical scientific and regulatory review by the FDA. If the candidate product is in legal terms 'substantially similar' to an existing, on the market product that has been issued a 510(k) [5], the device may be sold after filing a premarket notification (510(k)) with FDA. This process, if the submission includes the necessary information, may take as little as two to three months. If there are safety, efficacy or unanswered questions, the process can be indefinite.

If a substantially similar product does not exist, or if a substantially similar product was required to file a pre-market approval (PMA) [6] application, then the new manufacturer will also be required to do so. PMA applications require substantial additional effort and, depending on complexity, materials, device nature, technology, and other factors, may be as brief as three to four months or may take an extended time if safety, efficacy, or unanswered questions arise. February 2002 statistics from the FDA web site indicated an average review time of 126 days, with only five of 254 taking longer than 180 days. All clinical data to support a 510(k) or PMA must be collected under an approved Investigational Device Exemption (IDE) [7].

3. Investigational Device Exemption

In the FDA's own words, "Obtaining approval for an IDE application is not a simple process." The purpose of investigational device exemptions is to encourage discovery and development of new technologies, while protecting the clinical subjects and the public's health in general. IDEs provide the granting of exemptions to a researcher during the development of safety and effectiveness data for the device when clinical data in human subjects is needed. An approved IDE exempts a device that would otherwise be subject to premarketing clearance, to be legally shipped for the purpose of performing clinical studies. An IDE also exempts devices from registration, listing, premarket notification, premarket approval, performance standards, some records and reports, good manufacturing practice regulations, and some other clauses.

The manufacturer must make an assessment of the risk of the clinical investigation. If the risk is considered to be non-significant, then the manufacturer presents the proposal to an Institutional Review Board (IRB) [8]. If the IRB makes the same conclusion, then the clinical study is exempt from the IDE regulations and the study can proceed. If the manufacturer or IRB considers the clinical investigation a significant risk, then pre-approval from FDA and the IRB is necessary. An IDE also requires compliance with the Informed Consent regulations [9], Financial Disclosure by Clinical Investigators regulations [10], and the Design Controls section of the FDA Quality System Regulation [11] to assure the FDA that clinical studies have complied with Good Clinical Practices (GCP).

The manufacturer of a non-significant risk device may proceed with tacit (exempt) IDE approval if the device is:
- properly labeled as per the IDE regulations;
- obtains and retains IRB approval during the entire clinical investigation;
- obtains formal informed consent (IRB may waive) prior to study initiation;
- complies with all IDE monitoring requirements;
- keeps records and makes reports as required by the IDE regulations;
- assures that clinical investigators maintain records and make reports; and

- performs no promotion, test marketing, commercialization of investigational devices or unduly prolongs an investigation.

There are some valuable alternate routes for IDEs that can provide options for generation of safety and efficacy data. All veterinary use, custom devices, research with laboratory animals, diagnostic use if non-invasive, or invasive if the procedure is not a significant risk, diagnostic tests that are confirmed with other tests, certain non-risk consumer preference tests, and all pre-amendment devices are exempt from the IDE regulations.

Under certain circumstances, the Health Care Financing Administration [12] will consider Medicare coverage for devices with an FDA approved IDE that have been categorized as non-experimental or investigational (Category B). Category A devices are new technology devices (Class III) for which 'absolute risk' of the device type has not been determined. Category B are non-experimental/investigational devices in Class I or II, or a device in Class III for which underlying questions of safety and effectiveness of the device type have been resolved, or other manufacturers have been given FDA approval of the device type.

FDA approval of an IDE is often a rapid process and a training manual on IDEs [13] indicates that the process is normally approved or disapproved within 30 days. There are exceptions to most rules and the complexity of the device or the degree of risk may modify these time frames.

4. PMAs

The medical device amendments of 1992 define a Class III device as one that "supports or sustains human life or is of substantial importance in preventing impairment of human health or presents a potential, unreasonable risk of illness or injury." Class II devices require performance standards and Class I devices require general controls. All devices categorized as Class III require a PMA or an effort can be made in the form of a reclassification petition to move the device from Class III to Class II. These have, in our experience, rarely been successful unless the device has been on the market for some time and has experienced a low incidence of problems.

A PMA is not unlike a New Drug Application or a patent, in that it grants to the applicant a private license for marketing a specific medical device. The regulation handles pre-amendment and post-amendment devices differently; however, since there were so few neurological devices prior to 28 May 1976, only the post-amendment process will be reviewed. The PMA process will also be detailed more fully here since this will be the likely track for most neuroprosthetic devices, since by definition they will be new devices and automatically moved to Class III.

The PMA review process is summarized below.

1) FDA administrative and limited scientific review to determine completeness. This is called a filing review.

2) FDA scientific and compliance personnel in-depth review. Within this time frame, FDA will send the applicant an approval order under, an 'approvable letter', a 'not approvable letter', or an 'order denying approval'.

3) Advisory committee review and recommendation. This is called the panel review. The panel must also hold one public meeting to review the PMA.

4) FDA review of panel recommendation, documentation, and notification.

5) FDA Good Manufacturing Practices (GMP) inspection.

PMA content and format are clearly specified and include the following:

- Full disclosure of known information about the safety and effectiveness of the candidate and similar devices;
- Full disclosure of all components, ingredients and properties, concepts, and principles of operation;
- Manufacturing, packaging and, where relevant, installation, controls, methods, facilities, and processes;
- Designation and reference to any applicable aspect or performance standard if the device is a Class II, and data to demonstrate the candidate device meets those performance standards or justification for deviations;
- Samples of the device or address of one that can be examined and tested;
- Labeling;
- Other information which FDA or the panel may require.

All information submitted to FDA is considered confidential, including even the existence of a PMA file until final disposition (or at least near the end of the process). The summary of safety and effectiveness data and status are then published on the FDA website with considerable information from the PMA.

If changes to the device or manufacturing process are desired, they must normally be approved by a PMA supplement. Maintenance of a PMA requires batch testing of the device, continuing evaluation and reports to the FDA on the safety, effectiveness, and reliability of the device, unpublished reports of data from clinical investigations, and notification to the agency of reports in the scientific literature related to the approved device.

The FDA has written a training manual that helps with the process [14]. This is available from the FDA website.

5. Design Control

It is now mandatory that all aspects of the design of a medical device be critically reviewed by a formally established committee [11]. This process starts at concept and includes the research and development phase. A minimum design review would include software standards, biocompatibility, sterilization, packaging, electrical standards (IEEE, IEC), mechanical properties, manufacturing, and regulatory issues. While not required, legal, financial, and marketing aspects are typically also included. Design control greatly increases the probability of producing a device that is appropriate for its intended use and also provides a means to discover design deficiencies early in the process. The design control process involves the following:

- Design input: Review of the scientific literature, competitor products, user input, regulatory requirements.
- Design output: What are the deliverables, what is expected in the final product?
- Design transfer: Complete listing of specifications, production documents, quality control, and testing.
- Risk analysis: Completion and analysis of failure mode and effect analysis (FMEA), human factors engineering, etc.
- Design verification: The design input equals the design output, evaluated throughout the process.
- Design validation: Determine that the final product design is what user needs and matches the labeled use.

Manufacturers must also register their facility: 1) list all devices they make [15]; 2) comply with labeling regulations [16], reporting regulations [17] and Quality Systems Regulations [3] for many products, including many neuroprostheses; and 3) undergo post-market surveillance (PS) [17]. PS may be required for devices that are Class II or Class III when: 1) their failure would be reasonably likely to have serious health consequences; 2) the device is intended to be implanted for more than a year; or 3) the device is life-sustaining or life-supporting and used outside a device user (health care) facility.

6. Device Tracking

Devices which: 1) can fail and would likely result in serious adverse health consequences; 2) are intended for implantation in the human body for more than one year; or 3) are intended to be life-sustaining or life-supporting may need to be tracked throughout their life [2]. If the FDA initiates a tracking order, manufacturers must attempt to maintain individual patient information (patients can decline to be tracked). This typically requires a unique, sequential identifying number on each device. The addition of this identifier has resulted in biocompatibility test repeats.

7. Biocompatibility

The selection of the appropriate biocompatibility test battery in the U.S. is currently defined by the American National Standards Institute, Inc. (ANSI), Association for the Advancement of Medical Instrumentation (AAMI), and the International Standards Organization (ISO) 10993 series of standards as modified by the FDA. These guidance documents from ANSI/AAMI/ISO [18-33] presently number 20. The basic test selection guideline had its genesis in the Tripartite Guidance document [34]. Tripartite was a guidance document prepared by the Toxicology Sub-group of the Tripartite Sub-committee on Medical Devices. This sub-committee was represented by Canada, the United Kingdom, and the U.S.

The ISO is a federation of standards bodies from the various members. Standards documents are written by technical committees with representatives from interested countries who wish to provide input. Governmental and international organizations also take part in the work in liaison with ISO. Most standards undergo many drafts and additional input is sought, if not often integrated, and they are eventually voted upon as Draft International Standards (DIS). Publication of a final ISO standard requires approval by 75 percent of the member bodies who vote.

The test selection table is listed in ANSI/AAMI/ISO 10993-1, but is modified based on FDA guidance documents (Blue book memoranda G-95). This table is reproduced below as Table 1. In April of 2013, the FDA released a new draft guidance document the Use of International Standard ISO-10993, "Biological Evaluation of 3 Medical Devices Part 1: Evaluation and Testing". In this new draft guidance, new importance was put on risk evaluation and test selection and less emphasis on Table 1.

Table 1 shows the categories that must be assessed to determine the proper biological endpoints to perform and are divided by body contact type (skin, mucosal membranes, blood path direct, tissue/bone, etc.). After determining the body contact type, one must select the duration of contact. Category A contact is equal to or less than 24 hours, Category B contact is 24 hours to 30 days; and Category C is greater than 30 days. Repeat exposure of the medical device must be considered, for example, an intravenous (IV) bag might only have a few hours contact with the patient, but many IV bags may be used throughout the patient's hospital stay, therefore the total exposure time must be considered. An 'X' in the biological effect column indicates the ANSI/AAMI/ISO recommends that this category should be addressed. It does not mean that you must do this test (or only this test), it means that most products are expected to address the need. If you subject your product to a specific test or category, a defensible justification must be included. This is a guidance document and guidance documents all require input. Some biological endpoint categories are single tests, some comprise many possible options. An 'O' in the biological endpoint column indicates that FDA believes that this category should be also be addressed, in addition to those marked with an 'X' for consideration by ISO.

Materials used in medical devices should normally be characterized for their chemical properties before or concurrently with biocompatibility tests. Chemical characterization tests selection is based, much like the biocompatibility tests, on the materials selected for the device, the tissues contacted, and the duration of contact. The following list provides a range of options. Many of these tests are used to characterize device materials. The instruments necessary are based on the materials that make up the device, and its design and use.

- Gas Chromatography Mass Spectrometry (GC-MS);
- High Performance Liquid Chromatography Ultraviolet (HPLC - UV);
- Liquid Chromatography Mass Spectrometry (LC-MS);
- Inductively Coupled Plasma Mass Spectrometry (ICP-MS);
- Fourier transform infrared spectrophotometry (FTIR);
- USP physicochemicals test series;
- Total organic carbon (TOC);
- Differential scanning calorimetry (DSC);
- Thermogravimetry analysis (TGA);
- Mechanical/engineering properties (tensile, elongation, etc.);
- Density;
- Hardness (durometer);
- Ultraviolet spectrophotometry (UV);
- Moisture analysis;
- Surface analysis (contact angle);
- Scanning electron microscopy;
- Electron spectroscopy for chemical analysis (ESCA);
- Nuclear magnetic resonance (NMR);
- Molecular weight determination (GPC);
- Trace metal analysis.

Generally, when evaluating the quantitative amount of chemicals that may be extracted or leached from the device materials, GC-MS, LC-MS, and ICP-MS are used.

Table 1. FDA BIOCOMPATIBILITY (modified from Required Biocompatibility Training and Toxicology Profiles for Evaluation of Medical Devices, 5/1/95 (G95-1))

Device Type	Body Contact	Contact Duration A 24 Hrs, B > 24 Hrs < 30 Days, C > 30 Days	Cyto-toxic-ity	Sensi-tiza-tion	Irrita-tion	Sys-temic Toxic-ity	Sub-chron-ic Toxic-ity	Geno-toxic-ity	Im-plant-ation	Hemo-com-pat-ibility	Chron-ic Tox-icity	Car-cino-gen-icity
Surface Devices	Skin	A	X	X	X							
		B	X	X	X							
		C	X	X	X							
	Mucosal Membranes	A	X	X	X	O	O		O			
		B	X	X	X	O	O		O			
		C	X	X	X	O	X	X	O		O	
	Breached/Compromised Surfaces	A	X	X	X	O	O		O			
		B	X	X	X	O	O		O			
		C	X	X	X	O	X	X	O		O	
External Communicating Devices	Blood Path, Indirect	A	X	X	X	X	O			X		
		B	X	X	X	X	O			X		
		C	X	X	O	X	X	X	O	X	X	X
	Tissue/Bone Dentin Communicating +	A	X	X	X	O	O	X	X			
		B	X	X	O	O	O	X	X		O	X
		C	X	X	O	O	O	X	X		O	X
	Circulating Blood	A	X	X	X	X	O	O^	O	X	O	
		B	X	X	X	X	O	X	O	X	X	
		C	X	X	X	X	X	X	O	X	X	X
Implant Devices	Tissue/Bone	A	X	X	O	O	O	X	X		O	
		B	X	X	O	O	O	X	X		O	
		C	X	X	X	X	X	X	X		X	X
	Blood	A	X	X	X	X	O	X	X	X	X	X
		B	X	X	X	X		X	X	X	X	X
		C	X	X	X	X	X	X	X	X	X	X

X = ISO Evaluation Tests for Consideration

O = Additional Tests which may be applicable

Note + = Tissue includes tissue fluids and subcutaneous spaces

Note ^ = For all devices used in extracorporial circuits

For medical devices, biocompatibility tests should be performed:
- after sterilization;
- after all manufacturing processes (cleaning, welding, molding, etc);
- after ALL product development;
- before clinical trials;
- before marketing;
- before submission to FDA;
- after chemical characterization of materials; and
- usually only for initial qualification of materials and replacements.

Brain and brain stem tissues are among the most sensitive in the body. The selection of tests and interpretation of data must be made with this in mind. An example for which significant data and experience exists is endotoxin. Endotoxin is a potent, toxicologically active compound. Device materials or components may be more or less toxicologically active. This greater sensitivity of the spinal cord and brain must be understood and carefully considered in the selection of materials, medical device components, and in the interpretation of the biocompatibility results. The FDA bacterial endotoxins test guidance document [35] and USP 25 [36] have established 0.5 endotoxin units (EU)/ml or 20 EU/Device specification for most medical devices and 0.06 EU/ml or 2.15 EU/Device for devices that contact cerebrospinal fluid. This specification recognizes an 8+ fold greater sensitivity of the spinal cord and brain tissue.

Calculation of the endotoxin limits for drugs employs the formula K/M, where K = 5.0 EU/kg for parenteral drugs and M = maximum human dose/kg of body weight that would be administered in a single one-hour period. For radiopharmaceuticals, M equals the maximum human dose/kg at the product expiration date or time. Use 70 kg as the weight of the average human when calculating the maximum human does per kg. Also, if the pediatric dose/kg is higher than the adult dose, then it shall be the dose used in the formula. For products administered on a square meter (m^2) basis, use 1.80 m^2 to calculate the total dose, then divide by 70 kg to obtain the dose per kg.

The specification for intrathecal administration of drugs provides an even greater safety factor. For drugs administered intrathecally, the endotoxin limit is 0.2 EU/kg. The difference in sensitivity for intrathecal administration of drugs is 25 fold.

There are no specific neurological tissue contact tests in any of the guidance documents, but research models do exist. Dendritic cell culture is an example.

7.1. *Good laboratory practices (GLP)*

The FDA Good Laboratory Practice (GLP) regulations [37] and the corresponding Organization for Economic Cooperation and Development (OECD) GLP regulations [38], implemented in the European Community

(EC), define specific requirements, practices, monitoring, schedules, and formats for studies being performed for submission to a regulatory agency in support of a marketing permit. These regulations apply to both *in vitro* and *in vivo* studies designed to address safety or efficacy when lack of it makes the device unsafe.

All biocompatibility qualification tests should be performed under the GLP regulations. This will add to the cost of the tests, but is inexpensive compared to the time delays and issues raised by rejection of tests not performed under the GLP regulations. Regulatory guidance in the U.S. suggests that studies being submitted for a PMA, IDE, any drug-device combination, biological product, color additive, device development protocol, 510(k), or device classification petition be conducted under the GLPs. The ANSI/AAMI/ISO 10993 standards also recommend that all tests for regulatory approval be performed under GLP.

The following is taken directly from the FDA GLP regulations [37]: "When a sponsor conducting a nonclinical laboratory study intended to be submitted to or reviewed by the Food and Drug Administration utilizes the services of a consulting laboratory, contractor, or grantee to perform an analysis or other service, it shall notify the consulting laboratory, contractor, or grantee that the service is part of a nonclinical laboratory study that must be conducted in compliance with the provisions of this part." The consequences of noncompliance with the GLPs may include facility disqualification, fines, and imprisonment.

7.2. Animal tests

Most of the biocompatibility tests employ animal models. While there are many groups that are working to replace or reduce animal tests, these tests are still being validated and are not yet accepted by regulatory agencies worldwide. The greatest success has been in the area of genetic toxicity where it is now possible to screen and select polymeric, non-biodegradable materials for medical devices that virtually eliminate carcinogenicity potential by screening for the absence of mutational effects using a tiered series of DNA, chromosome, and gene mutation tests, with few or no animals. Chemical characterization of device materials has also shown great promise to evaluate the genotoxicity potential of biomaterials.

Facilities that perform animal tests are required to have an animal welfare committee that reviews study protocols, and the more aggressive committees review any modification or change to a protocol. Those who subcontract samples should confirm the existence of an active animal welfare committee at the contractor.

Animal facilities have the option of being accredited by the American Association of Laboratory Animal Care (AALAC). This currently represents the highest level of physical facility design, maintenance and care an animal facility can obtain and is a good qualifier for any facility to whom you consider subcontracting.

7.3. *Extraction media*

The media used to extract or leach biomaterials were borrowed from those used to evaluate medicine containers. The extraction media outlined in the USP include physiological saline, 5% ethanol in saline, vegetable oil, and polyethylene glycol 400 [39].

The current approach, modified by the ANSI/AAMI/ISO 10993 series of standards, normally employs only saline and oil; although there are product specific applications where a greater range of extraction solutions would be prudent. An example would be a catheter used to deliver drugs which contained alcohol or glycol excipients.

Extraction temperatures vary widely. It was previously standard, in USP, to extract the material at 121°C for 60 min; 70°C for 24 h, or 50°C for 72 h, using the highest temperature that would not distort the device materials. The 10993 series of standards generally recommend multiple extraction types based on device characteristics and conditions of use. Guidance documents require input and it is the responsibility of the manufacturer to evaluate the device use and tissue contact. In general, devices that have prolonged patient contact are recommended to extract at higher temperatures if that temperature does not impact the material. Knowledge of the biomaterials used, the catalysts, cross-linking agents, plasticizers, stabilizers, radiation absorbing additives, and the bonding agents may modify the extract selection.

7.4. *Cytotoxicity*

This category includes at various commonly used tests.

- Agar overlay (AO), in which test materials are placed onto agarose overlays of mouse embryo fibroblast cells. Cells are stained and cytopathic effects on the cells are scored after 24 to 72 hours. Results for known negative and positive controls are always included.
- Minimal essential media (MEM) elution test, in which extracts of the test materials are made, usually in MEM with 5% serum and placed onto monolayers of mouse embryo fibroblast cells. Cells are stained and cytopathic effects on the cells are scored after 24 to 72 hours. Results for known negative and positive controls are always included.
- Direct cell contact (DCC) tests, in which the device or device material is placed directly in contact with the cells in liquid media and then stained and scored as outlined above.

- Inhibition of cell growth (ICG) tests, in which measurement of total protein for cells in suspension culture is compared to time 0 refrigerated controls and known negative and positive controls. Negative controls are considered to be 100 percent and refrigerated cells prepared to the same density as test and negative controls are the percent protein baseline. Scores of from 0 to 100 percent inhibition of cell growth are possible. Tests are more valuable when performed with a predicate device for comparison.
- MTT/XTT assay, in which extracts of the test materials are made, usually in MEM with 5% serum and placed onto monolayers of mouse embryo fibroblast cells. Cells are stained using tetrazolium dye 3-(4,5-*dimethylthiazol*-2-yl)-2,5-di*phenyl*tetrazolium bromide (MTT) that NAD(P)H-dependent cellular oxidoreductase enzymes reduce the dye to its insoluble form, which has a purple color. Then a spectrophotometer can be used to determine cell viability based on the absorbance of color.

Most of the cytotoxicity tests can be modified to determine the extinction end-point of toxicity and, thus, a quantitative value. Most acceptable biomaterials do not cause any cytopathic effects.

The cytotoxicity test is the most inexpensive and the most sensitive. This test is required for all body contact types and all contact durations. It is also commonly used to screen candidate materials due to its sensitivity, rapid turnaround, and low cost. Devices or materials considered for neuroprostheses should not demonstrate any cell effects or cell growth inhibition.

7.5. Sensitization

Sensitization tests are performed to determine the immunogenicity potential for a material. There are several different methods of choice. Presently, most employ guinea pigs (e.g., guinea pig maximization) because of the generally recognized sensitivity of their immune system. Guinea pigs are often more sensitive than humans to immunogenic materials and thus provide a margin of safety for use of screened materials in humans. When inbred, the guinea pig is subject to nutritional deficiencies that can make it insensitive to immunogenic stimuli. It is important to assure that the facility that performs this test is knowledgeable about guinea pig husbandry and/or runs positive controls.

The use of positive controls in routine animal tests is an issue. Few animal tests employ positive controls since these increase the number of animals used. This issue is occasionally raised by the FDA during a submission. Most laboratories that perform these tests address this by performing a positive control periodically (quarterly, semi-annually, or annually) to demonstrate that animals in their care are capable of responding. The performance of positive controls as part of a routine test is discouraged, and many animal welfare committees will not approve them.

A method that employs mice for sensitization testing is increasing in use. The Local Lymph Node Assay (LLNA) test can produce results equivalent to guinea pigs (ask for equivalency data from the laboratory) and is more rapid and may be less expensive. However, the FDA has expressed concerns with medical devices and the mouse test, with any device that contains metal components or multiple types of materials. Due to approach used with LLNA test only the induction phase of sensitization can be measured, whereas, the guinea pig test also measures the elicitation phase.

Sensitization tests in guinea pigs typically take six to eight weeks to complete if the laboratories have no queue. This time includes time for acquisition and acclimation (quarantine) of animals, three weeks of dosing, a 10-day rest before the final challenge, two days to score, and time to write the final reports.

Since extractable/leachable chemicals may exhibit different solubilities in different solvents, it is expected that tests will be performed with both saline (polar) and vegetable oil (non-polar) extracts. Sensitization tests for any neuroprosthesis should demonstrate no sensitization. The consequences of antigen-antibody reactions in the brain or brain stem are substantial.

7.6. *Irritation tests*

This category may be addressed with a variety of different types of tests. Input is again necessary to select the proper procedure or the test which provides safety data most appropriate for the device. For a neuroprosthesis, the intracutaneous toxicity test would be expected.

The intracutaneous toxicity test employs extracts of materials injected intradermally in rabbits. The most commonly used extracts are saline and vegetable oil extracts, but others can be used. Devices used near or in the eyes would normally be expected to also do eye irritation tests. Neuroprosthetic devices should produce no responses in any of the test procedures. If reactions are seen, alternate device materials should be sought.

7.7. *Systemic toxicity tests*

The systemic toxicity test is performed in mice and employs from one to four of the standard extraction media previously discussed. Saline and vegetable oil extracts are expected by the FDA and are usually acceptable, however, every biocompatibility test procedure requires input.

The FDA believes that material mediated pyrogenicity of the device should also be addressed. This is typically included as part of the systemic toxicity test. The issue is to address whether or not a material can produce a fever. Pyrogenic reactions have been noted from blood tranfusion filters which were endotoxin negative. Investigation into non-endotoxin reactions may demonstrate residual solvent from the manufacturing process If a material appears to cause a fever in this test, and it is not from endotoxin contamination, then a cause should be exhaustively sought This concern can be addressed by extracting/washing the material with saline and injecting a series of rabbits and monitoring their core temperature. The rabbit pyrogen test is detailed in USP 25 [40].

7.8. Subchronic toxicity

Subchronic toxicity tests are designed to demonstrate safety from intermediate exposures times (up to 26 weeks). Subchronic tests are far from standardized and vary from facility to facility. They employ mice, rats, and occasionally larger animals; and typically integrate quantitative safety criteria and clinical chemistries into the procedure. These include weight gain percent, hematology values, or other measurable parameter compared to control groups. These studies should employ complete necropsy of the animals and examination and weights of internal organs. Histopathological evaluation of tissues should also be included. Tests of materials to be in contact with cerebrospinal fluid, brain, dura mater, or spinal column should include careful examination of these tissues in the subchronic studies. Implantation tests can be considered subchronic tests if the protocol is properly addressed. However, for dura substitute devices the FDA recommends [41], in addition, a 90-day subchronic toxicity test with histology of the surrounding tissue.

7.9. Genotoxicity

Genotoxicity tests should be performed on medical devices except when they are made only from materials where all major components of extracts have been identified and shown not to be genotoxic. Tests should be performed to address the three levels of genotoxic effects: DNA effects, chromosomal aberrations, and gene mutations. Tests are performed as extracts and typically employ saline and a solvent like dimethysulfoxide (DMSO) or polyethylene glycol (PEG), but this is dependent upon the device composition and application.

The following tests are good choices to address the three levels of genotoxic effects:

- DNA–Ames reverse mutation using *Salmonella typhimurium*;
- Chromosome–chromosomal aberrations w/Chinese Hamster ovary cells;

- Gene mutations–mouse lymphoma reverse mutation test.

The 10993-3 standard says that animal tests should be performed if *in vitro* tests are positive; the FDA is requiring the animal test along with the Ames test, and either the chromosomal aberration or the mouse lymphoma. Unless there is a very compelling reason for continued testing of a device, a positive result in any of these tests would suggest that another device material be selected. These tests can normally be performed in a few weeks.

7.10. *Implantation*

Implantation tests are among the most predictive tests for biocompatibility screening. The tissue device interface is normally the most important site. Implantation tests are commonly performed in a variety of laboratory animals including mice, rats, guinea pigs, rabbits, dogs, sheep, goats, and pigs. Short-term tests range from one to 12 weeks and long-term tests from 12 to 104 weeks. Implants may be in subcutaneous tissue, muscle, or bone. The ISO 10993-6 newest revision includes a neuro-implantation section. This along with the FDA dura substitute device guidance [41] suggests animal implantation at the anatomic site and evaluation of the following:

- cerebral spinal fluid leakage;
- adhesion formation;
- implant anchorage;
- device resorption and replacement by host tissue;
- device vascularization;
- incidence of infection;
- incidence of hydrocephalus;
- hemorrhage;
- foreign body reactions;
- other tissue reactions.

The selection of the animal species is based on the length of the study as a function of the life span of the animals. Biological responses in tissue vary in different species and the choice of animal should be made accordingly.

Exposure time is a big issue. It is valuable to determine that a device or material has reached a steady state in the tissue. This cannot normally be ascertained with a single time interval. Devices intended for long-term implantation will likely need to undergo animal implantation studies for 12, 26, and/or 52 weeks to demonstrate steady state biological response.

It is also important to note that the form, density, hardness, or surface structure may affect the tissue response of the implant. Specimens should be as close to the final product surface as possible to provide the most reliable data.

Implantation tests can, if the devices are functional, provide more valuable data and may also substitute for subchronic or chronic tests, depending upon duration. The use of functional implants is thus strongly encouraged.

7.11. *Hemocompatibility*

Hemocompatibility (ISO 10993-4) requires that five potential categories be addressed: thrombosis, coagulation, platelets, hematology and complement activation. Complement activation is normally performed on large, blood contact surfaces such as hemodialyzers and oxygenators, and the scientific literature contains reports of complement activation by some polymeric materials [42], but in the recent FDA draft guidance they are recommending complement activation on any device that contacts circulatory system. The greater sensitivity of the brain and brain stem mandates reviewing the published safety data on all materials used in a medical device contacting neuronal tissue. Thrombosis, coagulation or platelet effects studies may be considered based on the nature and site of device placement, but would not normally be necessary. Hemolysis is recommended in the FDA dura mater guidance document [41].

7.12. *Chronic toxicity*

Quoting from 10993-11, "Chronic toxicity or carcinogenicity testing for medical devices seems to be very rarely appropriate in relation to the health risk involved which arises from the exposure. In cases where it seems nevertheless necessary to answer such questions, experts should decide on a case-to-case basis on a proportionate test procedure." However, the FDA states in their dura substitute devices guidance document [41] that products which are designed to remain in the body for greater than 30 days should have a 180-day chronic toxicity test with histology of the surrounding tissue. Dura substitutes are Class II, 510(k) devices. This also serves to illustrate the differences in opinion that frequently occur when different standards writing organizations (ISO 10993-11), the FDA, and industry look at the same problem. A 180-day chronic toxicity study will add considerably to the device development costs.

7.13. *Carcinogenicity*

Carcinogenicity studies may be appropriate when components or devices are:
- resorbable;
- positive in genetic toxicity tests in mammalian cells;
- introduced into the body for 30 days or longer.

When unavoidable, studies are performed in at least one rodent species for the lifetime of the animal using typically two dose levels consisting of the maximum implantable dose (MID) and one half of the MID. Studies should include complete examination of the tissue at the implant site as well.

There is good developing evidence that two-step cell transformation assays may be able to detect non-genotoxic carcinogens [20]. At present, however, the data does not permit extension of the conclusions that all carcinogens will be detected.

Carcinogenicity tests may be avoided if there is significant human exposure data on all the materials used in the device. The use of materials known to be safe and supportable, with data from the scientific literature or by citing existing medical devices with human exposure history by 510(k) number or PMA number, may be possible and can certainly save project development dollars (and two and half years).

7.14. *Immunotoxicity*

Immunotoxicity testing guidance [43] was published by the FDA in the mid 1990s. The 1998 version picked up ISO/TC 194 annotations and should be required reading for all who develop novel biomaterials. Immunotoxicity includes any adverse effect on the structure or function of the immune system or any other system impacted consequently. This category includes humoral immunity, cellular immunity, immunosuppression, autoimmunity, hypersensitivity, and chronic inflammation. The immunotoxicity tests are summarized in Table 2.

The guidance document states "A decision on whether a material/device is immunotoxic must rely on the available evidence from pre-clinical test results and clinical evaluation, as well as prior history of use. Because the available data will often be less than conclusive, good judgment will play an important part in evaluating immunotoxic risk." The format of the immunotoxicity guidance document is similar in format to the general biocompatibility selection table, based on body contact and contact duration. This document suggests evaluation of five principle areas, including: 1) hypersensitivity, 2) chronic inflammation, 3) immunosuppression, 4) immunostimulation, and 5) autoimmunity. This document also specifies which tests should be performed for plastics and other polymers, metals, ceramics, glasses and composites; biological materials and other. Table 2 lists the immune response components of each of the five categories.

Cellular and T-cell responses include: Guinea pig maximization tests, mouse LLNA, mouse ear swelling test, lymphocyte proliferation, mixed lymphocyte reaction. Natural Killer Cells responses may be gauged with tumor cytotoxicity. Macrophage response criteria include phagocytosis and antigen presentation tests. Granulocyte responses are measured with degranulation and phagocytosis. Host resistance can be assessed by monitoring resistance to bacteria, viruses, and tumors. Those who broach the realm of device materials for which existing immunotoxicity data is not available should at least have good judgment.

Table 2. Potential immunotoxic effects of devices and constituent materials.

Body Contact		Contact Duration*	Immuno toxic Effects **				
			1	2	3	4	5
Surface Devices	Skin	A	pmbx		x	x	x
		B	pmbx	x	x	x	x
		C	pmbx	x	x	x	x
	Mucosal Membrane	A	pmbx		x	x	x
		B	pmbx	pmbx	mbx	x	x
		C	pmbx	pmbx	mbx	mbx	mbx
	Breached or Compromised Surface	A	pmbx		x	x	x
		B	pmbx	pmbx	mbx	mbx	mbx
		C	pmbx	pmbx	mbx	mbx	mbx
External Communicating Devices***	Blood Path, Direct and Indirect	A	pmbx		x	x	x
		B	pmbx	pmbx	mbx	pmbx	mbx
		C	pmbx	pmbx	mbx	pmbx	mbx
	Tissue/Bone/Dentin Communicating	A	pmbx		x	x	x
		B	pmbx	cpmbx	mbx	pmbx	mbx
		C	pmbx	cpmbx	mbx	pmbx	mbx
Implant Devices	Tissue/Bone, Blood, and other Body Fluids	A	pmbx		x	x	x
		B	pmbx	cpmbx	mbx	pmbx	mbx
		C	pmbx	cpmbx	mbx	pmbx	mbx

* A= Limited (< 24hrs); B= Prolonged (> 24 hrs to 30 days); C= Permanent (> 30 days).
** 1 = Hypersensitivity; 2 = Chronic Inflammation; 3 = Immunosuppression; 4 = Immunostimulation; 5 = Autoimmunity.
Effects Expected for Various Materials: p = Plastics and Other Polymers; m = Metals; c = Ceramics, Glasses, Composites; b = Biological Materials; x = Other Materials (Specify).
*** External devices that contact the circulating blood (e.g., dialyzers and immunoadsorbents) or the blood path indirectly at one point and serve as a conduit for entry into the vascular system (e.g., solution and blood administration sets) or tissue/bone/dentin (e.g., skin staples, laparoscopes, dental filling materials).

7.15. Sterilization

It is important to expose devices or components to the sterilant that will be used for the device if it is to be supplied sterile. Ethylene oxide is neurotoxic and the FDA requires [41], at least for dura substitutes, ethylene oxide residual data and additional tests on the finished device using intracranial implantation to assess irritation. It may be more wise to use another mode of sterilization.

Some medical devices in their final form that cannot be sterilized by conventional procedures. Devices to be processed with ethylene oxide need gas channels for the sterilant to penetrate. Peroxide or peroxide plasma systems typically need channels larger than for ethylene oxide. Many materials are not compatible with irradiation. As such, considerations for sterilization of the device should not be left until the end.

7.16. *Composite testing*

Many of these tests are expensive– some even outrageously so. If a device is comprised of eight materials (rather typical) and two bonding agents, the cost for testing each component will make development costs very high. The ISO 10993 documents recommend that composite testing be performed. Composite testing, while not possible for all tests (e.g., implantation), can significantly reduce development costs. In the example above, one would save about 80 percent of the cost of individual component tests. Composite testing, however, should be performed on completed, sterilized, final devices and this, depending upon device cost, may actually be more expensive.

8. Resource Materials

Some valuable resources and contact information is included below. Standards are available from AAMI, ANSI, ISO and FDA. American Society for Testing and Materials (ASTM) has consensus standard procedures that can save time and illustrate controls and protocol steps that have been carefully reviewed by others. The FDA website is actually rather extraordinary. The U.S. standards, laws, rules, regulations, manuals, guidance documents, and much more are available on-line. Facts on Demand Service allows those without internet access to use the telephone to call in and order documents to be sent via fax. The FDA will also provide redacted copies of previous submissions via their freedom of information service on-line. If time is not an issue, this service is free or carries a nominal charge. If you have more money than time, FOI services requests copies of PMAs, IDEs, 510(k)s, and other relevant documents from FDA, waits in the queue, then maintains a library of these previous submissions for sale. The charges are for the short-sightedness of those who failed to request the document six months before needing it.

PMA panel meetings, the FDA summary of safety and effectiveness data, and the basis for approval or rejection are posted on the FDA website. Those who need a more frequent dose of regulation can sign-up for daily FDA e-mail updates which include the PMA meeting minutes. The FDA Division of Small

Manufacturers, International and Consumer Assistance (DSMICA) was
mandated by congress and can be very helpful for the many questions that arise
in product development. This group can be reached via e-mail or by telephone.

AAMI: www.aami.org   800-332-2264
ASTM: www.ami.org   610-832-9585
ANSI: www.ansi.org   202-293-8020
FOI: www.foiservices.com   301-975-9400
ISO docs. www.global.ihs.com   800-854-7179 (Global Engineering)
FDA website: www.fda.org
FDA freedom of information: www.fda.gov/foi/foia2
                                                      888-INFO-FDA (888-463-6332)
FDA update service: http://list.nih.gov/archives/cdrhnew.html
FDA Division of Small Manufacturers, International and Consumer Assistance
(DSMICA):   http://www.fda.gov/cdrh/dsma/dsmamain.html
Telephone: 800.638.2041 or 301.443.6597
Fascimile: 301.443.8818
E-mail: dsma@cdrh.fda.gov

References

1. The Federal Food, Drug and Cosmetic Act. U.S.C. Title 21-Foods and Drugs; Chapter V
   Drugs and Devices, Subchapter A - Drugs and Devices (1999).
2. Safe Medical Devices Act, Public L. No. 101-629 (1990).
3. Quality Systems Regulation., 21 C.F.R. Part 820 (2002).
4. Food and Drug Administration Modernization Act of 1997, Public L. No. 105-115, 105th
   Cong. (1997).
5. Premarket Notification Procedures, 21 C.F.R. Part 807, Subpart E (2002).
6. Premarket Approval Of Medical Devices, 21 C.F.R. Part 814 (2002).
7. Investigational Device Exemptions, 21 C.F.R. Part 812 (2002).
8. Institutional Review Boards, 21 C.F.R. Part 56 (2002).
9. Informed Consent of Human Subjects, 21 C.F.R. Part 50 Protection of Human Subjects,
   Subpart B (2002).
10. Financial Disclosure by Clinical Investigators, 21 C.F.R. Part 54 (2002).
11. Design Controls , 21 C.F.R. 820 Quality System Regulation, Subpart C (2002).
12. Implementation of the FDA/HCFA Interagency Agreement Regarding Reimbursement
    Categorization of Investigational Devices, ODE Blue Book Memo #D95-2 (1995).
13. Investigational Device Exemptions Manual, U.S. Dept. HHS Publication FDA 92-4159
    (1992).
14. Premarket Approval Manual, U.S. Dept. HHS Publication FDA 97-4214 (1998).
15. U.S. Department of Health and Human Services, Public Health Service, Food and Drug
    Administration, Center for Devices and Radiological Health, Rockville, MD 20850.
16. Establishment Registration and Device Listing For Manufacturers and Initial Importers of
    Devices, 21 C.F.R. Part 807 (2002).
17. Labeling, 21 C.F.R. Part 801(2002).

18. Medical Device Reporting, 21 C.F.R. Part 803 (2002).
19. ANSI/AAMI/ISO 10993-1:2009/(R)2013 Biological evaluation of medical devices, Part 1: Evaluation and testing.
20. ANSI/AAMI/ISO 10993-2-2006/(R)2014 Biological evaluation of medical devices, Part 2: Animal protection requirements, 1ed.
21. ANSI/AAMI/ISO 10993-3:2014 Biological Evaluation of medical devices, Part 3: Tests for genotoxicity, carcinogenicity and reproductive toxicity, 1ed.
22. ANSI/AAMI/ISO 10993-4: 2002/(R)2013 & A1:2006/(R)2013 Biological evaluation of medical devices, Part 4: Selection of tests for interactions with blood, 1ed.
23. ANSI/AAMI/ISO 10993-5:2009/(R)2014 Biological evaluation of medical devices, Part 5: Tests for cytotoxicity: *in vitro* methods, 2ed.
24. ANSI/AAMI/ISO 10993-6-2007/(R)2014 Biological evaluation of medical devices, Part 6: Tests for local effects after implantation, 1ed.
25. AAMI ISO 10993-7:2008 (R2012) Biological evaluation of medical devices, Part 7: Ethylene oxide sterilization residuals, 2ed.
26. AAMI/ISO 10993-08/Ed.1 Biological evaluation of medical devices, Part 8: Selection and qualification of reference materials for biological tests, 1ed.
27. ANSI/AAMI/ISO 10993-9:2009/(R)2014 Biological evaluation of medical devices, Part 9: Framework for identification and quantification of potential degradation products, 2ed.
28. ANSI/AAMI/ISO 10993-10:2010/(R)2014 Biological evaluation of medical devices, Part 10: Tests for irritation and sensitization, 1ed.
29. ANSI/AAMI/ISO 10993-11:2006/(R)2014 Biological evaluation of medical devices, Part 11: Tests for systemic toxicity, 1ed.
30. ANSI/AAMI/ISO 10993-12:2012 Biological evaluation of medical devices, Part12: Sample preparation and reference materials, 1ed.
31. ANSI/AAMI/ISO 10993-13-2010/(R)2014 Biological evaluation of medical devices, Part 13: Identification and quantification of degradation products from polymeric medical devices, 1ed.
32. ANSI/AAMI/ISO 10993-14:2001/(R)2011 Biological evaluation of medical devices, Part 14: Identification and quantification of degradation products from ceramics, 1ed.
33. ANSI/AAMI/ISO 10993-15:2000/(R)2011 Biological evaluation of medical devices, Part 15: Identification and quantification of degradation products from metals and alloys, 1ed.
34. ANSI/AAMI/ISO 10993-16:2010/(R)2014 Biological evaluation of medical devices, Part 16: Toxicokinetic study design for degradation products and leachables from medical devices, 1ed.
35. Tripartite biocompatibility guidance for medical devices 1986, Toxicology Subgroup of the Tripartite Sub-Committee on Medical Devices.
36. Guideline on validation of the Limulus amebocyte lysate test as an end-product endotoxin test for human and animal parenterals, biological products, and medical devices. U.S. Department of Health and Human Services, Public Health Service, Food and Drug Administration, Rockville, MD (Dec 1987).
37. Bacterial Endotoxins Test <85>. 2001. United States Pharmacopeia 25. United States Pharmacopeial Convention, Inc. Rockville, MD.
38. Good Laboratory Practice Regulations for Nonclinical Laboratory Studies, 21 C.F.R., Part 58 (2002).
39. OECD Principles of Good Laboratory Practice. OECD Environmental Health and Safety Publications, Series of Principles of Good Laboratory Practice and Compliance Monitoring. No.1. Environmental Directorate, Organization for Economic Co-operation and Development, Paris (1998).

40. Biological Reactivity tests in vivo <88>. 2016. United States Pharmacopeia 25. United States Pharmacopeial Convention, Inc. Rockville, MD.

41. Biological Reactivity tests in vivo <87>. 2016. United States Pharmacopeia 25. United States Pharmacopeial Convention, Inc. Rockville, MD.

42. Draft guidance document for dura substitute devices, Guidance for industry and/or FDA reviewers/staff and/or compliance (13 Aug 1999), U.S. Department of Health and Human Services, Public Health Service, Food and Drug Administration, Center for Devices and Radiological Health, Plastic and Reconstructive Surgery Devices Branch, Division of General and Restorative Devices, Office of Device Evaluation, Rockville, MD.

43. Chenoweth, D. E., Complement activation produced by biomaterials, *Trans Am. Soc. Artif. Intern. Organs*, **22**, 226-232, 1986.

44. Draft Immunotoxicity Testing Guidance. ISO/TC 194 N291. Molecular Biology Branch, Division of Life Sciences, U.S. Department of Health and Human Services, Public Health Service, Office of Science and Technology, Food and Drug Administration, Center for Devices and Radiological Health, Rockville, MD.

Index